Menin Gate South

Menin Gate South

In Memory and In Mourning

Paul Chapman

Pen & Sword
MILITARY

First published in Great Britain in 2016 by
Pen & Sword Military
an imprint of
Pen & Sword Books Ltd
47 Church Street
Barnsley
South Yorkshire
S70 2AS

ISBN 978 1 47385 087 3

A CIP catalogue record for this book is available from the British Library

Typeset in Ehrhardt by
Mac Style Ltd, Bridlington, East Yorkshire
Printed and bound in the UK by CPI Group (UK) Ltd,
Croydon, CRO 4YY

Pen & Sword Books Ltd incorporates the imprints of Pen & Sword Archaeology, Atlas,
Aviation, Battleground, Discovery, Family History, History, Maritime, Military, Naval,
Politics, Railways, Select, Transport, True Crime, and Fiction, Frontline Books, Leo
Cooper, Praetorian Press, Seaforth Publishing and Wharncliffe.

For a complete list of Pen & Sword titles please contact
PEN & SWORD BOOKS LIMITED
47 Church Street, Barnsley, South Yorkshire, S70 2AS, England
E-mail: enquiries@pen-and-sword.co.uk
Website: www.pen-and-sword.co.uk

Contents

Author's Note

The role of the historian is to study, draw upon and interpret the narrative for the perception of the future.
Bishop, 1969

No matter how many times one visits the Western Front of France and Belgium, one cannot fail to be awed by the number of Commonwealth War Graves Commission cemeteries encountered at almost every turn. Some cemeteries are considerably larger than others but they all have one thing in common – the serried ranks of headstones, silently guarding the land in which they stand, paid for in the blood and self-sacrifice of those who lie beneath; their lives given that we might live in freedom. Every headstone and name on a memorial represents a personal tragedy; collectively they represent a lost generation of husbands, fathers, sons and brothers who answered their country's call to duty.

The visitor to these silent cities of the dead (all are easily accessible be it by foot or vehicle) usually falls into one of three categories – Personally related in some way to the casualty, historically minded, or casual. The relative, spurred by family connection, might be visiting for the first time, perhaps the very first time the casualty has received the comfort of a visit from home, or returning as part of annual pilgrimage; paying their respects to someone unknown to them personally yet ever remembered by the family. The historian, documenting his or her findings for personal interest or publication, might be researching a particular individual or action in which a certain division, brigade, regiment or battalion took part. The casual visitor is invariably someone passing through the vicinity, mildly curious, taking a brief break from his or her journey. But, for whatever reason the visit is made – and one can spend hours walking round – those who fail to be touched emotionally are few and far between.

Uniform in size and design the headstone informs the visitor of the casualty's name, rank, regiment, service number, date of death and (sometimes) age. Poignant epitaphs abound, but few give any insight into the man. The memorials to the thousands of missing record only regiment, rank and name. Examination of the appropriate cemetery or memorial register for further details will, with the exception of Victoria Cross recipients, rarely reveal more than next of kin. Whatever terminology one chooses, without additional information a list is just a list.

After over forty year's association with the Western Front, and, in particular the Ypres Salient, I have frequently asked myself the question who were these men, where did they come from, what happened? The answer to these questions can never be fully answered, the detail herein recorded began purely out of personal interest; researching a considerable number of casualties whose graves I had photographed. Initially drawing on the Marquis De Ruvigny's Rolls of Honour, published at the time and shortly thereafter in a series of parts, in time this expanded into page upon page of information bringing a personal aspect to the casualty – explaining and answering much more of the who, what, where and why than the norm.

Almost one hundred years after the Armistice the death toll of the First World War remains as a Roll of Honour, commanding as much respect today as it did at the time. Dubbed the Great War for Civilization it was the first total war in British history to affect every aspect of national life, and stands as the supreme icon of the horror and inhumanity of armed conflict. Our picture of the war is still vivid, the poems speak just as freshly to A–Level students today as they did to older generations, and the poignancy of the many photographs and newsreel footage touches us still.

Those smiling, young, unsuspecting faces marching into Flanders; those exhausted, shattered bodies struggling through the mud, the squalor and filth of the trenches where the ever present sense of death and the macabre were just another facet of everyday life – they could be our faces and bodies, or belong to those we know and love.

Throughout Great Britain and the Dominions there were few families who did not know of a husband, father, son, brother or uncle killed or wounded in the conflict. Behind the bald statistics of every account written at the time or years afterwards lie countless stories of individual tragedy. Drawn from a vast variety of sources, the accounts and casualty details (many at length) herein recorded, recount the gruesome horror of war in all its many facets. In an antidote to the adventure stories that pass for war in much of the literature of today mud, lice, rats, gas and death in every manner imaginable (and unimaginable). The biggest killer – shellfire – often buried men alive, or completely vaporised them, leaving no trace of their existence. Jagged chunks of red hot metal sliced through flesh in an obscene fashion, removing heads and limbs with ease. Snipers, grenades and the scything machine guns, skilfully used by well-trained specialists, all contributed to the horror; all get their due.

How soldiers endured all this is beyond comprehension, any part of the thin veneer of civilisation they had left behind was quickly eroded after a short time at the front. Men became dehumanised by the war, they brutalised and stripped the corpses of their enemies for souvenirs; snipers took special enjoyment in knocking off members of burial parties. But, it was a different matter when it came to their own dead. Under strict orders to ignore wounded comrades in an advance, soldiers repeatedly strove heroically to protect their own. Time and time again they risked their own lives to go out onto the bullet and shell swept battlefield to search for wounded and fallen comrades; bringing in the latter that they might be given 'the dignity of a decent burial' – rites that all too often proved short-lived. Some, hastily buried, re-emerged from the earth during the next rainstorm; countless numbers were exhumed or blown to pieces by bombardments. On reflection the question arises: 'Why bother at all?' In part the answer lies with those of the battalion who, after the fighting, answered the roll-call, heard the repeated silences that followed the reading of the names, only to be informed from higher up the attack had failed due to 'lack of pluck' on their part. When one takes all this into account one realises the importance of remembering the dead was often as much an act of tenderness by their comrades as it was in defiance.

Within the confines of the Ypres Salient are to be found one hundred and sixty nine Commonwealth War Grave Commission cemeteries and three memorials to the missing, honouring the memory of British and Commonwealth servicemen who gave their lives in the defence of this relatively small yet strategically important region of Belgium. Of the 210,000 casualties buried or commemorated in the Ypres Salient extended details relating to over 20,000 were drawn upon to compose these books. A small percentage of the total but who they were, where they came from, how they died are equally as important as the why. These men and the actions in which they gave their lives are a part of our history, our heritage; hopefully, by bringing something of the personal about them to the visitor, these books will ensure their memory never fades.

In Memory and In Mourning
Paul Chapman

Acknowledgements

First and foremost to my long suffering wife Sandra, who, without complaint over the almost thirteen years this work has taken, has not only put up with my spending days on end with my head stuck in one book or another, making copious quantities of notes (and leaving papers all over the house), typing or searching the internet at all hours, but has also endured alone my long periods away from home spent trekking the salient.

Secondly to the staff of the Commonwealth War Graves Commission, Maidenhead and Ypres, the Imperial War Museum, London, and the National Archives, Kew; for their many kindnesses and willing assistance. Also to the Australian War Memorial, Canberra, the Auckland Cenotaph, New Zealand and the Canadian National War Memorial, Ottawa, whose archival material greatly assisted in providing additional detail, clarified numerous points and answered many queries.

Special thanks to Gladys Lunn, MBE, for her continued interest and encouragement, without whose personal influence I would never have made the acquaintance of so many regimental associations: Royal Army Medical Corps; Royal Tank Regt.; Machine Gun Corps; Royal Berkshire, Wiltshire & Gloucestershire Regiments. Major A.R. McKinnell, Black Watch; Capt. A.W. Hughes – Cheshire Regt.; Corpl. Bingley and the late Major Louch – Coldstream Guards; Major T.W. Stipling – Duke of Cornwall's Light Infantry; Major P.R. Walton – King's Liverpool Regt., Manchester Regt.; Major C.M.J. Deedes – King's Own Yorkshire Light Infantry; Lieut.Col. G. Bennett – Lancashire Fusiliers; David Ball and Harry 'Aitch' Hogan – Prince of Wales's Leinster Regt. Association; Capt. Richard 'Dick' Hennessy-Walsh – The Life Guards; Major J.C. Rogerson – Middlesex Regt., Queen's Own (Royal West Kent Regt.); The Buffs (East Kent Regt.); George, Bob and J.P. – Northamptonshire Regt.; Leslie Frater – Northumberland Fusiliers; Major S.A. Kennedy – Prince of Wales's Own (West & East Yorkshire) Regt.; Major R.J.R. Campbell – Queen's Own Cameron Highlanders, Seaforth Highlanders; Capt. W.G. 'Bill' Sutherland – Royal Scots; Major A.W. Russell – Queen's Royal West Surrey Regt.; Major G. Correa – Royal Artillery; Lieut.Col. P.A. Roffey, Royal Army Veterinary Corps; Major R.G. Mills – Royal Warwickshire Regt; Major A. Ellingham – Royal Welch Fusiliers: And, Major John Baines and John Howells – New South Wales Lancers Museum (Australian Light Horse); Capt. Gary 'Poppa Holdfast' Silliker, Royal Canadian Air Force (Engineers); and Alison Taylor, Auckland Museum.

Also a big thank you to the many people whose contributions to this work have in various degrees, enhanced the whole. In particular the members of the internet sites 'The Great War Forum,' 'World War 1 Remembered' and 'The Aerodrome' whose knowledge (and resourcefulness) never ceased to amaze: My friend and work colleague Dick Atkins who, when my computer crashed at 1500 pages and all seemed lost, completely restored everything including my sanity: Steve 'One Shot' Clews for his photographic expertise: Steve 'For Canada' Douglas, The British Grenadier Bookshop, Ypres, for his untiring assistance with queries regarding the C.E.F.; often closing shop to check names and panel numbers on the Menin Gate: Sue Cox, Richard 'Daggers' Daglish, Ian 'Scoop' Davies, Derek 'Del' Doune, Pete Folwell, Frank 'The Oracle' Grande, Sandra Hanley, Bryan Harris, Tim Harrison & Anna Parker, Patricia Healey, John & Elizabeth Holbrook, Clive Hughes, Patricia Jackson (Jamaica), Carol Johnson, Ken Jones, the late Dr. John Laffin, Brian Little, Tony 'Squirrel' Nutkins, Dave Pain, Col. Graham Parker, Paul 'Nationwide' Smith, the late Ted Smith and the late Tony Spagnoly, Jennifer Spooner, Sandra Taylor, Colin & Geraldine Ward, Sylvia Watkins, my many colleagues 'in the job' who over the years have supplied copious quantities of notes and peripheral information gleaned from personal research and war memorials throughout the length and breadth of the British Isles, and – too numerous to mention – the many visitors I have had the pleasure to meet who kindly entrusted their stories to me in Flanders Fields.

In the years it took to compile and prepare this work, the like of which has never been attempted before, there were many times when it became necessary to call on local assistance – 'over there.' Particularly deserving of special mention: Dries Chaerle and Jacques Ryckebosch whose combined knowledge of the region, the obscure and little known is second to none. And 'Brother' Bart Engelen and An 'Girly' Van Der Smissen who, in response to many email (and postal) enquiries, always managed to find time out to visit (sometimes in atrocious weather) various sites, accurately recording and promptly supplying the information required. And, on my visits willingly continue to accompany me on my travels.

And finally, a special thank you to Laura Hirst and Jonathan Wright, Pen & Sword, for their support, interest, advice and attention throughout the seemingly unending days of editing, proof-reading, checking and cross-checking, embedding, the bits and pieces here and there that necessitated more than one delay: All this (and more) would have exhausted the patience of a saint. I thank you both.

Every reasonable effort has been made to trace copyright holders, but if there are any errors or omissions, the publishers will be pleased to insert the appropriate acknowledgement in any subsequent printings or editions.

Paul Chapman
January 2016

Ypres (Menin Gate) Memorial South

Who will Remember, passing through this Gate,
The unheroic dead who fed the guns?
Who shall absolve the foulness of their fate,-
Those doomed, conscripted, unvictorious ones?

Crudely renewed the Salient holds its own.
Paid are its dim defenders by this pomp;
Paid, with a pile of peace-complacent stone,
The armies who endured that sullen swamp.

Here was the world's worst wound. And here with pride,
'Their name liveth forever', the Gateway claims.
Was ever immolation so belied
As these intolerably nameless names?
Well might the Dead who struggled in the slime
Rise and deride this sepulchre of crime.

Siegfried Sassoon

Ypres (now known as Ieper) is one of the oldest towns in Flanders, indeed, eight centuries ago it was the greatest of them. Through changes in trade and industry, political disruptions, sieges and many changes of occupying powers, it decayed and lost importance.

By 1914 Ypres was, comparatively, one of the smaller towns of Belgian West Flanders; linked by canals and railways to the nearby French border and the coast. The town was situated in flat, intensively cultivated country, encircled by a low range of hills running from Kemmel in the southwest to Godewaersvelde and Cassel. To the north and east, a series of ridges, later known as the Pilckem, Passchendaele and Bellewaarde / Menin Road Ridges. In 1905 the town was described as dead, a ghost town, a cemetery, deserted of trade and industry; its only purpose, to guard its great and grandiose buildings for posterity. The town's defensive ramparts, built by Louis XIV's architect Vauban, were modernized by the Dutch Government prior to Belgian independence in 1830, and after being almost totally dismantled by the Belgian Government in 1854, remain only as two wide promenades on the eastern and southern sides.

There were two main gateways: the Lille Gate (Rijselsepoort) which retains its defensive flanking towers, and the Menin Gate (Meensepoort) which was only ever a passage between two wall ends.

Before the Great War was eighteen months old, Fabian Ware, founder and head of the Forces Graves Registration Unit, later to become the Imperial (now Commonwealth) War Graves Commission (CWGC), foresaw that there would come a time when the need would arise for memorials recording the names of the missing. The Graves Registration Unit saw the daily casualty lists and witnessed first-hand the destruction by subsequent fighting, of burial sites previously documented.

I should like us to acquire the whole of the ruins of Ypres. ... A more sacred place for the British race does not exist in the world.

Winston Churchill

At the end of the First World War Winston Churchill proposed the ruins of Ypres be left as a permanent memorial, a kind of Pompeii, in everlasting testimony to the destruction and sacrifice of war; further proposing that if the town were rebuilt it should be sited outside of its then boundaries. It was Churchill's sole decision that decided the largest 'British Memorial to the Missing' in the Ypres salient be situated where the Hangoart, or Antwerp, Gate had once been. Other sites suggested included Lille Gate and the 'Small Island.'

The Menin Gate set the standard for all other Commission memorials to the missing because at each stage of the planning for the Gate, problems arose that rebounded on other Commission plans. The Menin Gate was designed to accommodate up to 60,000 names, but it soon became evident that one memorial would not suffice for the Ypres salient. A second site was chosen at Tyne Cot (the largest CWGC cemetery in the world – 11,908 burials), and to commemorate the missing of the fighting in the Franco-Belgian border sector, the decision was taken to site a third memorial at Ploegsteert near Armentieres. The reshuffling of plans was due partly to geographical location, but mostly to the casualty figures – missing – that arose during the Battle of Messines and Third Ypres (Passchendaele) in 1917.

It should be borne in mind that the Indian Army figures and names recorded on the Menin Gate are not wholly representative, as their army records were inaccurately kept. Moreover, the Indian government, whilst wishing some form of commemoration for missing Indians, such as were known, requested they not be commemorated on a memorial outside of Europe. In the end some 13,500 names were saved for posterity by the construction and *engravure* of a memorial arch in Delhi, designed by Sir Edwin Lutyens.

The most direct route taken by the British soldier to the front line of the Ypres salient was the Menin Road. For those that knew this route it was both the road to Hell and 'Via Sacra.' Many of those who passed through here would have seen two stone lions flanking either side of the road; these were later donated to Australia in recognition of that young country's part in the defence of Ypres; they now reside in the National War Memorial, Canberra. Therefore, it is quite significant (yet indicative of the British Empire) that a recumbent lion, sculpted by Sir William Reid Dick, is situated atop the Menin Gate gazing serenely out across the salient. Situated on the 'town side' of the Gate; a sculpted, wreathed and flag-draped sarcophagus, signifying burial, 'and to remind the citizens of Ypres of the sacrifices made for them by the British Empire.' Beneath each sculpture a text reads:

TO THE ARMIES OF THE BRITISH EMPIRE
WHO STOOD HERE FROM 1914 TO 1918
AND TO THOSE OF THEIR DEAD
WHO HAVE NO KNOWN GRAVE

The Menin Gate was designed by Sir Reginald Blomfield together with Sir Herbert Baker, Charles Holden and Sir Edwin Lutyens; the four most highly respected British architects of the day. Lutyens, designer of the National War Memorial, The Cenotaph, Whitehall, was at the time heavily involved in the design and construction of the many military cemeteries, and the Thiepval Memorial to the Missing of the Somme battles. Sir Reginald Blomfield, born in London in 1856 to a family of clergy, studied architecture and art at Exeter College, Oxford, during the course of which he made a three-month study trip through France and Spain, where the Neo Gothic styles he encountered made little impression on him, whereas the linear qualities of Renaissance and classical architecture inspired him to such a degree that he often adopted them in his own works. Publishing a number of architectural books, he found employment in London where he designed a number of different buildings; his style noticeable by his propensity for flat roofs, cupolas and red bricks. He designed both the entrance building and Cross of Sacrifice for Lijssenthoek Military Cemetery, Poperinghe. He died in London in 1942.

The construction of the Menin Gate was proposed as early as 1919 for an estimated £150,000 and although the British High Command was more than well acquainted with the famous Yperian clay, they had dug out over five miles of tunnels in the area for the Messines Offensive alone, local architect Jules Coomans was requested to provide a sample of earth from the proposed construction site. Blomfield described the running sand found when excavations began in 1923, 'The worst possible ground for foundations. ...' At a depth of 3.5 metres the skeletons of twenty-eight Yprian civilians were discovered. They had taken shelter in a small café 'De Oude Wacht' when it was hit and destroyed by a shell on 22 April 1915, killing all the occupants. Construction of the memorial was initially projected for ninety weeks to completion, but due mostly to the foundation problems encountered, the contractors D.G. Somerville & Co. almost went bankrupt when the Belgian franc was devalued in 1926, causing a number of the workers to cross the border into France where wages were considerably higher. At this point only the foundations had been laid, consisting of 500 concrete pillars set 12 metres deep, capped by a 500 ton steel reinforced concrete raft. But after replenishing the workforce, construction of the monument continued and was completed using 6,000 tons of bricks, Euville stone, and 11,000 tons of white Portland cement. Each column bearing the Gate itself weighs 4 tons and the fascia stones between 4 and 8 tons apiece. The Portland Stone panels, carved by 120 stonemasons of the firm of Messrs A. Burslem & Sons, of Tunbridge Wells, Kent, number in excess of 1,200, in 30 different sizes. Prior to being shipped to Belgium and placed in-situ (by Ypres stonemasons De Plancke) they were erected, for perspective, on scaffolding at 82 Baker Street, London. Weighing in excess of 20,000 tons, the Menin Gate, from ground level to the top of the lion stands 25 metres high; the arches 9.5 metres wide and 14.8 metres high. The 'Hall of Memory', 36.5 metres long and 20 metres wide, is covered in by a coffered, half–elliptical arch, in a single span. The overall length of the memorial is 42.5 metres. The internal staircase arches measure 3.5 metres wide by 7 metres high. Above the entrance to the southern staircase is inscribed, 'Here are recorded names of officers and men who fell in Ypres Salient but to whom the fortunes of war denied the known and honoured burial given to their comrades in death' and 'They shall receive a crown of glory that fadeth not away' above the northern. At each corner two enormous Doric columns atop bloc form footings give access to pedestrian pathways above which, left and right, they are surmounted by entablatures inscribed 'Pro Patria' (For Kingdom) and 'Pro Rege' (For King).

'He is not missing. He is here.'

Sir Hubert Plumer

The Menin Gate was officially inaugurated on 24 July 1927, in a ceremony led by Sir Hubert Plumer in the presence of King Albert of the Belgians, British Ambassador Sir George Grahame, and M. Albert le Brun, President of France. Approximately 40,000 ex-British and Empire servicemen and women were in attendance including 700 mothers who had travelled courtesy of the St. Barnabas Hostels Association. The Archbishop of Canterbury composed a special prayer for the occasion. The ceremony was broadcast live by a contingent from the BBC. 'Last Post' was sounded by buglers of the Shropshire Light Infantry followed by 'Flowers of the Forest' played by pipers of 1st Battalion, Scots Guards.

'Then came a terrible minute of silence – a silence so absolute that it seemed as if the whole Salient must be standing hushed in prayer. ... As always, before the long minute was up it grew almost unendurable and the crash of bugles in the Reveille came as an immense relief. The Brabanconne was played, and then came a quite ineffaceable moment when once again the roll of British drums went out from the Menin Gate and the company sang God Save the King. They always make one shudder, those drums. But here, at such a place and in such surroundings, the splendour and the terror of them were beyond words.'

The Times

The memorial lists the names of officers and men, by date of death, regiment and rank of all British Dominion forces who fell in defence of Ypres, with the exception of New Zealand, whose missing are recorded at other locations. Of the 54,896 (this is the official figure excluding the addenda panels detailing approximately another 1,000) names listed here, there were initially believed to be 96 anomalies: 18 names of men listed or commemorated elsewhere by either burial or memorial (this figure is now known to be considerably higher) and 78 minor spelling mistakes. There was another error; a veteran who visited here after 1927 was surprised to find his name and details recorded – this has since been corrected!

During the First Battle of Ypres, late 1914, the Royal Welch Fusiliers suffered such enormous casualties they, quite literally, almost ceased to exist, and most of their bodies were lost due to shell-fire; their names are preserved here for posterity.

A unique soldier is recorded here – Pte. J. Smith, the Black Watch; his service number, '1'.

Captain Bruce Bairnsfather, officer and cartoonist, of the 6th Battalion Royal Warwickshire Regt., served in the Ypres salient. During his time here he created the famous walrus moustached character 'Old Bill' of 'If you knows of a better 'ole, go to it!' fame. The inspiration for 'Old Bill' can be found at the bottom of the Warwicks panel – L/Corpl. Thomas 'Pat' H. Rafferty. Other names with a literary connection include the poets, Lieut. Walter Scott-Lyon, Royal Scots and Lieut. John Collinson Hobson, MGC.; 2nd Lieut. William 'Billy' Grenfell, Rifle Brigade (brother of poet Julian Grenfell), 2nd Lieut. Arthur O. Hornung, 3rd attd. 2nd Bn. Essex Regiment, 6 July 1915 (son of E.W. Hornung, creator of *'Raffles'* and nephew of A. Conan-Doyle).

On 4 July 1917 the 7th Bn. King's (Liverpool) Regiment sent out a patrol commanded by Lieut. Aidan Chavasse. Lieut. Chavasse and eight other ranks were to patrol no man's land and report on the enemy trenches. Nearing the German wire they were fired upon by an enemy patrol, which was also out, and Lieut. Chavasse was wounded. This lieutenant was left in a shell hole covering the withdrawal of his men whilst they returned to their lines to summon assistance. Later a thorough search was made for the lieutenant, but no trace of him could be found. Exactly one month to the day later, his elder brother, Capt. Noel Chavasse, died and was posthumously awarded a Bar to his Victoria Cross (Noel is buried in nearby Brandhoek New Military Cemetery). Aidan Chavasse's name is near to the top of the panel commemorating the King's (Liverpool) Regiment. Incidentally, Edith Chavasse, their mother never accepted the fact that Aidan was dead; every year on the anniversary of his being reported 'missing' she heard him, in her sleep, calling to her across no man's land. On the tenth anniversary of his 'disappearance' Aidan called to her for the last time – Edith joined her beloved son.

There are seven holders of the Victoria Cross recorded here: – (Panel 24) L/Corpl. F. Fisher, Quebec Regt.; (Panel 3) Brigdr. Gen. C. Fitzclarence, Irish Guards; (Panel 24) Sergt.Major F.W. Hall, Manitoba Regt.; (Panel 35) 2nd Lieut. D.G.W. Hewitt, Hampshire Regt.; (Panel 35) Capt. J.F. Vallentin, South Staffordshire Regt.; (Panel 33) Pte. E. Warner, Bedfordshire Regt., and (Panel 46) 2nd Lieut. S.C. Woodroffe, Rifle Brigade. And three men who were executed: – Driver T. Moore, 24 Div. Train A.S.C. – shot for murder, Corpl. G. Povey, Cheshire Regiment and Pte. W. Scotton, Middlesex Regiment – both shot for desertion.

During the Second World War Ypres was occupied by the Germans and Adolf Hitler, whilst visiting the sector in which he had served over twenty years previously, passed through the Menin Gate and raised his arm in the characteristic Nazi salute in recognition of the dead recorded here; an act unrepeated anywhere else in occupied Europe. Also during WW2, a story, albeit unsubstantiated, relates a drunken German soldier, caught while in the act of urinating on the memorial, was promptly arrested by two SS officers who were drinking in a bar opposite, and shortly thereafter, found himself on the next transport to the Russian Front.

Visiting Ypres on 17 May 1985, during his famous world tour, prior to conducting a Mass on the Grote Markt, Pope John Paul II requested his driver stop beneath the Menin Gate. Alighting from the vehicle His Holiness ascended the steps of the northern portico where he knelt and kissed the floor. An engraving commemorates this act.

> *"What are you guarding, Man-at-Arms?*
> *Why do you watch and wait?"*
> *"I guard the graves," said the Man-at-Arms,*
> *"I guard the graves by Flanders Farms,*
> *Where the dead will rise at my call to arms,*
> *And march to the Menin Gate."*

When do they march then, Man-at-Arms?
Cold is the hour and late."
"They march tonight," said the Man-at-Arms,
"With the moon on the Menin Gate.
They march when the midnight bids them go,
With their rifles slung and their pipes aglow,
Along the roads – the roads they know,
The road to the Menin Gate."

"What are they singing Man-at-Arms
As they march to the Menin Gate?"
"The marching songs," said the Man-at-Arms,
"That let them laugh at Fate;
No more will the night be cold for them,
For the last tattoo has rolled for them;
And their souls will sing as old, for them,
As they march to the Menin Gate."

Anon.

In November 1929 the nightly 'Last Post' ceremony began. Every evening at 20.00 hours, 'Last Post' is sounded in commemoration of all who fell in Ypres Salient during the Great War. From its inception, it has continued virtually uninterrupted; the exception being the Second World War, when it ceased on the evening of 28 May 1940; beginning anew on 6 September 1944, the day Ypres was liberated by the Polish Army (the tradition was kept at Brookwood Cemetery, near London, during the occupation). The Buglers are mostly members of the local *Brandweer*: their forebears were taught the style in which they play 'Last Post' by the late Dick Collick, a Great War veteran and ex-IWGC gardener. Between 'Last Post' and 'Reveille' the 'Exhortation' (an extract from Laurence Binyon's poem 'For The Fallen') is given and a two-minute silence observed.

They shall grow not old, as we that are left grow old:
Age shall not weary them, nor the years condemn.
At the going down of the sun and in the morning
We will remember them.

Every year on Armistice Day, November 11, there is a 'Poppy Parade' through the town. Beginning in Van de Peerbloomplaats, between St Martin's Cathedral and St. George's Church, it makes its way slowly towards the Menin Gate, where all those participating in the Services of Remembrance are allocated places, forming one enormous congregation beneath the great arch of the Gate, which takes on a cathedral-like atmosphere (whether taking part in the ceremonies, or just attending out of respect; this is possibly the most evocative ceremony one will ever witness). Towards the end of the ceremonies, the hymns '*O Valiant Hearts*' and '*Abide With Me*' are sung during the course of which a million poppy petals, each one symbolizing a life given, are released from the roof to float down, softly carpeting the Menin Road, blood red.

If I should die, think only this of me:
That there's some corner of a foreign field
That is forever England. There shall be
In that rich earth a richer dust concealed;
A dust whom England bore, shaped, made aware,
Gave, once, her flowers to love, her ways to roam,
A body of England's, breathing English air,
Washed by the rivers, blest by suns of home.

Rupert Brooke

PANEL 2 BEGINS – JEMADAR KIRPA SINGH, 57TH WILDE'S RIFLES

Of all the regiments of the Indian Army, the Gurkhas were perhaps the most charismatic, and it was widely acknowledged that they regarded themselves as the elite of the country's military contingent. They were (and still are) tough fighters, particularly proud of their prowess and skill with their kukris; those lethal weapons whose curved blades were honed razor sharp and which, in the opinion of the Gurkhas, were miles better than any other weapon. Their almost irresponsible bravery and predilection for the use of this weapon was enough to strike fear into the heart of even the most resolute foe. One of their biggest problems in the wet and muddy landscape of Flanders were the trenches – the average Gurkha stands five feet three inches tall – being forced to stand on tip-toe in order to fire over the parapet in many instances. They hated shellfire as much as soldiers of any nationality, and they could not understand why they had to sit still under it without retaliation of a personal and murderous type. Killing Germans was what they were there for, and kill Germans was what they intended to do. But, their British officers, who also disliked shell fire, assured them that there would be ample opportunity for close and gory work with the kukri before long – and so it turned out to be. Particularly adept at scouting and patrolling, when they finally did meet the enemy in the alien landscape of Flanders, they took great delight in creeping up undetected to a German outpost, getting to grips with the enemy in hand-to hand combat, and dispatching him with a swift, silent swipe of the kukri. However, whilst second to none in this type of fighting, the Gurkhas, like every other unit of both sides, had no solution to the crossing of the bullet-swept killing zone of No Man's Land.

Following the abortive attack of 27th April 1915, on 1st May, 1st and 4th Gurkhas were ordered to renew the assault against the strong German position on Mauser Ridge. Advancing with great determination, at a range of 150 yards from their objective both battalions came under devastating machine gun and artillery fire. Two small parties of 4th Gurkhas, having managed to reach the German wire found it untouched by the preparatory British artillery fire preceding the attack. In frustration the gallant Nepalese tried to hack a path through the entanglements, with their beloved kukris reduced to little more than ineffective wire-cutters. The outcome was inevitable, the Gurkhas were cut down piecemeal; their bleeding and torn bodies hanging dead on the wire; among them:–

(Panel 2) Rfn. 4579, Ran Bahadur Bura, 1st Bn. 4th Prince of Wales' Own Gurkha Rifles, Indian Army: *s.* of Gauria Bura, of Huldi, Palpa, Parval, Nepal. Killed in action 1 May 1915

On 25 April 1915, after a hurried twenty-three mile march up to the salient from the region of Neuve Chapelle, the Lahore Division were given very little time to nurse their tired bodies and aching bodies, not to mention their blistered feet. Within twenty-four hours they were thrown into an attack on the right flank of the French Army above St. Jean. Although the attacking infantry did not realise it, the German positions were between 1,500 and 2,000 yards distant, across gently upward sloping fields for 500 yards to Hill Top Ridge – where knee-deep wheatfields, divided by dry ditches and small hedgerows – sloped down to a stream lined with willow trees, before gently rising up across open ground to the Mauser Ridge where the Germans were firmly entrenched. At 14.05 hrs., with ineffective artillery support of their own, the Indians came under enemy artillery fire almost as soon as they began to advance, and, as they crested Hill Top Ridge, the enemy's machine-gunners and riflemen cut them down in scores. German aircraft, with no British machines to harass them, were able to supply accurate details to their artillery batteries and, as the infantry moved down the slope, shells filled with lachrymatory gas began to fall, and the men of the Indian Corps having received no anti-gas instruction began to suffer increasing casualties from these also. Battalions became hopelessly intermingled, French, British, Indian, under the command of whoever happened to the most senior began digging themselves in, scraping out hollows in the ground, desperate to obtain whatever shelter they could find from the fire decimating their ranks. By 14.30 the advance had ground to a virtual standstill, and at 15.00 hrs the attack was cancelled. In this short space of time the Lahore Division had suffered over 1,200 killed or wounded. Incredibly, 57th Wilde's, in the centre of the Ferozepore Brigade's attack, managed to get to within 80 yards of the German positions, but their losses – 3 British officers, 3 Indian officers, 36 Indian Other Ranks killed, 4 British officers, 7 Indian officers, 215 Indian Other Ranks wounded – had virtually annihilated them:–

(Panel 2) Major Francis Taylor Duhan, 19th Punjabis, late 19th (Punjab) Bengal Infantry, attd. 57th Wilde's Rifles (Frontier Force), Indian Army: 4th *s.* of the late Harry Reilly Duhan: and brother to Col. W.T.T. Duhan, Royal Artillery: *b.* Calcutta, India, 3 January 1873: *educ.* Bedford Grammar School, DeParys Road, Bedford, where he was Head Boy, and Royal Military College, Sandhurst: gazetted 2nd Lieut., Unattd. List, Indian Army, October 1894: trained with the Hampshire Regt., afterwards joining 24th Punjabis, January 1896, subsequently transf'd. 19th Punjabis: promoted Lieut. January 1897: saw Active Service, 1897 – 98, on the North-West Frontier of India, being present at the Relief of Malakand, and Chakdara, the action at Landakai, and operations in the Bajaur, and Mohmand country: Medal, two clasps: promoted Capt. October 1903, served in Tibet: Medal: again on the North West Frontier 1908, taking part in operations in the Mohmand country: Medal with clasp: received his Majority October 1912. For Active Service in the Great War he was attached to 57th Wilde's Rifles (Frontier Force), and was killed in action 26 April 1915, near Ypres. Buried where he fell. He was a member of the United Service Club, a good cricketer, and a great fisherman: Age 42.

(Panel 2) Capt. Leonard De Lona Christopher, 40th Pathans, Indian Army: elder *s.* of Major-Gen. Leonard William Christopher, C.B., Indian Army (ret'd.), of Harcourt House, Camberley, co. Surrey, by his wife Florence, 4th *dau.* of the late Major-Gen. Charles Stuart Lane, C.B., and *gdson.* of the late Major-Gen. Leonard Raisbeck Christopher: *b.* Mansfield, Iver Heath, co. Bucks, 21 October 1883: *educ.* Wellington College, Crowthorne; and Royal Military College, Sandhurst: gazetted 2nd Lieut. North Staffordshire Regt., then in India, 9 January 1904: promoted Lieut. 2 March 1905, being transf'd. Indian Army, posted 40th Pathans, same month: obtained his Captaincy, 9 January 1913; Adjutant 12 April 1911 – April 1915, and took part in the operations in the Mohmand country (Medal with clasp) 1908. On the outbreak of the European War he came home with his regt., served in France and Flanders, and was killed in action in the Second Battle of Ypres 26 April 1915: Age 31. Buried in a farm three-quarters of a mile north-east of the village of St. Jean. His Colonel wrote, "The regt. was in the first line of attack, and had to cross over open ground for over 1,000 yards under a fearful fire of machine-guns and shells, both front and flank. A native officer of ours, near him, loosened his belt for him, and Chris said 'Mehbrahni' and died. He performed his duty nobly to the end." And a brother officer, "He was dearly loved in the regt., and died a very gallant death at the head of his men, and helped to make the regt. he loved so well famous in that reckless charge." Capt. Christopher *m.* East Barnet, co. Herts, 4 June 1913; Edith Marian, 4th *dau.* of Albert Robinson Bulman, of Trevor Hall, East Barnet, co. Herts, late Indian Civil Service.

PANEL 2 ENDS – BUGLER ZAMAN ALI, 40TH PATHANS

PANEL 2A BEGINS – MAJOR L.J. JONES, 9TH BHOPAL INFANTRY.

During the operations of the Ferozepore Brigade on the afternoon of 26 April 1915, 9th Bhopals had been in support and, having taken relatively few casualties, were warned for a night attack in conjunction with 15th Sikhs (Jullunder Brigade) and 1/4th Gurkhas (Sirhind Brigade), with the objective of linking up with Major Deacon, Connaught Rangers, who with a small group of men was holding out somewhere to the north. Just before 9.00 p.m., after a good deal of stumbling about in the dark, including finding themselves in a re-entrant overlooked on both sides by the Germans who were fortunately asleep, contact was made with Major Deacon. Unfortunately, there was no real idea as to the exact whereabouts of the main enemy positions, other than they were somewhere on the ridge in front protected by uncut wire. Armed with this information Brigade Headquarters ordered the attack should not be pressed further until the following day. Not that any of this would have concerned Capt. Etlinger; he was one of the 'relatively few casualties' incurred in the supports during the afternoon.

(Panel 2A) Capt. Henry Etlinger, 9th Bhopal Infantry, Indian Army: 4th *s.* of Edmund Etlinger, of Dublin, Civil Engineer, by his wife Charlotte Kincaid: and nephew to Gen. Kincaid, Indian Civil Service, and Joseph Kincaid, Civil Engineer, Westminster, London: *b.* 27, Cavendish Road West, London, S.W., 27 April 1880: *educ.* Preparatory School, Brighton College; Marlborough College, where he was Captain of the School XI, 1897, and Trinity College, Dublin, where he was also in the XI: joined 3rd (Militia) Battn. North Staffordshire Regt. during the South African War; gazetted from the Militia, 2nd Lieut. North Staffordshire Regt., January 1902: took part in operations in Transvaal, May 1902: Queen's Medal, two clasps: promoted Lieut. Regular Army, April 1904, receiving that rank in his regiment February 1906: Battalion Adjt. October 1909 – October 1912: promoted Capt. R.A., January 1911; transf'd. Indian Army with that rank November 1912, having served in India for ten years: came to Europe with 9th Bhopal Infantry, Lahore Divn., after the outbreak of war with Germany: took part in the heavy fighting around Ypres, 26 – 27 April 1915, and on the latter date – his 35th birthday – Capt. Etlinger was killed in action. A brother officer wrote, "I…knew him for the past two years, but never knew a better. I am unable to give you exact details of his death, but he was found in the trenches by one of our men, and an officer was on the spot immediately and applied first aid. He was quite unconscious, as the bullet had struck him in the head. He died right nobly in the attack. I am seeing to his grave, and am having a cross made to mark the spot. He was a good all-round sportsman, having won cups in India for football, tennis, and cricket, and was a member of the Junior Army and Navy Club. He was married to Miss Muriel Jelf, and left no family: Age 35.

PANEL 2A ENDS – FOLLOWER, SHEONARAIN TEWARI.

PANEL 4 BEGINS – PTE. T.S. LEIGH, KING'S LIVERPOOL REGT.

(Panel 4) Pte. 49763, Willie Lowe, 1/9th Bn. The King's (Liverpool) Regt. (T.F.): *s.* of Mr (& Mrs) Lowe, 2, Salmon Street, Sheffield, co. York: enlisted Sheffield. Killed in action 2 August 1917: Age 24. *unm.*

(Panel 4) Pte. 3076, Brisco Francis MacSwiney, 1/10th (Scottish) Bn. The King's (Liverpool) Regt. (T.F.): *s.* of Lieut.Col. Eugene Valentine MacSwiney, Royal Army Medical Corps, by his wife Florence Mary (7, Arnside Road, Oxton, Liverpool): and elder brother to Capt. J.R. MacSwiney, M.C., 10th King's (Liverpool) Regt., died 2 November 1918, at home; and Bmdr. 50762, D.Q. MacSwiney, Royal Field Artillery, died 20 March 1916, of wounds: *b.* Malta: a pre-war Territorial, undertook Imperial Service Obligations, Fraser Street, Liverpool: served with the Expeditionary Force in France from November 1914, and was killed in action 16 June 1915: Age 30.

His brother Joseph is buried in Birkenhead (Flaybrick Hill) Cemetery (2.R.C.23); Denis, Brandhoek Military Cemetery (I.J.10).

(Panel 4) Pte. 49766, Harold Mather, 1/9th Bn. The King's (Liverpool) Regt. (T.F.): formerly no.16927, Duke of Wellington's (West Riding) Regt.: *b.* Barnsley, co. York: enlisted Leeds. Died of wounds 2 August 1917.

(Panel 4) Pte. 2781, John William Mountford, 1/6th Bn. (Rifles) The King's (Liverpool) Regt. (T.F.): *s.* of the late James Mountford, by his wife Hannah: and late *husb.* to Muriel Mountford (35, Cowley Road, Uxbridge, co. Middlesex), late of Anfield, Liverpool: enlisted Liverpool: served with the Expeditionary Force in France from 25 February 1915, and was killed in action 26 March 1915, the only fatality incurred by his battalion that day: Age 25. Remains 'Unknown British Soldier' recovered unmarked grave (28.I.28.d.9.9); identified – Clothing, Titles; reinterred, registered 19 September 1927. *Buried in Sanctuary Wood Cemetery (IV.G.13).*

Dearly Loved Husband Of Muriel Mountford
Thy Will Be Done

(Panel 4) Pte. 2487, William Nicol, 'H' Coy., 1/10th Bn. (Scottish) The King's (Liverpool) Regt. (T.F.): formerly no.255, Royal Engineers (T.F.): *s.* of Alexander Nicol, of 133, Wistaston Road, Crewe, by his wife Louisa: enlisted Crewe, co. Chester: served with the Expeditionary Force in France and Flanders from November 1914. Reported missing after the fighting at Hooge 16 June 1915; believed killed: Age 22. *unm.*

(Panel 4) Pte. 33261, Andrew O'Shea, 1/9th Bn. The King's (Liverpool) Regt. (T.F.): formerly no.3573, Manchester Regt.: *s.* of T. (& Mrs M.) O'Shea, of 4, Olive Street, Ducal Street, Newtown, Manchester. Killed in action 8 February 1917: Age 23. *unm.* Buried Moston (St. Joseph's) Roman Catholic Cemetery (St. Anthony's Sect. 1976).

(Panel 4) Rfn. 2633, John Phillingham, 1/6th Bn. (Rifles) The King's (Liverpool) Regt. (T.F.): *s.* of the late Andrew Phillingham, by his wife Margaret (111, Bagot Street, Wavertree, Liverpool): enlisted Liverpool. Killed in action 24 March 1915 Buried nr. where he fell. Cross erected: Age 19. Remains 'Unknown British Soldier' recovered marked grave (28.I.28.d.9.9); identified – Burial Cross, Titles; reinterred, registered 19 September 1927. *Buried in Sanctuary Wood Cemetery (IV.G.12).*

(Panel 4) Pte. 57824, Thomas Bowerbank Pyburn, 19th (Service) Bn. The King's (Liverpool) Regt.: formerly no.429, Army Cyclists Corps: *s.* of Annie Pyburn, *née* Bowerbank (111, High Street, Carrville, Durham), and the late Philip Pyburn: *b.* Belmont, 1890: *educ.* Model School, Durham; Johnston Technical School (scholarship pupil); and Dundee Training College (1910 – 12) where he gained a 1st Class Certificate enabling him to enter Hettons Lyons Council School, as Student / Trainee Schoolmaster: enlisted Durham; proceeded to France mid-November 1916, and was killed in action 23 July 1917: Age 26. His Officer wrote, "He was killed by a direct hit from a shell, and as he died a soldier's death was given a soldier's grave, being buried by his comrades. He was one of the old boys of the Regiment, having been with us for some time."

(Panel 4) Pte. 51920, Frederick Rugen, 17th (Service) Bn. (1st City) The King's (Liverpool) Regt.: *s.* of H.E. (& Mrs) Rugen, of 42, Curate Road, Clubmoor, Liverpool: and brother to Pte. 46448, G. Rugen, South Wales Borderers, killed in action 11 April 1918, aged 19 years: *b.* Liverpool: enlisted there. Killed in action 31 July 1917, east of Stirling Castle.

His brother George also has no known grave; he is commemorated on the Ploegsteert Memorial (Panel 5).

(Panel 4) Pte. 14666, Joseph Southern, 12th (Service) Bn. The King's (Liverpool) Regt.: 9th *s.* of Thomas Southern, by his wife Annie (3, Rushton Place, Allerton Road, Woolton, Liverpool), *dau.* of William Byron: and yr. brother to Pte. R/4736, E. Southern, 19th (Queen Alexandra's Own Royal) Hussars, died 15 February 1916; and Pte. 25155, R. Southern, 1st King's Liverpool Regt., died 12 February 1919: *b.* Woolton, 24 March 1892: *educ.* there: Occupation – Gardener: enlisted Seaforth, co. Lancaster, 2 September 1914: served with the Expeditionary Force in France and Flanders, and was killed in action 9 April 1916. Buried at Ypres. An officer wrote, "Your son has done splendid work with the battalion, and his death is deeply deplored.": Age 24. *unm.*

His brother Edward is commemorated in Kensal Green (All Soul's) Cemetery (Screen Wall, 213.9.11); Robert is buried in Terlincthun British Cemetery, Wimille (XIII.C.38).

(Panel 4) Pte. 332556, Frank Tonge, 1/9th Bn. The King's (Liverpool) Regt. (T.F.): formerly no. 43235, Royal Welch Fusiliers: *s.* of Charles Tonge, of 80, Milton Street, Patricroft, Manchester, by his wife Sarah: enlisted Swinton. Killed in action 2 August 1917: Age 28. All personal effects and correspondence relating to the deceased should be forwarded to his widow, Annie Tonge (36, Bingham Street, Swinton, Manchester).

(Panel 4) Rfn. 49832, John Wark, 'D' Coy., 1/5th Bn. The King's (Liverpool) Regt. (T.F.): formerly no.16979, Duke of Wellington's (West Riding) Regt.: *s.* of Matthew Wark, of Astley Old Engine, Woodlesford, Leeds, by his wife Bertha: and brother to Pte. 44227, J. Wark, 27th Northumberland Fusiliers, died 29 April 1917, of wounds; and (his twin) Rfn. 49831, S. Wark, 1/5th King's (Liverpool) Regt., who fell one week previously: enlisted Leeds. Killed in action 31 July 1917: Age 26. *unm.*

His twin brother James is buried in Duisans British Cemetery, Etrun (III.H.6); Samuel has no known grave, he is recorded below.

(Panel 4) Rfn. 49831, Samuel Wark, 'A' Coy., 1/5th Bn. The King's (Liverpool) Regt. (T.F.): formerly no.16978, Duke of Wellington's (West Riding) Regt.: *s.* of Matthew Wark, of Astley Old Engine, Woodlesford, Leeds, by his wife Bertha: and brother to Pte. 44227, J. Wark, 27th Northumberland Fusiliers, died 29 April 1917, of wounds; and (his twin) Rfn. 49832, J. Wark, 1/5th King's (Liverpool) Regt., who fell one week later: enlisted Leeds. Killed in action 24 July 1917: Age 26. *unm.*

His twin brother James is buried in Duisans British Cemetery, Etrun (III.H.6); John has no known grave, he is recorded above.

(Panel 4) Lieut. Zouch Austin Turton, 3rd (Reserve) Bn. The Norfolk Regt. attd. 2nd Bn. (15th Foot) The East Yorkshire Regt.: eldest *s.* of the Rev. Zouch Horace Turton, formerly of 38, Primrose Mansions, Battersea Park, London, S.W.; formerly (for nearly 25 years) Vicar of St. Mary's, Southtown, Great Yarmouth, co. Norfolk; currently resident at 'Morsecot,' Lindon Avenue, Broadstairs, co. Kent, by his wife Alice Clara Elizabeth, *née* Austin. Although his father is in Holy Orders, Mr Turton is a descendant of a military family, both his grandfathers – Col. Edward Griffin Austin and Col. Joseph Turton – were in the Bengal Artillery, his only surviving uncle is Lieut.Col. Turton, D.S.O., late Royal Engineers; his maternal uncle, Col. G.B. Austin, late Indian Army, died November 1915: *b.* Hackleton Vicarage, nr. Northampton, 26 May 1886: gazetted 2nd Lieut. 3rd Norfolk Regt. 1905, intending to proceed into the Regular Army, but, owing to defective sight in one eye, this wish could not be realised at that time: went to Malay States, 1912, where he took up a successful career in the Rubber Plantation business, becoming manager of the Hong Kong Rubber Estate. Soon after the outbreak of war, much to the regret of his Directors, he resigned his position, and in due course rejoined his old battalion; Lieut. January 1915: served with the British Expeditionary Force in France attd. 2nd East Yorkshire Regt. On the afternoon of 23 April 1915 the Battalion was ordered to advance against some German trenches at Pilckem, nr. Ypres. Whilst leading his men to the attack Lieut. Turton was seen to fall seriously wounded and reported accordingly: subsequently reported 'missing;' after extensive enquiries, on 8 November 1915 he was unofficially reported as having been killed in action 23 April 1915: Age 28. *unm.* His younger brother Lieut. R.D. Turton, 9th York & Lancaster Regt., was killed in action at the Third Battle of Ypres 24 September 1917.

His brother Richard is buried in The Huts Cemetery (VII.A.5).

(Panel 4) Corpl. 3/8232, Horace Downes, 1st Bn. (9th Foot) The Norfolk Regt.: late *husb.* to Anna E. Downes (Wicklewood, Wymondham, co. Norfolk): *b.* Besthorpe, co. Norfolk, about 1872: enlisted Norwich. Killed in action 5 June 1915: Age 43. Remains 'Unknown British Corpl.' recovered unmarked grave (28.I.34.b.5.8); identified – 2 Medal Ribbons, Badge of Rank, Clothing; reinterred, registered 11 July 1927. *Buried in Sanctuary Wood Cemetery (IV.E.35).*

(Panel 4) L/Corpl. 3/7463, Joseph George Dixon, 1st Bn. (9th Foot) The Norfolk Regt.: *s.* of George Dixon, of 32, Hall Road, Norwich, by his wife Georgina: *b.* North Heigham: enlisted, 3rd (Reserve) Bn., Norwich: went to France with draft of reinforcements to 1st Bn., and was killed in action 5 May 1915, in the Ypres sector: Age 23. *unm.* Remains recovered; identified – Clothing, Disc; reinterred, registered 30 June 1927. *Buried in Sanctuary Wood Cemetery (IV.E.19).*

(Panel 4) L/Corpl. 8208, Charles Lamport, 1st Bn. (9th Foot) The Norfolk Regt.: *s.* of George Lamport, of 5, Stanley Villas, Shawfields, Ash, co. Surrey, by his wife Rose: and elder brother to 6900, A. Lamport, 23rd London Regt., killed in action 2 October 1916: *b.* 1881: enlisted Guildford: served with his regiment in India and, from 16 August 1914, in France and Flanders, and was killed in action 13 March 1915 at Ypres: Age 34.

His brother Arthur also has no known grave; he is commemorated on the Thiepval Memorial, Somme.

(Panel 4) Pte. 3/7438, Harry Butcher, 1st Bn. (9th Foot) The Norfolk Regt.: *s.* of Jonathan Butcher, of Fen Bank, Isleham, nr. Ely, co. Suffolk, by his wife Mary: and brother to Pte. 24488, D. Butcher, Northamptonshire Regt., killed in action 26 September 1916; and Pte. 30375, J.W. Butcher, Loyal North Lancashire Regt., killed in action 10 April 1918: and, by his sister's marriage, brother-in-law to Pte. 49148, H. Harvey, Royal Fusiliers, killed in action, vicinity Clapham Junction, 10 August 1917:

b. Isleham: enlisted Norwich, co. Norfolk: served with the Expeditionary Force in France and Flanders, and was killed in action 3 March 1915.

His brother David is buried in Vermelles British Cemetery (V.D.19), John is commemorated in Croix-du-Bac British Cemetery (Sp.Mem.A.3); brother-in-law Herbert has no known grave, he is recorded on the Menin Gate (Panel 6).

(Panel 4) Pte. 3/7976, Thomas Clabburn, 'B' Coy., 1st Bn. (9th Foot) The Norfolk Regt.: *s*. of Mrs M.A. Clabburn (1, Palace Yard, Barrack Street, Norwich): and brother to L/Corpl. 6260, W.J. Clabburn, Norfolk Regt., killed in action 27 July 1916: *b*. Islington, London, about 1877: enlisted Norwich: a pre-war Territorial, 3rd (Reserve) Battn., undertook Active Service obligations, transf'd. 1st Battn., proceeded to France, and was killed in action there 26 May 1915: Age 38. Pte. Clabburn leaves a widow, Mrs E. Clabburn (25, Palace Yard, Barrack Street, Norwich). *Buried in Sanctuary Wood Cemetery (IV.E.15)*.

His brother William also has no known grave; he is commemorated on the Thiepval Memorial, Somme.

(Panel 4) Pte. 14866, Harry Edwin Minns, 8th (Service) Bn. The Norfolk Regt.: *s*. of Harry Edwin Minns, of 3, Castle Lane, Bungay, co. Suffolk, by his wife Alice Victoria: and brother to Pte. 320242, C.W. Minns, 12th Norfolk Regt., killed in action 19 August 1918: *b*. Bungay: enlisted Norwich. Killed in action 11 August 1917: Age 23. *unm*.

His brother Charles is buried in Outtersteene Communal Cemetery Extension (II.C.58).

(Panel 4) Pte. 24211, Bertie Muteham, 8th (Service) Bn. The Norfolk Regt.: *s*. of George Muteham, of Thetford, co. Norfolk, by his wife Alice: and brother to Pte. 500993, G. Muteham, 435th Agricultural Coy., Labour Corps, died 20 December 1918, at home; and Pte. 104185, J. Muteham, Royal Fusiliers, died 4 March 1919: *b*. Thetford: enlisted Norwich. Killed in action 11 August 1917: Age 22. *unm*.

His brothers George and John are buried in Thetford Cemetery (I.M.565 / D.P.607).

(Panel 4) Pte. 5692, William Sanpher, 1st Bn. (9th Foot) The Norfolk Regt.: *s*. of Richard Jonas Sanpher, Farm Labourer; of Backhouse Lane, South Creake, Fakenham, by his wife Mary Ann Sanpher, *née* Shaul: and elder brother to Pte. 12898, A. Sanpher, 8th Norfolk Regt., killed in action 19 July 1916, at the Somme: *b*. South Creake, co. Norfolk: enlisted Colchester, co. Essex. Killed in action 21 April 1915; Hill 60, Ypres, Belgium: Age 31. Remembered on South Creake War Memorial.

His brother Arthur is buried in Sucrerie Military Cemetery, Colincamps (I.BB.49).

(Panel 4) Pte. 7021, Edgar Shearman, 1st Bn. (9th Foot) The Norfolk Regt.: *s*. of Mrs E.T. Shearman (Sugar Alms Houses, King's Lynn): late *husb*. to Jane E. Shearman (4, Wanford's Cottages, Wood Street, King's Lynn): and yr. brother to Corpl. 43723, E.T. Shearman, 8th Norfolk Regt., who fell 7 May 1917: served with the Expeditionary Force in France, and was killed in action 6 December 1914: Age 32.

His brother Edward is buried in Rookery British Cemetery, Heninel (C.28).

PANEL 4 ENDS – PTE. H.M. YOUNGS, NORFOLK REGT.

PANEL 6 BEGINS SERGT. S.E. WOODCOCK, ROYAL FUSILIERS.

(Panel 6) Corpl. SR/8364, Herbert Louis Johnson, 4th Bn. (7th Foot) The Royal Fusiliers (City of London Regt.): 2nd *s*. of the late H.L. Johnson, by his wife Alice Maud (44, Holly Street, Hackney, London, E.): *b*. Hackney: *educ*. Tottenham Road County Council School, Kingsland: enlisted Royal Fusiliers, 1908: served his time, and was called up on the outbreak of war August 1914: served with the Expeditionary Force in France and Flanders, and was killed in action at Hooge 16 June 1915. Buried where he fell. *unm*.

(Panel 6) Corpl. 14025, Albert Edward Napier, 3rd Bn. (7th Foot) The Royal Fusiliers (City of London Regt.): *s*. of James Napier, of Spinney House, Dunstable Road, Luton, co. Bedford, by his wife Ann: *b*. Kilburn, London, N.W.6: enlisted London. Killed in action 24 May 1915. One of seven brothers who served in the Great War.

(Panel 6) L/Corpl. 2092, James Belshaw, 1st Bn. (7th Foot) The Royal Fusiliers (City of London Regt.): *s.* of the late Sergt. 5668, H. Belshaw, 8th Royal Fusiliers: enlisted Brentford. Killed in action 31 July 1917.

His father Henry also has no known grave; he is commemorated on the Arras (Faubourg d'Amiens) Memorial (Bay 3).

(Panel 6) L/Corpl. 1/10277, Charles Chitty, 2nd Bn. (7th Foot) The Royal Fusiliers (City of London Regt.) attd. Oxford & Bucks Light Infantry: *s.* of William (& Mrs) Chitty, of 'Cliftonville', 6, Century Road, Staines, co. Middlesex: and elder brother to Pte. 11044, W. Chitty, East Surrey Regt., killed in action 8 May 1915: *b.* Chertsey, co. Surrey, *c.*1886: enlisted Staines: served with the Expeditionary Force, and died 29 September 1916, in Mesopotamia: Age 30. His widow, Alice Kate, has since remarried, now Mrs Hayhow (20, Princes Road, Jamalpur, Monghyr, Behar, India). Buried in Baghdad (North Gate) War Cemetery, Iraq (XXI.K.19).

His brother William has no known grave; he is recorded on Panel 34.

(Panel 6) L/Corpl. 60811, Richard Hammond, 12th (Service) Bn. The Royal Fusiliers (City of London Regt.): *s.* of the late Joseph Hammond, by his wife Annie, *dau.* of Richard Vaughan: *b.* Lambeth, London, S.E.: Occupation – Clerk: enlisted Royal Field Artillery, 13 May 1915: served with the Expeditionary Force in France and Flanders from October following: transf'd. Middlesex Regt.; subsequently Royal Fusiliers, and was killed in action 31 July 1917. An officer wrote, "He was a cheerful comrade, and an invaluable N.C.O." He *m.* St. Saviour's Church, Brixton, London, S.W., 11 August 1912; Mary (20, Pasley Road, Manor Place, Walworth, London, S.E.), *dau.* of Thomas Cox, and had a son, *b.* July 1913. (*IWGC record Pte.*)

(Panel 6) L/Corpl. 9611, Alfred Knight, 1st Bn. (7th Foot) The Royal Fusiliers (City of London Regt.): *b.* Whitechapel, London, E.: enlisted London. Killed in action 20 August 1915. Remains recovered 'Sanctuary Wood Old British Cemetery' (28.I.24.b.90.97) 'Unknown British Lance Corporal. Royal Fusiliers;' identified – Clothing, Titles, Badge of Rank; reinterred, registered 19 April 1928. Buried in Sanctuary Wood Cemetery (II.F.6).

(Panel 6) L/Corpl. L/12567, Leonard Alfred Lawrence, 4th Bn. (7th Foot) The Royal Fusiliers (City of London Regt.): served with the Expeditionary Force. Reported missing after the fighting at Zillebeke 10 November 1914; now assumed killed in action on that date.

(Panel 6) L/Corpl. 48340, Frank Pope, 26th (Service) Bn. (Bankers) The Royal Fusiliers (City of London Regt.): 5th *s.* of William Pope, of 25, Mikado Street, Penygraig, co. Glamorgan, by his wife Mary, *dau.* of John Conduit: and brother to Pte. 32719, A.W.H. Pope, 11th Welsh Regt., killed in action 14 November 1917, at Salonika; and Sergt. 8200, A.G. Pope, 7th King's (Shropshire Light Infantry), killed in action 21 August 1918, at Armentieres: *b.* Bridgwater, co. Somerset, 8 August 1889: *educ.* Tonypandy, co. Glamorgan: Occupation – Rider; Cambrian Collieries, Clydach Vale: enlisted Royal Army Medical Corps (no.46691) 18 October 1914: served with the Mediterranean Force at Gallipoli from April 1915; returned to England August following: proceeded to France the following month, where he served on a motor-ambulance: transf'd. Royal Fusiliers, November 1916: returned to England and underwent training at Dover: returned to France, and was killed in action at Ypres 7 June 1917. Buried in a shell hole at St. Eloi; 1½ miles west of Hollebeke, 2½ miles south of Ypres: Age 27. *unm.* (*IWGC record 46691*)

His brother Alfred is buried in Doiran Military Cemetery (VI.E.21); Arthur, Bucquoy Road Cemetery, Ficheux (VI.K.27).

(Panel 6) Pte. 9842, William John Alexander, 3rd Bn. (7th Foot) The Royal Fusiliers (City of London Regt.): *s.* of William John Alexander, Builder; of 336, Spring Road, Ipswich, by his wife Harriet, *dau.* of Edward Sharman: *b.* Ipswich, 15 February 1897: *educ.* St. Clement's School, Ipswich: Occupation – Surveyor's Office Messenger: enlisted 18 November 1914: served with the Expeditionary Force in France and Flanders from May 1915, and was killed at Ypres on the 24th of that month: 24 May 1915: Age 18.

(Panel 6) Pte. 9583, Ernest James Arnold, 1st Bn. (7th Foot) The Royal Fusiliers (City of London Regt.): late of Hayes End, co. Middlesex: enlisted Hounslow: served with the Expeditionary Force in France from September 1914, and was killed in action there 14 August 1915. Remains recovered unmarked grave 'Sanctuary Wood Old British Cemetery' (28.I.24.b.90.97) 'Unknown British Soldier. Royal Fusiliers;' identified – Clothing, Titles, No. on Underclothing; reinterred, registered 19 April 1928. *Buried in Sanctuary Wood Cemetery (II.F.8).*

Two days after moving up to the front near Klein Zillebeke, 32nd Royal Fusiliers 'had a strange experience on 5th August 1917. The Germans had delivered counter-attacks on various parts of the front, and on that day the blow fell to the left of the battalion front. At 4.10 a.m. the enemy barrage lifted and the Germans advanced under cover of fog and smoke bombs. Only half the front was involved; and there the attack was held up by rifle and machine-gun fire. But the Germans broke through the right flank of the battalion further north and a party of them got to the rear of the 32nd Royal Fusiliers. At mid-day it was ascertained that the enemy were holding 100 yards of Jehovah trench, which was sited in a strip of wood lying north of Klein Zillebeke road and some 500 yards east of the village. The situation was cleared up by the bold and decisive action of Major Robinson, Capt. H.L. Kirby and 2nd Lieut. G.W. Murrell, and when the battalion moved back on relief, the next day, the position was restored. Major Robinson led a few men against the German detachment who had got behind the centre post in the forward zone and succeeded in killing part of them and dispersing the rest.'

According to official records, on the day this 'strange experience' occurred 32nd Battalion suffered only one fatality; the action taken to restore the situation, however, cost the lives of 1 officer, and 37 other ranks who, with the exception of three, have no known grave.

(Panel 6) Pte. 66757, Thomas William Astle, 32nd (Service) Bn. (East Ham) The Royal Fusiliers (City of London Regt.): *s.* of Margaret Jones, *née* Astle (59, Teulon Street, Liverpool): enlisted Liverpool. One of 37 members of his battalion killed in action 7 August 1917: Age 19.

(Panel 6) Pte. G/3341, Christopher Umberto Balinari, 4th Bn. (7th Foot) The Royal Fusiliers (City of London Regt.): *s.* of Eliza Elizabeth Balinari (3, Porteous Road, Paddington): enlisted St. Paul's Churchyard. Killed in action 16 June 1915: Age 22. *unm.*

(Panel 6) Pte. SR/8488, Albert Beckett, 4th Bn. (7th Foot) The Royal Fusiliers (City of London Regt.): *s.* of John Thomas Beckett, of 4, Cross Street, Hampton Hill, co. Middlesex, by his wife Annie Susan: *b.* Teddington: enlisted Hounslow. Killed in action nr. Bellewaarde Ridge 16 June 1915, whilst assisting a wounded comrade along a trench: Age 22. *unm.*

(Panel 6) Pte. L/11854, William John Beer, 'A' Coy., 1st Bn. (7th Foot) The Royal Fusiliers (City of London Regt.): formerly no.5545, 5th Royal Fusiliers: late of West Ham, London: *s.* of Robert C. Beer, of 9, North Birkbeck Road, Leytonstone, co. Essex, and Emily Beer, his spouse: *b.* Bow, London, E., 1887: enlisted Stratford, co. Essex. Died 24 August 1915: Age 28. Remains recovered unmarked grave 'Sanctuary Wood Old British Cemetery' (28.I.24.b.90.97) 'Unknown British Soldier. Royal Fusiliers;' identified – Clothing, Titles; reinterred, registered 19 April 1928. *Buried in Sanctuary Wood Cemetery (II.F.4).*

(Panel 6) Pte. L/15991, Walter Henry Belcher, 4th Bn. (7th Foot) The Royal Fusiliers (City of London Regt.): late of New Kent Road, London, S.E.1: *b.* Walworth, London, S.E.: served with the Expeditionary Force in France, and was killed in action at Kemmel, Belgium, 17 January 1915; shot by a sniper.

(Panel 6) Pte. G/341, Frank Edward Benn, 4th Bn. (7th Foot) The Royal Fusiliers (City of London Regt.): *s.* of John Thomas Benn: *b.* Paddington, London, W., 18 May 1876: *educ.* St. Mary Magdalen C.E. School, there: enlisted, 2 August 1885: served seven years with the Colours, five in the Reserve, and four in Section D: rejoined 1 September 1914: served with the Expeditionary Force in France, and was killed in action at St. Eloi 26 August 1915: Age 38. He *m.* at Simon Zelotes, Bethnal Green, Elizabeth Mary, *née* Hammond (25, Huntsworth Terrace, Marylebone), and had five children – Amelia Elizabeth, *b.* 26 July 1907; Frank Edward, *b.* 26 May 1909; Amy Georgina, *b.* 18 March 1911; John Thomas, *b.* 31 August 1913; Daisy Beatrice, *b.* 18 December 1915. (*IWGC record SR/341, 26 April 1915*)

(Panel 6) Pte. 24215, Charles Herbert Bennett, 1st Bn. (7th Foot) The Royal Fusiliers (City of London Regt.): *s.* of Arthur Bennett, of 'Sharpthorne,' 4, Adelaide Road, Ashford, co. Middlesex, by his wife

Mary Ann: and yr. brother to Pte. G/10653, A.F. Bennett, Royal Fusiliers, killed in action 6 February 1916 at St. Eloi: *b.* Marlborough, co. Wilts: enlisted Staines, co. Middlesex. Killed in action 31 July 1917: Age 22. *unm.*

His brother Arthur is buried in Dickebusch New Military Cemetery (H.21).

(Panel 6) Pte. L/10037, Joseph Henry Betty, 4th Bn. (7th Foot) The Royal Fusiliers (City of London Regt.): late of Paddington, London, W.: served with the Expeditionary Force, and was killed in action 11 November 1914. (*IWGC record J.Betty*)

(Panel 6) Pte. G.2628, Charles Thomas Blackmore, 4th Bn. (7th Foot) The Royal Fusiliers (City of London Regt.): *s.* of Charles Richard Blackmore, Engineer; of 13, Alfred Street, Colebrook Road, Kingston, by his wife Martha: *b.* Stepney, 10 September 1890: *educ.* L.C.C. School, there: Occupation – Engineer: volunteered and enlisted 8 September 1914: served with the Expeditionary Force in France and Flanders, and was killed in action at Ypres 16 June 1915. Buried there. His Commanding Officer wrote that he showed himself to be courageous throughout and died a brave man whilst doing his duty to his country. His predominant features were pluck and determination, and many little incidents in his short career bear out this fact: Age 24. *unm.*

(Panel 6) Pte. L/14576, Warwick Spencer Blood, 4th Bn. (7th Foot) The Royal Fusiliers (City of London Regt.): *s.* of James Warwick Blood, of North Kensington, London, W., by his wife Clara: enlisted Hounslow, co. Middlesex: served with the Expeditionary Force, and was killed in action 11 November 1914: Age 20. *unm.*

(Panel 6) Pte. 42270, George Samuel Blunt, 32nd (Service) Bn. (East Ham) The Royal Fusiliers (City of London Regt.): late of 4, Lyme Regis Road, Banstead, co. Surrey: *s.* of the late William (& Annie) Blunt, of Banstead: and elder brother to S4/218557, P. Blunt, Army Service Corps, died in Macedonia, 17 October 1918: *b.* Goudhurst, 1881: Occupation – Decorator: enlisted Banstead, 7 December 1915: served with the Expeditionary Force in France and Flanders. Reported missing / believed killed in action 7 August 1917, on which date his battalion incurred the loss of 1 officer and 37 other ranks killed: Age 35. He was married to Nellie G. Blunt (63, Fishponds Road, Tooting Bec Road, London).

His brother Percy is buried in Beirut War Cemetery (36).

(Panel 6) Pte. L/15416, Henry Edward Boulton, 4th Bn. (7th Foot) The Royal Fusiliers (City of London Regt.): *s.* of William Henry Boulton, of 7, Newport Road, Walthamstow, London, E., by his wife Ellen Elizabeth: served with the Expeditionary Force. Killed in action 8 November 1914.

(Panel 6) Pte. L/16436, Albert William Bowley, 4th Bn. (7th Foot) The Royal Fusiliers (City of London Regt.): *s.* of Mary Debenham (5, Rose Cottages, Barnham, Bognor, co. Sussex): *b.* Slindon, Chichester, 1895: enlisted Edmonton. Killed in action at the Battle of Loos, 25 September 1915: Age 20. *unm.* Commemorated on the Loos Memorial (Dud Corner).

(Panel 6) Pte. SR/417, Albert William Charles Bowley, 'B' Coy., 4th Bn. (7th Foot) The Royal Fusiliers (City of London Regt.): *b.* Hampstead, London, N.W.: enlisted Fulham: served with the Expeditionary Force in France and Flanders from August 1914, and was killed in action 26 January 1915; Kemmel. War Diary records 'Foggy day. Several casualties from snipers.': Age 29. He was married to Sarah Ann Markham, *née* Bowley (23, Flask Walk, Hampstead).

(Panel 6) Pte. 12736, Harry William Bradley, 'B'Coy., 4th Bn. (7th Foot) The Royal Fusiliers (City of London Regt.): *s.* of Henry William Bradley, of 46, Arlington Street, New North Road, Islington, London, S.W.1: served with the Expeditionary Force. Reported wounded 11 November 1914; assumed killed: Age 25.

(Panel 6) Pte. 11209, Charles Edward Brighty, 4th Bn. (7th Foot) The Royal Fusiliers (City of London Regt.): *s.* of the late Charles Hudson Brighty, by his wife Ellen (Windmore Hall, South Mimms, Barnet, co. Hertford): served with the Expeditionary Force. Reported missing 11 November 1914, and now assumed killed: Age 25. (*IWGC record L/11309*)

(Panel 6) Pte. 37392, Ernest William Brown, 1st Bn. (7th Foot) The Royal Fusiliers (City of London Regt.): *s.* of Charles William Brown, of Hopton, Thetford, by his wife Mary: *b.* Shipdham, co. Norfolk,

27 September 1885: *educ*. Council School, there: Occupation – Butcher: enlisted Brandon, 31 May 1916: served with the Expeditionary Force in France and Flanders from December following. Reported missing after the fighting at Ypres, 31 July 1917; now assumed to have been killed in action on or since that date: Age 31. He *m*. Shipdham, 26 December 1908; Zoraida Garner, *née* Brown (since remarried), late of Church Road, Brandon (resident Brandon Road, Watton, Thetford, co. Norfolk,), *dau*. of Arthur Eastrick, and had three sons – Alec Charles, *b*. 4 April 1910; Stanley Eastrick, *b*. 24 September 1912; Ernest Frank, *b*. 2 July 1917.

(Panel 6) Pte. 11919, Sydney James Brown, 12th (Service) Bn. The Royal Fusiliers (City of London Regt.): 3rd *s*. of William Brown, of Hill Manor Cottages, Hinton Parva, Swindon, co. Wilts, Carter, by his wife Esther, *dau*. of George Grundy: *b*. co. Wilts, 5 March 1897: *educ*. Hinton Parva: enlisted January 1915: served with the Expeditionary Force in France from September 1915, and was killed in action there 8 January 1916. An officer wrote to his mother, "Your son was killed in action this morning and was laid to rest in the evening with two others that met their death the same morning; he did not lose any limbs, but passed peacefully away two hours after he was hit.": Age 18.

The two others laid to rest with Pte. Brown – Ptes. A.J. Inkpin and J. Wilson – also have no known grave; they are recorded below.

(Panel 6) Pte. 2662, Andrew Carter, 3rd Bn. (7th Foot) The Royal Fusiliers (City of London Regt.): late of Leigh-on-Sea: enlisted Southend. Died of wounds 14 April 1915. Buried in Bedford House Cemetery, Zillebeke (V.A.47/Enc.No.2).

(Panel 6) Pte. 9261, Montagu Cyril Castledine, 4th Bn. (7th Foot) The Royal Fusiliers (City of London Regt.): 3rd *s*. of George Henry Castledine, Lithographic Artist; of 55, Lyndhurst Grove, Peckham, London, S.E., by his wife Emma Eleanor, *dau*. of Thomas Austin Blake, H.M.C.: *b*. Camberwell, S.E., 16 February 1889: *educ*. Bancrofts School, Woodford, co. Essex: prior to the outbreak of war was, for eight years, employee London County & Westminster Bank, and at the time of his enlistment, 11 November 1914, Cashier; Sudbury branch, Suffolk. After four months' training at the Duke of York's Military School, Dover, was sent to the Front with a draft early March 1915, and was killed in action in the Battle of Hooge, nr. Ypres 16 June 1915: Age 26. *unm*.

(Panel 6) Pte. 5111, Frederick Cheney, 3rd Bn. (7th Foot) The Royal Fusiliers (City of London Regt.): *s*. of Benjamin Cheney, of 'Fieldgroves', Bryanston, Blandford, co. Dorset, by his wife Ruth: and *yr*. brother to Pte. 20625, G. Cheney, 2nd York & Lancaster Regt., killed in action 9 August 1915: *b*. Pimperne, co. Dorset, *c*.1890: enlisted Kingston-on-Thames, co. Surrey. Killed in action 22 April 1915: Age 25. *unm*.

His brother George also has no known grave; he is recorded on Panel 55.

(Panel 6) Pte. L/11137, Andrew Thomas Connor, 4th Bn. (7th Foot) The Royal Fusiliers (City of London Regt.): *s*. of Thomas Andrew Connor, of 21, St. Loys Road, Bruce Grove, Tottenham, London, N., by his wife Ellen: served with the Expeditionary Force. Reported missing 11 November 1914; now assumed killed: Age 26. *unm*.

(Panel 6) Pte. SR/400, Charles William Cooper, 4th Bn. (7th Foot) The Royal Fusiliers (City of London Regt.): *b*. Marylebone: enlisted London. Killed by hostile fire, 23 February 1915. See Pte. J. Pragnell, Ramparts Cemetery (C.1), also Pte. H. Warren, Poperinghe Old Military Cemetery (II.O.35).

(Panel 6) Pte. L/15297, Thomas David Edgar Cooper, 1st Bn. (7th Foot) The Royal Fusiliers (City of London Regt.): *s*. of the late Thomas George Cooper, by his wife Charlotte (74D, Evelina Mansions, New Church Road, Camberwell, London, S.E.): enlisted Hounslow, co. Middlesex: served with the Expeditionary Force, and was killed in action 14 August 1915: Age 18. Remains recovered unmarked grave 'Sanctuary Wood Old British Cemetery' (28.I.24.b.90.97) 'Unknown British Soldier. Royal Fusiliers;' identified – Clothing; reinterred, registered 19 April 1928. *Buried in Sanctuary Wood Cemetery (II.F.9).*

Lest We Forget

(Panel 6) Pte. L/9336, Harry Curtis, 4th Bn. (7th Foot) The Royal Fusiliers (City of London Regt.): *s.* of C. Curtis, of Brook Green, Hammersmith, London, W.: served with the Expeditionary Force. Killed in action 11 November 1914.

(Panel 6) Pte. 49624, Ernest Victor Dobney, 32nd (Service) Bn. (East Ham) The Royal Fusiliers (City of London Regt.) attd Machine Gun Corps: *yst. s.* of Joseph Dobney, of 10, Avondale Road, West Green, Tottenham, London, N., by his wife Mary Caroline, *dau.* of Nicholas Johns, Royal Navy: and brother to Bty.Sergt.-Major 33623, H.J. Dobney, 105th Bty., 22nd Bde., VIIth Divn., Royal Field Artillery, killed in action at Ginchy, 25 September 1916, aged 32 years: *b.* Cricklewood, London, N.W., 6 June 1887: *educ.* West Green Board School: Occupation – Upholsterer: enlisted Royal Fusiliers 29 May 1916; served with the Expeditionary Force in France and Flanders, attd. Machine Gun Corps, from 29 September, and was killed in action at Messines 7 June 1917: Age 30. He *m.* August 1914, Mary Anne, *dau.* of Thomas Hutton, and had a *dau.*, Lilian Ada, *b.* 10 October 1915.

His brother Henry also has no known grave; he is commemorated on the Thiepval Memorial, Somme.

(Panel 6) Pte. L/16122, Thomas Bertram Elcombe, 4th Bn. (7th Foot) The Royal Fusiliers (City of London Regt.): *s.* of Sydney Elcombe, of 21, Faraday Road, Acton, London, by his wife Sarah: and elder brother to Pte. 13496, D.A.R. Elcombe, Army Cyclist Corps, killed in action 17 April 1918, nr. Ypres: *b.* Paddington: enlisted Hounslow. Killed in action 11 November 1914: Age 19.

His brother David is buried in Abeele Aerodrome Cemetery (I.E.1).

(Panel 6) Pte. L/9894, George Etherington, 4th Bn. (7th Foot) The Royal Fusiliers (City of London Regt.): *s.* of the late J. Etherington, by his wife Ellen (51, Claremont Street, Greenwich, London, S.E.): and brother to Pte. S/6687, H. Etherington, The Queen's, died 29 October 1914 and L/Corpl. 11430, C. Etherington, Wiltshire Regt., killed in action 19 October 1917: served with the Expeditionary Force. Killed in action 11 November 1914: Age 28. *unm.*

His brother Henry also has no known grave, he is recorded on Panel 13; Charles is buried in Kemmel Chateau Military Cemetery (M.11).

(Panel 6) Pte. L/10609, Albert William Fenne, 4th Bn. (7th Foot) The Royal Fusiliers (City of London Regt.): *s.* of Frederick Henry Fenne, of Fulham, London, S.W., by his wife Charlotte Caroline: served with the Expeditionary Force. Reported missing 11 November 1914, now assumed killed: Age 28. *unm.*

(Panel 6) Pte. L/9589, Charles Fisher, 4th Bn. (7th Foot) The Royal Fusiliers (City of London Regt.): served with the Expeditionary Force. Reported missing 11 November 1914, now assumed killed.

(Panel 6) Pte. SR/2423, Albert Folwell, 4th Bn. (7th Foot) The Royal Fusiliers (City of London Regt.): *s.* of Annie Folwell, (8, Duckett Street, Stepney, London, E.1): *b.* Stepney. Killed in action 16 June 1915: Age 24.

(Panel 6) Pte. 11459, Thomas Richard Foster, 4th Bn. (7th Foot) The Royal Fusiliers (City of London Regt.): served with the Expeditionary Force. Reported missing 11 November 1914, now assumed killed. (*IWGC record L/11459*)

(Panel 6) Pte. G/1165, Dick Richard Fox, 3rd Bn. (7th Foot) The Royal Fusiliers (City of London Regt.): *s.* of Dick Fox, of 1, Keen's Cottages, Horton Bridge Road, Yiewsley: served with the Expeditionary Force in France. Killed in action 3 May 1915.

(Panel 6) Pte. 50396, William John Framingham, 11th (Service) Bn. The Royal Fusiliers (City of London Regt.): formerly no.41774, Royal Fusiliers: *s.* of Samuel Framingham, of Ringstead, King's Lynn, co. Norfolk, by his wife Elizabeth: *b.* Great Ryburgh, co. Norfolk: enlisted King's Lynn. Killed in action at the Battle of Arras, 3 May 1917: Age 27. *Commemorated on the Arras Memorial (Bay 3), Faubourg d'Amiens.*

(Panel 6) Pte. 9984, George Francis, 1st Bn. (7th Foot) The Royal Fusiliers (City of London Regt.): *s.* of Joseph Francis, of Fulham, London, S.W., by his wife Elizabeth: enlisted London: served with the Expeditionary Force in France and Flanders from September 1914, and was killed in action 18 August 1915: Age 33. He leaves a wife, Ellen (32, Rock Avenue, Fulham, London, S.W.6). Remains recovered

'Sanctuary Wood Old British Cemetery' (28.I.24.b.90.97) 'Unknown British Soldier;' identified – Clothing; reinterred, registered 19 April 1928. *Buried in Sanctuary Wood Cemetery (II.F.7)*.

(Panel 6) Pte. 6279, Walter Freeman, 1st Bn. (7th Foot) The Royal Fusiliers (City of London Regt.): late of Feltham, co. Middlesex: enlisted Hounslow. Died 16 July 1916. Buried in Feltham Cemetery (E.C.55).

(Panel 6) Pte. 11216, Herbert Frith, 4th Bn. (7th Foot) The Royal Fusiliers (City of London Regt.): *s*. of Cecilia Patten, *née* Frith (4, Sunnyside Road, Hazelville Road, Hornsey Rise, London): served with the Expeditionary Force. Reported missing 11 November 1914; now assumed killed: Age 32. (*IWGC record L/11216*)

(Panel 6) Pte. S/1632, Charles William Nelson Grimble, 4th Bn. (7th Foot) The Royal Fusiliers (City of London Regt.): served with the Expeditionary Force. Reported missing 11 November 1914; now assumed killed.

(Panel 6) Pte. G/9460, Samuel Hadgett, 4th Bn. (7th Foot) The Royal Fusiliers (City of London Regt.): *s*. of Daniel Hadgett, of Peel Street, Kidsgrove, co. Stafford: enlisted Macclesfield. Killed in action 17 September 1915: Age 28. *unm*. Remains exhumed Sanctuary Wood 'Unknown British Soldier. 9460. 5/Royal Fusiliers;' identified – Khaki, Boots; registered, reinterred 29 November 1928. *Buried in Sanctuary Wood Cemetery (II.M.6)*.

(Panel 6) Pte. 66919, Clement Haigh, 32nd (Service) Bn. (East Ham) The Royal Fusiliers (City of London Regt.): *s*. of David Haigh, of 17, Walton Street, King Cross, Liverpool, by his wife Emma. Killed in action 7 August 1917: Age 21. See Pte. 66922, F. Jagger, below.

(Panel 6) Pte. 3708, Thomas Henry Hancock, 'A' Coy., 3rd Bn. (7th Foot) The Royal Fusiliers (City of London Regt.): *s*. of Mr (& Mrs) Hancock, of Crown Street, Camberwell, London, S.E.5: late *husb*. to Alice Hancock (17, Royal Terrace, Kennington, London, S.E.11): *b*. Lambeth, *c*.1887: enlisted Willesden. Killed in action 3 May 1915: Age 28. Remains 'Unknown British Soldier' exhumed (28.D.15.c.2.9) unmarked grave 31 January 1929; identified – Khaki, Disc, Titles; reinterred, registered 6 February 1929. *Buried in Sanctuary Wood Cemetery (V.D.15)*.

Rest In Peace

(Panel 6) Pte. 49148, Herbert Harvey, 11th (Service) Bn. The Royal Fusiliers (City of London Regt.): late *husb*. to Rebecca Harvey (Fen Bank, Isleham), *dau*. of Jonathan Butcher, by his wife Mary: and brother-in-law to Pte. 2448, D. Butcher, Northamptonshire Regt., killed in action 26 September 1916; Pte. 3/7438, H. Butcher, Norfolk Regt., killed in action 3 March 1915, and Pte. 30375, J.W. Butcher, Loyal North Lancashire Regt., killed in action 10 April 1918: *b*. Isleham, nr. Ely, co. Suffolk: enlisted Newmarket: served with the Expeditionary Force, and was killed in action, vicinity Clapham Junction, 10 August 1917.

Brother-in-law David is buried in Vermelles British Cemetery (V.D.19); Harry has no known grave, he is recorded on the Menin Gate (Panel 4), and John is commemorated in Croix-du-Bac British Cemetery (Sp.Mem.A.3).

(Panel 6) Pte. L/10481, Thomas Haydon, 4th Bn. (7th Foot) The Royal Fusiliers (City of London Regt.): *s*. of Mary Ann Haydon: served with the Expeditionary Force, and was killed in action at Ypres 11 November 1914: Age 27. He leaves a wife, Jane (6, Blackhorse Road, Deptford, London, S.E.8).

(Panel 6) Pte. 12845, Thomas Hedderly, 3rd Bn. (7th Foot) The Royal Fusiliers (City of London Regt.): *s*. of Thomas Hedderly, of Steeple, Southminster, co. Essex, by his wife Margaret: and elder brother to L/Corpl. 41473, F. Hedderly, Base Depot. Machine Gun Corps, died 15 September 1918: *b*. Dublin: enlisted Stratford. Killed in action 24 May 1915: Age 25. *unm*.

His brother Fredrick is buried in Abbeville Communal Cemetery Extension (IV.F.6).

(Panel 6) Pte. L/10338, John Henry Hedgecock, 4th Bn. (7th Foot) The Royal Fusiliers (City of London Regt.): *b*. Kentish Town: enlisted Tottenham: served with the Expeditionary Force. Killed in action, 11 November 1914.

(Panel 6) Pte. L/10008, John Richard Hemmett, 4th Bn. (7th Foot) The Royal Fusiliers (City of London Regt.): late of South Tottenham: served with the Expeditionary Force. Reported missing 11 November 1914, now assumed killed. *m.*

(Panel 6) Pte. 13711, Albert Hives, 3rd Bn. (7th Foot) The Royal Fusiliers (City of London Regt.): late of Globe Road, Stratford, London, E.15: *s.* of Mrs M.A. Southam (14, Alexandra Road, Heeley, Sheffield): enlisted Dalston, London, E.8: served with the Expeditionary Force in France, and was killed in action 26 April 1915: **Age 16.** A comrade wrote, "On the day Albert was killed 1st Hants came up to establish connection with the left of the Royal Fusiliers, and 2nd Buffs carried out a partial relief but, in spite of all, the Germans penetrated to the left rear of the Royal Fusiliers. The battalion's position was almost intolerable. Even after the Germans were ejected they were absolutely plastered the whole time with shell and every other kind of fire from three sides at once, with practically no assistance at all from our guns, and nothing could exist or move over the ground in rear, as every yard of it was plastered without ceasing by enormous shells."

(Panel 6) Pte. L/16147, Frederick Holton, 4th Bn. (7th Foot) The Royal Fusiliers (City of London Regt.): served with the Expeditionary Force. Died 13 November 1914, from wounds received in action at Ypres.

(Panel 6) Pte. L/14925, Edward Honeyman, 4th Bn. (7th Foot) The Royal Fusiliers (City of London Regt.): *s.* of J. Honeyman, of Teddington, co. Middlesex: served with the Expeditionary Force. Reported missing 11 November 1914, and now assumed killed.

(Panel 6) Pte. L/15658, Walter Hopkins, 4th Bn. (7th Foot) The Royal Fusiliers (City of London Regt.): *s.* of Walter Hopkins, of 313, High Street, Brenford, co. Middlesex, by his wife Alice: enlisted Hounslow, co. Middlesex. Killed in action 28 August 1915: Age 21. *unm.* Remains exhumed, identified – Disc, Titles; registered, reinterred 29 November 1928. *Buried in Sanctuary Wood Cemetery (II.M.5).*

(Panel 6) Pte. L/15403, James Howell, 4th Bn. (7th Foot) The Royal Fusiliers (City of London Regt.): *s.* of J. Howell, of Bethnall Green, London, E.: served with the Expeditionary Force. Reported missing 10 November 1914; now assumed killed.

(Panel 6) Pte. 7437, Joseph Huggins, 3rd Bn. (7th Foot) The Royal Fusiliers: late of Chingford: enlisted Finsbury Barracks: on the outbreak of war was with his battalion in Lucknow, India: returned to England, December 1914, proceeded to France mid-January 1915, and was killed in action 8 February 1915. 3rd Battalion's first Active Service fatality.

(Panel 6) Pte. 17975, Alfred James Inkpin, 12th (Service) Bn. The Royal Fusiliers (City of London Regt.): *s.* of Alfred Inkpin, of 71, Franklin Road, Brighton, by his wife Susannah: *b.* Brighton, co. Sussex, 1891: enlisted Hove. Killed in action 8 January 1916: Age 24. *unm.* See Pte. 11919, S.J. Brown, above.

(Panel 6) Pte. 66922, Fred Jagger, 32nd (Service) Bn. (East Ham) The Royal Fusiliers (City of London Regt.): *s.* of John Jagger, of Towngate, Clifton, Brighouse, co. York, by his wife Sarah Ann: employee Messrs Ramsden, Camm & Co., Wireworks, Brighouse: enlisted Halifax, early 1917, (no.341393) Duke of Wellington's Regt.: transf'd. Royal Fusiliers, and served together, with his friends Clement Haigh and Maurice Heap. Killed in action 3 August 1917: Age 20. *unm.* Clement Haigh was killed in action four days later; Maurice Heap died 6 August, in the Casualty Clearing Station at Remy Siding, near Poperinghe, of wounds received in action near Ypres the previous day.

Clement Haigh also has no known grave he is recorded above; Maurice Heap is buried in Lijssenthoek Military Cemetery (XVII.D.4A).

(Panel 6) Pte. L/15940, William Jardine, 4th Bn. (7th Foot) The Royal Fusiliers (City of London Regt.): *s.* of J. Jardine, of Watford, co. Hertford: served with the Expeditionary Force. Reported missing 11 November 1914.

(Panel 6) Pte. L/15788, William Jewell, 4th Bn. (7th Foot) The Royal Fusiliers (City of London Regt.): *b.* Fulham, London, S.W.6: enlisted Hounslow, co. Middlesex: served with the Expeditionary Force in France. Reported missing 11 November 1914; assumed killed.

(Panel 6) Pte. 11890, Francis James Lockwood, 3rd Bn. (7th Foot) The Royal Fusiliers (City of London Regt.): *b*. Fulham, London, S.W.6: enlisted Hammersmith: served with the Expeditionary Force in France and Flanders from January 1915, and was killed in action 26 April 1915 at Gravenstafel. Remains recovered (28.D.16.b.9.1) unmarked grave 23 December 1926; identified – Damaged Disc, Gold Signet Ring; reinterred, registered 1 January 1927. *Buried in Sanctuary Wood Cemetery (III.B.2)*.

(Panel 6) Pte. 17674, John Malbon, 12th (Service) Bn. The Royal Fusiliers (City of London Regt.): late of Chesterton, co. Stafford: enlisted Newcastle, Stafford. Killed in action 7 July 1916: Age 25. *unm*. All correspondence regarding the deceased should be addressed c/o his brother, J. Malbon Esq., 61, Chell Heath, Smallthorne, Stoke-on-Trent. *Commemorated (as 8th Bn.) on the Thiepval Memorial, Somme.*

(Panel 6) Pte. SR/509, William Charles Moon, 4th Bn. (7th Foot) The Royal Fusiliers (City of London Regt.): late of Clerkenwell, London: *b*. Holborn: enlisted London. Killed while carrying out trench repairs 23 February 1915; one of 8 fatalities sustained by the battalion in twenty-four hours. See Pte. C.W. Cooper (above).

(Panel 6) Pte. 3509, William John Ollard, 'C' Coy., 3rd Bn. (7th Foot) The Royal Fusiliers (City of London Regt.): *s*. of Henry Ollard, of 9, Chester Road, Lower Edmonton, London, N.9, by his wife Amelia: and elder brother to Pte. L/13473, B.T. Ollard, 3rd Middlesex Regt., who fell the same day: *b*. Hoxton: enlisted Edmonton. Killed in action 3 May 1915: Age 30. Pte Ollard's widow has since remarried, now Daisy W.H. Clark (13, St. Mary's Road, Lower Edmonton).

His brother Benjamin also has no known grave; he is recorded on Panel 51.

(Panel 6) Pte. 7655, Edgar Pike, 3rd Bn. (7th Foot) The Royal Fusiliers (City of London Regt.): *b*. Islington: enlisted Finsbury Barracks: served with the Expeditionary Force in France and Flanders, and was killed in action 9 May 1915: Age 24. He was married to Emma Hetty Pike (55, Sutton Buildings, Upper Street, Islington, London), to whom all correspondence and information regarding the deceased should be addressed. Remains exhumed unmarked grave refers GRU Report, Zillebeke 5-60E (28.I.6.c.5.5); identified – Disc, Clothing; reinterred, registered 14 April 1927. *Buried in Sanctuary Wood Cemetery (IV.B.35)*.

Peace Perfect Peace

(Panel 6) Pte. L/15842, Alfred George Pines, 'Y' Coy., 4th Bn. (7th Foot) The Royal Fusiliers (City of London Regt.): *s*. of Henry C. (& Mrs) Pines, of 6, Houblon Road, Richmond, co. Surrey: *b*. Putney, London, S.W.: enlisted Guildford. Killed in action 17 January 1915; sniper, Kemmel: Age 19.

3rd Royal Fusiliers; Bellewaarde Ridge, 1915: On May 24th the enemy delivered a gas attack. This was the worst discharge of all. Five miles way, at Dickebusch, the 4th Battalion experienced its effects, many men suffering from sore eyes. The light north-easterly breeze carried the poisonous fumes across the British lines between Shell-Trap Farm, north of the St. Julien Road, and Bellewarde Lake. The surprise gained the enemy a considerable advantage, and as the men were searching for their respirators there began a violent bombardment. It was a terrible experience waking to this inferno; and some of the troops left their trenches. The 3rd Battalion, lying south of the Ypres-Roulers railway, at once found themselves not only obliged to cope with the poisonous fumes and the terrible bombardment, but also with the uncovering of their left flank, where the troops had left the trenches. Half of No.2 Company, under Lieuts. Sealy and Holleny (both killed later in the day), were sent to occupy the abandoned trenches north of the railway. After 5am. all telephone communication with Brigade H.Q. ceased to exist, Nos.1 and 4 Companies were cut off from Battalion H.Q. also, and the battle line appeared to fall to pieces with small islands of steadfast troops standing alone in the way of the German advance. Major Johnson received a message from Brigade ordering him to counter-attack with two companies of The Buffs in support, and the East Surreys co-operating north of the railway crossing. The remainder of No.2 Company and certain stragglers at once prepared to advance against the ridge from the road 200 yards south of the railway crossing, and, at the same time a half company of The Buffs moved up the sunken road south of the wood, close to the crossing. Major Baker crossed the railway and sent forward the other half of No.2 Company under Lieut. Sealy with orders to make good the old trench line 350 yards to the east. But, now disaster began to crowd upon disaster. Major Johnson's attack had not been successful, and he was wounded and had to go to the dressing station. Major Baker collected the remains of Major Johnson's party in the wood south of the railway and placed them in the third line trenches. But, before the Fusiliers had taken up their positions, the Germans had worked round to the south of Ridge 44 and were enfilading the road south of the railway. Baker got together some of his men and placed them in the ditch on this road, where they were able to return fire with less disadvantage. The Buffs reinforcements, when they arrived, were so thinned by shell fire that when the various small parties were collected, despite only numbering 200 men, they still formed a useful reinforcement. The Germans had been in possession of our fire trenches since 8am., but the surviving 150 (out of an original 880) Royal Fusiliers, with the assistance of The Buffs, succeeded in holding the third line to the end of the day. In final summing up the efforts of the Germans produced very little, despite the initial use of gas. Its effects, for the most part, did no worse than temporarily incapacitate the Fusiliers. They fought obstinately to retain their positions, make good the defection on the left and, even though weakened, bore a heavy onslaught from the Germans; and finally made a desperate counter-attack. By 8am. Major Baker was not only Commanding Officer, he was the only officer left out of 17. At the end of the day the battalion casualties amounted to 536, killed, missing, wounded; probably the worst loss in any days' battle of any Fusilier battalion in the entire war.

In the course of the day's mayhem John and Ann Racheil, of London, suffered probably the worst loss any family ever could. Their three sons, aged between 18 and 24 years, were numbered among over 130 of 3rd Battalion's other ranks killed. What made their loss even harder to bear is the fact that not one of the brothers had the honour of a known burial.

(Panel 6) Pte. 2314, Arthur Ernest Racheil, 3rd Bn. (7th Foot) The Royal Fusiliers (City of London Regt.): *s.* of John Racheil, of 23, Holme Road, East Ham, London, E., by his wife Ann. Killed in action 24 May 1915: Age 21. See below.

(Panel 6) Pte. 2237, Frank Albert Racheil, 3rd Bn. (7th Foot) The Royal Fusiliers (City of London Regt.): *s.* of John Racheil, of 23, Holme Road, East Ham, London, E., by his wife Ann. Killed in action 24 May 1915: Age 18. See above & below.

(Panel 6) Pte. 2269, Frederick George Racheil, 3rd Bn. (7th Foot) The Royal Fusiliers (City of London Regt.): *s.* of John Racheil, of 23, Holme Road, East Ham, London, E., by his wife Ann. Killed in action 24 May 1915: Age 24. See above.

(Panel 6) Pte. 7396, John Rynn, 1st Bn. (7th Foot) The Royal Fusiliers: *s.* of Thomas Rynn, of 15, School Street, Bury, co. Lancaster, by his wife Jane: and elder brother to Pte. 2553, J.L. Rynn, 1/7th Lancashgire Fusiliers, killed in action 5 June 1915, at Gallipoli: *b.* Bury: enlisted there. Killed in action 31 July 1917: Age 33.

His brother Joseph also has no known grave; he is commemorated on the Helles Memorial.

(Panel 6) Pte. G/9914, George Edward Smith, 4th Bn. The Royal Fusiliers (City of London Regt.): *s.* of William Smith, of 4, Rose Cottages, Beacontree Heath, Romford, co. Essex, and his spouse Elizabeth Smith: and brother to Pte. G/9915, H.S. Smith, 4th Royal Fusiliers, killed in action 27 March 1915: enlisted East Ham. Killed in action 16 June 1915: Age 21.

His brother Henry also has no known grave; he is recorded below.

(Panel 6) Pte. G/9915, Henry Samuel Smith, 4th Bn. The Royal Fusiliers (City of London Regt.): *s.* of William Smith, of 4, Rose Cottages, Beacontree Heath, Romford, co. Essex, and his spouse Elizabeth Smith: and brother to Pte. G/9914, G.E. Smith, 4th Royal Fusiliers, killed in action 16 June 1915: enlisted East Ham. Killed in action 27 March 1915: Age 21.

His brother George also has no known grave; he is recorded above.

(Panel 6) Pte. 13604, Thomas Talkington, 3rd Bn. (7th Foot) The Royal Fusiliers (City of London Regt.): *s.* of George Samuel Talkington, of 75, Eastcourt Road, Fulham, London, S.W.: and brother to L/Corpl. 7697, F. Talkington, East Surrey Regt., who fell five weeks later (29 June) in the vicinity of Hill 60: Killed in action at Bellewaarde Ridge, 24 May 1915.

His brother Frank is buried in Woods Cemetery (I.A.20).

(Panel 6) Pte. 65501, Edward Tompsett, 32nd (Service) Bn. (East Ham) The Royal Fusiliers (City of London Regt.): formerly no.21181, Royal Sussex Regt.: *s.* of Harriett Tompsett (95, Park Road, Sittingbourne, co. Kent). Died of wounds 5 August 1917, received in action at Klein Zillebeke the same day.: Age 19. See Pte. M.F. Heap, Lijssenthoek Military Cemetery (XVII.D.4A).

(Panel 6) Pte. L/11287, Edwin Albert Edward Triggs, 4th Bn. (7th Foot) The Royal Fusiliers (City of London Regt.): late of Hastings, co. Sussex: enlisted Hounslow, co. Middlesex. Killed in action 2 October 1915, at Loos: Age 27. He was married to Emily Triggs (49, Croydon Road, Anerley, London, S.E.20). *Commemorated on the Loos (Dud Corner) Memorial.*

(Panel 6) Pte. 2253, Walter David Webb, 3rd Bn. (7th Foot) The Royal Fusiliers (City of London Regt.): *s.* of Walter Webb, of 39, Wilmington Square, Spa Fields, London, by his wife Priscilla: *b.* Oxford, about 1900: enlisted Marylebone, London: served with the Expeditionary Force in France, and was killed in action 26 April 1915, south-west of St. Julien: **Age 15.** See comrade's note re. Pte. A. Hives, above.

(Panel 6) Pte. 4660, Charles John Wicks, 1st Bn. (7th Foot) The Royal Fusiliers (City of London Regt.): *s.* of Charles John Wicks, and late *husb.* to Kate Lydia Wicks (131, Midhope Buildings, Cromer Street, King's Cross, London, W.C.): *b.* Clerkenwell: enlisted Holborn. Killed in action 11 August 1915: Age 40. Remains recovered unmarked grave 'Sanctuary Wood Old Cemetery' (28.I.24.b.90.97) 'Unknown British Soldier. Royal Fusiliers;' identified – Clothing, Titles; reinterred, registered 30 April 1928. *Buried in Sanctuary Wood Cemetery (II.F.10).*

(Panel 6) Pte. 5221, James Wilson, No.2 Coy., 12th (Service) Bn. The Royal Fusiliers (City of London Regt.): late *husb.* to Mrs E. Wilson: enlisted Hackney, London, E.8. Killed in action 7 January 1916: Age 34. See Pte. 11919, S.J. Brown, above.

(Panel 6) Lieut.Col. William Stirling Bannatyne, 1st Bn. (8th Foot) The King's (Liverpool) Regt.: *s.* of Lieut.Col. John Millar Bannatyne, late King's Liverpool Regt.: *b.* Farme, Co. Limerick, 9 December 1868: *educ.* privately in Switzerland, and Royal Military College, Sandhurst: gazetted 2nd Lieut. King's Liverpool Regt. 22 August 1888: promoted Lieut. 7 May 1890; Capt. 22 January 1896; Major 17 February 1904; Lieut.Col. 17 February 1912: served in the South African War, 1899 – 1902, on the Staff, being Assistant Provost Marshal (graded D.A.A.G.), 29 March 1900 – 26 October 1902: took part in the operations in Natal, 1899, including actions at Reitfontein and Lombard's Kop: defence of Ladysmith, including sorties of 7 and 10 December 1899, and action of 6 January 1900: operations in Natal (March – June 1900), including action at Laing's Nek (6 – 9 June): operations in the Transvaal, May – June 1900: operations in Transvaal, east of Pretoria, July – 29 November 1900, including actions at Belfast (26 – 27 August), and Lydenberg (5 – 8 September): and the Transvaal again, 30 November 1900 – 31 May 1902: Mentioned in Despatches ('*London Gazette*,' 8 February 1901): Queen's Medal, three clasps; King's Medal, two clasps: D.A.A.G. and General Staff Officer (2nd Grade), 2nd London Division, London District, 2 January 1911 – 16 February 1912: served with the Expeditionary Force in France and Flanders from 12 August 1914: took part in the Retreat from Mons towards Paris, the Battles of the Marne and the Aisne, and finally in the actions in Flanders. Killed in action nr. Ypres, 24 October 1914, being shot through the heart from a loop-holed house in the village of Nord Westhoek, which village his battalion had orders to clear of Germans: Age 45. Twice Mentioned in Despatches ('*London Gazette*,' 19 October 1914; 17 February 1915) by F.M. Sir John (now Lord) French, for 'gallant and distinguished service in the field.' He *m.* 1889; Ethel Louisa (Avenue Lodge, Wellington College Station, co. Berks), *dau.* of the Rev. H.H. Winwood, of Bath, and sister to Lieut.Col. W.Q. Winwood, D.S.O., 5th (Princess Charlotte of Wales's) Dragoon Guards.: *s.p.*

(Panel 6) Major Andrew Stewart Anderson, 'B' Coy., 10th Bn. (Scottish) The King's (Liverpool) Regt. (T.F.): late of 24, Park Road South, Birkenhead, co. Chester: *s.* of Robert Anderson; Shipowner, Liverpool: *b.* Meikle, Pinkerton, Dunbar, 1878: Occupation – Solicitor (admitted July 1901), Messrs Harrison, Alcock, Burton & Anderson, Liverpool: joined 1/4th Cheshire Regt. (T.F.), 1909, obtained a commission, gazetted Lieut. 12 January 1911: transf'd. (1909) 1/10th King's (Liverpool) Regt., apptd.

'B' Coy.: promoted Capt. 17 September 1912: mobilised on the outbreak of war August 1914; served with the Expeditionary Force in France and Flanders from 1 November: apptd. Temp. Major, 5 January 1915: Mentioned in Despatches by Sir John (now Lord) French, 17 February 1915. Reported missing, believed killed 16 June 1915; leading his battalion in the attack at Bellewaarde, nr. Hooge: Age 37. The last man to see him alive was his orderly, Pte. White (Upton, Wirral), who, although he saw Major Anderson sitting in a trench with wounds to both legs, was unable to render assistance at that time. Later (that night), Pte. White went to look for him, but could find no trace. Thereafter followed some confusion; his father received a telegram from Chaplain Arndt, Dusseldorf, Germany, stating his son was wounded and in a hospital there, Messrs. Riley, Alcock & Anderson (Solicitors) notification to the effect Major Anderson had been killed in action. No identifiable remains were recovered.

(Panel 6) Capt. Bryden McKinnell, M.C., 1/10th Bn. (Scottish) The King's (Liverpool) Regt. (T.F.): eldest *s.* of the late W.J. McKinnell, of North Lawrieknowe, co. Dumfries, and Mrs. McKinnell ('Nithsdale,' Hoylake, co. Chester): *b.* Birkenhead, 24 July 1889: *educ.* Copenhagen, Denmark, and Dumfries Academy (boarded with English Master; A.C.E. Harris Esq.): commissioned 2nd Lieut. 5th King's Own Scottish Borderers (Galloway Rifles), June 1907: subsequently transf'd. Liverpool Scottish (1908): promoted Lieut. April 1910. A keen athlete and a member of the Birkenhead Football Club, in commercial life he was associated with Messrs Shipton, Anderson & Co., Corn Brokers, Liverpool: went with his battalion to France, 1 November 1914; Machine Gun Officer: promoted Capt. (Temp.) In the Field, January 1915 (subsequently confirmed): Mentioned in Sir John (now Lord) French's Despatch, 31 May 1915, and publicly thanked at the front by the Commanding Officer, Royal Scots Fusiliers and the Commanding Officer, Northumberland Fusiliers, for 'rescue work at two mine explosions.' Awarded the Military Cross ('*London Gazette*,' 23 June 1915) for 'distinguished service during the campaign,' and was killed in action, 16 June 1915, at Hooge, after the taking of the third German trench, as he was leading his men in the brilliant charge of the Liverpool Scottish, which a General afterwards said 'had saved the line.' He left a most interesting account of the doings of the 10th Battn. Liverpool Regt., written up to the night before the charge, and showing considerable literary merit. He won the Military Cross for showing courage, coolness, and resource on two separate occasions. The first took place in a trench just under Hill 60, 12 March 1915. At about 4 p.m. in the afternoon some heavy firing and some shelling began, directed at the trench. At the time Capt. McKinnell was over in a trench on the right near the railway cutting. Suddenly there was a tremendous explosion on the left of the trench, and masses of earth, sandbags, bricks, etc., went up into the air. He promptly ran down to the place, and found that a salient between our trench and the trench occupied by the Royal Scots Fusiliers had been literally blown away, burying a whole platoon of men, and exposing our left flank and the right flank of the Royal Scots Fusiliers. Capt. McKinnell at once did his best to put things right, and constantly exposed himself in broad daylight. Under heavy rifle fire he got the men together and helped to dig out some of the victims. Finally, he helped to dig a new trench behind a mine crater in a very exposed place. He worked until hours after dark, and his prompt work was of the greatest assistance at a critical period while many of the men were in a dazed condition and a great number wounded. He received the next day the thanks of the Officer Commanding the Royal Scots Fusiliers for his good work. The second occasion happened at St. Eloi, 14 April 1915, in trench Q2, a hundred yards or so behind the 'Mound.' About 9 pm. we had just received our letters, papers, etc., from England, when a heavy rifle fire commenced against the parapet of the trench followed by the heaviest shelling we had ever previously experienced. It all seemed directed on our trench and on trench Q3, manned by another of our companies. After the shelling had gone on for twenty minutes or so, there was a tremendous explosion in front of us, and it transpired the Germans had blown up trench Q1, just in front of us. As soon as this information was received from a telephone operator, who had run down to tell us of the occurrence, Capt. McKinnell was instructed to take a party up to man the trench that had been wrecked. This he promptly did, and under rifle and grenade fire he reorganised the whole trench very rapidly and assisted to dig out a large number of the Northumberland Fusiliers buried by the explosion. Without his prompt lead, which was splendidly backed up by the men, a very serious situation might have arisen, as the Germans had evidently intended to take the trench during the natural confusion and chaos caused by the explosion: Age 26. *unm.*

(Panel 6) Capt. John Henry Strode Batten, 1st Bn. (8th Foot) The King's (Liverpool) Regt.: elder *s.* of the late Col. John Mount Batten, of Upcerne, co. Dorset, and Mornington Lodge, West Kensington, C.B., J.P., Lord Lieutenant co. Dorset (*d.* 1916), by his 1st wife Margaret Annie (*d.*1893), *dau.* of the Rev. John Brooks, Rector of Walton-le-Dale, co. Lancaster: *b.* Aldon, nr. Yeovil, co. Somerset, 23 December 1875: *educ.* Rossall, and Trinity Hall, Cambridge, and after taking his B.A. degree was gazetted to his father's old corps – King's Liverpool Regt. – 20 May 1899: promoted Lieut. 21 March 1900; Capt. 1 December 1909: served through the South African War, 1899 – 1902, being employed with the Mounted Infantry; later as Supply Officer: took part in operations in Natal, 1899, including actions at Reitfontein and Lombard's Kop: defence of Ladysmith, including action of 6 January 1900: operations in Natal, March – June 1900: operations in the Transvaal, December 1900 – October 1901: Orange Free State, October 1901 – 31 May, 1902: Queen's medal, 2 clasps; King's medal, 2 clasps. After the outbreak of the European War, August 1914, he went to France with the 1st Expeditionary Force and consistently did good work, his name being Mentioned in Sir John (now Lord) French's Despatch, 8 October 1914 ('*London Gazette,*' 19 October) "On a particular occasion," 20 September, during the Battle of the Aisne, his Brigadier said, "quite regardless of himself, he encouraged and steadied the men on the right of his battn., and of the brigade, when very heavily attacked, and when the situation at that point was critical. It was owing to his very gallant conduct on that occasion that the portion of the line held its own." He was killed in action, 25 October 1914, being shot through the heart while on his way from the trench to confer with his Commanding Officer. Gen. R.H. Davies wrote, "I should like you to know that he was looked upon by all who knew him as one of the very bravest of the brave, and that by his exceedingly gallant and cool conduct at the Battle of the Aisne he did a great deal to stop a rush and prevent what easily might have proved to be a disaster to our part of the line." And Col. Stevenson, "He saved the whole line on 20 September just by his grit. Nothing would move him from the line he had to take up in that awful wood fight when Kyrke Smith and others were wounded...He was killed outright crossing a small gap in a hedge, by some men hidden in a house about 500 yards away...We buried him that night, beside the Colonel, in an orchard close to a farm outside the village where he was shot." "I owe him a debt I can never repay," wrote Lieut. P.C. Snatt, "If it had not been for his gallant work on 20 September I should now be a prisoner; I was wounded and unable to get away, and it was Strode who saved the line retiring." He *m.* Alberta, *yr. dau.* of P. Kavanagh, M.D., of 56, Queen's Gardens, Lancaster Gate.

(Panel 6) Capt. Edward Henry Brocklehurst, 6th Bn. (Rifles) The King's (Liverpool) Regt. (T.F.): 5th *s.* of the late Henry Brocklehurst, of 'Homesefton,' Aigburth Drive, Sefton Park, Liverpool, by his wife Ellen, *dau.* of William Hutchings: *b.* Waterloo, nr. Liverpool, 15 May 1878: *educ.* Harrow (Moreton's), 1892 – 96: thereafter joined his father's firm as Chartered Accountant: joined the Volunteers, as Subaltern, 1900; apptd. Capt. 6th King's Regt., 22 June 1910, when he secured the certificate of proficiency qualifying him for higher rank. Prior to August 1914, and volunteering for Foreign Service, Capt. Brocklehurst was on the Special Reserve of Officers (gazetted Regimental Instructor of Musketry a short time before war broke out): proceeded to France February 1915 where, on 5 May following, his company was ordered to advance and drive back the Germans who had captured part of their trench near Hill 60. While directing the operation he was instantaneously killed by a bullet from a machine gun: 5 May 1915. A brother officer wrote, "I need not tell you that he was really beloved by the Mess, and also by his Company.": Age 36. *unm.*

(Panel 6) Capt. Ronald Francis Bickersteth Dickinson, 'C' Coy., 10th Bn. (Scottish) The King's (Liverpool) Regt. (T.F.): 2nd *s.* of George Dickinson, of Red How, Cumberland, J.P., C.C., and 2, Sunnyside, Liverpool, by his wife Mary Florence, *dau.* of Edward Robert Bickersteth, F.R.C.S., of Liverpool: and brother to Capt. A.P. Dickinson, M.C., 10th King's (Liverpool) Regt., died 1 June 1918, of wounds received in action nr. Festubert; and Lieut. G.F. Dickinson, 10th King's (Liverpool) Regt., who (severely wounded at Hooge on the same day as his brother Ronald was killed), died in 1932 "as a result of wounds and ill-health contracted in the war": *b*. 23, Abercromby Square, Liverpool, 19 January 1888: *educ*. Rugby: admitted Solicitor, 1910, and at the time of his death was a Manager, Messrs Hill, Dickinson & Co., Liverpool: volunteered for Foreign Service following mobilisation on the outbreak of war; proceeded to France 1 November 1914. He was continuously engaged in the trenches, and trench fighting, until his death, which took place after the capture of four German trenches at Hooge, 16 June 1915. Owing to reinforcements not coming up in time, his men were eventually partially driven back by the German counter attack, and he was left lying wounded in six places, in the fourth German trench. It was believed that he died shortly after capture by the Germans. Eventually the first German line of trenches, and part of the second, were held, but only two officers and about 120 men of the battn. answered the roll call when they were relieved at night. Mentioned in F.M. Sir John (now Lord) French's Despatch of 31 May 1915. His Col. Wrote, "He was absolutely lion-hearted, and I think all will agree that he was pre-eminent in a battn. which I am proud to say numbers many brave men in its ranks. It was my duty on many occasions during the winter months to tramp round the front-line trenches at night, and invariably Ronald was to be found wherever a dirty or dangerous job had to be done." One of his men wrote, "As brave a man as ever held charge. The company idolised him; wherever there was danger he was there." Another, "We absolutely adored him. He was a leader worth following." Another said, "Time and again when any of his men were lying wounded outside the trench, he ordered his men to keep under cover while he himself ran the greatest risk in bringing the wounded in. If anyone deserved the V.C. it was Capt. Ronald Dickinson; he had won it over and over again. He was a little god to his men." And Capt. Noel Chavasse, V.C., "We all looked up to him, he was a byword for calmness and courage.": Age 27. *unm*.

His brother Alan is buried in Houchin British Cemetery (1.A.23); George, Lamplugh (St. Michael's) Parish Churchyard, Cumbria. Since the 1920's two cottages near St. Michael's Church have been utilised as charitable almshouses; one named 'Hooge' the other 'Le Plantin,' they were built by George in memoriam of his brothers. The brothers are also remembered on three brass plaques in Lamplugh (St. Michael's) Church; on George's, his daughter, who died in 1927 aged 8 years, is also remembered.

(Panel 6) Capt. John Graham, Jnr., 10th Bn. (Scottish) The King's (Liverpool) Regt. (T.F.): elder *s*. of John Graham, of 'Mohcroft,' Aigburth Drive, Liverpool, and 'The Croft,' Hoylake, Sugar Refiner, by his wife Mary Gilkison, *dau*. of James Allan, of Glasgow: *b*. Liverpool, 3 April 1877: *educ*. Marlborough: became partner Messrs Macfie & Sons, Sugar Refiners, Liverpool: joined Liverpool Scottish Volunteers (1900) and continued with them for 3 years after they became 10th Territorial Battn. King's Liverpool Regt., retiring with the rank of Captain: immediately rejoined (as Pte.) on the outbreak of war August 1914; given a commission as Lieut. 25 September; promoted Capt. 13 April 1915: went to France October 1914, and was killed in the great charge of the Liverpool Scottish, nr. Hooge, 16 June 1915. Mentioned in Despatches ('*London Gazette*,' 22 June, 1915) by F.M. Sir John (now Lord) French, for 'gallant and distinguished conduct in the field.' Though good at racquets and cricket, it was as a golfer that Capt. Graham was best known in the sporting world. He was in the first flight of amateur golfers, and had attained international honours, and while never getting further than the Amateur Championship semi-final, he had won most of the Club and open prizes. '*The Times*' reported – "Not only was he one of the very finest amateur golfers, but his most delightful and modest nature had endeared him to everyone who ever met him. 'Jack' Graham will be remembered in golfing history as the one really great player who never won a championship. It would not be right to call him an unlucky golfer. He had good chances and a natural genius for the game, but there was something in his temperament that prevented him from playing his best game in the crucial rounds towards the end of a championship. It was certainly not lack of courage in the ordinary sense of the word. No one who knew him could doubt that, and he has given the finest and most conclusive proof to the contrary. But the strain of hard matches day after day always proved too great a strain on his powers of endurance, and though he five times reached the final of the Amateur Championship he never got any farther. He was more successful as a score player than a match player. Only last year at Sandwich he won the St. George's Vase at Sandwich by truly magnificent golf; his record at the Hoylake Medals was one of many successes, and he several times finished first amateur on the list of the Open Championship. On one occasion in particular, at Muirfield, he finished immediately after the great 'triumvirate' and gave Taylor, who was drawn with him, one of the most agitating days of his long career. Capt. Graham was a great golfer. He could not but have been sometimes disappointed on account of his comparative lack of success, and he knew that his friends at Hoylake were more bitterly disappointed on his behalf than he ever was on his own. Not only did no word of complaint or excuse ever escape him, but he never for one moment fell into the opposite error of pretending that he did not care. He took his ups and downs with perfect modesty and quietness, and was always interested in the play and success of others. At Marlborough he distinguished himself at football, cricket and racquets, and if he had had time to play might have made a name for himself as a cricketer, but he always worked very hard at his business. Indeed, he played comparatively little golf, but it was remarkable how he could so constantly play a very fine game with so little practice – an occasional Saturday afternoon and perhaps an evening stroll on the links with two clubs under his arm, being apparently all the practice that he needed.": Age 38. *unm*.

(Panel 6) Capt. David Aitken Lumsden, 4th (Extra Reserve) attd. 1st Bn. (8th Foot) The King's (Liverpool) Regt.: only *s*. of the late David Lumsden, of 'Dalreoch, Dundee, by his wife Kate: *b*. 'Broomknowe,' Broughty Ferry, co. Forfar, 29 December 1887: *educ*. Harris Academy; St. Andrew's University, and University College, Dundee, where, for three years, between 1910 – 1912, he was one of the most popular members of the Union. Full of energy and enthusiasm, talented and of great versatility, he entered heartily into the various phases of college life, and was one of the most prominent members of his set. Above all he will be remembered for his work in the O.T.C. of which he was an original member of his company, and in which he found his greatest interest. He was one of the first batch of non-commissioned officers, and was the first Colour-Sergt. of 'B'Coy.: after taking his 'B' certificate, obtained his commission 2nd Lieut. 4th King's Liverpool Regt.; promoted Lieut. May 1914. Of fair physique, tall, with a commanding presence and bearing, he was in every way fitted for a military career, and most of his time was spent on courses of training at Aldershot, Hythe, and in Ireland: joined his battalion on mobilisation at the outbreak of war with Germany, attd. 1st Battn. for Active Service, and went to the Front, September 1914: wounded nr. Ypres late October following, and, after being at home for a short time, rejoined his battalion at Liverpool, January 1915; promoted Capt. same month: returned to France, March 1915, and was killed in action, 1 May following, nr. Ypres. Buried near St. Jean. The Adjutant of his battalion gave the following particulars of his death, "Capt. Lumsden was killed in action on Saturday, 1st. inst., in the fighting in which the battalion took part. He was shot through the head and killed instantly whilst gallantly leading his men, and his death is a great loss to the battalion, as in him we have lost a good officer and a very popular comrade. It will be a comfort to you to know that he had no suffering, and that he did his duty nobly and behaved in a most gallant way throughout the fighting for the good of his country, and we shall one and all miss him in every way." His Commanding Officer, in a letter to his parents, said, "I cannot tell you what a grief it was to me, and I feel he lost his life in order to save mine. We were in a trench together, and I was on the point of rushing forward to lead some men, who had stopped, under cover. Your son heard me say I was going, when he jumped over the parapet, saying, 'No, sir, I am going,' and rushed forward. His loss to the battalion is very great. I miss him very much – both as a friend and as an officer. He was a fine fellow, an excellent soldier, and was much loved by both officers and men.": Age 27. *unm*.

(Panel 6) Lieut. Edward Benjamin Baker, 3rd (Reserve) attd. 1st Bn. (8th Foot) The King's (Liverpool) Regt.: only *s*. of the late Edward Baker, Engineer, Indian State Railway, by his wife E.J. Baker, since remarried to Joseph Barnes-Boyle, Barrister-at-Law, of 22, Routh Road, Wandsworth Common, London, S.W.: *b*. Campbellpore, Punjab, India, 12 July 1894: *educ*. Grenville School, Guildford, co. Surrey: gazetted 2nd Lieut., Special Reserve, King's (Liverpool) Regt., 17 April 1914: promoted Lieut. 1 August following, attd. 1st Battn. for Active Service in the Great War: served with the Expeditionary Force in France and Flanders, and was killed 26 October 1914, while leading his platoon in an attack on a village: Age 20. *unm*. The following letter was received from his Commanding Officer, "Lieutenant Baker had done so well with the regiment since he joined, and his name had gone up for mention in despatches." Mentioned in F.M. Sir John (now Lord) French's Despatch, 31 May 1915 ('*London Gazette*,' 22 June), for 'gallant and distinguished service in the field.'

(Panel 6) Lieut. (A/Capt) Eric George Brock, M.C., 1/7th Bn. The King's (Liverpool) Regt. (T.F.): *s.* of the Rev. George Albert Brock, B.A., of 21, Harbord Road, Waterloo, Liverpool, Minister of Waterloo Congregational Church, Liverpool, by his wife Minnie Constance, *dau.* of G.I.W. Winzar, Sword Bearer to the Corporation of London: *b.* Liverpool, 19 March 1893: *educ.* Merchant Taylor's School, Crosby (Scholar); St. John's College, Cambridge (Scholar; took a First, Part I – Mathematical Tripos; Second, Part II), intending to compete for the Civil Service, but, on the outbreak of the European War applied for a commission: gazetted 2nd Lieut. Liverpool Regt. October 1914; subsequently promoted Lieut.; thereafter Actg. Capt.: served with the Expeditionary Force in France and Flanders from 1914, and was killed in action in Flanders, 31 July 1917. Awarded the Military Cross ('*London Gazette*,' 20 November 1916) for 'gallant and distinguished service in the field during the fighting on the Somme, when, at the attack on Guillemont, 'A' Coy. of the 7th Liverpool Regt. had advanced too far and had got into an isolated trench; he went in search of them, under fire, found them disorganized, rallied them, and held the trench four days till it was joined up on both flanks.' Mr H. Cradock Watson, Head Master of Merchant Taylor's School, wrote, "When he left he went up to Cambridge with a Mathematical Scholarship to St. John's College, a Lancashire County Scholarship, the 'Great Crosby' Scholarship, and the Exhibition awarded by the Oxford Local Examinations Delegates to the boy who took first place in England in the Senior Examination. This year will long be remembered in the school as 'Brock's year.' Mathematics were, of course, his forte, but he was no mean scholar beside. He achieved distinction in most school subjects, and almost swept the board of Foundation prizes in his last year. He played a prominent part in school life by his activity in the School Debating and Musical Societies.":Age 24. *unm.* (*IWGC record Capt.*)

At 12.15 a.m., on the night of 3 – 4 July 1917, 17th Bn. King's Liverpool Regt. sent out a fighting patrol from the trenches at Observatory Ridge, east of Zillebeke. The objective of the patrol, consisting of Lieut. Aidan Chavasse and eight men, was to gain information regarding the disposition of the German units opposite, obtain identification, and kill the occupants. "On nearing the enemy's wire, the patrol encountered a German patrol, which opened fire on Lieut. Chavasse and his men. A stiff fight ensued and the patrol withdrew, Lieut. Chavasse bringing up the rear, but on reaching our lines the officer was found to be missing. A search party was formed, consisting of Capt. A.I. Draper, Capt. C.E. Torrey, Capt. F.B. Chavasse, R.A.M.C. (brother of Lieut. Chavasse), 2nd Lieut. C.A. Peters, and L/Corpl. Dixon, then went out and searched No-Man's-Land. During the search Capt. Torrey was wounded and taken back to the trenches. 2nd Lieut. Peters and L/Corpl. 11531, H. Dixon then discovered Lieut. Chavasse, who had been wounded in the thigh, lying in a shell hole. Lieut. Peters returned for assistance, but was killed on his way back. Meanwhile, L/Corpl. Dixon had bandaged the wounded officer, and, after awaiting the arrival of necessary assistance, he too went back to our lines for stretcher-bearers to carry Lieut. Chavasse in. But, on returning, the party could not find the wounded officer and had to retire on account of the dawn breaking..." The following night 3 men under L/Corpl. Dixon left the Liverpool's trenches in an endeavour to find Lieut. Chavasse, but to no avail. The body of 2nd Lieut. C.A. Lieut. Peters was found and brought in by another party.

(Panel 6) Lieut. Aidan Chavasse, 'D' Coy., 17th (Service) Bn. (1st City) The King's (Liverpool) Regt.: 4th *s.* of The Right Rev. Francis James Chavasse, Bishop of Liverpool, of The Palace, 19, Abercromby Square, Liverpool, by his wife Edith Jane, *dau.* of the late Joseph Maude, Vicar of Chirk, co. Denbigh (*d.* 1874), by his marriage to the late Mary Fawler Hopper (*d.* 1913): and brother to Capt. Noel G. Chavasse, Royal Army Medical Corps attd. 10th (Liverpool Scottish) Bn. King's (Liverpool) Regt., V.C. & Bar, M.C., died of wounds, 4 August 1917: *b.* Wycliffe Hall, Banbury Road, Oxford, 26 July 1891: *educ.* Private Tutors; Liverpool College, and Corpus Christi College, Oxford, where he received a Second in Mathematics, and Third in History (1914): an active member of the Officer Training Corps at both Liverpool College and Oxford University: after the summer vacation of 1914 intended returning to University to study Theology: volunteered his services on the outbreak of war, August 1914, and applied for a commission gazetted 2nd Lieut. King's (Liverpool) Regt., posted 11th (Pioneer) Battn.: served with his Regiment in France from 1915, subsequently promoted Lieut.: sought and obtained transfer to 17th Battn., April 1917. After taking part in the fighting subsequent to the exploding of the mines at Messines, 7 June 1917, by 1 July 1917 the Battalion were holding the front-line at Observatory Ridge, spending much of their time in this sector taking part in trench raids, and night-time reconnaissance sorties into No-Man's-Land. After encountering, and coming under fire from, an enemy patrol on the night of 3 – 4 July 1917, Lieut. Chavasse was, subsequent to searches made at the time reported missing and wounded; believed killed. In February 1918, after exhausting all possible avenues of enquiry, Bishop Chavasse finally confirmed Aidan as having been killed on or about 4 July 1917. Further to enquiries through the British Red Cross his sister, May, received a letter from L/Corpl. Dixon, "Lieut. Chavasse was attached to 'D' Coy. I went out on patrol with him 3rd – 4th July. We were coming back from the German wire about 3 a.m. when Lieut. Chavasse was hit by a bullet in the right leg between the knee and thigh, I was alone with him, and told him that I could not carry him back myself, and left him lying in a shell hole about 10 yards from the German sap. I went back to him and bandaged him up, and he then told me to leave him as it was fast getting light. I did so, but the same evening, as soon as it was dark, I went back with his brother (Bernard) to the place where I had left Lieut. Chavasse but there was no sign of him. We searched again without success." Ironically the last surviving letter from Capt. N.G. Chavasse is one he wrote to Bernard thanking him for his efforts in trying to save Aidan, "Just a short letter to tell you how proud we all feel of you. Nobody could have done more to get poor old Aidan back. Your efforts seemed to me to have been almost superhuman. I am sorry you had to go through such a terrible experience. I never heard of such a chapter of horrors for a small fighting patrol. I am very sorry about the officer who lost his life trying to get a stretcher (C.A. Peters)...and the way you kept on looking for Aidan is beyond mere praise.": Age 25. *unm.* His brother Francis Bernard served with the Royal Army Medical Corps, and Christopher Maude (twin brother to Noel) served with the Royal Army Chaplain's Dept.

Edith Chavasse, their mother, doted on all her children but especially the youngest Aidan. Every year on the anniversary of his disappearance she dreamt of him, lying in no-man's-land, calling out to her. On the tenth anniversary (1927) she joined him.

His brother Noel is buried in Brandhoek New Military Cemetery (III.B.15). One of only three men to be awarded the Victoria Cross twice, his headstone is unique insomuch as it is the only one in the world engraved with two Victoria Crosses. 2nd Lieut. C.A. Peters is buried in Perth Cemetery (China Wall), Zillebeke (II.A.43).

(Panel 6) Lieut. Francis Robert Dimond, 17th (Service) Bn. (1st City) The King's (Liverpool) Regt.: only *s.* of Francis Dimond, of Tully House, Lenamore, Edgeworthstown, co. Longford, J.P., by his wife Lizzie, *dau.* of Robert Campbell: *b.* Tully House, Lenamore, 19 November 1895: *educ.* Mountjoy School, Dublin, where he gained the First Science Exhibition, Senior Grade, of the Irish Intermediate Education Board Examinations, and First Class Entrance Exhibition to Trinity College, Dublin: joined O.T.C., 1914; obtained his commission March 1915: served with the Expeditionary Force in France and Flanders from January 1916: sent to England May following, having been injured by a grenade; returned to his regiment in France December following, and was killed in action while leading his company against the German trenches, 31 July 1917. His Colonel wrote, "His death is a very great loss to the battalion in which he was so universally popular. His courage and cheerfulness, and good work, was an inspiration to all around him, and I cannot tell you how much his loss is felt by all ranks." And his Captain, "I cannot speak too highly of your son's gallant conduct during the whole time he had been with this battalion. He always set a smiling example of courage and cheerfulness, and this endeared himself to all his brother officers, while the men were devoted to him.": Age 21. *unm.*

(Panel 6) Lieut. Philip Walter Rudolph Doll, Machine Gun Officer, 1st Bn. (8th Foot) The King's (Liverpool) Regt.: 4th *s.* of Charles Fitzroy Doll, of Hadham Towers, Much Hadham, co. Herts.,

F.R.I.B.A., F.S.I., J.P. (London & Hertford), by his wife Emily Frances, *née* Tyler: *b.* 28 May 1890: *educ.* Charterhouse (Cricket XI), and Royal Military College, Sandhurst, where he was in the football team; played both sports in the Army, and, at the Army Rifle Association meeting (Aldershot), won the Lord Roberts Gold Cup for machine-gun practice with his squad: gazetted 2nd Lieut. King's Liverpool Regt. 6 November 1909; promoted Lieut. 10 April 1912: served with the Expeditionary Force in France and Flanders, and was killed in action at the First Battle of Ypres 31 October 1914; previously reported as missing: Age 24.

(Panel 6) Lieut. Philip Templer Furneaux, Asst. Adjt.; 1st Bn. (8th Foot) The King's (Liverpool) Regt.: only *s.* of the Rev. Walter C. Furneaux, Vicar of Dean, co. Bedford, Dean Vicarage, Kimbolton, formerly Chaplain (King's Regt., Mian Mir), by his wife Caroline Rosa: *gdson.* to the late Col. Templer, Lyndbridge, South Devon: *b.* 23 September 1889: *educ.* Rossall (1905 – 08): gazetted 2nd Lieut. Liverpool Regt. 18 September 1909; promoted Lieut. 6 May 1910: served with the Expeditionary Force in France and Flanders, and was killed in action 26 October 1914. At the time of his death he was Assistant Adjutant to his battalion: Age 25.

(Panel 6) Lieut. Kenneth Alexander Gemmell, 10th Bn. (Scottish) The King's (Liverpool) Regt. (T.F.): *s.* of John Edward Gemmell, Surgeon; of 28, Rodney Street, Liverpoool; and 'Beechlands,' Mossley Hill, by his wife Margaret Ann: and brother to 2nd Lieut. S.S. Gemmell, Cameron Highlanders, killed in action 21 March 1918: *b.* co. Ayr, 1895. Killed in action 16 June 1915, at the Battle of Bellewaarde: Age 20.

His brother Stewart is buried in Faubourg D'Amiens Cemetery, Arras (VII.B.8).

(Panel 6) Lieut. William Stewart Turner, 1/10th Bn. (Scottish) The King's (Liverpool) Regt. (T.F.): elder *s.* of William Neil Turner, of Mossley Hill Drive, Sefton Park, Liverpool, by his wife Jessie Stewart, *dau.* of the late Thomas Holder, of Liverpool, J.P.: *b.* Liverpool 19 March 1883: *educ.* Greenbank School, Liverpool, and Sedbergh (Mr Wilson's House, 1898 – 1901), and on leaving there entered the firm of Turner & Dunsett, Liverpool, of which his father was senior partner: enlisted Liverpool Scottish on the outbreak of war; received his commission – Reserve Battn. – 17 November, just before the Regt. left for the Front. In England when his *yr.* brother, Lieut. F.H. Turner, was killed in action at Kemmel, Belgium (10 January 1915), and it was immediately after this that he proceeded to the Front (18 January 1915), where, following upon a petition from the men, he was attached to the platoon with which his brother had been so popular an officer: promoted Lieut. May 1915, and was killed in action while leading his men in the advance on Bellewaarde Farm, Hooge, 16 June 1915. They had just captured a German trench when a heavy shell burst, killing him and Sergt. J.B. Jones instantly. The Liverpool Scottish lost heavily in this action, no fewer than twenty-one officers having been killed, wounded, or reported missing, while the casualties among the rank and file were proportionately heavy. Like his brother W.S. Turner was also a keen athlete. He was in the cricket and Rugby football teams at both Greenbank and Sedbergh, and gained both his cricket and football colours the year he left Sedbergh, being a useful three-quarter and a good cricketer. Afterwards he played regularly at cricket and football for the Liverpool Club, and was captain of the latter club in the season 1909 – 10. In 1908 the two brothers did a remarkable performance against Sedbergh in the Old Sedberghian Match; in the first innings W.S. took 5 wickets for 8 runs and F.H. 5 for 16, then after scoring 66 runs between them, they took 9 wickets in the second innings, F.H. taking 7 for 26 and W.S. 2 for 10 – in all taking 19 wickets for 60 runs. A memorial service to Lieut. Turner and his great friend, 2nd Lieut. C.D.H. Dunlop, of the same Battalion, was held at Sefton Park Church, Liverpool, 5 July 1915, when eloquent tribute was paid to the young officers' gallantry, and the loyalty and devotion to duty which led them at once to answer their country's call on the outbreak of war: Age 32. *unm.*

His brother Frederick is commemorated in Kemmel Churchyard (Sp.Mem.13), 2nd Lieut. Dunlop and Sergt. Jones have no known grave; both are recorded below.

(Panel 6) Lieut. Thomas Wilson, 'C'Coy., 1/6th Bn. (Rifles) The King's (Liverpool) Regt. (T.F.): 3rd *s.* of Col. George Adshead Wilson, V.D. (lately commanding the same battalion), by his wife Sarah Milne (6, Riversdale Road, Aigburth, Liverpool): *b.* Liverpool, 30 May 1891: *educ.* Rugby School; thereafter in

Germany: later entered his father's office: gazetted 2nd Lieut. King's (Liverpool Regt.) 1908: promoted Lieut. March 1911: went to France with his Battalion, and was killed in action between Zillebeke and Hill 60, nr. Ypres, while leading his Platoon in an attack, 5 May 1915. Fond of football and music, he took a keen interest in social work and, for some time prior to mobilisation, commanded a Company of the Christ Church (Liverpool) Lads Brigade: Age 23. *unm.*

(Panel 6) 2nd Lieut. George Bargh, The King's (Liverpool) Regt. attd. 1st Bn. (12th Foot) The Suffolk Regt.: *s.* of the late Isaac Bargh, by his wife Helen (Procter's Farm, Wray, co. Lancaster): *educ.* Halifax, and University College Reading, from whence he graduated B.Sc.: Occupation – Teacher, Hawes Council School: commissioned 2nd Lieut. King's (Liverpool) Regt. 1914: served with the Expeditionary Force, and was killed in action at Ypres 10 May 1915: Age 25. *unm.* In a letter to Mrs Bargh (written in a Prisoner of War Camp in Germany) Col. Wallace, 1st Suffolk Regt., said that on the date of his death – just before the Germans captured the trenches – her son was in the process of bandaging a wounded soldier when he was shot through the head and killed instantaneously.

(Panel 6) 2nd Lieut. William Francis Bullen, 10th Bn. (Scottish) The King's (Liverpool) Regt. (T.F.): *s.* of William Bullen, of Bidston, Birkenhead, co. Chester, by his wife Elizabeth Eleanor. Missing / believed killed in action 16 June 1915: Age 23. *unm.* The Bidston (St. Oswald's) War Memorial, is inscribed with the verse – O Valiant Hearts Who To Your Glory Came, Through Dust Of Conflict And Through Battle Flame, Tranquil You Lie Your Knightly Virtue Proved, Your Memory Hallowed In The Land You Loved – 2nd Lieut. Bullen is one of twenty parishioners who made the supreme sacrifice recorded in remembrance thereon. The memorial also records brothers 2nd Lieut. J.M. Bibby, East Yorkshire Regt., 3 May 1917 (Arras Memorial, Bay 7); Pte. C.L. Bibby, King's (Liverpool) Regt., 17 August 1916 (Abbeville Communal Cemetery, VI.J.4); 2nd Lieut. S.M. Harvie, King's Royal Rifle Corps, 1 June 1918 (Pernes British Cemetery, II.E.39); and Capt. E.F. Harvie, M.C., Gordon Highlanders, 15 June 1918 (Sandpits British Cemetery, II.F.3).

(Panel 6) 2nd Lieut. Christian Dalrymple Hamilton Dunlop, 10th Bn. (Scottish) The King's (Liverpool) Regt. (T.F.): only *s.* of the late Capt. Hamilton Dunlop, Royal Navy, by his wife Julia Robina (23, Murrayfield Avenue, Edinburgh), *dau.* of Patrick Gilmour, of The Grove, Londonderry: *b.* Southsea, co. Hants, 29 June 1880: *educ.* George Watson's College, Edinburgh, and Winchester College: afterwards received business training with Messrs John Warrack & Co., Shipowners, Leith: went to India for five years, eventually entering business with Messrs Pilkington & Dunlop, Liverpool, as Stockbroker: served 2 years with Mounted Coy., Queen's Edinburgh Volunteers (Royal Scots): joined Scottish Battn., King's Liverpool Regt., 31 August 1914 following the outbreak of war; gazetted 2nd Lieut. 17 November 1914: joined his battalion in Flanders 23 January 1915, and was killed in action, being shot through the heart while leading his platoon in an attack on the German trenches at Bellewaarde Farm, nr. Hooge, in the Ypres sector, 16 June following. Buried near where he fell. He was a member of the Royal Liverpool Golf Club, Hoylake, and Secretary of the Liverpool Rugby Football Club: 16 June 1915: Age 34. *unm.*

(Panel 6) 2nd Lieut. Harold Bruce Wallace, 3rd (Reserve) attd. 1st Bn. (8th Foot) The King's (Liverpool) Regt.: *s.* of Mrs E.J. Wallace (78, Thurlow Park Road, Dulwich, London), and the late Dr. James R. Wallace, M.D., F.R.C.S., late of Calcutta, India: *b.* Calcutta, 24 September 1893: *educ.* Dulwich College, where he was in the Second XV: joined 3rd Battn. of his regiment December 1913, attd. 1st Battn., gazetted 2nd Lieut. August 1914. Killed 26 October 1914 in the Great War, while leading the men of his platoon in an attack upon the village of Noord Westhoek, Belgium, a few miles from Ypres. The major of his battalion, writing to his relatives, said, "He had only been with us a short time, but had done well, showed great promise, and took such an interest in his work.": Age 21. *unm.*

(Panel 6) Sergt. 268883, Arthur Cooper, 1/9th Bn. The King's (Liverpool) Regt. (T.F.): formerly 7th Bn.: late *husb.* to Mary Ann Cooper (11, Attwood Street, Sleepers Hill, Anfield): enlisted Liverpool. Killed in action 2 August 1917: Age 38.

(Panel 6) Sergt. 357, Joseph George Alexander Donnan, 'B' Coy., 1/6th Bn. (Rifles) The King's (Liverpool) Regt. (T.F): eldest *s.* of the late Joseph Donnan, Merchant Tailor; of Aigburth, Liverpool, by his wife Margaret Webster (172, Upper Warwick Street, Liverpool) *dau.* of the late George Lawrenson, of Aigburth: *b.* Dingle, Liverpool, 1 November 1881: *educ.* Our Lady of Mount Carmel Roman Catholic School: prior to the outbreak of hostilities with the Central Powers was employed as Clerk; Messrs. J.H. & S. Johnson, Wholesale Druggists, Liverpool, and had completed his fifteenth year with this firm when war was declared: previously joined King's (Liverpool) Rifles, then 2nd Battn. King's Liverpools (T.F.), 1908, and, on the outbreak of war with Germany, volunteered for Foreign Service at once: undertook Imperial Service obligations and proceeded to France 24 February 1915; and was killed in action 30 March 1915, by a sniper while on duty in the trenches. Buried on the side of a railway cutting at Zillebeke. In a letter from one of his officers he was spoken of as being a "most conscientious N.C.O., and one of the best." During his twelve years of service with King's Liverpool Rifles he became one of its crack shots, and won many prizes in addition to two silver shooting cups. In July 1912 he won the 'Queen Mary' prize at Bisley: Age 33. *unm.* Remains 'Unknown British Soldier' recovered unmarked grave (28.I.28.d.9.9); identified – Clothing; reinterred, registered 16 September 1927. *Buried in Sanctuary Wood Cemetery (IV.G.9).*

O Merciful Jesus Have Mercy And Rest His Soul In Peace

(Panel 6) Sergt. 1538, John Blake Jones, 'D' Coy., 1/10th Bn. (Scottish) The King's (Liverpool) Regt. (T.F.): *s.* of J.H. (& Mrs) Jones, of 8, Windsor Road, Liverpool. Killed in action in the advance on Bellewaarde Farm, Hooge, 16 June 1915. The Battalion had just captured a German trench when a heavy shell burst, killing him and Lieut. R.W. Thornton instantly: Age 28.

Lieut. Thornton also has no known grave; he is recorded above.

(Panel 6) Sergt. 821, James Lindsay Marshall, 1/6th Bn. (Rifles) The King's (Liverpool) Regt. (T.F.): *b.* Liverpool: enlisted there. Killed in action 27 March 1915: Age 34. He leaves a wife, Jane Marshall (Mayfield, Penyffordd, co. Flint), to mourn his loss. Remains 'Unknown British Soldier' recovered unmarked grave (28.I.28.d.9.9); identified – Clothing; reinterred, registered 19 September 1927. (*IWGC record 221*) *Buried in Sanctuary Wood Cemetery (IV.G.14).*

Peace Perfect Peace With Loved Ones Far Away
In Jesus Keeping We Are Safe And They

(Panel 6) Corpl. 57607, Sidney Arthur Crane, 18th (Service) Bn. (2nd City) The King's (Liverpool) Regt.: *s.* of Edwin Crane, Storekeeper; of 22, Wheldrake Road, Pitsmoor, Sheffield, by his wife Lizzie, *dau.* of Edward Clarke: *b.* Sheffield, co. York, 11 March 1895: *educ.* Owler Lane Board School: Occupation – Clerk: enlisted West Riding Cyclists: transf'd. King's Liverpool Regt. 19 October 1915: served with the Expeditionary Force in France and Flanders from 1 January 1917, and was killed in action at Ypres 31 July following. Buried at Zillebeke. He was a good musician, and before the war had been for several years Deputy Organist at St. Cuthbert's, Sheffield, and subsequently at the Wesleyan Reformed Chapel: Age 22. *unm.*

(Panel 6) L/Corpl. 1225, Joseph Edward Thompson, 1/10th Bn. (Scottish) The King's (Liverpool) Regt.: *s.* of Annie Thompson (32, The Willows, Breck Road, Everton, Liverpool): *b.* Edge Hill, Liverpool: a pre-war Territorial, was, for nine years, Piper, Liverpool Scottish: undertook Active Service Obligations, Fraser Street, Liverpool, on the outbreak of war August 1914: proceeded to France 2 November following, and was killed in action 22 December 1914: Age 25. *unm.*

(Panel 6) Rfn. 49980, Arthur Adams, 1/6th Bn. (Rifles) The King's (Liverpool) Regt. (T.F.): formerly no.36538, The Prince of Wales's (North Staffordshire Regt.): *s.* of George Adams, of 369, Bilston Road, Wolverhampton, by his wife Agnes: and brother to L/Corpl. TS/7374, P. Adams, 17th Royal Fusiliers, died of wounds 27 July 1916: *b.* Burton, co. Stafford: enlisted Lichfield: served with the Expeditionary Force in France and Flanders, and was killed in action 31 July 1917, before Pommern Castle, Ypres.

His brother Percy also has no known grave; he is recorded on the Thiepval Memorial, Somme.

(Panel 6) Pte. 267894, Thomas Archer, 1/7th Bn. The King's (Liverpool) Regt. (T.F.): formerly no.38621, Royal Engineers: *s.* of the late William Archer, by his wife Annie (26, Bowring Road, Ramsey,

Isle of Man): and elder brother to Pte. G/11421, R. Archer, 23rd Middlesex Regt., killed in action 7 June 1917, aged 20 years: *b.* Douglas: enlisted Seaforth, co. Lancaster. Killed in action 31 July 1917: Age 25. *unm.*

His brother Robert is buried in Bus House Cemetery (A.13).

(Panel 6) Pte. 235213, Joseph Bailey, 19th (Service) Bn. (3rd City) The King's (Liverpool) Regt.: formerly no.6768, Alexandra, Princess of Wales's Own (Yorkshire Regt.): *s.* of John Bailey, of 61, Thursby Road, Burnley, co. Lancaster, by his wife Elizabeth: and elder brother to Pte. 201813, W. Bailey, 2nd Royal Welsh Fusiliers, killed in action 26 September 1917: enlisted Green Howards, Burnley. Missing / believed killed in action 24 July 1917: Age 38. He was married to Mary J. Bailey (61, Thursby Road, Burnley).

His brother William also has no known grave; he is commemorated on the Tyne Cot Memorial (Panel 64).

(Panel 6) Pte. 4290, William Black, 10th Bn.(Scottish) The King's (Liverpool) Regt. (T.F.): 3rd *s.* of the late John Charles Black, of 8, Neptune Street, Birkenhead, co. Chester, by his late wife Annie, *dau.* of J. Stowell: and stepson of Emily Black, of 8, Neptune Street, Birkenhead: *b.* Birkenhead, 10 November 1895: *educ.* Woodlands: Occupation – Railway Clerk: enlisted 12 January 1915: served with the Expeditionary Force in France and Flanders from March, and was killed in action at Hooge 16 June 1915. Buried in Flanders: Age 20. *unm.*

(Panel 6) Pte. 308967, Arthur Brady, 1/9th Bn. The King's (Liverpool) Regt. (T.F.): *s.* of Michael Brady, by his wife Mary: enlisted Liverpool. Killed in action 2 August 1917: Age 35. He leaves a wife Mrs M.E. Brady (15, William Moult Street, Liverpool).

(Panel 6) Pte. 49686, Harry Brook, 1/9th Bn. The King's (Liverpool) Regt. (T.F.): formerly no.30180, Duke of Wellington's (West Riding) Regt.: *s.* of Clara Brook (Delph Terrace, Manchester Road, Milnsbridge): enlisted Halifax, co. York. Killed in action 2 August 1917: Age 26. He leaves a wife, Sarah ('Casa Nova,' 334, Manchester Road, Milnsbridge, co. York). (*IWGC record 49689, 31 July 1917*)

(Panel 6) Pte. 3186, Alan Buchanan, 1/10th (Liverpool Scottish) Bn. The King's (Liverpool) Regt. (T.F.): *s.* of Robert Buchanan, J.P., of Bosbury House, Ledbury, co. Hereford, and Jeannie R. Buchanan, his wife. Killed in action at Hooge, Flanders, 16 June 1915: Age 25. *unm.* Pte. Buchanan (whose brother Robert also served) was the first member of Bosbury (Holy Trinity) Parish to give his life in the Great War.

(Panel 6) Rfn. 201483, Thomas Carey, 5th Bn. The King's (Liverpool) Regt. (T.F.): *s.* of Thomas Carey, of Liverpool. Killed in action 31 July 1917: Age 33. *Buried in Railway Dugouts Burial Ground (Transport Farm), Zillebeke (II.B.1).*

(Panel 6) Rfn. 2238, Colin Chappell, 'D' Coy., 1/6th Bn. (Rifles) The King's (Liverpool) Regt. (T.F.): *s.* of George Chappell, of Storrs Hill, Windermere, late of Brentwood, Hoylake, co. Chester, by his wife Emily: *b. c.*1888: enlisted Liverpool: served with the Expeditionary Force in France and Flanders, and was killed in action 23 March 1915 Buried near where he fell: Age 26. Remains 'Unknown British Soldier 6/ Liverpool' recovered unmarked grave (28.I.28.d.9.9); identified – Clothing, Titles; reinterred, registered 21 September 1927. *Buried in Sanctuary Wood Cemetery (IV.G.15).*

Crescat Crosbeia

(Panel 6) Pte. 350016, Walter Sidney Coleman, 1/9th Bn. The King's (Liverpool) Regt. (T.F.): formerly no.1049, Royal Engineers: *s.* of George Coleman, of 22, Fleet Street, Crewe, co. Chester, by his wife Emily: enlisted Birkenhead. Killed in action 2 August 1917: Age 22.

(Panel 6) Pte. 14952, Harry Felton, 4th (Extra Reserve) Bn. The King's (Liverpool) Regt.: *s.* of Henry Felton, of The Institute, Grange Lane, Gateacre, Woolton, Liverpool, by his wife Sarah: and brother to Pte. 61177, F. Felton, 18th Welsh Regt., killed in action 9 April 1918: *b.* Burslem, co. Stafford, *c.*1897: enlisted Liverpool: served with the Expeditionary Force in France and Flanders from 6 March 1915, and was killed in action 27 April following: Age 18.

His brother Frederick also has no known grave; he is commemorated on the Ploegsteert Memorial (Panel 7).

(Panel 6) Pte. 308136, John Finch, 1/9th Bn. The King's (Liverpool) Regt. (T.F.): *s.* of Job Finch, of 2, Caunce Street, Wigan, co. Lancaster: and *husb.* to Mary Jane Bottomley, *née* Finch (27, Trevor Street, Glodwick, Oldham): enlisted Oldham. Killed in action 2 August 1917: Age 39.

(Panel 6) Pte. 202872, William Ernest Gerrard, 1/9th Bn. The King's (Liverpool) Regt. (T.F.): *s.* of the late James Gerrard, by his wife Emma: late *husb.* to Jeannie McDougall Gerrard (46, Kingsway, Waterloo, Liverpool): enlisted Seaforth, co. Lancaster. Killed in action 2 August 1917: Age 33.

(Panel 6) Pte. 20235, James Goodliffe, 12th (Service) Bn. The King's (Liverpool) Regt.: *s.* of Godfrey Goodliffe, of Sebright House, Fairy Lane, Sale, co. Chester, by his wife Mary Ann: and *yr.* brother to Pte. 26189, J.T. Goodliffe, 3rd Cheshire Regt., died at home 15 November 1918; and Corpl. 14117, C.H. Goodliffe, East Lancashire Regt., killed in action 31 July 1917: *b.* Salford, 1895: enlisted Manchester. Killed in action 29 February 1916: Age 20. *unm.*

His brother John is buried in Sale Cemetery (X.5740); Charles has no known grave, he is recorded on Panel 34.

(Panel 6) Pte. 26437, David Greenhalgh, 4th (Extra Reserve) Bn. The King's (Liverpool) Regt.: *s.* of the late Thomas Greenhalgh, by his wife Elizabeth Sarah Alice (3, Mary Street, Darwen, Liverpool): and brother to L/Corpl. 25121, J. Greenhalgh, 11th King's (Liverpool) Regt., killed in action 18 August 1916; and Pte. 25118, J.W. Greenhalgh, 1st King's (Liverpool) Regt., killed in action 8 August 1916: enlisted Bolton, co. Lancaster: served with the Expeditionary Force in France and Flanders from 6 March 1915, and was killed in action 27 April 1915: Age 30. He leaves a wife Jane Alice Lucas Greenhalgh (23, Gladstone Street, Darwen).

His brother Joseph is buried in Delville Wood Cemetery (VI.K.8); John has no known grave, he is commemorated on the Thiepval Memorial (Addenda Panel).

(Panel 6) Pte. 3770, Douglas Buchanan Grossart, 10th Bn. (Scottish) The King's (Liverpool) Regt. (T.F.): *s.* of Alexander Grossart, of 36, College Road, Great Crosby, Liverpool, by his wife Mary Stuart: and yr. brother to Pte. 2200, R.R. Grossart, 1/7th King's (Liverpool) Regt., who fell the same day; and 2nd Lieut. A.C. Grossart, 10th King's (Liverpool) Regt. attd. Seaforth Highlanders, killed in action 23 July 1918, nr. Rheims: *b.* Waterloo, Liverpool. Killed in action 16 June 1915: Age 19.

His brother Robert also has no known grave, he is commemorated on the Le Touret Memorial; Archibald is buried in St. Imoges Churchyard (A.4).

(Panel 6) Pte. 26711, Joseph William Hannan, 12th (Service) Bn. The King's (Liverpool) Regt.: only *s.* of the late William Nicholas Hannan, J.P., of Calherelly Castle, Co. Limerick, by his wife M., *dau.* of Patrick Fitzgerald, of Tipperary, and nephew of Henry Hannan, of 'Ormskirk,' Alexandra Gardens, Belfast: *b.* Calherelly Castle, 21 January 1882: *educ.* Jesuit College, Mungrey, Limerick: enlisted Pte., 12th Liverpool Regt. March 1915: served with the Expeditionary Force in France from September following, and was killed in action 10 March 1916: Age 34. *unm.*

(Panel 6) Pte. 38470, Reginald Harrison, 20th (Service) Bn. (4th City) The King's (Liverpool) Regt.: *s.* of Livingstone Harrison, of 3, Castle Terrace, Central Promenade, Douglas, Isle of Man, by his wife Margaret Ann: and *yr.* brother to Pte. M2/097733, H. Harrison, Army Service Corps, died of wounds 27 June 1917 (four days before Reginald's death): enlisted Douglas: served with the Expeditionary Force in France from November 1915, and was killed in action 31 July 1917. Age 20. *unm.*

His brother Harold is buried in Brandhoek Military Cemetery (I.K.48).

(Panel 6) Pte. 332827, Thomas Harwood, 1/9th Bn. The King's (Liverpool) Regt. (T.F.): late *husb.* to Margaret Alice Harwood (24, Hull Street, Fulledge, Burnley): enlisted Burnley. Killed in action 2 August 1917: Age 38. (*IWGC record 332837, 31 July 1917*)

(Panel 6) Rfn. 2787, Arthur McGregor Hawitt, 'A' Coy., 1/6th Bn. (Rifles) The King's (Liverpool) Regt. (T.F.): *s.* of Richard Hawitt, of 16, Fitzclarence Street, Liverpool, by his wife Martha Jane: and elder brother to Pte. 29413, W. Hawitt, 1/4th Loyal North Lancashire Regt., killed in action 30 September

1918: *b.* about 1892: enlisted Liverpool: served with the Expeditionary Force, and was killed in action at Ypres 29 March 1915: Age 22. *unm.* Remains 'Unknown British Soldier' recovered unmarked grave (28.I.28.d.9.9); identified – Clothing; reinterred, registered 19 September 1927. *Buried in Sanctuary Wood Cemetery (IV.G.10).*

Never Forgotten

His brother Wilfred also has no known grave; he is commemorated on the Loos (Dud Corner) Memorial.

(Panel 6) Pte. 3305, Graham Thornton Henery, 1/10th Bn. (Scottish) The King's (Liverpool) Regt. (T.F.): *s.* of Perceval Jeffery Thornton Henery, of Spring Bank, Olive Grove, Wavertree, Liverpool, by his wife Maria, *née* Bullock: and brother to Lieut. H.W.L. Henery, 5th King's Own Scottish Borderers, killed in action 19 April 1917, in Palestine: *b.* Liverpool: Religion – Church of England: *educ.* Cothill House, Abingdon, and Harrow School (Church Hill), 1902 – 03: was in business, Messrs Duncan, Ewing & Co., Timber Brokers, Liverpool: enlisted Liverpool Scottish, August 1914: proceeded to France 1 November following, and served continuously in the trenches 29 November – 16 June 1915 on which latter date he was reported 'missing' after the fighting at Hooge and, nothing being heard or seen of him since, death has been presumed: Age 27. *unm.* Two other brothers P.D. and R.P. Henery also served. Remembered on Wavertree (Holy Trinity Church) Roll of Honour.

His brother Hewett is buried in Gaza War Cemetery (VII.C.15).

(Panel 6) Pte. 3583, Samuel Denys Hillis, 10th Bn. (Scottish) The King's (Liverpool) Regt. (T.F.): *s.* of Samuel Hillis, Cotton Broker; of 2, Green Lawn, Rock Ferry, co. Chester, by his wife Emma Melene, *dau.* of the late George Benjamin Keyworth, of Marr Grange, Doncaster: *b.* Liverpool, 9 October 1892: *educ.* Birkenhead School, and Liverpool University; graduated B.Sc., Chemistry Honours School, July 1913 and, after a year's research in Metallurgy, obtained degree M.Sc.: volunteered on the outbreak of war, joined Liverpool Scottish, September 1914: went to Flanders January 1915, and was killed in action in the great charge at Hooge, 16 June 1915: *unm.*

(Panel 6) Spr. 34992, Thomas Albert Hough, 1st (Cheshire) Field Coy., Royal Engineers attd. no.350042, 9th Bn. King's (Liverpool) Regt. (T.F.): *s.* of Daniel Hough, Coachman; of 28, Wilmer Road, Birkenhead, by his wife Mary: *b.* Birkenhead, 5 December 1889: *educ.* Woodlands School: Occupation – Van Driver; Birkenhead Corporation Gas Works: joined Territorials, May 1915: served with the Expeditionary Force in France and Flanders from February 1917, and was killed in action 31 July following. Buried where he fell. 2nd Lieut. J. Ebbetts wrote, "He was in my platoon, and ever since I have known him he has been a good soldier. He died on 31 July doing his duty to the last. You have every reason to be proud of him, and the only consolation I can offer you is that he died a soldier's death, game to the last.": Age 27. *unm.*

(Panel 6) Pte. 10378, Joseph Francis Houston, 4th (Extra Reserve) Bn. The King's (Liverpool) Regt.: *s.* of the late John (& Margaret) Houston, of Toxteth Park, Liverpool, co. Lancaster: and brother to Pte. S/43152, G. Houston, 2nd Gordon Highlanders, killed in action 5 September 1916: enlisted Liverpool: served with the Expeditionary Force in France and Flanders from 6 March 1915, and was killed in action 1 May 1915: Age 21. *unm.*

His brother George also has no known grave; he is commemorated on the Thiepval Memorial, Somme.

PANEL 6 ENDS PTE. J. LEES, KING'S LIVERPOOL REGT.

PANEL 8 BEGINS PTE. A. LLOYD, NORTHUMBERLAND FUSILIERS.

(Panel 8) Pte. 1899, Joseph Maloney, 1st Bn. (5th Foot) The Northumberland Fusiliers: enlisted Hull, co. York: served with the Expeditionary Force in France and Flanders from 14 August 1914, and died 8 November following, nr. Ypres. GRU Report, Zillebeke 5-314E refers remains 'Unknown British Soldier;' recovered unmarked grave (28.J.20.d.8.8); identified – Khaki, Disc; reinterred, registered 4 December 1928. *Buried in Sanctuary Wood Cemetery (IV.O.7).*

(Panel 8) Pte. 5938, James Elliott Mavin, 'X' Coy., 1st Bn. (5th Foot) The Northumberland Fusiliers: *s.* of the late Robert (& Sarah) Mavin: *b.* 1879: joined Regular Army 1899; took part in the South African Campaign: a pre-war Reservist; occupation Storekeeper (lately Engineers Labourer); Messrs Pyman-Bell; Coal Exporters, Coble Dene Dock, Newcastle: rejoined the Colours on mobilisation August 1914; apptd. Corpl., but returned to the ranks to proceed to France November following. Killed in action 16 June 1915; Bellewaarde: Age 36. He *m.* September 1904, Holy Trinity Church, Tynemouth; Miranda Amelia Mavin, *née* Vairy (11, Front Street, Milburn Place, North Shields); and was father to four children.

(Panel 8) Pte. 3096, William Mirrilees, 2nd Bn. (5th Foot) The Northumberland Fusiliers: 3rd *s.* of James Mirrilees, Plasterer; of 42, Coomassie Road, Crofton, Blyth, by his wife Mary, *dau.* of James Gilroy: and elder brother to Pte. 10228, S. Mirrilees, Northumberland Fusiliers, killed in action 11 February 1916, aged 18 years, being shot by a sniper while working in a triangle trench: *b.* Blyth, co. Northumberland, 14 February 1893: *educ.* Wright Street School: enlisted Northumberland Fusiliers 1910: went to France 18 January 1915, and was killed in action 16 February 1915, after delivering a message. Capt. O.B. Foster, Comdg. 'C' Coy, wrote, "He had volunteered to come back from the trenches in broad daylight under a heavy fire to take back a message to battn. headquarters, that ammunition was urgently required. He accomplished this dangerous duty successfully, being slightly wounded in the arm on the way. While at battn. headquarters, where his wound had been attended to by a doctor, a shell struck the building in which he was, a fragment of it hit him on the head, killing him instantly. Had he lived he would probably have been awarded the medal for Distinguished Conduct in the Field." And again, after saying that a "strong recommendation" had been forwarded to the authorities, giving full particulars of his brave act, added, "He certainly well deserved it. Since I wrote I found he took a further message by means of which our artillery, which had been firing in a wrong direction, was directed at the proper place; this was the means of saving a number of our men's lives. In any other war but this he would certainly have gained the V.C., but, as you can imagine, a terribly high standard of courage is required to win anything now. We had a very hard time with our company, but lately things have been a little easier. As we are not now in the same district I can give you the following information – Your son was buried by a farmhouse 2½ miles south of Ypres; the farm is south of the Ypres-Comines Canal, and is 1,200 yards south-east of the Chateau Lankhof. This may enable it to be traced after the war. A cross was erected over it.": Age 22 years. *unm.*

His brother Stuart is buried in Cité Bonjean Military Cemetery (IX.F.88).

(Panel 8) Pte. 88, Frank Newsome, 1st Bn. (5th Foot) The Northumberland Fusiliers: *s.* of Georgina Newsome (1, Heathfield Grove, Heath Lane, Halifax): and brother to Bmdr. L/5964, C. Newsome, 164th Bde. Royal Field Artillery, died of wounds 1 July 1916, aged 29 years: *b.* Ealing, co. Middlesex: enlisted Pontypool, co. Monmouth: served with the Expeditionary Force in France from 14 August 1914, and was killed in action at Ypres 11 November 1914: Age 31.

His brother Charles is buried in Bouzincourt Communal Cemetery Extension (I.C.16)

(Panel 8) Pte. 16715, Robert Oliver, 2nd Bn. (5th Foot) The Northumberland Fusiliers: *s.* of Thomas Oliver, of 13, Bents, Whitburn, Co. Durham, by his wife Jane: *b.* Whitburn, 1898: enlisted Sunderland: served with the Expeditionary Force in France from 18 January 1915, and was killed in action 8 May 1915: **Age 16.**

(Panel 8) Pte. 181, Alexander Paterson, 'W' Coy., 1st Bn. (5th Foot) The Northumberland Fusiliers: Killed in action 18 January 1915; Kemmel. See Pte. M. King (Panel 12).

(Panel 8) Pte. 1650, Ernest Pawson, 1st Bn. (5th Foot) The Northumberland Fusiliers: *b.* Shipton, co. York: enlisted Bradford: served with the Expeditionary Force in France and Flanders from 14 August 1914, and was killed in action at the First Battle of Ypres, 1 November following. Remains recovered unmarked grave (28.O.19.c.0.9); identified – Titles, Disc; reinterred, registered 17 May 1927. *Buried in Sanctuary Wood Cemetery (IV.D.11).*

On 5 June 1917 a platoon of 11th Northumberland Fusiliers were employed as a working party to the Australian Tunnelling Company in the vicinity of Hill 60. After being escorted through a labyrinth of underground galleries they were brought out into the open in an area behind a low ridge and out of direct enemy observation where a high breastwork of sandbags, stretching away for some considerable distance, was to be dismantled and carried into the tunnels beneath the hill for the purpose of tamping the explosive charge that lay there.

Initially the Fusiliers work went well, a human chain made the work easier and good progress was made. Unfortunately the working party was spotted by a German observation balloon and it was not long before shells began falling on the work party's position. Norman Gladden wrote, "…there was something in the approaching scream that marked us as the target. I cringed low as the first shell burst somewhere near the corner. Then we all began running like frightened rabbits back to the burrow, which now seemed so far away. As I turned the last bend a man a few yards ahead crashed to the ground. I recognised him as one of the youngsters of the recent draft and the very man who had taken my place at the corner I had vacated. Aided by the man just ahead, I attempted to lift our stricken comrade, but he was too stiff and heavy and we were now out there alone, some fifty yards or so from the sap entrance. A second salvo left the guns and terror took control of my senses. The next thing I knew I was leaning against the timbers of the opening, panting and frightened…Corpl. Bell of our company (on learning what had happened) demanded why we had not brought the casualty in. Our assertion that he was dead did not satisfy the corporal. 'Come on, one of you men,' he said; 'we must bring him in.' No one budged. .. The corporal lost patience; a last appeal and he started off alone…Against all reason I followed him. We raced along the breastwork. All was again quiet. We bent to raise the prostrate figure, but death had rendered the task of moving such a rigid corpse beyond our united strength .. Shelling recommenced, scattering bags from the breastwork all around us. 'Run!' shouted Corpl. Bell, and with my remaining energies I ran as I had never run before, as a tornado of bursts smashed down the breastwork under the shadow of which we had just been stooping. The enemy had really found his target and we two were lucky to survive. Later on it was reported that the stretcher-bearers, who eventually retrieved the body, were of the opinion that the dead man had been killed immediately, for he had shrapnel in his brain and about the heart. Yet I knew he had run a number of yards before he fell!"

(Panel 8) Pte. 22436, William Roach, 11th (Service) Bn. The Northumberland Fusiliers: *s.* of Joseph Roach, of 89, George Street, Newcastle-on-Tyne, by his wife Annie: enlisted Newcastle-on-Tyne: served with the British Expeditionary Force in France, and was killed by shellfire while engaged on a working party nr. Hill 60, Flanders, 5 June 1917: Age 23. *unm.*

(Panel 8) Pte. 2269, Joseph Sanderson, 2nd Bn. (5th Foot) The Northumberland Fusiliers: *s.* of William Sanderson, of 2, Millers Lane, Byker, Newcastle-on-Tyne, by his wife Mary Ann: and yr. brother to Pte. 7798, T.W. Sanderson, 1st Northumberland Fusiliers, killed in action 12 December 1914: *b.* Byker: enlisted Newcastle-on-Tyne: served with the Expeditionary Force in France from 18 January 1915, and was killed in action 19 February 1915: Age 24. *unm.*

His brother Thomas also has no known grave; he is recorded below.

(Panel 8) Pte. 7798, Thomas William Sanderson,, 1st Bn. (5th Foot) The Northumberland Fusiliers: *s.* of William Sanderson, of 2, Millers Lane, Byker, Newcastle-on-Tyne, by his wife Mary Ann: and elder brother to Pte. 2269, J. Sanderson, 2nd Northumberland Fusiliers, killed in action 19 February 1915: *b.* Byker: enlisted Newcastle-on-Tyne: served with the Expeditionary Force in France from 14 August 1914, and was killed in action 12 December 1914: Age 28. *unm.*

His brother Joseph also has no known grave; he is recorded above.

(Panel 8) Pte. 1698, Joseph Shaftoe, 1/7th Bn. The Northumberland Fusiliers (T.F.): *s.* of the late Joseph Shaftoe, by his marriage to Sarah Jane Rose, *née* Shaftoe (71, Matilda Street, Newcastle-on-Tyne): a pre-war Territorial, volunteered for Overseas Service on the outbreak of war: proceeded to France April 1915, and was killed in action on the 28th of that month: 28 April 1915: Age 30. He was married to Jane Shaftoe (11, Clavering Road, Bleach Green, Winlaton, Blaydon-on-Tyne, Co. Durham).

(Panel 8) Pte. 1320, William Simpson, 1/4th Bn. The Northumberland Fusiliers (T.F.): *s.* of the late William Simpson, by his wife Eliza (17, Warkworth Street, Lemington-on-Tyne), *dau.* of William

Tiplady, of Kibblesworth, Co. Durham: *b*. Dewley, Throckley, 2 January 1897: enlisted following the declaration of war: served with the Expeditionary Force in France and Flanders, and was killed in action west of Wieltje (vicinity Potijze) 25 May 1915. Sergt. R. Rewcastle, 'B' Coy., in forwarding to his mother a Bible taken from his pocket, wrote, "He died nobly while doing a duty that would have increased the safety of his comrades. He was buried the same day, and a cross marks the spot where he lies." Age 18.

(Panel 8) Pte. 19337, Charles Rae Small, 11th (Service) Bn. The Northumberland Fusiliers: brother to Pte. 18122, W.R. Small, 1st King's Own Scottish Borderers, killed in action 1 July 1916: *b*. Hampton, co. Lanark: enlisted Hamilton: served with the Expeditionary Force, and was killed in action at Messines 7 June 1917. (*IWGC record Rae-Small*)

His brother William also has no known grave; he is commemorated on the Thiepval Memorial, Somme.

(Panel 8) Pte. 2031, William Watson Smails, No.2 Coy., 1/7th Bn. The Northumberland Fusiliers (T.F.): *s*. of Joseph D. Smails, of Shilbottle, Lesbury, nr. Alnmouth, co. Northumberland, by his wife Jane Ann: and yr. brother to Pte. 36056, J. Smails, 4th King's Own Yorkshire Light Infantry, died of wounds 22 April 1918: *b*. Alnwick: enlisted there. Killed in action 26 April 1915: Age 29. *unm*. Dedicated – 'To The Glory OF God And In Memory Of The Men Of This Parish Who Gave Their Lives In The Great War 1914 – 1919,' the brothers Smails are remembered on the Shilbottle (St. James) Parish Church War Memorial. (*IWGC record Smalles*)

His brother John is buried in Etaples Military Cemetery (XXIX.K.6A).

(Panel 8) Pte. 2527, Edward Henderson Tait, 1/7th Bn. The Northumberland Fusiliers (T.F.): *s*. of Richard Tait, of 28, Hedgehope Terrace, Chevington Drift, Morpeth, co. Northumberland, by his wife Isabella: enlisted Alnwick. Killed in action 19 June 1915: Age 22. He was married to Eleanor Shotton Tait (17, Queen Street, Amble, co. Northumberland).

(Panel 8) Pte. 2458, David Kay Tulloch, 5th Bn. The Northumberland Fusiliers (T.F.): *yr*. *s*. of Capt. Thomas S. Tulloch, Master Mariner; of 32, Linkshill Terrace, North Shields, and his wife Helen: *b*. Tynemouth, 1894: enlisted Wallsend-on-Tyne: served with the Expeditionary Force in France from 20 April 1915; moved up to Ypres sector and into trenches Wieltje, 2 a.m., 25 April, and was killed in action nr. St. Julien, afternoon of 26 April 1915: Age 20. The Battalion War Diary records on the morning of 26 April 'the enemy were breaking through our line. Battalion ordered out to rectify this and make a counter-attack. Arrived at position 11.40 a.m. and ascertained report was incorrect. Message sent to Bde. Major to that effect.On the 26th of April, the 149th Brigade, with the support of Canadian Artillery, was instructed to attack St Julien 'astride the Wieltje road. The 4th, 5th and 6th Northumberland Fusiliers as been available for this, while the 5th Battalion had been sent up during the morning to Foruin where it had been reported, incorrectly, that the Germans were breaking in. The Diary notes that on the 26th, it was reported that the 'enemy were breaking through our line. Battalion ordered out to rectify this and make a counter attack. Arrived at position 11:40am and ascertained that report was not correct. Sent in message to Bde Major to that effect…. Battalion was being heavily shelled. The Brigade had made an attack on St Julian during the afternoon. Successful up to a point, but not being supported. Had to retire. Very heavy losses. Brigadier Riddell killed. Captain Nash and Lieut Bainbridge were also killed. Reported Battalion was being heavily shelled. Brigade made an attack on St. Julien in the afternoon, successful up to a point but, not being supported, had to retire. Very heavy losses. Officers – 2 killed, 1 Missing; O.R.- 9 killed, 68 wounded, 31 missing.'

(Panel 8) Pte. 1989, Thomas Henry Wake, 1/7th Bn. The Northumberland Fusiliers (T.F.): *s*. of Richard Wake, of The Gatehouse, Bamburgh Castle, co. Northumberland, by his wife Mary: and elder brother to Pte. 1598, W.H. Wake, Northumberland Fusiliers, killed in action the same day: *b*. Bamburgh: enlisted Alnwick. Killed in action 26 April 1915: Age 25.

His brother Wilfred also has no known grave; he is recorded below.

(Panel 8) Pte. 1598, Wilfred Hereward Wake, 1/7th Bn. The Northumberland Fusiliers (T.F.): *s*. of Richard Wake, of The Gatehouse, Bamburgh Castle, co. Northumberland, by his wife Mary: and yr.

brother to Pte. T.H. Wake, 1989, Northumberland Fusiliers, killed in action the same day: *b*. Belford: enlisted Anstead. Killed in action 26 April 1915: Age 20.

His brother Thomas also has no known grave; he is recorded above.

(Panel 8) Pte. 2972, Cecil Davies Wood, 1/5th Bn. The Northumberland Fusiliers (T.F.): *s*. of James L. (& Margaret S.) Wood, of 606, Wellbeck Road, Walker-on-Tyne: *b*. Newcastle-on-Tyne, *c*.1896: volunteered and undertook Active Service obligations following the outbreak of war: served with the Expeditionary Force in France and Flanders from 20 April 1915, and was killed thirteen days later (2 May 1915) by a high explosive shell bursting in the trench his battalion were occupying nr. Hill 60: Age 18. See Pte. J. Bain, Perth Cemetery (China Wall), (II.A.8) and Pte. T. Cuskern (I.L.40); also L/Corpl. T. Hardy and Pte. R. Heslop, Menin Gate Memorial (Panel 12); Pte. T. Cowen (Addenda Panel 59); and Pte. T.C. Dodds, Bailleul Communal Cemetery Extension (I.A.161).

(Panel 8) Lieut.Col. Walter Latham Loring, Comdg. 2nd Bn. (6th Foot) The Royal Warwickshire Regt.: 6th *s*. of the Rev. Edward Henry Loring, Rector of Gillingham, co. Suffolk: and brother to Major C.B. Loring, 37th Lancers (Baluch Horse), killed in action 21 December 1914; and Capt. W. Loring, Scottish Horse, killed in action 24 October 1915: *b*. Gillingham Rectory, 3 April 1868: *educ*. Fauconberge School, Beccles; Marlborough College, where he gained a scholarship; and Trinity Hall, Cambridge. As a boy he had lived with his mother at Ewshot, where all the members of the family were held in high esteem. He had the misfortune to lose his mother and sister by the foundering of the steamer in which they were going to Australia to visit a brother of the Colonel: joined Royal Warwickshire Regt. 1889, serving with it in India, Malta and, in the South African Campaign against the Boers, with the Mounted Infantry in the Transvaal: obtained his steps – Lieut. 1890; Capt. 1898; Major 3 November 1904: succeeded to O.C., 2nd Battn. 1914; antedated in his rank two years. The history of the 2nd Warwicks, led by their gallant Colonel, forms one of the many stirring episodes in the earlier part of the Great War. The battalion returned home from Malta in September 1914, and after a few weeks at home landed at Zeebrugge early in October. From the 19th of that month they were almost continually engaged with the enemy, near Ypres and Menin. On 23 October the Warwicks and Welsh Fusiliers were on the left of the line. A large force of the enemy unexpectedly appeared on the flank, and it was with difficulty, after severe fighting, that the Warwicks were liberated from a dangerous position. During this action Lieut. Col. Loring was struck on the foot by shrapnel, and though urged to go back to the hospital to have his wound attended to, refused to do so, and continued in his command with his foot bound up in a puttee, as he could no longer get a boot on. After the action the General commanding the Division came to see the battalion, and highly complimented their Colonel for his skill, and the battalion generally for its bravery and endurance. Next day, 24 October, the battalion was again hotly engaged, near Becelaere. The fighting was thus described by a General Officer:– "October 24. Again an attack on the line, and at 8 a.m. news that the line was broken. The Warwicks were sent up. They behaved splendidly: drove back the Germans, cleared a wood, and saved the situation. They lost one hundred and nine men and several officers, including the Colonel. Such a good sort, his death is a terrible loss to us." In this action, no longer being able to walk, Lieut. Col. Loring insisted on leading his battalion on horseback, thus, of course, exposing himself to far greater risk. Two of his chargers were shot under him, and he himself was killed instantaneously. A Staff Officer, who subsequently returned to England, and who was present during the fighting, described the general admiration among officers and men of Lieut.Col. Loring's courage and example, and the devotion of both officers and men of the Warwicks to their Colonel. A wounded N.C.O., who was in the action, wrote of him, "I am sorry to say our gallant Colonel was killed the same day, and, my word! he was a brave man. He was always in front of his regiment. I have only written what I have seen with my own eyes, and it is enough to make anyone's heart bleed.": Age 46. While in England Lieut.Col. Loring had been, 1908 – 1912, Staff Officer; Officers' Training Corps, Birmingham and Bristol Universities; and Royal Agricultural College, Cirencester. He was known as one of the best types of Englishman, a gallant soldier, a fine gentleman, and a Churchman who took his faith with him into everyday life. He was particularly interested in lads, and did much valuable work in connection with the C.E.M.S. For his services in the

Great War he was Mentioned in Sir John (now Lord) French's Despatch, 14 January 1915. He *m.* the *yst. dau.* of the Rev. (& Mrs) R.M. Marshall, late Rector of Hedenham, co. Norfolk, and left ten children – Constance & Grace (twins), *b.* 1899; Henry, *b.* 1900; Edward Christopher, *b.* 1901; Patience, *b.* 1904; Madeline, *b.* 1905; Faith, *b.* 1910; Marion, *b.* 1912; David & Joan (twins), *b.* 1914.

Both of Lieut.Col. Loring's brothers have no known grave; Charles is commemorated on the Neuve-Chapelle (Indian) Memorial (Panel 7), William, Helles Memorial, Gallipoli (Panel 21).

(Panel 8) Capt. William Maynard Carlisle Crowe, Reserve of Officers, The Royal Warwickshire Regt. attd 1st Bn. (48th Foot) The Northamptonshire Regt.: *s.* of Major-General Thomas Carlisle Crowe, late R.H.A. (ret'd.): *b.* Curragh Camp, 11 September 1870: *educ.* St. Paul's School, and Royal Military College, Sandhurst: gazetted 2nd Lieut. Royal Warwicks, 25 July 1891; promoted Lieut. 25 January 1893; Capt. 3 September 1898: retired 25 August 1907; joined Reserve of Officers: attd. 1st Northamptonshire Regt. after the outbreak of the European War: served with the Expeditionary Force in France and Flanders, and was killed in action nr. Ypres, 8 November 1914: Age 42. Capt. Crowe was a member of the United Service Club, and the Swiss Alpine and Ski Clubs. He *m.* 1904, Elizabeth Hannah Stanley, widow of C. Archer. (*IWGC record Carlisle-Crowe*)

(Panel 8) Capt. John Hugh Gardiner McCormick, 4th attd. 2nd Bn. (6th Foot) The Royal Warwickshire Regt.: *s.* of Samuel S. McCormick, of Shandon, Monkstown, Co. Dublin, and Emily, his spouse: and brother to Lieut. J.G. McCormick, 2nd Worcestershire Regt., killed in action 16 May 1915: *b.* 3 March 1886: *educ.* St. Lawrence College, Ramsgate, co. Kent. Killed in action 19 October 1914: Age 28. *unm.* Remembered on Monkstown Parish Church; St. Lawrence College, and St. Jude's Church (Kensington) Memorials.

His brother James also has no known grave; he is commemorated on the Le Touret Memorial.

(Panel 8) Capt. Cameron O'Bryen Harford Methuen, 2nd Bn. (6th Foot) The Royal Warwickshire Regt.: *s.* of the late Col. C.L. Methuen, Comdg. 1st City of Bristol Volunteers, late of the Cameron Highlanders (Old 79th), of 'Llystroyddn,' Pumpsaint, co. Carmarthen, and the late Mrs Methuen: *b.* Heidelberg, Germany, 7 May 1876: *educ.* Private School, Clifton; Harrow, and subsequently with military tutors: joined Warwickshire Militia, February 1895; becoming Lieut. March 1897: gazetted 2nd Lieut. 1st (Regular) Battn. January 1898: promoted Lieut. August the same year; Capt. February 1901: volunteered for Active Service on the outbreak of the South African War and attd. Royal Irish Fusiliers, with whom he sailed to South Africa: present at the relief of Ladysmith, including action at Colenso: operations in Orange Free State, including actions at the Vet and Zand Rivers: Transvaal, including actions nr. Johannesburg, Pretoria, and Diamond Hill: Transvaal east of Pretoria, including the action at Belfast (Queen's Medal, five clasps; King's Medal, two clasps). After Colenso he rejoined his own regiment, when that was sent out, and served with the Mounted Infantry through the remainder of the war. On the outbreak of the Great War his battalion was stationed at Malta, and brought to England, September 1914, leaving for the Front, 4 October following, as part of VIIth Division; disembarked Zeebrugge. Shot and killed instantaneously in the trenches before Ypres, while looking through his field glasses, 21 October 1914. Capt. Methuen was a relative of Field Marshal Lord Methuen, G.C.B.; 'a very distinguished soldier.' He was member of the Army & Navy Club: Age 38.

(Panel 8) Capt. Eric Charles Schooling, 2nd Bn. (6th Foot) The Royal Warwickshire Regt.: 2nd *s.* of Frederick Schooling, of 'Hollydene,' Bromley, co. Kent, by his wife Lily: and brother to the Rev. C.H. Schooling, Army Chaplain's Dept., died of wounds at Poperinghe, 21 June 1917: *b.* 27 June 1883: *educ.* Tonbridge School, and Royal Military College, Sandhurst: gazetted 2nd Lieut. Royal Warwickshire Regt. May 1901, just before his eighteenth birthday as, owing to the South African War, the time of instruction at the R.M.C. was shortened: promoted Lieut. April 1905; Capt. January 1913. On the outbreak of the Great War he was serving with 2nd Battn. of his regiment, part of VIIth Division, which landed at Zeebrugge, and, after forced marches in Belgium, lost many of its officers in the fighting around Ypres. Officially reported wounded November 1914, and 'missing' in the following March; no evidence as to his fate, except that of prisoners, could be obtained, and definite news only came to hand after many enquiries. Prisoners state that Capt. Schooling was shot in the head and killed instantaneously while fighting at Gheluvelt, Belgium, 31 October 1914: Age 31. At the time of his death he was in command of a trench, and no other officer was present, but a Sergeant, writing from Altdamn, wrote that his Captain's last words, just before he was shot, were, "Mind, no surrender." The letters received from prisoners of war, formerly in Captain Schooling's regiment, and with him when he was killed, tell frequently of his bravery and character. One writer says, "I shall never forget his last stand as long as I live. No man could ever set a more noble example;" another says, "He was a splendid officer, and encouraged us all to hold the trench up to the last, in spite of the terrific shell and rifle fire, and our very heavy losses. The few of us who are left regret him very much." He *m.*, April 1910, Edith McTaggart Gordon, *dau.* of J. (& Mrs) Nisbet Paton, of Radford Manor House, near Leamington, who survives him with one daughter.

His brother Cecil is buried in Lijssenthoek Military Cemetery (XIII.A.21).

On 22 April 1915 the Germans used poisonous gas for the first time in modern warfare. Unleashed against French Territorial troops its effect was devastating, causing the French to retire thus exposing the British line. Three days later, on 25 April, 1st Royal Warwicks were ordered to relieve the Canadians in the vicinity of St. Julien, near Ypres. Encountering heavy fire in their efforts to relive the Canadians, six of the Battalion's officers – Capt. H.J.I. Walker, Lieuts. G.S. MacLagan, J.O. Payne, R.B.B. Tillyer, C.H. Crowley, and 2nd Lieut. A. Jowitt – lost their lives. Of the six officers aforementioned only Lieut. J.O. Payne has a known grave – New Irish Farm Cemetery (II.F.6).

(Panel 8) Capt. Henry John Innes Walker, attd. 1st Bn. (6th Foot) The Royal Warwickshire Regt.: *s.* of the late Henry Charles Holden Walker (d.1918), by his wife Cecilia Kathleen, *née* Taylor (Victoria Avenue, Remuera, Auckland, New Zealand): *b.* 1890: *educ.* King's College, Auckland: joined Imperial Forces from New Zealand Forces, 1910; gazetted 2nd Lieut. attd. 1st Royal Warwickshire Regt. for Active Service: proceeded to France October 1914: promoted Capt. January 1915: Killed in action 25 April 1915: Age 25. Remembered on St. Aidan's Church War Memorial, Remuera. See Lieuts. G.S. Maclagan, R.B.B. Tillyer, and 2nd Lieut. A. Jowitt below; Lieut. C.H. Crowley (Panel 57), and Lieut. J.O. Payne; New Irish Farm Cemetery (II.F.6).

(Panel 8) Lieut. Gilchrist Stanley Maclagan, 3rd (Reserve) attd. 1st Bn. (6th Foot) The Royal Warwickshire Regt.: 3rd *s.* of the late T.J. Maclagan, M.D., of 9, Cadogan Place, London, S.W.: *b.* London, 5 October 1879: *educ.* Eton, and Magdalen College, Oxford (Third Class Hons., History): Member, London Stock Exchange (1904): gazetted 2nd Lieut. 3rd Royal Warwickshire Regt. August 1914: attd. 1st Battn. December following, leaving for France that month, and was killed in action near Pilckem Wood, Ypres, 25 April 1915, three days after the first German gas attack on the Canadians, whom his battalion relieved. Promoted Lieut. to date from 2 February 1915; promotion gazetted posthumously ('*London Gazette,*' 15 May 1915). While at Oxford he steered the University crew, 1899, 1900, 1901 and 1902 (winning 1901), and the Leander crew in the race for the Grand Challenge Cup eight times, winning six times. The 1902 crew rowed in the International Regatta at Cork, and won in the same summer as it lost the Grand. He also acted as coxswain for the Leander VIII, which won at the Olympia Regatta in 1908 against all comers. Mr Maclagan was undoubtedly the best (as he was the best known) cox in the last twenty-five years, and combined all the qualities for that post in a very marked degree. He was also a fine judge of rowing, crews and coaches alike setting great store by his opinion. On the committee of the Leander Club, and of the Henley Regatta, at the time of his death he was Hon. Secretary of the Amateur Rowing Association. He was a fine all round sportsman, an excellent shot, and a first class fisherman: Age 35. *unm.* See also Capt. H.J.I. Walker, above; Lieut. R.B.B. Tillyer, and 2nd Lieut. A. Jowitt, below; Lieut. C.H. Crowley (Panel 57), and Lieut. J.O. Payne New Irish Farm Cemetery (II.F.6).

(Panel 8) Lieut. Ronald Claude Nicolai, 1st Bn. (6th Foot) The Royal Warwickshire Regt.: *s.* of Adolfo Nicolai, formerly Major, Italian Army; of Forsham Cottages, Rolvenden, Cranbrook, co. Kent, and his wife Claudia Augusta Ormonde: and nephew to Henry Ormonde, of Leeds: Religion – Roman Catholic: obtained his commission 1914. Killed in action 25 April 1915, Kitchener's Wood, nr. St. Julien, Ypres: Age 22. *unm.*

(Panel 8) Lieut. Richard Bateson Blunt Tillyer, 'C' Coy., 1st Bn. (6th Foot) The Royal Warwickshire Regt.: *s.* of the late Richard Henry Tillyer, by his wife Florence Anna (Marston Gate, Brockenhurst, co. Hants): *b.* 27 November 1884: *educ.* Haileybury College. Killed while attacking German trenches nr. Pilckem Wood, Ypres, 25 April 1915: Age 20. Five brother officers also fell. See also Capt. H.J.I. Walker and Lieut. G.S. Maclagan, above; 2nd Lieut. A. Jowitt, below; Lieut. C.H. Crowley (Panel 57), and Lieut. J.O. Payne, New Irish Farm Cemetery (II.F.6).

(Panel 8) 2nd Lieut. John Arthur Christopher Croft, 4th (Extra Reserve) Bn. The Royal Warwickshire Regt. attd. 2nd Bn. (76th Foot) The Duke of Wellington's (West Riding) Regt: *yst. s.* of Henry Herbert Stephen Croft, Barrister-at-Law, Recorder of Tenterden; of Sussex Square, Brighton, by his wife Emma: *b.* 28, Royal Crescent, London, 15 April 1888: *educ.* Charterhouse; and Trinity College, Cambridge: gazetted 2nd Lieut. Royal Warwickshire Regt. August 1914: trained Isle of Wight: served with the Expeditionary Force in France and Flanders from November 1914, attd. 2nd West Riding Regt., until April 1915 when he was killed on the 18th. of that month in the first attack on Hill 60, Ypres, "while," in the words of his Commanding Officer, "leading his men with the greatest bravery in the successful charge on Hill 60 on Sunday last. We have lost a most capable and gallant officer and charming friend whose place will be hard to fill." Mr Croft was an international hockey player, Blackheath Club, champion of the Thames Punting Club (1912), and member of the New University Club, St. James's Street, London: 18 April 1915: Age 27. *unm.*

(Panel 8) 2nd Lieut. Denis Deane, 'C' Coy., 2nd Bn. (6th Foot) The Royal Warwickshire Regt: *s.* of Major C.L. Deane (Royal Warwickshire Regt.), of 'The Lodge,' Kent Road, Ellerslie, Fleet, co. Hants, and his wife: *educ.* Wellington College; Royal Military College, Sandhurst: gazetted 2nd Lieut. Royal Warwickshire Regt. 15 August 1914: served in the European War; killed in action 23 October 1914: Age 18.

(Panel 8) 2nd Lieut. Arthur Jowitt, 1st Bn. (6th Foot) The Royal Warwickshire Regt.: *s.* of the late Joseph Jowitt, of Tipping Street, Manchester: *b.* Leeds, co. York, 17 January 1878: *educ.* commercially: enlisted Pte., Royal Warwickshire Regt., 1895: served throughout the South African War (Queen's Medal, five clasps): commissioned (after 19 years in the ranks) 2nd Lieut. Royal Warwickshire Regt., December 1914; apptd. 1st Battn. for Active Service in the war against Germany: proceeded to France in the latter month, and was killed in action nr. Ypres, Flanders, 25 April 1915. His Company Commander, in writing to 2nd Lieut. Jowittt's widow, gave the following account of the circumstances under which he met his death, "We were to attack a wood; between us and the wood was a farm which we were told was unheld. I was told to extend the men close to the farm by the Commanding Officer, and did so. While doing so the enemy opened on us from the supposed unheld farm. We ran to some dead ground within twenty yards of their trench, and were under cover. Your husband charged with his platoon, but they were all killed except one man. He fell with his arms on the parapet of their trench, and the men say that the Germans pulled him into their trench, but I did not see this myself. I am very much afraid there is no doubt your husband was killed, as he was so very close, and must have been hit more than once. A magnificent soldier, officers and men were all devoted to him." His Colonel wrote, "He was the bravest of the brave, and, if he had to die, he died as he would have wished to do – bravely leading his men, who followed him everywhere.": Age 37. He *m.* Ethel Sarah, *dau.* of William Harwood, of Leamington Spa, and had a son, William Joseph, *b.* December 1911. See also Capt. H.J.I. Walker, Lieuts. G.S. MacLagan and R.B.B. Tillyer above; Lieut. C.H. Crowley (Panel 57), and Lieut. J.O. Payne (New Irish Farm Cemetery, II.F.6).

(Panel 8) 2nd Lieut. Frank Ricard, 4th (Extra Reserve) attd. 1st Bn. (6th Foot) The Royal Warwickshire Regt.: eldest *s.* of Charles Ricard, of 97, Westbourne Terrace, Hyde Park, London, W.: *b.* Amsterdam, 8 January 1888: *educ.* Harrow; and King's College, Cambridge (M.A., LL.B.): subsequently called to the Bar; Member – Inner Temple: member of O.T.C – Harrow & Cambridge: received his commission 4th Royal Warwickshire Regt., October 1914: served with the Expeditionary Force in France attd. 1st Battn., and was killed in action 25 April 1915, nr. St. Julien, Flanders. As an amateur musician he was a member of the Oxford & Cambridge Musical Club, being a perfect violin player. A very good rifle shot, he was in the Harrow team which shot at Bisley: Age 27. *unm.*

(Panel 8) L/Sergt. 2312, James Morris O'Callaghan, 1st Bn. (6th Foot) The Royal Warwickshire Regt.: elder brother to Rfn. A/3769, J. O'Callaghan, 8th King's Royal Rifle Corps, killed in action 24 July 1915; Hooge: *b.* Budbrooke, Warwick: enlisted Birmingham: served with the Expeditionary Force in France from 22 August 1914, and was killed in action 26 April 1915: Age 20. *unm.* All correspondence regarding James and Joseph should be addressed c/o their sister Mrs Kate Rachel (37, King's Street, Smethwick, co. Stafford).

His brother Joseph also has no known grave; he is recorded on Panel 53.

(Panel 8) L/Corpl. 9779, Harry Dennis, 1st Bn. (6th Foot) The Royal Warwickshire Regt.: *s.* of E. (& Mrs) Dennis, of 2 Court, 9 House, Alcock Street, Birmingham: and *yr.* brother to Pte. 8452, W. Dennis, 2nd Royal Warwickshire Regt., killed in action 19 October 1914: enlisted Birmingham, co. Warwick: served with the Expeditionary Force in France and Flanders from 22 August 1914, and was killed in action at the Second Battle of Ypres, 25 April 1915: Age 29.

His brother Walter also has no known grave; he is recorded below.

(Panel 8) Pte. 28727, Edgar Percy Baker, 11th (Service) Bn. The Royal Warwickshire Regt.: formerly no.S4/144931, Army Service Corps: twin *s.* of the late Albert Baker, Journeyman Bricklayer; of 41, Windsor Road, Bexhill, by his wife Kate Jane Willard, *née* Baker (Thornhill, Chillenden, Canterbury, co. Kent): *b.* 'The Honies,' Bexhill, 27 May 1894: enlisted A.S.C., Hastings: served with the Expeditionary Force in France and Flanders, subsequently transf'd. Royal Warwickshire Regt.: moved with his battalion 5 October 1917, into the front line at Tower Hamlets Ridge, and was killed there three days later, 8 October, by shell fire: Age 23. *unm.*

(Panel 8) Pte. 2446, Sidney Robert Bousfield, 'B' Coy., 2nd Bn. (6th Foot) The Royal Warwickshire Regt.: *s.* of George Bousfield, Gardener; of 10, King's Terrace, Southsea, Portsmouth (now 'The Lawns Cottage,' Lutterworth Road, Nuneaton), by his wife Sarah Jane, *dau.* of Robert Bateman: *b.* Coventry, co. Warwick: *educ.* Warwick Army School: Occupation – Collier: enlisted June 1913: served with the Expeditionary Force in France and Flanders from August 1914; wounded during the Retreat from Mons and invalided home: returned to France, and was killed in action at Hill 60 during the 2nd Battle of Ypres, 26 April 1915. Buried at Ypres: Age 19.

(Panel 8) Pte. 8452, Walter Dennis, 2nd Bn. (6th Foot) The Royal Warwickshire Regt.: *s.* of E. (& Mrs) Dennis, of 2 Court, 9 House, Alcock Street, Birmingham: and elder brother to L/Corpl. 9779, H. Dennis, 1st Royal Warwickshire Regt., killed in action 25 April 1915, nr. St. Julien: enlisted Birmingham, co. Warwick: served with the Expeditionary Force in France and Flanders from 6 October 1914, and was killed in action less than two weeks later, 19 October 1914: Age 31.

His brother Harry also has no known grave; he is recorded above.

(Panel 8) Pte. 956, Samuel Hateley, 2nd Bn. (6th Foot) The Royal Warwickshire Regt.: *s.* of Maria Hateley (2/100, Dolman Street, Vauxhall, Birmingham): and brother to Pte. 49741, H. Hateley, 2nd Northamptonshire Regt., killed in action 25 April 1918: *b.* Ashted, Birmingham: enlisted Warwick. Killed in action 7 November 1914: Age 19.

His brother Harry also has no known grave; he is commemorated on the Pozieres Memorial.

(Panel 8) Pte. 28751, John Hillier, 11th (Service) Bn. The Royal Warwickshire Regt.: formerly no.S/4/144977, Army Service Corps: eldest *s.* of John Henry Hillier, Baker, by his wife Catherine, *dau.* of Charles Spilsbury: *b.* Birmingham, co. Warwick, 12 October 1879: *educ.* Birmingham: joined A.S.C., 28 October 1915: transf'd. Royal Warwickshire Regt. about February 1917: served with the Expeditionary Force in France and Flanders from May following, and died at Ypres 25 July 1917 from wounds received in action: Age 37. He *m.* Birmingham, 12 April 1903; Alice Emily (Back of 95, Moland Street, Birmingham), *dau.* of William Gardiner, and had five children – George Leslie, *b.* 2 April 1904; John, *b.* 1 December 1907; Frank William, *b.* 17 May 1911; Nellie, *b.* 3 March 1913; Arthur *b.* 22 May 1915.

(Panel 8) Pte. 9620, William George Lilley, 'A' Coy., 1st Bn. (6th Foot) The Royal Warwickshire Regt.: *s.* of William Lilley, of 82, Conybere Street, Birmingham, by his wife Lucy: enlisted Birmingham: served with the Expeditionary Force in France, and was killed in action 24 May 1915: **Age 16.**

(Panel 8) Pte. 10528, Charles Paston, 11th (Service) Bn. The Royal Warwickshire Regt.: *s.* of George Paston, of Nuneaton, by his wife Ann: and yr. brother to Pte. 9702, W. Paston, Oxford & Bucks Light Infantry, killed in action 14 April 1917: enlisted Nuneaton. Killed in action 9 August 1917: Age 30. He leaves a wife, Bessie Paston (11, George Street, Attleborough, Nuneaton, co. Warwick).

His brother William also has no known grave; he is commemorated on the Arras (Faubourg d'Amiens) Memorial.

(Panel 8) Pte. 10225, Harry Paybody, 1st Bn. (6th Foot) The Royal Warwickshire Regt.: late of Nuneaton, co. Warwick. Killed in action nr. Wieltje, Flanders, 25 April 1915. Menin Gate, Bay 8, Stone J. Remembered, Jeremy (& Susannah) Paybody, Haselbech, Northants: November 2014.

(Panel 8) Pte. 10420, David 'Taff' Slaymaker, 1st Bn. (6th Foot) The Royal Warwickshire Regt.: late of Streatham, London, S.W.: *s.* of William Slaymaker, of St. John's Street, Carshalton, co. Surrey, by his wife Martha: and brother to former Seaman G. Slaymaker, R.N.V.R., died 8 September 1914, Guy's Hospital, London: *b.* Carshalton: enlisted Lambeth: served with Royal Warwicks in the Sudan Campaign and, in the war against the Boers in South Africa (wounded): a member of the Reserve, on the outbreak of war was gainfully employed as Builder's Labourer: rejoined his regiment on mobilisation, proceeded to France 22 August 1914. Reported wounded and missing, believed killed, after the attack on the German lines nr. Wieltje, 25 April 1915. He leaves a widow and three children.

(Panel 8) Pte. 498, William Wilkshire, 1st Bn. (6th Foot) The Royal Warwickshire Regt.: late of Upton-on-Severn, co. Warwick: *s.* of Charles Wilkshire, of Bridge Street, Kenilworth, co. Warwick: and brother to L/Sergt. R/3718, F.R. Wilkshire, 11th King's Royal Rifle Corps, died of wounds 4 April 1917, aged 20: enlisted Warwick. Killed in action 25 April 1915: Age 33.

His brother Frederick is buried in Bancourt British Cemetery (II.G.1).

(Panel 8) Lieut.Col. Arthur Percival Dearman Birchall, The Royal Fusiliers (City of London Regt.) attd. 4th Bn. Canadian Infantry (Central Ontario Regt.), C.E.F.: Killed in action 24 April 1915. RECORDED TWICE: See Panel 18.

(Panel 8) Capt. Wilfred John Hutton Curwen, 6th (Reserve) Bn. The Royal Fusiliers (City of London Regt.): only *s.* of John M. Curwen, of The High House, Thames Ditton, co. Surrey, and 53, Carlisle Mansions, London, S.W., by his wife Maria: and brother-in-law, by his sister's marriage, to the famous Charterhouse and Oxford half-back, C. Wreford-Brown: *b.* Beckenham, co. Kent, 14 April 1883: *educ.* Charterhouse; and Magdalen College, Oxford, where he obtained his Blue for Association Football: entered 2nd London Regt. (T.F.), April 1911: promoted Lieut. July 1912: sometime served as A.D.C. to Sir John Fuller, Bart., K.C.M.G., Governor of Victoria, and to the Right Hon. Lord Denman, when Governor-General, Australia: on the outbreak of war was serving as A.D.C. to the Right Hon. Sir R.C. Munro-Ferguson, Governor-General and Commander-in-Chief, Commonwealth of Australia: obtained permission to resign his appointment as A.D.C., and returned to England, where his offer of his services was immediately accepted: promoted Capt., joining 6th Battn. Royal Fusiliers, 25 December 1914: served with the Expeditionary Force in France and Flanders, and was killed in action at the Second Battle of Ypres, 13 May 1915, at a critical moment in the fighting, while gallantly directing some of his men. At the time of his death Capt. Curwen was Acting Adjutant to his battalion. His Commanding Officer wrote, "He died bravely while doing his duty." Buried close to where he fell: Age 32. He was an excellent cricketer, and a fine Association football player, and had represented his school and University at both games. A good batsman and a useful fast-medium bowler, he was in the Charterhouse XI, 1901 and 1902, averaging 22.66 in the former year, and 26.00 in the latter. In 1901 he was second in bowling, taking seventeen wickets for 18.23 runs each. In the 1906 match against Cambridge at Lords he scored 12 not out and 34 not out; in his second innings adding 90 runs in fifty-five minutes for the last wicket with E.G. Martin (56). Occasionally appearing for Surrey, in 1907-07 he was a member of the M.C.C. Team which toured New Zealand and, whilst in Australia, played for the M.C.C. at Geelong and Ballarat. He also belonged to the I Zingari, Free Foresters, Harlequins, represented Charterhouse at racquets, played football for the Old Carthusians on many occasions, and was a member of the Bath Club. (*IWGC record 9 May 1915*)

(Panel 8) Capt. Frederick Charles Day, 12th (Service) Bn. The Royal Fusiliers (City of London Regt.): *s.* of Emily A. Day (42, Fladgate Road, Leytonstone, London, E.11). Killed in action 31 July 1917. One of 9 officers, 170 other ranks of 12th Battn. killed and wounded on that date: Age 24. *unm.* Remembered on Leytonstone War Memorial.

(Panel 8) Capt. Hugh Densham Doudney, 'A' Coy., 12th (Service) Bn. The Royal Fusiliers (City of London Regt.): *s.* of Edwin Doudney, M.R.C.S., L.R.C.P., of 4B, Oxford & Cambridge Mansions, Marylebone Road, London, by his wife Ada. Killed in action 31 July 1917; vicinity of Jeffery Avenue, Bodmin Copse: Age 33. See account re. Capt. H.J. Cox, Hooge Crater Cemetery (IX.L.1).

(Panel 8) Capt. William Sigismund Friedberger, 5th (Reserve) attd. 3rd Bn. (7th Foot) The Royal Fusiliers (City of London Regt.): late partner J. Friedberger & Co.: served in the South African Campaign, commanding a battalion of Royal Fusiliers (Queen's and King's Medals with clasps; Mentioned in Despatches): retired rank Major: rejoined Royal Fusiliers on the outbreak of the European War; mobilised Hounslow, co. Middlesex, rank Capt. (vice Capt. Honorary Major), Royal Fusiliers, 4 September 1914 ('*London Gazette*,' no.28890, 1 September 1914); under Lieut.Col. Vivian Henry, Comdg.: served with the Expeditionary Force in France and Flanders and was killed 24 May 1915, in the fighting south of the Ypres – Roulers railway, nr. Bellewarde Ridge. In a letter to his widow the Adjutant wrote, "He was deeply respected and loved by his company and brother officers. I never met a man who was better fitted to command men, in fact, a born soldier;" and a brother officer, "He did quite enough for his country during the South African War without risking his life again…He was a keen officer, and a good comrade; his kindness to me in South Africa and at home I can never forget." And a Colonel under whom he served, "We soldiered in South Africa together and I knew what a good soldier he was. Her was most popular with all ranks, both officers and men, and I feel I have lost a good friend whom it is impossible to replace.": *m.*

(Panel 8) Capt. Clement Jesse Harter, 4th Bn. (7th Foot) The Royal Fusiliers (City of London Regt.): 3rd *s.* of Charles B. Hatfield Harter, of 5, Onslow Houses, South Kensington, London, S.W., by his wife Violet: and *yr.* brother to Capt. J.G. Harter, Durham Light Infantry, died of wounds 3 April 1916, received in action at Hooge: *b.* London, 4 December 1889: *educ.* Ladycross, Bournemouth; and Beaumont College, Old Windsor: originally served in the Royal Navy: gazetted 2nd Lieut. Royal Fusiliers from Special Reserve, August 1911; joined 3rd Battn., India: promoted Lieut. April 1914: served with the Expeditionary Force in France and Flanders with 4th Battn., IIIrd Divn., from March 1915, and was killed 16 June 1915 while leading his platoon at Hooge. In August it was officially notified that Lieut. C.J. Harter, who had been previously reported 'killed' was now 'reported wounded and missing.' The report of his death was, however, afterwards confirmed. He was a member of the Bath Club: Age 25. *unm.* (*IWGC record age 26*)

His brother John is buried in Lijssenthoek Military Cemetery, Poperinghe (V.A.13).

(Panel 8) Capt. Michael Reginald Kirkman Hodgson, 2nd Bn. (7th Foot) The Royal Fusiliers (City of London Regt.) attd. King's Own (Yorkshire Light Infantry): 2nd *s.* of Robert Kirkman Hodgson, of 77, Eaton Square, London, S.W.1, late of 7, Charles Street, Berkeley Square, London, by his wife Lady Honora 'Norah' Janet, *dau.* of 9th Earl of Cork: and elder brother to Capt. M.K. Hodgson, Sherwood Foresters, died of wounds 12 March 1915: *b.* Berkeley Square, 26 September 1879: *educ.* Eton, and Royal Military College, Sandhurst: received his commission 2nd Lieut. October 1899; promoted Lieut. September 1900: served throughout the Boer War: present at the Relief of Ladysmith, including action at Colenso: took part in operations on Tugela Heights, and Pieter's Hill: operations in Transvaal, Natal, and Cape Colony, including action at Ruidam: Mentioned in Despatches ('*London Gazette*,' 29 July 1902): Queen's Medal, 5 clasps; King's Medal, 2 clasps: subsequently served in India where his ponies ran first and second for the Lucknow Army Cup: also held the Indian Durbar Medal: promoted Capt. May 1907:

acted as A.D.C. to Lord Carmichael, Governor-General, Bengal, 1912: went to the Front at the beginning of the war with Germany, and, in October 1914, was transf'd. 1st King's Own Yorkshire Light Infantry, which he temporarily commanded; afterwards transf'd. 4th Battn. of his own regiment, with which he was serving when he was killed, being shot by an enemy sniper 17 March 1915, nr. Ypres. Buried that evening beside one of his subalterns, Lieut. B.F.G. Berrill. Capt. Hodgson was Mentioned in Sir John (now Lord) French's Despatch, 31 May 1915, for his services in the Great War: Age 35.

His brother Maurice is buried in Estaires Communal Cemetery (II.H.7); Lieut. Berrill also has no known grave he is recorded below.

(Panel 8) Capt. (Adjt.) George O'Donel Frederick Thomas-O'Donel, M.C., 4th Bn. (7th Foot) The Royal Fusiliers (City of London Regt.): only *s*. of Edwin Thomas-O'Donel, of Newport House, Newport, co. Mayo, J.P., D.L., by his wife Millicent Agnes, *dau*. of Capt. Richard Annesley O'Donel: *b*. Dublin, 21 October 1884: *educ*. Cheltenham College, and abroad: joined Royal Donegal Artillery Militia, 1902: gazetted 2nd Lieut. 4th Royal Fusiliers, 23 May 1906; promoted Lieut. 10 April 1909; Capt. 26 November 1914: apptd. Adjt., 15 January 1915: went to France with the Expeditionary Force 13 August 1914, and was killed in the attack on Bellewaarde Ridge, nr. Ypres, 16 June 1915: Age 30. Awarded the Military Cross ('*London Gazette*,' 19 February 1915); Twice Mentioned in Sir John (now Lord) French's Despatches ('*London Gazette*,' 19 October 1914; 18 February 1915). Brigdr.Gen. McMahon, Comdg. 4th Infantry Brigade, wrote, "5 November 1914. I think the Battn. has done very well out here, and I hope it will continue to do so. George is going strong and is fitter than when he started, and can claim a very large share in producing such good results as may have been attained." And Col. Hely-Hutchinson, "I cannot tell you what a shock the whole thing has been to me, we were the closest of friends, we slept together, we fed together, we rode together, and we fought together, and we never had a row for seven months, and the only time we had been separated, George goes and gets killed, and I get off. It is too sad after all the months he had been out and the good work he had done. I myself got a small touch of a shell on the head and have come home for a bit, thank God, as I don't think I could have carried on any longer out there without George and the rest – we lost six killed and nine wounded officers, and I had no heart and was just tired out and so was George, he just went on till he dropped.": Major F.R. Mallock, "His death is a great loss to his country and the regt. – he served so gallantly and so well; there are few of us left who went out with the Battn., George was the only one of the combatant officers left after the fighting at Ypres. I had a great affection and admiration for him, he did work splendidly right through." Brigdr.Gen. Reginald Pinney, formerly Comdg. 4th Battn. Royal Fusiliers, also wrote to Capt. Thomas-O'Donel's father, "I am most distressed for you and his mother at George's death – also for the regt. and the army, for he was fulfilling all the promise he showed when he joined; seeing his name gave me a special shock, for I had just heard of my getting a division, and had been talking of Staff and had hoped to get George appointed a G.S.O." He *m*. London, 26 November 1914; Florence Violet (Newlands, co. Wexford), only *dau*. of George Claud Flood Braddell, of Newlands, co Wexford, and Luckington, co. Wilts: *s.p.*

Killed in action east of Hooge, 11 November 1914, Brigdr.Gen. N.R. McMahon also has no known grave; he is incorrectly commemorated on the Ploegsteert Memorial (Panel 1).

(Panel 8) Capt. Arthur Kenneth Puzey, 4th Bn. (7th Foot) The Royal Fusiliers (City of London Regt.): only *s*. of Major Arthur Robert Puzey, Royal Engineers: *b*. Boaz Island, Bermuda, 11 March 1880: *educ*. Eastman's School, Stubbington: subsequently joined the Militia from which he transf'd., August 1910, 2nd Lieut., 1st Royal Fusiliers: promoted Lieut. February 1904; Capt. November 1909: Station Staff Officer, Mandalay, July 1902 – August 1903; held a similar appointment at Dum Dum, November 1903 – February 1904: Adjt., 8th Hampshire Regt. (Isle of Wight Rifles, Princess Beatrice's) (T.F.), February 1910 – February 1913: served with the Expeditionary Force in France and Flanders, and was killed in action nr. Ypres, Belgium, 11 November 1914: Age 34. He *m*. Olive Hunter Theobald, *née* Puzey (Kent House, Curzon Road, Weybridge, co. Surrey), *yr*. *dau*. of the late W. Pearce, and left two children – Eric, *b*. September 1911; Olga Desirée, *b*. (posthumously) July 1915.

(Panel 8) Lieut. Bernard Francis Gotch Berrill, 6th (Reserve) attd. 4th Bn. (7th Foot) The Royal Fusiliers (City of London Regt.): eldest *s.* of Arthur Berrill, of 'Wahringah,' Muswell Hill, London, N., late of Sydney, New South Wales, Australia: *b.* Sydney, 13 September 1894: *educ.* Beaumont College, Old Windsor, where he was Captain of the Boats, Prefect of the Sodality, Head of the Debating Society, and Captain of the School (2 years); also rowed stroke in the School Eight at Henley, and took a leading part in the theatricals for which the school is well known. Afterwards went to Balliol College, Oxford, where he was in the O.T.C.: at University for one year when war broke out; was given a commission 2nd Lieut. 6th London Regt. August 1914: promoted Lieut. February 1915, after one month in the fighting line: attd. 4th Battn. for Active Service, and was killed in action near Ypres 17 March 1915. His Commanding Officer described the circumstances of his death as follows, "It appears at the time he was hit he was kneeling down in the trench, and I think a bullet must have glanced off a tree and got him in the head. He was killed instantaneously. There was no attack. It was ordinary sniping. We had him carried down and buried at dusk, at the same time and place as his Captain, who, I regret to say, was also killed on that day. Your boy's death is a very great loss to me. He was always cheery and bright, made light of any work he had to do, and was absolutely without fear. Micky Hodgson, his Captain, told me, 'Young Berrill has a passion for putting wire out in front of the trenches' (which is not at all a pleasant job). He said it was a standing joke in the company, if they saw any wire on the roadside, to say, 'Where is Mr Berrill?'": Age 20. *unm.*

Capt. Hodgson also has no known grave, he is recorded above.

4th Royal Fusiliers, severely depleted in numbers during the fighting around Pont Logy – Neuve Chapelle (25 – 29 October 1914) were removed to Bailleul where several new drafts joined the battalion. Inspected on 4 November by General Sir Horace Smith-Dorrien who, after warmly congratulating the battalion on the fine work they had performed, closed his speech: "....I am here to tell you – and I'm afraid it will be a great disappointment to you – that, instead of the seven or eight days' rest you were looking forward to at Bailleul, I am very much afraid that in another twenty-four or forty-eight hours you will find yourselves back in the trenches again…"

His warning was soon fulfilled when, on the night of 6 November, the battalion took over positions from 6th Cavalry Brigade, east of Hooge, south of the Ypres-Menin road. After experiencing some difficulty in reaching the positions – the roads about Ypres being blocked with traffic – the Fusiliers settled down on the edge of Herenthage Wood; Northumberland Fusiliers on their right, French Zouaves on their left, who on 7 November were blown out of their trenches by a concentrated bombardment. The following day shellfire continued seemingly without cessation and several minor attacks – the most serious of which fell on Y Company – were successfully beaten off. But on the left the Zouaves were forced back which enabled the Germans to enter the wood and work round the Fusiliers open flank.

The Regimental History records:– "Stapleton-Bretherton and Jackson, with half of Y Company, delivered a violent counter-attack and penetrated the German trenches. Very few of these gallant fellows came back. The two officers and 62 men were seen no more. But, thanks to this charge and an advance by the West Riding Regt., the line was restored."

(Panel 8) Lieut. Wilfred Stanislaus Stapleton-Bretherton, 'Y' Coy., 4th Bn. (7th Foot) The Royal Fusiliers (City of London Regt.): 5th *s.* of Frederick Stapleton-Bretherton, of The Hall, Rainhill, nr. Prescot, co. Lancaster, by his wife the Hon. Isabella Mary, *dau.* of William Bernard Petre, 12th Baron Petre, and Mary Theresa, *née* Clifford: and brother-in-law to Admiral Sir E.F.B. Charlton, J.P., K.C.B., K.C.M.G., of Alverstoke, co. Hants: *b.* 26 November 1886: served with the Expeditionary Force in France and Flanders from August 1914. Reported missing after the fighting at Herenthage Wood, 8 November 1914: Age 27. *unm.*

Lieut. Jackson, previously wounded at Veuilly, 10 September 1914, is unrecorded by the CWGC.

(Panel 8) Lieut. Boyce Anthony Combe, 6th (Reserve) attd. 4th Bn. (7th Foot) The Royal Fusiliers (City of London Regt.): 2nd *s.* of Harvey Trewythen Brabazon Combe, of Oaklands, Sedlescombe, co. Sussex, late 3rd Royal Sussex Regt.: *b.* 1889: *educ.* Cheltenham: joined Royal Fusiliers, 2nd Lieut.:

promoted Lieut. 29 June 1913: served with the Expeditionary Force in France and Flanders, and was killed in action at the First Battle of Ypres 11 November 1914: Age 25.

(Panel 8) Lieut. Walter Joseph Dudley, 4th Bn. (7th Foot) The Royal Fusiliers (City of London Regt.): 4th *s.* of Henry Christopher Dudley, late Quartermaster-Sergt., Royal Engineers, of 'Appleton,' Park Road, Farnborough: *b.* Dundalk, Ireland, 22 January 1880: *educ.* military schools: joined Royal Fusiliers 1894: served in the ranks 2nd Battn., until 1901, then transf'd. 3rd Battn.: became Company Sergt. Major, 1905; Sergt.Major, 4th London Regt. (T.F.), January 1914, serving with them in Malta and France: awarded Long Service, and Good Conduct medals: gazetted 2nd Lieut. in his old regiment February 1915, for his services in the field; posted 4th Battn. Killed in action at Ypres, 16 June 1915, severely wounded while leading his platoon, he was subsequently killed by a shell. The Officer Commanding his battalion wrote, "He was with us during the most difficult part of our work, and his magnificent character made him beloved by us all. He died as he had always lived, a fine example of the British soldier." Another officer wrote, "We were all most awfully fond of him, and it was a geat shock to me when I heard the news of his death, as I had heard, earlier in the day, that he was wounded and coming back. He was a very brave and a very capable officer. I looked on him as one of my best platoon commanders, and I was always sure that anything he had to do would be very well done; and if there was a bit more he could do, it would be done. Only the day before the fight he did a very brave thing. He was coming back with 2nd Lieut. S.D.K. Rogers when the latter was hit by a sniper. They were outside of the communication trench. Your husband dressed Rogers' wound under very heavy sniper's fire, absolutely in the open, without assistance, and remained with him until he died." His servant also wrote, "I am very sorry to have to tell you that Mr Dudley has been killed in action, after being severely wounded, whilst most bravely leading his platoon against the enemy on the morning of the 16th.": Age 35. He was married to Annie, *dau.* of W. Raison, late 2nd Royal Scots Fusiliers, and left a *dau.*, Sybil Grace, aged five years.

Sheffield Rogers also has no known grave; he is recorded below.

(Panel 8) Lieut. Gilbert Colin Cunninghame Ferrier, 7th (Extra Reserve) attd. 4th Bn. (7th Foot) The Royal Fusiliers (City of London Regt.): *s.* of William Ferrier, of 71, Grey Road, Timaru, New Zealand, by his wife Eva Beatrice: gazetted 2nd Lieut. on probation from New Zealand Defence Forces, August 1914: served in the European War 1914. Reported wounded and missing after the fighting 11 November 1914. For some considerable time the fate of Lieut. Ferrier was a matter of uncertainty, in fact, it was not until the Casualty List published by the War Office, May 1915, that he was reported 'unofficially killed or died of wounds on or about 11 November 1914.' While his death was still in doubt, he was promoted Lieut. to date from February 1915: Age 24. *unm.*

In his book '*Anatomy of Courage*' Charles Moran, who served as an officer with 1st Royal Fusiliers, reflected on his conclusions regarding the mental state of fellow officer Lieut. A.M. Gordon, who – despite having been previously wounded – displayed an abnormal eagerness to return to the hazards of the front line:

> 'Most of us were quite content to do nothing; we were in no hurry to go back to the mud and monotony of the trenches, and I wanted to know if Gordon's restlessness was genuine, why he preferred the trenches to that peaceful existence in a village that might have been in England. I questioned Hill, but he was not very helpful. He told me that Gordon had been in his College Boat at Oxford; he seemed to have an idea at the back of his mind that he had not yet pulled his weight, though already, early in the war he had been severely wounded in the neck. Bow had done this, and Four that, and now the crew was down to three. He had an obsession about this boat; he was secretly bent on bringing some credit to it. Gordon was not an easy man to get to know, but when I saw more of him I was satisfied that this was the real aggressive spirit, so strange to some of us who had been out for some time and never went out of our way to look for trouble. There it was beneath the stolid exterior, covered up by all the negatives the average young Briton of his type thinks valuable.'

'One day after our return to the salient, while he was at the transport, his company was rather heavily shelled. When he returned and learnt what had happened he said nothing, but seemed put out; Hill thought he was brooding on it. Then one night, without a word to anyone, he went out on patrol taking a corporal with him. He did not come back. He had gone in his leather waistcoat, without his coat or anything that might give away his unit if he were captured. He had emptied his pockets of letters and papers. People said to go off like that was a silly thing to do, but that he was a good fellow and would be a loss. Months later a communication came from Germany through the American Red Cross. I print it because it gave me new heart at a time when I was less certain of things – "On the morning of the 24th January on the Ypern front, near four big holes caused by the bursting of shells, north-west of the Bellewarde Farm, and about 30 metres distant from the German front measuring from the west to the east, an Englishman was buried, a German officer in charge. The body had lain for a fortnight or three weeks before our front (here followed a full description with minute details about studs and underclothing). The wounds consisted of a shot in the heart so that death was instantaneous. Since the burial was carried out by the young officer in charge, although at a great personal risk as he was under fire at the time, and since his only object was to give his enemy an honourable burial, in the hope that this action would be of some comfort to the relatives of the dead man, I beg that this description may be sent to English troops on the Ypern front."

'Mark that minute description of the clothing, though Gordon was buried in no man's land after dark. Mark those comfortable words "The wounds consisted of a shot in the heart, so that death was instantaneous." I am glad to think that Gordon was decently buried by a gallant enemy. This was a man without fear who had brought from Oxford the young clean zest of his kind into the mixed business of war. Providence did well to revive the ancient chivalry of arms for his going out.'

(Panel 8) Lieut. Alexander Maurice Gordon, 1st Bn. (7th Foot) The Royal Fusiliers (City of London Regt.): *s.* of the late Alexander Duncan Gordon, by his wife Alice Elsie (Woodlands, Chalfont St. Giles, co. Buckingham). Missing while on patrol in no man's land; confirmed killed 23 January 1916: Age 21. *unm.* (*IWGC record 20 January*)

(Panel 8) Lieut. Sidney Eustace Laing Gordon, 5th attd. 4th Bn. (7th Foot) The Royal Fusiliers (City of London Regt.): elder *s.* of Henry Laing Gordon, M.D., formerly of Florence, Italy, by his wife Maud: *b.* Witheridge, co. Devon, 5 June 1892: *educ.* Pelham House, West Folkestone; Harrow (Druries, 1906 – 1911, Head of House, Monitor, Captain of House XI); Brazenose College, Oxford (1911 – 1914, Scholar, rowed College Eights 1913, graduated 3rd Class Honours, 1914): gazetted 2nd Lieut. 5th Bn. (Special Reserve of Officers) Royal Fusiliers, 15 August 1914; transf'd. 4th Battn. December following; proceeded to France on the 2nd. of the latter month, and was killed in action at Ypres, 13 March 1915. While giving an order to his platoon he was hit by a bullet, which striking a sandbag glanced off and shot him through the lung. He was buried outside the Regimental Headquarters dugout, Verbrandenmolen, Flanders. His Col. Wrote, "He was indeed a natural soldier. Such charming gentlemen are now becoming rare. His loss will be very much felt by the regt. He was greatly loved by his men, and had a happy tact in dealing with them which was a credit to his Harrow education." And his Major, "I cannot tell you how much I feel his loss. He was always cheery and bright; he had no fear of anything, and whatever work he had to do there was no fuss about it, he went off and did it. I looked on him as one of my most experienced young officers." His Capt. said, "He was an ideal subaltern in every way; always willing and reliable. Your son was a man without fear and on one or two occasions I had to check his wishes to do something which might have cost him his life.": Age 22. *unm.*

(Panel 8) Lieut. Hugo Molesworth Legge, 3rd Bn. (7th Foot) The Royal Fusiliers (City of London Regt.): *yst. s.* of the late Lieut.Col. the Hon. Edward Legge, late Coldstream Guards, and one time Asst. Sergt.-at-Arms, in the House of Commons; *s.* of 4th Earl of Dartmouth, by his wife the Hon. Mrs Legge, *née* Molesworth (Eversleigh House, Windsor): *b.* 29 July 1891: *educ.* Haileybury; Royal Military

College, Sandhurst: received his commission, Royal Fusiliers, March 1911; promoted Lieut. January 1913: served with his battalion in France, and was killed at Zonnebeke, Flanders, 3 May 1915, by a rifle shot in the head. His favourite recreations were cricket, polo and golf. Four other brothers of Lieut Legge are currently serving their country; two in their father's old regiment – Coldstream Guards; two in the Royal Navy: Age 23. *unm*.

(Panel 8) Lieut. Richard Kellock Stirling, 5th attd. 1st Bn. (7th Foot) The Royal Fusiliers (City of London Regt.): *s*. of the late Richard Stirling, of Southbrent, co. Devon (*d*.1895), by his wife Jane Emily, *née* Kellock ('Uphill,' Warren Road, Guildford, co. Surrey): *b*. 1893: *educ*. Exeter College, Oxford University (1912 – 14); played for the College Cricket XI; member of the O.T.C., obtained his commission 2nd Lieut., 5th Royal Fusiliers: proceeded to France attd. 1st Battn. and was killed in action 21 August 1915, at Hooge: Age 22. *unm*. Remains recovered 'Sanctuary Wood Old British Cemetery' (28.I.24.b.90.97) 'Unknown British Officer. Royal Fusiliers (Lieut.);' identified – Officers Clothing, Badge of Rank, Collar Badge; reinterred, registered 19 April 1928. *Buried in Sanctuary Wood Cemetery (II.F.5)*.

The Lord Make His Face To Shine Upon Thee

(Panel 8) Lieut. (Temp.) Robert West Thornton, 4th Bn. (7th Foot) The Royal Fusiliers (City of London Regt.): elder *s*. of Major Robert Lawrence Thornton, C.B.E., D.L., J.P., of High Cross, Uckfield, co. Sussex, by his wife Charlotte, J.P.: *b*. Uckfield, 26 January 1896: *educ*. Eton, where he was in the boats, and won his House Football Colours; and Royal Military College, Sandhurst (Corpl. Cadet): gazetted 2nd Lieut. October 1914; posted 4th Royal Fusiliers: left Dover for France, November following: promoted Temp. Lieut. February 1915. His Commanding Officer reported, "He was in Command of a Company for some weeks near Ypres, when he did most excellent work, and for his services was Mentioned in Sir John French's Despatch, 31 May 1915." Killed 16 June 1915, in an attack on Hooge, in Flanders, whilst acting as Machine Gun Officer. He fell beyond the line eventually held by the Germans. His Commanding Officer also said, "We were all most awfully fond of your boy, he was always so cheery and bright; I also had – as his Commanding Officer – the highest opinion of his abilities as an officer, and looked on him as quite in a class by himself. He was very clear-headed and quick at taking in a situation, and carrying on and doing the right thing." Another officer said, "When I was in Ypres I met a great friend of mine, and he told me of a certain young subaltern in his Battalion, 4th Royal Fusiliers, who at the age of nineteen was commanding a Company, and doing so well that although there were senior and older men available, the Colonel refused to put them over his head. I asked who the lad was, and was told it was Bobbie Thornton." And a Senior brother Officer wrote, "He had the knack of getting men to work and to fight." The Senior Officer left in the Battalion after the attack in which he was killed wrote, "He was a real good 'un and as brave as a lion." His Captain wrote from his Commanding Officer's bedside in Hospital, "The Commanding Officer would like you to know that he had sent in your boy's name for the Military Cross a couple of days before he died, and that he knows the General recommended it and sent it on. It will probably not have got through in time." His tutor at Eton wrote of him – "One of the cheeriest souls that ever lived.": Age 19.

(Panel 8) Lieut. Aubrey John Simon Waley, 12th (Service) Bn. The Royal Fusiliers (City of London Regt.): Killed in action 31 July 1917. (*IWGC record A.J. Waley*) See account re. Capt. H.J. Cox, Hooge Crater Cemetery (IX.L.1).

(Panel 8) Lieut. Brian Edmund Douglas Warde, 6th (Special Reserve) Bn. attd. 4th Bn. (7th Foot) The Royal Fusiliers (City of London Regt.): 2nd *s*. of Major Charles Aprilis Enthon Warde, of 2, Buckingham Mansions, Kensington, London, W., late 7th Dragoon Guards, and 6th Royal Fusiliers; currently 2.I.C., 15th (Reserve) Battn. Royal Fusiliers, by his wife Felicia, *dau*. of James Richard Alexander Douglas, F.R.C.S., of Treaty House, Hounslow: *b*. Hounslow, co. Middlesex, 29 July 1894: *educ*. Bilton Grange, Rugby, and Lancing College, Shoreham, where he was 2nd Classic and Captain of his House; thereafter intended to depart for Ceylon for a Plantation career but, on the day war was declared, applied for a commission and was gazetted 2nd Lieut. to his father's old battn. 15 August 1914; promoted Lieut. 2

February following. After training at Dover and taking part in the defences of the fortress, he left for the Front with a draft for 4th Battn. 29 December 1914: served with 4th Royal Fusiliers at Ypres, St. Eloi, and elsewhere in Flanders, until his death in action at Hooge, nr. Ypres, 16 June 1915. That day he was the last officer of his company unhurt. He had helped to take three lines of the enemy's trenches, had then fallen back to the 2nd line again, where his wounded Captain saw him quite calm and unconcerned, leading a handful of men down the trench. He jumped on the parapet to fire at and bomb a party of the enemy when he fell shot through the head. An hour later he died, never having recovered consciousness, and was buried in the trench where he was shot. His Commanding Officer wrote of him, "He will be great loss to us, he was always cheerful, was a very brave officer, and a good leader of men. ...He was sniped from the flank and killed dead." Lieut. Warde was a splendid game shot and devoted to field sports and to nature generally. He possessed an excellent knowledge of French: Age 20. *unm.*

His father, Major C.A.E. Warde, died 14 February 1920; he is buried in Heston (St. Leonard) Churchyard (I.24).

(Panel 8) 2nd Lieut. Charles Wilfrid Banister, 4th Bn. (7th Foot) The Royal Fusiliers (City of London Regt.): 3rd *s.* of Howard Cottrell Banister, of St. Catherine's, Cadogan Gardens, Tunbridge Wells: *b.* Blundellsands, Liverpool, 9 March 1893: *educ.* Merchant Taylors' School, Great Cosby; Jesus College, Cambridge: received a nomination to Royal Military College, Sandhurst on the outbreak of war; given his commission February 1915, posted 4th Royal Fusiliers attd. 5th (Reserve) Battn. for training: ordered to France 9 June 1915, and was killed one week later, 16 June 1915, at Hooge Chateau, nr. Ypres: Age 22. *unm.*

(Panel 8) 2nd Lieut. Edward Cohen, M.C., 12th (Service) Bn. The Royal Fusiliers (City of London Regt.). Died of wounds 31 July 1917, received in action in the advance at Bodmin Copse the same day. See account re. Capt. H.J. Cox, Hooge Crater Cemetery (IX.L.18).

(Panel 8) 2nd Lieut. Sydney Harold Lionel Douglas-Crompton, 1st Bn. (7th Foot) The Royal Fusiliers (City of London Regt.): first-born child of the late Sydney Douglas-Crompton, of Breightmet-Cromley, Beeson, nr. Stokenham, nr. Kingsbridge, co. South Devon, formerly of El Cipres, La Oratava, Tenerife, Canary Islands, by his wife Kathleen Louise Douglas-Robertson, *née* Douglas-Crompton (Lisbon, Portugal), *dau.* of Dr. Mordey Douglas, of Sunderland, and Salamanca, Santa Cruz, Tenerife, by his wife Emma, *dau.* of Sampson Payne, of Southampton, co. Hants: *b.* El Cipres, Tenerife, 2 June 1896: *educ.* Mr Haskin's School, Leatherhead, co. Surrey; and Sir Will Borlases's School, Great Marlow: joined First Surrey Rifles, Pte., 8 August 1914: served with the Expeditionary Force in France and Flanders from 15 March 1915: recommended for a commission July following: went to Cadet School, General Headquarters: gazetted 2nd Lieut. Royal Fusiliers, 27 August 1915. On 30 April 1916 he was slightly wounded, and after being in hospital at Camiers for three weeks, was invalided home: returned to France early September: transf'd. Royal Naval Air Service; rank Flight Sub.Lieut., June 1916, after which he was stationed at the Crystal Palace for a few days, joining H.M.S. 'Lightfoot' on the 8th. of that month. After a month at sea he underwent a nine months' course in flying, but it was subsequently found that his temperament was not suited to aviation, and rejoined Royal Fusiliers May 1917. Killed in action at Messines Ridge, 7 June following. An officer of his battalion wrote, "His end was as fine as it could possibly be. He tied a blue handkerchief to his stick and told his men to follow it. He was perfectly splendid, and seemed to forget there was any danger.": 7 June 1917: Age 21. *unm.*

(Panel 8) 2nd Lieut. Colin Gill, 12th (Service) Bn. The Royal Fusiliers (City of London Regt.): formerly Honourable Artillery Company: late of Antofagasta, Chile, South America: *s.* of J.H. (& Mrs) Gill, of Clapham, London. Killed in action 31 July 1917. One of 9 officers, 170 other ranks 12th Battn. killed and wounded on that date: Age 25. *unm.*

(Panel 8) 2nd Lieut. Walter Henry Grady, 6th (Reserve) attd. 3rd Bn. (7th Foot) The Royal Fusiliers (City of London Regt.): eldest *s.* of Walter Grady, of Eccleshall, Sheffield: *b.* Sheffield, co. York, 9 September 1886: *educ.* there, and Sheffield University, where he made a special study of Metallurgy at the Applied Science Department: Occupation – Analytical Chemist: previously a member of Sheffield

University O.T.C. for several years, was also Scoutmaster in connection with St. Mark's Church, of which he had been an honorary member of the choir for 16 years: offered and accepted a commission 2nd Lieut., Reserve of Officers, O.T.C., February 1914: gazetted 2nd Lieut. Reserve Battn. Royal Fusiliers, August 1914; attd. 3rd Battn. for Active Service: served with the Expeditionary Force in France and Flanders, and was killed at Zonnebeke, 25 April 1915, when a shell entered his dug-out, blowing it to pieces, killing him instantaneously. Buried on the battlefield. 2nd Lieut. Grady was a gymnast, and very fond of cricket. He *m.*, Ida (26, Thorney Hedge Road, Gunnersbury, London, W), only *dau.* of Colin (& Mrs) Bateman, of Gunnersbury: Age 28.

(Panel 8) 2nd Lieut. Wilfrid Mervyn Dunnington-Jefferson, 7th (Extra Reserve) attd. 3rd Bn. (7th Foot) The Royal Fusiliers (City of London Regt.): *yst. s.* of the late Capt. M. Dunnington-Jefferson, of Thicket Priory, nr. York, and his wife (Ashcroft, York): *b.* Middlethorpe Hall, York, 2 April 1893: *educ.* Radley, and Christ Church College, Oxford; graduated with honours in Law: entered for the Inner Temple, of which he was a member: received his commission 2nd Lieut. City of London Regt., August 1914, and proceeded to France: arrived at the firing line 20 April 1915, and was wounded at the Second Battle of Ypres, 25 April, only five days after his arrival, and died the next day. Buried at Gravenstafel: Age 22 years, 24 days. *unm.* (*IWGC record 27 April*)

(Panel 8) 2nd Lieut. Harold Martin (Temp./Lieut.), 12th (Service) Bn. The Royal Fusiliers (City of London Regt.): *s.* of Capt. H.C. (& Mrs M.H.) Martin, R.N., C.B.E., of 'Montpellier,' 82, Hermon Hill, Snaresbrook, co. Essex. Killed in action 31 July 1917, while advancing toward Jeffery Trench: Age 24. *unm.* (*IWGC record Lieut.*) See account re. Capt. H.J. Cox, Hooge Crtaer Cemetery (IX.L.1).

(Panel 8) 2nd Lieut. Alfred Geoffrey Newnham, 4th Bn. (7th Foot) The Royal Fusiliers (City of London Regt.): eldest *s.* of Alfred Newnham, of 163, Castelnau, Barnes, London, S.W.13, late of 14, Elm Grove, Barnes: *b.* Chelsea, London, S.W.3, 29 June 1892: *educ.* Latymer Foundation School, Hammersmith; Clark's College, Putney: enlisted May 1912: attended Higher Education Classes, Aldershot, September 1913 – March 1914: awarded Acting Schoolmaster's Certificate, February 1914: passed Officers Examination for promotion, April 1914: received his commission, 2nd Lieut., from rank Corpl., for 'service In the Field,' October following, and was killed in a charge by the Prussian Guard at Hooge, nr. Ypres, 11 November 1914. Fond of football and cricket, he was at one time secretary of the Barnes Icognito; later became a member of the Wasps' Football Club, Thames Ditton: Age 22. *unm.* (*IWGC record age 23*)

(Panel 8) 2nd Lieut. Harold George Patman, 12th (Service) Bn. The Royal Fusiliers (City of London Regt.): Killed in action 31 July 1917. One of 9 officers, 170 other ranks of 12th Battn. killed and wounded on that date.

(Panel 8) 2nd Lieut. (Temp.) Harold Strachan Price, 3rd Bn. (7th Foot) The Royal Fusiliers (City of London Regt.): 2nd *s.* of Edward G. Price, of No.1, Craven Hill, London, W., and Broadwater, Godalming, co. Surrey: *b.* 1881: *educ.* Charterhouse: prior to the outbreak of war had served 12 years with Artists' Rifles (L/Corpl. 292): went to France with his corps October 1914: accepted a commission, 2nd Lieut. (Temp.), General List, 23 April 1915, attd. 3rd Royal Fusiliers, and was killed in action one month later, 24 May 1915, while in command of a platoon holding an advanced position. Badly gassed, and ordered to retire, the greater number – 2nd Lieut. Price among them – were killed during the retirement. He was a tennis and golf player; cricket and shooting were among the sports he also took part in: Age 33. *unm.*

(Panel 8) 2nd Lieut. (Temp. Lieut) Sheffield Digby Kessine Rogers, 4th Bn. (7th Foot) The Royal Fusiliers (City of London Regt.) attd. 1st Bn. Northumberland Fusiliers. Killed in action by an enemy sniper 14 June 1915. See Lieut. W.J. Dudley (above).

(Panel 8) 2nd Lieut. Charles Frederic Noel Prince Sealy, 7th (Extra Reserve) attd. 3rd Bn. (7th Foot) The Royal Fusiliers (City of London Regt.): only *s.* of Lieut.Col. Charles William Henry Sealy, late Royal Artillery, and Political President, Kolhapur, India, of 6, Priory Grove, The Boltons, West Brompton, London, S.W., formerly of Hambledon House, Hambledon, co. Hants, by his marriage to the late Helena Louisa, *dau.* of Major.Gen. Noel Hamlyn Harris, Royal Artillery: and *gdson.* to the late Gen. George Prince Sealy, Royal Artillery: *b.* Southsea, co. Hants, 2 April 1892: *educ.* A.L. Bickmore's, M.A., Preparatory School, Yardley Court, Tonbridge; Wellington College (Combermere Dormitory), where he was a School Prefect, Head Prefect of his Dorm., and played in the 1st XV and 2nd XI; and Pembroke

College, Cambridge, where he was in the 1st XV, and 'tried' twice for the 'Varsity: in the O.T.C. at both Wellington and Cambridge. A good linguist, he played most games well, and as a Rugby footballer he played for his School, College, Richmond, Hampshire and the Trojans. He was a member of 'The Hawks,' Cambridge, and the Public Schools Club. He was to have gone up to Woolwich from Wellington, but was failed by the War Office Board on account of short sight: after leaving Cambridge, joined the firm of Alex Lawrie & Co., January 1914: sought, and obtained, his employers permission to offer his services when war with Germany was declared: enlisted 13th Princess Louise's Kensington Battn., London Regt., 7 August 1914: gazetted 2nd Lieut. 13th London Regt., October following, but, being transferred to 7th Battn. City of London Regt., November 1914, was ordered to join the latter at Falmouth: attd. 3rd Battn. for Active Service, with which he served in the British Expeditionary Force. In the early morning, 24 May 1915, he and his platoon were gassed at Ypres, and later in the day 2nd Lieut. Sealy was wounded in the shoulder. At night, when still in action, he was shot through the head and killed instantaneously. Buried next day near 'Y' Wood: Age 33. *unm.*

(Panel 8) 2nd Lieut. Harold Rolleston Stables, 5th (Reserve) Bn. The Royal Fusiliers (City of London Regt.): only *s.* of the late Henry Stables, of Horsforth, nr. Leeds, by his wife Mary: *b.* Horsforth, co. York, 1 July 1886: *educ.* Cheltenham College; New College, Oxford – rowed in the College VIII (1906, 1907 & 1908); took his degree (graduated B.A., 1909): subsequently studied for the Bar, and while so engaged joined Inns of Court O.T.C., 1911: called to the Bar at the Inner Temple, 1912. After the outbreak of war with Germany he obtained a commission 2nd Lieut. Royal Fusiliers, August 1914; soon afterwards, owing to the training he had received while a member of the Inns of Court O.T.C., was ordered to proceed to France for Active Service: served with the Expeditionary Force in France and Flanders, and was killed in action at the First Battle of Ypres. At the time of his death 2nd Lieut Stables was serving at the Front with 1st Battn. Cheshire Regt. He was shot through the head 15 November 1914, while helping to defend trenches three miles south of Ypres. He was a member of the Public Schools' and Leander Clubs, and of the Hardwicke Debating Society, a frequent speaker on eugenics and womens' suffrage; he was made a Freemason in the Apollo Lodge at Oxford, and in 1908 held the office of Assistant Grand Pursuivant in the Provincial Grand Lodge of Oxfordshire: Age 28. *unm.*

(Panel 8) 2nd Lieut. Henry Harman Young, 3rd Bn. (7th Foot) The Royal Fusiliers (City of London Regt.): *s.* of Major Henry Harman Young, of 'Balgowan,' Dorking, co. Surrey, by his wife Bessie: *b.* 2 September 1893: *educ.* Charterhouse: Occupation – Land Surveyor: joined Artist's Rifles: obtained a commission 3rd Royal Fusiliers. Killed in action 3 May 1915 Age 21. *unm.*

(Panel 8) A/Sergt. L/13789, Frederick William Thomas Farrant, 'A' Coy., 4th Bn. (7th Foot) The Royal Fusiliers (City of London Regt.): *s.* of Mary Ann Farrant (10, Park Cottages, Crown Road, St. Margaret's, East Twickenham): *b.* Twickenham, co. Middlesex, *c.*1891: enlisted Hounslow: served with the Expeditionary Force. Killed in action 11 November 1914: Age 23. *unm.*

(Panel 8) A/Sergt. L/11075, Samuel Gainey, 4th Bn. (7th Foot) The Royal Fusiliers (City of London Regt.): served with the Expeditionary Force. Reported missing 11 November 1914, and now assumed killed. (*IWGC record Sergt.*)

PANEL 8 ENDS SERGT. W.J. WINTER, ROYAL FUSILIERS.

South Portal:

> *Ad Majorem Dei Gloriam*
>
> *Here Are Recorded Names*
> *Of Officers And Men Who Fell*
> *In Ypres Salient But To Whom*
> *The Fortune Of War Denied*
> *The Known And Honoured Burial*
> *Given To Their Comrades*
> *In Death*

PANEL 10 BEGINS LIEUT. J. GALT, LORD STRATHCONA'S HORSE.

(Panel 10) Lieut. John Galt, Lord Strathcona's Horse (Royal Canadians), C.E.F.: *s.* of John (& Mabel Patton) Galt, of Victoria, British Columbia; late of 221, Rosslyn Road, Winnipeg: *b.* 1 May 1891: Religion – Church of England: *educ.* Proprietary School, Winnipeg; Upper Canada College, Toronto (1903 – 07); Lennoxville (1908 – 09); Royal Military College (1910 – 13), gazetted Lieut., Fort Garry Horse, April 1914: Occupation – Merchant: enlisted Lieut., Lord Strathcona's Horse, Pond Farm Camp, 2 October 1914: served with the Expeditionary Force in France from 4 May 1915: took part in operations at Festubert and south of Messines where, on the night of 9 December 1915, while commanding a night attack on the enemy trenches, Ploegsteert sector, Lieut. Galt and Pte. Chapman were reported missing / believed killed. No information regarding their deaths have been obtained. No remains recovered for burial: Age 24.

(Panel 10) Pte. 2469, George Blake, 'B' Sqdn., Lord Strathcona's Horse (Royal Canadians), C.E.F.: *b.* Charlton, co. Northampton, 17 July 1874: Religion – Wesleyan: Occupation – Teamster: 5'9½" tall, fair complexion, blue eyes, brown hair: prior to enlistment Valcartier, 23 September 1914, was five weeks member 106th Winnipeg Light Infantry (Militia): served with the Expeditionary Force in France from 4 May 1915, and was reported wounded and missing while on patrol 8 October 1915: Age 41. The Adjutant, 19th Battn. C.E.F. wrote, "18 October 1915. Last night at 11 p.m. one of our patrols found the body of Trooper George Blake, number 2469, of Second Troop B Squadron, Lord Strathcona's Horse at a point opposite right centre of M3 about 40 yds from the German lines. His serge and all his personal effects were brought in and an effort will be made to recover the body. Though a report found on body will be forwarded to Bde. Hdqrs." He leaves a wife, Elizabeth Blake (1428, Elain Avenue, Winnipeg).

(Panel 10) Pte. 2561, Willis Titus Chapman, Lord Strathcona's Horse (Royal Canadians), C.E.F.: c/o Greta Chapman (8, Howard Street, Maine, United States): *s.* of the late Charles Chapman, and his wife Margaret McCutcheon, *née* Chapman (Merrimac, Massachusetts): *b.* New Town, King's Co., 10 July 1887: Religion – Wesleyan: Occupation – Cook: previously served 2 yrs., 21st Alberta Hussars (Militia): joined C.E.F., Valcartier, 23 September 1914; apptd. Lord Strathcona's Horse, 25 September, proceeded to England; thence to France. Reported wounded and missing, 9 December 1915; believed killed (on or since the aforementioned date). 'A member of a party who went out to assault a barricade... The assaulting party was repulsed, and Pte. Chapman was last seen inside the enemy wire within a couple of yards of the barricade. Eleven out of the party became casualties, and no trace could be found of the missing. No information has since been received concerning Pte. Chapman.' Age 28. (*IWGC record age 27*)

(Panel 10) Pte. 2882, John Watt, Lord Strathcona's Horse (Royal Canadians), C.E.F.: *s.* of Mary Watt (22, Sussex Street, Cambridge, England), late of 2A, East Street: *b.* Sutton, co. Surrey, 9 October 1881: Occupation – Miner: previously served 12 years Royal Garrison Artillery: enlisted Pond Farm Camp, Salisbury Plain, 9 November 1914: served with the Expeditionary Force in France from 4 May 1915, and was shot and killed 4 October 1915, by a sniper; Vierstraat: Age 33. *unm.* (*IWGC record age 34*)

In Flanders fields the poppies blow
Between the crosses, row on row...

(Panel 10) Lieut. Alexis Hannum Helmer, 2nd Bty., Canadian Field Artillery, C.E.F.: only child of Colonel Richard Alexis (& Elizabeth I.) Helmer, of 122, Gilmour Street, Ottawa, Canada: *b.* Hull, Province of Quebec, 29 June 1892: graduated Royal Military College, Canada, 1912, afterwards entered McGill University, B.Sc. (Railways) 1914: commissioned 2nd Lieut., 2nd Field Bty., Canadian Militia, from Royal Military College, 1910: Capt., McGill University O.T.C., 1912 – 14: applied for a commission Canadian Expeditionary Force on the outbreak of the Great War: gazetted 2nd Lieut. Canadian Artillery, posted 2nd Bty., September 1914. Lieut. Helmer was present at the Second Battle of Ypres, when the Canadian Forces suffered so heavily from the German gas attack. After the battle he succeeded in bringing his guns and men out of action and rejoining the Canadian Artillery. He had just reported to his Commanding Officer, 2 May 1915, when a large German shell burst close to him and another officer with him (Lieut. O.C.F. Hague). Lieut. Helmer was buried north and slightly west of Ypres, near the Yser. His Commanding Officer wrote, "We have been through a very severe battle which started about 5 p.m. on 22nd April. Doubtless you have already heard through the Department of your loss, which is ours as well. During all the strenuous fighting from 22nd April to 2nd May Lex was in the middle of it, doing his duty in a most gallant and conspicuous manner. It seems hard that on 1st May I had sent his name in for gallantry under fire on 27th April, and also for his conduct on 24th April, when he was acting as Forward Observation Officer for the battery, and he was driven back by the poisonous fumes of the Germans, but still stuck to his post until I ordered him in. He was badly poisoned by the fumes, but begged and begged not to be sent to hospital, and after a period of twenty-four hours was once more in full charge of his section. He was full of pluck, and fought his guns time and again to a finish, at times when we all thought we were cut off and would never get through. His men adored him, and his section simply went to pieces when they saw what had happened. On the night of 1st – 2nd May we changed the position of Lex's section. One of my last recollections of him was on the afternoon of 1st May, when I saw him standing in the dug-out in the middle of his section doing his job with shells falling all around. I was passing about fifty yards away, and he waved his hand and smiled. He was always in the best of spirits and kept his men in fine shape. If I may say so, the battery has suffered a loss which cannot be remedied. Captain Cosgrave, who was at the Royal Military College and McGill with Lex, was near at hand when the shell came in, and immediately took charge of everything. You may know that Lex and the right section had been with me up in the salient, and when the Germans broke through our guns were the extreme left guns of the British Army. On the afternoon of the 24th April, Lex's section was run into the open at right angles to our usual line of fire, and opened fire on the Germans at 1,800 yards. The Germans were advancing out of a wood at the time, and we drove them back, and later in the day our Infantry occupied the woods. I could tell you of many instances of Lex's devotion to duty and care of his men.": Age 22. *unm*. See also Essex Farm Cemetery, Boesinghe.

Lieut. O.C.F. Hague died of wounds later the same day; he is buried in Hazebrouck Communal Cemetery (II.D.2).

(Panel 10) Lieut. Harold Louis Hull, 1st Trench Mortar Bty., Canadian Field Artillery, C.E.F.: *s*. of the Hon. H.C. Hull, of Muizenberg, Cape Province, South Africa, late of Johannesburg: *b*. Kimberley, South Africa, 1888: Religion – Church of England: *educ*. St. Andrew's College, Grahamstown; Repton School, England; McGill University (Engineering graduate): volunteered and enlisted at the outbreak of war: came over with 1st Canadian Contingent, October 1914: served with the Expeditionary Force in France and Flanders. Reported missing, presumed killed in action 3 June 1916, vicinity Sanctuary Wood: Age 27. He leaves a wife, Louise Hull (Muizenberg, Cape Province).

(Panel 10) Lieut. John William McDowell, 1st Siege Bty., Canadian Field Artillery, C.E.F.: *s*. of William McDowell, of Drayton, Ontario, by his wife Charlotte: *b*. Glen Allan, 9 December 1892: *educ*. Public School there; Drayton High School; Toronto University (Medicine), 1914 – 16: member C.O.T.C.: enlisted 67th (University of Toronto) Bty., Canadian Field Artillery, on its formation March 1916: departed Canada October following: received his commission June 1917, England: joined the Expeditionary Force in France October following: took part in the Battle of Passchendaele, and was killed on the Menin Road 13 December 1917 when the Divisional Headquarters was destroyed by a shell. Buried nearby: Age 25. *unm*.

(Panel 10) Bmdr. 315881, Roy Richard Hawkey, 3rd Bde. Canadian Field Artillery, C.E.F.: *s*. of Charles P. Hawkey, of Grimsby, Ontario, by his wife Mary D.: *b*. Grimsby, 28 March 1894: *educ*. Public (and High) Schools there; Hamilton College, Toronto University (Applied Science), 1913 – 16: enlisted 47th Bty., 12th Bde. Canadian Field Artillery, February 1916: departed Canada September following: trained in England throughout winter 1916 – 17: served with the Expeditionary Force in France from March 1917: took part in the Battle of Vimy Ridge and all subsequent engagements to Lens and Hill 70. On 28 October

1917, at Passchendaele, he was serving his gun with great coolness, answering S.O.S. calls, when the gun was hit by a shell killing three men instantly, fatally wounding his college colleague Gnr. 318008, J.R. Chapman and himself. Bmdr Hawkey succumbed to his wounds in the early hours of 29 October 1917, at the Dressing Station: Age 23. *unm.*

James Chapman is buried in Nine Elms British Cemetery (VIII.D.19).

(Panel 10) Gnr. 307729, Hugh Reid Kay, M.M., 43rd Bty., 8th Bde., Canadian Field Artillery: *s.* of William Kay, of Kirk Place, Bearsden, Glasgow, co. Lanark, by his late wife Isabella Haddow: *b.* Bearsden, 17 June 1890: *educ.* Public School, Glasgow; Ontario Agricultural College; University College, Toronto (Philosophy), 1911 – 15, B.A.; member of Y.M.C.A. (& Year) executive, 'Varsity' Staff; Knox College, Toronto; member C.O.T.C.: enlisted 43rd Howitzer Bty. with a number of Knox College colleagues early 1916: joined the Expeditionary Force in France July following: served on the Ypres and Kemmel fronts, thereafter at the Somme and, in the following year, took part in fighting at Vimy Ridge and Hill 70. Killed in action 6 November 1917: Age 27. On the day of his death he was detailed with two other signallers and an officer to go over with the infantry and, when the officer was wounded and accompanied back by one of the men, Gnr. Kay and the remaining man went forward through the fighting and continued to send back information. Later wounded himself, Gnr. Kay refused to leave the other man only later did he make his way back to a Dressing Station where he was killed by a shell. Buried nr. Passchendaele village. He was awarded the Military Medal in the summer of 1917 for his work as a linesman in keeping up telephone communication.

(Panel 10) Dvr. 42764, William Craigie (served as Warren, Walter), 3rd Bde. Canadian Field Artillery, C.E.F.: *s.* of James Craigie, of 34, Glebemount Avenue, Toronto, Ontario, by his wife Charlotte (Oak Ridge, Ontario): and brother to Pte. 250020, L. Craigie, 58th Bn. Canadian Infantry, died of wounds 28 August 1918: *b.* Toronto, 5 January 1887: Religion – Presbyterian: Occupation – Chainsman: 5'10" tall, light blue eyes, dark brown hair: volunteered and enlisted Valcartier 24 September 1914; posted 3rd C.F.A. Ammunition Col.: served with the Expeditionary Force in France from February 1915, and was killed in action 30 April 1915: Age 29. Remains recovered 'Unknown Canadian Soldier. Artillery' unmarked grave 2 December 1927; identified – Title, Cap Badge, Clothing, Gold Ring engrv. W.C.; reinterred, registered 26 December 1927. *Buried in Sanctuary Wood Cemetery (III.G.14).*

Honour Is Theirs Who For Their Country Died But For Us The Glorious Example

His brother Lewis is buried in Ligny-St. Flochel British Cemetery, Averdoingt (II.E.17).

(Panel 10) Dvr. 43913, James Joseph Miller, 1st Divn. Ammunition Col., Canadian Field Artillery attd. T.M. Bty., C.E.F.: *s.* of William G. Miller, of 129, North Street, Halifax, Nova Scotia, by his wife Elizabeth: elder brother to Pte. 415334, J.M. Miller, 24th Bn. Canadian Infantry, who fell the same day: Killed in action 7 June 1916: Age 21.

His brother James Mathias also has no known grave; he is recorded on Panel 24.

In 1915 and 1916 mine warfare was highly favoured by both sides. All along the Western Front both the Allies and Germans fought a desperate and treacherous battle underground with the dual objective of annihilating the opposition's miners and the total destruction of his front lines. Whilst at Ypres the low water table did not aid the miners, nor did it deter them. Beneath the salient men toiled day and night, excavating miles and miles of tunnels. On many occasions one side would break through into the other's tunnel system; often by the removal of walling timbers, and bitter hand-to-hand fighting would ensue in the darkness. To destroy or cause serious damage to the enemy's workings an explosive charge known as a camouflet would be stealthily placed by means of a boring tool and detonated at an opportune moment. On 1 June 1916 2nd Canadian Tunnelling Company were engaged on excavating deep dugouts near O'Grady Walk and The Tube, and shallow defensive galleries and listening posts in front of trenches at Armagh Wood; and, at Clonmel Copse, had begun 50 feet of gallery for a deep system of dugouts. The following morning a German camouflet, detonated beneath their position known locally as 'The Birdcage,' collapsed a length of Canadian gallery killing many of the party working there at the time. Above ground a hurricane bombardment and an infantry attack in overwhelming numbers resulted in the loss of the Canadian positions at both Armagh Wood and Clonmel Copse. The collapse of the gallery, initial bombardment and the fighting immediately thereafter, cost the Tunnellers heavily; exactly how heavily would not be realised until eleven days later when, on 13 June, after a pulverizing bombardment by Canadian guns, a counter-attack successfully recaptured most of the lost workings. Tunnelling Officer Lieut. John Westacott, the first to re-enter the systems, found them in a state of indescribable chaos, 'battered by the German mines and subsequent shellfire. Recent heavy rains had completed the disorder, filling parts with water and reducing the neatly cut clay to the formlessness of melting sugar. Some of the entrances were choked with dead soldiers. In a mined surface dug-out Westacott found the body of a brother officer, Lieut. George May (*sic*), pinned to the floor by a beam in an advanced state of decomposition and partially eaten by rats. He tried to pull the body out and, in a moment of exceptional ugliness, the legs and trunk parted. Outwardly calm Westacott ordered the pieces to be buried with the other corpses and set about the work of restoration.' Following the restoration under Westacott's direction an examination of the workings at Armagh Wood, by Lieut. Macaulay, 16 June 1916, reported them 'uninjured but half full of water. Traces of German occupation (clothing, equipment and a machine gun) were found. The machine gun was turned over to the Infantry O.C. Trenches. The saps in front of our old trenches 48 & 49 (28.I:30.c) were not reached. They are still within the enemy's lines.'

One month later, 16 July 1916, a board of enquiry held at Reninghelst into the loss of officers and men at Armagh Wood resulted in the exact fate of a substantial number of them as not being ascertainable, recording: 'Missing, since reported prisoners of war Lieut. J.D. Wilson, Lieut. A.J. Gaul, CSM. E. Massey-Cooke; Missing Lieut. R.G. Barnes; Killed 5 OR, Wounded 11 OR + 1 attd. Inf., Missing 75 OR + 19 attd. Inf., Wounded 1 OR, Killed 1 OR, Wounded 1 OR attd Inf.; Missing, since reported killed Lieut. R.B. Ford.'

Forty years passed before Lieut. Westacott spoke of this action and others after which time it is highly likely he substituted the name 'Lieut. May' to protect the family of Lieut. Ford from the true circumstances of his death. 2nd Tunnelling Company War Diary carries no mention of a Lieut. May; the Commonwealth War Graves Commission record no officer of that name having been killed on 2 June 1916.

(Panel 10) Lieut. Robert Bertram Ford, 2nd Tunnelling Coy., Canadian Engineers, C.E.F.: *s.* of Dr. R (& Mrs S.) Ford, of 2060, Lomax Street, Vancouver, British Columbia: *b.* London, 26 July 1873: Religion – Church of England: Occupation – Civil Engineer: enlisted 16 February 1916: served with the Expeditionary Force in France and Flanders. Reported missing at Clonmel Copse, Belgium, 2 June 1916; since confirmed killed in action: Age 31. He was married to Ethel Ford (232, Willesden Lane, London, N.W.), late of The Cottage, Enfield Road, Ealing, London, W.

(Panel 10) Corpl. 503216, William John Smith, 2nd Tunnelling Coy., Canadian Engineers, C.E.F.: *s.* of James Ed. Smith, of Elmwood Post Office, Ontario: *b.* Elmwood, 1 December 1882: Occupation – Teamster: enlisted Calgary, 19 October 1915: served with the Expeditionary Force in France and Flanders, and was killed in action 2 June 1916: Age 33.

(Panel 10) Spr. 503366, Henry Banks, 2nd Tunnelling Coy., Canadian Engineers, C.E.F.: *b.* 4 November 1880: brother to Georgina Young (Liverpool), and *husb.* to Mary Alice (91, Overbury Street, Edge Hill, Liverpool): Occupation – Labourer: enlisted Victoria, British Columbia, 10 December 1915. Killed in action 2 June 1916: Age 35.

(Panel 10) Spr. 625008, John Lawrence Budrow, 2nd Tunnelling Coy., Canadian Engineers, C.E.F.: late of Hastings, Coulee, Alberta: *s.* of Wallace Budrow, Cheboque Point, Nova Scotia: *b.* 2 February 1890: Religion – Roman Catholic: enlisted 1 March 1916. Killed in action 4 September 1917; Maple Copse: Age 27. *unm.*

(Panel 10) Spr. 503370, James Cochrane, 2nd Tunnelling Coy., Canadian Engineers, C.E.F.: *s.* of the late George Cochrane, by his wife Mary (24, Piddock Road, Litherland, Liverpool): Killed in action at

Mount Sorrel, 2 June 1916: Age 38. He leaves a wife, Catherine Cocharane (89, Ford Street, Vauxhall Road, Liverpool), to whom correspondence may be addressed.

(Panel 10) Spr. 503342, Henry Rowe Collins, 2nd Tunnelling Coy., Canadian Engineers, C.E.F.: brother to James Collins, of Rosendale Farm, Helston, co. Cornwall: *b*. Wendon Parish, co. Cornwall, 17 January 1877: Occupation – Miner: previously saw service with Gloucestershire Regt., South Africa, 1901 – 02 (Queen's & King's Medals with clasps); also 3 years, Australian Militia: prior to enlistment was serving member 2nd Grand Forks Militia: enlisted C.E.F., Vancouver, British Columbia, 6 October 1915: served with the Expeditionary Force in France and Flanders; Ypres sector from 7 April 1916, and was killed in action 2 June 1916: Age 39.

(Panel 10) Spr. 503401, James Leslie Cook, 2nd Tunnelling Coy., Canadian Engineers, C.E.F.: *s*. of George Cook, of Chesterfield Road, Mansfield, co. Nottingham, by his wife Charlotte: *b*. Swanwick, co. Derby, 7 November 1890: Occupation – Miner: enlisted Merritt, British Columbia, 6 January 1916: served with the Expeditionary Force in France and Flanders from April 1916. Killed in action 2 June 1916: Age 25. His widow Martha has since remarried, now Mrs M.A. Munro (403, 16th Avenue East, Vancouver, British Columbia).

(Panel 10) Spr. 55399, Henry Elliott Curtis, 2nd Tunnelling Coy., Canadian Engineers: *s*. of Martha (65, Daniel Hill Street, Walkley); late of 37, Forfar Square, Sheffield: *b*. Sheffield, co. York, 20 August 1894: Occupation – Farmer: enlisted Toronto, 12 November 1914: served with the Expeditionary Force in France and Flanders from April 1916; Ypres sector from the 7th of that month, and was killed at the Battle of Mount Sorrel, 2 June 1916: Age 21.

(Panel 10) Spr. 501045, Frank Everson, 2nd Tunnelling Coy., Canadian Engineers, C.E.F.: *b*. Glen William, Ontario, 6 May 1889: Occupation – Pastry Cook: served 3 yrs. Colour Sergt., Wellington Rifles (Militia), prior to enlisting Toronto, 3 November 1915: served with the Expeditionary Force in France from April 1916, and was killed in action 2 June following: Age 27. Spr. Everson leaves a wife, Lilly (18, Fenning Street, Toronto); all mails to be forwarded c/o R.W. Hall, Brampton Post Office, Ontario. (*IWGC record Eveson*)

(Panel 10) Spr. 503506, William Goacher, 2nd Tunnelling Coy., Canadian Engineers, C.E.F.: *s*. of Reuben Goacher, of New Villas, Meatham Road, Toll Gate, Moira, Burton-on-Trent, co. Stafford, by his wife Elizabeth: *b*. Moira, 31 October 1893: Occupation – Labourer: enlisted 4 February 1915. Killed in action 2 June 1916: Age 22.

(Panel 10) Spr. 503465, John Hailey, 2nd Tunnelling Coy., Canadian Engineers, C.E.F.: brother to Martin Hailey, of Boston, Massachusetts: *b*. St. John, New Brunswick, 6 March 1877: Occupation – Blacksmith: enlisted New Westminster, British Columbia, 1 December 1915: served with the Expeditionary Force in France and Flanders from April 1916; Ypres sector from the 7th of that month, and was killed in action nr. Ypres, 2 June 1916: Age 39. (*IWGC record 503405*)

(Panel 10) Spr. 503480, John Harris, 2nd Tunnelling Coy., Canadian Engineers, C.E.F.: c/o friend – John McMurray, of Conrad, Montana, United States: *b*. Cork, Ireland, 16 June 1878: Occupation – Miner: previously served 21st United States Cavalry: enlisted Lethbridge, Alberta, 26 November 1915. Killed in action 2 June 1916: Age 37.

(Panel 10) Spr. 503323, Harry McIvor Hepburn, 2nd Tunnelling Coy., Canadian Engineers, C.E.F.: *s*. of Mrs G.W.H. Hepburn (65, Skelton Road, Forest Gate, London, E.): *b*. Gypsy Hill, co. Surrey, 30 January 1872: Occupation – Mines Accountant: enlisted Vancouver, British Columbia, 1 January 1916: served with the Expeditionary Force in France, and was killed in action nr. Ypres 2 June following: Age 44.

(Panel 10) Spr. 503243, Robert Izatt, 2nd Tunnelling Coy., Canadian Engineers, C.E.F.: *s*. of James Izatt, of Kelty, Scotland: *b*. Kelty, 29 January 1889: Occupation – Miner: enlisted Calgary, 3 September 1915, and was killed in action 2 June 1916: Age 27.

(Panel 10) Spr. 67119, Nicholas Kennedy, 3rd Tunnelling Coy., Canadian Engineers, C.E.F.: *s*. of P. Kennedy, of Dominion, Cape Breton: *b*. Dominion, 9 July 1894: Occupation – Miner: joined 94th Regt. (Militia), 7 November 1914; enlisted C.E.F., Halifax, 9 November: served with the Expeditionary Force in France. Missing / believed killed in action between Tor Top and Stirling Castle on the night of 20 September 1917, having gone over the top with the infantry to search for enemy dugouts and booby traps: Age 23. *unm.* Remembered on the Dominion War Memorial, Cape Breton.

(Panel 10) Spr. 832573, Percy Leonard Mitton, 2nd Tunnelling Coy., Canadian Engineers, C.E.F.: *s.* of Lizzie Mitton (Berryton, Alberta Co., New Brunswick): *b.* 5 June 1895: Religion – Baptist: enlisted Moncton, 17 April 1916: Killed in action 4 September 1917; Maple Copse: Age 22.

(Panel 10) Spr. 409586, William Morris, 2nd Tunnelling Coy., Canadian Engineers, C.E.F.: *s.* of Peter Morris, of 8, Cowling Brow, Chorley, co. Lancaster, by his wife Jane: late *husb.* to Alice Ann Henry, *née* Morris (Thorold, Ontario): served with the Expeditionary Force in France from April 1916, and was killed in action at Mount Sorrel, nr. Ypres, 2 June 1916: Age 38.

(Panel 10) Spr. 503270, Edward Ellis Onions, 2nd Tunnelling Coy., Canadian Engineers, C.E.F.: *s.* of the late Thomas Onion, by his wife Mary: brother to Jane Ellis Onions (Cannock, co. Stafford): *b.* Cannock, 31 May 1883: previously served 38th South Staffordshire Infantry (Militia): sometime went to Canada, where he was employed as a Miner: enlisted Edmonton, 8 October 1915: served as Tunneller, Canadian Engineers, and was killed in action beneath Mount Sorrel, 2 June 1916: Age 34. (*IWGC record E.Onion*)

(Panel 10) Spr. 503450, William Polson (served as Thomas Wilson), 2nd Tunnelling Coy., Canadian Engineers, C.E.F.: *s.* of William Wilson, of 4, Holme Street, Edinburgh, co. Midlothian: *b.* Edinburgh, 7 December 1884: sometime went to Canada, and found employ as Miner: enlisted Calgary 11 January 1916: posted Canadian Engineers: served with the Expeditionary Force in France and Flanders, and was killed in action 2 June 1916: Age 31.

(Panel 10) Spr. 503392, Alexander Roy, 2nd Tunnelling Coy., Canadian Engineers, C.E.F.: *s.* of B. Swanson, of City Hotel, Vancouver, British Columbia: *b.* Mosstodloch, nr. Fochabers, co. Moray, 20 November 1886: Occupation – Ship's Fireman: volunteered and enlisted New Westminster, British Columbia, 7 December 1915, under the alias Robert Swanson, giving his place of birth as Nanaimo, Vancouver Island: posted 121st Overseas Battn., 29 December 1915. For reasons unknown he divulged his true identity and place of birth, 9 March 1916, shortly before his departure for France where he was killed in action 15 September following during fighting in a tunnel system which had fallen into the enemy's hands: Age 28. *unm.*

(Panel 10) Spr. 503409, Robert Clifton Singleton, 2nd Tunnelling Coy., Canadian Engineers, C.E.F.: *s.* of the late Robert Clifton Singleton, of Sunderland, by his wife Mary Ellen: *b.* Sunderland, 4 October 1887: Occupation – Miner: enlisted, Merritt, British Columbia, 6 January 1916, and was killed in action at Ypres 2 June following: Age 28. He was married to Eleanor (351, Aberdeen Street, Vancouver, British Columbia).

(Panel 10) Spr. 503389, Sydney Snow, 2nd Tunnelling Coy., Canadian Engineers, C.E.F.: c/o Mrs M. Doyle (23, Temple Street, Dublin, Ireland): *b.* Dublin, 6 May 1882: Occupation – Boilermaker: enlisted Vancouver, British Columbia, 24 November 1915: served with the Expeditionary Force in France from April 1916, and was killed in action 2 June 1916.

(Panel 10) Spr. 503412, John Wilcock, 2nd Tunnelling Coy., Canadian Engineers, C.E.F.: brother to Peter Wilcock, of Buckley, North Wales: *b.* Buckley, 7 May 1879: previously served with Royal Engineers, South Africa: prior to enlistment Merritt, British Coumbia, was employed as Miner: enlisted 5 January 1916: posted 2nd Tunnelling Company, 22 April 1916, and was killed in action 2 June following: Age 37.

(Panel 10) Spr. 503292, George Wilde, 2nd Tunnelling Coy., Canadian Engineers, C.E.F.: *b.* Ardsley, Barnsley, co. York, 25 March 1872: enlisted Pincher Creek, Alberta, 10 February 1915: served with the Expeditionary Force in France and Flanders. Reported missing / believed killed in action during the fighting at Sanctuary Wood, 2 June 1916: Age 44. He was married to Mary Ann Wilde (Hillcrest, Alberta).

(Panel 10) Pte. 733928, Roscoe Vaughan Trask, Royal Canadian Regt., C.E.F.: *s.* of the late Kilsey Trask, of Little River, Nova Scotia, by his marriage to Marion G. Pratt, *née* Trask (112, Jersey Street, Boston, Massachusetts): and yr. brother to Pte. 733929, R.K. Trask, 112th Battn. (surv'd.): *b.* Little River,

Digby County, 16 June 1897: Religion – Baptist: Occupation – Fisherman: 5'10" tall, fair complexion, brown eyes, dark hair: enlisted Digby, 31 January 1916: posted 112th (Overseas) Battn. 14 July. Killed by shellfire 16 November 1917; Passchendaele – Westroosebeke road: Age 18. Constructed in 1929 the Little River War Memorial honours Roscoe Trask, the only member of the local community to die in the Great War.

The P.P.C.L.I.

The trumpet sounded loud o'er hill and plain:
To Arms! To Arms! Our Empire is at war!
Come, join your Colours, on the land or main,
All Britons who have served the King before.

And in the mountain mine; by prairie plow,
They answered to the trumpet's brazen voice:
They who had served the Empire long enow
As soldiers by profession and from choice.

No conscripts, these, in whose unwilling hands
Weapons are thrust, to wage unwilling strife,
But – freemen all, who needed not commands
To volunteer their service, limb and life.

Thus rose a regiment, as 'neath a wand,
Of seasoned men, with medalled service too:
Soldiers from every corps throughout the land –
Britons beyond the seas; tried men and true.

This is indeed a princely gift to give
To our Imperial Realm in crisis sore –
Proud in the nation of the sturdy men,
And prouder yet of him who raised the Corps.

Then go, ye able sons of Britain's soil,
To take your place, wherever it may be;
God speed you in the glory – and the toil,
Princess Patricia's Canadian Infantry.

'Poet of the Pats'

Between 1914 – 1918 the lives of countless thousands of young men from the great powers and their colonies were spent with almost unthinking abandon, robbing many communities of their finest talent and thereby their future. Predominantly displayed casualty reports became a part of everyday life, bringing home both the sacrifice and sadness the war was exacting and the careless cruelty with which the war was being directed. Yet, even when they understood the possible consequences, young men continued to volunteer to serve a cause that was dubious to them, under leaders that were odious – but for a King and Empire that mattered to them in a manner incomprehensible by today's understanding.

Talbot Papineau – an articulate young man, a brilliant lawyer and orator with a promising career in politics before him (it is widely believed that had not the war intervened he would almost certainly have become a future prime minister of Canada) – went to war for reasons which over a century later we can analyse but never quite understand. Well connected in England and Canada Papineau engaged in debates with his cousin Henri Bourassa in defence of his country's participation in the First World War; he said, "It is true that Canada has not heard the roar of German guns, nor been struck by deadly zeppelins, but every shot fired against Belgium or France was aimed as much at Canada's heart as at the heart of our brave allies."

Joining Princess Patricia's Canadian Light Infantry (founded by his friend Hamilton Gault) in August 1914, he left Canada with the First Canadian Contingent and took part in the fighting at St. Eloi and Bellewaarde Ridge in 1915 before being transferred to London to work for Max Aitken as an eyewitness in the Canadian War Records Office throughout the summer of 1916 (contributing to the book '*Canada In Flanders*').

Uncomfortable with sitting on the sidelines as the Princess Patricia's fought at Mount Sorrel, on the Somme and at Vimy Ridge, Papineau's reason for rejoining the regiment for the Battle of Passchendaele was double edged – on the one hand he had seen enough action and filed enough reports to know it meant almost certain death, on the other – to be involved in one more big battle would almost certainly guarantee him political success after the war.

On 29 October 1917 he wrote to his mother about his experience in the trenches and his love and concern for her and his family, "Dearest Mother, After all, I have been able to write to you again before going over. We have been fortunate so far and all things are cheerful. I have even shaved this morning in a little dirty water. I was delighted last night to get two letters from you, and a box of candy which I have actually carried with me and have enjoyed. It was a cold night and I slept only about one hour. Also a noisy night, I can assure you, and the earth full of vibrations. I hope by the same mail you receive another letter from me to say all is successfully over. But of course it may be difficult or impossible to write for a few days, so don't worry. There seems so little to say when if only I knew what was to happen I might want to say so much. These would be poor letters to have as last ones but you must know with what a world of love they are written. Always remember that I could not love thee so well, or you love me, did I not love honour more. You have given me courage and strength to go very happily and cheerfully into the good fight. Love to all and a big hug for thee, my dear brave little mother."

The following day, from their position partway up the Passchendaele Ridge, the Princess Pats took part in 3rd Canadian Division's assault on the Meetcheele Ridge. With great difficulty in determining the exact direction of their attack – all roads, trees, villages and landmarks having been completely obliterated – the Pats encountered mud knee (and in places thigh) deep, uncut belts of wire, and pill-boxes that remained unsilenced due to ineffectual artillery fire. The whole attack was a complete shambles. With men falling everywhere Major Papineau encountered the battalion adjutant Capt. H.W. Niven sheltering in a shell-hole and after a brief consultation said, "Hughie, this is suicide," to which Capt. Niven replied, "I know, but we have to go on." Nodding in agreement Papineau pulled himself over the lip of the shell-hole only to be cut in half by a German shell moments later.

(Panel 10) Major Talbot Mercer Papineau, M.C., Comdg. No.3 Coy., Princess Patricia's Canadian Light Infantry (Eastern Ontario Regt.), C.E.F.: *s.* of Louis Joseph Papineau II, of The Manor House, Montebello, Quebec, by his wife Caroline, *née* Rogers (41, Queen's Gate Gardens, London, S.W.), formerly of Philadelphia, United States: and *gdson.* to Louis Joseph Papineau (1786 – 1871), Politician, Lawyer and leader of the reformist Patriote Movement: *b.* Montebello, 25 March 1883: *educ.* Montreal High School, and McGill University, from where (1905) he won a Rhodes Scholarship to Brasenose College, Oxford (Law student) and, after graduating, returned to Montreal (1908) and began practising in that profession: Religion – Presbyterian: enlisted P.P.C.L.I. as Lieut. 12 August 1914: served with the Expeditionary Force in France and Flanders from 23 January 1915, took part in the fighting at St. Eloi; awarded the Military Cross ('*London Gazette*,' 15 April 1915) for his part in a trench raid in that sector 28 February 1915 (the first trench raid of the war); and at Bellewaarde Ridge (8 May 1915) on which occasion the Patricia's 'held firm and counted not the loss.': appt'd. Staff Capt. 3 June 1916; General Staff Officer (Grade 3), vice Major A.D. Cameron, 25 November 1916; A/Major 26 May 1917: returned to his regiment 15 October 1917 after ten days leave, and was killed by a direct hit from a German shell after leaving the shelter of a shell-hole to lead an assault at Passchendaele on the 30th of that month: 30 October 1917: Age 34. Partial remains buried 17 November; grave marked with a cross.

For the third time in the war the Ypres Salient had proved to be the graveyard of the P.P.C.L.I. On October 30th – 31st the Regiment suffered 363 killed, wounded and missing for minor gains. Of the

600 men who took part in the attack 150 were killed. It was a shattering day for the Regiment and its Commanding Officer Lieut.Col. Agar Adamson who (on a scrap of paper) wrote to his wife Mabel from the front line, "31 October 1917. I am still alright and hanging on. Our attack was successful but both it and holding, have been awfully costly. Haggard, Papineau, Sulivan, Agar, Almon, Riddell, Williams, Morris, MacKenzie, killed. Wounded McKay, Lalor, Beeston, Gibson, Pike, Robins, Stevens, Reynolds, Macartney. Less men are left than on the historic 8th of May."

With no opportunity to pay any attention to the dying and the dead it was not until two weeks later that the Princess Pats returned to the vicinity of the Bellevue Spur to search for their fallen comrades and provide some semblance of a decent burial for as many as possible. The report of one party records finding 'a pair of feet with reversed puttees sticking out of a shell hole full of water,' and concludes, 'Major Papineau always wore his puttees that way. We pulled the legs out and by examining the contents of the pockets found it to be Papineau. Part of a shell had hit him in the stomach, blowing away everything else above. Poor fellow, he could not have known what hit him.'

Capt. R.L. Haggard, Lieuts. H.E. Agar and J.E. Almon are buried in Passchendaele New British Cemetery (VIII.A.19, X.E.22 and X.D.3), Capt. H.E. Sulivan, Oxford Road Cemetery (I.K.9), Lieut. J.R. Riddell, Brandhoek New Military Cemetery No.3 (I.M.11); Lieut. M.W. Williams and Capt. W.H. Morris have no known grave, they are recorded below.

(Panel 10) Capt. Harry Stuart Dennison, Princess Patricia's Canadian Light Infantry (Eastern Ontario Regt.), C.E.F.: *s.* of Ralph Abercrombie Dennison, of 90, Warrior Square, St. Leonards-on-Sea, co. Sussex, by his wife E.H.E. McTaggart Dennison: late *husb.* to Blanche D'Arcy Dennison (28, Portland Court, Portland Place, London): and brother to Lieut. R.E. McKie Dennison, 5th Royal Sussex Regt., who fell the following day: *b.* 1883: volunteered and enlisted as Pte. on the outbreak of war August 1914: came over with 1st Canadian Contingent, October following: promoted Temp. Lieut. November 1914: served with the Expeditionary Force in France from December 1914, being substantiated in his rank February 1915; promoted Capt. March 1915: took part in the fighting at the Second Battle of Ypres, and was reported missing after taking part in a rear-guard action in the front line during the fighting on Bellewaarde Ridge, 8 May 1915: Age 32.

His brother Ralph also has no known grave; he is commemorated on the Le Touret Memorial, France.

(Panel 10) Capt. William Hugoe Morris, M.C., No.1 Coy., Princess Patricia's Canadian Light Infantry (Eastern Ontario Regt.), C.E.F.: only *s.* of William Dawler Morris, of 11, Somerset Street, Ottawa, Ontario, by his wife Mary A.: *b.* 12 March 1894: Religion – Presbyterian: *educ.* McGill University; 3rd yr. Science Student: enlisted Ottawa, 26 February 1915: 5'7" tall, blue eyes, light brown hair: Killed in action 30 October 1917: Age 23. See Major T.M. Papineau (above).

(Panel 10) Lieut. Harold Edward Agar, 'A' Coy., Princess Patricia's Canadian Light Infantry (Eastern Ontario Regt.), C.E.F.: *s.* of Frederick Matthew Agar, of 28, Fountain Street, Hull, co. York, by his wife Margaret Anne: and brother to Pte. 52914, C.C. Agar, 2nd West Yorkshire Regt., died (prisoner of war) 1 August 1918: *b.* Howden, co. York, 28 September 1891: Occupation – School Teacher: previous to removing to Canada, served five years 5th East Yorkshire Regt. (T.F.): volunteered and enlisted, Edmonton, August 1914; came over with First Contingent 14 October following; crossed to France 20 December: served in the St. Eloi sector, nr. Ypres, from where, 15 January 1915, he was evacuated to hospital at St. Omer with frostbitten feet; returned to duty 24 January: hospitalised again after being slightly wounded in the arm during the counter-attack at The Mound, St. Eloi., 16 March 1915; returned to his regiment in the trenches at Polygon Wood, 18 April following: took part in the withdrawal from Polygon Wood to new positions on the Frezenberg and Bellewaerde Ridge where, on 4 May, he was struck in the head and right arm whilst digging new trenches: after recovery returned to his regiment in the Armentieres sector 7 July 1915: promoted L/Corpl. 3 January 1916: wounded in the shoulder during the Battle of Mount Sorrel, 2 June 1916, rejoining his regiment on the 29th of that month: promoted Corpl. 4 July; Sergt. three days later: took part in operations on the Somme, Courcelette, Regina Trench, September 1916: posted Seaford and O.T.C. Bexhill, 21 March 1917, for officer training: received his commission 7th Reserve

Battn. 1 July 1917: returned to France 10 October; joined Princess Patricia's L.I., Arras sector; shortly thereafter moved up to the Ypres salient, where he was killed in action 30 October 1917: Age 26. On the morning of 30 October 1917, the Patricia's assaulted Meetcheele Ridge, Lieut. Agar, with No.1 Company moving forward in support on the left, straight up the Bellevue Spur. In the face of murderous fire from machine guns housed in blockhouses, supported by troops entrenched in well placed positions, it was a battle of bloody-mindedness won by sheer guts and determination; a series of individual platoon actions against the strong German positions, which gained the regiment its first Victoria Crosses of the war. "... Out of the twenty-five officers who entered the battle, twenty were casualties including nine killed or missing. There were 150 other ranks killed or missing, along with a further 193 wounded... Lieut. Agar survived the assault and reached the objective. About an hour after doing so he was wounded in the head. With the line consolidated and being reinforced, Agar started back to the aid station, running from shell hole to shell hole across the exposed terrain. He was stopped by Capt. MacPherson who bound up his wound and stayed there for half an hour before deciding to take his chances in going back. Fifty yards later he was sniped in the head and killed." Recorded by the regiment as being buried on Meetcheele Ridge, 28.D.5.d.15.70, with Lieut. Almon and several other P.P.C.L.I., after the war a number of these bodies, "including Lieut. Almon were identified and accorded a named grave, another three were not so fortunate." Lieut. Agar would have to wait eighty-four years for his headstone; the identity of the other two – Ptes. Ruddy and Newell – remains undecided. *Buried in Passchendaele New British Cemetery (X.E.22).*

Your Sacrifice Gave Us Our Freedom
Always Remembered

His brother Cyril is buried in Valenciennes (St. Roch) Communal Cemetery (V.E.2).

(Panel 10) Lieut. Percy Edward Lane, Princess Patricia's Canadian Light Infantry (Eastern Ontario Regt.), C.E.F.: 2nd *s.* of the late Col. Cecil Newton Lane, C.M.G., resident Cephalonia, Greece, and Mrs Newton (Rycote House, Leamington, co. Warwick), *dau.* of the Hon. & Rev. F. Bertie: *b.* Boningale, co. Salop, January 1881: *educ.* Malvern College: served during the South African War 1899 – 1902 (Queen's Medal and clasp): went to Canada from thence: Occupation – Rancher: joined Princess Patricia's Canadian Light Infantry, 1914: gazetted Lieut.: arrived England October 1914: served with the Expeditionary Force in France and Flanders. Reported wounded and missing after the fighting at Bellewaarde Ridge, during the Second Battle of Ypres, 15 May 1915, being last seen in the forward fire trench before it was overwhelmed by the enemy assault, and is now assumed to have been killed in action on or about that date. Coy.-Quartermaster-Sergt. Allen, of Princess Patricia's Canadian Light Infantry, "The last seen of Lieut. Lane was in the firing trench leading his men on like the true soldier he was, for he was a man who knew not the word *fear*, and he was beloved by all who came in contact with him.": Age 34. *unm.*

(Panel 10) Lieut. George Stacey Stratford, 'A' Coy., Princess Patricia's Canadian Light Infantry (Eastern Ontario Regt.), C.E.F.: *s.* of Joseph E.H. (& Mrs) Stratford, of Brantford, Ontario: *b.* Brantford, 31 March 1892: *educ.* Brantford Public Schools and Collegiate; University of Toronto (Applied Science), 1911 – 12, 1913 – 15: member Beta Theta Pi fraternity, and C.O.T.C.: enlisted 2nd Universities Coy., P.P.C.L.I., June 1915: joined the regiment in France September following: served on the Somme and Armentieres fronts, and in the Ypres salient where he was wounded at Sanctuary Wood, June 1916: hospitalised six months, on recovery began training for a commission: rejoined P.P.C.L.I. May 1917, on the Vimy – Lens – Hill 70 front, and, after going through the Battle of Passchendaele, was killed 17 November 1917, when his battalion was holding the trenches at Meetcheele. Buried at Passchendaele: Age 25. *unm.*

(Panel 10) Lieut. Andrew Angus Wanklyn, Princess Patricia's Canadian Light Infantry (Eastern Ontario Regt.) , C.E.F.: *s.* of Frederic Lumb Wanklyn, late of 3453, Drummond Street, Montreal, Quebec; removed to 341, Drummond Street, and his late wife Edith Margaret: *b.* Montreal, 30 November

1890: *educ.* McGill University, member C.O.T.C., graduated B.A., B.C.L.: enlisted P.P.C.L.I., Lieut., 17 February 1915: served with the Expeditionary Force in France from March 1916, and was killed in action in the Sanctuary Wood sector, 2 June following. Buried nr. Kruistraat: Age 25. *unm.* Remains recovered unmarked grave (28.J.19.a.3.4); identified – Badge of Rank, Titles, Gold Watch engrvd. Sidney. DAYTON. 'Bye Ye Olde Firme HEINTZMAN & Co. Ltd. 1915;' reinterred, registered 4 October 1927. *Buried in Sanctuary Wood Cemetery (IV.H.1).*

"And To Give His Life A Ransom For Many"

Mark X.45

(Panel 10) Lieut. MC145, Mark Webber Williams, No.2 Coy., Princess Patricia's Canadian Light Infantry (Eastern Ontario Regt.), C.E.F.: *s.* of W.H. Williams, by his wife Emma (Maple Avenue, Burlington, Ontario): and yr. brother to Corpl. 89679, J.N. Williams, died 8 August 1920, consequent to wounds received on active service in France: *b.* Nelson Township, Halton Co., Ontario, 15 October 1893: Religion – Church of England: *educ.* Nelson Public School; Hamilton Collegiate; University of Toronto, 1912 – 15; member McGill University 2nd Regt., C.O.T.C.: enlisted Toronto, 26 May 1915: 5'6" tall, grey eyes, dark hair: posted 2nd University Coy., P.P.C.L.I., June 1915 and proceeded to France: initially served on the Somme front, thereafter Armentieres and the Ypres Salient: severely wounded (arm) at Sanctuary Wood – Mount Sorrel (Zillebeke), 3 June 1916: received his commission on recovery and rejoined P.P.C.L.I. early 1917, serving with the regiment at Vimy and Lens. Lieut. Williams was killed in action at Bellevue Spur (Passchendaele), 30 October 1917. The first line of enemy trenches had been captured, and he was leading his men on to the second line when he was hit by a sniper's bullet, and died of his injuries an hour later. Buried near where he fell, at Bellevue: Age 24. *unm.* See Major T.M. Papineau (above).

His brother Jack is buried in Burlington (Greenwood) Cemetery (Sect.22,Lot.5).

(Panel 10) Sergt. 21110, Francis Alderson, Princess Patricia's Canadian Light Infantry (Eastern Ontario Regt.), C.E.F.: *s.* of Christopher Alderson, of 15, Chapel Street, New Shildon, Co. Durham, England: *b.* 29 April 1888: Religion – Church of England: Occupation – Driver: previously served 4 yrs. Durham Light Infantry; joined C.E.F., Valcartier, 23 September 1914: served in France from 28 June 1915, and was killed in action 2 June 1916; Warrington Avenue, Sanctuary Wood. Buried where he fell: Age 28.

(Panel 10) Sergt. 48, John Percy Benham, No.1 Coy., Princess Patricia's Canadian Light Infantry (Eastern Ontario Regt.), C.E.F.: eldest *s.* of the late John Benham, Iron Founder; by his wife Helen Louisa (99, Warwick Gardens, Earl's Court, London, S.W.), *dau.* of John Jay: *b.* Earl's Court, 6 December 1872: *educ.* Salisbury: served as a volunteer with a Rail Detachment in the South African War and, on 5 August 1914, while out in Toronto, Ontario, Canada, enlisted Princess Patricia's L.I.: promoted L/Sergt.26 September: came over with 1st Canadian Contingent: served in France from 20 December 1914: wounded 22 March 1915, being shot in the arm, and lay in hospital in Boulogne for six weeks: thereafter returned to his company: took part in the Battle of Frezenberg, and was killed on the north-west side of Bellewaarde Lake, about 500 yards north-west of Hooge, 8 May 1915. Sergt. Benham had a good knowledge of French, and a comrade wrote, "Your son was held in great respect and his quiet cheerfulness was much appreciated by those who came in contact with him. He was very popular not only in No.1 Coy., but in the whole battn.": Age 43. *unm.*

(Panel 10) Sergt. 23630, Edouard Bourbonnais, Princess Patricia's Canadian Light Infantry (Eastern Ontario Regt.), C.E.F.: *s.* of Xavier Bourbonnais, of Aubrun, Ontario: and brother to Pte. 3796, A. Bourbonnais, Royal Canadian Dragoons, killed in action 23 March 1918: *b.* Aubrun, 3 October 1884: Religion – Roman Catholic: Occupation – Steamfitter: serving member of the Militia; enlisted Valcartier Camp, 27 August 1914, posted 12th (Overseas) Battn., 27 September: came over with 1st Canadian Contingent, October 1914, proceeded to France 17 February 1915, and was killed in action at Sanctuary Wood 2 June 1916: Age 31. *unm.* See account re. Pte. J.H. Miller, below.

His brother Arthur also has no known grave; he is commemorated on the Canadian National Memorial, Vimy.

(Panel 10) Sergt. 1246, Frank Smith Brown (*a.k.a.* 'Poet of the Pats'), Princess Patricia's Canadian Light Infantry (Eastern Ontario Regt.), C.E.F.: late *husb.* to Isobel Evelyn Vilma Brown ('The Manse,' Almonte, Ontario): *s.* of the Rev. S. Gorley Brown, of 200, Decarie Boulevard, Montreal, and Josephine Smith Brown, his wife: *b.* Waterford, Ontario, 8 December 1893: Religion – Presbyterian: previously served 9 months Royal Canadian Regt; 3 years, 2 months Canadian Engineers: Occupation – Soldier and Clerk: enlisted Ottawa, 26 August 1914; promoted Sergt. 11 September; posted P.P.C.L.I., 5 October: left Canada with First Contingent, 14 October 1914: crossed to France with reinforcement draft January 1915, and was killed on his first day in the trenches, 3 February following, being shot through the head by a German sniper. Reflecting on their brief acquaintance Holbrook Jackson, editor of Frank Brown's '*Contingent Ditties and other Soldier Songs of the Great War*' (Sampson, Law & Marston Ltd., London, 1915) wrote, "Fair, slight but sturdy, keen-eyed, self-confident but unassuming; such is my impression of the young soldier who came into my room on that grey January morning. He was the type of British soldier: healthy, cheerful, untroubled by mental subtlety or overwhelming ambition, but willing to square brain and brawn with the general attainment of an end known to be righteous and certain. All this was evident from the external view; but the intimacy of conversation revealed exceptional characteristics. It was evident that Sergeant Brown resembled the admirable average type of British soldier only by an effort of the will, born, probably of an equally British and equally admirable objection to being thought remarkable. On the three or four occasions upon which we met, I learned to value the mental qualities of this khaki-clad son of the Empire. His intellectual interests were wide, and, although backed up by a considerable bookish experience, they always sought a practical end. He was an Imperialist, but no jingo word escaped him in my hearing. On the contrary, his soldierly reticence was based in enthusiasm for personal endeavour…That was the man. He would talk, long and well, but the role was sincere rather than brilliant, and generally impersonal. I failed to get him to talk about himself. His two immediate concerns were to get to the Front where his comrades were fighting with undying heroism, and to have his poems published. Both wishes have now been gratified; but Sergeant Brown lived only to enjoy the first, and that for only a few brief hours." In a letter to Sergt. Brown's father, Capt. Talbot M. Papineau wrote, "You were right in assuming that I crossed to France with your son in the same draft for our regiment. I had, indeed, been closely associated with him from the beginning. We went immediately to the firing line, and he was actually in the trench of which I was in command when he was killed. As you know, he was an expert shot, and he showed at once the most commendable enthusiasm in his work. Indeed, it was this which caused his death. During the first day he fired nearly eighty rounds at the enemy, probably as much as the rest of the Company put together, and undoubtedly attracted the attention of the German sharpshooters to himself. About 3.30 that same afternoon he was struck in the head and died instantly and without pain. That evening we reverently buried him behind the firing line – a short distance – with his feet to a large tree and his head to the enemy. A wooden cross was erected to his memory. Either myself or Corporal Smithers of my Company could direct you to the exact spot. It lies between what were afterwards known as trenches 23B and 23C – in front of 'Shelley Farm' – and within sight of the famous 'mound of death' at St. Eloi. There are many of his comrades and many of his officers who are buried within a short distance of him. Had he lived I am sure he would have won signal distinction. He was a conscientious and reliable soldier, a skilful and courageous marksman. It is, indeed, one of the sad things of this war that those who will have done most and sacrificed most to bring it to a successful conclusion will not be there to receive their earthly reward nor share the glory of the achievement. It must be a comfort to you to know that your son died bravely and honourably in the discharge of his duties." Sergt. Brown's interests combined a love of outdoor life and intellectual pursuits, a good horseman, first-class shot; he was also a musician and writer of considerable promise. Helpful and cheerful, he won many friends, and his acquaintanceship was valued wherever he went. Prior to enlistment Sergt. Brown was acting District

Scoutmaster for the City of Quebec, and – during his short stay in England – was made a Honorary Member of the Veteran's Club, High Holborn, London: Age 21.

(Panel 10) Sergt.Major. 1315, James William Dames, D.C.M., M.S.M., Princess Patricia's Canadian Light Infantry: 2nd *s.* of John Joseph Dames. of London, England, by his wife Mary Ann, *dau.* of James Raybrook: *b.* London, 27 November 1871: enlisted Sherwood Foresters (Notts & Derby Regt.) 1885, aged 14 years: sent to India, 1897, as Sergt. in charge of a draft for 2nd Battn.; took part in the Tirah Campaign (Medal): on the Island of Malta, on the return journey to England, when the Boer War broke out; volunteered for Active Service without hesitation: proceeded to South Africa with Sherwood Foresters (attd. Malta Mounted Infantry); and served throughout that campaign; twice wounded, thrice Mentioned in Despatches, awarded Distinguished Conduct Medal & Queen's Medal (3 Bars): invalided home 1901; on recovery took employ as Clerk; The War Office: sometime removed to Canada; settled Derbytown, Alberta: volunteered and enlisted Levis Camp, 9 September 1914 after the outbreak of the European War; apptd. Princess Patricia's C.L.I., 5 October following: came over with 1st Canadian Contingent (14 October), proceeded to France 20 December 1914, and was killed in action at Bellewaarde Lake, nr. Ypres, 8 May 1915: Age 43. He *m.*, St. George's Church, Stonehouse, Plymouth, 26 July 1897; Florence (Derbytown, Mound P.O., Alberta, Canada), *yst. dau.* of the late John Coneybeer, of Ivybridge, co. Devon, and had two *s.* – Frank Coneybeer, *b.* 15 September 1899; Harold Victor, *b.* 28 September 1902. Remains 'Unknown British / Canadian Soldier;' recovered (GRU Report, Elverdinghe – 25/23E) unmarked grave (28.J.7.c.6.4) identified – D.C.M., Queen's, King's S.A. Medal Ribbons; registered, reinterred, GRU Cross 'Unknown British Soldier,' erected Hagle Dump Cemetery, 13 January 1925. Headstone replaced, detail amended 16 July 1993. *Buried in Hagle Dump Cemetery (III.H.12).*

(Panel 10) Corpl. 539, Albert Batten, Princess Patricia's Canadian Light Infantry (Eastern Ontario Regt.), C.E.F.: *s.* of Samuel Batten, of Liscard, co. Cornwall: *b.* there, *c.* 1883: served 3 years Duke of Cornwall's Light Infantry: removed to Canada; found employ as Labourer: served 2 years, Volunteers (Militia): joined P.P.C.L.I., 20 August 1914; promoted Corpl. September 1914: came to England with 1st Canadian Contingent, October following: reverted to Pte. 3 November 1914: promoted Corpl., proceeded to France; served with the Expeditionary Force there from 20 December 1914, and was killed in action on Bellewaarde Ridge, 4 May 1915, while digging in after the regiment's withdrawal from Polygon Wood: Age 31. He leaves a wife, Ada Batten (3, Salisbury Terrace, Bodmin, co. Cornwall).

In the early hours of 8 May 1915 the Germans, following up a whirlwind bombardment with a concentrated infantry attack, succeeded in pushing back a considerable portion of the Allied line around Frezenberg. Opening up, and leaving exposed, the flank of 80th Brigade situated to the immediate right, the defence of the flanking trench held by the Princess Pat's became the scene of one of the regiment's most outstanding achievements in the fighting at this time. By 6 a.m, with all telephone communication between Brigade Headquarters and the trenches having been severed, 'every single Canadian upon the strength was from that time forward in one or other of the trenches.' After an initial short but fierce struggle the German advance was checked 'and those of the enemy who were not either sheltered by buildings, dead or wounded, crawled back over the crest of the ridge to their own trenches.' But, throughout the remainder of the day the Pat's – continuously shelled by enemy howitzers, enfiladed by machine gun fire, fighting off counter-attacks – tenaciously stood their ground and paid dearly for their early success. When darkness fell and the Princess Pat's were relieved, after reading the service over their comrades, many of whom had already been buried by German shells, Lieuts. Niven, Papineau, Vanderburg and Niven led back the survivors – 150 men of a battalion that had gone into the line that morning 700 strong.

During the course of the day the Canadian's machine-guns and their crews, endeavouring to counter the German guns, were buried time and again by the enemy's artillery. Two were dug out, mounted and brought back into action; one was actually disinterred three times and kept in action until a shell annihilated the whole section – 'Corpl. Dover, stuck to this gun throughout and, although wounded, continued to discharge his duties with as much coolness as if on parade. In the explosion that destroyed his ill-fated gun he lost a leg and an arm and, rendered unconscious, was completely buried beneath the resultant debris. On regaining consciousness at dusk he crawled moaning for help out of what was left of the obliterated trench. On hearing his cries two of his comrades went to his assistance and succeeded in bringing in his mangled and bleeding body, but by this time there was very little hope for Corpl. Dover's survival, and as he was being lowered into the safety of the trench a sniper shot him in the head, putting an end to his sufferings.'

(Panel 10) Corpl. 1586, Crawford Dover, Princess Patricia's Canadian Light Infantry (Eastern Ontario Regt.), C.E.F.: *b*. Winchester, co. Hants, 1883: previously served Royal Naval Volunteer Reserve: sometime removed to Canada: on the outbreak of war volunteered for Imperial Service, enlisted P.P.C.L.I., 24 August 1914: came over with First Contingent, October 1914; promoted L/Corpl. 30th of that month; Corpl., Machine Gun Section, 11 December following: served with the Expeditionary Force in France from 20 December 1914: took part in the fighting at the Second Battle of Ypres, and was reported killed in action on Bellewaarde Ridge, 8 May 1915: Age 31.

(Panel 10) Corpl. 1529, John Brown Gallagher, Princess Patricia's Canadian Light Infantry (Eastern Ontario Regt.), C.E.F.: *s*. of James Gallagher, of 'Patricia,' Newmilns, co. Ayr, by his wife Agnes: *b*. September 1891: Occupation – Fireman: previously served 2 years, Army Service Corps: volunteered and enlisted 24 August 1914: came over with 1st Contingent, October 1914: served with the Expeditionary Force in France from 20 December following, and died in Warrington Avenue trench, Sanctuary Wood, 2 June 1916, after having both his legs blown off by the explosion of a shell: Age 24. *unm*. One of four brothers who served. (*IWGC record Gallacher*)

(Panel 10) Corpl. McG/127, Frederick Newton Read, Princess Patricia's Canadian Light Infantry (Eastern Ontario Regt.), C.E.F.: *s*. of Aaron Read: *b*. Owen Sound, 23 January 1891: Religion – Wesleyan: *educ*. Owen Sound Public School (& Collegiate), Applied Science, 1907 – 11, B.A.Sc. (Civil Engineering): Occupation – Civil Engineer, Kerrobert, Saskatchewan: served 1 year 2nd Field Coy., Engineers: enlisted 2nd Universities Coy., P.P.C.L.I., May 1915: joined his regiment at the Front, August following: served as Signaller throughout the autumn and winter on the Somme and Armentieres fronts: invalided to England (gas poisoning), Spring 1916: on recovery joined P.P.C.L.I. Depot, Seaford; employed as Regtl. Sergt. Major: three times offered a commission, Royal Engineers, but declined, preferring to remain with his own unit: reverted to Pte. and returned to France August 1917: promoted Corpl. September: received his papers for a commission with P.P.C.L.I., but chose to remain with his unit for the Battle of Passchendaele, during the course of which he was killed (30 October 1917), being shot by a sniper while attempting to rescue a comrade. Buried at point D.4.d.8.3.: Age 26.

(Panel 10) Corpl. McG/94, George Thomas Wilson, Princess Patricia's Canadian Light Infantry (Eastern Ontario Regt.), C.E.F.: *s*. of George (& Martha Tonkin) Wilson, of 34, Horsforth Avenue, Bridlington, co. York: *b*. Bridlington, 23 June 1893: Religion – Church of England: Occupation – Bank Clerk: enlisted Saskatoon, 23 May 1915: joined 2nd University Coy., C.E.F., 15 June: served with the Expeditionary Force in France and Flanders from September following, and was killed in action on the afternoon of 2 June 1916, when, after making his way down Warrington Avenue, Sanctuary Wood, with a party of bombers, he was shot in the head by a rifle bullet. Buried behind the trench where he fell: Age 22. *unm*. Remains 'Unknown Canadian Soldier. Canadian University Overseas Coy.' recovered unmarked grave (28.I.24.b.0.3) GRU Report, Zillebeke 5-125E; identified – Clothing, Badge, Titles, Spectacles; reinterred, registered 5 August 1927. *Buried in Sanctuary Wood Cemetery (IV.F.26).*

(Panel 10) L/Corpl. McG/159, Arthur Stuart Anderson, Princess Patricia's Canadian Light Infantry (Eastern Ontario Regt.), C.E.F.: *s*. of the Rev. John Anderson, of 462, Gilmour Street, Peterborough, Ontario: *b*. Nairn, Ontario, 16 May 1889: Religion – Presbyterian: *educ*. Peterborough Public School, from whence he won a Scholarship (Applied Science) to University of Toronto (1909 – 13), B.A.Sc., Mechanical Engineering (Hon.): after graduating took up positions – Mechanical Engineer – Messrs Ingersoll Rand Co., Sherbrooke, Quebec; and City Works Dept., Toronto: previously served 6 yrs. 57th (Peterborough) Rangers (N.C.O.); and Peterborough Collegiate Cadets (Capt.): enlisted 2nd Universities Coy., P.P.C.L.I., Toronto, 1 June 1915: served with the Expeditionary Force in France from August following: served in the Somme – Amiens sector throughout the autumn, and Kemmel sector through the winter until March 1916, when the battalion, as part of 3rd Canadian Divn., moved into the Ypres Salient. Recommended for a commission, May 1916, but, before he could leave to undertake officer training, the Battle of Sanctuary Wood began and, during the bombardment, he was killed 2 June 1916, by a shell which hit the front-line dugout in which he had volunteered to remain: Age 27. *unm.*

(Panel 10) L/Corpl. 1570, Alexander Bailey, No.4 Coy., Princess Patricia's Canadian Light Infantry (Eastern Ontario Regt.), C.E.F.: *s.* of the Rev. Robert Bailey, M.A., of 'The Manse,' Carlow, Ireland, by his wife Alice Magil: *b.* Strongford, Co. Down, 16 March 1887: Religion – Presbyterian: Occupation – Clerk / Sub-manager; Royal Trust Company, Winnipeg: member of the Legion of Frontiersmen; served 2 years, Royal North West Mounted Police: enlisted Ottawa, 24 August 1914; posted P.P.C.L.I., 1 October: came over with First Contingent: served with the Expeditionary Force in France and Flanders from 20 December 1914: hospitalised January 1915 (gastric enteritis); March (catarrh): after recovery rejoined his regiment in the Polygon Wood sector 28 April, and was killed in the trenches during the fighting on Bellewaerde Ridge 7 May 1915: Age 27. *unm.*

(Panel 10) L/Corpl. A/11004, Clayton Adam Bradley, Princess Patricia's Canadian Light Infantry (Eastern Ontario Regt.), C.E.F.: *s.* of the late Adam Bradley, of Cassonby, Ontario, by his wife Annie (North Gower, Ontario): *b.* Carleton County, 29 March 1889: Religion – Church of England: *educ.* Guelph University (O.T.C. member): Occupation – Student: enlisted C.E.F., Guelph, 16 March 1915, aged 26 years; posted 38th Battn.: served with the Expeditionary Force in France and Flanders from 16 July 1915, transf'd. P.P.C.L.I.; promoted L/Corpl. October following. Reported wounded and missing, 2 – 4 June 1916, while escorting a wounded officer (Lieut. Scott) to the dressing station near Lille Gate; since confirmed killed in action 2 June 1916: Age 28. Remains 'Unknown Canadian Soldier' recovered unmarked grave (28.I.24.c.9.8) refers GRU Report, Zillebeke 5-132E; identified – Button, Regtl. Badge; reinterred, registered 1 September 1927. *Buried in Sanctuary Wood Cemetery (IV.F.37).*

(Panel 10) L/Corpl. 51098, William John Causton, Princess Patricia's Canadian Light Infantry (Eastern Ontario Regt.), C.E.F.: *s.* of Mrs W.J. Causton (Chamberlain, Saskatchewan): *b.* co. Lanark, Scotland, 21 September 1880: Religion – Church of England: prior to enlistment served 1 yr. Lord Strathcona's Horse (Royal Canadians); 5 yrs. Cape Mounted Police; 2 yrs. Royal Canadian Regt. (Halifax): Occupation – Veterinary Surgeon: enlisted 28th Battn., Regina, 24 October 1914: subsequently transf'd. 1st P.P.C.L.I. Reinforcing Draft, January 1915: crossed to France, 24 February: joined his regiment in the trenches at St. Eloi, 1 March 1915: took part in the Battle of Frezenberg; and was killed in action during the fighting on Bellewaarde Ridge, 8 May 1915: Age 34.

(Panel 10) L/Corpl. McG/166, William Dalgleish Ford, Princess Patricia's Canadian Light Infantry (Eastern Ontario Regt.), C.E.F. *s.* of Joseph Ford, of Portneuf Station, Quebec, by his wife Mary Jessica D.: and elder brother to Pte. 110167, E.A. Ford, P.P.C.L.I., killed at the same moment: *b.* Portneuf, P.Q., 22 April 1890: Religion – Presbyterian: Occupation – Agricultural Instructor: previously served six months Home Guards: enlisted 2nd University Coy., Montreal, 15 June 1915: came to England, transf'd. 11th Battn., 18 July following; promoted L/Corpl.: served with the Expeditionary Force in France and Flanders from 24 August 1915; joined P.P.C.L.I., Armentieres sector, 1 September 1915. After a short period of leave, April 1916, returned to France, and was killed in action 3 p.m., 2 June 1916 in the forward trenches at Sanctuary Wood during a heavy German *minenwerfer* bombardment of 'The Loop.' The bay in the trench he was occupying with his brother and several other men being completely shattered by shell fire; there were no survivors: Age 26. *unm.*

His brother Eric also has no known grave; he is recorded below.

(Panel 10) L/Corpl. 22774, Joseph P Mahoney, Princess Patricia's Canadian Infantry (Eastern Ontario Regt.), C.E.F.: c/o Mrs R. James (1078, Saratoga Street, East Boston, Massachusetts): *b.* St. John, New Brunswick, 20 June 1884: Religion – Roman Catholic: Occupation – Brakeman; Trans Canadian Railroad: previously served 8 yrs. 62nd Regt., St. John: enlisted Valcartier, Quebec, 26 September 1914; apptd. P.P.C.L.I. 28 September: served with the Expeditionary Force In France. Killed instantly by a falling tree during a heavy bombardment east of Sanctuary Wood on the morning of 2 June 1916. No remains recovered for burial: Age 31.

(Panel 10) L/Corpl. 252, Norman Fry, Princess Patricia's Canadian Light Infantry (Eastern Ontario Regt.), C.E.F.: *s.* of John Fry, of 18, North Street, Wilton, by his wife Emma: *b.* Wilton, co. Wilts, 14 October 1887: Religion – Plymouth Brethren: Occupation – Clerk: previously served 10 yrs. 2nd Battn. Coldstream Guards: volunteered and enlisted P.P.C.L.I., Ottawa, 26 August 1914; came over with 1st Canadian Contingent, 14 October following: promoted L/Corpl., November 1914: served with the Expeditionary Force in France and Flanders, and was killed at Vierstraat 8 January 1915, by enemy shell-fire. Buried behind the trench where he fell: Age 27. The first member of the Princess Patricia's to be killed in the Great War.

(Panel 10) Pte. 51032, John James Abbott, Princess Patricia's Canadian Light Infantry (Eastern Ontario Regt.), C.E.F.: *s.* of the late John James Abbott, of North Devon, by his wife Elizabeth, *née* Holliday: *b.* London, June 1868: previously served Queen's Own (Royal West Kent Regt.); Waziristan and South Africa: sometime emigrated to Canada, and took up farming: enlisted 32nd Bn. C.E.F., 29 December 1914: crossed to France with Reinforcement Draft to P.P.C.L.I., joining his regiment in the Polygon Wood sector 14 April 1915; reported missing believed killed after taking part in the action at Bellewaerde Ridge, 8 May 1915; in that he failed to answer the roll-call held that evening and, since that time no information having been received concerning him, is now for official purposes presumed to have died on or about that date. No remains recovered for burial: Age 46. Pte. Abbott leaves a widow Alice Edith.

(Panel 10) Pte. 1711, Geoffrey Lloyd Adams, Princess Patricia's Canadian Light Infantry (Eastern Ontario Regt.), C.E.F.: 4th *s.* of the late George Frederick Adams, of Cardiff, M.Inst..E., by his wife Ellen Gertrude, Ty-Draw, Parkstone, co. Dorset; *dau.* of Frank Irwin, of Ebb Vale, co. Monmouth, M.D.: *b.* Penarth, co. Glamorgan, 9 August 1881: Religion – Plymouth Brethren: *educ.* Bedford Grammar School; Awarded Royal Humane Society Certificate for saving the life of a little girl at Carrington Mill, nr. Bedford: Occupation – Land & Timber Expert & Valuator: previously served 5½ years 2nd Dragoon Guards: enlisted Levis, Quebec, 12 September 1914, after the outbreak of war; posted Princess Patricia's L.I., Ottawa, 1 October following: proceeded to England with 1st Contingent; crossed to France with his regiment 20 December 1914: hospitalised N.Y.D. (incurred St. Eloi trenches) 15 January 1915, returned to his unit 13 February. Reported missing in action following the fighting at Bellewaerde Lake, nr. Ypres, 8 May 1915; presumed killed. His Commanding Officer wrote, "He was loved and respected by his comrades, and trusted by his officers. I say in all sincerity that no braver man ever lived than G. Lloyd Adams. He died facing the enemy with his rifle in his hands, and twice he drove them back.": Age 33. *unm.*

(Panel 10) Pte. 489851, Ernest Henry Aldwinckle, Actg.L/Corpl., No.2 Coy., Princess Patricia's Canadian Light Infantry (Eastern Ontario Regt.), C.E.F.: elder *s.* of Alfred Othniel Aldwinckle, of 54, Highbury Park, London, N., by his wife Emma: and brother to 2nd Lieut. R. Aldwinckle, 6th King's Own (Royal Lancaster Regt.) attd. 10th Loyal North Lancaster Regt., killed in action at Beaumont Hamel, 15 November 1916: *b.* Highbury, London, N., 3 November 1887: *educ.* Paradise House School there, and Guelph Agricultural College, University of Ontario, Canada: Occupation – Farmer; Alberta: volunteered for Imperial Service, joined 6th University Coy., Lacombe, Quebec, 24 October 1916; obtained his Crossed Swords; Instructor – Physical Training and Bayonet Fighting, proceeded overseas April 1917; to France May following: served with the Expeditionary Force there attd. 3rd Entrenching Bn.: joined Princess Patricia's Canadian L.I., Arras sector 14 October, and was killed in action at Passchendaele Ridge on the 30th (October 1917). Buried nr. Passchendaele: Age 29. He *m.* Lacombe, Alberta, 1915; Annah Coverdale, of Lacombe, and had a *dau.* Margaret, *b.* July, 1916.

His brother Ralph is buried in Frankfurt Trench British Cemetery (B.3).

(Panel 10) Pte. 2004502, Peter Allan, Princess Patricia's Canadian Light Infantry (Eastern Ontario Regt.), C.E.F.: late of Dawson, Yukon Territory: c/o Mrs Basille Bolduc (St. Étienne-de-Lauzon, Levis Co., Quebec): *b.* Levis, 8 February 1872: Religion – Roman Catholic: Occupation – Miner: joined Yukon Infantry Coy., C.E.F., Dawson, 28 September 1916; subsequently transf'd. P.P.C.L.I.. Reported wounded

/ missing 6 a.m., morning of 30 October 1917, just before his company jumped off in the attack on Passchendaele Ridge; presumed killed: Age 45. *unm.*

(Panel 10) Pte. 460004, Sidney James Allanson, Princess Patricia's Canadian Light Infantry (Eastern Ontario Regt.), C.E.F.: *s.* of Robert (& Elizabeth) Allanson, of 18, Sandringham Dive, New Brighton, Wallasey, co. Chester, England: *b.* Egremont, co. Chester, 12 May 1894: Religion – Presbyterian: Occupation – Clerk: serving member 106th Regt. (Militia); joined C.E.F., Winnipeg, 3 June 1915; apptd. P.P.C.L.I. Reported missing 18 July 1916; confirmed killed in action being 'practically blown to pieces by a German trench mortar shell': Age 22. Remembered on Wallasey Hospital War Memorial. (*IWGC record age 23*)

(Panel 10) Pte. 51040, Walter Frederick Angell, Princess Patricia's Canadian Light Infantry (Eastern Ontario Regt.), C.E.F.: *s.* of John (& Mrs) Angell, of Guelph, Ontario: *b.* Guelph, 24 January 1884: Religion – Church of England: Occupation – Steam Engineer: prior to the outbreak of war served with the Militia in both 103rd Calgary Rifles and 30th Guelph Rifles: enlisted 23rd Battn. C.E.F., Calgary, 3 November 1914: transf'd. P.P.C.L.I. (Rfts.) 1 January 1915; proceeded overseas later the same month: crossed to France, 23 February following; joined P.P.C.L.I., St. Eloi, nr. Ypres, 1 March 1915: took part in the Second Battle of Ypres: slightly wounded 29 April: Killed in action during the fighting at Bellewaarde, 8 May following. At the time of his death Pte. Angell was in a fire trench binding the wounds of a comrade when a high explosive shell burst nearby killing them both instantly. Buried in a collective grave behind the support trenches: 8 May 1915: Age 31.

(Panel 10) Pte. 51054, Henry John Bastable, Princess Patricia's Canadian Light Infantry (Eastern Ontario Regt.), C.E.F.: *s.* of the late George W.E. Bastable, by his wife Annie (23, St. James Street, Shaftesbury, co. Dorset): *b.* Shaftesbury, 20 August 1888: Religion – Methodist: Occupation – Labourer: enlisted Winnipeg, 17 December 1914; posted P.P.C.L.I. (Rfts.): proceeded to France March 1915, and was killed in action at Bellewaarde Ridge, 8 May 1915. Held the Long Service and Good Conduct Medal: Age 32.

(Panel 10) Pte. McG/205, Errol Stewart Bell, No.2 Coy., Princess Patricia's Canadian Light Infantry (Eastern Ontario Regt.), C.E.F.: *s.* of Robert John Bell, of Joggin Mines, Cumberland Co., Nova Scotia, by his wife Laura E.: *b.* Stellarton, Nova Scotia, 24 December 1895: Religion – Church of England: Occupation – Teller; Royal Bank of Montreal: enlisted 2nd University Coy., 15 June 1915, aged 19 years: posted 11th Battn. July following: served with the Expeditionary Force in France and Flanders, joining his unit In the Field 1 September 1915: took part in the fighting at Flers-Courcelette, and 1st Battle of Arras 1917 (Vimy Ridge), and was killed in action at the 3rd Battle of Ypres, in the assault on Meetcheele Ridge, 30 October 1917: Age 22. *unm.*

(Panel 10) Pte. 258, John Blackman, Princess Patricia's Canadian Light Infantry (Eastern Ontario Regt.), C.E.F.: *s.* of the late John Thomas Blackman, Sergt., 33rd West Riding Regt., by his wife Clara Mary E. (5, Coburg Place, Ilfracombe, England), formerly of 5, Best Town, Cage Lane, Chatham, *dau.* of Patrick Lyons: *b.* Lucknow, India, 11 April 1883: Religion – Roman Catholic: *educ.* Chatham, co. Kent: formerly served 6 years Grenadier Guards: removed to Canada, 4 April 1910: Occupation – Valet: volunteered for Imperial Service 25 August 1914, after the outbreak of war, and came over with First Canadian Contingent, 14 October 1914: served with the Expeditionary Force in France and Flanders: hospitalised sick (January 1915), returned to his unit after three weeks, and was killed while digging in near Hill 62, 4 May 1915, after the withdrawal from Polygon Wood: Age 32. *unm.*

(Panel 10) Pte. 51078, Charles Bradbury, Princess Patricia's Canadian Light Infantry (Eastern Ontario Regt.), C.E.F.: *b.* Liverpool, England, 7 May 1884: Religion – Church of England: Occupation – Ship's Carpenter: previously served R.M.C., Liverpool: 5'4¼" tall, grey-blue eyes, dark brown hair: enlisted Montreal, 31 October 1914; posted 23rd (Overseas) Battn., 10 January 1915: transf'd. Princess Patricia's (Rfts.), England: proceed to France 26 March 1915; joined P.P.C.L.I., Ypres sector, 28 March. Reported missing, presumed killed, 8 May 1915; Bellewaarde Lake: Age 31. He was married to Elizabeth Bradbury, *née* McDonald (11A, Alexander Street, Montreal).

(Panel 10) Pte. 11, Frederick Cavanagh, Princess Patricia's Canadian Light Infantry (Eastern Ontario Regt.), C.E.F.: c/o Mrs M.J. Griffiths (139½ Berkly-in-the-Rear, Toronto): *b.* co. Worcester, August 1885: Religion – Roman Catholic: Occupation – Labourer: previously served 3 years 2nd Bn. Worcestershire Regt.: volunteered for Imperial Service, enlisted Ottawa, 20 August 1914; came over with 1st Canadian Contingent, 14 October following: served with the Expeditionary Force in France from 20 December 1914: promoted L/Corpl., January 1915; Corpl. March following: reverted to Pte. 9 April: took part in the fighting at the Second Battle of Ypres and was killed while digging in on Bellewaarde Ridge, 4 May 1915: Age 29. (*IWGC record L/Corpl.*)

(Panel 10) Pte. McG/160, Russell Andrew Cross, Princess Patricia's Canadian Light Infantry (Eastern Ontario Regt.), C.E.F.: *s.* of Andrew Cross, of 20, Woodbine Crescent, Hamilton, Ontario, by his wife Sarah Catherine: *b.* Woodstock, Oxford Co., 31 May 1895: Religion – Congregationalist: *educ.* Hamilton Public School; University College, Toronto (Applied Science), 1912 – 15: enlisted 2nd University Coy., Toronto, 2 June 1915: departed Canada July following: trained England, posted 11th Battn.: proceeded to France 24 August 1915; joined Princess Patricia's 1 September: took part in engagements in the Armentieres and Ypres sectors. Killed in action at Sanctuary Wood on the morning of 2 June 1916, when the German bombardment began; a shell landed on the trench roof killing him instantly: Age 21. *unm.*

(Panel 10) Pte. 1233, Elson Petrie Cunningham, Princess Patricia's Canadian Light Infantry (Eastern Ontario Regt.), C.E.F.: *s.* of the late Rev. T.E. Cunningham, by his wife Jessie E. (Aylmer [East], Province of Quebec): *b.* Quebec, 9 June 1888: Religion – Church of England: Occupation – Contractor: volunteered for Imperial Service 26 August 1914, after the outbreak of war; posted P.P.C.L.I., 5 October: came over with 1st Canadian Contingent 14 October 1914: served in France and Flanders from 20 December following. Reported missing, believed killed in action, during the fighting on Bellewaarde Ridge, 8 May 1915: Age 26. (*IWGC record age 27*)

(Panel 10) Pte. 727564, George Davidson, 'D' Coy., Princess Patricia's Canadian Light Infantry (Eastern Ontario Regt.), C.E.F.: 3rd *s.* of David Davidson, Commercial Traveller; of 53, Gordon Street, Govan, Glasgow, by his wife Annie Elizabeth, *dau.* of John Ledingham, J.P.: *b.* Govan, Glasgow, 22 September 1896: Religion – Presbyterian: *educ.* Govan: employee Fairfield Shipbuilding Yard, Govan: removed to Canada 13 August 1913; settled Stratford, Ontario: Occupation – Pipe Fitter: enlisted 124th Bn., Stratford, Ontario, 14 February 1916: served with the Expeditionary Force in France from the following December, joining his regiment in the Vimy Ridge sector 4 January 1917: took part in the First Battle of Arras 9 – 10 April 1917, and was killed in action at Passchendaele, 30 October 1917, while acting as runner for Lieut. Chipman: Age 21. *unm.*

(Panel 10) Pte. 51129, Herbert William Walker Donaldson, Princess Patricia's Canadian Light Infantry (Eastern Ontario Regt.), C.E.F.: *s.* of the late Surgeon-Major James Donaldson (Madras Establishment), and his late wife Agnes Campbell: *b.* Nilgheary Hills, India, 17 September 1870: Religion – Presbyterian: trained Kingston Academy (from 1887) and served 20 years North West Mounted Police: at the time of his enlistment, Quebec, 19 November 1914, was gainfully employed as a Logger: posted Pte. 58th Battn. C.E.F.; transf'd. P.P.C.L.I. (Rfts.) 10 January 1915: served with the Expeditionary Force in France and Flanders from 18 March 1915; joined P.P.C.L.I. In the Field on the 21st.: took part in the Second Battle of Ypres, Battle of Frezenberg, and was reported missing in action during the fighting at Bellewaarde Ridge, 8 May 1915: Age 45. (*IWGC record age 48*)

(Panel 10) Pte. 1141, Horace Dowling, Princess Patricia's Canadian Light Infantry (Eastern Ontario Regt.), C.E.F.: *s.* of Frederick W. Dowling, of 7, Terront Road, South Tottenham, London, N., by his wife Agnes D.: *b.* St. Pancras, 1885: Religion – Roman Catholic: Occupation – Waiter: previously served Volunteer Bn., Queen's Own (Royal West Kent Regt.): enlisted 21 August 1914: posted P.P.C.L.I., 5 October, came over with 1st Canadian Contingent on the 14th of that month: served with the Expeditionary Force in France and Flanders from 20 December 1914: took part in the Second Battle of Ypres, the fighting at Frezenberg, and was killed in action on the Bellewaarde Ridge, 8 May 1915: Age

30. In 1907 Pte. Dowling was awarded a Royal Humane Society Certificate for saving a woman's life at Seabrook, co. Kent.

(Panel 10) Pte. 475433, Victor Archibald Ferrier, No.3 (University) Coy., Princess Patricia's Canadian Light Infantry, C.E.F.: *s.* of Chester Ferrier, Superintendant, Victoria Industrial School; of Main Street, Mimico, Ontario, by his wife Lillian: *b.* Toronto, 29 August 1893: Religion – Methodist: *educ.* Mimico Public School; Parkdale; University College, Toronto (Undergraduate), 1911 – 14: Occupation – Clerk: volunteered and enlisted 4th (University) Coy., P.P.C.L.I., Toronto, 6 October 1915: departed Canada November following: served with the Expeditionary Force in France from March 1916, transf'd 3rd Coy., and was reported wounded and missing after the Battle of Sanctuary Wood, 4 June 1916. Later a member of his Company, writing from a Prisoner of War Camp, Germany, stated that he had seen Pte. Ferrier killed on the aforementioned date: Age 22. *unm.*

(Panel 10) Pte. 110167, Eric Allan Ford, Princess Patricia's Canadian Light Infantry (Eastern Ontario Regt.), C.E.F.: *s.* of Joseph Ford, of Portneuf, Quebec, by his wife Mary Jessica D.: and *yr.* brother to L/ Cpl. McG/166, W.D. Ford, P.P.C.L.I., killed in action at Ypres 2 June 1916: *b.* Portneuf Station, P.Q., 27 January 1892: Religion – Presbyterian: prior to enlistment was Student, McGill University: enlisted 5th Canadian Mounted Rifles, 3 March 1915: promoted L/Cpl.: served with the Expeditionary Force in France and Flanders from 24 October 1915: transf'd. P.P.C.L.I., reverted to Pte., March 1916. At 3 p.m., 2 June 1916, during the Battle for Mount Sorrel, he was with his brother and several comrades in the advanced positions in Sanctuary Wood, when he was killed by German trench mortar fire at 'The Loop.': Age 24. *unm.*

His brother William also has no known grave; he is recorded above.

(Panel 10) Pte. 784937, Arthur Harold Foster, Princess Patricia's Canadian Light Infantry (Eastern Ontario Regt.), C.E.F.: *s.* of William Foster, of Ripple Vale, Ripple, Dover; late of Filmer House, Bridge, Canterbury, co. Kent, by his wife Emma: *b.* Stoney Creek, Ontario, 8 December 1881: Religion – Church of England: *educ.* Ashford Grammar School, 1895 – 99: sometime removed to Canada and took up farming: 5'11½" tall, dark complexion, blue eyes, dark brown hair: enlisted Dundas, Ontario, 11 March 1916: Killed in action 30 October 1917, at Passchendaele: Age 35. *unm.*

On the evening of 26 June 1916, the Princess Pat's relieved Royal Canadian Regiment in the front line and support trenches on the left of the Sanctuary Wood sector. The War Diary for the four day period spent in these positions – during which time they were treated to both intermittent and continuous bombardments of various calibres by the enemy – makes no mention of any casualties incurred by the regiment. Throughout the 29th, their penultimate day in the sector, the Pats received a small number of enemy shells without incident but, after dusk, when 'the enemy threw over a number of trench mortars at the Culvert' there occurred a curious incident.

Shortly after a soldier had vacated his place in a dug-out that brothers Hubert and Leonard Foster might shelter and share some time there together, the dug-out was struck by a 5.9 shell killing both men instantly. After removing their bodies from the wreckage, they were buried side by side behind the trench.

The Menin Gate records the names of 7,003 members of the Canadian Expeditionary Force (504 Princess Patricia's Canadian Light Infantry) of which number only two are recorded for 30 June 1916 – Tragic enough in itself, doubly tragic that they should be brothers:–

(Panel 10) Pte. 105947, Hubert Victor Foster, Princess Patricia's Canadian Light Infantry (Eastern Ontario Regt.), C.E.F.: *s.* of William John Foster, of 35, The Gardens, East Dulwich, London, S.E., by his wife Julia: and elder brother to Pte. 105582, L.C. Foster, P.P.C.L.I., who was killed by the same shell: *b.* London, 13 September 1892: Religion – Church of England: sometime went to Canada and found employ as a Farm Worker: enlisted 68th Battn., Regina, Saskatchewan, 13 March 1916: arrived in England, 8 May: crossed to France 8 June following, joining his regiment in Ypres salient two days later, and was killed by a 5.9 shell while sheltering in a dug-out with his brother in Trench 67, Sanctuary Wood sector, on the night of 29 – 30 June 1916. Buried beside his brother behind the trench where they were killed: Age 23. *unm.*

(Panel 10) Pte. 105582, Leonard Charles Foster, Princess Patricia's Canadian Light Infantry (Eastern Ontario Regt.), C.E.F.: *s.* of William John Foster, of 35, The Gardens, East Dulwich, London, S.E., by his wife Julia: and *yr.* brother to Pte. 105947, H.V. Foster, P.P.C.L.I., who was killed by the same shell: *b.* London, 22 August 1896: Religion – Church of England: sometime went to Canada and found employ as a Farm Worker: enlisted 68th Battn., Regina, Saskatchewan, 11 December 1915: arrived in England, 7 May 1916: crossed to France 8 June following, joining his regiment in Ypres salient two days later, and was killed by a 5.9 shell while sheltering in a dug-out with his brother in Trench 67, Sanctuary Wood sector, on the night of 29 – 30 June 1916. Buried beside his brother behind the trench where they were killed: Age 19.

(Panel 10) Pte. 23150, Alfred Cecil Henderson, Princess Patricia's Canadian Light Infantry (Eastern Ontario Regt.), formerly 12th Bn. Canadian Infantry, C.E.F.: *s.* of Henry William Henderson, of Union Road, Charlottetown, P.E.I., Canada, by his wife Eudevilla, *dau.* of Francis Simmonds, of Crapaud, P.E.I.: *b.* Royalty Junction, Prince Edward's Island, 12 April 1895: Occupation – Farmer: joined 3rd Militia (82nd Regt.), 1911; volunteered for Service Overseas on the outbreak of war, joined 12th Bn. C.E.F.: left P.E.I. for Valcartier, August 1914: came over with First Contingent, 14 October; drafted Princess Patricia's Canadian Light Infantry: crossed to France, 16 February 1915: sentenced to 28 days F.P. No.1 for drunkenness 26 March following, and was killed in action by the concussion of a shell at Hooge, during the Second Battle of Ypres, 8 May 1915: Age 20. *unm.*

(Panel 10) Pte. 475422, John Smith Hiddleston, No.4 (University) Coy., Princess Patricia's Canadian Light Infantry (Eastern Ontario Regt.), C.E.F.: *s.* of James Hiddleston, of Carronbank, Thornhill, co. Dumfries, by his wife Margaret: and brother to Pte. 30109, J. Hiddleston, 5/6th Cameronians (Sco.Rif.), killed in action 22 June 1918; and Pte. G/36733, R.D. Hiddleston, Queen's Own (Royal West Kent Regt.), posted 2/20th London Regt., killed in action 30 August 1918. Killed in action 2 June 1916; Sanctuary Wood: Age 30.

His brother James is buried in Nine Elms British Cemetery (XI.E.12); Robert is buried in H.A.C. Cemetery, Ecoust-St. Mein (IV.E.13).

(Panel 10) Pte. 51225, Frank Davenport Holland, No.1 Coy., Princess Patricia's Canadian Light Infantry (Eastern Ontario Regt.), C.E.F.: eldest *s.* of Frank Bernard Holland, of 6th Avenue East, Prince Rupert, British Columbia, by his wife Ada (1284, Monterey Avenue, Oak Bay, Victoria, B.C.), *dau.* of William Turner-Whitlow, and *gt-gdson.* to Peter Holland, Knutsford, co. Chester; Physician to Her late Majesty Queen Victoria: *b.* Great Warford, Alderley Edge, co. Chester, 13 September 1895: went to Canada with his parents, 11 April 1905: *educ.* Privately, Condover College; Imperial College, London (Pembridge), and King Edward School, Prince Rupert, and was on the Staff of the Bank of British North America when war began. He had joined Earl Grey's Own Rifles, November 1911, and immediately volunteered for Imperial Service: departed Canada with 30th Battn.; drafted Princess Patricia's L.I., January 1915. Arrived in France, 11 March, and was immediately sent up to the Front: took part in the fighting at St. Eloi, and was killed in action at Ypres, 4 May 1915, when trying to bind up the wounds of a comrade during the digging in on Bellewaarde Ridge. Buried to the rear of the trench the same night. The grave was not properly marked before the battalion was relieved that day, and consequently lost in later fighting. His Commanding Officer wrote that, "He was a splendid soldier;" and three comrades, "He was beloved by us all, and his behaviour when in action proved that he was both a son and a soldier to be proud of." He had a brilliant school career, was an expert shot and member of the rifle team that won the Corporation Cup and the Northern British Columbia Championship, 1913. A memorial tablet was erected in St. Andrew's Church, Prince Rupert: Age 19.

(Panel 10) Pte. 475886, George Stuart Wright Hough, No.3 (University) Coy., Princess Patricia's Canadian Light Infantry (Eastern Ontario Regt.), C.E.F.: *s.* of George L. Hough, D.D., of 70A, Melbourne Avenue, Toronto, by his wife Edith W. (707, Manning Avenue, Toronto): *b.* Picton, Ontario, 1 December 1896: *educ.* Picton Public School, and Harbord Collegiate Institute, Toronto. After completing his education gained employ as Clerk; West Toronto Branch, Bank of British North America, September

1914; served 1 year enlisted Montreal, 3 August 1915, Pte., 3rd University Coy., recruited to reinforce the Princess Patricia's Canadian Light Infantry; he went overseas with his unit and after a brief period of training in England arrived in France December following, and went at once into the firing line. During the spring of 1916 the regiment were almost continuously engaged in actions in the Ypres salient. Killed in action 2 June 1916, during the enemy attack at Sanctuary Wood, nr. Zillebeke, east of Ypres: Age 19.

(Panel 10) Pte. 806, Edward Stanley Jennings, Princess Patricia's Canadian Light Infantry (Eastern Ontario Regt.), C.E.F.: *s.* of John Jennings, of 'West View,' 35, Hartham Road, Holloway, London, by his late wife Ellen Eliza: *b.* London, August 1885: Occupation – Merchant: previously served 3 years, Royal Fusiliers: volunteered and enlisted August 1914: served with the Expeditionary Force in France and Flanders from 20 December 1914, and was killed at St. Eloi, nr. Ypres, 10 April 1915. His brother Sidney, serving in the same regiment wrote, "My brother Ted said to me, 'You make the tea, and I'll stand lookout for you.' A few minutes later he fell down against me, dead, after having been hit in the head by an exploding bullet. After dark we buried him behind the trench.": Age 29. (*IWGC record age 28*)

(Panel 10) Pte. 22591, Samuel Jones, Princess Patricia's Canadian Light Infantry (Eastern Ontario Regt.), C.E.F.: *s.* of Stephen Jones, of North Devon, New Brunswick, by his wife Levina: *b.* Fredericton, New Brunswick, 1870: served in the South African War: Occupation – Labourer: serving member 71st York Regt. (Militia); volunteered for Imperial Service and enlisted 12th Battn. Canadian Expeditionary Force, 13 September 1914, after the outbreak of war: came over with 1st Contingent, 14 October 1914: trained Salisbury Plain throughout winter 1914 – 15, during which time a series of infractions – absent without leave, vagrancy, drunkenness, breaking arrest – earned him a discharge from 12th Battn., 16 December 1914: joined 2nd P.P.C.L.I. Recruiting Draft, 1 February 1915: served in France and Flanders from 28 April following, joining his Regiment at Polygon Wood, nr. Ypres, and was killed in action at Bellewaarde Ridge, 8 May 1915: Age 45.

(Panel 10) Pte. 410924, William Henry Joyce, Princess Patricia's Canadian Light Infantry (Eastern Ontario Regt.), C.E.F.: *s.* of William John Joyce, of 158, Cherrier Street, Montreal, and the late Emily Elenore Joyce, *née* Bentley, his wife: and elder brother to Pte. 177109, R.R. Joyce, 87th Canadian Infantry, killed in action 18 November 1916, aged 16 years: *b.* Quebec, 8 February 1891: Religion – Wesleyan: Occupation – Shipper: 5'9" tall, dark complexion, brown eyes, black hair: serving member 3rd Victoria Rifles (Militia), enlisted Montreal, 1 March 1915: joined P.P.C.L.I. in France, 28 July 1915, and was killed in action, 2 June 1916; Sanctuary Wood: Age 25. *unm.* (*IWGC record age 24*)

His brother Robert also has no known grave; he is commemorated on the Canadian National Memorial, Vimy, France.

(Panel 10) Pte. 1152, Alfred Allen Keats, Princess Patricia's Canadian Light Infantry (Eastern Ontario Regt.), C.E.F.: *s.* of William Allen Keats, of 2, Victoria Road, Clapham Common, London: *b.* Stoke-on-Trent, co. Stafford, 3 December 1878: Religion – Church of England: Occupation – Messenger; Windsor Street Branch, Bank of Montreal: 6' tall, brown eyes, brown hair: previously served 10 years with the Colours; 7th Mountain Bty., Royal Horse Artillery, took part in the Tibet Expedition, 1901 – 04 (Medal): enlisted Ottawa, 25 August 1914: proceeded overseas with 1st Canadian Contingent: served with the Expeditionary Force in France and Flanders from 20 December 1914, and was killed in action 8 May 1915, during the fighting at Bellewaarde Ridge: Age 36. Correspondence regarding the deceased to be addressed c/o Nurse M. Couch, South Western Hospital, Stockwell, London. (*IWGC record Keates, age 37*)

At 8.30 a.m., 2 June 1916, the Germans began systematically shelling the Princess Patricia's front line and support trenches at Sanctuary Wood. This gradually increased to an intense bombardment from H.E. shells and trench mortars which, after continuing unabated for five hours, was lifted and followed by an infantry attack. The enemy succeeded in capturing the right front line held by No. 1 Coy., the garrison there being almost completely annihilated. The left company – No.2 – succeeded in holding on to their section of trench and effectively stopped a bombing attack. The supports held, on the right, the greater part of Warrington Avenue and Lovers Lane to Border Lane, and on the left, the 'R' series of trenches.

In conclusion the War Diary records – 'Our casualties were heavy. In the evening the enemy evidently suspected a counter-attack as they opened up a rapid machine-gun and rifle fire and an intense barrage on our rear. Water and food supply low.'

Of the 'heavy casualties' incurred by the regiment thirty-three have no known grave.

(Panel 10) Pte. 475939, James Harold Miller, Princess Patricia's Canadian Light Infantry (Eastern Ontario Regt.), C.E.F.: *s.* of John Miller, of 52, Dragon Avenue, Harrogate, co. York, England, by his wife Matilda: *b.* Co. Durham, 28 February 1889: Religion – Church of England: Occupation – Automobile Mechanic: 5'8" tall, blue eyes, fair hair: enlisted Calgary, 15 July 1915; posted 3rd University Coy. (McGill, 913), P.P.C.L.I., Montreal, 28 July: joined P.P.C.L.I. in France, 6 December 1915: wounded 18 April 1916. Reported missing, presumed killed 2 June 1916; Sanctuary Wood: Age 25. *unm.* (*IWGC record 4 June, age 28*)

(Panel 10) Pte. 765, Herbert Stirling Morgan, Princess Patricia's Canadian Light Infantry (Eastern Ontario Regt.), C.E.F.: *s.* of George Morgan, of 3, Acacia Road, Guildford, co. Surrey, by his wife Miranda: elder brother to Sergt. 432509, H.T. Morgan, 49th Bn. Canadian Infantry, killed during the fighting nr. Sanctuary Wood, 2 June 1916: *b.* London, England, August 1883: served 3 years, Royal Fusiliers (City of London Regt.); 4 years Berkshire Volunteers: Occupation – Electrician: enlisted P.P.C.L.I., 24 August 1914: came over with First Canadian Contingent: served with the Expeditionary Force in France and Flanders from 20 December 1914, and was killed in action on the Bellewaarde Ridge 8 May 1915: Age 31. (*IWGC record age 32*)

His brother Harold also has no known grave; he is recorded on Panel 28.

(Panel 10) Pte. 654, Edmond Fenning Parke, Princess Patricia's Canadian Light Infantry (Eastern Ontario Regt.), C.E.F.: *s.* of Edward Parke, of Wellesbourne, co. Warwick, by his wife Harriet Elizabeth: *b.* Pentre, Newtown, co. Montgomery, 20 June 1892: *educ.* Newtown Intermediate School; and County School: removed to Canada to take up an appointment as Clerk, Bank of Montreal; November 1910: previously served 2 years, 7th Royal Welsh Fusiliers (T.F.): enlisted Edmonton, 20 August 1914: came over with First Canadian Contingent: served with the Expeditionary Force in France and Flanders from 20 December 1914, and was killed in action 8 May 1915, at Bellewaarde: Age 22. *unm.*

(Panel 10) Pte. 475311, Roy Irvine Poast, Princess Patricia's Canadian Light Infantry (Eastern Ontario Regt.), C.E.F.: *s.* of Richard Poast, of Omemee, Ontario, by his wife Elizabeth Jane: *b.* Omemee, 29 March 1897: *educ.* Emily Public School; Omemee Public School, Lindsay Collegiate; Victoria College, Toronto, 1914 – 15, member C.O.T.C.: enlisted 4th University Coy., P.P.C.L.I., September 1915: proceeded to France, and joined his regiment in the Ypres salient May 1916, and, after going through the Battle of Sanctuary Wood, was killed in action at Mount Sorrel, 18 July 1916. With five others he had held an advanced part of the trench for four days until it became both isolated and untenable. As they were about to withdraw one of the party was buried by a shell explosion and, while helping to dig his comrade out of the broken trench, in full view of the enemy, another shell burst close by and killed him instantly: Age 19.

(Panel 10) Pte. 489784, John Stanley Richards, Princess Patricia's Canadian Light Infantry (Eastern Ontario Regt.), C.E.F.: late of 39, Sussex Street, Montreal: *s.* of John Richards, of the School House, Watton-at-Stone, co. Hertford, by his wife Ellen E.: *b.* Costock, co. Nottingham, 25 December 1892: Occupation – Clerk; Bank of British North America, London & Montreal: previously served 18 months, 48th Royal Highlanders of Canada (Militia): enlisted 5th University Coy., Montreal, 27 April 1916: proceeded to England July following from whence, after one month of training (during which period he qualified as Signaller), went to France (attd. Battn. Signal Sect.) and after more than one year of almost continuous front line service at the Somme, Vimy, and the Ypres salient, he was killed in action at Passchendaele, 30 October 1917, during an attack for the capture of the ridge: Age 25. *unm.*

(Panel 10) Pte. 21522, John Johnson Scott, Princess Patricia's Canadian Light Infantry (Eastern Ontario Regt.), C.E.F.: *s.* of William S. Scott, of Wadena, Saskatchewan, by his wife Lucinda: *b.* Lesbury, nr. Alnwick, co. Northumberland, 15 November 1890: educ. Lesbury School; Skerry's College, Newcastle-on-Tyne: on leaving entered service Messrs Barclays Bank; later removed to

Canada, taking appointment as Clerk, Bank of Montreal, Saskatoon: enlisted Valcartier, 25 September 1914: came over with 1st Canadian Contingent: trained Salisbury Plain, England: proceeded to France September 1915: took part in all the major engagements in which the Canadian Corps were involved throughout the winter and spring 1915 –16, and was killed in action, 2 June 1916; Sanctuary Wood, Ypres: Age 25. *unm.*

Writing to his sweetheart, Ethel Charlton, after the Battle of Mount Sorrel in which 3,000 Canadians were killed, Capt. Alan MacKenzie Gammel, Princess Patricia's Canadian Light Infantry, said,: "I came through our engagement without getting laid out. I was very lucky as we suffered very heavy casualties… it was too awful, and I want to forget it but I can't forget all the fellows of our bunch who are gone. They gave us a terrible bombardment for 11 hours. The worst ever launched against the British line. When we were given the order to go to our support line, our front line of trenches were completely gone…Fritz was coming over and we got a bunch before we got back…they were using liquid fire and smoke bombs. At our support line we made our stand and held them. The fight occurred in a small wood. It was a sorry looking place with the tops of the trees all off, and others were being knocked down with shells…My brother Norman was wounded in the back…Mrs Small's nephew, young Shearer, is reported missing, but I am afraid he is gone. I was in the same bay of the trench as he was, after we retired until night, and then I had to go farther down the trench in charge of another part of the trench; at that time we had no officers of our company. He isn't out with us now and nobody knows what happened to him. He must have been buried by a shell…"

(Panel 10) Pte. 475413, Harold Ross Shearer, 4th (University) Coy., Princess Patricia's Canadian Light Infantry (Eastern Ontario Regt.), C.E.F.: *s.* of the Rev. William Shearer, D.D., late of Pointe Claire, Quebec, and Isabella Reid Russell (924, 6th Avenue West, Calgary, Alberta), his wife: and yr. brother to Temp/Flt. Sub.Lieut. T.R. Shearer, 9th Sqdn. Royal Naval Air Service, killed in action 13 June 1917, aged 23 years: *b.* Sherbrooke, Quebec, 23 August 1896: Occupation – Student: enlisted 4th (Overseas) University Coy., Calgary, 2 October 1915; proceeded to France on the 11th of that month: joined P.P.C.L.I., Sanctuary Wood, 14 May 1916; and was killed by shellfire, 2 June 1916; Mount Sorrel. Buried where he fell: Age 19. Remains recovered Sanctuary Wood; identified – Disc; reinterred, registered March 1927. (*IWGC record age 20*) *Buried in Sanctuary Wood Cemetery (II.J.26).*

His brother Thomas is buried in Adinkerke Churchyard Extension (1713). Capt. Gammell's brother Norman suffered a fractured shoulder blade from a shell splinter; after treatment in a Base Hospital and a period of recuperation he returned to the front where he was mortally wounded in action two years later, and died 26 August 1918. Buried Vis-en-Artois British Cemetery, Havcourt (IV.E.16).

(Panel 10) Pte. 184, George Shepherd, Princess Patricia's Canadian Light Infantry (Eastern Ontario Regt.), C.E.F.: late *husb.* to Louisa J. Shepherd (6/21, Emily Street, Birmingham, England): *b.* 10 September 1893: Religion – Church of England: Occupation – Labourer: previously served 4 years Militia; volunteered and enlisted Ottawa, 25 August 1914; posted P.P.C.L.I., 2 October following: proceeded to France: present with his regiment at Bellewaarde Lake, 8 May 1915, and took part in the battle in that vicinity that day. At the Roll-Call held that evening he failed to answer his name and was reported missing. No tidings since have been received concerning him and, for official purposes, is presumed to have died on (or about) the aforementioned date: Age 21.

(Panel 10) Pte. McG/91, Alexander Ewing Tucker, No.1 Coy., Princess Patricia's Canadian Light Infantry (Eastern Ontario Regt.), C.E.F.: *s.* of Archdeacon (& Mrs) George Tucker, of Palmetto Grove, Bermuda: *yr.* brother to Sergt. 63869, G.S. Tucker, 3rd Bn. Canadian Infantry, killed in action at Mount Sorrel, 13 June 1916: *b.* Flats, Bermuda, November 1896: enlisted 2nd University Coy. 20 May 1915, subsequently posted 11th Battn., July following: joined P.P.C.L.I., Armentieres sector, September 1915. After occupying a position on the right flank of the battalion on the morning of 2 June 1916, the line being 'up in the air' at the time, he was seen to leave towards Warrington Avenue when a partial retirement was ordered, but failed to reach the rallying point: Age 19.

His brother George also has no known grave; he is recorded on Panel 30.

(Panel 10) Capt. Alfred Carburt Bastedo, 4th attd. 1st Bn. Canadian Infantry (Western Ontario Regt.), C.E.F.: *s.* of John M. (& Ida A.) Bastedo, of 4, Jean Street, Toronto: *b.* Milton, Ontario, 30 April 1886: *educ.* Milton Public School; University College, Toronto, 1911 – 14 (B.A. 1915): Capt. 20th Regt., during the vacation of his third University year, enlisted with 33 Miltonians and apptd. Capt., 4th Battn.: proceeded overseas with 1st Canadian Contingent, 14 October 1914: served with the Expeditionary Force in France from February 1915, attd. 1st Battn., and was killed in action on the morning of 23 April 1915, in the counter-attack at St. Julien. Buried north of Ypres: Age 29. One of the first members of Toronto University to fall in the Great War; his degree, B.A., was conferred posthumously.

(Panel 10) Lieut. Oswald Wetherald Grant, M.C., 1st Bn. Canadian Infantry (Western Ontario Regt.), C.E.F.: *s.* of the Rev. Dr. Andrew S. (& Mrs) Grant, of Toronto: *b.* Almonte, 27 December 1892: *educ.* Dawson Public School; Upper Canada College (1906 – 11); University College, Toronto (1911 – 14), B.A. (Law): Occupation – Student: serving Cadet Force (Lieut.), 27th (Lambton) Regt. (Militia); joined C.E.F., September 1914; apptd. 33rd Bn., St. Martin's Plain, November following: proceeded overseas with a draft of reinforcements to that unit 15 June 1915; transf'd. 12th Bn., Shorncliffe, same month; transf'd. joined 1st Bn., France, August following, serving with that unit for eight months, mostly in the Ypres sector: apptd. Brigade Bombing Officer, May 1916: rejoined 1st Battn., as Machine Gun Officer, for the drive to regain the lost ground following the German advance before Zillebeke. After the first and second German lines had been carried, 13 June 1916, he was killed instantaneously by a shell while holding an advanced machine gun emplacement. Lieut. Grant was posthumously (1 January 1917) awarded the Military Cross for consistent good work: Age 23. *unm.*

On 20 April 1915, after almost three months spent in camps behind the lines 1st Bn. Canadian Infantry (Western Ontario Regt.) were moved forward to the Ypres sector and accommodated in tents at 'B' Camp, Vlamertinghe. At 2.20 a.m., 23 April, the battalion received orders to move up to the front, and after marching via Brielen crossed the Yser at No.4 Bridge where at 9 a.m. orders were received to entrench themselves in preparation for an attack on the village of Pilkem. From 10am. onwards the hastily dug Canadian position, consisting of little more than scrapes in the ground, was subjected to a continuous bombardment by the enemy's artillery as well as machine gun and rifle fire, and it was not until nightfall, after tenaciously holding on all day, that the remnants of the battalion were able to withdraw to trenches thrown up by the local reserve the same day.

At 7 p.m. the following evening, such were the battalion's losses, the survivors were marched via Wieltje to Fortuin where, after constructing trenches during the night, they spent the following day – under intense fire for the second time in less than 24 hours – as support to a localised attack against some trenches in front of St. Julien which had recently been lost to the enemy.

Gallantly holding this position until 8 p.m. (25 April) the battalion was moved back to the west bank of the Yser Canal where, after another three days of bombardments, their sadly depleted ranks were withdrawn with what remained of 1st Infantry Brigade.

In recording the casualties for the period 23 – 30 April the Battalion War Diary states "...Officers killed 3, wounded 7, other ranks killed 56, wounded 306, missing 34. Nearly all these casualties occurred on 23rd inst."

Commenting on the battalion's baptism of fire, Lieut.Col. Hill, Comdg. 1st Battn. wrote, "The conduct of all ranks was all that could possibly be desired and their devotion to duty and steadiness remarkable."

(Panel 10) Sergt. 6285, William John Colson, 1st Bn. Canadian Infantry (Western Ontario Regt.), C.E.F.: eldest *s.* of Corpl. John Colson, R.F.A., by his wife Ellen, *dau.* of George Weller, of Wilmington: *b.* Erith, co. Kent, 25 November 1878: *educ.* Erith Board School: enlisted R.F.A. 1 December 1896: served 16 years – seven years with the Colours (Royal Field, Horse & Garrison Artillery); nine years with the Reserve – including four-and-a-half years abroad: obtained his discharge 30 November 1912: removed to Canada 30 October 1913: Occupation – Carmaker; Messrs Ford's Motor Works, Windsor, Ontario: volunteered and enlisted Valcartier, 31 August 1914, after the outbreak of war: 5'10½" tall, fair complexion, brown eyes, dark brown hair: scar on back of neck: posted 1st Battn. Western Ontario Regt.,

22 September, and apptd. Sergt.: left Valcartier by rail 25 September: embarked S.S. 'Laurentie,' Louisa Basin; departed Gaspe Bay, 3 October, and came over with First Contingent: arrived Devonport, 14 October following: underwent further training at Bustard Camp, Salisbury, during the winter of 1914 – 15: departed Avonmouth aboard Transport 'Architect' 8 February 1915: arrived St. Nazaire 11 February: moved up to the Front 20 April, and was killed in action at Ypres 24 April 1915, when the Canadians so gallantly "saved the situation." He was buried in a grave with 16 others on the east side of the Ypres to Pilckem Road, near the shrine, about 400 yards from where the pontoon bridge crosses the road: Age 36. He *m.* All Saints' Church, Belvedere, Kent, 5 August 1905, Emily (32, Upper Grove Road, Belvedere, co. Kent), *yst. dau.* of Richard Spicer, of Belvedere, and had five children – Cyril Arthur, *b.* 27 March 1906, Kathleen Adelaide, *b.* 13 December 1907, Winifred Emily, *b.* 10 August 1909, Margaret Ellen, *b.*21 July 1911, and Albert William, *b.* 10 April 1913. (*IWGC record 26 April*)

(Panel 10) Corpl. 6415, Albert Edward Thomas, 1st Bn. Canadian Infantry (Western Ontario Regt.), C.E.F.: *s.* of Charles M.S. Thomas, of Amherstburg, Ontario, by his wife Margaret Heard: and brother to Lieut. L.M. Thomas (Q.M., Actg.Major), 6th Welsh Regt., died 29 November 1915: *b.* 9 November 1891: serving member 'C' Sqdn. 1st (Amherstberg) Hussars (Militia); enlisted Valcartier, 22 September 1914: served in France from February 1915, and was killed in action at St. Julien, 23 April 1915: Age 23. (*IWGC record age 24*)

His brother Llewellyn is buried in Swansea (Oystermouth) Cemetery (F.265).

(Panel 10) L/Corpl. 6774, Thomas John Brennan, 1st Bn. Canadian Infantry (Western Ontario Regt.), C.E.F.: *s.* of John Brennan, of North Bay, Ontario, Canada, by his wife Annie, *dau.* of J. Gauthier: and brother to Pte. Martin Brennan: *b.* North Bay, 30 April 1897: *educ.* North Bay Collegiate Institute: volunteered on the outbreak of war; joined Canadian Expeditionary Force 15 August 1914: came over with First Contingent 14 October 1914: went to France 8 February following, and was killed at the Battle of Langemarck 23 April 1915. On this occasion 1st and 3rd Battns. were sent to recapture some trenches into which the Germans had forced their way. The Commanding Officer spoke highly of their conduct: Age 19.

(Panel 10) Pte. 189961, David Frederick Actworth, 1st Bn. Canadian Infantry (Western Ontario Regt.), C.E.F.: *s.* of John (& Rachael) Actworth, of 219, Centre Street, St. Thomas, Ontario: Religion – Salvation Army: joined 91st Bn. 25 February 1916. Killed in action 6 November 1917; Passchendaele: Age 18. Buried 28.D.6.a.20.20. Obituary '*St. Thomas Daily Times*,' 22 November 1917. (*pg.1,col.2; records age 22*).

(Panel 10) Pte. 406670, Charles Henry Belton, 1st Bn. Canadian Infantry (Western Ontario Regt.), C.E.F.: *s.* of George Belton, of Almhouses, Fetcham, co. Surrey, by his wife Jane: and elder brother to A/Bmdr. L/47104, T. Belton, 183rd Bde., Royal Field Artillery, killed in action 26 September 1916: *b.* Fetcham, 27 May 1889: Occupation – Gardener: enlisted Hamilton, Ontario, 20 April 1915. Killed in action 13 June 1916: Age 27. *unm.* Inscribed – 'True Love By Life, True Love By Death Is Tried, Live Thou For England, We For England Died' – the brothers are remembered on the Fetcham War Memorial.

His brother Thomas also has no known grave; he is commemorated on the Thiepval Memorial, Somme.

(Panel 10) Pte. 436815, Jean Paul Bordenave, 1st Bn. Canadian Infantry (Western Ontario Regt.) , C.E.F.: *s.* of Mrs B. Bordenave (Légunion, Pyrenees, France): *b.* 25 January 1883: Religion – Church of England: Occupation – Farmer: enlisted Edmonton, 9 February 1915. Killed in action 7 July 1916, when, between 4.30 and 10.20 p.m., the enemy fired fifteen 5.1 shells onto Halifax Street, and shrapnel into the front line and vicinity of Maple Copse, Zillebeke: Age 32. Remains recovered, identified – Clothing, Disc; reinterred, registered 5 October 1928. *Buried in Sanctuary Wood Cemetery (II.L.16).*

(Panel 10) Pte. 6301, Bertram Clare Cookson, 1st Bn. Canadian Infantry (Western Ontario Regt.), C.E.F.: *s.* of John Holland Cookson, of 197, Thames Street, Chatham, Ontario, by his wife Frances: served in France and Flanders, and was killed in action 30 April 1915: Age 31.

(Panel 10) Pte. 6793, John Andrew Fisher, 1st Bn. Canadian Infantry (Western Ontario Regt.), C.E.F.: *s.* of William Fisher, of Mountain Street, Merriton, Ontario: volunteered for Imperial Service, and enlisted after the outbreak of war August 1914: came over with First Canadian Contingent, 14 October 1914: served with the Expeditionary Force in France and Flanders, and was killed in action 22 – 30 April 1915: Age 30. (*IWGC record 22 April*)

(Panel 10) Pte. 7210, Frederick William Hull, 1st Bn. Canadian Infantry (Western Ontario Regt.), C.E.F.: *s.* of Frederick William (& Sarah Ellen) Hull, of 111, York Road, Dundas, Ontario: *b.* London, England, 7 July 1896: Religion – Methodist: Occupation – Tailor: serving member, 4 yrs., 77th Regt. (Militia): enlisted Valcartier, 22 September 1914: came over with First Canadian Contingent, October following: trained Salisbury Plain winter 1914 – 15: served with the Expeditionary Force in France from February 1915. Died of wounds 23 – 30 April 1915; 'While at duty at his Signal Post, vicinity of St. Julien, near the reserve trenches which one company of his Battalion occupied, he was severely wounded by shrapnel in the legs, right side and chest. Carried to the Dressing Station, he died soon afterwards from loss of blood.' Buried nr. Dressing Station, opposite side of canal, vicinity Langemarck: Age 19. (*IWGC record 24 April*)

(Panel 10) Pte. 6827, Angus LaForce, 1st Bn. Canadian Infantry (Western Ontario Regt.), C.E.F.: Mohawk; Six Nations: *s.* of Esther J. La Force: *b.* Caughnawaga, Montreal, 16 May 1874: Religion – Methodist: Occupation – Bridgeman: 5'7" tall, dark complexion, brown eyes, black-grey hair: enlisted Valcartier, 22 September 1914, apptd. 15th Battn.: served with the Expeditionary Force in France from February 1915, and was killed in action 22 April following: Age 40. *unm.* Believed to be the first Native Canadian to make the supreme sacrifice; an elder said, "For four short years our sons fought in European trenches beside their sons, our blood mingled with theirs, as for four hundred years in a different war our blood had mixed. Four thousand of our Native brothers and now grandfathers saw the European homeland through the sights of rifles and the roar of cannons. Hundreds are buried in that soil, away from the lands of their birth. These Native warriors accounted well for themselves, and the Allied cause… They were courageous, intelligent and proud carriers of the shield."

Believed to be the second Native Canadian killed in the Great War, Lieut. C.D. Brant, 4th Canadian Infantry, also has no known grave; he is recorded on Panel 18.

(Panel 10) Pte. 163662, Vernon Isaac Place, 1st Bn. Canadian Infantry (Western Ontario Regt.), C.E.F.: *s.* of Charles Place, of Fen Bank, Isleham, nr. Ely, co. Suffolk, by his wife Mary: and brother to Sergt. 6316, A.E. Place, Suffolk Regt., died of wounds 7 December 1914; and Corpl. 7544, T. Place, Suffolk Regt., died of wounds received at Loos 3 October 1915: *b.* Isleham, 11 April 1893: Religion – Church of England: Occupation – Labourer: 5'8½" tall, dark complexion, blue eyes, dark hair: sometime went to Canada: volunteered for Imperial Service, enlisted Toronto, 5 August 1915: served with the Expeditionary Force in France, and was killed at Ypres 13 June 1916: Age 23. *unm.*

His brother Arthur is buried in Bailleul Communal Cemetery (A.18); Thomas has no known grave, he is commemorated on the Loos Memorial.

(Panel 10) Capt. Walter Leslie Lockhart-Gordon, 2nd Bn. Canadian Infantry (Eastern Ontario Regt.), C.E.F.: formerly of 9th Mississauga Horse: 4th *s.* of William H. Lockhart Gordon, of 221, George Street, Toronto, Barrister-at-Law, by his wife Emily: and brother to Lieut.Col. H.D. Lockhart Gordon, 4th Mounted Rifles, 2nd Mounted Rifle Bde., 3rd Canadian Contingent; and Lieut. Maitland Lockhart Gordon, 3rd Gordon Highlanders: *b.* Toronto, 30 September 1890: *educ.* Toronto Church School; St. Alban's Cathedral School; Bishop Ridley College, and the Royal Military College, Canada, where he became Battn. Sergt.Major, and won the Sword of Honour in his last year: served with the Expeditionary Force in France, and was killed at the Battle of Langemarck, 23 April 1915, the following particulars being furnished to his brother by a Sergt.Major of the battalion, "On the morning of Friday, 23 April 1915, at about 3.30 a.m., we were about one hundred and fifty yards from the enemy trenches when we received an order to charge (this applies to No.1 Double Company only). As we commenced to charge, the Commander of my platoon, Lieut C.W. Day, was killed, and Capt. Gordon at once took his place. Owing to the intensity of the enemy fire, we had to advance on our knees, Capt. Gordon in front, encouraging the men by voice and gesture. We managed to get within thirty yards of the German trenches, and it was then that Capt. Gordon was hit through the neck and through the top of the head. At the time he died I was about six feet away from him, to the left rear." A Private of the Corps also wrote, "Just a line to let you know how Capt. Gordon died a hero's death. He was the bravest officer I saw in the engagement at Ypres. He went in front of his men, and led them into action. He certainly did his duty well. He was shot through the neck. Every man in the company thought the world of him for his bravery and skill. Where he went the men followed." He was a member of the Royal Canadian Yacht Club; and University Club, Toronto: Age 24. *unm.* (*IWGC record W.L.L. Gordon*)

Lieut. C.W. Day also has no known grave; he is recorded below.

(Panel 10) Lieut. Montague Lewis Farmar Cotgrave, 2nd Bn. Canadian Infantry (Eastern Ontario Regt.), C.E.F.: *yst. s.* of Richard de Malpas Farmar Cotgrave, of 'San Stefano,' Mannamead, Plymouth, and 13, Staverton Road, Brondesbury Park, London, by his wife Amelia, *dau.* of the late Capt. William Walsingham Morison, M.S.: and *gdson.* of the late Major-General William Roberts Farmar; and brother to 2nd Lieut. C.R. Farmar-Cotgrave, 2nd Worcestershire Regt. attd. 100th Trench Mortar Bty., killed in action 29 December 1917: *b.* Bedford, 23 December 1892: *educ.* St. Peter's School, Exmouth, and King's College, Taunton: removed to Canada (1912); settled at Saulte Ste. Marie, and was engaged in the Paper Mills: enlisted August 1914: came to England with First Contingent 14 October: served with the Expeditionary Force in France and Flanders from February 1915: severely wounded and gassed near St. Julien the following April: gazetted Lieut. the same month, in the autumn of 1915 returned to Canada for the benefit of his health; there apptd. to 227th Battalion then forming – subsequently promoted Capt. and Adjutant – returned to England, February 1917: proceeded to France, and was killed in action at Passchendaele 6 November following. Buried nr. Valour Farm. Lieut.-Col. McLoughlin wrote, "His gallantry and utter disregard for his own life were in a very large measure the factors which made for the great success of the engagement;" and again, "Your son fought bravely and conducted himself well in the battle." Lieut. Murray also wrote, "The history of this battalion is rich indeed with stories of bravery and devotion to duty, but few can equal those last few moments of Mr Cotgrave, whose influence lives in his old platoon." And Sergt. Moore, "Your son fell like a gentleman and a brave soldier that he was .. and we had the misfortune to lose the most popular officer of our unit." Lieut. Farmar Cotgrave was a fine footballer, and a prominent member of the Sons of Scotland football team, Canada: Age 25. *unm.*

His brother Christopher is buried in Winnezeele Churchyard (A.5).

(Panel 10) Lieut. Calvin Wellington Day, No.1 Coy., 2nd Bn. (Eastern Ontario Regt.), 1st Canadian Infantry Brigade, C.E.F.: 4th *s.* of Sidney Wellington Day, of 270, University Avenue, Kingston, Ontario, Canada, by his wife Adelaide Isabella, *dau.* of Charles Leslie Waggoner: *b.* Kingston, 19 April 1891: *educ.* Public Schools (& Collegiate Institute), Kingston; Collegiate Institute, Cobourg, Ontario, and Queen's University, Kingston, M.A., Honours, Physics & Mathematics, 1911; won University Medal (Physics), serving two years of his course as Physics Demonstrator: after graduation was for a time engaged at Queen's University with Professor Kalmus in research work, then took a post-graduate scholarship in Physics, Harvard University, 1912 – 13; secured Whiting (Physics) Fellowship, 1913 – 14, thereafter, having passed all the examinations, was preparing his thesis for a Doctorate in Philosophy: joined 14th Midland Bty., Cobourg, served three years (1907 – 10), attending camps at Petawawa, where he won First prize, Gun-Laying and Range-Finding: joined 14th Regt. Princess of Wales's Own Rifles, Kingston(1911), served a year, passed his examinations and was gazetted Lieut. 3 April 1912: volunteered for Imperial Service on the outbreak of war August 1914: came over with 1st Canadian Division October following: went to France with 2nd Battn. February 1915, and was killed in action, near St. Julien during the Second Battle of Ypres, 23 April following, when the 2nd Battn. fought so gallantly. Buried where he fell. Appreciative notices of the late Lieut. Day were published in several of the papers of his native country, giving accounts of his life and career. One gave the following account of the gallant charge of the 2nd Battalion – all Ontario men – at Ypres – "Creeping up in the early morning to within fifty yards of the German trenches, they charged. Major Bennett, who led the charge, fell badly wounded and died later. Lieut. C.W. Day fell dead with other officers and men. The regiment was decimated, but won the trenches, driving the Germans out. The 2nd Battalion held this position until relieved, though suffering from wounds and lack of food and water." An impressive memorial service to the late officer was held at Sydenham Street Methodist Church, the body of the church being reserved for the 21st Battn Canadian Expeditionary Force, while the galleries were crowded with people from every walk of life to pay their last tribute to their gallant young townsman. Several relatives of Lieut. Day are, or have been, serving with the Canadian Forces during this war, *viz.*, Lieuts. Lionel Baxter, Herchmer Stewart, George T. Richardson (Capt., died of wounds, 9 February 1916) and George Day. He was a member of the Kingston Yacht Club, Harvard Canadian Club, Cambridge, and fond of swimming, boating, canoeing, and walking: Age 24. *unm*. See also Capt. W.L. Lockhart-Gordon, above.

Capt. G.T. Richardson is buried in Bailleul Communal Cemetery Extension (II.B.74).

(Panel 10) Lieut. Herbert Norman Klotz, 'B' Coy., 2nd Bn. Canadian Infantry (Eastern Ontario Regt.), C.E.F.: *s*. of Emil W. Klotz, of 11, Harbord Street, Toronto, by his wife Leila A.: *b*. Hamilton, Ontario, 19 January 1887: *educ*. Huron Street Public School; Harbord Street Collegiate; University College, Toronto (Applied Science), 1912 – 16, B.A.Sc., Analytical & Applied Chemistry, Phi Kappa Pi: Occupation – Chemical Analyst, Gutta Percha & Rubber Co., Toronto: promoted Lieut. 9th Horse (Militia): apptd. 2nd Canadian Infantry, August 1914: departed Canada September following: trained in England throughout winter 1914 – 15: joined Expeditionary Force in France, February 1915, and was killed instantly at daybreak 23 April 1915, when leading his platoon in an attack on the German trenches nr. Langemarck, Belgium. Lieut. Klotz was one of the first members of Toronto University to fall in the Great War: Age 28. *unm*.

(Panel 10) Sergt. 8512, Albert John Brister, 2nd Bn. Canadian Infantry (Eastern Ontario Regt.), C.E.F.: *s*. of John Brister, of 57, Brock Street, Brockville, Ontario, by his wife Annie: volunteered for Imperial Service and enlisted on the outbreak of war, relinquishing rank of Lieut. 41st Regt. (Brockville Rifles) in order to proceed overseas with 1st Canadian Contingent October 1914: trained in England throughout winter 1914 – 15: went to France February 1915, and was killed in action 22 April following: Age 27. *unm*.

(Panel 10) Pte. 7813, Henry Charles Ablard, No.2 Coy., 2nd Bn. Canadian Infantry (Eastern Ontario Regt.), C.E.F.: *husb*. to Ethel Jane Ablard (136, Burnham Street, Bellville, Ontario): Religion – Church of England. Killed in action while sniping at the enemy, 22 April 1915, the battalion being engaged in attacking and repulsing counter-attacks in the vicinity of St. Julien. Buried, 28.C.17.b.10.3; Grave unmarked: Age 30. (*Archives Canada record Sergt*.)

(Panel 10) Pte. 7825, John Abrahamsen, 2nd Bn. Canadian Infantry (Eastern Ontario Regt.), C.E.F.: late of Woodroffe, Ontario: *husb*. to Anna D. Abrahamsen (92, Cambridge Street, Ottawa): *b*. Denmark, 8 October 1876: Religion – Church of England: Occupation – Bricklayer: serving member, 2yrs., Royal Canadian Regt., joined C.E.F., Valcartier, 22 September 1914. Killed in action 22 – 26 April 1915; repelling counter-attacks S.W. of St. Julien: Age 38.

PANEL 10 ENDS PTE. F.G. BACON, 2ND BN. CANADIAN INFANTRY.

PANEL 12 BEGINS PTE. F.H.A. PATRICK, EAST KENT REGT. (THE BUFFS).

(Panel 12) Pte. G/9198, Henry Quaife, 'B' Coy., 8th (Service) Bn. The Buffs (East Kent Regt.): *s*. of the late Thomas James Quaife, by his wife Jane (14, St. Hilda Road, Morehall, Folkestone): and yr. brother to Pte. G/9963, R.W. Quaife, 8th Buffs, who fell the following day: *b*. Hythe, co. Kent: enlisted Folkestone. Killed in action 14 June 1917: Age 23. *unm*.

His brother Robert also has no known grave; he recorded below.

(Panel 12) Pte. G/9963, Robert Walter Quaife, 8th (Service) Bn. The Buffs (East Kent Regt.): *s*. of the late Thomas James Quaife, by his wife Jane (14, St. Hilda Road, Morehall, Folkestone): and elder brother to Pte. G/9198, H. Quaife, 8th Buffs, who fell the previous day: *b*. Maple, co. Kent: enlisted Folkestone. Killed in action 15 June 1917: Age 32. He was married to Grace Quaife, resident at the same address as his parents.

His brother Henry also has no known grave; he is recorded above.

(Panel 12) Pte. G/5163, Frederick Setterfield, 2nd Bn. (3rd Foot) The Buffs (East Kent Regt.): *s*. of George Setterfield, by his wife Jane: *b*. Broadstairs, co. Kent: enlisted Ramsgate: served with the Expeditionary Force in France from 17 January 1915, and was one of five other ranks killed in action nr. Broodseinde Crossroads, Zonnebeke, 11 April 1915, by heavy trench mortar fire: Age 43. He was married to Louisa Jane Setterfield (II Townley Street, Ramsgate, co. Kent).

(Panel 12) Pte. G/1921, Henry Woodward, 2nd Bn. (3rd Foot) The Buffs (East Kent Regt.): late of Ramsgate: enlisted Canterbury. Killed by heavy trench mortar fire 11 April 1915; Broodseinde Crossroads.

(Panel 12) Lieut.Col. Aylmer Richard Sancton Martin, Comdg. 2nd Bn. (4th Foot) The King's Own (Royal Lancaster Regt.): *s*. of the late Rev. H. Martin, Vicar of Thatcham, Newbury: *b*. Newbury, co. Berks, 19 November 1870: *educ*. Bradfield College, and R.M.C. Sandhurst: gazetted 2nd Lieut. Royal Fusiliers, 4 March 1891; Lieut. 26 June 1892, transf'd. Royal Lancaster Regt. later the same year: became Capt. 25 January 1900; Brevet Major 29 November 1900; Major 8 September 1906; Lieut.Col. 13 December 1912: served through the South African War, 1899 – 1901, including the relief of Ladysmith and actions at Spion Kop, Vaal Kranz, Tugela Heights (14 – 22 February 1900; wounded) and Laing's Nek, and acted as Adjutant to 2nd Battn., 2 November 1899 – 8 January 1900, and 25 January – 15 September 1900 (Twice Mentioned in Despatches, '*London Gazette*,' 8 February & 10 September 1901; Queen's Medal, six clasps; Brevet of Major). On return to England, after passing through the Staff College, was attached General Staff, The War Office (1904 – 1906), and Deputy Assistant General, Scottish Command (1907 – 1912). In 1912 he was given the command of 2nd Battn. King's Own (Royal Lancaster Regt.), then in India. Lieut.Col. Martin was killed in action at Frezenberg, during the fighting around Ypres, 8 May 1915: Age 44. He *m*. at Surbiton, 21 July 1896, Mary Beatrice (3, St. Alban's Mansions, Kensington Court Place, London, W.), *dau*. of General Charles Terrington Aitchison, C.B., Indian Army, and had a *dau*., Eileen, *b*. 15 October 1898. (*IWGC record 9 May, 1915*)

(Panel 12) Capt. Frank Miller Bingham, 5th Bn. The King's Own (Royal Lancaster Regt.), (T.F.): 2nd *s*. of the late John Joseph Bingham, M.D., by his wife Kate Laura, *dau*. of John Yardley Robinson: *b*. Alfreton, co. Derby, 17 September 1874: *educ*. St. Peter's, York; obtained medical degree M.R.C.S., L.R.C.P., St. Thomas's Hospital, London: joined Territorial Force, 1909; gazetted Lieut., Royal Army Medical Corps, 24 March 1910; transf'd. 5th King's Own, 26 November following; promoted Capt. 2 May 1914: served in France and Flanders from 12 April 1915; took part in the fighting around Ypres in the early part of May and, following three days leave to visit his wife and children, was killed the day after returning to the Front when, while on reconnaissance work near Ypres, 22 May 1915, he stopped to assist in the rescue of a man who had been buried by a shell burst. Buried in Sanctuary Wood: Age 40. A well-known practitioner in Lancaster, Capt. Bingham formerly played cricket for Derbyshire County and Rugby football for Blackheath. He *m*. St. Margaret's, Westminster; 12 December 1900, Ruth Morley (Lindow Cottage, Lancaster), *dau*. of Alfred Evans Fletcher, late Chief Inspector of Abrali Works, and had three children –: Thomas Fletcher, *b*. 8 July 1902; Joan Fletcher, *b*. 15 July 1905; Jill Fletcher, *b*. 22 April 1911.

(Panel 12) Capt. Thomas Brittain Forwood, 2nd Bn. (4th Foot) The King's Own (Royal Lancaster Regt.): *s*. of Brittain Forwood, of Courtbourne, Farnborough, co. Hants, by his wife Edith Anne: *educ*. Northaw House, Harrow (Kendall's); Royal Military College, Sandhurst: gazetted King's Own, 1905; promoted Capt. 1915: proceeded to France January 1915. Killed in action, 8 May 1915, at Frezenberg, nr. Ypres. On the day of his death Capt. Forwood and his company were sent up to reinforce 3rd Monmouths, and was leading his men into their position under very heavy rifle fire when he was shot through the head and killed instantaneously: Age 28. He *m*. 1912; Constance M. Forwood, ('Mon Plaisir,' La Heule, Jersey, Channel Islands), eldest *dau*. of Col. W.F. Fairlie, of Middlewood, Jersey, and had one daughter.

Numerous letters of condolence have been received by his widow: "He was too brave – absolutely regardless of danger. The men would have followed him anywhere, he was always cheering them up and doing everything he could for them." " I have taken over T. B. F.'s old Company and assure you that I have a very hard task, if I am in any way to fill his position and keep up the standard of its last Company Commander. On all hands I am told by the N.C.O.'s and men of what was done when he commanded the Company, and can only say they make me feel very small. They were absolutely devoted to him and would have done anything for him." "He was always a hero and died a hero's death, encouraging his men to the end." " I know what he was as a soldier, and there are not many like him." His Colonel wrote, "The Regiment has lost one of its best Officers, and one who was not only an officer but a gentleman, in the best sense of the word; while I personally have lost a friend for whom I had the greatest liking and respect. Everyone in the Regiment is sharing his family's sorrow, for he was one of the best." Remembered by a memorial plaque in St. Andrew's (Frimley Green & Mytchett) parish church, it records 'Capt. Forwood, from 'Frimhurst' (near 'The King's Head' canal bridge Frimley Green) was killed nr. Ypres, May 1915;' Recorded on the village war memorial sited inside the lych-gate leading to the church; his medals and memorial plaque were donated to the Regimental Museum..

(Panel 12) Lieut. John Francis Bernal Greenwood, 'C' Coy., 1st Bn. (4th Foot) The King's Own (Royal Lancaster Regt.): eldest *s.* of Lieut.-Colonel Joseph Greenwood, R.E., by his wife Clara, *dau.* of John Bernal, of Albert Lodge, Limerick: *b.* Limerick, 22 March 1885: *educ.* Military College, Plymouth: joined Regular Army 13 July 1903; given a commission 18 January 1908; promoted Lieut. 21 May 1911: served in India, 1908 – November 1912; while there obtained Cavalry Higher Equitation (with Royal Dragoons, Lucknow, 1 October 1909); Mounted Infantry (Umballa, 1911 – 12); Supply & Transport (Rawal Pindi) Certificates; commanded a section Mounted Infantry School, Umballa: passed higher standard examinations in Hindustani (24 April 1911), Pushtu and Lower Standard Persian (13 July 1911), and held a certificate as an interpreter in French (gained June 1914): seconded, January 1913, for two years' service Army Pay Dept., but rejoined his regt. January 1915, being attd. 3rd Battn. from which he was drafted 1st Battn., France, April 1915. Killed in action at St. Julien, during the Second Battle of Ypres, Sunday, 2 May 1915; buried by the Germans about 2 miles N.E. of Ypres. Major Wilson wrote, "On 2 May, at about 3 p.m., the enemy used gas and under cover of the gas they advanced (about 700 strong) against a position (a farmhouse) held by 10 men of 'C' Coy., 1st Battn. Lieut. Greenwood, a Corpl, and three men, all 'C' Coy., rushed to the farmhouse (about 200 yards) to assist the 10 men holding the farm. The enemy continued their advance under rifle and machine gun fire to within 300 yards of our position and placed their maxim guns behind a hedge. During the attack Lieut. Greenwood, using his revolver, and the men with rifles accounted for a good number of the enemy. Lieut. Greenwood, after using all his revolver ammunition, took up a rifle and fired a few rounds, when he was shot in the head by the enemies' maxim gun. His death was instantaneous. The enemy having partly surrounded our small party we were eventually ordered to retire as it was impossible for so few men to hold the position any longer. His body was unavoidably left behind with about 10 men. He showed great gallantry during the fighting.": Age 30. He *m.* R.C. Garrison Church, Lucknow, India, 20 July, 1910, Frances Mary Georgina, eldest *dau.* of the late James Watson Anderson, of Saltburn-by-Sea, York, and of Bacon's Crescent, Exeter, Devon, and had one child – Henry Vincent Bernal, *b.* 16 August 1911.

(Panel 12) Lieut. Robert Arthur Douglas McCulloch, 1st Bn. (4th Foot) The King's Own (Royal Lancaster Regt.): eldest *s.* of Lieut.Col. T. McCulloch, M.B., Royal Army Medical Corps: and *gdson.* to the late Archdeacon French, of Mauritius: *b.* Dover, co. Kent, 17 July 1895: *educ.* Wellington College, and Royal Military College, Sandhurst: commissioned 2nd Lieut. October 1914; promoted Lieut. February 1915: served with the Expeditionary Force in France and Flanders from November 1914: apptd. Hand Grenade Officer to his company, March 1915, and was killed near Ypres, 1 May 1915, while gallantly leading his men in action. A brother officer, recounting the circumstances, said, "The advance trench was commanded by Lieut. Greenwood (also killed), and your gallant boy went forward with reinforcements and met his death in front of his men. It may be a consolation to you to know that death was instantaneous.

He was buried near the place where he fell. Your boy was beloved by us all, both for his personality and his splendid soldierly qualities. He was very happy in his all too short life with the regiment, and we shall miss him sadly." Another officer spoke of how universally popular he was, both with the 3rd and 1st Battalions of the regiment. One of the men, speaking of him, said, "Mr McCulloch is a fine young man, and a very gallant one too." His Commanding Officer said he had been doing real good work, and he had recently sent his name in for gallant conduct in helping to rescue men when the Germans blew in a (British) mine at Le Touquet. He went most gallantly, without any orders from his Commanding Officer, to get back a house out of which the Germans had driven our men by the use of gas: Age 19. (*IWGC record 2nd Lieut.*)

Lieut. Greenwood also has no known grave; he is recorded above.

(Panel 12) 2nd Lieut. Gerald William Beachcroft, 7th (Service) Bn. The King's Own (Royal Lancaster Regt.): *educ*. Dulwich College: joined King's Own, 29 May 1915. Killed in action 31 July 1917. Remembered on Heene Parish War Memorial, Sussex.

(Panel 12) 2nd Lieut. Thomas Hervey Hathaway, 3rd attd. 2nd Bn. (4th Foot) The King's Own (Royal Lancaster Regt.): formerly no.2028: obtained his commission 1914. Killed in action 17 February 1915. See Lieut. G.L. Harford, Tuileries British Cemetery (Sp.Mem.D.6).

(Panel 12) 2nd Lieut. George Knox, 8th attd. 6th (Service) Bn. The King's Own (Royal Lancaster Regt.): *b*. 11 September 1881: *educ*. Dulwich College, where he played rugby football for the Second XV, and Streatham-Croydon Club: travelled to South America on leaving Dulwich and, on returning to England took up residence and an appointment in the City of London: obtained a commission (Temp.) Royal Lancaster Regt., December 1914: trained Bournemouth, Winchester, Aldershot and, although wishing to proceed to France, departed with 6th Battn. of his regiment to Mesopotamia, March 1916. The whole of that month was spent getting into position and training for an attack on the Turkish positions near the Orah Canal. The first of these attacks came at 5 a.m., 5 April, with the King's Own successfully driving the enemy out of its front line trench "at the point of the bayonet" with very few casualties. By 7 a.m. the battalion were partaking of their breakfast! However, 12 hours later the Battalion was back in action again and captured a further three enemy trenches. On the 9th, the King's Own attacked again at 4.20 a.m. on the enemy positions at Sannaujat. The attack failed due to the Turkish troops being well prepared for an assault. After sending up flares they poured an accurate rifle and machine gun fire into the attackers, which continued until 8 a.m. The King's Own suffered 12 killed, 89 wounded, 91 missing; among the latter 2nd Lieut. Knox who was last seen leading his men. *Circumstances re. this casualty dictate commemoration on the Basra Memorial.*

(Panel 12) 2nd Lieut. George William Stewart Muchall, 2nd Bn. (4th Foot) The King's Own (Royal Lancaster Regt.): *s*. of the late Colour-Sergt. William Angus Muchall (served 21 years, 8th King's Liverpool Regt.): *b*. Orford Barracks, Warrington, 12 June 1881: enlisted King's Own, 4 January 1901; attained rank Colour-Sergt. Serving with his regt. in India when the European War broke out, August 1914; he came home with his regt., reaching England at Christmas: given a commission 2nd Lieut., 2nd King's Own, 9 January 1915: went to France, and was killed in action in the desperate fighting on the Frezenberg Ridge, nr. Ypres, 8 May 1915: Age 33. Lieut. Muchall was three years Battn. Champion Shot, won the J.H. Seward Jewel for judging distance at Bisley (1909), and was fourth in the grand aggregate. He *m*. Scotforth Church, Lancaster, 6 January 1906; Elizabeth (15, Cheltenham Road, Lancaster), *dau*. of William Jackson, of 15, Cheltenham Road, Lancaster, and had three children – William J., *b*. 18 February 1907; Lilian M., *b*. 6 April 1911; George, *b*. 13 August 1914. (*IWGC record 10 May 1915*)

(Panel 12) 2nd Lieut. George Prince Mountford Scudamore, 'A' Coy., 2nd Bn. (4th Foot) The King's Own (Royal Lancaster Regt.): *yst. s*. of the late Sergt.Major Robert Scudamore, late of 2nd King's Own Royal Lancaster Regt.; Sergt.Major, Royal Military College, Sandhurst; by his wife Katie (34, Tulse Hill, London, S.W.): *b*. Karachi, India, 24 October 1890: enlisted Royal Lancaster Regt., 1908: returned to England, from Lebong, India, late 1914, with rank of Sergt.: commissioned 2nd Lieut., in his old regiment, January 1915, posted 2nd Battn., and shortly thereafter proceeded to France. Reported missing, 8 May 1915, it has since been ascertained through the Red Cross Society that 2nd Lieut. Scudamore was killed in action on that date; a Corpl. in his Company having recently given the following account, "On May 8th 2nd Lieut. Scudamore was killed at Ypres by a bullet whilst in a trench near a wood. He was attached to 'A' Company at the time of his death. He was hit by the bullet through the side of the neck, and died about five minutes afterwards. The order had been given for him to hold the trench whilst the remainder retired. The Germans had already broken through in different parts of the line. Lieut. Scudamore was Commander of the trench, and was fighting, as it were, a rearguard action until the others got away. I was left under him in the same part of the trench. I was quite near to him and saw the whole affair. I knew him well." A brother officer wrote of him, "May I as one of your son's comrades and friends say how deeply distressed I am to see in the paper that he is reported killed. I would have written to you before, but I have only just found out your address in to-day's *Times*. I was for a time commanding 'A' Company, just after your son came out, and so we were together a good deal. I was awfully good pals with him, and he was always so cheery and bright, everybody liked him, both men and officers, and we always thought him in the Company the best of good fellows. I was in the next trench to him at that battle in Ypres, and we were laughing and chatting away at 3 a.m. on the morning of 8th May. We never dreamt such a battle would take place the next day. I can't tell you what a loss he is to me as a friend and companion. I always used to tell everyone in my Company, 'Go to Scudamore if you are in the blues, and he will cheer you up.'" His elder brother, R.C.R. Scudamore, is serving in the Army Service Corps, and his second brother, Lieut. A.A.V. Scudamore, 18th Battn. Yorkshire Light Infantry, is also serving in the war: Age 24. *unm.* (*IWGC record age 25*)

(Panel 12) Sergt. 376, James Sarginson Kirkby, 1/5th Bn. The King's Own (Royal Lancaster Regt.): *s.* of the late Richard Kirkby, of 93, Market Street, Carnforth, co. Lancaster, and Mary Kirkby: *b.* Carnforth, 1889: enlisted there. Killed in action 3 May 1915; Frezenberg: Age 25. A prominent football player (half-back) – Lancaster, Carnforth and Warton – he held office as Secretary, Carnforth Football and Cricket clubs. In a letter to his sister Sergt. W. Simpson informed that he had carried James back and buried him in the corner of a small churchyard. Capt. Evans wrote, "Sgt Kirby was killed whilst assisting in an advance by the Rifle Brigade who were in sore need of help. At the moment of his death he had been treating a wounded comrade; he had been hit in the neck by a shell and had died instantaneously. Colonel Lord Richard Cavendish has asked me to express his deepest sympathy. I cannot express to you any words which measure our sorrow at the loss of a true comrade, hero and friend. We laid him to rest in a soldiers grave in Verlorenhoek; the Colonel said a service. It must be some consolation to you that he gave his life to save you all at home from the horrors of this sorrowing land."

Towards the latter part of November 1916 a raiding party of 1/4th King's Own began organising a sudden descent on the German lines for the purpose of gathering information and determining the strength and quality of the enemy troops opposite the selected position. Rehearsals for the raid, extremely practical in their value, were carried out on a replica of the enemy position marked out by tapes on a practice ground at 'O' Camp, near Vlamertinghe, with times and distances carefully noted. On 21 December, after a full and final rehearsal the troops were inspected by General Sir Douglas Haig, dining the following evening in the great hall of Ypres prison.

At 1.30 a.m., 23 December, with their faces and hands blackened to minimise light reflection and facilitate recognition by their own side during the course of the raid, the 200 strong party were armed and inspected prior to departing in small groups at 3.15 a.m. to their jumping off position, a ditch running north and south in the St. Julien sub-sector.

Their objective was to enter the German trenches and penetrate to the Cameron support trench with a view to killing or taking prisoners and thereby secure identification. At 5.25 a.m., under cover of an accurately placed artillery barrage the raiders entered the enemy trenches according to plan, penetrating to the designated support line which were found to be very badly damaged by the artillery barrage and devoid of any Germans. Described as a brisk and well carried out minor action, the main result was, after all the preparation, more than a little disappointing; the reasoning being attributed to the enemy having withdrawn when the bombardment began and the fact that registering and bombarding of the position for more than a week had effectively advertised the intent of a raid, advocating the use of surprise methods which proved far more successful in future endeavours.

After returning to the safety of the British lines a roll-call of the raiders recorded two officers, 2nd Lieuts. Smith and Hart, wounded; Other Ranks, 3 killed; 3 missing; 30 wounded (4 died).

Of the three killed and three missing only L/Sergt. M. Caddy, and Pte. J. Millington, were confirmed; the bodies of all six were never recovered.

(Panel 12) L/Sergt. 200124, Matthew Caddy, 1/4th Bn. The King's Own (Royal Lancaster Regt.), (T.F.): *s.* of James Caddy, of 18, Burlington Street, Ulverston, co. Lancaster, by his wife Jane: *b.* St. Mary's, Ulverston, 1895: served with the Expeditionary Force in France and Flanders, and was killed in action during a raid in the St. Julien sub-sector, 23 December 1916. His Commanding Officer described him as 'a good experienced N.C.O. and a great loss to the battalion.': Age 21. *unm.* Remembered on Ulverston Great War Roll of Honour. See also L/Corpls. W. Douglas and T.H. Newby; Ptes. W. Finch and J. Halligan below; and Lijssenthoek Military Cemetery, Pte. J.H.Clarke (X.C.38A); Pte. A.Aked (X.C.39); L/Corpl. J.Little (X.C.39A), and Pte. T.Ashton (X.C.40).

(Panel 12) Corpl. 10349, Alfred Charles Joslin, 'A' Coy., 2nd Bn. (4th Foot) The King's Own (Royal Lancaster Regt.): *s.* of Alfred James Joslin, Boot Finisher; of 43, Grinstead Road, Deptford, London, S.E.8., by his wife Elizabeth Ann, *dau.* of Frederick Wilson: *b.* Old Kent Road, London, S.E., 16 September 1893: *educ.* Trundley's Road School, Deptford: enlisted 1910: served with the Expeditionary Force in France and Flanders. Reported wounded and missing after the fighting at Frezenberg, 8 May 1915; now assumed killed in action on that day: Age 21. *unm.* (*IWGC record age 22*)

On the afternoon of 22 April 1915 the first gas attack in the history of warfare descended on a portion of the front held by French colonial troops ('Zouaves') in the vicinity of St. Julien. Terror stricken by the strange yellow-green clouds as they approached and enveloped their trenches, the 'Zouaves' fled in complete panic; tearing at their throats, retching and choking as the gas attacked their lungs. A Canadian Division, hastily rushed forward, somehow managed – even though greatly outnumbered – to fill the gap left by tide of retreating Zouaves and check the ensuing German advance.

As part of a hastily planned and assembled counter-attack by the Canadians the following day, at 1 p.m. 5th King's Own moved toward Pilckem and on arrival dug in to support of the Canadian right flank. At 3.45 the attack began, 5th King's Own acting as reserve joining at 5 p.m. Within seconds of beginning their advance the ranks of the King's were met with a hail of machine-gun and rifle fire from three sides, which caused numerous casualties and forced the battalion to retire a couple of hundred yards, but with no artillery support and devoid of cover their position was hopeless. Witnessing soldiers attempting to find cover wherever they could, the King's Commanding Officer saw some seek safety behind a pile of manure only to be cut to pieces as bullets ripped through it. In the face of ever increasing losses he made his way to Brigade HQ where instead of receiving an order to effect a strategic withdrawal he was told, "Hold your position!"

A combination of the hastily contrived counter-attack and tenaciously holding onto their positions stemmed the German advance, but at great cost. Of the troops involved over fifty percent were killed; 5th King's Own alone lost 26 killed, 102 wounded; 1 gassed.

(Panel 12) L/Corpl. 1512, Thomas Burrow, 1/5th Bn. The King's Own (Royal Lancaster Regt.), (T.F.): *s.* of Edward Burrow, of Fern Bank, Halton, co. Lancaster, by his wife Sarah Alice: *b.* Halton: served with the Expeditionary Force in France and Flanders from 15 February 1915: underwent trench warfare instruction Neuve Eglise sector, March; took part in the fighting at Polygon Wood, 12 April 1915, and was killed in action nr. St. Julien on the afternoon of the 23rd of that month: Age 19.

(Panel 12) L/Corpl. 200438, William Douglas, 'C' Coy., 1/4th Bn. The King's Own (Royal Lancaster Regt.), (T.F.): *s.* of Joseph Douglas, of 24, Cameron Street, Barrow-in-Furness, co. Cumberland, by his wife Elizabeth: enlisted Ulverston, co. Lancaster: served with the Expeditionary Force in France and Flanders; reported missing / believed dead after a raid on the German trenches in the St. Julien sub-sector, 23 December 1916: Age 23. *unm.* See L/Sergt. M.Caddy, above.

(Panel 12) L/Corpl. 999, John Hirst Harper, 'C' Coy., 1/5th Bn. The King's Own (Royal Lancaster Regt.): *s.* of Alexander (& Ellen) Harper, of 29, Wellington Road, Lancaster: *b.* Christchurch: a pre-war Territorial, joined 1909, undertook Active Service obligations on the outbreak of war August 1914; Lancaster: served with the Expeditionary Force in France from 15 February 1915, and was killed in action 13 April following: Age 21.

(Panel 12) L/Corpl. 200179, Thomas H. Newby, 1/4th Bn. The King's Own (Royal Lancaster Regt.), (T.F.): *s.* of W. (& M.) Newby, of 8, Crellin Street, Barrow-in-Furness, co. Cumberland: *b.* Barrow-in-Furness, 1892: enlisted Ulverston, co. Lancaster: served with the Expeditionary Force in France and Flanders, and was reported missing / believed dead after a raid on the German trenches in the St. Julien sub-sector, 23 December 1916: Age 24. L/Corpl Newby was married to Mary Ethel Leahy, *née* Newby. See L/Sergt. M.Caddy, above.

At 8.20 p.m., 7 May 1915, 2nd King's Own relieved their 5th battalion in a section of uncompleted and barely tenable trenches before Frezenberg. Any work to improve these new trenches was continually interrupted throughout the night by intermittent shellfire, and at 7 a.m., 8 May, a hurricane bombardment, preliminary to an enemy advance, completely destroyed them altogether. 'A' and 'D' companies in the front line were quickly overwhelmed and the line captured. The Germans then advanced against 'B' and 'C' in support dugouts, from where 'B' was moved across the road to support 3rd Monmouths in some old trenches east of the burial ground. Stopped some 200 yards short in their advance against the support dugouts, at 11.30 the Germans diverted their advance to both flanks. At some point during these activities Lieut. Col. A.R.S. Martin, commanding the battalion, was killed and command now fell to Major Clough who, acting on a message received, ordered a retirement to Potijze and positions north of the Ypres – Zonnebeke road where the battalion remained throughout the remainder of the day. At the roll-call that evening very few of the battalion remained to answer, 15 officers killed, wounded, missing, over 400 other ranks killed, wounded, missing; among the latter brothers Richard and William Corfield, Charles and Thomas Phelps. Had they been able to sufficiently improve the trenches at Frezenberg would the action of 8 May have had a different outcome? The condition of the position at the time offered virtually no defensive capability whatsoever; they barely stood a chance.

(Panel 12) L/Corpl. 2594, Thomas Phelps, 2nd Bn. (4th Foot) The King's Own (Royal Lancaster Regt.): *s.* of John Randle Phelps, of Fulham, London, by his wife Kate: and elder brother to Pte. 2588, C. Phelps, 2nd King's Own, who fell in the same action. Killed in action 8 May 1915, at Frezenberg: Age 19.

His brother Charles, and Ptes. R. and W. Corfield also have no known grave; they are recorded below.

(Panel 12) Pte. 2069, Edward Adams, 1/5th Bn. The King's Own (Royal Lancaster Regt.), (T.F.): enlisted Lancaster: served with the Expeditionary Force in France and Flanders from 15 February 1915: underwent trench warfare instruction Neuve Eglise sector, March; took part in the fighting at Polygon Wood, 12 April, and was killed in action at St. Julien, 23 April 1915.

(Panel 12) Pte. 1386, George Edward Balderstone, 1/5th Bn. The King's Own (Royal Lancaster Regt.), (T.F.): *b.* Christchurch, Lancaster. Killed in action on the afternoon of 23 April 1915, nr. St. Julien.

(Panel 12) Pte. 3014, Thomas Bamber, 1/5th Bn. The King's Own (Royal Lancaster Regt.), (T.F.): *s.* of the late William Bamber, by his wife Sarah (10, High Street, Great Eccleston, Garstang): *b.* Singleton, co. Lancaster: enlisted Lancaster, 28 October 1914: served with the Expeditionary Force in France from 15 February 1915. Died of wounds 5 May 1915: Age 25. *unm.*

(Panel 12) Pte. 1363, George Beckett, 'A' Coy., 1/5th Bn. The King's Own (Royal Lancaster Regt.), (T.F.): *s.* of Richard Beckett, of Lancaster: *b.* St. Thomas, Lancaster. Killed in action on the afternoon of 23 April 1915, nr. St. Julien: Age 21.*unm.*

(Panel 12) Pte. 15908, Thomas Boyes, 8th (Service) Bn. The King's Own (Royal Lancaster Regt.): Officer's Servant to 2nd Lieut. R.C. Bowden. Killed in action at The Bluff, 2 March 1916. See Lijssenthoek Military Cemetery (II.A.43).

(Panel 12) Pte. 17367, James Brindle, 2nd Bn. (4th Foot) The King's Own (Royal Lancaster Regt.): *s.* of Hugh Brindle, of 29, Pickup Street, Blackburn, by his wife Jane Eliza, *dau.* of Henry Tomlinson:

b. Blackburn, 16 September 1893: *educ.* Holy Trinity School, Blackburn: prior to the outbreak of war was employed as Weaver; Sparrow's Mill, Quarry Street: joined the Army, 25 January 1915. Killed in action at Ypres, 8 May 1915: Age 21. *unm.* Five of his brothers are (1916), or were, on active service:– Pte. Joseph Brindle, 3rd Bn. East Lancashire Regt., Ewen, 4th Bn. East Lancashire Regt., and Alfred, Lancashire Fusiliers, are serving in France; George is in the Navy, and the *yst.*, Private Thomas Brindle, Scottish Rifles, has been discharged, having had his finger blown off at the Battle of the Aisne.

(Panel 12) Pte. 2093, George Cathcart, 1/5th Bn. The King's Own (Royal Lancaster Regt.), (T.F.): *s.* of John Cathcart, of 97, Dale Street, Lancaster, by his wife Mary: and elder brother to Pte. 2091, J. Cathcart, King's Own, who fell eleven days later: enlisted Lancaster, 4 September 1914: served with the Expeditionary Force in France and Flanders, and was killed in action 23 April 1915: Age 19.

His brother James also has no known grave; he is recorded below.

(Panel 12) Pte. 2091, James Cathcart, 1/5th Bn. The King's Own (Royal Lancaster Regt.), (T.F.): *s.* of John Cathcart, of 97, Dale Street, Lancaster, by his wife Mary: and *yr.* brother to Pte. 2093, G. Cathcart, King's Own, who fell eleven days previously: enlisted Lancaster, 4 September 1914: served with the Expeditionary Force in France and Flanders, and was killed in action 4 May 1915: Age 17.

His brother George also has no known grave; he is recorded above.

(Panel 12) Pte. 16077, Fred Clough, Machine Gun Section, 8th (Service) Bn. The King's Own (Royal Lancaster Regt.): 3rd *s.* of James Ernest Clough, of Rose Hill House, Westhoughton, by his wife Alice, *dau.* of J. Green: *b.* Aspull, Wigan, co. Lancaster: *educ.* Municipal Secondary School, Bolton: Occupation – Apprentice Mechanical Engineer: enlisted November 1914: served with the Expeditionary Force in France and Flanders from September 1915, and was killed in action at Ypres, 2 March 1916. The Rev. M.P.G. Leonard, Chaplain, wrote, "I cannot tell you how much we all mourn his loss, or how hard it will be to fill the gap which he leaves, but I am sure it would comfort you if you could hear how highly everybody speaks of him. His Officer told me he was the best man in his Machine Gun Section, always ready and eager to do his duty, fearless, cool and reliable, and a general favourite with all who knew him. The battalion can ill afford to lose such men as he.": Age 21. *unm.*

(Panel 12) Pte. 7609, William Connolly, 2nd Bn. (4th Foot) The King's Own (Royal Lancaster Regt.): *b.* Ballimore, Co. Galway: enlisted Manchester: served with the Expeditionary Force in France and Flanders from January 1915, and was killed in action 21 April following. (*IWGC record Connolly*) *Buried in Menin Road South Military Cemetery (II.K.20).*

(Panel 12) Pte. 20410, Christopher Constantine, 8th (Service) Bn. The King's Own (Royal Lancaster Regt.): *b.* Clapham, co. York, *c.* 1900: enlisted Nelson: served with the Expeditionary Force, and was killed in action at Ypres, 2 March 1916. All correspondence should be addressed c/o his aunt, Alice Constantine (7, Grey Street, Nelson, co. Lancaster): **Age 16.**

(Panel 12) Pte. 16386, Richard Corfield, 2nd Bn. (4th Foot) The King's Own (Royal Lancaster Regt.): *s.* of the late Alfred Corfield, by his wife Mary Jane (North Row, Bassenthwaite, Keswick): and elder brother to Pte. 17247, W. Corfield, King's Own, who fell the same day: *b.* Keswick, *c.*1885: enlisted Atherton: served with the Expeditionary Force in France from early 1915, and was killed in action 8 May 1915: Age 30. See account re. L/Corpl. T. Phelps, above.

His brother William also has no known grave; he is recorded below

(Panel 12) Pte. 17247, William Corfield, 2nd Bn. (4th Foot) The King's Own (Royal Lancaster Regt.): *s.* of the late Alfred Corfield, by his wife Mary Jane (North Row, Bassenthwaite, Keswick): and *yr.* brother to Pte. 16386. R. Corfield, King's Own, who fell the same day: *b.* Keswick, *c.*1893: enlisted Kingsbridge: served with the Expeditionary Force in France from early 1915, and was killed in action 8 May 1915: Age 22. See account re. L/Corpl. T. Phelps, above.

His brother Richard also has no known grave; he is recorded above.

(Panel 12) Pte. 10130, Robert Devenport, 2nd Bn. (4th Foot) The King's Own (Royal Lancaster Regt.): *s.* of Thomas Devenport, of Pendleton, co. Lancaster, by his wife Mary Ann: and elder brother to

L/Corpl. B/1366, J. Devenport, 7th Rifle Brigade, died, 7 May 1917, of wounds: enlisted Manchester. Killed in action 19 February 1915: Age 25.

His brother Joseph is buried in Warlincourt Halte British Cemetery (IX.G.15).

(Panel 12) Pte. 201388, Walter Finch, 1/4th Bn. The King's Own (Royal Lancaster Regt.), (T.F.): *s.* of Thomas Finch, of 24, Penn Street, Horwich, Bolton, by his wife Hannah: *b.* 1892: enlisted Bolton: served with the Expeditionary Force in France and Flanders. Reported missing / believed dead after a raid on the German trenches in the St. Julien sub-sector, 23 December 1916: Age 24. *unm.* See L/Sergt. M.Caddy, above.

(Panel 12) Pte. 1297, Fred Glover, 'B' Coy., 1/5th Bn. The King's Own (Royal Lancaster Regt.), (T.F.): *s.* of John Glover, of 1, Picadilly, Scotforth, co. Lancaster: and brother to Pte. 18235, J.T. Glover, 6th Royal Scots Fusiliers, killed in action 26 September 1915, at the Battle of Loos: *b.* Kendal: enlisted Lancaster. Killed in action 27 April 1915: Age 23. *unm.*

His brother John also has no known grave; he is commemorated on the Loos (Dud Corner) Memorial.

(Panel 12) Pte. 1675, Harry Grice, 1/5th Bn. The King's Own (Royal Lancaster Regt.), (T.F.): *s.* of Alfred Grice, of 7, Ripley Street, Lancaster, by his wife Jane: *b.* Scotforth, 1898 – 99: enlisted Lancaster: served with the Expeditionary Force in France, and was killed in action 27 April 1915: **Age 16**.

(Panel 12) Pte. 15613, John Griffin, 8th (Service) Bn. The King's Own (Royal Lancaster Regt.): eldest *s.* of the late William Griffin, Auctioneer, by his wife Mary (now Mrs John Eagles, 28, Westbourne Street, Everton, Liverpool), *dau.* of John Nolan: *b.* Gateshead-on-Tyne, Co. Durham, 13 April 1890: *educ.* St. Francis Xavier's Roman Catholic School, Liverpool: Occupation – Tobacco Presser: enlisted Liverpool, 11 November 1914, after the outbreak of war: went to France 25 August 1915, and was killed in action at The Bluff, north of the Ypres-Comines Canal, 2 March 1916. Buried at St. Eloi: Age 25. *unm.* Major C.W. West wrote, "I remember him well when I was commanding 'A' Company, and always found him so willing and capable. It is indeed a great sorrow to us all…In your sorrow it may be some little comfort to you to know that the action was a most brilliant one, and all behaved most splendidly, upholding well the traditions of the old regiment," and the Rev. M.P.G. Leonard, Chaplain to the Forces, "I know what a heavy blow this will be to you, and my heart goes out in sympathy; but nothing can take from you the pride you will always have that he gave his life in such a good cause. His is the death of a true man and a brave soldier, for he gave his life for England's honour and to protect our homes from German oppression."

(Panel 12) Pte. 200080, John Halligan, 1/4th Bn. The King's Own (Royal Lancaster Regt.), (T.F.): *s.* of Hugh Halligan, of 4A, Fay Street, Barrow-in-Furness, co. Cumberland, by his wife Sarah Jane: *b.* 1896: enlisted Barrow-in-Furness: served with the Expeditionary Force in France and Flanders; reported missing / believed dead after a raid on the German trenches in the St. Julien sub-sector, 23 December 1916: Age 20. *unm.* See L/Sergt. M.Caddy, above.

(Panel 12) Pte. 16050, Oliver Hingley, 8th (Service) Bn. The King's Own (Royal Lancaster Regt.): *s.* of the late William Hingley, by his wife Agnes (Haydock, co. Lancaster): Occupation – Collier; Messrs Richard Evans & Co. Ltd., Wood Pit, Haydock: enlisted Atherton. Killed in action 2 March 1916, while taking part in a bayonet charge at The Bluff: Age 22.

(Panel 12) Pte. 2384, Henry Huyton, 1/5th Bn. The King's Own (Royal Lancaster Regt.), (T.F.): *s.* of John Huyton, of 16, New Street, Halton, co. Lancaster, by his wife Harriet: enlisted Lancaster: served with the Expeditionary Force in France and Flanders from 15 February 1915: underwent trench warfare instruction in the Neuve Eglise sector, March; took part in the fighting at Polygon Wood, 12 April; killed in action nr. St. Julien, Ypres, on the 23rd of that month: Age 18.

(Panel 12) Pte. 1505, John Septimus Johnston, 1/5th Bn. The King's Own (Royal Lancaster Regt.), (T.F.): *s.* of Edward Johnston, of 22, Kirkby Terrace, Halton, co. Lancaster, by his wife Jane: enlisted Lancaster: served with the Expeditionary Force in France and Flanders from 15 February 1915, and was killed in action, 23 April 1915: Age 19. One of seven brothers who served.

(Panel 12) Pte. 201724, John Thomas Kay, 1/4th Bn. The King's Own (Royal Lancaster Regt.), (T.F.): enlisted Blackpool, co. Lancaster. Killed in action 14 July 1917. One of nine members of his battalion killed during the period 9 – 19 July 1917, described by the Battalion History as 'ten very trying days of intense strain,' carrying materials to forward dumps in the Potijze – St. Jean sector in preparation for the Third Battle of Ypres. See Vlamertinghe New Military Cemetery (I.F.26, I.G.20-21 & III.F.17-20), and L/Corpl. J. Collinson, Duhallow A.D.S. Cemetery (V.B.11).

(Panel 12) Pte. 3557, James Millington, 1/4th Bn. The King's Own (Royal Lancaster Regt.), (T.F.): *s.* of George Millington, of 36, Bradford Street, Barrow-in-Furness, co. Cumberland, by his wife Martha: *b.* 1897: a pre-war Territorial, volunteered at the outbreak of war August 1914; undertook Foreign Service obligations Barrow-in Furness: served with the Expeditionary Force in France and Flanders from 5 May 1915, and was killed in action during a raid on the German trenches in the St. Julien sub-sector, 23 December 1916: Age 19. See L/Sergt. M.Caddy, above.

(Panel 12) Pte. 2507, Samuel Milner, 1/5th Bn. The King's Own (Royal Lancaster Regt.), (T.F.): *s.* of George William Milner, of Whittingham, nr. Preston, co. Lancaster, by his wife Sarah. Died 6 June 1915, consequent to wounds received in action at Ypres: Age 24. *unm. Buried in Lancaster Cemetery, Lancashire (D.CE.832).*

(Panel 12) Pte. 2154, Joseph Nash, 'C' Coy., 1/5th Bn. The King's Own (Royal Lancaster Regt.): *b.* Lancaster: enlisted there, August 1914: served with the Expeditionary Force in France and Flanders from February 1915, and was killed in action 13 April 1915. The Battlion War Diary records:– "'C' Coy trenches heavily shelled by trench mortars, 2 men – L/Corpl. Harper, Pte. Nash – killed (died of wounds) Heavy shelling throughout the day. Great shortage of sandbags. Parapets unhealthy. Require strengthening."

(Panel 12) Pte. 8004, Walter Nutter, 2nd Bn. (4th Foot) The King's Own (Royal Lancaster Regt.): *s.* of Elkanah Nutter, of 21, Junction Street, Brierfield, nr. Nelson, by his wife Jane: and brother to Pte. 11228, B. Nutter, 6th East Lancashire Regt., who fell 9 August 1915, at Gallipoli, aged 26 years: *b.* Burnley: enlisted Lancaster. Killed in action 8 May 1915; Frezenberg: Age 30.

His brother Benjamin also has no known grave; he is commemorated on the Helles Memorial.

(Panel 12) Pte. 2588, Charles Phelps, 2nd Bn. (4th Foot) The King's Own (Royal Lancaster Regt.): *s.* of John Randle Phelps, of Fulham, London, by his wife Kate: and yr. brother to L/Corpl. 2594, T. Phelps, 2nd King's Own, who fell in the same action. Killed in action 8 May 1915; Frezenberg: Age 17.

His brother Thomas also has no known grave, he is recorded above.

(Panel 12) Pte. 240628, Reginald Stamper, 1/5th Bn. The King's Own (Royal Lancaster Regt.), (T.F.): *b.* Lancaster. Died of wounds 23 April 1915, received in action at St. Julien. All correspondence to be addressed c/o his brother, Henry Stamper Esq., Buxton Road, Chinley, Stockport.

(Panel 12) Pte. 1144, Walter W. Standen, 'A' Coy., 1/5th Bn. The King's Own (Royal Lancaster Regt.), (T.F.): *s.* of Robert Standen, of 6, Derby Road, Skerton, co. Lancaster, by his wife Rachel, *née* Saunders: enlisted Lancaster: served with the Expeditionary Force in France and Flanders from 15 February 1915, and was killed in action at St. Julien, nr. Ypres, 23 April 1915: Age 23. *unm.*

(Panel 12) Pte. 1324, William Henry Theobald, 'A' Coy., 1/5th Bn. The King's Own (Royal Lancaster Regt.), (T.F.): *s.* of Henry Theobald, of 6, Back, Marton Street, Lancaster, by his wife Mary Ann: enlisted Lancaster: served with the Expeditionary Force in France and Flanders from 15 February 1915: underwent trench warfare instruction Neuve Eglise sector, March; took part in the fighting at Polygon Wood, 12 April; killed in action at St. Julien, nr. Ypres, on the 23rd of that month: Age 19.

On 8 May 1915 2nd King's Own lost 15 officers killed, wounded, missing, and over 400 other ranks; among the latter three (of several) men who – although they shared the same surname – were totally unrelated. The fortunes of war dictated not only they share the same place and date of death, but deny them a known grave also.

(Panel 12) Pte. 17468, John Wilcock, 2nd Bn. (4th Foot) The King's Own (Royal Lancaster Regt.): *b.* Haslingden, co. Lancaster. Killed in action 8 May 1915; Frezenberg. See account re. L/Corpl. T. Phelps, above.

(Panel 12) Pte. 16956, Richard Wilcock, 2nd Bn. (4th Foot) The King's Own (Royal Lancaster Regt.): *b*. Preston, co. Lancaster. Killed in action 8 May 1915; Frezenberg: Age 37. He leaves a wife, Elizabeth Wilcock (38, Brookhouse Street, Preston, co. Lancaster). See account re. L/Corpl. T. Phelps, above.

(Panel 12) Pte. 7806, William Wilcock, 2nd Bn. (4th Foot) The King's Own (Royal Lancaster Regt.): *b*. Manchester. Killed in action at Frezenberg, 8 May 1915. He was married to Elizabeth Walton, *née* Wilcock (16, Beach Road, Heaton Mersey, Manchester).

(Panel 12) Capt. Claude Wreford-Brown, D.S.O., 2/5th Bn. The Northumberland Fusiliers (T.F.): 5th *s*. of the late William Wreford-Brown, by his wife Clara Jane (5, Litfield Place, Clifton, Bristol), *dau*. of Henry Clarke, M.D.: and brother to Capt. O.E. Wreford-Brown, 9th Northumberland Fusiliers, died 7 July 1916, of wounds received in action on the Somme: *b*. Clifton, 17 February 1876: *educ*. Waynflete, Durham Downs; Wells House, Malvern Wells, and Charterhouse: after serving in Royal Warwickshire Militia obtained his commission as 2nd Lieut., 1st Battn. 'Fighting Fifth,' 15 May 1897: promoted Lieut. 24 November 1899; Capt. 15 April 1901: took part in the Sudan Campaign (1898) under Lord Kitchener, being present at the Battle of Omdurman and the capture of Khartoum (Queen's Medal and Egyptian Medal with clasp): thereafter employed in the occupation of Crete, and, under Lord Methuen, served throughout the South African War, 1899 – 1902: took part in the advance on Kimberley, including the actions at Belmont, Enslin, Modder River and Magersfontein: operations in Orange Free State (March – May, 1900); the Transvaal (July – November 1900), including actions at Venterskroom and Rhenoster River. Twice Mentioned in Despatches ('*London Gazette*,' 9 July & 10 September 1901), received D.S.O. for his services at Lichtenburg; also Queen's Medal, four clasps; King's Medal, two clasps: selected to represent his regt. at the Coronation of King Edward VII. In April 1908, he was on the North-West Frontier of India, and while serving in the Mohmand Campaign was seriously wounded. On 4 September 1912 he was appointed an instructor at the Royal Military College, Sandhurst, which post he filled until 17 February 1915 when he joined the 2nd Battn. of his regt. then in France. Capt. Wreford-Brown was killed on the Menin Road, south of Ypres, 200 yards east of Wieltje Farm, north of Hooge, on Whit Monday, 24 May 1915. His regt. had been practically wiped out on the 13th, and when he heard of this he insisted on leaving Boulogne, where he was in hospital, and going back to reform the regt. He arrived at Headquarters, west of Ypres, Friday, 21 May, and there found 85 worn out men of his battn. and about 450 of the 5th Fusiliers and Durham L.I., and 15 officers, a new draft which had just arrived, all from the same depot. These he formed into a battn., and on Sunday, 23 May, was ordered to join the Brigade – only two clear days to form a new regt.! They marched between 15 and 29 miles, on a sweltering hot day, losing several men on the way under shellfire. They arrived at Menin Road on Monday (Empire Day) the 24th; and were ordered out into support at 6 a.m. Wreford-Brown was commanding. At about 1 p.m he received orders to advance to a certain point and attack a position which was allotted to him. The battn. shortly after leaving its support position came under heavy fire, and, for a distance of two and-a-half miles across country of open fields of buttercups, was continually under high-explosive fire and shrapnel, machine-gun and rifle fire. The regt. was formed up for the attack on the ridge which they took, but with very heavy casualties. Ten of the officers were wounded in this, leaving Wreford-Brown and two lieutenants. These, and the remaining men, dug themselves in and on getting to the ridge they found the Germans very strong in a farm called Wieltje; it looked as if the Germans were on three sides of them. The regt. on the right could not be found, and two companies of the 5th were taking on three miles of Germans. At 7 p.m. he sent word as to his position and the heavy casualties. The answer came back 'You must try and take it and hold it at all costs." One of the captains in the firing line who was wounded, and lying in a ditch, reports that Wreford-Brown told him to go back to hospital and congratulated him on getting back to England wounded, and said, "Good-bye, old fellow, I shall not see you again. I am ordered to attack the place, it is hopeless but I shall lead my men to it": and with that he turned to his men and called for a rifle and bayonet and said, "Now we wll make the final charge of the Mohicans," which he did, leading the men. The Germans had 20 to 25 machine-guns concentrated on them. Wreford-Brown fell 10 yards from the German trench mortally wounded. The remaining Lieut. reformed for a second attack and got wounded: the remaining few retired back to the trench behind the hedge, which they had dug after gaining the ridge. Only one officer got back safely, and he was with the machine-gun a long way behind which did not come into action. The regt. on the right had been delayed and came up afterwards. In the opinion of all he was shot several times and was certainly killed. Several attempts were made to recover his body, but it lay between two trenches of the Germans, and it was impossible owing to their withering fire. The Commander-in-Chief came round himself and thanked the survivors for their bravery. His brother officers bore general testimony to his capability and great courage: Age 39. *unm.*

His brother Oswald is buried in Corbie Communal Cemetery Extension (I.B.48).

(Panel 12) Capt. Roland Sackville Fletcher, 1st Bn. (5th Foot) The Northumberland Fusiliers: 2nd *s.* of Lionel Fletcher, of 'Elmscroft,' West Farleigh, Maidstone, co. Kent, by his wife Eleanor Mary, *née* Stopford Sackville: nephew to Col. Stopford Sackville, Drayton House, co. Northampton: *b.* London, 24 March 1882: *educ.* Charterhouse: gazetted 2nd Lieut Northumberland Fusiliers, from Northamptonshire Militia (with which he served when it was embodied for nearly nine months), 5 January 1901: promoted Lieut. 26 February 1902: employed with West African Frontier Force (Colonial Office) 5 November 1904 – 28 January 1910: promoted Capt., 4 September 1912: served with the Expeditionary Force in France and Flanders. On arrival at the front, 29 October 1914, he was sent, 1 November, with his company to help in holding Wytschaete against an overwhelming force of the enemy. After being seen to fall on the morning of 1st November, he was not seen again, but news of his death the following day (2 November), from wounds received in action, was obtained from one of the prisoners in a German camp in June 1915. Of a particularly literary turn of mind several articles by Capt. Fletcher, mainly regarding his experiences in Northern Nigeria, appeared in '*Blackwood's Magazine.*' He made a great study of the language and customs of the natives, and published a book entitled '*Hausa Sayings and Folklore.*' He qualified as a First-Class Interpreter (in Hausa) in 1912, as part of his examination for the Staff College. He was a member of the Wellington Club and very fond of all sports and games: Age 32. *unm.*

(Panel 12) Capt. Arthur Charles Hart, 2nd Bn. (5th Foot) The Northumberland Fusiliers: *s.* of the late Sir Israel Hart, J.P. (four times Mayor of Leicester); and Lady Hart (34, Holland Park, London, W.): *b.* 7 October 1881: *educ.* Cheltenham College: entered Leicestershire Militia, from which he was gazetted 2nd Lieut., Northumberland Fusiliers, January 1901: promoted Lieut. February 1902; Capt. March 1911: served in Antigua at the close of the South African War, afterwards in India: also with the Expeditionary Force in France and Flanders from January 1915, and, though twice wounded at duty, refused to leave the fighting line, and was killed in action at Zonnebeke, 9 May 1915, while gallantly rallying his men. He is known to have personally killed at least twenty of the enemy before he fell. For his services in the Great War he was Mentioned in Sir John (now Lord) French's Despatch, 31 May 1915. Capt. Hart was a member of the Junior Service, the Ranelagh, Roehampton, and Queen's Clubs: Age 33.

(Panel 12) Capt. George Edward Hunter, 6th Bn. The Northumberland Fusiliers (T.F.): elder *s.* of Edward Hunter, of Wentworth, Gosforth, co. Northumberland, by his wife Anne, *née* Cunningham: and brother to Capt. H.T. Hunter, Northumberland Fusiliers, killed on the same day: *b.* Newcastle-on-Tyne, 27 March 1887: *educ.* Aysgarth School, and Charterhouse: afterwards studied Architecture as a profession: served his articles with Messrs Cackett & Burns Dick, later taking his A.R.I.B.A.; thereafter joining his father's firm, Messrs Hunter & Henderson, Stockbrokers, Newcastle-on-Tyne; becoming partner, 1913: joined 3rd (Volunteer) Battn. Northumberland Fusiliers (now 6th Battn.), as 2nd Lieut. 1904: promoted Capt. June 1908: went to France with his regiment, some months after the outbreak of war, and was killed by a fragment of shell nr. St. Julien, 26 April 1915. A brother officer wrote, "He led his men with great courage and a total disregard for himself. He was right in front of the enemy's position, and was killed by a shell fired at short range." Age 28. *unm.*

His brother Howard also has no known grave; he is recorded below.

(Panel 12) Capt. Howard Tomlin Hunter, 6th Bn. The Northumberland Fusiliers (T.F.): *yr. s.* of Edward Hunter, of Wentworth, Gosforth, co. Northumberland, by his wife Anne, *née* Cunningham: and brother to Capt. G.E. Hunter, Northumberland Fusiliers, killed on the same day: *b.* Newcastle-on-

Tyne, 1 October 1888: *educ*. Royal Grammar School, Newcastle; Aysgarth, and Charterhouse: afterwards entered Durham University, graduating M.B., B.S., 1910: continued his post-graduate studies in surgery at the Royal Infirmary, Newcastle-on-Tyne; St. Bartholomew's Hospital, London, and in Vienna: joined 3rd (Vol.) Battn. Northumberland Fusiliers (now 6th Battn.), as 2nd Lieut. 1906; promoted Capt. January 1912: went to France with his regiment, and was killed in action nr. St. Julien, 26 April 1915. The following account of the circumstances attending Capt. H.T. Hunter's death was published in the Durham College of Medicine Gazette:– "We have all heard with pride and aching heart of his entry into action. The first torrent of bullet and shell only seemed to increase his absolute indifference to danger, and his example and courage infected the whole company. He led his men through a cross-fire of machine guns and shrapnel, trying to reach the German trenches by a series of rushes. When close to his objective he was struck in the leg, 'but stuck to his job, gamely cheering on his men.' We can imagine his bitter disappointment when he had to fall out so near the end of his task. While being helped to the rear he was struck again, in the chest, and almost immediately dropped dead." Age 26. *unm*.

His brother George also has no known grave; he is recorded above.

(Panel 12) Capt. Everard Joseph Lamb, 3rd (Reserve) Bn. The Northumberland Fusiliers attd. 2nd Bn. (105th Foot) The King's Own (Yorkshire Light Infantry): only *s*. of Robert Lamb, of Hayton House, How Mill, Carlisle, by his wife Helen: *b*. 1895: joined Northumberland Fusiliers, October 1905: promoted Lieut. June 1910; Capt. August 1914: served with the Expeditionary Force in France and Flanders, and was killed in action at the First Battle of Ypres 1 November 1914: Age 29. Capt. Lamb leaves a widow, Margery.

(Panel 12) Capt. George King Molineux, 2nd Bn. (5th Foot) The Northumberland Fusiliers: elder *s*. of Major Harold Parminter Molineux, of 'The Cottage,' Isfield, co. Sussex, late 56th (Essex) Regt., by his wife Ross Eugenie Katherine, 2nd *dau*. of the late Henry King, of Isfield Place, Sussex: *b*. Eastbourne, co. Sussex, 15 April 1887: *educ*. Winchester College, and Magdalen College, Oxford: after serving two years in 3rd South Staffordshire Regt. was gazetted 2nd Lieut. 2nd Northumberland Fusiliers, 11 December 1909, and served in England with his regt. until September 1913, when he proceeded with it to India, being promoted Lieut. 1 November 1913; Capt. 16 January 1915: apptd. Aide-de-Camp to Lord Hardinge of Penshurst, then Viceroy of India, August 1914, but resigned this appointment November following in order to accompany his regt. to France on Active Service. Landed in France in January 1915, and was engaged in transport work for a short time previous to going into the trenches in the Ypres district. On the 7 and 8 May, the Germans concentrated their guns on the salient held by the Brigade in advance of Ypres, the bombardment of the trenches being exceptionally severe. In the assault by the enemy which followed, owing to the giving way of a unit on the right of the Northumberland Fusiliers, the right flank of that regt. was overwhelmed, and Capt. Molineux was last seen wounded and unconscious in his trench, between Wieltje and Frezenberg, by the survivors who retired. He was most popular in his regt. and beloved by all who knew him. At Winchester he was in the cricket eleven (1906), and captain of Commoner Football. He gained his Harlequin colours at Oxford, and played in several matches for the University, also for Gentlemen of England against Oxford University and for the M.C.C. He was a first-class cricketer, shot, horseman, fisherman and a knowledgable naturalist: Age 28. *unm*. (*IWGC record 5 May 1915*)

(Panel 12) Capt. Robert Collingwood Roddam, 3rd (Reserve) attd. 1st Bn. (5th Foot) The Northumberland Fusiliers: only *s*. of Lieut.-Col. Roddam John Roddam, of Roddam, co. Northumberland, J.P., B.A., late comdg. 3rd Northumberland Fusiliers, now comdg. 15th Northumberland Fusiliers, by his wife Helen Fredericks, *yst. dau*. of Capt. Alexander Taubman Goldie, of The Hermitage, Isle of Man, late R.N.: *b*. Roddam Hall, nr. Alnwick, 10 January 1890: *educ*. Wellington College: joined 7th Northumberland Fusiliers (T.F.); 2nd Lieut., August 1908: transf'd. 3rd Special Reserve, commanded by his father, 1910; promoted Lieut., 2 December 1912: on the outbreak of war with Germany was in Ceylon: immediately returned to England, joined his Battn. September, proceeded to France (as Lieut.) December following – there attd. 1st Battn.; promoted Capt. – and was killed in action at Hooge, 16 June 1915, gallantly leading his Company in an attack on the German trenches. Buried there. Col. (now Brigdr.-Gen.) Ainslie wrote, "He will be a great loss as an officer, in fact I know of no one who shaped better or showed more soldier-like qualities. Over and over again he has been in very nasty situations and every time he has come out smiling, and kept his end up splendidly. It will be a consolation to you to know what a tip-top officer he was." Awarded the Military Cross ('*London Gazette*,' 23 June 1915) for 'gallantry with the handful of men in the trench left capable, after having had their trench mined at St. Eloi, 14 April': and Mentioned in F.M. Sir John (now Lord) French's Despatch of 31 May ('*London Gazette*,22 June 1915) for 'gallant and distinguished service in the field.': Age 25. *unm.*

(Panel 12) Lieut. Charles John McKinnon Thomson, Special Reserve of Officers attd. 1st Bn. (5th Foot) The Northumberland Fusiliers: 2nd *s.* of the Rev. S. McKinnon Thomson, Vicar of Northallerton, co. York, by his wife Edith Rose, *dau.* of the Ven. Edward Prest, Archdeacon and Canon of Durham: *b.* Tudhoe, Co. Durham, 10 January 1893: *educ.* The Abbey, Beckenham; Haileybury College; Armstrong College; Durham University (O.T.C. member); also with tutors at Tours, Hanover, and Lausanne: was studying for a degree in Civil Engineering: gazetted 2nd Lieut., Special Reserve of Officers, 18 April 1914; promoted Lieut., 12 August 1915: served with the Expeditionary Force in France and Flanders from 29 September 1914: acted as Assistant Town Major, Bailleul, March 1915 – 1916: recalled to his regiment, 15 March; and died at the Battle of St. Eloi on the 27th. of that month (March 1916), of wounds received in action the same day, being struck by a shell when in the second German trench. Buried on the battlefield. His Commanding Officer wrote, "At the time of his death he was leading his men very gallantly to victory. He was a capable and brave soldier." Age 23. *unm.*

(Panel 12) Lieut. Robert St.John Willans, 3rd (Reserve) attd. 1st Bn. (5th Foot) The Northumberland Fusiliers: only *s.* of the late Col. St.John Willans, by his wife Ethel D'Aragon: *gdson.* to the late Robert Courage, of Snowdenham, Bramley, co. Surrey: *b.* 8 September 1877: served in the South African War, 1899 – 1901, during which, after four months service with the embodied Militia, was gazetted 2nd Lieut. Northumberland Fusiliers, April 1900; promoted Lieut. June 1901: took part in operations in Transvaal, and Orange River Colony (Queen's Medal, 3 clasps): retired from the Army, 1905: on the outbreak of war with Germany, was re-gazetted to 3rd Battn. of his old regiment with the rank he held on retirement. Died nr. Ypres, 9 November 1914: Age 37.

(Panel 12) 2nd Lieut. Herbert Edward Hobbs, 2nd Bn. (5th Foot) The Northumberland Fusiliers: eldest *s.* of Herbert (& Mrs) Hobbs, of Riding Mill, co. Northumberland: and brother to Lieut. G.B. Hobbs, Northumberland Fusiliers attd. 9th Sqdn. Royal Flying Corps, killed nr. Martin Hill, Dover, while flying on military duty 7 September 1915: *b.* Merton Park, co. Surrey, 9 November 1894: *educ.* Newcastle Preparatory School; Malvern College; Keble College, Oxford, being there at the outbreak of war preparing to enter the Church. One of the first to be given a temporary commission, August 1914, he was sent for one month to the Officers' Training Camp, Churn: subsequently apptd. 8th Northumberland Fusiliers: after several months training, promoted Lieut. 25 January 1915 (rank to date from November 1914): attended Staff College, Camberley; gazetted, 2nd Lieut. 29 January 1915, to a permanent commission Regular Army, posted 2nd Northumberland Fusiliers: served with the Expeditionary Force in France and Flanders, going out with a draft for his regiment 2 May 1915, and was killed in action nr. Hooge on the 25th. of that month. He was a fine long-distance runner, and won the mile race for his College while at Oxford: 25 May 1915: Age 20. *unm.*

His brother Geoffrey is buried in St. Margaret's-at-Cliffe Churchyard, Sibertswold, Dover.

(Panel 12) 2nd Lieut. Kenneth Shann, 3rd (Reserve) attd. 2nd Bn. (5th Foot) The Northumberland Fusiliers: only *s.* of Lawrence Shann, of Farnham, Knaresborough, co. York, by his wife Lucy, *née* Fenwick: and nephew to Lieut.Col. Shann (ret'd.), 5th West Yorkshire Regt., Senior Medical Officer, Harrogate: *b.* Boston Spa, co. York, 22 April 1895: *educ.* St. Peter's School, York; Armstrong College, Newcastle-on-Tyne (2 yrs. member, Durham University O.T.C.): gazetted 3rd Northumberland Fusiliers, August 1914: served with the Expeditionary Force in France and Flanders, and was killed, 8 May 1915, in the trenches near St. Julien. His Company and two others of his battalion, while occupying poor and newly-constructed trenches, were surrounded by the enemy, and, in rising to look over the parapet towards the enemy on their original front, he was shot from behind: Age 20. *unm.*

(Panel 12) Coy.Q.M.Sergt. 869, Neville Benjamin Blythe Brook, 'A' Coy., 1/6th Bn. The Northumberland Fusiliers (T.F.): *s.* of Benjamin Blythe Brook, of 4, Cedars Road, Beckenham, co. Kent, by his late wife Martha Elizabeth: and elder brother to Pte. 3019, J.E.B. Brook, 28th Australian Infantry, killed in action 29 July 1916, at Pozieres: *b.* Wandsworth, London, 1889: a pre-war Territorial (joined 1908, Drill Hall, Newcastle-on-Tyne); undertook Active Service obligations on the outbreak of war: served with the Expeditionary Force in France from 21 April 1915, and was killed in action at St. Julien, nr. Ypres on the 27th of that month: 27 April 1915: Age 25. *unm.* Dedicated August 1920 by the Bishop of Woolwich, and lost when the church was destroyed in 1940, Neville and James Brook were among eighty-five parishioners remembered on Brockley (St. Cyprian's) War Memorial.

His brother James also has no known grave; he is commemorated on the Villers-Bretonneux Memorial.

(Panel 12) Sergt. 6931, John Clarke, D.C.M., 1st Bn. (5th Foot) The Northumberland Fusiliers: *s.* of Joseph Clarke, of Birkenhead, co. Chester, by his wife Annie: enlisted Liverpool: served with the Expeditionary Force in France and Flanders from August 1914. Died at Vierstraat, 18 June 1915, of wounds received in the vicinity of St. Julien: Age 36. *Buried in Kemmel No.1 French Cemetery (I.D.4).*

(Panel 12) L/Sergt. 9789, Henry Walter Richardson, 1st Bn. (5th Foot) The Northumberland Fusiliers: *s.* of Harry Richardson, of Islington, London, by his wife Catherine: 16 years with the Colours; served in the South African Campaign, and with the Expeditionary Force in France and Flanders (from 14 August 1914), and died 8 November 1914, of heart failure: Age 33. He was married to Rose Ethel Richardson (129, Armstead Walk, Dagenham, co. Essex).

(Panel 12) L/Sergt. 2625, Percy Webb, 2nd Bn. (5th Foot) The Northumberland Fusiliers: *s.* of the late Arthur Barnard Webb, of 27, King's Newton Street, Leicester, by his wife Susie. Died 8 May 1915. Remains recovered unmarked grave (28.C.23.d.05.85), refers GRU Report, Zillebeke 5.457E; identified – Clothing, Titles, Disc; reinterred, registered 16 January 1931. *Buried in Sanctuary Wood Cemetery (V.N.3).*

In Loving Memory At Rest

(Panel 12) L/Corpl. 1363, Thomas Hardy, 1/5th Bn. The Northumberland Fusiliers (T.F.): enlisted Walker-on-Tyne: served with the Expeditionary Force in France from 20 April 1915, and was killed in action nr. Zillebeke, Belgium, 2 May following. See Pte. J. Bain, Perth Cemetery (China Wall), (II.A.8) and Pte. T. Cuskern (I.L.40); also Pte. R. Heslop, Menin Gate Memorial (Panel 12); Pte. C. Wood (Panel 8); Pte. T. Cowen (Addenda Panel 59); and Pte. T. Dodds, Bailleul Communal Cemetery Extension (I.A.161).

(Panel 12) L/Corpl. 8976, John Headley Patterson, 1st Bn. (5th Foot) The Northumberland Fusiliers: *s.* of James Patterson, Joiner: *b.* Newcastle-on-Tyne, 7 February 1884: *educ.* Ouseburn Board Schools: a pre-war Reservist – occupation, Moulding Shop worker; Messrs. Henry Watson & Sons, High Bridge Works – called up on mobilisation, 5 August 1914: proceeded to France late November 1914, and was killed in action 4 March 1915. Buried at Ypres: Age 31. He *m.*, Newcastle-on-Tyne, 28 July 1907; Mary Pringle, *née* Melville, and had a son, John Headley, *b.* 24 September 1914, and three other children.

(Panel 12) Pte. 22271, Ernest Adams, 1st Bn. (5th Foot) The Northumberland Fusiliers: *s.* of Edward Adams, of Thorpe Willoughby, nr. Selby. co. York, by his wife Susannah: and yr. brother to Pte. 291263, J.E. Adams, Northumberland Fusiliers, killed in action 7 June 1917: *b.* Driffield: enlisted Selby: Died, 27 March 1916, at Ypres: Age 20. *unm.*

His brother John also has no known grave; he is recorded below.

(Panel 12) Pte. 291263, John Edward Adams, 11th (Service) Bn. The Northumberland Fusiliers: *s.* of Edward Adams, of Thorpe Willoughby, nr. Selby. co. York, by his wife Susannah: and elder brother to Pte. 22271, E. Adams, Northumberland Fusiliers, died 27 March 1916: *b.* Driffield: enlisted Goole. Killed in action 7 June 1917: Age 22. *unm.*

His brother Ernest also has no known grave; he is recorded above.

(Panel 12) Pte. 2235, Alexander Alderson, 1st Bn. (5th Foot) The Northumberland Fusiliers: *s.* of Mary Jane Alderson (Newcastle-on-Tyne): *gdson.* to Henry Alderson and Margaret Boyd: *b.* Lancaster, 1890: on the outbreak of war volunteered for Foreign Service: served with the Expeditionary Force in France and Flanders, and was killed at Ypres 15 November 1914: Age 24. 'While positioned in Herenthage Woods at Herenthage Chateau, enemy attacked and took Herenthage Stables. A party of 50 men, under CSM Gibbon, counter-attacked and regained the position. Headquarters, W and part of Y companies relieved and withdrawn. X and remainder of Y on 16th. 9 OR killed.'

> *He bravely answered duty's call,*
> *He gave his life for one and all,*
> *But the unknown grave is the bitterest blow,*
> *None but an aching heart can know.*

(Panel 12) Pte. 8726, James William Alderson, 1st Bn. (5th Foot) The Northumberland Fusiliers: *s.* of George Alderson, of 12, Durham Street, West Hartlepool, by his wife Hannah, *née* Spencer: and brother to Pte. 27991, C.G. Alderson, 1/4th King's Own, killed in action 16 September 1917: *b.* West Hartlepool, 1886: a pre-war Regular, served with the Expeditionary Force in France and Flanders from November 1914, and was killed in action 11 November 1917: Age 31.

His brother Charles is buried in Vlamertinghe New Military Cemetery (IX.G.3).

(Panel 12) Pte. 16982, Frank Allen, 1st Bn. (5th Foot) The Northumberland Fusiliers: *s.* of John Allen, of 258, Stockbrook Street, Derby, by his wife Elizabeth: and brother to Corpl. 8630, W. Allen, 1st South Staffordshire Regt., killed 27 March 1916; L/Corpl. 100976, T. Allen, 2nd Sherwood Foresters, killed 24 September 1915; and Pte. 14164, E. Allen, 11th Sherwood Foresters, killed 9 April 1917: *b.* Derby: enlisted there: served with the Expeditionary Force in France, and was killed in action at Ypres, 27 March 1916: Age 18. One of four brothers who fell.

His three brothers also have no known grave; they too are recorded on the Menin Gate – William (Panel 35), Thomas and Ernest (Panel 41).

(Panel 12) Pte. 5613, Joseph Ball, 'W' Coy., 1st Bn. (5th Foot) The Northumberland Fusiliers: late of Leeds: served with the Expeditionary Force in France from 14 August 1914, and was killed in action 18 January 1915; Kemmel. See Pte. M. King, below.

(Panel 12) Pte. 3387, Reuben Bezer, 'A' Coy., 1/6th Bn. The Northumberland Fusiliers (T.F.): *s.* Joseph Charles Bezer, of 9, Wolsley Gardens, Newcastle-on-Tyne, by his wife Isabella: *b.* Jesmond, Newcastle-on-Tyne: left Blyth for the Front, 20 April 1915; in action on the 26th, posted missing the following day (27 April 1915): Age 18.

(Panel 12) Pte. 1396, George Borthwick, 1/7th Bn. The Northumberland Fusiliers (T.F.): *s.* of the late S/Sergt. 63863, G. Borthwick, 'D' Bty., 175th Bde., Royal Garrison Artillery, who fell 3 September 1918; by his marriage to Mrs C.M. Young, *née* Borthwick (100, Juliet Street, Ashington, co. Northumberland): *gdson.* to John (& Louisa) Borthwick, of Hartlepool: enlisted Ashington. Killed in action, 16 June 1915: Age 19.

His father George is buried in Aubigny Communal Cemetery Extension (IV.A.32).

(Panel 12) Pte. 3295, John Butler, 2nd Bn. (5th Foot) The Northumberland Fusiliers: *s.* of the late John Butler, by his wife Edith Lucy: and brother to Pte. J. Butler, Army Service Corps, currently (1916) serving in India, and Pte. T. Butler, West Yorkshire Regt.: *b.* Tadcaster, co. York: enlisted York: served with the Expeditionary Force in France and Flanders from 16 January 1915, and was killed in action 22 February following: Age 19. His brothers both survived.

(Panel 12) Pte. 2808, Peter Byrne, 2nd Bn. (5th Foot) The Northumberland Fusiliers: *b.* Kelladeer, Co. Mayo: enlisted Middlesbrough, co. York. Died 8 May 1915. Remains recovered unmarked grave (28.C.23.d.05.85), refers GRU Report, Zillebeke 5.457E; identified – Clothing, Titles, Boots; reinterred, registered 16 January 1931. *Buried in Sanctuary Wood Cemetery (V.N.4).*

(Panel 12) Pte. 1610, William Carr, 1/7th Bn. The Northumberland Fusiliers (T.F.): late of Hepburn Lodge, Old Bewick: *s.* of John Carr, of Ellingham Home Farm, Chathill, co. Northumberland, by his wife Helen: and brother to Corpl. T. Carr, Northumberland Hussars (Yeomanry), who died of acute enteritis and pneumonia at Hepburn Lodge 17 February 1919, aged 28 years: *b.* Belford, co. Northumberland: enlisted Wooler, Glendale. Killed in action on the night of 16 June 1915, nr. Zouave Wood: Age 20. *unm.* Recorded on Chillingham War Memorial; William and Thomas are remembered on the headstone of their sister Margaret Helen who died 18 June 1901, aged 7 months.

(Panel 12) Pte. 3091, James Christie, 2nd Bn. (5th Foot) The Northumberland Fusiliers: enlisted Newcastle-on-Tyne. Died 8 May 1915. Remains recovered unmarked grave refers GRU Report, Zillebeke 5-398E; (28.I.36.b.25.60); identified – Clothing, Disc; reinterred, registered 12 February 1931. *Buried in Sanctuary Wood Cemetery (V.O.13).*

(Panel 12) Pte. 1948, Albert Coulthard, 1/7th Bn. The Northumberland Fusiliers (T.F.): 3rd *s.* of Robert Coulthard, Saddle & Harness Maker; of Market Street, Alnwick, co. Northumberland, by his wife Isabella, *dau.* of Andrew Swann: *b.* Alnwick, 19 September 1889: *educ.* Duke of Northumberland's School: Occupation – Decorator: enlisted 28 August 1914, after the outbreak of war: went to France 20 April 1915, and was killed in action at St. Julien on the 26th., during the Second Battle of Ypres: 26 April 1915: Age 25. *unm.*

(Panel 12) Pte. 430, William Crook, 1st Bn. (5th Foot) The Northumberland Fusiliers: *husb.* to Mary Ann Crook (53, Larcom Street, Walworth, London, S.E.): *b.* London: a pre-war Regular, served with the Expeditionary Force in France and Flanders from 14 August 1914, and died 8 November 1914, at Ypres: Age 27. Remains (two) recovered unmarked grave (28.J.20.d.8.8) 7 December 1928. GRU Report, Zillebeke 5-318E refers: 'Impossible to separate remains; identified – Khaki, Boots (size 8 & 10), Disc.' Reinterred, registered 12 December 1928. *Buried in Sanctuary Wood Cemetery (IV.P.1).*

(Panel 12) Pte. 3/9105, Thomas Dykes, 1st Bn. (5th Foot) The Northumberland Fusiliers: *s.* of the late William (& Jane) Dykes, of John Street, Cullercoats, Whitley Bay, co. Northumberland: enlisted 3rd (Reserve) Bn., Newcastle-on-Tyne, August 1914: served with the Expeditionary Force in France and Flanders, and was killed in action 14 April 1915: Age 50. Pte. Dykes leaves a wife, Sarah (8, Whitfield Road, West Benwell, Newcastle-on-Tyne) and family.

(Panel 12) Pte. 21014, Joseph Dyson, 2nd Bn. (5th Foot) The Northumberland Fusiliers: formerly no.10362, Durham Light Infantry: *s.* of Simeon Dyson, of 23, Seventh Avenue, Council Houses, Chester-le-Street, Co. Durham, by his wife Jane: and brother to Coy.Sergt.Major 25493, J. Dyson, Durham Light Infantry, killed in action 7 June 1917: *b.* Sunderland: served with the Expeditionary Force in France from January 1915; died there 26 May 1915: Age 29.

His brother James also has no known grave; he is recorded on Panel 36

(Panel 12) Pte. 17056, Alexander Ewins, 'Y' Coy., 1st Bn. (5th Foot) The Northumberland Fusiliers: 2nd *s.* of Christopher Ewins, Bricklayer; of 20, Church Way, North Shields, by his wife Mary, *dau.* of Dominick Rice: *b.* North Shields, co. Northumberland, 23 May 1884: *educ.* St. Cuthbert's R.C. School, North Shields: Occupation – Bricklayer: volunteered and enlisted 27 January 1915: served with the Expeditionary Force in France from 3 June 1915, and was killed in action at St. Julien, 27 July 1915: Age 35. *unm.*

(Panel 12) Pte. 1850, Clarence Royal Greathead, Machine Gun Section, 4th Bn. The Northumberland Fusiliers (T.F.): only *s.* of George William Greathead, of Cleadon, North Eastern Railway Official, by his wife Ada, *dau.* of William Greig, of West Hartlepool: *b.* West Hartlepool, 5 June 1897: *educ.* Henry Smith College there: Occupation – Apprentice; Messrs Grabham & Co., Newcastle-on-Tyne: enlisted September 1914, after the outbreak of war: proceeded to France April 1915, and was killed in action near Ypres, 5.30a.m., 16 June 1915, while in charge of a machine gun. Buried at Wieltje. His officer wrote, "He was a brave, fearless soldier, and will be missed by his battalion. We had him carefully buried and a cross bearing his inscription marks the place." Age 18.

(Panel 12) Pte. 3779, Thomas Ezra Joseph Hampden, 'W' Coy., 1st Bn. (5th Foot) The Northumberland Fusiliers: served in France from 14 August 1914,and was killed in action 18 January 1915, by shellfire; Kemmel. Ptes. 5613, J. Ball, 8013, M. King and 181, A. Paterson were also killed; Pte. 3511, D. Scales died of wounds the following day.

Pte. Scales is buried in Locre Churchyard (II.E.1).

(Panel 12) Pte. 2880, James Albert Hardy, 2nd Bn. (5th Foot) The Northumberland Fusiliers: *s.* of Emily Hardy (152, High Street, Poplar, London, E.): *b.* Stratford, London, 1892: enlisted Stratford: served with the Expeditionary Force in France and Flanders from 1 January 1915, and died 8 May following: Age 23. *unm. Buried in Sanctuary Wood Cemetery (V.P.6).*

(Panel 12) Pte. 5/1755, Robert Henderson, 1/5th Bn. The Northumberland Fusiliers (T.F.): formerly no.599, Royal Field Artillery: *s.* of Charles Henderson, by his wife Mary: *b.* Edinburgh: volunteered and enlisted Hebburn-on-Tyne: served with the Expeditionary Force in France and Flanders, and died of wounds 28 April 1915, received from shellfire while in dug-outs nr. Wieltje. He leaves a wife Selina Emily Henderson (6, Birch Terrace, Walker Estate, Newcastle-on-Tyne). (*IWGC record age 19*)

(Panel 12) Pte. 8937, Thomas Henderson, 'Y' Coy., 1st Bn. (5th Foot) The Northumberland Fusiliers: Killed in action 16 June 1915, at Bellewaarde: Age 38. He leaves a wife, Maggie Henderson (Lord Hood Yard, Morpeth), and nine children to mourn his loss. His widow wrote, "In the bloom of life death claimed him. In the prime of his manhood days, None knew him but to love him. None mentioned his name but with praise. His cheery face I'll never forget, Though, years may pass away. As I gaze on your photo that hangs on the wall, Your smiles and your welcome I often recall. I miss you and mourn you in sorrow unseen, And dwell on the memory of days that have been. He died for his country, And lies in a British soldier's grave. That unknown grave is the bitterest blow, None but an aching heart can know."

(Panel 12) Pte. 1229, Robert Heslop, 1/5th Bn. The Northumberland Fusiliers (T.F.): enlisted Walker-on-Tyne: served with the Expeditionary Force in France from 20 April 1915, and was killed in action 2 May 1915. See Pte. J. Bain, Perth Cemetery (China Wall), (II.A.8) and Pte. T. Cuskern (I.L.40); also L/Corpl. T. Hardy, Menin Gate Memorial (Panel 12); Pte. C.D. Wood (Panel 8); Pte. T. Cowen (Addenda Panel 59); and Pte. T. Dodds, Bailleul Communal Cemetery Extension (I.A.161).

(Panel 12) Pte. 8013, Michael King, 'W' Coy., 1st Bn. (5th Foot) The Northumberland Fusiliers: *s.* of Isabella King (4, Ridley Court, Newcastle-on-Tyne): and brother to Pte. 25/1052, C.T. King, 25th Northumberland Fusiliers, killed in action 24 April 1917: *b.* Newcastle-on-Tyne: enlisted there. Killed in action 18 January 1915, Kemmel. The noise from recently installed pumping apparatus (to remove liquid mud and slush from the trenches) drew the attention of the German troops opposite who, in turn, directed their artillery onto the company's trench. Ptes. 5613, J. Ball, 3779, T.E.J. Hampden and 181, A. Paterson were also killed; Pte. 3511, D. Scales died of wounds the following day. Pte. King leaves a wife, Emily, *née* Driscoll, and one child.

His brother Charles also has no known grave; he is commemorated on the Arras (Faubourg d'Amiens) Memorial. Joseph Ball and Thomas Hampden are recorded above, Alexander Paterson (Panel 8); David Scales is buried in Locre Churchyard (II.E.1).

(Panel 12) Pte. 2654, George Litchfield, 2nd Bn. (5th Foot) The Northumberland Fusiliers: *s.* of the late William Litchfield, by his wife Betsy (14, Brixton Road, Old Radford, Nottingham): *b.* Lichfield, co. Stafford: enlisted there. Died 8 May 1915: Age 22. Remains recovered unmarked grave (28.C.23.d.05.85), refers GRU Report, Zillebeke 5.457E; identified – Clothing, Titles, Disc; reinterred, registered 16 January 1931. *Buried in Sanctuary Wood Cemetery (V.N.2).*

For King And Country

PANEL 12 ENDS PTE. J. LITTLEFAIR, NORTHUMBERLAND FUSILIERS.

PANEL 14 BEGINS PTE. T.R. SAUNDERS, THE QUEEN'S.

(Panel 14) Pte. L/10105, Basil Thomas Treffry, 1st Bn. (2nd Foot) The Queen's (Royal West Surrey Regt.): *s.* of Thomas Alfred Treffry, of 16, Bensham Manor Road, Thornton Heath, co. Surrey, by his wife Helen: and brother to Rfn. 553186, R.H. Treffry, 1/16th London Regt. Died 16 August 1917 *b*. Peckham Rye, London, S.E., *c*.1895: enlisted Croydon: served with the Expeditionary Force in France and Flanders, and was killed in action at Ypres, 31 October 1914: Age 19.

His brother Richard also has no known grave; he is recorded on Panel 54.

(Panel 14) Pte. T/201144, Frederick Waterman, 8th (Service) Bn. The Queen's (Royal West Surrey Regt.): *s.* of the late Charles Melbourne Waterman, Fireman; by his wife Maria, *dau.* of William Lovatt: *b*. Croydon, co. Surrey, 17 November 1884: *educ*. Mitcham Road Council School: enlisted Royal West Surrey Regt., 13 October 1914: served with the Expeditionary Force in France and Flanders from 8 May 1917, and was killed in action in Belgium 14 June following. His officer wrote, "He was a splendid soldier and did his duty as such. Although only with my battalion a few weeks, he made many friends. We all sincerely sympathise with you in your great loss.": Age 32. He *m.* Rochester, New York, U.S.A., 27 September 1909, Rosina Alice (16, Cowper Avenue, Sutton, co. Surrey), *dau.* of Joseph Wood, and had two sons – Frederick Joseph Melbourne, *b*. 6 May 1911; Kenneth Albert, *b*. 12 November 1915.

(Panel 14) Pte. G/10377, Edward West, 10th (Service) Bn. The Queen's (Royal West Surrey Regt.): formerly no.22259, Northamptonshire Regt.: *s.* of Jonathan (& Mrs) West, of School Lane, Wymington, nr. Rushden, co. Northampton: and yr. brother to Pte. 43665, W. West, 1st Essex Regt., killed in action 14 April 1917; and Rfn. 7944, S. West, 12th London Regt. (Rangers), died 9 September 1916, of wounds: *b*. Wymington: enlisted Wellingborough. Killed in action 31 July 1917: Age 20.

His brother Wilberforce also has no known grave, he is commemorated on the Arras (Faubourg d'Amiens) Memorial (Bay 7); Stephen is buried in La Neuville British Cemetery (II.C.55).

(Panel 14) Pte. L/9591, Joseph Willows, 2nd Bn. (2nd Foot) The Queen's (Royal West Surrey Regt.): *s.* of H. (& Mrs) Willows, of 84, Hall Place, Paddington, London, W.2: and elder brother to Pte. S/6040, T. Willows, 2nd Queen's, killed in action 7 November 1914: *b*. Islington, *c*.1890: enlisted Guildford, co. Surrey. Killed in action 29 October 1914: Age 24. *unm.* See below.

(Panel 14) Pte. S/6040, Thomas Willows, 2nd Bn. (2nd Foot) The Queen's (Royal West Surrey Regt.): *s.* of H. (& Mrs) Wilows, of 84, Hall Place, Paddington, London, W.2: and yr. brother to Pte. L/9591, J. Willows, 2nd Queen's, killed in action 29 October 1914: *b*. Westminster, *c*.1893: enlisted London. Killed in action 7 November 1914: Age 21. *unm.* See above.

(Panel 14) Pte. T/207035, George Yole, 11th (Service) Bn. The Queen's (Royal West Surrey Regt.): formerly no.299775, Suffolk Regt.: late of Woburn Abbey, co. Bedford: *s.* of Matthew Yole, of 7 Taylor Square, Tavistock, co. Devon, by his wife Ann (34, Fitzford, Tavistock): and brother to Pte. 148536, F. Yole, 78th Canadian Infantry, killed in action 9 April 1917, at Vimy Ridge: *b*. Milton Abbott, co. Devon: enlisted Luton. Killed in action 1 August 1917: Age 35.

His brother Frederick also has no known grave; he is commemorated on the Canadian National Memorial, Vimy.

(Panel 14) Capt. Lawrence Fort, 'A' Coy., 2nd Bn. (3rd Foot) The Buffs (East Kent Regt.): *s.* of John (& Ianthe) Fort, of 48, Earlsfield Road, Hythe, co. Kent, late of 13, DeVere Gardens, Kensington, London, S.W.: and elder brother to Capt. R. Fort, King's Shropshire Light Infantry: *b*. Oswestry, co. Salop, 8 October 1881: *educ*. Cheltenham College; Royal Military College, Sandhurst: joined Army, August 1900: served in the South African War, January 1901 – May 1902, being present at operations in the Transvaal: Queen's Medal, 5 clasps: promoted Lieut. September 1903: received his company October 1911: after the South African War served with his regiment in India, where, as an ardent naturalist and fine shot with both rifle and gun, being specially devoted to big-game shooting, he secured many trophies from elephant downward; indeed, to further this hobby he had intended to leave the Service until the war with Germany interrupted his plans: returned from India, and proceeded to the Front, January 1915: Mentioned in

Despatches by Sir John French, 31 May 1915, and his name twice sent forward for recognition. On 15 February 1915, despite very heavy losses in officers and other ranks, the Buffs succeeded in capturing and holding a German trench. In an attempt to deal with enemy bombers causing nuisance from a further trench, Capt. Fort, with two other officers, ran up the communication trench and he was shot dead at the barricade. One of the other officers was wounded and subsequently taken prisoner. Capt. Fort's commanding officer, Lieut.Col. Geddes, who was himself killed shortly afterwards, wrote, "Your son met his death in a very gallant manner. He had previously distinguished himself by leading a very daring reconnaissance. For this he was Mentioned in Despatches, and I feel sure would have been awarded the D.S.O. had he survived." Age 33.

(Panel 14) Capt. (Adjt) Arthur Oswald Sherren, 4th Bn. The Buffs (East Kent Regt.), (T.F.): *s.* of the late Frederick G. Sherren, by his wife Ellie K. (31, Grange Road, Ramsgate): and brother to Major H.G. Sherren, Royal Army Medical Corps, died 28 February 1920, of typhus: *educ.* Dover College: Assistant Engineer & Surveyor, Dover until 1906, thereafter Surveyor, Cheriton Borough Council: on the outbreak of war was O.C. Dover Coy., 4th Bn. The Buffs, engaged in Coastal Defence with rank Major: served with the Expeditionary Force in France from April 1917, and was killed in action 3 August 1917: Age 38. He was married to Bessie Jane Sherren (118, Folkestone Road, Dover), to whom a fellow officer wrote, "It was while in command of my Company that your husband's portion of the line was subjected to the heaviest shelling from the enemy. He went out to see exactly what the situation was, when he was suddenly struck by a piece of shell. His death was instantaneous and in consequence there was no pain. We buried him as best we could where he fell. Your husband was one of the most popular and dearest officers in the Battalion. No one had anything but the very best opinion of him." He had three children.

His brother Hugh is buried in Haidar Pasha Cemetery, Turkey (I.J.10).

(Panel 14) Capt. Walter Neave Wells, 3rd (Reserve) Bn. The Buffs (East Kent Regt.) attd 'C' Coy., 1st Bn. (60th Foot) The King's Royal Rifle Corps: *s.* of the late Admiral Sir Richard Wells, K.C.B., by his marriage to Lady Augusta Jane Wells, *née* Norman (Warblington Lodge, Havant, co. Hants): *b.* June 1882: *educ.* Girdlestone School, Sunningdale: commissioned 2nd Lieut. The Buffs, November 1900: promoted Lieut. 1904; Capt. March 1906: served in the South African War: took part in operations in Orange River Colony, and Cape Colony (Queen's Medal, five clasps): served with the Expeditionary Force in France and Flanders from 1 October 1914 attd. 1st King's Royal Rifle Corps; joined battalion at Rifleman's Point, Verneuil, 8 October. Shot in the head and killed, nr. Zonnebeke, while leading his company on the 27th of that month. He was a member of the Junior Naval and Military Club, Piccadilly: 27 October 1914: Age 32.

(Panel 14) Lieut. John William Butts Archer, 2nd Bn. (3rd Foot) The Buffs (East Kent Regt.): only *s.* of the Rev. George Archer, Rector of Stilton, Peterborough; by his wife Beatrice, *dau.* of Capt. William Pitt Butts, The Buffs: *b.* Longfield, Halifax, co. York, 14 March 1890: *educ.* Stubbington, in France, and Royal Military Academy, Woolwich: gazetted 2nd Lieut. 5 October 1910; Lieut. 9 March 1912: served Singapore, 1910 – 12, and India, 1912 – 14. Recalled to England at the outbreak of war, arrived home late December and spent a few days at his home in Stilton before proceeding to France, 16 January 1915 The regt. was at once moved up to the firing line at Ypres, where he was wounded in the fighting, 15 February 1915, and died the following day. The story of his death is told in a letter written by his Commanding Officer. It appears that on the night of 15 February (almost exactly one month after he went to France) Lieut. Archer was sent out with his men to the relief of a regiment which was holding a trench which had been attacked by the Germans in the dark. He succeeded in fighting his way to the trench at the expense of half his men and of his own gallant life. The effort to hold the trench was successful. It was Lieut. Archer's task thus to take the lead in the counter-attack which the Brigade made to retake the trenches which had been lost, but the other regiments were so badly knocked about by a bitter shell-fire that they could not get up to support him and his gallant little handful of men, and so the work was splendidly done by this small company themselves. When he fell mortally wounded, they carried him at enormous risk to themselves, into a dug-out in the trench, and here he died about twenty-four hours afterwards, for it was impossible to get him out of the trench and into hospital in the face of the terrible fire which was maintained: Age 24. *unm.*

(Panel 14) Lieut. Arthur William Ramsey, 3rd (Reserve) Bn. The Buffs (East Kent Regt.) attd. 2nd Bn. (108th Foot) Royal Inniskilling Fusiliers: *s.* of H.L. Ramsey, of 16, West Side, Wandsworth Common, London, by his wife Mary: and brother to 2nd Lieut. C.O. Ramsey, 12/13th Northumberland Fusiliers, killed in action 21 March 1918. Killed in action 12 April 1915: Age 26. *unm.*

His brother Charles also has no known grave; he is commemorated on the Pozieres Memorial.

(Panel 14) 2nd Lieut. William Guy Cronk, 3rd (Reserve) Bn. The Buffs (East Kent Regt.) attd. 1st Bn. (60th Foot) The King's Royal Rifle Corps: only *s.* of William Henry Cronk, of Suffolk Place, Sevenoaks, by his wife Winifred Ruth, *dau.* of Lieut.Col. C.N. Kidd: *b.* Sevenoaks, co. Kent, 28 April 1893: *educ.* Eton, and Royal Military Academy, Woolwich: gazetted 2nd Lieut. 3rd Bn. East Kent Regt., 14 March 1914, attd. 1st King's Royal Rifle Corps: went to France early October, and was killed in action 2 miles S.E. of Zonnebeke, 26 October 1914, while leading his platoon in an attack on the enemy trenches: Age 31. *unm.*

(Panel 14) 2nd Lieut. Arthur Edwards, 4th Bn. The Buffs (East Kent Regt.), (T.F.): *s.* of Mr (& Mrs) Edwards, of Highbury, London: Occupation – Solicitor: enlisted London Rifle Bde.: served with the Expeditionary Force in France from November 1914: obtained a commission, and, after training in England returned to France, 2nd Lieut., East Kent Regt., December 1916. Killed in action 16 June 1917: Age 37. He was married to Helen Mary Mills, *née* Edwards ('Haseldene,' 11, Crossmead, Lynton, co. Devon).

(Panel 14) 2nd Lieut. Douglas William Hammond, 2nd Bn. (3rd Foot) The Buffs (East Kent Regt.): only *s.* of Egerton (& Ina) Hammond, of Old Court House, Nonington, co. Kent: and nephew to Lieut. Col. William Whitmore Hammond, of St. Alban's Court, co. Kent: *b.* 1897: *educ.* Castle Park School, Dalkey, Co. Dublin; Marlborough College, and Royal Military College, Sandhurst: gazetted 2nd Lieut., November 1914, attd. 3rd (Reserve) Bn. The Buffs, Dover: served with the Expeditionary Force in France and Flanders from January 1915, joining 2nd Battn. there: invalided home, February following, but rejoined his battalion at the Front in early May, and was killed in action on the 25th of that month, while leading his platoon to recover a trench near Ypres: 25 May 1915: Age 18.

(Panel 14) 2nd Lieut. Arthur Henry Webb, 8th (Service) Bn. The Buffs (East Kent Regt.): elder *s.* of the late Arthur Webb, of 'Dairy House,' Wix, Manningtree, co. Essex, by his wife Sarah Emily ('Oak Lawn,' Wivenhoe, Colchester), *dau.* of James Taylor: *b.* 'Dairy House,' Wix, 18 December 1891: *educ.* Colchester Grammar School (gained the Hewitt Scholarship), and Corpus Christi College, Cambridge (took First Class Honours, Modern Languages Tripos): Occupation – Master; Clifton College, Bristol: volunteered for Active Service on the outbreak of war, but was several times rejected as medically unfit: subsequently accepted; gazetted 2nd Lieut., The Buffs, 8 December 1916: served with the Expeditionary Force in France and Flanders from January 1917, and was killed in action at Hill 60 24 June following. Buried where he fell. Major P. Vaughan wrote, "Never have I known an officer held in more universal esteem, both by officers and men. This was the natural result of his conduct, which at all times was governed by the very highest sense of duty, and which led his Commanding Officer to have the greatest confidence in him. At the time of his death he was leading his men into action, when he was hit by a piece of shell and killed instantaneously." He was devoted to all games, and was a good shot and a good horseman. His knowledge of modern languages obtained for him the offer of a post on a Headquarters Staff, which he declined, preferring to take his chances in the firing line: Age 25. *unm.* (*IWGC record 4th Bn.*)

(Panel 14) Sergt. L/9310, Alfred George Glass, 2nd Bn. (3rd Foot) The Buffs (East Kent Regt.): *s.* of William Richard Glass, of 21, King Street, Milton Regis, Sittingbourne, by his wife Sarah Ann: and *yr.* brother to Pte. L/8659, W. Glass, 1st The Buffs, killed in action, 19 June 1915: *b.* Queensborough, co. Kent: enlisted Chatham: served with the Expeditionary Force in France and Flanders, and was killed in action, north of the Menin Road, 23 May 1915: Age 20. *unm.* Corpl. L. Parker wrote, "Dear Mrs Glass,

I am writing this to you to save delay of news of our son…I regret to inform you that Alfred was killed in action this morning, Sunday, May 23rd., at 7.30. He has been platoon commander for some time, and losing him is not only a great loss to his platoon or company, but to the whole Battalion. He was a man who knew his work, was a fearless man and could always be trusted, and I'm sure will be missed by the officers as well as the men. He was very popular with everyone, on duty or off. There is only one consolation that we have; he suffered no pain for he was killed instantly. I am sure you will feel very grieved at the loss of your son, and we are all very sorry for you here. The whole company sympathises with you. They all wish me to say how sorry they are for you. Should you require any more news of Alfred, I would be only too pleased to forward any information that I am able to, and his Company Officer, I know, would be only too pleased too. As I have no more to say at this time, I will conclude the sympathy of the whole Company being with you…P.S. Sergt. Glass has been buried in a small cemetery just behind the trenches, all comrades possible being at the graveside."

His brother William is buried in Potijze Chateau Wood Cemetery (B.5).

(Panel 14) A/Sergt. L/8406, John Harris, 2nd Bn. (3rd Foot) The Buffs (East Kent Regt.): *s.* of Elizabeth Harris (12, Artillery Hill, Ramsgate, co. Kent): enlisted Ramsgate: served with the Expeditionary Force. Killed in action 3 May 1915: Age 27. He was married to Amy Deverson, *née* Harris (18, Union Street, Canterbury).

(Panel 14) Corpl. L/8510, Thomas Dray, 2nd Bn. (3rd Foot) The Buffs (East Kent Regt.): *b.* Hythe: enlisted Shorncliffe, co. Kent: served with the Expeditionary Force in France from 17 January 1915, and was killed in action nr. Broodseinde Crossroads, Zonnebeke, 11 April 1915, by heavy trench mortar fire.

(Panel 14) L/Corpl. L/8163, James George Fuller, 'B' Coy., 1st Bn. (3rd Foot) The Buffs (East Kent Regt.): *s.* of the late James George Fuller, by his wife Minnie Anne Willett, *née* Fuller (High Street, Burwash, co. Sussex): *b.* Yalding, nr. Maidstone: enlisted Staplehurst, co. Kent: served nine years with his regiment in India, and with the Expeditionary Force in France and Flanders from 8 September 1914: took part in the fighting at the Aisne; Chateau de Flandres, nr. Radinghem (Battle of Armentieres); and is one of two men who have no known grave, killed in company with Lieut. W.F. Taylor and nine other men, 7 June 1915, by the same shell, when the hutted camp in which the men were resting between Poperinghe and Brielen was heavily shelled: Age 34. He was married to the late Jane Fuller, of Maidstone. See Pte. J. Hughes (below).

Lieut. W.F. Taylor is buried in Perth Cemetery (China Wall), (III.A.13).

(Panel 14) L/Corpl. L/8558, Charles Henry Goatham, 2nd Bn. (3rd Foot) The Buffs (East Kent Regt.): *s.* of Edward Goatham, of 23, The Wall, Sittingbourne, by his wife Emma: *b.* Sittingbourne, co. Kent, *c.*1888: enlisted Canterbury. Killed in action, 28 May 1915: Age 27. *unm.* Remains exhumed (GRU Report, Zillebeke 5-306E) unmarked grave (28.I.11.b.6.3); identified – Clothing, Titles, Certificate of Education; reinterred, registered 19 November 1928. *Buried in Sanctuary Wood Cemetery (II.N.10).*

Ever In Our Thoughts
Love Mum

(Panel 14) L/Corpl. L/8660, Stephen John Page, 1st Bn. (3rd Foot) The Buffs (East Kent Regt.): *s.* of the late James William Page, by his wife Frances Harriett (1, Admiralty House, Sittingbourne): and elder brother to Corpl. G/10421, A.G. Page, The Queen's (Royal West Surrey Regt.), killed in action 3 May 1917, at the Battle of Arras: *b.* Ospringe, nr. Faversham enlisted Sittingbourne. Killed in action at Hooge, 9 August 1915: Age 25. *unm.*

His brother Alfred also has no known grave; he is commemorated on the Arras (Faubourg d'Amiens) Memorial (Bay 2).

(Panel 14) Pte. 9548, George William Barnes, 2nd Bn. (3rd Foot) The Buffs (East Kent Regt.): *s.* of Edmund Barnes, of 75, Gibbon Road, Peckham, London, S.E., by his wife Annie (11, Tresco Road, Peckham Rye, London): served with the Expeditionary Force in France. Killed in action 25 May 1915: Age 35 (*IWGC record L/9548*)

(Panel 14) Pte. 180, John Thomas Bean, 2nd Bn. (3rd Foot) The Buffs (East Kent Regt.): eldest *s*. of William Bean, Fruiterer; of 72, Howdon Road, North Shields, by his wife Sarah (Redford): *b*. North Shields, co. Northumberland, 25 December 1872: *educ*. Council School: enlisted Royal Irish Rifles 20 October 1892: served 10 yrs., India: took his discharge 19 October 1904, thereafter worked as a Miner: enlisted The Buffs, Canterbury after the outbreak of war: went to the Front, 14 January 1915, and was killed in action 23 April following, at the 2nd Battle of Ypres, being shot in the abdomen: Age 42. He *m*. North Shields, 1 September 1907; Mary (33, Eastern Terrace, East Howdon, Newcastle-on-Tyne), *dau*. of John Gardner Allen, of Ringwould, nr. Dover, and had a *dau*., Doris Redford, *b*. 23 October 1908.

(Panel 14) Pte. 5120, Alfred George Beaney, 6th (Service) Bn. The Buffs (East Kent Regt.): *yst. s*. of Edward Beaney, of Rolvenden Lane, Rolvenden, by his wife Mary, *dau*. of Stanford Dann: *b*. Bodiam, co. Sussex, 15 November 1899: *educ*. Bodiam Village School: volunteered and enlisted 9th East Kent Regt. 14 December 1914: drafted 6th Battn. (France), October 1915, and was killed in action nr. Ypres 17 November following. A keen cricketer, he was a member of the Great Maytham Team: Age 26. *unm*. (*IWGC record G/5120, 8th Bn.*)

(Panel 14) Pte. G/21167, Sidney Arthur Beaumont, 8th (Service) Bn. The Buffs (East Kent Regt.): *s*. of John Beaumont, Engine Driver; of 51, Durban Road, White Hart Lane, Tottenham, London, N., by his wife Minnie, *dau*. of John Thurton: *b*. Tottenham, London, N., 5 January 1898: *educ*. Lancastrian School: Occupation – Munition Worker: enlisted The Buffs, 24 March 1917: served with the Expeditionary Force in France and Flanders from 1 July following, and was killed in action on the 27th of that month: 27 July 1917: Age 19.

(Panel 14) Pte. G/4930, Eli Chapman, 2nd Bn. (3rd Foot) The Buffs (East Kent Regt.): *s*. of the late George Chapman, of Highview Terrace, Cranbrook, co. Kent, by his wife Mary Ann (School Terrace, Bank Street, Cranbrook): served with the Expeditionary Force in France from 17 January 1915, and was killed in action 2 May 1915. *m*.

(Panel 14) Pte. G/860, Thomas Chittenden, 2nd Bn. (3rd Foot) The Buffs (East Kent Regt.): *s*. of Sylas Chittenden, by his wife Frances: *b*. Halling, co. Kent, 2 August 1875: *educ*. there: served 12 years with the Colours, four years in the Reserve: Occupation – Cement Labourer: rejoined October 1914, after the outbreak of war: went to France 17 January 1915, and was killed in action at Hill 60, Ypres, 1 May following: Age 39. He *m*. Wouldham, nr. Rochester; Louisa (New Road, Burham, near Rochester, co. Kent), *dau*. of Harry Carpenter, and had six children – Douglas, *b*. 20 October 1905; Violet, *b*. 17 April 1908; Thomas, *b*. 20 November 1909; John, *b*. 8 March 1911; Stanley, *b*. 14 May 1913; Francis, *b*. 3 February 1915. (*IWGC record S.860*)

(Panel 14) Pte. L/7787, Edwin Joseph Drew, 2nd Bn. (3rd Foot) The Buffs (East Kent Regt.): *s*. of Richard Drew, of Mill Lane, Upper Deal, co. Kent: *b*. Walmer, co. Kent: enlisted Dover, 1908: served with the Expeditionary Force in France and Flanders, and was killed in action 28 May 1915: Age 30. He was married to Emma Amelia Hammond, *née* Drew, *née* Whiddett (42, Devonshire Road, Dover), and had three children; a fourth child, Josephine, born seven months after her father's death, died 6 June 1916.

(Panel 14) Pte. G/3989, William James Edwards, 2nd Bn. The Buffs (East Kent Regt.): late of Goswell Road, Islington, co. Middlesex: *b*. Deptford: enlisted Walthamstow. Died in enemy hands 30 April 1915, of wounds received in action before Hill 60, Ypres. Buried Oostnieuwkerke Churchyard Cemetery (20.W.3.d.5.4). Remains (Grave 207) exhumed for identification purposes November 1920. The graves of three Unknown British Soldiers (ref. German Grave, 209a and 178) were paid particular attention to 'for the purposes of identification. None found. Dame Adelaide Livingstone informed.' Remains re-exhumed and removed to Langemarck, 7 February 1952. *Buried in Cement House Cemetery (XVII.C.5)*.

(Panel 14) Pte. L/9490, Charles Richard George, 2nd Bn. (3rd Foot) The Buffs (East Kent Regt.): eldest *s*. of Pte. Charles George, R.D. Corps, of 26, Littlewood Road, Lewisham, London, S.E., by his wife Catherine M., *dau*. of Richard Packman; for many years Sexton, Parish Church, Heston, co. Middlesex: and brother to Pte. B/21170, E.H. George, 2nd Highland Light Infantry, killed in action; Beaumont Hamel, Somme, 24 October 1916: *b*. Stratford, co. Essex, 21 August 1893: *educ*. Ennersdale

Road School, Lewisham: enlisted January 1910: served two years in Ireland with 1st Kent Regt.: transf'd. 2nd Battn. and went to India (1912): returned England, December 1914: proceeded to France, January 1915, and died en-route to hospital 14 February 1915, from wounds received in action at Ypres: Age 22. *unm.* (*IWGC record age 23*)

His brother Ernest is buried in Euston Road Cemetery, Colincamps (III.O.3).

(Panel 14) Pte. S/10770, Edward Aubrey Hickmott, 2nd Bn. (3rd Foot) The Buffs (East Kent Regt.): late of Cardiff, co. Glamorgan: *s.* of the late Edward Richard Hickmott, by his wife Fanny Flora (41, Victoria Road, Tunbridge Wells): *husb.* to the late Elizabeth Margaret Hickmott: and elder brother to 2nd Lieut. S.R. Hickmott, Queen's Own (Royal West Kent Regt.), died 1 October 1918, of wounds: *b.* Woolwich, co. Kent: enlisted there. Killed in action 14 April 1915: Age 35.

His brother Sydney also has no known grave, he is commemorated on the Tyne Cot Memorial (Panel 106).

(Panel 14) Pte. G/561, Haywood Thomas Holmes (served as Haywood, T.H.), 1st Bn (3rd Foot) The Buffs (East Kent Regt.): *s.* of Haywood Edward Holmes, of Margate, co. Kent, by his wife Jessie Alice: *b.* St. John's. Margate. Killed in action 9 April 1916: Age 18. *Buried in La Brique Military Cemetery No.2 (I.U.20).*

(Panel 14) Pte. L/9716, George Hoare, 2nd Bn. (3rd Foot) The Buffs (East Kent Regt.): 3rd *s.* of Alfred Hoare, Agricultural Labourer; of 'Whitehill Cottages,' Style Farm, Chilham, co. Kent, by his wife Fanny, *née* Hubbard: and elder brother to Pte. S/10552, D.P. Hoare, East Kent Regt. (surv'd.), and Pte. 503518, H. Hoare, Royal West Kent Regt. (surv'd.), and *yr.* brother to John Hoare, Munitions Worker, Explosives Loading Co. Ltd., Powder Mill, Upper Marshes, Faversham, died 2 April 1916: *b.* Chilham, September 1894: enlisted Canterbury: served with the Expeditionary Force in France and Flanders from 17 January 1915. Reported missing / believed killed in action following an enemy attack on the Buffs trenches, Verlorenhoek, 3 May 1915: Age 20. *unm.*

His brother John is commemorated on the Faversham Gunpowder Mill Explosion Memorial, Faversham Cemetery.

(Panel 14) Pte. S/108, John Hughes, 1st Bn. (3rd Foot) The Buffs (East Kent Regt): late of St. John's, Liverpool, co. Lancaster: enlisted Sittingbourne, co. Kent. One of two men who have no known grave, killed in company with Lieut. W.F. Taylor and nine other men, 7 June 1915, by the same shell, when the hutted camp in which the men were resting between Poperinghe and Brielen was heavily shelled. See. L/ Corpl. J.G. Fuller, above.

Lieut. W.F. Taylor is buried in Perth Cemetery (China Wall), (III.A.13).

(Panel 14) Pte. G/5186, Arthur John Jarvest, 2nd Bn. (3rd Foot) The Buffs (East Kent Regt.): *s.* of Mrs M. Jarvest (48, Tower Hamlets Road, Dover): enlisted Dover, co. Kent. Missing / believed killed in action 3 May 1915, at Verlorenhoek: Age 32.

(Panel 14) Pte. G/18243, Stanley Killick, 8th (Service) Bn. The Buffs (East Kent Regt.): *s.* of the late Francis Killick (*d.*1913), of Crawley, co. Sussex, by his wife Maria: and brother to Pte. 15950, J. Killick, 13th Royal Sussex Regt., killed in action 26 October 1916, in the closing stages of the Somme fighting; and R.S.M. 11032, F. Killick, Royal Field Artillery, who, after being invalided home (July 1918), was committed to Hellingly Asylum where he died 6 February 1919: *b.* Crawley, 1884: enlisted Horsham: served with the Expeditionary Force, and was killed in action at Messines 14 June 1917: Age 33.

His brother John also has no known grave, he is recorded on the Thiepval Memorial, Somme; Frank is buried in St. Michael's Churchyard, Lowfield Heath.

(Panel 14) Pte. G/4786, Albion Frederick Knott, 2nd Bn. (3rd Foot) The Buffs (East Kent Regt.): *s.* of the late Albion Knott, of Mill Lane, Eastry, co. Kent, by his wife Amy (22. Moat Sole, Sandwich): and brother to Pte. 17377, W.H. Knott, 8th Somerset Light Infantry, killed in action 15 November 1916: *b.* Eastry: enlisted Dover. Killed in action 24 May 1915: Age 20.

His brother William also has no known grave; he is commemorated on the Thiepval Memorial (Pier & Face 2A).

(Panel 14) Pte. L/9193, Bertie Moss, 2nd Bn. (3rd Foot) The Buffs (East Kent Regt.): late of Nunhead, co. Kent: *s.* of Jane Moss (Walden Road, Twyford Avenue, Portsmouth, co. Hants): and elder brother to Dvr. 2242, H.M. Moss, Royal Field Artillery, died 6 February 1916, at High Wycombe, co. Buckingham: *b.* Bury St. Edmunds, co. Suffolk: enlisted Shorncliffe, co. Kent: served with the Expeditionary Force in France and Flanders from 17 January 1915, and was one of five other ranks killed in action nr. Broodseinde Crossroads, Zonnebeke, 11 April following, by heavy trench mortar fire; the battalion's first experience of this weapon: Age 25. *unm.*

His brother Harold is buried in Dover (Charlton) Cemetery (Z.L.32).

PANEL 14 ENDS PTE. E.J. PARTRIDGE, EAST KENT REGT. (THE BUFFS).

PANEL 16 BEGINS PTE. R.C. MATHEWS, 2ND. REGT. SOUTH AFRICAN INF.

(Panel 16) Pte. 517, Cyril William Arnot, 3rd South African Infantry Regt., S.A.E.F.: 2nd *s.* of the late Frederick Stanley Arnot, F.R.G.S., Pioneer Missionary, Belgian Congo, Central Africa; by his wife Harriette Jane ('Raywood,' Westmeath Road, Park View, Johannesburg, Transvaal), *dau.* of William B. Fisher: *b.* Liverpool, 8 July 1896: *educ.* Redland Hill, Bristol, and Jeppe High School, Johannesburg: Occupation – Junior Clerk, National Bank, Johannesburg: enlisted, August 1915: arrived England, October 1915: served with the Egyptian Expeditionary Force, Egypt, January – May 1916, thereafter proceeding to France: wounded at Delville Wood, and Warlencourt: returned to France after four months in hospital, and was killed on the Ypres-Roulers Road, during the Third Battle of Ypres, 20 September 1917. Buried between Frezenberg Ridge and Zonnebeke Ridge. His Sergt. wrote, "There was no man in the battalion better liked by those who knew him, or more genuinely respected;" and another, "He had not much to say about religion, but let his daily life show it; he was a fellow who made one wish to be better while in his company and afterwards.": Age 21. *unm.*

The records of the Commonwealth War Graves Commission record 171 men with the surname England having made the supreme sacrifice during the Great War 1914–1919; of which 36 (32 UK, 3 Can., 1 S/Afr.) are buried or commemorated within the confines of the Ypres Salient. Rifleman Donald Cox wrote:–

> *If I should fall, grieve not that one so weak*
> *And poor as I*
> *Should die.*
> *Nay! Though thy heart should break*
> *Think only this: that when at dusk they speak*
> *Of sons and brothers of another one,*
> *Then thou canst say – 'I too had a son;*
> *He died for England's sake!'*

At 5.40 a.m., 20 September 1917, 3rd and 4th South African Infantry Regiments (supported by 1st and 2nd) were the leading battalions of the Brigade in 9th Division's attack towards Zonnebeke. Taking the Red Line in their stride, with the 3rd Regt. assisting the Royal Scots (right flank) in taking Potsdam, while 4th Battalion entered Borry Farm, the assault on the Blue and Green lines was carried on by 1st and 2nd Battalions. 1st Battalion reached their objective without any opposition, but the 2nd came under considerable fire from Waterend House, Tulip Cottages and Hill 37 in 55 Division's sector (left flank). Despite these difficulties the 2nd took the Bremen Redoubt and Zevenkote, and then threw out a defensive flank to the south of Zonnebeke until 55 Division caught up with them. During this action L/Corpl. W.H. Hewitt won the Victoria Cross, but many who took part never saw the close of day.

(Panel 16) Pte. 10996, Reginald England, 3rd South African Infantry Regt., S.A.E.F.: *s.* of William Edward Otway England, of 21, 30th Street, Malvern, Johannesburg, Transvaal, by his wife Florence

Charlotte. 'England by name, he died for England and our sake'. Killed in action 20 September 1917: Age 19.

(Panel 16) 2nd Lieut. Donald MacDonald, M.M., 4th South African (Scottish) Infantry Regt., S.A.E.F.: 5th *s.* of Donald MacDonald, of Market Hill, Glass, by his wife Margaret, *dau.* of Thomas Duncan: and brother to Pte. Duncan MacDonald (also killed in action): *b.* Glass, co. Aberdeen, 31 January 1881: *educ.* Public School, Glass: went to South Africa, age 21, and worked as a Carpenter; subsequently became a partner in the firm of F. Dey, Builders & Contractors, Pretoria: joined Transvaal Scottish, 1908; served four years: volunteered for Foreign Service 15 December 1915; joined 4th Bn. South African Infantry, rank Sergt.: served with the Expeditionary Force in France and Flanders from 25 July 1916: received a commission as 2nd Lieut. In the Field, and was killed in action nr. Langemarck, 22 October 1917. Buried there: Age 36. awarded the Military Medal ('*London Gazette*,' 9 April 1917), for 'bravery in the field.' He *m.* St. Andrew's Presbyterian Church, Pretoria, 18 December 1913, Miriam Rose (19, South Parade, Blossom Street, late of 15, Bishophill Senior, York), *dau.* of John Shepherdson: *s.p.*

(Panel 16) Sergt. 5304, Donald Gordon Douglas, 4th South African (Scottish) Infantry Regt., S.A.E.F.: *s.* of the late Richard Magenis Douglas, of Portballantrae, Bushmills, Co. Antrim, J.P., by his wife Julie (Ashby House, Hornsea, co. York), *dau.* of James Bonorandi: *b.* Portballantrae, Co. Antrim, 21 May 1886: *educ.* Moravian School, Ballymena; Foyle College, Londonderry: enlisted 1901: served in the South African War 1899 – 1902 (Queen's Medal, two clasps): took part in the Natal and Zulu Rebellions (Medal & Clasp): served in the German West African Campaign, 1914; afterwards returned to England: underwent further training at Borden Camp: sent to Egypt, 1915, thereafter to France, where he took part in the Delville Wood engagement, July 1916, and was killed in action nr. Zonnebeke 20 September 1917. Buried there. His Commanding Officer wrote, "It is my painful duty to inform you your son was fatally wounded at my side this morning (20 September). He fell to a sniper's bullet when the position was captured and victory complete for the moment. Your son was my right arm in the taking of the objective that fell to the lot of my platoon. A moment or so previously I had a marvellous escape myself, being struck by a bullet on the steel helmet. It was your son's great boldness and bravery that took him to the fatal spot to reconnoitre the resistance so as to deal with it. He was struck in the stomach and died almost immediately, but not before we had brought him into safety. Your son was buried in the neighbourhood of the 'strongpoint,' and a cross put up bearing his name and that of his regiment. Killed in action. I write you with a full heart, your son was a brave and great-hearted man. I feel his loss very much indeed; he came into action as Platoon Sergt., being there to take charge in the case of me falling. Sixteen men and me were all that came out of that action, and all these wish me to express their sincere sympathy with you in your bereavement." Age 31. *unm.* (*IWGC record L/Sergt.*)

(Panel 16) Corpl. 9160, Gordon Galletly Scott, 4th South African (Scottish) Infantry Regt., S.A.E.F.: *s.* of Major (& Mrs) M.A.J. Scott, of Scott Inverugie House, Kenilworth, Cape Province: and *yr.* brother to Major S. Scott, M.C., 19th Battn. Machine Gun Corps (Inf.), who fell 6 June 1918: *educ.* Wynberg Boys' High School, Cambridge Road (founded 1822): served with the Expeditionary Force in France and Flanders from March 1916, and was killed in action, 10 April 1918: Age 23.

His brother Stanley is buried in Terlincthun British Cemetery (XVI.B.15).

(Panel 16) L/Corpl. 8302, Robert Erskine Christie, 4th South African (Scottish) Infantry Regt., S.A.E.F.: 3rd *s.* of the late Dougall Christie, M.A., by his wife Mary (35, Mile End Avenue, Aberdeen), *dau.* of Alex Cran, M.D.: *b.* Kildrummy, co. Aberdeen, 13 January 1884: *educ.* Gordon's College, Aberdeen: went to South Africa, 1900; took part in the South African War, 1899 – 1902 (Queen's Medal, three clasps): served in German West Africa, 1914 – 15: came to England, March 1916: served with the Expeditionary Force in France from March, and was killed in action on the Messines Ridge,11 April 1918: Age 34. *unm.*

(Panel 16) L/Corpl. 11164, Alexander Methven, 4th South African (Scottish) Infantry Regt., S.A.E.F.: *s.* of the late Cathcart William Methven, of 'Bayswater,' 465, Bartle Road, Umbilo, by his wife

Amy ('Carwin,' Manderston, Natal): and elder brother to Pte. 9265, C.A. Methven, 2nd South African Infantry Regt., killed in action 25 September 1918. Killed in action 20 April 1917: Age 34.

His brother Charles is buried in Glageon Communal Cemetery Extension (I.H.6).

PANEL 16 ENDS PTE. W.H.M. SMITH, 4TH REGT. SOUTH AFRICAN INF.

PANEL 16A BEGINS PTE. O.E. SPILLER, 4TH REGT. SOUTH AFRICAN INF.

PANEL 16A ENDS PTE. W.A. WYLLIE, 4TH REGT. SOUTH AFRICAN INF.

South Portal (Left)

PANEL 18 BEGINS PTE. BANBROOK, 2ND BN. CANADIAN INFANTRY.

(Panel 18) Pte. 8525, George Eccles Bulleid, 2nd Bn. Canadian Infantry (Eastern Ontario Regt.), C.E.F.: *s.* of the late John Bulleid, of Plumstead, by his wife Lena (41, Lyndeoch Street, Greenock): *b.* Plumstead, co. Kent, 6 October 1895: sometime went to Canada, settled Smith's Falls, Ontario, found employ as Blacksmith: enlisted Base No.60, Valcartier, 22 September 1914, apparent age 18 years, 11 months, height 5'7", weight 184 pounds: embarked aboard S.S. Lassandra for England, 3 October 1914: went to France after a short period of training, and was with his battalion when it moved up to the front immediately before the German gas attack at St. Julien, 22 April 1915, subsequent upon which the men of 2nd, 3rd, 13th, and 15th battalions, unprepared and overwhelmed by enemy infantry and chlorine gas, suffered horrendous casualties. Reported missing, officially presumed killed, on that date; he had been a member of the Canadian Expeditionary Force for exactly seven months to the day: 22 April 1915: Age 20. *unm.* (*IWGC record age 15*)

(Panel 18) Pte. 8423, William Lockhard Campbell, 2nd Bn. Canadian Infantry (Eastern Ontario Regt.), C.E.F.: *s.* of William James Campbell, of Carleton Place, Ontario: *b.* Owen Sound, 10 May 1896: served with the Expeditionary Force in France, and was killed at the Battle of Ypres 25 April 1915. In a letter written to his mother the day before his death Pte. Campbell said, "I am writing to you again to let you know I am still alive and well, hoping everyone at home is same. Well, mother we are just beginning to realise what this war means to the Belgian people. There have been scores of people coming through this place this morning who have been chased out of house and home just this week back. You see old women, who have no other way of transporting their belongings, carrying larger and heavier packs than we carry on the march. Some of the farmers we had to get out and see them coming along with their horses and wagons loaded to the limit. I don't suppose any of them know where they are going to get a house of any kind to sleep in again. It makes a person vow vengeance on those who are causing their suffering. This week back we have been through a part of Belgium which has not been touched by the Germans and it certainly is a nice country. But still it isn't like it would be in peace time for there are refugees all through the country. There has been a lot of heavy fighting this last few days. There are loads of wounded coming through here all the time. It won't be long before we are at them, the Germans I mean, again, and there won't be any fun in it this time either, for the Germans seem to be determined to break through now or never...From your son, Lockhard." In reply to a letter from a friend, Samuel Crampton, a comrade Pte. 8476, James McGill, wrote, "In reference to your letter of June 9th, I am sorry to state that poor Lockhard is gone to a better land, dying the death of a brave soldier without a stain upon his conscience. He was always a good soldier and did all his work willingly and few ever heard him grumble. I have been with him since we left home and always found him ready to obey any command. As he was counted a good shot, with nerve enough to obey all orders, he was one of the picked men to go into this house between two firing lines for sniping purposes, or in other words to shoot off all stray Germans who were inclined to creep up for to study our positions. We held this house for three days till the enemy made his big advance on April 25th. By advancing on the French on our right, and driving them back by the use of that murderous mustard gas, part of our contingent were obliged to counter-attack the advance of the enemy which caused us a great deal of anxiety. In the meantime they also advanced on our left in an angling position, completely cutting us off in this house. A number of the boys being wounded we were obliged to get back to our trenches as quickly and quietly as possible so the Captain sent six of us out first and watched results. That was where poor Lockhard met his death by a bullet in the head. It was instant death, causing no pain, which was a blessing when we think of what some of the boys suffered on account of not being able to be moved. I cannot get any trace of many of the other boys, but I expect they are prisoners along with the Captain. I am in a lovely hospital in England getting the best of care and expect to be got out again before long. If there is any other information that you may want don't delay in writing to me and will do all I can to ease the wound it has caused to his kind parents whom I knew well. Please give my sincerest sympathy to his parents as his was a death to be proud of, dying for the honour of his country." (*IWGC record 22 April 1915*)

(Panel 18) Pte. 8536, Ezra Chard, 2nd Bn. Canadian Infantry (Eastern Ontario Regt.), C.E.F.: *s.* of John Chard, of Frankford, Ontario: and brother to Pte. 636293, J. Chard, 21st Canadian Infantry, killed in action 3 – 4 November 1917, at Passchendaele: *b.* Frankford, 12 April 1893: Occupation – Labourer: a serving member of 49th Regt. (Militia); enlisted 23 September 1914: came over with 2nd Canadian Contingent. Killed in action 22 April 1915, at St. Julien: Age 22. *unm.* (*IWGC record age 21*)

His brother John is buried in Tyne Cot Cemetery (XXXV.H.6).

(Panel 18) Pte. 7947, Thomas Elisha Coe, 2nd Bn. Canadian Infantry (Eastern Ontario Regt.), C.E.F.: *s.* of Leonard Burrell Coe, of 4, St. Mary's Avenue, Harrogate, co. York, by his wife Emma: *b.* Harrogate, 15 November 1885: *educ.* there: sometime employed as Clerk; Electrical Engineers' Office, Harrogate Corporation: removed to Canada, June 1912: prior to enlistment was Book-keeper; Hudson Bay Company: volunteered and enlisted, Valcartier, 1 September 1914: 5'4" tall, fair complexion, brown eyes, fair hair: 4 vaccination marks left arm, birthmark outside right leg: posted 6th Battn. 22 September 1914: came over with First Canadian Contingent October following: underwent further training in England during winter 1914 – 1915: subsequently transfd. 2nd Battn. serving with that unit in France and Flanders until his death. The exact circumstances regarding the fate of Pte. Coe are unknown; his father received a letter from the War Department, 15 May 1915, reporting his son recorded missing / seriously wounded, 22 April 1915. Shortly thereafter Mrs Coe received the following detailed letter from a comrade, "I think you will be somewhat prepared for the sad news I have to give. I have just been putting it off, hoping against hope that I might have some hope to give you, but I am afraid there is none. I did not take this duty upon myself as it was Tom's last request to me. He asked me to take your last letter to him out of his pocket, and let you become acquainted with the circumstances. You will no doubt think I have been dilatory, but when I explain you will absolve me. Up to the morning of the 23rd, the 10th Platoon had seen some fierce fighting, with Tom always to the fore. You would have been proud of him if you had seen him on that red day. But on the 23rd our platoon was taken out to reinforce the most advanced point on the line. To get there we had to cross a very exposed piece of ground under a very heavy fire from the German machine guns. We were dodging across singly at about 50 yard intervals. Tom was following me, suddenly I heard him call 'Bert, Bert! Oh, Bert!' I knew he was hurt and immediately dashed back. 'Where are you hit Tom?' I asked. 'In the stomach,' he replied. I took off his equipment etc. and pulled him into the shade, and made him as comfortable as possible. Then I examined his wound. I soon realised it was mortal. Tom himself had already realised it. Oh, how brave and cool he was. You may grieve for your own sake Mrs Coe, but never grieve for Tom's. If I can die and behave in the face of death as he did, I shall be quite content! He was quite conscious all the time I was with him, and though he suffered terribly at first, the pain soon left him. He asked me to write and tell you how it happened, and I promised I would. I had to leave him then. The position was critical and every man was needed. Later on our battalion was almost surrounded and we had to retire and fight our way through, but as we held the position for several hours and several of our men had been killed or wounded at the same place and time as Tom, I was hoping that he had been taken in by the stretcher bearers. Since then I have been badgering the powers that be and the hospital authorities trying to find him. The only record I could find said 'T. Coe, Wounded & Missing.' I got the Chaplain to help me but he could find nothing more. And now I have given you all the information I have. Oh, he just said as we shook hands. 'I have finished Bert, but I did my best.' .. I will close now. With my deepest sympathy. I remain Tom's friend and yours, Bert Holgate." A member of the Wesleyan Church, prior to emigrating Pte. Coe was a member of the Harrogate Y.M.C.A., and a chorister at St. Mary's Church: Age 29. *unm.*

(Panel 18) Pte. 7966, Michael Fox, 2nd Bn. Canadian Infantry (Eastern Ontario Regt.), C.E.F.: *s.* of the late Michael Fox, by his wife Mary: served in France and Flanders, and was killed in action 22 – 26 April 1915: Age 31. (*IWGC record 24 April*)

(Panel 18) Pte. 7969 William Gray, 2nd Bn. Canadian Infantry (Eastern Ontario Regt.), C.E.F.: 6th *s.* of the late Henry Gray, of 3, Queen's Road, Aberdeen, J.P., Merchant; by his wife Helen Mackay, *dau.* of George Mackay, Aberdeen: *b.* Aberdeen, 1 January 1882: *educ.* Aberdeen Grammar School, and University of Art Classes: went to Winnipeg, Canada, 1903, afterwards settled at Vancouver, B.C.: Occupation – Real Estate Agent: enlisted C.E.F. on the outbreak of war: left Valcartier for England with 2nd Battn., 1st Brigade Contingent: went to France, January 1915, and was killed by a bullet through the brain 23 April 1915: Age 33. *unm.* (*IWGC record 22 April, 1915*)

(Panel 18) Pte. 413117, George Heron, 2nd Bn. Canadian Infantry (Eastern Ontario Regt.), C.E.F.: *b.* Edinburgh, Scotland: removed to Canada with his parents: initially settled Trenton, Ontario, moved to Port Hope, 1902: prior to enlistment 39th Battn., March 1915, was employee Standard Ideal factory: proceeded overseas June 1915: subsequently transfd. 2nd Battn.: served with the Expeditionary Force in France and Flanders: took part in the fighting at Ypres, Somme, and other places. At the time of his death he was engaged on a work party putting out wire entanglements in front of the trenches when the enemy exploded a mine killing him and a number of his comrades 25 July 1916. Affectionately known as 'Scotty' his comrades spoke of him as most cheerful under all circumstances, and the life of every party with which he associated. An accomplished flute player and valued member of the Port Hope Band, he carried his flute into action with him, often playing it to good effect whenever those around him were of a despondent mind. On one occasion, when his flute was lost, such was his versatility he gave an impromptu imitation on a tin whistle. His loss is deeply felt by all who knew him.

(Panel 18) Pte. 402815, Thomas Irwin Earl Riddolls, 2nd Bn. Canadian Infantry (Eastern Ontario Regt.), C.E.F.: *s.* of Thomas Henry Riddolls, of Drayton, Ontario; *husb.* to the late Eliza Ann Riddolls: *b.* Drayton, 5 May 1895: Religion – Wesleyan / Presbyterian: Occupation – Student: Cadet Corps member; volunteered Guelph, 18 January 1915; apptd. 2nd Battn., 25 January: joined 2nd Battalion in France with a draft of reinforcements following losses at St. Julien. Reported missing / believed killed, since confirmed killed in action 26 April 1916. 'Whilst acting as a bomber at Hill 60, Zillebeke, the enemy detonated a mine immediately beneath his section, blowing up Pte. Riddolls and the comrades who were with him with the debris. Death is believed to have been instantaneous.' Buried 28.I.29.d.1.7; Cross erected Woods Cemetery: Age 19.

(Panel 18) Pte. 603266, Henry Victor Tarr, 2nd Bn. Canadian Infantry (Eastern Ontario Regt.), C.E.F.: *s.* of William Tarr, of West Monkton, Ontario: and *yr.* brother to L/Corpl. 401118, F. Tarr, 15th Canadian Infantry, killed 6 November. 1917, at Passchendaele. Killed in action 25 July 1916: Age 20.

His brother Frank also has no known grave; he is recorded on Panel 24.

(Panel 18) Pte. 7910, Rodolphe Tassé, 2nd Bn. Canadian Infantry (Eastern Ontario Regt.), C.E.F.: *s.* of Joseph Tassé, of 23C, St. Andrew Street, Ottawa: *b.* 10 November 1892. Killed in action 22 April 1915: Age 22. In May 2014, a young lady – Megan, of Ottawa, Canada – visited the Salient as part of a tour marking the 100th Anniversary of the outbreak of the Great War. Prior to departing from her home in Canada she penned – "Dear Rodolphe Tassé, I wanted to write you a letter to let you know you would be remembered. I don't really know much about you personally. I know your father lived in Ottawa, I know you fought in the second battalion of the Canadian Expeditionary Forces, and I know you died in Ypres, Belgium, on April 22nd. 1915 when you were only 21. I don't know what you looked like, or what you sounded like, or who you really were; I do know what you sacrificed. I know it was a time when many young men felt the excitement of going to war and were eager to join the fray without knowing how horrible it would be. I know not all men felt this way, and some were pressured to join by society. Regardless of how you came to be in the Army and regardless of your story or dreams, you joined, you helped to win a war believed to be an end to all wars; I think that a noble cause...It's funny that we were born over 100 years apart and would have never met. I'll see where you rest and will remember you." Unaware Rodolphe has no known resting place, appropriately Megan left the above letter at the Canadian Memorial, Vancouver Corner, St. Julien.

(Panel 18) Pte. 23063, George White, 2nd Bn. Canadian Infantry (Eastern Ontario Regt.), C.E.F.: *s.* of John White, of Niagara Falls, South Ontario, by his wife Esther: and elder brother to Pte. 2293, S.H. White, 2nd Bn., killed in action, 26 April 1915, at the Second Battle of Ypres,: killed in action, 11 June 1916: Age 21.

His brother Stanley also has no known grave; he is recorded below.

(Panel 18) Pte. 2293, Stanley Harding White, 2nd Bn. Canadian Infantry (Eastern Ontario Regt.), C.E.F.: *s.* of John White, of Niagara Falls, South Ontario, by his wife Esther: and yr. brother to Pte. 23063, G. White, 2nd Canadian Infantry, killed in action, 11 June 1916. Killed in action at the Second Battle of Ypres, 26 April 1915: Age 20.

His brother George also has no known grave; he is recorded above.

(Panel 18) Capt. George Crowther Ryerson, 3rd Bn. (Royal Grenadiers) Canadian Infantry (1st Central Ontario Regt.), C.E.F.: eldest *s.* of Surgeon Major-Gen. George Sterling Ryerson, of Niagara-on-the Lake, Toronto, Ontario; President, Red Cross Society, Canada; and his late wife Mary Amelia Ryerson, lost at sea when R.M.S. 'Lusitania' was torpedoed and sunk, 7 May 1915: and nephew to Chief Justice Sir William Mulock, former Postmaster-General, Canada; and Arthur L. Ryerson, of Haverford, lost at sea when R.M.S. 'Titanic' sank in the North Atlantic, 15 April 1912: *b.* Toronto, 21 October 1883: *educ.* Model School, Upper Canada College (Graduate); University of Toronto (Applied Science), 1902 – 05: Occupation – Insurance Broker, Messrs Mitchell & Ryerson: apptd. Lieut., Royal Grenadiers, 1903; promoted Capt. 1912: served with the Expeditionary Force in France and Flanders from 11 February 1915. Killed 4 a.m., 23 April 1915, leading his Company against overwhelming odds, and under heavy machine gun and artillery fire, from trench C.22 (nr. Brielen) to the attack at the Battle of St. Julien, nr. Ypres (wounded at the same instant, Pte. 9946, C.F. Payne died later that day). Capt. Ryerson belonged to the University Club, Canadian Military Institute, Royal Canadian Yacht Club, and the Alpha Delta Phi Fraternity: Age 31. *unm.* His sister Laura Mary, also aboard the Lusitania, was rescued. (*IWGC record age 32*)

Pte. C.F. Payne also has no known grave, he is recorded below.

(Panel 18) Capt. William Henry Victor Van der Smissen, 'C' Coy., 3rd Bn. Canadian Infantry (Central Ontario Regt.), C.E.F.: *s.* of William Henry Van der Smissen, of 15, Surrey Place, Toronto: served with the Expeditionary Force in France: took part in the fighting at St. Julien during the Second Battle of Ypres, Givenchy and Festubert: proceeded on leave 27 December 1915; returned to France 6 January 1916, and was killed at Mount Sorrel at the end of a hard day's fighting, 13 June 1916, by a shell which made a direct hit on the headquarters dug-out moments before handing over his trench to the relieving battalion (Lieut.Col. F.A. Creighton was fatally wounded by the same shell). A brother officer wrote, "We have just come out of a most splendid fight, they called out the old lot to get back the lost ground, and we got it. Victor was simply magnificent. We attacked shortly after 1 a.m., and had the Huns driven right out into their own lines in less than an hour. Then we had to hold on. Through the attack and throughout the day Victor was just an inspiration to everyone about him, cool-headed, absolutely self-controlled, and without a sign of fear or nervousness. But just before we were relieved a shell got him, and he died a soldier's death on the ground he had won and held. We shall miss him terribly. He was one of the very best, loved and respected by all of us, worshipped by his men. But he went out in a splendid and successful battle, knowing that we had succeeded, doing his duty and unafraid, the death he would have chosen." For many years prior to the outbreak of war an affectionate and brotherly friendship had existed between Capt. Van der Smissen and Lieut. G.L.B. Mackenzie; and in the home of Victor's parents, be it in the city or the summer retreat at Go Home Bay, George was always received as a son of the house: Age 23. *unm.*

Lieut.Col. Creighton died of his wounds three days later (*IWGC record 19th*), he is buried in Lijssenthoek Military Cemetery (VI.A.26); Lieut. George Mackenzie died one week previously of wounds received in action at Sanctuary Wood, he too is buried in Lijssenthoek Military Cemetery (VI.A.17).

(Panel 18) Lieut. Henry Russell Gordon, 3rd Bn. Canadian Infantry (1st Central Ontario Regt.), C.E.F.: *s.* of Henry B. Gordon, of 35, Kendal Avenue, Toronto, by his marriage to the late Mary Reynolds: *b.* Toronto, 10 April 1891: *educ.* Private Institution for Very Young Boys, Northern Toronto; St. Alban's School; University College, Toronto (English & History Classics), 1908 – 12, B.A.; Historical Club member: Occupation – Reporter; '*Toronto Daily Star*': member of 2nd Regt. (Militia); enlisted 3rd Bn. C.E.F., August 1914: came over with 1st Canadian Contingent, October following: served with the Expeditionary Force in France from February 1915: took part in the 2nd Battle of Ypres and fighting throughout 1915: subsequent to being promoted Corpl. he was selected for (and obtained) a commission 1916. Reported missing – last seen making his way toward the rear wounded – following the capture of Mount Sorrel on the night of 12 – 13 June 1916; later reported believed killed in the early hours of the 13th: Age 25. *unm.* His very good friends (from his days at the Private Institution for Very Young Boys) Lieuts. W.D.P. Jarvis and G.L.B. Mackenzie also made the supreme sacrifice.

Lieut. William 'Bill' Jarvis also has no known grave, he is recorded below; Lieut. George Mackenzie, died one week previously of wounds received in action, is buried in Lijssenthoek Military Cemetery (VI.A.17).

(Panel 18) Lieut. Hugh Mackay Grasett, 'B' Coy., 3rd Bn. Canadian Infantry (1st Central Ontario Regt.), C.E.F.: *s.* of Henry James Grasett, of Barrie, Ontario, by his wife Mary: *b.* Waterloo, 3 February 1894: *educ.* Barrie Public School; Barrie Collegiate; Bishop Ridley College, Toronto (Applied Science), 1912 – 14, Phi Kappa Pi: member 2nd Regt. (Militia); enlisted 3rd Bn. C.E.F., August 1914, apptd. L/Corpl.: served with the Expeditionary Force in France from February 1915, Armentieres sector: invalided to England, March following: returned to France, 2 May 1915: served through the battles of Festubert, Givenchy, and in the Ploegsteert sector: given a commission 3rd Battn., August 1915: after a period of training, England, returned to France, January 1916, and was killed in action 13 June 1916. During the attack on Mount Sorrel he was the first to bring up reinforcements to an advanced position held by an officer with a small party against an encircling movement by the enemy. Just as he reached this post he was wounded in the face, but remained at duty and was placed in command by the officer, who was wounded, and held the position until further reinforcements arrived. Shortly afterwards he was killed instantly, being shot through the head while leading a party of bombers in clearing the enemy out of shell holes. Buried where he fell: Age 22. *unm.* His friend and university fraternity colleague, Lieut. G.L.B. Mackenzie died one week previously of wounds received in the vicinity of Sanctuary Wood.

Lieut. George Mackenzie is buried in Lijssenthoek Military Cemetery (VI.A.17).

(Panel 18) Lieut. William 'Bill' Dummer Powell Jarvis, 'C' Coy., Toronto Regt., 3rd Bn. Canadian Infantry (1st Central Ontario Regt.), 1st Infantry Bde., C.E.F.: eldest *s.* of Æmilius Jarvis, of 34, Prince Arthur Avenue, Toronto, Canada, Banker, for many years Commodore, Royal Canadian Yacht Club, and Hon. Lieut.Col., Governor-General's Body Guard, by his wife Augusta, 2nd *dau.* of the late Sir Æmilius Irving, of Toronto, K.C.: *b.* Toronto, 31 March 1892: *educ.* Private Institution for Very Young Boys, Northern Toronto; Bishop Ridley College, St. Catherine's, Toronto: member Toronto Stock Exchange; representing his father's firm, Æmilius Jarvis & Co.; Bankers, Toronto: apptd. Lieut., Governor-General's Body Guard, 1911: on the outbreak of the European War he, with a company of this cavalry regiment, volunteered for infantry, and with a company of the Royal Grenadiers and two companies of Queen's Own Rifles, formed a Toronto Regt., 3rd Battn. C.E.F.: came over with 1st Contingent, October 1914: spent the winter, 1914 – 15, training Salisbury Plain: went to France, February 1915, and was killed in action near St. Julien during the Second Battle of Ypres, 24 April 1915. On 22 April, when the poisonous gases were first used by the Germans on the French Algerians and Canadians, the 3rd Battn. Toronto Regt. was in Reserve with 1st Canadian Brigade, and were brought up as reinforcements at mid-night on the 22nd. The right and left half of the regiment were separated; the left half 'C' Coy., composed of the Governor-General's Body Guard, and 'D' Coy., composed of 10th Royal Grenadiers, were sent to the support of 2nd Brigade, then occupying trenches near the wood to the west of St. Julien. Lieut. Jarvis was sent with a platoon to drive some German snipers from some buildings enfilading the position. This necessitated crossing the open. On arriving at the house, Lieut. Jarvis, with three others, were the only ones out of thirty uninjured. After returning to his Commanding Officer to make his report, he was then sent with the remainder of his company to close up the line and effect a juncture with the regiment then occupying St. Julien, which he did; the whole company dragging themselves along on their stomachs. Through loss of men and insufficient numbers it was found that a juncture could not be made, so Lieut. Jarvis proceeded alone into St. Julien and obtained from Col. Loomis, Royal Montreal Regt., enough men to take back and thus close the line. On the following day, 24 April, while occupying advanced trenches with his company, Lieut. Jarvis was killed instantly by a shot in the head while in the act of binding up the wounds of a Private. An hour or two afterwards this advance party were surrounded, and being without further ammunition, the forty that remained of 'C' and 'D' Companies surrendered. Lieut. Col. F.O.V. Loomis, Comdg., 13th Canadian Battn., wrote, "I will never forget the officer's conduct. He seemed so competent and full of resource. He had absolute confidence in himself, and evidently did not know what fear was. It was a great relief to me at the time he reported, as I had previously been unable to find out what was taking place on our left. I had sent out several small patrols previous to young Jarvis's appearance, but they were never able to return and report, as most of them were killed," and Capt. J.E.L. Streight, now a Prisoner of War, "Your son Bill was killed while defending his trench on the morning of 24 April .. At noon on the 23rd I received orders to get in touch with St. Julien, which was some 800 yards to my right. Your son Bill volunteered at once to take on this dangerous task, and as he was the only Platoon Commander I had left, I gave him instructions to get his platoon out and form a connective file between our trench and the town, which he cleverly did with only two losses. Every inch of this ground was covered by all pulling themselves along on their stomachs, as the enemy were alert at all times to snipe them, and in a few cases they did. Finding himself short of men before reaching the town; he proceeded by himself alone into the town and found Col. Loomis in command there. Col. Loomis, after hearing his case, gave him twelve men to complete the chain, and a perfect line of communication was kept up all day. Bill returned to my trench when he had satisfied himself and reported the line to Col. Loomis connected up. Several times he went back and forward across this opening, and kept this line of communication in perfect order. No one could have operated this movement better or braver than Bill had done and, had he lived, no doubt would have received some decoration for his services." Capt. Baptist L. Johnston also wrote, "I was deeply attached to your son, and never knew a man more chivalrous and with a higher sense of honour. I have not the slightest hesitation in stating that if God had spared him he would have been awarded a decoration for his gallant work. Energetic, resourceful, generous and gay, recklessly brave, he was a perfect soldier and a born leader, caring always for the welfare of his men, by whom he was not only greatly admired, but beloved." While at Ridley College he was Captain of the Cadet Corps, and on graduating awarded the Mason Medal for 'True Manliness.' A keen all-round sportsman and athlete, he won the 135lb. (Light-weight) Class, for boxing at Toronto University Boxing Tournament, 1911; and, for the Royal Canadian Yacht Club, of which he was a member, won the George Cup (an international yachting cup), with the yacht 'Swamba,' 1910. Successfully defending the Cup in 1914 with 'Nirvana,' he also won the Prince of Wales Cup twice, once with the 'Swamba,' and once with the 'Seneca.' He played quarter-back and centre scrimmage for the Argonaut Football Club, 1911 –1913, and was an excellent cross-country and show-ring rider. Lieut. Jarvis was a descendant of a Canadian pioneer family: his great-great-grandfather, William Jarvis, U.E.L., after fighting through the American Revolutionary War with the Queen's Rangers (or 1st American Regt.) under Col. John Grave Simcoe, was made First Secretary of State for the new Province of Upper Canada: his grandfather, Lieut.Col. Samuel Peters Jarvis, fought during the war of 1812 in the actions at Detroit, Queenston Heights and Stoney Creek, and was present at the cutting out of the Caroline at Fort Sclosser: his maternal great-grandfather, Jacob Æmilius Irving, was wounded at Waterloo while serving as a Lieut. in 13th Light Dragoons: Age 23. *unm*. His very good friends (from his days at the Private Institution for Very Young Boys), Lieuts. H.R. Gordon and G.L.B. Mackenzie, also made the supreme sacrifice.

Lieut. George Mackenzie is buried in Lijssenthoek Military Cemetery (VI.A.17).

(Panel 18) Lieut. Alexander Douglas Kirkpatrick, 'C' Coy., 3rd Bn. Canadian Infantry (1st Central Ontario Regt.), C.E.F.: *s*. of Alexander M.M. (& Caroline A.) Kirkpatrick, of 204, Rusholme Road, Toronto: *b*. 1 January 1891: *educ*. St. James Cathedral School, Toronto; Upper Canada College (1902 – 08): Occupation – Fire Insurance Inspector; Messrs Wood & Kirkpatrick: served 5 yrs., Governor General's Body Guard: transf'd. Lieut., Queen's Own Regt., August 1914: joined C.E.F., Valcartier, August 1914; apptd. Lieut., 3rd Bn., 22 September; proceeded overseas October: served with the Expeditionary Force in France from February 1915; missing, confirmed killed in action at St. Julien (2nd Battle of Ypres), 23 April 1915: Age 24.

(Panel 18) Sergt. 10191, Edwin Harold Mulloy, 3rd Bn. Canadian Infantry (1st Central Ontario Regt.), C.E.F.: *s*. of Charles Wesley Mulloy, B.A., of Aurora, Ontario, by his wife Gertrude Claflin: *b*. Grimsby, Ontario, 6 June 1887: Religion – Presbyterian: Occupation – Banker: a serving member of the Militia, enlisted Valcartier, 22 September 1914: 5'5¾" tall, fair complexion, blue eyes, light brown hair: served with the Expeditionary Force in France and Flanders, and was killed nr. Brielen, approximately 1.15 a.m., 23 April 1915, by the explosion of an enemy shell: Age 27. *unm*.

(Panel 18) Sergt. 63869, George Samuel Tucker, 3rd Bn. Canadian Infantry (1st Central Ontario Regt.), C.E.F.: *s*. of the late Archdeacon (& Mrs) George Tucker, of Palmetto Grove, Bermuda: elder brother to Pte. McG/91, A.E. Tucker, Princess Patricia's Canadian Light Infantry, killed in action 2 June 1916: *b*. Palmetto Grove, Bermuda, 17 July 1893: enlisted 23rd Battn., Montreal, subsequently joining 3rd Battn. in France, and was reported among the 137 men of his battalion missing / believed killed in action during the successful attack at Mount Sorrel, 13 June 1916: Age 22. *unm*.

His brother Alexander also has no known grave; he is recorded on Panel 10.

(Panel 18) L/Corpl. 10205, James Ross Binkley, 3rd Bn. Canadian Infantry (1st Central Ontario Regt.), C.E.F.: *s*. of Jemima Binkley (295, King Street West, Dundas, Ontario). One of 4 men killed approximately 1.15 a.m., 23 April 1915, when an enemy shell exploded over the company lines nr. Brielen: Age 32. See also Sergt. Mulloy and Ptes. E.M. Bickerstaff and D. Broughall.

(Panel 18) L/Corpl. 9467, Melville Elliot Lobb, 3rd Bn. Canadian Infantry (1st Central Ontario Regt.), C.E.F.: *s*. Sidney Wentworth Lobb, by his wife Adeline Noble Elliot (72, Queen Street West, Toronto): *b*. Nanaimo, British Columbia, 20 July 1892: Religion – Baptist: *educ*. Model School, Toronto; Woodstock College; University College, Toronto (Mathematics & Physics), B.A.: Occupation – Clerk; Canada Life Assurance Co.: member 2nd Regt. Queen's Own Rifles (Militia): 6'1½ tall, blue eyes, brown hair: enlisted 3rd Battn., Valcartier, 22 September 1914; proceeded overseas October following: went to France with his battn. February 1915, moved up to Armentieres sector. Last seen carrying ammunition up to the front line at the Battle of St. Julien 2 May 1915; reported missing, later reported killed in action: Age 22. *unm*.

(Panel 18) Corpl. 9877, William Ferguson, 3rd Bn. Canadian Infantry (1st Central Ontario Regt.), C.E.F.: *s*. of the late Sergt. William Ferguson, by his wife Charlotte Anne (Highgate, London). Killed in action 24 April 1915: Age 30. Two other brothers also served.

(Panel 18) Pte. 9746, Frederick George Arthur Adams, 3rd Bn. Canadian Infantry (1st Central Ontario Regt.), C.E.F.: *s*. of Rose Ellen Adams (1017, Shaw Street, Toronto: *b*. 7 March 1893: Religion – Church of England: enlisted Valcartier, 22 September 1914. Failed to answer the Battalion Roll-Call, Vlamertinghe, 30 April 1915, and, with no word or sight of him following the action at St. Julien, recorded missing believed killed, Ypres area, 23 – 24 April 1915. Subsequently recorded, following a Court of Enquiry (1916), believed to have died on or about the former date: Age 22. Prior to the outbreak of war

Pte. Adams was a member (Bugler), Queen's Own Rifles Bugle Band. (*IWGC record 23 April, age 21; CWG Register & Circumstances of Death Register, C.E.F., record 2 May*)

(Panel 18) Pte. 10009, Everard Moore Bickerstaff, 3rd Bn. Canadian Infantry (1st Central Ontario Regt.), C.E.F.: s. of Charlotte Bickerstaff (76, Dominion Street, Toronto): b. Toronto, 26 January 1889: Religion – Church of England: Occupation – Commercial Traveller: serving member 6 yrs, Royal Grenadiers (Militia): 5'8" tall, dark complexion, brown eyes, black hair: enlisted Valcartier, 22 September 1914: served with the Expeditionary Force in France and Flanders, and was killed nr. Brielen at approximately 1.15 a.m., 23 April 1915, by the explosion of an enemy shell: Age 26. *unm.* (*IWGC record 2 May 1915*)

(Panel 18) Pte. 426471, Charles Smith Bill, 3rd Bn. Canadian Infantry (1st Central Ontario Regt.), C.E.F.: s. of William Thomas Bill, of 'Beverley,' Hare Street, Romford, co. Essex, late of The Cottage, Havering Well; by his wife Selina: and brother to Pte. 10241, F.K. Bill, 1st Honourable Artillery Coy., died 17 November 1918, of wounds, aged 18 years: b. London, England, 7 June 1894: Occupation – Farmhand: joined C.E.F., Regina, Saskatchewan, 5 February 1915. Died of wounds 13 June 1916, Wulverghem Sector: Age 22.

His brother Frank is buried in Etaples Military Cemetery (L.D.6).

(Panel 18) Pte. 9175, Derrick Broughall, 3rd Bn. Canadian Infantry (1st Central Ontario Regt.), C.E.F.: s. of Fred W. (& Mrs L.M.) Broughall, of Warlingham, nr. Caterham, co. Surrey: b. Toronto, October 1895: Religion – Church of England: Occupation – Clerk: 5'10" tall, fair complexion, blue eyes, light brown hair: serving member of the Militia, previously served 6 months Queen's Own Regt.: enlisted Valcartier, 22 September 1914, posted 6th Battn.: served with the Expeditionary Force in France and Flanders, transf'd. 3rd Battn., and was killed by the explosion of an enemy shell nr. Brielen at approximately 1.15 a.m., 23 April 1915: Age 19. (*IWGC record 2 May 1915*)

(Panel 18) Pte. 404302, Alexander McW. Colquhoun, 3rd Bn. Canadian Infantry (1st Central Ontario Regt.), C.E.F.: s. of Anna Bella Colquhoun (122, Uxbridge Avenue, Toronto): and brother to Pte. 172141, C. Colquhoun, 5th Canadian Mounted Rifles, killed in action 2 October 1916; and Pte. 766554, G. Colquhoun (surv'd.): b. Clydebank, Scotland, 11 April 1893: Religion – Presbyterian: Occupation – Clerk: 5'4" tall, blue eyes, fair hair: enlisted Toronto, 5 April 1915. Killed in action 13 June 1916, at Sanctuary Wood: Age 23. *unm.* Remains recovered unmarked grave (28.I.30.a.30.15) 25 January 1927; identified – Damaged Disc; reinterred, registered 29 January 1927. *Buried in Sanctuary Wood Cemetery (III.E.5).*

His brother Charles is buried in Regina Trench Cemetery, Grandcourt (II.G.22)

(Panel 18) Pte. 10015, Ernest Charles Coles, 3rd Bn. Canadian Infantry (1st Central Ontario Regt.), C.E.F.: s. of George Charles Coles, of Barrie, Ontario, by his wife Sarah Ann: b. Barrie, 2 April 1887: Occupation – Carpenter: volunteered and enlisted 1 September 1914, posted 3rd Battn. 22nd of the same month: went to France, served with the Expeditionary Force there and in Flanders, and was killed in action at Ypres 23 – 24 April 1915: Age 28. *unm.*

(Panel 18) Pte. 171752, Benjamin Cossar, 3rd Bn. Canadian Infantry (Central Ontario Regt.), C.E.F.: s. of the late Private Alexander Cossar, Gordon Highlanders, by his wife Agnes F., *dau.* of John B. Ednie: b. Galashiels, co. Selkirk, 23 September 1890: *educ.* Glendinning School: removed to Canada, April 1913, settled Toronto, Ontario: Occupation – Motor Cycle Mechanic: joined Canadian Infantry, May 1915: served with the Expeditionary Force in France and Flanders. Reported wounded and missing after the fighting at Passchendaele Ridge 6 November 1917; now assumed killed in action on or about that date: Age 27. *unm.*

(Panel 18) Pte. 9311, Frederick John Davis, 3rd Bn. Canadian Infantry (1st Central Ontario Regt.), C.E.F.: *yst. s.* of the late James Davis, Carpenter (*d.*1896), by his wife Elizabeth Warren Davis, *née* Miller, Dressmaker (92, Bere Regis, Wareham, co. Dorset): b. Dorset, 12 January 1890: Occupation – Painter: enlisted Valcartier, 22 September 1914. Killed in the assault to recapture Mount Sorrel 13 June 1916: Age 26. *unm.* Remains recovered unmarked grave (28.I.30.a.5.0) 24 January 1927; identified – Disc; reinterred, registered 29 January 1927. *Buried in Sanctuary Wood Cemetery (III.D.36).*

(Panel 18) Pte. 416490, Ovila Dion, 3rd Bn. Canadian Infantry (1st Central Ontario Regt.), C.E.F.: *s.* of John Dion, of North Hatley, Quebec. Killed in action 13 June 1916: Age 40. *Buried in Sanctuary Wood Cemetery (V.U.9).*

(Panel 18) Pte. 140518, John Joseph Donoghue, 3rd Bn. Canadian Infantry (1st Central Ontario Regt.), C.E.F.: *s.* of Michael Joseph Donoghue, of 62, Borden Street, Toronto, Ontario, by his marriage to the late Mary Agnes Donoghue: *b.* 15 September 1885: Religion – Roman Catholic: Occupation – Labourer: serving member of the Militia, joined C.E.F., Toronto, 16 July 1915. Missing / believed killed 13 June 1916; trenches south-east of Zillebeke: Age 30. Remains recovered unmarked grave (28.I.30.a.30.15) 25 January 1927; identified – Disc; reinterred, registered 29 January 1927. *Buried in Sanctuary Wood Cemetery (III.E.4).*

(Panel 18) Pte. 211145, James Douglas, 'C' Coy., 3rd Bn. Canadian Infantry (1st Central Ontario Regt.), C.E.F.: *s.* of William Douglas, of 205, Ashworth Place, Syracuse, New York, United States of America, by his wife Hannah: previously served 8 years King's Royal Rifle Corps in South Africa, Egypt and India: served with the Expeditionary Force in France and Flanders, and was killed in action at Vapour Farm, Vimy *(q.v.)*, 6 November 1917: Age 33.

(Panel 18) Pte. 9677, Ernest Goodall, 3rd Bn. Canadian Infantry (1st Central Ontario Regt.), C.E.F.: *s.* of Sarah E. Goodall (5, Elliott House, Elliott Road, Thornton Heath, co. Surrey): and *yr.* brother to Pte. 20391, H. Goodall, 10th Canadian Infantry, who fell twelve days previously. Killed in action 2 May 1915

His brother Harold also has no known grave, he is recorded on Panel 24.

(Panel 18) Pte. 64055, Pierre Henri Lambert, M.M., 3rd Bn. Canadian Infantry (1st Central Ontario Regt.), C.E.F.: *s.* of Jules Lambert, of 3, Rue Emile Bonnet, Saint Leu-la-Forêt, Seine-et-Oise, Paris 78: *b.* Montreal, 29 August 1896: Religion – Roman Catholic: Occupation – Student: 5'6" tall, fair complexion, brown eyes, fair hair: volunteered and enlisted Dibgate Camp, 9 September 1915: posted 23rd (Reserve) Battn.: served with the Expeditionary Force in France and Flanders transf'd. 3rd Battn., and was killed in action at Zillebeke, 13 June 1916: Age 17.

(Panel 18) Pte. 9921, William John Howe, 3rd Bn. Canadian Infantry (1st Central Ontario Regt.), C.E.F.: left Valcartier with First Canadian Contingent, September 1914: trained England throughout winter 1914 – 15: went to France February 1915, and was killed in action 24 April 1915. Pte. Howe left a wife and five children to whom, two days before his death, he sent (enclosing some wild flowers picked in Belgium) the following letter:– "April 22nd 1915: Dear Wife & Children, Just a few lines hoping your are all quite well as it leaves me. At present…we are in a very dangerous place, the worst in the whole firing line….killed and wounded all around, it is awful to see the poor soldiers passing us on the road with bandages in all sorts of places but mostly in the head. We are out of France…at a place called Vlamertinghe in Belgium, the last place we was at in France…Winnezeele…the best place we had been to, we had six days rest there and now we have just arrived here and it is hot. No one could ever describe it without seeing the ruins of the towns and villages. The place we are at now the people have orders to be cleared out in 24 hours as there will be something doing at any minute. The poor things going along the road crying with 4,5,6 children and all with bundles, that was all they could take from their homes as the Germans had all-ready started firing on the town. It was awful, little babies in their arms and lots like that as they say the Germans was awful with the women when they first came through last October, killing them if they did not do what they wanted. Very old people could only just walk along but our transport…going the same way picked lots up and gave them a ride. I tell you…it hit lots of us fellows pretty hard to think what could happen to your own while you were away fighting. They are crowded up in barns sleeping anywhere, some of them have not seen or heard of their husbands since the war began and do not know if they are alive, prisoners or dead; nor do they know where to find them. I often think how thankful it is it is not our homes and towns. The places we have seen, but we are not allowed to tell or say. I have managed to get this envelope and I have said quite a lot that perhaps they would not like me to but I have took the chance…Dear Wife, we hear all kinds of rumour here but I must tell you that those who get through this are going to be very lucky, and I hope I shall be one of them, but what is to be will be. I do hope I shall have the chance to see all my children once more with you since I have seen these poor Belgians with their families it has made me think a lot of my three young ones the other two is not so bad as they are old enough to battle for themselves but I must tell them I want them to stand up and look to the others until they are old enough to look for themselves. I know you will do your best, but you may not be long enough upon the earth yourself and then what about the young ones; I want them to understand me, what I expect them to do but I hope we shall both see them grow off our hands and be able to look after themselves. I will now draw to a close. With best love and wishes from your ever loving Husband & Father, xxxxxx"

(Panel 18) Pte. 9686, George Latimer, 3rd Bn. Canadian Infantry (1st Central Ontario Regt.), C.E.F.: *s.* of the late Hugh Turner Latimer, by his wife Eliza Ann (2, Port Street, Burslem, co. Stafford): and elder brother to Pte. 11256, W. Turner, 4th Canadian Infantry, who fell the previous day: *b.* Burslem, Stoke-on-Trent, 16 August 1887: Occupation – Plumber: enlisted Valcartier, 22 September 1914: came over with First Contingent, October following: served with the Expeditionary Force in France from February 1915, and was killed in action 24 April 1915: Age 27.

His brother Walter also has no known grave; he is recorded below.

(Panel 18) Pte. 9946, Charles F. Payne, 3rd Bn. Canadian Infantry (1st Central Ontario Regt.), C.E.F.: *s.* of William Payne, of Kingsland Cottages, Faversham, co. Kent: *b.* Faversham, 21 September 1888: Religion – Church of England: Occupation – Labourer: 5'9½" tall, fair complexion, blue eyes, light brown hair: a serving member of the Militia; enlisted Valcartier, 22 September 1914: departed Canada aboard S.S. 'Tunisian': disembarked Devonport, 19 October 1914: trained Bustard Camp, Salisbury Plain, 20 October – 9 February 1915, on which latter date the battalion departed for France aboard S.S. 'City of Edinburgh': served with the Expeditionary Force in France and Flanders from 11 February 1915: underwent trench instruction, Armentieres sector: moved up to Canal Bank sector (via Poperinghe – Vlamertinghe) 19 – 22 April and died of wounds, 23 April 1915, received at approximately 4 a.m. the same day when leaving trench C.22 (nr. Brielen) in the attack on St Julien: Age 26. *unm.*

(Panel 18) Pte. 9246, Lawrence Scanlon Shields, 3rd Bn. Canadian Infantry (1st Central Ontario Regt.), C.E.F.: late of 80, Charles Street East, Toronto: *s.* of John (& Matilda) Shields, of 24, Maple Avenue, Hamilton: *b.* 19 May 1894: *educ.* Toronto University: Occupation – Clerk: enlisted 22 September 1914: came over with First Contingent: trained Salisbury Plain, winter 1914 – 15: served with the Expeditionary Force in France from February 1915, and was killed in action 24 April 1915, nr. St. Julien: Age 19. The first ex-Toronto University student to die in the Great War.

(Panel 18) Pte. 63855, Joseph Sime, 3rd Bn. Canadian Infantry (1st Central Ontario Regt.), C.E.F.: *s.* of Thomas Sime, of 39, North Church Street, Dundee, and Janet Y. Sime (18, King's Road, Dundee), his wife: and yr. brother to Pte. 180344, W. Sime, 28th Canadian Infantry, killed in action 29 September 1916; Somme, France: *b.* Church Street, Dundee, 24 June 1882: Religion – Presbyterian: Occupation – Labourer: 5'5" tall, hazel eyes, fair hair: joined C.E.F., 23 January 1915; posted 3rd Battn. 1 February. Killed in action 13 June 1916; Ypres, Belgium: Age 33. *unm.*

His brother William is buried in Adanac Military Cemetery, Miraumont (I.B.40).

(Panel 18) Pte. 9831, Harry Stevens, 3rd Bn. Canadian Infantry (1st Central Ontario Regt.), C.E.F.: *s.* of Robert Stevens, of Dover, co. Kent, by his wife Annie: and brother to Pte. 4331, A.R. Stevens, 15th London Regt., died of wounds 4 June 1916, Base Hospital, Le Treport: *b.* Spa, Belgium, 20 May 1893: Religion – Methodist: Occupation – Lithographer: 5'7" tall, blue eyes, light brown hair: previously served 2 yrs. Queen's Own; Canadian Militia member; enlisted Valcartier, 22 September 1914. Reported missing / believed killed in action 23 April – 2 May 1915: Age 21. *unm.* Correspondence should be addressed c/o his foster-mother, Mrs A.H. Peacock (163, Balsam Avenue, Barry Beach, Toronto). (*IWGC record 2 May 1915*)

His brother Alexander is buried in Le Treport Military Cemetery (I.N.7).

(Panel 18) Pte. 9733, Robert Henry White, 'C' Coy., 3rd Bn. Canadian Infantry (Toronto Regt.), C.E.F.: 2nd *s.* of the late Robert White, Master Roscrea (Ireland) Union, by his wife Elizabeth (44,

Dingwall Avenue, Toronto, Canada), *dau.* of William Proctor, of Glashare, Co. Kilkenny: *b.* Roscrea, Co. Tipperary, 8 July 1895: *educ.* National School, there: removed to Canada, May 1914: Occupation – Sales Clerk: volunteered on the outbreak of war; joined Canadian Expeditionary Force, Toronto, about 20 August 1914: left Valcartier for England with First Contingent, 9 October following: trained Salisbury Plain winter 1914 – 15: proceeded to France early February, and was killed in action 'in the field between St. Julien and St. Jean,' 23 April 1915, being shot through the head; death was instantaneous: Age 19.

(Panel 18 & 8) Lieut.-Col. Arthur Percival Dearman Birchall, Comdg. 4th Bn. Canadian Expeditionary Force, and Capt. Royal Fusiliers: 2nd *s.* of the late John Dearman Birchall, of Bowden Hall, co. Gloucester, by his wife Emily, *dau.* of John Towitt, of Harehills, Leeds: and brother to Capt. E.V.D. Birchall, D.S.O., Oxford & Bucks L.I., died 10 August 1916, of wounds in a Base Hospital: *b.* Bowden Hall, 7 March 1877: *educ.* Eton, and Magdalen College, Oxford: obtained a University Commission; gazetted 2nd Lieut. Royal Fusiliers (City of London Regt.), 23 May 1900; promoted Lieut. 11 April 1902; Adjt. 25 March 1904 – 24 March 1907; promoted Capt. 1 October 1908; Major and Lieut.Col. 22 September 1914: seconded for service with Royal Canadian Regt., 15 April 1910, was later on the Instructional Staff, Western Canada: invalided home from Canada, August 1914, but recovered sufficiently to rejoin 1st Canadian Contingent, November following, attd. as Staff Capt., 1st Brigade. Always a popular, keen and most efficient officer, he was appointed the colonelcy of 4th Canadians February 1915, and was killed in action in the attack on the Pilckem Ridge, nr. Ypres, 23 April 1915: Age 38. *unm.* Speaking of this action F.M. Sir John French said, "The Canadians had many casualties, but their gallantry and determination undoubtedly saved the situation. Their conduct has been magnificent throughout." And the Official Report from the Canadian Record Officer at the Front:– "The fighting continued without intermission all through the night, and to those who observed the indications that the attack was being pushed with ever-growing strength, it hardly seemed possible that the Canadians, fighting in positions so difficult to defend, and so little the subject of deliberate choice, could maintain their resistance for any long period. At 6 a.m. on Friday (April 23) it became apparent that the left was becoming more and more involved, and a powerful German attempt to outflank it developed rapidly. The consequences, if it had been broken or outflanked, need not be insisted upon. They were not merely local. It was therefore decided, formidable as the attempt undoubtedly was, to try and give relief by a counter-attack upon the first line of German trenches, now far, far advanced from those originally occupied by the French. This was carried out by the Ontario 1st and 4th Battns. of the 1st Brigade, under Brig.-Gen. Mercer, acting in combination with a British brigade. It is safe to say that the youngest private in the ranks, as he set his teeth for the advance, knew the task in front of him, and the youngest subaltern knew that all rested upon its success. It did not seem that any human being could live in the shower of shot and shell which began to play upon the advancing troops. They suffered terrible casualties. For a short time every other man seemed to fall, but the attack was pressed ever closer and closer. The 4th Canadian Battn. at one moment came under a particularly withering fire. For a moment – not more – it wavered. its most gallant commanding officer, Lieut.Col. Birchall, carrying, after an old fashion, a light cane, coolly and cheerfully rallied his men, and, at the very moment when his example had infected them, fell dead at the head of his battn. With a hoarse cry of anger they sprang forward (for indeed, they loved him) as if to avenge his death. The astonishing attack which followed, pushed home in direct frontal fire, made in broad daylight, by battns. whose names should live forever in the memories of soldiers, was carried to the first line of German trenches. After a hand-to-hand struggle the last German who resisted was bayoneted, and the trench was won. The measure of this success may be taken when it is pointed out that this trench represented, in the German advance, the apex in the breach which the enemy had made in the original line of the Allies, and that it was 2½ miles south of that line. This charge, made by men who looked death indifferently in the face – for no man who took part in it could think that he was likely to live – saved, and that was much, the Canadian left. But it did more. Up to the point where the assailants conquered or died, it secured and maintained, during the most critical moment of all, the Allied line. For the trench was not only taken, it was held thereafter against all comers, and in the teeth of every conceivable projectile, until the night of Sunday (25th) when all that remained of the war-broken, but victorious battns., was relieved by fresh troops." Major R.Hayter, Brigade Major, 1st Canadian Brigade wrote, "Your brother, Percy, fell on the 23rd leading his battn. in the first Canadian counter-attack on the 23rd made by the French, British, and 1st and 4th Canadian battns. just east of the Ypres Canal. His battn. lost all its officers but four, and some 560 casualties other ranks, but they never wavered and got into the enemy's line, saved the day, and prevented the enemy's advance south along the east bank of the canal. We are still being desperately engaged, and I cannot write much, but I am sure you will be glad to hear that he has been recommended for the Victoria Cross. He was wounded, had his wound dressed, was wounded again, yet would go on, and fell leading the charge which took the trenches. I had written a message from him, timed 4.20 pm., acknowledging an order, and I hope some-day to be able to give it to you. His loss has been the greatest blow the contingent could have had. Loved by all, and worshipped by his officers and men, we feel that it was his personal magnetism alone which kept his regt. together, and enabled them to hold what they had gained. All our deepest sympathies are with you and your family, but his end could not have been more glorious." And the following tribute, from an old friend, appeared in '*The Times*' (29 April 1915):– "The claim to have been the most popular officer in the Army is a large one, and may be advanced in the name of many a candidate. But it is probable that all who in any true sense had made Birchall's acquaintance will claim that no officer could have been more deeply, and probably none more widely, beloved and admired. At Eton, at Magdalen, and for fifteen years in the Army, he was for ever winning to himself friends by the simple, but irresistible, charm of his nature – by his manliness and sportsmanship, his humour and high spirits, his enthusiasm for his profession as in general for the better things of life. Joining the newly formed 4th Battn. of the Royal Fusiliers during the South African War, as a University Candidate, he became closely identified with its fortunes for some ten years; and was largely responsible for raising it to the high level of the older battns. of that famous regt. Beloved alike by his brother officers and men, he was equally prominent as a leader in soldiering and in sport: in the field of manoeuvre as in the football, the hockey, the hunting, but especially the cricket field, he always played a fine sporting game. After ably fulfilling the second adjutancy of his battn., he received the singular distinction of being selected – one of two officers from the whole Army – to be attached to the Canadian Forces, according to a scheme for the mutual benefit of both services. In Canada, he inevitably won through to the same affectionate and admiring popularity as at home. His period of appointment was extended, he was appointed to the Staff, and was given an almost transcontinental district of supervision. The characteristic energy which he threw into this work, in the unaccustomed climate, caused a temporary breakdown in his health, and bitter was his grief, on returning to England, shortly before the outbreak of war, to find himself entirely forbidden on medical grounds to take for the present the share in active service for which he had keenly prepared and eminently fitted himself. To such advantage, however, did he make use of his time, even of sickness, that, in the intervals of being visited by a constant stream of devoted friends from two continents, he compiled the admirable little manual for the use of regimental officers in the present emergency training, which he entitled 'Rapid Training of a Company for War' (Gale & Polden, Aldershot). This book rapidly attained a wide success, and was brought up to date in a second (and subsequent) edition, just as he himself, recently appointed Major, was appointed first a Staff Captain in the Canadian Expeditionary Force, and in immediate succession given command of the 4th Canadian Infantry a few days before it sailed for the Front." Col. Birchall resided at Saintbridge House, Gloucester; he was recommended for the Victoria Cross for his actions on the day of his death. Another brother, Capt. J. Dearman Birchall, is (1916) serving with the Royal Gloucestershire Hussars Yeomanry. Lieut.Col. Birchall is also recorded on Panel 8 (Royal Fusiliers).

His brother Edward is buried in Etaples Military Cemetery (I.B.42).

(Panel 18) Capt. John Donald Glover, (Adjt.) 4th Bn. Canadian Infantry (1st Central Ontario Regt.), C.E.F.: *s.* of William Glover, of Orillia, Ontario, by his wife Mary: and elder brother to Sergt. 20429, N. Glover, 10th Canadian Infantry, who also fell: volunteered and enlisted on the outbreak of war 4 August 1914: came over with First Canadian Contingent: underwent training in England, winter 1914 – 15:

served with the Expeditionary Force in France and Flanders, and was killed in action 23 April 1915, at the Second Battle of Ypres: Age 25.

His brother Norman also has no known grave; he is recorded on Panel 24.

(Panel 18) Lieut. William Henry Aggett, 4th Bn. Canadian Infantry (1st Central Ontario Regt.), C.E.F.: *s.* of John T. Aggett, of 10, Scollard Street, Toronto, by his wife Harriet A.: *b.* Toronto, 25 April 1895: Religion – Methodist: *educ.* Rosedale Public School, and University of Toronto (Applied Science, 1913 – 15); won Second Colours (Rugby, Hockey); member University O.T.C.: enlisted 25th Bty., 7th Canadian Field Artillery Bde. with a large number of his University colleagues, March 1915: departed Canada, July following: after training and transfer to 23rd Howitzer Bty., 5th Bde., England; proceeded to France, January 1916: served with his unit at Messines, St. Eloi and Mount Sorrel: wounded (knee, fractured ankle), Armentieres, July 1916: on recovery received his commission 4th Canadian Infantry, with which unit he served at Vimy and the fighting before Lens and Hill 70. Lieut. Aggett was killed instantaneously at Passchendaele, by the explosion of a shell 6 November 1917, while leading his platoon forward from Bellevue Spur to reinforce 1st Battalion. Body not recovered by unit: Age 22. *unm.*

Between 1914 and 1918 over 600,000 Canadians served in the C.E.F., among their number over 3,500 native Indians representing tribes from all over Canada – Delawares, Onondagas, Oneidas, Mohawks, Peguis, Saulteaux, Cree – who placed a greater cause above their own lives. Military historian Fred Gaffen wrote: "When Samuel de Champlain joined a Huron-Algonquin war party in 1609 and killed two Iroquois with the shot from his harquebus, a new era began. The only protection from the firearms and the greater killing power of the white man was in dispersion and ambush." Most native Canadians served as snipers or reconnaissance scouts, combining their traditional hunting and practice with newly acquired military skills to deadly effect. Their duties – straightforward and dangerous – instilled fear in the enemy, and legends of Indian stealth, cunning and ferocity were well renowned. Snipers, shooting from their well-concealed nests, kept the enemy unnerved by the accuracy of their rifle fire; scouts (reputedly often wearing 'war paint') slipping behind the enemy's front lines to determine their strength and capabilities regularly returned with 'traditional souvenirs' (scalps!). Privates 1295, Pat Riel, and 710, Philip McDonald served in both capacities, and Pte. 435684, Henry Norwest, with 115 'observed hits,' was considered to be the greatest sniper in the British Army.

Throughout the war the Department of Indian Affairs received countless letters from the front commending native marksmen and scouts. At least 50 decorations were awarded to native Canadians for bravery and other feats while sniping and scouting as well as for other acts of valour – Francis Pegahmagabow was awarded the Military Medal three times!

Over 320 Canadian Indians died during the war or as a direct result of their service – Pat Riel and Philip McDonald were both killed by shellfire in early 1916; in 1918 the intrepid Henry Norwest, firing on a German sniper, was killed by a bullet fired simultaneously by his adversary – both men fell dead.

The second Native Canadian to be killed in the Great War:–

(Panel 18) Lieut. Cameron Donald Brant, 4th Bn. Canadian Infantry (1st Central Ontario Regt.), C.E.F.: *s.* of Robert D. Brant, of Six Nations, Hagersville, Ontario, by his wife Lydia: and *gt.-gt.-gdson.* to the great Chief Thayendanaga, of the Six Nations: *b.* Brant County, Ontario, 12 August 1887: Religion – Church of England: Occupation – Sheet-metal Worker: 5'5½" tall, dark complexion, brown eyes, dark brown hair: vaccination scar left arm, tattoo, initials 'C.B.' left forearm, large oval surgical scar left breast: previously served 6 years (Militia); enlisted Valcartier, 4 September 1914; posted 4th Battn. 22 September: came over with First Contingent: undertook further training in England during winter 1914 – 15: promoted Lieut.: went to France, served with the Expeditionary Force there, and was killed in action while leading his platoon in a counter-attack at Ypres 24 April 1915. The following obituary notice appeared in '*Canada in Flanders, 1919*':– 'It is a singular coincidence that the first Brant county man to fall in action in the Great War was Capt. Cameron D. Brant, a great-great-grandson of Capt. Joseph Brant, from whom the county takes its name. This Indian officer went overseas with the 4th Battalion, and was killed at the Second Battle of Ypres, while gallantly leading his men in the heroic charge that earned historic renown for his battalion, and in which his commanding officer, Col. Birchall, and many other brave officers met their death. Capt. Brant had the instinctive Indian love for scouting, and he acquired a reputation for valuable services rendered in nocturnal reconnoitring in No Man's Land. Two other descendants of Capt. Joseph Brant, Corpl. Albert W.L. Crain, also of the 4th Battalion, and Pte. Nathan Monture, subsequently promoted to the rank of captain, were severely wounded at Ypres.' Lieut. Brant leaves a wife, Flossie (31, Spring Street, Hamilton, Ontario): Age 27. *unm.* (*IWGC record age 28*)

Ptes. P. Riel and P. McDonald are buried beside each other in (Royal) Berks Cemetery Extension (III.B.39 – 40); Pte. H. Norwest, Warvillers Churchyard Extension (A.30). The first Native Canadian killed, Pte. 6827, A. La Force, 1st Canadian Infantry, also has no known grave; he is recorded on Panel 10. Lieut.Col. A.P.D. Birchall holds the distinction of being twice recorded – Panel 18 above, and (Royal Fusiliers) Panel 8.

(Panel 18) Pte. 11216, Georges Cardozo, 4th Bn. Canadian Infantry (Central Ontario Regt.), C.E.F.: *s.* of Uriah Cardozo, of Aeux Cayes, Haiti, West Indies, and Marie Nicholson, his wife: *b.* Kingston, Jamaica: *educ.* Petit Seminaire College, St. Martial, Port-au-Prince, Haiti, and St. George's College, Kingston, Jamaica: served with the Expeditionary Force in France, and was killed in action 22 – 26 April 1915: Age 24.

(Panel 18) Pte. 11091, Harold Julius Clarke, 4th Bn. Canadian Infantry (Central Ontario Regt.), C.E.F.: *s.* of William (& Mrs) Clarke, of Station Road, Berkhampstead, co. Hertford: *b.* 9 December 1893: Religion – Church of England: Occupation – Riveter: 5'9" tall, dark complexion, blue eyes, brown hair: enlisted Valcartier, 22 September 1914. One of 407 other ranks killed in action 23 April 1915; Canal Bank sector, Ypres: Age 21. He was married to Ellen May Taylor, *née* Clarke (Winton, Saskatchewan).

(Panel 18) Pte. 11346, Frank Alfred Ellis, 4th Bn. Canadian Infantry (Central Ontario Regt.), C.E.F.: next of kin, Mrs Skett (5, Huron Street, Brantford, Ontario): *b.* Hampstead, London, N.W., 18 June 1892: Religion – Church of England: 5'6¼" tall, dark complexion, brown eyes, brown hair: sometime removed to Canada, finding gainful employ as a Labourer: previously served 5 years in the Militia: attested and enlisted Valcartier, 22 September 1914: quite possibly illiterate (Attestation Form bears three variant signatures): served with the Expeditionary Force in France and Flanders, and was killed in action 23 April 1915: Age 22. *unm.*

(Panel 18) Pte. 412592, Chester Joseph Ham, 4th Bn. Canadian Infantry (Central Ontario Regt.), C.E.F.: *s.* of James Ham, of Port Hope, Ontario, by his wife Susan: *b.* Port Hope, 4 August 1888: *educ.* Public School, and Port Hope High School (Graduate, 3 yrs.): self-employed Tinsmith & Plumber, Port Hope, similarly Saskatoon, March 1911- March 1915: returned Port Hope in latter month, volunteered for Imperial Service, enlisted 39th Battn., 6 March: transf'd. Headquarters, Belleville, shortly after enlistment, and after three months training embarked (July / August 1915) aboard S.S. 'Missinabie' for Europe. After a further five months training in England departed for France with First Draft, C.E.F. attd. 4th Battn.: served continuously with the Expeditionary Force there, at one time, following shellfire, being buried alive for over six hours before being rescued. Pte. Ham was killed while on sentry duty in the trenches 12 June 1916. Buried in a cemetery near Zillebeke: Age 27. *unm.* (*IWGC record age 26*)

(Panel 18) Pte. 10665, Thomas Ewart Kelly, 4th Bn. Canadian Infantry (Central Ontario Regt.), C.E.F.: *s.* of Thomas H. (& Margaret) Kelly: *b.* Toronto, 29 December 1889: *educ.* Park Public School; Dufferin Public School; Private School and Y.M.C.A.; University College, Toronto (Political Science), 1910 – 14, B.A.: Occupation – Student: serving member 12th York Rangers (Militia): enlisted 4th Battn., Valcartier, 23 September 1914, having but recently graduated: departed Canada with First Contingent, October following: served with the Expeditionary Force in France and Flanders from February 1915. Reported wounded and missing 23 April following, while serving as battalion runner at the Second Battle of Ypres; later confirmed killed in action: Age 25. *unm.*

(Panel 18) Pte. 11256, Walter Latimer, 4th Bn. Canadian Infantry (Central Ontario Regt.), C.E.F.: *s.* of the late Hugh Turner Latimer, by his wife Eliza Ann (2, Port Street, Burslem, co. Stafford): and *yr.* brother to Pte. 9686, G. Latimer, 3rd Canadian Infantry, who fell the following day: *b.* Burslem, Stoke-on-

Trent, 10 January 1893: Occupation – Car Repairer: a serving member of 36th (Militia) Regt., with 3 years previous service with 3rd North Staffordshire Regt.: volunteered and enlisted Valcartier, 22 September 1914: came over with First Contingent, October following: served with the Expeditionary Force in France from February 1915, and was killed in action 23 April 1915: Age 22. *unm.*

His brother George also has no known grave; he is recorded above.

(Panel 18) Pte. A/36301, Charles Pulley Maxey, 4th Bn. Canadian Infantry (Central Ontario Regt.), C.E.F.: c/o Frank R. Maxey Esq., 28, Cardigan Street, Ipswich: 3rd *s.* of the late John Thomas Maxey, Chemist; High Street, Wisbech, and his wife Lydia Mary Maxey (9, Henry Street, Wisbech, co. Cambridge, England), *dau.* of William Davis, of Dieppe, France: and brother to Sergt. 183433, W.D. Maxey, 31st Canadian Infantry (surv'd.): *b.* 30 May 1884: Religion – Church of England: *educ.* Wisbech Grammar School: removed to Canada, 1905: Occupation – Timekeeper; Northern Construction Co.: volunteered and enlisted C.E.F., Edmonton, 9 January 1915; proceeded overseas February following: trained Shorncliffe, England: joined 4th Bn., Ploegsteert, 7 August. Killed in action nr. Hill 60 on the night of 7 – 8 May 1916. A marksman (sniper) he was hit by a bullet from a sudden enemy machine-gun burst which swept across the parapet of the trench where he was at duty. His officer wrote, "He was one of our best men, always obedient and willing, and on the job when wanted." Buried Maple Copse Cemetery (28.I.23.a.9.5): Age 30.

(Panel 18) Pte. 10942, William John Sinclair, Machine Gun Section, 4th Bn. Canadian Infantry (Central Ontario Regt.), C.E.F.: *yr. s.* of Dr. George Thomas Sinclair, M.A., of 91, Coniston Road, Edinburgh, formerly of Craigengar, Culross, by his wife Marian, *dau.* of John McEwen, Register House, Edinburgh, and *gdson.* to the Rev. William Sinclair, of Kirkwall, Orkney: *b.* Sanquhar, co. Dumfries, 10 October 1889: *educ.* High School, Dunfermline; George Watson's College, Edinburgh, on leaving the latter took up employ with British Linen Co. Bank, Dunfermline: removed to Canada, 1910, to take up an appointment with Bank of Montreal, Hamilton, Ontario: a serving member of the Militia, volunteered for Imperial Service and enlisted Valcartier, 23 September 1914, after the outbreak of war: posted 4th Battn., came over with First Contingent October 1914: went to France, February 1915, and was killed in action at St. Julien, nr. Ypres, 23 April 1915. Buried at Vlamertinghe, three miles west of Ypres: Age 24. *unm.* Lieut. Washington wrote, "He died a hero's death. Rushing to the aid of a wounded comrade he was hit, and died shortly after. He was absolutely fearless and game to the last, and his behaviour under terrific fire was splendid. His memory is much honoured by myself and the Machine Gun Section." His brother, Lieut. Fraser McEwen Sinclair, of Glencraig, co. Fife, is now (1916) on active service in Egypt.

(Panel 18) Pte. A36313, George Tree, 4th Bn. Canadian Infantry (Central Ontario Regt.), C.E.F.: *s.* of the late Arthur Ernest Tree, of Carlstad, Alberta, and Kathleen Tree (9348, 104th Avenue, Edmonton): and yr. brother to Pte. 696474, E.A. Tree, 175th Canadian Infantry, died 25 January 1920, aged 25 years: *b.* Frelighsburg, Co. Missisquoi, Quebec, 6 March 1896: Religion – Wesleyan: Occupation – Elevator Driver: 5'7¼" tall, hazel eyes, brown hair: joined C.E.F., 9 January 1915. Killed in action 13 June 1916: Age 20. (*IWGC record age 18*)

His brother Ernest is buried in Edmonton Cemetery (BH.Sub.Div.E).

(Panel 18) Lieut. Charles George Dalegarth King-Mason, 5th Bn. Canadian Infantry (Saskatchewan Regt.), C.E.F.: *s.* of the late Capt. Charles T. King-Mason, 24th Battn. C.E.F. (*d.*1921), by his wife Annie Gertrude (Vancouver, British Columbia). Killed in action at Ypres 24 April 1915: Age 27. Remembered on St. Bees School Roll of Honour, Cumbria.

(Panel 18) Sergt. 424089, James Marr Brand, 5th Bn. Canadian Infantry (Saskatchewan Regt.), C.E.F.: *s.* of Mary Brand (90, Iona Street, Leith, co. Midlothian, Scotland): brother to W. Brand Esq., of 12 Jane Street, Leith; and Corpl. 3/6283, D. Brand, 1st Cameron Highlanders, killed in action 9 May 1915: *b.* 20 March 1882: Occupation – Farmer: previously served 2 years (18 months Active Service, South Africa) 5th Vol. Battn. Royal Scots: volunteered and enlisted Melville, Sask., 29 December 1914. Killed in action at Ypres 6 June 1916: Age 34. *unm.*

His brother David also has no known grave; he is commemorated on the Le Touret Memorial.

(Panel 18) Pte. 13507, Harold John Hulbert, No.3 Coy., 5th Bn. Canadian Infantry (Saskatchewan Regt.), C.E.F.: 2nd *s.* of George Reginald Hulbert, of Bethany, Manitoba, by his wife Amy, *dau.* of John Woodcock, of Netherhampton, co. Wilts: *b.* Bethany, 1 October 1894: *educ.* Minnedosa High School: enlisted Canadian Expeditionary Force directly war broke out: came over with 1st Contingent, October 1914: underwent further training on Salisbury Plain during the winter; went to the Front, January 1915, and was killed in action at the Battle of Ypres, 24 April 1915. Buried nr. St. Julien. Major Dyer, D.S.O. wrote, "Your boy was killed by shell fire on the hill of Gravenstafel, while his company was advancing to support the 8th Battn and help fill the gap left by the retiring Turcos. We were holding the trenches against 15,000 Germans with less than 1,000 men; for the last two days without food or water, but we were all there was between the Germans and Calais." Age 21. *unm.*

(Panel 18) Pte. 268105, Robert Laing, 'B' Coy., No.7 Platoon, 5th Bn. Canadian Infantry (Saskatchewan Regt.), C.E.F.: late of Nokomis, Saskatchewan: *s.* of John Laing, of Paisley, Scotland: *b.* Paisley, 15 November 1890: Religion – Presbyterian: Occupation – Carpenter: 5'2 ¼" tall, grey eyes, dark brown hair: joined C.E.F., Saskatoon, 7 February 1917. Killed in action 10 November 1917: Age 26. *unm.* Remains recovered unmarked grave (28.D.5.b.8.3) 22 December 1928; identified – Clothing, Titles, Badge, Divnl. Patch, Watch, Gold Ring engrvd. 'CANADA 214,' Aluminium Ring engrvd. 'LENS 1914 – 1917,' Waterproof Sheet mkd. 268105 R. Laing; reinterred, registered 3 January 1929. *Buried in Sanctuary Wood Cemetery (V.B.8).*

(Panel 18) Pte. A/40138, Stephen Hilliard Martin, 5th Bn. Canadian Infantry (Saskatchewan Regt.), C.E.F.: late of 493, 2nd Avenue, North Saskatoon: *husb.* to Elizabeth Martin (287, Hunter Street, Hamilton, Ontario): and elder brother to Pte. 474101, T.T. Martin, 5th Canadian Infantry, killed in action 8 September 1917, aged 24: *b.* Hamilton, 13 August 1882: Religion – Church of England: Occupation – Machinist: 5'7" tall, blue eyes, dark hair; tattooed both arms: enlisted Saskatoon, 21 December 1914, posted 5th Canadian Infantry, 24 December. Killed in action 2 June 1916: Age 34. An Officer wrote, "The Battalion had taken a new position at Hill 60, Zillebeke, as there were no trenches the men had to 'dig in' under heavy enemy artillery and machine–gun fire, and it was during this operation the Pte. Martin was killed. A search was made for his body but it could not be found, and it was presumed it was buried by shellfire." Remembered on Markdale Cenotaph, Ontario. (*IWGC record age 42, father of Pte. T.T. Martin*)

His brother Thomas 'Taylor' also has no known grave; he is commemorated on the Canadian National (Vimy) Memorial, France.

(Panel 18) Pte. 13779, Allan Murray, 'I' Coy., 5th Bn. Canadian Infantry (Saskatchewan Regt.), C.E.F.: *s.* of Angus (& Mrs) Murray, of 52, Keith Street, Stornoway, Lewis, Scotland: *yr.* brother to Pte. 13777, T. Murray, 5th Canadian Infantry, who fell at Ypres 10 May 1915. Killed in action 25 April 1915: Age 19.

His brother Thomas also has no known grave; he is recorded below.

(Panel 18) Pte. 13777, Thomas Murray, 'I' Coy., 5th Bn. Canadian Infantry (Saskatchewan Regt.), C.E.F.: *s.* of Angus (& Mrs) Murray, of 52, Keith Street, Stornoway, Lewis, Scotland: elder brother to Pte. 13779, A. Murray, 5th Canadian Infantry, who fell at Ypres 25 April 1915. Killed in action 10 May 1915: Age 22.

His brother Allan also has no known grave; he is recorded above.

(Panel 18) Pte. A/40193, Walter Pattenden, 5th Bn. Canadian Infantry (Saskatchewan Regt.), C.E.F.: *s.* of Ebenezer Pattenden, of Stonegate, co. Sussex, and Harriet Pattenden, his wife: and brother to Pte. L/7711, W. Pattenden, 2nd Royal Sussex Regt., killed in action 31 October 1914; and Pte. 242025, E. Pattenden, M.M., 2/6th Royal Warwickshire Regt., killed in action 21 March 1918. Killed in action 2 June 1916: Age 24. One of three brothers who fell.

His brothers also have no known grave William is recorded on Panel 20; Edwin, Pozieres Memorial, Somme.

(Panel 18) Capt. Cyril Knox Barrow Mogg, 7th Bn. Canadian Infantry (British Columbia Regt.), C.E.F.: *s.* of the Rev. Canon (& Mrs) Mogg, of The Vicarage, Bishop's Canning, Vale of Pewsey, co. Wilts: and brother to Pte. 703340, A.B. Mogg, 102nd Canadian Infantry, killed in action 19 August 1916, at

St. Eloi: *b.* Clifton, 8 May 1887: Religion – Church of England: Occupation – Banker: enlisted Vernon, British Columbia, 23 October 1915: 5'7" tall, fair complexion, blue eyes, light hair. Killed in action 11 November 1917, at Passchendaele: Age 30. *unm.* Capt. Mogg and his brother are commemorated on a brass Cross in Bishop's Canning (St. Mary the Virgin) Parish Church of which their father was vicar.

His brother Aubrey also has no known grave; he is recorded on Panel 30.

(Panel 18) Lieut. Herbert Assheton Bromley, No.3 Coy. 7th Bn. Canadian Infantry (1st British Columbia Regt.), C.E.F.: (Jett): *yst. s.* of the late Sir Henry Bromley, 5th Bt., by his wife Ada, only child of Westley Richards: *b.* Stoke Newark, 16 October 1879: *educ.* Farnborough and Eton: Occupation – Private Secretary to his brother, Sir Robert Bromley, Bt., Administrator of St. Christopher and Nevis (1905 – 06); afterwards to the Hon. James Dunsmuir, Lieut.-Gov. of British Columbia: joined 88th Fusiliers, Victoria, B.C., when that battn. was formed three years ago: volunteered for Overseas Service on the outbreak of war; gazetted Lieut. on formation of the Canadian Expeditionary Force, 21 September 1914, and was killed in action at the Second Battle of Ypres, 24 April 1915. Describing his death a comrade said, "He was badly wounded in the trenches but leaped out and led his men in a magnificent charge, calling out 'we have got to win, follow me.' He was quite alone away in front of his men and died a glorious death." His Company Commander, Major R.C. Cooper, wrote to the Editor as follows, "I would, as the late Lieut. H.A. Bromley's Company Commander, like to express my very high appreciation of him, both as an officer with the welfare of his men at heart, and as a personal friend. Mr Bromley was invaluable to me in France with his intimate knowledge of the language and customs. His men were devoted to him and missed him greatly when wounded in the head on the 16 March at Fleurbaix. He returned to us on 27 March and remained with the battn. up to 'Our Day' – doing duty in the trenches from the 14 to the 19 April, two days in billets and then the gas and subsequent heavy fighting. In Victoria, B.C., he was a member of the 88th Victoria Fusiliers, some time as a Company Officer and the remainder as Adjutant. He served with the regt. in the Civic Aid Force during the coal strikes at Nanaimo, Vancouver Island, 1913-14. On the outbreak of war he was one of the first officers selected for Active Service, being posted to my company, left for Valcartier, 28 August 1914, and for England, 27 September 1914, arriving at Plymouth, 15 October 1914 – four months of rain at Salisbury Plain and then to France. We all mourn 'Brom' as a pal and soldier. His last idea, and his was a forlorn hope, was to charge and scupper some of the Boches before going under himself. His platoon on 24 April lost twenty-one killed, sixteen wounded, three prisoners and eight wounded and prisoners. This record tells of his work." The following account of his death was published in the '*Daily Colonist*,' Victoria:– "Lieut. Bromley ... good sportsman and true friend, died as I think he would have wished to die. Wounded first in the head, he went to the supporting trench for first aid, and then, instead of going to the rear, as he might well have done, he preferred to return to the front line and 'carried on.' Soon he received another wound, this time in the left side – a bad wound that would have justified a stretcher party and hospital. Not troubling to even have this wound dressed, Bromley continued to fight on, and actually attempted to rally his men for a charge. Private Shaw, 104th Regiment of New Westminster, told me that Bromley came down his trench and asked how many men were left. Shaw told him 'two only.' 'Well, boys,' said Bromley, 'we have got to win the day; follow me.' These were his last words. He jumped out of the trench, waving his revolver, and ran towards the enemy's lines, but had not gone half a dozen yards before he fell." Another brother of Lieut. Bromley, Arthur, is a Captain in the Royal Navy, serving aboard H.M.S. Columbella: Age 36. *unm.*

(Panel 18) Lieut. Harry Carter, 7th Bn. Canadian Infantry (British Columbia Regt.), C.E.F.: late *husb.* to Sarah C. Carter, *née* Pretorius (Mountain View, Pretoria, Transvaal, South Africa): *s.* of Richard Carter, of Liverpool, United Kingdom, by his wife Ann Elisa: served with the Expeditionary Force in France and Flanders for 3 years and 3 months, and was killed in action 11 November 1917: Age 35.

(Panel 18) Lieut. Fred Fletcher Elliott, 7th Bn. Canadian Infantry (British Columbia Regt.), C.E.F.: 2nd *s.* of the Rev. William Elliott, of 'Jubilee,' 61, Dupplin Road, Victoria, British Columbia, Methodist Minister, formerly missionary Japan, by his wife Maria, *dau.* of George William Robinson: and brother to Pte. 16885, G.W. Elliott, 7th Canadian Infantry, who volunteered at the same time; killed in action 24

April 1915, at Langemarck: *b.* Kanazawa, Japan, 26 January 1891: Occupation – Bank Accountant: enlisted Valcartier, 19 September 1914; no.16302: left Canada with 1st Contingent, October 1914: underwent training on Salisbury Plain during the winter 1914 – 15: went to France February 1915, and was killed in action at Mount Sorrell, 3 June 1916: Age 25. *unm.*

His brother George also has no known grave; he is recorded on Panel 24.

(Panel 18) Lieut. Carleton Colquhoun Holmes, 7th Bn. Canadian Infantry (British Columbia Regt.), C.E.F.: only *s.* of the late Arthur Holmes, of 704, Esquimalt Road, Victoria, British Columbia) by his wife Adelaide (1502, Jubilee Avenue, Victoria): *b.* Shipley, co. York, 1 July 1886: *educ.* Streete Court, Westgate-on-Sea, and Haileybury College, where he was a member of the Cadet Corps affiliated with the Bedfordshire Regt.: on leaving school joined the Honourable Artillery Company, serving with that corps until emigrating to Canada, 1906: joined 88th Regiment, Victoria Fusiliers, on its formation, 1912, obtaining his commission as Lieut. in it, and was Acting Adjutant when the Nanaimo Coal Strikes necessitated the calling up of the Militia from Victoria: sent with the first draft to quell the disturbance, he remained as Quartermaster of the Civil Aid Force under Col. J.A. Hall until the outbreak of the European War: apptd. Lieut. 7th Canadian Infantry, 22 September 1914, and left with the first draft for Valcartier: served with the Expeditionary Force, and was killed in action at Langemarck, 24 April 1915, when the Canadians were retiring from the first to the second line of trenches: Age 28. *unm.*

(Panel 18) Lieut. Gerald Hamilton Peters, 7th Bn. Canadian Infantry (British Columbia Regt.), C.E.F.: *s.* of Frederick Peters, Premier; Prince Rupert, British Columbia, by his wife Roberta 'Bertha' Susan Hamilton, *dau.* of John Hamilton Gray, and Susan Ellen Bartley: and brother to Pte. 17417, J.F. Peters, 7th Canadian Infantry, killed in action 24 April 1915; cousin to 2nd Lieut., E.S. Poole, 11th West Yorkshire Regt., executed – Desertion, 11 December 1916: *b.* Charlottetown, Prince Edward Island, 8 November 1894: Occupation – Bank Clerk: enlisted Montreal, 9 February 1915. Killed in action 3 June 1916: Age 21. Another brother Capt. Frederic 'Fritz' T. Peters, Royal Navy, was awarded the Victoria Cross in World War II (he also held the D.S.O., D.S.C. & Bar); he was killed in an aerial collision 13 November 1942.

His brother John also has no known grave, he is recorded on Panel 24; cousin Eric is buried in Poperinghe New Military Cemetery (II.A.11). 'Fritz' Peters has no known grave; he is commemorated on the Portsmouth Naval Memorial (Panel 61, Col.3).

(Panel 18) Sergt. 16204, Frederick Cocroft, 7th Bn. Canadian Infantry (British Columbia Regt.), C.E.F.: late *husb.* to Florence Cocroft (644, Joyce Road, Collingwood East, Vancouver, British Columbia): *s.* of William Cocroft, of 41, York Road, Bowdon, co. Chester, by his wife Elizabeth: came over with 1st Canadian Contingent, October 1914: served with the Expeditionary Force in France and Flanders, and was killed in action north-east of St. Julien, 24 April 1915, at the Second Battle of Ypres: Age 32.

(Panel 18) Sergt. 16246, Hugh Nisbet Pearless, D.C.M., 7th Bn. Canadian Infantry (British Columbia Regt.), C.E.F.: *s.* of the late Reginald Wilson Pearless, by his wife Alice ('Heatherlea,' Gratwicke Road, Worthing, co. Sussex). Killed in action 24 April 1915, being shot while manning one of two Colt machine guns at the cross-roads north-east of St. Julien in company with Lieut. E. Nisbet who was awarded the Victoria Cross for his part in the action, and Sergt. Pearless the Distinguished Conduct Medal posthumously: Age 30. See Corpl. J.W. Odlum, Perth Cemetery (China Wall), XIII.B.5.

PANEL 18 ENDS CORPL. W.W. WATSON, 7TH BN. CANADIAN INFANTRY.

South Portal (Right)

PANEL 20 BEGINS CAPT. F.C.C. ROGERS, DUKE OF CORNWALL'S L.I.

(Panel 20) Lieut. Ronald Moseley Aston, 2nd Bn. (46th Foot) The Duke of Cornwall's Light Infantry: *s.* of the late Capt. Frederic Marriner Aston, 6th D.C.L.I., of 'Costislost,' Washaway, co. Cornwall, by his marriage to Florence Katherine Miller, *née* Aston (re-married), currently resident Great Trethew, Menheniot, co. Cornwall: *educ*. Rugby School: served with the Expeditionary Force in France from 21 December 1914, and was killed in action 14 March 1915, on which date the battalion were in trenches in the vicinity of 'The Mound,' St. Eloi. At 5 p.m. the enemy detonated a mine beneath the Cornwall's position, completing destroying trenches 17 and 18, and, following a heavy bombardment, commenced a strong attack. The official report of the action (despite the heavy losses incurred by the battalion) read:– "Our artillery opened fire at once, as well as our infantry, and inflicted considerable losses on the enemy during their advance. But chiefly owing to the explosion of the mines, and the surprise of the overwhelming artillery attack, the enemy penetrated the first line of trenches at some points. As a consequence of the garrisons of other units which had successfully resisted the assault, the Cornwall's were enfiladed and forced to retire just before it turned dark." Age 20. *unm*. A fair batsman, bowler and fieldsman, he was a member of the Rugby XI, 1911-12; heading the bowling average in the latter year with a record twenty wickets for 15.6 runs each. In the two matches he played in against Marlborough he made 47 runs in two completed innings and took ten wickets for 184 runs.

His father – killed at Hooge, 30 July 1915 – is buried in Sanctuary Wood Cemetery (I.C.4).

(Panel 20) Lieut. Charles Vivian DeGrete Edye, The Duke of Cornwall's Light Infantry attd. 1st Bn. Royal Welsh Fusiliers: *yr. s.* of Ernest Edye, of West Hill Lodge, Budleigh Salterton, formerly of Gifford Lodge, Twickenham, co. Middlesex, by his wife Kate S. He came from a very old Service family; going back only to his great-grandfather, who was one of five – two sons were in the Admiralty, two in Royal Navy, and a daughter married to a Commander, R.N. His great-grandfather had three sons – two post Captains, and one an Admiral – and three daughters – one married a sailor, one a soldier, and one an Admiralty official. Lieut. Edye's father was nominated a Naval cadet, but rejected by the doctors, and his only uncle is a retired Lieut.Col., Royal Marines. His only brother is in the Indian Civil Service. On his mother's side Huish was formerly a well-known naval name, but her father was in the 5th Lancers, subsequently transferring to 3rd Hussars.: *b*. 25 November 1886: *educ*. Stubbington; Sandroyd, and Bradfield College, from whence he passed into the Royal Military College, Sandhurst, where he won several cups and a revolver for topography: gazetted 2nd Lieut. Duke of Cornwall's Light Infantry, August 1905: promoted Lieut. January 1909: served in various stations abroad, including South Africa, attd. Mounted Infantry. In 1910, the Officer Commanding his battalion reported, "Commands his section well, is a good leader and instructor, a good horseman and horsemaster, has a very good eye for country, has tact, judgement, energy, and self-reliance; is quite reliable, has plenty of common sense, has influence over officers and men, lives quietly, is very fond of sport, is a very good scout officer, and has done very well.": apptd. A.D.C. to General Officer Commanding, China, but invalided home, July 1914, after enteric fever and pleurisy, at which time Major-General F.H. Kelly wrote, "We shall miss him very much. I found him a first-rate A.D.C. – neat, methodical, and always smart as paint." While on sick leave obtained permission to join the Depot of his regiment, and was almost immediately attached to 1st Royal Welsh Fusiliers, which he was in command of when it lost so many of its officers and other ranks during the First Battle of Ypres, 30 October 1914, and is believed to have been killed himself on that date. Confirmation has never been received, but owing to the lapse of time the War Office presume his death to have occurred on or about that date. He was a member of the Junior United Service Club, and good at all sports, but his favourite was polo, which he played wherever he was stationed. He was Secretary of the Hong Kong Polo Club when invalided home: Age 27. *unm*.

(Panel 20) 2nd Lieut. George John Lunnon, 'B' Coy., 2nd Bn. (46th Foot) The Duke of Cornwall's Light Infantry: *s*. of William Lunnon, Builder & Contractor; of 3, Portland Villas, Marlow, by his wife Marie Elizabeth: *b*. Great Marlow, co. Buckingham, 10 August 1887: assisted in his father's business until aged 18 when, having served 5 years as Bugler, 1st Bucks Rifle Volunteer Corps (in which his father served 27 years), he determined to join the Regular Army: joined 2nd Duke of Cornwall's Light Infantry, 10 November 1905, The Keep, Bodmin: went out with a draft to join 2nd Battn. at Gibraltar; rank L/Corpl.; two years thereafter proceeded to Bermuda (rank Corpl.), and two years later (apptd. Regimental

Schoolmaster Sergt.) went to Bloemfontein, South Africa: finding this work unsettling, applied to rejoin the battalion that – being six feet two inches tall, a splendid athlete, member of the regimental football and cricket teams; and while in Africa won the Regimental Rifle Championship – he might dedicate more time to these pursuits: proceeded with his battalion to Hong Kong late 1913: returned to England, November 1914, to take part in the Great War: on arrival in England, proceeded with his battalion to Hursley Park, Winchester, where his Colonel recommended him for a commission, requesting he remain with his own regiment: gazetted 2nd Lieut. December 1914, posted 2nd Duke of Cornwall's L.I.: went to France, December 1914; 82nd Bde., XXVIIth Divn.: eventually commanded 'B' Coy., and was killed at St. Jean, 23 April 1915, while leading an attack. A Captain wrote of him, "About poor Lunnon, he was wounded twice during that awful attack whilst at the head of his company. He kept up wonderfully well, but his Sergt.-Major advised him to leave the lines, but at that moment Lunnon was shot in the forehead. For several days he was missing. One night after we were fighting over that same ground his body was discovered in a ditch, quite five hundred yards from where he was shot. He had evidently struggled back towards the dressing station. I got some stretcher-bearers and buried his body by 2nd Lieut. H.G. Morris and Lieut. H. Stewart, of the Durham Light Infantry. We put up a little wooden cross and wrote the name on it. I had Lunnon's company afterwards, and I know how the men missed him." The officer now commanding the battalion wrote, "I only took over command of this battalion after the sad death of your son. I have asked the officers now left who were in the battalion at the time. Your son was in command of 'B' Company at the time of his death, and during the attack made by the regiment near St. Julien he was shot through the head. His company was one of the two leading companies of the battalion in the attack, and they came under a very rifle and machine-gun fire. I did not know your son personally, but from what I have heard he was a most excellent officer and his death was much regretted by all ranks, and had he been spared we are all sure he would have done very well." Age 27. *unm.*

Both 2nd Lieut. Henry G. Morris and Lieut. Herbert Stewart have no known grave; they are recorded on Addenda Panel 58, and Panel 36 respectively.

(Panel 20) 2nd Lieut. Edward Maxwell Vowler, 2nd Bn. (46th Foot) The Duke of Cornwall's Light Infantry: *b.* Marylebone, London, 1894: Occupation – Clerk; London Stock Exchange. Killed in action, 14 March 1915; The Mound, St. Eloi: Age 21. Remembered on a brass tablet in Marham Parish Church, Cornwall. Remains recovered unmarked grave (29.O.2.d.10.90); identified – Clothing, Disc; reinterred, registered 8 May 1930. *Buried in Sanctuary Wood Cemetery (V.M.9).*

(Panel 20) Corpl. 9680, Bert Alfred Corby, 2nd Bn. (46th Foot) The Duke of Cornwall's Light Infantry: late of Newport, co. Essex: elder brother to Pte. 10147, A.H. Corby, Duke of Cornwall's L.I., died of wounds 9 May 1915: *b.* St. Pancras, London, N.W.1: enlisted The Keep, Bodmin, co. Cornwall: served with the Expeditionary Force in France from December 1914, and was killed in action 14 March 1915, at The Mound, St. Eloi: Age 21. His sister, Mrs B.L. Ellis (21, Modbury Street, Kentish Town, London, N.W.5) would appreciate any information regarding her late brother.

His brother Albert also has no known grave; he is recorded below.

(Panel 20) L/Corpl. 9504, Frederick George Leonard Abrams, 2nd Bn. (46th Foot) The Duke of Cornwall's Light Infantry: 3rd *s.* of the late William J. Abrams, of Portsmouth, by his wife Caroline A. (5, Kent Street, Portsea, Portsmouth). Killed in action on the Western Front, 23 April 1915: Age 23. *unm.*

(Panel 20) L/Corpl. 13021, Walter Harold Dunn, 'D' Coy., 2nd Bn. (46th Foot) The Duke of Cornwall's Light Infantry: *s.* of Walter William Dunn, of 79, Sycamore Road, Handsworth, Birmingham, by his wife Ada: *b.* Small Heath, Birmingham: enlisted Birmingham. Killed in action on the evening of 14 March 1915, during the fighting at The Mound, St. Eloi: Age 17.

At 2.40 p.m., 23 April 1915, orders were issued for a general attack to be made between Kitchener's wood and the Yser Canal with the objective of regaining ground lost the previous day when the Germans first used poisonous gas against the Allies. On the right of the attack 2nd D.C.L.I. were to lead, supported by two companies of 9th Royal Scots on their right rear but, the attack – which had been ordered at the request of the French – never had any prospect of success. With 'B' and 'D' companies leading, 'A' and 'C' in support, the gallant Cornwall's set out in a northerly direction from Wieltje Farm; opening out at View Farm with 'B' Coy. extending east of the farm and 'D' extending west. No sooner had the leading lines of the attacking troops risen from the ground than they were met by a withering machine-gun and rifle fire. Yet on they went, against positions crammed with enemy troops whose fire swept the battlefield like a maelstrom. Carrying their attack into the smoke and dust the Cornwall's were soon lost from sight not only from observers but also from the enemy. 'B' Coy. reached Turco Farm, 'D' Coy. on the left reached some sheds left of the farm where they held on until 7 pm. and then joined 'B' Coy. until 9 pm. when both companies withdrew towards Foch Farm. On reaching Foch the two companies dug in just north of the farm, and were shortly thereafter joined by 'A' and 'C' companies who dug in south of the farm, with the York and Lancaster Regt. on their right just north of La Belle Alliance Farm.

The attack's lack of success, as foreseen before it began, was proven by the casualty figures:– "2nd Lieuts. G.J. Lunnon, H.G. Morris, H. Stewart, and 46 Other Ranks killed; Capts. A.P. Dene, R.H.G. Tatton, 2nd Lieuts. R.C. Jenkins, F.C.B. Savile, G.B. Howden, D.J. Tuck, A.F. Newbolt, and 216 Other Ranks wounded; 6 Other Ranks missing.

(Panel 20) L/Corpl. 3/5487, Albert English, 'C' Coy., 2nd Bn. (46th Foot) The Duke of Cornwall's Light Infantry: late of Hammersmith, London, W.: *s.* of the late Q.M.Sergt. Michael English, 19th Hussars, by his wife Margaret: *b.* Chapeltown, co. York, *c.*1874: enlisted D.C.L.I., The Keep, Bodmin, co. Cornwall: transf'd. from 3rd (Reserve) to 2nd Battn.: served with the Expeditionary Force in France and Flanders from late 1914. Recorded killed in action, 23 April 1915: Age 40.

(Panel 20) L/Corpl. 10771, Arthur Edward Jones, 'D' Coy., 6th (Service) Bn. The Duke of Cornwall's Light Infantry: *s.* of Henry Joseph Jones, of 127, Holmesdale Road, South Norwood, London, and Emma Ann Jones, his spouse: and brother to Corpl. 9589, H.V. Jones, 1st D.C.L.I., killed in action 8 May 1917, at Arras; and Pte. 683976, A.F. Jones, 1/22nd London Regt., killed in action 7 October 1916, at the Somme: *b.* Sydenham: enlisted St. Paul's Churchyard: served in France from 22 May 1915, and was killed in action at Hooge 30 July 1915: Age 26. One of three brothers who fell.

His brothers Herbert and Archibald also have no known grave, they are commemorated on the Arras Memorial (Bay 6), and Thiepval Memorial respectively.

(Panel 20) Pte. 10818, Robert Frederick Bliss, 2nd Bn. (46th Foot) The Duke of Cornwall's Light Infantry: *s.* of Robert E. Bliss, of 111, Victoria Parade, Moseley, co. Warwick, by his wife Alice Augusta: *b.* Ashford, co. Kent, *c.*1886: enlisted London. Died of wounds, 24 April 1915, at Poperinghe: Age 28. *Buried in Poperinghe Old Military Cemetery (II.K.23).*

Deep In Our Hearts
His Memory We Keep

(Panel 20) Pte. 17515 Thomas 'Tom' Brown, 1st Bn. (32nd Foot) The Duke of Cornwall's Light Infantry: One of two casualties sustained by the battalion, killed in action by enemy shell fire, 26 April 1915, while holding trenches between Hill 60 and the Ypres-Comines Canal. His Company Officer, Capt. Hingston, was also killed.

Capt. F.L. Hingston is buried in Poperinghe Old Military Cemetery (II.P.27).

(Panel 20) Pte. 12350, Edward Carlyle, Machine Gun Section, 6th (Service) Bn. The Duke of Cornwall's Light Infantry: *gdson.* of the late Edward Carlyle, of Milngate, Kirkmichael, Amisfield, co. Dumfries: Occupation – Footman; in employ to the Duke of Buccleuch & Queensberry, Montagu House, Whitehall: volunteered following the declaration of war August 1914, and enlisted in the 'Red Feathers': selected for Machine Gun Section: served with the Expeditionary Force in France and Flanders from May 1915, and was killed in action at Hooge, nr. Ypres, 30 July following. Buried at Zillebeke: Age 21. *unm.* (*IWGC record 31 July 1915*)

(Panel 20) Pte. 10147, Albert Harold Corby, 1st Bn. (32nd Foot) The Duke of Cornwall's Light Infantry: late of Newport, co. Essex: *yr.* brother to Corpl. 9680, B.A. Corby, Duke of Cornwall's L.I., killed in action at Ypres 14 March 1915: *b.* St. Pancras, London, N.W.1: enlisted Reading, co. Berks. Died of wounds, 9 May 1915, received from shellfire: Age 20. His sister, Mrs B.L. Ellis (21, Modbury Street, Kentish Town, London, N.W.5) would like to receive (and will reply to) correspondence from comrades of her late brothers.

His brother Bert also has no known grave; he is recorded above.

(Panel 20) Pte. 9409, John Huckle, 'D' Coy., 2nd Bn. (46th Foot) The Duke of Cornwall's Light Infantry: *s.* of John (& Mrs) Huckle of 7, Durrington Road, Homerton, London, E.5: *b.* Portland, co. Dorset: enlisted Stratford, London, E.15: served with the Expeditionary Force in France and Flanders from 21 December 1914, and was killed in action on the evening of 14 March 1915, when trenches 17 and 18 – occupied by 'D' Coy. – on the right of 'The Mound' (St. Eloi) were destroyed by the explosion of a mine: Age 22. *unm.*

(Panel 20) Pte. 16805, Charles Henry Libby, Machine-Gun Section, 7th (Service) Bn. The Duke of Cornwall's Light Infantry: late of Broadoak, co. Cornwall: *b.* Lostwithiel: enlisted Bodmin. Killed in action by the burst of a large shell which completely destroyed and buried the occupants of a machine-gun post; Boesinghe, opposite Brielen, 10 March 1916. See account re. Pte. H.J. Smith (below).

(Panel 20) Pte. 3/4906, Herbert Mancktelow, 1st Bn. (32nd Foot) The Duke of Cornwall's Light Infantry: *s.* of Alfred Mancktelow, of 4, St. Leonard's Avenue, Poplar, London, by his wife Isabella: and elder brother to Rfn. R/41297, H. Mancktelow, King's Royal Rifle Corps, posted Queen's Westminster Rifles, killed in action 28 September 1918: enlisted Stratford: killed in action 21 November 1914: Age 18.

His brother Horace is buried in Messines Ridge British Cemetery (II.B.39).

(Panel 20) Pte. 12118, Alfred John Pedel, 2nd Bn. (46th Foot) The Duke of Cornwall's Light Infantry: *s.* of Frederick John Pedel, Publican; 'The Railway Hotel,' Wendover, co. Buckingham, by his wife Emily: and elder brother to Sergt. 205080, F.W. Pedel, 1st Royal Buckinghamshire Hussars, died of wounds, 16 November 1917; Palestine: *b.* Halton, nr. Wendover, 7 February 1894: *educ.* Wendover Church of England School: Occupation – Clerk; London & Birmingham Railway Clearing House, Drummond Street, London: enlisted St. Pancras, London. Died 15 February 1915, of wounds: Age 21. *unm.*

His brother Frederick is buried in Ramleh War Cemetery (P.40).

On the night of 27 – 28 February 1916, 7th D.C.L.I. went into the line south of Boesinghe opposite Brielen, and remained in the sector throughout the following month. The Regimental History records:– "Life in the trenches during March was horrible. The weather did its best to make things utterly miserable – frost, rain, snow and sleet coming alternately. After heavy snow had fallen, the sun would come out and melt it, filling the trenches with snow-water. The enemy was also extremely active firing were those beastly things, aerial torpedoes, into the trenches, causing extensive damage. Retaliation shoots did something to cool his ardour, but still his guns of all calibres shelled the front line and local areas with unceasing energy....as an instance of the damage done by the enemy's shellfire – a machine-gun and its whole team, with the exception of an N.C.O., was buried by the burst of a large shell on 10th March." Ptes. H.J. Smith and C.H. Libby were killed.

(Panel 20) Pte. 15576, Harold James Smith, Machine-Gun Section, 7th (Service) Bn. The Duke of Cornwall's Light Infantry: *s.* of James Smith, of 95, Steward Street, Spring Hill, Birmingham, by his wife Frances K.: *b.* St. Peter's, Birmingham: enlisted Birmingham. Killed in action by the burst of a large shell which completely destroyed and buried the occupants of a machine-gun post; Boesinghe, opposite Brielen, 10 March 1916: Age 23. *unm.*

Pte. C.H. Libby also has no known grave, he is recorded above.

(Panel 20) Pte. 11723, Charles Edward Towner, 6th (Service) Bn. The Duke of Cornwall's Light Infantry: *yst. s.* of James Towner, of 95, High Street, Wapping, London, by his wife Harriet. Killed in action 31 July 1915; Hooge: Age 19. One of three brothers who served in the Great War.

(Panel 20) Lieut. Rowland Hely Owen, 3rd (Reserve) attd. 2nd Bn. (76th Foot) The Duke of Wellington's (West Riding) Regt.: *s.* of Mr (& Mrs) Hely Owen, of 35, Bath Street, Huddersfield: *b.* Huddersfield, co. York, 16 September 1892: *educ.* Stancliffe Hall Preparatory School, and Dover College, where he was Head of the School House, and had a scholarship, afterwards matriculating in 1st Division, London

University: joined 3rd Duke of Wellington's Regt., February 1911; completing 8 months training with 2nd Battn., November following; articled to his father (Solicitor) the same month: promoted Lieut. 1912. On the outbreak of war he was at Hythe, co. Kent, taking a musketry course under instructions, with a view to examination for promotion to Captain: to complete the establishment joined 2nd Battn. in accordance with previous instructions on mobilisation, departing for France August 13th. He was present at the Battles of Mons, Le Cateau, the Marne, the Aisne, La Bassée (October), and the First Defence of Ypres, where he was wounded, 7 November 1914. After recovery spent a short time with 3rd Battn., and left again for France, 17 February, to rejoin 2nd Battn. as Senior Subaltern. Present at St. Eloi, March 14 – 17, and was killed at Hill 60, 18 April following; leading the successful charge on the Hill. His Commanding Officer writes, "He was a great friend of my own, and extremely popular with everyone, and I can hardly tell you how sorry we are to lose him. He has been doing splendid work." Whilst at Dover College he was in the Football XV, and afterwards was Captain of the Huddersfield Rugby Union Football Club, and a member of the Yorkshire Rugby Union, playing for Yorkshire County in their match against Cumberland in the season before the war. He was also fond of swimming, golf, fishing and photography. During his time spent convalescing he wrote to the secretary of the Huddersfield Old Boys Club, "This year was going to be our great year. Well, so it is if we send as many men to the field of battle as we send to the field of play." Published in the '*Huddersfield Chronicle*,' his words inspired a cartoon, which appeared in a national newspaper, which in turn became the basis for the well-known recruiting poster – 'Will they never come?' After his death the Huddersfield Chronicle reported:– "There can be no doubt that that cartoon and Lieut. Owen's words, crystallised into the question 'Will they never come?', gave a great fillip to recruitment at the end of last year." Age 22. *unm.*

(Panel 20) Lieut. Douglas Fenton de Wend, 2nd Bn. (76th Foot) The Duke of Wellington's (West Riding) Regt.: *survg.* twin *s.* of the late Col. Douglas de Wend, 1st Duke of Wellington's (West Riding) Regt., of Aislaby Hall, Sleights, co. York, by his wife Alice Woodroffe de Wend, *née* Chester (Poyle Park, Tongham, co. Surrey): his grandfather served in the 44th Regt., and great-grandfather 60th Rifles: *b.* 1890: *educ.* Wellington College, Crowthorne, co. Berks (in the Wellesley, 1904 – 08, and a prominent member of the Rifle Club), and Royal Military College, Sandhurst (entered 1908): obtained his commission in his father's old regiment, December 1909: gazetted 2nd Lieut. West Riding Regt. 20 April 1910, promoted Lieut. 25 January 1914: served with the Expeditionary Force in France and Flanders, and was killed in action while fighting the Prussian Guard during the First Battle of Ypres, 10 – 11 November 1914. Lieut. de Wend was fond of football and hunting, and was a member of the Public Schools Club: Age 24.

(Panel 20) Lieut. Frederick Rennell Thackeray, M.C., 2nd Bn. (76th Foot) The Duke of Wellington's (West Riding Regt.) only *s.* of Col. Frederick Rennell Thackeray, 75th Bde. Royal Field Artillery, Guards Divn., who has since died (15 October 1915) on active service, by his wife Mary (Fleet, co. Hants), *dau.* of Col. J.O. Hasted, Royal Engineers: and *gdson.* of the late Capt. F.R. Thackeray, Highland Light Infantry: *b.* Campbellpore, Punjab, India, 24 March 1892: *educ.* St. Lawrence College, Ramsgate (1st Hockey Team and School XI); and Royal Military College, Sandhurst: gazetted 2nd Lieut. March 1912, posted 2nd West Riding Regt.: on the outbreak of war August 1914, was stationed at Dublin, and promoted Lieut.: went to France with his battalion, 13th Bde., Vth Divn.: took part in the engagement at Mons, and through the great retirement: present at the battles of Le Cateau, the Marne, the Aisne, and First Battle of Ypres (November 1914), after which he became Acting Adjutant: was invalided to Nice, March 1915, rejoining his battalion April following; reaching the trenches 17th. of that month. The following day (18 April 1915) he was sent for to take command of 'B' Coy., and was killed while leading his men in the charge on Hill 60, being shot through the head. The Regiment gallantly carried on the attack at the point of the bayonet, and, despite suffering very heavily in officers and men, held their position against all German counter-attacks until relieved. He was a general favourite, and much loved by his men. Just before their charge he spoke to them, saying, "Come on, boys; it's a tough job, but we've got to do it, so let's at it;" and his last words were, turning to his men, "Remember, you belong to the 'Duke's.'" His Commanding Officer wrote, "While he was Acting Adjutant, *i.e.*, after the Battle of Ypres, when the

Adjutant was wounded, until I left the Regiment after Xmas, we were together practically day and night, and, although many years younger than myself, I was always glad to have him with me. He was so bright and clever, and such a gallant young fellow, it is very hard that he should be taken away so young. He had done splendidly since the very beginning of the Campaign, and had seen more fighting than anyone else in the Battalion." The shell fire on Hill 60 was so great that the body of Lieut. Thackeray, and those of two others who had fallen, could not be removed, so they were buried side by side in a piece of land between the British and German trenches. For his services in the war he was Mentioned in Sir John (now Lord) French's Despatch, 14 January 1915, and awarded the Military Cross ('*London Gazette*,' 18 February 1915) for 'gallant and distinguished service in the field.' Age 23. *unm.*

His father, Col. F.R. Thackeray, is buried in Etretat Churchyard (I.C.17).

(Panel 20) 2nd Lieut. William Lyon Anderton, 4th Bn. The Duke of Wellington's (West Riding) Regt. (T.F.): elder *s.* of the Rev. William Edward Anderton, M.A., Congregational Minister, Woodford Green, Essex, by his wife Ellen, *dau.* of John Tyrer, of Liverpool: *b.* Woodford Green, 17 January 1885: *educ.* St Aubyn's School, Woodford Green, and Merchant Taylors' School, where he gained his colours for both cricket and football: Occupation – Director; Messrs George Anderton & Son Ltd., Cleckheaton Yorkshire: enlisted as Pte., West Riding Regt., 10 August 1914, following the declaration of war, and six months later, January 1915, was given a commission in his own regiment. He was shot by a sniper, while going his rounds as bombing officer, at 4.30 a.m., 21 August. 1915, about two miles north of Ypres, on the eastern bank of the Yser Canal. Writing to his father, Brig.-Gen. E. Brereton, Comdg. 147th Infantry Brigade, said, "I am able to send you the following particulars:– I left my headquarters at 4a.m. yesterday morning on my round of inspection. There is one corner where one has to leave a trench and be in the open more or less for about six paces, and then enter the trench again. At about 4.30 a.m. I came to this bit, and as I turned into the open found a small party with Mr. Law, of the 6th Battn., with your poor son lying at their feet. They said, 'For God's sake jump in quick; they have sniped Mr Anderton.' I saw at a glance his case was hopeless, poor boy. He was not suffering, of that I am sure, for practically the bullet had, I should imagine, passed through near the brain. I then proceeded on my rounds, and about three-quarters of an hour afterwards passed back, and found he had been moved to a first-aid post about 200 yards along the trench. He was still breathing as I passed, but quite unconscious. He died shortly afterwards, I understand. He died doing his duty. As you know, he was bombing officer to his battn. I knew him fairly well, and looked upon him as a very charming fellow, and an excellent officer." Other letters from his Company Officers and comrades unite in speaking of him in the highest terms. Gen. E.M. Perceval, 49th (West Riding) Divn., wrote, "Brig.-Gen. Brereton, who commands the 147th Infantry Brigade, told me that your son was one of his best officers, and I know that his brother officers and men were very fond of him." Lieut.-Col. E.P. Chambers, Commanding 4th West Riding Regt., "He was a most popular officer with the men, and everyone will feel his loss. Officers of his experience are difficult to replace, and our Battalion is much the poorer by his death." And Capt. W.F. Denning, "I was quite close to him when he was killed, at about 4.30a.m., being caught by a sniper. He was shot in the head and never regained consciousness, and I am thankful to be able to reassure you that he suffered no pain. We have been in perhaps the worst trench in the whole line, and have had a very hard and trying time, losing some good men, but I think poor Lyon's death was the last straw. I buried him on the canal bank in the afternoon, and we have put a cross over his grave, which adjoins the graves of several other soldiers. I'm afraid no words of mine can lessen your grief, but I should like you to know how much we all loved him, officers, N.C.O.'s, and men alike, and how terrible it feels to miss him." His cousin, German, Major H. Lyon Anderton, 1/6th West Yorkshire Regt., was wounded while in command of 11th West Yorkshire Regt., and is now (1916) on active service with the Expeditionary Force in France. Age 30. *unm.*

(Panel 20) 2nd Lieut. Thomas Wright Carson, 6th Bn. The Duke of Wellington's (West Riding) Regt. (T.F.): *yst. s.* of the late Rev. William Carson, Vicar of Girlington, Bradford, and Mrs Carson (Salisbury Street, Skipton, co. York): *educ.* Lancaster Grammar School, and Merchant Tailor's School, Liverpool: held an appointment with a firm of solicitors in North Wales but, on the outbreak of war, relinquished that position and joined 2/6th Duke of Wellington's Regt.: proceeded to France 1 November 1915 where, for a short while, he was attached to an entrenching battalion: subsequently transf'd. 6th Duke of Wellington's and was reported missing in action two weeks later; since confirmed killed on or about 27 – 28 December 1915: Age 31. Prior to enlistment he was also prominently involved with the Boy Scout movement. Remains recovered Langemarck German Cemetery No.9 (20.U.28.b.7.5), German Grave No.96/A. Identified – Burial List / Plan No.1283, Boots, Clothing; reinterred, registered 23 July 1929. *Buried in Sanctuary Wood Cemetery (V.J.6).*

(Panel 20) Coy.Sergt.Major 13453, William Swainston, 9th (Service) Bn. The Duke of Wellington's (West Riding) Regt.: Killed in action 2 March 1916. Remains 'Unknown British R.S. Major.;" recovered (28.I.34.b.4.3) unmarked grave; identified – Clothing, Badge of Rank, Crown, 'McC' on False Teeth; reinterred, registered 19 July 1927. *Buried in Sanctuary Wood Cemetery (IV.F.6).*

(Panel 20) Corpl. 13174, Dennis Bradbury, 10th (Service) Bn. The Duke of Wellington's (West Riding) Regt.: brother to Mrs E. Armitage (21, Hobson Terrace, Guiseley, Leeds): Killed in action 10 June 1917: Age 33. A comrade, Pnr. G. Ingle wrote, "Dear Friends, May we, the boys who were with him, offer you our deepest sympathy in your loss. He died nobly. Hearing a wounded man call, he at once went to assist, and I am sorry, very sorry, to say he was killed instantly. Surely no man could do more than this. We buried him near the spot, and will do our utmost to make him a cross (a proper one) when next we go that way. As I live near you (Ilkley), we had many talks of home and promised to see each other if we got back safely. After making inquiries I obtained this address, which I think is his sister's. We were together all the time and we realise that we have lost a good and faithful pal. He died bravely and nobly, doing his duty, helping his comrade. May this comfort all of you, his relatives at home. It reminds one of 'Greater love hath no man than this.' Anything I can tell you, or do, ask me. Someday, perhaps, I may see you. Please accept our deepest sympathy in your loss. May God give you strength to bear it bravely..."

(Panel 20) Corpl. 1318, Lewis Whiteley, 1/4th Bn. The Duke of Wellington's (West Riding) Regt. (T.F.): *s.* of Reuben Whiteley, of 2, Half House Lane, Hove Edge, Hipperholme, Halifax, co. York, by his wife Sarah Jane: and brother to Gnr. L/25880, F. Whiteley, 'D' Bty., 281st Bde. R.F.A., died of wounds 30 August 1918: a pre-war Territorial, prior to volunteering for Active Service and enlisting, August 1914, was employee to Messrs Craven & Pearson, Valley Dyeworks: proceeded to France April 1915, and was killed while in the process of preparing some food 31 July 1915; Lancashire Farm sector, Ypres: Age 20. Corpl. Whiteley was a regular attendee of St. Chad's Church and Sunday School.

His brother Fred is buried in Bucquoy Road Cemetery, Ficheux (VI.G.2).

(Panel 20) L/Corpl. 3/11878, Asa Clayton, 8th (Service) Bn. The Duke of Wellington's (West Riding) Regt.: *s.* of William Clayton, of 12, Rose Avenue, Horsforth, Leeds, and Ann, his spouse: and elder brother to Dvr. 795366, T. Clayton, Royal Field Artillery, killed in action 2 October 1917: *b.* Horsforth: enlisted Keighley, co. York. Killed in action 10 August 1917: Age 23. *unm.*

His brother Ted is buried in Vlamertinghe New Military Cemetery (V.H.15).

(Panel 20) L/Corpl. 7697, Arthur John William Maslen, 'G' Coy., 2nd Bn. (76th Foot) The Duke of Wellington's (West Riding) Regt.: *s.* of Arthur G. Maslen, of 31, Red Lion Street, Holborn, London, and the late Agnes Maslen: and brother to L/Corpl. 18256, W.A. Maslen, East Surrey Regt., died 19 September 1918, of wounds: *b.* Finsbury: enlisted London. Killed in action 18 April 1915, at Hill 60: Age 28. *unm.*

His brother William is buried in Doingt Communal Cemetery Extension (I.E.28).

(Panel 20) L/Corpl. 2440, Harold Naylor, 1/4th Bn. The Duke of Wellington's (West Riding) Regt. (T.F.): late of Howard House, Brighouse,. co. York: *s.* of B. (& Mrs) Naylor, of Cliffe House, Brighouse, co. York.: *b. c.*1890: *educ.* Rastrick Grammar School, 1901 – 1906: Occupation – Director, Messrs William Naylor & Sons, Removal Contractors & Coal Factors: enlisted September 1914, after the outbreak of war: served with the Expeditionary Force, and was killed near Thiepval Wood, during the Battle of the Somme, 27 August 1916: Age 26. *Circumstances re. this casualty dictate commemoration on the Thiepval Memorial.*

(Panel 20) Pte. 2664, Stephen Bishop, 1/6th Bn. The Duke of Wellington's (West Riding) Regt. (T.F.): late of 25, Rowland Street, Skipton, co. York: a well-known member of Skipton Rugby Football Club: enlisted Skipton: served with the Expeditionary Force in France from 14 April 1915, and was killed in action 18 July following: Age 37. He was married to Ellen Hudson, *née* Bishop (19, Otley Street, Skipton).

(Panel 20) Pte. 12613, James Brennan, 3rd (Reserve) attd. 9th (Service) Bn. The Duke of Wellington's (West Riding) Regt.: eldest *s.* of James Brennan, Labourer; of 8, Coach Fold, Haley Hill, Halifax, by his wife Catherine: *b.* Halifax, co. York, 9 April 1894: *educ.* St. Bernard School, Halifax: Occupation – Brick Moulder; Horley Green Brick Works: enlisted 27 September 1914, after the outbreak of war: served with the Expeditionary Force in France and Flanders from 19 June, 1915, and was killed in action at Ypres 2 March 1916: Age 21. *unm.*

(Panel 20) Pte. 2153, John Frederick 'Fred' Cocker: 1/4th Bn. The Duke of Wellington's (West Riding) Regt. (T.F.): late of 10, Halifax Road, Brighouse, co. York: *s.* of Fred Cocker, of 33, Grosvenor Terrace, Brighouse, and his spouse Mary Ellen: *b.* Grosvenor Terrace, *c.*1897: *educ.* Rastrick Grammar School, 1908 – 1912; thereafter was employee Messrs John Sykes & Co., Woollen Merchants, Huddersfield: volunteered and enlisted August 1914; proceeded to France April 1915, and was killed by a sniper whilst on sentry duty at Ypres, 25 August 1915: Age 19. He attended Bethel United Methodist Church and Sunday School.

(Panel 20) Pte. 11472, John Cogan, Machine Gun Section, 'C' Coy., 9th (Service) Bn. The Duke of Wellington's (West Riding) Regt.: resident with his wife and daughter at 9, Toothill Bank, Rastrick: *b.* Cork, *c.*1871: Occupation – Mason's Labourer: enlisted following the outbreak of war August 1914: served with the Expeditionary Force in France and Flanders, and was killed at Ypres, 2 March 1916: Age 41.

(Panel 20) Pte. 11511, William Harris, 2nd Bn. (76th Foot) The Duke of Wellington's (West Riding) Regt.: 2nd *s.* of the late William Harris, by his wife Mary (16, Radcliffe Road, Hough, Bolton): and elder brother to Rfn. R/9237, C. Harris, 9th King's Royal Rifle Corps, died Freidrichsfeld P.o.W. Camp, Germany, 26 September 1918: *b.* Salford, co. Lancaster: *educ.* Hough School: enlisted Huddersfield. Killed in action 5 May 1915; Hill 60. Four other brothers – Robert, Jack, Harry, Arthur – also served; all survived.

His brother Cyril is buried in Glageon Communal Cemetery Extension (II.H.6).

(Panel 20) Pte. 3/12716, James Mortimer, 9th (Service) Bn. The Duke of Wellington's (West Riding) Regt.: late of Milner Road, Luddenfoot: *b.* Bury, co. Lancaster, *c.*1881: Occupation – Spinner; Fairlea Mill: enlisted 1914: served with the Expeditionary Force in France and Flanders, and was killed in action 2 March 1916. A member of Luddenfoot Working Men's Club, and attendee St. Walburger Roman Catholic Church: Age 24. *unm.*

(Panel 20) Pte. 3/11052, James William Plaiter, 2nd Bn. (76th Foot) The Duke of Wellington's (West Riding) Regt.: *s.* of George Plaiter, of 8, Top-o-th'-Hill, New Hey, Rochdale, by his wife Isabella: and elder brother to L/Corpl. 30761, T. Plaiter, 2nd Green Howards, killed 31 July 1917, at the Third Battle of Ypres: *b.* Shipley, co. York: enlisted Huddersfield. Died of wounds 5 May 1915: Age 20. *unm.*

His brother Thomas also has no known grave; he is recorded on Panel 33.

(Panel 20) Pte. 3241, Fred Roberts, 'C' Coy., Machine Gun Section, 1/4th Bn. The Duke of Wellington's (West Riding) Regt. (T.F.): *s.* of the late Joseph Roberts 8, Firth Street, Rastrick, Brighouse, co. York, by his wife Emma: *b. c.*1890: *educ.* Rastrick Grammar School, 1901 – 1907: attended Park United Methodist Church and Sunday School; member of Bridge End Gymnasium: served with the Expeditionary Force, and was killed by a sniper, 27 September 1915, whilst using a periscope on sentry duty: Age 24.

(Panel 20) Pte. 3/10512, George Wilfred Robertshaw, 2nd Bn. (76th Foot) The Duke of Wellington's (West Riding) Regt.: *s.* of John Robertshaw, of Broad Head End, Hollock Lee, Mytholmroyd, co. York, by his wife Alice: b. Mytholmroyd, 1899: volunteered and enlisted 3rd (Reserve) Bn., Halifax, underage, August 1914; after the outbreak of war: subsequently transf'd. 2nd Battn.: proceeded to France with a draft of reinforcements, and was killed in action there 24 February 1915: **Age 16.**

(Panel 20) Pte. 4107, James Thornton, 1/4th Bn. The Duke of Wellington's (West Riding) Regt. (T.F.): s. of Martha Thornton (16, Birks Hall Terrace, Pellon Lane, Halifax): enlisted Halifax, co. York. Killed in action 17 August 1916, at the Somme: Age 25. *unm. Buried in Mill Road Cemetery, Thiepval (II.D.8).*

(Panel 20) Pte. 3/10545 John William Turpin, 2nd Bn. (76th Foot) The Duke of Wellington's (West Riding) Regt.: s. of the late Tom Turpin, of 8, New Street, Brighouse, co. York, by his wife Lily Ann: employee Messrs Jowetts Contractors, Brighouse: enlisted on the outbreak of war, 4 August 1914, and died of gas poisoning whilst in the process of retiring from Hill 60, Ypres sector, 5 May 1915: Age 21.

(Panel 20) Pte. 15306, Fred Wilcock, 9th (Service) Bn. The Duke of Wellington's (West Riding) Regt.: s. of William Wilcock, of Carterplace, Haslingden, co. Lancaster, and Jane Wilcock, his spouse: *b.* Longridge: enlisted Clitheroe, following the outbreak of war. Killed in action 2 March 1916: Age 26. *unm.* Remains recovered unmarked grave (28.I.34.b.4.3); identified – Sovereign Case mkd. 'F. Wilcock,' Clothing; reinterred, registered 18 July 1927. *Buried in Sanctuary Wood Cemetery (IV.F.4).*

Thy Will Be Done

(Panel 20) Pte. 3613, Jack Woodcock, 1/5th Bn. The Duke of Wellington's (West Riding) Regt. (T.F.): s. of John Woodcock, of Malling's Cottages, Ampthill Road, Bedford, by his wife Kate: *b.* Collingham, *c.*1899: enlisted Mirfield, co. York: served with the Expeditionary Force in France from April 1915, and was killed in action 9 November 1915; Canal Bank sector, Ypres: **Age 16.**

(Panel 20) Lieut.Col. Hugh Trevor Crispin, 2nd Bn. (107th Foot) The Royal Sussex Regt.: eldest s. of the late Trevor Crispin, of H.M. Treasury (Legal Department): *b.* London, 18 September 1868: *educ.* Bradfield College; Trinity College, Cambridge (graduated B.A.); Royal Military College, Sandhurst: gazetted 2nd Lieut., Leinster Regt., 18 May 1892; transf'd. Northumberland Fusiliers 14 December following: promoted Lieut. 21 July 1895; Capt. 17 February 1900; Major 8 February 1911: served in the Nile Expedition 1898 – took part in the Battle of Khartoum (Egyptian Medal with clasp: Medal): served in the South African War, 1899 – 1900; employed with Mounted Infantry: took part in the advance on Kimberley (severely wounded), including actions at Belmont, Enslin and Modder River: operations Orange Free State, February – May, 1900, including operations at Paardeberg (17 – 26 February): actions at Poplar Grove, Dreifontein, Vet River (5 – 6 May) and Zand River, and those in the Transvaal, May – June, 1900, including actions near Johannesburg, Pretoria and Diamond Hill (11 – 12 June), where he was severely wounded (Mentioned in Despatches ['*London Gazette*,' 10 September 1901], Queen's Medal, 6 clasps; Brevet of Major): apptd. to command 2nd Sussex Regt. 14 September 1914, after the outbreak of the European War: served with the Expeditionary Force in France and Flanders, and was killed in action nr. Ypres, Belgium, 30 October 1914: Age 46. *unm.*

(Panel 20) Lieut. Barry Pevensey Duke, 3rd attd 2nd Bn. (107th Foot) The Royal Sussex Regt.: eldest s. of the late Lieut.Col. O.T. Duke, by his wife Blanche (84, Bouverie Road West, Folkestone, co. Kent): *b.* 5 September 1889: *educ.* Wellington College; Royal Military College, Sandhurst: gazetted 2nd Lieut. Sussex Regt., October 1906; promoted Lieut. December 1909: served in the European War, and was killed in action 3 November 1914: Age 25. (*IWGC record age 27*)

(Panel 20) Lieut. Edward Arthur Lousada, 2nd Bn. (107th Foot) The Royal Sussex Regt.: s. of the late Capt. Simeon Charles Lousada, Norfolk Regt. (*d.*1905), of Shelburn Hall, Lansdowne Road, Cheltenham, co. Gloucester, and Charlotte Sophia Lousada (*née* Moysey), former wife of Thomas Marker: and twin brother to Lieut. B.C. Lousada, 1st York & Lancaster Regt., killed in action 9 May 1915: *b.* Cheltenham, 19 December 1888: *educ.* Cheltenham College; Royal Military College, Sandhurst: gazetted 2nd Lieut. Royal Sussex Regt., February 1909: promoted Lieut. October 1910: served with the Expeditionary Force in France and Flanders, and was shown in the Monthly Casualty List, published December 1914, as killed in action; no date or place being given: since confirmed 2 November 1914: Age 26. Remembered on Cheltenham War Memorial (North Panel), and his parents gravestone, St. Peter's Churchyard, Leckhampton.

His twin Bertie also has no known grave; he is recorded on Panel 55.

(Panel 20) 2nd Lieut. Leslie Robert Croft, 2nd Bn. (107th Foot) The Royal Sussex Regt.: *yst. s.* of Major G. (& Mrs) Croft, late Yorkshire and Royal Sussex Regiments, of Manor House, Hale, Farnham, co. Surrey: *b.* 1892: *educ.* Farnham Grammar School. The Head Master, Rev. G. Priestley, writing of him said, "All the boys of his time will remember his unfailing cheerfulness and his absolutely sterling character." He received his commission in the Royal Sussex Regt. from the ranks of the Cheshire Regt., 14 September 1912. The following account of his death was received from a Sergt. who was with him at the time:– "Lieut. Croft was in command of No.10 Platoon, which was leading 'C' Company of his battalion on the 30th October, when advancing against the Germans through a pine wood. As the enemy was found to be in force Lieut. Croft sent for reinforcements, and a few minutes after was wounded in the head. The Sergt. bandaged his head and selected a way for him to get away safely. Lieut. Croft, however, refused to leave, saying, 'I must see this job finished first.' These were his last words, for as he raised his head to give some command he was mortally wounded in the neck, death being practically instantaneous. "We all felt," said the Sergt., "that we had lost, not only an officer and a leader, but a great friend.": Age 22. *unm.*

(Panel 20) 2nd Lieut. Rolland Arthur Bazeley, 9th (Service) Bn. The Royal Sussex Regt.: *yr. s.* of Ernest A. Bazeley, of Woodland, Ottery St. Mary, co. Devon, by his wife Louisa Rolland, *dau.* of Major R.G. MacGregor: and nephew to the late Sir Charles Metcalfe MacGregor, K.C.B., Quartermaster-General, India: *b.* Ashwick Grange, nr. Bath, 11 October 1886: *educ.* Bedford Grammar School, and an Agricultural College: employed for two years in the teak forests, Burma, then acquired a ranch near Mara, British Columbia: on the outbreak of war he gave up everything and voluntarily enlisted: sent to England with a draft for Princess Patricia's C.L.I. Regt.: gazetted 2nd Lieut. 9th Sussex Regt., 20 March 1915: went to France, December following, and was killed in action 28 January 1916, nr. Hooge; being shot by a sniper. His Colonel wrote of him, "He was our Intelligence Officer and had charge of all our snipers. He was awfully keen on his job, very thorough and never spared himself; he had no fear, was as brave as the bravest and died like a hero." Age 29. *unm.*

(Panel 20) 2nd Lieut. Frederick Charles Jenner Marillier, D.C.M., 2nd Bn. (107th Foot) The Royal Sussex Regt.: only *s.* of Ernest Frank Jennens Marillier, Artist, of High Croft, Seaford, co. Sussex, late of Richmond, Malvern Link: *gdson.* to W. Marillier, one time Capt., Harrow XI; son of J.F. Marillier, for 50 years master at Harrow School: *b.* Fairlight, Hastings, 30 August 1888: *educ.* Privately: served in the ranks of the Army; went to the Front as Sergt. (no.9275): Mentioned in Despatches for having, on 1 October 1914, led a night attack on a German trench, which was captured and filled in: subsequently awarded the D.C.M. ('*London Gazette*,' 10 November 1914): after four and a half years in the ranks he was given his commission 2nd Lieut., Royal Sussex Regt., September 1914, and was killed in action, 30 October 1914, while leading his men in an attack on a wood near Ypres. A great favourite in his regiment, he was good at all sports, and played in the regimental football and cricket teams: Age 26. *unm.*

(Panel 20) 2nd Lieut. Gillachrist 'Gilla' Moore, 2nd Bn. (107th Foot) The Royal Sussex Regt.: *yr. s.* of Sir Norman Moore, M.D., F.R.C.P.S., 1st Bart., of Hancox in Whatlington, co. Sussex, and 94, Gloucester Place, London, W., by his wife Amy, *dau.* of William Leigh Smith, of Crowham: and brother-in-law (by the marriage of his sister, Ethne Philippa Moore, M.B.E., B.E.M.) to Lieut. Col. Walter M. Pryor, D.S.O.: *b.* London, 22 March 1894: *educ.* Oratory School, Birmingham; St. Catherine's College, Cambridge: received his commission August 1914; went to France September following, and was killed in action (being shot through the heart by a sniper) at the edge of a wood near Klein Zillebeke, a few yards from the German lines on the afternoon of 7 November 1914: Age 20. *unm.* Remembered on the Sedlescombe (St. John the Baptist) Church War Memorial.

(Panel 20) 2nd Lieut. Cuthbert Frank Shaw, Special Reserve attd. 'B' Coy., 2nd Bn. (107th Foot) The Royal Sussex Regt.: *s.* of Frank Herbert Shaw, of 'The Gables,' 60, London Road, St. Leonards-on-Sea, co. Sussex, by his wife Fanny Mary: *b.* 1894: *educ.* King's College, London (Student, Engineering Dept.), where he was a very active figure in the social life of the college during his three years there, being Secretary of the Rifle Club, Editor of the Engineering Faculty's section in '*The College Review*,' and

General Sub-Editor of the aforementioned publication; member of the College O.T.C. (attained Sergt.), having obtained the 'A' certificate while in Junior O.T.C., Gresham School, quickly qualified for his 'B' certificate: gazetted 2nd Lieut., Special Reserve of Officers, January 1914: proceeded to France, August 1914, and was killed in action in Flanders 31 October following: Age 20. *unm.*

(Panel 20) Sergt. 9490, Michael Delaney, 2nd Bn. (107th Foot) The Royal Sussex Regt.: *s.* of William Delaney, of Dublin Road, Carlow, by his wife Mary: served with the Expeditionary Force. Killed in action at Ypres, 30 October 1914: Age 25. *unm.*

(Panel 20) Sergt. L/6581, Arthur Hubert Kerswill, 2nd Bn. (107th Foot) The Royal Sussex Regt.: *s.* of the late John Edward Kerswill, by his wife Eliza: served with the Expeditionary Force in France. Killed in action at Ypres 30 October 1914: Age 30.

(Panel 20) Corpl. L/10203, Edward George Sangster, 2nd Bn. (107th Foot) The Royal Sussex Regt.: *s.* of H.P. (& Mrs) Sangster, of 19, Lumley Road, Horley, co. Surrey: and elder brother to Rfn. S/37658, H.A.M. Sangster, 2nd Rifle Brigade, died 17 October 1918, of wounds: *b.* Ipswich: enlisted East Grinstead: served with the Expeditionary Force, and was killed in action 6 November 1914: Age 19. (*MR.29,XXXI,pg.1280 records E. George, IWGC record E. Gregory*)

His brother Hugh is buried in Duisans British Cemetery, Etrun (VIII.B.4).

(Panel 20) L/Corpl. 15669, William Herbert Claude Bradbrook, 13th (Service) Bn. (3rd South Down) The Royal Sussex Regt.: eldest *s.* of John William Herbert Bradbrook, of 1, Winchester Street, Belgravia, London, S.W., by his wife Elizabeth Annie, *dau.* of Thomas Fenwick, of Chudleigh, co. Devon: *b.* Belgravia, 29 November 1886: *educ.* Westminster City School: Occupation – Butcher: enlisted Middlesex Regt., Piccadilly, 1 April 1916: later transf'd. Hertfordshire Regt.: served with the Expeditionary Force in France and Flanders from 18 August 1916, transf'd Royal Sussex Regt., and was killed in action 1 August 1917. Buried nr. St. Julien: Age 30. *unm.*

(Panel 20) L/Corpl. S/9964, Daniel Crowley, 2nd Bn. (107th Foot) The Royal Sussex Regt.: enlisted Eastbourne, co. Sussex: served with the Expeditionary Force. Reported missing; later confirmed killed in action 30 October 1914. *m.*

(Panel 20) L/Corpl. 8358, Edgar Gorringe, 2nd Bn. (107th Foot) The Royal Sussex Regt.: *s.* of John Gorringe, of 102, Ifield Road, Crawley, co. Sussex, by his wife Elizabeth: served with the Expeditionary Force, and was killed in action at Ypres, 30 October 1914: Age 30.

(Panel 20) L/Corpl. L/8030, Francis Hurst, 2nd Bn. (107th Foot) The Royal Sussex Regt.: served with the Expeditionary Force. Killed in action 30 October 1914.

(Panel 20) L/Corpl. L/10196, Wilfred John Jupp, 2nd Bn. (107th Foot) The Royal Sussex Regt.: *s.* of Charles Jupp, of 96, Elm Grove, Brighton, co. Sussex, by his wife Caroline: enlisted Chichester: served with the Expeditionary Force. Killed in action at Ypres 7 November 1914.

(Panel 20) L/Corpl. G/20566, Ernest Charles Wood, 9th (Service) Bn. The Royal Sussex Regt.: *s.* of James Wood, of The Forge House, Forge Hill, Pluckley, nr. Ashford, co. Kent, by his wife Elizabeth Rebecca: and brother to S/S. Corpl. SE/5648, J.W. Wood, Royal Army Veterinary Corps, died at Salonika, September 1918, of influenza; and Spr. 185773, H.H. Wood, Royal Engineers (surv'd.): enlisted Chelsea. Killed in action 3 August 1917: Age 23. *unm.*

His brother James is buried in Bralo British Cemetery, Greece (29).

(Panel 20) Pte. G/16616, James Edward Arundel, 9th (Service) Bn. The Royal Sussex Regt.: *s.* of Edwin Arundel, of 174, Ashford Road, Eastbourne, co. Sussex, by his wife Mary: and *yr.* brother to Corpl. 12532, J.W. Arundel, Wiltshire Regt., died 10 August 1915, at Gallipoli: *b.* Eastbourne, *c.*1888: Occupation – Clerk: enlisted Brighton. Killed in action 13 April 1917, at the Battle of Arras: Age 28.

His brother John also has no known grave; he is commemorated on the Helles Memorial.

(Panel 20) Pte. L/7701, Frederick Baker, 2nd Bn. (107th Foot) The Royal Sussex Regt.: *s.* of Henry Baker, of 149, Upton Lane, Forest Gate, London, E. (late of 38, Leslie Street, Eastbourne), by his wife Louisa: served with the Expeditionary Force in France, and was killed in action at Ypres, 30 October 1914: Age 30.

(Panel 20) Pte. 13466, Ernest Frank Berry, 13th (Service) Bn. (3rd South Down) The Royal Sussex Regt.: *s.* of Alfred Ernest Berry, of Ruckford, Hurstpierpoint, co. Sussex, by his wife Mary: *b.* Firle, Lewes, co. Sussex, 3 May 1898: *educ.* there: Occupation – County Accountant's Clerk: enlisted 25 June 1916: served with the Expeditionary Force in France and Flanders from 5 May 1917, and was killed in action at Ypres, 1 August following. An officer wrote, "He was a good soldier and very popular amongst his comrades and high in the esteem of the officers." Age 19. *unm.*

(Panel 20) Pte. S/414, Thomas Charles Bourne, 2nd Bn. (107th Foot) The Royal Sussex Regt.: *b.* Bolney, co. Sussex: served with the Expeditionary Force, and died while on Active Service at Ypres, 31 October 1914.

(Panel 20) Pte. L/6303, Frank Brown, 2nd Bn. (107th Foot) The Royal Sussex Regt.: *s.* of William Brown: *b.* Framfield, nr. Uckfield, co. Sussex, 1884: volunteered and enlisted 6 August 1914: served with the Expeditionary Force in France, and was killed in action at Ypres, 31 October 1914: Age 30. He *m.* Uckfield; Rosa (Red Crooke Cottage, Buxted, Uckfield), and had a son, Frank Frederick, *b.* 4 October 1914.

(Panel 20) Pte. S/416, George Burchell, 2nd Bn. (107th Foot) The Royal Sussex Regt.: *s.* of Albert Burchell, of Horsham: served with the Expeditionary Force. Killed in action at Ypres, 30 October 1914.

(Panel 20) Pte. L/9619, Thomas James Burton, 2nd Bn. (107th Foot) The Royal Sussex Regt.: *s.* of Thomas Burton, of 22, Janet Street, Milwall, Poplar, London, E., by his wife Julia Ann: served with the Expeditionary Force. Killed in action at Ypres, 30 October 1914: Age 19.

(Panel 20) Pte. L/6602, Frederick Bushby, 2nd Bn. (107th Foot) The Royal Sussex Regt.: served with the Expeditionary Force. Killed in action at Ypres, 30 October 1914.

(Panel 20) Pte. SD/5562, Stanley Button, 9th (Service) Bn. The Royal Sussex Regt.: *s.* of George Button, of Lime Kiln, Coddenham, Ipswich, by his wife Amelia, *dau.* of George Parker: *b.* Coddenham, 22 March 1894: *educ.* there: Occupation – Stockman: enlisted 7 April 1916: served with the Expeditionary Force in France and Flanders from 7 August following, and was killed in action 11 June 1917: Age 23. He *m.* Barking, co. Suffolk, 24 December 1914; Mary May Abbott, *née* Button (Ipswich Road, Needham Market), resident Bridge Street, Needham Market, *dau.* of John (& Eliza) Chaplin, and had a *dau.*, Ellen Mary, *b.* 29 January 1916.

(Panel 20) Pte. L/7331, John Collins, 2nd Bn. (107th Foot) The Royal Sussex Regt.: *s.* of the late James (& Fanny) Collins: served with the Expeditionary Force. Died 31 October 1914, from wounds received in action at Ypres: Age 32.

(Panel 20) Pte. L/10066, Reginald Coomber, 2nd Bn. (107th Foot) The Royal Sussex Regt.: *s.* of Frederick Coomber, of Hove, co. Sussex: served with the Expeditionary Force, and was killed in action at Ypres, 13 November 1914.

(Panel 20) Pte. L/8879, Frank Alfred Creed, 2nd Bn. (107th Foot) The Royal Sussex Regt. *s.* of the late William (& A.) Creed, of 52, Southwater Road, St. Leonards-on-Sea: served with the Expeditionary Force. Killed in action 31 October 1914: Age 26.

(Panel 20) Pte. G/3621, Jacob William Driver, 9th (Service) Bn. The Royal Sussex Regt.: eldest *s.* of the late James Driver, of Rottingdean, co. Sussex, by his wife Ellen (185, Bear Road, Brighton), *dau.* of J. Fensom: *b.* Connington, co. Cambridge, 10 December 1893: *educ.* Church of England School, Ovingdean, co. Sussex: enlisted Royal Sussex Regt. 4 September 1914: served with the Expeditionary Force in France and Flanders from January 1915: wounded 19 January 1916, and invalided home; returned to France 3 May following, and was killed in action at Ypres 29 July 1917. Buried in Larchwood Cemetery. His Commanding Officer wrote, "He was a fine lad, and I feel his loss personally, as I was with him when he was wounded last year, and it is another of the old ones gone, which fact, beyond his worth, which we all knew well, will make his loss felt by everyone in the company. You can well be proud of him, as I have seen his work in the line, and he did his bit and more." Age 33. *unm.* (*IWGC record age 34*)

(Panel 20) Pte. L/7778, John Joseph George Eckert, 2nd Bn. (107th Foot) The Royal Sussex Regt.: *s.* of Joseph Eckert, of Brighton, co. Sussex: served with the Expeditionary Force. Killed in action at Ypres, 1 November 1914.

(Panel 20) Pte. L/6315, Bartlett Cecil Elmes, 2nd Bn. (107th Foot) The Royal Sussex Regt.: late of the Soldiers & Sailors Home, 27, Upperton Road, Eastbourne: *s.* of Frederick Lonsdale Elmes, of Upper Holloway, London, E., by his wife Mary Rebecca: and yr. brother to Pte. L/6512, W.F. Elmes, 2nd Royal Sussex Regt., killed in action 9 May 1915, aged 34 years: a former Regular, served with 1st Battn. in the South African Campaign, re-enlisted Chichester, August 1914: served with the Expeditionary Force, and was killed in action 12 November 1914: Age 31. *m.* One other brother also served and made the supreme sacrifice.

His brother William also has no known grave; he is commemorated on the Le Touret Memorial.

(Panel 20) Pte. 794, George Froud, 'D' Coy., 11th (Service) Bn. (1st South Down) The Royal Sussex Regt.: *s.* of Sam Froud, Grocer's Assistan; of 10, Manor Villas, Wickham, co. Hants, by his wife Fanny, *dau.* of the late Alfred Bonford: *b.* Compton, nr. Petersfield, 12 May 1897: *educ.* there: Occupation – Painter: enlisted 8 September 1914: served with the Expeditionary Force in France and Flanders from March 1916, and was killed in action at Ypres, 31 July 1917. His Commanding Officer wrote, "He was a most trustworthy and gallant lad, a great loss to us all." Age 20. *unm.*

(Panel 20) Pte. TF/201445, William George Glaysher, 'C' Coy., 9th Bn. The Royal Sussex Regt.: *s.* of William George Glaysher, of Oak Villa, Perrymount Road, Hayward's Heath; late of 'The Dun Horse Inn,' Manning's Heath, by his wife Lucy: and brother to Pte. G/17842, F.M. Glaysher, died 14 May 1920: *b.* Horsham, co. Sussex: enlisted there. Killed in action 6 June 1917: Age 26. *unm.*

His brother Fred is buried in Nuthurst (St. Andrew's) Churchyard.

(Panel 20) Pte. L/10270, Ernest Herbert Grender, 2nd Bn. (107th Foot) The Royal Sussex Regt.: *s.* of John Grender, of Hook Lane, Aldingbourne, nr. Chichester, by his wife Annie: and brother to Pte. 727, S. Grender, 7th Royal Sussex Regt., died of wounds 4 March 1916: *b.* 1895 enlisted Chichester: served with the Expeditionary Force. Killed in action at Ypres, 14 November 1914: Age 19.

His brother Sidney is buried in Vermelles British Cemetery (II.G.14).

(Panel 20) Pte. L/6601, Alfred Henry Hall, 2nd Bn. (107th Foot) The Royal Sussex Regt.: *b.* Winchester, co. Hants: enlisted Poole, co. Dorset: served with the Expeditionary Force. Missing / believed killed in action 31 October 1914.

(Panel 20) Pte. L/7508, Robert James Heather, 2nd Bn. (107th Foot) The Royal Sussex Regt.: *s.* of Henry Heather, of Sutton, nr. Pulborough: enlisted Chichester, co. Sussex: served with the Expeditionary Force. Killed in action at Ypres, 30 October 1914.

(Panel 20) Pte. 16035, Richard Hellyer, 13th (Service) Bn. (3rd South Down) The Royal Sussex Regt.: *s.* of John Hellyer, of 'The Farm,' East Street, Littlehampton, co. Sussex, by his wife Eliza Down, *dau.* of Richard Weeks: *b.* Chagford, co. Devon, 19 June 1891: *educ.* Commercial School, Littlehampton: Occupation – Farmer: enlisted 20 March 1916: served with the Expeditionary Force in France and Flanders from 7 September following, and was killed in action in the advance at St. Julien, 31 July 1917. Buried at St. Julien: Age 26. *unm.*

(Panel 20) Pte. 6320, Frederick Curtis Holland, 2nd Bn. (107th Foot) The Royal Sussex Regt.: *s.* of George Holland, of Newland Road, Worthing, by his wife Harriett: enlisted Chichester, co. Sussex: served with the Expeditionary Force. Killed in action at Ypres, 30 October 1914: Age 30. He leaves a wife Elizabeth Emma Rose (30, Cottenham Road, Worthing).

(Panel 20) Pte. S/2130, Claude Gerald Hudson, 2nd Bn. (107th Foot) The Royal Sussex Regt.: *s.* of Mary Jane (1, Alma Villas, Cockfield Road, Hurstpierpoint, co. Sussex): served with the Expeditionary Force. Killed in action 23 December 1914: Age 20. *unm.*

(Panel 20) Pte. L/9867, Cornelius Coates Humphrey, 2nd Bn. (107th Foot) The Royal Sussex Regt.: *s.* of Harry Humphrey, of 3, Islingword Street, North Heath, Brighton, by his wife Rhoda A.: *b.* West

Chittington, co. Sussex, 1896: enlisted Petworth: served with the Expeditionary Force in France, and was killed in action at Ypres, 30 October 1914: Age 19.

(Panel 20) Pte. L/10112, Albert Charles Love, 'B' Coy, 2nd Bn. (107th Foot) The Royal Sussex Regt.: *s*. of Jemima Love (41, Shakespeare Road, Hove, Brighton): and brother to Pte. G/41303, P.G. Love, 4th Royal Fusiliers, killed in action 3 May 1917, at the Battle of Arras: *b*. Ryde, Isle of Wight, 1891. Killed in action 31 October 1914, nr. Ypres: Age 23. *unm*.

His brother Percy also has no known grave; he is commemorated on the Arras (Faubourg d'Amiens) Memorial (bay 3).

(Panel 20) Pte. G/19860, George Henry Mingay, 12th (Service) Bn. (2nd South Down) The Royal Sussex Regt.: *s*. of the late William Mingay, by his wife Emma Amelia (73, Chalk Lane, Bury St. Edmunds, co. Suffolk): and elder brother to Pte. 2052, A. Mingay, 5th Suffolk Regt., killed in action 7 October 1915, at Gallipoli: *b*. Bury St. Edmunds. Killed in action 3 February 1917: Age 31.

His brother Arthur is buried in Hill 60 Cemetery (I.E.4).

(Panel 20) Pte. L/7711, William Pattenden, 2nd Bn. (107th Foot) The Royal Sussex Regt.: *s*. of Ebenezer Pattenden, of Stonegate, co. Sussex, and Harriet Pattenden, his wife: and brother to Pte. A/40193, W. Pattenmden, 5th Canadian Infantry, killed in action 2 June 1916; and Pte. 242025, E. Pattenden, M.M., 2/6th Royal Warwickshire Regt., killed in action 21 March 1918: *b*. Wadhurst, 1892: enlisted Tunbridge Wells. Killed in action 31 October 1914: Age 26.

His brothers also have no known grave, Walter is recorded on (Panel 18); Edwin, the Pozieres Memorial, Somme.

PANEL 20 ENDS PTE. F.J. YOUNG, ROYAL SUSSEX REGT.

South Staircase (Facing)

PANEL 22 BEGINS PTE. A. HARDY, CHESHIRE REGT.

(Panel 22) Pte. 9782, Richard Hatton, 2nd Bn. (22nd Foot) The Cheshire Regt.: *s*. of James Hatton, of 37, St. Albans Road, Wallasey, co. Chester, by his wife Jane: and yr. brother to Corpl. 8560, J. Hatton, 21st King's Royal Rifle Corps, killed in action 5 August 1917: *b*. Birkenhead, *c*.1892: enlisted there. Killed in action 8 May 1915: Age 23. *unm*.

His brother James also has no known grave; he is recorded on Panel 53.

(Panel 22) Pte. 35568, Joseph Hockenhull, 13th (Service) Bn. The Cheshire Regt.: *s*. of the late Richard Hockenhull, by his wife Sarah Elizabeth (57, Moss Lane, Alderley Edge, co. Chester): and brother-in-law to Mary Jane Hatton (57, Moss Lane), by her marriage to his late brother Pte. 8691, H. Hockenhull, 1st Cheshire Regt., killed in action 3 September 1916: *b*. Alderley Edge: enlisted Wilmslow: served with the Expeditionary Force, and was killed in action 7 June 1917.

His brother Harry also has no known grave; he is commemorated on the Thiepval Memorial, Somme.

(Panel 22) Pte. 9001, Henry Ashcroft Jones, 1st Bn. (22nd Foot) The Cheshire Regt.: *s*. of Frederick Jones, of 13, Leigh Road, New Ferry, Coal Merchant, by his wife Ada, *dau*. of William Duffin: *b*. New Ferry, co. Chester, 2 July 1894: *educ*. Sunlight Schools: Occupation – Coal Merchant: enlisted 1911: served with the Expeditionary Force in France and Flanders from 26 January 1915, and was killed in action at Hill 60, Ypres, 22 June following. Buried near where he fell. Sergt. A. Cole wrote, "Your son was killed in action on the 22nd inst., and the Company wishes me to let you know how they all sympathise with you in your great loss. He has done so much good for the wounded since he has been a stretcher-bearer." Age 20. *unm*. (*IWGC record 23 June*)

(Panel 22) Pte. 202289, Clement Lockwood, 10th (Service) Bn. The Cheshire Regt.: brother to L/Sergt. 898, C.A. Lockwood, 2nd Grenadier Guards, killed in action, 15 September 1916, at the Somme; and Pte. 300157, C. Lockwood, 7th Essex Regt., killed in action 27 March 1917, Palestine: *b*. Fulham,

London: enlisted Northwich, co. Chester. Killed in action 1 August 1917. All three brothers are commemorated on the Chingford War Memorial, London, E.4.

Neither Cuthbert nor Cecil have known graves; they are commemorated on the Thiepval and Jerusalem Memorials respectively.

(Panel 22) Pte. 50665, George Henry Long, 11th (Service) Bn. The Cheshire Regt.: formerly no.27324, Bedfordshire Regt.: late of Attleborough, co. Norfolk: *s.* of George W. (& Eliza Ellen) Long, of Burfield Hall Farm Cottages, Wymondham: and brother to Pte. G/21055, A.G. Long, 2nd Queen's (Royal West Surrey), killed in action 14 July 1917: *b.* Long Stratton: enlisted Norwich. Killed in action 13 August 1917: Age 22.

His brother Arthur is buried in Croisilles British Cemetery (I.D.1).

(Panel 22) Pte. 12530, William McHugh, 9th (Service) Bn. The Cheshire Regt.: 3rd *s.* of James McHugh, of 1, Cambrian Row, Labourer; of Boundary Lane, Saltney, by his wife Jane, *dau.* of William Dobson: *b.* Saltney, co. Chester, 17 July 1894: *educ.* St. Anthony's Catholic Schools: Occupation – Forgeman: enlisted after the outbreak of war, August 1914: served with the Expeditionary Force in France and Flanders from 17 July 1915, and was killed in action 7 June 1917. Buried on the battlefield: Age 22. *unm.*

(Panel 22) Pte. 49927, James Brae Nolan, 11th (Service) Bn. The Cheshire Regt.: Occupation – Postman; Altrincham, co. Chester: served with the Expeditionary Force in France, and was killed in action 7 June 1917.

(Panel 22) Pte. 243796, Peter O'Kell, 13th (Service) Bn. The Cheshire Regt.: *s.* of William O'Kell: late *husb.* to Harriet O'Kell (41, Canal Street, Runcorn, co. Chester), and father to three children: *b.* Runcorn: enlisted there: served with the Expeditionary Force in France and Flanders, and was killed in action 10 June 1917: Age 33. As he lay dying his last words were, "I didn't think it would be like this."

(Panel 22) Pte. 266321, Ernest Salter, 6th Bn. The Cheshire Regt. (T.F.): *s.* of William Salter, of 115, Old Street, Ashton-under-Lyne, co. Lancaster: and yr. brother to L/Sergt. 352161, W.G. Salter, 2/9th Manchester Regt., killed in action 9 October 1917: *b.* Ashton: enlisted Stalybridge, co. Chester. Killed in action 31 July 1917.

His brother Walter also has no known grave; he is commemorated on the Tyne Cot Memorial (Panel 20).

(Panel 22) Pte. 49659, Arthur White, 13th (Service) Bn. The Cheshire Regt. attd. 195th Machine Gun Coy.: *yst. s.* of the late James White, of Crumpsall, nr. Manchester, by his wife Rebecca ('Fairholme,' 27, Westwood Avenue, Timperley, co. Chester), *dau.* of William Whitehead: *b.* Blackley, nr. Manchester, co. Lancaster, 4 July 1888: *educ.* Manchester Secondary School: 14 yrs. employee Messrs John Thomas & Co., Cotton Manufacturers, Manchester: enlisted Cheshire Regt., 7 April 1916: served with the Expeditionary Force in France and Flanders from 7 September following attd. Machine Gun Coy. Killed in action nr. Ypres, 5 August 1917. Buried nr. Zillebeke Lake. Lieut. A.E.G. Lewis wrote, "He was much respected by all his comrades in the section, both officers, N.C.O.'s and men being unanimous in their praise of him as a soldier and a man." Age 29 years, 1 month, 1 day. *unm.*

(Panel 22) Pte. 243732, Joseph William Woodfin, 13th (Service) Bn. The Cheshire Regt.: 2nd *s.* of the late William Woodfin, Baker, by his wife Ada (16, Earl Street, Rock Ferry, co. Chester): *b.* Bromborough, 1886: *educ.* there: Occupation – Coal Carter: joined 4th Cheshire Regt., 8 January 1917: served with the Expeditionary Force in France and Flanders from May following, transf'd. 13th Battn. Reported missing after the fighting 7 June of the same year; now assumed to have been killed in action on that date: Age 31. He *m.* St. Peter's Church, Rock Ferry; 18 April 1907, Florence (22, Earl Street, Rock Ferry), *dau.* of James Robinson, and had three children – Margaret Elizabeth, *b.* 13 June 1908; Hilda, *b.* 1 December 1911; Joseph William, *b.* 13 May 1915.

(Panel 22) Pte. 50195, John Henry Woodworth, 9th (Service) Bn. The Cheshire Regt.: 4th *s.* of William Ernest Woodworth, Shipyard Labourer; of 7, Kent Place, Birkenhead, by his wife Anne Elizabeth, *dau.* of John Cash: *b.* Birkenhead, co. Chester, 13 January 1896: *educ.* Cathcart Street Council School: Occupation – Labourer: joined 1/4th (Territorial) Battn. Cheshire Regt., 13 January 1915: served with the Expeditionary Force at Gallipoli, being present at the landing at Suvla Bay: contracted dysentery and appendicitis, and was invalided home: on recovery transf'd. 9th (Service) Battn.: served with the Expeditionary Force in France and Flanders from 5 December 1916, and was killed in action 19 July 1917. Buried on the field of action near Oostaverne: Age 21. *unm.*

(Panel 22) Capt. Richard Vincent Barker, 1st Bn. (23rd Foot) The Royal Welsh Fusiliers: *s.* of the late Rev. Frederick Barker, Rector of Wimborne St. Giles: *b.* Middleham, co. York, 13 June 1880: *educ.* Winchester (Scholar), and New College, Oxford: gazetted 2nd Lieut. Royal Welsh Fusiliers from the Militia, 5 January 1901; promoted Lieut. 29 October 1904; Capt. 9 September 1911: served in the South African War, 1901 – 02: took part in operations in Transvaal September – October 1901, and those in Orange River Colony, October 1901 – 31 May 1902 (Queen's Medal, four clasps): Adjutant to his regiment, 14 July 1904 – 13 January 1909; employed West African Frontier Force, 10 April 1909 – 2 April 1912. When the present war broke out Capt. Barker was with his battalion in Malta; returned England, subsequently apptd. Staff Captain, 22nd Brigade, VIIth Division, under Brigadier General Lawford: served with the Expeditionary Force in France and Flanders, and was killed in action during the First Battle of Ypres 31 October 1914, when, after two days of very severe fighting, nearly all the regimental officers had been killed and some men were seen to be falling back, Capt. Barker, who was then attending to wounded men under a heavy fire, asked permission to rally them, and while leading them forward, fell shot through the chest. His Brigadier reported of him, "Quite exceptional, a good friend and a splendid officer, no matter how hard the work and discomforts great, he was always cheerful." Posthumously Mentioned in Despatches ('*London Gazette*,' 17 February 1915) by F.M. Sir John (now Lord) French, for 'gallant and distinguished service in the field.' He was a keen rider to hounds, being well known in the South of Ireland with the United and other hunts: Age 34. *unm.*

(Panel 22) Capt. John Henry Brennan, 3rd (Reserve) attd 1st (23rd Foot) Bn. The Royal Welsh Fusiliers: only *s.* of the late T.C. Brennan, of Montreal, Canada: *b.* 14 May 1869: *educ.* St. Columba's, and Dublin University, where he was a prominent member of the cricket team: obtained a commission 4th (Vol.) Battn. Royal Welsh Fusiliers, 1902; promoted Capt. 3rd Battn., 1903: served with the Expeditionary Force in France and Flanders and was killed in action at Zonnebeke, 19, October 1914, while leading his men across an open field: Age 45. He *m.* K.C. *dau.* of the late T. Murray, of Milmount, co. Westmeath, and had three children – T. Henry L'Estrange; Gladys Evelyn H.; S. Charlotte.

(Panel 22) Capt. Bernard Digby Johns, 10th (Service) Bn. The Royal Welsh Fusiliers: only child of the late Digby Alexander Johns, Solicitor; of Carrickfergus, Co. Antrim, by his wife Honora (afterwards the wife of the late John A. French, of St. Ann's, Donnybrook, Dublin, LL.D: residing at 3, Sion Hill, Bristol), *dau.* of the Rev. J.W. Hardman, of Cadbury House, Yatton, co. Somerset, LL.D.: *b.* Bath, 13 May 1894: *educ.* Matfield Grange, co. Kent; Repton (1908), and Oriel College, Oxford (two Exhibitions and a History Scholarship, October 1913): gazetted on the outbreak of war, 2nd Lieut. 10th Royal Welsh Fusiliers; promoted Lieut. 23 November 1914; Capt. July 1915; being then 21 years of age: went to France the following September with his battalion: whilst supervising the strengthening of trenches at the salient at Ypres and encouraging his men was killed in action by a German sniper in an attack north of St. Eloi, nr. Ypres, 17 February 1916. Buried close to the trench where he fell, where within three weeks seven officers of his battalion had also fallen. His Colonel wrote of him, "He was the life and soul of the officers' mess," and Major E. Freeman (since killed), "He was an honour to have in any regiment, and showed the most brilliant promise of all those who had served with him in his soldiering.": Age 21. *unm.*

Seven other officers of the 10th Battalion fell between 17 February and 15 March 1916; three are recorded on Panel 22 of the Ypres (Menin Gate) Memorial – Lieut. Donald McBean, 15 March 1916; 2nd Lieut. Adrian Victor Cree, 17 February 1916, and 2nd Lieut. William Hughes, 3 March 1916. Three are buried in Spoilbank Cemetery – Lieut.Col. Steuart Scott Binny, D.S.O., 3 March 1916; Major Edward Freeman, 3 March 1916, and Capt. William Thomas Lyons, 3 March 1916. And Capt. John Arthur Walker, 19 February 1916, is buried in Reninghelst New Military Cemetery. (Lieut.Col. Binny, spelt Binney, ex 19th Hussars, is also recorded on Panel 5 of the Menin Gate).

(Panel 22) Capt. William Myles Kington, D.S.O., 1st Bn. (23rd Foot) The Royal Welsh Fusiliers: eldest *s*. of the late Col. W.M. Kington, 4th Hussars: *b*. Cheltenham, co. Gloucester, 25 April 1876: *educ*. Glenalmond College: gazetted 2nd Lieut. Royal Welsh Fusiliers, September 1896; promoted Lieut., January 1899: took part in the South African Campaign: Brigade Signalling Officer; Staff, November 1899 – December 1900: present at the relief of Ladysmith, and the Battle of Colenso: took part in operations at Vaal Kranz; Tugela Heights and action at Pieter's Hill: operations in the Transvaal (beginning and end of 1900), including the action at Frederickstad: in Cape Colony, including the action at Ruidam: in the Transvaal, 1901 and 1902, and in Orange River Colony: Four times Mentioned in Despatches ('*London Gazette*,' 8 February, 9 July, 10 September 1901; 29 July 1902): Awarded D.S.O.; Queen's Medal, 5 clasps; King's Medal, 4 clasps: employed with South African Constabulary, February 1902 – May 1904; Adjutant of Volunteers (& Territorial Force), April 1906 – September 1910, in which year he received his company: served with the Expeditionary Force in France and Flanders, and was killed by a shell at the First Battle of Ypres, where his battalion was in the VIIth Division, nr. Zonnebeke, Belgium, and was buried on the field in a trench. Many of the officers of his battalion were killed or wounded in the same battle. Capt. Kington was a very popular officer, and a man in his battalion who was present said in an account of the engagement, "For three days we remained in the trenches, firing and being fired at, without food or water. Lieut. Hoskyns, who commanded my platoon, was killed by a sniper, and about three hours later Capt. Kington, D.S.O., was killed. He was a fine officer, and would crack a joke in the trenches, which would set us all laughing our sides out. It made us all mad to avenge his death." Capt. Kington was married to Edith (Bryn Estyn, Wrexham, co. Denbigh), only *dau*. of F. (& Mrs) Soames, and left a son. A well-known cricketer, he was a member of the M.C.C., I Zingari, and Free Foresters. He was also an excellent shot, very artistic and something of a musical genius: Age 38.

(Panel 22) Capt. Meyricke Entwistle Lloyd, 1st Bn. (23rd Foot) The Royal Welsh Fusiliers: eldest *s*. of the late Henry Lloyd, of Pitsford Hall, co. Northampton, and 'Dolobran,' Isaf, co. Montgomery (whom he succeeded in 1902): *b*. 31 May 1880: after serving some months with the embodied Militia, joined Royal Welsh Fusiliers, June 1900; promoted Lieut. September 1907; Capt. April 1911: embarked for France 4 October 1914, served with the Expeditionary Force as part of VIIth Division, and was killed nr. Becelaere, 20 October, in the severe fighting which took place at the commencement of the First Battle of Ypres: Age 34. Mr Lloyd, a good horseman and keen follower of hounds, was married to Elizabeth ('Rosehill,' Ruabon, co. Denbigh).

(Panel 22) Capt. Clifford Nichols, 2/5th Bn. The Royal Welsh Fusiliers (T.F.), Comdg. 164th Machine Gun Coy. (Inf.).: *yr. s*. of Joseph Nichols, J.P., Manager, Messrs Lloyds Bank; of 'Furlong Cottage,' Hagley, Stourbridge, co. Worcester, late of 'Old Bank House,' Dudley, by his wife Emily, *dau*. of the late Henry Smyth: *b*. Harborne, Birmingham, 21 April 1890: *educ*. Dudley Grammar School, and King's Cathedral School, Worcester: passed his final examination for Chartered Accountant (1912), thereafter joined the staff of Messrs Price, Waterhouse & Co.: enlisted November 1914, after the outbreak of war: obtained a commission, 2nd Lieut. 9 December following; apptd. Adjutant: transf'd. 164th Machine Gun Coy. (Inf.) 1917: served with the Expeditionary Force in France and Flanders from January 1917: took part in the Battle of Arras, and was killed in action at Ypres, 31 July following. The Brigadier-General wrote, "He did a splendid work in command of the company, and instilled into them a new spirit and discipline, with the result that during the battle they all behaved magnificently. He lived up to the tradition of the great regiment to which he belonged, and fell whilst actually firing a gun. He was a splendid fellow and we all feel his loss very much." He was a keen sportsman, being well-known in the Midland hockey and golfing circles, and frequently represented his own and the Midland Counties Team: Age 27. *unm*.

(Panel 22) Lieut. Hugh Thomas Ackland-Allen, 1st Bn. (23rd Foot) The Royal Welsh Fusiliers: only *s*. of Charles Ackland-Allen, of St. Hilary Manor, Cowbridge, co. Glamorgan, by his wife Gertrude: *b*. 17 September 1893: *educ*. Wellington College, Crowthorne, co. Berks (Beresford, 1907 – 10); Royal Military College, Sandhurst (1912): received his commission 2nd Lieut., 1st Royal Welsh Fusiliers, 3 September 1913: went with the battn. to Malta, January 1914; returned to England, September: proceeded to France,

4 October, with VIIth Division, and was killed nr. Zonnebeke, nineteen days later, on the 23rd of that month:23 October 1914. Age 21. *unm.*

(Panel 22) Lieut. Guy Ogden De Peyster Chance, 1st Bn. (23rd Foot) The Royal Welsh Fusiliers: *yst. s.* of W.E. Chance, of Thurston Grange, Bury St. Edmunds: *b.* 28 February 1892: gazetted 2nd Lieut., Royal Welsh Fusiliers, 20 September 1911; promoted Lieut. 19 April 1913: served with the Expeditionary Force in France and Flanders, and was killed in action at Dadizeele, 19 October 1914: Age 22. *unm.*

(Panel 22) Lieut. Algernon Stuart Edwards, 17th (Service) Bn. The Royal Welsh Fusiliers: *s.* of Jobe Stevenson Edwards, of Achnashean, Ballgor: *husb.* to Kathleen Dora Edwards (Achnashean). Killed in action 31 July 1917, in the advance from Iron Cross Ridge toward the Steenbeek: Age 20. See Lieut. J.S.G. White, Canada Farm Cemetery (II.B.21).

(Panel 22) Lieut. Edwin Cecil Leigh Hoskyns, 1st Bn. (23rd Foot) The Royal Welsh Fusiliers: only *s.* & heir of Sir Leigh Hoskyns, Bart., Barrister-at-Law, J.P. for Oxford and High Sherriff, 1907, formerly Crown Prosecutor of Griqualand West, who succeeded his brother as 11th Bart., July 1914: *b.* Iffley, co. Oxon, 22 September 1890: *educ.* Eton, and Royal Military College, Sandhurst: gazetted 2nd Lieut. Royal Welsh Fusiliers, September 1911; promoted Lieut. April 1913: went to France with the Expeditionary Force, and was killed in action by a sniper nr. Zonnebeke, Belgium, 20 October 1914, when the gallant VIIth Division, of which his battalion formed part, without any reserves, held in check nearly one hundred thousand Germans. He was fond of hunting and polo: Age 24. *unm.*

(Panel 22) Lieut. Harold Madoc Jones, 'C' Coy., 17th (Service) Bn. The Royal Welsh Fusiliers: *s.* of the late John Roberts Jones, J.P., and his spouse Eunice Martha Jones (Bodfeirig, Anglesey): *educ.* Christ's College, Brecon; University College of Wales, Aberystwyth (graduated, B.A., Classical Hons.): volunteered and enlisted at the outbreak of war August 1914. Killed in action on the early afternoon of 31 July 1917, in the battalion advance toward the Steenbeek: Age 38. For his services in the Great War Lieut. H.M. Jones was twice Mentioned in Despatches. See Lieut. J.S.G. White, Canada Farm Cemetery (II.B.21).

During August 1914 a number of disgruntled young officer cadets at the Royal Military College, Sandhurst were convinced the fighting in France would be well and truly over before they would get anywhere near it. Among these young gentlemen, Francis Orme, who, during training, had committed more than his fair share of errors. His military career had, so far, not been distinguished; frequently called an 'idle gentleman' by the sergeant instructors, on one occasion he had been bawled out by a sergeant major of the Grenadier Guards with the condemnation, "Mr Horme, Sir, you're 'orrible!" However, his company commander, probably in the hope that Orme would speedily mend his ways and prove himself a credit to his regiment, convinced him his examiners must have been blind or drunk or a combination of both because he was now 2nd Lieut. Orme, Royal Welsh Fusiliers and despatched him to the Regimental Depot, Wrexham where he impatiently went on parade, inspected rifles, counted socks, prepared endless nominal rolls, dined in the mess and all the time heeded the Adjutant who reliably informed him the war would last some time yet.

News of the conduct of the war in France was scant at the Royal Welsh Fusiliers Depot, but with casualty lists all too frequent Francis Orme rapidly came to the conclusion that his days of counting socks and rifle inspections were numbered. The 1st Battalion had been blooded in circumstances of murderous ferocity as daily casualty lists of fallen officers sombrely revealed; page after page, listed under coldly impersonal headings: killed in action, died of wounds, wounded, missing believed killed, missing believed prisoner of war. And, with all these officers and men fighting and dying it is scarcely surprising that 2nd Lieut. Orme finally got his orders to proceed to France.

On arrival at the front with a draft of 109 other ranks, Orme reported to Capt. A. Roberts, 2nd Queen's and enquired, "I wonder if you could direct me to 1st Royal Welsh Fusiliers?" Roberts apparently jerked his thumb in the direction of about sixty or seventy mud covered men squatting in a ditch and said, "Over there." On further enquiry by Orme "Er, Who's in command?" Roberts simply replied, "I suspect that you are."

So, newly appointed 2nd Lieut. Orme, aged just eighteen years and nine months, found himself elevated to the command of 1st Royal Welsh Fusiliers; a tenure of command he was destined not to hold for long. The remnants of the Fusiliers went back into the line the following day and, before 24 hours had passed, yet another officer had been added to the long list of the regiment's fallen officers.

(Panel 22) Lieut. Francis Reginald Orme, 1st Bn. (23rd Foot) The Royal Welsh Fusiliers: *s.* of Francis H. Orme, by his wife Mary. Arrived at the front 5 November 1914; killed in action at about 6.15 a.m., 7 November 1914: Age 18 years, 9 months.

(Panel 22) 2nd Lieut. Geoffrey Philip Joseph, Snead-Cox, 1st Bn. (23rd Foot) The Royal Welsh Fusiliers: 2nd *s.* of John Snead-Cox, Lord of the Manor of Broxwood; Author, Biographer, Journalist; of Broxwood Court, nr. Kington, co. Hereford; and 38, Egerton Gardens, Eaton Bishop, by his wife Mary, *dau.* of George Porteous, of New Orleans: and brother to 2nd Lieut. R.M. Snead-Cox, 3rd Royal Scots, killed in action at Neuve Chapelle, 28 October 1914; and Midshipman H.A. Snead-Cox, H.M.S. 'Indefatigible,' R.N., killed in action at the Battle of Jutland, 31 May 1916, aged 16 years: *b.* 20 February 1895: Religion – Roman Catholic: *educ.* Downside School, nr. Bath; and Royal Military College, Sandhurst: gazetted 2nd Lieut. Royal Welsh Fusiliers 17 September 1913, after which he qualified as an Interpreter in French: served in Malta, also with the Expeditionary Force in France and Flanders, and was killed in action at Zonnebeke, during the First Battle of Ypres, 21 October 1914: Age 19. One of three brothers who fell. (*IWGC record 20 October*)

His brothers Richard and Herbert also have no known grave; they are commemorated on the Le Touret Memorial (Panel 4), and Plymouth Naval Memorial (Panel 10) respectively.

(Panel 22) 2nd Lieut. John Henry 'Harry' Hayes, 5th attd. 17th (Service) Bn. The Royal Welsh Fusiliers: *s.* of Walter Palmer Hayes, of 'Somerby,' Chester Road, Grappenhall, Warrington, and Elizabeth Allen Hayes, his wife. Killed in action at the Battle of Pilckem, 31 July 1917, in the battalion advance from positions held about Iron Cross Ridge toward the Steenbeek. Heavy casualties were sustained from fortified houses and concealed machine-gun posts: Age 28. He leaves a widow, Mabel Hayes (Ripon House, Seymour Rd., West Bridgford, Nottingham). See Lieut. J.S.G. White, Canada Farm Cemetery (II.B.21).

(Panel 22) 2nd Lieut. William Hughes, 10th (Service) Bn. The Royal Welsh Fusiliers: served with the Expeditionary Force in France and Flanders from 27 September 1915: underwent one week's trench instruction in the Ploegsteert area from 7 October; the battalion taking over trenches in the Hooge sector on the 15th of that month: saw action in the area of St. Eloi, November – December, and was killed 3 March 1916, in company with Lieut.Col. S. Binny, D.S.O., Major Freeman, Capt. (Adjt.) W.T. Lyons, 2 N.C.O.s and 10 other ranks when a stray shell landed on the Battalion Headquarters dug-out at Gordon Post, The Bluff, nr. Hill 60.

Lieut.Col. Binny, Major Freeman, and Capt. Lyons are buried in Spoilbank Cemetery, Zillebeke (I.M.3 – 5).

(Panel 22) A/Corpl. 15404, Walter Benedictus Davey, 10th (Service) Bn. The Royal Welsh Fusiliers: *s.* of George Benedictus Davey, by his wife Mary: *b.* co. Flint, *c.*1894: enlisted Mold, nr. Chester: served with the Expeditionary Force in France from 27 September 1915, and was killed in action at Gordon Post, 3 March 1916; nr. The Bluff, Hill 60: Age 22. *unm.* See 2nd Lieut. W. Hughes, above.

(Panel 22) L/Corpl. 15664, Benjamin Dallison, 10th (Service) Bn. The Royal Welsh Fusiliers: *s.* of George Benjamin Dallison, of Whitchurch, by his wife Rosa Ann: *b.* South Streatham, London, S.W.: enlisted Mountain Ash, co. Glamorgan: served with the Expeditionary Force in France and Flanders from 27 September 1915, and was killed in company with 4 officers, 1 N.C.O. and 10 other ranks, 3 March 1916, by the bursting of a stray shell which landed on the Headquarters dug-out at Gordon Post, nr. Hill 60: Age 21. *unm.* See 2nd Lieut. W. Hughes, above.

(Panel 22) Pte. 72834, Henry Pearson Adshead, 17th (Service) Bn. The Royal Welsh Fusiliers: formerly no.224810, Army Service Corps: late of Dunham, co. Norfolk: *s.* of the late Walter Adshead, of Altrincham, co. Chester, by his wife Mary (Ponteix, Saskatchewan, Canada): and elder brother to Pte.

50293, R. Adshead, 16th Cheshire Regt., who fell 29 April 1917, aged 19 years: *b*. Altrincham. Killed in action 31 July 1917: Age 23. *unm*.

His brother Robert also has no known grave; he is commemorated on the Thiepval Memorial, Somme.

(Panel 22) Pte. 60573, Harry Austin, 17th (Service) Bn. The Royal Welsh Fusiliers: *s*. of the late Robert (& Ellen) Austin, of Oakengates, co. Salop: and brother to Pte. 11813, E. Austin, King's Shropshire Light Infantry, who also fell: *b*. Oakengates, *c*.1893: enlisted Wellington. Killed in action, 31 July 1917: Age 24. *unm*.

His brother Edwin also has no known grave; he is commemorated on the Tyne Cot Memorial (Panel 112).

(Panel 22) Pte. 10753, Leonard Ralph Bradshaw, 1st Bn. (23rd Foot) The Royal Welsh Fusiliers: *s*. of the late Henry Bradshaw, by his wife Eliza (30, Chapel Road, Mitcham, co. Surrey): *b*. Mitcham, 1890: enlisted Royal Welsh Fusiliers, Mitcham. At the time of Pte. Bradshaw's death in action, 20 October 1914, his battalion and 2nd Seaforth Highlanders had been sent forward in a joint attack to capture positions via which communications across the River Lys might be greatly improved and, despite achieving limited success in the initial stages, this could not be exploited by either battalion due to a lack of high-explosive shells for the supporting artillery: Age 24. *unm*.

(Panel 22) Pte. 16114, William Collins, 10th (Service) Bn. The Royal Welsh Fusiliers: *b*. Balham, London, S.W.12: enlisted Aberavon. Killed in action by the bursting of a stray shell, Gordon Post, nr. Hill 60, 3 March 1916. See 2nd Lieut. W. Hughes (above).

(Panel 22) Pte. 60143, Arthur Coulson, 15th (Service) Bn. The Royal Welsh Fusiliers: formerly no.20867, East Lancashire Regt.: *s*. of Arthur Coulson, of 8, Birch Street, Accrington, by his wife Emma: and brother to Spr. 179454, H. Coulson, 99th Field Coy., Royal Engineers, died 18 September 1918: enlisted Accrington, co. Lancaster: served with the Expeditionary Force in France and Flanders, and was killed in action 25 July 1917.

His brother Henry is buried in Accrington Town Cemetery.

(Panel 22) Pte. 15131, Leonard Fred Devereux, 10th (Service) Bn. The Royal Welsh Fusiliers: 2nd *s*. of Frederick James Devereux, of Swilgate Road, Tewkesbury, by his wife Elizabeth Martha, *dau*. of Arthur William Rodway: *b*. Tewkesbury, co. Gloucester, 8 June 1896: *educ*. Holy Trinity School: Occupation – Labourer: enlisted 4 September 1914 (aged 17), after the outbreak of war: served with the Expeditionary Force in France and Flanders from 27 September 1915, and was killed in action 2 March 1916: Age 19.

(Panel 22) Pte. 15115, Thomas Griffiths, 10th (Service) Bn. The Royal Welsh Fusiliers: late of Mostyn, nr. Holywell: *b*. Picton, co. Flint: enlisted Rhyl: served with the Expeditionary Force in France and Flanders from 27 September 1915, and was killed 3 March 1916, in company with 4 officers, 2 N.C.O.s and 9 other ranks by the explosion of a shell which hit the Headquarters dug-out at Gordon Post: Age 34. Correspondence should be addressed c/o his sister, Mrs Ellen Williams (4, Dee View Terrace, Pen-Y-Fford, Fynnon Groew, Chester). See 2nd Lieut. W. Hughes, above.

(Panel 22) Pte. 9414, William George Hillier, 1st Bn. (23rd Foot) The Royal Welsh Fusiliers: *s*. of William George Hillier, Quarryman; of Conham Farm, Hanham, Bristol, by his wife Fanny, *dau*. of Alfred Coles: *b*. Bristol, 26 November 1887: *educ*. St. Anne's Board School, there: Occupation – Labourer; Great Western Railway: enlisted 1907, and after serving six years with the Colours, joined the Army Reserve: called up and rejoined on the outbreak of war; served with the Expeditionary Force in France and Flanders. Reported wounded and missing, 7 November 1914; now assumed, due to lack of further information or communication to the contrary, to have been killed in action on or about that date: Age 26. He *m*. St. Matthew's Church, Bristol, 4 January 1913; Gladys Elizabeth (42, Grove Park Terrace, Fishponds, Bristol, formerly, 9, Vera Road, Ridgway Road, Fishponds), *dau*. of Cecil Randolph Power: *s.p.*

"Under fierce shell fire and in driving rain, Thomas Jenkins bravely made his way across No Man's Land towards the enemy lines. An overnight barrage by more than 3,000 guns had briefly silenced the Germans. Poison gas sent over by the British billowed across the battlefield. But now murderous artillery salvoes roared back and machine- gun fire erupted from 300 enemy pill-boxes –mowing down hundreds of the assaulting troops. It was the early morning of Tuesday, July 31, 1917 and Private Jenkins, a 24-year-old soldier in the Royal Welch Fusiliers, did not have long to live. He became one of an eventual 270,000 British casualties of the Third Battle of Ypres, a First World War campaign grimly immortalised by the name of Passchendaele the Flemish village on a strategic ridge above Ypres that was the British objective. Like so many of those killed in the hell of Flanders, his heavily laden body disappeared into the deep quagmires of shell-blasted mud seemingly fated to be one of the thousands that would have no known grave...." '*Daily Mail*,' 2 March 2002.

Every year an average of twenty sets of soldier's remains are found and given a full military funeral, sadly the majority of those found are unidentifiable. In February 2002 an archaeological dig on the outskirts of Ypres uncovered the remains of a British soldier. Identified as being that of a member of the Royal Welsh Fusiliers by a RWF shoulder flash; other indicators to his identity were a battered steel helmet, three pieces of khaki tunic, a pair of infantryman's boots, and a pack full of kit including an entrenching tool, broken pipe, toothbrush, pencils, blue water bottle and an ampoule of iodine for treating wounds. Most compellingly the body was found near Boesinghe where at 3.50a.m, on the morning of 31 July 1917, 16 officers and 456 other ranks of 16th Royal Welsh Fusiliers began their assault on the Pilckem Ridge sector. The battalion lost a total of 36 men killed of which a number were subsequently recovered and buried giving, according to the Curator of the Regimental Museum, 'a better than one in five chance of identifying the remains found.' Investigation by the Commonwealth War Graves Commission with regard to the battalion's missing centred on the possibility of the soldier being identified as Pte. Thomas Jenkins but, with little other than circumstantial evidence to support this, no definite decision could be made.

(Panel 22) Pte. 45179, Thomas John Jenkins, 16th (Service) Bn. The Royal Welsh Fusiliers: late of Tooting, London, S.W.: 3rd *s.* of Jenkin Jenkins, Undertaker & Carpenter, of Butter Hall, Pontrhydfendigaid, Ystrad Meurig, co. Cardigan, by his wife Margaret: *b.* Pontrhydfendigaid, *c.*1893: Occupation – Trainee Undertaker: enlisted Wandsworth, August 1914: trained Llandudno and Winchester: served with the Expeditionary Force in France and Flanders from December 1915, and was killed in action 31 July 1917: Age 24. *unm.*

(Panel 22) Pte. 14991, Thomas Jones, 10th (Service) Bn. The Royal Welsh Fusiliers: *b.* Llanfechell, Anglesey: enlisted Menai Bridge. Killed in action in the vicinity of Hill 60, Ypres, 3 March 1916. See 2nd Lieut. W. Hughes, above.

(Panel 22) Pte. 15370, Thomas Jones, 10th (Service) Bn. The Royal Welsh Fusiliers: *s.* of Sidney Williams, of Cyllfelin, Aberdaron, Pwhelli, co. Caernarvon: *b.* Bryncroes, Caernarvon: enlisted Cefnamlwch. Killed in action at Gordon Post 3 March 1916: Age 23. See 2nd Lieut. W. Hughes, above.

(Panel 22) Pte. 23303, Bertram Knight, 10th (Service) Bn. The Royal Welsh Fusiliers: *s.* of Sophia Knight (Stockwell Cottage, Aylburton, Lydney, co. Gloucester): *b.* Lydney, *c.*1890: enlisted Newport, co. Monmouth. Killed in action at Gordon Post, nr. Hill 60, 3 March 1916: Age 25. *unm.* See 2nd Lieut. W. Hughes, above.

(Panel 22) Pte. 56332, Frederick Labram, 9th (Service) Bn. The Royal Welsh Fusiliers: formerly no.32207, Northamptonshire Regt.: *s.* of John Labram, of Grendon, co. Northampton, by his wife Rhoda: *b.* Grendon: enlisted Northampton. Killed in action 31 July 1917: Age 19. Frederick Labram is one of six men remembered on the Grendon War Memorial. Situated in St Mary's Churchyard it is inscribed – 'In Memory Of...Men Of Grendon Our Gallant Dead Who Fell In The Great War 1914-1918' – with the line: *Jesus Said 'I Am The Resurrection And The Life.' St. John XI* – on the plinth.

(Panel 22) Pte. 10963, David Maddox, 1st Bn. (23rd Foot) The Royal Welsh Fusiliers: *yst. s.* of John Maddox, of 27, Penrhyn Street, Liverpool; late of 4 House, 3 Court, Lawrence Street, by his wife Annie: and brother to Pte. 1969, G. Maddox, 1/7th King's (Liverpool) Regt., killed in action 16 May 1915, aged 24: *b.* St. Anthony's, Liverpool, 1894: enlisted Wrexham. Killed in action 30 October 1914: Age 20.

His brother George also has no known grave; he is commemorated on the Le Touret Memorial.

(Panel 22) Pte. 55477, Albert Mills, 17th (Service) Bn. The Royal Welsh Fusiliers: formerly no.2484, Montgomeryshire Yeomanry: s. of John Mills, of 11, Wansford, nr. Peterborough, by his wife Elizabeth: and yr. brother to Pte. 22507, F. Mills, 11th Hussars, killed in action 24 May 1915: b. Thornhaugh, co. Northampton: enlisted Welshpool. Killed in action 31 July 1917: Age 25. Commemorated on Thornhaugh and Sibson-cum-Stibbington War Memorials.

His brother Fred also has no known grave; he is recorded on Panel 5.

(Panel 22) Pte. 23486, Matthew Benjamin Morris, 10th (Service) Bn. The Royal Welsh Fusiliers: b. Blakenell, co. Stafford, 1885: enlisted Sutton-in-Ashfield, Nottingham, March 1915: served with the Expeditionary Force in France and Flanders from late September following, and was killed in action 2 March 1916: Age 30. He leaves a widow, Mrs M.B. Morris (15, Briggs Street, Forest Side, Sutton-in-Ashfield), and four children. In a letter to Mrs Morris his Lieut. Wrote, "I very much regret to say that your husband was killed in action the 2nd March. He was hit in the head by a piece of shell and died instantly. He was carried down and buried with a number of other men. The only consolation I can give is that he died instantly. I always found him an excellent man in the trenches, and one who never showed fear. We had made an attack and captured our lost trenches, and he was killed in the subsequent bombardment." A memorial service was conducted by Capt. Jessup at All Saints' Mission, and this was of an impressive and touching character. The subject of the preacher was 'Peace,' and he endeavoured to show that in spite of all the bitter warfare and its consequent bitter grief and suffering, the Saviour had purchased once and for all by the sacrifice of Himself an inward peace which it was His will that all should enjoy. The '*Notts Free Press*' 'In Memoriam,' 2 March 1917:–

> *A loving husband a faithful friend,*
> *One of the best God could lend;*
> *When nights are dark and friends are few,*
> *Dear husband, and dad, how we long for you.*

Sorrowing Wife & Little Ones.

(Panel 22) Pte. 15451, Patrick O'Brien, 10th (Service) Bn. The Royal Welsh Fusiliers: b. Tuam, Co. Galway: enlisted Ruthin. Killed in action by the bursting of a stray shell which hit the headquarters dugout at Gordon Post, The Bluff, nr. Hill 60, 3 March 1916. See 2nd Lieut. W. Hughes (above).

(Panel 22) Pte. 15371, Glyn Roberts, 10th (Service) Bn. The Royal Welsh Fusiliers: s. of Kate Roberts (Llys Eifion, Cilgain, Mold, co. Flint). Killed in action 3 March 1916, at Gordon Post, nr. Hill 60: Age 23. *unm.* See 2nd Lieut. W. Hughes (above).

(Panel 22) Pte. 14971, William Thomas Roberts, 10th (Service) Bn. The Royal Welsh Fusiliers: s. of the late Griffith Roberts, by his wife Elizabeth Alice (3, Garth Hill, Bangor, co. Caernarvon): served with the Expeditionary Force in France and Flanders from 27 September 1915: underwent trench training in the Ploegsteert sector from 7 October following: took part in actions in the Hooge sector and at St. Eloi, and was killed by the bursting of a stray shell at Gordon Post, nr. Hill 60, 3 March 1916: Age 27. See 2nd Lieut. W. Hughes (above).

(Panel 22) Pte. 18328, Hugh Rogers, 10th (Service) Bn. The Royal Welsh Fusiliers: s. of Edward Rogers, of Duke Terrace, Berwyn, Llangollen, co. Denbigh, by his wife Jane: b. Eglwysbach, Colwyn Bay, c.1896: served with the Expeditionary Force in France from September 1915, and was killed in action 3 March 1916, at Gordon Post: Age 20. *unm.* See 2nd Lieut. W. Hughes (above).

(Panel 22) Pte. 10661, John Boutcher Seldon, 1st Bn. (23rd Foot) The Royal Welsh Fusiliers: s. of William Seldon, of 'Green Tree,' Broad Clyst, Exeter, co. Devon, by his wife Eliza Ann: and brother to Sergt. 26061, J.S. Seldon, M.M., 2nd Devonshire Regt., killed in action 20 April 1918: b. Broad Clyst: enlisted London. Killed in action 20 October 1914: Age 20.

His brother Joseph is buried in Adelaide Cemetery, Villers-Bretonneux (II.L.22).

(Panel 22) Pte. 15132, Josiah Williams, 10th (Service) Bn. The Royal Welsh Fusiliers: s. of the late John Williams, by his wife Mary Jane (Llwest Park, Ystumen, co. Cardigan): b. Aberystwyth, c.1894: enlisted

Wrexham: served with the Expeditionary Force in France and Flanders from 27 September 1915. One of 10 other ranks killed by the bursting of a stray shell which hit the Headquarters dugout, Gordon Post, nr. Hill 60, 3 March 1916: Age 22. *unm*. Lieut.Col. Binny, Major Freeman, Capt. Lyons, 2nd Lieut. Hughes, and 2 N.C.O.s were also killed. See 2nd Lieut. W. Hughes (above), and Spoilbank Cemetery (I.M.3-5).

(Panel 22) Capt. Ian Bouverie Maxwell, 3rd (Reserve) attd. 1st Bn. (24th Foot) The South Wales Borderers: *s*. of Everard Ellis Maxwell, late Comdr. Royal Navy, by his wife Ethel Mary (214, Ashley Gardens, Westminster, London): and nephew to Lieut.Gen. Sir Ronald Maxwell, K.C.B.: *b*. London, 11 October 1890: *educ*. Radley, and Hertford College, Oxford (B.A.): after serving 18 months in the Army he resigned (April / May 1914), and was employed on the staff of the '*Burlington Magazine*': rejoined 3rd Battn. of his regiment on the outbreak of war August 1914; promoted Capt. September following; attd. 1st Battn. for Active Service on the Continent: served with the Expeditionary Force in France and Flanders from October 1914, and was killed in action at the Battle of Ypres on the 31st of that month: Age 24. *unm*. (*IWGC record 3rd attd. 2nd*)

(Panel 22) Lieut. John Richards Homfray, 1st Bn. (24th Foot) The South Wales Borderers: 2nd *s*. of Col. Herbert R. (& B.J.) Homfray, of Penllyn Castle, Cowbridge, co. Glamorgan: and nephew to Capt. J.G.R. Homfray: *b*. Penllyn Castle, 18 October 1893: *educ*. Haileybury College, co. Hertford; Royal Military College, Sandhurst: gazetted 2nd Lieut. South Wales Borderers, September 1912; promoted Lieut. September 1914: served with the Expeditionary Force in France and Flanders, and was killed by shellfire at Zillebeke; Belgium, 11 November 1914: Age 21. *unm*. Remains 'Unknown British Officer' recovered unmarked grave (28.I.30.a.5.0) 24 January 1927; identified – Officers Clothing, Collar Badges; reinterred, registered 29 January 1927. *Buried in Sanctuary Wood Cemetery (III.D.35)*.

The Lord Bless Thee And Keep Thee

(Panel 22) 2nd Lieut. Gervas Frederic Bullock, 3rd (Reserve) Bn. The South Wales Borderers: only *s*. of the late Frederic D'Olbert Bullock, LL.B., Cantab., Sessions Judge, Bengal Civil Service, by his wife Minnie Weir (59, Mount Park Road, Ealing, London, W.): *b*. Punjab, India, 24 March 1881: *educ*. Temple Grove, and Malvern, where he gained a scholarship and was head of the School House; afterwards went to Corpus Christi College, Cambridge: in Ceylon on the outbreak of war, returned home immediately; joined Inns of Court O.T.C., July 1915: obtained a commission 30 December following: served with the Expeditionary Force in France and Flanders, and was killed in action 31 July 1917, during the operations on Pilckem Ridge. Buried nr. Ypres. A brother officer wrote, "He was killed instantaneously by a sniper. He was in charge of the company at the time, and by his gallantry and coolness won the admiration of everyone. He was very highly esteemed by all, and his men positively loved him, and would have followed him anywhere. He died doing his duty nobly and well, as he had always done. I never knew him do a mean or ungentlemanly thing. He was a delightful friend and companion…He was a thorough sportsman, it was the very essence of his character." Age 36. *unm*.

(Panel 22) 2nd Lieut. (Temp.) Griffith Christmas Owen, 11th (Service) Bn. (2nd Gwent) The South Wales Borderers: *s*. of H. (& Mrs) Owen, of Bryngwenalt, Dolgelly, co. Merioneth: served with the Expeditionary Force. Killed in action 31 July 1917; Pilckem Ridge: Age 30. Remains 'Unknown British Officer. 2/Lieut.,' recovered (28.C.3.a.8.5); identified – G.S. Clothing, Badge of Rank; registered, reinterred 24 April 1928. *Buried in Sanctuary Wood Cemetery (II.J.11)*.

Of Bryngwenallt Dolgelly N. Wales
Addug Angau Ni Ddwg Angof

(Panel 22) 2nd Lieut. Horace Holmes Watkins, 3rd (Reserve) attd. 2nd Bn. (24th Foot) The South Wales Borderers: 6th *s*. of Thomas Watkins, Solicitor; of The Wern, Pontypool, co. Monmouth, by his wife Fanny Maria: *b*. Castle Parade House, Usk, co. Monmouth, 31 January 1891: *educ*. West Monmouth School, Pontypool; Monmouth Grammar School (won and held school scholarships), thence proceeded to Hertford College, Oxford, where he won an Exhibition and took a leaving one from Monmouth:

took second class honours in Moderations and Greats at Oxford (double second): previously 2nd Lieut. (Monmouth Grammar School Cadet Corps); Colour-Sergt. (Oxford O.T.C.), obtained certificates 'A' and 'B' qualifying him for a commission, also a qualification in Musketry, obtained at a course attended on his own initiative one summer. As a Recruiting Sergeant he had no equal, and, entering the O.T.C. as a real preparation for the crisis, his arguments explained to everyone in the College at personal interviews, doubled the size of the Hertford Detachment during the two years he worked in it: one of the first to appear before the Nominating Board, Oxford, August 1914, received his commission 2nd Lieut. (on probation), 3rd South Wales Borderers, in that month, attd. 1st Battn. for Active Service. Proceeded to France and was killed while leading his platoon, No.4, from Langemarck village to a frontal attack over some open ground, the only cover being that afforded by the beet and turnip leaves. He was hit by two bullets, both entering the abdomen, and the back of his neck was also blown away by a shell, but it is said this occurred after death. An athlete of some repute, at Monmouth he represented his school at cricket, Rugby football, and hockey, and rowed in the school boat. At Oxford he played hockey for the University, obtaining his Half-Blue, and playing for the winners in the Inter-'Varsity match the season before his death. He also represented his college at Rugby and Association football, hockey, tennis, and in the Torpid. 2nd Lieut. Watkins had no fewer than seven brothers serving or preparing to serve in His Majesty's Forces, one of whom – Capt. V.H.H. Watkins, 1/2nd Monmouthshire Regt., was wounded in the right upper side of his head by a bullet, 16 January 1915, and died in Empire Hospital, Westminster, 20 February 1915; a second – Capt. Herbert Holmes Watkins, 2/2nd Monmouth Regt. – was stationed at Bedford; a third, Colin, is a Private in 10th Canadian Mounted Rifles; two others applied for commissions – one in the Royal Engineers, and the other in the Royal Artillery; while a sixth was at Hertford College, Oxford, in the O.T.C., and also applied for a commission; a seventh was attested under Lord Derby's Scheme; and an eighth rejected on medical grounds. Age 23. *unm.*

His brother Vivian is buried in Pontypool (Panteg) Cemetery (A.6).

(Panel 22) Sergt. 18628, Robert Allen Blackwell, 'D' Coy., 11th (Service) Bn. (2nd Gwent) The South Wales Borderers: eldest *s.* of John Blackwell, Stonemason; of 6, Pitt Street, Rock Ferry, co. Chester, by his wife Annie, *dau.* of Owen Roberts: and brother to Pte. 22540, J.E. Blackwell, 11th South Wales Borderers, died of wounds received in action at Armentieres, 1 March 1916: *b.* Denbigh, 6 June 1894: *educ.* St. Paul's School, Rock Ferry: Occupation – General Dealer: enlisted August 1914: served with the Expeditionary Force in France from 7 November 1915. Reported wounded and missing after the fighting 3 August 1917, assumed killed in action on that date: Age 23. *unm.* (*IWGC record 31 July 1917*)

His brother John is buried in Bethune Town Cemetery (V.A.55).

(Panel 22) Sergt. 9311, Reuben Orman, 1st Bn. (24th Foot) The South Wales Borderers: *s.* of Simon Orman, of 143, Mill Street, Liverpool; late of 21, Gladstone Street, Cross Keys, co. Monmouth: and brother to Pte. L/13052, H. Orman, 4th Middlesex Regt., killed in action, 14 October 1914, aged 22 years: *b.* Aberstruth, Abertillery: enlisted Pontypool: served with the Expeditionary Force in France and Flanders from 13 August 1914, and was killed in action 31 October 1914, during the fighting to recapture Gheluvelt, at the Battle of Ypres: Age 26.

His brother Harry is buried in Vielle-Chapelle New Military Cemetery, Lacouture (VI.C.12).

(Panel 22) Corpl. 9334, Walter Bell, 1st Bn. (24th Foot) The South Wales Borderers: *s.* of the late Hewartson Bell, and his wife Frances (23, The Grove, Wandsworth, London, S.W.): formerly employee London County Council Asylums Dept.: *b.* Westminster: enlisted London: served with the Expeditionary Force in France from 13 August 1914, and was killed in action 31 October 1914, nr. Gheluvelt: Age 27.

(Panel 22) L/Corpl. 44380, Frederick Cheese, 'C' Coy., 11th (Service) Bn. (2nd Gwent) The South Wales Borderers: formerly no.187793, Royal Engineers: *s.* of John James Cheese, of 205, Great Brick Kiln Street, Wolverhampton, by his late wife Elizabeth: and brother to Pte. 27344, E. Cheese, 7th Loyal North Lancashire Regt., killed in action 7 June 1917: *b.* Wolverhampton, co. Stafford: enlisted Chatham, co. Kent. Killed in action 31 July 1917: Age 27. He was married to the late Nellie Cheese.

His brother Ernest is buried in Croonaert Chapel Cemetery (A.22).

(Panel 22) L/Corpl. 22429, Major Phillips, 11th (Service) Bn. The South Wales Borderers: s. of George Phillips, of Cinderhill Street, Monmouth, and his wife Sarah: and brother to Pte. 31304, R.G. Phillips, 19th Welsh Regt., killed in action 31 July 1917: enlisted Newport. Killed in action 31 July 1917: Age 32. He leaves a wife Florence Mary Phillips (20, Torfaen Terrace, Pontnewynydd), and five young children to mourn his loss.

His brother Richard also has no known grave; he is commemorated on the Thiepval Memorial, Somme.

(Panel 22) Pte. 10505, John Breeze, 1st Bn. (24th Foot) The South Wales Borderers: s. of John Breeze, Labourer; of 6, Durham Street, Grangetown, Cardiff, by his 1st wife, Caroline, dau. of Thomas Morris: b. Tenbury, co. Worcester, 9 March 1887: educ. National School, Monmouth. Killed in action at Langemarck 21 October 1914: Age 27. unm.

(Panel 22) Pte. 22253, Thomas Cousins, Machine Gun Section, 11th (Service) Bn. (2nd Gwent) The South Wales Borderers: s. of the late Thomas Cousins, by his wife Charlotte Rosina (28, Dean Street, Newport, co. Monmouth): b. Bristol, co. Gloucester, c.1892: enlisted Newport. Killed in action at Ypres, 31 July 1917: Age 24. unm. Remains 'Four Unknown British Soldiers' recovered unmarked grave (20.U.28.c.7.7); 20 September 1928. GRU Report, Zillebeke 5-291/E refers – '2 Titles, S.W.B. and M.G.C.; 2 Spoons marked 4 R.I.R. 3388 and 22253; 2 Forks marked R?E and 20950 S.W.B.; Gun-metal Ring initialed M.M. or W.W. The remains of these four men were so intermingled and broken up, apparently by shellfire, it was impossible to separate the bodies…The quantity of machine-gun ammunition found with these bodies would seem to indicate the five men buried in Graves 10 and 11 were a machine-gun team.' *Buried in Sanctuary Wood Cemetery (II.L.10).*

(Panel 22) Pte. 42131, Sydney Davies, 11th (Service) Bn. (2nd Gwent) The South Wales Borderers: s. of the late Henry John Davies, by his wife Edith (71, Etnam Street, Leominster), dau. of William Colledge: b. Clun, co. Salop, c. 1898: educ. Stratford-on-Avon: Occupation – Grocer's Assistant: enlisted 5 October 1914: served with the Expeditionary Force in France and Flanders. Reported missing after the fighting at Ypres, 1 August 1917; now assumed to have been killed in action on that date: Age 19.

(Panel 22) Pte. 8673, Louis Pelgrena Mazzei, 1st Bn. (24th Foot) The South Wales Borderers: s. of Frederick Mazzei, of Roath, Cardiff, by his wife Elizabeth: and elder brother to Pte. 17042, A. Mazzei, 6th South Wales Borderers, killed in action 27 May 1917: enlisted Cardiff. Killed in action 21 October 1914: Age 30.

His brother Alfred is buried in Nieuwkerke Churchyard (G.2).

(Panel 22) Pte. 10926, Frank Peskett, (Drmr), 1st Bn. (24th Foot) The South Wales Borderers: s. of the late George Peskett, of Leiston, co. Suffolk, by his wife Sarah: and yr. brother to L/Corpl. 35560, H.T. Peskett, Post Office Rifles, killed in action 30 October 1917: b. Leiston, c.1883: enlisted Chatham, co. Kent. Killed in action 4 November 1914: Age 31.

His brother Horace also has no known grave; he is commemorated on the Tyne Cot Memorial (Panel 150).

(Panel 22) Pte. 7812, Joseph Phillips Price, 1st Bn. (24th Foot) The South Wales Borderers: eldest s. of the late Thomas Price, Labourer, by his wife Jane (58, Ashville Road, Seacombe, co. Chester), dau. of Joseph Phillips: b. Broughton, co. Chester, 10 February 1880: educ. Church Road School, Seacombe: enlisted November 1898: served three years with the Colours, taking part in the South African War 1899 – 1902 (Queen's Medal, two clasps), and nine years with the Reserve: recalled on the outbreak of war August 1914: served with the Expeditionary Force in France and Flanders, and died at Ypres, 22 October following, from wounds received in action there: Age 34. unm.

(Panel 22) Pte. 33273, Joseph Henry Savage, 11th (Service) Bn. (2nd Gwent) The South Wales Borderers: s. of Selina Kirton, née Savage (14, High Town, Cradley, co. Worcester): and yr. brother to Sergt. 12563, W.H. Savage, 4th South Wales Borderers, killed in action 21 August 1915, at Gallipoli: b. Stafford: enlisted Abertillery. Killed in action 31 July 1917: Age 19.

His brother William also has no known grave; he is commemorated on the Helles Memorial, Gallipoli.

(Panel 22) Pte. 11472, Frederick Herbert Thomas, 1st Bn. (24th Foot) The South Wales Borderers: *s.* of William Henry Thomas, of 71, Blorange Terrace, Caependry, Abergavenny, by his wife Ellen. Killed in action 21 October 1914: Age 26. *unm.*

(Panel 22) Capt. Leonard Vale Bagshawe, 3rd (Reserve) Bn. The King's Own Scottish Borderers attd. 1st Bn. Northumberland Fusiliers.: *yr. s.* of Rev. William Vale Bagshawe, of Moorlands, Calver, Sheffield, formerly Assistant Master, Repton School; Master, Uppingham Lower School; Vicar of Isel; Rector of Pitchford; by his wife Alice Katherine, *dau.* of Edward Otto Partridge: *b.* Highfield, Uppingham, 30 November 1877: *educ.* Lower School, Uppingham; Shrewsbury, and Christ Church, Oxford. After taking his degree he entered the service of the Bombay – Burma Trading Corporation, and later became one of their forest managers. Being home on leave when war broke out he immediately applied, with three other members of the company's staff, for a commission in King's Own Scottish Borderers, and was gazetted 2nd Lieut. 30 August 1914; promoted Lieut. 6 November following: trained Portland and Sunderland; proceeded to France 4 December, being attd. 1st Northumberland Fusiliers nr. Ypres, where, having acted as Capt. of his company for several months, was gazetted to that rank 5 May 1915, and was killed in action at Hooge, Flanders, 16 June following. Lieut. Edward Partridge wrote from Ypres, "His example enabled his men to carry the position and retain it against counter-attacks, and they all speak so highly of his pluck and resource." And Pte. Pike, Northumberland Fusiliers, from the Base Hospital, Sheffield, "I was with your son when he got killed in the great charge at Hooge, near Ypres, on 16 June. I was very proud to be led by such a brave and noble man – for he led the Company as if he were in the streets of England." Pte. Pike also said that "Capt. Bagshawe and his men were in the fighting, in March, at St. Eloi, St. Julien, and Hill 60. One night he had 18 men in a trench which was shelled by the Germans preparatory to an attack; 16 men were killed or wounded. Capt. Bagshawe mounted the parapet and fired into the attacking enemy. He and his two men held the trench through the night until daylight caused the Germans to relinquish the attack." The Captain and Adjutant, 1st Bn. Northumberland Fusiliers, writing from King Edward VII Hospital, June 1915, said, "I am writing to tell you how much the loss of your son will be felt in my battalion. Although he did not belong to the regiment, he was as keen as anyone could be on its welfare, and was as popular with his men as he was with the officers. He joined the battalion when we were very short of officers, and what we had were most of them very young, so he was from the first in a very responsible position which he filled with great energy and tact. We were attacking, and I heard that he got into the first line of the enemy's trenches, and I think he was hit in the actual assault…Very little could be done in the way of clearing the field until night, and as we attacked at 4 a.m., this meant a long wait for the seriously wounded. Capt. Bagshawe will have been buried close to where he fell, which is just south of the Ypres – Roulers Railway, about three miles east of Ypres." Capt. Bagshawe was a keen and successful all-round sportsman. At college he rowed in the eight and represented Christ Church in the crew which competed for both Thames and Ladies in 1897 at Henley. They were beaten in the semi-final of the Ladies Plate by Emmanuel, and in the final of the Thames Cup by Kingston after a good race: Age 37. *unm.*

(Panel 22) Capt. Charles Ernest William Bland, D.S.O., 3rd (Reserve) attd. 2nd Bn. (25th Foot) The King's Own Scottish Borderers: *s.* of Horatio Bland, of Stretton House, nr. Alfreton, co. Derby, Capt. (ret'd) King's Own Scottish Borderers, by his wife Fanny Louisa (Stretton House, Alfreton, co. Derby), *dau.* of William Henry Duff: *b.* New Wandsworth, co. Surrey, 21 August 1881: *educ.* Marlborough, and Royal Military College, Sandhurst: joined Scottish Borderers, 20 January 1900: served in the Boer War, and was present at the actions at Vet River and Zand River, those near Johannesburg and Pretoria, and Zillikats Nek (Queen's Medal, three clasps; King's Medal, two clasps): became Capt. 9 March, 1908, and retired 26 October 1910; being gazetted 2nd Lieut., 3rd (Reserve) Battn. of his regt. On the outbreak of war he rejoined, was attached 2nd Battn. with which he went to the Front. Twice Mentioned in Despatches, 14 January 1915, by F.M. Sir John (now Lord) French, and awarded the D.S.O., 18 February 1915, and was killed in the action near St. Julien, Ypres, 23 April 1915, while attempting to save a wounded man. He is believed to have been buried near Pilckem. Major D'Ewes Coke wrote, "The actual event which gained him the D.S.O. was when we were holding trenches in Front of Ypres in November His trench was several times attacked by Prussian infantry, as well as being subjected to very heavy fire from *minenwerfers* and artillery, but he stuck to it and defended his trench with great bravery." A Sergeant of his company gave the following account of his death:– After expressing the sympathy of the men of his company, and saying how Capt. Bland was loved and respected by all ranks, he said that while advancing about twelve hundred yards from the enemy they lost heavily from machine-gun, and rifle fire, until they got to within two hundred yards of the enemy's trench. Capt. Bland and the Sergeant were alone in the open, and the officer went back about five yards to help a wounded man, when the enemy opened fire on him with their machine guns, and struck him down. After going through the thick of the fight, he met his death, when practically all was over, endeavouring to save the life of a comrade of his company. He *m*. Parish Church, Maynooth, Co. Kildare, Ireland, 22 October 1910, Isabella, *dau.* of William Browne-Lecky, of Ecclesville, Co. Tyrone, and had a *dau.* Patricia Ernest de Montmorency, *b.* 24 April, the day after her father was killed. Capt. Bland was a member of the Naval and Military and Caledonian Clubs, and was well known in the hunting field, frequently being out with the Cottesmore and Belvoir packs. He was also fond of racing, shooting, fishing, and golf: Age 33. (*IWGC record 3rd April, 1915*)

(Panel 22) Capt. James Robert Caird, 3rd (Reserve) attd 2nd Bn. (25th Foot) The King's Own Scottish Borderers: *s.* of Major Lindsay Henryson Caird (late Border Regt.), Assistant to Colonel in charge of Records, No. 2 District, by his wife the late Janet Laura, 5th *dau.* of the late Rowland Hunt, of Boreatton Park, co. Salop, and Kibworth Hall, co. Leicester, and grandson of the late Right Hon. Sir James Caird, of Cassencary, Kirkcudbrightshire: *b.* Dalhousie, India, 4 November 1892: *educ.* Bedford and Carlisle Grammar Schools: in the office of the Australian Mercantile Land & Finance Co. Ltd., when war broke out he at once applied for a commission, and being a Member of the Inns of Court O.T.C., was gazetted 2nd Lieut. 3rd Bn. K.O.S.B., 15 August 1914: promoted Lieut. 9 November following: went to France, December, being there attached 2nd Highland Light Infantry until March, when he came home on a short leave. On his return to the Front he was posted to 2nd Battn., and was killed in action while leading his platoon over open ground in the advance upon St. Julien, nr. Ypres, 23 April 1915. Major Hilton who was in command of the battalion during the action, and was himself seriously wounded, wrote, "Capt. Caird was a gallant fellow and we can ill afford to lose his kind. I didn't get much detail of the manner of his death as I was also knocked over, but I know enough to say that he died game and led his men well until killed." And Sgt. Hugh McMurchy, in a sworn statement, declared, "I saw Lieut. Caird killed on 23 April in the advance at St. Julien. He was advancing in front of me and was shot through the forehead, being killed instantaneously." Capt. Caird's experience of active service had brought him to the conviction that he preferred a military to a civil career, and his application for a permanent commission had been sent in before his death. His last letter to his father contained an interesting account of the assault, and capture, of Hill 60, in which he took part: Age 22. *unm.*

(Panel 22) Capt. Robert Gibson, 2nd Bn. (25th Foot) The King's Own Scottish Borderers: eldest *s.* of James Gibson, M.A., late Headmaster, Woodside Higher Grade School; of 28, Park Gardens, North Glasgow, by his wife Grace, *dau.* of William Gott: *b.* Glasgow, 30 November 1885: *educ.* Glasgow High School, and Glasgow University; graduated First Class Honours (Classics, 1908): gained Snell Exhibition and Newlands Scholarship, thereafter entered Balliol College, Oxford (graduated First Class – Mods. and Greats), and elected a Fellow and Tutor of Balliol: member of the O.T.C. there, and when war broke out was gazetted 2nd Lieut. 3rd K.O.S.B., 15 August 1914; subsequently attd. 2nd Battn. for Active Service: promoted Lieut. 9 November 1914, later promoted Capt. Killed in action nr. Hill 60, 5 – 6 May 1915. Mentioned in F.M. Sir John (now Lord) French's Despatch, 14 January. (*'London Gazette,'* 17 February 1915): Age 26. *unm.*

(Panel 22) Capt. Kenneth McDiarmid, 3rd (Reserve) attd. 'A' Coy., 2nd Bn. (25th Foot) The King's Own Scottish Borderers: *s.* of the late John McDiarmid, of Auchenvhin, Dalbeattie, Scotland, Ship owner, by his wife Mary A.J., *dau.* of the late James Hosack: *b.* 5, Devonshire Road, Liverpool, 26 October 1881: *educ.* Sedbergh School, and Royal Agricultural College, Cirencester: held an appointment in Burma with

Bombay Burma Trading Corporation Ltd., and being home on leave at the outbreak of war applied for a commission: gazetted 2nd Lieut., 3rd Battn., 4 September, subsequently transf'd. 2nd Battn.: promoted Lieut. 9 November 1914, and Capt. subsequent to his death, 5 May 1915, to date as from 2 February 1915: killed in action on Hill 60, nr. Ypres, 18 April 1915, while '… gallantly holding a hill we had captured.' Writing to his mother, his Commanding Officer said, "He not only showed a splendid example of leadership, but of great heroism. Though wounded he refused to go away from the fighting line, and, finally, when his platoon was very much reduced in numbers and the Germans were in consequence pressing on to the parapet, he leapt on to the parapet himself and met his end most valiantly fighting at close quarters. He was an officer whose brave deeds will never be forgotten in the regt. and whose charming personality made a great impression on me for the three short weeks I knew him." A brother officer wrote, " He was wounded through the arm first, but refused to leave the firing line. About 6 a.m., while cheering on the Scottish Borderers, he was shot clean through the head and killed instantaneously. Your son was beloved by his men and fellow officers, and in losing him the regt. has lost one of its best officers, and myself one of my best chums. It is some little consolation to know that his bravery pulled his men together at a very critical point, and his memory will never be forgotten." And another officer, "The conduct of 'A' Coy. was extraordinarily good. They had between 120 and 130 casualties out of 160. Lieut. McDiarmid did extraordinarily well there. Although severely wounded he kept up a rapid fire behind a blockade until he was killed. I was told his conduct was absolutely heroic, for he succeeded in holding a very important communication trench, thus saving a rather dangerous situation, as but for his action it might well have resulted in our communications being cut." Mentioned in F.M. Sir John French's Despatch of 31 May ('*London Gazette*,' 22 June 1915), for 'gallant and distinguished service in the field.': Age 33. *unm.*

(Panel 22) Capt. Hugh Vincent Corbett Turnbull, 2nd Bn. (25th Foot) The King's Own Scottish Borderers: only *s.* of the late Charles Corbett Turnbull, of Murvagh, Cheltenham, and Upper Colletts, Cleeve Hill, co. Gloucester: *b.* 20 July 1877: gazetted 2nd Lieut. King's Own Scottish Borderers from the Militia, 4 May 1898: promoted Lieut. 4 May 1900; Capt. 7 June 1908: Adjutant to his regiment, 22 January 1911 – 7 August 1912; detached for employ with Egyptian Army from 8 August 1912: returned to England on the outbreak of the European War: posted 2nd Battn. of his regiment; proceeded to France, and was killed in action there 13 November 1914: Age 37.

(Panel 22) Capt. Thomas Paterson Wingate, 2nd Bn. (25th Foot) The King's Own Scottish Borderers: only *s.* of the late Paterson Wingate, of Glasgow, Shipbuilder, by his wife Jessie Crawford (18, Westbourne Terrace, Glasgow), *dau.* of John Bruce Murray, of Glasgow: *b.* Woodcroft, Glasgow, 7 February 1877: *educ.* Kelvinside Academy, Glasgow, and Glasgow University (B.Sc., 1899): gazetted 2nd Lieut. 2nd King's Own Scottish Borderers, then in India, 4 May 1898: promoted Lieut. 21 April 1900; Capt. 24 January 1906: served in the South African War, 1899 – 1902, with King's Royal Rifle Corps: took part in operations in Natal, 1899, including actions at Rietfontein and Lombard's Kop: defence of Ladysmith, including action on 6 January 1900: operations in Natal, March – June 1900: Transvaal, east of Pretoria, July – 29 November 1900, and Transvaal, 30 November 1900 – March 1901: Railway Staff Officer (graded Staff Lieut.), 4 May 1900 – 4 May 1901; Military Landing Officer (graded Staff Capt.), 5 September 1901 – 30 June 1903 (Mentioned in Despatches ['*London Gazette*,' 8 February 1901], Queen's Medal, 2 clasps; King's Medal, 2 clasps). At the close of the war he joined his regt. in India and returned with it to Glasgow: Adjutant, 3rd (Reserve) Battn., 9 March 1912 – August 1914, Depot, Berwick-on-Tweed, and, after mobilisation (to 9 March 1915), Portland: proceeded to France, 16 March 1915, in charge of a draft to 2nd Battn., which had formed part of the First Expeditionary Force (13th Brigade, 5th Division), and was killed in action (shot through the head) at Hill 60, 18 April 1915, the day after 2nd King's Own Scottish Borderers and 1st Royal West Kents had stormed the Hill. Col. Sladen, D.S.O., Comdg. 2nd King's Own Scottish Borderers, himself wounded on this occasion, wrote, "He was such a brilliant soldier, and such a good comrade in every way. His loss is a great loss to the regt., and the Army can ill afford to lose such as he was. Hill 60 has indeed taken a heavy toll of this regt." Regimental Orders, 23

April 1915, recorded – "It is with very great regret that the commanding officer has to announce to the battn. the death of Captain T.P. Wingate, the late Adjutant, who was killed in action on 18 April 1915. In his magnificent soldierly qualities and his self-sacrificing devotion to duty the late Capt. Wingate has set a standard which all ranks may well endeavour to attain." Age 39. *unm.*

(Panel 22) Lieut. James Macpherson Gordon Brown, 3rd (Reserve) attd 2nd Bn. (25th Foot) The King's Own Scottish Borderers: *yr. s.* of James Rae Brown, of Thornidean Galashiels, co. Selkirk: *b.* Galashiels, 3 January 1888: *educ.* St. Mary's School, Melrose, and Edinburgh Academy: received a commission 2nd Lieut. (Temp.), 9th King's Own Scottish Borderers, September 1914: transf'd. 3rd (Reserve) Battn. on probation, December following: confirmed in rank, '*London Gazette*,' 5 May 1915, the day prior to his death, and in the same '*Gazette*,' promoted Lieut. to date from 2 February 1915. Killed 6 May 1915 near Ypres, being shot through the head in the charge to retake Hill 60. Mr Brown was a well-known Rugby footballer, having played in the First XV at Edinburgh Academy, was Captain of the Galashiels Football Club team, and had also played for the South of Scotland in an International Trial Match: Age 27. *unm.*

(Panel 22) Lieut. John Raphael Hamilton-Dalrymple, Adjt.; 2nd Bn. (25th Foot) The King's Own Scottish Borderers: 2nd *s.* of Sir Walter Hamilton-Dalrymple, 8th Baronet of North Berwick, by his wife Alice Mary, *dau.* of the late General the Hon. Sir Henry Hugh Clifford, V.C., and *grand-dau.* to Hugh Charles, 7th Lord Clifford of Chudleigh: *b.* 'The Lodge,' North Berwick, co. Haddington, 24 October 1889: Religion – Roman Catholic: *educ.* Ladycross, Bournemouth; Beaumont Old College, Windsor, and Royal Military College, Sandhurst: gazetted 2nd Lieut., King's Own Scottish Borderers, 18 September 1909; promoted Lieut. 8 May 1913: A.D.C. to Sir. H.H. Clifford, Governor & Commander-in-Chief, Gold Coast Colony, 11 December 1912 – 8 April 1914: went to France with the Expeditionary Force, 14 August 1914: served through the Retreat from Mons, the Battle of the Marne, the Aisne, etc.; wounded nr. Bethune, October and invalided home: returned to the Front, December following; reported wounded and missing near Pilckem, Flanders, 23 April 1915; on which day the enemy used poisonous gas for the first time. A brother officer wrote, "From what I can gather during some desperate fighting on April 23rd. north-east of Ypres he was slightly wounded, and went into a farm building just behind our firing line. Soon after he was seen to enter the farm four heavy shells fell into and round the building, completely wrecking it. All this occurred whilst our men were attacking, so there was a considerable amount of confusion at the time, and all the men to whom I have spoken seem a little vague as to what actually happened…That night the regiment was withdrawn from that portion of the line and taken right back… He had always behaved magnificently, always fearless and calm, with the keenest sense of duty. He was one of my greatest friends, and beloved by all who knew him. There is no man that I had a greater respect for. I hope it may be some comfort to you, in all your anxiety, to know that every officer and man who ever knew him would do anything to get him back again." His soldier servant said, "I went over the same ground where our battalion had been fighting in search of him. I lighted a match at each dead man I saw and also the poor wounded. I had been searching for him for three hours on the field when I met a man who told me that my master had been wounded; this man told me that when my master got wounded he crawled into a house for safety, which was knocked down and set on fire by the German big guns. He showed me the house, which was on fire, but I could not get near for the flames. I searched the ground among the dead and wounded until half-past eleven that night. He cannot be exactly a prisoner, because after he was wounded our battalion advanced 600 yards past where he was hit, so you see the Germans could not have got hold of him. I am more upset that I can say over his death, because he was such a good master to me, also a good officer at his work. If I can get to that house some-day I will go and inspect it, because he was carrying things about him that would not burn, and I could tell those things if I saw them among the ruins." Mentioned in Despatches ('*London Gazette*,' 19 October 1914) by F.M. Sir John (now Lord) French for, 'gallant and distinguished service in the field.': Age 25.

(Panel 22) Lieut. Hugh Arthur Grenville Malet, 'A' Coy., 2nd Bn. (25th Foot) The King's Own Scottish Borderers: elder *s.* of Allan Arthur Grenville Malet, of 'The Butts,' Harrow-on-the-Hill, M.I.C.E., Madras P.W.D. (ret'd.), Deputy Chief Engineering Inspector, Local Government Board, by his wife Elizabeth Anne, *dau*. of William Lysaght, of Beechmount, Co. Cork: and *gdson*. of the late Lieut.-Col. George Grenville Malet, 33rd (old 3rd) Queen's Own Bombay Light Cavalry (killed in action at Bushire; Persian War, 1857: 4th *s*. of Sir Charles Warre Malet, 1st Bart., F.R.S., F.S.A.): *b*. Duggirala, Kistua, India, 22 September 1892: *educ*. Harrow, and Caius College, Cambridge; in the O.T.C. at School and College, and on entering the Inner Temple (1913), joined Inns of Court Squadron: volunteered for Active Service the day war was declared, and obtained a Special Reserve commission in, and joined, 3rd Battn. King's Own Scottish Borderers, August 1914; given a commission as University Candidate, Connaught Rangers, 26 September following, but at the special request of the Col., 3rd King's Own Scottish Borderers, was transf'd. to them: promoted Lieut. 15 November following: joined 2nd Battn. of his regt. 26 November, and was killed in action at Hill 60, during the Second Battle of Ypres, 18 April 1915. Buried at Hill 60. An officer wrote, "Everyone here speaks very highly of him. And they all say he was absolutely fearless. I understand his name was sent in for 'Mention in Despatches' for some very useful work he did in scouting. Those who were present on Hill 60 say that he was killed while trying to take a communication trench which was held by German bomb throwers. I am told he was killed instantaneously, which is a blessing. I am really proud to have known him." A wounded Private of his platoon wrote from a Base Hospital, "At the request of Major Bindloss, R.A.M.C., I will endeavour to the best of my ability to describe to you how your son conducted himself during his period of active service. I cannot say for certain when he joined us out here, but it was either the end of November or the first days in December that he was posted to No.3 Platoon of 'A' Coy., which I belonged to. I know we were not exactly delighted at the time, for he looked just like a young boy, and we of No.3 did not like the idea of being led into action by a lad whom we thought had no experience, but he was not with us many days when we changed our opinion regarding him. It was our first turn in wet trenches when we began to take a little more notice of him. He came amongst us, cheering us all up and giving us all the help he possibly could to make things more comfortable until we were relieved. The next time we went in, your son, at a very great risk to himself, went about looking for different ways into the trench, so that we should not have to go through the communication trenches which were full of water, and he always found a way that took us into the trench with dry feet, which meant a great deal to our comfort. He was always the same, every time we went into the trenches. The comfort of the men came first; this continued during the hard winter which we put in. Spring came, and with it dangerous work. Your son was always the first to volunteer, in fact he was the only officer in 'A' Coy. who ever did any of that work. He used to go out in front of the trench scouting along with six men, perhaps he would stay out one hour, perhaps two, and then again I've known him to stay out from 8 o'clock at night until 4 in the morning, trying to find out who were in front of us. Then came the order we were to help at Hill 60. We lay in dug-outs while our artillery shelled the Hill; the Germans replied; the air seemed to be alive; it was awful, but we sat tight until the hour arrived, 7a.m. It was then the Hill went up; it was like a huge crater, and shook the earth for miles around. We then advanced on the Hill, and of course, we took it. We could not see a German anywhere, but bullets and bombs came amongst us, doing frightful damage. Your son then said, 'Follow me, men, I'll find the Germans for you.' We went after him, he found them, but I regret to say, they found him first. His death was instantaneous, he suffered no pain. Madam, your son died a hero, and he should have had the V.C., but unfortunately there was no one there to recommend him for same. His death was deeply regretted, not only by the men of his platoon, but by every man who was left alive in his Coy. We not only lost our best officer, but we had lost a friend." The Medical Officer, after taking a statement from two wounded men (a L/Corpl. and Pte.) of his platoon, wrote, "Lieut. Hugh Malet took command of the trench, and in less than an hour he was killed in an exactly similar way by a rifle bullet. His death was instantaneous. He fell within five yards of the place where Capt. Wingate was lying. Lieut. Malet was considered by these men to be a wonderfully brave officer, he invariably volunteered for all dangerous duties, quite recently he had gone out on four nights in command of scouts in front of the British trenches to try and capture German 'listening' posts and snipers who were suspected of using explosive bullets. The two men said that we men always said that he would either get a V.C. or be killed. Lieut. Malet used to come back from these night scouting expeditions covered from head to foot in mud, from the ditches he had crawled through." Age 23. *unm.*

(Panel 22) 2nd Lieut. George Baird Bayley, 2nd Bn. (25th Foot) The King's Own Scottish Borderers attd. 2nd Bn. Royal Scots Fusiliers: only *s.* of Isaac Fenton Bayley, of The Halls, Dunbar, East Lothian, by his wife Grace Jane, *dau.* of Gideon Pot, of Dod, co. Roxburgh: *b.* The Halls, 1 July 1894: *educ.* Cheltenham College, and Royal Military College, Sandhurst: gazetted 2nd Lieut., Scottish Borders, 24 January 1914. Killed in action at Ypres, 24 October 1914: slightly wounded at Le Cateau, 26 August 1914 – during the retirement from Mons – after being invalided home for a few weeks, Lieut. Bayley returned to the Front with VIIth Division, attd. 2nd Royal Scots Fusiliers. It was whilst with this battalion that he met his death at the Battle of Ypres, having only returned to the Front a short time before he fell. On the morning of 24th October the Royal Scots Fusiliers were holding a line of trenches running from the Ypres-Menin Road northwards towards the village of Reutel, 2nd Lieut. Bayley's company being in Reserve. On the Germans breaking through the line, his company was ordered up in support, and while running forward to the trenches he was shot, death being instantaneous. Mentioned in F.M. Sir John French's Despatch, 14 January 1915, for 'gallant and distinguished service in the field.': Age 20. *unm.* (*IWGC record 26 October*)

(Panel 22) 2nd Lieut. Samuel Eric Ditchfield, 4th Bn. (T.F.) attd. 7/8th (Service) Bn. The King's Own Scottish Borderers: only *s.* of Percy Ditchfield, of 'Holmgarth,' Thorn Lea, Menston-in-Wharfedale, by his wife Alice Barlow, *dau.* of Samuel H. Needham, of Manchester: *b.* Moston, nr. Manchester, 14 July 1895: *educ.* Ilkley Grammar School: Occupation – Staff; Scottish Widows' Fund Assurance Society, Leeds: joined Inns of Court O.T.C., 3 November 1916: gazetted 2nd Lieut. (Temp.), April 1917; substantiated 4 May 1917: trained Berkhampstead, co. Hertford: joined his battalion Catterick Bridge, Richmond, co. York, thereafter served with the Expeditionary Force in France and Flanders attd. 7/8th Bn. King's Own Scottish Borderers, and was killed in action near the Frezenberg Redoubt on the Ypres front, 31 July 1917. An officer wrote from Berkhampsted, "Though he was not in my platoon here, I got to know him well as he was one of my chief helpers in the production of the 'Bancroft Magazine.' I shall always remember his great keenness and unselfishness in that work, and, indeed, in everything he took up when he was here. He was one of our best cadets, and the Army can ill afford to lose him." And his Commanding Officer, "He had not been with us very long, but he was so keen on his work, and quick, and a most promising officer, that we are all deeply grieved with his loss. He died gallantly, going forward with his men. Please accept our sincere sympathy in the great loss you have sustained." A brother officer also wrote, "I feel I must write and tell you how sorry we are at the death of your son; he and I were very good friends and he was liked by everybody. He was doing fine work when unfortunately he got killed by a sniper, shot through the heart, and his death was instantaneous. Please accept my deepest sympathy in your loss.": Age 22. *unm.*

(Panel 22) 2nd Lieut. Kenneth Cortlandt MacGregor, 2nd Bn. (25th Foot) The King's Own Scottish Borderers: *yr. s.* of the late Cortlandt George MacGregor, of Llantrisant House, Llantrisant, co. Glamorgan, by his wife Margaret Josephine ('Glanwenny,' Bridgend, co. Glamorgan): *yr.* brother to Lieut. C.R. MacGregor, South Wales Borderers, killed in action on the Gallipoli Peninsula, 5 May 1915: *b.* Shooters Hill, Jamaica, 21 January 1896: *educ.* Lancing College, co. Sussex; private tutor Germany; and Royal Military College, Sandhurst: commissioned 2nd Lieut., King's Own Scottish Borderers, October 1914: served with the British Expeditionary Force in France, and was killed in action nr. Ypres, 26 February 1915: Age 19.

His brother Cortlandt also has no known grave; he is commemorated on the Helles Memorial, Gallipoli.

(Panel 22) Pte. 7505, James Allison, 'E' Coy., 2nd Bn. (25th Foot) The King's Own Scottish Borderers: *s.* of the late William Allison, of 14, Fewston Street, Leeds, co. York, and Mrs E. Allison (18, Fewston Terrace, Cross Lane, Leeds): *b.* Newcastle, co. Cumberland: enlisted Leeds: served with the Expeditionary Force in France. Killed in action at Hill 60, 18 April 1915: Age 30.

(Panel 22) Pte. 6674, Alexander Cameron, 2nd Bn. (25th Foot) The King's Own Scottish Borderers: *s.* of James Cameron, of 11, Summerlee Street, Coatbridge, by his wife Mary: *b.* Old Monkland, co. Lanark, 1898: served with the Expeditionary Force, and was killed in action 15 December 1914: **Age 16**.

(Panel 22) Pte. 6540, William Collingwood, 2nd Bn. (25th Foot) The King's Own Scottish Borderers: 3rd *s.* of the late John Collingwood, Coal Miner; of Denton Burn, Scotswood, co. Northumberland, by his wife Eleanor, *dau.* of William Millar: *b.* Newburn, co. Northumberland, 25 November 1876: *educ.* Denton Burn; afterwards employee Montagu Colliery, Denton Burn: enlisted K.O.S.B., Berwick-on-Tweed, 31 October 1898; served through the South African War, being present at operations in Paardeberg, Johannesburg and Cape Colony, received Queen's & King's medals, 5 clasps, also a certificate for good services in the Mounted Infantry, 26 May 1903: recalled to the Colours on the outbreak of the European War, 4 August 1914: proceeded to France with 2nd K.O.S.B., 15 August: took part in the Battle of Mons and the retreat to Compiegne, after which he returned home for a time on sick leave: returned to the Front in France at the end of October; took part in the First Battle of Ypres and several subsequent engagements in Belgium, and was killed in action by a shrapnel shell bursting in a trench at the Second Battle of Ypres, 5 March 1915. Buried at Zillebeke, nr. Ypres: Age 38. Pte. Collingwood *m.* Newcastle-on-Tyne, 6 March 1909; Mary Jane (98, Delaval Road, West Benwell, Newcastle), eldest *dau.* of Jacob Heslop, and had a *s.* and two *daus.* – Winifred, *b.* 11 October 1909; George Heslop, *b.* 13 November 1911; Eleanor, *b.* 1 April 1914.

(Panel 22) Pte. 11553, Joseph Edwards, 2nd Bn. (25th Foot) The King's Own Scottish Borderers: *b.* Everton, co. Lancaster, *c.*1899: enlisted Bedford: served with the Expeditionary Force. Killed in action at Ypres, 18 November 1914: **Age 15**. Correspondence should be addressed c/o Elizabeth Hardwick (38, Smollett Street, Kensington, London, S.W.); his aunt.

(Panel 22) Pte. 12001, Harry Holland, 2nd Bn. (25th Foot) The King's Own Scottish Borderers: enlisted Stockport, co. Lancaster: served with the Expeditionary Force: Died of wounds, 19 November. 1914.

(Panel 22) Pte. 6297, William Inglis, 2nd Bn. (25th Foot) The King's Own Scottish Borderers: *s.* of Mr (& Mrs) Inglis, of Galashiels, Selkirk: served with the Expeditionary Force. Killed in action 18 November 1914.

(Panel 22) Pte. 11523, John McWhirter, 2nd Bn. (25th Foot) The King's Own Scottish Borderers: *s.* of Peter McWhirter, of Burn Street, Dalbeattie; late of 100, Friars Vennel, Dumfries, by his wife Mary A.: and *yr.* brother to Pte. 9275, W. McWhirter, Gordon Highlanders, killed in action 14 December 1914; and Pte. A. McWhirter, Highland Light Infantry (surv'd.), and Pte. T. McWhirter, Canadian Infantry (surv'd.): *b.* Southwick, co. Kirkcudbright, *c.*1895: *educ.* Dalbeattie Higher Grade Public School: enlisted Berwick, co. Northumberland, December 1912; proceeded to France, August 1914, and was killed in action at Ypres, 2 June 1915: Age 19. The brothers McWhirter are remembered on the Southwick (Caulkerbush) War Memorial.

His brother William also has no known grave; he is recorded on Panel 38.

(Panel 22) Pte. 6337, John Morgan, 'C' Coy., 2nd Bn. (25th Foot) The King's Own Scottish Borderers: *s.* of James Morgan, of 3, Allars Bank, Hawick, by his wife Georgina: and brother to Pte. S/11286, G. Morgan, 2nd Black Watch, who fell 22 April 1916, in Mesopotamia: *b.* Cupar, co. Fife: enlisted Hawick, co. Roxburgh. Killed in action 18 April 1915: Age 19.

His brother George also has no known grave; he is commemorated on the Basra Memorial.

(Panel 22) Capt. Abdy Fellowes Anderson, 3rd (Reserve) Bn. The Cameronians (Scottish Rifles), attd. 2nd Bn. King's Own Scottish Borderers: 3rd *s.* of the late Col. James Alexander Anderson, 14th Regt. (West Yorkshire), by his wife Catherine (19, Gloucester Square, London, W.), *dau.* of William Campbell, of Victoria, Australia: *b.* nr. Melbourne, Australia, 3 October 1871: *educ.* Harrow, and Royal Military College, Sandhurst; from which (1892), he passed into 13th Hussars for five years: served Lieut., Queenstown Rifle Volunteers, during the South African Campaign: Queen's Medal, two clasps: later joined 4th Border Regt., (Capt.); ret'd. on disbandment, 1908. Offered his service on the outbreak of the

European War; given commission, Capt., 3rd Scottish Rifles. 5 September 1914: proceeded to France, attd. 2nd King's Own Scottish Borderers, October following, and was killed in action nr. the village of St. Jean, on the Yser Canal, 23 April 1915, while his battalion was supporting the Canadians following the first gas attack. Capt. Anderson's company was the first to reach Hill 60 when it was captured by us on 17–18 April 1915. On 23 April the battalion were ordered to support the French and Canadians who had been thrown back by the first use of poisonous gases. Capt. Anderson was leading his company in a charge to recapture some trenches when he was shot in the legs, but pluckily went on until he was shot through the lungs and killed about ten minutes later. The ground was so exposed and fire-swept that it was impossible to recover his body for two days and nights. Buried by one of his subalterns and two men near the village of St. Jean, close to the Yser Canal, and a rough cross put over his grave. During the fight for Hill 60, and the charge in which Capt. Anderson lost his life, all but two officers of 2nd King's Own Scottish Borderers were killed or wounded and at the close of the fighting only fifty men of the battalion answered the roll call: 23 April 1915: Age 43. In a letter home, written on the night prior to his death, he said he had been in a big fight that day and had to go through it again the following day, but could not possibly see how he could get through another day like it. A member of the Naval and Military Club, Piccadilly, London, Capt. Anderson *m.* St. George's, Hanover Square, London, W., Phyllis Evelyn Carr (32, Walpole St., Sloane Sq., London, S.W.), only child of William Morris Fletcher, Burley Beacon, co. Hants, J.P., late I.C.S., and *grand-dau.* to Henry Alworth Merewether, Bowden Hill, Lacock, nr. Chippenham, co. Wilts, Q.C., and had two *s.* David Allan Fletcher, *b.* 2 May 1904, and Gerald Donald, *b.* 29 January 1908.

(Panel 22) 2nd Lieut. William Sewell Calderwood, 8th Bn. The Cameronians (Scottish Rifles), (T.F.): 2nd *s.* of the Rev. Robert Sibbald Calderwood, of 'The Manse', Cambuslang, by his late wife Annie: *b.* Garelochead, co. Dumbarton, 31 July 1897: *educ.* George Watson's College, Edinburgh; Glasgow High School, and Glasgow University: enlisted 1 February 1916: obtained a commission 12 August following, afterwards attd. 11th (Service) Bn. Highland Light Infantry: served with the Expeditionary Force in France and Flanders, and was killed in action near Ypres 31 July 1917. His Colonel wrote, "He was a good and keen officer, much loved by all his comrades and men. He died while leading the charge…He did not know what fear was." Age 20. *unm.*

(Panel 22) 2nd Lieut. Harold Maxwell Currie, 10th (Service) Bn. The Cameronians (Scottish Rifles): only *s.* of the late Claude Maxwell Currie, by his wife Margaret Buchanan Gardener (184, Ledard Road, Langside, Glasgow): and *gdson.* of John Currie, F.F.S.: *b.* Glasgow, 26 July 1897: *educ.* Hamilton Academy: employee Messrs Nobel's' Explosives Company, Glasgow: joined Glasgow University O.T.C.; obtained a commission 21 January 1916: served with the Expeditionary Force in France and Flanders, and was killed in action nr. Frezenberg, north-east of Ypres, 1 August 1917. His Colonel wrote, "From what I know of the circumstances and conditions, he must have done extraordinarily fine work, and had he lived I should certainly have recommended him for an award of the Military Cross…I only hope that his gallantry and devotion to duty may be some slight consolation. All along he did wonderfully well, the more so considering his age;" and his Chaplain, "He was one of those who do not think of themselves, but of others. He had great gifts of comradeship, and endeared himself not only to those of his own company, but to us all." Age 20. *unm.*

(Panel 22) Sergt.10142, Thomas George Waker, 2nd Bn. (90th Foot) The Cameronians (Scottish Rifles): eldest *s.* of Private Thomas Waker, by his wife Mary (72, Kenninghall Road, Upper Edmonton, London, N.), *dau.* of A. Hennessy: *b.* Bethnal Green, London, E., 27 July 1890: enlisted Stratford, London, E., 8 September 1907: served with the Expeditionary Force in France and Flanders from January 1915, and was killed in action at Ypres 31 July 1917. Buried there: Age 27. *unm.*

(Panel 22) Pte. 43619, Charles Milligan, 10th (Service) Bn. The Cameronians (Scottish Rifles): *b.* Glasgow: enlisted there. Killed in action 3 June 1917: Age 20. *Buried in Canadian Cemetery No.2, Neuville-St. Vaast (XIX.A.14).*

(Panel 22) Pte. 27677, Fred Withers, 2nd Bn. (90th Foot) The Cameronians (Scottish Rifles): *s.* of James Withers, of 654, Shettleston Rd., Glasgow, and his wife Elizabeth: *gdson.* to Francis Palmer, of

Alexandra Place, Kilwinning. On 31 July 1917 2nd Bn. Scottish Rifles were support unit to 2nd Bn. West Yorkshire Regt., 23rd Bde. Attacking north of Hooge, south of the Ypres-Roulers railway, the West Yorks achieved their objectives. 2nd Sco. Rif. passed through the Yorkshires and went on to take the Black Line and Jaffa Trench, receiving some rifle fire from blockhouses on their right flank which was quickly dealt with. In all probability it was this rifle fire that cost 19 year old Fred Withers his life. His memoriam in the '*Ardrossan & Saltcoats Herald*' read:– 'No more news none at all / Killed in action that is all.' Quite appropriate really; his body was never found.

(Panel 22) Lieut. Clive Alfred Le Peton, 8th (Service) Bn. The Royal Inniskilling Fusiliers: *s.* of Alfred Edward Le Peton, of Earlsfort House School, 3-4, Earlsfort Place, Dublin, and Rose Le Peton, his wife: and brother to 2nd Lieut. D.A. Le Peton, Somerset Light Infantry, died of wounds (gas) 9 August 1916: served with the Expeditionary Force in France, and was killed in action 15 August 1917, at Ypres.

His brother Desmond is buried in Lijssenthoek Military Cemetery (IX.B.2).

(Panel 22) 2nd Lieut. Albert Bogle, 12th (Reserve) attd. 10th (Service) Bn. (Derry) The Royal Inniskilling Fusiliers: *s.* of William Bogle, of 7, Princes Street, Londonderry. Killed in action 10 August 1917: Age 30. *unm.*

(Panel 22) Sergt. 26205, Thomas Joseph Butterly, M.M., Lewis Gun Section, 8th (Service) Bn. The Royal Inniskilling Fusiliers: only *s.* of Thomas Butterly, of 14A, St. Anthony's Road, Rialto, Dublin, by his wife Lizzie: served with the Expeditionary Force in France: wounded 27 December 1916, and was killed in action 7 August 1917. Awarded the Military Medal 'for bravery and devotion to duty,' on 27 April 1916: Age 22. *unm.*

(Panel 22) Major Robert Stewart MacGregor Gardner, 1st Bn. (28th Foot) The Gloucestershire Regt.: 2nd *s.* of the late Francis William Gardner, of Thorpe, co. Surrey, Barrister-at-Law of the Middle Temple, by his wife Jane, sister of General Sir Robert MacGregor Stewart, G.C.B., R.A., and *dau.* of John Stewart: *b.* Hornsey, co. Middlesex, 25 August 1870: *educ.* Somerset College; entered Gloucestershire Regt. from the Militia 4 February 1891; promoted Lieut. 4 May 1892; Capt. 24 February 1900; Major 25 July 1914. Served with distinction through the South African War, 1899 – 1900, took part in the advance on, and relief of, Kimberley; operations in the Orange Free State, February – May 1900, including the actions at Paardeberg (17 – 26 February), and Poplar Grove and Dreifontein, and afterwards operations in Natal, May – June 1900. Mentioned in Despatches ('*London Gazette*,' 10 September 1901; Queen's medal, four clasps). On the outbreak of the European War, August 1914, Major Gardner went to France with the First Expeditionary Force, and was killed in action at Gheluvelt, nr. Ypres, 31 October 1914. His Colonel wrote, "We were heavily engaged on October 31, and had to go to the assistance of the remainder of the Brigade. He dashed to the front with his company and was hit badly while leading them most gallantly. The previous day he also displayed the greatest bravery in penetrating to the front in making a counter-attack." Another officer wrote of the valour and dash of his leading, adding, "He was always in front." He *m.* Clifton, 25 October 1910; Helen May Bridget, *dau.* of Charles Whitchurch Wasborough, of Clifton, and had two *daus.* – Stella Mary Bridget, *b.* 19 November 1911; Vere Daphne Stewart, *b.* posthumously, 11 February 1915.

(Panel 22) Capt. Stuart Duncan, 3rd (Reserve) Bn. The Gloucestershire Regt. attd 2nd Bn. Prince of Wales's Volunteers (South Lancashire Regt.): *yst. s.* of the late James Duncan, M.D., of 24, Chester Street, London, S.W.: *b.* 25 May 1865: obtained his commission, Lieut., 1st Gloucesters, 6 February 1891; promoted Capt. 31 December following: served through the South African War (1899 – 1900), taking part in operations in Natal (1899), including actions at Reitfontein and Lombards Kop (slightly wounded): subsequent operations in the Transvaal and Orange Free State (1900); received Queen's medal, three clasps: retired 16 April 1904; joined Reserve of Officers: volunteered his services August 1914, apptd. Capt., 3rd Gloucesters, from which he was sent out to 2nd South Lancashires at the Front, and was killed in action in France, 13 November. 1914: Age 49. *unm.*

(Panel 22) Capt. Archibald Alastair McLeod, 1st Bn. (28th Foot) The Gloucestershire Regt.: 3rd *s.* of the late Lieut.Gen. William Kelty McLeod, Col. The Highland L.I., by his wife Emilie Godfrey, *dau.* of the late James Thomson, of Gibraltar, nephew of the late Lieut.-Gen. Sir John McLeod, G.C.B., Col. The Black Watch, and *gdson.* of the late Col. Alexander McLeod, C.B., 61st Regt.: *b.* Singapore, 3 June 1877: *educ.* Wimbledon School; Oxford Military College; Royal Military College, Sandhurst: gazetted 2nd Lieut., 2nd Gloucestershire Regt., 8 September 1897; promoted Lieut. 24 February 1900; Capt. 13 October 1905: served (1) in the South African War, 1900 – 02, employed with Mounted Infantry: took part in relief of Kimberley, operations in Orange Free State, February – May 1900, including actions at Paardeberg (17 – 26 February), Poplar Grove, Dreifontein, Houtnek (Thoba Mountain), Vet River (5 – 6 May) and Zand River: operations in the Transvaal, May – June 1900, including actions near Johannesburg, Pretoria and Diamond Hill (11 – 12 June), operations in the Transvaal, west of Pretoria, July – 29 November 1900, operations in Orange River Colony, May – 29 November 1900, including actions at Wittebergen (1 – 29 July), Bothaville, Caledon River (27 – 29 November) Cape Colony, south of Orange River, 1900, and in Cape Colony, north of Orange River: operations in Orange River Colony, 30 November 1900 – August 1901, and October 1901 – 31 May 1902; and operations in Cape Colony, February. – March 1901, and September – October 1901 (Queen's Medal, six clasps; King's Medal, two clasps): (2) in Nigeria, being employed with West African Frontier Force, 29 September 1906 – 1908, when he joined 1st Battn.: and (3) with the Expeditionary Force in France and Flanders, 1914: went to the Front with 1st Division: present at the Battles of the Marne and Aisne, and was killed in action while leading his Coy. in an attack on a farm held by the Germans, 2 November 1914: Age 37. Capt. McLeod was distinguished in musketry, and had the Special Certificate of Signalling granted to him at Pretoria, June 1904. His Coy. were winners of the Douglas Shield (a regimental trophy), 1912. His recreations were hunting, polo and shooting. He *m.* Chapel Royal, Savoy, 18 June 1914; Marie Jeanette Amelia, *yst. dau.* of Lord Henry Fitzwarrine Chichester; *gdson.* of Edward, 4th Marquis of Donegal: *s.p.*

(Panel 22) Lieut. William Stanley Yalland, 1st Bn. (28th Foot) The Gloucestershire Regt.: *s.* of T.K. Yalland, The Manor House, Fishponds, Bristol: *b.* Fishponds, 27 June 1889: *educ.* Private School, and Clifton College: apptd. 3rd Leicestershire Regt. (Special Reserve), December 1910: given a commission, December 1912, 2nd Lieut. Gloucestershire Regt.: promoted Lieut. August 1914: served with the Expeditionary Force in France and Flanders with his battalion, 3rd Brigade, Ist Division, and died very gallantly at Langemarck, 23 October 1914. He was ordered to take his platoon to a trench to prevent the Germans making further ground. This he did, and his platoon, at considerable loss, drove the Germans back, and the trenches were reoccupied by the British. During this action he was killed. Lieut. Yalland was a good three-quarter back at football, and played for his regiment in the Regimental Cup, 1913 – 1914; he was also a good cricketer, having played for his county (Gloucestershire): Age 25. *unm.*

(Panel 22) 2nd Lieut. Herbert Knollys Foster, 1st Bn. (28th Foot) The Gloucestershire Regt.: *s.* of the Rev. Canon Foster, of St. Thomas' Vicarage, Groombridge, Tunbridge Wells, by his wife Edith Susan: *b.* All Saints' Vicarage, Gloucester, 18 October 1895: *educ.* Marlborough College; and Royal Military College, Sandhurst: gazetted to the Army, August 1914: proceeded with the Expeditionary Force to Belgium. Reported missing / believed killed in action at Gheluvelt, Flanders, on or about 29 October 1914: Age 19.

During the First Battle of Ypres the Germans, in a desperate effort to force a decisive victory in the west, threw many untried and untested units – often consisting of young students, fresh from the training depots – into their assaults. With their helmets adorned with flowers and laurel leaves, singing patriotically as they advanced, these young students were no match for the hardened professionals and rapid rifle fire of the British Expeditionary Force. Mown down in swathes, the slaughter was so great the Germans came to refer to the Battle of Langemarck as the '*Kindermord von Iepern*' – 'The Massacre of the Innocents at Ypres.' The slaughter was not, however, all one sided. Such was the numerical superiority and bravery of the German legions that the outnumbered British, suffering heavy losses themselves, were frequently forced to withdraw and regroup. Commanding a platoon of 1st Gloucesters, blocking the Langemarck-Koekuit Road, 2nd Lieut. Harold Hippisley and his men poured a murderous fire into the massed ranks of the enemy, shooting them down in hundreds – but they kept on coming, kept on falling, and at some point during this intense fighting 2nd Lieut. Hippisley joined the fallen.

(Panel 22) 2nd Lieut. Harold Edwin Hippisley, Special Reserve attd. 'A' Coy., 1st Bn. (28th Foot) The Gloucestershire Regt.: *s.* of W.J. (& Mrs) Hippisley, of Northam House, Wells, co. Somerset: *b.* Wells, 3 September 1890: *educ.* King's School, Bruton, co. Somerset; matriculated London University: a member of the Royal Agricultural College, Cirencester – Gold Medallist (Estate Management & Forestry), also gained National Diploma of Agriculture: Professional Associate of the Surveyor's Institution, and member of the O.T.C., Cirencester; subsequently joined Special Reserve of Officers: left for France on the despatch of the Expeditionary Force – 3rd Brigade, 1st Division – as 2nd Lieut., 1st Gloucestershire Regt., and was killed in action 23 October 1914, at Langemarck, Belgium. At the time of his death he was in command of one of the two platoons, which successfully held an exposed trench against a large force, despite the loss of all the officers and sixty percent of the men. One of the few survivors, Pte. Barton recalled, "About this time (10.30 a.m.) Lieut. Hippisley, the platoon commander, was hit. The bullet struck the middle of the forehead. He was attended by his servant Pte. Brown, who was under the impression that if he kept the brain from oozing out of the hole he would be all right. After a time he was convinced the wound was fatal and that his master had no chance. He then divided his time between the parapet, where he would fire a few rounds, and then return to Lieut. Hippisley. Between his concern for his master and his desire for revenge on the Germans, he seemed to have gone crazy." Age 24. At King's School Mr Hippisley was captain of the cricket and football teams, and at Cirencester of the cricket and hockey teams. He played cricket and hockey for his county, and cricket for the United Services. He leaves a widow, Ivy Gwendoline, *dau.* of the late J. (& Mrs) Hussey Cooper, of 'The Lodge,' Wheatley, Oxford.

(Panel 22) 2nd Lieut. Charles Basil Stanley Woodford, 15th (Reserve) attd. 1st Bn. (28th Foot) The Gloucestershire Regt.: Killed in action 22 August 1916, nr. Thiepval, Somme. *Details re. this casualty dictate commemoration on the Thiepval Memorial.*

(Panel 22) L/Corpl. 2051, Tom Purnell, 2nd Bn. (82nd Foot) The Gloucestershire Regt.: *s.* of S.C. (& Mrs) Purnell, of 18, Stratton Road, Gloucester: *b.* St. Paul's, Gloucester, *c.*1898: enlisted Gloucester: served with the Expeditionary Force in France and Flanders from 18 December 1914, and was killed in action 20 April 1915: **Age 16.**

(Panel 22) Pte. 19603, John Abbott, 8th (Service) Bn. The Gloucestershire Regt.: late of Waterford, Co. Cork: enlisted St. Paul's Churchyard, London. Killed in action 7 June 1917.

(Panel 22) Pte. 8389, William James Barnfield, 1st Bn. (28th Foot) The Gloucestershire Regt.: *s.* of James (& Emma) Barnfield, of Upper Lode Locks, Tewkesbury, co. Gloucester. Killed in action 29 October 1914: Age 25. Remains recovered; Kruiseecke German Military Cemetery, 18 March 1921. *Buried in Tyne Cot Cemetery (LXI.K.14).*

At Rest

(Panel 22) Pte. 9852, William Lewis Butcher, 2nd Bn. (82nd Foot) The Gloucestershire Regt.: *b.* Wotton-under-Edge, co. Gloucester: enlisted Bristol: served with the Expeditionary Force in France and Flanders from 18 December 1914, and was killed in action 10 May 1915. Remains 'Unknown British Soldier. Glosters' recovered unmarked grave (28.J.13.c.2.2), refers GRU Report, Zillebeke 5-122E; identified – Titles, Clothing, Spoon mkd. 9852 GR, Ring; reinterred, registered 1 August 1927. *Buried in Sanctuary Wood Cemetery (IV.F.17).*

(Panel 22) Pte. 7882, Frederick George Dowse, 1st Bn. (28th Foot) The Gloucestershire Regt.: brother to Pte. 756, T.H. Dowse, Gloucestershire Regt., killed 7 November 1914: *b.* Bristol: enlisted Dublin. Killed in action 22 October 1914, at Ypres: Age 29. All correspondence should be addressed c/o his brother, W.E. Dowse, Esq., 14, Grafton Street, St. Philip's Marsh, Bristol.

His brother Thomas also has no known grave; he is recorded below.

(Panel 22) Pte. 756, Thomas Henry Dowse, 1st Bn. (28th Foot) The Gloucestershire Regt.: brother to Pte. 7882, F.G. Dowse, Gloucestershire Regt., killed 22 October 1914: *b.* Stapleton, co. Gloucester:

enlisted Bristol. Killed in action 7 November 1914: Age 22. *unm*. All correspondence should addressed for the attention of his brother, W.E. Dowse, Esq., 14, Grafton Street, St. Philip's Marsh, Bristol.

His brother Frederick also has no known grave; he is recorded above.

(Panel 22) Pte. 10081, William Ernest Holbrow, 2nd Bn. (82nd Foot) The Gloucestershire Regt.: *s*. of George Holbrow, of Rowden Hazel Wood, Nailsworth, co. Gloucester, by his wife Ellen, *née* Scales: and brother to Stoker 1st Class, Z/23928, C. Holbrow, who lost his life aboard H.M.S. 'Black Prince,' when that ship was bombarded and sunk 31 May 1916, at the Battle of Jutland: *b*. Nailsworth: enlisted Stroud. Killed in action 10 May 1915: Age 17. The brothers are remembered on the Woodchester (Gloucestershire) War Memorial; unveiled August 1918, it is reputed to be the oldest war memorial in the British Isles. Also remembered thereon – Major R. Raymond-Barker, M.C., Royal Air Force, shot down and killed 20 April 1918; 79th victim of German Air Ace, Manfred von Richtofen 'The Red Baron' who was himself shot down and killed the following day; and Lieut. M.J. Dease, V.C., 4th Royal Fusiliers, killed in action 23 August 1914; one of the earliest British officer casualties of the Great War and first Victoria Cross recipient. (*IWGC record Holborow*)

Having no known grave but the sea his brother Charles is commemorated on the Portsmouth Naval Memorial (18); Major R. Raymond-Barker has no known grave, he is commemorated on the Flying Services Memorial, Arras; Lieut. Dease, V.C., is buried in St. Symphorien Military Cemetery (V.B.2).

(Panel 22) Pte. 17778, Albert Hughes, 'A' Coy., 2nd Bn. (82nd Foot) The Gloucestershire Regt.: *s*. of the late George Hughes, by his wife Annie ('The Wye,' Charfield, Wotton-under-Edge, co. Gloucester): and elder brother to Pte. 17777, H. Hughes, Gloucestershire Regt., who fell the same day: *b*. Charfield: enlisted Bristol. Killed in action 10 May 1915, at Sanctuary Wood: Age 19.

His brother Harry also has no known grave; he is recorded below.

(Panel 22) Pte. 17777, Harry Hughes, 'A' Coy., 2nd Bn. (82nd Foot) The Gloucestershire Regt.: *s*. of the late George Hughes, by his wife Annie ('The Wye,' Charfield, Wotton-under-Edge, co. Gloucester): and *yr*. brother to Pte. 17778, A. Hughes, Gloucestershire Regt., who fell the same day: *b*. Charfield: enlisted Bristol. Killed in action 10 May 1915, at Sanctuary Wood: Age 18.

His brother Albert also has no known grave; he is recorded above.

(Panel 22) Pte. 7207, Ernest Parker, 2nd Bn. (82nd Foot) The Gloucestershire Regt.: *s*. of John Parker, of 75, Marshall's Road, Raunds, nr. Wellingborough, co. Northampton, by his marriage to the late Mary Ann Parker: and (by his father's 2nd wife, Elizabeth Marie, *née* Coles) step-brother to Gnr. 102340, L.W. Coles, Royal Garrison Artillery, killed in action 26 July 1917; Spr. WR/273897, E.O. Coles, Royal Engineers, died 31 October 1918, in the Base Hospital, Etaples; and Pte. G/13879, J.J. Coles, East Kent Regt., died 29 March 1921, at home: *b*. Raunds, 1881: Occupation – Shoe-worker: enlisted Raunds, September 1914: proceeded to France, December following, and was killed in action 10 May 1915: Age 33.

His step-brother Luther is buried in Belgian Battery Corner Cemetery (I.G.6), Enos, Etaples Military Cemetery (LXXI.D.19), and John, Raunds Cemetery (Plot 315, Block1).

PANEL 22 ENDS PTE. J. PARKEY, GLOUCESTERSHIRE REGT.

South Staircase

PANEL 24 BEGINS L/CORPL. R.C. ALEXANDER, 7TH BN. CANADIAN INF.

(Panel 24) L/Corpl. 77081, Robert Campbell Alexander, 7th Bn. Canadian Infantry (British Columbia Regt.), C.E.F.: *s*. of Elizabeth M. Alexander (4, Rowald Place, Holywood, Co. Down, Ireland), formerly of 39, Orient Gardens, Belfast; and the late James Alexander: *b*. 16 May 1886: Religion – Church of England: Occupation – Surveyor: joined C.E.F., Victoria, British Columbia, 10 November 1914. Killed in action during a charge at Mount Sorrel, 3 June 1916; body recovered and buried where found two weeks later: Age 30. (*IWGC record age 31*)

(Panel 24) L/Corpl. 16775, William Ferguson Hay, 7th Bn. Canadian Infantry (British Columbia Regt.), C.E.F.: *s.* of the late James Hay, of Binghill, Murtle, co. Aberdeen, by his marriage to the late Janet Boyd: and yr. brother to Lieut.Col. J.B. Hay, D.S.O., A.P.M. Egyptian Military Police, GHQ Ismailia, died 2 August 1919: Occupation – Broker: volunteered for Imperial Service, and joined Canadian Infantry after the outbreak of war in August 1914: came over with 1st Canadian Contingent, October 1914: served with the Expeditionary Force in France and Flanders, and was killed in action at the Second Battle of Ypres 24 April 1915: Age 32.

His brother James is buried in Ismailia War Memorial Cemetery (C.42).

(Panel 24) L/Corpl. 23428, Sidney Oliver, 7th Bn. Canadian Infantry (British Columbia Regt.), C.E.F.: *s.* of James Oliver, of Hartington, Buxton, co. Derby, by his wife Dora: and father to Pte. 931564, J. Oliver, 54th Canadian Infantry, killed in action 9 April 1917, at Vimy Ridge, aged 19 years; and Pte. 23429, W.E. Oliver, 7th Canadian Infantry, killed in action 24 April 1915, aged 21 years: *b.* 27 July 1865 (attested 1870): Occupation Miner: previously served 2 years 45th Foot, Derby; 4 years 3rd Dragoon Guards: volunteered and enlisted Valcartier, 22 September 1914: came over with 1st Canadian Contingent October following: served with the Expeditionary Force in France from February 1915. Killed in action, 24 April 1915, Gravenstafel: Age 50. Married to Sophia Elizabeth Oliver, *née* Thomas (Trail, British Columbia); correspondence should be forwarded c/o his daughter, Mary Eileen Oliver (Greenwood, Trail). Remembered on the Hartington (St. Giles' Church) War Memorial, Derbyshire.

His son James is buried in Bois-Carré British Cemetery, Thelus (V.B.14); William has no known grave, he is recorded below.

(Panel 24) Pte. 21111, Antony Henry Adams, 7th Bn. Canadian Infantry, (British Columbia Regt.), C.E.F.: *s.* of Mrs H.E. Adams (19, St. Leonard's Road, Hull, England): Religion – Church of England. Missing, presumed died / killed in action on or about 24 April 1915, at or nr. St. Julien; 2nd Battle of Ypres.

(Panel 24) Pte. 442010, Aleksa Agish, 7th Bn. Canadian Infantry (British Columbia Regt.), C.E.F.: *s.* of the late Mina Agish, and his wife Fata O. Agish (Kolasin, Montenegro), c/o Consul General's Office, Consulate of Serbians, Croats & Slovenes, Montenegro: *b.* 14 January 1891: Religion – Greek Catholic: Occupation – Miner: joined C.E.F., Vernon, 31 May 1915. Reported wounded and missing during an attack at Mount Sorrel, 3 June 1916; now assumed killed: Age 25. (*IWGC record age 30*)

(Panel 24) Pte. 17195, Russell Kerby Arnold, 7th Bn. Canadian Infantry (British Columbia Regt.), C.E.F.: *s.* of Lewis F. Arnold, of Bold Avenue, Chilliwack, British Columbia, by his wife Mary: and brother to Pte. 28511, C. Arnold, 7th Battn. C.E.F., killed in action 6 May 1916, nr. Hill 60: *b.* Moose Jaw, Saskatchewan, 16 December 1895: Occupation – Fireman: serving member 104th Regt. (Militia); enlisted Valcartier, 23 September 1914. Killed in action 24 April 1915, at Gravenstafel: Age 19.

His brother Charles is buried in Chester Farm Cemetery (II.D.11).

(Panel 24) Pte. 23370, Henry Beaumont, 7th Bn. Canadian Infantry (British Columbia Regt.), C.E.F.: 2nd *s.* of the late Henry Beaumont, by his wife Charlotte Ann (Swavesey, co. Cambridge): and elder brother to Capt. G. Beaumont, M.C., 6th attd. 13th Bn. East Surrey Regt., killed in action 9 April 1918, aged 29: *b.* 16 August 1886: Occupation – Carpenter: serving member of the Militia; enlisted Valcartier, 18 September 1914: came over with First Canadian Contingent, October following: served with the Expeditionary Force in France from February 1915, and was killed in action, 24 April 1915, during the Canadian counter-attack at Gravenstafel Ridge, Ypres: Age 28.

His brother George also has no known grave; he is commemorated on the Ploegsteert Memorial (Panel 6).

(Panel 24) Pte. 21806, John Bewsher, 7th Bn. Canadian Infantry (British Columbia Regt.): *s.* of Benjamin Denton Bewsher, of 41, Cecil Road, Sheffield, and Susannah, his wife: and *yr.* brother to Pte. 205274, W. Bewsher, 8th Duke of Wellington's (West Riding) Regt., killed in action 9 October 1917: *b.* Sheffield, 5 December 1883: Occupation – Rail Worker: enlisted Valcartier, 23 September 1914: served with the Expeditionary Force in France from February 1915, and was killed in action 24 April following: Age 31. (*IWGC record age 32*)

His brother William also has no known grave; he is commemorated on the Tyne Cot Memorial (Panel 83).

(Panel 24) Pte. 428117, David Newton Bryenton, 7th Bn. Canadian Infantry (British Columbia Regt.), C.E.F.: *s.* of Albert Bryenton, of Bryenton, Northumberland Co., New Brunswick, and Annie, his wife: and brother to Pte. 444437, H.D. Bryenton, 26th Canadian Infantry, killed in action 9 April 1917, at Vimy Ridge: *b.* 19 February 1885: enlisted New Westminster, British Columbia, 18 March 1915. Killed in action during a two company counter-attack to recapture some lost trenches 3 June 1916; Zillebeke: Age 31.

His brother Howard also has no known grave; he is commemorated on the Canadian National (Vimy) Memorial.

(Panel 24) Pte. 17104, Basil Edward Clarke, 7th Bn. Canadian Infantry (British Columbia Regt.), C.E.F.: *s.* of the late Rev. James Sanderson Clarke, Vicar of Goudhurst, Co. Kent, England, and his wife Annie Clarke (198, Denmark Hill, Camberwell, London, S.E.): and elder brother to Sergt. G/2659, S.A. Clarke, 6th The Buffs (East Kent Regt.), killed in action 13 October 1915, at Hulluch: *b.* Goudhurst, 19 December 1877: Occupation – Cook: previously served 7th Middlesex Regt. and London Scottish (T.F.); was, at the outbreak of war, a serving member of 104th Regt. (Militia): volunteered and enlisted Vancouver, 23 September 1914: served with the Expeditionary Force in France from February 1915, and was killed in action at Gravenstafel, Ypres 24 April 1915: Age 37.

His brother Stewart also has no known grave; he is commemorated on the Loos (Dud Corner) Memorial.

(Panel 24) Pte. 78004, Walter James Davidson, 7th Bn. Canadian Infantry (British Columbia Regt.), C.E.F.: *s.* of Charles Britten Davidson, of 14, Park Avenue, Portobello, Scotland, by his wife Margaret, *née* Anderson: *b.* Leith, 21 February 1892: *educ.* James Gillespie, and George Heriot schools: entered employ of British Linen Bank, Edinburgh (1906), aged 14 years: removed to Canada (1910); joined staff of Bank of Montreal: previously served 2 years, 9 months, 4th Bn. Royal Scots (T.F.): enlisted Pte., 11th Canadian Mounted Rifles (Militia) 1915, but, after two months, impatient to proceed to France, took his discharge, paid his own passage to England, and re-enlisted Shorncliffe, 28 September 1915; joined a draft of reinforcements to 7th Battn. and went to France December following. During the winter of 1915 – 16 he was in action almost continuously with his unit. Instantly killed by shell fire at Hill 60 on 2 June 1916, during an enemy counter-attack in the Ypres salient: Age 24. *unm.* (*IWGC record 3 June*)

(Panel 24) Pte. 16885, George William Elliott, 7th Bn. Canadian Infantry (British Columbia Regt.), C.E.F.: 2nd *s.* of the Rev. William Elliott, of 'Jubilee,' 61, Dupplin Road, Victoria, British Columbia, Methodist Minister (formerly missionary, Japan); by his wife Maria, *dau.* of George William Robinson: and brother to Lieut. F.F. Elliott, who volunteered at the same time, and is now (1916) on active service with the same battn. in France (since killed in action): *b.* Toyama, Japan, 17 April 1893: *educ.* various public schools Manitoba, 1899 – 1902; privately in Japan, 1902 – 08, and Victoria and Vancouver (B.C.) High Schools, 1908 – 1910: for some time worked as a House Carpenter with a view to becoming an architect: enlisted 88th B.C. Fusiliers, November 1913, for special service (to assist in quelling the strike troubles at Vancouver Island) and, when nine months later, the European War broke out, volunteered for Imperial Service: left Canada with 1st Contingent, October 1914: underwent training on Salisbury Plain during the winter 1914 – 15: went to France February, and was killed in action at Langemarck, 24 April 1915, being shot through the head: Age 22 years, 7 days. *unm.*

His brother Fred, killed in action at Mount Sorrel, 3 June 1916, also has no known grave; he is recorded on Panel 18.

(Panel 24) Pte. 760781, Alexander Fletcher, 7th Bn. Canadian Infantry (British Columbia Regt.), C.E.F.: *b.* 8 July 1878: late *husb.* of Ellen Fletcher (743, Semlin Drive, Vancouver, British Columbia): previously served 13 years (4 Overseas, 9 Reserve) 21st (Empress of India's) Lancers: served in the South

African Campaign, and with the Expeditionary Force in France and Flanders, and was killed in action at Passchendaele, 10 November 1917: Age 39. *(IWGC record age 35)*

(Panel 24) Pte. 21600, William Henry Fowler, 7th Bn. Canadian Infantry (British Columbia Regt.), C.E.F.: 2nd *s.* of John Busteed Fowler, Member of Cork Stock Exchange and Insurance Agent; of 8, Sidneyville, Bellvue Park, Cork, by his wife Annie Louisa, *dau.* of William Henry Hill, B.E.: and brother to 2nd Lieut. F.R. Fowler, 3rd Leinster Regt. attd. 2nd Royal Irish Rifles, killed in action 18 October 1916: *b.* Summount, Cork, 7 August 1893: *educ.* Cork Grammar School, and University College, Cork: removed to Canada February 1912; settled Calgary, Alberta: Occupation – Official of the Bank of Commerce: volunteered on the outbreak of war, enlisted, 11 August 1914: left with 1st Contingent October 1914: trained on Salisbury Plain winter 1914 – 15: went to France March 1915, and was killed in action nr. Ypres, 27 April 1915. A comrade wrote, "I was right there when it happened, and we buried him. We had not time to do very much, for the bullets were flying all round us, but we wrapped him in his blanket and put a cross up.": Age 21. *unm.* Two other brothers also enlisted when war was declared and served with the Canadian Expeditionary Force in France – Pte. 656, Richard T. Fowler, Princess Patricia's Light Infantry, invalided home, November 1915; and Pte. 21595, John G. Fowler, 5th Battn., wounded at Festubert, May 1915.

His brother Frank also has no known grave; he is commemorated on the Thiepval Memorial, Somme.

(Panel 24) Pte. 16316, James Henderson, 7th Bn. Canadian Infantry (British Columbia Regt.), C.E.F.: *s.* of the late Pte. 703543, P. Henderson, 67th Bn., died (at home) 19 August 1917, of wounds, by his marriage to Joan Henderson (6210, Commercial Drive, Vancouver, British Columbia) late of 22, 8th Avenue West: *b.* Glasgow, co. Lanark, 29 December 1880: Religion – Presbyterian: Occupation – Shipping Clerk: 5'6" tall, grey eyes, brown hair: enlisted Valcartier, 19 September 1914: came over with 1st Contingent, October following. Killed in action 24 April 1915: Age 24. *(IWGC record father 102nd Bn.)*

His father Peter is buried in Vancouver (Mountain View) Cemetery (Jones.45.5.16).

(Panel 24) Pte. 443020, William Henry Jones, 7th Bn. Canadian Infantry (British Columbia Regt.), C.E.F.: *s.* of Philip Rogers Jones, of 'Vernon,' Richardson Road, Mount Albert, Auckland, New Zealand, by his wife Harriett Sarah: *b.* United Kingdom. Killed in action, 3 June 1916, nr. Sanctuary Wood, Ypres: Age 23. *unm. (IWGC:1935/CR.Belgium,453-455,pg.23; records H.W. Jones) Buried in Sanctuary Wood Cemetery (V.U.4).*

(Panel 24) Pte. A/28660, Archibald Henry McDiarmid, No.2 Coy., 7th Bn. Canadian Infantry (British Columbia Regt.): *s.* of Rev. Henry J. McDiarmid, of Kemptville, Ontario, by his wife Mary (Carleton Place, Ontario): and brother to Pte. 219202, V.L. McDiarmid, 75th Canadian Infantry, killed in action 9 April 1917, at Vimy Ridge: *b.* East Gloucester, Ontario, 17 May 1883: Religion – Presbyterian: Occupation – Engineer: 5'8½ tall, grey eyes, dark hair: previously served Royal Victoria Rifles; serving member 6th Duke of Connaught's (Militia), enlisted New Westminster, British Columbia, 15 March 1915. Killed in action on the morning of 3 June 1916, during a successful but costly, in terms of casualties, counter-attack: Age 33. *unm.* Correspondence regarding the deceased to be addressed c/o Miss Margaret McDiarmid (Suite 20, Grace Court, Vancouver).

His brother Victor also has no known grave; he is commemorated on the Canadian National (Vimy) Memorial.

According to Canadian historian G.G. Nasmith the Flanders winter 'is a period of rain, mist and general dreariness for weeks and even months on end' which effectively prohibited both sides from engaging in any large scale actions or movements of any kind. In November 1915 Brigadier General Lipsett, in order to counter the negative effect of these conditions and keep up the fighting spirit of the troops under his command, proposed that raiding parties, properly rehearsed, could enter the German lines, inflict large numbers of casualties and obtain valuable information without substantial loss to themselves. Accordingly a section of enemy trench near La Petit Douve Farm was carefully photographed and repeatedly reconnoitred until the exact details of the trench, the topography of the terrain, wire and other artificial (and natural) obstacles before the objective, were accurately known. Thereafter a detailed model of the position was constructed at Grand Munque Farm and the men who were to make the raid rehearsed until they knew their part by heart.

The first trench raid was made by two parties of 5th and 7th Canadians. One party entered the enemy trench, killed or took prisoner a large number of Germans and, despite coming under considerable enemy artillery and machine gun fire, carried on their work for twenty minutes passing their prisoners back over the parapet where they were taken charge of by scouts and led back to the Canadian lines. When the time was up the raiders duly returned to their own lines whereupon the Canadian artillery switched their range from the German supports to the section of raided trench in the hope of catching a number of the reinforcements which were sure to have been rushed forward.

Described as a most successful venture; the sector attacked by 7th battalion resulted in fifty enemy killed and twelve taken prisoner, parapets had been destroyed, dug-outs and machine gun emplacements bombed and, after returning to their own lines, the battalion's supporting artillery opened up on all sides. One member of the battalion was slightly wounded by enemy fire, and one killed by the accidental discharge of a rifle caused by a fellow raider stumbling over some wire.

(Panel 24) Pte. 4/29672, John Meade, No.4 Coy., 7th Bn. Canadian Infantry (British Columbia Regt.), C.E.F.: *b.* Queenstown, Co. Cork, 17 March 1877: Religion – Roman Catholic: Occupation – Logger: 5'6" tall, medium complexion, blue eyes, dark hair, 'True Love' tattoo right wrist: a serving member of the Militia, enlisted New Westminster, British Columbia, 16 March 1915: served with the Expeditionary Force in France and Flanders from September following, and was killed in action (accidentally) 17 November 1915, 'while taking part in an attack west of Messines. No further information as to the actual circumstances by which the deceased met his death are available.': Age 38. *unm.* All correspondence regarding the deceased should be addressed c/o his brother, J. Meade Esq., Pontypridd, South Wales, United Kingdom. (*Archives Canada record 29672*)

(Panel 24) Pte. 428678, Peter Morrison, 7th Bn. Canadian Infantry (British Columbia Regt.), C.E.F.: *s.* of Donald MacIntyre Morrison, by his wife Annie: *husb.* to Elizabeth Rowan Morrison (Hamilton, co. Lanark): *b.* 18 January 1887. Killed in action 3 June 1916: Age 41. Remembered on Kilchoman Parish (Port Charlotte, Islay) War Memorial. *Buried in Sanctuary Wood Cemetery (V.U.3).*

(Panel 24) Pte. 23429, William Evelyn Oliver, 7th Bn. Canadian Infantry (British Columbia Regt.), C.E.F.: *s.* of the late L/Corpl. 23428, S. Oliver, 7th Canadian Infantry, killed in action 24 April 1915; and his wife Sophia Elizabeth Oliver, *née* Thomas (Trail, British Columbia): *gdson.* to James (& Dora) Oliver, of Hartington, Buxton, co. Derby; and brother to Pte. 931564, J. Oliver, 54th Canadian Infantry, killed in action 9 April 1917, at Vimy Ridge, aged 19 years: *b.* New Westminster, 14 January 1893: Occupation – Rancher: enlisted Valcartier, 27 September 1914: came over with First Contingent October following: served with the Expeditionary Force in France from February 1915, and was killed in action 24 April 1915, at Gravenstafel: Age 21. *unm.* Correspondence should be forwarded c/o his sister, Mary Eileen Oliver (Greenwood, Trail). Remembered on St. Giles' Church War Memorial, Hartington, Derbyshire.

His father Sidney has no known grave, he is recorded above; his brother James is buried in Bois-Carré British Cemetery, Thelus (V.B.14).

(Panel 24) Pte. 17417, John Franklyn Peters, 7th Bn. Canadian Infantry (British Columbia Regt.), C.E.F.: *s.* of Premier Frederick Peters, of Prince Rupert, British Columbia, by his wife Bertha Hamilton Gray: and brother to Lieut. G.H. Peters, 7th Canadian Infantry, killed in action 3 June 1916; cousin to 2nd Lieut. E.S. Poole, 11th West Yorkshire Regt., executed – Desertion, 10 December 1916: *b.* Charlottetown, Prince Edward Island, 19 October 1892: Occupation – Bank Clerk: enlisted West Down South, 2 December 1914; apptd. 7th Battn. on the 22nd of that month: served in France from February 1915; moved up (from Ploegsteert; Franco – Belgian border) to Ypres, 14 April; reported missing 24 April 1915, since when, despite rumours of his being prisoner in Germany, no word or confirmation has been received and is now (29 May 1916) for official purposes presumed to have died on or since the former date: Age 22.

His brother Gerald also has no known grave, he is recorded on Panel 18; cousin Eric is buried in Poperinghe New Military Cemetery (II.A.11).

(Panel 24) Pte. 183173, Ernest Campbell Pope, 7th Bn. Canadian Infantry (British Columbia Regt.), C.E.F.: *s.* of Edwin Pope, of 552, St. John Street, Quebec, by his wife Margaret: and brother to Lieut. C.A. Pope, Princess Patricia's Canadian Light Infantry, who fell 7 May 1916, and Pte. 628075, H.B. Pope, 16th Canadian Infantry, who also fell: *b.* 27 June 1877: Occupation – Farmer: enlisted 13 November 1915: served with the Expeditionary Force in France and Flanders, and was killed in action 10 November 1917; Passchendaele: Age 40.

His brother Charles is commemorated in Maple Copse Cemetery (Sp.Mem.B.8); Henry, Railway Dugouts Burial Ground (Transport Farm) (VI.D.32).

(Panel 24) Pte. 16936, Alfred Gilbert Sivell, 7th Bn. Canadian Infantry (British Columbia Regt), C.E.F.: *s.* of the late Charles Henry Sivell, by his wife Alicia M. (15, Wolfington Road, West Norwood, London): *b.* 12 April 1876: Dulwich College Archives record;- 'On leaving school he joined H.M.S Conway, but after four years had to give up the sea, much to his sorrow, owing to eyesight. About 1900 he went to Canada, first to Alberta, then to British Columbia, being engaged in surveying land business and finally settling down on his own ranch in 1913 in Vancouver Island. At outbreak of war he was among the first to join up in the first Canadian Contingent. He served first in the 8th Victoria Fusiliers Battalion and then was transferred to 7th British Columbia Battalion, crossing to England, September 1914. After training at Salisbury Plain he proceeded to France February 1915. He refused to take a commission, preferring to serve in the ranks with "the boys" with whom he came across from Canada, and was killed in action 24 April 1915, at Ypres': Age 39. He leaves a wife, Elizabeth (19, Campden Hill Court, Kensington, London). Pte. Sivell was a member of Streatham-Croydon Rugby Football Club. (*IWGC record age 38*)

(Panel 24) Lieut. Wallace Alexander McKenzie, 8th Bn. Canadian Infantry (Manitoba Regt.), C.E.F.: *s.* of Alexander A. McKenzie, of 165, Albert Street West, Saulte St. Marie, Ontario, by his wife Martha: and brother to Sergt. 29287, N.J. McKenzie, 16th Bn. Canadian Infantry, who fell 25 April 1915. Missing / killed in action 23 April 1915: Age 27.

His brother Norman also has no known grave; he is recorded on Panel 26.

(Panel 24) Coy.Sergt.Major 81236, Ernest Blair Dymock, 8th Bn. Canadian Infantry (Manitoba Regt.), C.E.F.: *s.* of John D. Dymock, of 3, Holyrood Quadrant, Glasgow, co. Lanark, and Maria Jane Halliday Bell Dymock; his wife. Killed in action 5 July 1916: Age 28. *Buried in Poelcapelle British Cemetery*

(Panel 24) Sergt. 1228, Thomas Eccles, 8th Bn. Canadian Infantry (Manitoba Regt.), C.E.F.: *b.* co. Ayr, Scotland, 14 February 1879: Religion – Presbyterian: Occupation – Clerk: previously served 19 years, 2nd Royal Scots Fusiliers; India and South Africa: joined C.E.F., Valcartier, 27 August 1914; posted 8th Bn. 11 September: came over with First Canadian Contingent: served in France, and was killed in action 25 April 1915: Age 36. All correspondence should be addressed c/o his sister, Mrs George Millar (1868A, Chambord, Montreal); late of 363, Melbourne Avenue, Westmount. (*IWGC record age 35*)

"During the night of April 23rd the 8th Battalion of our 2nd Infantry Brigade relieved the 15th Battalion of the 3rd Brigade, in a section of our front line. In moving up to our fire trench the relieving troops had to cross a high bank which was fully exposed to the rifle and machine gun fire of the enemy in the positions opposite. This bank lay about fifteen yards in rear of our forward position at this point. Its crest was continually swept by bullets while the relief was taking place, and the incoming battalion suffered a number of casualties. In the darkness and the confusion of taking over a new trench under such adverse conditions, the exact extent of the casualties was not immediately known; but Sergt.Major Hall missed a member of his company on two separate occasions and, on two separate occasions, left the trench and went back to the top of the bank, under cover of the dark, returning each time with a wounded man. At nine o'clock in the morning of the 24th, the attention of the occupants of the trench was attracted to the top of the bank by groans of suffering. Hall immediately suggested a rescue, in spite of the fact that it was now high daylight, and Corporal Payne and Private Rogerson as promptly volunteered to accompany him.

The three went over the parados, with their backs to the enemy, and instantly drew a heavy fire. Before they could reach the sufferer, who lay somewhere just beyond their view on the top of the bank, both Payne and Rogerson were wounded. They crawled and scrambled back to the shelter of the trench with Hall's assistance. There the Sergeant-Major rested for a few minutes before attempting the rescue again. He refused to be accompanied the second time, knowing that as soon as he left the trench he would become the target for the excellent shooting that had already put Payne and Rogerson out of action. It was his duty as a non-commissioned officer to avoid making the same mistake twice. He had already permitted the risking of three lives in the attempt to save one life and had suffered two casualties; but doubtless he felt free to risk his own life again in the same adventure as he had already successfully accomplished two rescues over the same ground. He may be forgiven for not pausing to reflect that his own life was of more value to the cause than the life of the sufferer lying out behind the trench. The fire from the hostile positions in front and on the flanks of this point in our line was now hot and accurate. It was deliberate, aimed fire, discharged in broad daylight over adjusted sights at an expected target. Hall knew all this; but he crawled out of the trench. He moved slowly, squirming along very close to the ground. The bullets whispered past him, and over him, cut the earth around him, pinged and thudded upon the face of the bank before him. Very low shots, ricocheting off the top of the parados in his rear, whined and hummed in erratic flight. He reached and crawled up the slope of the bank without being hit. He quickly located and joined the wounded man, guided straight by the weakening groans of suffering. He lay flat and squirmed himself beneath the other's helpless body. Thus he got the sufferer on his back, in position to be moved; but in the act of raising his head slightly to glance over the way by which he must regain the shelter of the trench, he received a bullet in the brain. Other bullets immediately put an end to the sufferings of the man on his back."

(Panel 24) Coy.Sergt.Major 1539, Frederick William Hall, V.C., 8th Bn. Canadian Infantry (Manitoba Regt.), C.E.F.: late of Pine Street, Winnipeg: *s.* of the late Bmdr. F. Hall, by his wife Mary (43, Union Road, Leytonstone, London): *b.* Kilkenny, Ireland, 21 February 1885: Religion – Church of England: Occupation – Clerk: previously served 12 yrs. 1st Cameronians (Sco.Rif); serving member 106th Light Inf. Regt. (Militia); volunteered and enlisted Valcartier, 26 September 1914; posted 8th Battn. C.E.F.: served with the Expeditionary Force in France from February 1915. Awarded the Victoria Cross ('*London Gazette*,' No.29202, 23 June 1915) "On the 24th April 1915, in the neighbourhood of Ypres, when a wounded man who was lying some fifteen yards from the trench called for help, Company Sergt.-Major Hall endeavoured to reach him in the face of heavy enfilade fire which was being poured in by the enemy. The first attempt failed, and a non-commissioned officer and private soldier who were attempting to give assistance were both wounded. Company Sergt.-Major Hall then made a second most gallant attempt, and was in the act of lifting up the wounded man to bring him in when he fell mortally wounded in the head." He died of his wounds the following day.": 25 April 1915: Age 30. (*IWGC record age 28*)

Two other Canadian Victoria Cross recipients – Corpl. Leo Clarke and Lieut. Robert Shankland – also lived on Pine Street. Of the three only Lieut. Shankland survived the war and whilst the individual heroism of men like these, set against the background of the misery and horror of war, is something Canadians do not care to glorify – it is more characteristic of them to recognise the action of their soldiers in war as the unavoidable and accepted duty of courageous men in the face of global tragedy – as a mark of esteem and in recognition of these three men the City of Winnipeg renamed Pine Street 'Valour Road.'

(Panel 24) L/Sergt. 814, Weir Henry Acheson, M.M., 8th Bn. Canadian Infantry (Manitoba Regt.), C.E.F.: *s.* of the late Alexander Acheson, and his wife Sarah, *née* Bredin: c/o Miss Ethel Maude Acheson (Suite 'C,' Berkley Court, Winnipeg): *b.* St. James, Manitoba, 1 March 1886: Religion – Presbyterian: enlisted Wingham, 23 September 1914. Missing / believed killed 5 July 1916; since reported, "On the morning of the 5th. July, at about 4.30 a.m., Acheson was in charge of a party of bombers on Mount Sorrel on the Ypres front, on a bombing raid. He was killed in front of the German trench. Next night a party was detailed to bring in his body, and all that was found was the left arm of a thick grey Canadian sweater which was identified as that of Corpl. Acheson's. No further trace could be found of him." Posthumously awarded the Military Medal ('*London Gazette*,' 19 February 1917) "For general good service and devotion to duty since the battalion came to France." Age 30.

(Panel 24) Corpl. 131, Robert Whinry Harris, 8th Bn. Canadian Infantry (Manitoba Regt.), C.E.F.: late of 331, Edmonton Street, Winnipeg: *s.* of W.C. (& Mrs) Harris, of 3, Vincent Road, Wood Green, London: late *husb.* to Isabel Mary Munro, *née* Harris (5137, Baltimore Street, Los Angeles, California, United States of America): *b.* London, England, 15 November 1883: Religion – Church of England: Occupation – Electrician: previously served 1 year 38th Imperial Yeomanry; South African Campaign; 4 years 90th Regt.; 3 years 22nd Middlesex Volunteers; 3 years R.C.M.R.: volunteered and enlisted Lark Hill, England, 10 January 1915: served in France from February 1915, and was killed in action 24 April 1915, at the Battle of St. Julien: Age 31. (*IWGC record age 30*)

(Panel 24) L/Corpl. 432, Richard De Burgho Molyneux Bird, 8th Bn. (90th Winnipeg Rifles) Canadian Infantry (Manitoba Regt.), C.E.F.: *s.* of the late Henry Bird, by his wife A. Maud Katherine (9, Morrab Terrace, Penzance, co. Cornwall), *dau.* of Capt. Stanwell, 38th Regt.: and brother to Pte. 21571, H.G. Bird, 5th Canadian Infantry, who died at the Base Hospital, Wimereux, France, 23 April 1917, of wounds received in action at Vimy on the 9th of that month; and 2nd Lieut. C.E. Bird, 9th Royal Fusiliers, died of wounds 28 June 1917, aged 19 years: *b.* Plymouth, 21 February 1885: *educ.* Private school: removed to Canada, 1912; settled at Winnipeg and studied for the legal profession (Lawyer): enlisted Valcartier following the outbreak of war: came to England with First Contingent October 1914: served with the Expeditionary Force in France and Flanders from February 1915, and was killed in action at Ypres 25 April following: Age 30. *unm.* One of three brothers who fell.

His brother Harry is buried in Wimereux Communal Cemetery (II.I.6A); Clement, Monchy British Cemetery (I.F.15).

(Panel 24) L/Corpl. 1113, Alec Pasley Robertson, 12th Platoon, 3rd Coy., 8th Bn. Canadian Infantry (90th Winnipeg Rifles), C.E.F.: eldest *s.* of Edmund George Robertson, of Bridge Close, Holme-next-the-Sea, Kings Lynn, co. Norfolk, by his wife Ethel, *yr. dau.* of the late Henry Walter Barlow: *b.* Sydenham, co. Kent, 13 April 1890: *educ.* Brighton, and Hall's Grammar School, Snettisham, winning the 'King's Prize,' 1905, and playing cricket and football for the latter school. Removed to Canada (1906), settled Brandon, Manitoba; played cricket three seasons for his Province in the inter-Provincial Cricket Tournament, and was known as a fine football player and golfer: enlisted 99th Manitoba Rangers at the outbreak of war, he was included in the detachment furnished by that regiment to complete the strength of 90th Winnipeg Rifles ("Little Black Devils"), which became 8th Battn. Canadian Infantry, 2nd Bde., 1st Canadian Divn.: trained Valcartier and Salisbury Plain, thereafter proceeded to France, early February 1915, and rather than wait in England while his application for a commission was being considered L/Corpl. Robertson temporarily gave up his intention, and went with his battalion to the Western Front. L/Corpl. Robertson found trench life 'not so bad,' and scouting in 'No Man's Land' somewhat of a recreation. On 17 April the Division took over the lines of the French 11th Division on the Gravenstafel Ridge, north-east of Ypres; and on the afternoon of the 22nd, when the Germans made their first gas attack, 8th and 5th Battalions, 2nd Brigade, were occupying the fire trenches on the right of the Canadian lines, with 3rd (Highland) Brigade on their left, the latter in touch on their left with a French Division. After the French had given way to the gas attack, and the Highland Brigade had been swung round to protect the flank and rear of 2nd Brigade, and the British Divisions on the right and right rear, 8th and 5th Battalions found themselves at the very head of the narrowed salient, subjected to the enemy's repeated attacks on their front and enfiladed by fire on both flanks and on their left and right rear. In the early morning of the 24th, on detection of signs of the coming second gas attack, the officer commanding 12 Platoon, 8th Canadians, was ordered to take his men to support the Highlanders in the trenches at their left rear. The enemy did not follow up his gas attack with the expected infantry assault, but opened a very heavy artillery, machine-gun and rifle fire. Through a mistake, only about one-half of the platoon had followed the officer into the Highlanders' trenches; and L/Corpl. Robertson, one of those who had become detached, finding out what had happened, crawled out alone across a terrain swept from two sides by the enemy fire, and joined his platoon. "He was," wrote that officer, "the only one to come out and join us, and about seven hours afterwards, when we had orders to get back to our own battalion trenches, he and I waited until all the remainder had got away (there were several casualties getting away, for we were under fire from two sides), and then he wanted me to go while he kept a look-out – in fact, we nearly had an argument as to who was to go first." The Lance-Corporal went first, and was shortly afterwards wounded during a German infantry attack, but he refused to go back with the wounded at dark, and remained in the trenches taking his part in the fighting until the battalion were relieved at three o'clock in the morning of the 25th by the 8th Durhams. The 8th Canadians (with the exception of the isolated 4th Coy.) then went back to their support dug-outs, some 400 yards to the rear, and L/Corpl. Robertson, together with Ptes. F.C. Tunbridge and E. Caswell, turned into a dug-out on the extreme left of the line. The three were seen by several of their comrades at about 8 or 9 that morning; but two or three hours later the enemy broke through the Durhams, and it being impossible to organize a defence of the line of dug-outs (the shallow trench was without parapet or parados), a retirement was made some 800 yards up the ridge, and towards Headquarters. The retirement was so sudden and the advance of the Germans so rapid, that, wrote an N.C.O., "there was no time to alarm the men in the extreme left dug-out, to which there was no communication trench, and they were not seen again; but," he added, "I think the three of them would rather die fighting than be taken prisoners, as they were such splendid men." Evidence that Robertson and Tunbridge had been killed and buried appeared in a German list of August 1915; and the then Adjutant, 8th Canadians, wrote of L/Corpl. A.P. Robertson, "He was of the type one seldom sees nowadays – quiet, but thorough, most conscientious with his work and very popular with his section. His whole conduct during the fight was splendid, and on our return to rest billets I told the Commanding Officer about him, and he said he would recommend him for a commission when he got back from hospital (we thought then he had gone to the Dressing Station). You will believe me when I tell you that many a man has been decorated for deeds less worthy than those which Alec performed that day." An Order, limiting commissions for service in the field to men immediately available for duty, precluded the posthumous gift. Later, through the good offices of the American Embassy, his identification disc was obtained from Germany; while, in further evidence of his fate, his name and that of Tunbridge appeared in a very long German list (March 1916) of British killed buried by the enemy in a big unmarked grave at Verlorenhoek – a name which, it has been suggested, was given by the Germans to a wide district between Poelcapelle and Bellewaarde, and covering the Gravenstafel Ridge. Speaking to a wounded repatriated man of the 8th Canadians at the Q.A.M. Hospital in December 1916, Field Marshal Lord French referred to Robertson as "one of those who did such good work at Ypres." At a memorial service, held at St. Matthew's Church, Brandon, Manitoba, 25 April 1916, in honour of L/Corpl. A.P. Robertson, the Rector referred to the golden opinions Robertson had won "as a loyal and trustworthy colleague in the Bank of B.N.A.," and in concluding his address, said, "they knew their late friend in a threefold character, as a churchman, a sportsman and an English gentleman. As a churchman he was not only a worshipper but a worker. He did the difficult and disheartening work of a Sunday-school teacher. As a sportsman he played the game for the sake of the game, and was one of the best all-round cricketers Brandon ever possessed. As an English gentleman he had many of the outstanding features of that type. Without any trace of self-advertisement, he simply went on doing things, reserved, a little modest, but always where he was wanted and expected: Age 25. *unm.*

(Panel 24) Pte. 519, George Frederick Adams, 8th Bn. (90th Winnipeg Rifles) Canadian Infantry (Manitoba Regt.), C.E.F.: *s.* of George Henry (& Mary Alice) Adams, of 493, Corydon Avenue, Winnipeg, Manitoba: *b.* 18 June 1886: Religion – Presbyterian: Occupation – Painter. Missing, taken prisoner vicinity Gravenstafel, 24 – 25 April 1915; notified by the enemy died on the latter date, buried nr. Langemarck; no further particulars furnished: Age 18.

(Panel 24) Pte. 26, Charles Attwood, 8th Bn. Canadian Infantry (90th Winnipeg Rifles), C.E.F.: eldest *s.* of Henry Mark Attwood, Superintendent of Police, Somerton Division, Somerset, by his wife Emma Matilda, *dau*. of the late James Coles Taylor, of Weston-super-Mare: *b*. Bishopsworth, nr. Bristol, 5 October 1893: *educ*. various schools in Nailsea, Chard, where he learnt the trade of printing. At the termination of his indenture left for Canada, where at the outbreak of war he held a good position as a Printer, Winnipeg, Canada, Taunton, and Somerton, and was afterwards apprenticed to Mr J.G. Williams, Somerton: volunteered and enlisted 90th Winnipeg Rifles, 6 August 1914: came over with First Canadian Contingent: trained Salisbury winter 1914 – 15: proceeded to the Front, 10 February 1915 (sailed from Avonmouth): slightly wounded by a shell splinter at Neuve Chapelle, but in his own words, when writing home, "It was not enough to stop me," and took part in the memorable charge at Ypres, 23 April 1915, when the Canadians, in spite of heavy odds, recaptured the guns which the retirement of the French before the asphyxiating gas (then used for the first time) had left in the hands of the Germans. He was killed in action at Langemarck the following day, and as the trenches held by his company had to be evacuated shortly afterwards, his body was not recovered. Attwood was a fine athlete and a member of the Somerton Rifle Club, and later of the Winnipeg Rifle Club: Age 21. *unm*.

(Panel 24) Pte. 460717, Harry Beeny, 8th Bn. Canadian Infantry (90th Winnipeg Rifles, Manitoba Regt.), C.E.F.: *s*. of Lewis Beeny, Farm Stockman; of Manor Cottages, Faircrouch, Wadhurst, by his wife Annie: *b*. Wadhurst, 13 April 1894: emigrated to Canada, and took up farming: enlisted Winnipeg, 2 June 1915: after training embarked for England, arriving 20 September following: served with the Expeditionary Force in France and Flanders, 2nd Brigade, 1st Canadian Division, from 6 January 1916. On 12 June 1916 the battalion were in the front line at Zillebeke, in preparation for the attack to recapture Mount Sorrel. In the early hours of 13 June the battalion reached their objectives and dug in, holding the position throughout the remainder of the day and the next under continuous heavy bombardments from the enemy artillery. One officer and sixty-four other ranks were killed, 202 wounded and missing. Known to have been killed in action 14 June 1916: Age 22. *unm*.

(Panel 24) Pte. 100, William Joseph Blenner-Hassett (served as W. Sanders), 8th Bn. Canadian Infantry (Manitoba Regt.), C.E.F.: *s*. of the late Francis (& Margaret) Blenner-Hassett, of 364, Bathurst Street, Toronto, Ontario: *b*. Toronto, 9 May 1892: Religion – Wesleyan: Occupation – Clerk: 5'6½" tall, grey eyes, dark-brown hair: joined C.E.F., Valcartier, 23 September 1914. Died (gas poisoning) 23 April 1915: Age 24. *unm*.

(Panel 24) Pte. 81132, Frank Carlisle, 8th Bn. Canadian Infantry (Manitoba Regt.), C.E.F.: *s*. of F.J. (& Mrs) Carlisle, of 17, Warwick Drive, Wallasey, co. Chester: and yr. brother to Pte. 49459, F.J. Carlisle, 10th Bn. Cheshire Regt., who fell 9 October 1916, aged 36 years: *b*. Warrington, 26 December 1887: Religion – Church of England: Occupation – Solicitor: 5'5" tall, brown eyes, brown hair: enlisted Winnipeg, 24 December 1914. Killed in action 14 June 1916: Age 27. Pte. Carlisle leaves a wife, Frances Beatrice Carlisle (106, Edmonton Street, Alberta). Remembered on Grappenhall (St. Wilfred's) Church War Memorial.

His brother Frederick is buried in Grandcourt Road Cemetery, Grandcourt (C.11).

(Panel 24) Pte. 1098, Ernest Caswell, 12th Platoon, 3rd Coy., 8th Bn. Canadian Infantry (90th Winnipeg Rifles, Manitoba Regt.), C.E.F.: *s*. of Ernest Caswell, of 30, Cross Street, Southport, England, by his wife Susie Gertrude. Reported missing after the enemy attack 25 April 1915, now known to have been killed on that date: Age 21.

(Panel 24) Pte. 1122, Arthur Edwin Clarkson, 8th Bn. Canadian Infantry (90th Winnipeg Rifles, Manitoba Regt.), C.E.F.: *s*. of Annie (now wife of Maurice Barker, of St. Rose du Lac, East Bay, Manitoba, Canada, and relict of John Cahill, of Scarborough): and half-brother to Pte. 424638, J. Cahill, 45th Bn., who fell 15 September 1916: *b*. Scarborough, co. York, 24 May 1893: *educ*. Scarborough Board School: went to Canada with his mother, June 1903; subsequently found employ as Cook: volunteered on the outbreak of war; enlisted Portage la Prairie, Manitoba, 14 August 1914: left Canada with First Contingent October following: went to the Front February 1915, and was killed in action at Langemarck 25 April following: Age 21. He *m*. St. Mary's Church, Scarborough; Sarah Newcombe (21, Hadden Street, Aberdeen).

His half-brother John is buried in Albert Communal Cemetery Extension (I.O.53).

(Panel 24) Pte. 649, William Curley, 'C' Coy., 8th Bn. Canadian Infantry (Manitoba Regt.), C.E.F.: *s.* of Agnes Wood ('Lowlands,' Bracken Moor, Stocksbridge, Deepsae, nr. Sheffield): *b.* 16 August 1892: volunteered and enlisted 23 September 1914: served with the Expeditionary Force in France from 13 February 1915, and was killed by shellfire 15 April 1915, before Gravenstafel: Age 22. He was betrothed to be married to his cousin, Miss Alice Shaw (16a, Honoria Street, Fartown, Huddersfield, England). 8th Battalion's earliest recorded casualty on the Menin Gate; wounded at the same time Pte. 454, D. Gordon, died the following day.

Donald Gordon also has no known grave; he is recorded below.

(Panel 24) Pte. 666, Charles Dawson Evans, 8th Bn. Canadian Infantry (Manitoba Regt.), C.E.F.: *s.* of the late Joseph Evans, by his wife Henrietta (663, Mulvey Avenue, Winnipeg): *b.* 10 May 1895: Occupation – Stenographer: enlisted 21 September 1914. Died of wounds 24 April 1915: Age 19.

(Panel 24) Pte. 840, Edward Charles Ferg, 8th Bn. Canadian Infantry (90th Winnipeg Rifles, Manitoba Regt.), C.E.F.: 2nd *s.* of Fannin Ferg (born Germany, removed to Canada; age five), by his wife Sarah (Monkton, Ontario, Canada), *dau.* of William Blighton, of Newark, co. Nottingham: *b.* Elma Township, Perth co., Ontario, 23 July 1887: *educ.* Public School, Elma: Occupation – Locomotive Engineer: joined 90th Winnipeg Rifles, August 1914, after the outbreak of war: left Canada with First Contingent, and was killed in action at Langemarck, 22 April 1915. Buried at St. Julien: Age 28. *unm.* (*IWGC record 25 April 1915*)

(Panel 24) Pte. 1014, Frederick George Fletcher, 8th Bn. Canadian Infantry (90th Winnipeg Rifles, Manitoba Regt.), C.E.F.: *s.* of Richard Fletcher, Farm Labourer; of Hill Farm, Steventon, co. Berks, by his wife Sarah, *dau.* of William Denton, of Steventon: *b.* Hill Farm, 4 April 1891: *educ.* Steventon School: went to Canada, July 1913; settled Portage la Prairie, as Mill Hand: enlisted on the outbreak of war August 1914: came over with First Contingent, October: trained Salisbury Plain: proceeded to France, 17 February 1915: served through the Battles of Ypres and Langemarck, when the Canadians, to use Sir John French's words, "saved the situation," and was killed in action at Langemarck, 24 April 1915, while returning from binding up a comrade's wounds: Age 24. *unm.*

(Panel 24) Pte. 454, Donald Gordon, 'C' Coy., 8th Bn. Canadian Infantry (Manitoba Regt.), C.E.F.: *s.* of C. Gordon, of 260, Royal Avenue West, Kildonan, Manitoba: *b.* Glasgow, Scotland, 6 August 1896: volunteered and enlisted 23 September 1914: served with the Expeditionary Force in France from 13 February 1915, and died of wounds 16 April 1915, received in action before Gravenstafel the previous day: Age 18. See Pte. W. Curley, above.

(Panel 24) Pte. 81605, Cyril George Ettrick Moore, 8th Bn. Canadian Infantry (90th Winnipeg Rifles, Manitoba Regt.), C.E.F.: *s.* of the late Rev. George Moore, Vicar of Packington, co. Leicester, by his wife Mary Louisa (18, St. John's Road, St. Leonard's-on-Sea, co. Sussex): Killed in action 14 June 1916, at Ypres: Age 27. *unm.* 'Sons of the Anglican Clergy Who Fell in the Great War' record his brother 2nd Lieut. W.E. Moore, Lancashire Fusiliers, killed in action 8 November 1918, at Le Cateau; no record of this officer's death, place of commemoration or burial can be traced.

(Panel 24) Pte. 474, Reginald Alfred Minchinton, 8th Bn. Canadian Infantry (90th Winnipeg Rifles, Manitoba Regt.), C.E.F.: c/o Harriet Downer (265, Talbot Street, St. Thomas, Ontario): *s.* of James Minchinton, of Napanee, Ontario: and brother to Lieut. G.E. Minchinton, 27th Canadian Infantry, killed in action 9 April 1917, at Vimy Ridge: *b.* Napanee, 5 October 1894: Occupation – Stenographer: a pre-war member of the Militia, enlisted Valcartier 21 September 1914: served with the Expeditionary Force in France and Flanders; took part in the fighting at Neuve Chapelle, Second Battle of Ypres, St. Julien, Festubert, Givenchy, Battle of the Somme, Hill 70, and Passchendaele where, on 10 November 1917, he was shot through the head and killed by a sniper while assisting a wounded comrade: Age 23. *unm.* (*IWGC record age 24*)

His brother Gordon is buried in Ecoivres Military Cemetery, Mont-St. Eloi (VI.E.17).

(Panel 24) Pte. 1116, Fredrick Charles Tunbridge, 12th Platoon, 3rd Coy., 8th Bn. Canadian Infantry (90th Winnipeg Rifles, Manitoba Regt.), C.E.F.: *s.* of Arthur Tunbridge, of Chessins, Chignal Smealey, Chelmsford, co. Essex, by his wife Eliza. Reported missing after the enemy attack 25 April 1915, now known to have been killed in action on that date: Age 26.

On 8 November 1917, in preparation for an assault on the German lines in the vicinity of Mosselmarkt, 8th Battalion Canadian Infantry relieved the 13th Battalion in the front line trenches opposite the enemy. No sooner had the relief taken place than the Germans began a continuous heavy shelling on the battalion's position which, by the evening of the following day (9th), had caused them losses of 5 officers and 60 other ranks; 25% of the latter being buried by the shell fire. Nevertheless, despite these losses the 8th dutifully went over the top at 6.30 a.m. on the morning of November 10th, and almost immediately ran into difficulties.

At 7.00 a.m. observers reported large numbers of khaki clad figures returning from the direction of the battalion's objective. Fifteen minutes later the Officer Commanding 1st South Wales Borderers (the 8th Battalion's Support troops) reported that his men, disorientated by the terrain, had somehow lost their way and retired in order to advance. This seemingly simple error of judgement and manoeuvre had resulted in the exposure of the Canadian's left flank – from which direction they were now receiving heavy machine gun fire from enemy positions which should have been mopped up by the Borderers, and suffering large numbers of casualties as they desperately tried to consolidate, dig in and take cover.

The Menin Gate bears witness to thousands of men who lost their lives due to seemingly simple errors of judgement and manoeuvre; among them:–

(Panel 24) Pte. 829310, Raymond William Newbery, 8th Bn. Canadian Infantry (90th Winnipeg Rifles, Manitoba Regt.), C.E.F.: late of Winnipeg Coffee House, Winnipeg: *s.* of William Henry Newbery, of Acacia Lodge, Woodhall Spa, co. Lincoln, by his wife Mercy: *b.* London, 6 August 1879: Religion – Church of England: sometime emigrated to Canada, taking up residence and finding employ as Carpenter; Winnipeg, Manitoba: 5'11" tall, fair complexion, grey eyes, black hair: enlisted Winnipeg, 29 November 1915, after the outbreak of war: posted 144th Training Battn.: embarked for Europe aboard S.S. 'Olympic,' 18 September 1916, arrived Liverpool, 25th following: after completion of further training in England, proceeded to France, 21 April 1917; posted 8th Battn. C.E.F.. Reported missing on or about 10 November 1917: Age 38. *unm.*

(Panel 24) Pte. 21510, Daniel Robertson, 8th Bn. Canadian Infantry (Manitoba Regt.), C.E.F.: *s.* of the late Pte. 145841, D. Robertson, 87th Battn., by his wife Mary (8, Hazel Avenue, Ottawa, Ontario): *b.* Lauriston, co. Stirling, 1 June 1893: Religion – Presbyterian: Occupation – Plasterer: 5'8" tall, fair complexion, blue eyes, brown hair: enlisted Valcartier, 23 September 1914. Killed in action 14 June 1916: Age 24. *unm.*

His father Daniel also has no known grave, killed in action 18 November 1916, aged 44; he is recorded on the Canadian National Memorial, Vimy.

(Panel 24) Capt. Charles Telford Costigan, D.S.O., M.C., 10th (Calgary Highlanders) Bn. Canadian Infantry (Alberta Regt.), C.E.F.: *s.* of the late T.J. (& S.J.) Costigan: *b.* Surrey, 2 September 1880: *educ.* Halbrake College, Battersea, London: Occupation – Accountant; Mercantile Bank, 11, Queen's Road Central, Hong Kong: serving member 4 years Mounted Infantry (Militia); previously served 4th Queen's (Royal West Surrey Regt.): enlisted Valcartier, 27 September 1914; apptd. Capt. (Paymaster), Canadian Staff Hospital; proceeded overseas 7 November: transf'd. 10th Bn., France, 1915. Killed in action 11 November 1917: Age 37. *unm.* Awarded the Distinguished Service Order ('*London Gazette,*' 23 December 1915) 'For conspicuous gallantry near Messines on the night of 16-17 November 1915. He led a bombing party into the German trenches and, on encountering a party of three of the enemy, shot them with his revolver; he then led his bombers along the trench, which was filled with Germans.' And the Military Cross ('*London Gazette,*' 19 August 1916) 'For conspicuous gallantry during operations. He remained by his trench guns for two days and three nights, supporting the infantry. He was twice partially buried by shells and worked a gun himself when the detachment was thinned by casualties. On several occasions his gallantry has been brought to notice.' His medals – D.S.O., M.C., 1914 Star, War, Victory – were sold at auction October 2013 for the sum of £3,120.00. *Buried in Passchendaele New British Cemetery (XII.F.7).*

(Panel 24) Capt. James Thomas Hutchinson Nasmyth, 10th Bn. Canadian Infantry (Alberta Regt.), C.E.F.: 4th *s.* of John Nasmyth, of Mount Forest, by his wife Jane P., *dau.* of John Morrison: *b.* Mount Forest, Ontario, Canada, 23 August 1874: joined 46th Durham Regt. about 1900, and after going through a course of instruction at the Stanley Barracks, Toronto, was, two years later, given a commission as Lieut.; promoted Capt. 1912, after taking a second course: volunteered for Imperial Service on the outbreak of war; apptd. Lieut. 10th Battn. 22 September 1914: served with the Expeditionary Force in France and Flanders: promoted Capt. at the Front. Killed in action nr. St. Julien, 23 April 1915, during the heroic stand of the Canadians at the beginning of the Second Battle of Ypres: Age 39. He *m.* Janetville, Ontario, Canada, 22 October 1896; Emma Amelia (75, Glenelg Street West, Lindsay, Ontario), *dau.* of Christopher Armstrong, of Janetville: *s.p.*

(Panel 24) Lieut. Andrew Leslie Bell, 10th Bn. Canadian Infantry (Alberta Regt.), C.E.F.: *s.* of Andrew Bell, Manufacturer's Agent; of 301, St. James Street, Montreal, Province of Quebec, by his wife Louisa Leslie: *b.* Montreal, 1 September 1891: *educ.* Creighton School, Montreal; Upper Canada College (1902 – 04); St. Andrew's College, Toronto, Ontario (entered October 1906), passed through Middle and Upper Schools, leaving June 1910: beginning in the Lower, in 1908 and 1909, played in the First Football Team, and, in 1910 was in the Second Hockey Team: also in the Cadet Corps, attd. 48th Highlanders of Toronto, being Corpl. in the school year 1908 – 09, and 1st Cadet Lieut. 1909 – 1910: won the Ross Rifle, 1908; presented by the Governor of Canada for proficiency in shooting: Occupation – Cement Tester & Chemist; Messrs J.G. White & Co., New York (1910 – 11); Superintendent, Canadian Light, Heat & Power Co., Montreal; thereafter Chief Inspector & Tester, Montreal Tramway Co. (1912 – 13); afterwards took a position with Phoenix Construction Co., Salt Lake City, Utah: joined C.E.F., Montreal, October 1914: served with the Expeditionary Force in France, and was killed in action at the Battle of St. Julien following the German gas attack, 22 April 1915: Age 23. *unm.*

(Panel 24) Sergt. 20429, Norman Robert Glover, 10th Bn. Canadian Infantry (Alberta Regt.), C.E.F.: *s.* of William Glover, of Orillia, Ontario, by his wife Mary: and *yr.* brother to Capt. J.D. Glover, 4th Canadian Infantry, who fell the same day: volunteered for Overseas Service, and enlisted on the outbreak of war 4 August 1914: came over with 1st Canadian Contingent: underwent training on Salisbury Plain and at Shorncliffe throughout the winter 1914 – 15: served with the Expeditionary Force in France, and was killed in action at Ypres 23 April 1915: Age 23. *unm.*

His brother John also has no known grave; he is recorded on Panel 18.

(Panel 24) Corpl. 20738, Frederick Charles Abbott, 10th Bn. Canadian Infantry (Alberta Regt.), 1st Canadian Contingent, C.E.F.: *yr. s.* of Frederick Charles Abbott, Solicitor; of St. Mildred's, Salters Hill, Norwood, London, S.E.: *b.* Brixton, 2 February 1885: Religion – Church of England: *educ.* Dulwich College: Occupation – Assistant Baggage Master; Canadian Pacific Railway, Medicine Hat, Alberta: joined Canadian Contingent on the outbreak of war: promoted Corpl., April 1915, and was killed in action in the charge at Langemarck Wood, Second Battle of Ypres 23 April 1915. Body not recovered for burial: Age 30. *unm.*

(Panel 24) Corpl. 21901, Gordon Bickford West, 10th Bn. Canadian Infantry (Alberta Regt.), C.E.F.: brother to L/Corpl. 77569, B.M. West, 15th Canadian Infantry, who also fell: *b.* 4 January 1892: Occupation – Clerk: joined C.E.F., Valcartier, 23 September 1914. Killed in action 5 February 1916: Age 22. All correspondence should be addressed c/o their brother Gerald L. West Esq.; 350, Belmore Avenue, Montreal.

His brother Burton also has no known grave; he is recorded below.

(Panel 24) L/Corpl. 19616, George William Allan, D.C.M., 10th (Calgary Highlanders) Bn. Canadian Infantry (Alberta Regt.), C.E.F.: *s.* of Mary Allan (84, Huyston Road, Hamilton, Ontario): *b.* Rhode Island, United States, 12 January 1887: Religion – Presbyterian: Occupation – Electrician; Messrs W.L. McKenzie & Co., Lethbridge: previously served 91st Highlanders Regt., Hamilton (Militia): joined

C.E.F., Valcartier, Quebec, 27 September 1914. Killed in action 23 April 1915; vicinity Langemarck. Body not recovered for burial. 'This N.C.O. was in charge of a machine-gun crew. The enemy attacked the morning after the charge and advanced in face of our machine-gun fire. As the enemy advanced the crew fell one by one until only Allan remained; he fought his gun until it jammed then, finding he could not extract the shell, picked up his rifle and commenced firing over the parapet. Just afterwards he was shot in the head and killed instantly.' Awarded Distinguished Conduct Medal ('*London Gazette*,' no.29202, 30 June 1915) 'For conspicuous gallantry and devotion to duty on the night of 23rd – 24th April 1915, when he fought first one machine gun and then a second, until both were put out of action and their teams either killed or wounded, he then continued to fire with his rifle until killed at his post.': Age 28. *unm*.

(Panel 24) L/Corpl. 20789, Arthur Edward Lawrence, 10th Bn. Canadian Infantry (Alberta Regt.), C.E.F.: *s*. of Edwin Lawrence, of 26, Victoria Mansions, Lethbridge, Alberta, by his wife Fannie: and elder brother to Pte. 20500, R. Lawrence, 10th Battn., who fell the same day: *b*. Cheltenham, co. Gloucester, *c*.1880. Killed in action 22 April 1915: Age 34.

His brother Reginald also has no known grave; he is recorded below.

(Panel 24) Pte. 19676, Charles Henry Adams, 10th Bn. Canadian Infantry (Alberta Regt.), C.E.F.: *s*. of Charles Henry Adams, of 28, Pinewood Road, Toronto, Ontario: *b*. 13 October 1884: Religion – Baptist. Missing 23 April 1915: Age 30. Confirmed killed in action, vicinity Langemarck: "One of a crew of a machine–gun stationed in a house in St. Julien at the time of the German attack on the night of 22 – 23 April. The gun crew continued working the gun until the position became untenable, and the order was given for each man to look to himself. None of the gun crew surviving, or at present (1916), with the battalion appear to have seen or heard of him since. It was, however, definitely stated by one of the survivors when the roll of the battalion was called after the action that he had seen Pte. Adams lying dead." No record of grave or body removed for burial. (*IWGC record Adam, age 26*)

(Panel 24) Pte. 81010, Hugh Carter Allingham, 10th Bn. Canadian Infantry (Alberta Regt.), C.E.F.: *s*. of Arthur Wellesley Allingham, of Broadview, Saskatchewan: and brother to Pte. 276277, A.H. Allingham, 217th Battn. (surv'd.): *b*. Broadview, 14 June 1893: Occupation – Student: enlisted Winnipeg, 14 December 1914. Killed in action 3 June 1916: Age 23. *unm*.

It is impossible to even begin to imagine the anxiety endured by the families whose loved ones were on active service during the Great War; constantly worried about their circumstances and welfare. To be notified he was wounded or killed were awful enough, but to receive notification he was missing after the fighting somewhere was enough to drive one insane with worry. Had he been killed, had he fallen wounded and crawled off somewhere only to die alone on the battlefield, had he been blown to pieces, had he stumbled helpless into a water-filled shell-hole and drowned, had he been taken prisoner? The scenarios were endless.

Jane Allingham received notification her son John was missing after the fighting on 22 April 1915 but, because his name did not appear in the casualty lists, she could not be certain if he was alive or dead. Enquiries through official channels elicited no information. Only by placing a number of notices in newspapers requesting details regarding her son did she received that which she sought. Almost a year after John had been reported missing Mrs Allingham received a letter from a comrade Pte. V. Erickson, he said he had known 'Emerson' and was with him when he died. He went on to say that 'Emerson' had been slightly wounded the previous day and, after having the wound dressed, returned to duty the following day, April 23rd. On this day the battalion were again in the thick of the fighting and at some point during the afternoon 'Emerson' was shot in the head and, after uttering a few words to Erickson, died.

As the day drew to a close the Canadian's position was deemed untenable and, under cover of darkness, they were withdrawn; forced to leave their dead behind them. By virtue of this even though it was hoped the Germans would clear the battlefield of the dead, give them a proper burial, the whereabouts of the last resting place of Pte. Allingham being registered and notified would, like so many others, never be known. The only comfort, if any, that Mrs Allingham may have drawn from Pte. Erickson was that, in the madness of all that was happening as her son lay dying, in his last moments he was able to look into the face of a friend and utter a few words which in time would be conveyed to his sorrowing mother.

(Panel 24) Pte. 20741, John R. Emerson Allingham, 10th Bn. Canadian Infantry (Alberta Regt.), C.E.F.: *s.* of Jane Allingham (Leo, Alberta): *b.* Calgary, 16 February 1892: Religion – Methodist: Occupation – Brakeman: previously served 21st Alberta Hussars (Militia): enlisted Valcartier, Quebec, 23 September 1914. Reported missing 22 April 1915, at Langemarck (confirmed 17 April 1916 – killed in action 23 April 1915): Age 23. *unm.*

In the confusion of the fighting at the time it is not unreasonable to assume Pte. Allingham's temporary absence from the battalion on 22 April to have his wound dressed might easily have been overlooked, mistakenly providing reason for his being recorded as 'missing' on that date, and thereby account for the discrepancy in the date of his death.

(Panel 24) Pte. 20297, Joseph Maxwell Boultbee, 10th Bn. Canadian Infantry (Alberta Regt.), C.E.F.: *s.* of the Rev. Frederick Croxall Boultbee, of Hargrave Rectory, Huntingdon, England and 'Arnion Lodge,' The Avenue, Combe Down, Bath, co. Somerset, and Henrietta Eleanor Boultbee, *née* Molson, his spouse: and brother to Lieut. A.E. Boultbee, 25th Sqdn. Royal Flying Corps (& Northamptonshire Regt.), killed in action 17 March 1917; Pont-a-Verdun: *b.* co. Bedford, England, 8 May 1889: Religion – Church of England: Occupation – Rancher: 5'9" tall, blue eyes, fair hair: serving member of the Militia, enlisted Valcartier, Quebec, 26 September 1914. Missing / believed killed 22 April 1915: Age 25.

His brother Arthur is buried in Canadian Cemetery No.2, Neuville-St. Vaast (XI.A.2).

(Panel 24) Pte. 434511, James Farquhar, 10th Bn. Canadian Infantry (Alberta Regt.), C.E.F.: *s.* of the late James Farquhar, of Bower & Mains Farm, Forss, Caithness; by his wife Elizabeth (Rerneggy, Libster, Wick, co. Caithness): and brother to Pte. 68522, G. Farquhar, N.Z. Auckland Regt., killed in action 15 August 1918, at Bapaume; Pte. 12589, A.S. Farquhar, M.M., Norfolk Regt., killed in action 30 October 1917, at Bourlon Wood; and Pte. 434397, W. Farquhar, 10th Canadian Infantry, who fell in the same action: *b.* Wick, 10 November 1880: Occupation – Labourer: previously served 5 years, 1st Sutherland Highlanders (Vol.): enlisted Calgary, 25 January 1915. Killed in action at Mount Sorrel, 3 June 1916: Age 35. One of four brothers who fell. (*IWGC record age 38*)

His brother George is buried in Gommecourt Wood New Cemetery (III.B.25); Alexander and William have no known grave, they are recorded on the Cambrai Memorial (Panel 4) and below respectively.

(Panel 24) Pte. 434397, William Farquhar, 10th Bn. Canadian Infantry (Alberta Regt.), C.E.F.: *s.* of the late James Farquhar, of Bower & Mains Farm, Forss, Caithness; by his wife Elizabeth (Rerneggy, Libster, Wick, co. Caithness): and brother to Pte. 68522, G. Farquhar, N.Z. Auckland Regt., killed in action 15 August 1918, at Bapaume; Pte. 12589, A.S. Farquhar, M.M., Norfolk Regt., killed in action 30 October 1917, at Bourlon Wood; and Pte. 343511, J. Farquhar, 10th Canadian Infantry, who fell in the same action: *b.* Wick, 26 March 1885: Occupation – Salesman: previously served 5 years, 1st Sutherland Highlanders (Vol.): enlisted Calgary, 21 January 1915. Killed in action at Mount Sorrel, 3 June 1916: Age 31. One of four brothers who fell. (*IWGC record age 34*)

His brother George is buried in Gommecourt Wood New Cemetery (III.B.25); Alexander and James have no known grave, they are recorded on the Cambrai Memorial (Panel 4) and above respectively.

(Panel 24) Pte. 20391, Harold Goodall, 10th Bn. Canadian Infantry (Alberta Regt.), C.E.F.: *s.* of Sarah E. Goodall (5, Elliott House, Elliott Road, Thornton Heath, co. Surrey): and elder brother to Pte. 9677, E. Goodall, 3rd Canadian Infantry, who also fell: *b.* 17 December 1891. Killed in action 22 April 1915: Age 23.

His brother Ernest also has no known grave; he is recorded on Panel 18.

(Panel 24) Pte. 20500, Reginald Lawrence, 10th Bn. Canadian Infantry (Alberta Regt.), C.E.F.: *s.* of Edwin Lawrence, of 26, Victoria Mansions, Lethbridge, Alberta, by his wife Fannie: and *yr.* brother to L/ Corpl. 20789, A.E. Lawrence, 10th Battn., who fell the same day: *b.* Cheltenham, co. Gloucester, *c.*1882. Killed in action 22 April 1915: Age 32.

His brother Arthur also has no known grave; he is recorded above.

(Panel 24) Pte. 20330, William Alfred Lipsett, 10th Bn. Canadian Infantry (Alberta Regt.), C.E.F.: *yst. s.* of the late Robert Lipsett, Ballyshannon, Ireland: *b.* Ballyshannon, 29 January 1886: *educ.* St. Andrew's College, Dublin; Trinity College, Dublin: Occupation – Barrister at Law, member of the Irish Bar, removed to Canada (spring 1914) and took up legal work in Calgary, Alberta. Two days after war broke out he volunteered and enlisted as Pte.; refusing a commission: departed Canada with 1st Canadian Contingent and, after training on Salisbury Plain throughout the winter, proceeded to France, February 1915. Killed on the night of 22 – 23 April, 1915, at the Second Battle of Ypres, during the charge of the 10th and 16th Canadian Battns. on the wood to the west of St. Julien. It will be remembered that these regiments charged through the wood, against far superior numbers, under the heaviest machine-gun fire, and actually reached a point 500 yards in advance of the wood; retaking the four British guns which had been lost in the afternoon of 22 April. Unfortunately the casualties were very high. The 10th Battn. went into the wood 1,000 strong, and came out only 200 strong. Mr Lipsett played a gallant part in this attack. As Major Ormond, who took over command of the 10th Battn. after Col. Boyle was killed, wrote, "I saw Lipsett the night that he was killed; we went into action charging the wood west of St. Julien at 11.50p.m., April 22. The Grenadiers were grouped on our left flank and did exceptionally well, Lipsett being one of them. As soon as we had taken the trench, they continued along to the left until they were stopped. Lipsett, like the others, was very cool and appeared to have no fear. They were subjected to the most severe machine-gun fire I have known, but pressed on until all were killed or wounded. I regret to say that as he was killed 10 or 15 yards from the German redoubt at the corner of the wood we were unable to recover his body. He was an excellent soldier." His Adjutant also wrote, "He was a gallant soldier and is deeply regretted by all ranks," and again, "He rendered valuable service to his Battn. and is universally regretted." His eldest brother, Captain Lewis R. Lipsett, also a member of the Irish Bar, is (1916) serving in the Army Service Corps, with the Expeditionary Force in France. His cousin, Brigadier-General Lewis J. Lipsett, formerly of the Royal Irish Regt., was appointed a C.M.G. for his services at the Second Battle of Ypres, while in command of 8th Bn. Canadian Infantry: Age 29. (*IWGC record 22 April 1915*)

(Panel 24) Pte. 20660, John Furlow McConnell Sergeant, 10th Bn. Canadian Infantry (Alberta Regt.), C.E.F.: *s.* of Furlow Ross (& Mary Jane) Sergeant, of 3, Carisbrooke Drive, Mapperley Park, Nottingham, England: *b.* 14 January 1893: Religion – Church of England: *educ.* Nottingham University; 2 yrs. member O.T.C.: Occupation – Engineer: volunteered and enlisted Valcartier, 22 September 1914: came over with 1st. Contingent. Reported missing 5 June 1916; attd. 3rd Canadian Tunnelling Coy., when last seen he was on duty near a machine-gun crew in the trenches before Hill 60 which, at the time, was under a very heavy artillery bombardment. The machine-gun position was hit, the crew annihilated, and it was believed Pte. Sergeant was also killed. This was proven to be true when, about five weeks later, his body was found behind Trench 41 in a very advanced state of decomposition.: Age 23.

(Panel 24) Pte. 20824, John Charles Taylor, 10th Bn. Canadian Infantry (Alberta Regt.), C.E.F.: eldest *s.* of Charles Taylor, Farm Servant, Binscarth; of Woodbine Cottage, Finstown, Orkney, Scotland, by his late wife Elizabeth, *née* Brown (*d.* 1910): and brother to AbS. SS/4751, A. Taylor, H.M.S. 'Vindictive,' R.N., died of wounds 24 April 1918; received in the raid at Zeebrugge the previous day: *b.* Rusland, Harray, 28 May 1884: previous to removal to Canada was sometime Ploughman; Moan, Harray; subsequently Locomotive Engineer, Canadian Pacific Railway: joined 21st (Alberta) Hussars, Medicine Hat, 22 August 1914: joined 1st Contingent, Valcartier, apptd. 10th Battn., 26 September following: departed Quebec, SS 'Scandinavian,' 3 October: trained Salisbury Plain, 14 October – 14 February 1915; joined Expeditionary Force in France the following day: took part in the fighting at Kitchener's Wood, 22 – 23 April, and Gravenstafel the following day, and was killed in action (intermittent shellfire) 3 May 1915, on which date the battalion were in reserve guarding Bridges Nos. 3 and 4, Yser Canal Bank: Age 30.

His brother Alfred is buried in Gillingham (Woodlands) Cemetery, Kent (Naval.8.414).

(Panel 24) Capt. Gerald Oscar Lees, 13th Bn. Canadian Infantry (Quebec Regt.), C.E.F.: *s.* of William Lees, of 'Old Ivy House,' Tettenhall, Wolverhampton, by his wife Rosa: *b.* Wolverhampton, co. Stafford, 30 May 1877: Religion – Church of England: Occupation – Broker: served 5th Royal Highlanders of

Canada, 1907 – 10: enlisted Valcartier, 23 September 1914: served with the Expeditionary Force in France and Flanders from 15 February 1915. Killed in action at St. Julien, 24 April following: Age 37. *unm.* (*IWGC record 25 April*) See Capt. L.W. Whitehead, below.

(Panel 24) Capt. Lionel Ward Whitehead, 13th Bn. Canadian Infantry (Quebec Regt.), C.E.F.: *s.* of William Thomas Whitehead, of 99, Crescent Street, Montreal, by his wife Anne Lillian Ward: *b.* Montreal, 19 April 1890: Occupation – Manufacturer: previously served 8½ years, 5th Royal Highlanders of Canada: enlisted as Capt., Valcartier, 23 September 1914: came over with First Contingent, October 1914: served with the Expeditionary Force in France and Flanders from 15 February 1915. Died of wounds, 24 April 1915, received in action at St. Julien the same day. On 24 April 1915 the 13th Battalion were entrenched in the position to which they had retired the previous day, pivoting on the left flank of the 15th Battalion. Just after daybreak the Germans released gas which fell with particular severity on the 15th's trenches on the right, following this with an intense bombardment which wrecked the shallow trenches dug during the night and caused heavy losses. In an endeavour to overwhelm the remnants of the Highlanders German infantry, under cover of the bombardment, moved closer and closer to the Canadians and, in the desperate fighting that followed, Capt. Lees was killed and Capt. Whitehead mortally wounded. Both these officers had displayed resource and courage and their loss to the battalion was a heavy one.: Age 26. *unm.* (*IWGC record 22 April*)

(Panel 24) Sergt. 24898, William Ewart Stewart Caryer, 13th Bn. Canadian Infantry (5th Royal Highlanders of Canada), C.E.F.: *s.* of Isabella Emma Caryer (95, McCulloch Avenue, Ontario): *b.* Lee-Blackheath, co. Kent, 3 February 1887: Religion – Church of England: Occupation – Railway Agent: previously served 4 years 3rd Victoria Rifles of Canada, and 5½ years 5th Royal Highlanders of Canada: volunteered for Imperial Service following the outbreak of war: enlisted Valcartier, 29 August 1914: 5'6" tall, fair complexion, blue eyes, dark brown hair: came over with First Contingent October 1914: underwent training in England throughout the winter 1914 – 15: served in France and Flanders, and was killed in action 24 April 1915: Age 28. *unm.*

(Panel 24) Sergt. 63252, Matthew Brown Dunlop, 13th Bn. Canadian Infantry (Quebec Regt.), C.E.F.: *husb.* to Mrs Dunlop (614, Alma Street, Montreal): *b.* Glasgow, 12 June 1883: previously served 5 years, Royal Highlanders: volunteered and enlisted no.1549, 23rd Battn., 28 January 1915: subsequently transf'd. 13th Battn. Killed in action 13 June 1916 in an advance on the enemy's lines: Age 33. Remains recovered (28.D.16.b.9.1) unmarked grave Sanctuary Wood, 28 December 1926; identified – Disc; reinterred, registered 1 January 1927. *Buried in Sanctuary Wood Cemetery (III.B.3).*

(Panel 24) Sergt. 24079, George Wilfred Imrie, 13th Bn. Canadian Infantry (5th Royal Highlanders of Canada), C.E.F.: 2nd *s.* of the late David Imrie, Coal Merchant & Export Agent; Messrs Cory Brothers, Cardiff (*d.* 1903), by his wife Annie ('Hill Crest,' 10, Penrhyn Terrace, Brynmill, Swansea), *dau.* of John Finlay, Jeweller; of 72, Buchanan Street, Glasgow: *b.* Mumbles, nr. Swansea, co. Glamorgan, 8 September 1889: *educ.* Brynmill Board School, Swansea: removed to Canada, May 1910; settled Montreal: Occupation – Clerk; Messrs Nichols' Chemical Works, Montreal: joined 5th Highlanders of Canada, August 1914, on the outbreak of war: came over with 1st Contingent: went to France, March 1915, and was killed in action near the wood of St. Julien during the Second Battle of Ypres, 23 April 1915: Age 25. *unm.*

(Panel 24) Sergt. 24202, Peter McLeod, 13th Bn. Canadian Infantry (Quebec Regt.), C.E.F.: *s.* of Donald McLeod, of Breavis, Islivig, Stornoway, by his wife Catherine: *b.* co. Ross, Scotland, December 1888: sometime went to Canada finding gainful employ as Steam Fitter: previously served 3 years, 18th Highlanders; 1 year, 91st Argyll & Sutherland Highlanders: volunteered and enlisted 3rd Highlanders of Canada, Valcartier, 22 September 1914; posted 13th Battn.: came over with First Contingent, October 1914: underwent training West Downs and Larkhill, Salisbury Plain: served with the Expeditionary Force in France and Flanders from 15 February 1915, and was killed in action at the Battle of St. Julien, 24 April 1915, moments after taking over L/Corpl. F. Fisher's machine gun: Age 26. *unm.* (*IWGC record MacLeod, age 28*)

L/Corpl. F. Fisher, V.C., is recorded below.

(Panel 24) Corpl. 24397, Clifford Minchin Smith, 13th Bn. Canadian Infantry (Quebec Regt.), C.E.F.: *s*. of James Smith, of 13 Albert Street, Elland, co. York, England: *b*. Pateley Bridge, co. York, 21 July 1887: Religion – Church of England: Occupation – Mechanic: served 4½ years 4th (Territorial) Bn. West Riding Regt.: prior to emigrating was sometime employee to Messrs J. Smithies & Sons, Albert Mills: 5'7" tall, fair complexion, blue eyes, brown hair: tattoo of a flag on outside of left knee; vaccination scar, left arm: volunteered for Imperial Service, enlisted Valcartier, 23 September 1914; age 27 years, 1 month; declared medically fit, 29 August: mobilised, and left for France, with a draft to 5th Regt. Royal Highlanders of Canada. Reported missing / presumed killed in action, 24 April – 4 May 1915: Age 27. *unm*. A letter found on his body was later forwarded to his parents by a German lady. (*IWGC record 24 April 1915*)

(Panel 24) L/Corpl. 24686, John Baptist Adams, 13th Bn. Canadian Infantry (Quebec Regt.), C.E.F.: *s*. of Arnold S. Adams, of Trois Rivieres, Quebec, and his wife Elizabeth Boyce: *b*. Riviere aux Rats, Quebec, 22 May 1889: Religion – Presbyterian: Occupation – Lumberman: volunteered and enlisted Royal Highlanders of Canada, Valcartier, 29 August 1914: came over with First Canadian Contingent. Killed in action 24 April 1915; vicinity St. Julien – Langemarck: Age 26. 'Body not recovered for burial.' Remembered on stained-glass window War Memorial, St. Andrew's United Church, Rue Nerée-Beauchemin, Trois Rivieres.

"The Canadian 1st Division moved into the Ypres salient about a week before the Germans commenced their terrific and wanton bombardment of the unfortunate city of Ypres. They relieved troops of the 11th Division of the French Army in five thousand yards of undeveloped trenches. Fisher, a lance-corporal of the 13th Canadian Infantry Battalion, performed the deed of valour (at the cost of his life) for which he was granted the Victoria Cross, on the 23rd April 1915. He was our first V.C., in this war, by one day. On the afternoon of the 22nd of April the Germans projected their first use of asphyxiating gas against a point of our Allies' front. Turcos and Zouaves fell back, strangled, blinded and dismayed. The British left was exposed. A four-mile gap – a way to Calais – lay open to the enemy. The 1st Canadian Division, the only Canadian Division in the field in those early days, held the British left. It blocked the four mile gap and held up Germany, gas and all. There were no such things as gas masks in those days; but the Canadians were undismayed by that new and terrific form of murder. They had left their offices and shops, their schools and farms and mills, with the intention of fighting the Hun, and, in return, expecting the worst he could do to them. They did not expect him to fight like a sportsman, or even like a human being. So they accepted the gas as part of the day's work. It was the last day's work for hundreds of those good workmen. A battery of Canadian 18-pounders, commanded by Major W.B.M. King, C.F.A., maintained its original position well into the second day of the battle – the 23rd of April. The gunners were supported by a depleted Company of the 14th (Royal Montreal) Battalion, and kept up their fire on the approaching Germans until their final rounds were crashed into 'the brown' of the massed enemy at a range of less than two hundred yards. This is a class of performance which seems to make a particular appeal to courage, for technical difficulties in the matter of timing the fuses to a fraction of a second must be overcome under conditions peculiarly averse to the making of exact mathematical calculations. But this sort of thing is frequently done – always with gusto and sometimes with the loss of the guns and the lives of their crews. The gunner then feels all the primitive excitement of the infantryman in a bayonet charge. He clasps his gun, that complicated, high-priced and prodigious weapon, at the very head of the enemy, as if it were no more than a pistol. On this occasion the guns were not lost. They were extricated from beneath the very boots and bayonets of the enemy and withdrawn to open fire again from a more secure position and at a more customary range. They were 'man-handled' out and back by the survivors of their own crews and of the supporting company of infantry; but all those heroic and Herculean efforts would have availed nothing if Corporal Fisher had not played his part. Fisher was in command of a machine gun and four men of his battalion – the 13th. He saw and understood the situation of Major King's battery and instantly hastened to the rescue. He set up his gun in an exposed position and opened fire on the advancing Germans, choosing for his target the point of the attack which most immediately menaced the battery of field-guns. His four men were put out of action. They were replaced, as they fell, by men of the 14th, who were toiling near-by at the stubborn guns. Fisher and his Colt remained un-hit. The pressure of his finger did not relax from the trigger, nor did his eyes waver from the sights. Eager hands passed along the belts of ammunition and fed them into the devouring breach. So the good work was continued. The front of the attack was sprayed and ripped by bullets. Thus it was held until the 18-pounders were dragged back to safety. Not satisfied with this piece of invaluable work, Fisher advanced again, took up a yet more exposed position, and under the combined enemy fire of shrapnel, H.E., machine guns and rifles, continued to check and slay the Germans. The men who went up with him from his former firing position fell, one by one, crawled away or lay still in death. But the Lance-Corporal continued to fire. The pressure of his finger did not relax from the trigger until he was shot dead."

(Panel 24) L/Corpl. 24066, Frederick Fisher, V.C., 13th Bn. Canadian Infantry (Quebec Regt.), C.E.F.: *s.* of Mr W.H. Fisher, of 100, Fort Street, Montreal: *b.* St. Catherine's, Ontario, 3 August 1894: *educ.* McGill University, Montreal (Engineering): enlisted Valcartier, 23 September 1914: promoted L/Corpl. 22 December following: served with the Expeditionary Force in France and Flanders. Killed in action nr. St. Julien, 23 April 1915: Age 22. Awarded the Victoria Cross ('*London Gazette*,' No.29202, 22 June 1915), "On 23 April 1915, in the neighbourhood of St. Julien he went forward with the machine gun of which he was in charge, under heavy fire, and most gallantly assisted in covering the retreat of a battery, losing four of his gun-team. Later, after obtaining four more men, he went forward again to the firing line, and was himself killed while bringing his machine gun into action under very heavy fire, in order to cover the advance of supports."

(Panel 24) L/Corpl. 24023, William Francis Splatt, 13th Bn. Canadian Infantry (Quebec Regt.), C.E.F.: *s.* of William Francis Splatt, of 1, Ingleby Road, Wallasey, co. Chester, by his wife Rosa S.: *b.* St. Michael's-in-the-Hamlet, Liverpool, 12 April 1892: *educ.* Parkfield School, Sefton Park: sometime employee of Bank of Liverpool Ltd., removed to Canada, April 1913, having successfully applied for and obtained an appointment as Clerk, Bank of British North America, Montreal: previously served 3years 4th Cheshire Regt.: enlisted Royal Highlanders of Canada, Valcartier, 23 September 1914, having been twice previously vaccinated and invalidated: proceeded overseas with First Contingent October 1914: trained Salisbury Plain, winter 1914–1915, joined Expeditionary Force in France, February 1915, apptd. L/Corpl., Battalion Signal Section, and was killed in action 24 April 1915, during the resistance of the enemy attack in the Ypres salient: Age 23 years, 12 days. *unm.*

(Panel 24) Pte. 426744, William Robert Addinell, 13th Bn. Canadian Infantry (Quebec Regt.), C.E.F.: *s.* of William Addinell, of 24, King's Avenue, Muswell Hill, London, N.: *b.* Crouch Hill, 15 September 1888: Religion – Church of England: Occupation – Warehouseman: previously served 2years 10th Alberta Rifles; enlisted Regina, Saskatchewan, 8 April 1915. Killed during an intense enemy bombardment, 28 June 1916. Buried between Crab Crawl – St. Peter Street: Age 27. (*IWGC record Adinell*)

(Panel 24) Pte. 63105, John Blain, 13th Bn. Canadian Infantry (Royal Canadian Black Watch Highlanders), C.E.F.: *s.* of the late John Blain, of Mansion House, Brampton, Carlisle, by his late wife Jane, *dau.* of John Hetherington: *b.* Brampton, co. Cumberland, 23 June 1874: *educ.* Croft House, Brampton: removed to Canada, August 1914; settled Montreal: enlisted 10 November following: arrived in England with 2nd Contingent, Canadian Expeditionary Force, April 1915: served with the Expeditionary Force in France and Flanders from May following, and was killed in action at Passchendaele, 4 November 1917. Buried there: Age 43. His platoon officer wrote, "I always found him a good soldier, hard worker, willing and cheerful at all times to do his duty. He is greatly missed by all who knew him." He *m.* Barrowby, Grantham, co. Lincoln, 5 November 1904; Martha Elizabeth (5, Hull Road, Withersea, co. York), *dau.* of Arthur William Singleton, and had two sons – John Singleton, *b.* 28 October 1906; James, *b.* 22 December 1908.

(Panel 24) Pte. 24509, John Macdonald Carruthers, 13th Bn. Canadian Infantry (5th Royal Highlanders of Canada), C.E.F.: *s.* of Mrs. J. Carruthers (3, Peel Street, Carlisle, co. Cumberland): *b.* Carlisle, 18 November 1892: Religion – Church of England: sometime removed to Canada: Occupation – Fitter: 5'9" tall, fair complexion, blue eyes, fair hair: initials 'J.C.' tattooed on left arm: volunteered for Imperial Service on the outbreak of war: joined C.E.F., Valcartier, 25 September 1914; came over with First Contingent, October following: served in France and Flanders. Killed in action, 24 April 1915: Age 22. *unm.*

(Panel 24) Pte. 46819, Roland Hill Chapman, 13th Bn. Canadian Infantry (Quebec Regt.), C.E.F.: *s.* of Joseph Henry Chapman, of Amherst, Nova Scotia, and Agnes L. Chapman, *née* Rhor, his spouse: *b.* Amherst, 19 October 1894: Occupation – Clerk: a member of the Militia, enlisted 3rd (Nova Scotia) Battn., C.E.F., Valcartier, 26 September 1914: proceeded to France posted 13th Battn.. Missing / believed killed in action 24 April 1915: Age 20. He *m.* Springhill, Nova Scotia, 12 August 1914, Georgina, *née* Colburn.

(Panel 24) Pte. 46996, Walter Day, 13th Bn. Canadian Infantry (Quebec Regt.), C.E.F.: *s.* of John Day, of 2, Shakespeare Terrace, Shakespeare Street, Burmantoft, Leeds, by his wife Caroline: *b.* 3 November 1898 (attested as 1893): Religion – Wesleyan: Occupation – Clerk: volunteered and enlisted after the outbreak of war, Valcartier 22 September 1914: apparent age 21 years, 10 months: 5'7" tall, fair complexion, blue eyes, fair hair: posted 13th Battn., 28 September 1914: served in France, and was killed in action 24 April 1915; trenches vicinity St. Julien. No record of burial: **Age 16.** (*IWGC record age 18*)

(Panel 24) Pte. 24713, Thomas Charles Dixon, 13th Bn. Canadian Infantry (Quebec Regt.), C.E.F.: *b.* Newcastle-on-Tyne, 1892: *educ.* Alnmouth, and Tynemouth, from whence, after completing his education, he went to Canada and, entered service with Bank of British North America, Montreal; March 1913, later transf'd. Hamilton, Ontario branch: returned to Montreal, May 1914, and enlisted there on the outbreak of war August following; Pte. 13th (5th Royal Highlanders of Canada) Battn.: proceeded overseas with First Canadian Contingent, arrived in France with his unit February 1915, and immediately went into action with the battalion in Belgium, where the enemy offensive was in progress. He had been only two months in the line when he was listed as 'missing' after the German attack at Ypres, 22 April 1915. No information has been received with reference to the manner of his death: Age 22.

(Panel 24) Pte. 409721, James Hewitt, 13th Bn. Canadian Infantry (Quebec Regt.), C.E.F.: *s.* of James Hewitt, of Tunbridge Wells, co. Kent, by his wife Elizabeth: *b.* Kent, 8 August 1889: Occupation – Fireman: enlisted Niagara, 7 September 1915. Killed in action 13 June 1916, in the attack to recapture lost trenches at Sanctuary Wood: Age 26. (*IWGC:1926, record Howitt*)

(Panel 24) Pte. 24370, Robert Lowe, 13th Bn. Canadian Infantry (Quebec Regt.), C.E.F.: *s.* of David Lowe, of 24, West Holmes Gardens, Musselburgh, Scotland, and the late Annie Lowe, *née* Radcliffe: *b.* Edinburgh, 15 June 1893: *educ.* George Heriot School: briefly employed as Clerk, Union Bank of Scotland Ltd., removed to Canada 1913, for similar position Bank of Montreal: previously served 2 years, 3rd Royal Scots (Edinburgh); 2 years 5th Royal Highlanders of Canada (Militia); volunteered for Imperial Service on that unit being mobilised, enlisted Valcartier, 23 September 1914: proceeded overseas with 1st Canadian Contingent, October following: served with the Expeditionary Force in France and Flanders from February 1915, and was killed in action 24 April 1915, during the defence of the Ypres salient: Age 21. *unm.* (*IWGC record age 22*)

(Panel 24) Pte. 24634, Arthur Mayhew, 13th Bn. Canadian Infantry (Quebec Regt.), C.E.F.: *s.* of the late Henry (& Mary Hunt) Mayhew: late *husb.* to Nellie Mary Mexter Mayhew (2931, Holt Street, Rosemount, Montreal): *b.* Walthamstow, co. Essex, England, 16 February 1885: Religion – Church of England: Occupation – Bricklayer: joined C.E.F., Valcartier, 23 September 1914: served with the Expeditionary Force in France from February 1915, and was killed in action 24 April 1915, 'whilst taking part in the attack at St. Julien he was shot through the heart by an enemy rifle bullet. Buried in a trench at Ypres.': Age 30.

(Panel 24) Pte. 24640, James Edward Quin, 13th Bn. Canadian Infantry (5th Royal Highlanders of Canada), C.E.F.: elder *s.* of James Quin, of Corbally House, Limerick, J.P., Merchant, Head of the firm of John Quin & Co., of Limerick; by his wife Marian Frances, *dau.* of Nicholas James Lalor, J.P., of 33, Fitzwilliam Place, Dublin: *b.* 70, George Street, Limerick, 24 November 1888: *educ.* Stoneyhurst College, and Louvain University (obtained degree '*Faculté de Droit*'): removed to Canada, April 1912: Occupation – Salesman; Messrs Lindsay & Co., Montreal: proceeded to Valcartier following the outbreak of war, August 1914; joined 5th Royal Highlanders of Canada: came over with First Contingent, October 1914: trained Salisbury Plain, winter 1914 – 15: proceeded to the Front, February 1915. Reported missing after the Second Battle of Ypres, 22 April 1915, when his battn. defended the crossroads at Ypres, refusing to surrender, in spite of nearly all their number being killed, badly wounded, or taken prisoners, and he is now officially stated to have been killed in this action. A comrade wrote, "I don't think I ever met a more good-natured, generous hearted and unselfish fellow... No words of mine would fit tribute to his memory... I know he was thought a lot of by his superiors;" and another, "He was always given the most dangerous tasks to perform, and to my knowledge he always performed them ably and well." Age 26. *unm.* (*IWGC record 24 April 1915*)

(Panel 24) Capt. Richard Steacie, 14th Bn. Canadian Infantry (1st Royal Montreal Regt.), C.E.F.: 3rd *s.* of the late Edward Steacie: *b.* Ballinasloe, Co. Galway, 27 March 1868: *educ.* Ballinasloe: sometime went to Canada, where he took a keen interest in Military matters: joined 3rd Victoria Rifles of Canada (Militia): afterwards became Lieut., 6th Hussars (Militia): left to join 13th Scottish Light Dragoons (Militia), as Capt.: later joined 1st Grenadier Guards of Canada (Militia): volunteered for Active Service on the outbreak of war: came to England with 14th Bn. Canadian Infantry: served with the Expeditionary Force in France and Flanders, and was killed in action, at St. Julien, 22 April 1915. Buried in St. Julien Cemetery. One of his men gave the following account of his death, "The Major was wounded badly in a few minutes, so they called for Capt. Steacie to take command. He was at my side at the time handing out extra bandoliers, for we were using a great amount of ammunition; but jumped up at the command, but fell again in an instant, with a bullet through his heart. We turned him over, but he bravely replied 'Carry on, boys, I'm O.K.' Thus he died – a soldier and a hero. He was the most beloved Captain in the Royal Montreal Regt., and many a tear was shed by his boys when his death became known. We dragged his body to St. Julien Cemetery and buried him.": Age 47. He was a member of St. George's Club, Westmount; and the Westmount Bowling Club; Canadian Club, Montreal; National Club, Montreal; Rotary Club, Montreal, and Montreal Amateur Athletic Association. He *m.* Alice Kate, *dau.* of William McWood, and leaves a son, Edgar William, *b.* December 1900. Capt. Steacie was related to Col. Charles A. Smart, Comdg. 2nd Bde. Canadian Mounted Rifles.

(Panel 24) Sergt. 25911, John D'Auvergne Harris-Arundell, 14th Bn. Canadian Infantry (1st Royal Montreal Regt.), C.E.F.: 2nd *s.* of the late Robert Harris-Arundell, of Halifax, Nova Scotia, by his wife Elizabeth Blanche, *dau.* of the late John D'Auvergne Dumaresq, C.M.G., Acting Administrator of the Government of Lagos, West Africa, and *gdson.* to the late William Reinfred Harris-Arundell, of Lifton, co. Devon, England: *b.* Fairmont, Martin Co., Minnesota, U.S.A., 14 May, 1889: went to Halifax, Nova Scotia, with his family at the age of five: *educ.* Collegiate School, Windsor, N.S.; joined Staff, Royal Bank of Canada, 1905. In Montreal when war broke out, August 1914, he was at the time a Corpl., Victoria Rifles (Montreal), and volunteered at once for Active Service. On 24 August his regt., then called 1st Royal Montreal Regt., went into training at Valcartier Camp. On the night of 23 September they left for Quebec and embarked for England, arriving in Plymouth 14 October, and, after training at Salisbury, proceeded to France 5 February 1915. At the Battle of Langemarck, 24 April 1915, he was shot through the heart while assisting Lieut. Whitehead (wounded in the foot), to cross 200 yards under withering fire. The ground was captured by the enemy and Sergt. Arundell's body was never recovered: Age 25. *unm.* (*IWGC record 21.4.15, J.D.A.H. Arundell*)

(Panel 24) Sergt. 404372, Henry Hunt, No.4 Coy., 14th Bn. Canadian Infantry (Quebec Regt.), C.E.F.: *b.* Beeston, co. Nottingham, 23 January 1877: Religion – Church of England: Occupation – Teamster:

5'5½" tall, blue eyes, grey / brown hair: served in the South African Campaign: enlisted Toronto, 12 April 1915. Killed in action 3 June 1916; Hedge Street – Observatory Ridge: Age 39. On the day of his death Sergt. Hunt, in company with Lieut. Beaton and a small party of 35 other ranks, advanced on the far left of the battalion's frontage and came into contact with the enemy in the vicinity of Hedge Street. At 9 a.m. – cut off from the rest of the battalion and under enfilade fire from a machine-gun – Lieut. W.E. Beaton halted his party, faced the men to the left of the advance, posted sentries and kept patrols going, to keep touch with the enemy. The small force remained in this position throughout the day, their number being steadily decreased. At night the enemy concentrated trench mortars and artillery fire on the position, rendering it totally untenable, forcing the remnants of the small company to withdraw. Throughout the day Lieut. Beaton had been ably assisted by Sergt. Hunt who, after all the officers had become casualties, took over No.2 Coy, showed magnificent courage in leaving his trench time and again under heavy fire to recover wounded and dress their injuries. He was subsequently killed by a trench-mortar bomb. He leaves a wife, Anne Jane Hunt (11, Roden Place, Toronto).

Lieut. (Capt.) Beaton – killed in action 26 September 1916 – has no known grave, he is commemorated on the Canadian National (Vimy) Memorial, France.

(Panel 24) Corpl. 25931, Evan Stuart Cameron, 14th Bn. Canadian Infantry (1st Royal Montreal Regt.), C.E.F.: eldest *survg. s.* of Sir Edward John Cameron, K.C.M.G., Governor and Commander-in-Chief of Gambia, by his wife Lady Eva Selwyn Cameron, *dau.* of the late Robert Mackintosh Isaacs, LL.D., of New South Wales: *b.* Turks Island, West Indies, 21 September 1893: *educ.* Blundell's School, Tiverton (1905 – 12), where he was Head Boy for two years: on leaving there (September 1912) went to Montreal to take up an appointment with Royal Bank of Canada: enlisted Canadian Expeditionary Force, 21 September 1914, after the outbreak of war: came over with First Contingent; served in France and Flanders from late February 1915. In a letter to '*The Blundellian*,' 11 March 1915, he said, "I have had some very varied experiences. After leaving our first billet we marched some 12 to 15 miles, cobble-stones all the way, and two companies, nearly 500 men, were put in a large hall place in a fair sized town. From there we took our first turn in the firing line with some regulars; nothing exciting happened at all. After that we moved some five miles, and were billeted in a factory, the worst billet so far we have had. From there we took a longer turn in the firing line on our own; things were slightly more lively, and of course we had more to do. On our last afternoon our trenches received a little shelling, and I had a very miraculous escape when a shell burst over the dug-out which I was in, and tore a huge hole about a foot from my hand; there was another fellow with me and he got rather badly cut up, but beyond a slight shock and a few scratches on each hand I was none the worse, and except for being a bit deaf I have quite recovered. We are doing a turn in the reserve trenches; we carry up rations and ammunition, etc., to the front line at night, and there are some few fatigues in the day time. I managed to get a hot bath after our last turn but had to march three or four miles for it." Corpl. Cameron was killed in action near St. Julien, 24 April 1915: Age 21. Major Beatty, A.D.C. to Gen. Alderson, Comdg. 1st Canadian Contingent, wrote, "He was dearly loved by all his comrades, and he had earned the respect and admiration of all, and had behaved with the greatest gallantry all through that dreadful time from 5 p.m. on Thursday, 22 April, up to the time of his death." His Capt. said, "He handled his men wonderfully, and would have been given a commission in the field had he survived the battle." On a previous occasion, after being urged to take a commission in the British Army, Corpl Cameron declined, saying, "The Canadians brought me over and I must stick with them." The Headmaster of Blundell's said, "As I look back upon his school career I feel that we have lost one of the most sterling of the old pupils whom I remember in my long experience of 40 years. There has been no finer head of School, his character was marked by an unswerving honesty of purpose that made him, in his latter days, a true leader and a king of men. He held his views with unflinching courage; but could command the respect and confidence of those who differed from him. He was a sportsman and played the game in everything. In his old school his fame is secure, a great cricketer, a sterling football player, truly tolerant yet fired by the highest convictions, he ever laboured for the welfare of his House and School. He has died as honourably as he lived honoured by every Blundellian of his time and beloved by those who knew him best." He was a good cricketer, Capt. of Blundell's cricket eleven and football fifteen for two years, and won the average bat four years in succession. He played against the Australian XI (1913); at Lords in a Public Schools XI (1912), and made the first century of the season for the McGill Cricket Club, July 1914.

(Panel 24) L/Corpl. 23481, Alfred Leonard Bunnell, 14th Bn. Canadian Infantry (Quebec Regt.), C.E.F.: *s.* of Albert E. Bunnell, of 'Beechwood Farm,' Sussex, New Brunswick, and Mary J. Bunnell, his spouse: and brother to Pte. 23494, G.A. Bunnell, died of wounds 14 June 1916: enlisted 12th Battn., August 1914; joined a draft of reinforcements to 14th Battn. to proceed to France, and was killed in action at St. Julien, nr. Ypres, 22 April 1915: Age 25. *unm.*

His brother George is buried in Lijssenthoek Military Cemetery (VIII.A.13A).

(Panel 24) Pte. 448002, David Brown Adams, 14th (1st Royal Montreal) Bn. Canadian Infantry (Quebec Regt.), C.E.F. *s.* of the late Archibald Adams, by his wife Lily, *née* Brown (12, North Street, Anderston, Glasgow, Scotland): Religion – Presbyterian. Killed in action 3 June 1916; vicinity of Mount Sorrel, in a counter-attack on Maple Copse and Observatory Ridge positions: Age 34. 'Buried nearby; his name is inscribed on a large memorial cross erected in Railway Dugouts Cemetery.'

(Panel 24) Pte. 127376, Thomas Frederick Adcock, 14th Bn. Canadian Infantry (Quebec Regt.), C.E.F.: c/o Charles Adcock, Esq., of 49, Ansdell Road, London, S.E.: Religion – Church of England. Killed in action at Mount Sorrel – Maple Copse, 3 June 1916. Believed buried Railway Dugouts Burial Ground (Transport Farm), exact grave unknown; large Memorial Cross, with full particulars inscribed thereon, erected – Plot 6, Row Z, Grave 1.

(Panel 24) Pte. 140501, Robert Azoff Alford, 14th Bn. Canadian Infantry (Quebec Regiment), C.E.F.: *s.* of Thomas S. Alford, of 6, Symons Road, Saltash, co. Cornwall, England, and Susan S. Alford, his wife: *b.* Saltash, 18 April 1887: Religion – Church of England: removed to Canada, 1908: Occupation – Bridgeman: 5'8" tall, blue eyes, brown hair: enlisted 14th Royal Montreal Regt., Toronto, 6 August 1915: subsequently transf'd. 75th Battn.; transf'd 23rd Battn.: joined 14th Battn., January 1916. Killed in action 26 June 1916; Mount Sorrel, Ypres: Age 29. *unm.* Special Memorial Cross (No.3) erected (16 August 1921) Railway Dugouts Burial Ground (Transport Farm), inscribed with full particulars – Buried in this vicinity; exact grave unknown (VI.7).

(Panel 24) Pte. 457243, John Caine, 14th Bn. Canadian Infantry (Royal Montreal Regt.), C.E.F.: late *husb.* to Ellen Agnes Walker Caine (485, Valios St., Hochelaga, Montreal): and father to the late Pte. 25104, C.W. Caine, 13th Canadian Infantry: *b.* 10 February 1875: Religion – Presbyterian: Occupation – Quarryman: previously served 6 years King's Own Scottish Borderers; enlisted Montreal, 10 June 1915. Missing 3 – 4 June 1916; Mount Sorrel: Buried in the vicinity of Maple Copse; his name is inscribed on a large memorial cross erected in Railway Dugouts Cemetery: Age 40. (*IWGC record age 48*)

His son Carstairs is known to be buried in Maple Copse Cemetery, Zillebeke (Sp.Mem.G.12).

After taking over trenches from the French on the night of 16 – 17 April 1915, 14th Canadians spent five days in the left sub-sector of 3rd Canadian Brigade for which period the Battalion War Diary simply records:– 'Trenches St. Julien. Nothing special to report. Trenches in bad condition. Casualties 7 killed, 15 wounded,' and, on 21 April, after being relieved by the 13th Battalion between 9 p.m. and mid-night:– 'Left for reserve billets St. Jean, with the exception of No.2 Coy. which took over billets in St. Julien as a local reserve to 13th Battn.' No mention or details are recorded for the casualties sustained by No.2 Coy. on that date; 16 are recorded on the Menin Gate of which one was only fifteen years old:–

(Panel 24) Pte. 22722, Hector McDonald Cameron, No.2 Coy., 14th Bn. Canadian Infantry (1st Royal Montreal Regt.), C.E.F.: *s.* of Lachlan Cameron, of Lepreaux, New Brunswick, by his wife Annie: Religion – Presbyterian. 'During operations in the vicinity of St. Julien, nr. Ypres, 21 April 1915, he was shot through the head and killed.': No record of burial. **Age 15.**

(Panel 24) Pte. 919764, Magloire Charbonneau, 14th Bn. Canadian Infantry (1st Royal Montreal Regt.), C.E.F.: *s.* of Damien Charbonneau, of 72, College Street, St. Henri, Montreal: *b.* St. Paul, 17 October 1897: Occupation – Machine Runner: previously served 55th Irish Canadian Rangers (Militia), and 2½ months with a Composite Regt.: attested Montreal, 22 July 1916. Killed by shellfire on the night of 7 November 1917: Age 20. *unm.* See also Pte. J.I. Smith below.

(Panel 24) Pte. 25812, William Patrick Connors, 14th Bn. Canadian Infantry (1st Royal Montreal Regt.), C.E.F.: *s.* of John Connors, of 1456, St. Laurence Street, Montreal, by his wife Louisa: *b.* Montreal, 5 May 1887: Occupation – Painter: volunteered and enlisted Valcartier Camp, 28 August 1914: posted 14th Battn. 21 September following: served with the Expeditionary Force in France and Flanders, and was killed in action at the Second Battle of Ypres 21 – 27 April 1915: Age 27. *unm.*

(Panel 24) Pte. 63244, Edmond Cunningham, 14th Bn. Canadian Infantry (Quebec Regt.), C.E.F.: *s.* of Jane Cunningham (14, Albert Road, Paisley, Scotland): *b.* Paisley, 2 July 1893: Religion – Presbyterian: 5'3½" tall, fair complexion, blue eyes, fair hair: sometime removed to Canada; found gainful employ as Carpenter: volunteered for Imperial Service after the outbreak of war August 1914; enlisted 23rd Battn., Calgary, 3 November following; apptd. 14th Battn., 23 November. 1914: served with the Expeditionary Force in France and Flanders, and was killed in action 21 May 1915: Age 21. *unm.*

(Panel 24) Pte. 164078, Lewis Evers, 14th Bn. Canadian Infantry (Quebec Regt.), C.E.F.: *s.* of the late John Henry Evers, of 3, Oddfellow Street, Brighouse, co. York, by his wife Elsie (490, Billington Street, Hamilton, Ontario): *b.* 10 December 1894: Religion – Church of England: *educ.* St Andrew's School, where he was also a member of the Sunday School; after leaving there he entered the employ of Messrs T.F. Firth, Carpet Mill, Bailiff Bridge: removed to Canada with his mother (1912); settled Hamilton, Ontario, finding gainful employ as Labourer; Messrs Thornhill Briggs: enlisted Niagara, 3 September 1915, one year after the outbreak of the European War: went to France, and was killed in action nr. Ypres, Belgium, 12 June 1916: Age 21.

(Panel 24) Pte. 25734, John Hempenstall Kearney, 14th Bn. Canadian Infantry (Quebec Regt.), C.E.F.: *s.* of James Kearney, of West Street, Callan, Co. Kilkenny, by his wife Frances: *b.* Bangor, Ireland, 12 March 1892: Religion – Church of England: removed to Canada, 1911, aged 19 years: Occupation – Clerk; Quebec Bank, Montreal: serving member (1 yr.) Canadian Militia; volunteered and enlisted Royal Montreal Regt., Valcartier, 21 September 1914, after the outbreak of war: came over with 1st Canadian Contingent, October following: underwent further training Salisbury Plain, England (winter 1914 – 15), proceeded to France, 15 February 1915; served with the Expeditionary Force there from the 16th., and was killed in action at Mount Sorrel, nr. Sanctuary Wood, 3 June 1916: Age 24. *unm.*

(Panel 26) Pte. 25625, William Officer, 14th Bn. Canadian Infantry (Quebec Regt.), C.E.F.: *s.* of Arthur Officer, of 135, Manor Street, Belfast, Ireland, by his wife Margaret: and brother to Pte. 63694, A. Officer, 3rd Canadian Infantry, killed in action 17 June 1915: *b.* Belfast, 1887: Religion – Church of England: Occupation – Tinsmith: serving member of the Militia; enlisted Valcartier, 22 September 1914: served with the Expeditionary Force in France and Flanders from 16 February 1915. Missing / believed killed in action 3 June 1916: Age 28. *unm.*

His brother Arthur also has no known grave; he is commemorated on the Canadian National (Vimy) Memorial.

(Panel 24) Pte. 26237, Bert Arthur Presant, 14th Bn. Canadian Infantry (Quebec Regt.), C.E.F.: *s.* of Philip H. Presant, of 27, Eighth Avenue, Toronto, by his wife Emma A.: and brother to Pte. 9516, C.H. Presant, C.E.F. (surv'd.); and (by his brother's marriage to Lucy Madeleine Presant; sister-in-law) nephew to Pte. B/31837, R.A. Presant, Canadian Army Medical Corps, killed in action 14 August 1944, at Bayeux, France: winner of Strathcona Gold Medal, Toronto, for Cadet School Shooting Contest: Religion – Wesleyan: Occupation – Factory Hand: 5'6"tall, blue eyes, brown hair: enlisted Valcartier, 22 September 1914: came over with 1st Contingent, October following: served in France from 16 February 1915, and was killed in action at the Battle of Ypres, 26 April 1915: **Age 16**. At his enlistment he gave date of birth 17 October 1895; his brother Cecil gave 6 December 1895; clearly one of them was not being entirely truthful.

His uncle Philip also has no known grave; he is commemorated on the Bayeux Memorial (Panel 27, Col.2).

(Panel 24) Pte. 603246, Edward Riggall, 14th Bn. Canadian Infantry (Quebec Regt.), C.E.F.: late of Dr. Barnado's Home, 51 – 52, St. Peter's Street, Toronto: next-of-kin Miss Lottie Riggall, c/o Mrs King (507 – 509, Lordship Lane, East Dulwich, London): *b*. Spalding, co. Lincoln, England, 18 December 1890: Religion – Church of England: Occupation – Labourer: joined C.E.F., Mitchell, 8 September 1915. Killed in action Sanctuary Wood, nr. Ypres, 12 – 13 June 1916. Buried nr. Mount Sorrel. Recorded on Memorial Cross; Railway Dugouts: Age 25. *unm.*

(Panel 24) Pte. 26001, Richard Ingersoll 'Jack' Sanders, 14th Bn. Canadian Infantry (1st Royal Montreal Regt.), C.E.F.: 2nd *s*. of James Harris Sanders, Merchant; of 110, Cannon Street, London, E.C., by his wife Marie Louise, *dau.* of James Ingersoll Day, of U.S.A.: *b*. Shenley, co. Hertford, 21 April 1891: Religion – Church of England: *educ.* Temple Grove, East Sheen, and Wellington College, Crowthorne, co. Berks; on leaving went to Germany, where he remained for just over a year. On return to England he started in business with Messrs Jardine, Mathesons, Merchants, London: went to Canada, December 1911, where for a short time he was employee to the Bank of Montreal, thereafter British Trade Commissioners' Office, Montreal, and, on the outbreak of war, August 1914, was employed as Student Labourer; Messr A.K. Drury, Montreal: volunteered for Imperial Service, Valcartier, 23 August 1914; apptd. 'D' Coy., 14th Battn., 22 September: came over with First Contingent, October 1914: went to France, 14 February 1915. Reported 'wounded and missing' after the fighting nr. St. Julien during the Second Battle of Ypres, 24 April 1915; now (1916) assumed to have been killed in action on or about that date: Age 24. *unm.*

On 7 November 1917, as the battle for Passchendaele approached its climax, 14th Battalion Canadian Infantry were in Brigade Reserve at Wieltje prior to moving up to the Bellevue Spur; the Battalion War Diary records:– 'No untoward events occurred and preparations were made to move forward again, and at 8.30 p.m. the entire battalion moved forward to reserve in the Bellevue Spur area. The companies were occupying funk holes in the area D.4.d.8 and D.10.b. relieving 3rd Canadian Battn. Battn. HQrs being established at Waterloo D.9.d.8.9., relief being completed at 2 a.m. Track No.5 was used during the relief, and sporadic shelling by heavy guns caused casualties of two other ranks killed.' That neither of the two men – Ptes. M. Charbonneau and J. Smith – have a known grave is probably due to the fact that the salient at that time was one enormous shell-cratered morass into which their bodies, like so many others, would have sunk without trace.

(Panel 24) Pte. 889787, John I. Smith, 14th Bn. (1st Royal Montreal Regt.) Canadian Infantry, C.E.F.: *s*. of the late Nicholas Smith, by his marriage to Sarah McWhirter, *née* Smith, *née* Long (New Richmond, Quebec): *b*. New Richmond, Province of Quebec, 5 March 1902: Religion — Church of England: attested by Lieut. C.L.R. Caldwell, New Richmond, 7 April 1916, giving date of birth 5 March 1898: apparent age 18 years, 1 month; occupation Farmer; the form bearing – X – ('his mark') as signature. Killed by shellfire in the vicinity of Bellevue, 7 November 1917: **Age 15.**

Pte. Charbonneau is recorded above.

(Panel 24) Pte.25773, Donald Morrison Trapnell, 14th Bn. Canadian Infantry (1st Royal Montreal Regt.), C.E.F.: elder *s*. of Robert Henry Trapnell, Jeweller & Optician; by his wife Jessie Wainwright (St. John's, Newfoundland); *dau.* of the late Fraser Wylie Dakin: and brother to Gnr. G.S. Trapnell, Canadian Field Artillery (surv'd.): *b*. Windsor, Nova Scotia, 17 February 1891: Religion – Presbyterian: *educ.* McGill University, Montreal (Applied Science; 1911-14); graduated BA (Engineering): Occupation – Engineer: enlisted Valcartier, 21 September 1914: came over with 1st Canadian Contingent, October following. Killed in action 23 April 1915: Age 24.

(Panel 24) Pte. 26022, Charles Barry Douglas Whitby, 14th Bn. Canadian Infantry (1st Royal Montreal Regt.), C.E.F.: eldest *s*. of Charles Joseph Whitby, of 9, The Paragon, Bath, M.D. (Cantab.), by his wife Clare, *dau.* of Joseph Hayden: *b*. Cambridge, 13 November 1884: *educ.* Reading School: went to Canada about 1904, residing first in Montreal, later in Emerson and other places, then returning to Montreal where, at the outbreak of war, August 1914, he held a position on the Staff of the '*Montreal Gazette.*' He at once enlisted and went into training at Valcartier, came to England with First Canadian Contingent, and completed his training on Salisbury Plain. Crossed to Flanders with his Division early 1915, and took part in the action at Neuve Chapelle. On 22 April 1915, the Second Battle of Ypres was opened by the discharge of poison gas against the French Turcos, who were driven back leaving the Canadian left exposed. On the morning of the 24th. the 14th Battn., shelled out of a shallow dug-out they had prepared overnight in a field near St. Julien, retreated uphill under very heavy fire. Near the summit Pte. Whitby was hit and fell in a ditch, joking as he fell. He was never seen again by his comrades but was officially reported as 'wounded and missing.' Later a report by the enemy stated that he had been picked up by them, had died on May 8 or 9, and was buried on Hill 20 (Kerselaere), not far from where he fell. In letters received from his comrades he was described as "a splendid soldier, always among the first to offer himself for any dangerous duty." While at the Front Private Whitby contributed several descriptive articles on life in the trenches to the '*Montreal Gazette.*': Age 30. *unm.* (*IWGC record C.D.B. Whitby, 13 July 1915*)

(Panel 24) Lieut. Geoffrey Barron Taylor, 15th Bn. Canadian Infantry (48th Highlanders of Canada), C.E.F.: *s.* of William John Mahaffy Taylor, of 49, Heath Street West, Toronto, by his wife Stella Bertha: *b.* Toronto, 4 February 1890: *educ.* Model School, Harbord Street Collegiate, Toronto (Applied Science), 1910 – 13; and, on the outbreak of war, Trinity College, Oxford: joined 15th Battn. on its arrival in England: went to France, February 1915. Reported missing at the Battle of St. Julien, 24 April 1915; believed to have died from the inhalation of poisonous gas. Last seen making his way to a deserted farmhouse a short distance behind the trenches: Age 25. *unm.*

Between 23rd and 24th April 1915, immediately after the first German gas attack, (22nd April) a rumour circulated regarding the shocking discovery of a Canadian soldier, captured by the Germans and crucified on a barn door or tree; most reports identified the soldier as a Canadian sergeant. Atrocity stories abounded during the war but the image of a crucifixion stirred up the worst possible public outrage. In 1919 investigations with the German government brought strong denials of the event, and the Allies were unable to prove the matter was anything more than a myth. Eyewitness accounts were inconclusive since no one had been able to put a name to the victim, and eventually the case was closed. Proof of this atrocity was a long time in coming, in fact over eighty years passed before the forgotten notes of a British Red Cross nurse and the accounts of four soldiers settled the matter.

One of the earliest accounts comes from Pte. Leonard Vivian, 3rd Bn. Middlesex Regt.: "...I was in charge of No.1 Stretcher Section, which made several trips bringing in wounded from the line in front of St. Julien. We had made about five journeys, and on the sixth journey I saw, on the right hand side of the road, on a barn door, what appeared to be a Canadian sergeant crucified to the door. There was a bayonet through each hand and his head was hanging forward as if he were dead or unconscious. I did not stop as the Army was retiring and I had a wounded man on the stretcher. I later learned he had been captured by the enemy and crucified for protecting an old woman..."

About the same time, L/Corpl. William Metcalf, V.C., M.M. & Bar, related: "...On or about April 23rd. my platoon was proceeding along the St. Jean road when I noticed a soldier pinned to a barn door with bayonets. There was a bayonet through each wrist, his head hung forward on his breast as though he were dead. I could not see any bullet wounds, but did notice the maple leaf badges on his collar. We were told later that this man belonged to the 16th Canadian Battn. The platoon sergeant, whose name I cannot remember, examined the body and we moved on..."

On 11th. July 1915 British Red Cross nurse Ursula Challoner was questioning a wounded Canadian soldier. Her job was to find out what had happened to missing men. Now, just twelve weeks after the battle at Ypres, L/Corpl. Clement Brown passed on the story of the crucified soldier, but he also came up with a name: "...There was a Sergt. Bain, or Band, but I cannot remember the number. He was crucified after the battle of Ypres on one of the doors of a barn with five bayonets in him. I cannot quite remember the name of the place."

On 1st June 1916, Pte. William Freeman wrote to Harry Band's sister, Mrs Elizabeth Petrie:– "...As a Private in Sergt. Band's platoon in France, and one who went through the battle at St. Julien in April 1915, and seeing Sergt. Band's picture in '*The Mirror*' as missing, I thought it my duty to write and let you know that Sergt. Band was killed 24th April at St. Julien, as most of his platoon and the men of his C Coy. were captured. I am sorry for you all and you have my deepest sympathy. He died as he always wished to, a soldier's and a hero's death…"

Since the disappearance of her brother, and the stories of the crucified soldier reported in the press, Elizabeth Petrie had an uneasy feeling, some sixth sense, that her brother was the soldier in question. Writing to Freeman, querying his account, she received the following:– "…I am very sorry to say it is perfectly true, Harry was crucified, but whether he was alive at the time I don't think anyone can say for sure. When I wrote to you about Harry's death I didn't want to tell you all the horrible details, I thought it best not to tell you how they found him; it would only have caused you more worrying and I did it for the best. As other soldiers have told you I expect you know all about it now. I think Harry must have thought a lot about you, because he was always good to his men, and he always saw that his platoon got everything they had coming to them. He treated everyone the same and never had any favourites…"

Elizabeth Petrie kept the circumstances surrounding her brother's death to herself; she revealed her secret to her daughter in 1940.

(Panel 24) Sergt. 27286, Harry Band, 15th Bn. Canadian Infantry (48th Highlanders of Canada), C.E.F.: *s.* of Martin Band, House-builder; Box 101, Kilowna, British Columbia: *b.* Montrose, co. Kincardine, Scotland, 12 August 1885: Religion – Presbyterian: Occupation – Lineman: 5'11" tall, of proportionate build, fair complexion, brown eyes, brown hair; vaccination scar on left forearm, tattoo spots back of fingers: served 3 yrs. 1st Forfar Volunteers, 3 yrs. 48th Highlanders of Canada (Militia); enlisted Valcartier, 18 September 1914: came over with First Canadian Contingent, October following; trained Salisbury Plain, winter 1914–15: served with the Expeditionary Force in France from 15 February 1915. 'Reported missing in the field, 24 April 1915; St. Julien, for official purposes presumed killed': Age 29. *unm.* At attestation he requested his pay be sent to Miss Isabella Ritchie (93, King Street, Dundee).

(Panel 24) Sergt. 47129, William Isadore Groshow, 15th Bn. Canadian Infantry (48th Highlanders of Canada), C.E.F.: *s.* of the late Nicholas Groshow, by his wife Janet B. (418½, Talbot Street, London, Ontario): *b.* 26 July 1894: Religion – Presbyterian: Occupation – Accountant. Reported missing, presumed died / killed in action on or since 24 April 1915; vicinity St. Julien: Age 20. (*IWGC record age 18*)

(Panel 24) Sergt. 47870, Ernest Hoyles, 15th Bn. Canadian Infantry (48th Canadian Highlanders, Central Ontario Regt.), C.E.F.: *s.* of George Hoyles, of 14, Montgomery Street, Skipton, by his wife Alice, *dau.* of Richard Birch, of Grassington, co. York: and brother to Pte. 34186, R. Hoyles, 8th East Lancashire Regt., killed in action 5 October 1917; and Corpl. 266968, G. Hoyles, 1/6th Duke of Wellington's (West Riding Regt.), died of wounds 23 March 1917: *b.* Hebden, co. York, 5 June 1885: *educ.* Skipton: enlisted 6th Liverpool Regt., 1901: took part in the South African War (South African Medal, 3 Bars). On leaving the Army he went to Canada, and settled near Markdale, Ontario, being employed as a Farm Servant: on the outbreak of war he immediately joined the Canadian Contingent: served with the Expeditionary Force in France from 17 July 1915, and was killed in action 3 June 1916. Buried where he fell: Age 29. He *m.* Baptist Church, Skipton; Agnes (97, Newmarket Street, Skipton), *dau.* of Joseph Simpson, and had a son – Wilfrid, *b.* 1 April 1907. (*IWGC record L/Sergt., Age 30*)

His brother George is buried in Merville Communal Cemetery Extension (III.A.1); Richard has no known grave, he is commemorated on the Tyne Cot Memorial (Panel 78).

(Panel 24) Sergt. 77726, James Campbell Kempston, 15th Bn. Canadian Infantry (48th Canadian Highlanders), C.E.F.: *s.* of the late Rev. Augustus Kempston, Rector of Bally, Vurly, King's Co., by his wife Mary, *dau.* of Henry Campbell: *b.* Dublin, 15 March 1871: *educ.* Benson's School, Rathmines, Dublin: enlisted Seaforth Highlanders, May 1892: served in India and the Sudan (Medal); afterwards the South African War 1899 – 1902 (Medal and clasps): re-enlisted on the outbreak of the European War: served with the Expeditionary Force in France and Flanders, and was killed in action at Ypres 3 June 1916: Age 43. Capt. Spottiswoode wrote, "I have always liked him and he has invariably borne an excellent character in the regiment." He *m.* Fernie, British Columbia, 1906, Olive Georgina, *dau.* of William Earls, of Dublin, and had three children – Vera Agnes, *b.* 4 July 1907; Iris Mabel, *b.* 29 August 1908; Lancelot Campbell, *b.* 4 June 1911. (*IWGC record Corpl.*)

(Panel 24) L/Sergt. 27845, John Dawson Hannah, 'G' Coy., 15th Bn. Canadian Infantry (1st Central Ontario Regt.), C.E.F.: *s.* of the late James Hannah, by his wife Agnes (85, Great King Street, Edinburgh): *b.* Edinburgh, 4 November 1878: Occupation – Postman: previously served 6 years, Royal Army Medical Corps: enlisted Valcartier, 22 September 1914: came over with 1st Canadian Contingent, October following: trained Salisbury Plain throughout the winter 1914 – 15: proceeded to France, February 1915; served with the Expeditionary Force there, and was killed in action 24 April 1915: Age 36.

(Panel 24) Corpl. 27598, Charles Daniel Eyles, 15th Bn. Canadian Infantry (1st Central Ontario Regt.), C.E.F.: *s.* of Charles Daniel (& Mary Ann) Eyles, of 99, Gamble Avenue, Todmorden, Ontario: *b.* 25 April 1893: Religion – Wesleyan: Occupation – Cutter: enlisted Valcartier Camp, 19 September 1914; posted 15th Battn. 22 September: came over with 1st Canadian Contingent: served in France from February 1915, and was killed in action 24 April 1915: Age 22 years, 1 day.

(Panel 24) Corpl. 27715, Gordon Cameron Freeland, 15th Bn. Canadian Infantry (48th Highlanders of Canada), C.E.F.: *s.* of Fred C. Freeland, of 307, Fourteenth Street, Buffalo, New York, U.S.A., by his wife Edith: *b.* Hamilton, Ontario, 11 September 1891: Religion – Presbyterian: Occupation – Telegraph Operator: serving member of the Militia, 1 year 57th Peterborough, Ontario; 2 years 91st Hamilton, Ontario; volunteered for Imperial Service, Valcartier, 20 September 1914. Killed in action 24 April 1915: Age 23. (*IWGC record age 24*)

(Panel 24) Corpl. 27011, William George Early Wyatt, 15th Bn. Canadian Infantry (48th Highlanders of Canada), C.E.F.: *s.* of the late William George Early Wyatt, by his marriage to Ann Elizabeth Tucker, *née* Wyatt (33, Melinda Street, Toronto): *b.* 3 May 1886: enlisted Valcartier, 22 September 1914: served with the Expeditionary Force, and was killed in action (gas) 24 April 1915: Age 28. *unm.*

(Panel 24) L/Corpl. 27061, John Joseph Delaney, 'A' Coy., 15th Bn. Canadian Infantry (1st Central Ontario Regt.), C.E.F.: *s.* of Mrs A.J. Delaney (14, Underley Street, Smithdown Road, Liverpool): *b.* 9 August 1891: Religion – Church of England: Occupation – Bank Messenger: previously served 5th King's Liverpool Regt. (2 years, 291 days); serving member (1 year) 48th Highlanders of Canada (Militia); enlisted Valcartier, 22 September 1914: came over with 1st Canadian Contingent, October following: trained Salisbury Plain, winter 1914 – 15: proceeded to France February 1915. Reported missing / believed killed (after the attack at St. Julien); now, for official purposes presumed to have died on or since 24 April 1915: Age 23.

(Panel 24) L/Corpl. 27086, John Duncan McColl, 15th Bn. Canadian Infantry (1st Central Ontario Regt.), C.E.F.: *s.* of the late John Duncan McColl, by his wife Alice (145, Central Avenue, London, Ontario): brother to Pte. 37309, B.J. McColl, and Pte. 27087, D. McColl, 15th Bn. Canadian Infantry, who both fell at Ypres, 29 April 1915: *b.* Park Hill, Ontario, 26 April 1886: Religion – Presbyterian: Occupation – Commercial Traveller: previously served 5 yrs., 7th Regt. (Fusiliers), London, Ontario (Militia): volunteered and enlisted C.E.F., Valcartier, 22 September 1914: came over with First Canadian Contingent, October following: trained Salisbury Plain, England, throughout winter 1914 – 1915; proceeded to France February 1915, and was killed in action there 24 April 1915; St. Julien: Age 27. One of three brothers who fell.

His brothers Bruce and Duncan also have no known grave; both are recorded below.

(Panel 24) L/Corpl. 401118, Frank Tarr, 15th Bn. Canadian Infantry (1st Central Ontario Regt.), C.E.F.: *s.* of William Tarr, of West Monkton, Ontario: and brother to Pte. 603266, H.V. Tarr, 2nd Canadian Infantry, killed in action 25 July 1916: *b.* Logan, Perth, Ontario, 24 February 1893: enlisted London, Ontario, 5 July 1915. Killed in action at Passchendaele, 6 November 1917: Age 24.

His brother Henry also has no known grave; he is recorded on Panel 18.

(Panel 24) L/Corpl. 27410, Wilbur Charles Vandervoort, 15th Bn. Canadian Infantry (48th Highlanders of Canada), C.E.F.: *s.* of Charles Wilbur Vandervoort, of Napanee, Ontario, by his wife Francis Victoria: prior to enlistment was employee Messrs Bell Telephone Co., Toronto: volunteered and enlisted on the outbreak of war: came over with 1st Canadian Contingent, October 1914: trained on Salisbury Plain winter 1914 – 15: went to France February 1915, and was killed in action at the Battle of Ypres, 24 April following: Age 22. *unm.*

(Panel 24) L/Corpl. 77569, Burton Montcalm West, 15th Bn. Canadian Infantry (1st Central Ontario Regt.), C.E.F.: brother to Corpl. 21901, G.B. West, 10th Canadian Infantry, died 5 February 1916: *b*. Georgeville, 25 September 1893: Occupation – Bank Clerk: joined C.E.F., Valcartier, 9 November 1914. Killed in action 3 June 1916. All correspondence should be addressed c/o their brother G.L. West Esq., 350, Belmore Avenue, Montreal.

His brother Gordon also has no known grave; he is recorded above.

(Panel 24) Pte. 27853, Robert Aikenhead, 15th Bn. Canadian Infantry (48th Canadian Highlanders), C.E.F.: elder *s*. of Major Frank Aikenhead, Comdg. The (Somerset) R.H.A., by his wife Mabel, *dau*. of the late Major-Gen. Edward Andree Wylde, R.M.L.I.; and *gdson*. to the late Robert Aikenhead, of Otterington Hall, nr. Northallerton: *b*. Southsea, 22 April 1892: *educ*. Cheltenham College: Occupation – Commercial Editor, '*Toronto News*': volunteered and enlisted 48th Highlanders on the outbreak of war. Killed in action at the Second Battle of Ypres, 24 April 1915. His Commanding Officer wrote, "He displayed the greatest gallantry and courage, and though severely wounded and gassed, continued fighting till killed by a bullet in the head. He was always brave and cheerful, and one of the best." A memorial tablet has been erected to his memory in the Great Elm Parish Church, Somerset: Age 23. *unm.*

It is a common tendency to regard the First World War as being primarily an Anglo-German conflict. However, it should, be remembered the term 'World War' meant precisely what it said; this was the first ever truly global conflict, with combatants from Albania to Afghanistan; Cuba to the Cameroons. Similarly, it should be borne in mind that men from many countries, other than the warring nations, chose to enlist in either the British or German armies, and to fight for a cause they believed to be just. One such man was Carl Barnard, enlisting in September 1914 he was one of the first American volunteers to join the Canadian Forces.

(Panel 24) Pte. 27302, Carl Montford Barnard, 15th Bn. Canadian Infantry (48th Highlanders of Toronto), C.E.F.: *s*. of the late John Barnard, by his wife Sarah F. Smith, *née* Barnard (Apt. 5, 45, Berlamond Avenue, Toronto); late of 31, Main Street East: *b*. Summerville, Massachusetts, U.S.A., 29 August 1893: Occupation – Student: 5'9" tall, fair complexion, blue eyes, fair hair; ship tattoo left arm: prior to enlistment served 3 years Queen's Own Rifles (Militia): enlisted Valcartier, 22 September 1914: came over with First Contingent: served with the Expeditionary Force in France and Flanders, and is believed to have been killed in action in the vicinity of Ypres, on or about 29 April 1915: Age 21.

(Panel 24) Pte. 27310, Augustus Brooks, 'C' Coy., 15th Bn. Canadian Infantry (48th Highlanders of Toronto), C.E.F.: *b*. *c*.1889: admitted Dr. Barnardo's Homes, 16 October 1895: removed to Canada, July 1898; settled Riga, North-West Territory; reports received concerning him being "uniformly good over the whole period of his stay in Canada": volunteered for Overseas Service on the outbreak of the European War, August 1914: departed Canada with First Contingent, October following: proceeded to France, February 1915: wounded (Lt. shoulder) at Langemarck; after a brief period of hospitalisation returned to his unit, and was killed in action at Ypres, 23 April 1915: Age 26. *unm.*

At 4.00 a.m., 24 April 1915, a poisonous gas attack swallowed up the landscape like a heavy fog as it rolled across the entire Canadian front. With little experience of how to combat the effects of gas the men had been told to wet a handkerchief and tie it over their mouth and nose, or to stand on the parapet as the gas, being heavier than air, would cling to the ground – completely untrue and an action which, if taken, was to step into a solid wall of machine-gun and rifle fire, guaranteed to invite instant death! Followed within seconds by a concentrated artillery barrage, the Germans launched massed infantry attacks behind the cover of the gas and artillery, only to be cut down by a withering fire from the choking Canadians.

At the apex of the Canadian lines on the extreme left of the Gravenstafel Ridge (known as Locality C), the trenches held by 15th (48th Highlanders of Canada) Battalion disappeared from view, smothered by the noxious gas cloud and exploding shellfire. After ten minutes pounding the position with artillery and trench mortars the enemy attacked. Taking the Canadians completely by surprise, the 15th had no idea the enemy were advancing on them, their makeshift gas masks were totally ineffective, shouted orders died in green frothing mouths, blinded eyes failed to see hand signals otherwise only discernible a few yards away, and the savage screaming and ear-splitting explosions of shells completely obliterated all other sights and sounds.

In the face of the advancing infantry men cursed in frustration as their Ross rifles jammed – instructed to lay their entrenching tool handles by their side to slap the bolt with in the event of a jam or, if this failed, to place the butt of the rifle on the ground and stamp on the bolt with their heel – most threw them aside, to hastily pick up and fire a fallen one. Blinded and choking the beleaguered battalion continued to pour fire into the advancing Germans, the dying and the wounded lying in the mud freeing and loading rifles for their comrades; the 15th held their ground, living or dying where they stood.

An S.O.S. sent by the battalion to their supporting artillery batteries; drew the following reply:– "4.01 a.m. We have to admit that it is impossible for us to respond to your S.O.S. and along the entire original front, as the trenches are out of range of our present positions."

What remained of the doomed companies in the front line never received the reply. From a shell hole 100 yards away to the right a soldier of the 8th Battalion, who were fighting their own battle, witnessed "...a line of men on our left leaving the line, casting away equipment, rifles, clothing as they ran. Some managed to get halfway to where they were going only to fall writhing to the ground, clutching at their throats, tearing open their shirts in a last struggle and lying still while a greenish foam formed over their mouths and lips."

These were the shattered remnants of the 15th. What happened beneath that gas cloud, in those ten minutes of shellfire? During the ensuing fire-fight? No one will ever know for certain. No officer survived to submit a report, 'A' and 'C' Coys. were virtually annihilated; fighting it out to the choking finish in a maelstrom of death.

The Menin Gate records the names of 497 Canadians who died on 24 April 1915 and have no known grave; 129 of these are officers and men of the 15th Battalion.

(Panel 24) Pte,. 27053, Hugh Campbell, 15th Bn. Canadian Infantry (48th Highlanders of Canada), C.E.F.: *s.* of Hugh Campbell, of 577, St. Clair Avenue West, Toronto, by his wife Georgina (95, Dupont Street): and *yr.* brother to Pte. 27056, R. Campbell, 15th Bn., who fell the same day: *b.* Edinburgh, 29 January 1889: Religion – Presbyterian: Occupation – Photographer: 5'10" tall, dark complexion, brown eyes, dark hair: previously served Queen's Own Cameron Highlanders: enlisted Valcartier 18 September 1914; posted 15th Battn.: came over with 1st Contingent, October following: served with the Expeditionary Force in France from February 1915, and was killed in action 24 April following: Age 26.

(Panel 24) Pte. 27056, Robert Campbell, 15th Bn. Canadian Infantry (48th Highlanders of Canada), C.E.F.: *s.* of Hugh Campbell, of 577, St. Clair Avenue West, Toronto, by his wife Georgina: and elder brother to Pte. 27053, H. Campbell, 15th Bn. who fell the same day: *b.* Edinburgh, 1 December 1884: Religion – Baptist: Occupation – Tailor: 5'11" tall, fair complexion, blue eyes, fair hair: previously served Queen's Own Cameron Highlanders: enlisted Valcartier 18 September 1914; posted 15th Battn.: came over with 1st Contingent, October following: served with the Expeditionary Force in France from February 1915, and was killed in action 24 April following: Age 30.

(Panel 24) Pte. 27052, George Hugh Cleal, 'A' Coy., 15th Bn. Canadian Infantry (48th Highlanders of Canada), C.E.F.: late of 25, Nanton Avenue, Toronto: *s.* of Joseph Pacey Cleal, of 56, Clifton Road, Moore Park, Toronto, by his marriage to the late Margaret Robinson Cleal, *née* McDonald: and brother to Sergt. 193279, D.McD. Cleal, 92nd Battn.; discharged (wounded); and Q.M.Sergt. 799216, P.E. Cleal, 134th Battn.; discharged (inflammatory rheumatism): *b.* Dayton, Ohio, 15 December 1894: Religion – Church of England: *educ.* Toronto University: Occupation – Insurance Agent; Western Insurance Co.: 5'7" tall, fair complexion, grey eyes, fair hair: enlisted Valcartier 9 September 1914; posted 15th Battn. (18 September): proceeded overseas with First Canadian Contingent: served with the Expeditionary Force in France from February 1915, and was killed in action 24 April following, at Langemarck: Age 20. *unm.*

In a letter to Pte. Cleal's father Corpl. G.H. Beaver, Somerset Light Infantry, wrote, "It is with deep regret that I am writing to let you know that your son George is dead. He was in the glorious charge of the Canadians, and the Germans sent over a lot of gas, which gave a lot of our boys no chance. He was amongst them. I have had him buried and a cross made, which we did by moonlight."

(Panel 24) Pte. 27458, Archibald Wilson Corson, 15th Bn. Canadian Infantry (48th Highlanders of Toronto), C.E.F.: *s.* of the late John (& Sarah) Corson, of 10, Dunard Road, Rutherglen: *b.* Rutherglen, nr. Glasgow, 1 August 1891: *educ.* Stonelaw School: joined Canadian Expeditionary Force, 11 September 1914; came over with 1st Contingent and, after training on Salisbury Plain during the winter, 1914 – 15, served with the Expeditionary Force in France from February, and was killed in action at the Battle of St. Julien, 25 April 1915: Age 22. *unm.* (*IWGC record 24 April 1915*)

(Panel 24) Pte. 27054, Emerson Crosby, No.1 Coy., 15th Bn. Canadian Infantry (48th Highlanders of Canada), C.E.F.: *s.* of Samuel J. Crosby, of 62, Shannon Street, Toronto, by his wife Emillie B. (281, Augusta Avenue): *b.* 14 January 1892: Religion – Baptist: Occupation – Wireman: 5'8" tall, dark complexion, grey eyes, dark hair: enlisted Valcartier, 9 September 1914; posted 15th Battn (18 September): came over with First Canadian Contingent, October following; served with the Expeditionary Force in France and Flanders from February 1915, and was killed in action at Langemarck, 24 April following: Age 23. *unm.*

(Panel 24) Pte. 46131, John McLean Currie, 15th Bn. Canadian Infantry (1st Central Ontario Regt.), C.E.F.: 3rd *s.* of John David Currie, High Sheriff, Hants Co.; of Windsor, Nova Scotia, by his wife Bessie, *dau.* of the late James Cutting, of Truro, N.P.: and *gdson.* to the late John Currie, D.D., Professor of Hebrew, Pine Hill Theological College, Halifax, Nova Scotia: *b.* Maitland, Hants Co., 18 October 1896: *educ.* Maitland High School, and Windsor Academy: enlisted No.1 Coy., Royal Nova Scotia Regt. (17th C.E.F.), on the declaration of war August 1914; left Windsor for Valcartier on the 20th of that month: proceeded to England with First Contingent, October: trained throughout the winter, 1914 – 15, Salisbury Plain, England: on disbandment of 17th Battn. joined 15th (48th Highlanders) under Col. John Currie: served in France from 15 February 1915, and was killed at Langemarck 23 April following: Age 19. (*IWGC record age 18*)

(Panel 24) Pte. 27600, Alexander Daubert, 15th Bn. Canadian Infantry (1st Central Ontario Regt.), C.E.F.: *b.* co. Surrey, England, 31 August 1894: removed to Canada, settled Ontario: Occupation – Tailor: prior to enlistment served 1 yr. 22nd Oxford Rifles, Ontario (Militia); volunteered and enlisted Valcartier Camp, 19 September 1914, after the outbreak of war; posted 15th Battn. the following day: came over with 1st Contingent, October 1914: trained in England during the winter of 1914 – 15: served with the Expeditionary Force in France from 15 February, and was killed in action 22 April 1915: Age 20. *unm.*

(Panel 24) Pte. 27354, Douglas McN. Hannah, 15th Bn. Canadian Infantry (1st Central Ontario Regt.), C.E.F.: *s.* of the late James Hannah, by his wife Mary (16, Sandholes, Paisley, co. Renfrew): *b.* Paisley, 1 August 1895: Occupation – Clerk: previously served 2 years, 6th Argyll & Sutherland Highlanders (Volunteers): enlisted Valcartier, 22 September 1914: came over with First Contingent, October following: underwent further training Salisbury Plain, winter 1914 – 15: served with the Expeditionary Force in France from February 1915, and was killed in action 24 April 1915: Age 19.

(Panel 24) Pte. 27349, William Benjamin Hodges, 15th Bn. Canadian Infantry (48th Highlanders of Canada), C.E.F.: 2nd *s.* of Ephraim Alphaeus Hodges, Farmer; of Stanstead, Quebec, by his wife Myra Jane (Hatley, Quebec), *dau.* of Benjamin Frederick Bowen: and brother to Pte. 27348, R.B. Hodges, 15th Battn., died at Bailleul, 27 April 1915, of wounds received at the Second Battle of Ypres: *b.* Hatley, Quebec, 24 May 1894: Religion – Wesleyan: *educ.* Model School, Hatley: subsequently assisted his father on the farm: enlisted 26th Stanstead Dragoons, as Orderly, 1911: promoted Corpl. 1913; Sergt. 1914: volunteered for Imperial Service; joined 48th Highlanders of Toronto, September 1914, after the outbreak of the European War: came over with 1st Canadian Contingent, October 1914: trained Salisbury Plain winter, 1914 – 15: served with the Expeditionary Force in France and Flanders from February. Reported wounded and missing after the fighting at the Second Battle of Ypres, 24 April 1915; now assumed killed in action on or about this date: Age 20. *unm.*

His brother Ray is buried in Bailleul Communal Cemetery Extension (I.D.1).

(Panel 24) Pte. 27352, Herbert Hopley, 15th (48th Highlanders of Canada) Bn. Canadian Infantry (1st Central Ontario Regt.), C.E.F.: *s.* of Stephen Hopley, of 35, Bloomsbury Road, Ramsgate, by his wife Mary Ann, *dau.* of William Wilmott, of Ramsgate: *b.* Ramsgate, co. Kent, England, 15 May 1888: Religion – Church of England: *educ.* Christ Church School, Ramsgate: formerly 8 yrs. employee Messrs Tucker & Sons; Smack Owners & Sail Makers: removed to Canada (c.1912) where he was 2 yrs. employee Messrs Turner & Sons; Tent Makers, Peterborough, Ontario: removed to Toronto shortly before the outbreak of war: volunteered and joined Canadian Expeditionary Force, 22 September 1914: left Valcartier Camp for England, October following: trained Salisbury Plain during the winter of 1914 – 15: went to France, February 1915. Died (gas poisoning) at the Battle of St. Julien, 26 April 1915: Age 26. *unm.*

(Panel 24) Pte. 27813, Harry Hyde, 15th (48th Highlanders of Canada) Bn. Canadian Infantry (1st Central Ontario Regt.), C.E.F.: *s.* of Mary Hyde ('Northleigh,' 370, Bury New Road, Whitefield, Manchester, co. Lancaster): *b.* London, England, 22 February 1897 (attested 22 February 1895): Religion – Church of England: Occupation – Paper maker: enlisted (under-age) Valcartier, Quebec, 22 September 1914. Killed in action 24 April 1915: Age 18.

(Panel 24) Pte. 46028, William John Hyde, 15th (48th Highlanders of Canada) Bn. Canadian Infantry (1st Central Ontario Regt.), C.E.F.: late of 226, Richmond Street, Toronto: *s.* of the late Charles Hyde, of 'Rowes Cottage,' Everton, Lymington, and his wife Caroline E. Hyde (The Cottage, Burley Beacon, Brockenhurst, co. Hants): *b.* Milford-on-Sea, 11 September 1886: Religion – Salvation Army: Occupation – Storeman / Clerk: previously served 6 years, 28 weeks, 2nd Dorsetshire Regt.; volunteered and enlisted 78th Highlanders (Nova Scotia Bn.), Toronto, 8 p.m., 24 September 1914; subsequently apptd. / transf'd. 48th Highlanders (15th Battn.): came over with 1st Canadian Contingent, October 1914. Killed in action 24 April 1915: Age 28. *unm.*

(Panel 24) Pte. 27360, Robert Crawford Jamieson, 15th Bn. Canadian Infantry (1st Central Ontario Regt.), C.E.F.: *s.* of the late Robert Crawford Jamieson, and his wife (41, Herkimer Street, Apartment 10, Hamilton, Ontario): *b.* Toronto, 4 May 1892: Religion – Presbyterian: *educ.* Rose Avenue Public School; Jarvis Street Collegiate; Farquharson School; University College, Toronto (1910 – 11): Occupation – Clerk: member 48th Regt. (Militia); enlisted Valcartier, 19 September 1914; apptd. 15th Battn., 22 September: came over with First Contingent: served with the Expeditionary Force in France from February 1915. Reported missing after the Battle of St. Julien, 24 April 1915; later confirmed killed in action: Age 22.

(Panel 24) Pte. 602701, William Charles Last, 15th (48th Highlanders of Canada) Bn. Canadian Infantry (1st Central Ontario Regt.), C.E.F.: *s.* of Arthur Albert Last, of Nedging, co. Suffolk, by his marriage to the late Susannah Last: and brother to Pte. 03664, P.A. Last, C.E.F. (surv'd.); and Gnr. 334128, A. Last, 4th Bde. Canadian Field Artillery, killed in action 27 September 1918, aged 17 years: *b.* Ipswich, 17 February 1896: Religion – Wesleyan: Occupation – Farmer: 6' tall, grey eyes, dark brown hair: enlisted C.E.F., London, Ontario, 19 July 1915. Killed in action 3 June 1916; Mount Sorrel: Age 19. Correspondence should be addressed c/o his sister-in-law, Lily Last (202, Wharncliffe Road, London, Ontario).

His brother Arthur also has no known grave; he is commemorated on the Canadian National (Vimy) Memorial.

(Panel 24) Pte. 37309, Bruce J. McColl, 15th Bn. Canadian Infantry (1st Central Ontario Regt.), C.E.F.: *s.* of the late John Duncan McColl, by his wife Alice (145, Central Avenue, London, Ontario): brother to L/Corpl. 27086, J.D. McColl, 15th Bn. Canadian Infantry, killed at Ypres, 24 April 1915; and Pte. 27087, D. McColl, 15th Bn. Canadian Infantry, killed the same day as Bruce: *b.* Park Hill, Ontario, 24 September 1896: Religion – Presbyterian: Occupation – Student: enlisted Valcartier, 23 September 1914. Killed in action 29 April 1915, during the Battle of Ypres. No further information as to the actual circumstances under which he met his death is available': Age 18. One of three brothers who fell.

His brothers John and Duncan both have no known grave, Duncan is recorded below; John above.

(Panel 24) Pte. 27087, Duncan McColl, 15th Bn. Canadian Infantry (1st Central Ontario Regt.), C.E.F.: *s.* of the late John Duncan McColl, by his wife Alice (145, Central Avenue, London, Ontario): *husb.* to Mary Alice McColl (274, Jones Avenue, Toronto): and brother to L/Corpl. 27086, J.D. McColl, 15th Bn. Canadian Infantry, killed at Ypres, 24 April 1915; and Pte. 37309, B.J. McColl, 15th Bn. Canadian Infantry, killed the same day as Duncan: *b.* Oban, Scotland, 5 April 1877: Religion – Presbyterian: Occupation – Stonemason: previously served Scots Greys; prior to enlistment (Valcartier, 22 September 1914) serving member of the Militia. Killed in action 29 April 1915; St. Julien: Age 38. One of three brothers who fell.

Both John and Bruce have no known grave, they are recorded above.

(Panel 24) Pte. 27590, Harold Walton Mooney, 15th Bn. Canadian Infantry (48th Highlanders of Canada), C.E.F.: *s.* of John Mooney, of Cowansville, Quebec, by his wife Candice. Killed in action at the Battle of Ypres, 24 April 1915: Age 24

(Panel 24) Pte. 28055, William Henry Moore, 15th Bn. Canadian Infantry (1st Central Ontario Regt.), C.E.F.: *husb.* to Heather May Moore: *b.* 31 August 1877: Religion – Church of England: Occupation – Labour Foreman: serving member 48th Highlanders of Canada, enlisted C.E.F., Valcartier, 22 September 1914: served with the Expeditionary Force in France from February 1915. Killed in action 24 April 1915: Age 37. All correspondence to be addressed c/o his son, Frederick C. Moore Esq., 782, Ossington Avenue, Toronto, Canada.

(Panel 24) Pte. 27381, Alexander Murray, 'C' Coy., 15th Bn. Canadian Infantry (1st Central Ontario Regt.), C.E.F.: *s.* of the late Francis R. Murray, by his wife Anne Mackay: *b.* Inverness, Scotland, *c.*1888. Killed in action at Gravenstafel, Ypres, 24 April 1915: Age 27.

(Panel 24) Pte. 27391, Frank Page, 15th Bn. Canadian Infantry (48th Highlanders of Canada), C.E.F.: *s.* of John Henry Page, of 205, Portland Street, Ashton-under-Lyne, Manchester, by his wife Emily Jane (Ellesmere, co. Chester): and *yr.* brother to Pte. 425177, N.J. Page, 43rd Battn., who also fell: *b.* 22 May 1897. Died of wounds (gas) 24 April 1915: Age 17. (*IWGC record age 18*)

His brother Newton is buried in Roye New British Cemetery (II.A.16).

(Panel 24) Pte. 28038, John George Palethorpe (*a.k.a.* Holt, J.G.) 15th Bn. Canadian Infantry (48th Highlanders of Canada), C.E.F.: *s.* of Julia Holt (65, Francis Road, Haymills, Birmingham, England): *b.* Liverpool, 7 December 1885: Religion – Church of England: Occupation – Prospector: 5'4½" tall, fresh complexion, blue eyes, fair hair: previously served 3 yrs., 4th King' s Liverpool Regt. (Vol.): enlisted Valcartier, Quebec, 19 September 1914: served with the Expeditionary Force in France from February 1915. Missing, believed killed in action 24 April 1915, following the gas attack at St. Julien: Age 29. His medals – 1914-15 Star, British War, Victory; and Memorial Plaque sold at auction for £620, April 2004. (*IWGC record Palethorpe*)

(Panel 24) Pte. 28078, John Forbes Philip, 15th Bn. Canadian Infantry (48th Highlanders of Canada), C.E.F.: *s.* of John Forbes Philip, of Hawthorn Cottage, Strathdon, Aberdeen, by his wife Annie, *née* McHardy: and brother to L/Corpl. 1025, G. Philip, 6th Gordon Highlanders, died of wounds 17 June 1915, aged 21 years: *b.* 24 May 1891: Occupation – Grocer: enlisted Valcartier, 22 September 1914. Died of wounds 24 April 1915: Age 23. His father and four other brothers also served; of the latter one other was killed. (*IWGC record age 24*)

His brother George is buried in Longuenesse (St. Omer) Souvenir Cemetery (I.A.158).

(Panel 24) Pte. 27006, James Robertson, 'A' Coy., 15th Bn. Canadian Infantry (48th Highlanders of Canada), C.E.F.: *s.* of William Edmonston Robertson, of 3, Lily Bank, Burntisland, Scotland, by his wife Elizabeth. Killed in action (gas) 24 April 1915: Age 31. He was married to Jessie (173, Wolverleigh Road, Toronto). On the day of his death there were reports of a soldier of the 15th Battalion having been crucified by the Germans, and speculation surrounding whether or not this actually took place went on for many years afterwards. However, in 1996, it was established from contemporary sources (a transcript of an interview between L/Corpl. C. Brown and Red Cross nurse, Ursula Challoner) that the soldier in question was Sergt. Harry Band, 15th Bn. C.E.F.

Harry Band has no known grave; he is recorded above.

PANEL 24 ENDS PTE. J.W. TIMSON, 15TH BN. CANADIAN INF.

PANEL 26 BEGINS PTE. G. TODD, 15TH BN. CANADIAN INF.

(Panel 26) Capt. Hamilton Maxwell Fleming, 16th (Canadian Scottish) Bn. Canadian Infantry (Manitoba Regt.), C.E.F.: 8th *s.* of the late John Fleming, C.S.I., by his wife Mary: *b.* 'Homewood,' Chiselhurst, co. Kent, 4 March 1876: *educ.* Dulwich College; Lieut. in the School Corps, and one year won the Public Schools' Fencing Competition, Aldershot: in the Argentine at the outbreak of the South Africa War, he at once went to South Africa, enlisting as Trooper, Brabant's Horse: eventually became Quartermaster: unable to remain for the duration of the campaign, owing to recurring rheumatic fever from which he had suffered twice previously: Queen's Medal, three clasps: went to Vancouver, British Columbia, 1909: on their formation, joined 72nd Seaforth Highlanders of Canada, as Lieut., being promoted Capt. six months later: volunteered for Foreign Service on the outbreak of war with Germany: came over with First Contingent, Canadian Expeditionary Force: stationed on Salisbury Plain for preliminary training. On the Force being ordered to France, he was sent on ahead, with others, to act as Landing Officer, and make general arrangements. Capt. Fleming was killed nr. Ypres, 23 April 1915, after being shot through the leg while leading his men in a charge on the German trenches. One of his men who was with him wrote, "I tied up his leg and wanted him to go back to the dressing station, but he was too good an officer and too brave a gentleman to do that as he thought the boys needed him." He struggled on and shortly after was shot through the head and killed instantly.: Age 39.

(Panel 26) Capt. John Geddes, 16th (Canadian Scottish) Bn. Canadian Infantry (Manitoba Regt.), C.E.F.: *s.* of Alexander Geddes, of Blairmore, Huntly, co. Aberdeen, Scotland, by his wife Frances: and elder brother to 2nd Lieut. A.F. Geddes, 3rd attd. 2nd Royal Scots Fusiliers, killed in action 16 June 1915; and brother-in-law (by the marriage of his sister Rachel) to Lieut. E.A. Cameron, Royal Garrison Artillery (surv'd.); and Capt. W.H.V. Cameron, 1st Highland Light Infantry, killed in action 20 December 1914: *b.* Glass Parish, co. Aberdeen, 6 November 1878: Occupation – Agent: enlisted Valcartier, 23 September 1914. Killed in action 24 April 1915: Age 37. He leaves a widow, Helen Geddes (1045, Lexham Gardens, Kensington, London, England); late of Central Avenue, Winnipeg. His brother-in-law Ewan was great-grandfather to British Prime Minister David Cameron.

His brother Alastair and in-law William also have no known grave; both are commemorated on the Le Touret Memorial.

(Panel 26) Capt. Cecil Mack Merritt, 16th (Canadian Scottish) Bn. Canadian Infantry (Manitoba Regt.), C.E.F.: last *survg. s.* of Lieut.-Col. William Ingersoll Merritt, of 6, Sumner Place, South Kensington, London, late 30th (East Lancashire) and 4th Manchester Regts., by his wife Mary Beatrice, 3rd *dau.* of Major-Gen. Frank Adams, C.B., and *grand-dau.* of Henry Cadwaller Adams, of Anstey Hall, co. Warwick, J.P., D.L.: *b.* St. Catherine's, Ontario, Canada, 6 January 1877: *educ.* St. Paul's School, London: went to Canada, 1895; joined Royal Grenadier (Militia) Regt., 1896. He was one of the few who went into Dawson in the rush of '98 over the Edmonton trail, the journey taking him two years. After leaving the Yukon he returned to England and was for a short time on the London Stock Exchange. Went to Vancouver, 1904, and when 72nd Seaforth Highlanders Regiment of Canada was formed, November 1910, was appointed one of its senior Capts.; received his Majority, 13 October 1914. On Major-Gen. Sir Sam Hughes's Staff during his visit to the Imperial Army manoeuvres, 1912, and on the outbreak of war immediately volunteered for Imperial Service, and was given command of a Coy., 16th Battn. 'Canadian Scottish,' 1st Canadian Division: went with them to France, February 1915, and was present at the Battle of Neuve Chapelle. On 22 April 1915, during the Second Battle of Ypres, he was leading his Coy. in the charge made by the Canadian Scottish near St. Julien, to check the first rush of the Germans after their gas attack, when he was wounded in the leg. He refused to leave his men, and with them occupied the German trenches. Next morning he was killed while encouraging his men during a counter-attack. Mentioned in F.M. Sir John (now Lord) French's Despatch of 31 May 1915, for 'gallant and distinguished service in the field.' His commanding officer, Col. R.E. Edwards Leckey, wrote, "Cecil Merritt was one of the finest officers I ever knew. He was wounded in the charge, but not severely and still continued to lead his men on. He remained in the trenches we had captured, and when a counter-attack was threatened he got up to shoot over the parapet with his revolver. It was then he received his fatal wound. No one could have been braver, and no one could have lead his men better than he did. His name has been submitted for the Military Cross." Brother officers speak of his "personal bravery and spirit of dash and tenacity," and of the admiration which his men had for him. And a Private wrote, "He was wounded twice but would not expose his men to be carried back to the Dressing Station, and after some hours in the captured trenches heard there was a counter-charge from the Germans, and it was then he received the fatal shot in his head.": Age 38. At St. Paul's he took a leading part in the school life, being captain of the football XV. He was one of the first captains of the well-known Harlequin Rugby Football Club. He *m.* Vancouver, B.C., 4 December 1905, Sophie Almon, eldest *dau.* of the Hon. Sir Charles Hibbert Tupper, K.C.M.G., and had one daughter and two sons – Beatrice Ormonde, *b.* 14 February 1907; Charles Cecil Ingersoll, *b.* 10 November 1908; Francis William, *b.* 16 August 1913. (*IWGC record 23 April, 1915*)

(Panel 26) Lieut. Charles Cecil Ogden MacFee Adams, 16th (Canadian Scottish) Bn. Canadian Infantry (Manitoba Regt.), C.E.F.: *s.* of Julie O. Adams (886, Broughton Street, West Vancouver): *b.* Westminster, London, 23 February 1891. Religion – Church of England: Occupation – Surveyor: previously served 3 years, Officer Training Corps: joined Lord Strathcona's Horse, 7 November 1914; volunteered and transf'd. 16th Battn., Pond Farm, on the 26th of that month: proceeded overseas January 1915. One of ten men of the battalion who, on the morning of 13 June 1916, were killed near Zillebeke by a high-explosive shell; death was instantaneous. Buried 28.I.30.a.8.5.: Age 25. *unm.* On the day of Lieut. Adams death the battalion took part in the large scale Canadian attack which, while successful in the recapture of trenches lost during the Battle of Mount Sorrel one week previously, cost 16th Battalion casualties of 5 officers – Capt. S.W. Wood, Lieuts. C.C.O.M. Adams, H.J. McLaurin, W.N. McLennan, R.T. Sachs – killed; 5 officers wounded (1 died); and 257 other ranks killed, wounded and missing. See Lijssenthoek Military Cemetery (VI.A.30).

(Panel 26) Lieut. George Samuel Ager, 16th (Canadian Scottish) Bn. Canadian Infantry (Manitoba Regt.), C.E.F.: *husb.* to Mary Ager (516, Trutch Street, Victoria, British Columbia): Religion – Church of England. Missing, presumed died on or since 22 April 1915; 2nd Battle of Ypres, St. Julien '…wounded in the stomach, when in a wood during the advance. He was brought in with the rest on an improvised stretcher, but when they had reached the open beyond the wood they were ordered to retire and it was impossible to bring him away. Several men tried to carry him but failed. This was the last that was seen of him.'

(Panel 26) Lieut. John Gibson Kenworthy, 16th (Canadian Scottish) Bn. Canadian Infantry (Manitoba Regt.), C.E.F.: *s.* of John Kenworthy, of Tenby, co. Pembroke, South Wales, by his wife Mary: and brother to Lieut. D. Kenworthy, Somerset Light Infantry, who fell at Ypres, one week previously: *b.* Hurst, co. Lancaster, 27 August 1881: previously served 10 years, Lancashire Fusiliers: enlisted, Lieut., Valcartier, 7 September 1914: came over with First Contingent, October following: proceeded to France February 1915, and was reported wounded and missing following the fighting at St. Julien 24 April 1915, later confirmed killed: Age 33. He leaves a wife, Iris J. Kenworthy. Another brother, Capt. W. Kenworthy, 33rd Light Cavalry, Indian Army, formerly Capt., Governor of Bengal's Body-Guard, is with his regiment, fighting in Mesopotamia.

His brother Donald is buried in New Irish Farm Cemetery (XXVII.A.14).

(Panel 26) Sergt. 29287, Norman James McKenzie, 16th (Canadian Scottish) Bn. Canadian Infantry (Manitoba Regt.), C.E.F.: *s.* of Alexander A McKenzie, of 165, Murray Street, Saulte St. Marie, Ontario, by his wife Martha: and brother to Lieut. W.A. McKenzie, 8th Canadian Infantry, who fell 25 April 1915: *b.* Greenville, Plumas Co., California, 3 September 1884: Occupation – Insurance Clerk: a serving member of the Militia, 4 years Cameron Highlanders of Canada; enlisted Valcartier, 23 September 1914:

served with the Expeditionary Force in France from 17 February 1915. Killed in action 23 April 1915: Age 30. *unm.*

His brother Wallace also has no known grave; he is recorded on Panel 24.

(Panel 26) Corpl. 29524, Gerald Coussmaker Heath, 16th (Canadian Scottish) Bn. Canadian Infantry (Manitoba Regt.), C.E.F.: 3rd *s.* of the late Col. Lewis Forbes Heath, Indian Army, formerly commanding 10th (now 110th) Mahrattas, by his wife Susan Wilhelmina (Failand, Grosvenor, Paignton, co. Devon), *dau.* of Ezekiel Charles Petgrave: *b.* Mount Abu, Rajputana, India, 3 May 1888: *educ.* Wellington College, co. Berks, and on leaving there went out to Canada (aged 17), and for the five years before the war had been in Vancouver City, where he joined 72nd Seaforths, 1911. On the declaration of war, August 1914, he volunteered for service overseas, and left Canada with the First Canadian Contingent, 3 October 1914: went to France early February 1915, and was mortally wounded in action at Langemarck, 25 April 1915. He was carried off the field, but died shortly afterwards without regaining consciousness. The Major of his regt. wrote, "His work in the hard fighting in which we were engaged on 22 April, and afterwards, was most excellent, and he had been noted for distinction for his gallant conduct." Another officer, who joined with reinforcements after the action, wrote, "Major Rae and all his comrades have nothing but praise for his work. Several times he volunteered and took out stretcher parties with wounded officers and men, always under fire. His efforts were evidently of the finest. He has been recommended for distinguished service recognition." Heath was a fine athlete and won many medals and prizes for hurdling and the broad jump. In 1912 he won the championship of British Columbia for hurdling, and the following year became champion hurdler of Canada. Mentioned in F.M. Sir John French's Despatches ('*London Gazette*,' 22 June 1915): Age 26. *unm.* (*IWGC record 22nd April 1915*)

(Panel 26) L/Corpl. 28951, Charles Byron Amos, 'E' Coy. 16th (Canadian Scottish) Bn. Canadian Infantry (Manitoba Regt.), 3rd Bde., 1st Canadian Contingent, C.E.F.: *yst. s.* of Henry Amos, of New House Farm, Sheldwich, Faversham, Kent, by his wife Ellen Mary, *dau.* of John Byron, of Kirkby Green, Sleaford, co. Lincoln: *b.* Littles Manor, Sheldwich, 12 August 1886: Religion – Church of England: *educ.* Felstead School, Essex, and Crystal Palace School of Engineering: removed to Canada, April 1913: Occupation – Engineer: enlisted Vancouver, B.C., 23 September 1914, after the outbreak of war. Killed in action nr. Ypres, 25 April 1915. A comrade wrote, "Charlie was shot after we had recaptured the guns and were returning. We were sent out of one small fort and had to dig ourselves in about 100 yards in advance of the fort, and it was whilst doing this that Charlie got hit: in fact we had just received the order to get back to the fort, and he and I were making our way down a small ditch when he fell; his death was instantaneous, as he was shot in the head. Our ranks were, indeed, terribly thinned by that attack, but as we have been told by Gen. Anderson that it was our Brigade that stopped the whole of the German line advancing, we feel very proud, and my deepest regret is that Charlie was not spared to share the honours; but you can all feel proud of him. He died like a man, and a better friend or braver soldier there was not.": Age 29. At Felstead he made a name for athletics, winning the junior steeplechase one year and the senior twice. He also took the championship for sports. He *m.* Hillingdon, West Uxbridge, 25 October 1911, Brenda Grant (9, Chatsworth Gardens, Acton Hill, London), *dau.* of Edmund Bailey, 9 Belmont Road, Uxbridge, and had issue a *dau.* Angela Mary, *b.* 1 November 1913.

(Panel 26) L/Corpl. 51141, Edgar Street Denison, 16th Bn. Canadian Infantry (Manitoba Regt.), C.E.F.: *s.* of the late Lieut.Col. Frederick Charles Denison, 58th & 61st Regt., C.M.G., M.P. (*d.*1896), and his wife Julia A. Denison (4, Rusholme Road, Toronto): *b.* 13 August 1879: Religion – Church of England: *educ.* Upper Canada College (1891 – 97): Occupation – Clerk, Imperial Bank of Canada: served 3 yrs., Tpr., Governor General's Body Guard; enlisted Victoria, British Columbia, 17 November 1914; Pte., 50th Canadian Gordon Highlanders; transf'd. Rft. Draft P.P.C.L.I., proceeded overseas: transf'd. apptd. L/Corpl., 16th Battn., Lark Hill, 9 February 1915: served with the Expeditionary Force in France (from 15 February), and was killed in action, 23 April 1915; Trenches south of Wood, 2 miles west of St. Julien: Age 35.

(Panel 26) Pte. 29178, Charles John Adams, 16th Bn. Canadian Infantry (Manitoba Regt.), C.E.F.: *s.* of the late Robert Adams, by his wife Jane (55, Castlegate, Penrith): *b.* Greenock, Scotland, 26 August 1884: Religion – Presbyterian: Occupation – Carpenter: joined C.E.F., Valcartier, 23 September 1914; posted 16th Battn.: served with the Expeditionary Force in France from 17 February 1915. Died of wounds in German hands, 23 April 1915. Buried nr. Langemarck: Age 28. Correspondence to be addressed c/o his sister; Alice L. Adams, 55, Castlegate, Penrith, co. Cumberland, England.

(Panel 26) Pte. 29298, Hugh (*a.k.a.* Henry) Aitken, 16th Bn. Canadian Infantry (Manitoba Regt.), C.E.F.: *s.* of Henry Aitken, c/o Mrs J.E. Barclay (1916, 8th Avenue, Lethbridge, Alberta): *b.* 10 April 1890: Religion – Presbyterian. Missing wounded, reported by Stretcher Bearer (since killed) Pte. Aitken was shot through the body and, while this stretcher-bearer was attending him, was hit a second time – shot through the head, and killed instantly; 23 April 1915. Information received states casualty occurred in the woods nr. Langemarck: Age 25. Correspondence c/o Miss Agnes Jarrett (14, Patterson Street, Hamilton, Ontario).

(Panel 26) Pte. 29299, George Aitkens, No.4 Coy., 16th (Canadian Scottish) Bn. Canadian Infantry (Manitoba Regt.), C.E.F.: *s.* of Johnston Aitkens, of 178, McIntosh Avenue, Elmwood, Winnipeg: elder brother to Pte. 29300, J. Aitkens, 16th Canadian Infantry, who fell the same day, and *yr.* brother to Pte. 71777, J. Aitkens, 27th Canadian Infantry, who fell at St. Eloi, 6 April 1916: *b.* 13 December 1893: Religion – Presbyterian. Killed in action between St. Julien and Langemarck, 23 April 1915: Age 21. (*IWGC record age 22*)

Both James and John have no known grave; both are recorded below.

(Panel 26) Pte. 29300, James Aitkens, No.4 Coy., 16th (Canadian Scottish) Bn. Canadian Infantry (Manitoba Regt.), C.E.F.: *s.* of Johnston Aitkens, of 178, McIntosh Avenue, Elmwood, Winnipeg: *yr.* brother to Pte. 29299, G. Aitkens, 16th Canadian Infantry, who fell the same day, and Pte. 71777, J. Aitkens, 27th Canadian Infantry, who fell at St. Eloi, 6 April 1916: *b.* 9 June 1895: Religion – Presbyterian. Killed in action between St. Julien and Langemarck, last seen lying dead on the battlefield 23 April 1915: Age 19. No details available concerning the death of this soldier; no record of burial.

Both George and John have no known grave; George is recorded above, John below.

(Panel 26) Pte. 28905, Wilfred Beley, 16th (Canadian Scottish) Bn. Canadian Infantry (Manitoba Regt.), C.E.F.: *s.* of Hannah Beley: *b.* Ottery St. Mary, Exeter, 7 November 1880: *educ.* Blundell's School (School House, 1897 – 98), Tiverton, co. Devon: after leaving school served 3 years, 20th Middlesex Regt.: went to Canada: volunteered for Imperial Service, and enlisted 23 September 1914: served with the Expeditionary Force in France. Reported missing after the fighting 23 April 1915. In reply to a request for information made in June, his sister received a letter from the Company Paymaster, "Unfortunately, even his own personal friends and those who were near him on the night of April 22nd. cannot give me any details about him. Like a great many of our boys, he simply vanished into the darkness and amongst the trees during the charge we made. He may have been taken prisoner; but at this date, unless he has written to you, that is a slender possibility. The other alternative, and that is a very sad one for you, is that he died in the field. He was personally known to me and was very popular with his comrades. At all times and under the most trying circumstances he showed the greatest courage and the Colonel is sorry to have lost such an excellent soldier. You may feel proud of your brother's memory; he did his duty nobly for his King and Country." Dedicated "The years go by, the generations pass but out of the homes of England, out of our Public Schools, there has poured in these five years a band of noble brothers whose memory we shall never willingly let die," Pte. Beley's name is inscribed on the Blundell's School War Memorial: Age 24. *unm.*

At 1.30 a.m., 13 June 1916, an attack by four battalions of 1st Canadian Division was launched against the German positions at Mount Sorrel and Observatory Ridge with the objective of recapturing the Canadian positions so recently lost thereabouts. Carried out in pitch darkness, the attack was so sudden, the Germans were completely taken unawares and the old Canadian lines regained with very few casualties. 3rd (Toronto) and 1st (Western Ontario) Battalions recaptured Mount Sorrel, 13th (Black

Watch of Montreal) and 16th (Canadian Scottish) attacked Observatory Ridge, and recaptured all the ground between Hill 62 and Mount Sorrel. Immediately after the attack the enemy mercilessly pounded the front lines with artillery, and whilst the attack was a resounding success, and the casualties slight, under the artillery fire the statistics altered dramatically. Among the dead, fallen somewhere in the attack on Observatory Ridge, blown to smithereens or buried by the shellfire, was Colin Biggs. Given the nature of his father's post-war employ it is highly likely he would ultimately be responsible for submitting his own son's name to be engraved on the Menin Gate.

(Panel 26) Pte. 420827, Colin Biggs, 16th (Canadian Scottish) Bn. Canadian Infantry (Manitoba Regt.), C.E.F.: s. of Capt. Thomas J. Biggs, formerly Royal Engineers; of The Imperial War Graves Commission, Camp Anglaise, Armentieres, Nord, France: b. Curragh Camp, Co. Kildare, Ireland, 6 December 1893: Religion – Church of England: Occupation – Farmer: enlisted Winnipeg, 31 December 1914. Killed in action in the early hours of 13 June 1916, during the surprise attack on Observatory Ridge: Age 19.

(Panel 26) Pte. 29426, Alexander Campbell, 16th Bn. (Canadian Scottish) Bn. Canadian Infantry (Manitoba Regt.), C.E.F.: s. of William Campbell, of 206, Balmoral Avenue North, Hamilton, Ontario, by his wife Jeannie: served with the Expeditionary Force in France and Flanders, and was killed in action 23 April 1915: Age 24. unm.

(Panel 26) Pte. 29430, Peter James Carrol, 16th (Canadian Scottish) Bn. Canadian Infantry (72nd Seaforth Highlanders of Canada), C.E.F.: s. of James Carrol, Machinist; of 156, Cannon Street West, Hamilton, Ontario (b. Lariston, Scotland), by his wife Mary, dau. of John Jardine: b. Terra Cotta, Peel Co., Ontario, 16 October 1881: educ. Hamilton: joined 4th Field Battery, 1898 with which he served 3 years: joined 91st Highlanders, 1914: volunteered for Imperial Service on the outbreak of the European War, August 1914: came over with 1st Contingent, October: went to France February 1915, and was killed in action at St. Julien, 23 April 1915, while on a sniping expedition immediately after the Battle of St. Julien. Buried about 30 yards from the wood of St. Julien: Age 32. The Corpl. in charge of the expedition wrote from hospital in England, "On the night of 22 April we made a charge, and on the morning of 23 April, just at daybreak, I was sent about 20 yards from the German trench to dig ourselves in with seven men, and Private Peter Carrol, 29430, was one of the men who went with me. It was close to the wood we had taken the night before, so we did not go so far down in the ground when we found we were being fired at from all sides, and there were only three of us left in five minutes, so we tried to move round to the main tunnel, and it was in doing that that Private Carrol was shot through the head. He was as cool under fire as he always was, and had his pipe in his mouth when he left the trench to go out, and sat joking when we were under heavy fire." Pte. Carrol m. Hamilton, 21 December 1903, Margaret Ethel (1, Birch Avenue, Hamilton, Ontario, Canada), dau. of Alexander McIsaac, and had issue two daus. – Florence, b. 14 July 1905; Auralie, b. 9 May 1908. (IWGC record L/Cpl, Carroll)

(Panel 26) Pte. 29200, Stuart Carter, 16th (Canadian Scottish) Bn. Canadian Infantry (Manitoba Regt.), C.E.F.: b. Cambridge, England, 9 November 1895: sometime went to Canada, finding gainful employ as Clerk: volunteered for Imperial Service; joined Canadian Expeditionary Force, Valcartier, 23 September 1914: came over with First Contingent, October following: served in France and Flanders, and was killed in action 23 April 1915, nr. St. Julien: Age 19.

(Panel 26) Pte. 29036, Joseph Henry De Paiva, 16th (Canadian Scottish) Bn. Canadian Infantry (Manitoba Regt.), C.E.F.: s. of S.J. De Paiva, of 24, Edith Road, Ramsgate, co. Kent, England: b. co. Middlesex, England, 21 March 1888: Religion – Roman Catholic: Occupation – Electrician: previously served 6 yrs, Duke of Cambridge's Own (Middlesex Regt.): volunteered and enlisted Valcartier, 23 September 1914. Reported wounded and missing, since, for official purposes, presumed to have died on or about 24 April 1915; available information indicating he was shot while bringing in a wounded comrade and left in a trench in the vicinity of St. Julien: Age 27.

(Panel 26) Pte. 29089, Douglas Arthur J. Dunn, 16th (Canadian Scottish) Bn. Canadian Infantry (Manitoba Regt.), C.E.F.: b. Brondesbury, nr, London, England, 19 August 1894: saw previous service with Officers' Training Corps, Berkhampstead: went to Canada finding employ as Surveyor: volunteered and enlisted, Valcartier, 7 September 1914: posted 16th Battn., 4th Canadian Infantry Bde., 23 September: went to France, served with the Expeditionary Force there and in Flanders, and was killed in action 23 April 1915, nr. Ypres, Belgium: Age 20. *unm.*

(Panel 26) Pte. 29546, Oliver Fyson, 'D' Coy., 16th (Canadian Scottish) Bn. Canadian Infantry (Manitoba Regt.), 3rd Canadian Infantry Brigade, C.E.F.: *s.* of the Rt. Rev. Philip Kemball Fyson, formerly Bishop, Hokaido, Japan; currently Rector, Elmley Lovett, Droitwich, by his wife Eleanor, *dau.* of Richard Lee Furley: and brother to Lieut. G. Fyson, 3rd attd. 1st Royal Scots, killed in action 4 September 1918; Macedonia: *b.* Hull, 25 October 1884: *educ.* C.M.S.H. Limpsfield, and Loretto School: removed to Canada, 1906; settled at Vancouver: volunteered on the outbreak of war, 5 August 1914: came over with First Canadian Contingent, October 1914: trained Salisbury Plain, winter 1914 – 15: proceeded to France, February 1915, and was killed in action nr. Langemarck, 22 April 1915: Age 30. *unm.* Dedicated – "God Was Not Ashamed To Be Called Their God For He Hath Prepared For Them A City" – the brothers Fyson are among nine parishioners of St. Michael's Church, Elmley Lovett who gave their lives 1914 – 1918 remembered on the church roll of honour.

His brother Geoffrey also has no known grave; he is commemorated on the Doiran Memorial, Greece.

(Panel 26) Pte. 28860, John Saint Claire Gunning, 'C' Coy., 16th (Canadian Scottish) Bn. Canadian Infantry (Manitoba Regt.), C.E.F.: *s.* of Samuel Gunning, of 3642, 35th Avenue West, Vancouver, British Columbia, by his wife Margaret Elizabeth: and *yr.* brother to Corpl. 75188, B.T. Gunning, 29th Canadian Infantry, who fell before Passchendaele, 6 November 1917: *b.* 21 December 1893: enlisted Valcartier, 23 September 1914. Killed in action 22 April 1915, at the Second Battle of Ypres: Age 21. *unm.*

His brother Benjamin also has no known grave; he is recorded on Panel 28.

(Panel 26) Pte. 28862, Ralph Ewart Herald, 16th (Canadian Scottish) Bn. Canadian Infantry (Manitoba Regt.), C.E.F.: *s.* of Capt. Wilson Herald, Medical Officer, 16th C.E.F., and his wife Ellen E. Herald (Kelowna, British Columbia): *b.* Vancouver, 1895. Killed in action 23 April 1915: Age 20. *unm.*

(Panel 26) Pte. 51370, William Olliff, 16th (Canadian Scottish) Bn. Canadian Infantry (Manitoba Regt.), C.E.F.: elder *s.* of William Olliff, of 13, Grainger Street West, Newcastle-on-Tyne, Motor & Cycle Agent, by his wife Isabella: *b.* Newcastle-on-Tyne, 29 March 1888: *educ.* Royal Grammar School: served his apprenticeship with Messrs. C.A. Parsons & Co. Ltd., Heaton Works, Newcastle-on-Tyne: went to sea as Engineer, and took a 2nd Engineer's certificate, afterwards going to British Columbia, February 1913: worked for a time at the Esquimault Dockyard, leaving there to enter the motor trade in Victoria: volunteered on the outbreak of war; joined Victoria Rifles: came over Febrary 1915, being one of a hundred picked men for the P.P.L.I., but was drafted 16th Canadian Scottish (Gordon Highlanders), and after only a fortnight in England, went with his regt. to the Front. Came unscathed through the heavy fighting at Ypres, 22 – 25 April, and was killed by a high explosive shell while resting by the roadside on the night of 26 – 27 April 1915. Pte. Olliff was offered a commission, but as this entailed a return to Canada, he refused: Age 27. *unm.* (*IWGC record 22 April, 1915*)

(Panel 26) Pte. 29019, Charles Thomas Wentworth Sarel, 16th Bn. Canadian Infantry (Manitoba Regt.), C.E.F.: *s.* of Charles Wentworth Sarel, of Ottawa, and his wife Adelaide Minnie (1244, Ridway Avenue, North Vancouver): and brother to Pte. 169017, M.W. Sarel (surv'd.); and Pte. 29039, I.D.W. Sarel, 30th Canadian Infantry, died 10 May 1915: *b.* Wrangell Island, Alaska, 24 February 1892: *educ.* Dollar Academy, Scotland: enlisted Valcartier, 23 September 1914: proceeded to France February 1915, and was killed in action 22 April following: 22 April 1915: Age 23. *unm.* Remembered on Dollar Academy (Clackmannan) War Memorial Roll of Honour.

His brother Ian is commemorated in Bristol (Arnos Vale) Cemetery (Screen Wall, 7-725).

(Panel 26) Pte. 53892, Emerald Brittain Broadwell, Scout; 18th Bn. Canadian Infantry (Western Ontario Regt.), C.E.F.: *s.* of Amos (& Elizabeth S.) Broadwell, of Pincher Creek, Alberta: *b.* Kingsville, Ontario, 31 October 1896: Occupation – Fitter: serving member 29th Regt. (Militia); enlisted Galt, 23 October 1914. Reported missing (lost) on night patrol 30 – 31 January 1916; assumed killed: Age 19. (*IWGC record 30 January, age 21*)

(Panel 26) Pte. 53847, Albert James Reeves, Scout; 18th Bn. Canadian Infantry (Western Ontario Regt.), C.E.F.: s. of Martha Elizabeth Emma Reeves (co. Essex): b. St. Albans, co. Hertford, 4 September 1896: Occupation – Machinist: enlisted Stratford, Ontario, 31 October 1914. Reported missing (lost) on night patrol 30 – 31 January 1916; assumed killed: Age 19. (*IWGC record 30 January*)

(Panel 26) Pte. 799277, Charles Walter Hopkins, No.2 Coy., 19th Bn. Canadian Infantry (1st Central Ontario Regt.), C.E.F.: formerly Corpl. 'A' Coy., 134th Bn., C.E.F.: s. of Robert E. Hopkins, of 107, Clinton Street, Toronto, Ontario, by his wife Mary Ann: Religion – Baptist. Died of wounds, 3 November 1917, received in 'trenches south of Passchendaele.' Buried 28.D.11.d.6.7: Age 26.

The Old Score
Here is to fame, and a lasting name
And loud may the Twentieth shout
"May it take the Huns a thousand guns
To wipe the Old Score out!"

Anon

(Panel 26) Pte. 210055, William John Alkins, 20th Bn. Canadian Infantry (Central Ontario Regt.), C.E.F.: s. of William Alkins, and his wife Esther (Sugarleaf Street, Port Colborne, Ontario): b. 2 September 1886: Religion – Church of England: Occupation – Dredgeman: joined 98th (Overseas) Bn., C.E.F., Welland, Ontario, 24 November 1915. Severely wounded by a piece of enemy shell during operations at Passchendaele, 11 November 1917; despite being immediately attended to, he died shortly afterwards: Age 31. Grave unlocated.

(Panel 26) Pte. 58170, Bert H. Baker, 20th Bn. Canadian Infantry (Central Ontario Regt.), C.E.F.: s. of William Henry Baker: b. Tiverton, co. Devon, 9 July 1895: Occupation – Electrician: previously served 3 years, 23rd Northern Pioneers: enlisted Toronto, 23 March 1915. Reported missing 28 June 1916, when a raiding party to which he was attached, after being observed and fired on by the enemy, was forced to retire. (Struck off strength 30 June 1916): Age 20. See account re. Lieut. D.S. Anderson, Lijssenthoek Military Cemetery (VI.A.40).

(Panel 26) Pte. 58189, Frederick Burns, 20th Bn. Canadian Infantry (Central Ontario Regt.), C.E.F.: s. of Richard (& Bridget) Burns, of 193, York Street, Ottawa: b. 14 July 1889: joined 20th C.E.F., Toronto, 27 March 1915. Shot and killed, shortly after midnight, 27 – 28 June 1916; being observed by a German working party while engaged in a raid on the enemy trenches at The Bluff: Age 26. *unm.* See account re. Lieut. D.S. Anderson, Lijssenthoek Military Cemetery (VI.A.40).

(Panel 26) Pte. 58195, Albert Waterfield, 20th Bn. Canadian Infantry (1st Central Ontario Regt.) attd. 2nd Tunnelling Coy., Canadian Engineers, C.E.F.: s. of Albert Waterfield, of 83, Argyle Street, Toronto, by his wife Elizabeth: b. Jersey, Channel Islands, 15 October 1894: enlisted Toronto, 31 March 1915. Killed in action at Mount Sorrel, 2 June 1916: Age 20. See Panel 10.

(Panel 26) Lieut. John Francis Maloney, 'C' Coy., 21st Bn. Canadian Infantry (Eastern Ontario Regt.), C.E.F.: s. of Ellen Maloney (Britannia, Ottawa): b. Calgary, Alberta, 22 December 1895: *educ.* Ottawa University: Occupation – Clerk, Bank of Montreal: enlisted Ottawa, 5 August 1916; Gnr. 1258264, 72nd Bty. Ammunition Col. (Depot), Canadian Field Artillery: transf'd. Infantry, with which, after a period of training (England), he qualified for, and obtained, his commission: proceeded to France with reinforcement draft to 2nd Battn., July 1917; seconded 21st Battn. shortly thereafter, and was killed in action 9 November 1917, while on a working party in the vicinity of Potijze: Age 21. *unm.* A fellow officer recorded:– "On the afternoon of November 9th. 1917, a carrying party of 200 other ranks was detailed to meet the Division Signal Officer at a specified point on the plank road south of Passchendaele. Lieut. Maloney was in charge of the men of 'C' Company. The party reached the appointed spot at 3.30 p.m. and received the order to sit down and wait for the orders. At 3.45 p.m. the officer in charge of the party passed the word along that the Signal Officer was ready for the men to commence work. 'A' Company was the first to move and when they had cleared the ground where 'C' Company was halted two high explosive shells came over on the road. The first one did not cause any casualties but the second, which struck the road in the centre of 'C' Company, caused about twenty casualties; Lieut. Maloney's left leg and right arm being blown off, making him scarcely recognisable, and causing instantaneous death." Remembered on the In Memoriam Roll of Honour, St. Patrick's Basilica, Ottawa, Ontario. *Buried in White House Cemetery (I.A.23).*

(Panel 26) Pte. 210057, Roy Ernest Acton, 21st Bn. Canadian Infantry (Eastern Ontario Regt.), C.E.F.: *s.* of the late James (& Maria) Acton, of Watford, Ontario: *b.* 29 March 1895: Religion – Methodist: joined 98th Bn. C.E.F., St. Catherines, December 1915; transf'd. 21st Battn.: Killed instantaneously by the bursting of a shrapnel shell, close support trenches, west of Passchendaele; morning of 3 November 1917: Age 22. Buried 28.D.6.c.35.05.

(Panel 26) L/Corpl. 61755, Emmanuel Pelletier, 22nd (Canadien Francais) Bn. Canadian Infantry (Quebec Regt.), C.E.F.: *s.* of Phileas Pelletier, of 111, St. Peter Street, Toronto, Ontario, by his wife Elizabeth: served with Canadian Army prior to the outbreak of war, discharged 1914 due to injuries: re-enlisted 1915: served with the Expeditionary Force in France, and was killed in action 11 June 1916: Age 26.

(Panel 26) Pte. 61589, Paul Adrien Lambert, D.C.M., Machine Gun Section, 22nd (Canadien Francais) Bn. Canadian Infantry (Quebec Regt.), C.E.F.: *s.* of the late Joseph Lambert, by his wife Eugenie Beauchamp: and brother to Joseph A. Lambert, of Montreal: *b.* 9 July 1894. Killed in action 8 April 1916: Age 22. *unm.* Awarded the Distinguished Conduct Medal, and Médaille Militaire (France), '*London Gazette,*' 11 March 1916 "For conspicuous gallantry and devotion to duty when, with another man, he carried in a severely wounded comrade under heavy fire. Having no stretcher they carried him on their shoulders, and in doing so had to cross barbed wire and several trenches. Their bravery and physical energy was most marked."

(Panel 26) Pte. 65003, Charles Adams, 24th Bn. Canadian Infantry (Quebec Regt.), C.E.F.: c/o The Superintendent, Protestant Orphan Home, Montreal, Quebec: *b.* 13 July 1896: Religion – Church of England. Killed in action 23 May 1916; St. Eloi Craters. Buried rear of Trench 19: Age 19. (*IWGC record age 20*)

(Panel 26) Pte. 445160, William John Croft, No.5 Platoon, 24th Bn. Canadian Infantry (Quebec Regt.), C.E.F.: *s.* of William Croft, of Chatham, New Brunswick, by his wife Sarah. One of eleven men killed by the explosion of an enemy shell while passing Zillebeke Church on the night of 6 – 7 June 1916: Age 19. *Buried in Zillebeke Churchyard (B.3).*

(Panel 26) Pte. 65453, Walter James Hobday, 24th Bn. Canadian Infantry (Quebec Regt.), C.E.F.: *s.* of Benjamin Thomas Hobday, of Brunces Farm, Ashburnham, Battle, co. Sussex, by his wife Elizabeth: and brother to Lieut. S.G. Hobday, D.C.M., 3rd C.E.F., who also fell: served with the Expeditionary Force in France and Flanders, and was killed in action 16 June 1916, at Zillebeke: Age 26.

His brother Stephen also has no known grave; he is commemorated on the Canadian National Memorial, Vimy.

(Panel 26) Pte. 415334, James Mathias Miller, No.5 Platoon, 24th Bn. Canadian Infantry (Quebec Regt.), C.E.F.: *s.* of William G. Miller, of 129, North Street, Halifax, Nova Scotia, by his wife Elizabeth (15, St. Alban Street, Halifax): and *yr.* brother to Dvr. 43913, J.J. Miller, 1st Divn. Ammunition Col., Canadian Field Artillery, who fell the same day: *b.* 24 February 1896: enlisted 30 July 1915. Killed in action at Zillebeke, 7 June 1916: Age 20.

His brother James Joseph also has no known grave; he is recorded on Panel 10.

(Panel 26) Corpl. 68041, Adam Allan, 25th Bn. Canadian Infantry (Nova Scotia Regt.), C.E.F.: *husb.* to Clementine Allan (Atlantic Street, Sydney Mines, Nova Scotia): *b.* Colburn, Scotland, 7 February 1879: Religion – Presbyterian: Occupation – Miner: previously served 4 yrs., Highland Light Infantry (Vol.); joined C.E.F., Halifax, 3 December 1914. Killed in action 17 June 1916, Hill 60; buried Front Line there (Front I.29.c.): Age 37. No remains recovered.

In the late spring of 1917, 42nd Bn. Canadian Infantry, moved back from the trenches on Vimy Ridge to the village of Vimy itself, relieving the Canadian Mounted Rifles, taking on fatigue duties such as trench digging, wiring, ration carrying etc. William Bird was one of them. He later recorded:–

> "Getting our party together had taken so long that I had no chance to prepare any sort of shelter. As we went back and drew near the railway embankment someone called in a low voice. I went over and found two men from the 73rd had dug a neat bivvy into the embankment. They were very decent chaps and insisted they had made the place wide enough to accommodate the three of us. We snuggled in, and with a ground sheet pegged to hold over our heads we were really comfortable. In seconds I was dead to the world.
>
> The ground sheet pegged over our heads was pulled free and fell on my face, rousing me. Then a firm hand seized one of mine and pulled me up to a sitting position. It was very early, as first sunshine was glittering on the dew-wet grass. I was annoyed that I should have to do some chore after being out so late. I tried to pull free. But the grip held, and as I came to a sitting-up position my other hand was seized and I had a look at my visitor.
>
> In an instant I was out of the bivvy, so surprised I could not speak. I was face to face with my brother Steve, who had been killed in 1915! The first notice from the War Office had said: "Missing, believed dead." After a time one of his mates wrote and said a boot had been found with his name on it. The Germans had mined the Canadian trench and blown it up.
>
> Steve grinned and he released my hands, then put his warm hand over my mouth as I started to shout my happiness. He pointed to the sleepers in the bivvy and to my rifle and equipment. "Get your gear," he said softly. ...."

Will Bird followed his brother away from the two sleeping men in the bivvy, into the ruins of the village at which point he dropped his rifle, stooping to retrieve it he found his brother had disappeared. Will searched for his brother for some considerable time until, eventually, he sat down on his kit and fell asleep.

Roughly awakened by two of his mates, who were extremely pleased to find him in one piece, he was informed the bivvy in which he had been sleeping had taken a direct hit; all that remained was one man's helmet and the legs of the other.

Steve had saved his life.

(Panel 26) Pte. 67193, Stephen Carmen Bird, 'B' Coy., 25th Bn. Canadian Infantry (Nova Scotia Regt.), 2nd Division, C.E.F.: *s.* of the late Stephen Bird, Lieut. 93rd Battn. (*d.* 9 December 1895), by his wife Augusta (Amherst, Nova Scotia), *dau.* of William Bird: *b.* Mapleton, Nova Scotia, posthumous, 24 April 1896: *educ.* Amherst High School: employee Canada Car Co., Amherst: volunteered following the outbreak of war, August 1914; joined Canadian Expeditionary Force, 9 November 1914: came over with 2nd Contingent, 29 May 1915: went to France, 15 September, and was killed in action there, 8 October 1915, by the explosion of a mine. A comrade wrote, "He was a friend at all times and under all circumstances, no one need wish a better friend, we all loved him and we all mourn his loss." And another, "He had splendid courage, and when urged to fall back a little further a few minutes before the explosion occurred his reply was 'I am staying right here.'" Private Bird was a keen athlete and base-ball player: Age 19.

(Panel 26) Pte. 406863, William Christopher Kewley, 25th Bn. Canadian Infantry (Nova Scotia Regt.), C.E.F.: only *s.* of the late Rev. William Kewley, Vicar of Millom, co. Northumberland, by his wife Margaret Ada (10, Vicarage Terrace, Kendal, co. Westmoreland), *dau.* of John Sharpe: *b.* Ulpha Vicarage, co. Cumberland, 12 July 1892: *educ.* Kendal and Warrington Grammar Schools; Selwyn College, Cambridge (member O.T.C.): went to Canada, March 1914, settled at Cardale, Manitoba, and took up Farming: volunteered for Imperial Service after the outbreak of war; joined 36th Battn. C.E.F., January 1915: came over with the June 1915 Contingent, drafted 25th Battn.: served with the Expeditionary Force in France and Flanders from December 1915, and was killed in action at St. Eloi, 13 April 1916, being shot through the head while trying to save a wounded comrade. Buried there. His officer wrote, "It was a noble sacrifice; one of the other boys was badly wounded and he volunteered to carry him out, and it was in doing this noble act that he was killed. He was a fine fellow, always willing to do more than his share of work, no matter how unpleasant it was, and he will be greatly missed by all who knew him.": Age 23. *unm.*

(Panel 26) Pte. 67347, William Ellis McKim, 25th Bn. Canadian Infantry (Nova Scotia Regt.), C.E.F.: *s.* of Elias McKim, of Amherst, Nova Scotia, by his wife Mary: elder brother to Pte. 444543, A.I. McKim, 60th Bn. Canadian Infantry, who died of wounds received at the Battle of Ypres, 3 June 1916: Killed in action 8 October 1915: Age 31. William leaves a widow Mary.

His brother Allan also has no known grave; he is recorded on Panel 30.

(Panel 26) Pte. 414963, Roland Judson Swaine, 25th Bn. Canadian Infantry (Nova Scotia Regt.), C.E.F.: *s.* of Samuel Swaine, of Canso, Nova Scotia, by his wife Emma: and brother to Pte. 415903, A.E. Swaine, 43rd Canadian Infantry, killed in action 21 September 1916; and Pte. 902431, B.W. Swaine, 85th Canadian Infantry, who fell 24 March 1918: *b.* Canso, 6 Februay 1893: Religion – Baptist: Occupation – Lumberman: 5'9" tall, blue eyes, fair hair: enlisted Aldershot Camp, 10 August 1915. Killed in action 14 April 1916: Age 22. *unm.* Unveiled 7 September 1925, the Canso War Memorial is inscribed 'To The Glory Of God, And In Loving Memory Of Those Who Made The Supreme Sacrifice In The World War, 1914-1918;' brothers Arthur, Benjamin and Roland Swaine are among those remembered thereon.

His brother Arthur also has no known grave, he is commemorated on the Canadian National Memorial, Vimy; Benjamin is buried in Aix-Noulette Communal Cemetery Extension (II.D.10).

(Panel 26) Sergt. 69157, Francis Louis Cotter, 'A' Coy., 26th Bn. Canadian Infantry (New Brunswick Regt.), C.E.F.: late of 16, Orange Street, St. John: *s.* of Richard J. Cotter, of 184, Duke Street, St. John, New Brunswick, and Elizabeth Cotter, his wife: *b.* 22 May 1892: Occupation – Clerk: joined 26th Battn., St. John, 30 November 1914: served in France from 15 September 1915, and was killed in action 13 October 1915; machine-gun fire. Age 23. (*IWGC record age 25*) See La Laiterie Military Cemetery (II.A.5-20).

Formed at St. John, New Brunswick, 2 November 1914, the 'Fighting 26th' formed part of 2nd Canadian Contingent, C.E.F. Commanded by Lieut. Col. J.L. McAviry, at full strength the battalion numbered some 35 officers and 996 other ranks. The originals of the battalion left St. John 13 June 1915 and, after arriving in England, spent most of the summer training at Shorncliffe Camp before sailing to France as part of 5th Infantry Brigade, 2nd Canadian Division, comprised of 22nd French Canadian Battn., 24th Victoria Rifles of Canada Battn., 25th Nova Scotia Rifles Battn. and 5th Trench Mortar Battery. By late September 1915 the Division was in the thick of the action at the front.

Harry Darkes enlisted in March 1916 and, before (as well as after) being transferred to the 26th as a replacement, a number of recurrent illnesses might well have kept him out of harm's way indefinitely. Finally rejoining his battalion in late October 1917, he was just in time to take part in the Canadian assault on Passchendaele.

At 4 a.m., 6 November 1917, 2nd Canadian Division were assembled in their positions on the right of the line facing Passchendaele, ready to assault the Germans in the shattered ruins of what had once been the village. Just after 6 a.m. the division, with the 'Fighting 26th' on the far right flank, went over the top. The advance through mud and water waist deep in places, under heavy enemy artillery and machine gun fire, was described thus:– 'In front were our officers, every one of them from junior to senior, well ahead of their men…A wave of the hand, a quarter right turn, one long blast of the whistle and we were off. We made mad rushes of fifty or sixty yards at a time, then down we would go…at the signal from our captain with two short blasts on his whistle. No place to seek cover, only to hug Mother Earth. Our lads were falling pretty fast; our officers even faster…We were about two hundred yards from the enemy's trench and my estimation is that easily one third of our fighting men were gone. Easily eighty per cent of our officers were out of the immediate game…The machine gun fire was hellish. The infantry fire was blinding. A bullet would flash through the sleeve of a tunic, rip off the brim of a cap, bang against a water-bottle, bury itself in the mass of a knap-sack. It seemed as though no one could live in such a hail of lead… Each battalion was advancing, with slowness and awful pain, but all were advancing.'

By 7.40 am. Passchendaele was in Canadian hands but the cost in lives had been great. Of the 'Fighting 26th,' 'A' Company had started the day with 130 men and finished with only 30; most of them lost to shell fire. More than one in three soldiers of the battalion had been either killed, wounded or reported missing. Among the latter Pte. Harry Darkes, hit sometime during the attack amid the smoke and noise of the battle – swallowed up by the mud, blown apart and scattered on the wind – he simply vanished 'in the hell on earth that was fought in the mud and horrors of Flanders fields.'

(Panel 26) Pte. 742978, Harry William Darkes, 26th Bn. Canadian Infantry (New Brunswick Regt.), C.E.F.: *s.* of Henry Dierks (Darkes), Widower, of Petersen, Victoria Co., New Brunswick, by his marriage to the late, Laurine 'Lena' Hansena (New Denmark, N.B.): *b.* Petersen, 18 June 1897: Religion – Danish Lutheran: Occupation – Labourer: enlisted St. John, New Brunswick, 11 March 1916: 5'11½", dark complexion, brown eyes, brown hair: hospitalised (tonsillitis) 4 – 16 April 1916: enlistment approved 6 April, posted 'D' Coy., 115th Battn.: incapacitated at St. John (measles), 9 – 27 May: after a brief period of basic training left Halifax, Nova Scotia, aboard S.S. 'Olympic,' 23 July 1916: arrived England, 31 July: stationed Bramshott Camp for further training, transf'd. 112th Battn., 15 October: put into isolation, Aldershot (repeat tonsillitis) 27 December 1916 – 23 January 1917: transf'd. 13th Battn. 2 February 1917: Admonished by Capt. Berry, Shoreham Camp, 12 April 1917 – 'Dirty mess-kit while on active service': transf'd. 26th Battn., 30 May 1917; proceeded to France same day: hospitalised 86th Field Ambulance, 'bad case of impetigo – face and arms,' 4 – 17 July: subsequently attd. 5th Machine Gun Coy., 15 September – 13 October, thereafter rejoined 26th Battn.: 'Reported missing believed dead, in the hell on earth that was fought in the mud and horrors of Flanders fields,' 6 November 1917: Age 20. *unm.*

(Panel 26) Pte. 69311, Jerome Gallant, 26th Bn. Canadian Infantry (New Brunswick Regt.), C.E.F.: *s.* of Moses (& Mrs) Gallant, of South Rustico, Prince Edward Island: and brother to Pte. 69344, M. Gallant, 26th Canadian Infantry, killed in action 30 September 1915, aged 27 years: *b.* Wheatley River, 18 October 1885: Occupation – Labourer: enlisted St. John, 5 November 1914: served with the Expeditionary Force in France and Flanders from 15 September 1915, and was killed in action 16 June 1916: Age 30. *unm.* Correspondence to be addressed c/o Mrs H.J. McKinnon (110, Queen Street, Charlottetown, Prince Edward Island). (*IWGC record age 19*)

His brother Moses is buried in La Laiterie Military Cemetery (II.A.23).

(Panel 26) Pte. 69353, Henry Wilbert Graham, 'C' Coy., 26th Bn. Canadian Infantry (New Brunswick Regt.), C.E.F.: *s.* of the late Philip C. (& Margaret) Graham, of 260, Brussels Street, St. John's: *b.* St. John's, New Brunswick, 7 May 1889: Occupation – Labourer: a serving member of the Militia, 71st (Sussex) Bn.; enlisted St. John's, 25 November 1914. Killed in action, 14 June 1916: Age 27. *unm.* His brothers, Walter and Chester, also served. All correspondence should be addressed c/o Miss Edna Graham (260, Brussels Street, St. John's, New Brunswick).

(Panel 26) Pte. 412475, Harold Albert Henry, 26th Bn. Canadian Infantry (New Brunswick Regt.), C.E.F.: *s.* of the late William Henry, of 143, London Street, Peterborough, Ontario, by his wife Margaret Elizabeth (1013, Water Street, Peterborough): *b.* 7 November 1899: enlisted Peterborough, Ontario, 24 February 1915, aged 15 years; providing date of birth 7 November 1896; occupation Labourer: went to France and was killed in action there 18 June 1916: **Age 16.**

(Panel 26) Lieut. Reginald Stellwagen Black, 27th Bn. Canadian Infantry (Manitoba Regt.), C.E.F.: *s.* of Dr. Henry Hambleton Black, of Manitou, Manitoba, by his wife Miriam Stellwagen: Occupation – Manager; Bank of Hamilton, Miami, Manitoba: enlisted November 1914: served with the Expeditionary Force in France and Flanders, and died of wounds, 6 November 1917, received at Passchendaele: Age 31. Remembered on Manitou Village War Memorial.

(Panel 26) Lieut. Ralph Egerton Norris Jones, 27th (City of Winnipeg) Bn. Canadian Infantry (Manitoba Regt.), C.E.F.: *s.* of Charles S.L. (& Helen A. McDougall) Jones, of St. Mary's, Ontario: *b.* 3 June 1877: Religion – Presbyterian: *educ.* Huron Street Public School; Upper Canada College (1891 – 92): Occupation – Bank Manager, Canadian Bank of Commerce, Alexander Avenue, Winnipeg: previously served 100th Winnipeg Grenadiers (Militia); joined C.E.F., November 1914: apptd. Lieut., 27th Bn., 16

February 1915; served with the Expeditionary Force in France from 15 September following. Killed in action 26 April 1916 'while gallantly leading his men in an endeavour to capture a mine crater and thus restore a breach in the line at St. Eloi.' Buried with a number of his men, close to the reserve line of trenches at St. Eloi. Grave subsequently obliterated by shellfire; not located since: Age 38. *unm.*

(Panel 26) Pte. 71777, John Aitkens, 'D' Coy., 27th Bn. Canadian Infantry (Manitoba Regt), C.E.F.: *s.* of Johnston Aitkens, of 178, McIntosh Avenue, Elmwood, Winnipeg: and elder brother to Pte. 29299, G. Aitkens, and Pte. 29300, J. Aitkens, 16th Bn. Canadian Infantry, both of whom fell in the fighting between St. Julien and Langemarck, 23 April 1915: *b.* Aberdeen, Scotland, 21 November 1884: enlisted 24 October 1914. Killed in action 6 April 1916, in the fighting at St. Eloi: Age 29.

His brothers George and James both have no known grave; both are recorded above.

(Panel 26) Pte. 294080, Carl Emil Albrectsen, 27th Bn. Canadian Infantry (Manitoba Regt.), C.E.F.: *s.* of Emil Albrectsen, of Svinget 28, Kjobenhaven C, Denmark, by his wife Martha: *b.* Svendborg, Denmark, 1893: enlisted Winnipeg, 1915. Voluntarily reverted from officer's rank (Lieut.) to proceed overseas, and was killed in action at Passchendaele 7 November 1917: Age 24.

(Panel 26) Pte. 21136, Arthur Joseph Chislett, 27th Bn. Canadian Infantry (Manitoba Regt.), C.E.F.: *s.* of James Chislett, of Deddington, co. Oxford, England, by his wife Emily (Clay Hill House, Enfield, co. Middlesex): and brother to Rfn. R/31261, N. Chislett, 18th King's Royal Rifle Corps, killed in action 31 July 1917, at Pilckem Ridge: *b.* Deddington, 18 January 1890: Occupation – Clerk: enlisted Valcartier, 23 September 1914. Killed in action 6 November 1917, at Passchendaele: Age 27.

His brother Norman also has no known grave, he is recorded on Panel 53.

(Panel 26) Pte. 622395, Walter George Cowell, 27th (City of Winnipeg) Bn. Canadian Infantry (Manitoba Regt.), C.E.F. *s.* of Walter Cowell, of Castle Camps, co. Cambridge, England: and brother to Pte. 622394, C. Cowell, 27th Canadian Infantry, died of wounds 18 June 1916, at Poperinghe: *b.* South Taunton, 8 July 1891: Religion – Methodist: Occupation – Labourer: 5'8" tall, blue eyes, brown hair: enlisted Portage la Prairie, apptd. 44th (Overseas) Battn., 24 April 1915: departed Quebec, S.S. 'Carpathia,' 17 May (transf'd. 27th Battn.); trained Dibgate, Shorncliffe, and Otterpool, England from the 28th of that month: served with the Expeditionary Force in France and Flanders from 19 September 1915, and was killed in action 11 June 1916; Zillebeke: Age 24. *unm.*

His brother Clement is buried in Lijssenthoek Military Cemetery (VIII.A.36A).

(Panel 26) Pte. 72082, George Frederick Heldt, 'D' Coy., 27th (City of Winnipeg) Bn. Canadian Infantry (Manitoba Regt.), C.E.F.: *s.* of George Heldt, of 52, Humberstone Road, Grimsby, co. Lincoln, by his wife Ellen: previously served 8 years, 3rd Lincolnshire Regt. (Volunteers); South African Campaign (1900): *b.* 17 October 1874: enlisted Fort Frances, Ontario, 26 October 1914. Killed in action 6 April 1916, at St. Eloi: Age 41.

(Panel 26) Pte. 71275, Albert Kelly, 27th (City of Winnipeg) Bn. Canadian Infantry (Manitoba Regt.), C.E.F.: *s.* of Frederick John Kelly, of Hulton, St. Vital, Manitoba, by his wife Louise (40, Barry Street, Norwood): *b.* London, England, 13 June 1896: Religion Church of England: Occupation – Printer: serving member 79th Cameron Highlanders of Canada (Militia): enlisted Winnipeg, 25 October 1914: 5'8" tall, sallow complexion, grey eyes, dark hair: served with the Expeditionary Force in France and Flanders from 18 September 1915, and was killed in action 9 October 1915, while assisting in the removal of some bales of wire from his company's trench: Age 19. At his enlistment Pte. Kelly falsified his date of birth, the attesting officer recording age 21; the battalion's second Active Service fatality, his true age was only revealed after his death.

(Panel 26) Pte. 871553, Stanley Richard Shore, 27th (City of Winnipeg) Bn. Canadian Infantry (Manitoba Regt.), C.E.F.: *s.* of Thomas Edward Shore, of 429, 9th Street, Nutana, Saskatoon: *b.* Manitou, Manitoba, 16 December 1897: *educ.* Brandon School; King Edward School, Saskatoon: sometime briefly employed with National Trust Co., Saskatchewan; resigned to return to education (Nutana Collegiate) and resume his studies: entered employ Bank of British North America, Saskatoon; Clerk, October 1915: prior to the outbreak of war was Bugler, 105th Saskatoon Fusiliers (Militia): enlisted 9 March 1916; Pte.

183rd Battn. and proceeded to England from whence, after training and disbandment of that unit, he went to France with a reinforcement draft to 27th Battn. and was killed in action, 6 November 1917, in the attack at Passchendaele Ridge: Age 19.

(Panel 26) Pte. 2114885, Jack Smith, 27th (City of Winnipeg) Bn. Canadian Infantry (Manitoba Regt.), C.E.F.: late of 210, Whytewold Road, St. James, Manitoba: *s.* of John Henry Smith, of 25, The Baulk, Biggleswade, co. Bedford, by his wife Rose: and yr. brother to Pte. 187163, E.J. Smith, 8th Canadian Infantry, died 29 September 1918: *b.* 4 February 1897: enlisted Winnipeg, 2 January 1917. Killed in action 6 November 1917, while with a bombing party in the Canadian assault at Passchendaele Ridge: Age 20.

His brother Ernest is buried in Sancourt British Cemetery (I.B.30).

(Panel 26) Pte. 267562, Leo Alexander Bunnah, 28th Bn. Canadian Infantry (Saskatchewan Regt.), C.E.F.: late of Kermaria, Saskatchewan: *s.* of the late Joseph Bunnah, by his wife Bridget Flod Bunnah (Fort Coulonge, Quebec): and brother to Pte. 267561, C. Bunnah, 5th Canadian Infantry, died of wounds (gas) 12 March 1918; received vicinity Hill 70; and Pte. 267560, C. Bunnah (surv'd.): *b.* Fort Coulonge, 28 April 1894: enlisted Watson, 27 March 1916. Killed in action 6 November 1917; Passchendaele Front: Age 23.

His brother Cardinal is buried in Aix-Noulette Communal Cemetery Extension (II.C.1).

(Panel 26) Pte. 446565, Hugh Melville Carmichael, 28th Bn. Canadian Infantry (Saskatchewan Regt.), C.E.F.: *s.* of Angus (& Minnie H.) Carmichael, of Kenora, Ontario: *b.* 12 April 1887: Religion – Presbyterian: *educ.* Kenora High School; Upper Canada College (1904 – 05); McGill University (Undergrad.); Queen's University (member 1yr., Queen's University Rifles): Occupation – Civil Engineer: joined C.E.F., Sarcee Camp, Calgary, 4 May 1915; Pte. 56th Bn.; proceeded overseas, 1 September: apptd. L/Corpl. East Sandling, England, Machine Gun Sect., 9th Reserve Bn.: proceeded to France, 15 May 1916, attd. M.G. Coy., 28th Bn.: Reported missing, presumed killed, 6 June 1916; vicinity Hooge. An officer wrote, "The enemy exploded four mines under the trenches held by the Company to which this soldier was attached."

(Panel 26) Pte. 74007, Edgar Henry Cutler, 'D' Coy., 28th Bn. Canadian Infantry (Saskatchewan Regt.), C.E.F.: *s.* of Thomas Cutler, by his wife Catherine (15, Greystone Flats, Eastbourne, England): *b.* Nottingham, 17 October 1873: served 5 years Coldstream Guards; served in the South African Campaign, and with the Expeditionary Force in France and Flanders, and was killed in action at the Second Battle of Ypres, 26 April 1915: Age 41. *unm.* (*IWGC record age 44*)

(Panel 26) Pte. 74291, Thomas Dawson, 28th Bn. Canadian Infantry (Saskatchewan Regt.), C.E.F.: *s.* of Albert Dawson, Rail Coach Painter; of 45, Buckingham Road, Wolverton, England, by his marriage to the late Mary Ann Dawson: and brother to Gnr. 33078, B. Dawson, Royal Garrison Artillery transf'd. Royal Engineers (discharged, May 1918): *b.* Wolverton, 11 November 1888: Religion – Church of England: Occupation – Carpenter: 5'5" tall, grey eyes, light brown hair: previously served six years 1/1st Oxford & Bucks Light Infantry; joined C.E.F., Winnipeg, 31 March 1915, apptd. 29th Battn.: Killed in action 6 June 1916: Age 28. He leaves a widow, Mrs A.A. Dawson (596, Kylemore Avenue, Fort Rouge, Winnipeg).

PANEL 26 ENDS – PTE. W.W. GAY, 28TH BN. CANADIAN INF.

PANEL 28 BEGINS – PTE. F.W. GIBSON, 28TH BN. CANADIAN INF.

(Panel 28) Pte. 426190, Reuben George Gillespie, 28th Bn. Canadian Infantry (Saskatchewan Regt.), C.E.F.: *s.* of Andrew Gillespie, of Mawer, Saskatchewan, and Eva Gillespie (202, Caribou Street, Moose Jaw); his wife: and yr. brother to Pte. 426117, W.J. Gillespie, 28th Canadian Infantry, killed the same day: *b.* East Garafraxa, Ontario, 11 September 1892: Religion – Methodist: Occupation – Carpenter: previously served 1 year Militia: joined C.E.F., Moose Jaw, 29 December 1914: served with the Expeditionary Force in France and Flanders from 18 September 1915, and was killed in action on the afternoon of 6 June 1916; Mount Sorrel: Age 24. See below.

(Panel 28) Pte. 426117, William James Gillespie, 28th Bn. Canadian Infantry (Saskatchewan Regt.), C.E.F.: *s.* of Andrew Gillespie, of Mawer, Saskatchewan, and Eva Gillespie (202, Caribou Street, Moose Jaw); his wife: and elder brother to Pte. 426190, R.G. Gillespie, killed the same day: *b.* East Garafraxa, Ontario, 2 June 1888: Religion – Methodist: Occupation – Tinsmith: previously served 6 months Militia: joined C.E.F., Moose Jaw, 21 December 1914: served with the Expeditionary Force in France from 18 September. 1915, and was killed in action 6 June 1916, Mount Sorrel: Age 28. See above.

(Panel 28) Pte. 424858, Arthur Stanley Gurnett, 28th Bn. Canadian Infantry (Saskatchewan Regt.), C.E.F.: c/o Miss E. Gurnett (N. Sanatorium, Gravenhurst, Ontario): *s.* of Mrs A.L. Gurnett (Ancaster, Ontario), by her marriage to the late William F. Gurnett: *b.* 19 August 1890: enlisted 12 February 1915: departed Canada, March 1916; rank Coy.Sergt.Major; reverted to Pte. to proceed to France, and was killed in action 8 June 1916, nr. Ypres: Age 25.

(Panel 28) Pte. 73174, John Finlay MacInnes, 28th Bn. Canadian infantry, C.E.F.: *s.* of Finlay MacInnes, of 38, Lawrence Place, Downhill, Glasgow, Scotland: and elder brother to Pte. 79182, F.D. MacInnes, 31st Canadian Infantry, killed in action 13 October 1915; Kemmel: *b.* Glasgow, co. Lanark, 30 July 1887: Religion – Presbyterian: *educ.* Hillhead High School, Glasgow: apprenticed to Union Castle Line, Shipping Agents; on leaving there removed to America: Occupation – Teamster: previously served 9 months United States Forces; 1 year Canadian Mounted Rifles, joined 28th C.E.F., Moose Jaw, Saskatchewan, 28 October 1914: served in France from 18 September 1915, and was killed in action 7 April 1916: Age 28. "The gallant brothers were typical pioneers of Empire, industrious in the arts of peace, but not 'too proud to fight' for the right."

His brother Finlay also has no known grave; he is recorded below.

(Panel 28) Pte. 424487, Alex Scott, 28th Bn. Canadian Infantry (Saskatchewan Regt.), C.E.F.: *s.* of Robert Scott, of 85, Maxwell Street, Pollokshaws, Glasgow, by his wife Agnes: and yr. brother to Pte. R. Scott, 28th Canadian Infantry, killed the same day: *b.* Glasgow, 28 March 1896: Religion – Presbyterian: Occupation – Labourer: joined C.E.F., Minnedosa, Manitoba, 18 December 1914: departed Canada, 28 May 1915: trained England, June – September: joined Expeditionary Force in France on the 18th. of the latter month: took part in the actions at St. Eloi, March – April 1916, and was killed in action, 6 June 1916, at Mount Sorrel when, at approximately 3 p.m. the battalion's frontage was subjected to a veritable whirlwind of artillery and trench mortar fire; two companies were virtually annihilated: Age 20. *unm.* See below.

(Panel 28) Pte. 424488, Robert Scott, 28th Bn. Canadian Infantry (Saskatchewan Regt.), C.E.F.: *s.* of Robert Scott, of 85, Maxwell Street, Pollokshaws, Glasgow, by his wife Agnes and elder brother to Pte. 424487, A. Scott, 28th Canadian Infantry, killed the same day: *b.* Glasgow, 3 August 1882: Religion – Presbyterian: Occupation – Labourer: joined C.E.F., Minnedosa, Manitoba, 18 December 1914. Killed in action 6 June 1916: Age 34. *unm.* See above.

(Panel 28) Pte. 73965, Charles Robert Spooner, 28th Bn. (North West Regt.) Canadian Infantry (Saskatchewan Regt.), C.E.F.: *s.* of William John Spooner, of 6, Pasley Road, Newington, London, S.E., by his wife Mary: *b.* Newington, 3 October 1885: *educ.* there: Occupation – Checker; Canadian Pacific Railway: enlisted Fort William 23 October 1914: served with the Expeditionary Force in France and Flanders. Reported missing after the fighting on 6 June 1916, and is now assumed to have been killed in action on or about that date.: Age 30. *unm.*

(Panel 28) Pte. 73864, Robert Anderson Waring, 'D' Coy., 28th Bn. Canadian Infantry (Saskatchewan Regt.), C.E.F.: *s.* of Elizabeth Meakin, *née* Waring (Cambray Chambers, Cambray, Cheltenham, co. Gloucester), late of Salisbury House, Swindon Road; wife to the late George Bruyne Waring: *b.* Cheltenham, 20 November 1886: Occupation – Butcher: a serving member of the Militia; enlisted Regina, 24 October 1914: served with the Expeditionary Force in France from 18 September 1915; shot and killed by a sniper on the 28th. (September 1915); the battalion's second fatality attributable to this German soldier's marksmanship: Age 29.

(Panel 28) Pte. 430860, George Williams, 28th Bn. (North West Regt.) Canadian Infantry (Saskatchewan Regt.), C.E.F.: *s.* of George Williams, of Newton Crossing, Manorbier, co. Pembroke: *b.* Pembroke, South Wales, 14 August 1883: Religion – none: previously served Royal Navy: sometime removed to Canada: Occupation – Labourer: 5'4" tall, dark complexion, brown eyes, black hair; tattoos on both arms and neck: prior to enlistment was a serving member of 88th Victoria Rifles (Militia): volunteered and enlisted Victoria, British Columbia, 31 March 1915, posted 28th Battn. C.E.F.: served with the Expeditionary Force in France and Flanders from September 1915, wintering in the region of Ploegsteert Wood before moving up to the St. Eloi sector, and was reported missing, believed killed in action, 6 June 1916, during the fighting at Mount Sorrel, Zillebeke. Age 32. *unm.*

(Panel 28) Pte. 73417, Allen Ray Woodside, 28th Bn. Canadian Infantry (Saskatchewan Regt.), C.E.F.: *s.* of John Henry Woodside, of 'The Algoma Hotel,' 21, Centre Street, Port Arthur, Ontario: and elder brother to Pte. 73415, J.M. Woodside, 28th Canadian Infantry, killed the same day: *b.* Port Arthur, 25 February 1892: Religion – Church of England: Occupation – Street Railway Motorman: serving member of the Militia, enlisted Port Arthur, 23 October 1914. Killed in action on the afternoon of 6 June 1916, during the fighting at Mount Sorrel in which two companies of the battalion were virtually wiped out: Age 24. Among the battalion's dead that day six brothers – Reuben and William Gillespie, Alex and Robert Scott, John and Allen Woodside. (*IWGC record age 25*) See below.

(Panel 28) Pte. 73415, John Morris Woodside, 28th Bn. Canadian Infantry (Saskatchewan Regt.), C.E.F.: *s.* of John Henry Woodside, of 'The Algoma Hotel,' 21, Centre Street, Port Arthur, Ontario: and yr. brother to Pte. 73417, A.R. Woodside, 28th Canadian Infantry, killed the same day: *b.* Port Arthur, 28 April 1894: Religion – Church of England: Occupation – Machinist: serving member of the Militia, enlisted Port Arthur, 23 October 1914. Killed in action 6 June 1916, Mount Sorrel: Age 22. (*IWGC record age 23*) See above.

(Panel 28) Corpl. 76115, Wilfred Kirkpatrick Bramwell Ellis, 'D' Coy., 29th (Vancouver) Bn. Canadian Infantry (British Columbia Regt.), C.E.F.: *s.* of the late Ralph Arthur Frederick William Ellis, retired Military Officer; by his wife Ella Augusta (Coverack Cottage, Cookham), *dau.* of the late N.C.C. Bramwell: and late *husb.* to Priscilla Ellis (342, Garden Drive, Vancouver, British Columbia): *b.* London, 11 August 1892: *educ.* Durlston Court, Swanage, co. Dorset, and H.M.S. 'Worcester': went to Canada, 1912: joined 29th Canadian Infantry, September 1914: served with the Expeditionary Force in France and Flanders from 1915, and was killed in action at St. Eloi, 20 April 1916. Buried where he fell: Age 23. (*Archives Canada record unmarried*)

(Panel 28) Corpl. 75188, Benjamin Thomas Gunning, 'A' Coy., 29th (Vancouver) Bn. Canadian Infantry (British Columbia Regt.), C.E.F.: *s.* of Samuel Gunning, of 3642, 35th Avenue West, Vancouver, British Columbia, by his wife Margaret Elizabeth: and elder brother to Pte. 28860, J.St.C. Gunning, 16th Canadian Infantry, who fell 22 April 1915, at the Second Battle of Ypres. Killed in action before Passchendaele, 6 November 1917: Age 25. *unm.*

His brother John also has no known grave; he is recorded on Panel 26.

(Panel 28) Pte. 75370, Colin McDonald (*a.k.a.* C.A. Fairbairn), 29th (Vancouver) Bn. Canadian Infantry (British Columbia Regt.), C.E.F.: c/o J.A. McDonald Esq., Chilliwack, British Columbia: *s.* of James Fairbairn, of Hunt Street, Anderson's Bay, Dunedin, New Zealand, and his late wife Amelia (*d.*1910): and brother to Pte. 8/197, H.P. Fairbairn, Otago Regt., N.Z.E.F., wounded at Gallipoli, died, and buried at sea, 3 May 1915, en-route to Alexandria: *b.* Dunedin, New Zealand, 20 January 1892: Occupation – Farmer: previously served 3½ years New Zealand Mounted Rifles; serving member Canadian Mounted Rifles, enlisted Vancouver, 18 March 1915. Shot and killed by a German sniper, 26 September. 1915; Wytschaete Ridge: Age 23.

Having no known grave but the sea his brother Hunter is commemorated on the Lone Pine Memorial (75).

(Panel 28) Pte. 430164, Herbert Arthur Raincock, 29th (Vancouver) Bn. Canadian Infantry (British Columbia Regt.), C.E.F.: *s.* of George R. Raincock, of Penticton, British Columbia: and brother to Pte.

2021544, W.B. Raincock, 1st Depot Bn. (surv'd.): *b.* Gladstone, Manitoba, 27 December 1892: Religion – Church of England: Occupation – Plate Fitter: serving member 132nd Regt. (Militia); enlisted C.E.F. Willows Camp, Victoria, 3 March 1915; apptd. 29th Bn.. Killed in action 6 June 1916, 'during a heavy bombardment of our trenches at Hooge, prior to an enemy attack, a high-velocity shell penetrated the dugout occupied by Pte. Raincock killing him instantly.': Age 23.

(Panel 28) Pte. 76319, Eustace Pelham Rooff, 29th (Vancouver) Bn. Canadian Infantry (British Columbia Regt.), C.E.F.: *s.* of the late Pelham Hales Roof; London Stock Exchange, by his wife Fanny Maud (24, Lewisham Road, Kentish Town, London, N.W.): *b.* Highgate, London, N.W., 25 April 1890: Religion – Roman Catholic: *educ.* Burstow School, Horley, and Highgate School, London: Occupation – Mechanical Engineer: volunteered for Imperial Service; joined Canadian Expeditionary Force, Vancouver, 13 November 1914; after the outbreak of the European War; apptd. 29th Battn., 31 November: served with the Expeditionary Force in France and Flanders, and was killed in action at St. Eloi, 19 – 20 April 1916. His Captain wrote saying he died very bravely, having volunteered to deliver a message involving great risk; this he did, and a few hours after was killed by a shell while holding a crater: Age 25. *unm.* (*IWGC record age 26*)

(Panel 28) Pte. 75971, Amyas Henry Whipple, 29th (Vancouver) Bn. Canadian Infantry (British Columbia Regt.): *s.* of Ernest George Whipple, of 59, Junction Road, Sheffield, co. York, England, and Rose Hannah Whipple, his wife: and brother to Pte. 205471, L.O. Whipple, York & Lancaster Regt., died of wounds 9 July 1918, nr. Poperinghe: *b.* Grantham, co. Lincoln, 6 February 1890: Occupation – Salesman: formerly served 5 yrs 6th Dragoon Guards; a serving member (Bandsman) of the Militia; enlisted 29th Battn., Vancouver, 6 May 1915. Killed in action 19 April 1916: Age 26. *unm.* His parents have since removed to 14 – 16, Barnsley Road, Goldthorpe, Rotherham.

His brother Lancelot is buried in Hagle Dump Cemetery (I.J.8).

Sidney Winterbottom was a prolific writer, keenly observant, somewhat philosophical, he corresponded with his family almost every other week. Always cheerful, his letters were full of all manner of observations, snippets of news, and comments on matters at home, army and otherwise. On 30 October 1917 he wrote what would be his last letter; it contained no mention of the day spent in training over taped areas near Cassel or the Brigade inspection by the Army Commander, and no indication as to the Canadians impending part in the battle for Passchendaele. With apologies for not writing for two weeks, a request for tobacco and the quality of army bread, he commented on the Flanders landscape and scenery:– "… The part of the country we are now in reminds one of the fairy stories. Every little knoll has a quaint windmill on it which is no doubt hundreds of years old. They still work full speed whenever there is any wind – that is they can always work as it blows steadily here. The farms are occupied by quaint looking people who look like the pictures you see of people in Holland. The farm implements are as usual a century behind the time. The wagons are awfully clumsy affairs weighing hundreds of more pounds than our light serviceable wagons. The double trees are connected on to the tongue of the wagon and are about eight feet from the box. On to these the horses are connected by long chains. By heck you would laugh to see them. One thing these quaint people have is good horses. It would make a fellow in B.C. stare to see the size of some of these horses. I saw one of them haul a heavily loaded wagon through a muddy piece of ground. In B.C. it would take a good team to do the same stunt. The country is as flat as a pancake and very wet. Here and there are small hills dotted over with windmills. At present all the farmers are busy threshing wheat and carting in sugar beet and mangels. Believe me they know how to grow the latter here. The mangels often look like small stumps in size…"

Within a few days Sidney's idyllic impression of the picturesque 'fairy story' landscape and Flanders lifestyle would be replaced by a nightmare world of mud, filth, decay and every abomination known to man. At Passchendaele he would witness hell on earth, and death would find him.

(Panel 28) Pte. 116506, Sidney Amyas Winterbottom, 'C' Coy., 29th (Vancouver) Bn. Canadian Infantry (British Columbia Regt.), C.E.F.: *s.* of Arthur Winterbottom, of 136, Columbia Street, Kamloops, British Columbia, by his wife Jennie Louise: *b.* Calgary, Alberta, 22 November 1896: Religion – Church of

England: Occupation – Student: 5'8" tall, blue eyes, fair hair: enlisted Vernon, British Columbia, 15 July 1915: departed Halifax; White Star liner SS 'Lapland,' 16 July 1916: trained Cheriton Camp, England, July – October 1916; served with the Expeditionary Force in France and Flanders from the middle of the latter month, took part in the fighting at Vimy Ridge, and was killed in action 6 November 1917, at Abraham Heights, Passchendaele: Age 20. *unm.* (*IWGC record age 21*)

(Panel 28) Lieut. Myles Earl Merkley, 31st Bn. Canadian Infantry (Alberta Regt.), C.E.F.: *s.* of the late Frederick W. (& O.C.) Merkley, of Chesterville, Ontario: and elder brother to Pte. 113393, C.A. Merkley, 4th Canadian Mounted Rifles, killed in action 2 June 1916, at Sanctuary Wood: *b.* 16 February 1890: Religion – Presbyterian: Occupation Accountant: serving member 103rd Calgary Rifles (Militia); enlisted Capt., Calgary, 22 July 1916. Killed in action in the attack south of Passchendaele, 6 November 1917: Age 28. No remains recovered. He was married to Eva Merkley (922, 14th Avenue West, Calgary, Alberta).

His brother Clifford; recorded on Panel 32, is buried in Bedford House Cemetery (I.A.15/Enc.No.6).

(Panel 28) Lieut. Paul George Tofft, 'C' Coy., 31st Bn. Canadian Infantry (Alberta Regt.), C.E.F.: *b.* Copenhagen, Denmark, 18 May 1871: Religion – Lutheran: Occupation – Clerk, Supreme Court (Winnipeg): prior to emigrating to Canada served in Royal Danish Army; sometime served Royal North West Mounted Police, and, at the time of his enlistment, was a serving member of 16th Light Horse (Militia): enlisted 15th Avenue East, Calgary, 18 November 1914: 6' tall, fair complexion, blue eyes, brown hair: departed Calgary, May 1915: served with the Expeditionary Force in France from 18 September following, and was killed by shellfire 13 October 1915, nr. Kemmel, Belgium, while attempting to rescue a number of men buried by the explosion of a previous shell: Age 44. He leaves a wife, Mary Elizabeth Law Tofft (287, Colony Street, Winnipeg, Manitoba), and family. Capt. H.W. McGill said, "…I have only to close my eyes in order to recall many a scene about the old mess. As if it were yesterday, I can see Lieut. P.G. Tofft walking down the corridor and pausing outside the door of a room wherein he could hear the sound of voices or the clink of glasses. Very politely Tofft would tap on the door, and when bidden to enter, would merely thrust in his head and shoulders, asking in the most courtly tone, 'Gentlemen, may I be permitted to become your guest?' Tofft was always welcome and thoroughly appreciated any proffered hospitality. He was a Dane by birth. He had been in the Mounted Police and I believe possessed a military education obtained in his mother country. At any rate we all had great respect for his military knowledge, especially in matters of mess propriety and of general military deportment and etiquette. He was by many years the oldest of the subalterns, and by a strange irony of fate was the first to die in action. Tofft took his position as an officer with the utmost earnestness and was a striking and likeable character. Rightly or wrongly I have always thought of him in connection with the appellation, 'soldier of the old school,' whatever that phrase may mean." Corpl. 80039, T. Henderson, Ptes. 79083, A.J. Groves, 79182, F.D. McInnes, 79484, S. Sheridan and 79054, L.E. Callaghan were also killed.

Corpl. Henderson, Ptes. Groves, McInnes and Sheridan also have no known grave, all are recorded below; Pte. Callaghan is buried in Wulverghem-Lindenhoek Road Military Cemetery (III.C.17).

(Panel 28) Sergt. 79235, William Atkin Crossland, 31st Bn. Canadian Infantry (Alberta Regt.), C.E.F.: *s.* of J. Crossland, of 135, Gibraltar Street, Sheffield: *b.* Sheffield, England, 25 November 1892: Occupation Meat Cutter: attested 17 November 1914: dark complexion, black hair, grey eyes: served with the Expeditionary Force, and was killed in action at St. Eloi, 4 April 1916: Age 23. *unm.*

(Panel 28) Sergt. 79230, Walter Dalziel, D.C.M., Grenade Section, 31st Bn. Canadian Infantry (Alberta Regt.), C.E.F.: eldest *s.* of the late Walter Dalziel, by his wife Emma Annie (37, East Street, Brighton), formerly of 54A, Grand Parade; *dau.* of Thomas Austen: *b.* Tunbridge Wells, 7 October 1889: Religion – Church of England: *educ.* Elm Grove School, Brighton: Occupation – Topographer: volunteered and enlisted 16 September 1914; attested Calgary, 17 November 1914: served with the Expeditionary Force in France and Flanders, and was killed in action at Ypres, 6 June 1916. Buried there. He was awarded the D.C.M., the notification of which was received on the day of his death ('*London Gazette*,' 28 July 1916), for 'conspicuous gallantry. When his two officers were wounded he took charge of a bombing party, advanced under heavy firing to seize a point on which the enemy were advancing, and when he met them, forced them to retire; he then held his position all night until relieved.": Age 26. *unm.*

(Panel 28) Sergt. 80141, Leonard Edward Stump, 31st Bn. Canadian Infantry (Alberta Regt.), 2nd Infantry Bde., C.E.F.: *yst. s.* of George Stump, Hotel Proprietor; of Leigh Place, Cobham, co. Surrey, by his wife Harriett, *dau.* of Miles Allison, of Attleborough, co. Norfolk: *b.* Bayswater, London, W., 9 November 1890: *educ.* Thanet College, Margate; St. Pierre College, Calais: removed to Canada, June 1913; settled Chateau Frontenac, Quebec: Occupation – Chief Clerk: joined Canadian Infantry, February 1915: served with the Expeditionary Force in France and Flanders from September following, and was killed in action at Passchendaele 6 November 1917, three days before his 27th. birthday. Buried there. Lieut. E.A.C. Herbert wrote, "His comrades in the platoon have asked me to tell you how much they appreciated his sterling qualities; he was unselfish to a fault, and his cheerfulness at all times was a fine example to the other boys.": Age 26. *unm.* (*IWGC record age 27*)

(Panel 28) Corpl. 79033, John Martin Allan, 31st Bn. Canadian Infantry (Alberta Regt.), C.E.F.: late of 424, Sunnyside Boulevard, Calgary: *s.* of the late James Allan, of 'Woodlands,' Tillicoultry, Scotland, by his wife Jessie (Westerton Farm, Tillicoultry): *b.* 16 July 1886: Religion – Presbyterian: Occupation – Clerk: serving member 103rd (Calgary Rifles) Regt. (Militia); joined C.E.F., Calgary, 16 November 1914; apptd. 31st Bn., 30 January 1915: served with the Expeditionary Force in France from 18 September 1915. Shot and killed by a sniper during the attack on Passchendaele village, 6 November 1917; death was instantaneous. Buried near where he fell: Age 30. In 1922 Sunnyside Boulevard was renamed Memorial Drive in remembrance of the many men of Calgary who gave their lives in the Great War.

(Panel 28) Corpl. 79577, Desmond St.Clair George, 31st Bn. Canadian Infantry (Alberta Regt.), C.E.F.: *s.* of Capt. Henry George, M.R.C.S. (Canadian Army Medical Corps), and Mrs. B.M. George (2524, Fernwood Road, Victoria, British Columbia): *b.* 16 February 1894: Religion – Church of England: *educ.* Lindsay Thurber High School, Red Deer: Occupation – Law Student: attested 18 November 1914: fair complexion, blue eyes, brown hair: served with the Expeditionary Force and was killed in action at St. Eloi, 4 April 1916: Age 22. *unm.* One of thirteen former students remembered on the Lindsay Comprehensive High School Memorial Plaque, dedicated – 'To The Glory Of God And In Loving Memory Of The Students Of Red Deer Schools Who Were Killed In Action During The Great War 1914-1918: Full Of Promise Noble And Fearless They Gave Their Lives In Defence Of Their Country.'

(Panel 28) Corpl. 80039, Thomas Henderson, 31st Bn. Canadian Infantry (Alberta Regt.), C.E.F.: *husb.* to Jessie Henderson (759, Athabasca Avenue, Edmonton): *b.* Tinewald Parish, Dumfries, 5 June 1886: Occupation – Mechanical Engineer: previously served 18 months, 9th (Glasgow Highlanders) Bn. Highland Light Infantry (T.F.), Scotland: enlisted Calgary, 16 December 1914. Killed by shellfire 13 October 1915, at Kemmel, while attempting to rescue comrades buried by a previous explosion: Age 29. Lieut. P.G. Tofft, Ptes. 79083, A.J. Groves, 79182, F.D. McInnes, 79484, S. Sheridan and 79054, L.E. Callaghan were also killed.

(Panel 28) L/Corpl. 80138, George Francis Allan, 31st Bn. Canadian Infantry (Alberta Regt.), C.E.F.: *s.* of the late Major Matthew A. Allan, and his wife Elizabeth (81, Fitzroy Street, Charlottetown, Prince Edward Island): *b.* 19 December 1888: Religion – Presbyterian: Occupation – Bank Clerk: serving member 103rd (Calgary Rifles) Regt. (Militia); previously served 2 yrs. Artillery, 2 yrs. Army Medical Corps, 2 yrs. Infantry; joined C.E.F., Calgary, 15 February 1915; apptd. 31st Bn., 26 February: served with the Expeditionary Force in France from 18 September 1915. Killed in action 13 June 1916, nr. Zillebeke, Ypres. Buried 20 yards behind Trench R70, just left of Armagh Wood. Actual grave not located; Memorial Cross erected (between rows D & E) Reninghelst New Military Cemetery (16 June 1919): Age 25.

(Panel 28) L/Corpl. 79858, Arthur William Milne, 'B' Coy., 31st Bn. Canadian Infantry (Alberta Regt.), 6th Brigade, 2nd Division, C.E.F.: only *s.* of Frederick Law Milne, of 'Ochiltrie', Chelston, Torquay, Retired Engineer, by his wife Amy Beatrice, *dau.* of John Beevor Prest, of York: *b.* Carlsdahl, Kortfors, Sweden, 31 July 1885: *educ.* Weston, Torquay, and Mittweida, Saxony: removed to Canada, March 1911; settled Colinton, Alberta, as Homesteader: volunteered for Imperial Service, enlisted

Canadian Expeditionary Force, November 1914: came over with 2nd Contingent, May 1915: served with the Expeditionary Force in France and Flanders from 13 September following, and was killed in action at Ypres, 13 June 1916. Buried in Sanctuary Wood: Grave unlocated. Age 30. *unm.*

(Panel 28) Pte. 446906, Graham Edward Adam, 31st Bn. Canadian Infantry (Alberta Regt.), C.E.F.: *s.* of James Graham Adam, of 1805, 17th Street West, Calgary, Alberta, and his wife Beatrice Eleanor: Religion – Church of England. Missing, presumed killed on or about 6 November 1917; Passchendaele: Age 20. No remains recovered.

(Panel 28) Pte. 80009, Hugh Burney, 31st Bn. Canadian Infantry (Alberta Regt.), C.E.F.: *s.* of Paul Burney, of Rockmount, Whitewall, Belfast: *b.* Belfast, Ireland, 21 November 1888: Religion – Presbyterian: Occupation – Teamster: fair complexion, blue eyes, medium fair hair: attested Edmonton, 12 December 1914: served with the Expeditionary Force, and was killed in action at St. Eloi, Belgium, 4 April 1916: Age 27. *unm.*

(Panel 28) Pte. 79083, Arthur John Groves, 31st Bn. Canadian Infantry (Alberta Regt.), C.E.F.: stepson to Mrs M.A. MacDonald (Dundas, Ontario): *b.* Markham, Ontario, 25 May 1892: Occupation – Printer: enlisted Claresholm, Alberta, 18 November 1914. Killed by the bursting of an enemy shell 13 October 1915, at Kemmel, while digging out comrades buried by a previous explosion; Lieut. P.G. Tofft, Corpl. 80039, T. Henderson, Ptes. 79054, L.E. Callaghan, 79182, F.D. McInnes and 79484, S. Sheridan were also killed: Age 23. *unm.*

(Panel 28) Pte. 79940, William James Imrie, 31st Bn. Canadian Infantry (Alberta Regt.), C.E.F.: *s.* of Alexander Imrie, of Hayfield, Kinross, Scotland, by his wife Emily: *b.* Kinross, 5 November 1893: Religion – Presbyterian: *educ.* Locally, thereafter entered an apprenticeship with a firm of Solicitors: removed to Canada, took up an appointment as Clerk; Bank of Montreal, Medicine Hat, Alberta: volunteered and enlisted Medicine Hat, 11 November 1914: proceeded to England after a brief period of training, from whence, after further training, he went to France, autumn 1915, and almost immediately took part in his first action; thereafter took part in all the operations in which his battalion was engaged during the spring of 1916, and was killed instantaneously on the night of 5 June 1916, with two of his comrades when, during a heavy enemy artillery bombardment, a shell struck and demolished the dug-out in which they were sleeping: Age 22. *unm.* Correspondence should be addressed c/o W.J. Imrie, Esq., Abergavenny, Wales. (*IWGC record age 23*)

(Panel 28) Pte. 79182, Finlay D. MacInnes, 31st Bn. Canadian Infantry (Alberta Regt.), C.E.F.: *s.* of Finlay MacInnes, of 38, Lawrence Place, Downhill, Glasgow, Scotland: and yr. brother to Pte. 73174, J.F. MacInnes, 28th Canadian Infantry, killed in action 7 April 1916: *b.* Glasgow, co. Lanark, 22 December 1888: Religion – Presbyterian: *educ.* Hillhead High School, Glasgow: Occupation – Surveyor: previously served 6th Highland Light Infantry: enlisted C.E.F., Edmonton, 16 November 1914: served in France and Flanders from September 1915, and was killed in action at Kemmel, 13 October 1915, by shellfire while attempting to dig out comrades buried by a previous shell burst: Age 25. *unm.* Lieut. P.G. Tofft, Corpl. 80039, T. Henderson, Ptes. 79054, L.E. Callaghan, 79083, A.J. Groves and 79484, S. Sheridan were also killed.

His brother John also has no known grave; he is recorded above.

(Panel 28) Pte. 79102, Alex Moncrieff, 31st Bn. Canadian Infantry (Alberta Regt.), C.E.F.: *s.* of George Moncrieff, of 8, George Street, Cellardyke, co. Fife: *b.* co. Fife, Scotland, 23 June, 1881: Religion – Presbyterian: Occupation – Cooper: fair complexion, grey eyes, light brown hair: previously served six years Black Watch: attested 16 November 1914: served with the Expeditionary Force, and was killed in action at St. Eloi, 5 April 1916: Age 34. *unm.*

(Panel 28) Pte. 80227, Leonard Godfrey Rope, 31st Bn. Canadian Infantry (Alberta Regt.), C.E.F: *s.* of Aaron (& Ellen Alice) Rope, of 1, Bergh Apton, co. Norfolk, England: and brother to Pte. CH/1472/S, H.A. Rope, Royal Marine Light Infantry, died of wounds 5 May 1917: *b.* Bergh Apton, 8 April 1888: Religion – Church of England: Occupation – Farmer: 5'9" tall, fair complexion, blue eyes, brown hair:

joined C.E.F., Calgary, 8 April 1915; posted 31st Battn., 23 April: proceeded to France, and was killed in action there on the eve of his 28th. birthday; 7 April 1916.

His brother Hubert is buried in Etaples Military Cemetery (XVIII.H.8).

(Panel 28) Pte. 80084, Frank Elson Rowley, 31st Bn. Canadian Infantry (Alberta Regt.), C.E.F.: *s.* of John Rowley, of 31, Walsall Street, Willenhall, co. Stafford, England: *b.* 9 October 1890: served with the Expeditionary Force, and was killed in action at St. Eloi, 6 April 1916.

(Panel 28) Pte. 79484, Stanley Sheridan, 31st Bn. Canadian Infantry (Alberta Regt.), C.E.F.: c/o Joseph Sheridan, Washington, United States: *b.* Liverpool, England, 4 March 1885: Occupation – Car Man: enlisted Edmonton, Alberta, 16 November 1914. Killed by shellfire 13 October 1915, at Kemmel, Belgium, while in the process of attempting to rescue comrades buried by a previous shell: Age 30. Lieut. P.G. Tofft, Corpl. 80039, T. Henderson, Ptes. 79054, L.E. Callaghan, 79083, A.J. Groves and 79182, F.D. McInnes were also killed.

Lieut. Tofft, Corpl. Henderson, Ptes. Groves and McInnes also have no known grave, all are recorded above; Pte. Callaghan is buried in Wulverghem-Lindenhoek Road Military Cemetery (III.C.17).

(Panel 28) Pte. 439000, Alfred Ernest Steels, 31st Bn. Canadian Infantry (Alberta Regt.), C.E.F.: *s.* of Philip Steels, of Dungammon, Ontario: *b.* London, Ontario, 10 February 1883: Religion – Church of England: Occupation – Woodsman: attested 15 February 1915; served with the Expeditionary Force, and was killed in action at St. Eloi, 6 April 1916: Age 35. *unm.*

"Monday, April 17, 1916: Our battalion was out on fatigue again last night, digging a communication trench at the back of T16, near Shelley Lane. Unfortunately the enemy got wind of us and opened up with shells and machine-gun fire. Being in the open a few of our number got caught. Miller, a Scot from Wick, had his arm almost blown off, his legs broken, and other injuries, and died on the way out. He was buried at Voormezeele, to the south of the road. The two of us were together, immediately before he left for the line. Grimes and Sharp were also wounded, whilst Webber is missing…A brother of Rowley who was killed at St. Eloi, was here making enquiries. He was quite a youngster and belonged to an English battalion. He appeared down in the mouth over his errand. Poor Miller, amongst his personal effects was his pocket book, with on one side an identification card, stating his next of kin, and on the other side a photo of his girl in the north of Scotland…A search party has been organized to look for Webber."

"Tuesday, April 18, 1916: Webber has been found. He was half buried by a shell, and lay in the shell hole. He was in pieces, even his badges and knife being bent or broken. His tunic was in threads. Being torn to ribbons, he had to be left where he was. His personal effects and identification disc were removed. An Englishman, a minister's son, he was farming near Langdon, Alta.": *Pte. Fraser, 31st Battn.*

(Panel 28) Pte. 80069, Frederic William Webber, 31st Bn. Canadian Infantry (Alberta Regt.), C.E.F.: *s.* of George Henry (& Fanny) Webber, of 'Laburnum View,' West Malvern, co. Worcester; previously resident 5, Dean Street, Coventry: *b.* Port Glasgow, Scotland, 3 August 1892: joined C.E.F., Calgary, 14 December 1914; posted 31st Bn. 30 January 1915. Killed in action at St. Eloi, 16 April 1916: Age 23.

(Panel 28) Corpl. 639413, William Henry Gibbins, 38th Bn. Canadian Infantry (Eastern Ontario Regt.), C.E.F.: *s.* of George Gibbins, of Godmanchester, co. Huntingdon, England, by his wife Mary, *née* Edwards: brother to John W. Gibbins, of Godmanchester; and L/Sergt. 152423, E.J. Gibbins, 43rd Canadian Infantry, killed in action 8 August 1918: *b.* Godmanchester, 20 February 1890: Religion – Church of England: Occupation – Farmer: 5'3¼" tall, dark complexion, brown eyes, black hair: enlisted Brockville, Ontario, 21 December 1915. Killed in action 30 October 1917; Passchendaele, Belgium: Age 28. He was married to Emma Jane Gibbins (Wellington Street, Gananoque, Ontario).

His brother Ellis (*IWGC record Gibbons*) also has no known grave; he is commemorated on the Canadian National (Vimy) Memorial.

(Panel 28) Pte. 633382, Clifford Shaver, No.3 Platoon, 'A' Coy., 38th Bn. Canadian Infantry (Eastern Ontario Regt.), C.E.F.: 6th *s.* of William Shaver, of Mountain, Ontario, by his wife Jessie: *b.* 30 June 1896: Religion – Methodist: Occupation – Farmer: 5'10" tall, dark complexion, brown eyes, brown hair: enlisted 1 February 1916, aged 19 years: went to Barriefield; trained there until 25 October following; thereafter sailed from Halifax with 154th Battn.:trained England, until 24 May 1917; proceeded to France: served with the Expeditionary Force there, enduring five long months of hardship; being on one occasion 41 days in the trenches without rest, and was killed in action at Ypres 30 October 1917. In writing to Pte. Shaver's mother, his Platoon Officer, Lieut. Arthur G. Starkings, said, "It is with sorrow that I write to say how deeply I sympathise with you in the sad loss of your son Clifford. I find it difficult to do this however, first because I feel that words are so cheap at such a time and again because, although we shall miss him, we know that you will miss him more. Believe me when I say that he was loved and respected by all. His comrades valued his friendship and mourn his loss, while for myself I can only add that he was one of my best and bravest men. It was during a heavy barrage when we were expecting a counter attack that he met his death, nobly standing by his Lewis gun, coolly awaiting the expected attack. His conduct was an example to us all and it may comfort you to know that his death was a painless one. We buried him near the spot where he gallantly fell, which we could give you sometime in the near future should you desire it. His personal effects, a testament, two fountain pens, a pair of scissors and a ring, I have enclosed. His pay roll has been handed in to the orderly room. For us it remains to carry on, following his example, and while we continue this struggle we trust that strength may come to you to help you in your bitter loss. May God be with you in your sad bereavement." Sergt. 410076, John A. Delaney wrote, "No doubt you have been informed of the death of your son Clifford by this time, so this will not be a surprise. All the boys of No. 3 Platoon wish me to express their deep regret to you for the loss of so fine a son and comrade. He was well liked throughout the Battalion and I suppose the God of all wars had a better place for him. I suppose he has told you that he was in the Lewis Gun Section. I can assure you we were sorry to lose so fine a boy, always devoted to his duty and willing to do everything possible to help others along. I can give you some consolation in the fact that he did not suffer. He was killed instantly. I was not more than ten feet away from him when it happened. He was buried on Passchendaele Ridge and if you wish for any further particulars let me know and I will be only too glad to help you all I can." The Ontario newspaper reported:– "It is our painful duty this week to chronicle the death of Clifford Shaver, sixth son of Mr and Mrs Wm. Shaver, of Vancamp. On Friday 16th. inst., they received a telegram saying Clifford was killed by a shell on October 30th, somewhere in Belgium…Clifford was of a quiet unassuming disposition, and endeared himself to all with whom he came in contact. He was a good brother and an exceptionally kind and loving son. He will be very much missed both in the home circle and in the community. He leaves to mourn his demise, his father and mother, three sisters and six brothers as follows; Mrs Edgar Brown, of Inkerman; Mrs Arnold Suffel, of Inkerman; and Miss Nellie at home; Ernest, of Winchester; Russell and Ira (somewhere in France); Harry of North Dakota; Daniel and Frank at home. The sympathy of the entire community is extended to the bereaved and sorrowing ones.": Age 21. *unm.*

(Panel 28) Corpl. 873, George Hope Whitelaw, 42nd (Canadian Highlanders) Bn. Canadian Infantry (Quebec Regt.), C.E.F.: only *s.* of Alexander Francis Whitelaw, Shepherd; of 'Marchcleugh,' Oxnam, Jedburgh, co. Roxburgh, by his late wife Margaret, *dau.* of James Patterson: *b.* Crailing, co. Roxburgh, 6 November 1888: *educ.* Jedburgh: went to Canada, May 1914; settled at Ottawa: Occupation – Constable: enlisted Canadian Army Service Corps, 9 December following: came to England with 2nd Canadian Contingent, February 1915: served with the Expeditionary Force in France and Flanders from September following: transf'd. Canadian Highlanders, October 1917, and was killed in action at Passchendaele Ridge 16 November of the same year. Buried where he fell: Age 29 years, 10 days. *unm.*

(Panel 28) Pte. 841615, Alexander Forrester, 42nd (Canadian Highlanders) Bn. Canadian Infantry (Quebec Regt.), C.E.F.: *s.* of Alexander Forrester, of Dundee, Scotland: *b.* Dundee, 23 May 1873: Religion – Presbyterian: Occupation – Driller: previously served 8 yrs. Cameronians (Sco. Rif.); (2 yrs. South Africa): joined C.E.F., Montreal, 24 February 1916; apptd. 148th (Overseas) Bn., 3 March 1916. Killed in action 16 November 1917; Trenches nr. Passchendaele: Age 44. He was married to Annie L. Forrester (5519, Ninth Avenue, Rosemount, Montreal), and all effects / correspondence should be forwarded to that address. He was father to six children. Remains 'Unknown Canadian Soldier. 42' recovered unmarked grave (20.V.30.c.71.40); identified – 2 Damaged Discs, Collar Badge; reinterred, registered 16 March 1927. (*IWGC record age 48*) *Buried in Sanctuary Wood Cemetery (III.H.7).*

Ever To Be Remembered

(Panel 28) Pte. 135832, Albert Riddlesworth, 42nd (Canadian Highlanders) Bn. Canadian Infantry (Quebec Regt.), C.E.F.: *s.* of William Henry (& Lydia) Riddlesworth, of 122, Symon Street, Mimico, Ontario: *b.* Stockport, England, 10 June 1895: Religion – Church of England: Occupation – Colour Maker: joined C.E.F., Toronto, 27 July 1915; proceeded overseas 11 August: served with the Expeditionary Force in France, and was killed in action 10 a.m, 9 April 1916, Trench 65, Sanctuary Wood, 'being hit by a fragment from an enemy shell.' Age 20.

(Panel 28) Pte. 445138, Francis Savoie (*a.k.a.* Frank Savoy), 42nd (Canadian Highlanders) Bn. Canadian Infantry (Quebec Regt.), C.E.F.: *s.* of Henri Savoie, of Paquetville, New Brunswick, by his wife Marie Obeline: *b.* 15 September 1899: Religion – Roman Catholic: 5'7" tall, brown eyes, brown hair; large birth mark (4"x5") across lower ribs and abdomen: enlisted 55th Battn., Sussex, New Brunswick, 30 June 1915; aged 15 years: served with the Expeditionary Force in France from 9 October 1915, transf'd. 42nd Battn. Reported missing / believed killed in action, on or since 2 – 3 June 1916; trenches Maple Copse – Sanctuary Wood. No remains recovered for burial: **Age 16.**

(Panel 28) Lieut. William Arnold Palmer, 43rd (Cameron Highlanders) Bn. Canadian Infantry (Manitoba Regt.), C.E.F.: late of 631, Croydon Avenue, Winnipeg: *s.* of Rev. Frederick William Henry Palmer, M.A., Headmaster, Hall's Grammar School; of Snettisham, King's Lynn, co. Norfolk, by his wife Charlotte Vilbois: *b.* Snettisham, 18 October 1887: *educ.* Privately, and Hall's Grammar School: Occupation – nine years Bank Clerk, Messrs Lloyds Bank Ltd.; removed to Canada (1913), joined Bank of Montreal, Winnipeg: previously served 1 year, 2nd Gloucestershire Regt.; enlisted 43rd Battn., Winnipeg, 12 March 1915; Pte. 421040: served with the Expeditionary Force in France from mid-summer of that year: wounded at Courcelette, during the heavy fighting at the Somme, 1916, and evacuated to England: following treatment and recuperation, trained for and received his commission: returned to his battalion as Lieut., July 1917, and was killed in action 14 November 1917, during operations at Passchendaele: Age 30. Erected by public subscription in memory of those who sacrificed their lives in the Great War, Lieut. Palmer is remembered on the Snettisham War Memorial. He was married to Janet Elizabeth Palmer (106, Noble Avenue, Elmwood, Winnipeg).

(Panel 28) Corpl. 420977, Frederick Percival Bousfield, 43rd Bn. Canadian Infantry (Manitoba Regt.), C.E.F.: *s.* of Frederick Ladlay Bousfield, of 844, Home Street, Winnipeg, Manitoba, and 'Rusticana,' Winnipeg Beach, by his wife Hannah: *b.* Cotehill, co. Cumberland, 8 March 1896: Occupation – Carpenter: previously served 1 year, 79th Cameron Highlanders of Canada; enlisted C.E.F., Winnipeg, 29 January 1915. One of four 43rd Battn. men killed in action 7 June 1916, by shellfire; Zillebeke trenches: Age 20. *unm.*

(Panel 28) L/Corpl. 153341, James Courage Hunter, 43rd (Cameron Highlanders) Bn. Canadian Infantry (Manitoba Regt.), C.E.F.: *s.* of Mary A. Hunter (596, Warsaw Avenue, Winnipeg): *b.* Woodside, Aberdeen, 25 February 1886: Religion – Presbyterian: Occupation – Policeman: 6'4" tall, dark complexion, blue eyes, brown hair: member 79th Cameron Highlanders of Canada (Militia); joined 43rd Battn. C.E.F., Winnipeg, 5 July 1915: served with the Expeditionary Force in France from 22 February 1916, and was shot and killed at Sanctuary Wood, 10.45 (10–50) a.m., on the morning of 31 March 1916, by a sniper. Buried in Sanctuary Wood: Age 30. *unm.* Although 43rd Battn. lost a further three men killed on 31 March 1916, the time of L/Corpl. Hunter's death distinguishes him as the battalion's second Active Service fatality attributable to enemy action.

(Panel 28) Pte. 153557, Frederic Edwards, 43rd (Cameron Highlanders) Bn. Canadian Infantry (Manitoba Regt.), C.E.F.: *s.* of William Edwards, of 13, Perthy, Ellesmere, co. Salop, by his wife Annie: *b.* 5 December 1892: Occupation – Farmer: member 79th Cameron Highlanders of Canada (Militia); enlisted Winnipeg, 26 July 1915. Killed by shellfire (shrapnel) 24 April 1916; Pte. Hurrell was also killed, and 5 others wounded: Age 23. *unm.*

(Panel 28) Pte. 421121, Donald Scott Ellis, 43rd (Cameron Highlanders) Bn. Canadian Infantry (Manitoba Regt.), C.E.F.: *s.* of David Ellis, of 'The Poplars,' Fossoway, Rumbling Bridge, co. Kinross, by his wife Catherine, *née* Scott: *b.* Fossoway, 19 April 1887: Religion – Presbyterian: Occupation – Accountant: 5'11" tall, fresh complexion, blue eyes, red-brown hair: enlisted Shorncliffe Camp, co. Kent, 16 September 1915; posted 43rd Battn.: served with the Expeditionary Force in France and Flanders from 22 February 1916, and was killed by shellfire 31 March 1916, while on a carrying party to the front line, Sanctuary Wood – Mount Sorrel; two other men were wounded: Age 28. *unm.*

(Panel 28) Pte. 420404, Douglas Hurrell, 43rd (Cameron Highlanders) Bn. Canadian Infantry (Manitoba Regt.), C.E.F.: *b.* Malden, co. Surrey, 3 June 1896: Occupation – Clerk: enlisted Winnipeg, 9 January 1915: served with the Expeditionary Force in France and Flanders from February 1916, and was killed by shellfire (shrapnel) 24 April 1916; Pte. Edwards was also killed, and 5 other men wounded: Age 19. Correspondence should be addressed c/o his brother William Hurrell, Esq., 489, Newman Street, Winnipeg.

(Panel 28) Pte. 420747, Thomas Lumsden, 43rd Bn. Canadian Infantry (Manitoba Regt.), C.E.F.: late of 588, Warsaw Avenue, Winnipeg: *s.* of Charles M. Lumsden, of 59, Essex Avenue, St. Vital, Manitoba, by his wife Grace: and *yr.* brother to Gnr. 87029, J. Lumsden, Canadian Field Artillery, killed in action 24 April 1917, at the Battle of Arras: *b.* Winnipeg, 5 January 1894: Occupation – Railway Brakeman: enlisted Winnipeg, 6 January 1915. Killed by shell fire 7 June 1916; Zillebeke trenches: Age 22. *unm.*

His brother John is buried in Ecoivres Military Cemetery, Mont-St.-Eloi (VI.G.3).

(Panel 28) Pte. 153448, Archibald MacDonald, 43rd Bn. Canadian Infantry (Manitoba Regt.), C.E.F.: *s.* of William MacDonald, of Balvicar, co. Argyll, by his wife Elizabeth: late *husb.* to Mary MacDonald (346, Lipton Street, Winnipeg): *b.* Kildrandon, co. Argyll, 8 February 1886: Religion – Methodist: Occupation – Police Officer: previously served 6 yrs, Royal Argyle & Bute (T.F.), serving member 79th (Cameron Highlanders of Canada); enlisted Winnipeg, 19 July 1915. Killed in action 11 June 1916: Age 29. Remains 'Unknown Canadian L/Corpl. 43' recovered unmarked grave (28.I.24.b.55.15); Sanctuary Wood Cemetery; identified – 2 Damaged Discs, Collar Badge; reinterred, registered 17 March 1927. These remains were discovered during the work of excavation for the re-interment of isolated remains in this cemetery. *Buried in Sanctuary Wood Cemetery (III.H.13).*

(Panel 28) Pte. 153783, Murdoch 'Murdo' MacLeod, 'B' Coy., 43rd Bn. Canadian Infantry (Manitoba Regt.), C.E.F.: *s.* of Duncan J. MacLeod, of 7, Ranich, Stornoway, Isle of Lewis, by his wife Betsy: *b.* Stornoway, 14 October 1888: Occupation – Dredgeman: serving member 79th Cameron Highlanders of Canada (Militia); enlisted Winnipeg, 29 September 1915. Killed by shellfire 7 June 1916: Age 27. *unm.* Corpl. 420977, F.P. Bousfield, Ptes. 420747, T. Lumsden, and 420871, K.W. MacLeod were also killed.

Corpl. Bousfield and Pte. Lumsden also have no known grave, they are recorded above. Buried at the time in Valley Cottages Cemetery; after the war the grave of Pte. K.W. MacLeod could not be located, he is commemorated by a Special Memorial in Railway Dugouts Burial Ground (Transport Farm).

(Panel 28) Pte. 153261, Robert Moscrop, 43rd (Cameron Highlanders) Bn. Canadian Infantry (Manitoba Regt.), C.E.F.: *s.* of Richard Moscrop, of 11, New Street, Cockermouth, co. Cumberland, by his wife Grace: and elder brother to L/Corpl. 71908, C. Moscrop, 9th Coy., Machine Gun Corps (Inf.), killed in action 5 June 1917, at Arras: *b.* Tallentire, 24 July 1879: Occupation – Labourer: serving member 79th Cameron Highlanders of Canada (Militia); enlisted Winnipeg, 18 June 1915: served with the Expeditionary Force in France and Flanders from 22 February 1916, and was killed in action (shellfire) 26 April following: Age 36. Inscribed – 'Our Glorious Dead Who Died In The Great War 1914-1919. Let Those Who Come After See To It That These Names Be Not Forgotten…They Found Death In The

Path Of Duty' – The brothers Moscrop are remembered on the Cockermouth War Memorial. (*IWGC record age 42*)

His brother Clark also has no known grave; he is commemorated on the Arras (Faubourg d'Amiens) Memorial (Bay 10).

(Panel 28) Pte. 722071, William Thain, 43rd (Cameron Highlanders) Bn. Canadian Infantry (Manitoba Regt.), C.E.F.: *s.* of the late William Thain, Baker; of Aberdeen, by his wife Margaret, *dau.* of John Robertson: *b.* Newtownhill, co. Kincardine, 26 December 1894: *educ.* Aberdeen: went to Canada, April 1913: settled Aneroid, Saskatchewan: Occupation – Farmer: enlisted June 1915: served with the Expeditionary Force in France and Flanders from March 1917, and was killed in action at Passchendaele 26 October following. Buried there: Age 22. *unm.*

(Panel 28) Pte. 153695, Frederick Armados Varrin, 43rd (Cameron Highlanders) Bn. Canadian Infantry (Manitoba Regt.), C.E.F.: *s.* of the late Joseph Varrin, of Dacre, Ontario, by his marriage to Catherine Scully, *née* Varrin (Griffith, Ontario): *b.* Griffith, 5 March 1892: Occupation – Locomotive Fireman: serving member 79th Cameron Highlanders of Canada (Militia); enlisted Winnipeg, 18 August 1915: served with the Expeditionary Force in France from 22 February 1916, and died of wounds (shrapnel) 23 April 1916; Maple Copse – Sanctuary Wood.: Age 24. *unm.*

(Panel 28) Lieut. Charles Lucas Jeffrey, 44th Bn. Canadian Infantry (New Brunswick Regt.), C.E.F.: *s.* of Charles W. Lucas, of 90, Powell Avenue, Ottawa, by his wife Laura Halifax: *b.* 1897: *educ.* Queen's University. Killed in action in the vicinity of Bannf House, 27 October 1917, at the 2nd Battle of Passchendaele: Age 20. *unm.*

(Panel 28) Pte. 830571, James Fraser Moore, 44th Bn. Canadian Infantry (New Brunswick Regt.), C.E.F.: late of 68, Grace Street, Winnipeg: *husb.* to Jessie K. Arbuthnot, *née* Moore, (513, Spence Street, Winnipeg, Manitoba): and father to Pte. 147566, R. Moore, 78th Canadian Infantry, died No. 44. C.C.S., Poperinghe, two weeks previously: *b.* Montrose, Scotland, 1 July 1873: Religion – Presbyterian: Occupation – Boilermaker: 5'3" tall, fresh complexion, brown eyes, and fair hair: previously served 5 years, 1st Bn. Highland Light Infantry; enlisted Winnipeg, 3 January 1916. Killed by shellfire on the evening of, 14 November 1917, while at work digging new support line east of Ypres: Age 44. (*IWGC record 15 November*)

His son Robert is buried in Nine Elms British Cemetery (VIII.F.12).

(Panel 28) Pte. 198390, John Ervine Bourns, 46th Bn. Canadian Infantry (Saskatchewan Regt.), C.E.F.: late of Fort William, Ontario: *s.* of the late John Henry Bourns, by his wife Sarah Jane (Whitewood, Saskatchewan): and yr. brother to Pte. 104133, R.H. Bourns, 68th Canadian Infantry, died 22 January 1916: *b.* Ireland, 1 July 1884: Occupation – Locomotive Engineer: enlisted Fort William, 2 December 1915. Killed in action 26 October 1917; Passchendaele, Belgium: Age 33. He was married to Nellie Bourns (59, Third Estate, Barlby Road, Selby, co. York). (*IWGC record age 34*)

His brother Robert is buried in Whitewood Cemetery, Saskatchewan.

(Panel 28) Pte. 782459, John Campbell Buchanan, 46th Bn. Canadian Infantry (Saskatchewan Regt.), C.E.F.: 4th *s.* of the late Donald Buchanan, of Lichentuim, Glencoe, by his wife Margaret ('Khedive,' 222, Fairford Street West., Moose Jaw, Saskatchewan), *dau.* of M. McDougall, of Kilmuir, Skye: *b.* Glencoe, co. Argyle, 31 January 1895: *educ.* Ballacuish Public School, and Oban High School: joined Canadian Forces, June 1916: came to England with 128th (Moose Jaw's Own) Battn., August following: subsequently transf'd. 46th Battn.: served with the Expeditionary Force in France and Flanders from May 1917. Reported wounded and missing after the fighting at Passchendaele, 26 October following; now assumed to have been killed in action on or about that date: Age 22. *unm.*

(Panel 28) Pte. 910790, Campbell Arnott Matheson, 46th Bn. Canadian Infantry (Saskatchewan Regt.), C.E.F.: late of Humboldt, Saskatchewan: *s.* of the late Alexander Matheson, Farmer; by his wife Jennie (435, 13th Street, Brandon, Manitoba): and brother to Lieut. F.A. Matheson, M.C., Canadian Light Horse (surv'd.): *b.* Chelmsford, Ontario, 1 February 1898: *educ.* Brandon Collegiate: Occupation – Clerk; Canadian Bank of Commerce: member 99th Regt., Brandon (Militia): enlisted 196th (Western Universities) Battn.,

Humboldt, 7 April 1916: transf'd. 46th Battn., France, March 1917. Killed in action at Passchendaele 26 October 1917, while acting as Company Runner: Age 19. In a letter to Mrs Matheson, his Company Commander wrote, "A very dependable and good soldier. I shall miss him more than any man we lost in the last attack. Please accept my most sincere sympathy in the loss of a very brave and God-fearing son."

(Panel 28) Lieut. John William Hinckesman, 47th (British Columbia) Bn., Canadian Infantry (Western Ontario Regt.), C.E.F.: *s.* of the late John William Hinckesman, of Charlcotte, Bridgnorth, co. Salop, by his wife Marion Margaret (Hadley, Droitwich, co. Worcester), *dau.* of the Rev. David Vaughan: *b.* Bridgnorth, 15 September 1891: *educ.* there: removed to Canada, 1907; settled at Penticton: Occupation – Rancher: joined Canadian Forces, Penticton, British Columbia, 10 August 1914: came to England with 2nd Canadian Contingent: served with the Expeditionary Force in France and Flanders from September 1915: gazetted Lieut. 28 November 1916, and was killed in action at Passchendaele 27 October 1917. Buried there. An officer wrote, "In his death the battalion has sustained a great loss, as he was looked upon as one of the most promising officers, and was actually due for immediate promotion for the good work he has done in this unit. By all he was looked upon as a thoroughly efficient, courageous and reliable officer, and the men of B. Coy., with whom he was more familiar, feel his loss particularly. During the whole of his connection with this battalion his relationship with all ranks was one of a most pleasant character. The operation in which the battalion was engaged at the time resulted very successfully, and the work done by Lieut. J.W. Hinckesman on the night of the 27th was most creditably performed, and the information he obtained was of great value, the situation being very precarious at the time.": Age 26. Lieut. Hinckesman had three brothers on active service. Remains 'Unknown Canadian Officer, Lt. 47 Cans.;' recovered unmarked grave 28.D.12.c.40.15; identified, reinterred Tyne Cot, 29 July 1921. (*IWGC record...husband of Eva C. Hutchison (formerly Hinckesman), of 19, Ingleston Place, Greenock, Scotland, and Age 27.) Buried in Tyne Cot Cemetery (XXXVI.E.24).*

(Panel 28) Corpl. 628614, George Ernest Foskett, 47th Bn. Canadian Infantry (Western Ontario Regt.), C.E.F.: *s.* of Joseph M. Foskett, Carpenter; of Harris, Saskatchewan, late of 18, Raunds Road, Stanwick, nr. Wellingborough, co. Northampton, by his wife Mary: and yr. brother to Corpl. 7815, C.W. Foskett, 1st Duke of Cornwall's Light Infantry, who fell four days later: *b.* Northampton, England, 7 October 1887: Religion – Church of England: removed, with his parents, to Canada, 1907: Occupation – Machinist: 5'5¼" tall, dark complexion, brown eyes, black hair: serving member of the Militia, enlisted Vernon, British Columbia, 29 June 1915: served with the Expeditionary Force in France and Flanders from 1916: took part in the fighting on the Ancre Heights, Somme, October – November 1916; Vimy Ridge, April – May 1917; and was killed in action 26 October 1917 on which date his battalion was attacking in a north-easterly direction from the vicinity of Zonnebeke toward Crest Farm and Passchendaele: Age 30. *unm.* Shortly before his death Corpl. Foskett enjoyed a period of leave with his aunt, Mrs. Clarke, 'Rose Cottage,' Grange Road, Stanwick.

His brother Charles also has no known grave; he is commemorated on the Tyne Cot Memorial (Panel 81).

(Panel 28) Pte. 629396, Fred (*a.k.a* 'General') Booth, 'D' Coy., 47th Bn. Canadian Infantry (Western Ontario Regt.), C.E.F.: *s.* of the late James Henry Booth, by his wife Sarah (36A, Bertram Road, Bertrams, Johannesburg, Transvaal, South Africa): *b.* 3 November 1894: Occupation – Labourer: enlisted Vernon, British Columbia, 18 August 1915: served with the Expeditionary Force in France and Flanders from 11 August 1916, and was killed in action 17 September 1916: Age 21. *unm.* (*IWGC record age 32*)

(Panel 28) Pte. 629592, William Maurice Davin, 47th Bn. Canadian Infantry (Western Ontario Regt.), C.E.F.: 3rd *s.* of George Davin, Manufacturing Stationer; of 21, Aubrey Street, Londonderry, by his wife Elizabeth: *b.* Londonderry, 19 April 1893: *educ.* Foyle College, there: removed to Canada, 1914; settled Whonnock, British Columbia: Occupation – Fruit Farmer: enlisted October 1914: served with the Expeditionary Force in France and Flanders from August 1916: wounded at the taking of Regina Trench, 10 November following, and was killed in action at Passchendaele, 27 October 1917. Buried there. A comrade wrote, "Billy was one of the finest boys I have ever met, a good soldier, always willing to do his share, and fearing nothing. He died the noblest death possible, fighting for his country in the name of freedom." Age 23. *unm. (IWGC record 26 October 1917)*

(Panel 28) Lieut. John Lloyd Bishopric, 49th Bn. Canadian Infantry (Alberta Regt.), C.E.F.: *s.* of Oscar William Bishopric, of 8717, 99th Street, Edmonton, Alberta, by his late wife Sarah *née* Hutchison: *b.* Toronto, 3 August 1885: Occupation – Gentleman: serving member 101st Edmonton Fusiliers (Militia); joined C.E.F., Edmonton, 4 January 1915: prior to leaving Canada was Capt., 218th Battn. Alberta Regt.; apptd. 63rd Overseas Bn; reverted to Lieut. (in England) to proceed to France, and was killed in action before Passchendaele, 29 October 1917: Age 32. (*IWGC record age 30*)

(Panel 28) Lieut. Robert John Gunn Dow, 49th Bn. Canadian Infantry (Alberta Regt.), C.E.F.: late of Whitby, Ontario: *s.* of the late John Ball Dow, by his wife Mary A. (17, College Terrace, Brighton, co. Sussex): *b.* Whitby, 2 October 1883: *educ.* Whitby; Trinity College, Toronto University (Political Science, History), B.A., 1902 – 06; member College Athletic Executive, and Association Football team: serving member 101st Regt. (Militia): enlisted as Pte., 151st Battn.; attained rank of Capt., but prior to leaving Edmonton, Alberta, reverted to Lieut. to join 49th Battn., France. At Passchendaele his battalion had been in the attack for three days, and he had served in command of his company with great skill and courage. On 30 October 1917 he was hit by a sniper, but remained at duty for some time until forced to retire. He insisted on walking to the Dressing Station, as so many needed carrying, and had almost reached a place of safety when he was hit by a shell and died almost instantly: Age 33.

(Panel 28) Sergt. 432509, Harold Thomas Morgan, 49th Bn. Canadian Infantry (Alberta Regt.), C.E.F.: *s.* of George Morgan, of 3, Acacia Road, Guildford, co. Surrey, by his wife Miranda: and yr. brother to Pte. 765, H.S. Morgan, Princess Patricia's Canadian Light Infantry, who fell 8 May 1915; Gravenstafel when the Patricia's 'counted not the cost.' Killed in action during the fighting near Sanctuary Wood, 2 June 1916: Age 30.

His brother Herbert also has no known grave; he is recorded on Panel 10.

At the beginning of June 1916 the Canadian Corps held the southern sector of the Ypres Salient between Hooge and St. Eloi. The northern (left) flank was held by the 3rd Division; the Royal Canadian Regiment holding the left of the line 500 metres north of Hooge to just south of the Menin Road. This sector, the easternmost apex of the salient, was the most vulnerable to German fire. The front line trenches, whose parapets had been badly knocked about by shellfire, 'consisted of eight outposts inaccessible by daylight, the intervening space being both open to view and waist deep in water and slime' was approached by a long and exposed communication trench...Between the lines were the remains of French and German soldiers killed months before, while it was a common occurrence to turn up bodies when endeavouring to repair the trenches...Sniping, machine gun fire and shelling were constant, enfilading the whole position.' In the Sanctuary Wood sector, 350 metres south, both front lines ran very close together, but the Germans had by far the more commanding position. The Birdcage, a heavily wired German strongpoint built on the grounds of Stirling Castle, easily enabling enfilade fire of the Canadian positions meant that the overall strength of the defence fell heavily to the troops manning the support trenches.

Shortly after 8.00 a.m., 2 June 1916, the German guns opened up on the 3rd Canadian Division positions at Mount Sorrel. Guns of all calibre literally ripped the front apart, demolishing the trenches and dug-outs, scattering the shattered remains of men everywhere. With communication to the front line completely cut off, orders were given to the support troops to 'Stand To!' At 1.00 p.m. the firing stopped, and the positions further rent by the explosion of huge mines. With the firing of these mines the Germans, in overwhelming numbers, easily moved forward and passed through the remains of the Canadian lines; mopping up small pockets of resistance. The centre of the line had fallen, the flanks held, but the Germans had achieved their objective Observatory Ridge. The battle raged continually throughout the remainder of the day, ferociously fighting hand-to-hand the Canadians were forced back, trench-block by trench-block, into Sanctuary Wood.

The following day a counter-attack was ordered by General Byng. On the left flank three battalions of the 3rd Division – 60th (Queen Victoria's Rifles), 52nd (New Ontario), and 49th (Alberta) – the latter being the only one properly assembled and prepared for the attack, resulted in failure. Hurriedly executed, without adequate artillery support, it succeeded only in developing a better defensive line. Over the next few days the 3rd Division was relieved by the 2nd, the remnants of the P.P.C.L.I., the 42nd and 49th in Sanctuary Wood being relieved by 31st and 43rd (Cameron Highlanders of Canada). Once out of the line the battalions of the 3rd Division began counting their losses. P.P.C.L.I. – 407 killed, wounded or prisoners, including their C.O., Lieut.Col. Buller; 4th C.M.R. – 626 killed, wounded or prisoner, including their C.O., Lieut.Col. Ussher (taken prisoner); 1st C.M.R. lost their C.O., Lieut. Col. Shaw, killed near Tor Top, 5th C.M.R . Lieut.Col. Baker, 52nd Bn. Lieut.Col. Hay. The R.C.R. at Hooge, 158 killed, wounded, missing; 42nd Bn. – 283, killed, wounded, missing; and the 49th Bn. – 366 killed, wounded, missing. Added to these General Mercer had been killed by shellfire (the highest ranking Canadian killed in the war), and Brigadier-General Williams taken prisoner.

The bodies of most of those killed in the fighting around Mount Sorrell and Sanctuary Wood over the course of those three days were never recovered. A large number were torn to atoms by the incessant shellfire or buried in the collapse of trenches and dug-outs; for these there would be no honoured burial, their names instead recorded in memory and in mourning on the Menin Gate Memorial.

(Panel 28) L/Corpl. 432397, David Miller, 49th Bn. Canadian Infantry (Edmonton Regt.), C.E.F.: 5th child of the late William Miller, by his wife Isabella (Uddingston, Glasgow, co. Lanark), *dau.* of Mr (& Mrs) Campbell: and brother to Margaret Miller: *b.* 1876: removed to Canada, 1906: Occupation – Lumber Camp worker; Canadian Pacific Railway: enlisted 5 January 1915: previously served 11 years 2nd Scottish Rifles (Militia), 1894 – 1905, attained rank Sergt.: departed Canada 3 June 1915, arrived England ten days later (13 June): served with the Expeditionary Force in France and Flanders from October following. Reported missing / believed killed after the fighting at Mount Sorrel between 3rd – 5th June 1916, later confirmed killed in action on the former date: Age 40. *unm. (IWGC record 31st Bn.)*

(Panel 28) Pte. 432051, Albert Edward Allen, 49th Bn. Canadian Infantry (Alberta Regt.), C.E.F.: *s.* of Robert Allen, of 38, Fallsbrook Road, Streatham, London: *b.* Carlisle, England, 3 May 1890: Religion – Presbyterian: Occupation – Assistant Tinsmith: enlisted Edmonton, 4 January 1915: apptd. 49th Battn. Reported missing, presumed died, on or about 5 June 1916, vicinity Maple Copse, Zillebeke: Age 26. *unm.*

(Panel 28) Pte. 832412, Herbert William Fenwick Blackall, 49th Bn. Canadian Infantry (Alberta Regt.), C.E.F.: *s.* of Dr. W.W. Blackall, of St. John's, Newfoundland, by his wife Ida: departed Canada, Coy.Sergt.Major, 9th (Reserve) Battn.; reverted to Pte. to proceed to France with all possible haste, and was killed in action before Passchendaele, 30 October 1917: Age 23. *unm.*

49th Battalion C.E.F.: "From 4 – 9 April 1916 the battalion occupied the trenches Shrapnel Corner, Gordon House, Halfway House, and Trench 71 (Zillebeke sector) where virtually every day saw the battalion's strength depleted by the ever active enemy artillery. On the night of 9 April, Sergt. Caine and Pte. Southern went out from Trench 71 and located the body of Pte. Carr which had been lying out for a number of days. It being impossible to bring the body in owing to enemy flares, they buried him in no man's land."

(Panel 28) Pte. 432240, Julian St. Thomas Carr, 49th Bn. Canadian Infantry (Edmonton Regt.), C.E.F.: *s.* of the late Thomas Carr, of Hurworth-on-Lees, Darlington, England, by his wife Jane: *b.* South Shields, 24 September 1894: Religion – Church of England: Occupation – Lumber Worker; Axeman: 5'5½" tall, dark complexion, blue eyes, brown hair: enlisted Edmonton, 5 January 1915. Killed in action 6 April 1916. Buried where he fell: Age 31. *unm.*

PANEL 28 ENDS – PTE. G. COLLING, 49TH BN. CANADIAN INF.

PANEL 30 BEGINS – PTE. E.M. COVE, 49TH BN. CANADIAN INF.

(Panel 30) Pte. 435613, John Burt Dunlop, 49th Bn. Canadian Infantry (Alberta Regt.), C.E.F.: *s.* of Daniel Dunlop, of Frank, Alberta, by his wife Annie: and *yr.* brother to Pte. 438651, J. Dunlop, 52nd

Canadian Infantry., killed in action 27 May 1916: *b*. 25 August 1899 (added two years at attestation – 25 August 1897): Religion – Church of England: enlisted Blairmore, Alberta, 25 August 1915, aged 16 years. Reported missing after the fighting 2 – 5 June 1916, since confirmed killed in action; the circumstances being 'whilst on duty as a company runner in the trenches at Sanctuary Wood, Ypres salient, an enemy shell exploded nearby. Death was instantaneous.' No record of burial. **Age 16.**

His brother James also has no known grave, he is recorded below.

(Panel 30) Pte. 432128, Frederick Taylor Knock, 49th Bn. Canadian Infantry (Alberta Regt.), C.E.F.: *s*. of George Knock, of Meanwood Grove, Leeds, co. York, by his wife Annie: *b*. Leeds, 11 April 1875: Religion – Church of England: Occupation – Labourer: joined C.E.F., Edmonton, 4 January 1915. Killed in action 3 June 1916 when, while taking part in operations at Sanctuary wood, nr. Ypres, he was wounded in the arm and, as he was making his way back to a dressing station, he was killed by the nearby explosion of an enemy shell and buried by the resultant debris: Age 41. Pte. Knock leaves a widow, Annie Elizabeth (12, Wharfedale Street, Meanwood Grove, Leeds). Remains recovered unmarked grave Sanctuary Wood, 3 January 1927; identified – Clothing, Titles, Gold Watch mkd. FTK, Medallion, mkd. F. Knock; reinterred, registered 8 January 1927. *Buried in Sanctuary Wood Cemetery (III.B.27).*

(Panel 30) Pte. 425747, Ian MacMillan, 49th Bn. Canadian Infantry (Alberta Regt.), C.E.F.: 2nd *s*. of David MacMillan, of 125 Wellington Crescent, Winnipeg, Canada, late of Chanque Barr, co. Ayr, Scotland, by his wife Agnes Turner (19, Argyle Place, Edinburgh), *dau*. of John McCulloch, of Laggan, Ballantrae: and brother to Pte. W.McC. Macmillan, Alberta Regt., reported wounded and missing after the fighting on the Somme 8 October 1916: *b*. Barr, co. Ayr, 26 October 1897: *educ*. Barr, and Girvan Academies: went to Canada, 1912, entered employ with the Union Bank, Winnipeg: volunteered for Active Service, January 1916, and joined Canadian Infantry: served with the Expeditionary Force in France and Flanders from April 1916, and was killed in action at Passchendaele 30 October 1917. Buried in Nine Elms Cemetery, there: Age 20 years, 4 days. *unm*.

(Panel 30) Pte. 183686, Sidney Reygate, 49th Bn. Canadian Infantry (Alberta Regt.), C.E.F.: *s*. of the late George Reygate, by his wife Emily (Sutton Lane, Banstead, co. Surrey): and *yr*. brother to Pte. G/58216, C.H. Reygate, Middlesex Regt., died of wounds, 28 September 1918, at Ypres: *b*. Banstead, 1 February 1883: Religion – Church of England: Occupation – Farmer: 5'3½" tall, dark complexion, blue eyes, dark hair: enlisted Calgary, 1 December 1915: served with the Expeditionary Force in France and Flanders, and was killed in action before Passchendaele, 30 October 1917: Age 34. *unm*.

His brother Charles is buried in Belgian Battery Corner Cemetery (III.B.22).

(Panel 30) Pte. 404564, Rupert Elwyn Rivers, 49th Bn. Canadian Infantry (Alberta Regt.), C.E.F.: *s*. of James Rivers: *b*. Perth Co., 1 May 1892: *educ*. Hibbert Public School; Seaforth Collegiate, University of Toronto (Medicine), 1914 – 15; member C.O.T.C.: Occupation – School Teacher; Hagersville: enlisted 35th Battn., April 1915; proceeded overseas October following: served with the Expeditionary Force in France, joined 49th Battn., Ypres, 29 May 1916. Reported missing, believed killed 2 – 5 June 1916. On 3 June the battalion counter-attacked at Sanctuary Wood and suffered heavy losses, but held on to the ground gained until relieved on the 5th; it is thought Pte. Rivers was a casualty of the counter-attack: Age 24. (*IWGC record 5 June*)

(Panel 30) Pte. 696469, William Clare Sample, 49th Bn. Canadian Infantry (Alberta Regt.), C.E.F.: known as 'Clare': *s*. of Matilda Ann (Quackenbusch) Sample (Blenheim, Ontario): and brother to Pte. 523031, H.B. Sample, 50th Bn. Canadian Infantry, who also fell: *b*. Harwich Township, Kent co., Ontario, 26 October 1889. After completing his education Clare moved to western Canada to take up teaching, initially in Saskatchewan, later in Irvine, Alberta, where he was joined by his brother Harry: enlisted Alberta Regt., CE.F., Medicine Hat, 4 March 1916: trained Calgary: embarked aboard SS 'Saxonia,' Halifax, Nova Scotia: disembarked Liverpool, England: transf'd. Signallers Depot, Seaford, Sussex, 10 November 1916: briefly stationed with 175th Bn. (31 December 1916 – 10 January 1917), transf'd. 21st (Reserve) Battn. Alberta Regt. on the latter date: posted 9th (Reserve) Battn., Bramshott, 1 June 1917: joined draft for 49th Battn. Alberta Regt. (also stationed Bramshott), for service at the Front, 5 June following: served with the Expeditionary Force in France from 7 June 1917, joining his unit 12 June, and was killed during a German artillery barrage 30 October 1917, four days after his brother Harry: Age 28. *unm.* A memorial stone honouring both brothers was erected by Mrs Sample in Evergreen Cemetery, Blenheim; also a memorial plaque in Blenheim Presbyterian Church.

His brother Harry also has no known grave, he is recorded below.

(Panel 30) Pte. 904468, William Niven Steadman, 49th Bn. Canadian Infantry (Alberta Regt.), C.E.F.: *s.* of Rev. William Steadman, of 53, Dudley Street, Leighton Buzzard, co. Bedford, by his wife Frances Sophia Anne: and brother to Pte. 871056, J.N. Steadman, 78th Bn. C.E.F., killed in action 21 September 1917: *b.* Thornborough, 22 January 1890: *educ.* Buckingham Royal Latin School: Occupation – Farmer: joined C.E.F., Edmonton, 6 March 1916; apptd. 194th Overseas Battn. (Highland Regt.). Killed in action 30 October 1917: Age 27. *unm.*

His brother John also has no known grave; he is commemorated on the Canadian National Memorial, Vimy.

(Panel 30) Pte. 447922, Gordon Howard Thorpe (served as Turner), 49th Bn. Canadian Infantry (Alberta Regt.), C.E.F.: *s.* of Charles Stuart Thorpe, of 126, Salisbury Road, Brondesbury, London, by his wife Ellen. Killed in action 5 June 1916: Age 29. Remains 'Unknown Canadian Soldier' recovered unmarked grave (28.I.24.a.8.8); identified – Titles, Clothing, Gold Ring engrvd. G.H.T.; reinterred, registered, 11 October 1927. Buried in Sanctuary Wood Cemetery (IV.J.3).

It Is Raised In Glory

(Panel 30) Pte. 811876, Herbert James Weal, 49th Bn. Canadian Infantry (Alberta Regt.), C.E.F.: *yst. s.* of the late Charles Weal, by his wife Emily (50, St. Stephen's Almshouses, Castlebar Road, Ealing, London, W.): *b.* Ealing, 21 November 1885: Religion – Church of England: *educ.* St. Stephen's Schools, Winchester Road, Twickenham: Occupation – Gardener; Kew Garden Road Nurseries, Twickenham: removed to Canada, June 1911; settled Saskatchewan; found gainful employ as Porter: volunteered for Foreign Service, enlisted 138th (Overseas) Bn., C.E.F., Edmonton, 3 February 1916: served with the Expeditionary Force in France and Flanders from February 1917, and was killed in action 30 October following. Buried where he fell: Age 31. *unm.*

(Panel 30) Pte. 432049, Harold 'Harry' Edgar White, 49th Bn. Canadian Infantry (Alberta Regt.), C.E.F.: *s.* of William Harold White, of Orangeville, Ontario, by his wife Margaret Jane: and brother to Pte. 261359, H.A. White, who fell fifteen months later: *b.* 28 December 1893: Religion – Wesleyan: Occupation – Clerk: serving member (2 months) 19th Regt. (Militia), joined C.E.F., Edmonton, 4 January 1915. Killed in action 1 May 1916: Age 19. *(IWGC record father – Edward)*

His brother Howard also has no known grave; he is commemorated on the Canadian National Memorial, Vimy.

(Panel 30) Pte. 432719, Arthur Wesley Young, 49th Bn. Canadian Infantry (Alberta Regt.), C.E.F.: *s.* of George R. Young, c/o Box 135, Picton, Ontario: attested / joined 49th Battn. C.E.F., Edmonton, 12 January 1915; provided Date of Birth – 30 November 1893; occupation – Buttermaker: Religion – Methodist: 5'4" tall, fair complexion, grey eyes, fair hair. Killed in action 2 June 1916; Sanctuary Wood: **Age 16.** Inscribed – 'In Memory of the men of Prince Edward County who fought and fell in the Great War 1914-1919' – Pte. Young is remembered on the section dedicated to the four men of Athol municipality; Picton War Memorial.

(Panel 30) Pte. 895068, John Edwin Barrett, 50th Bn. Canadian Infantry (Alberta Regt.), C.E.F.: eldest *s.* of Richard William Barrett, of White House, Munsley, Ledbury, co. Hereford, by his late wife Susannah, *dau.* of William Fennell: *b.* Munsley, 22 June 1890: Religion – Church of England: *educ.* Broomy Hill Academy, Hereford: removed to Canada, 1913; settled High River, Alberta: Occupation – Farm Assistant: enlisted Calgary, 1 June 1916; apptd. 50th Battn., 13 June: arrived England, February 1917: served with the Expeditionary Force in France from June following; and was killed in action at Ypres, 23 October

1917. A comrade wrote, "His death is a great loss to all his many comrades…He was greatly beloved by all who knew him…a most straightforward, upright, honest lad." Age 27. *unm.*

Situated in support trenches at Levi Cottage in readiness for an attack scheduled for 26th October 1917, 50th Canadians utilised much of the 23rd making familiarisation patrols of the ground between them and the enemy with all companies ordered to pay special attention to Decline Copse. Within moments of moving out a patrol under Lieut. Corley came under fire from a position less than fifteen feet away and, after forcing the enemy back with bombs and fire from eight separate positions, was forced to retire after thirty minutes. Thirty minutes during which the battalion lost one of its best scouts.

(Panel 30) Pte. 895403, Mike Foxhead, 50th Bn. Canadian Infantry (Alberta Regt.), C.E.F.: *s.* of the late Fox Head, of the Blackfoot Indian Reservation, Alberta, by his wife Mary Many Shots: *b.* 16 August 1898: Religion – Roman Catholic: Occupation – Cowboy: 5'8" tall, dark complexion, brown eyes, black hair: enlisted Calgary, 9 October 1916: apptd. 191st Overseas Battn.; departed Canada, 19 March 1917: served with the Expeditionary Force in France and Flanders; reported missing while on reconnaissance patrol 23 October 1917. Age 19. Buried 28.D.17.a.9.2. Grave unlocated. A Blackfoot Indian, one of 3,500 native Canadians who served with the C.E.F. *(IWGC record age 20)*

(Panel 30) Pte. 895029, Joseph William Jones, 50th Bn. Canadian Infantry (Alberta Regt.), C.E.F.: c/o Mrs Prince (27, Hardy Street, Garston, Liverpool, England): *s.* of the late Edward Jones, by his wife Caroline (13, Brunswick Street, Garston): *b.* Holywell, North Wales, 19 January 1877: Religion – Church of England: Occupation – Music Teacher: 5'4¼" tall; medium complexion, hazel eyes, dark hair; depressed facial scar, left cheek: enlisted 50th Battn., Macleod, Alberta, 19 May 1916: served with the Expeditionary Force in France from 11 August 1916, and was killed in action 24 October 1917, 'by shellfire while on duty at a bombing post in front of Passchendaele. Death was instantaneous.' Buried 250 yards North of Hamburg; 28.D.10.d.40.30: Age 40. *(IWGC record age 43)*

The first wave of Japanese immigrants to Canada arrived in 1877. Known as *Issei* – first generation – by 1914 over 10,000 people of Japanese descent had settled in Canada. The Issei, predominantly educated young males, were, for the most part, from fishing and farming villages on the southern islands of Kyushu and Honshu; a minority migrated from other parts of Japan. Many settled in what became known as 'Japantowns,' the suburbs of Vancouver and Victoria, farms in the Fraser Valley, fishing villages, and pulp-mill and mining towns along the Pacific coast. A minority settled and found work on farms and in the coal-mining towns of Alberta, near Lethbridge and Edmonton. Japanese Canadians, both *Issei* immigrants and their Canadian-born children, called *Nisei* (second generation) were forced to endure, unrelenting prejudice and discrimination. Beginning in 1874, politicians in British Columbia pandered to white supremacists, passing a series of laws whereby conditions imposed would make life so unbearable for Asians they would be forced to leave Canada rather than stay. Beginning with the Chinese in 1874; followed by the Japanese in 1895; and 'Hindoos' (South Asians) 1907, all Asians were denied the right to vote. Exclusion laws were introduced whereby Asians were barred from employ in underground mining, the civil service and professions such as the practice of law, which required the practitioner to be listed on the provincial voting lists. Labour and minimum-wage laws ensured that Asian Canadians be employed only for menial jobs or farm labour, and be paid at lower rates than Caucasian workers. Asians who worked harder and longer to earn a living wage, were accused by white labour unions of unfair competition, stealing jobs and undermining the efforts of the unions to raise the living standards of white workers.

The discrimination continued during the First World War. Hoping to prove their loyalty to Canada over 200 volunteers attempted to enlist only to be refused by recruitment offices throughout British Columbia who would not accept Asians for military service. To circumvent this practice 195 *Issei* men, and one *Nisei* (Pte. G. Uyehara) travelled from British Columbia to Alberta to enlist. Of the 196 who served, 54 were killed, 92 wounded; 13 of them received the Military Medal for acts of gallantry.

(Panel 30) Pte. 697078, Hikotaro Koyanagi, 50th Bn. Canadian Infantry (Alberta Regt.), C.E.F.: late of 240, Alexander Street, Vancouver: *s.* of Haya Koyanagi, of 1144, Mikawawachi, Ken, Japan: *b.* 26 March 1885: Religion – Methodist: Occupation – Fisherman: volunteered, enlisted C.E.F., Calgary, 1 September

1916; apptd. 175th Bn.: proceeded to France with a draft of reinforcements to 50th Battn.; served with the Expeditionary Force there, and was killed by shellfire, 26 October 1917, while in support trenches at Levi Cottage, Passchendaele: Age 22.

In April 1920, marking the third anniversary of the Battle of Vimy Ridge, the Japanese Canadian War Memorial cenotaph was officially unveiled in Vancouver's Stanley Park, near Lumberman's Arch. Situated atop of the sandstone column is a marble lantern containing an eternal flame. Veteran, Sergt. Yasuzo Shoji, 52nd Battalion, C.E.F., said "We don't forget what we owe to Canada and we were proud to fight when Britain declared war on the common enemy."

(Panel 30) Pte. 523031, Harry Bertrand Sample, 50th Bn. Canadian Infantry (Alberta Regt.), C.E.F.: *s.* of Matilda Ann (Quackenbush) Sample (Blenheim, Ontario): and brother to Pte. 696469, W.C. Sample, 49th Bn. Canadian Infantry, killed in action 30 October 1917: *b.* London Township, Middlesex Co., Ontario, 7 March 1897 (lived Kent Co. most of his life): *educ.* Blenheim School (graduated 1912), thence to Teacher Training College; thereafter removed to Irvine, Alberta, to take up a career in teaching: volunteered and enlisted Calgary, when General Mobilisation was announced as the war in Europe intensified and the need for more troops developed, 1 January 1916; posted Section C, No.1 Field Ambulance Depot, Canadian Army Medical Corps, Edmonton, for training: embarked aboard S.S. 'Baltic,' Halifax, Nova Scotia, 22 May 1916: arrived Liverpool one week later: stationed Dibgate, 31 May – 18 June; transf'd. Shorncliffe Military Hospital on the latter date: remained there until transf'd. 21st (Reserve) Battn., Seaford, co. Sussex, 15 March 1917: assigned 50th Battn., 5 July 1917, for service at the front: joined his unit 1 September 1917, and was killed by an enemy barrage during the Battle of Passchendaele (26 October 1917); his death occurring, by a curious twist of fate, on the birthday of his elder brother, Pte. William Clare Sample (49th Bn.) who fell four days later in similar circumstances: Age 20. *unm.* The '*Blenheim News Tribune*' (Vol.50, No.45, pg.1, November 14, 1917) reported;- "Killed in action was the dread message that came Monday morning to Mrs. Sample concerning her second eldest son, who has been serving at the front, Pte. Harry Sample, signaller in the 49th Battalion, France. Harry was 23 years of age and was brought up in the Samson's school community, Centre Line. After graduating from School here he went west to engage in teaching and enlisted in a western battalion. He was sent overseas without being able to get leave to see his mother. His eldest brother, Clare, is a signaller with the 50th Battalion in France. The deep sympathy of the entire community will go to his mother, who was completely prostrated at the news." (*q.v*).

Thomas Sample, the younger brother of Harry and Clare, recalled. When word of Harry's death was received, Charles Clement, a prominent merchant and cousin by marriage, came to his school in Chatham to break the sad news to him and to drive him back to the family home, to be with his mother and younger sister. Entering Blenheim they observed the town hall flag had been lowered to half-mast in Harry's honour. After a few days Mr Clement came to take him back to school, on the way they noticed the flag being lowered again. Thomas recalled thinking to himself that some other family would be mourning the loss of a loved one. He was unaware until he returned home later in the day that this time the flag was being lowered in honour of his other brother Clare.

His brother William also has no known grave; he is recorded above.

(Panel 30) Major Alexander Young, 52nd (New Ontario) Bn. Canadian Infantry (Manitoba Regt.), C.E.F.: *s.* of the late Robert Young, of Aberdeen: served 24 years Royal Canadian Regt, Toronto and Quebec: served in the South African Campaign, and with the Expeditionary Force in France and Flanders, and was killed in action nr. Ypres, 3 June 1916: Age 46. Major Young held both the Long Service and Good Conduct medals. He was married to Annie Gardiner, *née* Young (89, Lockwell Avenue, Quebec).

(Panel 30) Sergt. 439486, Walter Hart, M.M., 52nd Bn. Canadian Infantry (New Ontario Regt.), C.E.F.: *s.* of Lewis Hart, of Heighway Avenue, Goydon, Ontario, and his wife Joanna Rebecca Hart (Crown Street, Surrey Hill, Sydney, Australia): *b.* New South Wales, 11 July 1888: Religion – Church of England: Occupation – Teamster: 5'4" tall, fair complexion, grey eyes, brown hair: joined 52nd C.E.F., Port Arthur, July 1915: served with the Expeditionary Force in France from February 1916, and was killed in action 28 October 1917; Abraham Heights, Passchendaele: Age 26. Awarded the Military Medal (Daily Orders, Winnipeg Camp, 1 October 1917) – 'Commanding a Platoon in a raid on German positions, near Lens, on the night of September 3rd – 4th 1917. Personally blew up with a mobile charge a dug-out from which the enemy was endeavouring to obstruct the advance. Afterwards he showed great courage in the evacuation of the wounded under heavy fire.'

(Panel 30) Pte. 438651, James Dunlop, 52nd (New Ontario) Bn. Canadian Infantry (Manitoba Regt), C.E.F.: *s.* of Daniel Dunlop, of Frank, Alberta, by his wife Annie: and elder brother to Pte. 435613, J.B. Dunlop, 49th Bn., reported missing after the fighting 2 June 1916; confirmed killed in action at Sanctuary Wood on that date (aged 16 years): *b.* Scotland, 21 February 1890: Religion – Presbyterian: Occupation – Labourer: joined C.E.F., Port Arthur, 27 April 1915: served with the Expeditionary Force in France, and was 'killed in action whilst in trenches at Zillebeke, 5 p.m., 27 May 1916; he was hit by an enemy high-explosive shell. Death was instantaneous.' Buried in Maple Copse Cemetery, nr. Ypres. Age 26. (*IWGC record age 20*)

His brother John also has no known grave; he is recorded above.

(Panel 30) Pte. 439667, Henry Edward Percy Hannon, 52nd (New Ontario) Bn. Canadian Infantry (Manitoba Regt.), C.E.F.: only *s.* of the late Henry Percy Hannon, of Ardreigh House, Athy, co. Kildare, by his wife Kathleen (84, Kensington Gardens Square, London, W.): *b.* Ardreigh House, 1 August 1891: *educ.* Trinity House School, Colwyn Bay, and Avoca School, Co. Dublin: removed to Canada; settled Avonlea, Saskatchewan: Occupation – Ledger Keeper (Staff), Bank of Ottawa: joined New Ontario Regt., on formation, 25 August 1915: served with the Canadian Expeditionary Force in France and Flanders from 1 February 1916, and was killed in action at Sanctuary Wood, nr. Ypres, 9 June following. Buried on the battlefield. A comrade wrote, "We mourn the loss of a good comrade, one who was always willing to share all things with us." Age 23. *unm.*

(Panel 30) Pte. 439474, Joe Sebastian, 52nd (New Ontario) Bn. Canadian Infantry, C.E.F.: *s.* of F. Sebastian, of Kiev, Russia: *b.* Kiev, 17 October 1880: Occupation – Blacksmith: volunteered and enlisted Port Arthur, 22 July 1915; posted 52nd Battn.: served with the Expeditionary Force in France from 21 February 1916, and after going out on patrol on the night of 10 – 11 March 1916, did not return. His comrade, with whom he shared the patrol, stated that it was his belief Pte. Sebastian had been hit by machine-gun fire and killed and, no word of him having been received since that date, death is assumed: Age 35. *unm.* 52nd Battalion's first Active Service fatality.

(Panel 30) Pte. 442655, Peter Stuart Farquharson, 54th Bn. Canadian Infantry, C.E.F.: *s.* of James Farquharson, of Tomdarroch, Inchmarnoch, Dinnet, co. Aberdeen, by his wife Margaret Stewart, *dau.* of George Stewart Aldehe: and yr. brother to Gnr. 145700, J. Farquharson, died of wounds 11 April 1918: *b.* Ballater, 6 March 1893: Religion – Presbyterian: Occupation – Labourer: 6'3" tall, blue eyes, light brown hair: enlisted 54th (Kootenay O.S.) Battn., Vernon Camp, August 1915; apptd. L/Corpl.: trained Bramshott Park, England: reverted to Pte. at own volition to proceed more rapidly to France; joined the Expeditionary Force there 14 August 1916, and was killed in action 17 September following: Age 23.

His brother John is buried in Godewaersvelde British Cemetery (I.M.36).

(Panel 30) Lieut. Edgar William Galbraith Patten, 'C' Coy., 58th Bn. Canadian Infantry (2nd Central Ontario Regt.), C.E.F.: *s.* of Charles Galbraith Patten, of St. George, Ontario, by his wife Millicent: *b.* Morriston, 21 March 1891: *educ.* Morriston Public School; St. George Continental School; Brantford Collegiate; University College, Toronto, 1912 – 16 (Mathematics & Physics), B.A., Edward Blake Scholar, Alexander T. Fulton Scholar, William Mulock Scholar, A.A.A. Gold Medallist, and member C.O.T.C.: enlisted 215th Battn. March 1916: promoted Corpl. June 1916; Sergt. July following: received his commission, having passed his examinations with distinction, August 1916: proceeded overseas with a draft of officers September following, and crossed to France, July 1917: joined 58th Battn., Lens sector, and was killed in action at Bellevue Spur, Passchendaele, 26 October 1917: Age 26. *unm.* On the day of his death, as he went forward with his platoon, the officer on the left was killed and the advance was held up. After rallying his men he found that in order to make further progress it was necessary to bring forward a machine gun, the crew of which had all been killed or wounded. He carried it up and was in the process of getting it into position when he was shot and killed instantly by a sniper. Buried where he fell. All sixteen of the officers who went over with him that morning became casualties.

(Panel 30) Coy.Sergt.Major 451160, Dudley Gordon Wright, 58th Bn. Canadian Infantry (2nd Central Ontario Regt.), C.E.F.: *s.* of 1069, Robert Wright, No.6 Sqdn. King Edward's Horse: *b.* Stockport, 1 August 1885: Religion – Church of England: Occupation – Furniture Packer: previously served 3rd Loyal North Lancashire Regt.: volunteered and enlisted Niagara, 30 June 1915. Missing / believed killed 3 June 1916: Age 30. *unm.* Remains recovered 3 January 1927 unmarked grave (28.I.24.d.1.8), Sanctuary Wood; identified – Clothing, Badge of Rank, Titles, reinterred, registered 8 January 1927. *Buried in Sanctuary Wood Cemetery (III.B.25).*

(Panel 30) Pte. 451181, Hector Blake Beaton, 58th Bn. Canadian Infantry (2nd Central Ontario Regt.), C.E.F.: *s.* of Charles K. Beaton, Caretaker, Star Theatre; by his wife Annie (88, Rhodes Avenue, Toronto): *b.* Toronto, 14 August 1899 (attested 14 August 1896): Occupation – Steel Worker: 5'4½" tall; dark complexion, hazel eyes, dark hair: enlisted Niagara (against the express wishes of his parents), 30 June 1915. Missing / believed killed in action 12 – 14 June 1916; Zillebeke sector. No remains recovered: **Age 16.** Since receiving notification of his son being reported missing Mr Beaton, despite information indicating he was probably buried or blown to pieces by a heavy bombardment on 12 – 13 June, has been trying to discover the whereabouts of his son. The Adjutant wrote, "I am sorry to state that during a heavy bombardment on the night of the 12th and the morning of the 13th your son was reported 'missing.' There is very little doubt but that he was killed, as the bombardment was followed by an attack. Of course, the case was very carefully investigated at the time, and every possible effort made to locate your son." Confirmed (March 1917) killed in action on or about 13 June 1916. (*IWGC record 14 June 1916, age 17*)

(Panel 30) Pte. 452428, Holman Roy French, 58th Bn. Canadian Infantry (2nd Central Ontario Regt.), C.E.F.: *s.* of Mrs T.B. French (Humberstone, Ontario): *b.* 24 April 1893: Occupation – Flour Packer: joined 58th C.E.F., Niagara Camp, 28 June 1915. One of five 58th Battn. O.R. killed during a continuous bombardment of the battalion's trenches near Rifle Pits, Maple Copse, 6 June 1916: Age 23. *unm.* (*IWGC record Herman*)

Severely wounded during the same bombardment, Pte. Parkhurst died later the same day in the Casualty Clearing Station, Poperinghe; he is buried in Lijssenthoek Military Cemetery (VII.B.34).

(Panel 30) Pte. 135780, William Ewart Mawson, 58th Bn. Canadian Infantry (2nd Central Ontario Regt.), C.E.F.: 3rd *s.* of the late William Mawson, by his wife Jane (Flatt House, St. Bees, co. Cumberland): *b.* St. Bees, 7 October 1888: Religion – Church of England: sometime Clerk, Furness Railway Co., Pte. Mawson emigrated to Canada, 1912, finding employ in Toronto, as Accountant: enlisted Toronto, 27 July 1915: 5'7½" tall, grey eyes, brown hair: posted 74th Battn., subsequently transf'd. 58th Battn.: served with the Expeditionary Force in France from June 1916, and was killed in action on the 10th of that month, which, it is believed, was his first time in the trenches and had only been there about one hour. Greatly esteemed; during his time in St. Bees, Pte. Mawson was Secretary to the Sancta Bega Lodge of Oddfellows, Hodgetts Club, and the local Technical Committee; he was also a member of St. Bees Cricket Club and played for them on many occasions: Age 27. *unm.* (*IWGC record age 30*)

(Panel 30) Pte. 451267, Arthur Henry Miles, 58th Bn. Canadian Infantry (2nd Central Ontario Regt.), C.E.F.: late *husb.* to Annie Smith, *née* Miles (8, Low Skellgate, Ripon, co. York). Killed in action 14 June 1916. Remains recovered unmarked grave (28.I.24.b.0.3) 18 January 1927; identified – Disc; reinterred, registered 22 January 1927. Buried in Sanctuary Wood Cemetery (III.D.1).

(Panel 30) Pte. 835209, James Russell Strachan, 58th Bn. Canadian Infantry (2nd Central Ontario Regt.), C.E.F.: *s.* of the late James Shaw Strachan, by his wife Christina (13, Queen Street, Perth), *dau.* of Thomas Russell: *b.* Perth, 16 February 1882: *educ.* Craigie School, and Perth Academy: went to Canada, 1904; settled Vancouver, British Columbia: Occupation – Stockbroker's Clerk: joined Canadian Infantry, April 1915: served with the Expeditionary Force in France and Flanders from June 1917, and was killed in action at Passchendaele 26 October following. Buried at Bellevue Spur there: Age 32. *unm.*

(Panel 30) L/Corpl. 458038, Michael Gilligan, 'B' Coy., 60th (Victoria Rifles of Montreal) Bn. Canadian Infantry, C.E.F.: c/o John Gilligan Esq., of 270, St. Patrick's Street, Montreal: *b.* Dundee, Scotland, 8 August 1881: Religion – Roman Catholic: Occupation – Plater's Assistant; C.P.R.: previously served 4 yrs. Connaught Rangers; 10 yrs Reserve; volunteered and enlisted Montreal, 15 July 1915. Killed in action 26 April 1916; trenches Hooge. Remains 'Unknown Canadian Soldier. 60 Canadians,' recovered unmarked grave Sanctuary Wood (GRU Report, Zillebeke, 5-283/E); identified – Good Conduct Stripe (or Badge of Rank), Numerals. Reinterred, registered 13 July 1928. *Buried in Sanctuary Wood Cemetery (II.K.20).*

(Panel 30) Pte. 444543, Allan Inglis McKim, 60th (Victoria Rifles of Montreal) Bn. Canadian Infantry, C.E.F.: *s.* of Elias McKim, of Amherst, Nova Scotia, by his wife Mary: and *yr.* brother to Pte. 67347, W.E. McKim, 25th Bn. Canadian Infantry, killed in action at Ypres, 8 October 1915. Died of wounds received at the Battle of Ypres, 3 June 1916: Age 20. *unm.*

His brother William also has no known grave; he is recorded on Panel 26.

(Panel 30) Lieut. Roy Cairman Gillespie, 72nd Bn. Canadian Infantry (British Columbia Regt.), C.E.F.: *s.* of David H. Gillespie, of 2221, Stephens Street, Vancouver, British Columbia, by his wife Isabella Jane: *b.* Marvesville, 24 March 1890: Religion – Methodist: Occupation – Wholesale Grocer: serving member 6th Duke of Connaught's Own (Militia); enlisted (as Lieut.) Vancouver; apptd. 158th Overseas Bn., 2 March 1916; subsequently transf'd. 72nd: served with the Expeditionary Force in France from 13 August 1916. 'On the morning of 31 October 1917, after an attack on Passchendaele Ridge, whilst endeavouring to get some prisoners into a trench, he was shot through the throat and killed instantly by a bullet fired by an enemy sniper.' Age 27. *Buried in Passchendaele New British Cemetery (XV.C.5).*

(Panel 30) Corpl. 130014, Alexander 'Sandy' Muir Lyon, 72nd (Canadian Seaforth Highlanders) Bn. Canadian Infantry (British Columbia Regt.), C.E.F.: 4th *s.* of Thomas Lyon, of 49, South Hamilton Street, Kilmarnock, co. Ayr, by his wife Margaret Sturrock, *dau.* of the late Gavin Walker: *b.* Kilmarnock, 26 August 1889: *educ.* there: removed to Canada, 1912, settled Vancouver, B.C.: Occupation – Clerk; Royal Bank of Canada: enlisted October 1915, after having been rejected for military service three times: served with the Expeditionary Force in France and Flanders from 12 August 1916, and was killed in action at Passchendaele, 28 October 1917. Buried there. His Commanding Officer wrote, "Your son was in charge of a Lewis Gun Section in 'C' Coy. I would like to take this opportunity of expressing to you my appreciation of his gallant conduct throughout his service with us in France. His example has always been an inspiration to all his comrades; he was the most popular man in the whole company, possessing qualities of an exceptional nature;" and another officer, "He was an excellent gunner, absolutely fearless, an ideal man to lead a Lewis Gun section in the field; out of the line he was a good, steady soldier, bearing an excellent character; always of a bright and cheery disposition that made him one of the most popular men in the company." A comrade wrote, "Alexander was a great favourite among all the boys, and many a weary mile has been shortened by Sandy striking up a chorus or speaking a word of cheer." Age 28. *unm.*

(Panel 30) Pte. 687529, Ernest Joseph Hereron, 72nd (Canadian Seaforth Highlanders) Bn. Canadian Infantry (British Columbia Regt.), C.E.F.: *s.* of Mary Hereron (R.R. No.1, Kelowna, British Columbia): and brother to Lieut. C. Hereron, M.M., 2nd Canadian Mounted Rifles, died 6 November 1918; and Pte. 2204244, J.J. Hereron, Forestry Dept. (surv'd.): *b.* 16 August 1897: Occupation – Rancher: joined 102nd Regt., C.E.F, Kelowna, 13 December 1915; transf'd. 72nd Battn. Killed in action 30 October 1917, at Passchendaele. Age 20. *unm.*

His brother Charles is buried in Quievrain Communal Cemetery (A.1).

(Panel 30) Lieut. Henry Lyman Devlin, 75th Bn. Canadian Infantry (Central Ontario Regt.), C.E.F.: *s.* of Samuel Lyman Devlin, of 71, Delaware Avenue, Toronto, by his wife Margaret J.: *b.* Stayner, Ontario, 18 January 1896: *educ.* Stayner Public (& High) School; St. Andrew's College (1911 – 12); and University College, Toronto University (Kappa Alpha, 1913 – 15): member of '*The Varsity*' (University newspaper) staff, and journalist for '*The Toronto Star*': prior to enlistment served with 9th Mississauga Horse (Militia): enlisted Toronto, 29 July 1915, posted 75th Battn.: served with the Expeditionary Force in

France and Flanders from late July 1916. Reported missing / known to have been killed while taking part in a raid on the enemy trenches at St. Eloi, Belgium, 9 September 1916; the circumstances being recorded thus:– "On the night of 9 September 1916 Lieut. Devlin's battalion was in the line before St. Eloi, and, in company with Lieut. F.C. Howard, 'A' Coy., he took a party out for a raid on the German trenches. When they reached the enemy trench they were fired upon by machine guns and rifles; Lieut. Devlin was killed instantly and Lieut. Howard fatally wounded. The following morning a party went out to retrieve Lieut. Devlin's body, but despite a thorough search his body could not be found. It is thought that he was taken in by the Germans and buried beside his brother officer at Comines." Age 20. *unm.*

Lieut. Francis C. Howard is buried in Pont-Du-Hem Military Cemetery, La Gorgue (IV.H.7).

(Panel 30) Corpl. 147247, John 'Jack' Howard Pounds, 78th Bn. Canadian Infantry (Manitoba Regt.), C.E.F.: *s.* of Robert Pounds, of Southampton, England, by his wife Eliza: *b.* London, 20 January 1892: Religion – Church of England: removed to Canada; found employ as Transport Conductor: 5'9¾" tall, dark complexion, brown hair, brown eyes: member 100th Winnipeg Grenadiers (Militia); 2 years Military School experience, enlisted Winnipeg, 1 July 1915: served with the Expeditionary Force in France and Flanders from 15 August 1916, and was killed in action (sniper) 13 September 1916, while at work on trench drainage at Kemmel: Age 24. 78th Battalion's first Active Service fatality.

(Panel 30) Lieut. Frederick John Anderson, 85th Bn. Canadian Infantry (Nova Scotia Regt.), C.E.F.: *s.* of Frank Anderson, of 12, Ellis Street, Niagara Falls, Ontario, by his wife Clara: *b.* Niagara Falls, 14 March 1886: *educ.* Public School there; University of Toronto (Applied Science), 1903 – 07, B.A.Sc., Civil Engineering: Occupation – City Engineer, Niagara Falls: enlisted November 1915; apptd. 98th Battn.: departed Canada, July 1916: served with the Expeditionary Force in France from 1917, transf'd. 85th Battn., with which unit he served as Works Officer, Lens sector. Killed in action 28 October 1917; Passchendaele. On the date of his death his company had just arrived to take over the line preparatory to an attack and found the battalion they were to relieve had been compelled to fall back. The company immediately launched a counter-attack to restore the situation and was killed leading his men just as their objective was won: Age 31. *unm.*

On 28 October 1917, 85th Canadians left Brandhoek and proceeded to Potijze from whence, after partaking of supper and being issued with bombs and trench stores, they departed at 4.45 p.m. and began their approach to the front line before Passchendaele. Proceeding by way of H and X Tracks to Seine Corner where Battalion Headquarters was established in a pill-box previously occupied by 47th Battalion; 'D' Company continued to the front line to take over the frontage held by 44th Battalion. When passing advanced Headquarters at Hillside Farm it was found a counter-attack had driven in the right front line platoon of the 44th and a section of the flank lay open. Capt. Martin (2nd in Command, 44th Battn.) immediately reorganised his battalion and, with the assistance of the two leading platoons of 'D' Company, ordered by Capt. Mackenzie (85th Battn.) to extend across the frontage covered by the counter-attack, this combined force managed to drive out the Germans to their original positions and enable the Canadians to reoccupy their front line.

In the process of this engagement Capt. MacKenzie was mortally wounded in the abdomen but carried on reorganising his men until, after seeing his outposts established, he fell dead. Lieuts. Martell and Anderson were also killed, and Lieut. Christie, after being wounded, was carried to the Regimental Aid Post only to be killed by a shell while awaiting treatment.

(Panel 30) Lieut. Ross McAulay MacKenzie (T/Capt.), Comd'g. 'D' Coy, 85th Bn. Canadian Infantry (Nova Scotia Regt.), C.E.F.: *s.* of Maud Mackenzie (Baddeck, Cape Breton, Nova Scotia): *b.* 29 December 1890: Occupation – Locomotive Fireman: previously served 3½ years Royal Newfoundland Mounted Police; a serving member of 14th Kentville C.A. (Militia), and 1 year 85th (Overseas) Battn. in which unit he held his commission, volunteered for Overseas Active Service, Camp Aldershot, Nova Scotia, 10 October 1916: served with the Expeditionary Force in France and Flanders from 10 February 1917, and died of wounds (abdominal) 28 October 1917; vicinity Hillside Farm, Seine Corner, Passchendaele Ridge: Age 26. *unm.*

Lieut. N.C. Christie is buried in Tyne Cot Cemetery (XXXVII.F.20).

(Panel 30) Lieut. Walter Urban Martell, M.M., 85th Bn. Canadian Infantry (Nova Scotia Regt.), C.E.F.: *s.* of Fred A. Martell, of L'Ardoise, Nova Scotia, by his wife Maria Louise: *b.* L'Ardoise, 5 November 1892: Religion – Roman Catholic: Occupation – Student: 5'4" tall, grey eyes, brown hair: enlisted Sydney, Cape Breton, 19 August 1915; apptd. Lieut., 85th (Nova Scotia Highlanders), 20 December following. Killed in action 28 October 1917: Age 23. *unm.* (*IWGC record age 27*)

(Panel 30) Pte. 901869, Forest Charles Benner, 85th Bn. Canadian Infantry (Nova Scotia Regt.), C.E.F.: *s.* of Charles Benner, of Shubenacadie, Hants Co., Nova Scotia, by his wife Kate: *b.* 12 April 1899 (attested 1897): Religion – Presbyterian: Occupation – Fireman: 5'7" tall, hazel eyes, brown hair: enlisted Shubenacadie, 31 March 1916 (aged 15 years, 11 months). Killed in action 30 October 1917: Age 18. Standing on a plot of ground donated by the Canadian National Railroad the Shubenacadie War Memorial (unveiled July 1921) records the names of nineteen local men who gave their lives in the Great War; the first name inscribed thereon – Pte. F.C. Benner.

(Panel 30) Pte. 282425, Ralph Yorke, 85th Bn. Canadian Infantry (Nova Scotia Regt.), C.E.F.: *s.* of Hattie Yorke (Bear River, Nova Scotia): and brother to L/Corpl. 515637, C.M. Yorke, 5th Canadian Mounted Rifles, who fell the same day: *b.* Bear River, Annapolis Co., 7 November 1897: Religion – Baptist: Occupation – Farmer: 5'8¾" tall, grey eyes, black hair: enlisted 85th Battn., Bear River, 10 March 1916; joined the Expeditionary Force in France, 10 February 1917, and was killed in action 30 October 1917, at Passchendaele: Age 19. Remembered on Bear River War Memorial, Nova Scotia.

His brother Curtiss also has no known grave; he is recorded on Panel 32.

(Panel 30) Pte. 775273, James Charles Donaghy, 87th (Canadian Grenadier Guards) Bn. Canadian Infantry (Quebec Regt.), C.E.F.: *husb.* to Laura Hamilton Donaghy (165, Franklin Avenue, Toronto): *b.* Alma, Wellington Co., 18 May 1887: Religion – Presbyterian: Occupation – Machinist: previously served 11th Howitzer Bty., Guelph: joined C.E.F., Toronto, 10 December 1915: proceeded overseas 28 June 1916. 'Previously, for official purposes presumed to have died, now reported killed in action. Information available states he was on duty with a Lewis gun, during an action in the vicinity of Passchendaele church, 17 November 1917, when an enemy shell exploded, shattering the gun and blowing him to pieces.' Age 30.

(Panel 30) Pte. 144504, Arthur John Duff, 87th (Canadian Grenadier Guards) Bn. Canadian Infantry (Quebec Regt.), C.E.F.: *s.* of John Duff, of Savana Grande, Trinidad, British West Indies: and brother to Dvr. T4/124243, A.H. Duff, Army Service Corps, died of wounds 11 April 1918; Poperinghe: *b.* Princes Town, Trinidad, 25 November 1895: Occupation – Planter: volunteered and enlisted Smith Falls, 7 August 1915: departed Halifax, S.S. 'Empress of Britain,' 25 April 1916; trained England from 5 May following: served in France and Flanders from 11 August 1916: took part in the fighting – 21 October – when the battalion successfully blocked Regina Trench east of the Courcelette-Pys road (Somme); at Vimy Ridge (April 1917) when half the battalion's leading wave was cut-down by machine-gun fire; and was killed in action at Passchendaele 16 November 1917: Age 21. Correspondence to be forwarded c/o of his sister, Ms. Ada Duff (Trinidad).

His brother Alfredo is buried in Lijssenthoek Military Cemetery (XXVI.H.7).

(Panel 30) Corpl. 703504, James Wright, 102nd Bn. Canadian Infantry (2nd Central Ontario Regt.), C.E.F.: *s.* of James Wright, of 44, Cobbler Street, Dalton: *b.* Dalton, co. Lancaster, 26 February 1886: emigrated to Canada, taking up residence Smithers, British Columbia: Occupation – Miner: enlisted Smithers, 26 January 1916. Killed in action, Passchendaele Ridge, 17 November 1917: Age 31. *unm.* Remains 'Unknown Canadian Corpl. 102' recovered unmarked grave (28.D.6.c.0.8) 27 January 1927; identified – Badge of Rank, Collar Badges; reinterred, registered 29 January 1927. *Buried in Sanctuary Wood Cemetery (III.E.20).*

At 11.50 a.m., 30 October 1917, 102nd Battalion received sudden orders to move up from their camp near Brandhoek in support of 12th Brigade. On arrival at Potijze, with insufficient winter clothing, the battalion was kept waiting in the cold and rain for orders as to its ultimate destination. Eventually ordered to proceed to (and dig in on) Abraham Heights, from whence they were to relieve the 87th in the front line later that day. Advancing along a duck-board track laid precariously over the mud and water-filled shell-holes, under heavy fire all the way, the battalion incurred 13 casualties and on arrival the only shelter the men could take was that which they had to dig for themselves.

Remaining in the front line for just one day and night under a continuous enemy barrage which included gas – from the effects of which they lost their medical officer, Major Bapty – the battalion's casualty report for their first of two tours in the Passchendaele sector recorded:– 28 Other Ranks killed, 3 officers wounded, 74 Other Ranks wounded or gassed.

It is worthy of mention that the 102nd Battalion was the last Canadian unit to leave the Passchendaele Ridge, the Battalion History records ;- "We had gained no particular honour or glory there. Our tours in the line had been short and had involved no offensives; they had entailed much hard work in burying cable, digging trenches and putting the line in better shape, and they had called for the staying quality which enables men to lie down for long hours in ill-protected positions under incessant bombardments. We had just done the little that we had been set to do, but had suffered casualties out of all proportion to our task, and that it is which makes the memory of Passchendaele a nightmare in the minds of all those who had a share in a particularly odious experience."

Such was the nature of the battlefield and fighting at Passchendaele it was considered unreasonable to put men's lives at risk to perform an honoured burial; the majority of those who died remained where they fell, either in shell holes or sucked down into the all absorbing mud.

(Panel 30) L/Corpl. 103234, Herbert Charles French, 102nd Bn. Canadian Infantry (2nd Central Ontario Regt.), C.E.F.: s. of Albert E. French: b. Brantford, Ontario, 1 January 1889: Occupation – Clerk: previously served 50th London Regt., Ontario (Militia): volunteered for Overseas Service, 31 October 1915: served with the Expeditionary Force in France and Flanders, and was killed in action at Passchendaele, 1 November 1917: Age 28.

(Panel 30) Pte. 225830, George Henry Barnard, 102nd Bn. Canadian Infantry (2nd Central Ontario Regt.), C.E.F.: s. of W. (& Mrs) Barnard: b. Cliffe, co. Kent, 20 November 1894: Occupation – Electrician: previously served 6 months Canadian Engineers: volunteered and enlisted Toronto, 13 May 1916. Killed in action 1 November 1917: Age 22. He leaves a widow, Emily Barnard (95, Sussex Avenue, Toronto); late of 3½, Morse Street, Toronto.

(Panel 30) Pte. 267016, Arthur James Billington, 102nd Bn. Canadian Infantry (2nd Central Ontario Regt.), C.E.F.: late of Saskatoon, Saskatchewan: s. of Edward Billington, of 349, Gladstone Street, Peterborough, co. Northampton, by his wife Annie: b. Willesden, London, N.W., 18 May 1894: Occupation – Farmer: enlisted Waldena, Saskatchewan, 10 December 1915: posted 195th Overseas Battn.: served with the Expeditionary Force in France and Flanders transf'd. 102nd Battn, and was killed in action 1 November 1917: Age 23.

(Panel 30) Pte. 135450, Ernest Charles Chapman, 102nd Bn. Canadian Infantry (2nd Central Ontario Regt.), C.E.F.: s. of Harry Pledge Chapman, of 130, Woodland Avenue, Ilford, co. Essex: b. London, England, 23 November 1894: Occupation – Upholsterer: enlisted Toronto, 22 July 1915. Killed in action 31 October 1917: Age 22.

(Panel 30) Pte. 727114, Frank Cobb, 102nd Bn. Canadian (2nd Central Ontario Regt.), C.E.F.: late husb. to Iva Cobb (Factory House, Great William Street, Stratford-on-Avon, co. Warwick): s. of Ruth Cobb (Heckington, co. Lincoln). Killed in action during the final stages of his battalion's second tour on the Passchendaele Ridge, 18 November 1917: Age 32.

(Panel 30) Pte. 104230, John Ferguson, 102nd Bn. Canadian Infantry (2nd Central Ontario Regt.), C.E.F.: b. Dallas, co. Moray, 23 June 1889: Occupation – Clerk: enlisted Regina, Saskatchewan, 23 July 1915; given Actg. Sergt. rank: reverted to Private to proceed overseas, and was killed in action 31 October 1917: Age 28. He leaves a wife, Minnie (2326, 16th Avenue, Regina).

(Panel 30) Pte. 755067, Albert Giverman, 102nd Bn. Canadian Infantry (2nd Central Ontario Regt.), C.E.F.: b. Hull, Quebec, 23 July 1893: Occupation – Labourer: enlisted Thessalon, Ontario, 30 March 1916: posted 119th Overseas Battn.: transfd. 102nd Battn. before proceeding to France, and was killed in action 1 November 1917: Age 24. All correspondence should be addressed c/o his brother, Harry Giverman Esq., Hull, Quebec.

(Panel 30) Pte. 200200, Bruce Glenn, 102nd Bn. Canadian Infantry (2nd Central Ontario Regt.), C.E.F.: *s.* of John Gilbert Glenn, of 1956, 43rd Avenue West, Vancouver, British Columbia, late of 1416, 10th Avenue East, Vancouver, by his wife Charlotte: *b.* St. Mary's, Ontario, 22 October 1894: Occupation – Printer: enlisted Vancouver, 15 January 1917; apptd. No.3 Rft. Draft.: transf'd. No.1 Canadian Army Service Corps Training, 16 February 1917: posted overseas, 22 February 1917: served with the Expeditionary Force in France and Flanders, and was killed in action 31 October 1917: Age 23.

(Panel 30) Pte. 704154, Charles Hansen, 102nd Bn. Canadian Infantry (2nd Central Ontario Regt.), C.E.F.: late of Courtenay, British Columbia: *s.* of Margaret Hansen (51, Albert Street, Ottawa): *b.* Copenhagen, Denmark, 6 June 1886: Occupation – Logger: enlisted Courtenay, 25 April 1916, posted 102nd Battn. Killed in action 31 October 1917: Age 31.

(Panel 30) Pte. 226877, Adelard Houle, 102nd Bn. Canadian Infantry (2nd Central Ontario Regt.), C.E.F.: late of 10, Haynes Street, St. Catherine, Ontario: *b.* Quebec, 22 July 1898: Occupation – Labourer: enlisted St. Catherine's, 9 January 1917. Killed in action 1 November 1917: Age 29.

(Panel 30) Pte. 1003078, Russell Courtney McIntyre, 102nd Bn. Canadian Infantry (2nd Central Ontario Regt.), C.E.F.: *s.* of Mrs Wm. McIntyre (Sudbury, Ontario): *b.* Mattawa, Ontario, 17 September 1898: Occupation – Clerk: previously served 97th Algonquin Rifles (Militia); enlisted Sudbury, 20 April 1916; posted 227th Overseas Battn.: subsequently transf'd. 102nd Battn., and was killed in action in France, 31 October 1917: Age 29.

(Panel 30) Pte. 907520, Edward Martin, 102nd Bn. Canadian Infantry (2nd Central Ontario Regt.), C.E.F.: *s.* of Henrietta Martin (1225, Dufferin Street, Toronto); late of Evesham, co. Suffolk, England: *b.* Huntsville, Muskoka, Ontario, 27 July 1892: Occupation Farmer: enlisted Regina, Saskatchewan, 22 March 1916. Killed in action 1 November 1917: Age 25.

(Panel 30) Pte. 102657, Alfred James Mills, 102nd Bn. Canadian Infantry (2nd Central Ontario Regt.), C.E.F.: *b.* London, N.W., 27 July 1885: Occupation – Fireman: prior to emigrating saw previous service with 6th Bn. Duke of Cornwall's Light Infantry: enlisted Victoria, 14 September 1915: served with the Expeditionary Force in France and Flanders, and was killed in action 30 October 1917; Passchendaele: Age 32. All correspondence should be addressed c/o his sister, Miss Mabel Mills (10, Star Street, Edgeware Road, London, N.W.).

(Panel 30) Pte. 703340, Aubrey Barrow Mogg, 102nd Bn. Canadian Infantry (2nd Central Ontario Regt.), C.E.F.: late of Sandwich, British Columbia: *s.* of the Rev. Canon (& Mrs) Mogg, of The Vicarage, Bishop's Canning, Vale of Pewsey, co. Wilts: and brother to Capt. C.K.B. Mogg, British Columbia Regt., killed in action 11 November 1917, at Passchendaele: *b.* Chittoe, Bromham, co. Wilts, 29 July 1889: Religion – Church of England: Occupation – Poultry Farmer: 6' tall, dark complexion, grey eyes, black hair: enlisted Comox, British Columbia, 27 January 1916. Killed in action 19 August 1916, at St. Eloi: Age 28. *unm.* Pte. Mogg and his brother are commemorated on a brass Cross in Bishop's Canning (St. Mary the Virgin) Parish Church of which their father was vicar.

His brother Cyril also has no known grave; he is recorded on Panel 18.

(Panel 30) Pte. 1003024, Joseph Paquette, 102nd Bn. Canadian Infantry (2nd Central Ontario Regt.), C.E.F.: *s.* of Peter Paquette, of Korah Road, Ontario: *b.* Vernick Hill, Ottawa, 10 May 1892: Occupation Labourer; Ship Canal, Saulte St. Marie: previously served 9 months, 51st Scottish Rifles (Militia): volunteered and enlisted Saulte St. Marie, 28 March 1916; being illiterate, signing – X – his mark: posted 227th Overseas Battn.: went to France, transf'd. 102nd Battn., and was killed in action 31 October 1917: Age 25.

(Panel 30) Pte. 129882, Arthur Walker Peters, 102nd Bn. Canadian Infantry (2nd Central Ontario Regt.), C.E.F.: *s.* of the late William Peters, of 3672, 15th Avenue West, Vancouver, by his wife Alice M. (6536, East Boulevard, Vancouver, British Columbia): *b.* St. John, New Brunswick, 31 March 1894:

Occupation Banker: enlisted Vancouver, 1 October 1915; apptd. 72nd Battn.; subsequently transf'd. 102nd Battn., and was killed in action at Passchendaele, 1 November 1917: Age 23. *unm.*

(Panel 30) Pte. 908041, Harry Gilbert Ransom, 102nd Bn. Canadian Infantry (2nd Central Ontario Regt.), C.E.F.: late of Waldena, Saskatchewan: *s.* of Jane Ann Marks, *née* Ransom ('Iona,' Park Lane, Harefield, Uxbridge, co. Middlesex): *b.* London, England, 15 February 1894: enlisted Regina, Saskatchewan, 5 July 1916: proceeded to France, 31 December following, and was killed in action 1 November 1917: Age 23. *unm.*

(Panel 30) Pte. 100530, Joseph Roscoe, 102nd Bn. Canadian Infantry (2nd Central Ontario Regt.), C.E.F.: late of Sudbury, Ontario: *s.* of Joseph Roscoe, of 202, Sumack Street, Nortonia, Toronto, by his wife Elsie: *b.* Wahnapitae, Ontario, 29 March 1894: Occupation Prospector: enlisted Sudbury, 24 June 1916. Killed in action 1 November 1917: Age 22. *unm.*

(Panel 30) L/Sergt. 745607, Walter James Blunden, 116th Bn. Canadian Infantry (Central Ontario Regt.), C.E.F.: *s.* of Sarah Blunden (Eastern Road, Lindfield, co. Sussex): and brother to L/Corpl. G/8697, P.C. Blunden, 6th East Kent Regt., killed in action 7 October 1916; Guedecourt, Somme: *b.* co. Sussex, 28 June 1892: Religion – Methodist: 5'5½" tall, fair complexion, blue eyes, brown hair: Occupation Farmer: enlisted Uxbridge, Ontario, 17 November 1915; apptd. 116th Battn., Whitby, Ontario 15 March 1916; proceeded overseas April following: served with the Expeditionary Force in France and Flanders, and was killed in action 27 October 1917; Passchendaele Ridge: Age 25. He leaves a wife, Mrs. A. Blunden ('Three Furnaces Inn,' Madeley, co. Salop).

His brother Percy also has no known grave, he is commemorated on the Thiepval Memorial (Pier & Face 5D).

(Panel 30) Lieut.Col. Alfred Ernest Shaw, Comdg. 1st Canadian Mounted Rifles (Saskatchewan Regt.), C.E.F.: late *husb.* of Katherine Shaw (732, 13th Avenue West, Calgary, Alberta). Killed in action, 1.15 p.m., 2 June 1916, while making a determined stand against an enemy attack; 1st C.M.R. Headquarters, Vigo Street trench, Sanctuary Wood – Mount Sorrel sector. *(IWGC record 3 June)*

4th Canadian Mounted Rifles, Trenches Sanctuary Wood – Mount Sorrel: "1st June 1916: The enemy was generally quiet, a few trench mortars were put over into the right company which had two casualties. About 2 p.m. the enemy shelled our S.P.12 with about twenty rounds 4.2 and 5.9 and got several direct hits on the communication trench. Our guns retaliated to a certain degree. About 4 p.m. we observed a large working party of the enemy digging very wide shelter trenches opposite 51 and 52. We managed to disperse this working party with our Lewis and Stokes guns. The night of 1st and 2nd was very quiet. We had a large working party on the sap and new trench in front of 51.

2nd June: The enemy fired over about 20 or 30 trench mortars about 7 a.m. Gen. Mercer and Gen. Williams, Capt. Fraser and Lieut. Gooderham arrived at Battn. Hdqrs. About 7.45 a.m. on a tour of inspection of the front line with special reference to the new work on the sap. The C.O. accompanied them. At 8.30 the enemy commenced a bombardment and a shell burst opposite the party, deafening Gen Mercer almost completely, slightly wounding Gen. Williams, and deafening Lieut. Gooderham. Gen. Mercer with two aides was brought to Battn. H.Q. Gen. Williams was taken to the Dressing Station where the C.O. remained with him. The bombardment increased, and we were bombarded in the front line, supports and reserves, by thousands of shells of every description. This bombardment was most intense. The front line was also bombarded by trench mortars. The O.C. of the platoon in S.P.12 held his position until about 11.30 a.m. when he sent out his remaining men who were mostly wounded and when his last man had left, came out himself. A mine exploded on the battalion front about 1 p.m. and an order came down the line to withdraw. At this time the whole front line was flattened and there were no trenches of any description, and very few of the battn. that were able to carry on. Capt. Symons and the SinC remained at Battn H.Q. throughout the bombardment; Col. Ussher remaining with Gen. Williams. Gen. Mercer and his staff also remained at Battn. H.Q. throughout the bombardment, and were not further injured when the order came to withdraw.

The SinC gathered about 20 men together and started for Maple Copse where the supportng battn. was situated. When he reached the copse he had only three men with him, the others having become casualties through enemy shells, machine-gun and rifle fire. He proceeded down the C.T. to Bde. H.Q. at Zillebeke where he reported. He was given permission to take up 6 men and try to discover news of the battn. He remained in the neighbourhood of Zillebeke village for about 2 hours, but could get no word of any men in the battn. He then reported back to Bde. During the afternoon and evening of the 2nd about 45 men reported at Bde. H.Q. from the front and support lines. During the day the scouts of the battn. who had survived made numerous trips through the area, acting under the Bde. Intelligence Officer. A few more men reported, making 56 in all. The SinC received orders to move back with the men he had to Camp B at 8 p.m. He reached Camp B that evening with 64 men from the front line. During the day the survivors of the battn. furnished a carrying party for water to the front line."

At a muster parade held on the morning of 4th June only 73 out of 702 men from the front line answered their names; a further 56 men were reported as having passed through the dressing stations as casualties of varying degree. Of the officers in the trenches, only the SinC and Capt. Coleman survived, 17 officers were unaccounted for, and Lieut. Rutter had been evacuated to hospital.

Panels 30 and 32 record the names of 717 officers and men of the Canadian Mounted Rifles; among them 165 of 4th C.M.R. who lost their lives 2-3 June 1916.

(Panel 30) Capt. John Hannaford Symons, 4th Canadian Mounted Rifles (1st Central Ontario Regt.), C.E.F.: *s.* of William Linbury Symons, by his wife Georgia Lutz: *husb.* to E. Marion Douglas Symons (64, South Drive, Toronto). Missing / believed killed in action 2 June 1916: Age 25.

(Panel 30) Lieut. Herbert Hallowell Bourne, 4th Canadian Mounted Rifles (1st Central Ontario Regt.), C.E.F.: *b.* 20 September 1886: Occupation Banker: enlisted 17 June 1915: posted 54th Battn. 1 October following, and proceeded to Europe: served with the Expeditionary Force in France and Flanders, transf'd. 4th Mounted Rifles, and was reported missing believed killed in action 3 June 1916: Age 29. He was married to Margaret Agnes Bourne; all correspondence should be addressed c/o Miss Moran (Suite 501, 1086, Bale Street, Vancouver, British Columbia).

(Panel 30) Lieut. Lionel Esmonde Clarke, 4th Canadian Mounted Rifles (1st Central Ontario Regt.), C.E.F.: *s.* of Lionel H. (& Annie C.G.) Clarke, of 6, Clarendon Crescent, Toronto: *b.* Toronto, 8 March 1894: Occupation – Clerk: enlisted Valcartier. Missing / believed killed in action 3 June 1916: Age 22.

(Panel 30) Lieut. Jaffray Eaton, 4th Canadian Mounted Rifles (1st Central Ontario Regt.), C.E.F.: only *s.* of the late Christopher Eaton, by his wife Annie E. Jaffray Eaton (Eagles Nest, Owen Sound, Ontario): *b.* Owen Sound, 6 June 1886: *educ.* Public School there; University College, Toronto, 1902 – 07, where he was a member of the Gymnasium team: on the Staff – '*The Toronto Globe*,' a member of the Press Executive, and Newspapermen's Rifle Association: attained rank of Major, 31st Regt. (Militia), as Adjt. to which unit he was active in recruiting and training 100 men from Owen Sound who joined 1st Canadian Contingent: apptd. Adjt. 86th Machine Gun Battn. 1915: transf'd. 147th (Grey County) Battn., January 1916, as Major and Second-in-Command: reverted from rank to Capt. (Q.M.) to proceed overseas; serving in that capacity to 8th Battn. in England until August 1917: reverted to Lieut. that he might proceed to France, joining 4th Mounted Rifles there, and was killed in action at Passchendaele 26 October 1917, on which date his platoon was on the extreme flank and suffered so severely that only two returned: Age 30. *unm.*

(Panel 30) Lieut. Charles Edward Kilcoursie Lambart, 'B' Coy., 1st Canadian Mounted Rifles (Saskatchewan Regt.), C.E.F.: *s.* of the late Major Frederick Lambart. Missing / believed killed in action, Sanctuary Wood – Mount Sorrel sector, 2 – 5 June 1916: Age 38. Lieut. Lambart leaves a wife, Isabel Dora Lambart, and was one of three brothers who served in the Great War. *(IWGC record 5 June 1916)*

(Panel 30) Lieut. George Morrisey, 4th Canadian Mounted Rifles (1st Central Ontario Regt.), C.E.F.: *s.* of Alfred Morrisey, of 58, Hazen Street, St. John, New Brunswick, by his wife Lilian: *b.* St. John, New Brunswick, 4 May 1892: Occupation Clerk: prior to enlistment served 10 yrs. Cadet Corps (no.173), 1 yr. 62nd Regt., 3 yrs. C of C, 2 yrs. 28th New Brunswick Dragoons: enlisted Amherst, 30 March 1915:

served with the Expeditionary Force in France and Flanders, and was reported missing, believed killed in action, 3 June 1916: Age 24. *(IWGC record age 22)*

After a little over two months acclimatisation in the Ploegsteert – Messines area attached to General Seely's Cavalry Division, 3rd and 6th Canadian Mounted Rifles were withdrawn from the trenches and, after reorganisation, placed under the command of Brigadier General V.A.S. Williams as part of the newly formed 8th Canadian Infantry Brigade. From the beginning of January until March 1916 all ranks of the C.M.R., in their new role as dismounted infantry, underwent intensive training in infantry tactics and drill 'in dead earnest' before moving up to Ypres to take over part of the line between Hill 60 and Hooge.

On the morning of 2 June 1916 5th C.M.R., Battalion Headquarters, and three companies were in support at Maple Copse when, at about 8am. the enemy began a heavy bombardment coinciding with information that an attack was in progress on the sector held by 7th and 8th Brigades. At mid-day the explosion of mines was observed and, as the shelling continued unabatingly, it was quite clear that the whole area held by the two brigades was being systematically destroyed. With all communications to the rear cut it was not until 2pm. that Capt. B.W. Roscoe received orders – despite there being no specified route – to reinforce with his Company what remained of Battalion Headquarters at Maple Copse; the officer conveying the order adding that he hoped Roscoe would get through.

The only other officer with Roscoe's Company at this time was Lieut. Otty but it developed that the N.C.O's had the requisite requirements of leadership and judgement. Led by Capt. Roscoe, the Company advanced to the support of what remained of the Battalion in full view of the enemy, through an extremely heavy barrage and reached Maple Copse with surprisingly few casualties where, shortly after arrival, further orders were received requesting the Company make contact with 7th Brigade on the left, dig in and hold the Copse to the last. It was at this point that the N.C.O's displayed qualities of leadership and judgement which were later substantially rewarded. C.S.M. Gill, with twenty men, occupied and held a position whose garrison had all been killed; Sergts. Chase, McGarry and Martin led detachments through the Copse and dug in on the edge nearest to the enemy. Lieut. Otty showed absolute fearlessness in assisting with the disposition of the Company, refusing to avail himself of anything that might afford him shelter. Shortly after remarking to Capt. Roscoe that if he were to be killed it would happen anyway – the safety of his men was his main consideration – Lieut. Otty was hit and killed outright.

(Panel 30) Lieut. George Nugent Dickson Otty, 'D' Coy., 5th Canadian Mounted Rifles, C.E.F.: formerly 'A' Sqdn., 6th C.M.R.: *s.* of George O. Otty, of Hampton, Kings Co., New Brunswick, by his wife Emily Dickson: *educ.* McGill University (Graduate): mobilised Amherst, Nova Scotia, 17 March 1915: transf'd. Valcartier, May, embarked Quebec, aboard troopship 'Herschel,' for the European War early July: after further training in England, proceeded to France, 24 October 1915, being there attd. Gen. Seely's Cavalry Divn., as Corps Troops; Ploegsteert – Messines sector, and was killed in action 3 June 1916, at Maple Copse, Zillebeke: Age 30.

(Panel 30) Lieut. Cecil Howard Peaker, 4th Canadian Mounted Rifles (1st Central Ontario Regt.), C.E.F.: *s.* of the late W.J. Peaker, by his wife Rose (411, Riverdale Avenue, Ottawa). Missing / believed killed in action, 2 June 1916: Age 22.

(Panel 30) Lieut. Howard Vincent Pickering, 4th Bn. Canadian Mounted Rifles, C.E.F.: *s.* of the late Joseph Pickering, by his marriage to Emily J. Freel, *née* Pickering (Winona, Ontario): *b.* Arkona, 5 September 1884: *educ.* Tapleytown Public School, Hamilton Collegiate; University College, Toronto, 1906 – 10, B.A (English & History Mods); Columbia University (Ph.D. studies), 1910 – 11, graduated M.A.: Occupation Teacher; Grimsby School: joined 110th Battn.; Lieut., Stratford, 5 May 1915: apptd. Adjt., November following; proceeded overseas 1916: joined 4th C.M.R., Vimy sector April 1917, served in the engagements before Lens and Hill 70, and was killed in action at Passchendaele, being shot by a sniper as he was leading his men in the attack on the morning of 26 October 1917: Age 33. Buried where he fell.

In August 1914, Lieut. Harry Colebourn, a veterinary officer with 34th Fort Garry Home Brigade, was travelling on the Canadian Pacific Railway from his home in Winnipeg to Valcartier, Quebec, to enlist in the Canadian Army and, whilst waiting to change trains at White River Bend, Ontario, he noticed a man with an American black bear cub. Engaging the man in conversation Colebourn discovered he was a trapper who had shot and killed the cub's mother and after offering him $20 for the young bear – which the trapper immediately accepted – travelled onward with the cub to Quebec where 2nd Infantry Brigade adopted it as their mascot and took it to England with them. In December 1915 as the Brigade prepared to move to France, Colebourn decided it would be both unwise and unsafe to take the cub with him and perhaps thinking, as many at the time also thought, that this year the war would definitely be over by Christmas, he visited London Zoo requesting they care for the cub for 'no longer than two weeks.' Unfortunately the war was not destined to end quite so quickly and although Colebourn visited her on numerous occasions during the course of the war almost four years passed before he was in a position to reclaim her; four years during which time she been given the name 'Winnipeg' – in recognition of Colebourn's hometown in Canada – and become so popular with visitors to the zoo that he decided to leave her there.

After the war 'Winnipeg' became the inspiration for A.A. Milne's 'Winnie the Pooh,' stories; a regular visitor to the zoo he shortened her name to 'Winnie' and combined it with the name of his son, Christopher Robin's, pet swan 'Pooh.'

Perhaps not so famous but worthy of note nonetheless is 'Teddy,' a stuffed bear sent out to France in a care package by Aileen Rogers to protect her father Lieut. Lawrence B. Rogers. In a letter to his wife dated September 1916 he asks her to inform Aileen that Teddy is still with him despite it being rather dirty and its legs having almost fallen off. One year later, after Lieut. Rogers' death at Passchendaele, Teddy was found among his effects along with his wedding ring and letters from his family and, almost eighty years later Aileen's niece, Roberta Rogers Innes, rediscovered Teddy in an old briefcase with over 200 letters written by Lieut. Rogers to his wife May.

In 2003, to commemorate the 90th Anniversary of the Armistice, 'The Memory Project' – an initiative of The Dominion Institute, Toronto; The '*Globe and Mail*' and the government of France – launched a national request for letters, photographs and artefacts from the front lines of the First World War. Submitted by Roberta Rogers 'Teddy' was among 100 of the most significant items selected, appearing on CBC's '*The Journal*' and the '*Vicki Gabereau Show*.' He was the subject of an article in '*The Globe and Mail*' – "*It Went to Hell and Back: Mr Rogers' Teddy Bear*," and another article entitled "*Longing and Loss from Canada's Great War*" which appeared in the Winter 2007 edition of Wilfred Laurier University's '*Canadian Military History*,' written by Canadian War Museum historian Tim Cook and Carleton University Honours History graduate Natascha Morrison. Donated to the Canadian War Museum by the Rogers family, the legless and dirty little bear now sits in a glass case as part of the World War I exhibition. 'Teddy' is the subject of a book '*A Bear In War*' by Stephanie Innes and Harry Endrulat.

(Panel 30) Lieut. Lawrence Browning Rogers, M.M., 5th Canadian Mounted Rifles, C.E.F.: *s.* of the late Major John Duncan Rogers, by his wife Hattie (Montreal): *b.* 17 December 1878: Religion – Church of England: Occupation – Dairy Farmer; East Farnham: 5'10" tall, fair complexion, blue eyes, light brown hair: small scar below right knee, callous on left wrist: enlisted Sweetsburg, Quebec, 11 February 1915: underwent Infantry training, Valcartier; departed Canada, R.M.S. 'Hesperian,' June 1915: underwent further training in England before proceeding to France later that year, where he served as a Medic to his regiment in all the major engagements of the Canadian Corps, and was killed in action 30 October 1917, at the Battle of Passchendaele: Age 38. His widow, Janet May Weaver Rogers, 'May' (106, Madison Avenue, Montreal), received the following letter from his Commanding Officer detailing the circumstances of her husband's death, "29 November 1917: It is with the deepest regret that I have to inform you of the death of your husband, Lieut. L. B. Rogers. Besides being one of the best Officers in our Battalion, he was a gentleman of the highest order and most popular in this Battalion. He was killed in action on 30th October, 1917, while assisting to care for the wounded. A dressing station had been provided but being a brave Officer he chose to fill it with the wounded and dress the cases as they came along in the open, totally disregarding all danger to himself. He was buried near where he fell. His personal effects have been collected and forwarded to you. All of my Officers join me in extending to you heartfelt sympathy in your sad bereavement." Lieut. Browning had two children, a *dau.*, Aileen (*b.* 1905) and *s.* Howard (*b.* 1908). (*IWGC record age 40*)

(Panel 30) Lieut. Edwin Charles Shepherd, 4th Canadian Mounted Rifles (1st Central Ontario Regt.), C.E.F.: *s.* of Mrs E.H. Shepherd (Niagara-on-the-Lake, Ontario): *husb.* to Ellen 'Nellie' Elizabeth Shepherd (123, Jane Street, North Bay, Ontario): *b.* Toronto, 11 November 1879: Religion – Anglican: Occupation – Plumber: previously served 23rd Regt. (Militia); serving member (5 yrs) 27th Regt., volunteered and enlisted 159th (Overseas) Bn., as Capt., North Bay, 10 March 1916: subsequently promoted Major, but relinquished this rank at his own request that he might proceed to France with a draft of reinforcements to 4th Mounted Rifles. Killed in action, being shot by a sniper while leading his platoon to the attack on Bellevue Spur, nr. Passchendaele, on the morning of 26 October 1917: Age 37.

(Panel 30) Lieut. Henry Wright Uglow, 4th Canadian Mounted Rifles (1st Central Ontario Regt.), C.E.F.: *s.* of Georgina Jane Uglow (164, Barrie Street, Kingston, Ontario): *b.* Ottawa, 27 April 1886: Occupation – Banker: volunteered and enlisted Ottawa, 21 May 1915: served with the Expeditionary Force in France. Reported missing / believed killed in action, 3 June 1916: Age 30.

PANEL 30 ENDS – LT. L.F. WEBSTER, CANADIAN MOUNTED RIFLES.

PANEL 32 BEGINS – CSM. J.A.P. SCARTH, CANADIAN MOUNTED RIFLES

(Panel 32) Sergt. 415679, Percy Earl Benjamin, 5th Canadian Mounted Rifles (Quebec Regt.), C.E.F.: *s.* of J.N. Benjamin, of Pugwash, Cumberland Co., Nova Scotia, and the late Mrs D.H. Benjamin: elder brother to Pte. 111031, H.E. Benjamin, 5th Mounted Rifles, killed in action, Battle of Mount Sorrel, 2 June 1916: *b.* Pugwash, 4 September 1891: Occupation – Steam Engineer: served 2 years 93rd Militia Regt.; enlisted 14 July 1915; served with the Expeditionary Force in France and Flanders, and was killed in action 30 October 1917: Age 26.

His brother Harold also has no known grave; he is recorded below.

(Panel 32) Sergt. 106648, John Biller, 1st Canadian Mounted Rifles (Saskatchewan Regt.), C.E.F.: *s.* of the late John Biller, by his wife Susannah: *b.* London, 1876: served with the Imperial Yeomanry in the South African Campaign: enlisted 1914: came over with 2nd Contingent: served with the Expeditionary Force in France and Flanders, and was killed in action at Sanctuary Wood, 2 June 1916: Age 39. He was married to Olive (since remarried), now Mrs Allen (James Island, British Columbia).

(Panel 32) Sergt. 835683, Hugh Buie, 4th Canadian Mounted Rifles (1st Central Ontario Regt.), C.E.F.: eldest *s.* of the late Archibald Buie, of Colonsay, by his wife Marion (63, Belvedere Road, Montreal): *b.* Colonsay, co. Argyle, 25 August 1898: *educ.* Oban, and Sandbank: went to Canada, September 1913; settled Montreal: employee Grand Trunk Railway Company: volunteered for Foreign Service and enlisted 145th (Kensington) Battn., March 1916: subsequently transferring Canadian Mounted Rifles: served with the Expeditionary Force in France and Flanders from December following, and was killed in action by the explosion of a shell at Passchendaele, 26 October 1917. Buried where he fell: Age 19.

(Panel 32) Sergt. 430787, Edward Harold Kemp, 4th Canadian Mounted Rifles (1st Central Ontario Regt.), C.E.F.: 9th *s.* of the late Rev. John Kemp, of Ilkley, co. York: *b.* 20 June 1883: previously reported missing, 8 September 1916, now officially confirmed killed in action 2 June 1916: Age 32.

(Panel 32) Sergt. 117043, Arthur Owen Philipps, 'B'Coy., 1st Canadian Mounted Rifles (Saskatchewan Regt.), C.E.F.: *s.* of the late Rev. James J. Philipps, by his wife Emma (Windrath, Manorbier, co. Pembroke): *b.* Tenby, 26 June 1879: Religion – Church of England: 5'11" tall, fair complexion, blue eyes, dark brown hair: previously served 14 yrs. (took part in the South African Campaign with) 102nd Yeomanry: sometime thereafter removed to Canada; gainfully employed as Rancher: enlisted 1st C.M.R., Calgary, 4 January 1915: after infantry training at Bordon Camp, co. Hants (late spring – early summer

1915) crossed to France as part of 3rd Canadian Divn., and was killed in action at the Battle of Mount Sorrel, 2 June 1916: Age 37. *unm. (IWGC record age 38)*

(Panel 32) L/Corpl. 117456, John C. Oxborough, 2nd Canadian Mounted Rifles (British Columbia Regt.), C.E.F.: Killed in action by enemy shell fire, Passchendaele Ridge, 31 October 1917. In reply to a letter from Miss Joy Smith, a fellow N.C.O., J.K. Moffat, wrote, "23.11.17: Your very kind letter was most welcome and I do appreciate your past esteem and consequent sorrow at the loss of our gallant comrade John C. Oxborough. To properly put together a letter extending sympathy and condolence I have ever considered beyond my efforts, and as in most cases, we find it a great boon to hand to our padre the known facts of each casualty, by doing so we feel assured that those who mourn are informed and possibly comforted. Where you so bravely ask for the bare facts of how it happened; you remove the greatest difficulty coupled with a natural desire to do everything possible when it has to do with 'little Chauncey.' I shall do my best to oblige.: October 31st. Wed. – about 5.30 p.m. Vapour Farm, Passchendaele Ridge. In an advanced outpost. A 4.5 Howitzer shell landed on the ground about three feet distant. A small particle of shrapnel penetrated the head. The body was otherwise unmarked. Death was instantaneous. At the time we were expecting a counter-attack on that (then newly-won) position. About two hours later when the bombardment had quieted down we buried our dead.: I found it extremely difficult to remove the identification disk and other personal effects from my splendid pal. Possibly you can understand. The body was in a kneeling attitude, with the left arm encircling the head. The moon came out clear from behind the dark cloudbank. Getting down beside him, in the hastily erected breastworks, in the mud, I turned the body over, the eyes were closed. His dear kind face that ever bore a sunny smile was strangely white and calm. When we lifted him up we could not believe it possible that he was gone from us, and lest there should be any possible mistake, we took ten minutes or so to make sure. We had gone through so much together, when we came back to find him still kneeling, it seemed so awe-inspiring and in such perfect keeping with his life and spotless ideals. When he could no longer serve in the body, he could make supplication in spirit. True indeed he was a genuine favourite wherever he went. So clean living, clean minded, and willing to serve others. It is one of our most highly cherished memories that shall ever remain fresh and green."

(Panel 32) L/Corpl. 415637, Curtiss M. Yorke, 5th Bn. Canadian Mounted Rifles, C.E.F.: *s.* of Hattie Yorke (Bear River, Nova Scotia): and brother to Pte. 282425, R. Yorke, 85th Canadian Infantry, who fell the same day: *b.* Bear River, Annapolis Co., 14 January 1894: Religion – Baptist: Occupation – Farmer: 5'5" tall, blue eyes, dark hair: previously served 69th Infantry Regt., and 27th Artillery Bty., enlisted Digby, 10 May 1915. Killed in action 30 October 1917, at Passchendaele: Age 23. *unm.* Remembered on Bear River War Memorial, Nova Scotia.

His brother Ralph also has no known grave; he is recorded on Panel 30.

(Panel 32) Pte. 114416, Geoffrey Gerald Adames, 1st Canadian Mounted Rifles (Saskatchewan Regt.), C.E.F.: c/o Mrs B.E. Mills ('Hayfield Lodge,' 120, Orchard Street, Chichester, co. Sussex, England): Religion – Church of England. Missing, presumed killed / died of wounds on or about 5 June 1916; failing to answer Roll Call, Divnl. Rest., St Lawrence Camp, following attack by the enemy at Sanctuary Wood, Ypres.

(Panel 32) Pte. 907911, Joseph Adeline, 1st Canadian Mounted Rifles (Saskatchewan Regt.), C.E.F.: *s.* of Stefan (& Mary) Adeline, of 1911, Quebec Street, Regina, Saskatchewan: *b.* 24 September 1897: Religion – Roman Catholic. Killed in action 24 October 1917, when standing close to the entrance of a captured German pill-box – Capricorn Keep, Passchendaele – in company with a comrade (Pte. Binch); he was killed instantaneously by the concussive blast from a heavy enemy shell: Age 21. Buried – Map. Loc. C.C.4/28.D.13.a.9.8.

(Panel 32) Pte. 106053, Charles Augustus Aldridge, 1st Canadian Mounted Rifles (Saskatchewan Regt.), C.E.F.: c/o Mrs E.L. Clifford (307, Main Street East, Toronto, Ontario): *s.* of the late David (& Elizabeth) Aldridge: *b.* 17 November 1886: Religion – Methodist: Occupation – Jeweller's Buyer: serving member, 6 months, 34th Fort Garry Horse (Militia); joined C.E.F., Brandon, Manitoba, 11 January 1915.

Reported missing, presumed killed in action 2 June 1916. After a heavy enemy bombardment of his battalion's front-line trench – Sanctuary Wood, Ypres – Pte. Aldridge was found lying at the bottom of the trench suffering from shell-shock. Shortly afterwards the trench was completely wrecked and taken by the Germans; nothing further was seen of him: Age 29. *unm.* (*IWGC record age 30*)

(Panel 32) Pte. 106071, John Robertson Baird, 1st Canadian Mounted Rifles (Saskatchewan Regt.), C.E.F.: late of 108, Royal Street, Winnipeg: 2nd *s.* of Alex Baird, of 942, North Drive, Fort Garry, Winnipeg, and his wife Jessie Louise, *née* Robertson: *b.* Glasgow, Scotland, 2 February 1891: Religion – Presbyterian: *educ.* Hillhead High School (Cadet Corps member): removed to Canada, 1905: 5'9½" tall, dark complexion, blue eyes, light brown hair: sometime Bank Clerk, Winnipeg; lately Book-keeper in his father's business: volunteered and enlisted Brandon, Manitoba, 11 January 1915; apptd. 1st C.M.R., departed Canada, April following: trained Shorncliffe, England (from June 1915); thereafter proceeded to join the Expeditionary Force in France: spent winter months 1915 – 16 in Ypres Salient sector, where – 'in the fierce fighting that raged around the trenches in the vicinity of Sanctuary Wood and Hooge Farm – during the month of June 1916 – the entire 1st Canadian Mounted Rifles were virtually wiped out. Pte. J.R. Baird is believed to have been among those killed in action, 5 June 1916, but, such was the intensity and prolonged nature of the fighting and so few survivors came back, the exact date of death has not be ascertained.': Age 25. Sometime afterwards Mr & Mrs Baird received a letter from a German soldier who said that while occupying the trenches previously held by the Canadian Mounted Rifles he had found, and had in his possession, Pte. Baird's bible; he offered to return this to them. 'Needless to say they gratefully accepted, and sent a letter thanking this soldier for his kindness.' 'Pte. Baird dearly loved his adoptive land, and was loud in its praises, but responded at once to his native country's call in its hour of need.'

(Panel 32) Pte. 111031, Harold Esty Benjamin, 5th Canadian Mounted Rifles (Quebec Regt.), C.E.F.: *s.* of J.N. Benjamin, of Pugwash, Cumberland Co., Nova Scotia, and the late Mrs D.H. Benjamin: and *yr.* brother to Sergt. 415679, P.E. Benjamin, 5th Mounted Rifles, killed 30 October 1917: *b.* 2 March 1896: Occupation – Student: enlisted Amherst, Nova Scotia, 7 June 1915: served with the Expeditionary Force in France and Flanders, and was killed in action at the Battle of Mount Sorrel, 2 June 1916: Age 20.

His brother Percy also has no known grave; he is recorded above.

(Panel 32) Pte. 255184, Charles Langton Binch, 1st Canadian Mounted Rifles (Saskatchewan Regt.), C.E.F.: *s.* of Charles (& Mrs) Binch, of Laura, Saskatchewan: Religion – Church of England. Killed instantaneously by the explosion of a heavy German shell, 24 October 1917; at the time of his death he was standing close to the entrance of a captured German pill-box – Capricorn Keep, Passchendaele. Buried – 28.D.13.a.9.8.: Age 23. Pte Adeline was also killed.

(Panel 32) Pte. 106102, George Hume Keese Bradshaw, 1st Canadian Mounted Rifles (Saskatchewan Regt.), C.E.F.: *s.* of George Hume Bradshaw, of Binscarth, Manitoba, by his wife Katherine: *b.* Moosomin, Saskatchewan, 15 March 1890: Religion – Church of England: Occupation – Farmer: joined C.E.F., 23 December 1914: served with the Expeditionary Force in France from 23 September 1915, and was killed in action 5 June 1916: Age 26. Remains recovered unmarked grave (28.J.19.c.0.6); identified – Disc, Titles, Clothing; reinterred, registered 15 March 1927. *Buried in Sanctuary Wood Cemetery (III.K.18).*

(Panel 32) Pte. 109235, Geoffrey Bertram Brake, 4th Canadian Mounted Rifles (1st Central Ontario Regt.), C.E.F.: *s.* of the late Henry F. Brake, by his wife Mary C. Missing / believed killed in action 2 June 1916: Age 19. *Buried in Sanctuary Wood Cemetery (V.U.17).*

Not Dead. Oh No! But Bourne Beyond The Shadows Into The Full Clear Light

(Panel 32) Pte. 111078, John William Carr, 5th Canadian Mounted Rifles (Quebec Regt.), C.E.F.: *s.* of Benjamin (& Annie) Carr, of 995, Barrington Street, Halifax, Nova Scotia: *b.* Aldershot, England, 15 August 1899 (attested 1896): Religion – Church of England: 5'2" tall, fair complexion, blue eyes, light red hair: Occupation Pipe Fitter: enlisted Halifax, 2 June 1915. Reported missing 2 June 1916, now assumed killed in action: **Age 16.**

(Panel 32) Pte. 623046, Edward Campbell Currie, 1st Canadian Mounted Rifles (Saskatchewan Regt.), C.E.F.: *s.* of the late Archibald Currie: and late *husb.* to Myrtle F. Johnston-Williams, *née* Currie (2123, Pleasant Avenue, Minneapolis, United States): *b.* Collingwood, Ontario, 18 March 1871: Occupation – Merchant: joined C.E.F., Camp Hughes, Fort William, 17 September 1915; posted 44th (Overseas) Battn., 30 September: subsequently transf'd. 1st C.M.R. Reported missing, believed killed 5 – 6 June 1916; Roll-Call, St Lawrence Camp (after being in trenches Sanctuary Wood) now, for official purposes presumed to have died: Age 45. Identity disc inscribed with Pte. Currie's name, number and unit was found, September 1928, by a farmer near to the exhumation site of Pte. 622326, J. MacKay, 1st C.M.R.

Pte. Mackay (served as Martin, T.), buried in Sanctuary Wood Cemetery (II.L.9), is recorded below.

At 8.30 a.m. on the morning of 2 June 1916, trenches T54-60 – manned by 1st Canadian Mounted Rifles – in the Sanctuary Wood – Mount Sorrel sector were subjected to a heavy bombardment, followed at 1.15 p.m. by a massed infantry attack. 1st C.M.R. War Diary records:– "Lieut.Col. A.E. Shaw killed at Battn. HQrs during a determined stand made by him and about 80 others of the battn. against enemy's troops who had succeeded in piercing our line to right of T52 occupied by 4th C.M.R. Battn. The company of this battn. occupying the trenches on our right being completely destroyed by being blown up by one of the enemy's mines. After Col. Shaw was killed Major Palmer took command and defended the position at Vigo Street at Battn. HQrs until there were only two officers and eight other ranks remaining alive and unwounded. The enemy having bombed the survivors to one end of the trench, and having no ammunition or bombs to reply to the enemy's fire, he issued orders for the remainder to get out if they could and retire to SP14. As far as it is known only one officer, Lieut. F.A. Ley, and about four or five others were the only ones who arrived at this point which they found occupied by by Lieut. A.V. Evans and a few men with a Colt Machine Gun. This position was held by them until relieved, and has since remained in our possession."

Throughout the following three days the War Diary records no action, only their relief (6 June) when the battalion Roll Call revealed:– "Out of 21 Officers and 671 Other Ranks who went into the trenches during this tour, 5 Officers are reported as killed, 5 wounded and 10 missing, Other Ranks total casualties 536 killed, wounded and missing; 135 returning."

Among the missing were two men who, although they had consecutive service numbers and a shared surname, were totally unrelated:

(Panel 32) Pte. 106179, George Andrew Davidson, 1st Canadian Mounted Rifles (Saskatchewan Regt.), C.E.F.: *s.* of George Davidson, of Brae Cottage, Longside, co. Aberdeen: *b.* Longside, 6 December 1885: Occupation – Farmer: previously served 3 years, Peterhead Garrison Artillery: enlisted Yorkton, 24 December 1914. Reported missing / believed killed in action 2 – 5 June 1916: Age 30. *unm.* (*IWGC record 5 June 1916, Age 31*)

(Panel 32) Pte. 106180, Nelson Davidson, 1st Canadian Mounted Rifles (Saskatchewan Regt.), C.E.F.: *s.* of Mrs W.C. Davidson (Russell, Manitoba): *b.* 19 December 1888: Occupation – Farmer: previously served 1 year, 32nd Montreal Light Horse: enlisted Brandon, 1 December 1914. Reported missing / believed killed in action 2 – 5 June 1916: Age 27. *unm.* (*IWGC record 5 June 1916*)

(Panel 32) Pte. 109325, Albert Edward Elford, M.G. Coy.; 4th Canadian Mounted Rifles (1st Central Ontario Regt.), C.E.F.: *s.* of James Elford, of Oak Ridges, Toronto, Ontario, by his wife Elizabeth (6, Lawton Avenue, Toronto); late of Weston-Super-Mare, co. Somerset, England: and brother to Pte. 404328, S. Elford, 3rd Canadian Infantry, died of wounds 13 April 1917: *b.* Pontypridd, Wales, 29 December 1892: removed to Canada shortly before the outbreak of war: Occupation – Gardener: joined C.E.F. 27 November 1914: proceeded overseas June 1915; to France 19 October following. Missing / believed killed in action 2 June 1916: Age 24. *unm.* Previous to removing to Canada Pte. Elford was, for some time, employed on the staff of the '*Clevedon Mercury & Courier*,' co. Somerset. Remains recovered unmarked grave refers GRU Report, Zillebeke 5-398E; (28.I.30.a.80.90); identified – Clothing, Disc, Titles; reinterred, registered 12 February 1931. *Buried in Sanctuary Wood Cemetery (V.O.10).* (*IWGC record age 25*)

Dearly Loved Never Forgotten

His brother Stanley is buried in Barlin Communal Cemetery Extension (I.H.53).

(Panel 32) Pte. 109342, Walter Grant Forbes, 4th Canadian Mounted Rifles (Quebec Regt.), C.E.F.: *s.* of the late James Forbes, of Bleachfield House, Persleyden, Woodside, co. Aberdeen, by his wife Elizabeth ('Gownlea,' Fauldhouse, co. West Lothian): and brother to Pte. 1661, G. Forbes, 4th Gordon Highlanders, killed in action 25 September 1915; and AB. (Clyde) Z/800, J.G. Forbes, Howe Bn. R.N.V.R., killed in action 26 October 1917: *b.* Aberdeen, 26 August 1893: Occupation – Machinist: a serving member of the Militia prior to enlistment, 28 November 1914. Killed in action 2 June 1916: Age 23. *unm.*

Neither of his brothers have a known grave; Gilbert is recorded on Panel 38; Joseph, Tyne Cot Memorial (Panel 2).

(Panel 32) Pte. 110240, Robert Thomas Hewitt, 5th Canadian Mounted Rifles (Quebec Regt.), C.E.F.: late of 12, Meadow Street, Sherbrooke, Quebec: *s.* of the late Gnr. 43528, G.H. Hewitt, 10th Bty., Canadian Field Artillery, late of 10, Thorold Road, St. Catherine's; died 5 April 1920, consequent to wounds received, and Emma Sylvester, his wife (6, Ida Street South, St. Catherine's, Ontario): *b.* Surrey, United Kingdom, 11 January 1896: Religion – Church of England: Occupation – Horseman: 5'6" tall, blue eyes, fair hair: 2 yrs. member 23rd Regt. (Militia), enlisted Sherbrooke, 9 February 1915. Killed in action 2 – 3 June 1916; Mount Sorrel: Age 20. *unm.* (*IWGC record age 18*)

His father George is buried in Montreal (Mount Royal) Cemetery (Soldiers S.G.G.937/M).

(Panel 32) Pte. 113323, William Hodson Johnson, 4th Canadian Mounted Rifles (Quebec Regt.), C.E.F.: *s.* of William Johnson, by his wife Elizabeth (427, Clarence Street, Ottawa): *b.* Peterborough, 30 June 1899 (attested 1898): Religion – Church of England: 5'3" tall, fair complexion, grey eyes, light brown hair: Occupation – Unemployed: enlisted 5th Light Dragoon Guards, Ottawa, 29 June 1915: served with the Expeditionary Force in France posted 4th C.M.R. Reported missing believed killed in action 2 June 1916: **Age 16.**

(Panel 32) Pte. 458314, Andrew Kalfas, 5th Canadian Mounted Rifles (Quebec Regt.), C.E.F.: *s.* of Artemios Kalfas, of Galagado, Acroteri, Canea, Crete, Greece, by his wife Sophia. Missing, believed killed in action, 30 October 1917; Woodland Marshes, before Source Farm and Vapour Farm: Age 26.

(Panel 32) Pte. 110327, James Alexander Lobban, 5th Canadian Mounted Rifles (Quebec Regt.), C.E.F.: *s.* of W. Lobban, of Golden Stream, Manitoba: and brother to Pte. 3346485, F. Lobban (surv'd.): *b.* Keyes, Manitoba, 26 September 1888: Religion – Church of England: Occupation – Student: 5'5" tall, blue eyes, dark hair: enlisted Sherbrooke, 6 March 1915. Killed in action 2 June 1916; Mount Sorrel: Age 27. *unm.*

(Panel 32) Pte. 622326, John MacKay (served as Martin, Tom), 1st Canadian Mounted Rifles (Saskatchewan Regt.), C.E.F.: *s.* of Donald MacKay, of 12, Keose Lochs, Stornoway, by his wife Margaret: *b.* Stornoway, 14 April 1889: Religion – Presbyterian: Occupation – Bridgeman: previously served 3 yrs. 42nd Cameron Highlanders: joined C.E.F., Winnipeg, 3 May 1915; posted 44th (Overseas) Bn.; subsequently transf'd. 1st C.M.R. Reported missing, believed killed 5 June 1916; Roll-Call, St Lawrence Camp (after being in trenches Sanctuary Wood) now, for official purposes presumed to have died on or since that date: Age 30. Remains exhumed unmarked grave (28.I.24.d.7.7) 19 September 1928; identified – Clothing, Disc; registered, reinterred 21 September 1928. Disc found by a farmer near exhumation site inscribed '623… E.C. Currie, 44/Bn. Canadian Inf.' *Buried in Sanctuary Wood Cemetery (II.L.9).*

"Dean Subhach Sinn A Reir Nan La Chraidh Thu Sinn Gu Gourt"

PS. XV.15

Pte. E.C. Currie, 44th C.E.F., transf'd. 1st C.M.R., killed in action 6 June 1916, has no known grave; he is recorded above.

(Panel 32) Pte. 113393, Clifford Alexander Merkley, 4th Canadian Mounted Rifles (1st Central Ontario Regt.), C.E.F.: *s.* of the late Frederick W. (& O.C.) Merkley, of Chesterville, Ontario: and *yr.* brother to Lieut. M.E. Merkley, 31st Bn., who fell at Passchendaele: *b.* Maryville, Ontario, 11 January

1894: Religion – Presbyterian: Occupation Labourer: enlisted Ottawa, 17 January 1915. Killed in action at Sanctuary Wood, nr. Ypres, 2 June 1916: Age 21. *m. Buried in Bedford House Cemetery (I.A.15/Enc.No.6).* His brother Miles has no known grave; he is recorded on Panel 28.

(Panel 32) Pte. 195174, Robert Alonzo Micks, 5th Canadian Mounted Rifles (Quebec Regt.), C.E.F.: *s.* of Alonzo Robert Micks, of Port Hope, Ontario, by his wife Ellen: *b.* Port Hope, *c.*1897: *educ.* Public School, there: prior to enlistment, October 1915, was employed at Peterborough; trained there and Bariefield: embarked for Europe July 1916: drafted 5th Canadian Mounted Rifles during further training England: served with the Expeditionary Force in France: took part in the fighting at Vimy Ridge, Somme, Hill 70, and Passchendaele. Orderly to Lieut. A.W. Logie, in the attack on Source Farm Pte. Micks was partially buried by the explosive effect of a nearby shell. After extrication he continued forward with his comrades and was one of five men to gain and secure the objective – Source Farm. Observed to be in a dazed condition from the previously mentioned explosive shock his officer ordered Pte. Micks to return to the rear with some prisoners. He was never seen or heard of again. Lieut. Logie, believing he was killed by a shell on his way to headquarters as no trace was ever found, wrote of him to his sister, "I feel honoured in having known him, and you should feel proud of having such a brother." Age 20. *unm.*

(Panel 32) Pte. 109503, Edward Clarence Morgan, (Actg. L/Corpl.), 4th Canadian Mounted Rifles (1st Central Ontario Regt.), C.E.F.: *s.* of Rev. John W. Morgan, of 24, Sykes Avenue, Weston, Ontario: *b.* Cookstown, 16 December 1894: *educ.* Weston High School; University of Toronto, 1914 – 15, member C.O.T.C.: enlisted 4th C.M.R., May 1915: served with the Expeditionary Force in France and Flanders, attd. Machine Gun section, from October following in the Ploegsteert – St. Eloi sector, and Ypres salient. When the Battle of Sanctuary Wood began his machine gun was blown to pieces and all the crew buried by shellfire. It appears, from the report of one of his companions, who was eventually dug out by the Germans, that he was either instantly killed or died shortly afterwards. He had been badly wounded at the beginning of the fighting, but being in charge of the gun, refused to leave his post. Recorded, missing believed killed in action 2 June 1916: Age 21. Remains recovered unmarked grave, refers GRU Report, Zillebeke 5-398E; (28.I.30.a.80.90); identified – Clothing, Disc, Titles; reinterred, registered 12 February 1931. *Buried in Sanctuary Wood Cemetery (V.O.11).*

His Bow Abode In Strength
He Was Made Strong By The Mighty God

(Panel 32) Pte. 633768, Cecil Ouderkirk, 4th Canadian Mounted Rifles, C.E.F.: *s.* of Peter Ouderkirk, c/o P.O. Box 59, Berwick, Ontario, by his wife Mary Jane: and brother to Pte. 437651, W.S. Ouderkirk (surv'd.), Pte. 633976, G. Ouderkirk (surv'd.), Gnr. 345833, A. Ouderkirk (surv'd); and 2nd Corpl. 486625, W.L. Ouderkirk, 2nd Canadian Tunnelling Coy., killed in action 23 December 1916, beneath Hill 60: *b.* Finch, North Stormont, 14 November 1898: Occupation – Farmer: enlisted Finch, 15 March 1916. Killed in action 26 October 1917, at Passchendaele: Age 18. Cecil and William are remembered on the Berwick (Finch Township) War Memorial.

His brother William, whose grave was lost in later fighting, is commemorated in Railway Dugouts Burial Ground (Transport Farm), (Valley Cottages Sp.Mem.A.10).

(Panel 32) Pte. 106513, Vincent Lionel Wright Ridout, 1st Bn. Canadian Mounted Rifles (Saskatchewan Regt.), C.E.F.: *s.* of Joseph Lionel Ridout, of Stonewall, Manitoba, and the late Emily Ada Ridout; his wife: and elder brother to Pte. 106512, W.C. Ridout, 1st C.M.R., killed in the same action: *b.* Solsgirth, Manitoba, 7 July 1890: Occupation – Engineer: enlisted Brandon, 21 December 1914. Killed in action 5 June 1916: Age 25. *unm.* See below.

(Panel 32) Pte. 106512, Walter Colin Ridout, 1st Bn. Canadian Mounted Rifles (Saskatchewan Regt.), C.E.F.: *s.* of Joseph Lionel Ridout, of Stonewall, Manitoba, and the late Emily Ada Ridout; his wife: and yr. brother to Pte. 106513, V.L.W. Ridout, 1st C.M.R., killed in the same action: *b.* Solsgirth, Manitoba, 11 October 1896: Occupation – Farmer: enlisted Brandon, 9 February 1915. Killed in action 5 June 1916: Age 20. *unm.* See above.

(Panel 32) Pte. 491222, William Smoker, 4th Bn. Canadian Mounted Rifles (1st Central Ontario Regt.), C.E.F.: *s.* of the late William Smoker, and his wife Mary Smoker (411, West Chalmers, Youngstown, Ohio, United States): *b.* Newcastle, Jamaica, 23 November 1874: Religion – Church of England: Occupation – Plumber: 5'9" tall, fresh complexion, brown eyes, dark brown hair: joined 21st Regt., Windsor, Ontario, 28 January 1915; posted C.M.R. for service overseas: departed Canada, 10 July 1915; trained Dibgate, Shorncliffe, from the 29th of that month: joined the Expeditionary Force in France and Flanders 25 October following. Missing / believed killed 2 June 1916; no word having been received since that date, and no trace of Pte. Smoker found, it is with regret assumed he was one of a considerable number lost when, during the fighting at Mount Sorrel on the aforementioned date, a mine was detonated beneath the battalion's front-line trench: Age 41. *unm.*

(Panel 32) Pte. 110535, William Arthur Stoddart, 5th Canadian Mounted Rifles (Quebec Regt.), C.E.F.: 1st & only child of the late William George Stoddart, Furniture Dealer (*d.* 1918); by his marriage to Eliza Ellen (Mrs N.H.) Petrie (*m.* 1923), *née* Stoddart (8, Fourth Street South, St. Petersburg, Florida, U.S.A.): *b.* Thorold, Ontario, 25 August 1898 (attested 1896): *educ.* Grand Valley Public School, Toronto; Cornwall Public School, Ontario, and Montreal, Quebec: joined 5th C.M.R., Montreal, 10 May 1915 (aged 16 years): attd. 8th Canadian Inf. Bde., 3rd Divn., C.E.F., 1 January 1916: took part in the fighting at Ypres, and was killed in action at the Battle of Mount Sorrel there 2 June 1916: Age 17.

(Panel 32) Pte. 931535, Jonathan Wade, 2nd Canadian Mounted Rifles (British Columbia Regt.), C.E.F.: formerly 16th (Reserve) Bn.: *s.* of William Wade, of 22, Stratton Street, Biggleswade: *b.* Biggleswade, co. Bedford, 28 January 1891: *educ.* Church School, there: removed to Canada, 1909; settled Nelson: Occupation – Farmer: enlisted July 1916: came to England with Canadian Contingent, January 1917: served with the Expeditionary Force in France and Flanders from April, and was killed in action at Passchendaele 30 October 1917: Age 26. *unm.*

(Panel 32) Pte. 113613, Frederick David Walker, 4th Canadian Mounted Rifles (1st Central Ontario Regt.), C.E.F.: *s.* of F. Ernest Walker, of Thomas Street, West Napanee, Ontario, by his wife Mary Elizabeth: *b.* 4 October 1897: Religion – Methodist: Occupation – Student: joined C.E.F., 9 a.m., 3 August 1915, Barriefield, Ontario, posted 8th C.M.R.: proceeded overseas transf'd. reinforcement draft to 4th C.M.R. Missing / believed killed in action 2 June 1916: Age 18. Remains exhumed 12 March 1929; identified – Clothing, Disc; reinterred, registered 12 March 1929. *Buried in Sanctuary Wood Cemetery (V.C.6).*

(Panel 32) Pte. 144969, Ernest Wood, 4th Canadian Mounted Rifles (1st Central Ontario Regt.), C.E.F.: *s.* of Frederick Peace Wood, of 177, Gowan Avenue, Todmorden, Toronto, by his wife Louisa Mary (93, Hastings Avenue, Toronto): *b.* Chelsea, London, 19 March 1897 (added three years, *b.* 1900): enlisted Smith Falls, 23 August 1915; the Medical Officer noting 'a somewhat undersized lad, will come up to standard': 5'3" tall, ruddy complexion, grey eyes, light hair: Religion – Church of England: 4 vaccination marks left arm. One of 165 members of his regiment reported missing believed killed in action 2 June 1916, recorded as having no known grave: **Age 16.**

(Panel 32) Sergt. 430994, Stuart Milne Tees, Machine Gun Section, 3rd Bn. Canadian Pioneers, C.E.F.: *s.* of David T. Tees, of Montreal Trust Co., and the late Elizabeth Anne Milne Tees: *b.* Montreal, 2 August 1887: Occupation – Clerk; Bank of Montreal, Vernon, British Columbia branch: prior to the outbreak of war was a serving member of 30th British Columbia Horse (Militia), in which he held a commission, rank Lieut.: resigned his commission; enlisted Pte., 48th Battn., Victoria, 12 April 1915, apptd. 3rd Pioneers: subsequently promoted Corpl., thereafter Sergt.: served with the Expeditionary Force in France and Flanders from 10 March 1916, attd. Machine Gun Section (3rd Pioneers), and was killed in action at about 8 p.m., 3 June 1916. On this date, virtually wiped out when their positions in the front-line at Maple Copse were blown in and destroyed by shellfire, the surviving members of the machine-gun section were withdrawn to new positions in Sanctuary Wood. Coming under intense shellfire in the process further losses were incurred when a dug-out in which a number had sought refuge was hit and destroyed by a shell: Age 28. *unm.* Correspondence to be addressed c/o Dr. Thomas Tees, Mount Dora, Florida, United States of America.

(Panel 32) Pte. 431129, Thomas Lorne Beamish, 3rd Bn. Canadian Pioneers, C.E.F.: late of Kenyon Apts., Seattle, Washington, United States: *s.* of the late R.F. Beamish: *b.* Pembroke, Ontario, 20 November 1882: Occupation – Real Estate Broker: previously served 3rd Mounted Rifles: enlisted Victoria, British Columbia, 9 June 1915: served with the Expeditionary Force in France from 10 March 1916, and was killed in action 3 June 1916. He leaves a wife, Lillian Beamish (Amaranth, Manitoba).

(Panel 32) Pte. 430299, Henry Branch, 3rd Bn. Canadian Pioneers, C.E.F.: *s.* of Mrs A.J. Branch (18, Mid Street, Whitehaven, co. Cumberland): *b.* Whitehaven, 21 March 1885: Occupation – Iron Moulder: enlisted 48th Battn., Victoria, British Columbia, 3 March 1915, posted 3rd Pioneers. Killed in action 3 June 1916: Age 31. *unm.*

(Panel 32) Pte. 430453, Albert Griffiths, 3rd Bn. Canadian Pioneers, C.E.F.: *s.* of Edward Griffiths, of Pentrebach, Pontardulais, co. Glamorgan: *b.* Pontardulais, 20 January 1890: Occupation – Miner: previously served 50th Gordon Highlanders: enlisted Victoria, British Columbia, 11 March 1915; 48th Battn., posted 3rd Pioneers. Killed in action 3 June 1916: Age 26. *unm.*

(Panel 32) Pte. 104293, Anthony 'Tony' Leonard Hart, 3rd Bn. Canadian Pioneers, C.E.F.: *s.* of the late Anthony E. Hart, and Mary A.C. Hart (Moosomin, Saskatchewan), his wife: *b.* Moosomin, 6 January 1897: Occupation – Auto Repairman: enlisted Moosomin, 16 August 1915: served with the Expeditionary Force in France and Flanders from 10 March 1916, and was killed in action 3 June 1916: Age 19.

(Panel 32) Pte. 166345, Bennett John Horne, 1st Bn. Canadian Pioneers, C.E.F.: *s.* of Andrew P. Horne, of Enfield, Nova Scotia, by his wife Agnes: and *yr.* brother to Sergt. 223467, L.A. Horne, M.M., 85th Canadian Infantry, died 20 November 1918, Base Hospital, Etaples: *b.* Enfield, 20 August 1891: Religion – Roman Catholic: Occupation – Machinist: 5'9¾" tall, black eyes, black hair: enlisted 5 October 1915; posted 2nd Pioneer Battn., 25 November. Killed in action 6 June 1916: Age 24. *unm.* Two of four men who made the supreme sacrifice in the Great War remembered on the Enfield (Hants County) War Memorial.

His brother Leo is buried in Etaples Military Cemetery (L.F.2).

(Panel 32) Pte. 431159, Sidney Norris Rich, 3rd Bn. Canadian Pioneers, C.E.F.: *s.* of Norris H. Rich, of Ladner, British Columbia, by his wife May: *b.* Ladner, 27 June 1892: Occupation – Surveyor: previously served University Cadet Corps: enlisted Victoria, British Columbia, 21 June 1915. Killed in action 3 June 1916: Age 23. *unm.* (*IWGC record age 22*)

(Panel 32) Pte. 463352, Frederick Orlando Roberts, 3rd Bn. Canadian Pioneers, C.E.F.: *s.* of Frederick William (& Martha Louise) Roberts, of Langley Prairie, British Columbia: *b.* Kensington, London, W., 25 December 1897: Occupation – Student; Duke of Connaught's High School, New Westminster, British Columbia, from whence he enlisted – Vernon, 30 July 1915: proceeded overseas 29 August, trained Salisbury Plain, England: served with the Expeditionary Force in France and Flanders from 10 March 1916, and was killed in action 3 June 1916: Age 18.

(Panel 32) Pte. 104549, William John Sinclair, 3rd Bn. Canadian Pioneers, C.E.F.: *s.* of John Sinclair, of Stravithie R.S.O., co. Fife: *b.* North Berwick, Haddington, co. East Lothian, 4 March 1889: Occupation – Farmer: enlisted 17 August 1915: served with the Expeditionary Force in France from 10 March 1916, and was killed in action 3 June 1916: Age 27. *unm.*

(Panel 32) Pte. 430246, George Smith, 3rd Bn. Canadian Pioneers, C.E.F.: *s.* of John Smith, of Lavington, Vernon, British Columbia: *b.* Aberdeen, Scotland, 17 October 1892: Occupation – Fireman: serving member 102nd Regt. (Militia), enlisted 48th Battn., posted 3rd Pioneers, Victoria, 3 March 1915. Killed in action 3 June 1916: Age 25. *unm.*

(Panel 32) Pte. 414631, Charles D. Stewart, 3rd Bn. Canadian Pioneers, C.E.F.: served with the Expeditionary Force in France and Flanders from 10 March 1916, and was killed in action 3 June following.

(Panel 32) Pte. 463567, John Scott Watt, 3rd Bn. Canadian Pioneers, C.E.F.: *s.* of John Watt, of 'Ellangowan,' Gladstone Road, Huntly, co. Aberdeen: *b.* Huntly, 12 December 1886: Occupation –

Watchmaker: previously served 2 years Militia; enlisted Vernon, British Columbia, 15 July 1915. Killed in action on the night of 2 – 3 June 1916, while at duty on a working party assisting the Engineers to strengthen and repair positions to which the infantry had returned following a retirement before an earlier enemy attack; 14 O.R. were also wounded: Age 29. *unm.* (*IWGC record 2 June*)

(Panel 32) Lieut. 1158, Hugh McDonald McKenzie, V.C., D.C.M., Canadian Machine Gun Corps attd. Princess Patricia's Canadian Light Infantry (Eastern Ontario Regt.), C.E.F.: *s.* of the late Jane McDonald McKenzie, of 23, James Street, Dundee, Scotland: *b.* Inverness, 5 December 1896: Religion – Presbyterian: Occupation – Teamster: previously served 4 years Royal Garrison Artillery, 2 years Field Artillery (Special Reserve): enlisted Ottawa, 24 August 1914: 5'7" tall, grey eyes, brown hair: served with the Expeditionary Force in France and Flanders from 20 December 1914: took part in the fighting at 2nd Ypres, the Somme, Vimy Ridge and was killed in action 30 October 1917, being shot through the head while leading an assault by the Princess Patricia's on the Meetcheele Ridge pill-box. Awarded the Victoria Cross ('*London Gazette,*' 12 February 1918), "For most conspicuous bravery and leading when in charge of a section of four machine guns accompanying the infantry in an attack. Seeing that all the officers and most of the non-commissioned officers of an infantry company had become casualties, and that the men were hesitating before a nest of enemy machine guns, which were on commanding ground and causing them severe casualties, he handed over command of his guns to an N.C.O., rallied the infantry, organised an attack, and captured the strong point. Finding that the position was swept by machine-gun fire from a 'pill-box' which dominated all the ground over which the troops were advancing, Lt. McKenzie made a reconnaissance and detailed flanking and frontal attacking parties which captured the 'pill-box,' he himself being killed while leading the frontal attack. By his valour and leadership this gallant officer ensured the capture of these strong points and so saved the lives of many men and enabled the objectives to be attained.": Age 30. Awarded the Distinguished Conduct Medal ('*London Gazette,*' 14 January 1916) for his actions in the fighting at Bellewaerde Ridge, 8 May 1915, and Croix de Guerre (France), 24 February 1916. He was married to Mrs H. McKenzie (297, Gertrude Street, Verdun, Quebec), to whom his Victoria Cross (awarded posthumously) was presented.

(Panel 32) Lieut. 642, Albert Edward Kill, Borden Motor Machine Gun Bty., Canadian Machine Gun Corps, C.E.F.: c/o Mining Records Office, Matheson, Ontario: *s.* of George Kill, of 25, King Edward Street, Whitstable, co. Kent, by his wife Annie: *b.* West London, England, 9 January 1884: Religion – Church of England: Occupation – Prospector (Gold): joined C.E.F., Toronto, 12 November 1914: proceeded overseas 17 May 1915; joined the Expeditionary Force in France 15 September following, and was killed in action at Passchendaele, Belgium, 6.35 a.m., 10 November 1917; shellfire: Age 32.

(Panel 32) Sergt. 45507, Robert Bellas, 1st Canadian Motor Machine Gun Bde., C.E.F.: *s.* of Robert Bellas, of 'Glentonvale,' Morland, co. Westmorland, England, and Mary Bellas, his wife: *b.* Morland, 1 August 1886: Occupation – Chauffeur: previously served 4 yrs., Westmorland & Cumbria Imperial Yeomanry (T.F., Cav.): enlisted Toronto, 24 August 1914: served with the Expeditionary Force in France from 18 June 1915. Killed in action 30 October 1917; shellfire, Passchendaele Ridge: Age 31. *Buried in Cement House Cemetery (XVI.A.21-23).*

(Panel 32) Corpl. 701209, William Edward Bolton, 13th Coy., Canadian Machine Gun Corps, C.E.F.: *s.* of the late George Bolton, of 472, Stradbrooke Place, Winnipeg, Manitoba, by his wife Annie (749, Fleet Avenue, Winnipeg): and brother to Pte. 701210, G.E. Bolton, 16th Canadian Infantry, killed in action 9 October 1916, aged 20 years: *b.* 4 April 1896: Occupation – Printer: joined C.E.F., Winnipeg, 24 February 1916. Killed in action 2 November 1917; shellfire, above Nile House, before Passchendaele: Age 20.

His brother George also has no known grave; he is commemorated on the Canadian National (Vimy) Memorial.

(Panel 32) Corpl. 114106, Harold Hathaway, 9th Coy., Canadian Machine Gun Corps, C.E.F.: *s.* of Alfred Edward Hathaway, of Lloydminster, Saskatchewan, and the late Mary Hathaway, his wife: and elder brother to Pte. 624478, H.H. Hathaway, 78th Canadian Infantry, who fell 12 January 1917: *b.* London,

England, 21 February 1891: Religion – Church of England: Occupation – Farmer: 5'6" tall, blue eyes, fair hair: enlisted Lloydminster, 1 May 1915. Killed in action 26 October 1917: Age 26. *unm.* Remembered on the Marwayne Legion Cenotaph, Alberta.

His brother Herbert is buried in Cabaret-Rouge British Cemetery, Souchez (II.D.3).

(Panel 32) L/Corpl. 427091, Herbert Harradon Fletcher, 10th Coy., Canadian Machine Gun Corps, C.E.F.: *s.* of Jonathan Fletcher, of Inglewood, California, United States of America: Occupation – Barrister, Messrs Allen & Gordon, Regina, Saskatchewan: enlisted May 1915: served with the Expeditionary Force in France and Flanders, and was killed in action at Passchendaele, Belgium, 26 October 1917. He leaves a wife, Henrietta Pepperell Fletcher.

(Panel 32) Pte. 696183, George Clinton Adams, No.1 Coy., Canadian Machine Gun Corps, C.E.F.: c/o James Adams Esq., of Tide Lake, Alberta: *b.* Prince Edward County, Ontario, 23 April 1891: Religion – Methodist: Occupation – Farmer: joined C.E.F., Medicine Hat, 11 February 1916; apptd. 175th Battn.: transf'd. Machine Gun Corps, England: served with the Expeditionary Force, and was killed in action on the morning of 6 November 1917, shortly before the advance on Passchendaele, the enemy laid down a heavy barrage on the Canadian lines; he received severe wounds which proved fatal almost immediately: Age 26. No remains recovered for burial.

On 11 February 1939 the remains of three Canadian Soldiers were recovered, buried together in a collective grave (Ref. 28.D.15.b.8.4.). They were reinterred side by side in Cement House Cemetery (Extension). Of the three only the remains of Pte. Carr could be identified with any degree of certainty. Sergt. Bellas and Pte. Willson could not be individually identified.

(Panel 32) Pte. 444791, Vincent Carr, 1st Canadian Motor Machine Gun Bde., C.E.F.: *s.* of Robert Carr, of Cape Traverse, Prince Edward Island: *b.* 3 May 1894: Religion – Methodist: Occupation – Labourer: joined C.E.F., Sussex, New Brunswick, 3 June 1915. Killed in action 30 October 1917: Age 23. Buried where he fell. Remains 'Unknown Canadian Soldier' one of three recovered (28.D.15.b.8.4) 11 February 1939; identified – G.S. uniform, field boots, titles, damaged disc. *Buried in Cement House Cemetery (XVI.A.22).*

(Panel 32) Pte. 463765, Sydney William Giles, 6th Coy., Canadian Machine Gun Corps, C.E.F.: *s.* of Charles Samuel Giles, of 20, Wyndham Street, Brighton, co. Sussex, by his wife Sarah Ann: *b.* London, 25 January 1885: Religion – Church of England: sometime emigrated to Canada, finding gainful employ as Woodcarver: served 9 months Duke of Connaughts Own Regt. (from November 1914), joined C.E.F., Vernon, British Columbia, 7 August 1915, apptd. 6th Bn., 21 August: reverted from rank of Corpl. that he might proceed to France (October 1915): served with the Expeditionary Force there, and was killed in action before Passchendaele, 8 November 1917; the sap-hole he was occupying being blown in by a high-explosive shell: Age 32. All correspondence should be forwarded to Pte. Giles widow, Edna May Giles, *née* Durling ('Myrtle Cottage,' Common Road, Stanmore, London, N., Great Britain). *Buried in Sanctuary Wood Cemetery (III.B.34).*

Remembrance

(Panel 32) Pte. 829250, Ernest Vivian Hare, 6th Coy., Canadian Machine Gun Corps, C.E.F.: *s.* of the late Ernest Hare, Accountant; by his wife Ellen Louisa (The Gables, Blisworth, co. Northampton), *dau.* of George Goode: *b.* Blisworth, 28 August 1893: *educ.* Town and County School, Northampton: went to Canada, February 1913; settled Winnipeg: Occupation – Engineer: enlisted 13 October 1914: came to England with 144th Battn. Machine Gun Coy., 90th Winnipeg Rifles, Canadian Contingent: served with the Expeditionary Force in France and Flanders, and was killed in action at Passchendaele, 11 November 1917: Age 24. *unm.*

(Panel 32) Pte. 863147, William Kee, Borden Motor Machine Gun Bty., Canadian Machine Gun Corps, C.E.F.: late of 1832, Dufferin Street, Toronto: *s.* of the late Joseph Kee, by his wife Isabella Jardine Kee (128, Pacific Avenue, Toronto): *b.* Streetville, Ontario, 7 September 1884: Religion – Presbyterian: Occupation – Labourer: joined C.E.F., Toronto, 31 March 1916; apptd. 180th Overseas Bn., 1 April.

Killed in action at Passchendaele, 1.30 p.m., 10 November 1917; shellfire: Age 33. Pte. 911972, W.J. McVicar was also killed.

Pte. McVicar is buried in Passchendaele New British Cemetery (X.C.17).

(Panel 32) Pte. 818221, Earl Winifred Mathie, 15th Coy., Canadian Machine Gun Corps, C.E.F.: *s.* of Joseph Winifred (& Nettie) Mathie, of Dennysville, Maine, United States of America: *b.* Edmunds, Maine, 14 July 1890: Religion – Congregationalist: Occupation – Sailor: enlisted West St. John, New Brunswick, 6 May 1916. Killed in action 24 October 1917, while on duty at his gun position during operations south-east of Passchendaele; in the course of an enemy bombardment a shell burst in front of his gun and shrapnel from it penetrated his head. Death was instantaneous: Age 27. *unm.*

(Panel 32) Pte. 174381, Albert Rhodes, 16th Coy., Canadian Machine Gun Corps, C.E.F.: late of 282, Catherine Street, Hamilton, Ontario: *s.* of Thomas Edmund Rhodes, of 810, Harrogate Road, Greengates, Bradford, co. York, by his wife Martha Ann: and brother to Pte. 690757, F. Rhodes, 116th Canadian Infantry, died 19 November 1917: *b.* 23 March 1881: Occupation – Labourer: enlisted Hamilton, 28 August 1915. Killed in action 31 October 1917, at Passchendaele: Age 36. He was married to Letitia Mary Rhodes (141, Bold Street, Hamilton, Ontario).

His brother Fred is buried in Eccleshill Methodist Burial Ground (New Pt.2).

(Panel 32) Pte. 337823, William Alexander Denison Sutterby, 1st Motor Machine Gun Bde., Canadian Machine Gun Corps, C.E.F.: *s.* of William John Sutterby: *b.* Hamilton, Ontario, 19 February 1879: Religion – Methodist: *educ.* Hamilton (Hess Street) Public School; Hamilton Collegiate; Victoria College, Toronto University, 1915 – 16, where he was Year Secretary and C.O.T.C. member: enlisted 67th (University of Toronto) Bty., Canadian Field Artillery on its formation, March 1916: departed Canada, July following: underwent training England, where he was promoted Corpl., acted as Instructor and was offered a commission but declined: reverted, at his own request, to Pte. that he might proceed to France; served with the Expeditionary Force there from August 1917, and joined 1st Motor Machine Gun Bde. He was killed at the battle of Passchendaele 31 October 1917, when the members of his unit were serving dismounted and he was struck in the forehead by a piece of shrapnel. Death was almost instantaneous. Buried where he fell: Age 38. Remembered on Hamilton First Methodist Church War Memorial.

(Panel 32) Pte. 864, Jack Bingham Willson, 1st Canadian Motor Machine Gun Bde., C.E.F.: *s.* of Dr. A. Willson, of Plattsville, Ontario: *b.* 17 January 1897: Religion – Wesleyan: Occupation – Chauffeur: joined C.E.F., Toronto, 1 February 1915. Killed by shellfire, Passchendaele Ridge, 30 October 1917: Age 20. Buried nr. where he fell. One of three sets of remains recovered 'Unknown Canadian Soldier,' 28.D.15.b.8.4., 11 February 1939; identified – G.S. uniform, boots, titles. *Buried in Cement House Cemetery (XVI.A.21-23).*

(Panel 32) Corpl. 115335, Stanley Alfred Bales, 9th Bn. Canadian Railway Troops, C.E.F.: *s.* of Capt. Frank Alfred Bales, V.D., of 'Auckland House,' 812, Woodbridge Road, Ipswich, by his wife Ellen Mary: and brother to Pte. 14601, F.P. Bales, 8th Suffolk Regt., killed in action 18 July 1916: *b.* Ipswich, 16 May 1893: Religion – Church of England: Occuipation – Farm Hand: 5'9" tall, fair complexion, blue eyes, light hair: enlisted Grenfell, Saskatchewan, 22 December 1914. Killed by shellfire 31 July 1917, at duty ballasting, ditching and track-laying; Westhoek sector: Age 24. *unm.*

His brother Frank has no known grave, he is commemorated on the Thiepval Memorial, Somme.

(Panel 32) Capt. Richard Alfred Ireland, Canadian Army Medical Corps attd. 5th Canadian Mounted Rifles (Quebec Regt.), C.E.F.: *s.* of the late William Henry Ireland, by his wife Caroline: *b.* Trenton, 13 January 1889: *educ.* Trenton Public (& High) Schools; University of Toronto (Medicine), 1907 – 11, M.B.: prior to enlistment was House Surgeon, Toronto General Hospital, practising St. John's, Newfoundland, and on the Staff, Homewood Sanatorium, Guelph: apptd. Medical Officer 76th Battn., summer 1915: departed Canada April 1916: briefly attd. 36th and 39th Reserve Battns., England: went to France, August 1916: initially served with No.3 General Hospital, thereafter No.7 Stationary Hospital and No.10 Field Ambulance: later apptd. M.O., 5th Mounted Rifles: served at the Battle of the Somme and at Vimy Ridge, and was killed in action at Passchendaele 30 October 1917. Having filled his Dressing Station he left it to tend the wounded lying outside and was killed instantly by a shell. Buried near where he fell: Age 28. *unm.*

(Panel 32) Pte. 322936, Charles Hilton Stewart, 2nd Field Amb., Canadian Army Medical Corps, C.E.F.: *s.* of the late John (& Laura J.) Stewart, of Guelph, Ontario: *b.* Eramosa, 22 November 1892: *educ.* Guelph Public Schools and Collegiate: sometime apprenticed to Messrs Alexander Stewart Drug Stores; studied Toronto University Pharmaceutical College, graduated PH.M.B., 1914: lately Manager, Pharmacy Hockey Team, Carnahan Drug Stores, Toronto: enlisted 55th Bty., Canadian Field Artillery, April 1916: proceeded overseas with a draft from the aforementioned unit, and transf'd. C.A.M.C., England: went to France, September following, and, after a period working at the Base Hospital, Rouen, joined No.2 Canadian Field Ambulance: served on the Somme front at Courcelette, Le Trouslay, Montay (1916); Vimy and Hill 70 (1917). Took part in the Passchendaele Offensive from late October 1917. On the day of his death, 3 November 1917, he was initially on duty at Dressing Stations but, owing to the difficulty in carrying out the wounded, additional stretcher bearers were called for and it was while engaged in this work that a shell struck killing all six bearers and the man being carried. Buried Waterloo Pill Box, Passchendaele Road: Age 24. (*IWGC record age 25*)

(Panel 32) Capt. (Hon.) De Witt Oscar Irwin, Canadian Young Men's Christian Association attd. 10th Bn. Canadian Infantry (Alberta Regt.), C.E.F.: *s.* of the late John Irwin, by his wife Mary L. (Collingwood, Ontario): *b.* Collingwood, 1 October 1885: *educ.* Redwing Public School; Collingwood Public School (& Collegiate); University College, Toronto, 1908 – 12; Knox College: Occupation – Assistant; Victoria Church, West Toronto, and Mount Albert Presbyterian Church: departed Canada October 1914 as Hon. Lieut., Y.M.C.A., First Contingent; later promoted Capt.: served chiefly with 10th Battn. with which unit he crossed to France February 1915. Reported wounded and missing after the fighting for Kitchener's Wood, nr. St. Julien, 23 April 1915, later confirmed killed: Age 29. *unm.* (*IWGC record 28 April*)

PANEL 32 ENDS – CAPT. DE.W.O. IRWIN, CANADIAN Y.M.C.A.

PANEL 34 BEGINS – PTE. H.F. PASS, GLOUCESTERSHIRE REGT.

(Panel 34) Pte. 16367, William Harold Saxton, 2nd Bn. (61st Foot) The Gloucestershire Regt.: *s.* of George Saxton, of Hazel Cot, Rudgeway, Bristol, by his wife Edith: and elder brother to Pte. 24803, J.W. Saxton, 1st Royal Berkshire Regt., killed in action 14 November 1916; and Pte. PLY/7942, 2nd Royal Marine Light Infantry, died of wounds 30 December 1915, received at Gallipoli: *b.* Wortley: enlisted Bristol. Killed in action 10 May 1915: Age 36. He was married to Florence Lucinda Frankcon, née Saxton (Brook Cottages, Ozleworth, Wotton-under-Edge).

His brother James also has no known grave, he is commemorated on the Thiepval Memorial (Pier/Face 11D); Charles is buried in Malta (Capuccini) Naval Cemetery (Prot.298).

On 6 November 1914 the Germans, having pushed back the French holding part of the line near Zillebeke, were threatening to break through. At 4 o'clock that afternoon 1st Gloucesters left the position they had been holding for the previous two days and moved up to new positions north of the village of Zwarteleen, arriving in darkness and amid much confusion. The frontage the battalion occupied was lengthy, too large really for an already depleted battalion which nevertheless did its best by dividing the line up roughly into sectors and posting batches of men throughout. What few officers remained were distributed amongst the scattered outposts as effectively as their limited numbers allowed. The Official History records 7th November "…was misty and marked the definite commencement of winter weather: mud henceforth seriously interfered with operations and cold at night made sleeping in the open difficult, if not impossible." Certainly, there had been little sleep for the Gloucesters on the eastern edges of Zwarteleen and in the woods further to the north and, as the morning advanced, an order to assist the neighbouring 22nd Brigade in a counter attack on the left was cancelled because thick fog presented a serious problem in the event of concentrated fire being encountered. However, the 22nd Brigade, having pushed ahead and secured its objectives, reported back that the trenches opposite the Gloucesters were empty and orders issued (with the remainder of 3rd Brigade in support) for an immediate advance to seize the vacated enemy trenches. Pushing forward in two lines the battalion had scarcely left Zwarteleen when they were met with intense rifle and machine gun fire from German troops still holding on to some of the houses in the village. The Battalion Historian recorded: "The whole advance had been far too hurried and no definite orders had ever been given. Officers and men were much too exhausted to do more than clear a few of the houses. Most of the men had to lie down in the open all day and only a few could get back to the trenches they had dug the night before." At roll call that night, only three officers and 213 men answered their names. Sixteen year old Harold Wellbelove, arrived three days previously, was not among their number.

(Panel 34) Pte. 9821, Harold Charles Wellbelove, 'B'Coy., 1st Bn. (28th Foot) The Gloucestershire Regt.: s. of Amelia E. Turner (19, Bessborough Gardens, Westminster, London): b. Kingston-on-Thames: enlisted Bristol: proceeded to France with a draft of reinforcements, joining 3rd Battn. at Ypres 3 November 1914, and was killed in action three days later, on the 7th of that month: Age 16.

(Panel 34) Capt. Eric Wilson Buckler, M.C., 6th (Reserve) attd. 3rd Bn. The Worcestershire Regt.: 2nd s. of the late John Henry Buckler, Capt. R.M.S.S. Co., by his marriage to Mrs Adelaide Maud Ashwin, formerly Buckler ('Brackleys,' Wickham Bishops, co. Essex): b. Southampton, 11 June 1885: educ. Leeds Grammar School, and Kelso: sometime served in King's Own Scottish Borderers, and Royal Army Medical Corps: afterwards went to Canada, where he was engaged in Ranching and Real Estate business in the west: while there served with 15th Canadian Light Horse, and was a member of the Ranchers' Club, Calgary. On the outbreak of war he was in England on business, and sent a cable to Canada enquiring if his regiment was coming over, and finding it was uncertain enlisted King Edward's Horse as a Trooper whilst awaiting developments: subsequently given a commission Lieut. 6th Bn. Worcestershire Regt., October 1914; promoted Capt. February 1915: served with the Expeditionary Force in France and Flanders, and, with the exception of ten days when he was in hospital wounded, served with his battalion continuously till his death at Hooge, where he was killed while leading his company, 16 June 1915: Age 30 years, 5 days. For his services at St. Eloi he was Mentioned in Sir John (now Lord) French's Despatch, 31 May 1915, and awarded the Military Cross. He was married to Muriel Irene, dau. of E.R. Frost, of Calgary: s.p.

Throughout the 6th November 1914 the low-lying valley of the River Lys was blanketed by a thick fog through which great shells hurtled continuously. For the men in the waterlogged trenches there was nothing to do but stare ahead and hope against hope that one of the shells did not land on their particular section. Between 3 and 4 am of the following day, the enemy utilised both the continued fog and the cover of darkness to subject the British line east of Ploegsteert Wood to a very heavy bombardment which was followed, at 5 am., by a massed infantry attack. The ensuing fighting accounted for over 200 of the Worcesters – killed, wounded, missing – among them Capt. Arnold Nesbitt, one of 17 members of Worcestershire County Cricket Club to die in the Great War.

(Panel 34) Capt. Arnold Stearns Nesbitt, 3rd Bn. The Worcestershire Regt.: eldest s. of the late William Henry (& Mrs) Nesbitt, of Oatlands Drive, Weybridge: b. Walton-on-Thames, co. Surrey, 16 November 1878: educ. Bradfield College, co. Berks: joined Worcestershire Regt. from the Militia, 1900, becoming Lieut. the same year; promoted Capt. November 1904: as Adjutant to 6th Battn., at the Depot, Norton Barracks, Worcester, he organised a Military Tournament at the Skating Rink which, owing to his energies and foresight, as well as his tact and courtesy, was a great success: employed with Egyptian Army, 1907 – 1908. He was a good cricketer, having been a member of the Icognito, the Worcestershire County (First Team), and the Gentlemen of Worcester's Crickets Clubs. In 1914 he played for Worcestershire against Middlesex at Lord's: went to France with his battalion, 16 August 1914, and was killed in action at Ploegsteert, Belgium, in the early hours of 7 November 1914, when, after a very heavy shellfire, between 3 and 4 a.m., a massed German attack was launched against the British line east of Ploegsteert Wood. An officer who had known him throughout his military career said he was one of the best officers the regiment ever had. The news of his death was received with the greatest regret by his numerous military and civilian friends. For his services in the Great War he was Mentioned in Sir John (now Lord) French's Despatch, 14 January 1915 ('*London Gazette*,' 17 January 1915): Age 35. *unm.*

(Panel 34) Capt. Francis Joseph O'Brien (2nd Lieut. Actg.), 1st Bn. (29th Foot) The Worcestershire Regt.: *s.* of Thomas O'Brien, of 'Melrose,' Sansome Walk, Worcester, and Elizabeth, his wife: and yr. brother to Major W.H. O'Brien, Royal Engineers, killed in action 7 February 1917, aged 33 years: Religion – Roman Catholic. Killed in action 31 July 1917: Age 31. Mentioned in Despatches for his services.

His brother Wulstan is buried in La Gorgue Communal Cemetery (III.C.6).

(Panel 34) Lieut. Campbell Greenhill, M.C., 3rd Bn. The Worcestershire Regt.: *s.* of Dr. Robert Greenhill, of 1, Rodger Drive, Rutherglen, Glasgow, by his wife Flora, *née* Fletcher: *b.* Glencairn Terrace, Rutherglen, 4 November 1885: *educ.* Rutherglen, and Glasgow University (O.T.C. member): Occupation – Commercial Traveller: joined Lowland Divn., Royal Engineers, as Dvr., on the outbreak of war: obtained a commission 2nd Lieut., 12th Worcestershire Regt., 14 May 1915: proceeded to France, 14 March 1916; promoted Lieut. posted 3rd Battn., December following. For his actions when a member of a raiding and reconnaissance party at Wulverghem (2 – 3 June 1917), during preparations for the forthcoming Battle of Messines Ridge which took place a few days later, he was awarded the Military Cross ('*London Gazette*,' 26 July 1917), 'For conspicuous gallantry and devotion to duty during a raid upon enemy trenches. Finding his party suddenly attacked by a machine gun he attacked it with bombs down the flank and front, putting it out of action and saving his company from many casualties.' Killed in action 10 August 1917, when, in attacking at Westhoek, the battalion was met by heavy machine-gun fire: Age 31. He was Scoutmaster to 113th Glasgow Scout Group. (*IWGC record age 34*)

(Panel 34) Lieut. Richard Bowen Woosnam, 6th (Reserve) attd. 4th Bn. The Worcestershire Regt.: *s.* of Bowen Pottinger Woosnam, of 41, Warwick Gardens, Kensington, London, by his wife Kate: proceeded overseas 21 March 1915: served with the Expeditionary Force in the Dardanelles (landed Cape Helles, 25 April), and was killed in action 4 June 1915, at the Battle of Krithia, Gallipoli: Age 34. IWGC/1926, MR.29,XXXVI,pg.1613. *Known to be recorded on the Helles Memorial (Addenda Panel).*

(Panel 34) 2nd Lieut. William Bingham Barling, 3rd Bn. The Worcestershire Regt.: only *s.* of William Barling, of The Paddocks, Newnham-on-Severn, by his wife Millicent, *dau.* of Seymour Bingham: *b.* Newnham, co. Gloucester, 8 July 1892: *educ.* Beresford House, Gloucester; The Priory, Great Malvern; and Dean's Close, Cheltenham: on leaving the latter became a student at Wye College: elected to a Fellowship of the Surveyor's Institute, and became a member of the Inland Revenue Valuation Department, Gloucester; a post he held for three years. Following the declaration of war enlisted Pte., 5th Gloucestershire Regt. (on or about 12 August): received his commission 2nd Lieut. 6th Worcestershire Regt., 2 December 1914; placed on Officers' Reserve: went to France, 19 February 1915, reaching the firing line on the 23rd. (attd. 3rd Battn.), and was killed in action seventeen days later, 12 March 1915. A wire from the War Office came on 16 March:– "reported missing believed killed," and the last authoritative information concerning his death was contained in a letter from his Colonel. It informed that when last seen Lieut. Barling was very bravely leading his platoon in a determined assault against an enemy's trench, near Kemmel, Belgium, and was believed to have been killed, as were all the other officers concerned. As the attack unfortunately failed, no other examination of the ground could be made, and no further news was received, but a Corpl. concerned in this particular advance reported he stumbled over an officer whom he believed to be Lieut. Barling. The trench, which a very few men succeeded in reaching, had to be evacuated at nightfall, and is still (1916) in the enemy's hands: Age 22. *unm.* (*IWGC record 6th Bn.*)

(Panel 34) 2nd Lieut. Ronald Anderson Budden, 1st Bn. (29th Foot) The Worcestershire Regt.: only *s.* of Horace Budden, formerly of 35, Marlborough Road, Wimbledon Park, London, S.W., now 52, Hillcrest Road, Acton, by his wife Laura Evangeline, *dau.* of Capt. John Anderson, of Brighton and Burton-on-Trent: *b.* Bournemouth, co. Hants, 16 October 1897: *educ.* Bournemouth School; Royal Military College, Sandhurst: gazetted 2nd Lieut., Worcestershire Regt., 7 April 1916: served with the Expeditionary Force in France and Flanders from the following September, and was killed in action near

Hooge, east of Ypres, 31 July 1917. Lieut.Col. G. Davidge wrote, "He was a most gallant young officer, and had frequently distinguished himself previously to his death, and died as he would have wished, at the head of his company. The N.C.O.'s and men of his company looked up to him with great admiration, respect and affection, and they speak of his good qualities in glowing terms;" and Capt. Urwick, "He was shot through the head by a German sniper and died instantly. He met his death in the most gallant fashion. The company of which his platoon formed part had already attacked and captured the front and second lines of the front trench system held by the enemy. While attacking the third line they were checked for a moment by machine-gun fire. Your son very promptly organized a small party from his platoon, and led them forward from shell-hole to shell-hole, with a view to attacking and silencing the nearest of these machine guns. While within point-blank range of the gun, he raised himself on the lip of the crater to throw a bomb, and was shot at that instant. The men with him immediately rushed the gun and bayoneted the crew, including the man who sniped your son. The gun was captured, and the line went forward to its further objectives. I cannot hope to express the extreme value of such leading as was displayed by your son. Apart altogether from the personal gallantry of the deed, the initiative, the quick grasp of opportunity in the face of momentary checks, are exactly those qualities which are needed to make the full use of the arms and equipment which are at last ours. The fact that the regiment fulfilled every task which had been set it to the letter, despite strong opposition, is in itself sufficient testimony to the value of the work done by him...The Colonel and all his brother officers cannot speak too highly of him, while more important still, the men of his own platoon seem to miss him sorely." The Chaplain of his battalion also wrote, "I had come to know him very well indeed, and his death has come as a great blow to all of us, for he was a general favourite in the battalion...He always proved himself a fearless soldier... he lived a good life, and died a noble death in the greatest effort that England has made for the freedom of the world." He was awarded a Parchment Certificate for gallant conduct and devotion to duty by the General Officer Commanding the 8th Division, the official record stating, "He was in charge of a patrol which entered the German lines nr. Hooge, east of Ypres, on the night of 27 – 28 July 1917. He carried out his reconnaissance with skill, judgement and determination. He handled his men well and returned with valuable information." Age 19.

(Panel 34) 2nd Lieut. **Frederick John Noel Clarke**, 6th (Reserve) attd. 3rd Bn. The Worcestershire Regt.: *s.* of Frederick Charles Philip Clarke, of Runnymede, Jersey, by his wife Minnie Jane: *b.* 21 October 1895: *educ.* Victoria College, Jersey: on leaving there, obtained a commission, April 1913, 3rd Battn. Royal Militia, Island of Jersey: mobilised with his battalion on the outbreak of war: entered R.M.C. Sandhurst, expressing a wish to take a more active part in the war: subsequently gained a commission, 2nd Lieut., 12 May 1915, posted 6th (Reserve) Bn. Worcestershire Regt.: joined his battalion at Devonport, proceeding to France shortly thereafter, where he was posted to 3rd Battn., serving in front of Ypres, and was killed at Hooge, 30 June 1915, while taking his men out of a trench which had been blown up by German shellfire, and was the first officer of 3rd Jersey Militia to fall in the war. The following appeared in Battalion Orders, 6 July 1915, "The Commanding Officer learned with deep regret that 2nd Lieut. F.J.N. Clarke, Worcestershire Regt., who resigned his commission in the battalion at the end of last year in order to join the Regular Army, has been killed in action in Flanders. He feels sure that his regret at the loss of this gallant young officer will be shared by the officers and all ranks of the battalion...2nd Lieut. Clarke has set a fine example of devotion to duty and sacrifice, which might well be followed by many young men in the island." The Adjutant of the Reserve Battalion wrote, "I was very much impressed by him...Very bright and active, with a career in front of him...a most promising soldier." He was a keen sportsman, and had played for the Jersey Island Rugby Football XV: Age 19. Remains recovered unmarked grave, partially destroyed by shellfire, 'Sanctuary Wood Old Cemetery' (28.I.24.b.90.97) 'Unknown British Officer.;' identified – Officers Clothing; reinterred, registered 4 May 1928. *Buried in Sanctuary Wood Cemetery (II.F.36).*

(Panel 34) 2nd Lieut. **Wakefield Waldo Meade**, 6th (Reserve) attd. 3rd Bn. The Worcestershire Regt.: only *survg. s.* of Hannah Meade ('Kingscliffe,' Hale Lane, Mill Hill, London, N.W.), late of 95,

Broadway, Kettering, co. Northampton, by her marriage to the late Rev. Wakefield Suft Meade, Rector of Loddington, Kettering, who was cousin to the late Edmund Waldo-Meade-Waldo, of Hever Castle, and Stonewell Park, co. Kent: *b*. Loddington Rectory, 15 November 1895: *educ*. St. Edmund's School, Canterbury, co. Kent (September 1905 – April 1913), O.T.C. member: Occupation – Clerk; Capital & Counties Bank, Rushden, co. Northampton: enlisted 4th Northamptonshire Regt., September 1914, after the declaration of war: gazetted 2nd Lieut., 6th (Reserve) Bn. Worcestershire Regt., January 1915, attd. 3rd Battn. in Flanders, March following, and was shot by a sniper, 20 June 1915, while endeavouring to assist a wounded brother officer (2nd Lieut. Barfoot, also killed) at Hooge, near Ypres. Buried in Sanctuary Wood, Ypres: Age 19. Remains recovered 'Sanctuary Wood Old Cemetery' (28.I.24.b.90.97) 'Unknown British Officer. 2/Lieut.;' identified – Officers Clothing, Badge of Rank; reinterred, registered 4 May 1928. See Sergt. H. Brightmore, Hooge Crater Cemetery (XVI.H.I). *Buried in Sanctuary Wood Cemetery (II.F.34)*.

"Death Is Swallowed Up In Victory"

I. Cor. XV.54

2nd Lieut. G.A. Barfoot is buried in Hooge Crater Cemetery (XV.H.14).

(Panel 34) 2nd Lieut. Basil Muir, 6th (Reserve) attd. 3rd Bn. The Worcestershire Regt.: eldest *survg*. *s*. of the late T.J. Muir, of Michaelstow House, St. Teath, co. Cornwall, by his marriage to Mrs Batchelor, *née* Muir (Whitstone Rectory, Exeter): *b*. Musselburgh, co. Midlothian, 2 March 1896: *educ*. St. Andrew's, Eastbourne, and Malvern College, where he was in the Cricket XI: left Malvern, Christmas 1914: gazetted 2nd Lieut., 6th Worcestershire Regt., January 1915, attd. 3rd Battn. for Active Service: served with the Expeditionary Force in France and Flanders from March 1915, and fell in action, 16 June following, in the fighting to straighten the line at Hooge. Buried with other officers and men behind the trenches near the Ypres-Menin road: Age 19.

(Panel 34) 2nd Lieut. Edward Ernest Vaile, 3rd Bn. The Worcestershire Regt.: formerly 1st Bn. Honourable Artillery Coy.: *s*. of Philip (& Amy) Vaile, of 10, Ormonde Terrace, Regent's Park, London: and elder brother to 2nd Lieut. P.A. Vaile, 2/19th London Regt., died of wounds 14 October 1916, in the Base Hospital, Le Havre. Killed in action 5 October 1915: Age 24. *unm*.

His brother Philip is buried in St. Marie Cemetery, Le Havre (Div.3.L.8).

(Panel 34) Sergt. 9551, John Hicks, 'A' Coy., 3rd Bn. The Worcestershire Regt.: *s*. of George (& Catherine A.) Hicks, of 4, Grove Houses, Guarlford, Malvern: *b*. Malvern: enlisted Worcester. Killed in the attack at Spanbroek Mill, Lindenhoek, 12 March 1915: Age 23. An envelope bearing the address of his fiancée, Miss Phipps (Malvern Commons), was found on his body; Coy.Sergt.-Major P.T. Blond wrote, "Dear Miss Phipps, I am sorry to have to tell you that Sergt. Hicks, whose hand-writing you will recognise on the envelope containing this letter, was killed at about 4.30 pm. on the 12th inst. It was in the course of an attack which we made on the enemy's trenches. He was shot through the head and killed instantaneously. I cannot express my sorrow at his untimely end sufficiently, for we all liked him. As a leader of his platoon he was an example. In the care for the welfare of his men he was most diligent; as a comrade he was one of the best, and in losing him we suffer a loss which, I am sure, is only excelled by yours and his people, of whom he so often spoke of in terms of affection. I must ask you to let his people know, as I cannot write direct, having only your address."

(Panel 34) L/Sergt. 13080, John Gordon, 3rd Bn. The Worcestershire Regt.: Shot and killed 20 June 1915, by a German sniper who had already accounted for Sergt. Brightmore, 2nd Lieut. G.A. Barfoot and 2nd Lieut. W.W. Meade.

Sergt. Brightmore and 2nd Lieut. Barfoot are buried in Hooge Crater Cemetery (XVI.H.1 & XV.H.14); 2nd Lieut. Meade, buried in Sanctuary Wood Cemetery (II.F.34) is also recorded above.

(Panel 34) L/Corpl. 13511, George Sidaway, 3rd Bn. The Worcestershire Regt.: *s*. of Ephraim Sidaway, of 30, High Street, Cradley, Malvern, co. Worcester, by his wife Sarah: *b*. Dudley, co. Stafford: enlisted Wolverhampton, May 1914. Died of wounds 18 June 1915, received in action two days previously from the bursting of a shell above his trench: Age 19. *Buried in Bailleul Communal Cemetery Extension (I.E.82).* (*Headstone records Siddaway*).

> *God Gave His Only Son*
> *And I Gave Thee For Honour Life And Liberty*

(Panel 34) Pte. 10133, Joseph Bissell, 2nd Bn. (45th Foot) The Worcestershire Regt.: *s.* of Joseph Bissell, of 120, Lupin Street, Ashted, Birmingham, and the late Leah Rebecca, his wife: and brother to Pte. 18963, W. Bissell, 1st Worcestershire Regt., killed in action 26 March 1918: served with the Expeditionary Force in France from 14 August 1914, and was killed in action 21 October following, at Gheluvelt: Age 25. *unm.*

His brother William also has no known grave; he is commemorated on the Pozieres Memorial (Panel 41).

In the early hours of 12 March 1915, after a night march from their billets at Locre, three companies of 3rd Worcesters filed into their assembly positions near Kemmel in readiness for an attack on the German lines at Spanbroekmolen scheduled for 8.40a.m. Due to a dense morning fog, which under any other circumstances would have greatly aided the attackers, the attack was postponed until the mid-afternoon by which time the fog had dispersed. As soon as the Worcesters rose out of their waterlogged trenches to begin their assault the enemy opened a fierce and deadly fire into them, cutting down officers and men like a scythe. In places small parties of men from one company managed to breach the enemy lines and seize a group of farm buildings; the other two companies lay between the lines dead, dying, wounded. As the attack lost momentum so the Germans concentrated on regaining control of the breached sector of their lines, bombing their way toward the farm buildings. Effectively trapped with no means of withdrawal and no chance of reinforcements reaching them, after three hours of tenaciously holding out against the enemy and their number being steadily depleted, the end came when the artillery – misinformed regarding the position – laid a heavy bombardment on the buildings and completely annihilated what remained of the gallant Worcesters.

A roll-call held later back at Locre revealed 2 officers and 77 other ranks would never answer their names again.

(Panel 34) Pte. 16423, Cornelius Richard Careless, 3rd Bn. The Worcestershire Regt.: *s.* of the late Richard Careless, by his wife Susan ('The Elm,' Newtown, Offenham, Evesham, co. Worcester): Offenham, 1895: enlisted Evesham: served with the Expeditionary Force in France and Flanders from 19 February 1915, and was killed in action at Spanbroek Mill, nr. Kemmel, three weeks later, 13 March 1915: Age 19.

(Panel 34) Pte. 23778, Clement Cyril Carter, 3rd Bn. The Worcestershire Regt. (Lewis Gun Section): *yst. s.* of the late Rev. William David Carter, of St. John's, Stand Lane, by his wife Mary Emma (Holland House, Crumpsall, Manchester), *dau.* of the late William Openshaw, of Redvales: *b.* Stand Lane, nr. Manchester, 12 June 1888: *educ.* Grammar School, Bromyard, and The College, Llandovery: removed to Canada, 1905, where he spent several years farming in Alberta and New Brunswick, living for some months at the Mission House, Edmonton: returned to England at the outbreak of war, and became a lay-brother at Pershore Abbey: volunteered to join the Army, but was refused owing to defective eyesight, and joined the Volunteer Force during the winter of 1914 – 15; accepted in the Worcestershire Regt., 22 July 1915, proceeded to (and served with) the Mediterranean Expeditionary Force, Gallipoli from the following October: evacuated to Alexandria, December, suffering from an attack of enteric fever, subsequently repatriated to England; thence, after treatment and recuperation, proceeded to France, 30 August 1916: slightly wounded at the Battle of Messines Ridge (June 1917), and was killed in action nr. Hooge, 21 July 1917, while on patrol duty. Buried at Hooge: Age 29. *unm.*

(Panel 34) Pte. 9656, Isaac Cooper, 'A' Coy., 3rd Bn. The Worcestershire Regt.: *s.* of William (& Mary) Cooper, of Angel Street, Dudley, co. Worcester: served with the Expeditionary Force in France, and died of wounds 21 February 1915. He was married to Mary Sutton, *née* Cooper (5, House, Court 1, Abeerley Street, Dudley). *Buried in Locre Churchyard (II.A.5).*

(Panel 34) Pte. 30742, Bertie Dix, 1st Bn. (29th Foot) The Worcestershire Regt.: *s.* of Alfred Dix, of Pettygrove Road, Mont Hill, Kingswood, Bristol, by his wife Ellen: *b.* 1894: enlisted Bristol. Killed in action in the vicinity of Westhoek, 15 August 1917: Age 23. *unm. Buried in Sanctuary Wood Cemetery (V.F.26).*

(Panel 34) Pte. 34690, Percy Ewins, 3rd Bn. The Worcestershire Regt.: *s.* of the late Harry George Ewins, by his wife Sarah (217,Trinity Road, Aston, Birmingham): and yr. brother to Pte. 2350, J. Ewins, 2nd Royal Warwickshire Regt., fell 19 December 1914: *b.* Brighton, co. Sussex: enlisted Birmingham. Killed in action 10 August 1917: Age 26. He was married to Hannah Sanders, *née* Ewins (1, Tower Place, Tower Road, Aston).

His brother John also has no known grave; he is commemorated on the Ploegsteert Memorial (Panel 2).

(Panel 34) Pte. 8675, Charles Frederick Hadley, 'C' Coy., 2nd Bn. (45th Foot) The Worcestershire Regt.: *s.* of William John Hadley: *b.* Birmingham, 6 October 1887: *educ.* St. Joseph's, Aston, Birmingham: served some years with the Colours then joined the Reserve: called up on the outbreak of war, August 1914: served with the Expeditionary Force in France. Reported missing after the Battle of Ypres; now assumed killed in action 31 October. 1914: Age 27. He *m.* Birmingham, 27 December 1911; Minnie (7, Temperance Square, Wilton Street, Lozells, Aston), *dau.* of James Perry, and had two sons – Charles Frederick, *b.* 4 January 1913; Arthur John, *b.* 27 March 1914.

(Panel 34) Pte. 17778, Edward Harrington, 3rd Bn. The Worcestershire Regt.: *s.* of William Harrington, of 150, Summer Row, Dudley Port, Tipton, co. Stafford: *b.* Dudley, co. Worcester: enlisted Worcester. Killed in action 20 June 1915: Age 19. Remains recovered 'Sanctuary Wood Old Cemetery' (28.I.24.b.90.97) 'Unknown British Soldier,' identified – Clothing, Titles; reinterred, registered 4 May 1928. *Buried in Sanctuary Wood Cemetery (II.F.35).*

Gone But Not Forgotten

(Panel 34) Pte. 9997, John Hayes, 2nd Bn. (45th Foot) The Worcestershire Regt.: *b.* London, about 1886: enlisted Stratford, London, E.: served with the Expeditionary Force in France from August 1914. Reported missing, believed killed in action 31 October following: Age 28. *unm.* All correspondence should be addressed c/o his sister, Mrs C. Thake (16, John's Hill, St. George Street, London Dock, London). Remains recovered unmarked grave (28.J.22.b.6.1) Gheluvelt Chateau; identified – Clothing, Disc; reinterred, registered 19 May 1927. *Buried in Sanctuary Wood Cemetery (IV.D.18).*

(Panel 34) Pte. 13565, George William Pollard, 3rd Bn. The Worcestershire Regt.: *s.* of the late Sergt. G.W.J. Pollard, 9th Royal Warwickshire Regt., died of wounds 9 April 1916, in Mesopotamia; and Mrs M. Pollard (68, Chesterton Terrace, Plaistow, London): *b.* Plaistow: enlisted Birmingham. Killed in action 16 June 1915: Age 20. *unm.*

His father George also has no known grave; he is commemorated on the Basra Memorial (Panel 9).

(Panel 34) Pte. 6298, Thomas Arthur Richardson, 3rd Bn. The Worcestershire Regt.: late of Bidford-on-Avon, co. Warwick: enlisted Worcester. Severely wounded in the thigh near Spanbroek Mill, and died in a Casualty Clearing Station, 12 March 1915, nr. Chocques: Age 35.

(Panel 34) Pte. 235039, William Swift, 1st Bn. (29th Foot) The Worcestershire Regt.: *b.* Wolverhampton: enlisted there: Killed in action 24 July 1917; shellfire (gas), Lille Gate, Ypres.

(Panel 34) Pte. 9262, Alfred Ernest Vidler, 3rd Bn. The Worcestershire Regt.: *s.* of William Vidler, of 49, Limekiln Street, Dover, co. Kent, by his wife Harriet: Occupation – Railway Worker; Staplehurst Station: enlisted Dover, 24 May 1905: served with the Expeditionary Force in France from 15 August 1914, and was reported missing, believed killed in action 7 November. 1914: Age 28. *unm.* He was betrothed to Miss Daisy Rigden (28, Limekiln Street, Dover).

(Panel 34) Lieut. Herbert Westrup Canton, 1st Bn. (30th Foot) The East Lancashire Regt.: only *s.* of Frank Canton, Merchant (of a Huguenot family), by his wife Florence: *b.* Walton-on-Thames, 6 March 1892: *educ.* Magdalen College School, Oxford; R.M.C. Sandhurst: gazetted 2nd Lieut., 13 March 1912: went to the Front with the Expeditionary Force, August 1914: first came under fire at Le Cateau where his platoon suffered heavy casualties: took part in the retreat from Mons, and was present at the Battles of the Marne and the Aisne: with his regt. through the winter of 1914 in the trenches near Armentieres, and was killed in action near Ypres, 13 May 1915, after repelling a strong German attack. Buried at Wieltje. Though promoted to the command of his company from 5 March 1915, his appointment to rank as from 31 March 1915, was posthumously gazetted after his death: Age 23. *unm.*

(Panel 34) Lieut. Hector Alan Lane, 1st Bn. (30th Foot) The East Lancashire Regt.: only *s.* of John Lane, of Cullisse, Parkstone, co. Dorset: *b.* Decorah, Iowa, United States, 2 June 1889: *educ.* Newton College, Newton Abbot; obtained a scholarship from the Law Society: Occupation – Solicitor: received a commission, Dorsetshire Royal Garrison Artillery Volunteers, March 1907, and served with them until 1911, when he went to Singapore to practise his profession: joined Singapore Volunteer Artillery and, on the outbreak of war he, with two other officers, was put in charge of a fort: offered his services to the War Office, in England gazetted 2nd Lieut. East Lancashire Regt., September 1914, as 'a candidate from the self-governing Dominions & Crown Colonies': promoted Temp. Lieut. November following; Lieut. December 1914: arrived London, January 1915, posted 1st East Lancashire Regt.: served with the Expeditionary Force in Flanders, and was killed instantaneously by a bullet in the head 13 May 1915. His Colonel wrote of him, "I am very grieved to inform you that your son, Lieut. H.A. Lane, was killed on the 13th inst. On the evening of that day he led his platoon against a farm occupied by the Germans; he got in all-right with his men, and was exchanging shots with them in the farm buildings when he was shot in the head and died at once. He was only with us a short time, but quite long enough to show what stuff he was made of. He was a valuable officer, and did his work very well, and I am very sorry to lose him. He made himself very popular with all ranks. He is buried at the farm he took, which is 1,200 yards north of Wieltje, a village north-east of Ypres." Age 25. *unm.*

(Panel 34) 2nd Lieut. Francis William Hambley, 2nd Bn. (59th Foot) The East Lancashire Regt.: Killed in action 31 July 1917. See account ref. Sergt. T.H. Briggs, M.M., below.

(Panel 34) 2nd Lieut. Cecil Leigh Hutchinson, 3rd (Reserve) Bn. The East Lancashire Regt.: elder *s.* of Christopher Edward Hutchinson, of Moss Side, near Lytham, co. Lancaster, by his wife Leonora Cecil Maud, *dau.* of Carl Goetz: *b.* Manchester, 9 July 1896: *educ.* Collegiate School, St. Anne's-on-Sea; and King Edward VII's School, Lytham: enlisted 18 January 1915: served with the Expeditionary Force in France and Flanders from March 1916: invalided home June; returned to France, September: took part in the operations on the Somme, and again invalided home November: took part in the spring offensive of 1917, and was killed in action at Westhoek, nr. Ypres, 31 July 1917. Buried there. A brother officer wrote, "We had reached our objective, and he was giving orders for the consolidation of the position gained, when he was hit in the stomach by a sniper a few minutes after I had left him. He did splendidly and led his men through with total disregard of danger." He was captain of his school football club: Age 21. *unm.* See account ref. Sergt. T.H. Briggs, M.M., below.

(Panel 34) 2nd Lieut. George McMillan, 2nd Bn. (59th Foot) The East Lancashire Regt.: *s.* of John McMillan, of 11, King's Drive, Heaton Moor, Stockport, co. Chester, by his wife Mary Ellen: served with the Expeditionary Force in France and Flanders from November 1914, and was killed in action 31 July 1917: Age 31. In civilian life Mr McMillan was Honorary Secretary to the Heaton Mersey Lad's Club. See account ref. Sergt. T.H. Briggs, M.M., below.

(Panel 34) 2nd Lieut. Paul Reichardt, 3rd attd. 2nd Bn. (59th Foot) The East Lancashire Regt.: Killed in action 31 July 1917. See account ref. Sergt. T.H. Briggs, M.M., below.

(Panel 34) 2nd Lieut. William Harold Vyvyan Smith, 2nd Bn. (59th Foot) The East Lancashire Regt.: *s.* of Harold Oxley Chamberlain Smith, of Grange Court, 40, Grange Road, Ealing, London, W., Solicitor, by his wife Kate Courtenay, *dau.* of William Courtenay Vyvyan, formerly of the 4th Foot: *b.* Ealing, London, W., 4 June 1897: *educ.* Harrow View, Ealing, London, W., and Epsom College: enlisted 16th (Queen's Westminster Rifles) Bn. London Regt. (T.F.), 6 August 1914: served with the Expeditionary Force in France and Flanders from 1 November following: took part in the operations at Armentieres and Ypres: invalided home, March 1915, suffering from scarlet fever: on recovery rejoined his regiment at Hooge, where he saw severe fighting, and subsequently went to the Officers' Cadet Corps, General Headquarters: obtained a commission, 2nd Lieut. East Lancashire Regt., 23 October 1915: took part in several engagements, including Armentieres, Souchez, Vimy Ridge, Hulluch, the Hohenzollern Redoubt, Hooge, Battle of the Somme, and Contalmaison: again invalided home, suffering from pyorrhoea and septic throat, October 1916: returned to France, May 1917, and was killed in action 31 July following, by a sniper while organising his platoon outside Glencorse Wood, north of Ypres, after a successful advance of 2,000 yards. Buried south-west of Glencorse Wood. His Colonel wrote, "He always did his job well, and was doing well at the time of his death;" and another officer, "He was always so cheerful under all circumstances, and he was magnificent under fire, the men would follow him anywhere. I do not think that any Platoon Commander on that day kept his men better together. He led them first through a heavy barrage and then right on to their final objective, altogether about 2,000 yards. I saw him a few minutes before he was hit, and he was full of how well his men had done. He was shot by a sniper and died instantaneously, and was buried that night close to where he fell. I feel sure he would not have wished to die otherwise than leading his men in battle." He was recommended for the Military Cross (not recognised) after action at Contalmaison, during operations on the Somme: Age 20. *unm*. See account ref. Sergt. T.H. Briggs, M.M., below.

At 3.50 a.m., zero hour 31 July 1917, 8th Division (advancing in four waves with 1st Worcesters on the left, 2nd Northamptons on the right) began its attack against the enemy positions on the Bellewaarde Ridge. At zero plus twenty 2nd East Lancashires on the right and 1st Sherwood Foresters on the left moved up in artillery formation to the Bellewaarde Ridge where they formed up in preparation to advance (at zero plus one hour fifteen) through the preceding battalions to the Westhoek Ridge. For the most part the battalion's advance was successfully carried out, although their right flank was left 'in the air' due to 11th Manchesters encountering difficulties in their sector. Unable to gain touch with the Manchesters the East Lancs kept touch with the Sherwoods and, despite stiff opposition and heavy casualties from machine gun fire due to the open right flank, managed to reach, take and consolidate their objective. An attack on the open flank later that morning was driven off by the courage and initiative of Corpl. Hyndman who, seeing the attack coming, took his Lewis gun section well out into the exposed area, laid down a heavy field of fire and brought the attack to a standstill. Later still, during the afternoon, two further counterattacks were successfully beaten off with the use of stokes mortars and rifle grenades. Although the Division's attack had not been entirely successful, the East Lancs part in the action was deemed satisfactory; it had done all that had it had been tasked with. The War Diary concluded with:– "...all ranks worked splendidly and were absolutely untiring." The battalion's casualty toll, however, had been heavy: Lieuts. Reichardt, Smith, McMillan, Hambley, Hutchinson, and 47 Other Ranks killed; Capt. Craig (R.A.M.C.), Lieuts. Duffy, Short, Gordon, Giles, and 137 Other Ranks wounded; 40 Other Ranks missing. Among the other ranks Sergt. Busfield was wounded, CSM. Hamilton, D.C.M., died of wounds and Sergts. Wade, Young, Pinfield and Briggs were killed; all had served with the battalion since the 1914.

(Panel 34) Sergt. 10513, Thomas Herbert Briggs, M.M., 2nd Bn. (59th Foot) The East Lancashire Regt.: late of 10, St. Paul's Terrace, Hoddlesden, nr. Darwen, co. Lancaster: eldest *s*. of John Briggs, of 17, Clifden Terrace, Hoddlesden, by his wife Alice: and brother to Sergt. 12319, R.W. Briggs, 7th East Lancashire Regt., killed 14 November 1916, aged 20 years: *b*. Hoddlesden, 1894: a pre-war Regular, prior to enlistment was a Weaver, Messrs Carus' Mill, Hoddlesden: stationed at Wynberg Camp, South Africa on the outbreak of war, departed Capetown, 1 October 1914; disembarked Southampton on the 30th of that month: served with the Expeditionary Force in France and Flanders from 6 November 1914: took part in many actions including the Battle of Contalmaison, July 1916, for his actions during which he was awarded the Military Medal ('*London Gazette*,' September 1916): was wounded, losing one eye; returned to duty after a period of hospitalisation and convalescence, and was killed in action 31 July 1917, in the vicinity of Westhoek Ridge: Age 23. *unm*.

His brother Robert also has no known grave; he is commemorated on the Thiepval Memorial, Somme.

(Panel 34) Sergt. 10679, John Elijah Pinfield, 2nd Bn. (59th Foot) The East Lancashire Regt.: *s.* of John Pinfield, of Fairfield, Bromsgrove, co. Worcester: *b.* Birmingham, *c.*1872: enlisted Rifle Brigade, no.4441, Gosport, co. Hants, 14 February 1896: served in the Sudan, 1898; South African Campaigns, 1899 – 1902; Malta, Crete, Egypt (Cairo), India: transf'd. 2nd East Lancashire Regt. February 1912 and, on the outbreak of war August 1914, was stationed with his battalion at Wynberg Camp, nr. Capetown, South Africa: served with the Expeditionary Force in France and Flanders from 6 November 1914, and was killed in action at Westhoek Ridge, 31 July 1917: Age 44. He leaves a wife, Sarah Pinfield (Osborne Villa, Windsor Road, Totton, Southampton), and family. See account ref. Sergt. T.H. Briggs, M.M., above.

(Panel 34) Sergt. 10048, Edward Wade, 2nd Bn. (59th Foot) The East Lancashire Regt.: *b.* Aldeburgh, co. Suffolk: enlisted Kingston-on-Thames: served with the Expeditionary Force in France and Flanders, and was killed in action 31 July 1917. See account ref. Sergt. T.H. Briggs, M.M., above.

(Panel 34) Sergt. 18404, Robert Stanton Young, 2nd Bn. (59th Foot) The East Lancashire Regt.: *s.* of T. (& Mrs) Young, of 36, Eckersley Road, Bolton, co. Lancaster: *b.* Hawkshaw: enlisted Ramsbottom. Killed in action 31 July 1917: Age 22. *unm.* See account ref. Sergt. T.H. Briggs, M.M., above.

(Panel 34) Corpl. 14117, Charles Henry Goodliffe, 8th Bn. The East Lancashire Regt.: *s.* of Godfrey Goodliffe, of Sebright Cottage, Fairy Lane, Sale, co. Chester, by his wife Mary Ann: and elder brother to Pte. 26189, J.T. Goodliffe, 3rd Cheshire Regt., died at home 15 November 1918; and Pte. 20235, J. Goodliffe, King's (Liverpool) Regt., killed in action 29 February 1916: *b.* Hulme, 1888: enlisted Manchester. Killed in action 31 July 1917: Age 29. *unm.*

His brother John is buried in Sale Cemetery (X.5740); James has no known grave, he is recorded on Panel 6.

(Panel 34) L/Corpl. 8778, Thomas Catlow, 1st Bn. (30th Foot) The East Lancashire Regt.: *s.* of Sophia A. Catlow (3, Orchard Street, Barnoldswick, Colne): and brother to Pte. 18574, E. Catlow, 7th East Lancashire Regt., died of wounds 2 August 1917, at Bailleul: *b.* Burnley, co. Lancaster: enlisted Preston. Killed in action 9 May 1915, at Ypres: Age 29. *unm.*

His brother Edward is buried in Bailleul Communal Cemetery Extension (III.E.274).

(Panel 34) Pte. 26600, William Whiteside, 1st Bn. (30th Foot) The East Lancashire Regt.: late of Blackpool, co. Lancaster: *s.* of William Whiteside, by his wife Arabella: and elder brother to Pte. 7594, J. Whiteside, Scots Guards, who also fell: *b.* Blackburn: enlisted there. Killed in action 4 August 1916: Age 38.

His brother John also has no known grave; he is recorded on Panel 11.

(Panel 34) Pte. 28633, William Henry Woods, 2nd Bn. (59th Foot) The East Lancashire Regt.: late of 30, Grimshaw Street, Great Harwood: *s.* of John William Woods, of 6, Albert Street, Great Harwood, co. Lancaster, by his wife Annie Maria: and brother to Pte. 23181, T.E. Woods, 9th East Lancashire Regt., died of wounds 26 September 1918, aged 29 years. Killed in action 31 July 1917: Age 29. He was married to Jane Elizabeth Hanson, *née* Woods (2, St. Hubert's Road, Great Harwood).

His brother Thomas is buried in Doiran Military Cemetery (V.E.25).

(Panel 34) Capt. Arthur George McCausland Burn, 2nd Bn. (70th Foot) The East Surrey Regt. attd. 1st Bn. Gloucestershire Regt.: only *s.* of Lieut.-Col. A.G. Burn, of Mansel Lacy, co. Hertford, Indian Army: *b.* Dorunda, Chota Nagpore, India, 22 December 1882: *educ.* Wellington College, Crowthorne, co. Berks, and Royal Military College, Sandhurst: gazetted 2nd Lieut. East Surrey Regt. 18 January 1902: promoted Lieut. 29 January 1904; Capt. 5 March 1910: served in India: home on leave when the European War broke out, and was then ordered to join 1st Gloucestershire Regt.: served with the Expeditionary Force in France and Flanders: took part in the Retreat from Mons, the Battles of the Marne and the Aisne, and was killed in action during the first Battle of Ypres, 29 October 1914: Age 31. *unm.*

(Panel 34) Capt. the Hon. Archibald Rodney Hewitt, D.S.O., 2nd Bn. (70th Foot) The East Surrey Regt.: of Hill House, Lyndhurst, co. Hants: *yr. s.* of Archibald Robert Hewitt, 6th Viscount Lifford, of The Court, Crondall, co. Hants: and *yr.* brother to Capt. the Hon. E. Hewitt, Dorsetshire Regt.:

b. Torquay, co. Devon, 25 May 1883: *educ*. Private Schools; Dulwich, and Royal Military College, Sandhurst: gazetted 2nd Lieut., East Surrey Regt., October 1902; posted 1st Battn., serving with it in India, 1903 – 1910: promoted Lieut. June 1904; Capt. May 1910: apptd. Adjutant, 1st Battn., June 1911 – May 1914: went to Belgium with his regiment, August 1914, and was seriously wounded at the Battle of the Marne, 9 September following: Mentioned in Despatches by Sir John (now Lord) French, 8 October 1914, for his services, and awarded the D.S.O. ('*London Gazette*,' 9 November 1914)'..for moving out of the trenches at Le Cateau, under heavy shell fire, and bringing back men who were dribbling to the rear.' By the end of December 1914, having sufficiently recovered from his wounds to fit him for home duty, in February 1915 he returned to the Front, and was killed at Zonnebeke, Flanders, 25 April following, while leading his men in a charge against a German trench. Buried near Zonnebeke. He was a member of the Naval and Military Club, London, and his recreations were hunting, shooting, fishing, golf and football: 25 April 1915: Age 31. *unm*.

(Panel 34) Capt. Adam Gordon Howitt, M.C., 12th (Service) Bn. (Bermondsey) The East Surrey Regt.: *s*. of Adam Howitt, and brother to Mrs A.G. Bulmer (81, Duthie Terrace, Aberdeen): *b*. Ellon, co. Aberdeen, 11 June 1884: *educ*. Gordon's College; B.Sc. (Agr., 1910), thereafter entered service of the Potash Syndicate and, after a period in their offices in Germany, went to South Africa (1912) in the capacity of Director of Propaganda: joined Cape Town Highlanders on the outbreak of war, August 1914: took part in General Botha's Campaign in German West Africa, 1914 – 15, during which he rose through the ranks and gained a commission: came to England on conclusion of that campaign and obtained a commission; Lieut., East Surrey Regt., October 1915: served in Ireland during the rebellion; proceeded to France, May 1916, was wounded on the Somme: removed to England from whence after treatment and a period of convalescence he returned to France, March 1917: promoted Capt., and awarded the Military Cross, for services on the field of battle, June 1917: 'The success of the raid was due to his good leadership and cool judgment.' Killed in action during the repulse of a sudden counter-attack at Hollebeke, 5 August 1917. His Colonel wrote, "Although outnumbered, and under climatic conditions impossible to adequately describe, Captain Howitt and his men beat the enemy back in the fierce hand-to-hand fighting. 'Jock' Howitt died fighting to the last, one of the bravest of the brave…Had he survived he would have secured another well-earned decoration.": Age 33.

(Panel 34) Capt. Austin Henry Huth, 4th (Extra Reserve) attd. 1st Bn. (31st Foot) The East Surrey Regt.: late (60th Foot) The King's Royal Rifle Corps: *yr. s*. of the late Edward Huth, J.P., D.L., of Wykehurst Park, co. Sussex, by his wife Edith (Avenue House, Bear Wood, Wokingham, co. Surrey): *b*. Hertford Street, Mayfair, London, W., 13 October 1881: *educ*. Eton, and Royal Military College, Sandhurst: received his commission 2nd Lieut. King's Royal Rifle Corps, 1900: served in the South African War: Queen's Medal with clasp; King's Medal, two clasps: on the cessation of hostilities, retired from the Army, rank Lieut.: entered Magdalen College, Oxford (member Oxford & Cambridge Club, rowed in the Torpids); graduated 1909: enlisted Public Schools' Bn., Middlesex Regt., on the outbreak of war with Germany: received a commission Capt., 4th East Surrey Regt., October 1914: served with the Expeditionary Force in France and Flanders from January 1915, and was killed in action at the famous Hill 60, nr. Ypres, 20 April 1915. The Brigadier-General commanding the brigade of which his regiment formed part wrote, "I am fortunate enough to have in my brigade five splendid battalions, none of which I would change for any other in the Service, and amongst these battalions the East Surreys are second to none. In such a battalion it is necessary that the officers should set the highest possible example, and this was brilliantly the case in the work done by your son (Capt. A. Huth). I was wounded just a week before he was killed, and had a long talk to him in the trench that night. I was much impressed at the time with his zeal, keenness, and thoroughness and with the measures he was taking to put his trench on a thoroughly sound footing…His life was given in the hour of victory for King and country, in the performance of a magnificent exploit in capturing and consolidating our hold on Hill 60, a point of extreme importance to the well-being of the Allied front." Age 33.

In the spring of 1916, when the Canadians held the St. Eloi sector, four mines were exploded beneath the German positions resulting in four large craters, which were held by the enemy; the lips forming a considerable portion of their front line. Only forty yards at this point separated the combatants, and a good bomber could easily toss a Mills bomb into the crater. Usually held by 18th King's Royal Rifle Corps, between 29 October 1916 and September 1917 the 'distinctly unhealthy' front line hereabouts was, for the most part, held by 12th (Bermondsey) Bn. East Surrey Regt. The nightly patrolling of 'No Man's Land' – checking on the condition of their own defences, looking for signs of enemy activity, and familiarising themselves with their surroundings – was the responsibility of all front line troops, by the end of their time in this sector the East Surreys knew the area intimately but in the early days they had much to learn:– "The 11th. November 1916 marks a tragedy in the history of the Battalion. The day had been quiet and everyone had prepared for a restful night, when suddenly the stillness was disturbed by bombing and machine-gun fire. No orders out of the ordinary appeared to have been issued from Battalion H.Q., and the Adjutant, who was in the H.Q. dugout at Dead Dog Farm at the time, was at a loss to understand what was taking place. Some little time later Sergt. C. Turner of B Company, entered H.Q. dugout and gave a report of what had happened. Sergt. Turner stated that at 10 p.m. Acting Capt. C.O. Slacke, O.C. B Company, who had recently returned from leave, had taken out a patrol consisting of 2nd Lieut. J.F. Walton and four others to reconnoitre the enemy wire on the left of No.1 Crater. On arriving at the wire the patrol was heavily bombed and fired on with machine-guns, as a result of which one man was wounded. Stretcher-bearers were sent for, and on their arrival the party was again fired on by machine-guns, sustaining more casualties and being dispersed. In consequence, Capt. Slacke was missing, believed wounded, 2nd Lieut. Walton was wounded and missing, and four other ranks, including Ptes. Budd and Brenton, stretcher-bearers, were missing. The matter was reported to the Colonel, who at once began to investigate. Patrols went out to try to locate the bodies without success. Pte. J. Kirk, who was in the front line at the time, states that he vividly remembers the figure of Capt. Slacke looming over his sentry post and calling out the pass-words, "Is Mrs May in?" and then in the next breath, "For God's sake get the stretcher-bearers!" He then went back into No Man's Land and never returned. From the account of one of the survivors it appears that, when 2nd Lieut. Walton was wounded, Sergt. T.G. Mackenzie, who was with the patrol, got the assistance of Lce-Cpl. A. Kitchen and Pte. T.J. Young in order to bring him in. It was then discovered that Capt. Slacke was also wounded. This little party endeavoured to get both the officers back, but it was found that 2nd Lieut. Walton was again wounded (this time mortally) and that Capt. Slacke had disappeared. Two of the men were known to have been killed. The firing became such that Mackenzie and his gallant assistants had to get back to the trench. The next day instructions were issued to the observation posts in the sector to scan No Man's Land thoroughly for any vestige of the bodies. No trace was ever found of them…In Capt. Slacke's case it was presumed that he fell into a large shell hole and was drowned…For their services, Sergt. Mackenzie, Lce.-Cpl. Kitchen and Pte. Young were subsequently awarded the Military Medal. The loss of both the officers was serious to B Company, as they were the senior company officers and generally popular."

(Panel 34) Capt. Clulow Orme Slacke, 12th (Bermondsey) Bn. The East Surrey Regt.: *s.* of Francis Alexander Slacke, C.S.I., by his wife Caroline Elizabeth: Occupation – Assistant Accountant General; Financial Department, Government of India. Reported missing / believed wounded 12 November 1916, now thought drowned on or about that date: Age 35.

(Panel 34) Capt. Damer Wynyard, 1st Bn. (31st Foot) The East Surrey Regt.: Adjt. and Battn. Medical Officer: *s.* of Lieut.Col. Richard Damer Wynyard, late East Surrey Regt., and his wife (2, South Belfield, Weymouth, co. Dorset): served with the Expeditionary Force in France and Flanders, from August 1914, and was mortally wounded by a shell, while tending to wounded men in an exposed section of trench near Hill 60, 20 April 1915, dying shortly thereafter: Age 25. He was previously wounded at Mons, 23 August 1914. Capt. Wynyard was married to Olive Wakely, since re-married, now the wife of Lieut. Comdr. Brind, Royal Navy. See also Lieut.Col. W.H. Paterson, Bedford House Cemetery (V.A.39/Enc.

No.2); Capt. P.C. Wynter, Railway Dugouts Burial Ground (IV.K.17); Lieut. G.L. Watson, and Corpl. F.W. Adams (below).

(Panel 34) Lieut. Cecil Frederick Featherstone, 3rd attd. 2nd Bn. (70th Foot) The East Surrey Regt.: eldest *s.* of Frederick Featherstone, of Mount Pleasant, Plough Lane, Purley, Member; London Stock Exchange, by his wife Minnie Elizabeth, *dau.* of Thomas W. Dean: *b.* Lewisham, 13 February 1897: *educ.* Holmwood, Bexhill-on-Sea (1906 – 10), joining School Cadet Corps (1907) which was affiliated with 2nd Home Counties Royal Engineers (T.F.), after leaving Holmwood went to Dover College (1911 – 14), where he won prizes in English, Latin, and other subjects, joined O.T.C., attained rank Sergt.: gazetted 2nd Lieut. 3rd (Special Reserve) Bn. East Surrey Regt., 16 December 1914: joined his regt. January 1915, left for France, 20 March following, briefly attd. 'C' Coy., 1st Dorsetshire Regt., thereafter transf'd. 2nd East Surrey Regt., being confirmed in rank 9 April 1915, and was killed in action, being shot through the heart while bravely leading his men in the repulse of the German attack on the British trenches near Ypres, 25 April 1915. Buried in the Officer's Graveyard, 1½ miles east of Zonnebeke. Sergt. Buckingham, of the East Surreys, gave the following graphic account of the incidents from 17 to 27 April – "Our headquarters were at Zonnebeke, near Ypres. About 3p.m. on the 17th an order was given to pack up and move. There was some heavy shelling at the time, and it took about one hour to get everything on to the transport. We were then given another 150 rounds of ammunition to carry and about 4.30 the order to move was given. We took a road to the left of Ypres. Our Company Officer, Capt. Fuller, was sick, so he was not with us, but Lieut. Rottman took charge. We had only three officers – Lieuts. Rottman, Featherstone, and Ward – and we reached our destination, about a mile from Langemarck, about 7p.m. We were then under heavy shellfire. A, B and C Companies were put into position and we were to be the supports, we were in position all that night, but nothing happened. As it was getting daylight we retired a bit further back – this was the 18th – but had to stand to nearly all day as there was heavy rifle fire and shells. About 5 p.m. we pushed forward, going through the Canadians and some French infantry who had been pushed back, and we had to retake their trenches, which we did without much trouble. The French were made secure and got their trenches, and we took the Canadian's and had orders to stop in them. We worked all night repairing the breastworks with sandbags, the officers and sergts. relieving one another for a rest. At dawn on the 19th the enemy started with their trench mortars, which were dropping just in rear of our trenches. We were expecting a big shelling then, but they must have been laying their guns or had brought more up for we were only getting a shell here and there and were pretty quiet and remained so until the afternoon of the 20th. From the 17th to the 20th we had no casualties amongst the officers and not many men. On the afternoon of the 20th the bombardment started, but they did not have a good range that day. At night the Middlesex brought our rations up and a working party, who made us a bit stronger. They left us about 3 a.m. on the 21st. Toward dawn we were bombarded again, this time a little closer. As it got lighter we saw about half-a-dozen German aeroplanes coming towards our trenches, they flew up and down dropping smoke bombs, and the shells were dropping all round us, so we had to lay close up to the parapets. Here we stayed all day, this night – 21st, or rather early 22nd – no rations could be brought to us and no working party, so we dug ourselves right in as messages came that we were to hold on at all cost. We still had all our officers. As day dawned it was a bit quiet. That night we had our rations and hot soup brought up and were told we were going to be relieved the next night, 23rd. On the morning of the 23rd it was still quiet, but about 3p.m. they started something terrible, only taking our regiment. They were then using gas shells and breaking our parapets and shelling the roads. Again a message came to hold on, and that we would not be relieved; we then lost a few men. This lasted all day. On the early morning of the 24th Lieut. Fardell was killed, and gas was used all day. Lieut. Featherstone got some handkerchiefs and soaked them with water and handed them around, and we lost about 40 men that day. As night came on, I think it was about 2a.m. on the 25th, Mr Featherstone, who was then taking his rest, came, and he looked very upset, and said to me, "Poor Mr Rottman is killed." I said, "I am very sorry to hear that," and went and had a look at him. I came back and he was still standing, and I and Sergt. Lower said, "Why don't you go and finish your rest, we will come and get you and let you know if anything is wrong." So he went, but he did not stop long as it was getting on time to stand to arms, so we stood, and when it was light they sent shells in front of our trench, and smashed the barbed wire, therefore we knew that they were going to attack, and while we were getting ready a shell struck the parapet, and me and Mr Featherstone had the sandbags over us. We got out of that and laughed at one another. As it went on, the parapets were being blown to bits, so an order came to get the men to the right and at some parts we had to crawl. Sergt. Lower led the way and Mr Featherstone and I saw every man safe. It was while we were crawling past a gap in the parapet that a piece of shell struck me, I did not stop, but he saw I was hit and said, "Are you all right?" I said, "Yes, come on." We got past the gap and he said, "Where are you hit?" I thought it was my arm and dropped my rifle. He picked it up and said, "We must get out of this," and we went on a bit and found we were in the Northumberlands, and stayed there, and then the enemy were in our trenches. I had had my shoulder dressed, and the order to spread out came. I then saw Mr Featherstone had lost his hat and, getting close up to him, I said, the supports are driving them out so they were all shouting hurrah. Mr Featherstone was then firing out of my rifle and I gave him another clip. I then saw him go up a little way further and fall. He was struck by a bullet and we sent for the stretcher bearers. He was then dead." The Adjutant of his Battn. wrote to his father, "Like all our young officers he carried out his duty to the end and by his example the men remained steadfast and the trenches were held in spite of the poisonous gases and rifle and shell fire. We have been so fortunate in having such good officers that the battn. has earned special praise from all, and general French thanked us yesterday for the good work of 25 April, during which your son fell. " And a subaltern, "2nd Lieut. Featherstone was killed during the German attack on 25 April under circumstances which proved him a very brave officer. The enemy having got all round us, our men were firing in all directions, generally at no particular object as often happens in times of excitement. It was in trying to stop the men wasting their munitions that Lieut. Featherstone was twice wounded. He still continued, however, to calm his men till he was shot in the heart by a stray bullet." While at Holmwood School, Lieut. Featherstone was a sapper and shot in the School XI, winning the Sheffield Trophy on outdoor competition at 200 and 500 yards with the service rifle; he also shot in the team for the Holman Cup, an indoor competition at 20 yards. At Dover College he was in the 1st Football XI, as well as playing cricket; and shot for his school at Bisley, in 1913, in the Cadet Pairs, likewise in the Team of the Ashburton Shield in 1914. Lieut. Featherstone was promoted Lieut. subsequent to his death: Age 18.

(Panel 34) Lieut. Geoffrey Launcelot Watson, 3rd Bn. attd 'A' Coy., 1st Bn. (31st Foot) The East Surrey Regt.: *s.* of the Rev. C.S. Watson. Killed with 20 of his men while attempting to hold a battered stretch of trench nr. Hill 60, 20 April 1915: Age 35. See also Lieut.Col. W.H. Paterson, Bedford House Cemetery (V.A.39/Enc.No.2); Capt. P.C. Wynter, Railway Dugouts Burial Ground (IV.K.17); Capt. D. Wynyard (above), and Corpl. F.W. Adams (below).

(Panel 34) 2nd Lieut. Edward John Wilfred Birnie, Special Reserve attd. 2nd Bn. (70th Foot) The East Surrey Regt.: *s.* of the late Major William Jones Birnie, Deputy Commissary, Commissariat & Transport Staff: *b.* Holland Road, London, 19 December 1881: *educ.* Home, Private tutorage: after completing his education was, for about eight years, in the employ of the National Provincial Bank, obtaining an appointment in Bank of Bengal, September 1906. During his stay in Bengal he joined Indian Light Horse, serving for 6 ½ years, stationed in Calcutta, Lucknow, and Cawnpore, qualifying for his first commission shortly before his first leave in England, January 1913. After arriving in England he applied for a commission in a British Infantry Regt., and was gazetted 2nd Lieut. East Surrey Regt., June 1913. As that battalion was returning to the Depot after its training, he desired more active work and was attached to South Wales Borderers, being with them during manoeuvres until finishing his attachment at Bordon Camp, December 1913. Left England for India, early January 1914, and went through annual training with Royal Fusiliers, Fort William, Calcutta: gazetted to Special Reserve of his regt. May 1914: on the outbreak of hostilities with Germany, reported to 2nd East Surrey Regt., then in India, joining them on mobilisation: left India, November 1914, arrived England 24 December following. By virtue of his training, in 1913, was qualified to serve with the battalion at once without any further preparatory course: after a short time at Winchester embarked Southampton with his battalion for France, January 1915. In his anxiety to fit himself for service in every way, Lieut. Birnie seemed to have prescience of the war; an idea confirmed by a remark he made to his mother when on leave in England. He was heart and soul a soldier in the truest sense of the word. A Sergt. of the regiment gave the following details of his death:– "The late officer was killed on Sunday, 14 February, near Ypres, whilst leading his platoon into action. He was hit in the chest whilst walking up and down the trench, cheering everybody up, and also looking for a better forward position. I myself was the Platoon Sergt., assisting Mr Birnie. He took over the platoon at Jhansi, India, just prior to the battalion leaving for England. He was well respected by all the company because of his happy-go-lucky ways and for his bravery. His last words were, 'Sergeant Oliver, cheer the platoon up and look well after them. Good-bye; I have done my best.' His loss was felt by everyone. He was removed the same night by a party of men, who I took to be Royal Army Medical Corps, and buried near the spot where he fell." He was a member of the Junior Naval and Military Club, and the 'Cocoa Tree' Club, St. James's, London, S.W.: Age 32. *unm.*

(Panel 34) 2nd Lieut. Cyril Bernard Dix, 8th (Service) Bn. The East Surrey Regt.: *s.* of Arthur Dix, of 11, Doveridge Gardens, Palmer's Green, London, N.13, by his wife C. Ethel: prior to enlistment was, fourteen months, Medical Student, Guy's Hospital, London, S.E.1: volunteered and enlisted Artist's Rifles O.T.C., no.760962: gazetted 2nd Lieut., 8th East Surrey Regt., 1 July 1917, and was killed in action at Zillebeke, 10 August following: Age 20. *unm.*

(Panel 34) 2nd Lieut. Joseph Frank Walton, 11th (Reserve) Bn. The East Surrey Regt.: *s.* of Joseph Wallis Walton, by his wife Josephine Jane: served in the South African Campaign. Missing, believed drowned after being wounded whilst patrolling with Capt. C.O. Slacke, 12 November 1916: Age 35. See Capt. C.O. Slacke (above); Ptes. W.J. Brenton and P.J. Budd, M.M. (below).

(Panel 34) Sergt. 9914, Joseph Robert Adcock, 1st Bn. (31st Foot) attd. 2nd Bn. (70th Foot) The East Surrey Regt.: *s.* of Joseph Adcock, of Worcester Park, formerly soldier in the same regiment, by his wife Margaret, *dau.* of James Moore: *b.* Wandsworth, 1 October 1891: *educ.* Cheam Council School: enlisted 17 January 1910: apptd. L/Corpl., 1911; promoted Corpl., 1912; Sergt., 27 September 1914: served with the Expeditionary Force in France from 6 March 1915, and was killed in action at the Battle of Ypres, 9 May following: Age 22. A comrade of Sergt. Adcock's wrote that both of them were in an advanced trench of the line and were ordered to retire, and that he (Adcock) was seen to fall after running a short distance. He *m.* Worcester Park Catholic Church, 14 February 1914; Ann Elizabeth (294 Kingston Road, Raynes Park), *dau.* of Horace George Goulding, of Raynes Park, and had a *s.* Joseph William, *b.* 17 July 1914.

(Panel 34) Sergt. 1140, Thomas Ball, 1st Bn. (31st Foot) The East Surrey Regt.: *s.* of Robert Ball, of 32, Ferrier Street, Wandsworth, London, S.W., by his wife Rebecca: *b.* Battersea, London, S.W., 1882: enlisted, Gosport, co. Hants: served in the South African Campaign, and with the Expeditionary Force in France. Killed in action 22 November 1914: Age 32. He leaves a wife Alice Ball (7, Musgrave Road, Fulham).

(Panel 34) Sergt. 3948, Robert William Briggs, 2nd Bn. (70th Foot) The East Surrey Regt.: enlisted Shorncliffe, co. Kent: served with the Expeditionary Force in France, and was killed in action 25 April 1915. *m.*

(Panel 34) Sergt. 17442, Edward Hambleton, 12th (Bermondsey) Bn. The East Surrey Regt.: *s.* of Albert Hambleton, of 63, Seely Road, Tooting, London, S.W., by his wife Susannah: and *yr.* brother to Pte. 301998, C. Hambleton, Durham Light Infantry, who fell 14 April 1917, during the advance on Wancourt: *b.* Walworth, London, S.E., 1896: enlisted East Surrey Regt., Kingston, co. Surrey. Missing / believed killed in action 5 August 1917, on which date the enemy – under cover of a thick mist – successfully attacked and captured the trenches held by the East Surreys between Hollebeke and Forret Farm: Age 21. *unm.*

His brother Charles is buried in Heninel Communal Cemetery Extension (F.7).

(Panel 34) Sergt. 9597, Edward Rose, 'C' Coy., 2nd Bn. (70th Foot) The East Surrey Regt.: *s.* of the late George (& Louisa) Rose: *b.* Beckenham, co. Kent: enlisted London. Killed in action 24 May 1915:

Age 26. Remains (three) recovered (28.I.6.c.40.45), unmarked grave (shell-hole) 23 April 1929; close to a large concrete German dug-out. Identified – Clothing, Boots, Sergt. Stripes, Disc.; reinterred Sanctuary Wood. Of the three sets of remains recovered only those of Sergt. Rose could be identified with any degree of certainty. The other two were an unknown British Major (V.H.26) and Tpr. Leicestershire Yeomanry (V.H.28). *Buried in Sanctuary Wood Cemetery (V.H.27).*

(Panel 34) Corpl. 9940, Frederick William Adams, 1st Bn. (31st Foot) The East Surrey Regt.: *s.* of Jane (1, Lock Cottages, New Road, Ham, Richmond). With his comrades dead, and part of his jaw shot away, continued to work his machine-gun single-handedly until shot through the head and killed, 20 April 1915, nr. Hill 60: Age 23. *unm.* See also Lieut.Col.W.H. Paterson, Bedford House Cemetery (V.A.39/Enc. No.2); Capt. P.C. Wynter, Railway Dugouts Burial Ground (IV.K.17); Capt. D. Wynyard, and Lieut. G.L. Watson (above).

(Panel 34) Corpl. 7248, Henry Brackstone, 1st Bn. (31st Foot) The East Surrey Regt.: served with the Expeditionary Force in France and Flanders. Killed in action 20 April 1915. *m.* (*IWGC record Brackston*)

(Panel 34) Corpl. 1959, Frederick Cobbold, 2nd Bn. (70th Foot) The East Surrey Regt.: *s.* of the late William Cobbold, by his wife Sarah (Free Wood Street, Bradfield St. George, nr. Bury St. Edmunds): and *yr.* brother to Pte. 17770. W. Cobbold, Suffolk Regt., who fell, 8 May 1915, at the Second Battle of Ypres: *b.* Bradfield St. George, *c.*1880: enlisted Kingston-on-Thames, co. Surrey: served in the South African Campaign against the Boers (1899 – 1902), and with the Expeditionary Force in France and Flanders from January 1915, and was killed in action 25 April following: Age 35. He was married to Mrs G.J. Baldry, *née* Cobbold (Oak Lane, Rougham, Bury St. Edmunds). One of two brothers who fell.

His brother William also has no known grave; he is recorded on Panel 21.

(Panel 34) L/Corpl. 10003, Arthur Charles Chandler, 'B' Coy., 2nd Bn. (70th Foot) The East Surrey Regt.: *s.* of Mrs R.J. Dale (17, St. James' Road, Carshalton, co. Surrey): served with the Expeditionary Force. Killed in action 25 April 1915: Age 24. *unm.*

(Panel 34) L/Corpl. 9341, John Christopher Gardiner, 2nd Bn. (70th Foot) The East Surrey Regt.: *s.* of Mrs L. (& the late Mr) Gardiner (86, Amity Grove, Cottenham Park, Wimbledon, London, S.W.): *b.* Sunbury, co. Middlesex: enlisted London. Killed in action 25 April 1915: Age 23. *unm.* Remains (4th of six exhumed) 21 December 1928 unmarked (collective) grave (28.D.16.d.65.05); identified – Disc, Badge, L/Corpl. Stripe, Khaki; reinterred, registered 28 January 1929. *Buried in Sanctuary Wood Cemetery (V.B.1).*

(Panel 34) Pte. 5860, Edward Ainslie, 1st Bn. (31st Foot) The East Surrey Regt.: Killed in action on the Western Front 15 December 1914. *m.*

(Panel 34) Pte. 8211, William Allard, 1st Bn. (31st Foot) The East Surrey Regt.: served with the Expeditionary Force in France. Killed in action there, 22 January 1915.

(Panel 34) Pte. 6322, Charles Allen, 2nd Bn. (70th Foot) The East Surrey Regt.: *s.* of Charles Quinn, of 39, Cirencester Street, Paddington, London, W., by his wife Bella: enlisted Mill Hill, London, N.W.: served with the Expeditionary Force in France. Killed in action 25 April 1915: Age 34.

(Panel 34) Pte. 10948, Albert Ansell, 2nd Bn. (70th Foot) The East Surrey Regt.: *s.* of George Ansell, of Maple Road, Ashtead: served with the Expeditionary Force in France and Flanders: Killed in action, 25 April 1915.

(Panel 34) Pte. G/1043, Sidney Herbert Ansell, 2nd Bn. (70th Foot) The East Surrey Regt.: *s.* of the late Charles M. Ansell, by his wife Amelia (24, Whitehall Road, Grays, co. Essex): served with the Expeditionary Force in France, and was killed in action there 25 April 1915: Age 26. *unm.*

(Panel 34) Pte. 11002, Albert Richard Ashley, 2nd Bn. (70th Foot) The East Surrey Regt.: *s.* of the late James William Ashley, Groom; of 14, Dane Road, Merton, co. Surrey, by his wife Minnie Ford, *née* Ashley (1, Putland Terrace, Denton, Newhaven, co. Sussex): *b.* Worth, co. Sussex, 15 May 1899: *educ.* Pound Hill C.E. School, Worth, and C. of E. Boys' School, Merton: volunteered after the outbreak of war, enlisted Merton, co. Surrey, 11 November 1914: went to the Front in France. Reported as wounded 25 April; and was afterwards killed in action on or about the 27th. Buried at Zonnebeke, Flanders. A L/

Corpl. of the Battn. wrote Ashley was sent out of the trenches with two thumbs badly wounded, and a Private stated that he found him in a trench with his thumbs bound up and that he buried him: **Age 15**.

(Panel 34) Pte. 9583, William James Atterbury, 1st Bn. (31st Foot) The East Surrey Regt.: eldest *s*. of William Atterbury, of 3, Spencer Terrace, Spencer Road, Mitcham, co. Surrey, by his wife Mary: *b*. Carshalton, co. Surrey, 7 October 1888: enlisted 5 June 1908: served with the Expeditionary Force in France from 7 October 1914. Killed in action there, 24 November. following: Age 26.

(Panel 34) Pte. G.6328, Robert Bettney, 2nd Bn. (70th Foot) The East Surrey Regt.: *s*. of Thomas Bettney, Commercial Traveller: *b*. Handsworth, Birmingham, 11 May 1878: *educ*. King Edward's Grammar School, Handsworth: enlisted 22 November 1914: served with the Expeditionary Force in France, and was killed in action at Zonnebeke, Flanders, 25 April 1915. Buried behind the trenches there. He *m*. Croydon, 1 November 1900; Florence M. (18, Trevelyan Road, Tooting, London, S.W.), *dau*. of the late William White, of Mitcham, co. Surrey, and had three *daus*. – Dora, *b*. 11 October 1901, Marjorie, *b*. 23 July 1903; Iris, *b*. 2 March 1906:

(Panel 34) Pte. 9499, Horace Alfred Brazier, 2nd Bn. (70th Foot) The East Surrey Regt.: *s*. of James Brazier, of 22, Stewart's Lane, Battersea: served with the Expeditionary Force in France and Flanders. Killed in action, 25 April 1915.

(Panel 34) Pte. 12042, William John Brenton, 12th (Service) Bn. (Bermondsey) The East Surrey Regt.: Killed in action with Pte. P.J. Budd whilst patrolling with officers, Capt. C.O. Slacke and 2nd Lieut. J.F. Walton; 12 November 1916.

(Panel 34) Pte. G/127, Thomas Bristow, 1st Bn. (31st Foot) The East Surrey Regt.: *s*. of Jesse Bristow, of 2, Distillery Cottages, Collingwood Road, Luton: *b*. North Cheam, *c*.1878: *educ*. Sutton: served in the South African War with The Rifle Brigade (King's & Queen's Medal; four clasps): re-enlisted Kingston-on-Thames, after the outbreak of war, 26 August 1914: served with the Expeditionary Force in France and Flanders, and was killed in action 1 January 1915, by the explosion of a large shell which completely collapsed a section of trench and buried him alive: Age 36. *unm*. See Pte. C. Owen (below).

(Panel 34) Pte. 8123, George Thomas Brockwell, 1st Bn. (31st Foot) The East Surrey Regt.: *s*. of George Brockwell, of 36, Hawks Road, Norbiton, Kingston-on-Thames, by his wife Sarah: served with the Expeditionary Force. Killed in action 24 November 1914: Age 29.

(Panel 34) Pte. 6633, George Percy Brown, 1st Bn. (31st Foot) The East Surrey Regt.: *s*. of the late Charles Brown, and his wife (since remarried) now Mrs Jones (151, Carlisle Street, Edgware Road, London): *b*. Marylebone, 22 July 1891: enlisted on the outbreak of war, 4 August 1914: served with the Expeditionary Force in France, and was killed in action 29 November 1914: Age 23. He *m*. 22 October 1909, Florence Jane Snowden, *née* Brown (39, Lyons Place, Edgware Road) late of 11, Richmond Street, and had three children – Leonard George, *b*. 28 February 1911; Henry Thomas, *b*. 2 July 1913; Percy Charles, *b*. 31 January 1915. (*IWGC record age 25*)

(Panel 34) Pte. 14848, Percy James Budd, M.M., 12th (Service) Bn. (Bermondsey) The East Surrey Regt.: Killed in action with Pte. W.J. Brenton whilst patrolling with officers, Capt. C.O. Slacke and 2nd Lieut. J.F. Walton; 12 November 1916.

(Panel 34) Pte. 10491, John Thomas Bunker, 1st Bn. (31st Foot) The East Surrey Regt.: 2nd *s*. of John Thomas Bunker, Skilled Labourer; of 20, Burford Road, Perry Hill, Catford, London, S.E.6, by his wife Ada, *dau*. of Charles (& Emma) Bryden: *b*. Catford, 27 June 1894: *educ*. Kilmorie Road Council School, Forest Hill: enlisted 1912: went to the Front with the Expeditionary Force, 13 August 1914, and was killed in action when on outpost duty, nr. Hill 60, Flanders, 20 April 1915: *unm*.

(Panel 34) Pte. 1809, Samuel George Burge, 2nd Bn. (70th Foot) The East Surrey Regt.: *s*. of the late Samuel Burge (*d*.1924), by his wife Clara, *née* Hills: *b*. Tooting, London, S.W., 1893: Occupation – Painter & Decorator: enlisted Kingston, 6 September 1914, in company with his brother Reuben (surv'd.): served with the Expeditionary Force in France from 26 April 1915, and was killed in action twelve days later, 8 May 1915, at the Battle of Frezenberg: Age 21. Pte. Burge *m*. 1913; Alice, *née* Sallis, and had a son, Reuben George, *b*. 1913.

(Panel 34) Pte. 7841, George Bye, 1st Bn. (31st Foot) The East Surrey Regt.: *b.* Fulham: enlisted London. Killed in action 1 January 1915, by the explosion of a large shell which collapsed a section of trench burying him and four other men. See Pte. C. Owen (below)

(Panel 34) Pte. 25387, John Thomas Cansdale, 'B' Coy., 12th (Service) Bn. (Bermondsey) The East Surrey Regt.: *s.* of the late Robert Cansdale, by his wife Emily (4, Brand's Yard, Church Street, Sudbury, co. Suffolk): and brother to Pte. G/15148, A.A. Cansdale, 6th Queen's Own (Royal West Kent Regt.), killed in action 7 October 1916; and Pte. 18715, C.J. Cansdale, 11th Essex Regt., killed in action 13 June 1916: *b.* Bures St. Mary, co. Suffolk, 1888: enlisted Bury St. Edmunds. Killed in action 5 August 1917: Age 30. He leaves a wife Mary Ann Cansdale (4, Mount Place, Sudbury), and two sons – John Gordon and Reginald George (killed in action in the Second World War).

His brother Arthur also has no known grave, he is commemorated on the Thiepval Memorial, Somme (Pier & Face 11C); Charles is buried in Essex Farm Cemetery (II.R.17). His son Pte. 5827402, R.G. Cansdale, Suffolk Regt., killed in action 15 February 1942 has no known grave; he is commemorated on the Singapore (Kranji War Cemetery) Memorial (Col.54).

(Panel 34) Pte. 6450, William Carroll, 2nd Bn. (70th Foot) The East Surrey Regt.: *s.* of Bartholomew Carroll, of 39, Albion Street, King's Cross, London, N.: served with the Expeditionary Force. Killed in action 25 April 1915.

(Panel 34) Pte. G/2617, George Frederick Cavendish, 2nd Bn. (70th Foot) The East Surrey Regt.: *s.* of John Cavendish, of 10, Hornshay Road, Deptford, London, S.E.: served with the Expeditionary Force in France. Killed in action 25 April 1915.

(Panel 34) Pte. 6907, Thomas William Chitty, 2nd Bn. (70th Foot) The East Surrey Regt.: *yr. s.* of Thomas Chitty, Labourer; by his wife Eliza: *b.* Eton Wick, nr. Windsor, 22 January 1880: *educ.* Eton Wick: Occupation – Cowman; Beaumont College Farm: enlisted 7 January 1915: served with the Expeditionary Force in France and Flanders from 1 May, and was killed in action at Hill 60 during the Second Battle of Ypres, 8 May 1915. Buried there: Age 35. He *m.* Boveney New Town, co. Bucks, 16 September 1905; Jane Isabel (17, Albert Road, Englefield Green, Egham, co. Surrey), *dau.* of Thomas William Pardoe, and had five children – Mabel Helen, *b.* 9 February 1907, Thomas Charles, *b.* 10 March 1908, Emily Louise, *b.* 2 April 1909, Albert Victor, *b.* 22 July 1910; George Edward, *b.* 1 February 1912.

(Panel 34) Pte. 11044, William Chitty, 2nd Bn. (70th Foot) The East Surrey Regt.: *s.* of William (& Mrs) Chitty, of 'Cliftonville,' 6, Century Road, Staines, co. Middlesex: and *yr.* brother to L/Corpl. 1/10277, C. Chitty, Royal Fusiliers, died 29 September 1916, in Mesopotamia: *b.* Chertsey, *c.*1896: enlisted Egham, co. Surrey. Killed in action, 8 May 1915, at Frezenberg: Age 19.

His brother Charles, recorded on Panel 6 of the Menin Gate, is buried in Baghdad (North Gate) War Cemetery (XXI.K.19).

(Panel 34) Pte. G/7102, James Coles, 1st Bn. (31st Foot) The East Surrey Regt.: *s.* of Thomas Coles, Labourer; of Toddington, co. Bedford: and brother to Mrs J. Chance (Chalton, Dunstable, co. Bedford): *b.* Toddington, 1879: *educ.* Wesleyan Day School, Toddington: served seven years in the Militia, taking his discharge with a Good Conduct Certificate: volunteered and enlisted 10 October 1914: served with the Expeditionary Force in France, and was killed in action on Hill 60, 19 April 1915. A letter was received from Coy.Q.M.Sergt. W.A. Butler, expressing the sincere sympathy of the N.C.O.'s and men of his company, with whom he was very popular: Age 26. *unm.* (*IWGC record 20 April 1915*)

(Panel 34) Pte. G/1170, John Hugh Compton, 2nd Bn. (70th Foot) The East Surrey Regt.: *s.* of Hugh Compton, of 'Rosedale,' Central Avenue, Southchurch, Southend-on-Sea, late of 2, Sydney Terrace, Meadow Road, Hadleigh, by his wife Flora: served with the Expeditionary Force in France. Killed in action 25 April 1915: Age 17.

(Panel 34) Pte. G/3597, Gilbert Granville Coole, 2nd Bn. (70th Foot) The East Surrey Regt.: *s.* of Granville A. Coole, of 9, Cambridge Road, New Malden, co. Surrey, by his wife Annie: served with the Expeditionary Force in France, and was killed in action 25 April 1915: Age 21. *unm.*

(Panel 34) Pte. G/2756, John Cooling, 2nd Bn. (70th Foot) The East Surrey Regt.: served with the Expeditionary Force. Killed in action 24 April 1915. *m.*

(Panel 34) Pte. G/5717, Ernest John Cousins, 2nd Bn. (70th Foot) The East Surrey Regt.: enlisted Battersea, London, S.W.: served with the Expeditionary Force. Killed in action 25 April 1915. *m.*

(Panel 34) Pte. 9921, Thomas Peter Elliott, 'C' Coy., 2nd Bn. (70th Foot) The East Surrey Regt.: *s.* of the late Peter Hyde Elliott, by his wife Mary Jane: *b.* Kennington, London, S.E.: enlisted Kingston-on-Thames, co. Surrey. Killed in action 27 April 1915: Age 21. Remains recovered (refers GRU Report, Zillebeke 5-86E) unmarked grave (28.D.23.a.25.33); identified – Disc, Clothing; reinterred, registered 8 April 1927. *Buried in Sanctuary Wood Cemetery (IV.B.20).*

(Panel 34) Pte. 1090, Alfred John Flexman, 2nd Bn. (70th Foot) The East Surrey Regt.: *s.* of the late Spr. 61719, A.E. Flexman, Royal Engineers (former Bricklayer); by his wife Sarah Jane (62, Heaton Road, Peckham, London, S.E.), *dau.* of William John Freebury, of Bermondsey Brewery: *b.* Peckham, London, S.E., 6 September 1895: *educ.* Choumert Road Schools: subsequently employee Messrs Barclay & Fry, Tin Printers; Blackfriars, London, S.E.: enlisted September 1914, after the outbreak of war: served with the Expeditionary Force in France and Flanders, and was killed in action at Hill 60, during the Second Battle of Ypres, 25 April 1915: Age 19. Remains 'Unknown British Soldier' recovered unmarked grave (28.D.23.a.25.33); identified – Clothing, Boots mkd. 1090; reinterred, registered 5 April 1927. *Buried in Sanctuary Wood Cemetery (IV.B.6).*

His father Alfred, killed in action 1 July 1916, is buried in Warlincourt Halte British Cemetery, Somme (XII.C.17).

(Panel 34) Pte. 10764, William Arthur Foulger, 1st Bn. (31st Foot) The East Surrey Regt.: *s.* of Alfred William Foulger, of Saunders Cottages, Epsom Common, co. Surrey, by his wife Mary, *née* Taylor: and brother to Dvr. 217147, A.E. Foulger, Royal Field Artillery, died November 1921: *b.* 29 March 1894: Religion – Church of England: Occupation – Barman; Wellington Hotel, Epsom: enlisted 4 December 1913: served Dublin, Ireland, 18 April – 22 August 1914, and with the Expeditionary Force in France from 7 October following. Killed in action 19 November 1914; shellfire, support trenches Lindenhoek, nr. Kemmel: Age 20. All correspondence and / or articles of personal property to be forwarded c/o Miss Florence Foulger (47, Woodlands Road, Epsom).

His brother Alfred is buried in Epsom Cemetery (unmarked grave).

(Panel 34) Pte. 3107, Albert Harry Gent, 2nd Bn. (70th Foot) The East Surrey Regt.: late of 557, Lincoln Road, Peterborough: brother to Pte. 203243, F.W. Gent, 2nd Dorsetshire Regt., died of pneumonia, 7 October 1917, at Baghdad: volunteered and enlisted at the outbreak of war: served with the Expeditionary Force in France and Flanders, and was killed in action 25 April 1915.

His brother William is buried in Baghdad War Cemetery, Iraq (XII.D.9).

(Panel 34) Pte. 122, Henry Gravestock, 1st Bn. (31st Foot) The East Surrey Regt.: *s.* of the late John Gravestock: *b.* Fulham, London, S.W., 1876: *educ.* there: Occupation – Saw-Mill Plane Machine Operator: enlisted 1st Devonshire Regt., 22 August 1895: served 20 years with the Colours; joined the Reserve: time expired on the outbreak of war; re-enlisted East Surrey Regt., August 1914: served with the Expeditionary Force in France and Flanders. Reported missing after the fighting at Hill 60, 21 April 1915, and is now assumed to have been killed in action by the explosion of a shell on or about that date: Age 38. He *m.* Lewisham, London, S.E., 11 February 1910; Mary (46, Stanton Street, Peckham, London, S.E.), *dau.* of Henry Wiseman, and had three children – William Henry, *b.* 20 March 1910; Arthur Henry, *b.* 21 November 1911; Phyllis Louise, *b.* 11 November 1913. (*IWGC record 20 April*)

(Panel 34) Pte. 8620, John William Haley, 1st Bn. (31st Foot) The East Surrey Regt.: *b.* Holborn: enlisted London. Killed in action New Year's Day, 1 January 1915, by the explosion of a large shell which collapsed a portion of trench burying him and four other men. See Pte. C. Owen (below).

(Panel 34) Pte. 10476, James Hoare, 1st Bn. (31st Foot) The East Surrey Regt.: *s.* of Samuel Hoare, of 24, Halliburton Road, St. Margaret's, Twickenham, co. Middlesex, by his wife Mary: enlisted Kingston-on-Thames, co. Surrey: served with the Expeditionary Force, and was killed in action at the Battle of Ypres, 1 November 1914: Age 19.

(Panel 34) Pte. 5722, Albert Hudson, 2nd Bn. (70th Foot) The East Surrey Regt.: *s.* of William Hudson, of 33, Tooting Grove, Tooting, London, S.W.17, by his wife Alice: enlisted Kingston-on-Thames: served with the Expeditionary Force in France, and was killed in action there 25 April 1915: Age 20.

(Panel 34) Pte. 25030, John Hybart, 9th (Service) Bn. The East Surrey Regt.: adopted *s.* of Albert John Hybart, Timber Merchant; 26, Conway Road, Cardiff: *b.* Barry, co. Glamorgan, 21 April 1896: *educ.* Grammar School, Cowbridge: formerly engaged in business at Cardiff Docks, on the outbreak of war was employee Messrs Lloyds Bank Ltd., Salisbury: enlisted 31st Royal Fusiliers, 24 January 1916: served with the Expeditionary Force in France and Flanders from 6 September following: transf'd. East Surrey Regt., acting as Company Runner for eight months, and was killed in action by shellfire during the operations at Messines Ridge and Hill 60, 17 June 1917. Buried there. His Commanding Officer wrote, "He was selected for this duty because of his intelligence and the keen way in which he had been doing his work in the trenches, and for eight months he was my faithful follower and friend. I say 'friend' because many were the talks we had, as we went round on our rounds, on current events of the day, and sometimes on politics, political economy etc. As a runner he was always reliable, and showed a keen intelligence, and never once during the whole period he was with me had I occasion to find fault with him." Age 21. *unm.*

(Panel 34) Pte. 7134, George Litchfield, 2nd Bn. (70th Foot) The East Surrey Regt.: *s.* of George Litchfield, of 3, Old Road, Walgrave St. Peter, co. Northampton, by his wife Maria: and brother to Siglr. Bristol Z/5611, L.H. Litchfield, H.M.S. 'Tartar,' Royal Naval Volunteer Reserve, died 17 June 1917: *b.* Walgrave, 1891: enlisted Kettering: served with the Expeditionary Force in France and Flanders from January 1915, and was killed in action 25 April 1915, at the Battle of Ypres: Age 24. Remembered on Walgrave War Memorial.

His brother Leonard is buried in Calais Southern Cemetery (V.G.14).

(Panel 34) Pte. 9966, James William Malcher, 2nd Bn. (70th Foot) The East Surrey Regt.: *s.* of Charles Edwin Malcher, of Station House, North Ealing, London, W., by his wife Bessie Florence: enlisted Kingston-on-Thames, co. Surrey. Killed in action 29 April 1915: Age 22. Remains 'Unknown British Soldier' recovered unmarked grave (28.D.23.a.25.33); identified – Clothing, Braces mkd. 9966; reinterred, registered 5 April 1927. *Buried in Sanctuary Wood Cemetery (IV.B.7).* (*CR.Belgium,453-455,pg.25,records 25 April*)

(Panel 34) Pte. G/2941, Percy Malkin, 2nd Bn. (70th Foot) The East Surrey Regt.: *s.* of Elisha Malkin, of 11, Barngate Street, Leek, co. Stafford, by his wife Harriet: served with the Expeditionary Force in France and Flanders, and was killed in action 8 May 1915: Age 19.

(Panel 34) Pte. 10374, James Merricks, 2nd Bn. (70th Foot) The East Surrey Regt.: *s.* of Sarah Merricks (10, Union Road, St. John's, Redhill, co. Surrey), and the late Pte. G/37493, J. Merricks, 11th Queen's (Royal West Surrey Regt.), killed in action 7 June 1917: *b.* Caterham, co. Surrey: enlisted Kingston-on-Thames. Killed in action 11 February 1915: Age 18.

His father James also has no known grave; he is recorded on Panel 13.

(Panel 34) Pte. 9543, Charles Moss, 2nd Bn. (70th Foot) The East Surrey Regt.: *s.* of the late Mr (& Mrs) Moss, of Brixton, London, S.W.2: enlisted Kingston-on-Thames, co. Surrey. Killed in action 25 April 1915: Age 25. Remains recovered (refers GRU Report, Zillebeke 5-86E) unmarked grave (28.D.23.a.25.33); identified – Clothing, Badge of Rank, Spoon mkd. 9543.E.S., Piece of Braces mkd. 9543, Underclothing mkd. RAY; reinterred, registered 8 April 1927. *Buried in Sanctuary Wood Cemetery (IV.B.21).*

On New Years' Day 1915 1st East Surreys trenches north-east of Wulverghem were sporadically bombarded with high explosive by the enemy in response to heavy shelling of their positions at Messines. One shell exploded in the support trench of 'A' Company collapsing part of the trench and burying five men. Pte. Owen and another man immediately began to dig these men out, but when another shell landed near by the other man stopped work and sought shelter. Regardless of the danger he was exposed to Pte. Owen continued digging and was in the process of pulling out one of the buried men when a third shell fell and blew him to pieces.

(Panel 34) Pte. 9004, Charles Owen, 1st Bn. (31st Foot) The East Surrey Regt.: *s.* of Mary Owen (35, Orford Street, Draycott Avenue, Chelsea, London): served with the Expeditionary Force in France and Flanders. Killed in action, 1 January 1915: Age 40.

(Panel 34) Pte. 16305, Edward Perrin, 12th (Service) Bn. (Bermondsey) The East Surrey Regt.: *s.* of William Perrin, of 74, Rockingham Street, New Kent Road, London, S.E.1: and brother to Pte. S/6142, W. Perrin (served as Bradley), who fell at the First Battle of Ypres: enlisted Rotherhithe, London, S.E.: served with the Expeditionary Force in France and Flanders, and was killed in action 7 June 1917.

His brother William is buried in Poelcapelle British Cemetery (LIII.B.10).

(Panel 34) Pte. 3504, Thomas Charles Ebery Piggott, 2nd Bn. (70th Foot) The East Surrey Regt.: *yst. s.* of Emma Piggott (25, Lowell Terrace, Park Lane, Tottenham, London, N.): *b.* Tottenham, *c.*1895: *educ.* Raynham Road School: enlisted 5 September 1914: served with the Expeditionary Force in France and Flanders, and was killed in action at Hill 60, Ypres, 25 April 1915: Age 20. *unm.*

(Panel 34) Pte. 9784, Arthur Price, 2nd Bn. (70th Foot) The East Surrey Regt.: enlisted London. Killed in action 25 April 1915, nr. Zonnebeke. Remains 'Unknown British Soldier. E.Surrey' recovered unmarked grave (28.D.23.a.25.33); identified – Clothing, Title, Braces; reinterred, registered 5 April 1927. *Buried in Sanctuary Wood Cemetery (IV.B.13).*

(Panel 34) Pte. 7593, William Arthur Prior, 1st Bn. (31st Foot) The East Surrey Regt.: *b.* Newbury, co. Berks: enlisted Kingston-on-Thames, co. Surrey. Killed by the explosion of a shell which collapsed his section of trench burying him and four other men, 1 January 1915. See Pte. C. Owen (above).

(Panel 34) Pte. 10988, Alfred Rowland, 2nd Bn. (70th Foot) The East Surrey Regt.: *s.* of the late Alfred Rowland, by his wife Ellen (26, Story Street, Caledonian Road, King's Cross, London): and brother to Rfn. 6193, T. Rowland, 4th King's Royal Rifle Corps, killed in action 6 August 1915: *b.* Islington, London. Killed in action 9 May 1915: Age 22. *unm.*

His brother Thomas is buried in Chapelle-D'Armentieres Old Military Cemetery (D.8).

(Panel 34) Pte. 7260, Frederick Ernest Rush, 2nd Bn. (70th Foot) The East Surrey Regt.: 3rd *s.* of Walter Samuel Rush, of Malling Farm, Bentley, Ipswich, and Ellen Jane Rush, his spouse: and *yr.* brother to Pte. 40160, C.D. Rush, 9th Norfolk Regt., killed in action 19 April 1917: *b.* Ipswich: enlisted there: served with the Expeditionary Force in France, and was killed in action 24 May 1915; Ypres, Belgium: Age 19.

His brother Charles is buried in Vermelles British Cemetery (VI.B.3).

(Panel 34) Pte. 10301, Charles Tibbles, 1st Bn. (31st Foot) The East Surrey Regt.: *s.* of Edward T. Tibbles, of 57, Fountain Road, Tooting, London, by his wife Elizabeth: *b.* Bermondsey, 1890: enlisted Kingston-on-Thames, co. Surrey. Killed in company with four other men – Ptes. Bristow, Bye, Haley and Prior – on New Year's Day, 1 January 1915 – by a large shell which exploded in the section of trench they were occupying at the time. See Pte. C. Owen (above).

> *What passing–bells for these who die as cattle?*
> *Only the monstrous anger of the guns.*
> *Only the stuttering rifles' rapid rattle*
> *Can patter out their hasty orisons.*
>
> *No mockeries now for them; no prayers nor bells,*
> *Nor any voice of mourning save the choirs –*
> *The shrill, demented choirs of wailing shells;*
> *And bugles calling them from sad shires.*
>
> *What candles may be held to speed them all?*
> *Not in the hands of boys, but in their eyes*
> *Shall shine the holy glimmers of good-byes*
> *The pallor of girls' brows shall be their pall;*
> *Their flowers the tenderness of patient minds,*
> *And each slow dusk a drawing-down of blinds.*

The above poem '*Anthem For Doomed Youth*' by Wilfred Owen is to be found with a framed photograph of Pte. Joseph Toms beside the memorial at St. Eloi. Placed there by his nephew, Derek Doune, it is cared for by the local municipality.

(Panel 34) Pte. 30847, Joseph Edward Toms, 'B' Coy., 12th (Service) Bn. (Bermondsey) The East Surrey Regt.: (17th Section, No.8 Platoon): *s.* of John Toms, Labourer; of 110, East Street, Epsom, co. Surrey, by his wife Harriet, *dau.* of Charles Dearcey, by his wife Ann: *b.* Epsom, *c.*1897: *educ.* Epsom Junior Council School (to age 9): prior to the outbreak of war was member 1/5th (Territorial) Battn. East Surrey Regt.: undertook Imperial Service obligations on the outbreak of war; subsequently transf'd. 3rd Battn., Grand Shaft Barracks, Dover, thence to 12th Battn. for Active Service: served with the Expeditionary Force in France and Flanders from November 1916, and was reported missing in the vicinity of St. Eloi, nr. Ypres, sometime between 12 April and 3 May 1917; later reported as having been killed in action on or about the latter date, aged 19 years. His former C.O., Capt. N. Legge, 1/5th Battn., in writing from Mesopotamia to Pte. Toms' father (9 May 1918), said, "I was deeply grieved to read in the 'Epsom Herald' about the death of your son, Pte. 30847, J.E. Toms, and hasten to express to you and Mrs Toms my very real sympathy and sorrow in your loss. Your son joined my Company before the war – one of the keen youngsters who helped to save the country in the early days of it – and I always regretted he was too young to come out to India with his brother and the rest of us. He was so cheery and willing and would certainly have done well with us. There are still a few of his old friends in what was the original Epsom Company and they, I know, would wish me to add to my own an expression of their sincere sympathy with you. I trust your other son, J.C., is doing well and will be spared to you and his wife." Pte Toms, believed by his surviving family to have been a member of a Lewis Gun section, was almost certainly killed by enemy shellfire during the battalion's relief on 12 April 1917. His brother, Pte. J.C. Toms, survived the war. Their nephew regularly visits the Ypres salient, retracing his uncle Joe's footsteps.

(Panel 34) Pte. 202984, Douglas Aymos White, 12th (Service) Bn. (Bermondsey) The East Surrey Regt.: *s.* of Henry White, of 5, Park Road, South Harting, Petersfield, by his wife Alice: and *yr.* brother to Pte. PO/2011, H.G. White, Royal Marine Light Infantry, who fell, 20 August 1915, at Gallipoli. Killed in action 2 August 1917: Age 20. *unm.*

His brother Henry is buried in Lancashire Landing Cemetery (G.73).

(Panel 34) Pte. 9296, James 'Jack' White, 1st Bn. (31st Foot) The East Surrey Regt.: brother to Pte. 6130, C. White, 1st East Surrey Regt., killed in action 28 October 1914: *b.* Addlestone, co. Surrey: Occupation – Brick Maker: 5'7" tall, brown hair, grey eyes: enlisted after the outbreak of war, 7 September 1914, Weybridge, co. Surrey: served with the Expeditionary Force in France, and was killed in action there 23 November 1914. Remembered on Addlestone War Memorial.

His brother Charles is commemorated in Pont-Du-Hem Military Cemetery, La Gorgue (Edward Road Cem.Mem.21).

(Panel 34) Pte. 204311, George Whitehorn, 9th (Service) Bn. The East Surrey Regt.: *s.* of George Whitehorn, of Woolstone Road, Uffington, nr. Faringdon, co. Berks, by his wife Ellen: enlisted Faringdon: served with the Expeditionary Force, and was killed in action 3 August 1917: Age 19.

South Loggia:

PANEL 36 BEGINS PTE. E.McL. SHEARER. – YORK & LANCS

(Panel 36) Pte. 3/2093, Charles Uttley, 2nd Bn. (84th Foot) The York & Lancaster Regt.: *b.* Bradgate: enlisted Rotherham. Killed in action 9 August 1915. *Buried in Bedford House Cemetery (IV.C.16/Enc. No.6).*

(Panel 36) Major Stanley Edgar Badcock, 6th Bn. The Durham Light Infantry (T.F.): *s.* of Frederick Badcock, Solicitor; of Thornfield, Bishop Auckland, Co. Durham, by his wife Fanny: *b.* Bishop Auckland, 28 February 1881: *educ.* Bishop Auckland; Pocklington, co. York; matriculated London University: afterwards practiced as Solicitor, Bishop Auckland: joined 2nd Volunteer Battn., Durham Light Infantry (now 6th Battn.), as 2nd Lieut. May 1900: promoted Lieut. June 1901; gazetted Capt. June 1906: received his Majority, April 1915. Major Badcock, had qualified at the Musketry Course, held a certificate of proficiency for his rank and, having undertaken Imperial Service obligations, proceeded to France with his battalion, 19 April 1915, and was killed seven days later while leading his men into action, at the Second Battle of Ypres, 26 April 1915. He was a good athlete, and played cricket and football, and was also a member of the Durham City Hockey Club: Age 34. *unm.*

(Panel 36) Capt. Richard Wilfred Braithwaite, 10th (Service) Bn. The Durham Light Infantry: *s.* of the late Rev. John Masterman Braithwaite, Vicar and Rural Dean, of Croydon, co. Surrey, by his wife Elizabeth Jane: *educ.* Marlborough College, after which he took up business as Tea Planter; Ceylon: served in South Africa; Tpr., Ceylon Mounted Infantry, during which campaign he was wounded: joined London Stock Exchange, Member (1910), and was a partner in the firm Messrs Foster & Braithwaite: received a commission, Capt. 10th Durham Light Infantry, on the outbreak of war: went to France; wounded near Sanctuary Wood, Ypres, 27 July 1915, but refused to leave the trenches and was killed four days later (30 July): Age 38. He was married (1907) to Sybil Deans, *née* Braithwaite (6, Basil Mansions, Knightsbridge, London), *dau.* of Mr (& Mrs) Brodhurst Hill.

(Panel 36) Capt. Luther Vincent Burgoyne Johnson, 1/8th Bn. The Durham Light Infantry (T.F.): eldest *s.* of Lieut.Col. John Burgoyne Johnson, 8th (Reserve) Bn. Durham Light Infantry, of 'Brockley,' Saltburn-by-the-Sea, J.P., County of Durham: *b.* Middlemoor, nr. Richmond, co. York, 5 September 1890: *educ.* Charterhouse; King's College, Cambridge (B.A.): gazetted 2nd Lieut. (T.F.), April 1910: promoted Lieut. May 1912; Capt. September 1914: qualified with distinction in musketry and machine-gun courses at Hythe: undertook Imperial Service obligations on the outbreak of war; went to France, 19 April 1915, and was killed in action at Gravenstafel Ridge, Ypres sector, 25 April 1915: Age 24. *unm.*

(Panel 36) Lieut. Herbert Stewart, 3rd (Reserve) Bn. The Durham Light Infantry attd. 2nd Bn. Duke of Cornwall's Light Infantry: 2nd *s.* of James Reid Stewart, of Millfield House, Eldon Place, Newcastle-on-Tyne, by his wife Eleanor: *b.* Newcastle, 22 February 1887: *educ.* Bow, Durham, and Durham School, where he distinguished as an oarsman: joined the Army, as 2nd Lieut., on the outbreak of war August 1914: promoted Lieut. February 1915: served with the Expeditionary Force in France, and was killed in action, 23 April 1915, while making an attack north of St. Jean, nr. Ypres, Flanders. Buried beside Lieut. H.G. Morris and 2nd Lieut. G.J. Lunnon. of the Duke of Cornwall's Light Infantry. Lieut. Stewart was a member of the Tyne Amateur Rowing Club: Age 28. *unm.*

Both 2nd Lieut. Henry Morris and George Lunnon have no known grave; they are recorded on Addenda Panel 58, and Panel 20 respectively.

(Panel 36) 2nd Lieut. Colin Smith Kynoch, 6th Bn. The Durham Light Infantry (T.F.): 2nd *s.* of Robert Kynoch, of Stocksfield-on-Tyne, by his wife Jennie, *dau.* of Silvanus Smith: *b.* Newcastle-on-Tyne, 8 September 1883: *educ.* Private School, Newcastle-on-Tyne: Occupation – Traveller; Corn & Flour Trade: volunteered on the outbreak of war: gazetted 2nd Lieut., 6 October 1914: proceeded to France 19 April, 1915, and was killed in action nr. St. Julien, Ypres, seven days later, 26 April 1915. Buried nr. Hill 60: Age 30. *unm.*

(Panel 36) 2nd Lieut. Andrew Little, 1/9th Bn. The Durham Light Infantry (T.F.): *s.* of the late Andrew Little, by his wife Sarah (Oakfield, Newcastle-on-Tyne): *b.* 25 May 1886: *educ.* Bilton Grange, Harrogate: gazetted 2nd Lieut., Territorial Force, November 1914: went to France, 19 April 1915, and was killed outright by a shell exactly one week later, 26 April, while leading his men into action at the Second Battle of Ypres. Buried nr. Verlorenhoek: Age 29. *unm.*

(Panel 36) Coy.Sergt.Major 25493, James Dyson, 12th (Service) Bn. The Durham Light Infantry: *s.* of Simeon Dyson, of 23, Seventh Avenue, Council Houses, Chester-le-Street, Co. Durham, by his wife Jane: and brother to Pte. 21014, J. Dyson, Northumberland Fusiliers, died 26 May 1915: enlisted Newcastle-on-Tyne: served with the Expeditionary Force in France and Flanders from August 1915, and was killed in action 7 June 1917, at Messines, Belgium: Age 31. He leaves a wife Agnes Dyson (12, Co-operative Street, Chester-le-Street, Co. Durham).

His brother Joseph also has no known grave; he is recorded on Panel 12.

(Panel 36) Sergt. 856, George Ernest White, 1/5th Bn. The Durham Light Infantry (T.F.): *s.* of Henry A. White, of Haughton House, Haughton-le-Skerne, Darlington, Co. Durham, by his wife Emily A.: *b.* Derby: enlisted Darlington: served with the Expeditionary Force in France and Flanders from 18 April 1915, and was killed in action at Hooge, nr. Ypres, 25 May following: Age 25. Remains recovered unmarked grave 'Sanctuary Wood Old Cemetery' (29.I.24.b.90.97), 'Unknown British Sergeant. D.L.I.;' identified – Clothing, Titles, Badge of Rank; reinterred, registered 10 May 1928. *Buried in Sanctuary Wood Cemetery (II.G.26).*

(Panel 36) Corpl. 9688, Frank Brown, 2nd Bn. (106th Foot) The Durham Light Infantry: eldest *s.* of Charles Brown, of Choppington Station, by his wife Mary Jane, *dau.* of Frank Robinson: *b.* Barrington Colliery, 22 July 1889: *educ.* Barrington Council School: enlisted 6 October 1906; served some years in Ireland, completing his service with 3rd Bn. (2nd Durham Militia) at Newcastle: Occupation – Motorman; Newcastle Tramways: called up on mobilization, 4 August 1914; proceeded to France, 7 September, and was killed in action while digging himself in, being shot through the head, nr. Hooge, 9 August 1915: Age 26. He *m.* North Shields, 24 December 1910, Euphemia (Hedley's Old Buildings, New York, Shiremoor: *re-m.* now Logan, of 35, Brookland Terrace, New York, Shiremoor, Northumberland), *dau.* of the late Robert (& Margaret) Crossley, and had two *daus.* – Margaret, *b.* 11 October 1912; Mary Jane, *b.* 31 October 1914.

(Panel 36) Corpl. 2126, Harold Finlay Punshon, 'C' Coy., 8th Bn. The Durham Light Infantry (T.F.): 2nd *s.* of Thomas Punshon, of Ashley Terrace, Chester-le-Street, Co. Durham, by his wife Agnes Kershaw, *dau.* of the late Richard Finlay: *b.* Chester-le-Street, 23 February 1892: *educ.* Higher Grade School, Gateshead: employee Priestman Colliery Office: joined Durham L.I. Territorials, April 1912: in training in camp when war was declared August 1914, and volunteered for Foreign Service: went to France, 19 April 1915, and was killed in action near Ypres on the 26th, being shot by a sniper. Buried about ½ mile S.E. of St. Julien. Capt. John Turnbull, in a letter to his brother, wrote, "I regret very deeply to have to inform you that your poor brother Harry was killed on Monday the 26th. I was not with him when he met his death, but saw him an hour before, when, I am sure you will be proud to know, he was doing his bit in a splendidly cool manner, under most trying circumstances. I got separated from the body of men with whom he was, but have since learned that he with two or three other N.C.Os., and a few men, were cut off by a large body of Germans. Some of our chaps had to surrender, but Harry and a few others made a dash for it and got clear. He was killed soon after this while going between trenches with ammunition." Age 23. *unm.*

(Panel 36) L/Corpl. 12374, John Thomas Foster, 10th (Service) Bn. The Durham Light Infantry: eldest *s.* of Robert Foster, Shipwright; of 28, Wear Street, Southwick-on-Wear, by his wife Dorothy Ann, *dau.* of John Rames: *b.* Southwick, Co. Durham, 15 July 1886: *educ.* Southwick National School: Occupation – Shipyard worker; Sunderland: enlisted 10 August 1914: trained Surrey: went to the Front, 21 May 1915, and was killed in action in France, 31 July following. Buried at Sanctuary Wood, nr. the Dressing Station: Age 29. *unm.*

(Panel 36) L/Corpl. 1592, Herbert Pallas, 1/7th Bn. The Durham Light Infantry (T.F.): *s.* of Lawson Pallas, of 55, Washington Street, Millfield, Sunderland, by his wife Annie: and brother to Pte. 2200, J. Pallas, 1/7th Durham Light Infantry, killed in action 28 July 1916; and Pte. 7/3488, M. Pallas, 1/7th Durham Light Infantry, killed in action 3 July 1916: *b.* Sunderland: enlisted there. Killed in action 24 May 1915: Age 19.

His brother John also has no known grave, he is recorded below; Mark is buried in Ridge Wood Military Cemetery (I.V.5).

On 31 July 1917 20th Durham Light Infantry were support battalion to 123rd Brigade's attack north of the Yser Canal. Despite strong resistance the brigade managed to take their first objective, but owing to the state of the ground over which the attack had to be made progress was slow and, as the covering barrage got further and further ahead of the troops, attempts to reach their second objective were foiled by a series of heavily defended pill boxes which defied all attempts to take them.

(Panel 36) Pte. 20/908, Thomas Alderson, 20th (Service) Bn. (Wearside) The Durham Light Infantry: *s.* of John Alderson, of 1, Graham Terrace, Shildon, Co. Durham, by his wife Ann, *née* Swinglehurst: *b.* Shilson, *c.*1885: enlisted Bishop Auckland: served with the Expeditionary Force in France and Flanders from 5 May 1916, and was killed in action 31 July 1917: Age 31.

(Panel 36) Pte. 9474, John Atcheson, 2nd Bn. (106th Foot) The Durham Light Infantry: 2nd *s.* of the late Hugh Atcheson, of Jarrow, Machine Planer; by his wife Mary (Carley Place, Southwick, Sunderland), *dau.* of Michael Benson: *b.* Monkwearmouth, Sunderland, co. York, 24 May 1894: *educ.* St. Barnett's, Sunderland: enlisted October 1910: after serving his time with the Colours joined the Special Reserve, and was employed at Thomson's Yard, Sunderland: called up on mobilisation, 5 August 1914, and was killed in action at Ypres, 1 June 1915. His brother, Pte. Samuel Atcheson, is now (1916) serving with the Expeditionary Force in France: Age 21. *unm.* (*IWGC record 3/9474; brother survived*)

(Panel 36) Pte. 2280, John James Bailey, 1/7th Bn. The Durham Light Infantry (T.F.): *b.* Sunderland, Co. Durham, August 1887: prior to enlistment was employee Foster's Forge, Sunderland: pre-war member 7th (Territorial) Bn. Durham Light Infantry, volunteered for Active Service on the outbreak of war, Sunderland, August 1914: trained Gateshead: disembarked Boulogne, 19 April 1915, and was killed in action "somewhere in France," 15 May 1915: Age 27. He *m.* Sunderland, 24 August 1912, Elizabeth Jane (who died 16 June 1914), *dau.* of William Chambers Farley, Machine Druiller; of Sunderland, and had issue one child, Catherine (15, Victoria St., Southwick, Sunderland).

(Panel 36) Pte. 2383, Thomas Chilton, 1/5th Bn. The Durham Light Infantry (T.F.): *s.* of John William Chilton, of 65, Wellington Street, Stockton-on-Tees, by his wife Ellen: enlisted Stockton-on-Tees: served with the Expeditionary Force in France and Flanders from 18 April 1915, and was killed in action 16 June 1915: Age 25. *unm.* Remains exhumed 'Unknown British Soldier.' unmarked grave (28.I.24.d.15.45), 28 January 1929; identified – Khaki, Boots size 7/4; reinterred, registered 31 January 1929. *Buried in Sanctuary Wood Cemetery (V.C.30).*

(Panel 36) Pte. 2642, James Edward Cook, 1/7th Bn. The Durham Light Infantry (T.F.): 2nd *s.* of George Cook, Fruiterer & Florist; of Thornley, by his wife Annie, *dau.* of John Peel: and elder brother to Pte. 18/1432, P. Cook, Durham Light Infantry (also a trained teacher), killed in action 27 July 1916, during the fighting on the Somme: *b.* Thornley, Co. Durham, 12 January 1891: *educ.* Council School there; Henry Smith's Secondary School, Hartlepool, and the Teachers Training College, Sunderland (1909 – 11), from whence, having obtained his certificate, was appointed Assistant Master, Thornley Council School, which post he held at the outbreak of war. While going through his course at Sunderland Training College he had joined the Durham Light Infantry Territorial Battn. and, on 9 September 1914, volunteered for Imperial Service: left Gateshead for France, 19 April, and on arrival the Durham L.I. were immediately sent up to the trenches at Ypres, where he was killed in action on Whit Monday, 24 May 1915. His body, in an advanced state of decomposition, was found six weeks afterwards in front of the first line trenches and buried by a comrade: Age 24. *unm.*

His brother Percy is buried in St. Vaast Post Military Cemetery, Richebourg-L'Avoue (III.K.14).

(Panel 36) Pte. 13022, James Albert Dixon, 14th (Service) Bn. The Durham Light Infantry: eldest *s.* of Harry Robson Dixon, Grocer; by his wife Emily, *dau.* of James Dean: *b.* Birtley, Co. Durham, 19 June 1887: *educ.* Public School, there: Occupation – Coal Miner: enlisted 26 September 1914, after the outbreak of war: crossed to France 4 October 1915, and was killed in action 31 December following, being shot by a German sniper while out with a working party: 31 December 1915. Age 27. He was well known as a Violinist and Entertainer in the Chester-le-Street district. He *m.* Parish Church, Chester-le-Street, 15 October 1908; Isabel (Stuart Street, Chester-le-Street, Co. Durham), *dau.* of James Sterling, and had three children – Nancy, *b.* 30 April 1910; Emily, *b.* 23 October 1911; James Albert, *b.* 19 January 1916 (*d.* 17 December 1916).

(Panel 36) Pte. 1552, John Earls, 1/5th Bn. The Durham Light Infantry (T.F.): *s*. of the late William Earls, and his wife Annie J. (5, Vulcan Steet, Albert Hill, Darlington): and brother to Pte. 1568, W. Earls, 4th Yorkshire Regt., who fell the same day: *b*. Darlington: enlisted there. Killed in action 24 May 1915. Remembered on Coxhoe (St. Mary's) Church (and village) War Memorial. (*IWGC record Earles*)

His brother William also has no known grave; he is recorded on Panel 33.

(Panel 36) Pte. 2127, Ernest Stuart Livingstone Fenton, 1/7th Bn. The Durham Light Infantry (T.F.): enlisted Sunderland: served with the Expeditionary Force in France and Flanders from 19 April 1915, and was killed in action 16 June 1915. Remains 'Unknown British Soldier. Durham L.I.;' recovered unmarked grave (28.I.24.d.15.45); identified – Khaki, Titles; reinterred, registered 3 January 1929. *Buried in Sanctuary Wood Cemetery (IV.T.9).*

(Panel 36) Pte. 7737, John Ferry, 2nd Bn. (106th Foot) The Durham Light Infantry: 2nd *s*. of George Clark Ferry, by his wife Margaret, *dau*. of William Gill: *b*. Deptford, Sunderland: *educ*. Simpson Street Schools: enlisted 1908: served with the Expeditionary Force in France from 1 November 1914, and was killed in action at Hooge, 9 August 1915. *unm*.

(Panel 36) Pte. 3/10692, Thomas Ferry, 'B' Coy., 2nd Bn. (106th Foot) The Durham Light Infantry: *s*. of William Ferry: *b*. Sunderland: served with the Expeditionary Force. Killed in action at Hooge, nr. Ypres, 9 August 1915. Age 23. He was married to Hannah Stephenson, *née* Ferry (5, Back, Aylmer Street, Deptford, Sunderland).

(Panel 36) Pte. 2066, Thomas William Fox, 7th Bn. The Durham Light Infantry (T.F.): 2nd *s*. of Peter Fox, Driller; of 10, Hylton Road, Sunderland, by his wife Mary, *dau*. of David Cockburn: *b*. Sunderland, Co. Durham, 8 April 1895: *educ*. St. Mary's R.C. Schools: employee Engineering Dept., Messrs Lynn's Forge, Pallion, Sunderland: joined Durham L.I. (T.F.) 12 May 1914: volunteered for Foreign Service on the outbreak of war August: went to France 20 April 1915, and was killed in action during the Second Battle of Ypres 24 May following: Age 20. *unm*. (*IWGC record 26 May 1915*)

(Panel 36) Pte. 2623, Arnold John Green, 'B' Coy., 1/7th Bn. The Durham Light Infantry (T.F.): *yr*. *s*. of John Green, Manager; of 41, Otto Terrace, Sunderland, by his wife Isabella Elliot, *dau*. of Robert Lowson: *b*. Sunderland, Co. Durham, 27 June 1892: *educ*. Ackworth Friends' School, nr. Pontefract: joined North Eastern Railway, Chief Passenger Agents' Dept., 8 October 1908, where his capacity for study made him exceptionally successful in the company's secondary examinations, and during 1914 obtained a first-class pass in 'Railway and Commercial Geography,' and a second-class pass in 'Railway Operating': subsequently transferred General Manager's Office, York, and while there took a prominent part in the affairs of the local Y.M.C.A.: volunteered and joined 7th Durham Light Infantry, September 1914, after the outbreak of war: trained Gateshead: served with the Expeditionary Force in France and Flanders from 19 April 1915, and was killed in action nr. Ypres, 24 May following. While at York he frequently contributed articles to the North Eastern Railway Magazine – '*Bonnie Blanchland*' (October 1913), and '*A Peep At Durham*' (May 1914), being among their number: Age 22. *unm*.

(Panel 36) Pte. 2724, John Roland Hannan, 1/5th Bn. The Durham Light Infantry (T.F.): enlisted Darlington: served with the Expeditionary Force in France and Flanders from 18 April 1915, and was killed in action 21 May following. Remains recovered unmarked grave 'Sanctuary Wood Old Cemetery' (29.I.24.b.90.97), 'Unknown British Soldier. D.L.I.;' identified – Clothing, Titles; reinterred, registered 10 May 1928. *Buried in Sanctuary Wood Cemetery (II.G.25).*

(Panel 36) Pte. 9669, John George Hills, 'C'Coy., 2nd Bn. (106th Foot) The Durham Light Infantry: *s*. of John Hills, of Benwell, Newcastle-on-Tyne: *b*. Benwell, 31 January 1889: *educ*. there: enlisted 17 September 1906: served two years Cork, Ireland, and four years in India, where he was on duty at the Delhi Durbar: returned to England on mobilisation, 5 August 1914: undertook Imperial Service obligations; proceeded to France with the Expeditionary Force, 22 October 1914: ten months in the thick of the fighting, and was killed in action at Hooge, 9 August 1915: Age 26. He *m*., St. Peter's Church, Wallsend, Newcastle-on-Tyne, 31 March 1914, Florence (13, Third Street, Wallsend), *dau*. of Mr (& Mrs) Maine, and had a son, John George Robson, *b*. 14 March 1915.

(Panel 36) Pte. 14118, Martin O'Donnell, 14th (Service) Bn. The Durham Light Infantry: *b*. Roundstone, Co. Galway: Occupation – 15 years, Shipyard Worker; Messrs Short Brothers, Pallion, Sunderland: enlisted Sunderland: served with the Expeditionary Force in France from October 1915, and died there, 26 January 1916, shortly after being shot through the head by a sniper. Sergts. Brammer and Halpin, 'D' Coy., wrote to his widow, Catherine (22, Hart Street, Deptford, Sunderland), "Dear Madam, I regret to have to break this sad news to you regarding your husband, whom I'm sorry to tell you was shot through the head this morning by a sniper, he was unconscious until he died, it has been a sad blow to me and all his chums for he was well respected by all with whom he came into contact with, we did the best we could for him when we saw there was no hope of recovery, his platoon sergeant and chums said the Rosary and De Profundas and a few acts of contrition, as we were Roman Catholics like himself. He died the death of a hero, he was a soldier and a man. Please accept the sympathy of myself and all his comrades. Gone but not forgotten…Enclosed you will find his Rosary beads, Sacred Heart badge and two rings." Father to two children. Pte. O'Donnell was one of the 'souls of the parish' remembered by a special Requiem Mass held at the instance of the teachers and schoolchildren of St. Joseph's, Millfield, 28 November 1918.

(Panel 36) Pte. 2200, John Pallas, 1/7th Bn. The Durham Light Infantry (T.F.): *s*. of Lawson Pallas, of 55, Washington Street, Millfield, Sunderland, by his wife Annie: and brother to L/Corpl. 1592, H. Pallas, 1/7th Durham Light Infantry, killed in action 24 May 1915; and Pte. 7/3488, M. Pallas, 1/7th Durham Light Infantry, killed in action 3 July 1916: *b*. Sunderland: enlisted there. Killed in action 28 July 1916: Age 18.

His brother Herbert also has no known grave, he is recorded above; Mark is buried in Ridge Wood Military Cemetery (I.V.5).

(Panel 36) Pte. 11278, Francis Albert Millard, 2nd Bn. (106th Foot) The Durham Light Infantry: late of Bath, co. Somerset: *b*. Bath: enlisted Newcastle. Died 18 August 1915, of wounds. Commemorated on Bath City War Memorial. *Buried in Bath (St. James's) Cemetery.*

(Panel 36) Pte. 1689, John Thornton, 'D' Coy., 1/5th Bn. The Durham Light Infantry (T.F.): *s*. of John Thornton, of 59, Wynyard Street, Horden Colliery, Seaham Harbour, Co. Durham, by his wife Isabella: *b*. Brandon, Durham: enlisted Spennymoor. Killed in action 19 June 1915: Age 27. *unm*. Remains 'Unknown British Soldier. Durham L.I.;' recovered unmarked grave (28.I.24.d.15.45); identified – Khaki; reinterred, registered 9 January 1929. *Buried in Sanctuary Wood Cemetery (IV.U.2).*

PANEL 36 ENDS PTE. L. TULLY – DURHAM LIGHT INFANTRY.

PANEL 38 BEGINS PTE. F. TUNNEY – DURHAM LIGHT INFANTRY.

(Panel 38) Pte. 1839, Samuel Tuttle, 1/5th Bn. The Durham Light Infantry (T.F.): late of Thornaby-on-Tees, co. York: *s*. of S. (& Mrs) Tuttle of 7, Kingston Street, Tilery Road, Stockton-on-Tees: and brother to Pte. 42417, J.W. Tuttle, 15th Bn. Durham Light Infantry, killed in action 10 September 1916, at the Somme: *b*. Sand Hutton, co. York: Occupation – Fireman, North Eastern Railway Co.: enlisted Stockton-on-Tees. Killed in action 27 April 1915: Age 21. Pte. Tuttle is remembered in the '5th D.L.I. Book of Remembrance,' and (with his brother) in the 'Stockton-on-Tees Book of Remembrance;' both held in St. Thomas' Parish Church, Stockton.

His brother John also has no known grave, he is commemorated on the Thiepval Memorial, Somme.

(Panel 38) Pte. 2316, Dennis Unitt, 1/5th Bn. The Durham Light Infantry (T.F.): late of Blackhall Colliery, Castle Eden: *s*. of the late A.E. Unitt, by his wife Margaret (4, Fairfield Street, Darlington): and brother to Pte. 200390, L. Unitt, Durham Light Infantry, killed in action 28 October 1917: *b*. Ladywood, Birmingham: enlisted Stockton-on-Tees. Killed in action 23 June 1915. Remains 'Unknown British Soldier. Durham L.I.;' recovered unmarked grave (28.I.24.d.15.45); identified – Khaki, Titles; reinterred, registered 9 January 1929. *Buried in Sanctuary Wood Cemetery (IV.U.3).*

His brother Lawrence has no known grave, he is commemorated on the Tyne Cot Memorial (130).

(Panel 38) Pte. 2878, Robert Percy Waller, 'D' Coy., 1/5th Bn. The Durham Light Infantry (T.F.): *s.* of Thomas (& Mrs) Waller, of 85, Windsor Road, Stockton-on-Tees: served with the Expeditionary Force in France from 18 April 1915, and was killed in action 16 May 1915: **Age 16.**

(Panel 38) Pte. 3389, John Winn, 1/8th Bn. The Durham Light Infantry (T.F.): *s.* of Joseph Winn, of 9, Dale Street, Ushaw Moor, Co. Durham: enlisted Durham: served with the Expeditionary Force in France from 17 April 1915, and was killed in action on the 26th of that month: **Age 16.**

(Panel 38) Capt. Robert Guy Incledon Chichester, 2nd Bn. (74th Foot) The Highland Light Infantry: 2nd *s.* of the Rev. Richard Chichester, Rector of Drewsteignton, co. Devon: *b.* 28 January 1873: gazetted 2nd Lieut., Highland Light Infantry, 29 May 1895: promoted Lieut. 8 September 1898; Capt. 27 March 1901: served (1) North-West Frontier of India 1897 – 98, with Malakand and Buner Field Forces, when he took part in the attack and capture of the Tanga Pass (Medal with clasp): (2) South African War 1901 – 02, being employed with the Mounted Infantry: took part in the operations in Cape Colony, January – March 1901: operations in Orange River Colony, March 1901 – April 1902; and those in the Transvaal, April – 31 May 1902 (Queen's Medal, five clasps): (3) with the Expeditionary Force in France and Flanders, and was killed in action nr. Ypres 13 November 1914: Age 41. Capt. Chichester was a descendant of Sir John Chichester (knighted after the Siege of Calais, 1348) who took part in the Battle of Poitiers, 1356, and Sir John Chichester who fought at the Battle of Agincourt, 1415.

(Panel 38) Capt. Thomas Booth Myles, M.C., 12th (Service) Bn. The Highland Light Infantry: 4th *s.* of Charles Y. Myles, of Wellbank, Arbroath: *b.* Arbroath, 25 December 1892: *educ.* Arbroath, thereafter studied Agriculture, Aberdeen University (entered 1911), where he became well-known as a skilful cricketer, and his good nature and cheerfulness made him a general favourite; a contemporary remarked, "No Varsity function was complete without him.": joined 4th (University Detachment) Gordon Highlanders on the outbreak of war: commissioned 12th Highland Light Infantry, February 1915: served with the Expeditionary Force in France and Flanders from late 1915: promoted Capt. 1916; posthumously awarded the Military Cross for bravery ('*London Gazette*') '...when commanding two companies in a raid was a fine example to the men, and was largely responsible for the success of the raid, during which 79 prisoners were taken and valuable information obtained was obtained.': Killed in action 1 August 1917, being shot by a sniper while attempting to get in touch with another company to ascertain the dispositions of the enemy. His Commanding Officer wrote, "He was one of my most valued company commanders, and his place will be hard to refill...": Age 24. One of four brothers who served. He was married to Bella Shand Hill (Aberdeen), and left one son. Remembered on Abbey (Parish) Church War Memorial, Arbroath. (*IWGC record 31 July*)

(Panel 38) Lieut. Charles Lawson Cornish, 2nd Bn. (74th Foot) The Highland Light Infantry: *s.* of the late Henry Cornish, by his wife Emily Henrietta ('Glastonbury,' Lovelace Road, Surbiton, co. Surrey): *b.* Brighton, co. Sussex, 13 August 1887: *educ.* Stoke House, Slough; Charterhouse, and Trinity College, Cambridge (graduated B.A.): gazetted 2nd Highland Light Infantry, 1910; promoted Lieut. 1912, afterwards resigned his commission – voluntarily joined Reserve of Officers, spring 1914. On the outbreak of war in August of that year he rejoined his battalion, which was one of the first units of the First Army Corps to go to the relief of the VIIth Division near Ypres, and was almost continually engaged till the enemy's assaults were broken in November. Lieut. Cornish took part in the retirement from Mons, the Battles of the Marne and the Aisne, being killed at last by a shell in the Battle of Ypres, 13 November 1914, while his company was taking up its position in the trenches. Buried alongside the Passchendaele-Becelaere Road: Age 27. *unm.*

(Panel 38) Lieut. Alan James Dickson, 2nd Bn. (74th Foot) The Highland Light Infantry: *s.* of Patrick Dickson, J.P., of Barnhill, co. Kincardine, by his wife R.I. Dickson ('Sunnyside House,' Montrose): *b.* Laurencekirk, 28 February 1892: *educ.* Fettes College, Edinburgh; Merton College, Oxford (B.A., 1914): received his commission from University O.T.C.; gazetted 2nd Lieut., Highland Light Infantry, July 1914: ordered to the Front on the outbreak of war, August 1914; served with the Expeditionary Force in France and Flanders from the 14th. of that month: promoted Lieut. November, and was killed in the trenches by a sniper, when looking out in an attempt to locate same, 16 November 1914: Age 22. *unm.*

(Panel 38) Lieut. John Duncan, 10th (Service) Bn. The Highland Light Infantry: eldest *s.* of John Duncan, Journalist; of 25, Buccleuch Place, Edinburgh, by his wife Mary. J., *dau.* of James Wilson, Railway Contractor: and brother to Pte. W. Duncan: *b.* Edinburgh, 11 May 1886: *educ.* George Watson's College, where he had a successful college career, carrying off prizes in German and Drawing: subsequently apprenticed to Messrs Cousin, Ormiston & Taylor, Architects & Surveyors, attended for the prescribed period the School of Art classes under the Board of Manufacturers. He also distinguished himself at the Heriot Watt College, where in two successive sessions he gained the Bronze Medal, first in the Junior and next in the Senior Class of Building Construction. Employed with the British Aluminium Co. on the outbreak of the European War; resigned September 1914, and joined 9th Royal Scots: gazetted 2nd Lieut. Highland Light Infantry, November following; promoted Lieut. January 1916: served with the Expeditionary Force in France and Flanders from 1 July 1915, taking part in the fighting on the Ypres front: invalided home, July 1916, suffering from severe shell shock: returned to the Front January 1917, and was killed in action at Ypres 31 July following, while gallantly leading his men against their second objective in the face of determined opposition and heavy machine-gun fire. His superior officer wrote, "His work has at all times born the stamp of excellence. He was beloved by us all. I feel his loss deeply.": 31 July 1917: Age 31. *unm.*

(Panel 38) Lieut. James Young Milne-Henderson, 11th (Service) Bn. The Highland Light Infantry: *s.* of John Milne-Henderson, of 15, Merchiston Park, Edinburgh, by his wife Ina: and elder brother to 2nd Lieut. J.M. Milne-Henderson, Royal Engineers attd. Royal Flying Corps, killed in action 28 January 1918: Occupation – Works Manager; Messrs McVitie & Price, Willesden, London. Killed in action 31 July 1917: Age 26. *unm.* A Watsonian, International Rugby Football player and member of the Madras Rugby team, he was also Junior East of Scotland Swimming Champion. Mentioned in Despatches by F.M. Sir Douglas Haig for his services in the Great War.

His brother John also has no known grave; he is commemorated on the Arras Flying Services Memorial.

(Panel 38) Sergt. 11302, William Black, 2nd Bn. (74th Foot) The Highland Light Infantry: 4th *s.* of Jeremiah Black, by his wife Matilda, *dau.* of Joseph Lowry: *b.* Craigywarren, Ballymena, Co. Antrim, Ireland, 28 January 1890: *educ.* Craigywarren National School: enlisted Hamilton, April 1909: promoted Sergt. November 1914: served with the Expeditionary Force in France and Flanders, and was killed in action on the Rossitier Road (*q.v*) in the village of Zonnebeke, five or six miles from Ypres, 14 November 1914: Age 24. *unm.* (*IWGC record Corpl.*)

His brother Robert also has no known grave; he is recorded below.

(Panel 38) Sergt. 8540, Joseph A. McL.S. Britten, 2nd Bn. (74th Foot) The Highland Light Infantry: *b.* Rickmansworth, co. Buckingham: served with the Expeditionary Force, and was killed in action at St. Julien, 23 October 1914.

(Panel 38) L/Corpl. 12109, Robert Black, 2nd Bn. (74th Foot) The Highland Light Infantry: late of Dunfane, Ballymena: *s.* of Jeremiah Black, by his wife Matilda, *dau.* of Joseph Lowry: and brother to Sergt. 11302, W. Black, Highland Light Infantry, who also fell: *b.* Craigywarren, Ballymena, Co. Antrim: enlisted Paisley: served with the Expeditionary Force in France and Flanders. Reported wounded and missing after the trench he was in was hit by a shell, 24 October 1914; now assumed killed in action. L/Corpl. Black has kin-folk resident at Ballygarvey, Ballymena.

His brother William also has no known grave; he is recorded above.

(Panel 38) Pte. 9608, James Agnew, 2nd Bn. (74th Foot) The Highland Light Infantry: *s.* of Charles Agnew, of 270, East Wellington Street, Parkhead, Glasgow (late of 424, Westmuir Street, Parkhead), and his late wife Mary: *b.* Wishaw, co. Lanark, 1894: enlisted Glasgow. Killed in action at Poperinghe (*q.v.*), 7 November 1914: Age 20. *unm.*

(Panel 38) Pte. 9370, John Aldington, 2nd Bn. (74th Foot) The Highland Light Infantry: served with the Expeditionary Force. Killed in action 3 November 1914.

(Panel 38) Pte. 10132, Alfred H. Amos, 2nd Bn. (74th Foot) The Highland Light Infantry: *s.* of Mr (& Mrs) Amos, 25, Lyndhurst Road, Upper Edmonton, London, N.: enlisted London: served with the Expeditionary Force. Killed in action at Ypres, 21 October 1914.

(Panel 38) Pte. 5463, William Anderson, 2nd Bn. (74th Foot) The Highland Light Infantry: *s.* of Robert Anderson, by his wife Eliza Young: served with the Expeditionary Force. Killed in action at Poperinghe (*q.v.*), 7 November 1914: Age 34. (*IWGC record 5465*)

(Panel 38) Pte. 11758, James Arthurs, 2nd Bn. (74th Foot) The Highland Light Infantry: *s.* of Andrew Arthurs, of 15, Langlands Road, Govan, Glasgow: served with the Expeditionary Force. Killed in action at Poperinghe (*q.v.*), 7 November 1914: Age 20. *unm.* (*IWGC record R/758*)

(Panel 38) Pte. 11908, John Bateman, 2nd Bn. (74th Foot) The Highland Light Infantry: enlisted Hamilton, co. Lanark: served with the Expeditionary Force. Killed in action at Ypres, 21 October 1914.

(Panel 38) Pte. 12078, John Briggs, 2nd Bn. (74th Foot) The Highland Light Infantry: *s.* of James Briggs, of 12, High Vennel, Wigtown: served with the Expeditionary Force. Died 31 October 1914, from wounds received in action at Ypres.

(Panel 38) Pte. 12250, John Brown, 2nd Bn. (74th Foot) The Highland Light Infantry: served with the Expeditionary Force. Died 21 October 1914, from wounds received in action at Ypres.

(Panel 38) Pte. 11675, Thomas Burke, 2nd Bn. (74th Foot) The Highland Light Infantry: *s.* of the late John Burke, by his wife Catherine: *b.* Edinburgh, *c.*1895: served with the Expeditionary Force. Killed in action at Poperinghe (*q.v.*), 27 November 1914: Age 19.

(Panel 38) Pte. 9064, James Burns, 2nd Bn. (74th Foot) The Highland Light Infantry: served with the Expeditionary Force. Killed in action at Poperinghe (*q.v.*), 14 November 1914.

(Panel 38) Pte. 9533, Hugh Fraser Campbell, 2nd Bn. (74th Foot) The Highland Light Infantry: *s.* of the late David Campbell, of Edinburgh, by his wife Mary, *née* Fraser: *b.* Edinburgh, *c.*1886: served with the Expeditionary Force, and died of wounds received in action at Ypres, 27 October 1914: Age 26. *unm.*

(Panel 38) Pte. 12238, John Campbell, 2nd Bn. (74th Foot) The Highland Light Infantry: late of Glasgow: served with the Expeditionary Force. Killed in action 14 November 1914.

(Panel 38) Pte. 7654, Stephen Campbell, 2nd Bn. (74th Foot) The Highland Light Infantry: served with the Expeditionary Force. Killed in action at Poperinghe (*q.v.*), 14 November 1914: *m.*

(Panel 38) Pte. 9319, Daniel Carney, 'C' Coy., 2nd Bn. (74th Foot) The Highland Light Infantry: *s.* of Patrick Carney, of 61, Queen Street, Galashiels, by his wife Isabella: served with the Expeditionary Force. Killed in action 21 December 1914: Age 27. *unm.*

(Panel 38) Pte. 9829, George Chandler, 2nd Bn. (74th Foot) The Highland Light Infantry: *s.* of Frederick Chandler, of The Grove Lodge, Prince's Road, Wimbledon Park, London, S.W., by his wife Elizabeth: served with the Expeditionary Force. Killed in action 24 – 27 October 1914: Age 25. *unm.*

(Panel 38) Pte. 8908, William Clarke, 'G' Coy., 2nd Bn. (74th Foot) The Highland Light Infantry: *s.* of William John Clarke, of Bow Yetts, Torpichen: served with the Expeditionary Force. Killed in action at Ypres 29 October 1914: Age 29. He left a wife, Maggie Young McKenzie, *née* Clarke (27, Deans Rows, Bathgate).

(Panel 38) Pte. 7767, Joseph Clayton, 2nd Bn. (74th Foot) The Highland Light Infantry: late of Glencairn, co. Dumfries: *s.* of the late Thomas Clayton, and his wife Jemima (1, Teviot Row, Hawick, co. Roxburgh): and brother to Pte. S/12389, J.W. Clayton, 8/10th Gordon Highlanders, killed in action 17 June 1916; and Pte. G/17058, J. Clayton, 10th Royal West Kent Regt., died of wounds 4 August 1917: *b.* Hawick: enlisted there: served with the Expeditionary Force, and was killed in action at Poperinghe (*q.v.*), 14 November 1914.

His brother James is buried in Vermelles British Cemetery (III.C.9); John, Lijssenthoek Military Cemetery (XVII.G.5).

(Panel 38) Pte. 9623, John Conaghan, 2nd Bn. (74th Foot) The Highland Light Infantry: served with the Expeditionary Force. Reported missing, 13 November 1914; now (1916) assumed killed.

(Panel 38) Pte. 9376, Joseph Cullen, 2nd Bn. (74th Foot) The Highland Light Infantry: *s.* of Mr. (& Mrs) Cullen, of Penicuik, co. Midlothian: enlisted Edinburgh: served with the Expeditionary Force, and was killed in action at Poperinghe (*q.v.*), 11 November 1914.

(Panel 38) Pte. 11515, Robert Devine, 2nd Bn. (74th Foot) The Highland Light Infantry: *s.* of B. Devine, of Glasgow: served with the Expeditionary Force. Killed in action at Poperinghe (*q.v.*), 7 November 1914.

(Panel 38) Pte. 7914, Harry Dick, 2nd Bn. (74th Foot) The Highland Light Infantry: served with the Expeditionary Force: killed in action at Poperinghe (*q.v.*), 13 November 1914.

(Panel 38) Pte. 7987, Cornelius Docherty, 2nd Bn. (74th Foot) The Highland Light Infantry: eldest *s.* of the late William Docherty, Miner (38, New Orbiston, Bellshill): and brother to Pte. 8300, W. Docherty, 2nd Argyll & Sutherland Highlanders, killed in action 12 April 1916, and Corpl. 8082, A. Docherty, 2nd Argyll & Sutherland Highlanders, killed in action at Loos 25 September 1915: *b.* Wishaw, co. Lanark, 25 December 1880: *educ.* Public School, there: served a number of years with the Colours thereafter joined the Reserve, during which time and the outbreak of war he was employed as Miner; Parkhead Colliery, Bellshill: recalled on mobilization 4 August 1914: served with the Expeditionary Force in France, and was killed in action 22 October 1914. Buried there: Age 33. One of three brothers who fell.

His brothers William and Andrew are buried in Cambrin Churchyard Extension (L2.10 & C.4 respectively).

(Panel 38) Pte. 8687, Daniel Docherty, 2nd Bn. (74th Foot) The Highland Light Infantry: *b.* Dundee: enlisted Cupar, co. Fife: served with the Expeditionary Force in France. Killed in action at Poperinghe (*q.v.*), 14 November 1914. *m.*

(Panel 38) Pte. 9301, Frank Duffey, 2nd Bn. (74th Foot) The Highland Light Infantry: served with the Expeditionary Force. Killed in action at Ypres, 1 November 1914.

(Panel 38) Pte. 7263, William Dunlop, 2nd Bn. (74th Foot) The Highland Light Infantry: served with the Expeditionary Force. Killed in action at Poperinghe (*q.v.*), 3 November 1914.

(Panel 38) Pte. 7998, William Farey, 2nd Bn. (74th Foot) The Highland Light Infantry: served with the Expeditionary Force. Killed in action at Poperinghe (*q.v.*), 13 November 1914.

(Panel 38) Pte. 11555, Robert Fitzsimmons, 2nd Bn. (74th Foot) The Highland Light Infantry: *s.* of John Fitzsimmons, of Partick, Glasgow: enlisted Hamilton, co.Lanark: served with the Expeditionary Force, and was killed in action at St. Julien 21 October 1914.

(Panel 38) Pte. 10255, John Gaffney, 2nd Bn. (74th Foot) The Highland Light Infantry: *s.* of Charles Gaffney, of Dundee: served with the Expeditionary Force, and was killed in action at St. Julien, 31 October 1914. (*IWGC record 1 November 1914*)

(Panel 38) Pte. 9760, Patrick Gallagher, 2nd Bn. (74th Foot) The Highland Light Infantry: *s.* of Mr (& Mrs) Gallagher, of Townhead, Glasgow: enlisted Hamilton, co. Lanark: served with the Expeditionary Force, and was killed in action at Poperinghe (*q.v.*), 2 November 1914.

(Panel 38) Pte. 6824, John Graham, 2nd Bn. (74th Foot) The Highland Light Infantry: *s.* of Mr (& Mrs) Graham, of Edinburgh; and brother to John Bogie Esq., 70, West Port, Edinburgh: served with the Expeditionary Force. Killed in action at Poperinghe (*q.v.*), 14 November 1914: Age 33. *m.*

(Panel 38) Pte. 10084, Arthur A. Gulland, 2nd Bn. (74th Foot) The Highland Light Infantry: *b.* Plumstead, co. Kent: served with the Expeditionary Force. Killed in action at Poperinghe (*q.v.*), 14 November 1914.

(Panel 38) Pte. 12185, John Guy, 2nd Bn. (74th Foot) The Highland Light Infantry: *s.* of Samuel Guy, of 43, Thornwood Rows, Uddingston, co. Lanark: served with the Expeditionary Force. Killed in action at Poperinghe (*q.v.*), 13 November 1914: Age 19.

(Panel 38) Pte. 11921, Cecil W. Hearn, 2nd Bn. (74th Foot) The Highland Light Infantry: *s.* of James Hearn, of 30, Elmwood Terrace, Leith, Edinburgh, by his wife Elizabeth: served with the Expeditionary Force. Killed in action at St. Julien, 21 October 1914: Age 19.

(Panel 38) Pte. 12140, George Houston, 2nd Bn. (74th Foot) The Highland Light Infantry: *s*. of Robert Houston, of 8, Finnieston Street, Anderton, Glasgow, by his wife Annie: served with the Expeditionary Force. Killed in action at Poperinghe (*q.v.*), 13 November 1914: Age 21. *unm*.

(Panel 38) Pte. 4716, Thomas Houston, 2nd Bn. (74th Foot) The Highland Light Infantry: *s*. of the late Thomas Houston, of Calton, Glasgow: served with the Expeditionary Force. Killed in action at Poperinghe (*q.v.*), 14 November 1914. Pte Houston leaves a wife Marion, *née* Paterson (1, Buchanan Lane, Bell Street, Calton): Age 29.

(Panel 38) Pte. 6854, John Hughes, 2nd Bn. (74th Foot) The Highland Light Infantry: *b*. Glasgow, co. Lanark: served with the Expeditionary Force. Killed in action at Poperinghe (*q.v.*), 11 November 1914.

(Panel 38) Pte. 9089, Daniel Kelty, 2nd Bn. (74th Foot) The Highland Light Infantry: served with the Expeditionary Force, and was killed in action 12 November 1914: Age 29. Pte. Kelty leaves a wife, Elizabeth (56, Duke Street, Edinburgh).

(Panel 38) Pte. 9674, George Kennedy, 2nd Bn. (74th Foot) The Highland Light Infantry: served with the Expeditionary Force. Killed in action at Poperinghe (*q.v.*), 13 November 1914: Age 26. He leaves a widow, Jesse Leslie Kennedy, *née* Innes (72, Dudhope Street, Dundee, co. Forfar).

(Panel 38) Pte. 9493, Allan Kerr, 2nd Bn. (74th Foot) The Highland Light Infantry: enlisted Hamilton, co. Lanark: served with the Expeditionary Force. Killed in action at St. Julien, 31 October 1914. (*IWGC record 1 November 1914*)

(Panel 38) Pte. 9389, John Hofmeister Master, 2nd Bn. (74th Foot) The Highland Light Infantry: *s*. of Mr (& Mrs) Hofmeister, of 163, Tiverton Road, South Tottenham, London: *b*. Marylebone: enlisted London. Killed in action 3 November 1914: Age 27. He leaves a widow, A.M. Hofmeister (148, Arlington Road, Camden Town, London), to mourn his loss.

(Panel 38) Pte. 8622, Donald McQueen, 2nd Bn. (74th Foot) The Highland Light Infantry: *s*. of the late Charles McQueen, of 110, Lauriston Place, Edinburgh: *b*. 1882: served in the South African Campaign against the Boers, and with South African Constabulary: a pre-war Regular, mobilised on the outbreak of war, served with the Expeditionary Force in France from 14 August 1914, and was killed in action 1 November following: Age 32. Pte. McQueen was married to Mrs Minnie Sutherland McLean, *née* McQueen (34, 'C' Block, Highland Light Infantry Married Quarters, Abbassia, Cairo, Egypt).

(Panel 38) Capt. Keith Bethune Mackenzie, 2nd Bn. (78th Foot) attd. 1st Bn. (72nd Foot) The Seaforth Highlanders (Ross-shire Buffs, The Duke of Albany's), attd. 1st Bn. Gordon Highlanders: elder *s*. of the late James Mackenzie, of Daresbury, Malvern, co. Worcester, by his wife Jane (Woodham House, Horsell, Woking, co. Surrey), only *dau*. of the Rev. Neil Bethune, of Thamesford, Ontario, Canada: *b*. Shanghai, China, 1 December 1879: *educ*. Malvern College: gazetted 2nd Lieut. from the Militia, 5 January 1901: promoted Lieut. 5 April 1904; Capt. 3 June 1911: served in the South African War, 1900 – 02, taking part in the operations in Cape Colony, August 1900 – January 1902: Orange Free State, January – March 1902: Transvaal, March – May 1902 (Queen's Medal, five clasps): and with the Expeditionary Force in France and Flanders, 14 October – 12 November 1914, on which latter date he was killed in action at Hooge, nr. Ypres when the dugout he was sharing with two other officers was hit by a sixty-pound shell. Buried at Hooge: Age 34. Capt. Mackenzie was a Knight of the Saxe Ernestine Family Order. He *m*. St. Giles' Cathedral, Edinburgh, 22 January 1912, Louise, *dau*. of the late James Scott, of Craigholme, Edinburgh: *s.p.* See Capt. D.C.W. Thomas, Argyll & Sutherland Highlanders (Panel 42).

(Panel 38) Lieut. William Noel Lawson Boyd, 2nd Bn. (78th Foot) The Seaforth Highlanders (Ross-shire Buffs, The Duke of Albany's): only *survg*. child of William Boyd, of 26, Inverleith Place, Edinburgh, Writer to '*The Signet*,' Member; King's Body Guard for Scotland (R.C.A.), by his wife Laura, *dau*. of the late John Crerar of Halifax, Nova Scotia, and *gdson*. of the late Sir John Boyd, of Maxpoffle, co. Roxburgh, by his wife Lady Isabella, 2nd *dau*. of John Lawson, 14th Laird of Cairnmuir, co. Peebles: and brother to 2nd Lieut. N.J.L. Boyd, died from wounds received in action at the Battle of the Aisne, 14 September 1914: *b*. Edinburgh, 26 December 1892: *educ*. Cargilfield, Midlothian; Clifton College, and Exeter College, Oxford, being a member of the O.T.C., both at Clifton and Oxford. When war broke out he was in Norway, visiting friends there, and at once telegraphed that he was returning to take up a commission, after considerable difficulties he arrived in Scotland, 14 August 1914; immediately reported himself to the Headquarters of the O.T.C., Oxford: gazetted 2nd Lieut., 7th Seaforth Highlanders at the beginning of the following month, and after a period of training at Churn Camp, joined his battalion at Aldershot, October: subsequently applied for transfer to 3rd (Special Reserve) Battn. Seaforth Highlanders; which he subsequently joined early January 1915. When training with 3rd Seaforths, he definitely decided to adopt the Army as a profession, and on a recommendation from the University at Oxford obtained a commission in the Regular Army, being posted to 2nd Battn. of his regiment: served with the Expeditionary Force in France and Flanders from March 1915 when he joined his battn., with which he was in the trenches near Messines, and took part in other operations in which it was concerned including the Second Battle of Ypres. 'He was reported wounded and missing, 25 April 1915, and from the evidence which was afterwards obtained, it has been concluded that he was killed in action on that day. It appears that on 25 April his company was the leading company of the battalion in an attack upon the German trenches north-east of Ypres, near St. Julien, and came under very severe fire. He was reported to have been seen leading his platoon with fine gallantry throughout the attack, and got to within about 20 yards of the enemy's lines when he was observed to be wounded. He was believed to be hit again, and, as stated, it has been decided from the testimony received that he must have been killed in action on that day. From the battalions of the regiment with which he had been connected came expressions of the estimation in which he had been held, and special appreciation of the fearless devotion to duty displayed on the day he fell. Warm-hearted and generous, he had many friends among whom he was a great favourite.' He was a keen sportsman, being specially devoted to shooting and fishing, and he rowed for his college in 1913 and 1914: Age 22. *unm.*

His brother Nigel is buried in Edinburgh (Dean or Western) Cemetery (I.110).

(Panel 38) Lieut. Charles Napier Lipp, 1/6th Bn. (Morayshire) The Seaforth Highlanders (Ross-shire Buffs, The Duke of Albany's), (T.F.): *s.* of George (& Mary A.) Lipp, of The Square, Fochabers, co. Moray. Killed in action on the same day as Capt. J. Bliss, and 58 other ranks of his battalion, 31 July 1917: Age 23. *unm.*

Capt. J. Bliss is buried in Gwalia Cemetery (I.G.32); see also 2nd Lieut. H.B. Lendrum, Dozinghem Military Cemetery (II.H.1).

After 15th Scottish Division had successfully achieved their first two objectives on 31 July 1917, Orderly Runner, Pte. 24819, Bill Morgan, Highland Light Infantry, was sent back to Battalion H.Q. with a message from Capt. Campbel – "He scribbled on a paper and gave it to me and he said, 'Just tell them that we're getting on fine, Morgan. If you happen to lose the message, tell them that we're getting on fine. We're over the first two lines.' Back across the battlefield. Back through the clouds of crashing explosions, the sniper fire, the crackling machine-guns. Dodging shell-holes, sidestepping the bodies of wounded and dead, detouring to avoid the hottest spots where the succeeding waves were still mopping up and flushing the enemy out – even back at the first objective, where machine-guns and snipers were still firing from hidden hollows in the tumbled earth."

By the time Morgan had delivered the message and returned to his company they were pressing toward their third objective, well forward from where he had left them almost three hours previously. And, surrounded by dead bodies, with shells exploding all around and bullets flying everywhere, Morgan crawled, ran, jumped and dodged from the cover of shell-holes and folds in the ground until he eventually caught up with Sergt. McCormack and Lieut. Burns, pinned down by heavy fire from Beck House and Borry Farm. "We were really held up at this place but the bombers were at it, attacking it from the flanks. There were boys there with buckets of bombs…They were all going at it, hammer and tongs. They were still going at it when it started to rain. They were still going at it an hour later, and by that time we were practically up to our knees in water. Lieut. Burns said to me, 'You'd better get a message back, Morgan, and let them know what's happening. We must have reinforcements.' We were standing in this wet shell-hole and he was just handing me the message when the machine-gun bullet got him. He fell right over on to me and we both went right down into the water. I managed to pull him a bit up the side of this crater and laid him down and knelt down beside him. His eyes were open and he looked straight up at me and he said, 'I'm all right, Mum.' And then he died."

(Panel 38) 2nd Lieut. Francis Burns, M.C., attd. 8th (Service) Bn. The Seaforth Highlanders (Ross-shire Buffs, The Duke of Albany's): Killed in action 31 July 1917: Age about 19.

(Panel 38) Corpl. 416, Alexander Sutherland, 2nd Bn. (78th Foot) The Seaforth Highlanders (Ross-shire Buffs, The Duke of Albany's): s. of G. (& Mrs) Sutherland, of Myrons Lane, Golspie, co. Sutherland: and brother to Pte. 669, R.J. Sutherland, 1/5th Seaforth Highlanders, killed in action 24 March 1916: *b.* Golspie: enlisted Fort George, Inverness. Killed in action 24 April 1915; St. Julien: Age 26.

His brother Roderick is buried in Maroeuil British Cemetery (II.A.1).

(Panel 38) L/Corpl. 3/7204, Malcolm Campbell, 2nd Bn. (78th Foot) The Seaforth Highlanders (Ross-shire Buffs, The Duke of Albany's): *s.* of Finlay McLean Campbell, of 16, Habost, Port of Ness, Stornoway, by his wife Marghed: and brother to Pte. 3/7174, A. Campbell, 1st Seaforth Highlanders, killed in action 9 May 1915: *b.* Barvas, Stornoway: enlisted Fort George, co. Inverness. Killed in action 24 April 1915; St. Julien. (*IWGC record Cambell, 317204*)

His brother Angus also has no known grave; he is commemorated on the Le Touret Memorial.

(Panel 38) Pte. 3/7049, Roderick MacLeay, 2nd Bn. (78th Foot) The Seaforth Highlanders (Ross-shire Buffs, Duke of Albany's): *s.* of Roderick MacLeay, of 14, Ballantrushal Shader, Barvas, Stornoway, Lewis, by his wife Margaret: and elder brother to Pte. 204506, L. Macleay, 7th Seaforth Highlanders, died 10 January 1918, of wounds, aged 19 years: *b.* Barvas, *c.*1893: enlisted Stornoway: served with the Expeditionary Force in France and Flanders from August 1914, and was killed in action 18 May 1915: Age 21. *unm.*

His brother Louis is buried in Tincourt New British Cemetery (IV.E.10).

(Panel 38) Pte. S/6906, James McPherson, 2nd Bn. (78th Foot) The Seaforth Highlanders (Ross-shire Buffs, The Duke of Albany's): *s.* of the late John (& Mrs) McPherson, of 14, Church Street, Coatbridge, co. Lanark: *b.* Falkirk, co. Stirling, *c.*1896: enlisted Coatbridge. Killed in action 16 May 1915: Age 19. Pte. McPherson was one of eight brothers who served.

(Panel 38) Pte. 265083, Alexander Younie, 6th Bn. (Morayshire) The Seaforth Highlanders (Ross-shire Buffs, The Duke of Albany's), (T.F.): *s.* of the late James Younie, Police Officer; of 50, Main Street, New Elgin, and his wife Jane Ann, *née* Grant (Verabank, Findhorn, Forres): and yr. brother to L/Corpl. 9057, J. Younie, 3rd Scots Guards (discharged April 1916), died 19 August 1918, of Phthisis Pulmonalis (tuberculosis of the lungs & progressive bodily degeneration), aged 31 years: *b.* Elgin, co. Moray, 9 March 1894: Occupation – Clerk: enlisted Elgin. Reported missing / believed killed in action 31 July 1917: Age 23.

His brother James is buried in Elgin New Cemetery (Sec.E., Grave 206); inadvertently omitted, his details were added to the Commonwealth War Graves Debt of Honour Register, 13 March 2012.

(Panel 38) Capt. George Michael Monteith, 3rd attd. 1st Bn. (75th Foot) The Gordon Highlanders: *s.* of Joseph Monteith, of Carstairs House, co. Lanark: and yr. brother to Chaplain IVth Class, R.J. Monteith, Army Chaplain's Dept. attd. Royal Field Artillery, died 27 November 1917, of wounds. Killed in action 25 September 1915: Age 28. *unm.*

His brother Robert is buried in Ribecourt British Cemetery (I.D.11).

(Panel 38) Lieut. Cyril Cochrane, 1st Bn. (75th Foot) The Gordon Highlanders: only child of Alexander Cochrane, of 37, Drayton Court, London, S.W., by his wife Sarah: *b.* London, 6 September 1890: *educ.* France, Switzerland, and Royal Military College, Sandhurst: gazetted 2nd Lieut., 2nd Bn. (92nd Foot) Gordon Highlanders, 20 September 1911: served with 2nd Battn. in India and Egypt. Invalided home, August 1913, put on half-pay lists 12 August 1914, shortly thereafter diagnosed and operated on (appendectomy) to correct his malady, thereafter proceeded to and joined Regimental Depot, Aberdeen: went to France joining 1st Battn. of his Regt., February 1915: after some time in the trenches was invalided home (German measles), and again went to the Depot, Aberdeen: returned to France, rejoined 1st Battn., August 1915, and was killed in action nr. Hooge, 25 September following, during the great attack on the German lines. Buried about a mile and a half south-east of Hooge, in a cemetery between Maple Copse and Sanctuary Wood. Posthumously promoted Lieut. to rank as from 14 March 1915, and Temp. Capt. from 27 August to 2 September (inclusive) (*'London Gazette,'* 19 February 1916). His Colonel wrote to his father, "His loss is sadly felt by us all, as he was a general favourite;" and Capt. Dinwiddie, Adjutant 'A' Coy., 1st Battn., "My company was in support, and went up after the bombardment to hold our old front line. Your son was going along to try and get into touch with another part of the line when he was shot, as he was passing through a shallow part of the trench. The company and myself are terribly sorry to lose him. He was a good soldier and a brave officer. A great help to me in the work of the company." He was fond of all sports, being a good oar and keen on polo; also rode to hounds, and was a good motor-car driver, in addition to driving horses. While in the Army he qualified as a first-class shot: Age 25. *unm.*

(Panel 38) Lieut. James Howie Fraser, 2nd Bn. (92nd Foot) The Gordon Highlanders: *s.* of Edward Cleather Fraser, C.M.G., M.L.C., of Mauritius: *b.* Blackheath, London, S.E., 4 April 1888: *educ.* Rugby: gazetted Gordon Highlanders, October 1907: served with his battalion in India and Egypt: promoted Lieut. March 1909: on the outbreak of war proceeded with his regiment to the Front, and was killed in action 30 October 1914, while advancing on Klein Zillebeke Farmhouse. Mentioned in Sir John (now Lord) French's Despatch (14 January 1915), for his services: Age 26. *unm.*

(Panel 38) Lieut. Archibald Stuart Bulloch Graham, 2nd Bn. (92nd Foot) The Gordon Highlanders: *s.* of Archibald Bulloch Graham, of 3, Park Gardens, Glasgow, W., formerly Capt. Glasgow Highlanders (T.F.): *b.* 28 April 1891: *educ.* Glasgow Academy, Rossall School; Royal Military College, Sandhurst: gazetted 2nd Lieut. Gordon Highlanders, joining 1st Battn., Colchester, 25 March 1911: transf'd. 2nd Battn., Cawnpore, India, October 1911, proceeding with the battalion from that place to Cairo, Egypt, December 1912: promoted Lieut., July 1914: left Cairo for Southampton with his battalion September 1914, and, after a few days at Lyndhurst, left for Zeebrugge as part of VIIth Division. During the latter days of October, Lieut. Graham frequently attracted attention by his bravery and cheeriness under trying conditions, and especially in the charge after which he was treacherously killed. Several officers wrote saying how well he had done, and in 1915 his father received a parchment certificate to the effect that Lieut. Graham's conduct on 29 – 31 October 1914, had been brought to the notice of the Commanding Officer, who had much pleasure in bringing it to the notice of higher authority. He was killed on the afternoon of 31 October 1914, the following account having been received from his soldier servant, "At the time of his death he was one of three officers left with the remains of the battalion, which after the recent severe fighting had been largely reduced in numbers. They were ordered to take a wood, and this they did in such a manner that the enemy thought they were overpowered by numbers, and threw up their hands to surrender. While the officers were seeing that the enemy's arms were given up a wounded German officer, pretending to be dead, waited till Lieut. Graham was close in front of him, and then shot him in the back of the head with his revolver. Our men were so enraged that they gave the Germans no quarter." His Commanding Officer, writing on 12 November 1914, said, "The Gordons had charged through the Germans, and had them in full retreat when your boy (Stuart) was hit from behind, and has not been heard of from that time. I can tell you that he was a splendid officer and a great loss to his country, the Army, and his regiment. When he had to do a thing I knew it would be well done, and it always was well done. I cannot tell you how much I regret his loss." And writing again on the 15th he said; "His popularity with the men was very great, and he proved himself a born leader of men. He is a great loss to us and the Army at large.": Age 23. *unm.* (*IWGC record Bullock*)

(Panel 38) Lieut. Alexander Rennie Henderson, 4th Bn. The Gordon Highlanders (T.F.): elder *s.* of Alexander Rennie Henderson, of 46, Beaconsfield Place, Aberdeen; Teacher, Robert Gordon's Technical College, Aberdeen, by his wife Elizabeth Jane, *dau.* of James Thomson, of Aberdeen: *b.* Aberdeen, 8 November 1888: *educ.* Robert Gordon's Technical College, and Aberdeen University; M.A. (1911): Occupation – Teacher; Aboyne Higher Grade School: joined University Coy., 4th Gordon Highlanders

(T.F.); Pte., November 1907: promoted Colour-Sergt. 1910; resigned 1912: volunteered for Foreign Service, and undertook Imperial Service obligations on the outbreak of war: obtained a commission, 2nd Lieut., 4th Gordon Highlanders, 2 September 1914; promoted Lieut., 15 May 1915: served with the Expeditionary Force in France and Flanders from 19 February 1915. Reported wounded and missing after the Battle of Loos (*q.v.*), 25 September following, and is now assumed to have been killed in action on that date at Hooge, when he led his platoon into action, and at the third line of German trenches was blinded by the explosion of a shell. His Commanding Officer wrote, "The courage and pluck shown by him and his men that day is beyond words of mine.": Age 26. *unm.*

(Panel 38) Lieut. Charles Keith Latta, 2nd Bn. (92nd Foot) The Gordon Highlanders: 3rd *s.* of the late John Latta, of 17, Royal Circus, Edinburgh, by his wife Margaret, *dau.* of the late John Jopp, Writer to '*The Signet*,' Edinburgh: *b.* Edinburgh, 2 December 1889: *educ.* Edinburgh Academy, and Royal Military College, Sandhurst: received his commission 2nd Lieut. 2nd Gordon Highlanders, November 1909; promoted Lieut., August 1911: served with 2nd Battn. in India, until 1912, thereafter proceeded to Egypt, where the battalion was stationed when war with Germany broke out: accompanied his battalion to the Front, where it formed part of VIIth Division, and was killed in action, 29 October 1914, in the neighbourhood of Ypres. The Colonel of his battalion, intimating his death to his relatives, said, "He gave his life for his country in a gallant fight, which was necessary for the safety, not only of his own regiment, but of a large force...He has always proved himself a fine example, and you may well be proud of him, as we are, and also all those of his own command. He is a great loss to us and the Army.": Age 24. *unm.*

(Panel 38) 2nd Lieut. the Hon. Simon Fraser, 3rd (Reserve) attd. 2nd Bn. (92nd Foot) The Gordon Highlanders: 3rd *s.* of Alexander William Frederick Fraser, 18th Baron Saltoun of Abernethy, J.P., D.L., by his wife Lady Mary Helena Saltoun (Philorth, Fraserburgh, co. Aberdeen), only *dau.* of Thomas Arthur Grattan-Bellew, M.P.: *b.* 7 September 1888: *educ.* Winton House, Winchester (preparatory school), and Charterhouse, afterwards entered the business of Messrs Greenwell & Co; became Member; London Stock Exchange, 1912: gazetted 2nd Lieut. 3rd Gordon Highlanders, 7 September 1914, and at the end of that month attached 2nd Battn. (at Lyndhurst), leaving for the Front, 4 October following: served with the Expeditionary Force in France and Flanders, and was killed in action nr. Ypres on the 29th of that month. Lieut. Col. H.P. Uniacke, C.B., Commdg. 2nd Bn. Gordon Highlanders, wrote, "3 November 1914, It is with the deepest regret that I write to tell you that poor Simon was killed on the 28th October when fighting a difficult rearguard action. Willie (his yr. brother William) buried him on the morning of the 29th in the grounds of an old chateau. The Army has lost an officer of rare quality and we a brother officer, who in a very short space of time, gained not only our affection but won from us our greatest admiration by his soldier-like qualities. Both your boys have done the most gallant and splendid work, which has made them an example to all. Under the most severe conditions they have been always cheery and helped to keep up the spirits of the men. Twice only have I seen Willie anything but the soul of fearless content; once when he lost one of his guns and then when we lost Simon. Our grief at losing Simon is very great, so you both have all the sympathy of the whole battalion. I only trust that the record of their splendid work may help in some way to alleviate your grief. Forgive this very hurried letter, but you will understand that I have much sad news to write, and have only just arrived in England rather weak after losing a good deal of blood from a shell, although very slightly wounded...The fighting has been the severest of the war, and their artillery work is marvellous. There is no doubt that their very best troops and finest artillery has been concentrated against our immediate front. Our losses have been very heavy, and I regret to say amongst them Lieut. J.A. Otho Brooke. The last two days, 31st October and 1st November., were the severest of them all...We are all with you both in your grief over the loss of your son, whose death means so much to us and also to the Army." And a brother officer, 2nd Lieut. Peter Duguid, "You will have already have had information about what happened on the 29th of last month, but I think you will like to hear what I know. In the morning, your son Simon and I were with our platoons in a trench on the left of the Gordons' position. The Germans came up on our left and drove back the troops there, and we had to take up new positions as we were enfiladed by a machine gun. In doing this I got a bullet through the flesh of my left arm. When we had time Simon put on a field dressing for me, and also attended to two of his own men who were hit. We had to fall back to the village of Zandvoorde, where we helped to organize the men. About noon Simon very gallantly carried a box of ammunition to a machine gun over an open field under fire. I rejoined him later and we took cover in a ditch during some very heavy shelling about 2 pm. He had just offered me a drink of water and had changed his position to further down the ditch when a shell burst near him and though I ran to him at once there was nothing I could do. I am sure he did not suffer. I had to go to the hospital but Capt. Huggins told me his body was brought in that night. Although I knew him so short a time, I regarded him as my best friend in the battalion. We were the only two reserve officers and were in the same Company. I shall always think of his cheerfulness and fortitude whatever had to be done. He had an extraordinary aptitude for the work, and all his men liked him. The first questions of two wounded at Ypres hospital were for him… My slight wound is nearly healed, and I hope to return to duty by the end of the month." Two of his brothers are serving in the Gordon Highlanders as Lieuts. – the Master of Saltoun, and the Hon. William 'Willie' Fraser, 6th Bn. Gordon Highlanders, who, shortly after the death of his brother, was temporarily captured, 1 – 2 November 1914, after his shoulder had been smashed by a shell splinter – 'At first he heard a yelled German order to shoot him, after capture. He was still in the German front line, the situation was confused, the atmosphere feverish and vengeful. Willie managed to attract the attention of a German officer. The latter snapped a question to his NCOs who had threatened Willie and Willie recognised the accent – he spoke good German, having spent a happy time in Frankfurt before going to Sandhurst in 1909. He managed to force a question on the German officer. "Do you come from Frankfurt?" There was surprise. "Yes. Was –?" "Don't you wish you were there now?" Willie said. "On a Saturday night?" He was in a lot of pain but he managed, somehow, to exchange a grin with his captor. It worked. The German, clearly a Reserve officer and no very military figure, said firmly to his soldiers, "You shan't shoot him! He's a British officer, he speaks German, he knows Frankfurt!" And shortly afterwards in the general melee the Germans withdrew and Willie managed to get lost and drop into a ditch where he lay in some agony, covered with mud and unrecognisable, until he saw British troops return and advance against the same Germans moving through a wood. Then an English and a Scottish soldier came running along either side of Willie's ditch. Willie tried to lever himself up and the English soldier yelled, "There's one of the bastards!" and aimed a ferocious kick at Willie's mud-covered figure. The boot landed on the wounded shoulder and Willie – a man who rarely swore – let out a stream – or scream – of the strongest language he ever remembered using. The Scottish soldier stopped, his ear attentive, "That's no Jerry bastard," he said, "it's one of our officers.'": Age 26.

After convalescing in England Willie Fraser returned to France, later promoted Lieut.Col. of his battalion; he survived the war. Lieut. James A. Otho Brooke, 2nd Gordon Highlanders, was posthumously awarded the Victoria Cross; he is buried in Zandvoorde British Cemetery (VI.E.2). Lieut.Col. Uniacke died of wounds 13 March 1915; he lies in Estaires Communal Cemetery (II.F.8).

(Panel 38) 2nd Lieut. John Cook Macpherson, 11th (Reserve) attd. 1st Bn. (75th Foot) The Gordon Highlanders: *s.* of Rev. Robert Macpherson, D.D., V.D., late Senior Collegiate Minister, Elgin, and his wife Catherine Duff: *b.* 1885: *educ.* Aberdeen University, where he took the Gladstone Memorial Prize; Hunter Gold Medal (Roman Law), and graduated M.A., LL.B.: took a prominent role in the literary life of his university, a member of the S.R.C., Secretary 1909 and, for a period, Editor of the University Magazine '*Alma Mater*': prior to the outbreak of war was employed as Assistant, Solicitor's Dept., North British Railway Co.: obtained a commission 11th Gordon Highlanders, went out with a draft of reinforcements attd. 1st Battn., and was killed in action 25 September 1915: Age 30.

(Panel 38) 2nd Lieut. William Stewart Robertson, D.C.M., 2nd Bn. (75th Foot) The Gordon Highlanders: *s.* of William Robertson, by his wife Barbara, *née* Stewart: served in the South African Campaign, for distinguished conduct in which he was awarded the D.C.M., twice Mentioned in Despatches: Regtl.Sergt.Major, 1904 – 1914: served with the Expeditionary Force in France and Flanders from 14 August 1914, and was killed in action 31 October 1914: Age 41. Mentioned in Despatches by Sir

John (now Lord) French for his services in the Great War. He was married to Janet Barclay Robertson (Holly Cottage, West Newport, co. Fife)

(Panel 38) 2nd Lieut. Luke Taylor Sinclair, 11th (Reserve) Bn. The Gordon Highlanders: only *s*. of the late William Sinclair, Stonecutter; of Aberdeen, by his wife Isabella (19, Thomson Street, Aberdeen), *dau*. of James Samson: *b*. Aberdeen, 16 June 1892: *educ*. United Free Church Normal School, and Robert Gordon's College, Aberdeen: previously connected with East India Company's Office, London; voluntarily enlisted as Tpr., 17th Lancers, 5 September 1914: stationed Curragh Camp, Ireland, for seven months, thereafter gazetted 2nd Lieut. 11th Battn. Gordon Highlanders, 29 March 1915; transf'd. 3rd Battn.: crossed to France 20 September 1915, attd. 1st Battn., and was killed in action by the explosion of a shell 15 yards from the German trenches, south-south-east of Ypres, Flanders, 2 March 1916. Buried near the trenches, and it was reported later that his body was removed to La Clytte Cemetery. His Colonel wrote that he was killed instantaneously by a shell whilst nobly leading his platoon against the German trenches; his company suffered severely, all of its officers being hit. A Company Officer also wrote that he was bravely leading his men in a bombing attack; he was the first over the parapet, and was within 15 yards of the German trenches when he was killed: Age 23. He *m*. Trinity Presbyterian Church, Clapham, London, S.W., 3 January 1916, Jessie Maud (3, Glendall Street, Perndale Road, Stockwell, London), *yst*. *dau*. of Henry Pratt, of Brixton, London, S.W.: *s.p.*

(Panel 38) Coy.Sergt.Major 1493, William Lawson Crichton, 1st Bn. (75th Foot) The Gordon Highlanders: *b*. Stirling: *educ*. Hibernian School, Dublin, and Queen Victoria School, Dunblane; being one of two Scottish boys transferred to the school when it opened (June 1909): a member of Q.V.S.O.T.C., he went (as Col. Corpl.) to Balmoral with 11 other pupils to receive the School Colours from Edward VII; he also attended the Coronation of King George V. (Primus, Queen Victoria's): gained entry to Trinity College, Dublin (June 1914) but, on the outbreak of war, put his studies aside and joined Gordon Highlanders, Stirling, 14 August 1914: served with the Expeditionary Force in France and Flanders from October following (promoted L/Corpl. same month): promoted Sergt. June 1915; C.S.M. September following (after the Battle of Loos), and was killed in action 2 March 1916, during the fighting to recapture The Bluff. C.S.M. Crichton is commemorated on the Roll of Honour in the Memorial Chapel of Holy Trinity (Scottish Episcopal) Church, Stirling.

(Panel 38) Sergt. S/5617, Alexander Spence, 10th (Service) Bn. The Gordon Highlanders: eldest *s*. of the Rev. Alexander Easton Spence, of The Manse, Dollar, co. Clackmannan, by his wife Barbara Milne, *dau*. of the Rev. Robert Cowan: *b*. Insch, co. Aberdeen, 4 February 1891: *educ*. Walker's Academy, Aberdeen; Stirling High School; Technical College, Glasgow, and Agricultural College, Glasgow: Occupation – Assistant Surveyor, co. Lanark: enlisted 3 September 1914: served with the Expeditionary Force in France and Flanders from July 1915. Reported missing after the fighting nr. Ypres 31 July 1917, now assumed to have been killed in action on that date: Age 26. *unm*.

(Panel 38) L/Sergt. S/7765, William Edward George Smith, D.C.M., 1st Bn. (75th Foot) The Gordon Highlanders: eldest *s*. of John Edward Smith, of Gorsebrook Lodge, Pembury Rd., Tunbridge Wells, by his wife Annie Harriet, *dau*. of William Creasy: and brother to L/Corpl. 265219, C.G. Smith, 1st West Kent Cyclist Bn., died Dalhousie Hospital, 10 November 1918, of influenza contracted while on active service: *b*. Thorpe, Norwich, 17 April 1890: *educ*. Higher Grade School, Norwich; Victoria School, Tunbridge Wells: went to South Africa, 1904; joined Western Light Horse; returned home (1906); thereafter removed to Australia from whence, after 3 years, returned to England: joined Royal West Kent Regt. (T.F.), 1910: removed to Canada, 1912, where, shortly after the outbreak of war (4 August 1914) he volunteered for Foreign Service with Canadian Expeditionary Force, but was rejected medically unfit: returned to England immediately, enlisted 1st Gordon Highlanders, November 1914: served with the Expeditionary Force in France and Flanders from December following: took part in considerable severe fighting. Died at Hooge, 25 September 1915, from wounds received in action there the same day. Buried near where he fell. His Commanding Officer wrote, "I deeply regret that L/Sergt. W. Smith was among those who fell at the Battle of Hooge. It was a very terrible battle but the Gordons did all that men could do, and died rather than fail;" and a L/Corpl., "I am sorry for the loss of his company, as he was such a nice fellow, and a good soldier. He always did his duty, and all the boys are sorry for the loss of the sergeant." Awarded the Distinguished Conduct Medal ('*London Gazette*,' August 1915) "For conspicuous gallantry on the night of 16th – 17th August 1915, near Ypres. When on patrol duty with an officer and two men between the British and the German trenches, the officer was wounded and unable to move. While the two men went for a stretcher Sergt. Smith dragged the officer towards our lines. On reaching the wire, with the assistance of one of the two men who had returned, he placed the wounded officer in a shell hole, cut a passage through the wire, and then carried him into safety, being the whole time under very heavy rifle fire.": Age 25. *unm.*

(Panel 38) Corpl. S/3273, Hugh Gourlay, 1st Bn. (75th Foot) The Gordon Highlanders: *s.* of Hugh McKail Gourlay, of 271, Hamilton Road, Cambuslang, Glasgow, by his wife Jeannie, *née* Wilson: *b.* Ayr, *c.*1895: Occupation – Crane Driver; Hallside Steelworks: volunteered and enlisted Cambuslang, co. Lanark, on the outbreak of war: proceeded to France with a draft of reinforcements, and was killed in action 5 March 1915; by a sniper's bullet which ricocheted off a tree, hit him in the chest and penetrated his lung: Age 19.

(Panel 38) Corpl. 290222, Easton McPherson Pope, 7th Bn. (Deeside Highland) The Gordon Highlanders (T.F.): *s.* of the late William Pope, of Aberdeen: enlisted Skene. Killed south-east of Langemarck, 3.50 a.m., 29 July 1917, when a section of the Gordon's assembly trench was directly hit by a German shell: Age 22. The same shell also killed Bde.-Major, Capt. H.H. Lean, L/Corpl. W. Lockerby, Pte. Whannell; and mortally wounded Brigdr.-Gen. A.F. Gordon, Comdg. 153rd Inf.Bde. (51st Divn.), who was visiting the Gordon's front-line trenches at the time.

Capt. Lean is buried in Poperinghe New Military Cemetery (II.G.35); L/Corpl. Lockerby and Pte. Whannell have no known grave, they are recorded below; Brigdr.Gen. Gordon died of his wounds two days later; he is buried in Lijssenthoek Military Cemetery (XIV.A.13).

(Panel 38) L/Corpl. S/11944, Lewis George Duncan, 8/10th (Service) Bn. The Gordon Highlanders: *s.* of William Duncan, Ploughman; of Morrone Cottage, Ballater, co. Aberdeen, by his wife Anne, *née* Young: and brother to Pte. 202830, C. Duncan, 8th Black Watch, killed in action 12 October 1917; and Pte. 290652, M. Duncan, Gordon Highlanders, died of wounds 7 October 1918: *b.* Glenmuick: enlisted Huntingdon. Killed in action 31 July 1917.

His brother Charles also has no known grave; he is commemorated on the Tyne Cot Memorial (Panel 95), Murray is buried in Bucquoy Road Cemetery, Ficheux (IV.E.20).

(Panel 38) L/Corpl. 266325, John Martin Ingram, 6th (Banff & Donside) Bn. The Gordon Highlanders (T.F.): *s.* of James Ingram, of Waulkmill Cottage, Insch, co. Aberdeen, Railwayman, by his wife Elsie (*née* Martin): *b.* Leslie, co. Aberdeen, *c.*May 1898: served with the Expeditionary Force in France and Flanders from 1917, and was killed in action at Ypres 31 July 1917. Shortly before zero hour on the morning of 31 July the front line trenches held by 6th Bn. Gordon Highlanders came under increasingly heavy enemy shelling, and the Gordons, steadily sustaining casualties, were forced to abandon their positions and move out into No Man's Land. At 5.13 a.m. the battalion began its advance towards Pilckem behind a creeping barrage. Encountering, and successfully eliminating, several enemy machine gun posts in the vicinity of Adam's Farm, Hurst Wood, Francois Farm and Racecourse Farm, all the battalion objectives were reached and consolidation begun by 7.30 a.m. Sometime between 3.50 a.m. and consolidation, nineteen year old L/Corpl. Ingram lost his life.

(Panel 38) L/Corpl. S/4367, William Lockerby, 'M' Coy., 8/10th (Service) Bn. The Gordon Highlanders: *s.* of the late William Lockerby, and Catherine McMillan Lockerby: *b.* Govan, co. Lanark: enlisted Whiteinch, Glasgow. Killed south-east of Langemarck, 3.50 a.m., 29 July 1917, when a section of the Gordon's assembly trench was directly hit by a German shell: Age 21. See Corpl. E.M. Pope, above.

(Panel 38) L/Corpl. 3431, James S. Young, 1st Bn. (75th Foot) The Gordon Highlanders: *b.* Stewarton, co. Ayr: enlisted Hamilton. Shot and killed by a sniper on the night of 2 – 3 March 1916, in the trenches

St. Eloi, France: Age 32. He was married to Margaret Lindsay Young (140, Low Waters, Hamilton, co. Lanark), and father to one child Laurence (died January 1917, aged six years).

(Panel 38) Pte. 2550, Robert Grant Beattie, 1/4th Bn. The Gordon Highlanders (T.F.): *s.* of Alexander Beattie, Carriage Cleaner, Joint Station, Aberdeen; by his wife Margaret, *dau.* of John Clark: *b.* Aberdeen, 12 January 1896: *educ.* Frederick Street Public Schools: Occupation – Labourer; Northern Agricultural Company, Aberdeen: joined Gordon Highlanders 15 October 1914: served with the Expeditionary Force in France and Flanders from 18 February. Killed in action at the Battle of Loos (*q.v.*), 25 September 1915. Buried to the south of Hooge: Age 19.

(Panel 38) Pte. 7789, Charles S. Bethell, 2nd Bn. (75th Foot) The Gordon Highlanders: *s.* of the late Henry Bethell, by his wife Helen Mary (57, Stanley Road, West Green, South Tottenham, London): and elder brother to Pte. SE/27127, H.E. Bethell, Army Veterinary Corps, died 27 June 1918: *b.* King's Langley, co. Kent: enlisted London. Killed in action 29 October 1914: Age 29.

His brother Herbert is commemorated in Tottenham Cemetery (Gen.7369, Screen Wall).

(Panel 38) Pte. 3/6818, Malcolm Brodie, 1st Bn. (75th Foot) The Gordon Highlanders: *b.* Bridge-of-Weir, co. Renfrew, *c.*1883: enlisted 3rd (Reserve) Bn. Gordon Highlanders, Glasgow, co. Lanark: proceeded to France with a draft of reinforcements to 1st Bn., and was killed in action 21 February 1916: Age 33. He leaves a widow, Agnes Brodie (Beechwood, Bridge-of-Weir). *Buried Perth Cemetery (China Wall), Zillebeke (I.G.17).*

(Panel 38) Pte. 702, Henry Cattanach, 2nd Bn. (75th Foot) The Gordon Highlanders: *s.* of James Cattanach, of Wellhouse, Birse, Aboyne, co. Aberdeen, by his wife Jessie: and elder brother to Pte. 2780, G. Cattanach, 1/7th Gordon Highlanders, killed in action 26 July 1916: *b.* Birse: enlisted Tarland: served with the Expeditionary Force in France from 7 October 1914, and was killed in action at Ypres on the 29th. of that month: Age 22. *unm.* Remembered on Invergowrie War Memorial.

His brother George is buried in Flatiron Copse Cemetery (VII.F.4).

(Panel 38) Pte. 2362, George Simpson Coutts, 1/4th Bn. The Gordon Highlanders (T.F.): 3rd *s.* of Edward Mitchell Coutts, Engineer; of 57, Union Grove, Aberdeen, by his wife Mary, *dau.* of Alexander Simpson: *b.* London, 10 December 1889: *educ.* Broomhill Public School, Aberdeen: Occupation – Stonecutter: served eight years R.A.M.C. (T.F.); obtaining rank Sergt.: joined Gordon Highlanders, September 1914; after the outbreak of war: went to France 14 February 1915, and was killed in action at Hooge, 25 September following. Buried at Ypres. He was a well-known member of Aberdeen Boys' Brigade: Age 25. *unm.*

(Panel 38) Pte. 4119, James Paterson Dargie, 1/4th Bn. The Gordon Highlanders (T.F.): eldest *s.* of Thomas Dargie, Fireman; of 27, Gordon Street, Aberdeen, by his wife Mary Ann, *dau.* of James Fox: *b.* Aberdeen, 25 December 1893: *educ.* Marywell Public School, Aberdeen: Occupation – Apprentice Ironbound Cooper: joined Gordon Highlanders, 13 April 1915: went to France 15 July. Killed in action at Hooge, 25 September following. Buried at Hooge: Age 20. He *m.* Aberdeen, 26 June 1915, Mary Ann, *dau.* of Harry Fraser. (*IWGC record age 21*)

(Panel 38) Pte. 3/7292, Alexander Dowall, 1st Bn. (75th Foot) The Gordon Highlanders: *s.* of James Dowall, of 5, Mount Pleasant Street, Greenock, co. Renfrew, by his late wife Jessie: and brother to A/ Corpl. S/6771, J. Dowall, Gordon Highlanders, killed in action 27 September 1918: *b.* Greenock, 1889: enlisted Glasgow, posted 3rd (Reserve) Battn.: subsequent to heavy losses incurred by 1st Battn. at Le Cateau, proceeded to France with a draft of reinforcements 14 February 1915; and was killed in action four days later 18 February 1915: Age 26.

His brother James is buried in Ruyaulcourt Military Cemetery (N.20).

(Panel 38) Pte. 254, David McLeod Duncan, Signaller; 2nd Bn. (92nd Foot) The Gordon Highlanders: *yst. s.* of the late Donaldson Rose Duncan, by his wife Jane, *dau.* of William Leiper (late of 27, Short Loanings, Aberdeen): *b.* Farmer's Hall Lane, Aberdeen, 20 December 1888: *educ.* there: enlisted 2 February 1907: served with the Expeditionary Force in France and Flanders from 7 October 1914, and was reported missing 4 November following, during the First Battle of Ypres assumed killed on or about that date: Age 25. *unm.* (*IWGC record 11 November 1914*)

(Panel 38) Pte. S/3316, John Dunn, 'B' Coy., 1st Bn. (75th Foot) The Gordon Highlanders: *s.* of Mr (& Mrs) Dunn, of 52, Barrowfield Street, Bridgeton, Glasgow: *husb.* to the late Agnes Christie Dunn: served in the South African Campaign (Silver medal), and with the Expeditionary Force in France and Flanders. Died 2 March 1916, of wounds received on the field of battle: Age 27.

(Panel 38) Pte. 1661, Gilbert Forbes, 'B' Coy., 4th Bn. The Gordon Highlanders (T.F.): *s.* of the late James Forbes, of Bleachfield House, Persleyden, Woodside, co. Aberdeen, by his wife Elizabeth ('Gownlea,' Fauldhouse, co. West Lothian): and *yr.* brother to Pte. 109342, W.G. Forbes, 4th Canadian Mounted Rifles, killed in action at Mount Sorrel, 2 June 1916, aged 22; and AB. (Clyde) Z/800, J.G. Forbes, Howe Bn., R.N.V.R., killed in action 26 October 1917: *b.* Woodside, *c.*1896: enlisted Aberdeen: served with the Expeditionary Force. Killed in action 25 September 1915: Age 19.

His brothers Walter and Joseph also have no known grave; Walter is recorded Panel 32; Joseph, Tyne Cot Memorial (Panel 2).

(Panel 38) Pte. S/7055, Robert Gardiner, 1st Bn. (75th Foot) The Gordon Highlanders: *b.* Kilmarnock, co. Ayr: served with the Expeditionary Force in France from July 1915. Killed in action 25 September 1915. *Commemorated on the Loos Memorial, Dud Corner. IWGC/MR19, Pt.V., pg.263.*

(Panel 38) Pte. S/2385, Robert Gray, 1st Bn. (75th Foot) The Gordon Highlanders: eldest *s.* of George Gray, Engineer; by his wife Martha, *dau.* of John Johnson: *b.* Newcastle-on-Tyne, 1 September 1882: *educ.* there: Occupation – Cloth Industry employee: enlisted Glasgow, 1 September 1914, after the outbreak of war: served with the Expeditionary Force in France and Flanders from 4 December following, and was killed in action 3 March 1916, being hit by a fragment of a shell after the bayonet charge in which the Gordons took the International Trench from the Germans. Buried where he fell: Age 33. He *m.* St. Aiden's Church, Gateshead-on-Tyne, 1 February 1901; Eleanor (2, Northbank Terrace, Kelvinside North, Glasgow), *dau.* of Charles John Rowley, and had a son – John Robert, *b.* 4 May 1902.

(Panel 38) Pte. 2956, James Kidd, 1/4th Bn. The Gordon Highlanders (T.F.): eldest *s.* of James Kidd, Gamekeeper; of Wardes Road, Inverurie, co. Aberdeen, by his wife Elizabeth Jane, *dau.* of Robert Watson: *b.* Belhelvie, co. Aberdeen, 16 February 1895: *educ.* Inverurie Public School, and, on leaving school was Apprentice Draper, afterwards being employed with an Aberdeen firm: enlisted Gordon Highlanders, Aberdeen, October 1914, after the outbreak of war: proceeded to France, served with the Expeditionary Force there and in Flanders from 19 February 1915. Wounded – returned to front line duty July 1915, and was killed in action 23 December 1915. Buried in the Dorsets' Cemetery, south of Verbrand-Molen: Age 20. *unm.*

(Panel 38) Pte. S/3343, Martin Charles Lyden, 'B' Coy., 1st Bn. (75th Foot) The Gordon Highlanders: eldest *s.* of Martin Lyden, by his 2nd wife Agnes (47, Kirk Street, Calton, Glasgow), eldest *dau.* of Hugh Biggart, of Glasgow: *b.* Calton, 9 June 1891: *educ.* St. Alphonsus's School, Glasgow: Occupation – Shipbuilding yard worker: enlisted 1 September 1914, after the outbreak of war: served with the Expeditionary Force in France and Flanders from December following, and was killed in action at Ypres, 2 March 1916, while charging a communication trench. Buried there behind the trenches. The Chaplain wrote, "Early that morning he took part in an engagement with his battalion, and was killed while charging a communication trench by himself. For this gallant act I understand he is being recommended for distinction;" and 2nd Lieut. W.R. Watt, "He was killed on the morning of the 2nd in the attack made by the battalion on the German trenches. He had shown conspicuous bravery all through, and died fighting bravely in a trench full of Germans. I have recommended him to Headquarters for his distinguished services, and I have every hope of his being awarded the D.C.M. I feel his loss keenly, as well as his comrades do, with whom he was a general favourite, and I always found him a most obliging and willing lad." Age 25. *unm.*

(Panel 38) Pte. 7707, James Maxwell, 2nd Bn. (92nd Foot) The Gordon Highlanders: late of Kilwinning, co. Ayr: On the outbreak of war, August 1914, was with his Battn. at its peacetime depot in

Egypt: arrived Zeebrugge, France 7 October 1914, went to the Front line at Ypres, 23 October and was killed in action near the Menin Road, during the First Battle of Ypres, 29 October 1914. Three weeks after his arrival in France; six days after arrival at Ypres.

(Panel 38) Pte. S/3218, Charles McKerracher, 'C' Coy., 1st Bn. (75th Foot) The Gordon Highlanders: *s.* of Peter McKerracher, of 72, Lumley Street, Grangemouth, by his wife Alice: and brother to Pnr. WR/267810, P. McKerracher, Royal Engineers, died 14 November 1918, aged 24 years: *b.* Grangemouth, co. Stirling: enlisted there. Killed in action, 2 March 1916: Age 21. *unm.*

His brother Peter is buried in Terlincthun British Cemetery (X.E.24).

(Panel 38) Pte. 3/5655, Alick McLeod, 1st Bn. (75th Foot) The Gordon Highlanders: brother to Pte. 3/5667, D. McLeod, Gordon Highlanders, died of wounds received the same day: *b.* Point, co. Ross: enlisted Stornoway. Killed in action during an ill-conceived attack on a German strongpoint at Wytschaete, 14 December 1914. See also Irish House Cemetery.

His brother Donald is known to be buried in Kemmel Churchyard (Sp.Mem.11).

(Panel 38) Pte. 9275, William McWhirter, 1st Bn. (75th Foot) The Gordon Highlanders: *s.* of Peter McWhirter, of Burn Street, Dalbeattie; late of 100, Friars Vennel, Dumfries, by his wife Mary A.: and elder brother to Pte. 11523, J. McWhirter, King's Own Scottish Borderers, killed in action 2 June 1915; and Pte. A. McWhirter, Highland Light Infantry (surv'd.), and Pte. T. McWhirter, Canadian Infantry (surv'd.): *b.* Lochmaben, co. Dumfries, *c.*1883: enlisted Kilmarnock: served with his regiment in India, South Africa; with the Expeditionary Force in France and Flanders from August 1914. Missing believed killed in action 14 December 1914, on which date 1st Gordons were tasked with attacking a strongly wired and highly fortified German position in the vicinity of Maedelstade Farm. Attacking up hill, through mud – in places over a foot deep – the battalion suffered casualties of 260 killed, wounded and missing from a force which began 560 strong: Age 31. The brothers McWhirter are remembered on the Southwick (Caulkerbush) War Memorial.

His brother John also has no known grave; he is recorded on Panel 22.

(Panel 38) Pte. 1736, Robert H. Middleton, 4th Bn. The Gordon Highlanders (T.F.): *s.* of David Middleton, Farmer; of Cockley, Maryculter, Aberdeen, by his wife Isabella: and yr. brother to 2nd Lieut. E.R.R. Middleton, 6th Seaforth Highlanders, killed in action 9 April 1917: *b.* Anfield, Liverpool, 5 December 1892: *educ.* Robert Gorrillege, Aberdeen University (matriculated Arts, 1912): enlisted University Coy., 4th Gordon Highlanders, Aberdeen 1913: trained Bedford: proceeded to France, February 1915, and was killed in action 1 June following, nr. Hooge: Age 22. *unm.* A University friend who was with him in the trenches wrote, "He was not one of those who grow less lovable as they grow more intimately known, because he had sympathy, taste and understanding. With his eyes open, realising all the sacrifice he might be called upon to make, he yet was eager for the glorious glad adventure, and, following the path of duty, joined the ranks of those whose life was all tomorrow and they died to-day."

His brother Edwin is buried in Maroeuil British Cemetery (IV.D.14).

(Panel 38) Pte. 6619, William Mills, 2nd Bn. The Gordon Highlanders: late of 12, Kilsyth Road, Kirkintilloch, co. Dumbarton: a pre-war Reservist, served in the South African Campaign, rejoined the Colours on mobilisation 4 August 1914; proceeded to France 7 October, and died of wounds on the 31st. of that month received at the Battle of Ypres; the circumstances being that after being wounded he was conveyed to an ambulance wagon but so serious were the nature of his wounds he died shortly thereafter in the hands of the ambulance men, and was buried at Ypres on the same date. He leaves a widow and two sons, the eldest of whom attended school for the first time on the day of his father's departure for France.

(Panel 38) Pte. 1750, David Mitchell, 4th Bn. The Gordon Highlanders (T.F.): *s.* of James (& the late Mrs.) Mitchell, of 38, Don Street, Aberdeen: and yr. brother to Pte. 2664, J. Mitchell, 4th Gordon Highlanders, killed in action 19 July 1915: *b.* Aberdeen: enlisted there. Killed in action 16 June 1915: Age 20. *unm.*

His brother James also has no known grave; he is recorded below.

(Panel 38) Pte. 2664, James Mitchell, 4th Bn. The Gordon Highlanders (T.F.): *s.* of James (& the late Mrs.) Mitchell, of 38, Don Street, Aberdeen: and elder brother to Pte. 1750, D. Mitchell, 4th Gordon Highlanders, killed in action 16 June 1915: *b.* Aberdeen: enlisted there. Killed in action 19 July 1915:Age 22. *unm.*

His brother David also has no known grave; he is recorded above.

(Panel 38) Pte. 285086, John Purves, 6th Bn.(Banff & Donside) The Gordon Highlanders (T.F.): *s.* of John Purves, of 25, Lingerwood Road, Newton Grange, co. Midlothian, by his wife Margaret: and brother to L/Corpl. S/11079, J. Purves, 2nd Cameron Highlanders, who also fell: *b.* Reston, co. Berwick: enlisted Coatbridge, co. Lanark. Killed in action 31 July 1917: Age 21. *unm.*

His brother James also has no known grave; he is recorded below.

(Panel 38) Pte. 6186, Scott Robertson, 1st Bn. (75th Foot) The Gordon Highlanders: *s.* of the late Henry Robertson, by his wife Louisa Ann (Edinburgh): served 17 years with the Colours: served in the South African Campaign; and with the Expeditionary Force in France and Flanders, and was killed in action 14 December 1914: Age 34.

(Panel 38) Pte. S/41066, William Hercules Todd, 8/10th Bn. The Gordon Highlanders: *s.* of William Todd, of 51, Millgate, Friockheim, co. Forfar, and Mary Ann Norrie, his wife: Occupation – Yarn Bleacher; Robert Wood, Friockheim: joined 3rd Black Watch, October 1916; transf'd. 10th Gordon Highlanders, proceeded to France early 1917: took part in the fighting at Arras (wounded), April 1917, and was killed in action at Ypres 31 July following: Age 27. His brother served in France with the Royal Field Artillery.

(Panel 38) Pte. S/7664, John Torrance, 1st Bn. (75th Foot) The Gordon Highlanders: *s.* of Alexander Torrance, of 44, Barrowfield Street, Bridgeton, Glasgow, co. Lanark, by his wife Isabella: and brother to Pte. 100, J. Torrance, Argyll & Sutherland Highlanders; killed in action 25 February 1915, at Ypres: *b.* Bridgeton: enlisted Glasgow: served in France from February 1915, and was killed in action 17 June 1915: Age 33.

His brother James also has no known grave; he is recorded on Panel 44.

(Panel 38) Pte. 291136, Andrew Whannell, 7th Bn. (Deeside Highland) The Gordon Highlanders (T.F.): *s.* of Hugh Whannell, of 30, Ann Street, Stonehaven, co. Kincardine: enlisted Banchory. Killed south-east of Langemarck, 3.50 a.m., 29 July 1917, when a section of the Gordon's assembly trench was directly hit by a German shell: Age 21. The same shell also killed Brigade-Major, Capt. H.H. Lean, Corpl. E.M. Pope, L/Corpl. W. Lockerby; and mortally wounded Brigadier-General A.F. Gordon, Comdg. 153rd Inf.Bde. (51st Divn.) who was visiting the Gordon's front-line trenches at the time. Pte. Whannell is remembered on the Black Hill (Stonehaven) War Memorial, Aberdeenshire; the interior lintel of which is engraved with a quotation from Donald Hankey's '*Student in Arms*':–

'One By One Death Challenged Them,
They Smiled In His Grim Visage And Refused To Be Dismayed'

Capt. Lean is buried in Poperinghe New Military Cemetery (II.G.35); Corpl. Pope and L/Corpl. Lockerby have no known grave, they are recorded above; Brigdr.Gen. Gordon died of his wounds two days later and is buried in Lijssenthoek Military Cemetery (XIV.A.13). Donald Hankey (2nd Lieut., Royal Warwickshire Regt.) was killed at the Somme, 12 October 1916; he too has no known grave and is commemorated on the Thiepval Memorial.

(Panel 38) Capt. Ewen James Brodie, 1st Bn. (79th Foot) The Queen's Own (Cameron Highlanders): 11th Laird of Lethen and Coulmony: 2nd & only *survg s.* of the late James Campbell John Brodie, 9th Laird of Lethen and Coulmony, Lord Lieut. of co. Nairn, by his wife Fanny Sophia Constance, *dau.* of Edmund Thomas Wedgwood Wood, of Henley Hall, co. Salop.: *b.* Lethen, 17 July 1878: *educ.* Harrow, and Trinity College, Cambridge: gazetted 2nd Lieut., 2nd Cameron Highlanders, from the Militia, 26 May 1900; promoted Lieut. 22 January 1902; Capt. 3 May 1911: served in the Mediterranean, Africa and China, and from 1909 to 1913 was Adjutant, Lovat Scouts (T.F.), when he rejoined 1st Cameron Highlanders, Edinburgh Castle. Went to the Front, August 1914, with the Expeditionary Force; took part in the Battle of the Aisne, and all the fighting preliminary to the First Battle of Ypres, and fell in action in the encounter with the Prussian Guard at Ypres, 11 November 1914. Acting Adjt. 1st Battn., at the time of his death; he was one of only three surviving officers of the regiment who, only ten weeks previously, had proudly marched away from Edinburgh Castle. Buried near to some men of his regt.; close to the spot where he fell: Age 36. He *m.* 4 January 1911; Marion Louisa, eldest *dau.* of William Stirling, of Fairburn and Monar, co. Ross, and had three children – David James, *b.* 27 October 1911; Helen Charlotte, *b.* 22 June 1913; Peter Ewen, *b.* 6 May 1914. (*IWGC record 12 November 1914*)

The weather on 31 July 1917 had begun slightly overcast, but by mid-afternoon torrential rain (heralding the wettest August in living memory) had begun to fall. The battlefield surrounding Ypres, which three years of continuous bombardment and fighting on both sides had turned into a scene of devastation even Dante's wildest nightmares could not match had, by the end of the day, begun to resemble a swamp. After all day attacking the enemy in their heavily fortified positions and concrete pill-boxes, taking enormous numbers of casualties in the process, the exhausted survivors of the attacking British units found whatever shelter their objective afforded them (or where-ever fate had decreed they end up) and 'held on' as best they could. Throughout the night with the sound of machine-gun bullets whipping and snapping all around them and shells hurtling through the night sky, men huddled in shell-holes, surrounded by the wounded, dying and dead, waiting for the light of dawn to assess their situation. In the vicinity of Iberian Farm at dawn Pte. W. Morgan, 'dozing in a shell-hole, awoke with the rain still beating on his face. It was a large shell-hole, half-full of water…opposite Bill was an officer of the Cameron Highlanders who had crawled in during the night. He lay at an awkward angle, his mud-coated legs sticking out from beneath a bedraggled kilt. There wasn't a mark on his body, but his head lay under the water. Bill could see his face quite clearly. The eyes were closed. He had slipped in and drowned in his sleep."

It is believed the Cameron Highlander officer referred to was:–

(Panel 38) Capt. Cameron Roy Carruthers, 4th Bn. The Queen's Own (Cameron Highlanders): *s.* of Sir William Carruthers, of Beckenham, co. Kent; formerly of the British Linen Bank; National & Provincial Bank; and (from 1918) Deputy General Manager, Barclays Bank Ltd. Missing / believed killed 31 July 1917: Age 28. He leaves a widow Maud Carruthers (Bedford).

(Panel 38) Capt. Alan Arthur Fowler, 'B' Coy., 2nd Bn. (79th Foot) The Queen's Own (Cameron Highlanders): 2nd & *yst. s.* of the late Sir John Arthur Fowler, 2nd Bart.; of Inverbroom House, Lochbroom, Braemore, co. Ross, by his marriage to Alice Janet Clive Bayley, Lady Fowler; *dau.* of Sir Edward Clive Bayley, by his wife Emily Ann Theophilia Metcalfe: *gdson.* to the late Sir John Fowler (*d.* 1898), Engineer-in-Chief, Forth Bridge: and brother to Capt. Sir J.E. Fowler, 2nd attd. 1/4th Seaforth Highlanders, killed in action 22 June 1915, nr. Richebourg L'Avoue: *b.* Inverbroom, Lochbroom, co. Ross, 27 February 1887: *educ.* Harrow (Elmfield), and Royal Military College, Sandhurst: gazetted 2nd Lieut. Cameron Highlanders, May 1907; promoted Lieut. April 1911; Capt. February 1915: served with the Expeditionary Force in France and Flanders, and was killed in action, about noon, 28 April 1915, while in command of his company which was occupying the front trench on the lip of a huge crater 40 feet deep, formed by the explosion of a mine. It was the last day the Battalion occupied these trenches, and he, his subaltern, and several men were killed by the same shell – a *minenwerfer* bomb: Age 28. Brigdr.-Gen. MacFarlane, Comdg. 81st Bde., said, "He was a first-rate soldier and a dear good fellow, for whom I had a great regard, and I always wished I had him on my Staff. He will be dreadfully missed, both in his Regiment and in the Brigade." Col. J. Campbell, Comdg. 2nd Cameron Highlanders, wrote, "He died a soldier's death about 12 noon to-day, when holding a trench in a difficult and important position. I cannot speak too highly of the truly gallant way in which he has behaved and kept his men together and cheerful." And a brother-officer, "During the week on Hill 60 he was never once depressed, though all of them, and his Company in particular, were having a very rough time." Capt. Fowler was a keen sportsman, especially fond of shooting and all games. He *m.* Bankipore, India, December 1912; Alice

Mary, *yst. dau.* of Sir Charles Bayley, G.C.S.I., by his wife Lady Bayley, and leaves a *dau.* Marjorie Mary, *b.* Bangalore, India, September 1913.

His brother John's remains were repatriated to the family estate (Braemore, nr. Garve) and buried with full military honours in Foich Burial Ground; the private cemetery there. Prior to mid-1915 the repatriation of remains was permitted, and the bodies of a small number of officers, the cost borne by their families, are known to have been returned to the U.K. The ban forbidding repatriation was put in place for a number of reasons; primarily due to issues of logistics, health and the effect the repatriation of thousands of bodies would have on national morale.

(Panel 38) Lieut. James Richard Haig Anderson, 'A' Coy., 2nd Bn. (79th Foot) The Queen's Own (Cameron Highlanders): 2nd *s.* of Alexander Cunningham Anderson, of 'The Homestead,' Prestwick, co. Ayr, by his wife Jessie Cunningham, *dau.* of the late James Richard Haig, of Blairhill, co. Perth: and yr. brother to Capt. R.C. Anderson, 1st Black Watch, died of wounds 26 September 1915: *b.* 22 February 1893: *educ.* Bilton Grange, Rugby, and Royal Military College, Sandhurst, out of which he passed fifth; took prize for Military Administration: gazetted 2nd Lieut. Indian Army (Unatt'd. List), January 1912: exchanged November 1912, 2nd Cameron Highlanders; joined Bangalore, India: promoted Lieut. December 1914, and went to the Front in France the same month, and was killed at Hooge, nr. Ypres, 11 May 1915. His Captain wrote, "Your son Dick was in command of 'A' Company, and on Tuesday, the 11th May, 'A' and 'B' Companies were holding the advanced fire of our position. About 10 a.m. both companies were forced to evacuate the trenches by reason of the appalling shell-fire, bombing and gassing. Your son, together with the Captain of 'B' Company, collected their men in the rear of the trench and charged, forcing the Germans to retreat at the point of the bayonet. The Captain of 'B' Company told me that never in his life had he seen, or imagined possible, conduct so magnificent as that of your son. Knowing Dick as I did, this is only what I and his brother officers expected of him." Lieut. J.R.H. Anderson was a fine shot and a promising golfer, having made a reputation for himself at Ootacamund, and also at Prestwick in the open championship of 1914. He was a member of Prestwick Golf Club, and the Caledonian Club, London: Age 22. *unm.*

His brother Robert is buried in Noeux-Les-Mines Communal Cemetery (I.K.7).

(Panel 38) Lieut. Ronald Mosse Macdonald, 1st Bn. (79th Foot) The Queen's Own (Cameron Highlanders): elder *s.* of William Mosse Macdonald, late Capt. 3rd Cameron Highlanders; of Glenmore, Isle of Skye, and Mrs Macdonald (Glenmore Cottage, East Avenue, Bournemouth): *b.* Bombay, India, 9 December 1890: *educ.* Horris Hill, Newbury; Winchester College; Royal Military College, Sandhurst, from whence he obtained his commission 2nd Lieut., Cameron Highlanders, November 1910: Signalling Officer to his battalion, 1913: promoted Lieut. August 1914: left Edinburgh Castle with his battalion on the 12th of that month, with twenty-five officers, of whom, when he fell, he was the last one remaining: wounded 14 September following, at the Battle of the Aisne: after recovery rejoined his battalion 8 October, and fell in action at Veldhoek, nr. Ypres, 2 November 1914. Lieut. Macdonald was an accomplished violinist. He was a member of the Aldershot Cricket XI, 1911 – 12, and The Caledonian Club, London: Age 24. *unm.*

(Panel 38) 2nd Lieut. Harry Lawson Fairbairn, 4th Bn. The Queen's Own (Cameron Highlanders), (T.F.) attd. 10th (Scottish) Bn. King's (Liverpool) Regt. (T.F.): *s.* of Mrs Catherine Fairbairn (29, Brougham Street, Edinburgh), late of 7, Gayfield Square, Edinburgh: and brother to Pte. 201451, D.H. Fairbairn, Cameron Highlanders, killed in action 31 July 1917: enlisted 4th Bn. (Queen's Edinburgh Rifles) Royal Scots, 1914: served with the Expeditionary Force at Gallipoli from June 1915; wounded there: on recovery obtained a commission Cameron Highlanders, and was killed in action at Ypres, attd. King's Liverpool Regt., 2 August 1917: Age 26.

His brother Donald also has no known grave; he is recorded below.

(Panel 38) 2nd Lieut. Robert Rae McIntosh, 2nd Bn. (79th Foot) The Queen's Own (Cameron Highlanders): *yst. s.* of the Rev. Robert McIntosh, D.D. (Senior Minister, Alva West United Free Church), of 92, Craiglea Drive, Edinburgh, by his wife Helen, *dau.* of the late Thomas Stevens, of Ardline,

Helensburgh: *b.* The West Manse, Alva, Stirling, 8 May 1888: *educ.* Dollar Academy, and Edinburgh University (graduated M.A., 1908): on the outbreak of war was studying for LL.B. degree: gazetted 2nd Lieut. (Special Reserve) Cameron Highlanders, 14 April 1914; joined his regt. 1 July following: went to France 20 February 1915, and was killed in action at Hill 60, during the night of 23 – 24 April 1915. Buried nr. Hill 60, to the east of the Ypres-Lille railway: Age 26. *unm.* Remembered on his parents' headstone Alva Cemetery, Clamannan. (*IWGC record 24 April 1915*)

(Panel 38) Sergt. 7203, Archibald 'Archie' Bowie, 1st Bn. (79th Foot) The Queen's Own (Cameron Highlanders): *s.* of John Bowie, of 'Carnan,' Fochar, Lochboisdale, South Uist: and brother to Pte. 3220, A. Bowie, Cameron Highlanders, who also fell: served with the Expeditionary Force. Killed in action at Ypres, 22 October 1914: Age 29. *unm.*

His brother Angus also has no known grave; he is recorded below.

(Panel 38) Sergt. 9215, David McGillivray, 6th (Service) Bn. The Queen's Own (Cameron Highlanders): *s.* of the late John McGillivray, of 35, Ferry Road, Leith, co. Midlothian, and Helen Fraser McGillivray, his wife: and yr. brother to Pte. S/7854, J. McGillivray, 2nd Seaforth Highlanders, killed in action 11 April 1917: *b.* Inverness: enlisted there: served with the Expeditionary Force in France from 1915. Missing / presumed killed 31 July 1917: Age 25.

His brother John also has no known grave; he is commemorated on the Arras Memorial (Bay 8).

Prior to the outbreak of war in 1914 West Calder, fourteen miles west of Edinburgh, was a prosperous and lively village; most of its inhabitants being employed in farming, mining and oil processing. By 1918 over 180 men from the village had volunteered to serve their country and joined the ranks of the fallen. Reflecting on their sacrifice the parish priest, Reverend Anderson, said, "One of the most remarkable things about the present war, one of the glories that swim up through all its horrors and atrocities, and for the moment submerges them, is the courage which is manifested not merely by the saint or hero, but by just the average ordinary man. They have gone out from our shops and offices, from our factories and farms, and mines and they are just the kind of men you and I are accustomed to meet from day to day in our common life and all for the cause of King and Country." One such man, local mine worker, Thomas Torrance:–

(Panel 38) Sergt. S/15620, Thomas Torrance, 'B' Coy., 7th (Service) Bn. The Queen's Own (Cameron Highlanders): *yst. s.* of Mrs Torrance (Dickson Street, West Calder, co. Midlothian) and the late Alexander Torrance, of Drummonds Buildings, West Calder: served with the Expeditionary Force in France and Flanders from May 1915. Killed in action 28 July 1917. The local press recorded:– "We regret to announce the sad news which reached West Calder yesterday that Sergt. Thomas Torrance of the Cameron Highlanders…was killed in action on the 28th July. Sergt. Torrance early answered his country's call for men, having enlisted in December 1914. After a period of training he was sent to France, and had been in active service for two years and two months, during which time he had taken part in many of the big engagements. He was home on leave during the summer, and was in fine health and spirits. In civil life he worked as a dispatch clerk with Young's Oil Company, and at a later date was employed with the Fife Coal Company at Cowdenbeath. Sincere sympathy will be felt for Mrs Torrance and the family circle in the sad bereavement they have sustained. The sad news was conveyed in the following letter received from Lieut. ….., 'Sergt. Torrance was killed whilst coming out of the trenches near…on the night of 28th July by shell fire. It may be some small consolation to you to know that death was instantaneous and your son had not suffered. The matter was the more unfortunate in that we had just been relieved from a spell in the trenches and were on our way back for a short rest. Such is the fortune of war.'"

(Panel 38) Corpl. 5391, James Aberdeen, 'B' Coy. 2nd Bn. (79th Foot) The Queen's Own (Cameron Highlanders): *b.* Durham, 8 June 1880: joined Army, 10 July 1900: served nine years with the Colours; five years Reserve, and held the South African Campaign medal with 4 clasps; called up on the outbreak of war and, after going through the Battle of Ypres, was killed by a shell, 30 April 1915, while resting in a wood: Age 32. He *m.* 26 March 1900; Brandon, Co. Durham, Margaret Hannah, *dau.* of George Stringer, of New Brancepeth, Durham, and had two children – Vera Rebecca, *b.* 19 October 1911; James Gordon, *b.* 16 May 1913.

(Panel 38) Corpl. S/11312, Thomas Adamson, 2nd Bn. (79th Foot) The Queen's Own (Cameron Highlanders): *yst. s.* of Robert Adamson, of Garfield, Cardross, co. Dumbarton: and brother to Gnr. 810715, A. Adamson, Royal Field Artillery, killed in action 30 July 1917, at Ypres: *b.* Cardross: former employee Bank of Scotland: enlisted Edinburgh: went to France and was killed in action there 11 May 1915: Age 24. *unm.* The brothers Adamson are remembered on Cardross (Dumbarton; Helensburgh District) War Memorial. (*IWGC record S/1312*)

His brother Archibald also has no known grave; he is recorded on Panel 5.

(Panel 38) Corpl. 8440, John Dick Hutton, 2nd Bn. (79th Foot) The Queen's Own (Cameron Highlanders): *s.* of the late James Hutton, Chartered Accountant; of Glasgow: and *gdson.* of the late Rev. Harper, D.D., of Edinburgh: and *yr.* brother to Lieut. F.R.H. Hutton, Argyll & Sutherland Highlanders, died 10 May 1915: *b.* Cadder, co. Dumbarton, *c.*1876: enlisted Edinburgh, co. Midlothian: served with the Expeditionary Force in France and Flanders from 20 December 1914, and was killed in action 6 February 1915: Age 38.

His brother Frederick also has no known grave; he is recorded on Panel 42.

(Panel 38) L/Corpl. 8040, Henry Cuthbertson, 2nd Bn. (79th Foot) The Queen's Own (Cameron Highlanders): *s.* of Malcolm Cuthbertson, of 24, Mid Arthur Place, Edinburgh, by his wife Helen: and elder brother to Pte. S/16277, M. Cuthbertson, 2nd Cameron Highlanders, killed in the same action: *b.* Edinburgh: enlisted Glencorse. Killed in action 11 May 1915: Age 27.

His brother Malcolm also has no known grave; he is recorded below.

(Panel 38) L/Corpl. S/16266, John Murray, 2nd Bn. (79th Foot) The Queen's Own (Cameron Highlanders): *s.* of Alexander Murray, of 16, Milbrae Crescent, Langside, Glasgow, co. Lanark, by his wife Elizabeth: *b.* Mount Florida, co. Lanark, *c.*1891: enlisted Glasgow. Killed in action 11 May 1915: Age 24. *unm.* Remains recovered Small Battle Cemetery, Sanctuary Wood; 'Unknown British Soldier. Cameron Hdrs.,' identified – Titles, Kilt mkd. 16266; reinterred, registered 28 February 1928. *Buried in Sanctuary Wood Cemetery (II.D.3).*

(Panel 38) L/Corpl. S/11079, James Purves, 2nd Bn. (79th Foot) The Queen's Own (Cameron Highlanders): *s.* of John Purves, of 25, Lingerwood Road, Newton Grange, co. Midlothian, by his wife Margaret: and elder brother to Pte. 285086, J. Purves, 6th Gordon Highlanders, killed in action 31 July 1917: *b.* Coldingham, co. Berwick: enlisted Cambuslang, co. Lanark. Killed in action 8 May 1915: Age 25. *unm.*

His brother John also has no known grave; he is recorded above.

(Panel 38) Pte. 3220, Angus Bowie, 1st Bn. (79th Foot) The Queen's Own (Cameron Highlanders): *s.* of John Bowie, of 'Carnan,' Fochar, Lochboisdale, South Uist: and brother to Sergt. 7203, A. Bowie, 1st Cameron Highlanders, killed in action the same day: served with the Expeditionary Force in France. Killed in action at Ypres, 11 November 1914: Age 31. *unm.*

His brother Archibald also has no known grave; he is recorded above.

(Panel 38) Pte. S/15723, John Briggs Dunlop, 2nd Bn. (79th Foot) The Queen's Own (Cameron Highlanders): *s.* of Archibald Dunlop, of 6, Melville Place, Carluke, co. Lanark, by his wife Mary Briggs: and *yr.* brother to Pte. S/30005, W. Dunlop, 1st Cameron Highlanders, killed in action 17 September 1918, aged 25 years: *b.* Maybole, co. Ayr: enlisted Carluke. Killed in action 10 May 1915: Age 20. *unm.*

His brother William is buried in Roisel Communal Cemetery Extension (III.L.10).

(Panel 38) Pte. S/16277, Malcolm Cuthbertson, 2nd Bn. (79th Foot) The Queen's Own (Cameron Highlanders): *s.* of Malcolm Cuthbertson, of 24, Mid Arthur Place, Edinburgh, by his wife Helen: and *yr.* brother to L/Corpl. 8040, H. Cuthbertson, 2nd Cameron Highlanders, killed in the same action: *b.* St. Leonards: enlisted Edinburgh: served with the Expeditionary Force, and was killed in action 11 May 1915: Age 23.

His brother Henry also has no known grave; he is recorded above.

(Panel 38) Pte. 201451, Donald Hugh Fairburn, 7th (Service) Bn. The Queen's Own (Cameron Highlanders): late of Colinton, co. Midlothian: *s.* of Mrs Catherine Fairburn (29, Brougham Street, Edinburgh), late of 7, Gayfield Square, Edinburgh: and brother to 2nd Lieut. H.L. Lawson, Cameron Highlanders attd. King's (Liverpool) Regt., killed 2 August 1917: enlisted Edinburgh: served with the Expeditionary Force in France and Flanders, and was killed in action 31 July 1917: Age 30.

His brother Harry also has no known grave; he is recorded above.

(Panel 38) Pte. 5122, David Millar, 'A' Coy., 1st Bn. (79th Foot) The Queen's Own (Cameron Highlanders): late of 34, New Street, Stevenston: *b.* Rutherglen, co. Lanark: a pre-war Reservist (previously served in the South African Campaign) was, on the outbreak of war, employee to Messrs Nobel (Explosive Manufacturers): re-called on mobilisation, re-joined the regiment at Edinburgh and proceeded to France: served with the Expeditionary Force there from 14 August 1914, and has been missing since 11 November following. Any information regarding him will be thankfully received by his wife and / or sister, Mrs D. Millar (258 Nuneaton Street, Bridgeton); Mrs Gilmour (188 French Street, Bridgeton). Remembered on Stevenston War Memorial.

(Panel 38) Pte. 8358, Thomas Laing Ramsay, 2nd Bn. (79th Foot) The Queen's Own (Cameron Highlanders): *s.* of the late Thomas Alexander Ramsay, by his wife Jessie, *née* McMillan (37, Harrybrook Street, Belfast): a pre-war Regular, on the outbreak of war was detached from his battn. to Military Telegraphist duties, Bangalore, India, rejoined his battn. October 1914, at Poona, and departing from Bombay for the European War on the 16th of that month: served with the Expeditionary Force in France from December 1914, and was killed in action 28 April 1915: Age 24. *unm.*

PANEL 38 ENDS PTE. J. SPENCE – CAMERON HIGHLANDERS.

PANEL 40 BEGINS PTE. T. SPICER – CAMERON HIGHLANDERS.

(Panel 40) Pte. 8098, Samuel Henderson Stallard, 2nd Bn. (79th Foot) The Queen's Own (Cameron Highlanders): late of Coatdyke, Airdrie: previously served in India. Found dead in the trenches 11 January 1915; died of exposure – froze to death.

(Panel 40) Pte. 9902, William Stroyan, 1st Bn. (79th Foot) The Queen's Own (Cameron Highlanders): late of Drunmore, co. Wigtown: *s.* of William Stroyan, Police Constable; of Path Cottage, Blackcraig, Newton Stewart, co. Wigtown, by his 1st wife Lillian McLelland Stroyan, *née* Kelly: stepson to Mary Stroyan, *née* Galloway: and elder brother to Sergt. 200489, C.F. Stroyan, 1st Cameron Highlanders, killed in action 18 April 1918; and L/Corpl. 18257, J. Stroyan, 11th Highland Light Infantry, killed in action 11 March 1916: *b.* Mainsriddle, Southwick, co. Kirkcudbright, 1882: previously served 12 years; served in the South African Campaign, and in France and Flanders: re-enlisted Leven, co. Fife, August 1914. Missing (believed killed) in action 11 November 1914, at Ypres: Age 32.

His brother Charles also has no known grave, he is commemorated on the Loos Memorial; John is buried in Tancrez Farm Cemetery (I.E.7).

(Panel 40) Pte. 7268, James Whigham, 1st Bn. (79th Foot) The Queen's Own (Cameron Highlanders): late of West Calder, co. Midlothian: *s.* of Robert F. Whigham, 13, Blair Street, Edinburgh: enlisted Edinburgh. Reported missing / believed taken prisoner, 11 November 1914, now confirmed as having been killed in action on or about that date: Age 36.

(Panel 40) Major Hazlett Samuel Allison, 7th (Service) Bn. The Royal Irish Rifles: eldest *s.* of Lieut.-Col. Hazlett Allison, of The Shola, Portrush, M.D., Indian Medical Service (ret'd), by his wife Mary Hunter, *dau.* of Michael Woods: *b.* Fort St. George, Madras, India, 6 January 1894: *educ.* Campbell College, Belfast, and Jesus College, Cambridge; graduated B.A., 1914: gazetted 2nd Lieut. Royal Irish Rifles, September 1914; promoted Lieut. 31 December 1914; Capt. 4 April 1916; Major December 1916: served with the Expeditionary Force in France and Flanders from 20 December 1915, and was killed in action at Frezenberg Ridge, 9 August 1917; buried there. His Commanding Officer wrote, "He was a most valuable officer to me, and richly deserved his rapid promotion. He was most popular with all ranks;" and the Battalion Chaplain, "I have been with him since April 1915, and knew him very well. We were all proud of him, and he was beloved by all who knew him; his battalion miss him sorely, especially the men of his own company." Another Chaplain also wrote, "He was in the trenches holding a most difficult part of the line. I am in a position to know that he was beloved and most popular with both officers and men. The fact of his having obtained his majority so soon bears ample testimony to his efficiency as an officer in a division which has covered itself with glory. He was a fine character – most unassuming, but a firm and steadfast friend." Mentioned in Despatches ('*London Gazette*,' 4 January 1917) by General Sir Douglas Haig for 'gallant and distinguished service in the field', the official record stating:– "Near Hulluch, on the night of 31 July – 1 August, he was in charge of an enterprise against the German trenches. Shortly after the return of his party, the enemy made a bombing attack on our saps. Capt. Allison immediately returned to the saps and organized a counter-attack, which not only drove off the Germans, but followed them up and bombed them back into their own trenches. During the past nine months Capt. Allison has repeatedly shown great courage and resource whilst leading patrols, and has set a splendid example to all ranks." Age 23. *unm.*

(Panel 40) Capt. Valentine Knox Gilliland, 2nd Bn. (86th Foot) The Royal Irish Rifles: *yst. s.* of the late George Knox Gilliland (*d.* 22 May 1915), of Brook Hall, Londonderry, by his wife the late Frances Jane (*d.* October 1921), *dau.* of Joseph Cooke, and Frances, *née* Walker: *b.* 15 February 1889. Killed in action 8 May 1915: Age 25. *unm.*

(Panel 40) Capt. Samuel Valentine Morgan, 2nd Bn. (86th Foot) The Royal Irish Rifles: formerly Adjt., 3rd Bn., Portobello Barracks: eldest *s.* of the late Col.Sergt. John Morgan, Instr. (Musketry) Royal Irish Rifles (*d.*1904); by his wife Anna Elizabeth, *née* Caldwell (Newtownards, Co. Down): and brother to Lieut. J.J.L. Morgan, 2nd Royal Inniskilling Fusiliers, died of wounds 16 May 1915: *b.* 5 June 1880: Religion – Roman Catholic: served with the Expeditionary Force. Killed in action 10 August 1917: Age 37. He was married to Rose Gertrude Morgan, *née* Marquess (53, Southwell Road, Bangor, Co. Down), and leaves two children – John Leo, b. 1912, and Gertrude Elizabeth, b. 1917.

His brother John is buried in Bethune Town Cemetery (II.G.16).

(Panel 40) Lieut. William La Nauze, 4th (Extra Reserve) Bn. The Royal Irish Rifles attd 1st Bn. Princess Victoria's (Royal Irish Fusiliers): 5th *s.* of Thomas Storey La Nauze, of 'Manor,' Highgate, Co. Fermanagh: and brother to Lieut. G.M. La Nauze, Royal Irish Rifles, killed in action at Fromelles, one week previously: *b.* 21 May 1895: *educ.* Abbey School, Tipperary; and Trinity College, Dublin, where he was studying for his degree: gazetted 2nd Lieut., 20 May 1914, joining 4th Battn. Royal Irish Rifles, Tidworth, where he served three months on a course attached 2nd Battn. On the outbreak of war 4th Battn. were immediately embodied, and sent to Hollywood, near Belfast, where he joined for duty: promoted Lieut. 16 January 1915: served with the Expeditionary Force in France and Flanders, attd. Royal Irish Fusiliers, from 2 May 1915, immediately taking up his duties in the front line trenches near Ypres, and was killed in action a few days later, 16 May 1915, five days before his twentieth birthday. His Company Commander commented most favourably concerning his bravery and gallant conduct: Age 19.

His brother George also has no known grave; he is commemorated on the Ploegsteert Memorial (Panel 9).

(Panel 40) Lieut. Arthur Augustus Raymond, 2nd Bn. (86th Foot) The Royal Irish Rifles: *s.* of the late Capt. H.W. Raymond, Royal Irish Rifles: served with the Expeditionary Force in France, and was killed in action 1 August 1915, when, while observing artillery fire on the German positions at Hooge, 'an unlucky shell pitched into the trench.': Age 19. Lieut. (Temp/Capt.) W.E. Andrews, L/Corpl. J.W. Tatam and Rfn. J. Kearney were also killed.

Buried at the time in Lankhof Chateau, after the armistice the grave of Capt. Andrews could not be located; he is commemorated in White House Cemetery (Sp.Mem). L/Corpl. Tatam and Rfn. Kearney have no known grave, they are recorded below.

On the evening of 19 September 1916, 2nd Lieut. Amy, 9th Royal Irish Rifles, with a small party of men crept out from their positions into no man's land towards the German lines. Previously accused of lying about finding a gap in the enemy wire, Lieut. Amy had been offered the chance to redeem himself by obtaining a sample of the enemy's defensive wire at the Horseshoe, south of Ypres. The following morning he was reported missing. His commanding officer, Brigadier General Frank Crozier, later wrote, "Amy, I find, went forward on patrol, left his men lying down and went forward to the Horseshoe. There was a good deal of stray firing at the time and no unusual sound was heard. He simply disappeared. Nine months later, when Second Army launched its successful attack at Messines, over the very spot where Amy fell, his skeleton and watch were found in a lonely furrow near the Horseshoe – for good luck perhaps. He had died for more than a bit of wire. He had saved his soul."

(Panel 40) 2nd Lieut. Adolphe Barbier Amy, 9th (Service) Bn. (West Belfast) The Royal Irish Rifles: *s.* of Adolphus Barbier, of St. Clements Road, Jersey, Channel Islands, by his wife Louisa, *née* Le Petevin Dit Le Roux: *b.* 1883: *educ.* Victoria College: a pre-war member of 3rd Bn. Royal (Island of Jersey) Militia, with which he held a commission; volunteered and enlisted apptd. 2nd Lieut. 9th Royal Irish Rifles, September 1914: served in Dublin during the suppression of the revolt, Easter 1916; thereafter proceeded to France. Reported missing 19 September 1916, subsequently (August 1917) confirmed killed in action. In a letter to his widow his officer wrote, "Dear Mrs Amy, It is my sad duty to let you know that news has at last been heard of your husband. A letter from an Australian officer, Lieut. Vallence, received by me yesterday states that while clearing the battlefield after the Messines battle he found the body of a British officer north west of Messines and on the left wrist was an identity disc bearing your husband's name and Regiment. The remains were buried on the old No Mans' Land near to which Amy did his last unfortunate patrol, the exact spot will be notified to you by the Graves Registration Committee in due course. I am afraid there is now no doubt that you husband is dead; he was probably killed by a German bomb whilst on patrol and his body carried into the German lines and buried. The bombardment by our Artillery prior to the assault on 7 June was so violent that he might easily have been disinterred, which would account for his body being recognisable after being so long dead. All that remains is for me to offer my most heartfelt sympathy and that of all the other officers of the 9th who were here last year and knew your husband's sterling worth." Age 33.

(Panel 40) 2nd Lieut. Kenneth Ross, 4th (Extra Reserve) Bn. The Royal Irish Rifles: *s.* of George Harrison Ross, of Cultra, Co. Down, by his wife Henrietta: and yr. brother to 2nd Lieut. M. Ross, Royal Irish Rifles, who fell the same day. Killed in action 25 September. 1915: Age 25. *unm.*

His brother Melbourne also has no known grave; he is recorded below.

(Panel 40) 2nd Lieut. Melbourne Ross, 4th (Extra Reserve) attd 2nd Bn. (86th Foot) The Royal Irish Rifles: *s.* of George Harrison Ross, of Cultra, Co. Down, by his wife Henrietta: and elder brother to 2nd Lieut. K. Ross, Royal Irish Rifles, who fell the same day. Killed in action 25 September 1915: Age 30. *unm.*

His brother Kenneth also has no known grave; he is recorded above.

(Panel 40) Corpl. 16191, Thomas Bingham, 10th (Service) Bn. The Royal Irish Rifles: father to L/Corpl. 11650, T. Bingham, 6th Royal Inniskilling Fusiliers, killed in action 17 August 1915, at Gallipoli, aged 16 years: *b.* Banbridge, Co. Down: volunteered and enlisted Belfast to serve his country and avenge the death of his son. Killed in action 6 August 1917. He leaves a widow Janet Bingham (16, Medway Street, Belfast).

His son Thomas also has no known grave; he is commemorated on the Helles Memorial.

(Panel 40) L/Corpl. 42311, Michael Bernard Hosey, 8th (Service) Bn. (East Belfast) The Royal Irish Rifles: formerly no.R/30799, King's Royal Rifle Corps: *s.* of Michael Bernard Hosey, by his wife Emma, of Kensington, London, S.E.11. Died of wounds 6 August 1917: Age 19. Remains 'Unknown British Soldier. 8/R.I.R.' recovered unmarked grave (28.C.18.c.95.30); identified – Clothing, Boots, Badge; reinterred, registered 23 March 1929. *Buried in Sanctuary Wood Cemetery (V.G.8).*

(Panel 40) L/Corpl. 5147, Joseph William Tatam, 2nd Bn. (86th Foot) The Royal Irish Rifles: formerly no.4059, Lancers: *s.* of William John Tatam, of Little Eaton, co. Derby, by his wife Mary: enlisted

Woolwich, co. Kent. Killed in action 1 August 1915, when 'an unlucky shell pitched into the trench;' Lieut. (Temp/Capt.) W.E. Andrews, Lieut. A.A. Raymond (observing artillery fire on the German positions at Hooge) and Rfn. J. Kearney were also killed: Age 32.

Buried at the time in Lankhof Chateau, after the armistice the grave of Capt. Andrews could not be located; he is commemorated in White House Cemetery (Sp.Mem). Lieut. Raymond and Rfn. Kearney have no known grave, they are recorded above and below respectively.

(Panel 40) Rfn. 8955, Robert James Adair, 2nd Bn. (86th Foot) The Royal Irish Rifles: *s.* of Robert Hunter Adair, of 84, Brussels Street, Belfast, by his wife the late Elizabeth Adair: and elder brother to Pte. 27699, J. Adair, Wiltshire Regt., died in service 13 March 1919. Killed in action 11 November 1914: Age 24.

His brother John is buried in Belfast City Cemetery (AI.606).

(Panel 40) Rfn. 4956, James Bland, 2nd Bn. (86th Foot) The Royal Irish Rifles: formerly no.7065, Lancers: *s.* of Joseph Gill (& Margaret) Bland, of Grange Fell, Grange-over-Sands, co. Lancaster: *b.* Cartnel: enlisted Morecambe. Killed in action 25 September 1915: Age 28. On 10 November 2014 a school party from Rfn. Bland's home town visited the Menin Gate; one of the students – Lorna Hamilton – left the following, dedicated to his memory:–

> **"For Rfn. Jimmie Bland"**
> *Gun shots rain the air*
> *Too young we all think*
> *Too young*
> *Your life a road twisting and turning,*
> *The options of children, a wife, a house,*
> *The feel of sunshine on your face,*
> *Gone.*
> *Gone, like the thousands of others*
> *Who talk their last breath in a hail of pain and gasps;*
> *Stolen from you – like your future.*
>
> *'Shush' your mother whispers, 'rest your eyes,'*
> *For you are lost and she will find you.*

(Panel 40) Rfn. 44604, Frederick William Butcher, 12th (Service) Bn. The Royal Irish Rifles: *s.* of the late Frank Butcher, Member, London Stock Exchange; by his wife Elizabeth (9, Park Lane, Aldeburgh, co. Suffolk), *dau.* of Thomas Hardisty: *b.* London, 12 August 1896: *educ.* Oundle School, co. Northampton: joined Inns of Court O.T.C., October 1915: served with the Expeditionary Force in France, from January 1917, and was killed in action at Frezenberg, 9 August following. Buried there. The Chaplain wrote, "He lived a noble life, and died an heroic death." Age 20. *unm.*

(Panel 40) Rfn. 4816, Robert Close, 2nd Bn. (86th Foot) The Royal Irish Rifles: *s.* of the late Joseph Close, of Scarva Street, Newry Road, Banbridge, Co. Down, and Elizabeth, his spouse: and brother to Rfn. 3973, W. Close, 1st Royal Irish Rifles, killed in action 29 May 1915, at Hooge: *b.* Seapatrick, Co. Down: enlisted Banbridge: served with the Expeditionary Force in France and Flanders from 14 August 1914; moved up with his unit into the trenches near Hill 60, 6 May 1915, and was killed in action the following day: 7 May 1915: Age 20. His brother Hugh, one of two other brothers who also served, was seriously wounded at Gallipoli.

His brother William also has no known grave; he is commemorated on the Ploegsteert Memorial (Panel 9).

(Panel 40) Rfn. 10358, William Fitzpatrick, 2nd Bn. (86th Foot) The Royal Irish Rifles: *s.* of John Fitzpatrick, of 87, Rialto Buildings, South Circular Road, Dublin, by his wife Mary: and *yr.* brother to Pte. 9768, J. Fitzpatrick, Royal Irish Rifles, killed in action two months later: enlisted Dublin. Killed in action 10 March 1915: Age 19.

His brother Joseph also has no known grave; he is commemorated on the Ploegsteert Memorial (Panel 9).

(Panel 40) Rfn. 6322, Patrick Fitzsimmons, 2nd Bn. (86th Foot) The Royal Irish Rifles: late *husb.* to Bridget Fitzsimmons (9, Raphael Street, Belfast): *b.* Ballymacarrett, Co. Down, *c.*1880: enlisted 4th Bn., Ballykinlar, on the outbreak of war: served with the Expeditionary Force in France transf'd. 2nd Bn. from April 1915, and was killed in action at Railway Wood, 16 June 1915 on which date two companies of 2 R.I.R. took part in the Battle of Bellewaarde. In an attack on the German trenches, 'after starting from good cover on the eastern edge of Railway Wood, they went forward most gallantly until destroyed' by an exceptionally heavy artillery bombardment which caused over 300 casualties; killed, missing, wounded. Buried near where he fell: Age 35. Remains 'Unknown British Soldier, 4R.I.R.' recovered (July 1923) from an unmarked collective grave (28.I.11.b.15.45) were identified by clothing and a piece of boot marked 6322/4RIR and taken to be those of 6322 4th Royal Irish Regt. The question as to why the remains of an eighteen (reputed fourteen) year-old soldier of 2nd (previously 3rd) Royal Irish Regt. who fell in the vicinity of Mouse Trap Farm should be mistakenly identified and attributed to the remains of a thirty-five year-old soldier of 2nd (previously 4th) Royal Irish Rifles recovered almost two miles away in the vicinity of Railway Wood is something of an enigma. The recognised standard abbreviation utilised for Royal Irish Regt. was (and is) R.I.Regt.; Royal Irish Rifles – R.I.R.

The remains recovered, buried in Poelcapelle British Cemetery (LVI.F.8), were attributed to Pte. John Condon; reputed to be the youngest British casualty of the Great War (irrefutable evidence disproves this). Possibly, with few exceptions, the most visited grave in the Ypres Salient.

One hundred years to the day after Patrick Fitzsimmons died the grave at Poelcapelle, Railway Wood and the Menin Gate were visited by his great-nephew Kenneth Hanna and his son Adrian. Kenneth said, "Clearly from the stamping identified and because of the regimental battle histories, it cannot possibly be John Condon. I'm convinced those remains buried in John Condon's grave are Patrick Fitzsimmons." To resolve the issue irrefutably would involve an exhumation of the remains and a DNA test which Kenneth said would not only be very controversial but hurtful to the Condon family who are entirely blameless. "My honest feeling is that both soldiers gave their lives for the cause of freedom. That they are commemorated in error is a fact of history. To switch now would create a huge controversy."

(Panel 40) Rfn. 5623, John Foster, 2nd Bn. (86th Foot) The Royal Irish Rifles: late *husb.* to Rose Ann Foster (26, Bells Yard, White House, Co. Antrim): *b.* Carlisle, Co. Cumberland, 1858. Killed in action 18 December 1914: **Age 56.**

(Panel 40) Rfn. 42402, Albert Edwin Hopkins, 1st Bn. (83rd Foot) The Royal Irish Rifles: *yst. s.* of Joseph William Hopkins, Coffee House Keeper; by his wife Harriet (14, Nelson Square, Peckham, London, S.E.), *dau.* of James Coster: *b.* 18 July 1891: *educ.* St. Michael's School, Chester Square, London, S.W.: Occupation – Baker: enlisted 8 March 1917: served with the Expeditionary Force in France and Flanders from 29 May 1917, and was killed in action 31 July following: Age 26. *unm.* (*IWGC record age 28*)

(Panel 40) Pte. 5055, George William Jessop, 2nd Bn. (86th Foot) The Royal Irish Rifles: formerly no.8274, 16th Lancers: *s.* of William Jessop, of 1, The Retreat, Horn Lane, Woodford Green, co. Essex, by his wife Zilah: and yr. brother to Pte. 41976, C.J.E. Jessop, 12th Suffolk Regt., killed in action 21 March 1918: *b.* Woodford, *c.*1897: volunteered and enlisted Walthamstow, September 1914: served with the Expeditionary Force in France transf'd. Royal Irish Rifles, and was killed in action 11 October 1915: Age 18.

His brother Charles also has no known grave; he is commemorated on the Arras (Faubourg d'Amiens) Memorial (Bay 4).

(Panel 40) Rfn. 5645, John Kearney, 2nd Bn. (86th Foot) The Royal Irish Rifles. Killed in action 1 August 1915, when 'an unlucky shell pitched into the trench;' Lieut. (Temp/Capt.) W.E. Andrews, Lieut. A.A. Raymond (observing artillery fire on the German positions at Hooge) and L/Corpl. J.W. Tatam were also killed.

Buried at the time in Lankhof Chateau, after the armistice the grave of Capt. Andrews could not be located; he is commemorated in White House Cemetery (Sp.Mem). Lieut. Raymond and L/Corpl. Tatam have no known grave, they are recorded above.

(Panel 40) Rfn. 673, Francis Killips, 12th (Service) Bn. (Central Antrim) The Royal Irish Rifles: *s.* of John Killips, of Delamont, Killyleagh, Co. Down, by his wife Margaret Jane: and yr. brother to Rfn. 776, J. Killips, 12th Royal Irish Rifles, killed in action 1 July 1916, aged 29 years: *b.* Killyleagh: enlisted Belfast: served with the Expeditionary Force in France and Flanders from October 1915, and was killed in action 15 August 1917: Age 22.

His brother John also has no known grave; he is commemorated on the Thiepval Memorial, Somme.

(Panel 40) Rfn. 10276, Daniel McFall, 2nd Bn. (86th Foot) The Royal Irish Rifles: *s.* of Thomas McFall, of Garfield Place, Ballymena, by his wife Rosetta: and nephew to Rfn. 626, D. McFall, 8th Royal Irish Rifles, who fell, 2 July 1916, at the Battle of the Somme, aged 28. Killed in action 10 July 1915: Age 19. His cousin, Rfn. 10277, J. McFall, with whom he enlisted, served in the same battalion and is believed to have been killed in action at Ypres on or about 8 May 1915. All three men are commemorated on the Cloughwater Presbyterian Church Roll of Honour. Another nephew, Rfn. Robert McFall, Royal Irish Rifles, spent almost three years in a German P.o.W. camp.

His nephew Daniel and cousin James have no known grave; they are recorded on the Thiepval Memorial (Pier & Face 15) and the Menin Gate (below) respectively.

(Panel 40) Rfn. 10277, James McFall, 2nd Bn. (86th Foot) The Royal Irish Rifles: *s.* of the late James McFall, of Craigywarren, whose brother Rfn. 626, D. McFall, 8th Royal Irish Rifles, fell at the Battle of the Somme, 2 July 1916, aged 28. Missing / believed killed in action on or about 8 May 1915: Age 20. *unm.* His cousin Rfn. 10276, D. McFall, with whom he enlisted, served in the same battalion and was killed in action at Ypres, 10 July 1915. All three men are commemorated on the Cloughwater Presbyterian Church Roll of Honour. Another uncle, Rfn. Robert McFall, Royal Irish Rifles, spent almost three years in a German P.o.W. camp.

His uncle and cousin – both named Daniel – have no known grave; they are recorded on the Thiepval Memorial (Pier & Face 15) and the Menin Gate (above) respectively.

(Panel 40) Rfn. 7518, George McFarland, 2nd Bn. (86th Foot) The Royal Irish Rifles: *s.* of the late Robert McFarland, of Ballymena, and his wife Margaret 'Maggie': *gdson.* to George (& Eliza) McFarland: and brother to Pte. 18728, J. McFarland, Machine Gun Corps, killed 1 July 1916: *b.* Ballymena, Co. Antrim, 1886: enlisted Ballykinlar, Co. Down. Killed in action at La Bassée, France, 14 January 1915. He leaves a wife, Agnes (7, Roseberry Street, Connswater, Belfast): Age 28.

His brother James also has no known grave; he is recorded on the Thiepval Memorial (Pier & Face 5C)

(Panel 40) Rfn. 7528, William John McReavie, 15th (Service) Bn. (North Belfast) The Royal Irish Rifles: *s.* of Hugh McReavie, of 10, Weir Street, Belfast, by his wife Elizabeth: *b.* Shankill, Co. Antrim: enlisted Belfast. Killed in action 31 October 1916: Age 25. *unm. Buried in Pont-du-Hem Military Cemetery, La Gorgue (IV.H.8).*

(Panel 40) Rfn. 203, Thomas Matthews, 12th (Service) Bn. (Central Antrim) The Royal Irish Rifles: late of 19, Witham Street, Belfast: *b.* Ballymacarrett, Co. Down: enlisted Belfast. Thought to have been killed by the same bullet that killed 2nd Lieut. J.A.P. Bill, whilst attempting to dress this officer's wounds in front of the company's wire at the Battle of Langemarck, 15 August 1917.

2nd Lieut. Bill also has no known grave (recorded as 16 August 1917); he is commemorated on the Tyne Cot Memorial (Panel 138).

(Panel 40) Rfn. 9202, David Millar, 'A' Coy., 1st Bn. (83rd Foot) The Royal Irish Rifles: *s.* of the late John Millar, of Carrickfergus, Co. Antrim, by his wife Jane: *b.* Carrickfergus, 1890: enlisted Belfast: served with the Expeditionary Force, and was killed in action 21 December 1914: Age 24. (*IWGC:1926/ MR.29,XXVII,pg.1005 records 2nd Bn.*) *Buried in Rue-du-Bacquerot (13th London) Graveyard, Laventie (G.3).*

(Panel 40) Pte. 5088, Robert Mitchell, 'D' Coy., 2nd Bn. (86th Foot) The Royal Irish Rifles: formerly no.4550, Lancers: *s.* of Richard Mitchell, of 24, Clarence Street, Ballymena, Co. Antrim, by his wife Mary Christie: and brother to Pte. 59642, W. Mitchell, Royal Scots, who fell 28 October 1918, aged 19: *b.* Ballymena, *c.*1893: enlisted Glasgow, co. Lanark. Killed in action 25 September 1915: Age 22. *unm.*
His brother William is buried in Heestert Military Cemetery (A.6).

(Panel 40) Rfn. 45126, James Henry Thomson, 8th (Service) Bn. (East Belfast) The Royal Irish Rifles: formerly no.6620, London Regt. (T.F.): *s.* of the late Robert Murray Thomson, by his wife Alice Victoria (21, Cambridge Buildings, Westminster, London). Killed in action 6 August 1917: Age 22. *unm.* Remains 'Unknown British Soldier. 8/R.I.R.' recovered unmarked grave (28.C.18.c.95.30); identified – Disc, Clothing, Boots; reinterred, registered 23 March 1929. *Buried in Sanctuary Wood Cemetery (V.G.9).*

A Loss So Great A Shock Severe
To Part With One We Loved So Dear

(Panel 40) Rfn. 9629, George Webster, 8th (Service) Bn. (East Belfast) The Royal Irish Rifles: late of London: enlisted Cork. Killed in action 6 August 1917. Remains 'Unknown British Soldier. R.I.R.' recovered unmarked grave (28.C.18.c.95.30); identified – Clothing, Boots, Title, Badge; reinterred, registered 23 March 1929. *Buried in Sanctuary Wood Cemetery (V.G.10).*

PANEL 40 ENDS PTE. J. YOUNG – ROYAL IRISH RIFLES.

PANEL 42 BEGINS CAPT. A.J. MILLAR – ROYAL IRISH FUSILIERS.

(Panel 42) Capt. Arthur James Millar, 3rd attd. 1st Bn. (87th Foot) The Princess Victoria's (Royal Irish Fusiliers): 2nd *s.* of James Millar, of 87, Eglantine Avenue, Belfast, F.C.I.S., by his wife Jane Isabella, *dau.* of William Hardie, of Edinburgh: *b.* Belfast, 10 September 1890: *educ.* Methodist College, Belfast, and Queen's University, there, attended Medical Course, and served over three years O.T.C., from which he joined Special Reserve of Officers; attd. 2nd Lieut., 3rd Royal Irish Fusiliers, 25 May 1912; promoted Lieut. 21 November 1910; Capt. 10 April 1915: joined his regt. on the outbreak of war, August 1914: went to France with a draft September following: served in the trenches during the winter 1914 – 15, and was killed in action 25 April 1915, nr. St. Julien. An officer wrote, "He met his soldier's death gallantly leading his platoon forward against very heavy rifle and machine-gun fire – the way he led his platoon was splendid. Almost the last act he performed under this fire was to crawl over and bandage a man of his platoon who had been wounded, and was certainly one of the most gallant things I have ever seen done. It was almost immediately after this that he was so very unfortunately killed. His name was sent forward prior to the 25th for his excellent work during the whole time he was out here, and has now been sent forward for his most gallant conduct on the 25th, and I only hope he will get the reward he so thoroughly deserves. He is buried with his men where he fell on the field, between the villages of Fortuin and St. Julien, north-east of Ypres. His name will be remembered in the regt. and its glorious annals." Age 24. *unm.*

(Panel 42) Lieut. William Leonard Ringrose Hatch, 2nd Bn. (89th Foot) The Princess Victoria's (Royal Irish Fusiliers): elder *s.* of Lieut.Col. William K. Hatch, Indian Medical Service (ret'd); of 8, Earlham Road, Norwich: and *gdson.* to Gen. William Sparks Hatch, Royal Artillery, Inspector-General of Ordnance, Bombay Presidency: *b.* 27 November 1890: *educ.* Shrewsbury School, and Royal Military College, Sandhurst: gazetted 2nd Lieut. Royal Irish Fusiliers, March 1911: joined 2nd Battn., Quetta (Malta), autumn 1911: promoted Lieut. April 1913: remained with his battalion at Quetta until October 1914 when it departed for Active Service in France: served with the Expeditionary Force there from December 1914, and, after being wounded early on the morning of 25 January 1915, was killed later that day by a shell while lying in a dug-out somewhere in Flanders. Lieut. Hatch was very keen on sport, and took a leading part in all the regimental games and sports: Age 25. *unm.*

On the night of 25 May 1915, in the aftermath of the concentrated German attack against the Faugh-a Ballaghs positions near Potijze, the battalion had to mourn the loss of a particularly fine young officer, 2nd Lieut. C.E. Cooke, who was shot dead while out with a covering party. He had already been wounded once, and many times mentioned for gallant conduct in action. A quiet unassuming young officer, he devoted himself unsparingly to the performance of his duties, and the welfare of his men who affectionately dubbed him 'The Sand-bag King.' As was necessarily the case during prolonged actions such as the battalion had just been through, he was buried in the bottom of the muddy trench near where he fell, but before covering him over each and every man in his platoon knelt down and shook him by hand.

(Panel 42) 2nd Lieut. **Charles Ernest Cooke**, 3rd (Reserve) attd. 1st Bn. (87th Foot) The Princess Victoria's (Royal Irish Fusiliers): *s.* of Alexander Cooke, of Notting Hill House, Belfast: *b.* Belfast, 11 October 1884: *educ.* Malvern College: afterwards removed to South Africa; served three years South African Police Force: on the outbreak of war, August 1914, was Asst. Adjt., Ulster Volunteer Force, and immediately applied for a Regular Army commission: gazetted 2nd Lieut. (on probation), 3rd Royal Irish Fusiliers, the same month: after a brief training went to France, September 1914, attd. 1st Battn. of his regiment, and was present at the First Battle of Ypres, and was killed in action 26 May 1915, shot dead whilst out with a covering party. Buried nr. Wieltje: Age 30. *unm.* Previously wounded once, several times mentioned regarding his gallant conduct in action; for his services in the war he was Mentioned in Sir John (now Lord) French's Despatch, 14 January 1915:– "A quiet unassuming, particularly fine young officer, his death is deeply mourned. He devoted himself unsparingly to the performance of his duties and was known to his men as 'the sand-bag king.' As was necessarily the case during these prolonged battles, he was buried in the mud near where he fell, and before covering him up every man in his platoon knelt down and shook him by the hand."

(Panel 42) 2nd Lieut. **Edwin James Macmillan**, 4th (Extra Reserve) attd. 8th (Service) Bn. The Princess Victoria's (Royal Irish Fusiliers): *s.* of Isaac Macmillan, of 'Morvyn,' 642, Burwood Road, Auburn, Victoria, Australia, by his wife Mary: served in the South African Campaign, and in France and Flanders where he was killed in action 12 January 1917: Age 37. *Buried in Pont du Hem Military Cemetery, La Gorgue (IV.H.10).*

At 2.45 a.m., 24 May 1915, gas clouds were seen issuing from the German trenches opposite those held by 1st Royal Irish Fusiliers, and at almost the same time the enemy opened a heavy artillery and rifle fire. Immediately adjusting their respirators, the Faugh-a-Ballaghs poured a heavy machine gun and rifle fire into the advancing gas clouds and, as the clouds gradually rolled back behind the fire trenches, the Irishmen saw that the Germans were within a short distance of their wire entanglements. The Faughs met the enemy with such an effective fire that they not only fell back, but did not succeed in making another attack on the battalion front throughout the remainder of the day. On this occasion, chiefly in the vicinity of Potijze Chateau, in addition to poison gas, the enemy also used lachrymatory shells. With only rudimentary protection against gas and none against this type, which caused pain to the eyes and made it extremely difficult to carry on the fight, the success of the battalion 'during this trying day was due to the excellent leading of the officers and N.C.O.'s, and to the discipline and excellent spirit of the men.' The Battalion were fortunate in having few killed that day, but amongst them were:–

(Panel 42) 2nd Lieut. **Hugh Patrick Shine**, 1st Bn. (87th Foot) The Princess Victoria's (Royal Irish Fusiliers): *yst. s.* of Col. J.M.F. Shine, C.B., Army Medical Services; of Abbeyside, Dungarvan, Co. Waterford, by his marriage to the late Kathleen Mary Shine: and brother to 2nd Lieut. John D. Shine, Royal Irish Regt., killed at the Battle of Mons, 25 August 1914; and Capt. James O.W. Shine, Royal Dublin Fusiliers, killed 16 August 1917: *b.* Corradino House, Malta, 20 August 1896: Religion – Roman Catholic: *educ.* Downside School, and Royal Military College, Sandhurst: gazetted 2nd Lieut., Royal Irish Fusiliers, October 1914, posted 1st Battn.: served with the Expeditionary Force in France, and was killed by shell fire in the trenches near Ypres, 25 May 1915. Buried near the road running south-east from Wieltje. His Company Commander reported him as "fearless" and "...risked his life to save others." He was a good all-round athlete and was in the Sandhurst 1st Hockey XI, 1914: Age 18.

His brother John is buried in Mons Communal Cemetery (IV.B.18); James has no known grave; he is commemorated on the Tyne Cot Memorial (Panel 144).

(Panel 42) Sergt. 9108, John Sproule, 2nd Bn. (89th Foot) The Princess Victoria's (Royal Irish Fusiliers): *s.* of the late Robert Sproule, by his wife Catherine (28, Ellsworth Avenue, Toronto, Canada): and yr. brother to Sergt. 7917, J. Sproule, 1st Royal Irish Fusiliers, killed in action 8 December 1914, aged 31 years; and Pte. 3032014, R. Sproule, Canadian Infantry, died 11 February 1918, aged 30 years: *b.* Clones, Co. Monaghan: enlisted Clones. Killed in action 14 February 1915: Age 25. *unm.*

His brother Joseph also has no known grave, he is commemorated on the Ploegsteert Memorial (Panel 9); Robert is buried in Toronto (Prospect) Cemetery (Sec.18.4558).

(Panel 42) Pte. 9818, Daniel McCarthy, 'A' Coy., 2nd Bn. (89th Foot) The Princess Victoria's (Royal Irish Fusiliers): *s.* of William (& Mrs N.) McCarthy, of 25, Argyle Gardens, Upminster, co. Essex: *b.* Monaghan: enlisted Enniskillen. Killed in action 2 May 1915: Age 25. *unm.* His brother also fell.

(Panel 42) Capt. Frank Harrison Saker, 4th (Reserve) attd. 2nd Bn. (94th Foot) The Connaught Rangers: *yst. s.* of the late Edward Saker, of Liverpool: *b.* 1880: entered 5th (afterwards 4th) Battn. Connaught Rangers, 2nd Lieut. February 1904; promoted Lieut. June 1906: passed through a School of Instruction; qualified as Instructor of Musketry: promoted Capt. September 1914: served with the Expeditionary Force in France from the 24th. of the latter month. Sergt. J. McIlwain, 2nd Connaught Rangers, said, "On the night of 30 – 31 October 1914 Capt. Saker, who brought up the last of the reserves from home, decided to attack the German lines opposite and – with about 90 men – got up a raid of his own undertaking. Advancing beyond the objective he got into difficulty and, surrounded by the enemy, was forced to surrender himself and those of his men who were left alive. He was last seen surrendering and being carried away wounded by the Germans." Reported ('*The Times*,' 13 November) wounded and taken prisoner – 30 October 1914 – there having been, despite extensive enquiries, no further word of Capt. Saker, it is believed he died shortly after being taken prisoner. Whether as a consequence of his wounds or killed by subsequent shelling of the enemy lines by our guns is unknown: Age 30. *m.* A talented amateur thespian, Capt. Saker was a respected member of The Green Room Club, Leicester Square, London. (*IWGC record 30 October 1914*)

(Panel 42) Capt. Montagu Hill Clephane di Cristoforo de Bouillon Wickham, 'B' Coy., 2nd Bn. (94th Foot) The Connaught Rangers: *s.* of Lieut.Col. Edmund Hill Wickham, R.A., of 34, Charleville Road, West Kensington, London, and Horsington, co. Somerset; by his wife The Princess Eugenie Paleologue: commissioned 5th Connaught Rangers, May 1898: served in the South African Campaign, 1900; West African Frontier Force, 1908 – 14. Killed in action 9 May 1915: Age 36. Mentioned in Despatches for his services in the Great War.

From the outbreak of war until his discharge in 1919 Sergt. 6757, James McIlwain, Connaught Rangers, kept a diary recording his experiences in France, Flanders, Gallipoli and Salonika. His entry for 30 October – 7 November 1914 reads:– "About this time we hear much talk of Ypres; a place most of us had never seen and knew nothing of. We now learn how important it is – our transport men tell us it is a big town, that the Germans are striving fiercely for it, and that our job is its defence. The shelling becomes heavier daily, the pressure on our troops greater; in places we are but fifty yards from the enemy. On going up with rations one night, in the front line where talk was carried on in whispers because of the German bombing, I came across a party of Royal Engineers making bombs with jam tins! A futile effort to retaliate upon the Germans with their efficient rifle and hand grenades. Relief from the trenches these times consists of parties of troops going back for a few hundred yards to the shelter of the woods where they throw themselves exhausted. Those of us behind the line join them. Everyone understands that at the signal being given all must rush forward and fight to the last if the Germans break through. Seldom is there more than 24 hours of such so-called relief. Day by day the British army grows less but still hangs on. By day and night the dead and wounded are brought back, but many more being on the German side cannot be recovered. Reinforcements for most regiments arrive but the Rangers have exhausted their reserves…I soon discover the position of Ypres when, one dreary evening, in waking up to the realisation that the intensified shelling is coming from three sides of us, I begin to fear that soon we shall al be surrounded. Lying facing the enemy who are shelling us I observe the shells are coming also from my right rear; that is Ypres..."

During the period narrated above the Connaughts, consistently attacked and bombarded by the enemy, lost three officers killed – Lieuts. C.J.O'C. Mallins, A.T.C. Wickham and 2nd Lieut. A. Winspear, 4 officers wounded, and over 100 other ranks killed and wounded.

(Panel 42) Lieut. Claude Joseph O'Conor Mallins, 2nd Bn. (94th Foot) The Connaught Rangers: *s.* of Capt. Frederic William Mallins, 3rd East Lancashire Regt., by his wife Eliza O'Conor-Fitzsimons (31, Pembroke Road, Dublin), *yst. dau.* of Roderic Joseph O'Conor, J.P., of Milton, Co. Roscommon: and nephew to Lieut.Col. J.R. Mallins, R.A.M.C., of 'Tigh-na-Mara,' Alverstoke, co. Hants: *b.* 23, Raglan Road, Dublin, 3 October 1894: *educ.* Stoneyhurst College; Wimbledon Army College; Royal Military College, Sandhurst: gazetted 2nd Lieut. Connaught Rangers, August 1914; proceeded on Active Service, September: was, for a short time, Acting Adjutant to his battalion – which shows the losses in officers suffered by our regiments in this war. Lieut. Mallins was killed at Molenaarelshoek, not far from Ypres, between Becelaere and Passchendaele, 2 November 1914, when it was said of him, "He was the soul of the defence of his part of the line, and had just succeeded in beating off a German attack (a remarkable commendation for so young an officer), when he fell by a sniper's bullet," being shot through the forehead. He was buried with another officer in a small garden in the village of Molenaarshoek, where he was killed. His Commanding Officer wrote of him, "Your brave son was as promising a young officer as I have ever met." Age 20. *unm.*

(Panel 42) Lieut. Anthony Theodore Clephane Wickham, 4th (Special Reserve) attd. 2nd Bn. (94th Foot) The Connaught Rangers: only *s.* of the Rev. James Douglas Clephane Wickham, of Holcombe Manor, co. Somerset, by his wife Alice Matilda, 2nd *dau.* of William Neal: joined 4th Prince Albert's Somerset Light Infantry, 1904: transf'd. 4th Connaught Rangers, October 1907: was Musketry Instructor and Machine Gun Officer to his Battalion for three or four years: served with the Expeditionary Force in France and Flanders, attd. 2nd Battn. of his Regiment, and was killed near Ypres, 2 November 1914; being shot by a German sniper whilst trying to effect the rescue of a wounded officer, who was lying outside the trenches. The Officer Commanding his Battalion wrote of him that he was a most promising officer, beloved by all ranks, and would have been promoted Captain, December 1914, had he lived. He was a member of the Hibernian United Service Club, Dublin, the Kilkenny County Club, a keen follower of hounds – hunted with the Royal Meath for three years – and a talented amateur actor: Age 27. *unm.* Remains 'Unknown British Officer' recovered unmarked grave (28.J.5.b.2.0) refers GRU Report, Zillebeke 5-102E; identified – Officers Clothing, Gold Signet Ring with Crest; reinterred, registered 17 June 1927. *Buried in Sanctuary Wood Cemetery (IV.E.7).*

In Sacred Memory Of One Who Died
To Rescue a Brother Officer

(Panel 42) 2nd Lieut. Arthur Winspear, 'B' Coy., 2nd Bn. (94th Foot) The Connaught Rangers: previously served Coy. Sergt.-Major, Irish Guards: gazetted 2nd Lieut. October 1914: while Sergt., Irish Guards, he was Mentioned in Sir John (now Lord) French's Despatch, 8 October 1914. Killed repulsing an enemy attack made under cover of darkness, 5 – 6 November 1914, nr. Molenaarelsthoek. L/Corpl. 10867, M.J. Dalby, and 5 Other Ranks were also killed. (*IWGC record 5 November*)

L/Corpl. Dalby also has no known grave; he is recorded below.

(Panel 42) Sergt. 3780, Michael O'Hara, 'A' Coy., 2nd Bn. (94th Foot) The Connaught Rangers: *s.* of the late William O'Hara, by his wife Ann: served with the Expeditionary Force in France and Flanders from August 1914, and was killed in action 1 November 1914, being decapitated by a shell: Age 23. He was married to Ellen O'Hara (Kilbride Cottages, Swinford, Co. Mayo). See Pte. J. Moyles (below)

(Panel 42) L/Corpl. 10867, Michael James Dalby, 2nd Bn. (94th Foot) The Connaught Rangers: late of Castlerea, Co. Roscommon: enlisted there. Killed in action late evening, 5 – 6 November 1914; Molenaarelsthoek. Lieut. Winspear and 5 Other Ranks were also killed.

2nd Lieut. Winspear also has no known grave; he is recorded above.

(Panel 42) L/Corpl. 3567, Thomas Mulligan, 2nd Bn. (94th Foot) The Connaught Rangers: *s*. of Patrick Mulligan, of Mill Street, Ballymote, Co. Sligo, by his wife Mary: proceeded to France, 4 October 1914, with a draft of 191 Other Ranks from 4th Battn.: joined 2nd Battn. In the Field, 14 October and was killed in action on the 21st. of that month: 21 October 1914: Age 25.

(Panel 42) Pte. 4072, John Delaney, 2nd Bn. (94th Foot) The Connaught Rangers: late of Loughrae, Co. Galway: enlisted Oranmore. Killed in action 2 November 1914. Remains recovered unmarked grave (28.J.5.b.2.0); identified – Clothing, Boots mkd. 318 – 3rd CT.; reinterred, registered 13 June 1927. *Buried in Sanctuary Wood Cemetery (IV.E.4/6).*

(Panel 42) Pte. 10966, Reginald Flook, 2nd Bn. (94th Foot) The Connaught Rangers: *b*. Bristol: enlisted Seaforth. Killed in action 11 November 1914, north-east of Polygon Wood.

(Panel 42) Pte. 8973, Patrick Moloney, 2nd Bn. (94th Foot) The Connaught Rangers: late of Tullamore, King's Co.: *b*. Boyle, Co. Roscommon: enlisted Tullamore. Killed in action 29 October 1914, nr. Zonnebeke. Remains recovered unmarked grave (28.J.5.b.2.0); identified – Clothing, Boots mkd. 141 – 3rd CT.; reinterred, registered 13 June 1927. *Buried in Sanctuary Wood Cemetery (IV.E.4/6).*

The Ballina Volunteer Corps was part of the paramilitary organisation that sprung up throughout Ireland in 1913 in support of devolution. After hundreds of years of British domination Parliament was finally poised to give Ireland more autonomy within the United Kingdom in the form of Home Rule, but Protestant Unionists in the north opposed it and began training with weapons. In the south the head of the Irish Home Rule Party, John Redmond, rallied a force to protect the Home Rule Bill; 150,000 Catholic Nationalists answered the call, among them James Moyles. Less than one year later Britain declared war on Germany and along with thousands of his fellow countrymen James went off to fight for the British.

(Panel 42) Pte. 3479, James Moyles, 2nd Bn. (94th Foot) The Connaught Rangers: a pre-war member of 3rd (Reserve) Bn. (enlisted Galway 1892), and Instructor, Ballina Volunteer Corps: mobilised with his battn. on the outbreak of war 4 August 1914: departed Crosshaven, Cork Harbour and went to France with Lieut. A.W.T.P. Whyte and a draft of 93 other ranks (reinforcements) from 3rd Battn. 31 August, and was killed in action near Zonnebeke at the First Battle of Ypres, 2 November 1914: Age 39. A comrade, Pte. 4015, Michael Gavaghan, wrote, "I saw Michael O'Hara of Ballina walking up and down the trench to keep himself warm when his head was taken clean off him by a shell. I was quite near poor Jimmy Moyles, another Ballina man, when he peeped over the trench and fell back quite dead…a bullet had cut clean through his forehead. He was one of the pleasantest men in the trench…" Pte. Moyles was 5'3½" tall, religion – Roman Catholic; he bore tattooed crosses on both thumbs, and an anchor on his left wrist. One of the first Ballina men to be killed in the Great War; he leaves a widow, Mary Ann, *née* Ormsby (Shambles Street, Ballina, Co. Mayo), and eight children. He was a relative of former B.B.C. radio presenter Chris Moyles. Remains recovered unmarked grave (28.J.5.b.2.0); identified – Clothing; reinterred, registered 13 June 1927. *Buried in Sanctuary Wood Cemetery (IV.E.4/6).*

Sergt. Michael O'Hara also has no known grave; he is recorded above.

(Panel 42) Capt. Dick Macdonald Porteous, D.S.O., 1st Bn. (91st Foot) The Princess Louise's (Argyll & Sutherland Highlanders): only *s*. of Col. John James Porteous, of 7, Sloane Street, London, S.W., late R.A.: *b*. Dublin, 15 June 1883: *educ*. Wellington College, and R.M.C. Sandhurst: gazetted 2nd Lieut. Argyll & Sutherland Highlanders (the 'Old 91st') 22 October 1902, Lieut. 19 October 1907; Capt. 13 September 1913: served with the Expeditionary Force in France and Flanders, greatly distinguishing himself. Awarded the D.S.O. for conspicuous gallantry on many occasions throughout the campaign ('*London Gazette*,' 15 April 1915), the official record stating:– "His very great daring and total disregard of danger on reconnaissance duty, especially at St. Eloi on 19 February 1915, were noticeable," and was Mentioned again in F.M. Sir John (now Lord) French's Despatch of 31 May ('*London Gazette*,' 22 June) 1915, for 'distinguished service in the field': killed in action, 10 May 1915, being shot through the head, in the trenches nr. Ypres: Age 31. *unm*.

(Panel 42) Capt. Duncan Collisson Willey Thomas, 4th (Extra Reserve) Bn. The Princess Louise's (Argyll & Sutherland Highlanders) attd. 1st Bn. Gordon Highlanders: only *s.* of Lieut.Col. W.F. Thomas, *yr.* and *jnr.* branch of Ap Thomas, 1st Bart., of Wenvoe Castle, co. Glamorgan, by his wife Jane ('Dunmere,' 17, Eaton Road, Branksome Park, Bournemouth): *b.* Quilon, India, 19 November 1890: *educ.* Holm Leigh, Buxton; Uppingham School; Caius College, Cambridge, and Royal Military College, Sandhurst: received his commission February 1911, 2nd Lieut., Army Service Corps: resigned from that Corps and joined Special Reserve, Argyll & Sutherland Highlanders, April 1914: promoted Lieut. August 1914: on the outbreak of war was, for Active Service, attd. 1st Gordon Highlanders, with which he was serving when he met his death. The battalion (8th Brigade, IIIrd Division) was present at the Battle of Mons and subsequent fighting. He had been recommended for promotion in his own battalion, in the hope that it would go out as a complete unit, but before his promotion was gazetted a draft of junior officers was called for, and Capt. (then Lieut.) Thomas (promoted 15 September 1914) was one of four Subalterns selected to go. An account of the circumstances attending his death was given by Capt. Paterson, Gordon Highlanders, "Duncan (Capt. Thomas) was back that day in some trenches in reserve to our position, which was at the time in some woods near Ypres. These reserve trenches were a line of small dug-outs roofed in with straw, and were very rarely shelled. Duncan, Capt. K.B. McKenzie (Seaforth Highlanders), and 2nd Lieut. Cook (3rd Black Watch), were in the same dug-out. A shell burst right on top, one of these big 60 lb explosives. The trench was completely buried. Their Coy.Sergt.-Major and their cook – Pte. Huggins – dug them out at once, but found that Duncan had been struck on the head by a piece of shell, and McKenzie was dead too, either from shock or suffocation. Cook was untouched, but had concussion of the brain. I believe he may recover. They were buried together in a place quite close." Though Capt. Thomas had been such a short time with the Gordon Highlanders he had already made many friends, for, as one of his young brother officers said, ".. it would have been difficult for anyone *not* to get on well with him." From his old masters also, Lieut.Col. Thomas received many sympathetic and appreciatory letters. A letter of the officer promoted to the command of the Gordon Highlanders indicated the appalling losses in officers we are suffering in this war. Writing in March 1915, he said, "Since I took command on 1st November no less than fifty-two officers have served under me at various times, and of these thirty-two have come and gone, and yet I have never at one time had more than eighteen officers present. Of the seventeen officers now serving, I am the only one that has been here continuously for over four months." A winner of many prizes for athletic and sporting ability during his school and college career, Capt. Thomas was a good rider, a first-class football player (centre-forward), good cricketer, excellent at tennis, and generally fond of sports of all kinds. He was killed, 12 November 1914, one week before his twenty-fourth birthday. *unm.*

Capt. Mackenzie also has no known grave; he is recorded on Panel 38.

(Panel 42) Lieut. Andrew Douglas MacArthur Anderson, 9th Bn. (Dumbartonshire) The Princess Louise's (Argyll & Sutherland Highlanders), (T.F.): *s.* of James Scott Anderson, of Tullichewan Castle, Balloch, co. Dumbarton, and Blairmuckhill, co. Lanark, by his wife Margaret Chiene: *b.* Glasgow, 25 March 1895: *educ.* Glasgow Academy: joined Argyll & Sutherland Highlanders (T.F.), April 1914: promoted Lieut. September 1914: Machine Gun Officer of his battalion, and having undertaken Imperial Service obligations, was sent to the seat of war, where he was killed in action by a high explosive shell near Ypres 10 May 1915: Age 20. *unm.* (*IWGC record 8 May 1915*)

(Panel 42) Lieut. George Gordon Chrystal, 1/9th Bn. (Dumbartonshire) The Princess Louise's (Argyll & Sutherland Highlanders), (T.F.): only *s.* of John Gordon (& Mrs) Chrystal, of Bloomhill, Cardross, co. Dumbarton: *educ.* Oxford University: a pre-war Territorial Officer, undertook Overseas Service obligations Stirling, August 1914: served with the Expeditionary Force in France and Flanders from February 1915, and was killed in action 25 May 1915, vicinity Sanctuary Wood: Age 29. Of the fighting in which he was killed a survivor wrote, "We were up against overwhelming odds for days, the Germans were trying to break our lines. The 9th kept up a brisk rate of fire on the advancing Germans who lost a terrible amount of men but we ourselves lost heavily. The wood was raked by shelling which seemed to scorch every yard of it – trees were smashed like matches. When the shelling ceased hardly a tree remained standing, all was a jumble of broken timber beneath which lay dead men, broken rifles, equipment and torn sandbags."

(Panel 42) Lieut. Montague Christian Cuthbert Clarke, 'B' Coy., 1st Bn. (91st Foot) The Princess Louise's (Argyll & Sutherland Highlanders): only *s.* of the late Montague Charles Clarke; Southern Mahratta Railway, India; by his wife Ada Georgina (Belgaum, India): *gdson.* of the late Dr. Vans Christian Clarke, Royal Navy, formerly Governor of Woking Prison: *b.* Lindfield, co. Sussex, 3 October 1893: *educ.* Brunswick School, Haywards Heath (eight years); Radley College, Abingdon (May 1907 – July 1910), and Royal Military College, Sandhurst: apptd. 2nd Lieut. Argyll & Sutherland Highlanders, September 1912: served two years 1st Battn., Dinapore, India, and was there on the outbreak of war: promoted Lieut. December 1914: served with the Expeditionary Force in France, and was killed in action nr. Ypres, 8 May 1915, by shrapnel while assisting a wounded soldier. A fair bowler, oar and keen fisherman, Mr Clarke spent much time big-game shooting while in India: Age 21. *unm.*

(Panel 42) Lieut. Frederick Robert Hughes Hutton, 1/9th Bn. (Dumbartonshire) The Princess Louises's (Argyll & Sutherland Highlanders), (T.F.): *yst. s.* of the late James Hutton, of Glasgow, Chartered Accountant: and *gdson.* of the late Rev. Harper, D.D., of Edinburgh: and brother to Corpl. 8440, J.D. Hutton, 2nd Cameron Highlanders, killed in action 6 February 1915: *b. c.*1882: *educ.* Glasgow Academy, and Glasgow University (graduated M.A.): subsequently became a partner in his father's firm: gazetted 2nd Lieut., Territorial Force, June 1913: promoted Lieut. September 1914: undertook Imperial Service obligations, with almost the whole of his battalion, on the outbreak of war: served with the Expeditionary Force in France and Flanders, and met his death at the Second Battle of Ypres. On that day, 10 May 1915, the Germans, in great force and supported by powerful artillery, made a determined attempt to break through the British lines, which resulted at one point in the temporary retirement of an English regiment, and two companies of 9th Argylls were thrown into the breach. The rest of the battalion was coming up in support under very heavy fire when Lieut. Hutton, who was in command of his company at the time, was killed by a shell. The Argylls on that day lost several of their officers, including the Colonel of the regiment. A short time previously Lieut Hutton had been engaged on important reconnaissance duty, and had brought in valuable information regarding the enemy's movements. Age 33.

His brother John also has no known grave; he is recorded on Panel 38.

(Panel 42) Lieut. Geoffrey Howel Scratton, M.C., 13th (Reserve) Bn. The Princess Louise's (Argyll & Sutherland Highlanders): *s.* of the late William Howel Scratton, M.A., by his wife Edith (18, Homefield Road, Wimbledon, London, S.W.), *dau.* of Sir Michael Kennedy, K.C.S.I.: *b.* Grahamstown, South Africa, 25 July 1893: *educ.* St. Paul's School: Occupation – Rubber Planter; Malay States: joined Malay States Contingent on the outbreak of war, and returned to England; joined Inns of Court O.T.C., January 1915: obtained a commission 2nd Lieut. Argyll & Sutherland Highlanders, March following: served with the Expeditionary Force in France and Flanders from November 1915, attd. 4th Battn. Black Watch (apptd. Adjt. January 1916), and was killed in action near St. Julien 1 August 1917. Buried in Kitchener's Wood. Awarded the Military Cross for 'conspicuous gallantry in action,' and Mentioned in F.M. Sir Douglas Haig's Despatch, January 1918, for 'gallant and distinguished service in the field.' His Commanding Officer wrote, "I cannot conceive a greater loss to his battalion or myself. Always reliable, willing, enthusiastic and hard-working…even-tempered and exceptionally cool, loyal, true and trustworthy." Age 34. *unm.*

(Panel 42) Lieut. John George Sheriff, 7th Bn. The Princess Louise's (Argyll & Sutherland Highlanders), (T.F.): eldest *s.* of the late George Sheriff, of Carronvale, Stenhouse, and Kersie, co. Stirling, by his wife Catherine J. (Carronvale, Larbert): and brother to 2nd Lieut. A. Nimmo, Northamptonshire Regt., who fell at the First Battle of Ypres: *b.* 24 August 1890: *educ.* Merchiston School, Edinburgh; Wadham College, Oxford: commissioned 2nd Lieut., Territorial Force, June 1914: undertook Imperial Service obligations on the outbreak of war, August 1914: promoted Lieut. September following: served with the British Expeditionary Force in France from December 1914, and was killed in action, 26 April 1915, nr. St. Julien, Flanders, at the Second Battle of Ypres: Age 24. *unm.*

His brother Alexander also has no known grave; he is recorded on Panel 43.

(Panel 42) Lieut. Colin Hunter Stein, 7th Bn. The Princess Louise's (Argyll & Sutherland Highlanders), (T.F.): *yst. s.* of John G. Stein, of Millfield, Pollmont, Falkirk: *b.* Bonnybridge, 21 November 1894: *educ.* Glasgow High School, where he was five years a member of the O.T.C. (Cadet Officer in his last year); and Glasgow University, where, on the outbreak of war, August 1914, he was studying Engineering: immediately volunteered and enlisted as Pte., 6th (Service) Battn. Cameron Highlanders: given his commission, 2nd Lieut., 7th Argyll & Sutherland Highlanders, January 1915: undertook Imperial Service obligations, went to France and was killed, 24 May 1915, at the village of Wieltje, nr. Ypres. 'At the time of his death he was Machine Gun Officer, and kept his gun going through a severe German attack and clouds of gas. The German attack, begun at 3 a.m., was not successful. Lieut. Stein was killed by a shell during a heavy bombardment in the afternoon, and a few hours later orders were received to evacuate the trench, which had become untenable through our trenches on either flank having been captured by the enemy. Buried in the trench where he fell.' Age 20. *unm.* A keen motor cyclist, and fond of Rugby football. Promoted Lieut. shortly before his death, gazetted posthumously. (*IWGC record 2nd Lieut.*)

(Panel 42) 2nd Lieut. George Henry Gordon Birrell, 9th Bn. (Dumbartonshire) The Princess Louise's (Argyll & Sutherland Highlanders), (T.F.): eldest *s.* of Col. John Birrell, of Allander House, Milngavie, co. Dumbarton, late 9th Argyll & Sutherland Highlanders and Army Service Corps (Highland Division), by his wife Grace Marguerite, *dau.* of George William Masson Buish, of Salto, B.O.: *b.* Milngavie, 2 February 1893: *educ.* Loretto College: gazetted to his father's old regt., 3 November 1914; joined at the Front February 1915. On 10 May 1915, during the Second Battle of Ypres, the Battn., which formed part of the 81st Brigade, received orders to take and hold a line of trenches near Hooge; this they did, but at a considerable loss. Lieut. Birrell was killed during the advance, while gallantly leading his platoon under heavy shellfire. He was buried in Zouave Wood, nr. Hooge: Age 22. *unm.* Remembered on Milngavie war Memorial.

(Panel 42) 2nd Lieut. Kenneth James Campbell, 9th Bn. (Dumbartonshire) The Princess Louise's (Argyll & Sutherland Highlanders), (T.F.): only *s.* of Robert Story Campbell, of Achnashie, Rosneath, co. Dumbarton, retired East Indian Merchant, by his wife Evelyn Rose, *dau.* of the late Rev. William Henry Stokes, Vicar of Goring; a nephew of the late Sir James Campbell, K.C.I.E. (Bombay Civil Service; Compositor, '*Bombay Gazetteer*'), and *gdson.* of the late Rev. John McLeod Campbell, D.D.: *b.* Bombay, 4 January 1891: *educ.* Rottingdean; Marlborough; Magdalen College, Oxford (scholarship student), where he took his degree with honours in History (1912), and 'Greats' (1914). He had originally intended to take orders in the Church of England, and on leaving the University (1913) joined Magdalen College Mission, Euston Road: on the outbreak of war having been 8 years O.T.C. cadet (Marlborough and Oxford), he applied for a commission; gazetted (2 September 1914) 2nd Lieut., 1/9th Argyll & Sutherland Highlanders, leaving Bedford with his regt. 19 February 1915 for France. Killed in action near Ypres, being struck by a shell while in charge of machine guns, 10 May 1915. His commanding officer wrote that he died "doing his duty nobly." His Platoon Sergt. said that "He was a brave young officer and the pride of all the platoon." A brother officer, writing on 13 May, stated, " I was myself slightly wounded the same day, so was not on the spot when he was killed, but I understand that he was wounded by a shell, but that he continued to serve the gun until a second shell killed him." He was stroke of his college boat in the Torpids when Magdalen was head of the river in 1913: Age 24. *unm.* (*IWGC record 12 May 1915*)

(Panel 42) 2nd Lieut. Richard Gibb, 1st Bn. (91st Foot) The Princess Louise's (Argyll & Sutherland Highlanders): 4th *s.* of the late Francis Moray Gibb, of Cowdenbeath: *b.* Fordell, Aberdour, co. Fife, 4 January 1876: *educ.* Cowdenbeath: enlisted 1st Argyll & Sutherland Highlanders, January 1892: served throughout the South African War, with rank of Sergt. (Queen's Medal, 4 clasps; King's Medal, 2 clasps); awarded Good Conduct Medal: accompanied his battalion to Malta, 1909, thence to India, 1912: had risen to rank of Sergt.-Major when the outbreak of war with Germany was declared: received his commission, 2nd Lieut., December 1914, after twenty-three years' service in the regiment; posted to his old battalion: served with the Expeditionary Force in France and Flanders, and was killed in action at Ypres, 12 May 1915: Age 39. Mentioned in Sir John French's Despatch, 31 May 1915, for 'gallant and distinguished service in the field.' He was married to Alice, *dau.* of John Davies, late of the Prison Commission, Scotland.

(Panel 42) 2nd Lieut. William Campbell Suttie, 2/7th Bn. The Princess Louise's (Argyll & Sutherland Highlanders), (T.F.): only *s.* of John Suttie, of 'Levenbank,' Bawhirley Road, Greenock, by his wife Jeannie: *b.* Greenock, 3 April 1891: *educ.* Greenock Higher Grade School – thereafter took up an appointment in the banking profession; Member, Institute of Bankers: applied for a commission on the outbreak of war, August 1914: gazetted 2nd Lieut., 7th Argyll & Sutherland Highlanders, October 1914: after training proceeded to France 3 May 1915. Three weeks later, 24 May, he was killed by shell splinters near Ypres. Buried at St. Jean: 24 May 1915: Age 24. *unm.* (*IWGC record age 23*)

(Panel 42) Sergt. S/3392, Harry Cassidy Doyle, 'C' Coy., 10th (Service) Bn. The Princess Louise's (Argyll & Sutherland Highlanders): *s.* of James Doyle, of 27, Charles Street, Greenock, co. Renfrew: *b.* Rothesay, Isle of Bute, 1888: proceeded to France May 1915, and was killed in action 20 November 1915: Age 27. Remains recovered (GRU Report, Zillebeke – 5/269E) unmarked grave 'Sanctuary Wood Old Cemetery' (29.I.24.b.90.97), 'Unknown British Soldier. Highlander;' identified – Clothing, Kilt; reinterred, registered 16 May 1928. *Buried in Sanctuary Wood Cemetery (II.H.11).*

(Panel 42) Sergt. 2273, David Hulme, 10th (Service) Bn. The Princess Louise's (Argyll & Sutherland Highlanders): *s.* of Arthur Hulme, of Port Glasgow, by his wife Bridget: *husb.* to Lilian May Hulme (Temperance Hall, Bonnybridge, co. Stirling): *b.* Gourock, co. Renfrew, 1879: enlisted Stirling: served with the Expeditionary Force in France and Flanders from 11 May 1915, and was killed in action 14 November following: Age 36. Remains recovered unmarked grave 'Sanctuary Wood Old Cemetery' (29.I.24.b.90.97), 'Unknown British Soldier. Highlander;' identified – Clothing, Kilt; reinterred, registered 16 May 1928. (*IWGC record 14 November 1914*). *Buried in Sanctuary Wood Cemetery (II.H.7).*

(Panel 42) Corpl. 1061, James McNair, 1/9th Bn. (Dumbartonshire) The Princess Louise's (Argyll & Sutherland Highlanders), (T.F.): *s.* of William McNair, of Canniesburn, Bearsden, Glasgow, co. Lanark, and Elizabeth, his wife: Occupation – Warehouseman; Messrs Stewart, Moir & Muir, Miller Street, Glasgow: served with the Expeditionary Force in France from February 1915. Killed while on sentry duty 6 – 7 April 1915. In the four days up to Corpl. McNair's death 'the Argylls were under almost continuous fire from the Germans who were only 50 yards away; their casualties were 10 killed and 36 wounded.' Age 23. He was married to the late Agnes Park McNair (Main Street, Milngavie, co. Dumbarton), and left two small children.

(Panel 42) L/Corpl. 783, James Owens, 1st Bn. (91st Foot) The Princess Louise's (Argyll & Sutherland Highlanders): *s.* of James Owens, of Govan, co. Lanark, by his wife Annie: enlisted Glasgow, 1910. Killed in action 26 April 1915: Age 22. *unm.* See Pte. T. Dolan, below.

(Panel 42) Pte. S/20354, William James Birse, Lewis Gun Section, 1/8th Bn. (Argyllshire) The Princess Louise's (Argyll & Sutherland Highlanders), (T.F.): *s.* of the late William Eddie Birse, Farmer; of Woodfield, Coull, Tarland, co. Aberdeen, by his wife Ann, *dau.* of the late James Dunn, Farmer; of Warkbraes, Leochel-Cushnie, co. Aberdeen: *b.* 19 October 1897: *educ.* Coull Public School: Occupation – Farmer: enlisted 18 December 1916: served with the Expeditionary Force in France and Flanders from 10 May 1917, being employed in the Lewis Gun Section of his battalion; and was killed in action at Ypres 31 July following. Buried where he fell. His Commanding Officer, 2nd Lieut. James Beveridge, wrote, "He was cheery and made a fine comrade. The fact that he was in the Lewis Gun Section proves that, as that section is always specially picked men." Age 19.

(Panel 42) Pte. S/9629, John Burns, 10th (Service) Bn. The Princess Louise's (Argyll & Sutherland Highlanders): late of Liverpool, co. Lancaster: *b.* Lambeth: enlisted Southwark, London, S.E. Killed in action 15 November 1915. Remains recovered unmarked grave 'Sanctuary Wood Old Cemetery' (29.I.24.b.90.97), 'Unknown British Soldier;' identified – Clothing; reinterred, registered 16 May 1928. *Buried in Sanctuary Wood Cemetery (II.H.9).*

(Panel 42) Pte. 10823, Charles Campbell, 1st Bn. (91st Foot) The Princess Louises's (Argyll & Sutherland Highlanders): *s.* of Robert Campbell, of 67, Bridge Street, Strabane, Co. Tyrone, by his wife Martha: enlisted Paisley, co. Renfrew, 1907. Killed in action 26 April 1915: Age 26. *unm.* See Pte. T. Dolan, below.

(Panel 42) Pte. 1586, Alexander Doig, 'G' Coy., 1/7th Bn. The Princess Louise's (Argyll & Sutherland Highlanders), (T.F.): *s.* of the late Alex Doig, by his wife Janet (4, Brandfield Street, Edinburgh, co. Midlothian): and brother to Pte. 1573. A. Doig, 1/7th Argyll & Sutherland Highlanders, died of wounds 27 April 1915: *b.* Edinburgh, *c.*1894: Occupation – Signalman; North British Railway: enlisted Kinross, August 1914: served with the Expeditionary Force in France and Flanders from 6 January 1915, and was killed in action 2 May 1915: Age 21. *unm.*

His brother Andrew is buried in Hazebrouck Communal Cemetery (II.E.31).

(Panel 42) Pte. S/3331, Thomas Dolan, 1st Bn. (91st Foot) The Princess Louise's (Argyll & Sutherland Highlanders): *s.* of Mrs Dolan, late of Linlithgow: enlisted West Calder, co. Midlothian, August 1914: served with the Expeditionary Force in France, and was killed in action at the Second Battle of Ypres, 26 April 1915. His Company Officer said Pte. Dolan was killed by a bullet when firing over the parapet, death being instantaneous and without pain, and his cheerful obedience to duty and the respect in which he was held by his comrades was a great loss to the Company as a whole; concluding that Pte. Dolan 'and another hero were buried together.' No name was given for the 'hero' buried beside Pte. Dolan; five members of 1st Argylls were killed in action that day, none have a known grave.

(Panel 42) Pte. 2076, James Duchart, 1/7th Bn. The Princess Louise's (Argyll & Sutherland Highlanders), (T.F.): *s.* of Alexander Duchart, of 16, Church Square, Grahamston, Falkirk, co. Stirling, by his wife Elizabeth Sorley: and brother to Pte. S/6010, A. Duchart, Argyll & Sutherland Highlanders, died of wounds 8 October 1915: enlisted Falkirk: served with the Expeditionary Force in France and Flanders, and was killed in action 25 April 1915: **Age 16**.

His brother Alexander is buried in Etaples Military Cemetery (III.D.1A).

(Panel 42) Pte. 5944, Arthur Neil Gillespie, 'A' Coy., 10th (Service) Bn. The Princess Louise's (Argyll & Sutherland Highlanders): 3rd *s.* of David Gillespie, Moulder, now (1917) on active service, by his wife Agnes (16, Boyd Street, Falkirk), *dau.* of Hugh Neil: *b.* Falkirk, 10 March 1891: *educ.* Comely Park School, Falkirk: Occupation – Moulder (deferred), but enlisted 15 October 1914: went to France, May 1915, and was killed in action 15 October following. Buried at Ypres: Age 24. He *m.* Wolf Craig, Stirling; Maggie (now wife of George Jamieson, of 220, East Wallace Street, Grahamston, Falkirk), *dau.* of Hugh Douglas, and had a son, David, *b.* 17 March 1915 (*d.* 11 January 1917).

PANEL 42 ENDS PTE. P. LAMBERT, ARGYLL & SUTH. HIGHLANDERS.

PANEL 44 BEGINS PTE. J. LAWRIE – ARGYLL & SUTH. HIGHLANDERS.

(Panel 44) Pte. 6521, William Moir, 1st Bn. (91st Foot) The Princess Louise's (Argyll & Sutherland Highlanders): late of Falkirk: *b.* Edinburgh: enlisted Stirling, 1914. Killed in action 26 April 1915. See Pte. T. Dolan (Panel 42).

(Panel 44) Pte. 196, Robert Paul, 'A' Coy., 1st Bn. (91st Foot) The Princess Louise's (Argyll & Sutherland Highlanders): 2nd *s.* of Robert Paul, Plumber; of 22, Lutton Place, Edinburgh, by his wife Eliza: *b.* Edinburgh, 28 May 1889: *educ.* Preston Street Public School: enlisted September 1908: served at Chatham, Malta, India, and with the Expeditionary Force in France and Flanders. Killed in action nr. Hooge, 10 May 1915. Writing to his father, his Chief Officer, Capt. J.R. Couper, said, "He was killed instantaneously by a shell which burst on the parapet in front of him, and two others with him. The company was heavily engaged at the time and later had to evacuate the trench by order of our General. At night we went back and buried your son along with ten others. The company lost on this date 11 killed and 22 wounded. The place was close to Hooge, which is east of Ypres, and the exact spot of his grave is not marked by any special feature or by a cross as the burial had to be done very hurriedly. Your son was a splendid 'sticker,' and though he suffered from very bad feet, always refused to 'go sick,' and on one occasion, when ordered to go to the Dressing Station to have his feet treated, as he could not keep up with his company, he very reluctantly went, but rejoined us within three hours, having found his way to the trench at his own pace." Age 25. *unm.*

(Panel 44) Pte. S/9511, Andrew Radcliffe, 10th (Service) Bn. The Princess Louise's (Argyll & Sutherland Highlanders): adopted *s.* of Mr (& Mrs) Thomson, of Fallhills Toll, Penicuik, co, Midlothian: enlisted Edinburgh. Killed in action 15 November 1915: Age 21. *unm.* Remains recovered unmarked grave 'Sanctuary Wood Old Cemetery' (29.I.24.b.90.97), 'Unknown British Soldier. Highlander;' identified Clothing, Kilt; reinterred – registered 16 May 1928. *Buried in Sanctuary Wood Cemetery (II.H.10).*

Time Rolls On
Memories Remain

(Panel 44) Pte. 100, James Torrance, 1st Bn. (91st Foot) The Princess Louise's (Argyll & Sutherland Highlanders): *s.* of Alexander Torrance, of 44, Barrowfield Street, Bridgeton, Glasgow, co. Lanark, by his wife Isabella: and brother to Pte. S/7764, J. Torrance, Gordon Highlanders, killed in action 17 June 1915, at Ypres: *b.* Barony, co. Lanark: enlisted Glasgow. Killed in action 25 February 1915: Age 33.

His brother John also has no known grave; he is recorded on Panel 38.

(Panel 44) Pte. S/709, Robert Turner, 1st Bn. (91st Foot) The Princess Louise's (Argyll & Sutherland Highlanders): *s.* of Adam Turner, of 7, Anchor Buildings, Paisley, co. Renfrew, by his wife Williamina: enlisted Paisley, 1914. Killed in action 26 April 1915: Age 18. See Pte. T. Dolan (Panel 42).

(Panel 44) Capt. John Goold Adams, 1st Bn. (100th Foot) The Leinster Regt. (Prince of Wales' Royal Canadians): *s.* of the Ven. John Michael Goold Adams, Rector of Clonleigh, Co. Donegal, and Archdeacon of Derry, by his wife Emma, 4th *dau.* of Robert McClintock, of Dunmore, Carrigans, Co. Donegal, D.L.: *b.* Rossdowney Vicarage, Londonderry, 10 October 1883: *educ.* Bilton Grange Preparatory School, Rugby; R.M.C. Sandhurst: gazetted 2nd Lieut., Leinster Regt. 22 April 1903; promoted Lieut. 15 December 1904; Capt. 21 September 1912: served Pretoria, 1903 – 04; with Mounted Infantry; Harrysmith, 1904 – 05; Mauritius, 1905 – 06; West African Frontier Force, Northern Nigeria, 1908 – November 1913. After the outbreak of war, August 1914, he accompanied his regiment (which had been brought home from India) to France, 23 December following: wounded, February 1915: rejoined his regiment April, and was killed in action at Hill 60, nr. Ypres, 4 May following, by the same shell that also killed one of his subalterns, 2nd Lieut. E. Kahn: Age 33. He *m.* Moneyguyneen, Birr, King's Co., 5 August 1913; Irene Grace, eldest *dau.* of Assheton Biddulph, M.F.H., of Moneyguyneen: *s.p.* (*IWGC record 5 May 1915*)

2nd Lieut. Kahn also has no known grave; he is recorded below.

(Panel 44) Capt. William George Henry Bates, 1st Bn. (100th Foot) The Leinster Regt. (Prince of Wales' Royal Canadians): 2nd *s.* of the Rev. William Wheatley Bates, M.A., of Toronto, by his wife Emily, *dau.* of Manasseh (& Emma) Leeson, Extensive Landowner, Canada: *b.* Thornhill, Toronto, 12 October 1878: *educ.* Privately, and Trinity College, Toronto: enlisted Lancashire Fusiliers, 1901, hoping to see active service in South Africa, but the regt. was ordered to Crete and kept there until the conclusion of that campaign: after serving over two years in the ranks, was commissioned 2nd Lieut., Leinster Regt., 7 November 1903; promoted Lieut. 15 Decemebr 1906; Capt. 21 September 1912: saw much foreign service, serving in Crete, Malta, Gibraltar, South Africa, Mauritius and India: was Instructor, School of Musketry, South Africa, and invented an automatic elevating and traversing gun gear, which is now (1916) being tested in the Hythe School of Musketry. On the outbreak of war Capt. Bates was in India, and arrived with his regt. in Flanders, 21 December 1914, holding the double command of Company and Brigade Machine Gun Officer. He went through all the heavy fighting for Ypres, and served continuously until he was killed in action, shot through the head (Hill 60 – Zillebeke sector) nr. Ypres, 26 April 1915: Age 36. His Commanding Officer wrote, "Your husband was one of the bravest and most gallant men I know, and his death leaves a gap which cannot be filled. I can only add that he died like the gallant man he was." A brother officer wrote, "The regt. can say of him that he never asked a man to do a thing he would not do himself. He simply did not know fear, and would always tell us that dying was part of the game. It isn't only we officers who admired him, but every man who knew him would have followed him anywhere – everywhere he led." He *m.* St. Margaret's Church, Warnham, co. Sussex, 10 August 1912; Mabel (Dent, Warnham, West Sussex), *yst. dau.* of Hastings Castor Draper, and left a *s.* and *dau.* – Lionel William Leeson, *b.* 25 May 1913; Pamela Dorcas, *b.* 2 June 1914.

(Panel 44) Capt. Robert Macgregor Bowen-Colthurst, 4th (Special Reserve), attd. 1st Bn. (100th Foot) The Leinster Regt. (Prince of Wales' Royal Canadians): 2nd *s.* of the late Robert Walter Travers Bowen-Colthurst, of Oak Grove, Killinardish, Co. Cork, J.P., by his wife Georgina de Bellasis, only *dau.* of Alfred Greet, of Dripsey House, Co. Cork, J.P.: *b.* Oak Grove, Killinardish, Co. Cork, 15 September 1883: *educ.* Harrow, and Trinity College, Cambridge (graduated 1905); thereafter took a Staff appointment; Lord Lieutenant of Ireland, initially as Assistant Private Secretary; later Vice-Chamberlain, which latter post he held until 1912. He then undertook work in connection with the Irish Department of Agriculture, and later succeeded the Earl of Carrick as Inspector for Irish Agricultural interests in Great Britain, which post he held until the outbreak of war. Acting on his conviction that every man ought to be trained in time of peace for the defence of the country, he had joined 4th (Special Reserve) Bn. Leinster Regt., 1910: received his Lieutenancy, 12 March 1912, and, volunteering for Imperial Service, was gazetted Capt. 14 August 1914; proceeded to the Front in France, 5 March 1915, and was killed in action on the 15th. of that month at St. Eloi. Lieut.Col. C.B. Prowse, Comdg. 1st Leinster Regt., wrote, "The battn. had to retake some trenches which had been lost by another regt., and your husband bravely led his men and took and occupied the trench as he was ordered to. But early the following morning he was shot through the head over the parapet of a trench and died, I hear without pain – in fact death was instantaneous. During the few days he was with us he had done splendid work and behaved most gallantly, and the men would follow him anywhere, and I do greatly sympathise with you and yours in your loss, and the regt's. loss, too. I am sending your husband's name to the General for 'gallant conduct' and I also enclose a note which he wrote previous to the night attack, which was to be given to you." And a brother officer, "I know Col. Prowse has written to you, but I think, perhaps, you might like to hear a second account of everything that happened. It might throw fresh light on details you have heard from the commanding officer. Your husband arrived up here last Thursday week, 11 March. We were just going to start our eight days' tour of duty in the trenches and were marching to them. He, with Capt. Radcliffe from the 5th Battn., joined us about 5 p.m., when we were having a halt for tea. I remember how delighted I was to see him again, as he had always been so good to me, and it was just like a link with home seeing him again. He and Capt. Radcliffe came with us into the trenches, your husband taking command of 'A' Coy. We came out of the trenches again on Saturday night, arriving in our billets about 2 a.m. on Sunday morning, the 14th. I did not see much of him that day as we were all sleeping off the effects of the 48 hours in the trenches. About 4.30 p.m., in the afternoon of Sunday, the 14th, a tremendous bombardment by our guns started. We were very soon turned out and hurried up to a ruined village not far behind the trenches. We learned that the Germans had captured our trenches, and it was decided that we must counter-attack at 2 a.m. on Monday morning. Your husband was detailed with his company to recapture a trench, No.20. He was full of keenness and enthusiasm about it, as he was always about everything. Just before midnight, before we started off, I met him in the Dressing Station, where he gave a letter to Dr. Kenny, our Medical Officer, asking him to send it to you by registered post if he was killed. The Medical Officer said, 'Nonsense,' not to talk that way, as he would not be killed. Your husband replied cheerfully that it did not worry him a bit, only he wanted the letter sent if he were. After that we started off. He was ahead of me. About 12.45 I caught him up with my company, and gave him a lot of empty sandbags we had been carrying for his company. This was about 500 yards from the enemy's trenches, and the bullets were flying about. I said, 'Good-night,' wishing him the best of luck. He was very cheery and happy then, that is the last time I saw him alive. From Coy.Sergt.Major Kershaw, whose home address is 22, Clarendon Street, Bradford, I got the following details. He was with your husband the whole time. At 2 a.m. they charged and captured the trench, any Germans who were in it running away; but after some time they found they were being so hotly fired on into the trench from the right flank that they decided to fall back into a trench just behind. As they did this a young subaltern, named Buchanan, of the Irish Fusiliers, who was attached to 'A' Coy., was badly wounded. As soon as your husband got his company into a trench behind, he, with the Coy.Sergt.-Major and a volunteer, went back under heavy fire and brought Buchanan into the trench. By the time it was 5.15 a.m., just day-light. At 5.30 a.m. the Sergt.-Major saw a lot of men retiring out of the left flank of the trench they were in, and went to see what it meant. Your husband followed him. They were walking along inside the trench, but your husband's head must have been exposed (his height was 6 feet 4 inches), for a bullet came over the parapet and went through his head. He knew nothing about it, but just dropped, death being instantaneous. It would seem almost as if he had a premonition of his death, as several times he repeated to his Coy. Sergt.-Major, 'Be sure, if I am shot, that you bury me where I fall, as I am too big and heavy for the men to carry in.' Up to the end he was always thinking of others. He was buried as soon as it was dark, on Monday evening, 15 March, in a little plot of ground on the left-hand side of the road, just as you leave the ruined village of St. Eloi for Ypres. This spot is exactly opposite the last ruined cottage on the right as you leave the village. We are going back to this post tomorrow evening for another eight days' work. I am getting the Battn Sergt.Major – Sergt.Major Shaw – who buried him, to point out the spot so that I will know it should I ever return alive. I can then tell you exactly. A wooden cross with his name and regt. will be put up to mark the place. I am very glad to say the commanding officer is recommending your husband for the D.S.O. for the good work he did that night.": 15 March 1915: Age 31. He *m.*, Bilton, nr. Rugby, 7 December 1907; Winifred ('The Gable House,' Layer de la Haye, Essex), *dau.* of the late Rev. Charles Frederick Cumber West, Vicar of Charlbury, Oxford, and had issue a *s.* and three *daus.* – Peggy Winifred Isabel, *b.* 2 August 1909; Honor Georgina Beatrice, *b.* 13 September 1911; Charles Patrick Russell, *b.* 25 February 1913; Marian Elizabeth Hope, *b.* 12 October 1914.

(Panel 44) Capt. Herbert Travers Radcliff, 5th (Reserve) attd. 1st Bn. (100th Foot) The Leinster Regt. (Prince of Wales' Royal Canadians): 2nd *s.* of the late George Edward Radcliff, of Willmount, Kells, Co. Meath, by his wife Emma May Alexandria, *dau.* of John Travers Madden, of Inch House, Balbriggan: *b.* Kells, 11 August 1882: *educ.* Royal School, Armagh: gazetted 2nd Lieut. Leinster Regt., 27 October 1906: promoted Lieut., and Capt. 10 February 1913: went to France 6 March 1915, attd. 1st Battn., and was killed in action at St. Eloi, 15 March following. Lieut.Col. A.B. Prowse, commanding 1st Leinster Regt., wrote, "He was holding a trench which had a garrison of 30 men, and which was attacked by 100 Germans at, or soon after, dawn. He was killed instantaneously by a bullet which struck him in the head, and could have suffered no pain. I may add that the Germans were beaten off with a loss of 34 killed alone. During the few days he has been with us he has proved himself a brave and gallant officer, and we deplore the loss of a good comrade, and offer you a whole hearted sympathy." And Lieut. C.I. McKay, 5th Battn., "I was with him when he was killed. He was my company commander both here and in Passage, and, like all the men of the company, I would have done anything for him. He always thought of the men first and afterwards himself, and it was through his unselfishness he met his death. Someone said the Germans were leaving their trench to attack, and no one looked out, so he looked over and was hit. He suffered no pain whatever. He was buried on Monday night, and we have handed all his things to the Quartermaster, who will send them to you in a few weeks. I only know too well how useless it is to express sympathy, but I have taken this opportunity of expressing not only my own sympathy, but that of all the men of the company, who had grown to love him, even in the few days under his command.": Age 32. *unm.*

(Panel 44) Lieut. Andrew Buckland Hodge, 3rd attd. 2nd Bn. (109th Foot) The Leinster Regt. (Prince of Wales' Royal Canadians): *s.* of the late Rev. John Mackey Hodge, M.A. (Oxon.), Vicar of St. Luke's, Plymouth, and Chaplain of the Old Cemetery, by his wife Jenny (Exeter), *dau.* of Isaac Lang, J.P.: *b.* Plymouth, 7 September 1892: *educ.* Plymouth College; won the Dyke Exhibition, the only one from this school to do so since 1898; also the Dean Boyd Exhibition: entered Exeter College, Oxford, October 1911; won Honours in Moderations, and was reading for 'Greats' with a view to entering the I.C.S.: joined Oxford University O.T.C.: obtained a commission, 2nd Lieut., 26 January 1915; promoted Lieut., October following: served in Ireland; Musketry Officer & Adjutant, Cork; and with the Expeditionary

Force in France and Flanders, and was killed in action at Shrewsbury Forest, south-east of Zillebeke, 31 July 1917. Buried there. His Colonel wrote, "He was leading his company in the front of our attack. He was a fine officer and, in common with a number of his comrades, has died a fine death. The battalion has suffered severely, but the individual acts of so many gallant leaders have left an impression which can never die. Your brother fell in the hour of victory, and died soon after he got his mortal wound." And a brother officer, "He died a truly heroic death, leading his company into action, and so has won for himself the immortal praise of all ranks. He was, in my estimation, the most conscientious, hard-working, thorough soldier I have ever met, and the success of his company is due to his untiring energy in explaining and working out the most minute details of what his company were entrusted to do under his most able leadership." Age 24. *unm.*

(Panel 44) Lieut. Spencer Ruscombe Westmacott, 2nd (109th Foot) attd. 1st Bn. (100th Foot) The Leinster Regt. (Prince of Wales' Royal Canadians): *s.* of Canon (& Mrs) Westmacott, of The Sanctuary, Probus, co. Cornwall: and elder brother to 2nd Lieut. F.C. Westmacott, Royal West Kent Regt., who fell 31 July 1917, at the Third Battle of Ypres. Killed in action 8 May 1915: Age 25. *unm.*

His brother Frederick also has no known grave; he is recorded on Panel 45.

(Panel 44) 2nd Lieut. Edgar Kahn, General List attd. 1st Bn. (100th Foot) The Leinster Regt. (Prince of Wales' Royal Canadians): *s.* of Emil Kahn, of 49, Harley House, Regent's Park, late of 53, Compayne Gardens, Hampstead, London, N.W., by his wife Frances: *b.* London, 21 March 1892: *educ.* University College, and abroad: joined Honourable Artillery Coy., Armoury House, on the outbreak of war: served with the Expeditionary Force in France from 18 September 1914: gazetted Temp. 2nd Lieut., General List, February 1915, attd. 1st Leinster Regt. for Active Service. Killed in the attack on Hill 60, 4 May following, by a shell which also killed Capt. J.G. Adams. He was, for many years, a member of the Hendon Golf Club: 4 May 1915: Age 23. *unm.* Capt. Adams also has no known grave; he is recorded above.

(Panel 44) 2nd Lieut. Kenneth Kemble Pelton, M.C., 5th (Extra Reserve) Bn. The Leinster Regt. (Prince of Wales' Royal Canadians) attd. 7th (Service) Bn. Princess Victoria's (Royal Irish Rifles): elder *s.* of the Rev. William Frederick Pelton, Vicar of Ullenhall, Henley-on-Arden, by his wife Susan Lena, *dau.* of George Lock: *b.* North Walsham, co. Norfolk, 15 June 1897: *educ.* Hazelwood; Limpsfield, and Dover College: Occupation – Articled Chartered Accountant: volunteered for Foreign Service following the declaration of war, 4 August 1914: gazetted 2nd Lieut., Leinster Regt., 31 July 1915: served with the Expeditionary Force in France and Flanders from 20 July 1916, attd. 7th Royal Irish Rifles: present at the fighting at Ginchy, and was killed in action between Ypres and Zonnebeke, 1 August 1917. Buried where he fell. Lieut.Col. S.E. Francis, Officer Comdg., wrote, "I want to tell you how sorry we all are at the death of your son. He has been with this battalion just a year, and we were all very fond of him. His splendid courage and cheery disposition made him a general favourite;" and the Chaplain, "The dear lad was the bravest of the brave, and passed through two Hun barrages. He was killed practically instantly." Sergt. Frank Hendrey also wrote, "It was your son's unselfishness and thought for others before himself which finally cost him his life. A wounded artillery officer came up just as the shelling, if possible, became worse than ever. He was going to drop down, as he was in the open, but your son insisted in changing places with him, thereby giving up what cover he had got. A few minutes after there came the rushing whistle of a shell on arrival – an ear-splitting crash, and a rain of earth, mud and pieces of brick from the explosion. I was somewhat dazed by the shock for a moment, but directly the rain of pieces stopped, I saw that your son had been hit." Mentioned in Despatches ('*London Gazette*,' 25 May 1917), by F.M. Sir Douglas Haig, and awarded the Military Cross ('*London Gazette*,' 26 April 1917), for 'conspicuous gallantry and devotion to duty.' He also received the thanks of the General Commanding 16th (Irish) Division, for gallant conduct on the field of battle, 'worthy of permanent record on the annals of the regiment.': Age 20. *unm.*

(Panel 44) Sergt. 9337, Robert Martin O'Connor, 'A' Coy., 2nd Bn. (109th Foot) The Leinster Regt. (Prince of Wales' Royal Canadians): formerly no.6560, Seaforth Highlanders: 16th child of Martin O'Connor, of 46 – 47, Bridge Street, Tralee, Co. Kerry, by his wife Catherine, *née* Counihan: and brother-in-law to Capt. D.D. Sheehan, M.P., 9th Royal Munster Fusiliers (surv'd.): a pre-war Reservist, served with Seaforth Highlanders, South African Campaign: returned to the Colours on the outbreak of war, posted Leinster Regt. Killed in action 31 July 1917: Age 36. He *m*. April 1916; Mary (1, Lower Browne Street, Youghal, Co. Cork), *dau*. of Mr (& Mrs) Hennessey, of Middleton, Co. Cork, and had a *s*. Robert Martin, *b*. 19 August 1917.

(Panel 44) L/Sergt. 10765, Richard Morrissey, 2nd Bn. (109th Foot) The Leinster Regt. (Prince of Wales' Royal Canadians): formerly no.8533, 8th Hussars: *s*. of the late Matthew Morrissey, by his wife Mary (8, Albert Place, Fermoy, Co. Cork): and brother to Sergt. RTS/4245, W. Morrissey, Army Service Corps, died 11 November 1918; and Drmr. 7794, M. Morrissey, 2nd Leinster Regt., died 5 April 1916: enlisted Cork . Killed in action 21 July 1917: Age 25. One of three brothers who fell.

His brother William is buried in St. Sever Cemetery Extension, Rouen (S.II.GG.29); Matthew, Ration Farm (La Plus Douve) Annexe (II.C.17).

(Panel 44) Corpl. 8865, John Harrington, 2nd Bn. (109th Foot) The Leinster Regt. (Prince of Wales' Royal Canadians): *s*. of Paul Harrington, of 4, Davitt Place, Kenmare, and Bridget, his spouse: *b*. Kenmare, Co. Kerry: enlisted Tralee. Killed by shellfire 13 March 1916, at Hooge: Age 26. *unm*. See Menin Road South Military Cemetery (I.J.1-5; I.K.6-16).

(Panel 44) Corpl. 8131, Eugene O'Callaghan, 'A' Coy., 1st Bn. (100th Foot) The Leinster Regt. (Prince of Wales' Royal Canadians): *s*. of Denis (& Mrs) O'Callaghan, of Model Farm, Bishopstown, Co. Cork: enlisted Cork. Killed in action 12 May 1915 Age 28. *Buried in Sanctuary Wood Cemetery (V.R.7)*.

(Panel 44) Pte. 5470, Charles Barham, 7th (Service) Bn. The Leinster Regt. (Prince of Wales' Royal Canadians): *s*. of the late William Barham, Wheelwright; of 6, Woods Green, Wadhurst, co. Sussex, by his wife Laura, *née* Smith (Marlpit, Wadhurst): *b*. Wadhurst, 20 September 1883: Occupation – Grocer's Assistant: enlisted Royal Sussex Regt. (no.13179), Tonbridge, co. Kent: served with the Expeditionary Force in France and Flanders: previously wounded and after recovery transf'd. Leinster Regt. Immediately after the detonation of the mines beneath the Messines Ridge, 7 June 1917, his battalion advanced amidst a dense fog of fumes towards their objectives. Successfully taken by the end of the day the battalion suffered 'slight casualties' in the process. Fifteen other ranks killed, over 100 wounded, a newspaper report stated:– 'Charles Barham was killed by shrapnel and buried in a military cemetery behind the lines.': Age 33. He *m*., 10 July 1907, Wesleyan Mission Hall, Hill Street, Tunbridge Wells; Anne Jarvis, spinster (Stationer's Assistant),

(Panel 44) Pte. 4450, John Bowes, 2nd Bn. (109th Foot) The Leinster Regt. (Prince of Wales' Royal Canadians): *b*. Dublin: enlisted Mosney Camp, Co. Louth: served in France from September 1914, and was killed in action nr. Hooge, 4.00 – 4.30 a.m., 12 August 1915, by an explosive bullet in the head. Buried in a disused trench.

(Panel 44) Pte. 5422, James Brighton (*a.k.a.* Jim Lincoln), 2nd Bn. (109th Foot) The Leinster Regt. (Prince of Wales' Royal Canadians): formerly no.146731, Royal Field Artillery: *s*. of the late Thomas Brighton, of Norwich, by his wife Mary. Died 16 June 1917: Age 36. He was married to Mary Ann Brighton (226, Silver Road, Norwich).

(Panel 44) Pte. 3551, Patrick Burlace, Machine Gun Section, 2nd Bn. (109th Foot) The Leinster Regt. (Prince of Wales's, Royal Canadians): *s*. of the late Pte. 4335, T. Burlace, 2nd Connaught Rangers, died 9 December 1914, aged 50 years; and his late wife Mary: *b*. Athlone, Co. Westmeath: enlisted there: served in France and Flanders from September 1914; killed by the direct hit of a 5.9 shell on the gun position 12 August 1915, nr. Hooge: **Age 16**. Ptes. J. Scully and P. Cleary were also killed.

His father Thomas is buried in Beuvry Communal Cemetery Extension (III.D.15). Pte. Scully has no known grave, he is recorded below; Pte. Cleary is buried in Birr Cross Roads Cemetery (II.D.30).

(Panel 44) Pte. 5852, Patrick Condon, 2nd Bn. (109th Foot) The Leinster Regt. (Prince of Wales' Royal Canadians): *s*. of James Condon, of Chapel Street, Kilfinane, Co. Limerick, by his wife Johanna: *b*. Kilfinane, *c*.1898: enlisted Mallow, Co. Cork. Killed in action 16 June 1917: Age 19

(Panel 44) Pte. 4563, Patrick Daly, 'A' Coy., 1st Bn. (100th Foot) The Leinster Regt. (Prince of Wales' Royal Canadians): *s.* of James Daly, of Clara Road, Moate, Co. Westmeath, by his wife Mary: *b.* Dublin: enlisted Athlone, Co. Westmeath. In a letter to Mrs Daly, Sergt. 6387, J. Matthews, 'A' Coy., 1st Leinster Regt, wrote, "I deeply regret to have to announce the death of your brave son, Private P. Daly, of my platoon, who was killed in action this morning at 5.30 a.m. We were holding a trench, and your son was on watch duty. The enemy opened upon us a heavy, rapid fire. Upon your son's vigilance depended our lives. Though bullets were falling fast around him, he never flinched from the duty entrusted to him. It was in the performance of this duty he was struck in the head, and received such shocking injuries that his death was instantaneous. Although I did not know him long, I found him to be one of the best men in my platoon. He was fearless. His death is much regretted by the Officers, N.C.O.'s and men of his company. Well may you be proud of him. By his noble act he has kept up the traditions of an Irishman and the British army. He is laid to rest a short distance from the firing line, and a cross has been erected in his memory. You can rest assured that he is happy in heaven, for next to his breast was the crucifix of his Redeemer, which I buried with him. Other little articles which I found upon him I have given to his young brother, who I am indeed very sorry for. Dear Mrs Daly, on behalf of the N.C.O.'s and men of this platoon, we extend to you our deepest sympathy in this your great loss." 24 April 1915: Age 23. *unm.*

(Panel 44) Pte. 6032, James 'Jimmy' Fay, 2nd Bn. (109th Foot) The Leinster Regt. (Prince of Wales's, Royal Canadians): *s.* of Mary Fay (Garlowcross, Navan, Co. Meath). Killed in action nr. Hooge 12 August 1915, by shellfire: Age 35. Strongly believed to be one of two unknown soldiers of the Leinster Regt. buried in Birr Cross Roads Cemetery, Plot II, Row D. In recognition of Pte. Fay his great-nephew David Ball reformed the Leinster Regiment Association, 2001.

(Panel 44) Pte. 9570, William Halligan, 1st Bn. (100th Foot) The Leinster Regt. (Prince of Wales's, Royal Canadians): *s.* of John Halligan, of 70, Paul Street, Dublin, by his wife Mary: and brother to Pte. 7938, P. Halligan, Irish Guards, died 10 October 1918, consequent to wounds received in France; and Pte. 1471, M. Halligan, Australian Infantry, killed in action 20 August 1915, at Gallipoli: *b.* Dublin, 1892: enlisted there. Killed in action 7 February 1915: Age 22. *unm.* One of three brothers who fell.

Neither of his brothers have a known grave, Patrick is commemorated on the Hollybrook Memorial, Southampton; Michael, Lone Pine Memorial (Panel 14).

(Panel 44) Pte. 3642, Patrick Lysaght, 2nd Bn. (109th Foot) The Leinster Regt. (Prince of Wales's, Royal Canadians): *s.* of John Lysaght, of Ballyclough, Mallow, Co. Cork, and Ellen, his wife. Killed in action nr. Hooge 12 August 1915, by shellfire: Age 21. Strongly believed to be one of two unknown soldiers of the Leinster Regt. buried in Birr Cross Roads Cemetery, Plot II, Row D.

(Panel 44) Pte. 15255, Walter Milner, 2nd Bn. (109th Foot) The Leinster Regt. (Prince of Wales's, Royal Canadians): formerly no.64650, Training Reserve Battn.: *s.* of John William Milner, of 29, Bowman Place, Hanson Lane, Halifax, by his wife Sarah Jane: and yr. brother to Pte. 203140, W. Milner, 1/4th York and Lancaster Regt., died 15 April 1918, of wounds: *b.* Halifax, co. York: enlisted there: killed in action 31 July 1917: Age 19.

His brother Wilfred is buried in Haringhe (Bandagehem) Military Cemetery (II.C.8).

(Panel 44) Pte. 9785, Michael Mooney, 2nd Bn. (109th Foot) The Leinster Regt. (Prince of Wales's, Royal Canadians): *s.* of James Mooney, of 7, Parson's Street, Maynooth, Co. Kildare, and Ellen, his spouse: *b.* Trim, Co. Meath: enlisted Drogheda, Co. Louth, 1912. Killed by shellfire, 15 March 1916, at Hooge: Age 20. See Menin Road South Military Cemetery (I.J.6-16; I.K.1-5).

(Panel 44) Pte. 5588, Charles Alfred Rickwood, 2nd Bn. (109th Foot) The Leinster Regt. (Prince of Wales's, Royal Canadians): formerly no.124076, Royal Field Artillery: late of Broadstairs, co. Kent: *s.* of Albert Edward Rickwood, of 9, Belmont Terrace, Church Road, Whitstable, by his wife Charlotte, *née* Rutland: and elder brother to Telegraphist J/47053, A.H. Rickwood, H..M. Tug 'Charm,' R.N., died 28 June 1919: enlisted Marylebone, London. Killed in action 31 July 1917: Age 28. *unm.*

His brother Alfred is buried in Whitstable Cemetery (H.6).

(Panel 44) Pte. 10132, John Scully, Machine Gun Section, 2nd Bn. (109th Foot) The Leinster Regt. (Prince of Wales's, Royal Canadians): *s.* of Joseph Scully, of 3, Cottagewell Road, Maryborough, Queen's Co., and Ellen Scully, his wife: *b.* Maryborough: enlisted Naas, Co. Kildare. Killed by the direct hit of a 5.9 shell on the gun position 12 August 1915, nr. Hooge: Age 28. Ptes. P. Burlace and P. Cleary were also killed.

Pte. Burlace also has no known grave, he is recorded above; Pte. Cleary is buried in Birr Cross Roads Cemetery (II.D.30).

(Panel 44) Capt. Hugh Mortimer Travers, D.S.O., 5th (Extra Reserve) Bn. The Royal Munster Fusiliers attd. 2nd Bn. Duke of Wellington's (West Riding) Regt.: elder *s.* of the late Lieut.Col. Joseph Oates Travers, C.M.G., D.S.O., Leicestershire Regt., Chevalier Legion of Honour (received for the Crimean Campaign); by his wife Elinor, *dau.* of Major-General Sir Henry Marion Durand, K.C.S.I., C.B., Royal Engineers: *gdson.* of General Sir Robert Travers, Rifle Brigade: *b.* 2 September 1873: *educ.* Wellington College, Crowthorne, co. Berks: gazetted 2nd Lieut. 1st Leicestershire Regt., from the Militia, 9 December 1896: joined his battalion at the Cape, 1897; remained there until 1902: served in the South African War 1899 – 1902: took part in operations in Natal 1899, including actions at Talana Hill, the retreat from Dundee, and Lombard's Kop, Defence of Ladysmith: promoted Lieut. October, 1899: operations in Natal, March – June 1900, including action at Laing's Nek (6 – 9 June): operations in the Transvaal, east of Pretoria, including actions at Belfast (26 – 27 August), and in Sir Reivers Buller's advance on Lydenberg (5 – 8 September): operations in Transvaal 30 November 1900 – 31 May 1902, under Field Marshal (then General) Sir John French: and Orange River Colony, April 1901 – March 1902: for the last thirteen months of the war was on an armoured train, and received the thanks of Lord Kitchener: Queen's Medal, five claps; King's Medal, two clasps: Coronation Medal: promoted Capt. 26 April 1902: selected for the Egyptian Army, but retired (1907), having contracted black-water fever: joined 5th Royal Munster Fusiliers November of that year. At the outbreak of the Great War was attd. 2nd Duke of Wellington's Regt. and was present at the Battle of the Aisne, La Bassée, and Givenchy, at all of which he did exceedingly well. Killed in action 8 November 1914, being shot through the head gallantly leading his men in a bayonet charge nr. Hooge, a small village nr. Ypres. For his conduct in this action he was awarded the D.S.O., the official record stating that it was bestowed for 'conspicuous gallantry and ability on November 8th near Ypres in organising an attack and recapturing a trench from the enemy, and subsequently for leading a second attack and capturing another position 50 yards farther to the front. Captain Travers was killed while maintaining his post on this occasion." Several officers of his regiment wrote to the effect that it was entirely owing to his skill and gallantry that the operation was successful, and that his death had cast a gloom over them all. The Adjutant of his battalion, in a letter, said that he, ".. died the death of a soldier and a very gallant gentleman," and a Sergeant described his behaviour as, ".. the coolest deed I have ever seen. It was gloriously brave." His grandfather, Sir Robert Travers, was one of six brothers, four of whom were in The Rifle Brigade, and two in the Navy, and the six brothers had between them 24 sons, all of whom went into the Army. At the time Sir Robert and three of his brothers were in The Rifle Brigade there were also two first cousins in it, making no fewer than six officers by the name of Travers in the regiment at one time. It is doubtful if any family has produced so many soldiers, and they well deserved their nickname of 'the fighting Travers.' In their crest is a cockle shell, indicating that their ancestors took part in the Crusades. Their name is carved at Battle Abbey, and is on the Battle Abbey roll. They trace their descent from Baron Robert de Travers, who in 1067 married the heiress of Nateby, co. Lancaster. Another ancestor – Admiral Sir Eaton Travers – was engaged with the enemy over one hundred times, and was eight times mentioned for gallant conduct. One member of the family, Robert W. Travers, eldest son of Sir Robert, was Captain of 1st Company, 24th Foot, at Chillianwallah, and among the thirteen officers of the Regiment killed on that day; and another Travers only missed the catastrophe at Isandhlwana, in the Zulu War, 1879, owing to his having left his Regiment for the command of the 48th a short time previously. One of Capt. H.M. Travers' cousins – R.L. Travers, is currently serving in the Queen's Own Royal West Kent Regt.; another cousin – Lieut. H.H. Travers, South Wales

Borderers, died of wounds at Bethune, 28 March 1915. At the time of his death Capt. H.M. Travers was engaged to be married to Wilhelmina Annette, 2nd *dau.* of Surgeon General Sir William Taylor, M.D., K.C.B., and Lady Taylor, the marriage having been postponed owing to Capt. Travers having to leave for the Front at twenty-four hours' notice: Age 41. *unm.*

His cousin Hamilton is buried in Bethune Town Cemetery (II.B.11).

(Panel 44) L/Corpl. 2786, Michael Murphy, 1st Bn. (101st Foot) The Royal Munster Fusiliers: *s.* of John Murphy, of 6, Keane's Lane, Boherbee, Tralee, Co. Kerry: and brother to Pte. 10158, M. Murphy, Royal Munster Fusiliers, killed in action 27 August 1914, at Etreux; and uncle to Pte. 189, J. Murphy, 25th Australian Infantry, killed in action 7 October 1915, at Apex Chailak Dere, Gallipoli: *b.* Tralee, *c.*1884: *educ.* Christian Brothers School, Tralee. Killed in action at Ypres, 12 November. 1914: Age 30. He *m.* Tralee; Ellenor Hannah (2, Keane's Lane, Boherbee, Tralee), *dau.* of John Murphy, and had two children. (*IWGC record 2nd Battn., Age 50*)

His brother Maurice is buried in Etreux British Cemetery (I.14); John is believed to be buried in Lone Pine Cemetery (Sp.Mem.A.15);

(Panel 44) Capt. Edward Nugent Bankes, 3rd (Reserve) attd 2nd Bn. (103rd Foot) The Royal Dublin Fusiliers: 5th & *yst. s.* of the late Henry Hyde Nugent Bankes, of Wraysbury, co. Bucks., by his wife the Hon. Lalage Letitia Caroline, *née* Vivian, *dau.* of Richard Hussey, 1st Lord Vivian, P.C., G.C.B., and *gdson.* to the Right Hon. George Bankes, M.P., of Kingston Hall, Dorset: *b.* Wraysbury, 3 October 1875: *educ.* Charterhouse: served in the ranks during the South African War Lumsden's Horse; afterwards employed with Imperial Yeomanry: took part in operations in Orange Free State and Transvaal, May 1900, including action near Johannesburg, and in those in the Transvaal, March 1901 – 1902: Mentioned in Despatches ('*London Gazette,*' 20. August 1901): Queen's Medal, five clasps: given a commission 2nd Lieut., 2nd Dragoon Guards (the Queen's Bays), 25 December 1901; promoted Lieut. 25 December 1902; Capt. 12 September. 1908: Remount Officer, South Africa, 29 September 1905 – 12 March 1907, and Staff Officer there, 13 March 1907: retired 4 December 1912, and joined 3rd (Special Reserve) Bn. Dublin Fusiliers: called up on the outbreak of the European War and rejoined at the depot, Naas, from which he was sent to 2nd Bn. in France, 16 March 1915, and was killed in action at St. Julien, 26 April following. Buried close to a farm, about 500 yards on the Ypres side of St. Julien. His Commanding Officer wrote, "He came safely through our big action on 25 April against the village of St. Julien, some three miles north of Ypres. He was with me throughout the day of the 25th, while we dug in on the ground gained that day, I left him in command of the battn. on the night of the 25th, as I was slightly wounded myself. He was instantaneously killed by a rifle bullet on April 26th, during an attack made by another Brigade sent up to our assistance. He behaved with the greatest gallantry on the 25th, leading his men all the time." He *m.* at Pietermaritzburg, Natal, 19 February 1906; Lettice Adelaide, eldest *dau.* of Charles Wrothesley Digby, of Meriden Hall, nr. Coventry (*gt.-gt.-gt.-gdson.* of William, 5th Lord Digby), and had issue a *s.* and two *daus.* – John Digby Hyde, *b.* 16 November 1906; Adelaide Margery Dora, *b.* 21 February 1908; Lettice Monica, *b.* 12 April 1909. Captain Bankes, who was a member of the Naval & Military Club, was descended from ancestors who were settled in Dorsetshire as long ago as the reign of James I. He resided at Meriden Hall, Warwickshire, and was a prominent supporter of the North Warwickshire and Atherstone Hunts: Age 39.

(Panel 44) Capt. Bertram Walter Bourke, 5th (Extra Reserve) attd 2nd Bn. (103rd Foot) The Royal Dublin Fusiliers: only *survg. s.* of the late Major William Henry Bourke, Connaught Rangers; of Heathfield, Ballymena, Co. Mayo, by his wife Sarah Louisa, *dau.* of James John Young: *b.* 9 December 1882: *educ.* St. Servant, France: served with Royal Engineers (Militia); transf'd. 5th Royal Dublin Fusiliers, 1904: passed School of Instruction Examination for Regular Forces employ, and obtained rank Capt., 24 February 1912: proceeded to France 2 May 1915, attd. 2nd Royal Dublin Fusiliers, and was killed in action while gallantly leading his men near Ypres one week later, 9 May 1915: Age 33. Capt. Bourke *m.* Stapletown, Carlow, 19 April 1913; Eileen, *dau.* of George Neville Usher, of Carlow, and had two *daus.* – Vivienne Neville, *b.* 29 January 1914; Patricia Bertram, *b.* 4 November 1915.

(Panel 44) Capt. Frederick Neil Le Mesurier, Reserve of Officers attd. 2nd Bn. (103rd Foot) The Royal Dublin Fusiliers: *yst. s.* of Col. F.A. Le Mesurier, C.B., late Royal Engineers; of 31, St. Margaret's Road, Oxford: *b.* Brighton, co. Sussex, 7 March 1875: *educ.* Marlborough, 1886 – 91; and Royal Military College, Sandhurst, 1894 – 95, where he won the two mile race with a sprained foot: joined Royal Dublin Fusiliers, September 1895, and went with them to Bombay, and, in 1897, Natal: promoted Lieut. October of that year: served with the Mounted Infantry of his regiment in the South African War, 1899: taken prisoner at Pretoria; escaped, March 1900, and after an arduous tramp (sprained his foot on the second day) reached Delagoa Bay: subsequently rejoined his regiment, but was invalided home after a bad fever: promoted Capt. March 1900: returned to South Africa the same year: took part in the operations in the Transvaal, December 1900 – May 1901, and January – May 1902: Mentioned in Despatches ('*London Gazette*,' 10 September 1901): Queen's Medal, four clasps; King's Medal, two clasps: seconded from his regiment, 1904, on appointment to Sierra Leone Battn., West African Frontier Force: took part as Second-in-Command, in the operations against the Kissis, 1904. During a retirement he was commanding the rear-guard, and on his own initiative halted in a favourable position and lay in ambush until the enemy came to within a few yards of him, when he charged and defeated them in a hand-to-hand fight. This engagement ended the campaign, and the Kissis submitted to British protection: Frontier medal and clasp. Succeeding to the command of his battalion, the remainder of his five years' service was occupied in teaching the conquered tribes to live in peace, establishing markets for the exchange of their commodities in place of their raids on one another's territories: retired from the Army, October 1909: continued working in Sierra Leone, employed as Assistant Commissioner, Colonial Service, having long since established a good reputation with the natives: rejoined the Army on the outbreak of war, August 1914, posted to a company in 2nd Battn. of his old regiment: served in the trenches throughout the winter of 1914 – 15. In April 1915 the division was ordered to relieve the Canadians, who had been gassed in the Ypres salient. In the early morning of 25 April 1915 he led his company in the attack on St. Julien until they were brought up at the village by a wire entanglement enfiladed by machine guns. Ordering his men to lie down, Capt. Le Mesurier went forward to cut a way through the wire for them and, while making a second attempt to do this he was killed. At the same time as his death his old battalion, 1st Royal Dublin Fusiliers, were suffering heavy losses landing at the Gallipoli Peninsula. Throughout his service it was his first care to see to the welfare, in every sense, of his men, and their love and willing service were his reward. He used to speak of (and with) them as his friends, and a brother officer wrote, "The men spoke of him as their friend, worshipped him and followed him anywhere." Age 40. Capt. Le Mesurier *m.*, 1906, Rachel, *dau.* of the late Frederick (& Mrs) Gilham, of Bushey, co. Hertford.

(Panel 44) Capt. Basil Maclear, 2nd Bn. (103rd Foot) The Royal Dublin Fusiliers: *yst. s.* of the late Major Henry Wallich Maclear, 'The Buffs;' of Bedford: and brother to Lieut.Col. P. MacLear, Royal Dublin Fusiliers, Comdg. 2nd Nigeria Regt., West African F.F., killed in action 30 August 1914: *educ.* Bedford School, and Royal Military College, Sandhurst (awarded Sword of Honour, 1900): gazetted 2nd Lieut. Royal Dublin Fusiliers, August 1900; promoted Lieut. July 1904: served as Battn. Adjutant, May 1905 – May 1908: obtained his company, February 1911; apptd. Instructor on the Staff, Royal Military College, where he also took charge of the gymnasia – which post he held until 1915, when he rejoined his battalion in France: served during the South African War, where he saw much active service: took part in operations in Orange River Colony, December 1900 – February 1901: Transvaal, February 1901 – January 1902: Queen's Medal, five clasps: also saw service in the Hinterland, Aden, 1903. In the European War he was Mentioned in Sir John French's Despatch, 30 November 1915, and recommended for honours. Capt. Maclear was killed at Ypres, 24 May 1915, while gallantly leading a bombing attack. Known best in sport as the famous Irish International, Capt. Maclear was a great all-round athlete, excelling in all branches of sport he took up. At school, besides being a good bowler, he also showed his capabilities as a batsman by making 133 *v.* the M.C.C., and in later years 143 for the Royal Dublin Fusiliers against Cork, and 98 against Cork County. He also played for Bedfordshire County whenever possible. He won eight events at the School sports, 1898, and later won the 100 yards in 10½ seconds, and the 120 yards hurdles in 16¾ seconds, both on grass, at the Bedford County Championship meeting. Amongst other events at the Royal Military College sports, he won the long jump at 20 feet 6½ inches, and represented the College against Woolwich at athletics, as well as football and cricket, being Captain of the latter. But it was Rugby football of which he was most fond, and he became the most famous of all Ireland's Rugby Internationals, with a reputation that was world-wide, not only for the great game that he played, but the spirit in which he always played the game, and for his whole-hearted courage and chivalry. He started his football career in the 'pack,' but soon became a three-quarter, a position he afterwards never left, and where his great weight and speed, and keen knowledge of the game, made him so difficult an opponent, both in attack and defence. He played for Ireland in the Internationals *v.* England, Scotland, and Wales in the seasons 1905 – 06 – 07, gaining eleven International caps. He also appeared three times against the famous New Zealand team of 1906, and for Ireland against South Africa the following season. His best known performance was the memorable try he scored for Ireland *v.* South Africa at Belfast, 1906. Playing on the left wing, he saw the ball lying close on the right, near his own goal line, and dashing across and picking it up, he ran through the whole South African team and scored, after an eighty yards' run. He was also a great 'kick,' and once converted eleven out of twelve tries against the Old Paulines, and invariably took the 'kicks' for Ireland. The way he 'handed off' will long be remembered.

His brother Percy also has no known grave; he is commemorated on the Lokoja Memorial, Nigeria.

(Panel 44) Lieut. Maurice O'Connor Cuffey, 2nd Bn. (103rd Foot) The Royal Dublin Fusiliers: elder *s.* of Dr. (& Mrs) Edward Cuffey, of Port Said, Egypt: *gdson.* of the late J.C. O'Connor, of Ballyglass House, Sligo: *b.* 14 December 1896: *educ.* Stonyhurst College, where he took part in many of the gymnastic displays of late years, and won the King's Cup at the athletic sports, 1913, for best athlete in his division: entered Royal Military College, Sandhurst, on the outbreak of war, receiving his commission on his eighteenth birthday, 14 December 1914: attd. 3rd Royal Dublin Fusiliers, Cork, for training until 3 May 1915, when he was appointed to 2nd Battn. for Active Service in France: served with the Expeditionary Force in France and Flanders, and was officially reported killed in action 20 May 1915. He was a very promising soldier, and most popular with all ranks of his regiment. His loss is deeply regretted in his battalion, and among his friends and relations: Age 18.

(Panel 44) Lieut. Charles Stockley French, 2nd Bn. (103rd Foot) The Royal Dublin Fusiliers: *s.* of the late John Alexander French, LLD. (*d.* November 1916), by his first wife, Elizabeth Mary, *née* Stockley (St. Ann's, Donnybrook, Co. Dublin), *dau.* of the late John Surtees (& Alicia) Stockley: and yr. brother to Capt. C.A. French, 2nd Royal Irish Regt., died of wounds 1 June 1915: *b.* 4 July 1892: *educ.* Shrewsbury School, and Trinity College, Dublin University (graduated B.A., 1914): served with the Expeditionary Force in France and Flanders from August 1914: wounded at Armentieres, December following, and was killed in action 25 April 1915, at St. Julien: Age 22. Remembered on St. Mary's Church of Ireland War Memorial, Donnybrook.

His brother Claude is buried in Wimereux Communal Cemetery (III.P.2).

(Panel 44) 2nd Lieut. Christopher Daniel Considine, 5th (Extra Reserve) attd. 2nd Bn. (103rd Foot) The Royal Dublin Fusiliers: 3rd *s.* of the late Sir Heffernan Considine, C.B., M.V.O., D.L., of Derk, Pallasgreen, Co. Limerick (*d.*1912), by his wife Emily Mary, *dau.* of the late John Hyacinth Talbot, M.P., D.L., of Castle Talbot, and Ballytrent, Co. Wexford: and brother to Capt. H.J. Considine, Royal Irish Regt., killed in action 27 October 1916: *b.* 'New Park,' Co. Kilkenny, 21 December 1887: *educ.* Beaumont College, Old Windsor, where he was a member of both the cricket and football XI's, rowed for the college, a fine golfer, keen sportsman, and good at all games: volunteered for service on the outbreak of war: received his commission, 2nd Lieut., 5th Royal Dublin Fusiliers, August 1914: served with the Expeditionary Force in France and Flanders from early May 1915, attd. 2nd Battn., and was killed near Ypres by a shell early in the morning of 24 May, during a strong German attack which was delivered under dense clouds of poisonous gas. He gave his life in a noble attempt to save his Major, who had been gassed. He was buried by the Germans, with his men, where he fell – 'Shell Trap Farm.' A Chaplain to the Forces wrote of him, "I knew him for a brave officer and a true gentleman even in the few days I was with him, and his death was just like what I knew of him. Under a murderous artillery and machine-gun fire he tried to bring the Major Commanding his company out of danger. Your dear brother was killed instantaneously, and the Major died shortly afterwards. It was a fine and chivalrous thing to do, worthy of the man and the old regiment. I don't think anyone who wasn't with them could understand the full heroism of our officers, men like your brother. The horrors of gas and heavy artillery and raking machine-gun fire seemed to matter nothing to them. They did the right thing, coolly and collectedly, in the face of certain death. They died like Christian gentlemen" Age 27. *unm.*

His brother Heffernan is buried in Kemmel Chateau Military Cemetery (X.34).

(Panel 44) 2nd Lieut. James Neville Herbert Murphy, 5th (Extra Reserve) attd. 2nd Bn. (103rd Foot) The Royal Dublin Fusiliers: only *s.* of the late Rev. W.A.E. Murphy, M.A., Rector of Desertmartin, Co. Derry, by his wife Isabella (2, Waltham Terrace, Blackrock, Co. Dublin: *b.* Cardonagh, Co. Donegal, 5 February 1895: *educ.* St. Columba's College, Rathfarnham, and Trinity College, Dublin, where he was studying medicine, and a member of the O.T.C.: volunteered on the outbreak of war, and received his commission, 2nd Lieut. Royal Dublin Fusiliers, from the O.T.C.: served with the Expeditionary Force from May 1915, attd. 2nd Battn. of his regiment, and was killed in action on the 9th or 10th of that month, while resting in a reserve trench two miles north of Ypres. Prior to the outbreak of war he had been a member of the Monkstown Football Club, and Captain of the Third XV, 1913: Age 20. *unm.*

(Panel 44) 2nd Lieut. Edward Maxwell Salvesen, 4th (Extra Reserve) attd. 2nd Bn. (103rd Foot) The Royal Dublin Fusiliers: 2nd *s.* of Lord Salvesen, Senator of the College of Justice, by his wife Lady Salvesen, *dau.* of Lord Trayner, Senator of the College of Justice, Dean Park, Edinburgh: and brother to Capt. F.M.R. Salvesen, 82nd Punjabis, Indian Army, who died 21 December 1919: *b.* Crawford Priory, co. Fife, 30 August 1891: *educ.* Cargilfield, co. Midlothian, and Clifton College. Being at first intended for the Diplomatic Service, he spent a year in France and a year in Germany to acquire the languages. In 1912 he entered University College, Oxford, where he took his degree of B.A. (1914), with second class Honours in Law, with the intention of completing his legal studies in Edinburgh before joining the Scottish Bar. On the outbreak of war he returned from Norway, where he had been on holiday, and as he could not at once get a commission he enlisted in Lovat's Scouts. After training with that Corps for two months he was given a commission as 2nd Lieut. 4th Battn. Royal Dublin Fusiliers, October 1914, joined 2nd Battn., at the Front, 1 January 1915; having been previously in the O.T.C. his training period was shortened. At the time he joined his battalion they were in the trenches, and continued to be so until about a fortnight before the action in which he was killed; near St. Julien, 25 April 1915. A brother officer, Lieut. Dickie, gave the following account of the circumstances, "He was in the same Company as myself and very popular indeed with both officers and men. Early on Sunday morning we received orders to attack the Germans in and just each side of the village of St. Julien, where some Canadians were still believed to be holding out. Very early in the attack my Company Commander was slightly hit, and I took command of the Company. We reached a farm about 350 yards from the village with very few casualties, and I received orders from the Colonel as to my exact objective, and told Maxwell Salvesen and the other platoon commanders exactly what to do. We then went forward with the rest of the Battalion for about 60 yards, when the Colonel said that my Company would have to go forward and support the attack by the remainder of the Battalion. He asked me if I could make good the village, and I said I would try. Up to this time the fire from our front was almost negligible, but there was a good deal of machine gun fire from a hill called 20 on our flank. As we moved for the next rush we were met with a perfectly devastating fire at close range from the village! At first I could not make out where it came from. Maxwell came on with his Platoon after me, and got down at the end of the rush, about 50 yards, I should think, unhurt. We only lost ten men in the rush. The fire on our front and flank became like a hailstorm, but we could not retire unless the right moved, as we were supposed to be supporting their advance. Just as I realised which houses the fire was coming from (it was impossible to see through our glasses as they were all wet and muddy), I saw your son turn over. I called out, 'Are you hit?' but got no answer. Before I could move one got me in the right shoulder, coming out under the shoulder blade, but doing no damage. I slipped out of my equipment and went over to where your son lay. He was dead. One of the flanking bullets had hit him in the back of the neck. He did his job splendidly, and died a man's death. He went forward in that attack as well as if it was company training, and the men followed him to a man." In a letter of sympathy to his parents, Dr. Macan, of University College, Oxford, thus describes the deceased officer, "I am sure I speak for all who knew him here, where he bore with us not merely a blameless, but an excellent character and reputation. He was really a splendid young fellow with the promise of a most useful and distinguished career in times of peace. We thought very well indeed of his abilities and no less well of his character, and with his industry, determination, splendid and attractive personality and good manners, he would, I am sure, have made a mark in the world. He has, indeed, done that now: 'being made perfect in a short time, he has fulfilled a long time.'" Mr Salvesen was a very good tennis and football player, and also a very good shot and fisherman. Lieut. Dickie recovered from his wound after being invalided: Age 23. *unm.*

His brother Frederick, buried in Jandola Cemetery (15), is commemorated on the Delhi (India Gate) Memorial (Face 4).

After receiving orders to be ready to move off at half an hour's notice, at 7.30 p.m., 23 April 1915, 2nd Royal Dublin Fusiliers left Bailleul and marched north to overnight billets at Westoutre, before departing early the following morning by way of Hensken, Zevecoten, Ouderdom, and Vlamertinghe; reaching the outskirts of Ypres at 8 p.m. At Ypres packs were discarded, and at midnight the Battalion marched on St. Jean, deploying at 4 a.m. on the 25th west of the Wieltje St. Julien road. The need that had arisen to call for the 10th Brigade to take hurriedly its part in what is known as the Second Battle of Ypres, was due to the success which had been won by the Germans in their attack on the 22nd upon the position held by the Canadians and the French between Bixschoote and Langemarck, owing to their unexpected employment of gas, resulting in the forcing of a gap five miles wide in the front of the Allied position. It was a desperately difficult undertaking, the night was extremely dark, the ground, which had not been reconnoitred, was honeycombed with trenches and strewn with barbed wire, and, moreover, the artillery had not been able to 'register' – get its range of the terrain. Just before the attack was launched word came back that some Canadians were still holding out in the village of St. Julien; whence a fresh gas attack had driven the Canadian left on the morning of the 24th. "Therefore the place could not be shelled. The guns, however, opened on the wood west of the village. The 7th Argyll and Sutherland Highlanders, a Territorial battalion that was on its trial that day, led with splendid dash on the right, the 1st Warwicks on the left. They were followed on right and left respectively by the 1st Royal Irish Fusiliers and the 2nd Dublins, while the 2nd Seaforths were ordered to connect with General Riddell's brigade of the Northumberland Division, which had been sent up to relieve the Canadians. As soon as our men got out of their trenches they were met by a terrific machine gun and rifle fire at close quarters, whilst the German heavy guns in the rear spouted a continual torrent of shells over the fields through which the assault was delivered. Our men dropped left and right, but they never wavered, and the Irish Fusiliers and the Dublins, Irishmen all, fighting shoulder to shoulder, actually got into the outskirts of St. Julien. The scattered ruins, the maze of trenches, and the barbed wire strung out everywhere, seriously delayed these two battalions and checked our advance. Two battalions of a brigade of the Northumberland Division, supporting the Dublins, lost their direction…On the left the Warwicks and on the other flank the Highlanders got to within 70 yards of the German trenches in front of the wood. Here they were hung up and were 'properly hammered,' in the words of one who was there, by German high explosive shells. Nevertheless, by this gallant attack the gap between the Canadians east of St. Julien and north of Fortuin was filled." Lieut.Col. Loveband was wounded at the close of the first day's fighting, and handed over command of the Battalion to Captain Bankes, and the Royal Dublin Fusiliers dug themselves in on a line facing, and a quarter of a mile from St. Julien."

(Panel 44) Sergt. 10595, Samuel Rattle, 2nd Bn. (103rd Foot, Royal Bombay Fusiliers) The Royal Dublin Fusiliers: *s.* of John Rattle, of 45, Surbiton Road, Ipswich, by his wife Sarah Ann, *née* Land: *b.* Bredfield Street. Woodbridge, 27 November 1891: enlisted Ipswich, co. Suffolk, 1908: served with the

Expeditionary Force in France and Flanders from 22 August 1914, and was killed in action, 25 April 1915, nr. St. Julien, Ypres: Age 24.

On the night of 23 – 24 May 1915, 2nd Royal Dublin Fusiliers were in the front line near St. Julien when, at around 2.45 a.m., the Germans launched a poison gas attack. By 9.30 p.m., when the battalion retired to headquarters, all that remained out of an initial strength of 666 men was 1 officer and 20 other ranks. In just under 19 hours the Dublins had been virtually annihilated, suffering a loss of 645 men most of whom were killed by the poisonous gas fumes or blown to pieces by the hurricane bombardment that followed. For years after the war many men who had been wounded by the various types of gases suffered long bouts of illness, eventually dying a slow and agonising death from weakened lungs. The German gas attack in the early hours of 24 May 1915 was described as being 'about three miles wide and forty feet deep; bleaching the grass, blighting the trees and leaving a broad scar of destruction in its wake.' The Allied troops in the trenches had little hope of escape from its effects. The bodies of 143 members of 2nd Royal Dublin Fusiliers who died that night were never found.

(Panel 44) Pte. 16694, George Alderson, 2nd Bn. (103rd Foot) The Royal Dublin Fusiliers: *b*. South Shields, Co. Durham, 1894: *husb*. to Hannah Simpson, *née* Alderson (10, Galt Street, Thornley, Co. Durham). Killed in action at St. Julien, 24 May 1915: Age 21.

PANEL 44 ENDS PTE. R. BYRNE – ROYAL DUBLIN FUSILIERS.

PANEL 46 BEGINS PTE. 7823, T. BYRNE – ROYAL DUBLIN FUSILIERS.

(Panel 46) Pte. 8753, Christopher Devitt, 2nd Bn. (103rd Foot) The Royal Dublin Fusiliers: *s*. of Peter Devitt, of 27, Convent Road, Dalkey, Co. Dublin, by his wife Mary: and yr. brother to Pte. 10137, A. Devitt, 1st Royal Dublin Fusiliers, killed in action 29 June 1915, at Gallipoli: *b*. Dalkey: enlisted there: served with the Expeditionary Force in France, and was killed in action 24 May 1915: Age 22. *unm*.

His brother Anthony also has no known grave; he is commemorated on the Helles Memorial.

(Panel 46) Pte. 8643, John Hackett, 2nd Bn. (103rd Foot) The Royal Dublin Fusiliers: *s*. of Arthur Hackett, of 7, Hardwicke Place, Dublin: *b*. Dublin. Killed in action 9 May 1915: Age 19. Buried in Sanctuary Wood Cemetery (V.O.20).

(Panel 46) Pte. 8982, John McDonnell, 2nd Bn. (103rd Foot) The Royal Dublin Fusiliers: *s*. of Edward McDonnell, of 46, Bride Street, Dublin, by his wife Anne: and *yr*. brother to Pte. 9443, P. McDonnell, 2nd Royal Dublin Fusiliers, who fell four weeks previously; and Pte. 8848, P. McDonnell, 2nd Royal Dublin Fusiliers, killed in action at St. Julien, 24 May 1915: enlisted Dublin: served with the Expeditionary Force in France from 22 August 1914, and was killed in action beside his brother Patrick at St. Julien 24 May 1915: Age 22. One of three brothers who fell.

His brothers Peter and Patrick also have no known grave, Peter is recorded below; Patrick, Addenda Panel 59.

(Panel 46) Pte. 9443, Peter McDonnell, 2nd Bn. (103rd Foot) The Royal Dublin Fusiliers: *s*. of Edward McDonnell, of 46, Bride Street, Dublin, by his wife Anne: and elder brother to Pte. 8982, J. McDonnell, 2nd Royal Dublin Fusiliers, who fell the following month; and Pte. 8848, P. McDonnell, 2nd Royal Dublin Fusiliers, killed in action beside his brother Patrick, at St. Julien, 24 May 1915: enlisted Dublin: served with the Expeditionary Force in France from 22 August 1914, and was killed in action 26 April 1915: Age 42. One of three brothers who fell.

His brothers John and Patrick also have no known grave, John is recorded above; Patrick, Addenda Panel 59.

(Panel 46) Pte. 5701, Myles Mahoney, 2nd Bn. (103rd Foot) The Royal Dublin Fusiliers: *s*. of James Mahoney, of 10, Lower Bridge Street, Dublin: *b*. Dublin: enlisted there: served with the Expeditionary Force in France, and was killed in action there 10 May 1915: **Age 16**.

(Panel 46) Capt. Hugh Montagu Butterworth, 9th (Service) Bn. The Prince Consort's Own (The Rifle Brigade): eldest & only *survg. s.* of George Montagu Butterworth, Solicitor; of Christchurch, New Zealand; formerly Swindon, co. Wilts, by his wife Catherine Lucie, *dau.* of Major Charles Warde: *b.* Saffron Walden, co. Essex, 1 November 1885: *educ.* Hazelwood, Limpsfield; Marlborough, and University College, Oxford: went to New Zealand (1907) and became Assistant Master, Collegiate School, Wanganui; returned to England early 1915, in order to serve his country: gazetted 2nd Lieut., Rifle Brigade, 11 March 1915; promoted Lieut.; and Capt. (posthumous): went to France 22 May, and was killed in action at Hooge 25 – 26 September following. His Colonel wrote, "He showed throughout the most conspicuous courage and coolness, and can never be replaced as an officer." While at Marlborough he was Capt. of the Cadet Corps, a member of the cricket, football, and hockey teams, racquet representative, and winner of the Athletic Championship Cup. At Oxford he was one of the most brilliant all-round athletes of his day, where he represented his University at cricket, football, hockey and racquets, and won the Freshmen's 100 yards, but a bad knee and ankle only permitted him to obtain his Blue at racquets; J.J. Astor and G.N. Foster being his partners. In 1906 he made 130 in the Seniors' Cricket Match, and played many big innings for his college and for Wiltshire: Age 29. *unm.* (*IWGC record 25 September 1915*)

(Panel 46) Capt. Douglas Carmichael, 9th (Service) Bn. The Prince Consort's Own (The Rifle Brigade): eldest *s.* of James Carmichael, J.P., of Redclyffe, Streatham Park, London, by his wife Annie Reid, *dau.* of James Reid Ruthvin, of co. Perth: *b.* Wandsworth, London, S.W., 17 January 1894: *educ.* Leys School, Cambridge; Jesus College, Cambridge (graduated B.A.): volunteered his services on the outbreak of war, gazetted 2nd Lieut., Rifle Brigade, 9 September 1914; promoted Lieut. 1 October following; Capt., 4 March 1915: went to France, May 1915, and was killed in action at Hooge, 26 September following. Lieut.Col. W. Villers-Stuart wrote, 29 August 1915, "I am taking the liberty of writing to tell you about Douglas. From the very beginning he was quite exceptionally valuable, and his capacity and industry were amazing. But he has in the last month been compelled to show himself as he really is – no longer to hide his magnificent qualities under his modest demeanour. The battalion was very badly knocked about in the fighting at Hooge. Your son's first act was to collect men of another regiment, who, by his personality and fearlessness, he rallied and kept with him till long afterwards they were able to rejoin their unit. As time wore on, the incessant bombardment and continued drain in wounded officers began to affect the battalion, and so your son, who had already organized in the most excellent way everything within reach, was sent to steady two companies. Many of the N.C.O.'s and riflemen have told me that while your son was near they were perfectly happy. He carried out every kind of duty under incessant shellfire until we were relieved, and I don't think he can have slept at all for many days. Since then I have had more opportunity than before of seeing his work, and the more I see, the more extraordinarily capable I know (not think) him to be. I have recommended him for some mark of distinction, and he thoroughly deserves such a mark. I would much like you to know that I, an old soldier of many years' service in wild and rough places, would give command of the battalion over to your son today, with the knowledge that he is a better and more capable soldier than I have seen in twenty-five years service. His capacity you would know; his coolness is phenomenal, and his bravery quite exceptional;" and again after his death, "He was killed on 25 September in action near Hooge. I saw him last at twelve o'clock midnight, and he was killed next morning about nine o'clock. His bravery is a byword in the division. He fought that day with infinite courage. I have no words, and no one else would have any, to express his magnificent bravery. For long he has done everything for me, and he knew he was absolutely trusted. I shall never see a soldier like him again. It is quite impossible that anyone so fearless could ever be found. He carried four lines of trenches with his company under a most desperate artillery and machine-gun fire, and when masses of Germans came against him, by his wonderful personality he kept his men, now reduced to a handful, in good spirit, and led them again and again to the attack. They say it was glorious to see him throw himself on the packed masses of Germans and almost alone forced them back. He rallied the men over and over again, and they stuck to him till the end. He was wounded early in the day, about 5 a.m., but, just like him, made nothing of it. He was killed instantaneously by a bullet in the forehead as he was once more leading a bomb charge. We tried to bring in his body in the evening, but it had been completely destroyed by high-explosive German shells. I will try and tell you better in a few days about it all, but we are so worn out just now that words will not come. He would have earned the V.C. ten times had he lived. He was the most capable and bravest officer of the old army or the new army I have ever or shall ever see, and I can never look on his like again. It is heartrendingly sad that he had to go. Two divisions were attacking. You will know that Douglas carried more German trenches than any other officer on the whole front. Others could not carry any. He at one time carried five lines. If it is possible for you to have any consolation in losing your son, he had become well known for his devotion to duty, bravery and capacity, and I have lost my very best officer and my great friend who I admired so greatly." Sergt. W. Walker, Machine Gun Section, also wrote, "There was not a man in our battalion who would not have followed him anywhere. To cut a long story short, he was in command of the whole attack on the morning of the 25th, and right well did he lead us until he was hit in the leg. Then we pushed forward alone, as he refused to have any assistance; but just after I saw him hopping on one leg towards the next line of German trenches under a murderous fire. We took three lines in all, but had to retire. Your son was still in command, absolutely refusing to be taken back. On reaching the original German front line he rallied the small handful of men left, and told us to hold it at all costs, which we did against masses of Germans until almost every man was either killed or wounded. Your son was killed with a machine gun, and I was twice wounded at the same time. It was instantaneous, and his last words were, 'For God's sake hold them back!' He earned the V.C. 50 times over. No officer could be loved more, or held in higher esteem by his men, than your gallant son. A more gallant leader or fearless man never led men on the field of battle." Age 21. *unm.*

At 7 o'clock, on the evening of 19 July 1915, 175 Tunnelling Company, Royal Engineers, detonated a mine, the largest thus far exploded by the British, consisting of 3,500 lbs. of ammonal, twenty feet beneath the heavily fortified German positions at Hooge. The resultant explosive force hurled stones, trees, bricks, concrete, shattered equipment and bodies 500 feet skywards. Even as the debris was falling so the British artillery opened up a terrific bombardment on the enemy trenches beyond, as the 4th Middlesex rushed to occupy the position. The resultant crater formed by the explosion measured some twenty feet deep, twelve feet high at the lip, and one hundred and twenty feet in width – it was to become one of the most fought over, deadly and fearsome places in the salient.

The tactical advantage this position afforded was of extreme importance to both sides. From the British point of view it gave them a position not only overlooking part of the German line, but also affording a point from where an attempt to break through to the German rear might achieve success. Similarly, it afforded the same advantage to the enemy if they could gain control of the crater and surrounding defences.

For the next seven days and nights the task of denying the advantage to the enemy 126th and 132nd German Infantry regiments fell to 8th Bn. King's Royal Rifle Corps – holding the trenches to the extreme right of the crater; the crater itself and the trenches to the immediate left and right of it being the responsibility of 7th Bn. The Rifle Brigade. Although a bombing post was established either side, the crater itself was untenable owing to continual enemy bombardments of its confines. The front line, support and communication trenches did not escape this attention either, and gradually as the trenches caved in, with no available cover to withdraw to, whole sections of men at a time were simply blown to pieces. One who suffered this fate was '*The Beloved Captain*' – Ronald Hardy:

(Panel 46) Capt. Ronald Montague Hardy, 'D' Coy., 7th (Service) Bn. The Prince Consort's Own (The Rifle Brigade): *yst. s.* of the late Herbert Carey Hardy, J.P., of Danehurst, co. Sussex, by his wife A. Louisa C. (Chilworth Manor, co. Surrey): and cousin to Capt. Alfred Cecil Gathorne Hardy, The Cameronians (Sco.Rif.), killed at the Battle of Loos, 25 September 1915; and Lieut. Alan Herbert Hardy, Royal Flying Corps, killed whilst flying 14 October 1915: *b.* Danehurst, 12 April 1882: *educ.* Eton College (Mr E.C. Austen-Leigh's House): enlisted Royal Sussex Regt. Territorials, 7 August 1914: gazetted Temp. Lieut., 7th Rifle Brigade, then being raised at Aldershot, October 1914; promoted Temp. Capt. November following: served with the Expeditionary Force in France and Flanders from May 1915, and was killed in action at Hooge, 23 July following, while his company were holding the trench in front of the crater made on 19 July. Donald Hankey, at the time a Corpl., 7th Rifle Brigade, under the pseudonym '*A Student At Arms*' wrote of Capt. Hardy – '*The Beloved Captain*':– "We were holding some trenches which were as about as unhealthy as trenches could be. The enemy were only a few yards away, and were well supplied with trench mortars. We hadn't got any at that time. Bombs were dropping round us all day. Of course, the Captain was there. It seemed as if he could not keep away. A torpedo fell into the trench and buried some of our chaps. The fellows next to them ran to dig them out. Of course, he was one of the first. Then came another torpedo in the same place. That was the end. .." Age 33.

His cousin Alfred also has no known grave, he is commemorated on the Loos (Dud Corner) Memorial (Panel 57); Alan is buried in St. Mary's Churchyard, Chilham.

(Panel 46) Capt. Charles Harry Norman 'Sam' Scholey, 9th (Service) Bn. The Prince Consort's Own (The Rifle Brigade): only *s.* of Harry Scholey, of 14, Sidney House, Bedford Park, London, W., and 56, Victoria Street, S.W.1, by his wife Frances Edna: *b.* 19 August 1892: *educ.* Uppingham, co. Leicester (September 1907 – December. 1911); Clare College, Cambridge (Undergraduate), O.T.C. member: gazetted 2nd Lieut., 9th Rifle Brigade, September 1914; promoted Lieut., February 1915; Capt. (Temp), August following: served with the Expeditionary Force in France and Flanders from May 1915, and died of wounds 26 September following, received in action nr. Bellewaarde Farm the same day: Age 23. *unm.* His Commanding Officer wrote, "His company led the assault on the East Force. He did splendidly and carried two lines of German trenches. It was while he was consolidating the position won that he was badly wounded by a bomb. Although we lost the position he had so bravely won he was not abandoned but brought back to the first line, where he died later in the day. Of his Company only one NCO and six Riflemen returned to the British lines." Whilst at Uppingham he won his School colours for Rugby, and at Cambridge obtained the college colours for Cricket, Rugby and Hockey.

(Panel 46) Capt. Bingham Alexander Turner, D.S.O., 6th (Reserve) Bn. The Prince Consort's Own (The Rifle Brigade) attd. 2nd Bn. King's Royal Rifle Corps: *s.* of the late Gen. E.P. Bingham Turner, of Milesdown, Winchester, by his wife Helen, *dau.* of Sir Casimir Gzowski, A.D.G., K.C.M.G.: *b.* 30 May 1877: *educ.* Wellington College, and R.M.C. Sandhurst: gazetted 2nd Lieut., Rifle Brigade, 22 January 1898: served in the Nile Expedition, 1898; took part in the Battle of Khartoum (Medal & Egyptian Medal with clasp): promoted Lieut. 11 December 1899: served in the South African Campaign, 1899 – 1902, taking part in operations in Natal, 1899, including the action at Lombard's Kop: took part in the defence of Ladysmith, sortie 10 December 1899, and action 6 January 1900: operations in Natal, March – June 1900, including the action at Laing's Nek, 6 – 9 June; operations in Transvaal, east of Pretoria, July – 29 November 1900, including actions at Belfast, 26 – 27 August, where he was slightly wounded; and Lydenberg, 5 – 8 September: subsequently employed with Mounted Infantry; taking part in operations in Transvaal, 30 November 1900 – 31 May 1902. Mentioned in Despatches ('*London Gazette*,' 25 April 1902); Queen's Medal, three clasps; King's Medal, two clasps; created Companion of the Distinguished Service Order ('*London Gazette*,' 26 June 1902) "In recognition of services during the operations in South Africa;" invested by H.M. the King, 24 October 1902: retired from Regular Army, July 1909; joined 6th (Reserve) Battn. of his regiment, attd. 2nd Battn. 60th Rifles (K.R.R.C.) for active service: served with the Expeditionary Force in France, and was killed in action 2 November 1914: Age 37. He m. 1906; Gladys Gooch, *née* Turner (Hodcott House, West Ilsley, Newbury, co. Berks), *dau.* of J.S. St Vincent Jervis.

(Panel 46) Capt. the Hon. Francis George Godfrey Willoughby, 9th (Service) Bn. The Prince Consort's Own (The Rifle Brigade): 3rd *s.* of Godfrey Ernest Willoughby, 10th Baron Middleton, of Birdsall, Malton, co. York, by his wife Ida Eleanora Constance, *dau.* of Col. George William Holmes Ross, of Cromarty House, co. Argyll, and Adelaide Lucy, *née* Davidson, his wife: and brother to Comdr. H.E.D.H. Willoughby, R.N., H.M.S. 'Indefatigable,' killed 31 May 1916, at the Battle of Jutland: *b.* 29 August 1890: served with 9th Rifle Brigade in France from 20 May 1915, and was killed in action at Hooge, 9 August 1915, being hit by a shell which completely obliterated him leaving no part to bury: Age 24. *unm.* (*IWGC record age 25*)

His brother Henry has no known grave but the sea; he is commemorated on the Plymouth Naval Memorial (Panel 10).

(Panel 46) Lieut. Hugh Cecil Benson, 9th (Service) Bn. The Prince Consort's Own (The Rifle Brigade): elder *s.* of Cecil Benson, of 35, Bedford Square, London, W.C., by his wife Constance, *dau.* of George Bernard O'Neill: *b.* 16, Young Street, Kensington Square, London, W., 3 July 1883: *educ.* Eton: Occupation – Architect: volunteered for Imperial Service on the declaration of war: given a commission 2nd Lieut., Rifle Brigade, 30 December 1914: proceeded to the Western Front with his regt., 20 May 1915, and was killed in action at Hooge, nr. Ypres, 22 June following: Age 31. *unm.*

(Panel 46) Lieut. Charles Bourns, 6th (Reserve) attd. 4th Bn. The Prince Consort's Own (The Rifle Brigade): *yr. s.* of Charles Bourns, of Boley, Lichfield, formerly of West Hill, Oxted, Physician, by his wife Florence, *dau.* of Edward Walker, of West Hill, Oxted, and Araluen, Eastbourne: *b.* West Hill, Oxted, 7 August 1881: *educ.* Merchant Taylor's School, and St. John's College, Oxford (M.A.); Assistant Master (member O.T.C.) at Repton when war was declared, he obtained a commission, 2nd Lieut., October 1914: promoted Lieut., Rifle Brigade, 22 January 1915, and was killed in action nr. Hooge, 25 May 1915. He was an Oxford (Rugby football) Blue (1903): Age 34. *unm.*

On 6 July 1915, 11th Brigade, 4th Division, were ordered, at the behest of 2nd Army H.Q to attack part of the German line east of the Yser Canal, south-west of Pilckem – 'to improve the tactical situation to the left of VI Corps line, and to distract the enemy's attention from operations near Hooge.' When the operations at Hooge were cancelled it was argued locally that the planned attack was now superfluous, furthermore, it was almost certain to inflict heavier casualties on the attackers than the defenders. The objections were overruled, the attack was to go ahead as planned; the prophecy with regard to casualties was to prove sadly justified. In the initial stages of the attack good progress was made largely due to a single field gun having been rafted across the canal during the night and stealthily manoeuvred up to a position sixty yards in front of the German trenches by 2nd Lieut. P.A. Robinson, R.F.A. and Lieut. R.L. Withington, R.E. and "The British found the trench choked with German dead and littered with letters and parcels. Evidently the mail had just arrived. Some kind of meal had been in progress, for there was an abundance of coffee, which was eagerly consumed by the raiders who in addition fortified themselves with cigars. Thirty prisoners, mostly of the 215th Regt. (Schleswig-Holstein) were captured, together with two machine-guns, two trench mortars and a considerable amount of trench stores. But German machine gun fire continued with unabated accuracy and by 11 am. the British casualties were becoming severe…At 3 pm. a more deliberate counter-attack developed on the left. It was easily driven off, but two companies of the Hampshire Regt. who had been sent forward in support were stood-to in case of emergency. By 3.30 pm. the shelling had become so severe that the old British front line had to be evacuated. The captured trenches received their share of the bombardment, under cover of which another attempt was made at counter-attacking on the left – the enemy endeavouring to work along a communication trench instead of advancing over the open. The attack was checked and defeated – in part by the artillery, in part by 2nd Lieut. C.A. Gould of the Somerset Light Infantry who, with his Platoon Sergeant and some of his men went to the help of a 1st Battn. post of three bombers, and engaged the enemy with them, whilst the remainder of the platoon worked feverishly at deepening and improving the trench. This was the last attempt at re-capturing the position. Shortly after 5 p.m. the firing died down. Late at night the captured ground was handed over to the 2nd Battn. Lancashire Fusiliers. The officers and men who had been engaged were, as they had every right to be, in high spirits over their achievement. The Brigadier professed himself to be delighted. But the gain of some seventy-five yards of ground on a frontage of three hundred yards had been made at the expense to the Somerset Light Infantry of 2nd Lieut. H.V. Webber and 27 other ranks killed, 3 officers and 102 other ranks wounded, and 5 men missing; to the 1st Battn. of Lieut. Brandt, 2nd Lieuts. Gibbs, Blair and Juckes, and 33 other ranks killed, Capts. Downes and Ellis, 2nd Lieuts. Bullock and Boyle, and 176 other ranks wounded, and 37 other ranks missing; and it is safe to assume that the great majority, if not all of the missing were killed."

Talana Farm Cemetery, Boesinghe, contains 529 burials with 88 headstones bearing the date 6 July 1915, among them 2nd Lieuts. H.V. Webber (I.D.7), B. Gibbs (I.D.8), G.F. Juckes (I.D.9), P.C.B. Blair (Sp.Mem.I.E.10), and the aforementioned 33 other ranks; Lieut. Brandt has no known grave:–

(Panel 46) Lieut. Druce Robert Brandt, 6th (Reserve) Bn. attd. 1st Bn. The Prince Consort's Own (The Rifle Brigade): late of 15, Lennox Gardens, London, S.W.: *yr. s.* of the late Robert E. Brandt, of 23, Brompton Square, London, by his wife Florence: *educ.* Harrow (Elmfield), 1903 – 06; Balliol College (Exhibitioner, 1st Class Mods.), and Oxford University (Lecturer, Brasenose, 1910), B.A.: member of Brasenose College O.T.C: left Oxford (1913); took up social work with Settlement Movement, Bermondsey; joined Special Reserve of Officers the same year: mobilised on the outbreak of war August 1914; posted Training Depot, Sheerness: apptd. 6th (Reserve) Battn., attd. 1st Rifle Brigade for Active service; proceeded to France, May 1915. Died of wounds, 6 July 1915. His Commanding Officer wrote, "At about 6.30 a.m., during the successful assault on a line of German trenches, 6 July 1915, your son fell, wounded in two places. The attack had been gallantly led by your son with his company on this section of the front assaulted, and he had reached the German parapet and was engaged in cheering on his men to renewed efforts when he fell, and, it seems, died almost immediately." Reflecting on the fact that Lieut. Brandt has no known grave, his mother said, "The surge of heavy fighting swept back and forward over the spot where he fell, and an unknown grave adds to the grief of some who loved him best." Strongly believed to be the Unknown British Soldier buried in Talana Farm Cemetery (I.D.12).

(Panel 46) Lieut. William Buckworth, 10th (Service) Bn. The Prince Consort's Own (The Rifle Brigade): late of Harrow-on-the-Hill: *s.* of the late Benjamin Buckworth, of Croydon, co. Surrey, by his wife Ellen. Killed in action 14 August. 1917: Age 40. His younger brothers 2nd Lieut. W.A. Buckworth, 1st Royal Inniskilling Fusiliers, and Rfn. 592334, H. T. Buckworth, 18th (London Irish Rifles) London Regt., were both killed in action; their nephew 2nd Lieut. A.B. Buckworth, 3rd Royal Inniskilling Fusiliers, also fell. All correspondence should be addressed c/o Ernest B. Buckworth, Esq., 47, Devonshire Road, Harrow-on-the-Hill, co. Middlesex. Remains recovered 20.U.28.a.5.7, 2 December 1926, 'Unknown British Officer, Rifle Brigade;' identified – Buttons, Officers clothing, Boots, Watch, Compass. Buried Oosttaverne Wood Cemetery, Wytschaete (IV.A.3).

His brother Wallace fell at Gallipoli leaving a wife, Evelyn Maria (33, Hosack Road, Balham, London, S.W.12), he has no known grave and is commemorated on the Helles Memorial; Horace is buried in Bedford House Cemetery (I.C.5/Enc.No.4); their nephew Alan is buried in Tyne Cot Cemetery (IX.F.1).

(Panel 46) Lieut. George Ashwin Curnock, 6th (Reserve) attd. 4th and 10th (Service) Bn. The Prince Consort's Own (The Rifle Brigade): eldest *s.* of Clement Corderoy Curnock, of Woolton Hill, Newbury, co. Berks, by his wife Mary Elizabeth, only *dau.* of Manley Ashwin, of Honeybourne, by his wife Sarah Elizabeth, *née* Godfrey: *b.* Honeybourne, co. Worcester, 5 July 1893: *educ.* St. Bartholomew's Grammar School, Newbury (entered 1905, Senior Prefect, Librarian, Editor of '*The Newburian*'): elected for an open Scholarship (Classics) to Pembroke College, Cambridge (December 1911), awarded (July 1912) Senior Scholarship by Hampshire County Council; went up to Cambridge, October 1912 (top of the list of classical men for the year, elected for the Stewart of Rannock Exhibition, 1913; also obtained a college prize for Greek verse), joined University O.T.C. on the outbreak of war: obtained a commission, 16 December 1914: served with the Expeditionary Force in France and Flanders, and was killed in action nr. Langemarck, 14 August 1917. His Commanding Officer wrote, "It is with the very deepest of regret I am writing to tell you your son was killed in action on the morning of 14 August. He was gallantly leading his men in a big attack by the battalion, when he was killed by machine-gun and rifle fire. I cannot tell you how sorry I am to lose such a splendid and plucky officer. We all miss him so very much." Age 24. *unm.*

(Panel 46) Lieut. the Hon. Gerald William Grenfell, 8th (Service) Bn. The Prince Consort's Own (The Rifle Brigade): 2nd (& at the time of his death, elder *survg.*) *s.* of William Henry, 1st Baron Desborough, K.C.V.O., by his wife Ethel Anne Priscilla, Lady of the Bedchamber to H.M. the Queen, *dau.* of the Hon. Julian Henry Charles Fane, and *grand-dau.* of John, 11th Earl of Westmoreland: *b.* 4 St. James's Square, London, S.W.: *educ.* Eton (gained an entrance scholarship and Newcastle scholarship);

and Balliol College, Oxford (obtained the Craven scholarship, 1911), and was about to be called to the Bar: volunteered after the outbreak of war; gazetted 2nd Lieut. 8th Rifle Brigade, 12 September 1914: served with the Expeditionary Force in France and Flanders from May 1915, and was killed instantaneously by machine gun fire at Hooge, Flanders, 30 July 1915, while leading a counter attack. Capt. A.C. Sheepshanks wrote, "He died splendidly leading his men over open ground up hill in the face of a tremendous fire from machine guns. His Platoon Sergt. saw him pitch forward with a bullet in the head, and thinks he was hit again, in the side, as he fell. He must have been killed instantaneously as he was not seen to move afterwards. Both as his company commander and his friend I shall miss him enormously. His platoon all loved him, and he had somehow inspired them with a fighting spirit, and it was only a few days ago that I told the Col. that Bill's platoon was the best fighting platoon I had." And A.A. Tod, 2nd In Command, 8th Battn., "We were great friends, and though I didn't know him before he joined, I, like all the others, was immediately drawn to him by his delightful personality. I know you must be inundated with letters, so feel rather diffident adding to the number, but somehow it seems to help to write about a dear friend that has gone. We all loved Billy, and his men, to my certain knowledge, adored him. It couldn't have been otherwise, because ever since he went to France he was always to the fore, and what the men always like, never expected them to do anything he couldn't do himself. His gallantry was remarkable, and fear was a word he didn't know the meaning of. As you know he died at the head of his men leading a counter-attack. It's poor consolation, but I am positive of all the deaths it is the one he would have chosen. That was a fearful day, and no one can describe the horror of seeing 20 officers and well over 500 men fall in one Battn. in about 14 hours." His elder brother, Capt. J.H.F. Grenfell, 1st Royal Dragoons, and twin cousins, Capt. F. Grenfell, V.C., 9th (Queen's Royal) Lancers, and Capt. R.N. Grenfell, Royal Buckinghamshire Hussars, were also killed in action, and his *yst.* and only *survg.* brother, the Hon. Ivo G.W. Grenfell, is now with the Coldstream Guards. His sister, the Hon. Monica Grenfell, is a Red Cross Nurse in France: Age 25. *unm.*

His brother Julian is buried in Boulogne Eastern Cemetery (II.A.18); cousins Francis and Riversdale are buried in Vlamertinghe Military Cemetery (II.B.14) and Vendresse Churchyard (1), respectively.

(Panel 46) Lieut. Sidney Milsom, 8th (Service) Bn. The Prince Consort's Own (The Rifle Brigade): late of Cliff Lawn Esplanade, Fowey, co. Cornwall: *s.* of Francis Henry Milsom, of Audley Lodge, Bath, co. Gloucester, by his wife Kate Isobel: and brother to Lieut. E.W. Milsom, HMS 'Defence,' R.N., killed in action 31 May 1916, when that ship was lost with all hands (903) at the Battle of Jutland: Occupation – Chemistry Student: served with the Expeditionary Force in France from 19 May 1915, and was killed in action at Hooge, 30 July following: Age 29. *unm.* The following day his Colonel wrote, "It is a cruel story; it was a sudden attack under cover of liquid gases that set the trench aflame. In spite of all the horror and confusion, your boy, apparently with two other officers, Rae and Pawle, rallied the men at once, and firing hard through the flames, held their ground. It was simply heroic, and just what we all knew and could be done by your boy in a tight corner. He had already proved himself quite fearless, and what is more quite cool under fire, and his platoon loved him – a roughish set of men who followed him anywhere – and he was always chosen for any particular difficult digging task. He had a genius for getting work done – and done well. I was very fond of him personally, and I feel I've lost a friend as well as an efficient officer. He was popular with everyone, generous and open-handed to an extraordinary degree."

With no known grave but the sea his brother Edward is commemorated on the Plymouth Naval Memorial (10).

(Panel 46) 2nd Lieut. Peter Adam, M.C., 3rd Bn. The Prince Consort's Own (The Rifle Brigade): *s.* of Peter Adam, of 'Cairndhu,' Kidderminster, co. Worcester, by his wife Isabella Neilson: *b.* 1893: *educ.* The Leys School, Cambridge (West House, 1907), where he won second Colours for cricket and football, was a member of the Bisley VIII, and Cadet Corpl. in the School O.T.C.; and Birmingham University, reading Civil Engineering: enlisted Public Schools Battn. on the outbreak of war, attaining rank of Sergt.: gained a commission and joined Prince Consort's Own, 1916: served with the Expeditionary Force in France and

Flanders, being awarded the Military Cross for 'distinguished service,' and was killed in action on the first day of the Third Battle of Ypres, 31 July 1917: Age 24. *unm.* (*IWGC record age 33*)

(Panel 46) 2nd Lieut. Thomas Samuel Gent, 7th (Service) Bn. The Prince Consort's Own (The Rifle Brigade): *s.* of the late His Honour Judge John Gent, by his wife Harriet F. Gent (Little Sutton, Churchill Road, Thames Ditton): *educ.* Surbiton School; Rossall College; Oxford University. Killed in action, 24 July 1915; Hooge: Age 21. Remains 'Unknown British Officer. 2/Lieut. Rifle Bde.' exhumed, identified – Khaki Clothing, Buttons, 1 Piece of Boot, marked Salter & Sons, Aldershot; reinterred, registered, 7 February 1928. *Buried in Sanctuary Wood Cemetery (II.B.13).*

(Panel 46) 2nd Lieut. Alan Godsal, 7th (Service) Bn. The Prince Consort's Own (The Rifle Brigade): 2nd *s.* of Edward Hugh Godsal, of Winnersh Lodge, Wokingham, by his wife Marion Grace, *dau.* of the Rev. Florence Thomas Wethered, Vicar of Hurley, co. Berks: *b.* Hawera, New Zealand, 4 May 1894: *educ.* Oundle School: gazetted 2nd Lieut. 7th Rifle Brigade, 22 September 1914: went to France, May 1915: apptd. Battn. Machine-Gun Officer, July 1915, and was killed in action at Hooge, 30 July 1915. Buried in Sanctuary Wood, Hooge. His Col. wrote speaking of him as a most promising officer. The circumstances of Lieut. Godsal's death were:– "The battn., on leaving the trenches for rest, had left their machine-guns for the use of the relieving battns., from whom they were captured by a sudden enemy assault, and on the 7th Battn. being brought back from their billets seven miles away to recover the trenches the Col. ordered Lieut. Godsal to take up a position with his machine-gun men, from whence, when opportunity offered, to advance and regain possession of the guns. It is now clear from the statement of Corpl. Molloy, who was within 20 yards of Lieut. Godsal when he was killed, that Lieut. Godsal did himself advance from this position and get possession of at least one of the guns, for the Corpl. saw him firing it at the enemy, and later saw him firing his revolver – probably when he recovered the gun he only picked up a small amount of ammunition – and later still heard a shout that he was killed, a shell having struck him in the face. Private King gallantly endeavoured to pull his body back into the trench and was himself killed instantaneously. Corpl. Molloy accounts for Lieut. Godsal's recovering the gun by saying that he knew every yard of trench and ground as he was out frequently, day and night, making daring reconnaissances. The Corpl. added that if ever anyone deserved the V.C. he did.": *unm.*

(Panel 46) 2nd Lieut. Edward Henry Lovett Henn, 9th (Service) Bn. The Prince Consort's Own (The Rifle Brigade): *s.* of Edward Lovett-Henn, of Campagne Sidi-Merzoug, El-Biar, Algiers, by his wife Margaret Agnes Vaughan Henry: *educ.* Freiburg University, Baden; Trinity College, Cambridge; graduated B.A. (1913): qualified for entry (2nd in competition) to the Foreign Office, August 1914; relinquishing that opportunity to volunteer and enlist September following: served with the Expeditionary Force in France and Flanders from August 1915, and was killed in action 25 September 1915, in the attack on Bellewaarde Farm: Age 23. *unm.*

Thomas Keith Hedley Rae, known to family and friends as Keith, was born in Birkenhead into a family of middle-class income. His early life was plagued with bouts of illness and it was thought he would never realise his aspirations to attend public school and college. However, in 1907 he won a scholarship to Balliol College, Oxford where he proved himself a hard-working student, eager to learn and, as his physique developed, took a keen interest in sports and outdoor pursuits. In 1913 he was awarded a teaching diploma with the promise of a tutorial at Marlborough College ahead of him when war broke out in August 1914. Through personal influence with Lieut.Col. R. MacLachalan Keith was commissioned into 8th Battalion The Rifle Brigade, 15 December 1914, which at the time was forming at Aldershot and, after training went to France with his battalion in mid-May 1915 as part of 41st Brigade, 14th (Light) Division. Moved around Ypres for general instruction in trench warfare the 7th soon found themselves in the notorious Railway Wood sector where they would spend the next month manning the trenches around Hooge; experience their first baptism of fire and learn a very costly lesson in the process. Keith Rae, having proved himself an efficient and valuable platoon officer in 'C' Company was destined to play a full and gallant part in these events.

The area around Hooge formed a salient jutting into the British line above the Menin Road and had only recently been captured from the enemy by the exploding of a large mine beneath their defences. The Germans responsible for this sector desperately wanted to win back the lost ground and their retaliation was not slow in coming. In the early hours of 30 July Keith Rae's platoon were part of the 'C' Company garrison manning the fire-trench on the right of the mine crater ('A' Company on the left). In an attack of massive proportions, preceded by a violent barrage, a new and fearsome weapon – the flamethrower – was unleashed on the hapless defenders. 2nd Lieut. G.V. Carey later wrote, "I remember having a strong presentiment, as I plodded up the line that night, that I should never come back from it alive; in the event I was the only officer in my Company to survive the next twenty-four hours…The night was ominously quiet. There had been very little shelling on the way up for which we were duly thankful; but the absence of the sniper's bullet as we filed up the communication trench from Zouave Wood was something more surprising. The continued silence, after we got into the line, became uncanny. .. About half an hour before dawn .. there was a sudden hissing sound, and a bright crimson glare over the crater turned the whole scene red. As I looked I saw three or four distinct jets of flame – like a line of powerful fire hoses spraying fire instead of water – shoot across my fire trench. How long this lasted it is impossible to say – probably not more than a minute…I remember catching hold of a rifle with fixed bayonet of a man standing next to me…when there was a terrific explosion, and almost immediately afterwards one of my men, with blood running down his face, stumbled into me, coming from the direction of the crater…The *Minenwerfer* had started, and such men as had survived the *Flammenwerfer* were, in accordance with orders, giving the crater a wide berth. Then broke out every noise under heaven: 'Minnie' and bombs in our front trench, machine-guns from places unseen, shrapnel over the communication trenches and open ground between us and Zouave Wood, and high explosive on the wood and its vicinity…It was a death trap to stay where we were… About a dozen men of No.2 Platoon were all that I could find – those that had faced the flame attack were never seen again."

(Panel 46) 2nd Lieut. Thomas Keith Hedley Rae, No.10 Platoon, 'C' Coy., 8th (Service) Bn. The Prince Consort's Own (The Rifle Brigade): *yst. s.* of Edward Rae, Stockbroker; of Courthill, Devonshire Place, Birkenhead, by his wife Margaret: *b.* Birkenhead, co. Chester, 24 May 1889: *educ.* Privately (due to ill health), and Balliol College, Oxford (Scholarship, 1907), where he gained 2nd Class Honours in History (1912) and, taking a great interest in the well-being and education of the young, founded a Boys' Club in Oxford: thereafter (1913) gained his Teaching Diploma, took up a position as Assistant Master, Marlborough College: volunteered and enlisted on the outbreak of war, August 1914; obtained a commission, 8th Rifle Brigade, 15 December following: went to France, 14 May 1915, and was killed in action at Hooge, 30 July following. Rfn. B1416, E. Griffiths wrote, "16 August 1915. While we were in the firing trench at Hooge on July 19th (?) at about 3 a.m. the Germans attacked us with liquid fire. I was doing Trench Police at the time. The last I saw Lt. Rae was firing his revolver over the parapet of the firing trench. He was struck and he fell. We were retiring along the fighting trench at the time and, of course, had to leave him behind. I feel almost sure he was killed outright.": Age 26. *unm.* See also Sanctuary Wood Cemetery.

Be Thou Faithful Unto Death And I Will Give Thee A Crown Of Life
Christ's Faithful Soldier And Servant Unto His Life's End

(Panel 46) 2nd Lieut. (Temp.) Bernhard Rissik, 9th (Service) Bn. The Prince Consort's Own (The Rifle Brigade): eldest *s.* of the Hon. Johann Friedrich Bernhardt Rissik, Administrator of the Transvaal, of 'Linschoten,' Park Street, Pretoria, South Africa: *b.* Pretoria, 8 March 1892: *educ.* Diocesan School, Pretoria; St. Andrew's College, Grahamstown, and Trinity College, Oxford (entered 1912). In the long summer of 1914 he went to South Africa for his vacation, and when he returned to England (October) joined Oxford O.T.C.: gazetted 2nd Lieut., 13th (Service) Bn. Middlesex Regt.; subsequently transf'd. 9th Rifle Brigade, in which he served as a platoon officer: went to Flanders with his battalion, and was killed by shrapnel in the trenches, 23 June 1915, eleven miles from Poperinghe. Fond of all sports, he played football, tennis and golf; and was also a good shot: Age 23. *unm.*

(Panel 46) 2nd Lieut. Kenneth Stuart Trotter, 6th (Reserve) attd. 1st Bn. The Prince Consort's Own (The Rifle Brigade): 3rd *s.* of the late John Trotter, by his wife Louisa (Brickindon Grange, Hertford): *b.* 26 January 1893: *educ.* Eton, and Trinity College, Cambridge: volunteered and enlisted on the outbreak of war, August 1914: gazetted 2nd Lieut. 6th Battn. Prince Consort's Own, the same month: served with the Expeditionary Force in France and Flanders, attd. 1st Battn., and was killed in the vicinity of Hill 37, Fortuin – Gravenstafel, 27 April 1915, by a direct hit from a shell: Age 22. *unm.*

(Panel 46) 2nd Lieut. Charles Aubrey Vintcent, 5th (Reserve) attd. 4th Bn. The Prince Consort's Own (The Rifle Brigade): *s.* of Charles Vintcent, of Cape Province, South Africa, by his wife Lilian: *b.* Oudtshoorn, South Africa, 16 November 1892: *educ.* St. Andrew's College, Grahamstown, South Africa; Boxgrove School, Guildford (H.F. Caldwell), where he was Head Boy for his last four terms; Uppingham School, where he got his Colours for Rugby Football, being conspicuous as a dashing forward, and Pembroke College, Cambridge, 1913 – 14: joined the Army on the outbreak of war, having been given a commission, 5th Rifle Brigade, August 1914: served with the British Expeditionary Force in France from January 1915, and was shot through the heart, 13 April following, while reconnoitring a trench near Ypres. Buried with other officers of the Rifle Brigade, near the Polygon Wood. His Commanding Officer said, "He did exceptionally well at the Battle of St. Eloi. He was in charge of the bomb throwers and snipers at the time of his death." His former Headmaster and Tutors at Cambridge wrote most appreciative letters to his father, sympathising with him in his loss, and deploring the early death of such "a fine specimen of manhood – with such promise." His father and three uncles were at Charterhouse, and all four made their mark in athletics and outdoor sports. 2nd Lieut. Vintcent went to Cambridge University with a great reputation for forward play, Uppingham being noted as one of the best Rugby schools for learning the groundwork, and, as he was a big, powerful man, his value in a team was considerable. During his first year at Pembroke College he received his Rugby Blue; and, like his father and three uncles, was a good all-round athlete. Age 22. *unm.*

(Panel 46) 2nd Lieut. Anthony Thornton Walker, 8th (Service) Bn. The Prince Consort's Own (The Rifle Brigade): 2nd *s.* of John Walker, of Bank House, Bawtry, co. York, by his wife Dorothy Mary, *dau.* of Thomas Taplin Wickham, of Bideford, N. Devon: *b.* Bawtry, 9 May 1894: *educ.* Dulwich Preparatory School, from which he obtained a scholarship to Uppingham School, from whence he secured an open scholarship and exhibition University College, Oxford: joined Public Schools Battn., Middlesex Regt., August 1914; given a commission 2nd Lieut., 8th Rifle Brigade, 2 December following: left for France, 25 July 1915, and was killed in action at Hooge on the 30th. of that month; the day after he joined his battn. in the trenches. At Uppingham he was captain of football, and played for his college at Oxford. He was also very musical, and was leader of the orchestra at Uppingham: 30 July 1915: Age 21. *unm.*

(Panel 46) 2nd Lieut. Sidney Clayton Woodroffe, V.C., 8th (Service) Bn. The Prince Consort's Own (The Rifle Brigade): 4th & *yst. s.* of Henry Long Woodroffe, of Thorpewood, Branksome Avenue, Bournemouth, co. Dorset, by his wife Clara, *dau.* of the late Henry Clayton: *b.* Lewes, co. Sussex, 17 December 1895: *educ.* Rose Hill School, Banstead; Marlborough College, Devizes (Senior Prefect, Captain of the O.T.C., winner of the Curzon-Wyllie Medal; member of the Football XV, 1912 – 1914, Hockey XI, Cricket XXII): gained a Classical Scholarship, Pembroke College, Cambridge: gazetted 2nd Lieut., 8th Rifle Brigade, 23 December 1914: went to France 25 May 1915, and was killed in action at Hooge, Flanders, 30 July 1915. Mentioned in Despatches, and posthumously awarded the Victoria Cross ('*London Gazette*,' 6 September 1915) "For most conspicuous bravery on 30 July 1915, at Hooge. The enemy having broken through the centre of our trenches, consequent on the use of burning liquids, this officer's position was heavily attacked with bombs from the flank and subsequently from the rear, but he managed to defend his post until all his bombs were exhausted, and then skilfully withdrew his remaining men. This very gallant officer immediately led his party forward in a counter-attack under an intense rifle and machine-gun fire, and was killed whilst in the act of cutting wire obstacles in the open." Lieut.-Col.

R.C. Maclachlan wrote to his father, "Your younger boy was simply one of the bravest of the brave, and the work he did that day will stand out as a record hard to beat; later I will try to get you a more or less definite account. When the line was attacked and broken on his right he still held his trench, and only when the Germans were discovered to be in rear of him did he leave it. He then withdrew his remaining men very skilfully right away to a flank and worked his way alone back to me to report. He finally brought his command back and then took part in the counter-attack. He was killed out in front, in the open, cutting the wire to enable the attack to be continued. This is the bald statement of his part of that day's action. He risked his life for others right through the day and finally gave it for the sake of his men. He was a splendid type of young officer, always bold as a lion, confident and sure of himself too. The loss he is to me personally is very great, as I had learnt to appreciate what a sterling fine lad he was. His men would have followed him anywhere.": Age 19. On 24 January 1919 the Graves Registration Office notified Sidney Woodroffe's parents their son was buried 600 yards south-east of Hooge (Sanctuary Wood); his grave 'marked by a durable wooden cross bearing full particulars.' Mr & Mrs Woodroffe lost their two elder sons also in the European War. Lieut. K.H.C. Woodroffe, 6th attd 3rd Rifle Brigade, killed in action 9 May 1915. (He was also Senior Prefect at Marlborough, and Capt. (1912) of the cricket team. He took six wickets for Cambridge in his first (1913) Oxford & Cambridge Match, Lord's; played cricket as a fast bowler for Hants C.C.C. (1912) *v.* South Africans (5 wickets), and for Sussex C.C.C. in 1913.) Capt. L. Woodroffe, M.C., 8th Rifle Brigade, was, while at Marlborough College, head of the school, in the Cricket XI and football XV. At Oxford he took a 1st. in Mods, and 2nd. in Lit.Hum. Severely wounded at Hooge, July 1915, on the same day as brother Sidney was killed; he rejoined his regiment 1 June 1916 and, wounded again later that day, died three days later.

Two days after Sidney's Victoria Cross was gazetted his friend the poet Charles Sorley wrote:–

In Memoriam SCW, VC.
There is no fitter end than this.
No need is now to yearn nor sigh.
We know the glory that is his,
A glory that can never die.

His brother Kenneth has no known grave, he is commemorated on the Le Touret Memorial (Panel 44); Leslie is buried in Barlin Communal Cemetery Extension (I.J.66).

(Panel 46) Sergt. Z/421, Philip Heacock Baynes, 1st Bn. The Prince Consort's Own (The Rifle Brigade): *s.* of the late Thomas Hutton Baynes, M.A., by his wife Margaret (72, Coleherne Court, Earl's Court, London): Occupation – Black & White Humourist: enlisted 1914. Killed in action nr. St. Julien, 6 July 1915: Age 34.

(Panel 46) Sergt. 5428, Alfred James Cross, D.C.M., 2nd Bn. The Prince Consort's Own (The Rifle Brigade): *s.* of Charles William Cross, of Ellen's Lodge, Dytchley, Enstone, by his wife Harriett: *b.* Spelsbury, co. Oxford: enlisted Oxford. Killed in action 31 July 1917: Age 21. In a letter to Mrs Cross the Chaplain, J. Kitson, wrote, "20 August 1917…I am afraid you will have heard by now of the great loss that you have incurred by the death of your son Sergt. Cross of this battalion, killed in action on July 31st. I know that at times like these words are of very little use, but I am writing because I should like you to know that your loss is shared by the whole battalion; your son was one of the bravest men in the whole battalion and was immensely respected and admired by every officer and man in it. We are all so proud of him because of the splendid example that he has given us, because he has done the finest thing a man can do – his duty – giving his life in the defence of his country and those at home against a cruel enemy. I am so very sorry for you, but I trust you will be able to feel this same sense of pride, for being the mother of such a man – and that this may help to take a little of the weight off the blow. I hope that you will have strength to bear this great trial, and that God in His goodness will give you this strength and comfort you in your sorrow." Awarded the Distinguished Conduct Medal ('*London Gazette,*' 18 June 1917), 'For Conspicuous gallantry and devotion to duty…his example of courage and initiative;' at Gouzeaucourt,

5 April 1917. "A Stokes Mortar was brought up to fire on the Mill at 10 a.m. and after about 30 rounds had been fired Sergt. Cross in charge of the two patrols of Battle Patrol Platoon worked their way forward and drove the Germans out of their strong post and pushed on down the slope and caused the enemy many casualties in the low ground. The enemy retaliated by bringing heavy shell fire on these troops in an exposed condition and after dark Sergt. Cross, after suffering five or six casualties, brought his detachment back to the enemy trench on the crest by the Mill buildings."

(Panel 46) Sergt. S/4980, Thomas Andrew Goodwin, 'D' Coy., 7th (Service) Bn. The Prince Consort's Own (The Rifle Brigade): *s.* of Mary Goodwin (34, Abbey Terrace, St. John's Green, Colchester, co. Essex): *b.* Plymouth, co. Devon, *c.*1886: enlisted Birmingham: served with the Expeditionary Force in France and Flanders from May 1915, and was killed in action 23 July 1915, at Hooge: Age 29. *unm.* Remains recovered (28.I.24.b.1.8, Sanctuary Wood) 'Unknown British Sergeant. 7 Rifle Bde.' exhumed, identified – Clothing, Titles, Badge of Rank; reinterred, registered, 9 February 1928. Buried in Sanctuary Wood Cemetery (II.B.20).

Greater Love Hath No Man
R.I.P.

(Panel 46) Sergt. Z/746, John Apps Harrison, 'B' Coy., 11th (Service) Bn. The Prince Consort's Own (The Rifle Brigade): *s.* of Mrs Harrison (18, Pentyla, Aberavon, co. Glamorgan): *b.* Keswick, co. Cumberland, *c.*1883: served with Welch Regt. in the South African Campaign, and with the Rifle Brigade in India: joined Calcutta Police on expiry of his service: rejoined the Prince Consort's Own on the outbreak of war, August 1914: served with the Expeditionary Force in France and Flanders from May 1915, and was killed in action 14 August 1917, before Au Bon Gite, Langemarck: Age 34.

(Panel 46) Sergt. Z/1460, Arthur 'Pat' Paterson, 4th Bn. The Prince Consort's Own (The Rifle Brigade): *s.* of Adam Paterson, Music Teacher, of 72, Prospect Road, Scarborough, co. York; by his wife Rosa: *b.* Rochester, co. Kent, 1883: Religion – Roman Catholic: *educ.* St. Martin's, Scarborough: sometime employee Borough Engineer's Office; Scarborough Town Hall; Messrs Watts, Kitching & Donner, Solicitors; and, after removing to the south coast, took up Acting: enlisted Marylebone, September 1914; posted 6th Rifle Brigade (transf'd. 4th on its return from India): proceeded to France, December 1914, took part in the battalion's baptism of fire at St. Eloi,, and was killed in action 26 April 1915, east of Potijze Chateau, nr. Ypres: Age 32. In a letter to Sergt. Paterson's father a comrade wrote, "He was killed on the 26th April 1915, about 1pm, while on observation duty. The Regiment at the time were lying in support of the French Turco troops who were making an attack. Pat and a party were sent along the Yser Canal to watch the advance and report anything to headquarters…From what I gathered, Pat was continuously assisting the sentries on observation, and while doing so a shrapnel shell burst overhead killing him and wounding the sentry. One bullet penetrated his brain and another his shoulder. The same afternoon he was buried alongside the once beautiful Yser Canal, and his grave is marked by two crosses…."

(Panel 46) L/Sergt. S/2403, George Appleton, 9th (Service) Bn. The Prince Consort's Own (The Rifle Brigade): *s.* of Thomas Appleton, of Cross Bow, Statham, Warrington, co. Chester, by his wife Ann: and brother to Rfn. 415278, S. Appleton, 1/9th London Regt. (Q.V.R.), who fell 28 November 1917, at Cambrai: enlisted Manchester. Killed in action 24 August 1915, near La Brique: Age 21. *unm.* (*IWGC record B/2403*)

His brother Sydney also has no known grave; he is commemorated on the Cambrai Memorial (Panel 11).

(Panel 46) Corpl. B/2801, John Basnett, 'D'Coy., 8th (Service) Bn. The Prince Consort's Own (The Rifle Brigade): *s.* of John Basnett, Labourer; of 14, Clement Street, Taylorson Street, Salford, Manchester, by his wife Emily, *dau.* of John Gallop: *b.* Bristol, 1 September 1890: *educ.* Ordsall Board School, Salford: employee Messrs British Westinghouse, Trafford Park: joined Rifle Brigade, 31 August 1914, after the outbreak of war: served with the Expeditionary Force in France from May 1915, and was killed in action at Hooge, 30 July 1915. His Capt., A.C. Sheepshanks, wrote that after the action he was found to be missing and must have been struck down in the charge that day, adding, "He was turning out a most useful and reliable N.C.O." Age 25. *unm.*

(Panel 46) Corpl. S/6837, John Thomas Bateman, 10th (Service) Bn. The Prince Consort's Own (The Rifle Brigade): *s.* of Mr (& Mrs) Bateman, of 4, Victoria Terrace, Langley Mill, co. Derby: *b.* 1892: enlisted Ilkeston, November 1914: served with the Expeditionary Force in France and Flanders for two years, during which time he was twice wounded, and was killed in action, 14 August 1917. His Commanding Officer, in a letter to his parents, wrote, "21 August 1917, Your son died gallantly while taking part in the attack on the 14th inst. He will be missed, for he was a good soldier and always to the fore in any games when we were out of the lines. Speaking as his Company Commander I can ill afford to lose such a good N.C.O." '*Langley Mill & Aldercar's Part in the Victory*' records, 'The death of so gallant a fellow at the early age of 25 years is to be deplored, for his name is still mentioned with pride by many in connection with a plucky rescue he effected of a young girl by death from drowning in the canal, for which he awarded a sum of money and certificate by the Royal Humane Society. Not only was his reputation as a swimmer well-known, but he will also be remembered as a footballer of some prowess, having been a member of the Wesleyan and Rovers Clubs.': Age 25. *unm.* (*IWGC record 11 August 1917*)

(Panel 46) Corpl. 2111, Walter Bulldeath, 3rd Bn. The Prince Consort's Own (The Rifle Brigade): *s.* of Seth Bulldeath, of 12, Back Road, Spitalfields, Kitts Hil, Norwich, by his wife Mary Ann: and yr. brother to Rfn. 1609, G.P. Bulldeath, 2nd Rifle Brigade, killed in action 8 December 1914: *b.* Thorpe Hamlet, co. Norfolk: enlisted Norwich: Killed in action 11 August 1917: Age 29. *unm.*

His brother George is buried in Fauquissart Military Cemetery, Laventie (B.7).

Panel 46) Corpl. B/2988, Charles High Chatten, 9th (Service) Bn. The Prince Consort's Own (The Rifle Brigade): *s.* of Annie Chatten (The Row, Tendring, Clacton-on-Sea): and yr. brother to Pte. G/36691, E.H. Chatten, Queen's Own (Royal West Kent Regt.), posted 2/20th London Regt., killed in action 14 September 1918; and AB/236650, J.S. Chatten, H.M.S. 'Kale,' R.N., lost at sea 27 March 1918, when that ship was sunk by a mine: *b.* Tendring, co. Essex: enlisted London. Killed in action 25 September 1915: Age 22. *unm.*

His brother Edward is buried in Hermies Hill British Cemetery (II.E.26); with no known grave but the sea his brother James is commemorated on the Chatham Naval Memorial (28).

(Panel 46) Corpl. 3077, Frederick George Fuller, 4th Bn. The Prince Consort's Own (The Rifle Brigade): *s.* of Henry Fuller, of 18, King's Road, Caversham, Reading, by his wife Emily: and *yr.* brother to Pte. 7888, A. Fuller, Oxford & Bucks Light Infantry, killed in action 11 November 1914: *b. c.*1892: enlisted Caversham. Killed in action 10 May 1915: Age 23. *unm.*

His brother Albert also has no known grave; he is recorded on Panel 39.

(Panel 46) Corpl. B/3306, Basil Raymond, 8th (Service) Bn. The Prince Consort's Own (The Rifle Brigade): *s.* of Richard Lewis Raymond, of Watlington, co. Oxford, by his wife Emily: and *yr.* brother to Rfn. S/9710, B. Raymond, 8th Rifle Brigade, killed in action at Hooge the following day: *b.* Watlington: enlisted London. Killed in action 29 July 1915, at Hooge: Age 19. Remembered on the Watlington Village War Memorial.

His brother Bertie also has no known grave, he is recorded on Panel 48.

(Panel 46) Corpl. 6513, John Sumner, 7th (Service) Bn. The Prince Consort's Own (The Rifle Brigade): late of Caversham, co. Berks: *s.* of John Sumner, of Old Club House, Sonning, co. Berks, and Sarah, his spouse: enlisted Reading: served in the South African Campaign (Queen's & King's medals), and with the Expeditionary Force in France from May 1915, and was killed in action at Sanctuary Wood, nr. Ypres, 23 July following: Age 34. He leaves a wife, Florence Emma Sumner (130, Belmont Road, Reading), to mourn his loss. Remains recovered (28.I.24.b.1.8, Sanctuary Wood) 'Unknown British Corporal. 7 Rifle Bde.' exhumed, identified – Clothing, Titles, Badge of Rank, 3 Medal Ribbons; reinterred, registered, 8 February 1928. *Buried in Sanctuary Wood Cemetery (II.B.11).*

(Panel 46) L/Corpl. B/1835, George Cowley, Machine Gun Section, 7th (Service) Bn. The Prince Consort's Own (The Rifle Brigade): *b.* Castle Northwich, co. Chester: enlisted Manchester. Killed in action (nr. La Belle Alliance) 7 December 1915, when the machine-gun dugout was blown in by a shell: Age 32. He was married to Mrs F. Jacks, *née* Cowley (8, Offershaw Lane, Marston, Northwich). Rfn. A. Bailey and J.D. Burk were also killed.

The two riflemen also have no known grave, Albert Bailey is recorded below; James Burk, Panel 48.

(Panel 46) L/Corpl. S/424, Walter James Grass, 8th (Service) Bn. The Prince Consort's Own (The Rifle Brigade): *s.* of Eliza Grass (64, Bury Road, Brandon, co. Suffolk): and elder brother to Rfn. R/10559, J. Grass, 1st King's Royal Rifle Corps, who fell at Loos 3 October 1915, aged 19 years: *b.* Brandon, *c.*1887: enlisted Reading, co. Berks: served with the Expeditionary Force in France and Flanders from May 1915, and was killed in action, at Hooge 30 July following: Age 28. *unm.*

His brother James also has no known grave; he is commemorated on the Loos Memorial

(Panel 46) L/Corpl. B/1747, William Arthur Norris, 7th (Service) Bn. The Prince Consort's Own (The Rifle Brigade): formerly no.7206, Staffordshire Regt.: *s.* of Samuel Norris, of 203, Great Colmore Street, Edgbaston, co. Warwick, by his wife Alice Mary: enlisted Birmingham, co. Stafford: served with the Expeditionary Force in France, and died there 29 December 1915: Age 30. Remains exhumed (28.C.14.c.00.05) 'Unknown British Soldier, Rifle Brigade;' identified – Titles, Clothing; 26 January 1928. *Buried in Sanctuary Wood Cemetery (IV.N.22).*

(Panel 46) L/Corpl. S/5080, Ralph Max Warren, 7th (Service) Bn. The Prince Consort's Own (The Rifle Brigade): *s.* of Amos Warren, of Buca, Smyrna, Asia Minor, by his wife Madeline: cousin to Corpl. S/5085, P. Rice, 7th Rifle Brigade, died of wounds 7 July 1915; and brother to Sydney and John Warren, of Linthorpe, Middlesbrough, to whom Lieut. J. Maxwell, 7th Rifle Brigade, wrote, "Your brother was in my platoon, and I regret his loss very much indeed. He was a gallant soldier, and had every quality which I would wish for in a N.C.O. His perfect coolness and reliability would certainly have got him rapid promotion and distinction. His death took place in an attack we had to make through a wood. I can only regret that England has lost a very gallant soldier, whilst I have lost my best N.C.O. and a very good friend.": *b.* Smyrna: enlisted London: served with the Expeditionary Force in France from May 1915, and was killed in action 30 July 1915, at Hooge.

His cousin Percy is buried in Wimereux Communal Cemetery (I.J.8).

(Panel 46) Rfn. S/2062, Gilbert Angelinetta, M.M., 7th (Service) Bn. The Prince Consort's Own (The Rifle Brigade): *s.* of Albert George Angelinetta, of 120, High Street, Wootton Bassett, co. Wilts, by his wife Sarah Emily: and brother to Pte. 22450, O.E. Angelinetta, 6th Wiltshire Regt., killed in action, 8 July 1916; Somme: *b.* Wootton Bassett: enlisted Swansea, co. Glamorgan: served with the Expeditionary Force in France from May 1915, and was killed in action at Hooge, 30 July following: Age 20. *unm.*

His brother Oliver is buried in Serre Road Cemetery No.2 (XXXVI.M.1/12).

(Panel 46) Rfn. Z/1077, Joseph Henry Anlezark, 1st Bn. The Prince Consort's Own (The Rifle Brigade): *s.* of William Henry Anlezark, of 50, Gloucester Street, Salford, Manchester, by his wife Martha: *b.* St. Bart's, Lancaster: enlisted Manchester. Killed in action at Mousetrap Farm, north of Wieltje, 14 May 1915: Age 20. *unm.*

(Panel 46) Rfn. S/16820, Frederick Alfred Ansell, 1st Bn. The Prince Consort's Own (The Rifle Brigade): eldest *s.* of Frederick W. Ansell, Printer's Compositor; of 30, Arlesford Road, Stockwell, London, by his wife Clara: *b.* Stockwell, 1892. Killed in action 24 August 1916: Age 24. *unm.*

(Panel 46) Rfn. 3115, Charles George Baldock-Apps, 4th Bn. The Prince Consort's Own (The Rifle Brigade): *s.* of Mr (& Mrs) Baldock-Apps, of Hurst Green, co. Sussex: and brother to Rfn. 2725, H. Baldock-Apps, 4th Rifle Brigade, lost at sea 21 February 1917, whilst crossing the Mediterranean; Pte. TF/315357, H.E.V. Baldock-Apps, 16th Royal Sussex Regt., died 14 September 1918, of wounds; Pte. 14215, W.J. Baldock-Apps, 3rd Grenadier Guards, died 30 September 1915, of wounds received in action at Loos; and Pte. SD/2075, P.D. Baldock-Apps, 12th Royal Sussex Regt., killed in action 3 March 1917, nr. Ypres: *b.* Robertsbridge, *c.*1890: enlisted Tonbridge. Killed in action 4 May 1915, at the Second Battle of Ypres: Age 24. *unm.* Commemorated Hurst Green (Holy Trinity) Parish Church Memorial. One of five brothers who fell.

His brother Horace has no known grave but the sea, he is commemorated on the Mikra Memorial; Herbert is buried in Etretat Churchyard Extension (II.G.4); William, Bethune Town Cemetery (IV.E.57); Percy is commemorated in Maple Copse Cemetery (Sp.Mem.J.2).

(Panel 46) Rfn. Z/2367, Joseph Clarke Argue, 'A' Coy., 1st Bn. The Prince Consort's Own (The Rifle Brigade): 7th *s.* of Thomas Argue, of 'Urcher House,' Bailie Borough, Co. Cavan, by his wife Essie: and brother to L/Corpl. B/7470, J. Argue, 2nd Cameronians (Sco.Rif.), died, 3 June 1915, of wounds: enlisted Battersea, August 1914. Killed in action, 26 April 1915, nr. Fortuin: Age 25. *unm.*

His brother James is buried in Sailly-sur-la-Lys Canadian Cemetery (II.E.98) (*IWGC record L. Argue*)

(Panel 46) Rfn. B/1602, Albert Bailey, Machine Gun Section, 7th (Service) Bn. The Prince Consort's Own (The Rifle Brigade): *s.* of the late Edward Bailey, by his wife Sarah (24, Lower Cross Street, Smethwick, co. Stafford): *b.* Smethwick: enlisted there. Killed in action (nr. La Belle Alliance) 7 December 1915, when the machine-gun dugout was blown in by shellfire: Age 21. L/Corpl. G. Cowley and Rfn. J.D. Burk were also killed.

George Cowley and James Burk also have no known grave, they are recorded above and on Panel 48 respectively.

(Panel 46) Rfn. S/11631, Joseph Robert Bailey, 1st Bn. The Prince Consort's Own (The Rifle Brigade): *s.* of Frederick Bailey, of 3, Tomlin's Terrace, Limehouse, London, by his wife Elizabeth. Killed in the attack at Boesinghe, 6 July 1915: Age 17.

(Panel 46) Rfn. 3253, Mark Barnard, 1st Bn. The Prince Consort's Own (The Rifle Brigade): *s.* of David Barnard, of 17, Beltring Road, Eastbourne, co. Sussex, by his wife Eliza: and elder brother to Coy. Sergt.Major L/10145, F. Barnard, D.C.M., Royal Sussex Regt., killed in action 12 – 13 April 1917, at Arras: enlisted Brighton. Killed in action 13 May 1915: Age 24. *unm.*

His brother Frederick also has no known grave; he is commemorated on the Arras (Faubourg d'Amiens) Memorial (Addenda Panel).

(Panel 46) Rfn. S/11013, Arthur Edward Battle, 12th (Service) Bn. The Prince Consort's Own (The Rifle Brigade): *s.* of Frederick Battle, of Blunham, Sandy, co. Bedford, and his wife Jane: late *husb.* to Lucy Emma Battle (46, Valnay Street, Tooting, London). Killed in action 12 February 1916: Age 31.

(Panel 46) Rfn. S/13026, Walter Frederick Bessant, 9th (Service) Bn. The Prince Consort's Own (The Rifle Brigade): *s.* of Tom Edward, of 18, Doncaster Road, Eastleigh, co. Hants, by his wife Mary: and *yr.* brother to Corpl. S/6482, A. Bessant, 4th Rifle Brigade, who also fell: *b.* Eastleigh, 1894: enlisted Southampton. Killed in action, 25 September 1915: Age 21. *unm.*

His brother Archibald also has no known grave; he is commemorated on the Doiran Memorial, Greece.

(Panel 46) Rfn. S/13019, William Bird, 9th (Service) Bn. The Prince Consort's Own (The Rifle Brigade): 4th *s.* of Eli Thomas Bird, of High Cross, Aldenham, co. Hertford, by his wife Louisa, *dau.* of William Humbles: *b.* 15 February 1899: *educ.* Boys' Elementary Church of England School, Delrow: Occupation – Gardener: enlisted 9th Rifle Brigade, 11 June 1915: served with the Expeditionary Force in France, from 17 September 1915, and was killed in action 17 January 1916. His Captain wrote, "We were digging a new trench, connecting two other trenches, and Bird was hit in the neck by a stray bullet; we managed to get him down on a stretcher to the Dressing Station, but he died almost as soon as he got there, and within an hour of being hit. We buried him just behind our second line. I am very sorry to lose Bird; he had been in my company some time." **Age 16.** (*IWGC record 18 January*)

PANEL 46 ENDS RFN. A. BOWERY, THE RIFLE BRIGADE.

PANEL 48 BEGINS RFN. J.BOWIE, THE RIFLE BRIGADE.

(Panel 48) Rfn. S/8686, Thomas Bradford, 7th (Service) Bn. The Prince Consort's Own (The Rifle Brigade): Missing believed killed in action at Hooge 30 July 1915: Age 32. He leaves a wife Elizabeth Bradford (37, Crown Street, Sutton-in-Ashfield), and children the youngest of which, May, *b.* 26 June

1915, at her baptism (St. Mary's Church, 6 September 1915) her father was recorded 'Soldier, Missing in action. *'Notts Free Press,'* 9 August 1918:–

> *He left his home in perfect health, He looked so strong and brave;*
> *He little thought how soon he would be laid in a hero's grave.*

(Panel 48) Rfn. 96, Charles Bryant, 4th Bn. The Prince Consort's Own (The Rifle Brigade): *s.* of Joseph Bryant, by his wife Susan Jane Amelia: *b.* Upavon, nr. Pewsey, co. Wilts: enlisted Hartley Wintney, nr. Basingstoke, co. Hants. Died of wounds 20 April 1915: Age 31. Remains recovered Asylum British Cemetery, 28.H.12.d.9.7., Row D., Grave 8, 29 April 1924; identified – Cross, Clothing. *Buried in Bedford House Cemetery (V.A.33/Enc.No.2).*

(Panel 48) Rfn. S/11176, James Davey Burk, Machine Gun Section, 7th (Service) Bn. The Prince Consort's Own (The Rifle Brigade): *s.* of the late James D. Burke by his wife Elizabeth Ann (5, Neale Street, Dean Bank, Ferryhill, Co. Durham): *b.* Ferryhill: enlisted there. Killed in action (nr. La Belle Alliance) 7 December 1915, when the machine-gun dugout was blown in by a shell: Age 30. L/Corpl. G. Cowley and Rfn. A. Bailey were also killed.

George Cowley and Albert Bailey also have no known grave; they are recorded on Panel 46.

(Panel 48) Rfn. S/17556, Herbert William Carvell, 16th (Service) Bn. (St. Pancras) The Prince Consort's Own (The Rifle Brigade): *s.* of Frederick Carvell: enlisted Highbury. Missing / confirmed killed during the battalion's raid on 'The Mound.' 15 February 1917: Age 27. He was married to Lily Foskett, *née* Carvell (163, Liverpool Buildings, Highbury Station Road, London, N.1). See account re. 2nd Lieut. J.C. MacLehose, Brandhoek Military Cemetery (II.K.15).

(Panel 48) Rfn. S/10229, Albert John Cootes, 8th (Service) Bn. The Prince Consort's Own (The Rifle Brigade): *s.* of John Cootes, of 53, Cirencester Street, Paddington, London, W.2, by his wife Ellen: and yr. brother to Pte. 3/6518, J.T. Cootes, 3rd Bedfordshire Regt., died 28 October 1918, aged 29 years: *b.* Marylebone, London: enlisted there. Killed in action 4 February 1916: Age 19.

His brother James is buried in Paddington Cemetery (S.P.14452).

(Panel 48) Rfn. S/18317, Arthur David, 16th (Service) Bn. (St. Pancras) The Prince Consort's Own (The Rifle Brigade): *s.* of Thomas John David, of 43, Newport Road, Leyton, London, and Isabella his wife: enlisted Leyton. Missing / confirmed killed during the battalion's raid on 'The Mound.' 15 February 1917: Age 31. See account re. 2nd Lieut. J.C. MacLehose, Brandhoek Military Cemetery (II.K.15).

(Panel 48) Rfn. S/27042, George Donovan, 16th (Service) Bn. (St. Pancras) The Prince Consort's Own (The Rifle Brigade): late of St. Pancras, London, W.C.: enlisted London. One of eight Other Ranks, 16th Battn., missing / confirmed killed during a raid on 'The Mound.' 15 February 1917. See account re. 2nd Lieut. J.C. MacLehose, Brandhoek Military Cemetery (II.K.15).

(Panel 48) Rfn. S/6717, Richard Henry Dowswell, 4th Bn. The Prince Consort's Own (The Rifle Brigade): only child of Richard Dowswell, by his wife Mary: *b.* London, April 1872: served several years with the Colours; thereafter joined the Reserve: Occupation – Clerk; Camberwell Town Hall: recalled on mobilisation following the outbreak of war and rejoined Prince Consort's Own, August 1914: served with the Expeditionary Force in France and Flanders from 21 December, and was killed in action 29 April 1915: Age 43.. He *m.* St. Peter's Church, Camberwell; Elizabeth (31, Linden Grove, Nunhead, London, S.E.), *dau.* of John Bartholomew, Builder; and fathered seven children.

(Panel 48) Rfn. S/141, John Eastment, 9th (Service) Bn. The Prince Consort's Own (The Rifle Brigade): *s.* of Robert Eastment, of Puddletown, Haselbury, Crewkerne, co. Somerset, by his wife Maria: and brother to Pte. 17493, W. Eastment, 9th Bn. Devonshire Regt., who fell 2 April 1917: *b.* Hardington, co. Somerset, *c.*1890. Killed in action 24 June 1915: Age 25.

His brother also has no known grave; he is commemorated on the Arras (Faubourg d'Amiens) Memorial (Bay 3).

(Panel 48) Rfn. S/27314, Harold Eggington, 16th (Service) Bn. (St. Pancras) The Prince Consort's Own (The Rifle Brigade): *s.* of Francis Eggington, of 8, Claremont Road, Forest Gate, London, and his spouse Martha Selina Eggington: enlisted Stratford, co. Essex. Missing / confirmed killed during the battalion's raid on 'The Mound.' 15 February 1917: Age 19. See account re. 2nd Lieut. J.C. MacLehose, Brandhoek Military Cemetery (II.K.15).

(Panel 48) Rfn. B/1222, Alfred Harry Emmett, 9th (Service) Bn. The Prince Consort's Own (The Rifle Brigade): 5th *s.* of William Emmett, Chimney Sweep; of Basingwell Street, Bishop's Waltham, by his wife Eliza Jane (Farrell): *b.* Bishop's Waltham, co. Hants, 1 June 1894: *educ.* Eastleigh Boys' School: Occupation – Chimney Sweep: enlisted 4 September 1914, after the outbreak of war: went to France, May 1915, and was killed in action at Hooge, 31 July 1915: Age 21. *unm.*

(Panel 48) Rfn. S/18440, William Flintham, 16th (Service) Bn. (St. Pancras) The Prince Consort's Own (The Rifle Brigade): late of Kennington: enlisted Lambeth, co. Surrey. One of eight Other Ranks, 16th Battn., missing / confirmed killed during the battalion's raid on 'The Mound.' 15 February 1917. See account re. 2nd Lieut. J.C. MacLehose, Brandhoek Military Cemetery (II.K.15).

(Panel 48) Rfn. S/31588, Frederick Charles George, 3rd Bn. The Prince Consort's Own (The Rifle Brigade): *s.* of William George, of 27A, Goldsboro' Road, Springfield Estate, Wandsworth, London, SW.8, by his wife Sarah E.: *b.* South Lambeth, SE.: enlisted early 1917, and, after a short period of training, proceeded to France, March 1917, and was killed in action 31 July following. During his brief service on the Western Front he took part in many engagements, did very good work with his Battalion; and gave his life for the freedom of England nr. Hill 60, Ypres sector: Age 19.

And Doubtless He Went
In Splendid Company

(Panel 48) Rfn. S/6063, William George Gibbs, 'D' Coy., 7th (Service) Bn. The Prince Consort's Own (The Rifle Brigade): *s.* of John Gibbs, of 69, Huntingdon Road, East Finchley, London, N., by his wife Amy Ann: *b.* Lewes, co. Sussex: enlisted St. Pancras, London, N.: served with the Expeditionary Force in France and Flanders from May 1915, and was killed in action at Hooge, 23 July following: Age 20. *unm.* Remains recovered (28.I.24.b.1.8, Sanctuary Wood) 'Unknown British Soldier. 7 Rifle Bde.' exhumed, identified – Clothing, Titles; reinterred, registered, 10 February 1928. *Buried in Sanctuary Wood Cemetery (II.B.24).*

Faithful Unto Death

(Panel 48) Rfn. B/1914, Alfred Gilbert, 7th (Service) Bn. The Prince Consort's Own (The Rifle Brigade): *b.* Salford, co. Lancaster: enlisted Pendleton: served with the Expeditionary Force in France, and was killed in action 23 July 1915, at Hooge, Belgium: Age 47. He leaves a wife, Rosanna (138, Cook Street, Whit Lane, Pendleton, Manchester). Remains recovered (28.I.24.b.1.8, Sanctuary Wood) 'Unknown British Soldier. 7 Rifle Bde.' exhumed, identified – Clothing, Titles; reinterred, registered, 9 February 1928. *Buried in Sanctuary Wood Cemetery (II.B.22).*

Rest In Peace

(Panel 48) Rfn. Z/629, William Goode, 1st Bn. The Prince Consort's Own (The Rifle Brigade): *s.* of the late Henry Goode, by his wife Amy (11, Tunnel Cottages, Galley Common, Nuneaton, co. Warwick): and elder brother to Pte. 19633, H. Goode, Wiltshire Regt., who fell almost six weeks later: enlisted Nuneaton, co. Warwick. Killed in action 1 May 1915: Age 24. *unm.*

His brother Harry also has no known grave; he is recorded on Panel 53.

(Panel 48) Rfn. 2473, Cecil William Gurney, 4th Bn. The Prince Consort's Own (The Rifle Brigade): *s.* of John Henry Gurney, of 95, East Street, Eastbourne, by his wife Mercy Ellen: and yr. brother to Sergt. 1195, P.J. Gurney, 2nd Rifle Brigade, killed in action 24 October 1916, at the Somme: *b. c.*1890: enlisted Eastbourne. Killed in action 4 May 1915: Age 24. *unm.*

His brother Philip also has no known grave; he is commemorated on the Thiepval Memorial.

(Panel 48) Rfn. S/14268, Gordon Harris, 16th (Service) Bn. (St. Pancras) The Prince Consort's Own (The Rifle Brigade): *s.* of George Harris, of 'Montreux,' Kingsbridge Road, Newbury, co. Berks, by his wife Kate: enlisted Reading. Missing / confirmed killed during the battalion's raid on 'The Mound.' 15 February 1917: Age 28. (*IWGC record 14 February*) See account re. 2nd Lieut. J.C. MacLehose, Brandhoek Military Cemetery (II.K.15).

(Panel 48) Rfn. S/27902, Albert Henry Hemmings, 16th (Service) Bn. (St. Pancras) The Prince Consort's Own (The Rifle Brigade): formerly no.28220, Gloucestershire Regt.: *s.* of Heneage Hemmings, of 'The Mason's Arms,' Pebworth, nr. Stratford-on-Avon, and his wife Mary Hemmings: enlisted Chipping Campden, co. Gloucester. Missing / confirmed killed during the battalion's raid on 'The Mound.' 15 February 1917: Age 19. See account re. 2nd Lieut. J.C. MacLehose, Brandhoek Military Cemetery (II.K.15).

(Panel 48) Rfn. S/10080, George William Hussey, 2nd Bn. The Prince Consort's Own (The Rifle Brigade): *s.* of Alfred Hussey, of 6, Laurie Grove, New Cross, London, S.E., by his wife Annie, *dau.* of William T. Kempster: *b.* Peckham, London, S.E.: *educ.* there: Occupation – Electrical Instrument Winder: enlisted Woolwich, co. Kent, March 1915: served with the Expeditionary Force in France and Flanders from the following October: invalided home: returned to France, February 1917. Reported wounded / missing after the fighting 30 July following; now assumed killed in action on that date: *unm.*

(Panel 48) Rfn. S/6205, John Marriott, 12th (Service) Bn. The Prince Consort's Own (The Rifle Brigade): 1st *s.* of the late John William Marriott, of 13, Belfield Lane, Firgrove, Milnrow, Rochdale (*d.*1934), by his wife Naomi (*d.*1953): and brother to Pte. 10769, H. Marriott, 2nd Border Regt., killed in action at the battle of Loos, September 1915; and Pte. 78781, W.B. Marriott, Royal Fusiliers, killed in action October 1918: *b.* Hollingworth, co. Lancaster, *c.*1892: Occupation – Weft Carrier; Lowfield Spinning Co.: enlisted Rochdale, 18 November 1914: served with the Expeditionary Force in France, and was killed 6 June 1916, by the explosion of a German mine. Following the explosion his comrades dug for two days in an endeavour to recover his body; no trace of Rifleman Marriott was found. Recorded on Belfield (St. Ann's) Church, War Memorial: Age 23. *unm.*

His brother Harry has no known grave, he is commemorated on the Loos Memorial (Dud Corner); William is buried in Wellington Cemetery, Rieux-en-Cambresis (I.D.6).

(Panel 48) Rfn. S/10418, Joseph Charles Mignot, 7th (Service) Bn. The Prince Consort's Own (The Rifle Brigade): *s.* of Joseph Mignot, Bootmaker; of Roman Road, Bethnal Green, London, E.2: *b.* Bethnal Green: enlisted Shoreditch, London, E.C. Killed in action 29 December 1915. Remains recovered 'Unknown British Soldier. 7/RB.;' unmarked grave (28.C.14.c.00.05); identified – Badge of Rank, Titles, Clothing; reinterred, registered 26 January 1928. *Buried in Sanctuary Wood Cemetery (IV.N.21).*

(Panel 48) Rfn. S/7045, Harold Mills, 1st Bn. The Prince Consort's Own (The Rifle Brigade): *s.* of Mary Mills (Mount Street, Breaston, Derby): and elder brother to Pte. 3898, H. Mills, 2nd Sherwood Foresters, killed in action 9 August 1915: *b.* Sheffield: enlisted Nottingham. Killed in action 13 May 1915: Age 22. *unm.*

His brother Horace also has no known grave; he is recorded on Panel 41.

(Panel 48) Rfn. S/11081, Harold William Morton, 9th (Service) Bn. The Prince Consort's Own (The Rifle Brigade): *s.* of the late George Maddison Morton, by his wife Mary Ann (28, Chapel Place, Dover): enlisted Woolwich: served with the Expeditionary Force in France and Flanders from 12 December 1915, and was killed in action 5 January 1916; St. Jean sector, Ypres: Age 31. His officer wrote, "He had gone out with a party to assist in getting away a man who had been wounded, and was himself hit in this work of mercy. He only lived a few minutes, and then passed peacefully away." And a comrade, "He died a beautiful death, the death of a hero, and his last words were 'Goodbye Rosie.'" He was married to Rose Ellen Bradley, *née* Tracy, *née* Morton (1990, Haultain Street, Victoria, British Columbia, Canada), and had two children.

(Panel 48) Rfn. 1171, Percy Harold Mountain, 3rd Bn. The Prince Consort's Own (The Rifle Brigade): *s.* of Mrs H. Mountain (Lovick's Yard, Mariners Lane, Norwich): and yr. brother to Pte. 6732,

B. Mountain, 1st Norfolk Regt., who fell 24 August 1914, aged 30 years: *b*. Norwich: enlisted there. Killed in action 31 July 1917: Age 29. *unm*.

His brother Bertie also has no known grave; he is commemorated on the La Ferte-Sous-Jouarre Memorial.

(Panel 48) Rfn. S/8685, Edward Organ, 11th (Service) Bn. The Prince Consort's Own (The Rifle Brigade): late of 11, Millpond Street, Baptist Mills, Bristol: *s*. of Joseph Stephen Organ, of 21, Fox Road, Mina Road, Bristol, by his wife Eliza: and yr. brother to Gnr. 54980, J.S. Organ, Royal Horse Artillery, died 14 July 1918, aged 28 years: *b*. Gloucester: enlisted Bristol. Killed in action 7 August 1917: Age 22. *unm*.

His brother Joseph is commemorated in Bristol (Arnos Vale) Cemetery (Screen Wall 1.679).

(Panel 48) Rfn. 4614, Henry Lewis Osborne, 4th Bn. The Prince Consort's Own (The Rifle Brigade): *s*. of Lewis Henry Osborne, of 94, Barton Hill Road, Barton Hill, Bristol: *b*. Rotherhithe, co. Kent: enlisted Bristol. Killed in action 10 May 1915: Age 24. *unm*. Remains exhumed 28.J.13.a.35.40, 15 December 1936; identified – G.S. Uniform, Boots, Titles & Disc. *Buried in Bedford House Cemetery (I.H.15/Enc.No.6)*.

(Panel 48) Rfn. Z/2905, John Pearce, 1st Bn. The Prince Consort's Own (The Rifle Brigade): *s*. of the late John Pearce, by his wife Emma (9, Longley Road, Harrow, co. Middlesex): and yr. brother to Rfn. 3128, H. Pearce, 12th London Regt., killed in action 8 May 1915: *b*. Lambeth: enlisted London. Killed in action 13 May 1915: Age 28.

His brother Herbert also has no known grave; he is recorded on Panel 54.

(Panel 48) Rfn. B/1358, Percy Price, 7th (Service) Bn. The Prince Consort's Own (The Rifle Brigade): *s*. of the late John Price, by his wife Sarah (37, Corser Street, West Smethwick, co. Stafford). Killed in action at Hooge, 30 July 1915: **Age 16**.

(Panel 48) Rfn. S/8981, Bernard Thomas Quinn, 9th (Service) Bn. The Prince Consort's Own (The Rifle Brigade): late of Sheinton, co. Salop: *s*. of Annie Quinn (7, Stone Terrace, Storer Street, Nottingham): enlisted Nottingham. Killed in action 25 September. 1915: **Age 16**.

(Panel 48) Rfn. S/9710, Bertie Raymond, 8th (Service) Bn. The Prince Consort's Own (The Rifle Brigade): *s*. of Richard Lewis Raymond, of Watlington, co. Oxford, by his wife Emily: and elder brother to Corpl. B/3306, B. Raymond, 8th Rifle Brigade, killed in action at Hooge the previous day: *b*. Watlington: enlisted Worthing, co. Sussex: served with the Expeditionary Force in France from May 1915, and was killed in action 30 July 1915, at Hooge: Age 26. *unm*. Remembered on Watlington Village War Memorial.

His brother Basil also has no known grave; he is recorded on Panel 46.

(Panel 48) Rfn. S/27961, Ernest Rivett, 16th (Service) Bn. (St. Pancras) The Prince Consort's Own (The Rifle Brigade): *s*. of Albert Henry Rivett, of 86, Albany Road, Old Kent Road, Camberwell, London, by his wife Mary Ann: and yr. brother to Rfn. S/9750, C. Rivett, 3rd Rifle Brigade, died 12 February 1916, of wounds: *b*. Camberwell: enlisted St. Paul's Churchyard. Killed in action 31 July 1917: Age 19.

His brother Christopher is buried in Lijssenthoek Military Cemetery (II.D.40A).

(Panel 48) Rfn. S/8937, Thomas Edgar Rushbrooke, 8th (Service) Bn. The Prince Consort's Own (The Rifle Brigade): *s*. of George Rushbrooke, of 100, Bridge Street, Stowmarket, co. Suffolk, by his wife Hannah: and yr. brother to L/Corpl. 47797, A.L.J. Rushbrooke, 17th Royal Fusiliers, killed in action 24 March 1918: served with the Expeditionary Force in France from May 1915, and was killed in action 30 July 1915, at Hooge, nr. Ypres: Age 17.

His brother Arthur also has no known grave; he is commemorated on the Arras (Faubourg d'Amiens) Memorial (Bay 3).

(Panel 48) Rfn. B/3203, William Skinner, 7th (Service) Bn. The Prince Consort's Own (The Rifle Brigade): *b*. Erdington, co. Warwick: enlisted Birmingham. Killed in action at Hooge, 23 July 1915. Remains recovered (28.I.24.b.1.8, Sanctuary Wood) 'Unknown British Soldier. 7 Rifle Bde.' exhumed, identified – Clothing, Titles; reinterred, registered, 10 February 1928. *Buried in Sanctuary Wood Cemetery (II.B.23)*.

In Loving Memory
Nobly He Did His Duty And Died A Briton

(Panel 48) Rfn. Z/2928, Albert Leonard Smith, 1st Bn. The Prince Consort's Own (The Rifle Brigade): *s.* of William (& Alice) Cheshire Smith, of Upper Clapton, London, E.5: *b.* Leicester, *c.*1890: Occupation – Clerk, London Stock Exchange: enlisted London. Killed in action 3 May 1915: Age 24.

PANEL 48 ENDS RFN. E.W. SPELLER, THE RIFLE BRIGADE.

PANEL 50 BEGINS RFN. J. SPRATT, THE RIFLE BRIGADE.

(Panel 50) Rfn. S/7337, Arthur John Stilton, 7th (Service) Bn. The Prince Consort's Own (The Rifle Brigade): *s.* of Luke Stilton, of 4, California, Aylesbury, co. Buckingham, by his first wife Sarah: and (by his second wife Hannah) half-brother to Pte. 37797, F. Stilton, 8th Royal Berkshire Regt., died of wounds 28 February 1918; and L/Corpl. 18946, G.F. Stilton, 6th King's Own Yorkshire Light Infantry, killed in action 13 January 1916: *b.* 18 June 1883: Occupation – Book Binder; Messrs Hazell, Watson & Viney, Printers: enlisted Lambeth, London. Killed in action 23 July 1915: Age 32. Remains recovered (28.I.24.b.1.8, Sanctuary Wood) 'Unknown British Soldier. 7 Rifle Bde.' exhumed, identified – Clothing, Titles, Wallet; reinterred, registered, 9 February 1928. *Buried in Sanctuary Wood Cemetery (II.B.21).*

His half-brothers Fred and George are buried in Montescourt-Lizerolles Communal Cemetery (163); and New Irish Farm Cemetery (VI.D.13) respectively.

(Panel 50) Rfn. 1299, George Thumwood, 4th Bn. The Prince Consort's Own (The Rifle Brigade): *s.* of John Thumwood, of 25, Summerley Street, Earlsfield, London, by his wife Emily: *b.* Ashford, co. Middlesex: enlisted Guildford, co. Surrey. Killed in action 14 May 1915: Age 27.

(Panel 50) Rfn. S/27860, Albert Watts, 16th (Service) Bn. (St. Pancras) The Prince Consort's Own (The Rifle Brigade): *s.* of Mrs Watts (70, Rutland Road, Forest Gate, London): late *husb.* to Daisy Edith Watts (4, Blenheim Road, East Ham, London): enlisted East Ham. Missing / confirmed killed during the battalion's raid on 'The Mound.' 15 February 1917: Age 26. (*IWGC record 14 February*) See account re. 2nd Lieut. J.C. MacLehose, Brandhoek Military Cemetery (II.K.15).

Rfn. H.W. Carvell, A. David, G. Donovan, H. Eggington, W. Flintham, G. Harris, and A.H. Hemmings were also killed, none has a known grave; they are recorded on Panel 48.

(Panel 50) Rfn. S/9462, Douglas Wilcockson, 16th (Service) Bn. (St. Pancras) The Prince Consort's Own (The Rifle Brigade): *s.* of Joseph Wilcockson, Coal Miner; of 102, St. Michael's Street, Sutton-in-Ashfield, Nottingham, by his wife Emma: *b.* Chatsworth Street, Sutton-in-Ashfield, *c.*1894. Killed in action 31 July 1917: Age 22. *unm.* '*The Notts Free Press*,' 'In Memoriam,' 2 August 1918:–

> One year has gone and still we miss him, Friends may think the wound has healed;
> Little do they know the sorrow, That's within our hearts concealed.
> Loving Mother, Father, Brothers & Sisters.

(Panel 50) Rfn. S/7377, Herbert Wood, M.M., 1st Bn. The Prince Consort's Own (The Rifle Brigade): *s.* of Hartley Wood, Engineer-in-Charge, Denholme Mills; of Denholme, Bradford, co. York, by his wife Anna: *b.* Grünberg, Silesia, 1891: *educ.* Breslau, Bad Harzburg, and Petrograd, Russia (Engineering Academy) from whence he returned to enlist; London, October 1914. Killed in the attack on International Trench, Mauser Ridge, 6 July 1915: Age 24. *unm.* Mentioned in Despatches (posthumously); awarded the Military Medal ('*London Gazette*,' November 1916), for 'distinguished service and devotion to duty.' See also Talana Farm Cemetery.

His brother Harry was also killed in 1915, vicinity Hill 60; his commemoration is not recorded.

(Panel 50) Rfn. S/13677, Bertram William Wyner, 2nd Bn. The Prince Consort's Own (The Rifle Brigade): *yst. s.* of William Wyner, Sign Writer; of 27, Union Street, Rochester, co. Kent, by his wife Ellen, *dau.* of Richard Pettman, of Whitstable: *b.* Canterbury, 15 February 1896: *educ.* Gillingham, co. Kent: Occupation – Decorator: enlisted 4 August 1915: served with the Expeditionary Force in France and Flanders from December following: invalided to England, frozen feet March 1916: returned to

France, March 1917. Reported wounded and missing after the fighting near Ypres 31 July following, and is now assumed to have been killed in action on or since that date: Age 21. *unm.*

(Panel 50) Capt. James Lancaster, 3rd Bn. The Monmouthshire Regt. (T.F.): *yr. s.* of the late Robert Lancaster, by his wife Euphemia (Allesley, co. Warwick): *gdson.* to the late John Lancaster, M.P., of Bilton Grange, Rugby: *b.* Wolston Heath, Rugby, 18 December 1877: *educ.* Shrewsbury School: Member; Institute of Mining Engineers: gazetted Lieut. February 1910; promoted Capt. October 1914: undertook Imperial Service obligations at the outbreak of the Great War: served with the Expeditionary Force in France and Flanders, and was killed in action at Ypres, 9 May 1915: Age 37. Capt. Lancaster's main recreations were cricket and golf. He *m.* Margaret Ormonde, *dau.* of Clermont Livingstone, of Cowichan, Vancouver Island, British Columbia, and had three children – Robert Clermont, *b.* January 1906; James Donald, *b.* March 1910, and John Stewart, *b.* June 1914.

(Panel 50) Capt. Benjamin Lewis Perry, 1/1st Bn. The Monmouthshire Regt. (T.F.): elder *s.* of the late Benjamin Perry, J.P. (Monmouth County), of Caldicot Hall, and his wife (The Glen, Caerleon, co. Monmouth): *b.* Chepstow, co. Monmouth, 2 July 1878: joined Monmouthshire Regt., 1903; obtained his company, October 1910: on the outbreak of war – having previously passed through a school of musketry instruction, and qualified for promotion to Field rank – undertook Imperial Service obligations and went to France, where he was shot through the head and killed instantaneously, 25 April 1915, while leading his men. Buried in the vicinity of Zonnebeke: Age 36. A Military Member of the Monmouthshire Territorial Force Association, he was very keen on hunting, and belonged to the Llangibby Hunt; his horse 'Bill Bailey' won the Monmouthshire Point-to-Point Race three times. He *m.* Elizabeth 'Elsie' (72, Cross Oak Road, Berkhampstead, co. Hertford), *dau.* of J. Flexman, The Manor House, Gunnersbury, and left a son, Benjamin Richard, aged six years at the time of his father's death.

(Panel 50) Capt. Iltyd Edwin Maitland Watkins, 2nd Bn. The Monmouthshire Regt. (T.F.): only *s.* of John Maitland Watkins, Solicitor; of Usk, co. Monmouth, by his wife Frances: *b.* Usk, 25 March 1890: *educ.* Downside School, nr. Bath, co. Gloucester, and King's College, Cambridge, where he took his degree of LL.B. and B.A. (Law Tripos), 1911: articled to his father's firm the same year: passed Solicitors Final Examination, 1914: gazetted 2nd Lieut., Monmouthshire Regt., 29 March 1909: promoted Lieut. September 1912; Capt. July 1914: volunteered for Active Service on the outbreak of war; apptd. Command, No.4 Welsh Divisional Signal Coy.: rejoined Monmouthshire Regt., January 1915: served with the Expeditionary Force in France and Flanders from February 1915, and was killed in action, 7 May following, between Ypres and St. Julien. Buried on the battlefield, La Brique, St. Jean, north of Ypres. His Commanding Officer, Col. Cuthbertson, C.M.G., M.V.O., wrote expressing to his father his deep sympathy on the loss of his gallant son adding, "He was killed on the morning of the German attack, and his death was instantaneous and painless. Of his qualities as a soldier and a gentleman, I cannot speak too highly; cheerful, gallant and unselfish, he died as he would have chosen to die, with his face to the enemy and in the middle of the men whom he loved and commanded so well. We buried him on the battlefield... his loss is deeply deplored by all ranks." While at College Mr Watkins rowed each year in the Lent, and May Races. He was fond of riding, hunting, swimming, and all outdoor pursuits, but had a particular talent for artistic work and literacy; showing great promise in the former as a painter of portraits in oils, and in the latter being well read in the best of both English and French literature: Age 25. *unm.*

(Panel 50) Lieut. Charles Herbert George Martin, 1/3rd Bn. The Monmouthshire Regt. (T.F.): only *s.* of the late Edward Pritchard Martin, Mining Engineer & Colliery Owner; of 'The Hill,' Abergavenny, by his wife Margaret, *dau.* of C.H. James, of Merthyr: *b.* Dowlais, co. Glamorgan, 5 October 1882: *educ.* Eton, and Magdalen College, Oxford, where he obtained a high standard of efficiency in biology and obtained his degrees (M.A., F.Z.S.): prior to the outbreak of war was demonstrator in Zoology, University of Glasgow; Lecturer, Oxford, and well-known at Cambridge and Naples, and was a scientist of European reputation: joined Glasgow University O.T.C.: gazetted 2nd Lieut. Unatt'd. (T.F.), 12 October 1909; posted 3rd Monmouths, 5 June 1912: promoted Lieut. 29 August 1914; subsequently apptd. Machine Gun Officer: volunteered for Foreign Service on the outbreak of war, and was killed in action N.E. of

Ypres, 2 May 1915: Age 33. Buried between St. Julien and Frezenberg. The published author of several books on protozoology, he was preparing papers for the Rothamstead Experimental Station, Harpenden when war broke out. An ardent all-round sportsman, keen follower of the Monmouthshire Hounds, and Master of the Cricklewell Harriers; he *m*. St. Mary's Church, Abergavenny, 11 June 1912, Beatrice Elsie ('The Hill,' Abergavenny), only child of Ferdinand Packington John Hanbury, J.P., D.L., of Nantoer, Abergavenny, co. Monmouth, and had a son, Charles Edward Capel, *b*. 21 April 1913. Mrs Martin re-married; now Mrs Solly-Flood (Manor House, Butters Marston, co. Warwick). Remains 'Unknown British Lieut.' recovered (28.J.4.a.70.10) unmarked grave; identified – Officers Clothing, Collar Badge, Badge of Rank; reinterred, registered 2 May 1930. *Buried in Sanctuary Wood Cemetery (V.L.16).*

(Panel 50) 2nd Lieut. William Victor Stewart, 1st Bn. The Monmouthshire Regt. (T.F.): only *s*. of William Stewart, Mining Engineer, ex-President, South Wales Coal Owners Association; of Brodawel, Caerleon, co. Monmouth: *b*. Abertillery, co. Monmouth, 10 January 1897: *educ*. Oakfield House Preparatory School; Blundell's School, Tiverton (Junior House, September 1909, North Close, 1910 – 14), where he sang alto and bass in the school choir, and was an active member of the O.T.C. (1910 – 14), played in the Corps band, went to camp (1912 – 13), promoted L/Sergt. (1913), in the shooting VIII (twice representing his school at Bisley), and played in the third XV: 'universally beloved he stood for everything that was sound and honourable in relation with his school and his fellows': commissioned 2nd Lieut., August 1914, aged 17 years: served with the Expeditionary Force in France and Flanders from February 1915, and was killed in action at Frezenberg, between Zonnebeke and Ypres, 8 May 1915. Having moved into the trenches the previous night, the Battalion was fiercely bombarded by the enemy the following morning. 2nd Lieut. Stewart was killed after the enemy had broken through the line to the right of the Monmouthshires and got in rear of the Battalion. The following account of an incident that occurred on the day of the charge at Neuve Chapelle was sent by a Private of the battalion to his wife, "I expect you will read of the very plucky action of Lieut. W.V. Stewart (son of Mr W. Stewart, Brodawel, Caerleon) and a party of men. We were running short of ammunition in the trenches, and the Captain and his Company were at a farm about a mile away. They were telephoned to, and volunteers were asked for to bring the ammunition up. The party, under Lieut. Stewart, came up with it in broad daylight, and were almost up to their knees in mud and slush. They had the ammunition strung round their necks. It was a daring deed, and not one of them was struck. They got to the trenches about 1 pm., and had to stay there wet through till dark. We shared what food we had with them, and gave them our dirty, but dry, socks to put on. They all deserve recognition, and we hope they will get it." Another man wrote the following account of the Officer's death, "It was about 8.30 a.m. when Lieut. Stewart, with a few other officers, came to breakfast…After this Lieut. Stewart went out and joined his Platoon. It was about 11.30 when I saw him next. It happened thus. The Regiment on our right got cut off and captured. Lieut. Stewart then came running up and took a rifle from a man who seemed to be helpless owing to shock. He then dashed into the firing line, and I never saw him again. It was about 12.45 when I heard news of him again, and then it was to hear that he had been killed. This upset me more than I can say, as Lieut. Stewart had been more than good to me." Age 18.

(Panel 50) Sergt. 2030, Henry Morgan, 1st Bn. The Monmouthshire Regt. (T.F.): late of Shire Newton: *s*. of Elijah Morgan, of 13, Shop Row, Blaina, co. Monmouth, and Louisa, his wife: and brother to Pte. 1508, F.W. Morgan, 3rd Monmouthshire Regt., killed in action the same day: *b*. Chepstow: enlisted there. Killed in action 8 May 1915.

His brother Frederick also has no known grave; he is recorded below.

(Panel 50) Sergt. 111, William Pritchard, 3rd Bn. The Monmouthshire Regt (T.F.): late *husb*. to Mary Pritchard ('Sunnymeade,' Mardy, Abergavenny, co. Monmouth): and father to Pte. 1653, R.J. Pritchard, 3rd Bn. Monmouthshire Regt., who was killed in the same action: 2 May 1915: Age 42.

His son Reginald also has no known grave; he is recorded below.

(Panel 50) Sergt. 1115, James Herbert Spencer, 1st Bn. The Monmouthshire Regt. (T.F.) attd. 171st Tunnelling Coy., Royal Engineers: *s*. of F. (& Mrs M.) Spencer, of 'Brynteg,' Cefn Road, Blackwood, co.

Monmouth: Occupation – Miner: a pre-war Territorial, Corpl., 'H' Coy., 1st Monmouth: served with the Expeditionary Force in France from 14 February 1915, shortly thereafter (at the call for volunteers with mining experience) transf'd. 171 Tunnelling Coy., R.E., and was killed in action 2 June following, at Hill 60: Age 27. In a letter to Sergt. Spencer's mother his Commanding Officer, Capt. E. Wellesley, R.E., wrote, "I am writing to express my sympathy with you and to inform you how he was killed. Your son was in charge of a party working up at the trenches on Wednesday evening. The Germans blew in one of our mines, burying one man and partly burying another. There was a large amount of poisonous gas in the mine at the time. Your son very gallantly went down to this end of the gallery to try and rescue one other man., but was overcome by the fumes, and, when he was brought out of the gallery, was dead. He has been buried behind the trenches, and his grave marked by a cross. He was always conspicuous in the trenches for his zealousness, and he met his end fearlessly doing his duty as a soldier should. I can only again express my sympathy with you in your loss…" Manufactured by Messrs Mears & Stainbank, London, the bell of Blackwood (St. Margaret's) Church bears the inscription 'To The Glory Of God In Memory Of Sergt. J.H. Spencer Who Was Gassed At Hill 60, France, June 2nd 1915, When Nobly Attempting To Save A Comrade.'

(Panel 50) Pte. 2143, Charles Henry Bishop, 1/3rd Bn. The Monmouthshire Regt. (T.F.): *s.* of William Bishop, Coachman; of 15, Westminster Road, Malvern Wells, by his wife Annie Elizabeth: *b.* Ledbury, 1889: Occupation – Miner; Tredegar Colliery: volunteered and enlisted, Abergavenny, August 1914: served with the Expeditionary Force in France and Flanders, and was killed 2 April 1915, by the explosion of a shell. Capt. Gattie, 3rd Battn., wrote, "I regret that I have not had the opportunity of writing to you sooner to express my deep sympathy with you in the loss of your son. He had proved himself a keen, hard-working and capable soldier; and I had more than once occasion to congratulate him particularly on his work. I was quite close when the shell burst which fatally wounded him and as he became unconscious almost at once, he did not, I am sure, suffer much pain. He has been laid to rest in a very beautiful pinewood, close to the spot where he fell." Age 24. *unm.*

(Panel 50) Rfn. 2113, William Blackmore, 'B' Coy., 1st Bn. The Monmouthshire Regt.: *s.* of William Blackmore, of Milton Cottage, Llanwern, Newport, co. Monmouth, by his wife Rosa: and elder brother to Pte. 9541, J.A. Blackmore, 1st Scots Guards, killed in action 25 January 1915, aged 33 years: *b.* Swansea, co. Glamorgan: enlisted Newport. Killed in action 8 May 1915: Age 35. Remembered on the Christchurch (Newport) War Memorial.

His brother James also has no known grave; he is commemorated on the Le Touret Memorial.

(Panel 50) Pte. 1963, William Edwards, 'C' Coy., 3rd Bn. The Monmouthshire Regt. (T.F.): *s.* of John Richard Edwards, Engine Driver; by his wife Catherine, *dau.* of David Thomas, Colliery Manager: *b.* Cwmback, Aberdare, 17 April 1879: *educ.* National School, Bassaleg, Newport, co. Monmouth: joined 2nd Volunteer Battn. South Wales Borderers, 19 May 1896; served 12 years, retiring 31 March 1908: rejoined on the outbreak of war with the contingent from Messrs Whitehead's Iron & Steel Works, Tredegar, where he had been employed as an Ironworker: went to France 15 February 1915, and was killed in action at Messines Ridge, 27 March following. Buried in Wulverghem Churchyard. His Commanding Officer, Capt. O.W.D. Steel, wrote, "Private Edwards had been in my company for some six months, and we all had come to regard him as a thoroughly reliable and excellent soldier. He was most popular with the company, and despite the fact that he had taken up soldiering somewhat late in life, had made himself most efficient in every way. I was with your husband soon after he was wounded, and was with him till his death. He lived only a few minutes and his end was quite painless." Age 36. He *m.* at Bassaleg, Monmouth, 29 September 1906, Rose (3 Varteg Place, Sirhowy, South Wales), *dau.* of William Clift.

(Panel 50) Pte. 2586, Thomas Benjamin Havard, 2nd Bn. The Monmouthshire Regt. (T.F.): *s.* of Sarah Havard (Gwrhay Fawr Cottage, Argoed, Newport): and brother to L/Corpl. 265827, E. Havard, 2nd Monmouthshire Regt., killed in action 2 December 1917: *b.* Pontypool, co. Monmouth: enlisted there. Killed in action 8 May 1915. Age 22. *unm.*

His brother Ernest also has no known grave; he is commemorated on the Cambrai Memorial (Panel 11).

(Panel 50) Rfn. 2401, Alwyn Joseph Lewis, 1st Bn. The Monmouthshire Regt.: *s.* of Joseph Lewis, of 1, Bolt Street, Newport, co. Monmouth, by his wife Esther: *b.* Barry, co. Glamorgan: employee Alexandra Dock Co.: a pre-war Territorial; undertook Active Service Obligations, Newport, August 1914: proceeded to France, 13 February 1915. Missing / believed killed in action 8 May 1915: Age 25. *unm.* Deeply mourned by his father, mother, sister and brothers; In Memoriam:– 'Could we have raised his dying head, Or heard his last farewell, The pain would not have been so hard, For those who loved him well.' (*IWGC record age 24*)

(Panel 50) Pte. 1717, Albert Mifflin, 3rd Bn. The Monmouthshire Regt. (T.F.): brother to Pte. 1715, J.T Mifflin, 3rd Monmouthshire Regt., who fell the same day: *b.* Suckley, co. Worcester: enlisted Abertillery: served with the Expeditionary Force in France from 14 February 1915, and was killed in action 2 May following. Buried between St. Julien and Frezenberg. Inscribed "These Men Were Very Good Unto Us, And We Were Not Lost," (I Samuel, 23.15); Albert and Thomas are remembered on the Suckley (St. John the Baptist) Church War Memorial.

His brother John also has no known grave; he is recorded below.

(Panel 50) Pte. 1715, James Thomas Mifflin, 3rd Bn. The Monmouthshire Regt. (T.F.): brother to Pte. 1717, A. Mifflin, 3rd Monmouthshire Regt., who fell the same day: *b.* Suckley, co. Worcester: enlisted Abertillery: served with the Expeditionary Force in France from 14 February 1915, and was killed in action 2 May following. Buried between St. Julien and Frezenberg. Inscribed "These Men Were Very Good Unto Us, And We Were Not Lost," (I Samuel, 23.15); Albert and Thomas are remembered on the Suckley (St. John the Baptist) Church War Memorial.

His brother Albert also has no known grave; he is recorded above.

(Panel 50) Pte. 1508, Frederick William Morgan, 3rd Bn. The Monmouthshire Regt. (T.F.): *s.* of Elijah (& Louisa) Morgan, of 13, Shop Row, Blaina, co. Monmouth: and brother to Sergt. 2030, H. Morgan, 1st Monmouthshire Regt., killed in action the same day: *b.* Blaina: enlisted there. Killed in action 8 May 1915: Age 18.

His brother Henry also has no known grave; he is recorded above.

(Panel 50) Pte. 2024, David Smith Nekrewes, 'A' Coy., 3rd Bn. The Monmouthshire Regt. (T.F.): 2nd *s.* of the late David Smith Nekrewes, of 3, Carisbrook Road, Maindee, Newport, Monmouth, by his wife Ellen, *dau.* of Michael Buckley: *b.* Newport, 20 July, 1883: *educ.* Shaftesbury School, Newport: enlisted at Abergavenny on the outbreak of war, proceeded with his regt. to France 14 February 1915, and was killed in action at Frezenberg, 16 May 1915. Private Nekrewes was well known in South Wales as an athlete. He represented his school on two occasions in the School's Swimming Championship, and also in the School's Gymnastic Competition; he also played Rugby football for Bridgend, Glam., and (three-quarter), Pontypridd, Mountain Ash, Pontypool, and Glamorgan County. He met with considerable success as a sprinter: Age 31. *unm.*

(Panel 50) Rfn. 2581, Victor Gordon Pearce, 1st Bn. The Monmouthshire Regt. (T.F.): only child of Edwin Victor Pearce, of 38 Devon Place, Newport: enlisted Newport, August 1914: served with the Expeditionary Force in France from 13 February 1915, and was killed in action 8 May following, 'when his regiment was so terribly cut up near Ypres.' Age 21.

(Panel 50) Pte. 1653, Reginald James Pritchard, 3rd Bn. The Monmouthshire Regt. (T.F.): *s.* of the late Sergt. 111, W. Pritchard, 3rd Bn. Monmouthshire Regt., by his wife Mary ('Sunnymeade,' Mardy, Abergavenny) . Killed in action 2 May 1915: Age 19.

His father William (killed the same day) also has no known grave, he is recorded above.

(Panel 50) Sergt. 849, John William Purell, 1st Bn. The Cambridgeshire Regt. (T.F.): *s.* of Mrs Purell (Witcham, co. Cambridge): Occupation – Asst. Overseer, Wentworth Estate: a pre-war Territorial; volunteered and enlisted Sutton, August 1914: served with the Expeditionary Force in France from 15 February 1915. Missing / believed prisoner; confirmed killed in action 13 March 1915, by the bursting of a shell which collapsed and destroyed the section of trench he was in at the time. In a letter to his mother Capt. Keenlyside said on the evening of the 13th. Sergt. Purell went up with 2nd D.C.L.I. to gain experience in the front-line, and was killed at about 5.30 p.m. when the trench he was in was heavily bombarded by the enemy with the result it had to be evacuated. Subsequently what remained of this trench and those on either side were captured by the enemy. (*IWGC record 21 March*).

(Panel 50) L/Corpl. 326095, Walter Dilley, 'A' Coy., 1st Bn. The Cambridgeshire Regt. (T.F.): formerly no.3048: *s*. of Frederick (& Phoebe) Dilley, of Grantchester, co. Cambridge: *b*. Grantchester, 1895: sometime Garden Boy; West House; thereafter Assistant to Dr. H.B. Roderick, Surgeon & University Demonstrator; Trumpington Street: enlisted Cambridge, 1914; proceeded to France, February 1915. Killed in action 31 July 1917: Age 24. In a letter to his mother his officer wrote, "My dear Mrs Dilley, I am writing to convey to you on behalf of the officers, non-commissioned officers and men of this company our sympathy on the sad loss of your son. Walter Dilley was one of the most popular men of the company. He was a fine soldier and as a man was British to the backbone. As his platoon officer for several months I soon realised what a fine boy he was, so cheery and willing, and we all sadly miss him and the other brave men of the Cambridgeshires who made the great sacrifice on July 31st."

(Panel 50) Pte. 1633, George Harry Cross, 1st Bn. The Cambridgeshire Regt. (T.F.): *s*. of George Peter Cross, of 9, New Barnes Road, Ely, co. Cambridge, by his wife Emma: and elder brother to Pte. G/69048, A.C. Cross, The Queen's (Royal West Surrey Regt.), who fell 21 September 1918: *b*. Prickwillow, co. Cambridge, *c*.1896: enlisted Ely. Killed in action 11 May 1915: Age 19. Mr and Mrs Cross have since removed to 9, Council Cottages, Mirbarn's Road, Ely, and all correspondence regarding their sons should be addressed accordingly.

His brother Arthur is buried in Meath Cemetery, Villers-Guislain (II.B.2).

(Panel 50) Pte. 325302, Alfred Walter Wayman, D.C.M., 1st Bn. The Cambridgeshire Regt. (T.F.): formerly no.1673, Cambridgeshire Regt.: *s*. of Betsy Wayman (6, Potters Lane, Ely, co. Cambridge): and yr. brother to Pte. 220461, G.T. Wayman, 1st East Yorkshire Regt., died 25 April 1918: enlisted Ely. Killed in action 31 July 1917: Age 21. *unm*.

His brother George also has no known grave; he is commemorated on the Tyne Cot Memorial (Panel 48).

PANEL 50 ENDS – PTE. A.W. WAYMAN, CAMBRIDGESHIRE REGT.

PANEL 52 BEGINS – PTE. H.F. WHITE, CAMBRIDGESHIRE REGT.

(Panel 52) Pte. 225100, Ormond Edwin Meppem, 1st (City of London) attd. 12th Bn. (Royal Fusiliers) The London Regt. (T.F.): *s*. of Ormond Edwin Meppem, of Rose Cottage, Imberhorne Lane, Felbridge, East Grinstead, co. Sussex, by his wife Isabella, *née* Banister: and brother to Pte. 6192, S.C. Meppem, Royal Fusiliers, killed near the Butte de Warlencourt, Somme, during the autumn fighting, 8 October 1916: *b*. Ewhurst, co. Surrey, 9 February 1882: conscripted East Surrey Regt. (no.6023), Horsham, co. Surrey: posted 12th Royal Fusiliers: subsequently transf'd. 1st Battn.: served with the Expeditionary Force in France and Flanders from February 1917. Reported missing / presumed killed, at Ypres, 15 June 1917. He *m*. St. John's Church, Felbridge, 17 February 1917; Lillian Annie, *dau*. of Fred (& Salome) Creasey; four months later she was a widow: Age 35. A memorial plaque was erected to his memory in St. John's Church, recording his regiment as the East Surrey Regt.

His brother Sydney is buried in Warlencourt British Cemetery (V.F.4).

(Panel 52) Coy.Sergt.Major 230911, Walter Evershed Gardner, 2/2nd (City of London) Bn. (Royal Fusiliers) The London Regt. (T.F.): eldest *s*. of John Gardner, of Hatfield Grange, Harlow, co. Essex, Granary Keeper, by his wife Eleanor Charlotte, *dau*. of Thomas Walter: *b*. Rotherhithe, 14 March 1888: *educ*. Ardingly College, nr. Haywards Heath, co. Sussex: joined 2nd London Regt., September 1914: served with the Expeditionary Force in France and Flanders from 1915, and was killed in action by a shell, 15 September 1917. His Commanding Officer wrote, "It is with great regret that I have to inform you that your son was killed while we were in the line last. On Saturday night, the 15th inst., he was in charge of a party laying duck-board track when a shell landed near and killed him outright, wounding several others. A wooden cross, in a neighbouring valley, marks where he was buried. Everyone regrets that his long service with the battalion has ended so abruptly. The position of Acting Regtl.Sergt.Major, which he filled so ably, can hardly be replaced;" and a comrade, "At no time out here did he try to shelve responsibility, and notwithstanding the fact that he was offered a Base billet, he preferred to rejoin the battalion and go forward." Age 29. *unm.*

(Panel 52) Sergt. 230396, Harry Albert Berry, M.M., 1/2nd (City of London) Bn. (Royal Fusiliers) The London Regt. (T.F.): eldest *s.* of James William Berry, of Loughcrew, Old Castle, co. Meath, by his wife Mary Ellen, *dau.* of Joseph Coggins, of Sunningdale, co. Berks: *b.* Loughcrew, 9 December 1894: *educ.* there, and Skerry's College, Dublin: Occupation – Civil Service Clerk: enlisted 5 August 1914; went to Malta, 4 September following: served with the Expeditionary Force in France and Flanders from 6 January 1915: wounded at Hooge, July following: on recovery (December 1915) proceeded to Egypt, served with the Expeditionary Force there, and in Palestine: returned to France, May 1916, and was reported missing after the fighting at Glencorse Wood, 16 August 1917; now assumed to have been killed in action on that date. Mentioned in Despatches for 'gallant and distinguished service in the field,' and awarded the Military Medal for 'his assistance to the wounded under heavy shell fire, while severely wounded himself.' Age 23. *unm.*

(Panel 52) Pte. 232795,William Henry Bye, 2nd attd. 1/1st (City of London) Bn. (Royal Fusiliers) The London Regt. (T.F.): *s.* of Richard William Bye, of 267, Church Road, Leyton, London, by his wife Harriet Kate: and brother to Pte. CH/17389, F.E. Bye, Royal Marine Light Infantry, lost at sea 15 October 1914, aboard H.M.S. 'Hawke': *b.* Shoreditch: enlisted Hackney. Killed in action 16 August 1917.

His brother Frank has no known grave but the sea; he is commemorated on the Chatham Naval Memorial (7).

(Panel 52) Pte. 232171, Albert Markworth, 1/2nd (City of London) Bn. (Royal Fusiliers) The London Regt. (T.F.): *s.* of Thomas Birch Markworth,, of 62, Alscot Road, Bermondsey, London, S.E., by his wife Elizabeth: and brother to Pte. 28053, G.E. Markworth, Cheshire Regt., killed in action 9 January 1917: *b.* Bermondsey: enlisted Westminster. Killed in action 16 August 1917: Age 18.

His brother George is buried in Karasouli Military Cemetery (A.61).

(Panel 52) Pte. 233283, Richard Eldon Thorp, 1/2nd (City of London) Bn. (Royal Fusiliers) The London Regt. (T.F.): formerly No.6670, 1st London Regt.: *s.* of Emily Thorp (18, Devonshire Road, Hackney, London): *b.* Stepney: enlisted Leyton. Killed in action 16 August 1917: Age 34. He was married to Rosetta Weaver, *née* Thorp (103, Warren Road, Leyton, London).

(Panel 52) Pte. 253239, Ernest Achille Boudrie, 'B' Coy., 1/3rd (City of London) Bn. The London Regt. (Royal Fusiliers): formerly no.1798, 4th Queen's Own (Royal West Kent Regt.): late of 22, Barham Road, Dartford, co. Kent: eldest *s.* of Ernest Boudrie, Carpenter; of Beechworth, Victoria, Australia, and his wife (*m.*1894) Frances Mary, *dau.* of Edmund Russell, of Hythe Street: *gdson.* to the late Achille Boudrie (*a.k.a.* Baudry, *d.*1913), of Anderlecht, Belgium: *b.* Dartford, 6 October 1897: joined R.W.K., June 1915 proceeded to France with a draft of reinforcements to 3rd London Regt. (T.F.), summer 1917, and was killed in action 16 August 1917; Battle of Langemarck (Third Battle of Ypres); Menin Road Ridge, vicinity Glencorse – Polygon woods: Age 19. His brother Leonard also served; Pte. (Bdsmn.) Royal West Kent Regt. (surv'd.). Inscribed – 'Splendid You Passed, The Great Surrender Made, Into The Light That Nevermore Shall Fade;' 'All You Had Hoped For, All You Had You Gave, To Save Mankind – Yourselves You Scorned To Save;' 'Tranquil You Lie, Your Knightly Virtue Proved Your Memory Hallowed In The Land You Loved' – Pte. Boudrie is remembered on Dartford War Memorial (Face 1, Col.2).

(Panel 52) Lieut. Clement Jesse Harter, 4th (City of London) Bn. (Royal Fusiliers) The London Regt. (T.F): 3rd *s.* of Charles B.H. Harter, Esq., of 5, Onslow Houses, Kensington, London, S.W.: *b.* London, 4 December 1889: brother to Capt. J.G. Harter, Durham Light Infantry, died of wounds 3 April 1916: *educ.* Ladycross, Bournemouth, and Beaumont College, Old Windsor: previously served Royal Navy; gazetted 2nd Lieut., Royal Fusiliers, from Special Reserve, August 1911, and joined 3rd Battn., India: promoted

Lieut., April 1914: went to France with 4th Battn., 3rd Divn., March 1915, and was killed in action 16 June 1915, while leading his platoon at Hooge. In August 1915 it was officially notified that Lieut. J.C. Harter, who had previously been reported 'killed' was now reported 'wounded and missing.' The report of his death was, however, afterwards confirmed. Lieut. Harter was a member of the Bath Club: Age 25. *unm.*

His brother John is buried in Lijssenthoek Military Cemetery, Poperinghe (V.A.13)

(Panel 52) 2nd Lieut. Charles Wilfred Banister, 4th (City of London) Bn. (Royal Fusiliers) The London Regt. (T.F.): 3rd *s.* of Howard Cottrell Banister, of St. Catherine's, Cadogan Gardens, Tunbridge Wells: *b.* Blundellsands, nr. Liverpool, 9 March 1893: *educ.* Merchant Taylors' School, Great Crosby; Jesus College, Cambridge: received a nomination to Royal Military College, Sandhurst on the outbreak of war: given his commission 2nd Lieut., posted 4th (Royal Fusiliers) London Regt. (T.F.): attd. 5th Battn. for training: ordered to France, 9 June 1915 – exactly one week before he fell in action: 16 June 1915: Age 22. *unm.*

(Panel 52) Sergt. 281267, Eric Pleydell Gough Brand, D.C.M., 2/4th (City of London) Bn. (Royal Fusiliers) The London Regt. (T.F.): *s.* of Charles Frederic Brand, of 28, Dovercourt Road, East Dulwich, London, by his wife Ruth Constance: *educ.* Alleyn's School (Roper's House): *b.* Pimlico: enlisted Shaftesbury Street, London, N. Killed in action 20 September 1917. Capt. S. Davies wrote, "You must know in what esteem he was held by all ranks in his Regiment. He had charge of a platoon and led them with great courage, determination and skill, and the success of the day was due in no small measure to his good work. He was easily my best NCO. I was about to recommend him for a commission; he deserved it." Age 20. Captain of Roper's House, the House Book recorded:– "One of the very best type of boy. Straightforward and gentlemanly to a degree, and popular with all."

(Panel 52) Corpl. 295251, Horace Nicholls, 2/4th (City of London) Bn. (Royal Fusiliers) The London Regt. (T.F.): formerly no.36, 5th Bedfordshire Regt. (T.F.): 2nd *s.* of Albert Nicholls, of 147, Fletton Avenue, Peterborough, Old Fletton, co. Northampton, by his wife Elizabeth: *b.* Peterborough: Occupation – Clerk; Messrs. Buckle (Solicitors), Priestgate, Peterborough: a pre-war member 5th Bedfords; transf'd. Huntingdon Cyclists Battn. on absorption of that unit February 1914: undertook Active Service obligations (Fletton) on mobilisation August 1914; apptd. L/Corpl. October: stationed Grimsby, attd. Eastern Command (Coastal Defence), thereafter Scarborough: proceeded to France with a draft of reinforcements July 1916, on arrival attd. 4th London Regt. Reported missing 20 September 1917, since confirmed killed in action: Age 25. Well known as a comedian in his home region, he was a member of the 'Dandy Pigs' concert party. His widow, Florence Emily Nicholls (1, Fairfax Road, Filey, co. York), and family would be most grateful to receive correspondence from any of Corpl. Nicholls' comrades regarding him. One of three brothers who served, Albert is (1918) serving with the Royal Garrison Artillery; Percy, Royal Warwickshire Regt., was discharged after the amputation of one leg. (*IWGC record 21 September*)

(Panel 52) L/Corpl. 1411, Alfred Elsom, 1/4th (City of London) Bn. (Royal Fusiliers) The London Regt. (T.F.): *s.* of the late Edward Elsom, by his wife Eliza (Shoreditch, London, E.C.): *b.* London, *c.*1895: enlisted Shaftesbury Street, London, N.: served with the Expeditionary Force in France and Flanders from 6 January 1915, and was killed in action 26 April 1915, nr. La Brique, Ypres: Age 19.

(Panel 52) L/Corpl. 1123, George William Orton, 1/4th (City of London) Bn. (Royal Fusiliers) The London Regt. (T.F.): late of Hackney, London, E.8: eldest *s.* of George James Orton, of 50, Templar Road, Lower Clapton, London, E.5, by his wife Mary: and brother to Pte. G/11672, W.F. Orton, 1st Royal West Surrey, killed in action 8 June 1916; and Pte. 1603, S.T. Orton, 1/4th London Regt., died of wounds 3 May 1915, aged 19 years: *b.* Bethnal Green, *c.*1880: enlisted Shaftesbury Street, City Road, London, N.1: served with the Mediterranean Expeditionary Force at Malta (from September 1914), and in France and Flanders (from January 1915), and was killed in action 27 April 1915, at the Second Battle of Ypres: Age 35.

His brother William also has no known grave, he is commemorated on the Loos Memorial; Sidney is buried in Wimereux Communal Cemetery (I.F.27).

(Panel 52) Pte. 295157, Herbert Alfred Blick, 2/4th (City of London) Bn. (Royal Fusiliers) The London Regt. (T.F.): formerly no.553758, Queen's Westminster Rifles: *s.* of John Blick, of 128, Grove Road, Balham, London, by his wife Jessie: served with City Imperial Volunteers in the South African Campaign, and with the Expeditionary Force in France and Flanders, and was killed in action 21 September 1917: Age 37. He leaves a wife, Emily Elizabeth Blick (202, Clapham Road, Stockwell, London).

(Panel 52) Pte. 1652, William George Alfred Bone, 1/4th (City of London) Bn. (Royal Fusiliers) The London Regt. (T.F.): 1st *s.* of William George Bone, of 253, Seward Street Buildings, Goswell Road, London, E.C., by his wife Ada Rose: *b.* St. Luke's, London, E.C., 29 August 1895: *educ.* L.C.C. Central School: enlisted, August 1914: went to Malta with his battalion 4 September following: served with the Expeditionary Force in France from 6 January 1915, and was killed in action in Flanders, 27 April following: Age 19.

(Panel 52) Pte. 3555, Jeffrey Huelin Carey, 1/4th (City of London) Bn. (Royal Fusiliers) The London Regt. (T.F.): eldest *s.* of Ernest Rutherford Carey, Accountant; of Melbourne, Australia, by his wife Mabel Marion, (6, Park Rd., Brentwood, Middlesex), *dau.* of Thomas Shann Detham, of Leeds, Yorks: *b.* Melbourne, Victoria, 13 October 1898: *educ.* Merivale, Bexhill-on-Sea, City of London School (1909 – 11), and Brentwood Grammar School (1911 – 14): joined 1/4th London Regt. 6 January 1915, and was killed in action at Ypres, 27 April 1915: **Age 16**. His major wrote, in a letter of sympathy, "Your son was a good boy, and faced the fire without fear. He was unfortunately hit, death being instantaneous. I enclose you a small sketch map, showing the spot where I had him buried by the side of a comrade who was killed at the same time. I hope the map will be clear to you; the grave lies in the corner of the field, about 3 yards from the hedge, and at present has a small cross at its head bearing his name, number and regt."

On 25 April 1915, after three days of almost continuous forced marching from Merville, 4th Londons (Ferozepore Bde., 3rd Lahore Divn.) arrived at Ouderdom with orders to billet in huts. Most were already occupied and the exhausted Londons, compelled to bivouac in the adjoining fields, could plainly hear the storm raging in the salient. Throughout the afternoon and into the night the air vibrated with the continuous thunder of artillery in which the distinctive retorts of the French seventy-fives were clearly discernible. Shortly after midnight orders were received denoting the Division would be entering the firing line that day (26th), and at dawn the battalion was formed up. Issued with shovels, picks and instructions to dig themselves in to whatever position they could gain; each platoon was issued with a yellow flag for signalling purposes and, leaving packs and superfluous equipment behind, the companies moved off at five minute intervals.

Due to the exhaustion of the men progress was understandably slow and although Ypres was being steadily bombarded by predominantly heavy calibre shells, the approach roads received very little attention from the enemy artillery. By about 9.30 a.m. the battalion were concentrated in a field adjoining Outskirt Farm, La Brique and began digging in to assembly trenches. This position, behind the crest of the spur running west from St. Jean, past La Brique towards the Canal, although out of site of the enemy was clearly visible to aerial reconnaissance and, combined with the close proximity of a number of British and French batteries, drew a considerable amount of attention from German batteries. Surprisingly, the storms of shrapnel that tore into the Londons assembly position, seemingly coming from north and south at the same time, throughout the morning caused few casualties.

(Panel 52) Pte. 1354, John Cole, 1/4th (City of London) Bn. (Royal Fusiliers) The London Regt. (T.F.): *b.* Islington: enlisted Shaftesbury Street, London, N.: served at Malta (14 September. 1914 – 2 January 1915), and with the Expeditionary Force in France and Flanders from 6 January following, and was killed in action 26 April 1915, nr. La Brique, Ypres.

(Panel 52) Pte. 232975, Alfred William Forse, 1/2nd (City of London) Bn. (Royal Fusiliers) The London Regt. (T.F.): *s.* of Joseph Robert Forse, of 5, Kingston Road, Crownfield Road, Leytonstone, by his wife Mary Jane: and elder brother to Rfn. R/16850, C.A. Forse, 16th King's Royal Rifle Corps, died

23 April 1917, of wounds; and Rfn. R/35597, B.A. Forse, 8th King's Royal Rifle Corps, died in Germany 28 September 1918, a Prisoner of War: *b.* St. Pancras, London, W.C.: former employee London County Council Tramways Dept.: enlisted London. Killed in action 16 August 1917: Age 29.

His brother Charles also has no known grave, he is commemorated on the Arras Memorial (Panel 7); Benjamin is buried in Hamburg Cemetery (I.B.10).

(Panel 52) Pte. 281318, Frederick Marnes, 'B' Coy., 1/4th (City of London) Bn. (Royal Fusiliers) The London Regt. (T.F.): *s.* of Frederick Marnes, of 52, Westlake Road, Rotherhithe, London, by his wife Matilda: and brother to L/Corpl. 41857, W.T. Marnes, West Yorkshire Regt., killed in action 21 March 1918: *b.* Rotherhithe: enlisted Shaftesbury Street, London, N. Killed in action 16 August 1917: Age 27. *unm.*

His brother William also has no known grave; he is commemorated on the Arras (Faubourg d'Amiens) Memorial (Bay 4).

(Panel 52) Pte. 295027, William Walter Short, 2/4th (City of London) Bn (Royal Fusiliers) The London Regt. (T.F.): formerly no.9049, 7th London Regt.: *b.* Islington: enlisted Whitehall. Killed in action 20 September 1917, in the vicinity of Winnipeg Crossroads. See account re. Pte. J. Mudd, Tyne Cot Memorial (Panel 149).

(Panel 52) Pte. 282893, Henniker Ernest Thorp, 4th attd. 1/3rd (City of London) Bn. (Royal Fusiliers) The London Regt. (T.F.): *s.* of Henniker (& Mrs) Thorp, of 4, Rojack Road, Forest Hill, London, S.E.23: *b.* Wood Green: enlisted Lewisham. Killed in action 16 August 1917: Age 30. He was married to Mary Ellen Thorp (140, Malham Road, Forest Hill, London, S.E.).

To My Mother – 1916

If I should fall, grieve not that one so weak
And poor as I
Should die.
Nay! Though thy heart should break
Think only this: that when at dusk they speak
Of sons and brothers of another one,
Then thou canst say – "I too had a son;
He died for England's sake!"

Rfn. Donald Cox, London Rifle Brigade.

(Panel 52) Capt. William Guy Deane Butcher, 'A' Coy., 1/5th (City of London) Bn. (London Rifle Brigade) The London Regt. (T.F.: *yst. s.* of William Deane Butcher, of Holyrood, Cleveland Road, Ealing, London, W., M.R.C.S., by his wife Fanny, *dau.* of Lieut.Col. Bazett, 9th Bengal Cavalry (ret'd.): *b.* Windsor, co. Berks, 29 October 1891: *educ.* Harrow View School, and Stoke House, Slough; gained (1904), foundation Scholarship at Eton, entered there as King's Scholar: took minor Scholarship (Classics), Trinity College, Cambridge (1908), also the Reynold's Scholarship, and Newcastle Scholarship: became resident at Trinity, 1910, and in 1913 took First Class in Classical Tripos; 1914, First Class in Part II of the Classical Tripos, and in the same year gained the Craven Scholarship and Chancellor's Medal: reading for a Trinity Fellowship, August 1914: member Cambridge O.T.C., three years; gazetted 2nd Lieut., London Rifle Brigade, October 1914: promoted Lieut.; Capt. 1916: served with the Expeditionary Force in France from May 1917, and was killed in action at Glencorse Wood, 16 August following. Buried near where he fell. His Colonel wrote, "Capt. Butcher had not been with us very long, but in the actions he had taken part, he had always displayed a complete fearlessness and disregard of danger. He encouraged his men by his example and cheerfulness, and we have lost a splendid officer," and an officer, "I cannot tell you what a loss he is to us. Our company was composed of officers, whose sole aim was to help each other cheerfully to perform our duty, and to make our hardships and inconveniences more bearable. To say that Capt. Butcher was the one person who, more than anyone else, succeeded in that aim, is not exaggerating a bit. He was tremendously popular with his fellow officers, and was respected and loved by the men of our company. He will always remain in my memory as one of the finest types of men I have ever known – as a man who had high ideals and tried to live them. He is spoken of by the men with the greatest respect. In him they saw a man they felt they could trust, and that trust was never misplaced." Another also wrote, "I learned to respect, admire and love old 'Butch.' His straightness, keenness, loyalty and invariable good temper, together with an infinite capacity for fun, made him a companion and friend that stood out in my mind, even in this war of innumerable associations. It was most noteworthy how he was liked by all; I have heard his men cheer him to the echo when a draft left." The late Dr. Butler, of Trinity, wrote, "Your dear son's Eton and Trinity career was indeed a brilliant one, and his character was not unworthy of his fine mental powers. He will not soon be forgotten at Trinity. He seemed to have fullness of life before him, and no common unfruitful life…His loss is not only a personal but a national loss." And a school and college friend, "Guy Butcher died as he had lived, showing both in his life and in his death that he was on the side of all that was honourable and just and right. Guy's memory to me will always be that of a gentleman and a scholar, who, in his manhood and his scholarship, was fighting not for self-interest, but to make the world better than he found it. His men had learned to love and respect him, and no man could wish for more, for to win the love and respect of the British Tommy is worth death itself, for the Tommy is a hard judge, rightly respecting the just and the brave. I have lost a very dear friend, but Guy's memory will always be an inspiration to me; I hope I may always be able to live up to his high standard of honour and scholarship.": 16 August 1917: Age 25. *unm.*

(Panel 52) Capt. Frederic Furze, 2/5th (City of London) Bn. (London Rifle Brigade) The London Regt. (T.F): elder *s.* of Frederic Furze, of 10, Chiswick Place, Eastbourne, formerly of 6, Welbeck House, London, W., by his wife Helen, *dau.* of W.A. Hubbuck: *b.* Beckenham, co. Kent, 29 April 1881: *educ.* Charterhouse: obtained a commission London Rifle Brigade, August 1914: served two years Adjt.; apptd. Coy. Comdr., April 1917: served with the Expeditionary Force in France and Flanders. Killed in action, Menin Road Battle, 20 September 1917. Buried Hubner Farm; between Poelcapelle and St. Julien: Age 36. His Commanding Officer wrote, "His behaviour during the attack was splendid, and it is due to his fine example and great gallantry that the attack was the great success it was. He was shot three times but still carried on, and was finally killed by a sniper at the final objective. His loss to us is immense; he was most popular with all ranks." He *m.* Beckenham, 27 October 1898; Alice Duthie, *dau.* of J. Trimmer.

(Panel 52) Capt. George Whitaker, 5th (City of London) Bn. (London Rifle Brigade) The London Regt. (T.F.): *s.* of George Whitaker, of 2, Albemarle Mansions, Kingsway, Hove, co. Sussex, by his wife Eliza Annie: Occupation – Clerk; London Stock Exchange. Killed in action 20 September 1917: Age 25. *unm.*

(Panel 52) 2nd Lieut. Sidney Martin Lines, 1/5th (City of London) Bn. (London Rifle Brigade) The London Regt. (T.F.): *s.* of Ellen Lines (41, Mayfield Avenue, Southgate, co. Middlesex), wife of the late Richard Lines: pre-war member L.R.B.; volunteered and undertook Active Service Obligations, Bunhill Row, London, on the outbreak of war, August 1914, proceeded to France 5 November: promoted (from N.C.O.) to commission at St. Jean, two days prior to his death, being killed in action 13 May 1915, nr. Shell Trap Farm, Wieltje: Age 29. *unm.* GRU Report, Zillebeke 5-356E refers remains exhumed unmarked grave (28.C.23.c.00.70); identified – Disc, Clothing, Boots; reinterred, registered 28 March 1929. *Buried in Sanctuary Wood Cemetery (V.G.20).*

(Panel 52) 2nd Lieut. Richard Lintott, 2/5th (City of London) Bn. (London Rifle Brigade) The London Regt. (T.F.): eldest *s.* of Bernard Lintott, of 11, The Carfax, Horsham, co. Surrey, by his wife Alice Lisle: *b.* Horsham, 13 July 1896: *educ.* Hurstpierpoint School, 1907 – 1914, where he was a Prefect, and O.T.C. Sergt., holding certificate 'A': on the outbreak of war was with his School Corps in camp, which was struck as the government stores were required elsewhere: attempted to join a Regular regiment, but failed as his youthful appearance and age, 18, were against him: joined Public Schools' Special Corps; Paddock Camp, Epsom: after a month transf'd. Pte., 2/5th London Rifle Brigade; two weeks later obtained transfer to 1/5th Battn. who were under orders for France. By all accounts he took very kindly to soldiering, and all through the long dreary winter of 1914 – 15 he was one of the most cheerful of men, and many a stew was enriched by rabbits he got by digging and wiring in Ploegsteert Wood. Commissioned 2nd Lieut., 2/5th London Rifle Brigade, April 1915, but went into the line to fight with 6th Battn as every available man was wanted to fill the breach in the line made by the German gas attack at Ypres. 2nd Lieut. Lintott was killed at Fortuin, 3 May 1915, by one of our own shells, whilst asleep in a reserve trench, after four days' action at the Second Battle of Ypres. Buried at Fortuin: Age 18. Whilst at Hurstpierpoint Mr Lintott was a member of the First Cricket XI, won the Fives Cup, and, in 1914, took the part of Octavius in 'Julius Caesar.' At cricket he was the best bat in the School team of 1914. Referring to the match versus M.C.C., the '*Johnian*' records:– 'Lintott was very daring, for he hit three fours in the first over and settled down to enjoy himself.' His best score was against Whitgift, when he made 87 runs. Two of his uncles joined the Forces – Sub. Lieut. W. Lintott, R.N.V.R., Royal Naval Division, since killed in action at the Dardanelles, and Lieut. A.J.C. Lintott, 2/5th London Rifle Brigade. (*IWGC record age 19*)

His uncle William also has no known grave; he is commemorated on the Helles Memorial, Gallipoli.

(Panel 52) Sergt. 300269, Harold Oscar Saunders, 1/5th (City of London) Bn. (London Rifle Brigade) The London Regt. (T.F.): *s.* of the late Edward George Saunders, by his marriage to Mrs E.A. Saunders (55, Alexandra Road, Wimbledon, London, S.W.): *b.* Ryde, Isle of Wight, *c.*1890: Occupation – Clerk; London Stock Exchange: enlisted London. Killed in action 16 August 1917: Age 27.

(Panel 52) Corpl. 370, Fred Lakeman Banks, 5th (City of London) Bn. (London Rifle Brigade) The London Regt. (T.F.): 2nd *s.* of Frederick Seymour Banks, Commission Agent; of 4, St. John Street, Bedford Row, London, W.C., by his wife Elizabeth: *b.* Doughty Street, Mecklenburgh Square, London, 20 January 1874: *educ.* Whitgift Grammar School; entering his father's business on leaving: joined London Rifle Brigade, 1892, and served all through the South African War with C.I.V. Mounted Infantry, receiving the medal with four bars: rejoined the Brigade with his old schoolfellow, J.L. Hampton, on the outbreak of the European War and arrived in the trenches about the middle of November. Shot, and died within moments 13 May 1915, nr. Ypres. Writing to his parents the Officer Commanding his company stated that Hampton (who met his death ten days before Banks did) and he well helped to maintain a fine tradition by their spirit and experience, and that it was almost impossible to write any sort of appreciation of what those two men were to their company. There were many occasions when they gave their officer comfort and courage in difficult times; he added, "When we get into the tight places again I know that many of us who had been taught by him will think of Freddy Banks and his cheery confidence, and take courage." On more than one occasion he was offered a commission but preferred to remain in the ranks alongside his comrades. At the Whitgift Grammar School athletic sports he won the mile on three occasions, 1889, 1890, and 1891. A fourth win was obtained in 1893 when he secured the Old Boys' Mile. He joined the Cadet Corps, and won the Spencer Cup for the champion shot of the Public Schools at Bisley in 1891, scoring 33 out of a possible 35 at 500 yards. He also won the Easty silver medal. He won the Whitgift Veterans in 1896. In 1892 he made a brave attempt to rescue a boy who had fallen into the river at Rainham. He was competing for his Regimental Bronze Badge at the time, and was waiting for his turn to fire, when he plunged into the river and, after diving repeatedly, recovered the lifeless body of the boy. He afterwards resumed his shooting, and obtained second place, being beaten by only one point. He received the Royal Humane Society's certificate on vellum, and a bronze medal, being also complimented by Lord E Pelham-Clinton (at an inspection by the Duke of Cambridge) on his deed. Corpl. Banks won the 'D' Coy. Waldegrave Challenge Cup three times, when it became his, as also did the Moger Cup similarly thrice won. He shot in the winning team for the '*Daily Telegraph*' Cup, 1897 and 1898. On his return from the South African War the late Sir Walter Gilbey, Bt. presented him with a massive silver cup "as a token in appreciation of services rendered to his country." Age 43. *unm.*

John Hampton also has no known grave, he is recorded below.

(Panel 52) Corpl. 316, Albert Augustus Claridge, 1/5th (City of London) Bn. (London Rifle Brigade) The London Regt. (T.F.): late of Gerard's Cross, co. Buckingham: *s.* of the late Henry Claridge, by his wife Mary Ann (12, Holland Terrace, Acton, London): and elder brother to Sergt. 800454, A.B.

Claridge, London Regt., who fell 20 September 1917, at the Battle of the Menin Road; Corpl. Z/104, S.H. Claridge, 2nd Rifle Brigade, killed in action 3 March 1916; and Pte. L/13839, A. Claridge, 3rd Royal Fusiliers, killed in action 7 March 1915: *b.* 1883: enlisted Bunhill Row, London, E.C.: served with the Expeditionary Force in France and Flanders from 5 November 1914, and was killed in action 13 May 1915, nr. Wieltje: Age 32.

His brother Archibald also has no known grave; he is recorded on Panel 54; Sydney is buried in Rue-du-Bois Military Cemetery, Fleurbaix (I.C.26); Alfred, Kemmel Chateau Military Cemetery (G.46).

(Panel 52) Corpl. 300454, Madgewick John Rhodes, 2/5th (City of London) Bn. (London Rifle Brigade) The London Regt. (T.F.): *s.* of the late Henry Rhodes, by his wife Ellen ('Crossways,' Little Kimble, Princes Risborough, co. Buckingham): *educ.* Alleyn's School, Dulwich: enlisted London. Reported wounded and missing / believed killed in action 20 September 1917: Age 37. '*Alleyn's Magazine*' (October 1917) recorded:– "'Among those recently reported missing is one of the best known and most popular of our Old Boys, Corpl. M.J. Rhodes…We have not yet given up hope that he is alive and well."

(Panel 52) Corpl. 614, Leonard Hawkins, 1/5th (City of London) Bn. (London Rifle Brigade) The London Regt. (T.F.): 3rd *s.* of Samuel James Hawkins, Printer; of 109, Whipps Cross Road, Leytonstone, by his wife Lizzie, *dau.* of the late Thomas Hunt: *b.* Walthamstow, co. Essex, 13 January 1891: *educ.* Newport Road Council School, and Worshipful Company of Carpenters School, Stratford: Occupation – Accountant's Clerk: enlisted 15 September 1914, after the outbreak of war: promoted Corpl. February 1915: went out to France with a draft 14 March, and was killed in action at Wieltje, during the Second Battle of Ypres, 13 May 1915. Buried near the front trenches at Wieltje. Letters speak of his having "done extremely well" and having "died fighting bravely.": Age 24. *unm.*

(Panel 52) L/Corpl. 199, John Latham Hampton, 1/5th (City of London) Bn. (London Rifle Brigade) The London Regt. (T.F.): *s.* of Charles Alfred Hampton, of 'Seleng House,' Epsom Road, Ewell, co. Surrey, by his wife Emma, *née* Latham: and brother to Pte. 9794, W. Hampton, London Rifle Brigade, died 14 May 1915, of wounds (G.S. neck) received in action 16 January previously: *b.* Brixton, London, 1877: *educ.* Uplands House School, Downs Road, and Whitgift Grammar School, South Croydon: on leaving school entered the offices of Messrs Le Blanc, Smith & Co., becoming Member, London Stock Exchange, 1901, and partner in the former 1904: volunteered on the outbreak of the South African War, and, in early 1900, served in that campaign with City Imperial Volunteers Mounted Infantry until invalided home with enteric dysentery: first joined London Rifle Brigade, 1897, and, on the outbreak of war, August 1914, rejoined L.R.B. with old school-friend F.L. Banks (Corpl., killed 13 May 1915): served with the Expeditionary Force in France and Flanders from November 1914, and was killed (shot through the head) by a sniper nr. Fortuin, 3 May 1915; a few days before he was to receive a commission with East Surrey Regt.: Age 38. His Company Officer wrote, "There is no one whom we shall miss more than your son. The men have been absolutely magnificent all through, and it is to your son and Banks that I have put down the credit for most of it. They have always been so cheery and full of confidence, that they have infected the younger and less experienced men round them with something of their own spirit." All correspondence should be addressed c/o his brother, George C. Hampton, Esq., 'The Firs,' College Road, Epsom, co. Surrey.

His brother Walter is buried in Ewell (St. Mary) Churchyard (Old Ground 182A); Fred Banks has no known grave, he is recorded above.

(Panel 52) L/Corpl. 9594, James William Charles Reading, 'D' Coy., 1/5th (City of London) Bn. (London Rifle Brigade) The London Regt. (T.F.): *b.* Marlow, co. Buckingham: enlisted London. Killed at St. Jean, 28 April 1915, in company with three other men when the house in which they were breakfasting was hit by a shell. See also Rfn. A.J. Foster and J.G. Newell (Panel 54), and R.S.M. A.G. Harrington, King's Royal Rifle Corps attd. London Rifle Brigade (Addenda Panel 57).

(Panel 52) L/Corpl. 302194, Henry Charles Stembridge, 1/5th (City of London) Bn. (London Rifle Brigade) The London Regt. (T.F.): *s.* of Samuel Eastman Stembridge, of Home Cottage, Beckenham, co. Kent, by his wife Emily: and elder brother to Pte. 1488, O.S. Stembridge, Honourable Artillery Coy., killed in action 2 May 1915: *b*. Gunnersbury, London: enlisted Bromley, co. Kent. Killed in action 16 August 1917: Age 40.

His brother Oscar 'Pickles' is buried in Voormezeele Enclosure No.3 (XIV.L.1).

(Panel 52) L/Corpl. 768, Gilbert Townsend, 1/5th (City of London) Bn. (London Rifle Brigade) The London Regt. (T.F.): *s*. of William Henry (& Emily) Townsend, of 134, Tenison Road, Cambridge: *educ.* Perse School: Occupation – Clerk; Messrs Barclays Bank: enlisted 130, Bunhill Row, London: served with the Expeditionary Force in France from 5 November 1914, and was killed in action 13 May 1915; vicinity Mouse Trap Farm, Wieltje: Age 25. *unm.*

(Panel 52) Rfn. 303973, Roger George Alabaster, 1/5th (City of London) Bn. (London Rifle Brigade) The London Regt. (T.F.): formerly no.5091, 12th Essex Regt.: *s*. of Roger George Alabaster, of 257, Crown Road, Romford, co. Essex, by his wife Mary Ellen Ann. Killed in action 16 August 1917: Age 25. *unm.*

(Panel 52) Pte. 887, William George Allison, 2/5th (City of London) Bn. (London Rifle Brigade) The London Regt. (T.F.): eldest *s*. of George William Allison, of the Central Telegraph Office, London, and 30, Cavendish Flats, Gilbert St., Grosvenor Square, by his wife Georgina Rose, *dau*. of the late William Dean: *b*. St. George's, Hanover Square, London, W., 20 November 1890: *educ*. Polytechnic, Regent Street: when war broke out he was on the clerical staff of a City shipping firm: joined 2nd Bn. London Rifle Brigade, 2 September 1914; left for France, 27 March 1915. The London Rifle Brigade supported the Canadians at Ypres when they retook the guns which had been temporarily captured by the Germans, and after nine days in the trenches he fell victim the very day they were being relieved, being killed by shrapnel, 3 May 1915. Sir John (now Lord) French, in his report, stated that the 5th City of London Regt. (London Rifle Brigade), although their losses were heavy, unfalteringly retained their position: Age 24. *unm*. (*IWGC record 1st Bn.*)

PANEL 52 ENDS – RFN. B.F. BISHOP, LONDON RIFLE BRIGADE.

PANEL 54 BEGINS RFN. T.M. BOND, LONDON RIFLE BRIGADE.

(Panel 54) Rfn. 9973, Thomas M. Bond, 1/5th (City of London) Bn. (London Rifle Brigade) The London Regt. (T.F.): *b*. Belfast, Ireland, 12 October 1896: *educ*. Christ's Hospital School, London: on completion of his studies joined the staff of Bank of British North America (London branch): a pre-war Territorial, undertook Active Service obligations on mobilisation, Bunhill Row, August 1914: served with the Expeditionary Force in France and Flanders from 5 November following and was killed in action during an enemy attack at Ypres, 3 May 1915: Age 18.

(Panel 54) Rfn. 305557, Stuart Botterill, 2/5th (City of London) Bn. (London Rifle Brigade) The London Regt. (T.F.): *yst. s*. of the late William Richard Botterill, of Croydon, by his wife Amy ('Killarney,' Purley): *b*. Croydon, co. Surrey, 1 July 1879: *educ*. Whitgift Grammar School, Croydon: Occupation – Local Manager; Red Hand Composition Company, Southampton, being for several years volunteer, London Rifle Brigade: rejoined 12 April 1917: served with the Expeditionary Force in France and Flanders from 1 July, and was killed in action north-east of St. Julien 20 September 1917. Buried nr. Ypres: Age 38. He *m*. at Southampton, 29 April 1915, Ethel Elizabeth (82, late of 74, Belmont Road, Portswood, Southampton), *dau*. of Henry William Hoare, of Southampton.

(Panel 54) Rfn. 1069, William Arthur Bradbury, 1/5th (City of London) Bn. (London Rifle Brigade) The London Regt. (T.F.): eldest *s*. of James Arthur Bradbury, of Rosemorran, Kent Gardens, Ealing, London, W. (late of Strawberry Hill, co. Middlesex): *b*. Brentford, co. Middlesex, 28 November 1892: *educ*. King's College School, Wimbledon, and on leaving there entered his father's business (Wholesale Provision Merchant): joined London Rifle Brigade, September 1914, after the outbreak of war: served with the Expeditionary Force in France and Flanders from June, 1915, and was killed in action near St. Eloi, 2 December following. Buried on the battlefield. Capt. A.L. Lintott wrote, "I was in command of

No.2 Coy. up to almost the end of November, and I had often noticed your two boys. They were both very good and keen on their work and always took the cheerful side of things. W.A.B. will be a sad loss to the company and to the regiment, and he will be another who has laid down his life for King and Country and Regiment;" and Rfn. W.E. Callow, "I cannot in mere words tell you how I feel the loss of such a comrade. After a year's continual friendship, working together under all conditions, it seems that I have lost one who was more than a brother." Age 23. *unm.*

(Panel 54) Rfn. 5704, Philip George Mortimer Brown, 1/5th (City of London) Bn. (London Rifle Brigade) The London Regt. (T.F.): only *s.* of the late Frederick Robert Brown, Solicitor; by his wife Emily Louisa (Thirlmere, Dukesthorpe Rd., Sydenham, London, S.E.), *dau.* of George Phillips, of 4, Styles Way, Parklangley, Beckenham: *b.* Sundridge Park, co. Kent, 15 October 1896: *educ.* The Hall, Sydenham Preparatory School, and Dulwich College: joined London Rifle Brigade early 1914: on the outbreak of war was with his regt. at Eastbourne for the midsummer manoeuvres. Volunteering for foreign service, he left with his regt. for France early November 1914, and was killed in action at Ypres, 3 May 1915. His Commanding Officer wrote, "He died doing his duty to the last, and was buried the same night. After he was slightly wounded himself he spent all his time attending to other wounded friends, and it was whilst performing this duty that he was killed." Age 18.

(Panel 54) Rfn. 302040, Henry Edward Burnham, Gnr. Lewis Gun Section, 1/5th (City of London) Bn. (London Rifle Brigade) The London Regt. (T.F.): late of Dulwich, London, S.E.: *s.* of Richard Henry (& Clara) Burnham: *b.* Buxton, January 1888: Occupation – Clerk, Securities Dept., Coutts Bank, 440, The Strand, London, W.C.2 (joined 18 November 1908): enlisted Bunhill Row, 17 November 1915: served with the Expeditionary Force in France and Flanders from 1916; took part in the fighting at Arras and Combles. Reported missing 15 August 1917 at the Third Battle of Ypres; subsequently (1918) confirmed killed in action on that date: Age 29. *unm.*

(Panel 54) Rfn. 301709, Luther William Dancey, 1/5th (City of London) Bn. (London Rifle Brigade) The London Regt., (T.F.): *s.* of Thomas Dancey, of Beanacre, Melksham, co. Wilts, and Lydia Dancey, his spouse: *educ.* Dauntsey Agricultural School. Shot through the head and killed instantaneously 16 August 1917. Buried where he fell: Age 36.

(Panel 54) Pte. 9551, Ernest William Fairs, 1/5th (City of London) Bn. (London Rifle Brigade) The London Regt. (T.F.): eldest *s.* of William Fairs, of 32, Beaconsfield Road, Croydon, Surrey, Joiner, by his wife Ellen Sarah, *dau.* of Skillington Medwell: *b.* Banstead, co. Surrey, 15 December 1895: *educ.* Sydenham Road Council Schools, Croydon: employee Messrs. Giddy & Giddy, Auctioneers & Estate Agents, Regent Street: joined London Rifle Brigade, August 1913: volunteered for Foreign Service on the outbreak of war, August 1914: went to France, 5 November 1914, and was killed in action at Ypres, 3 May 1915. Buried at Fortuin: Age 19.

(Panel 54) Rfn. 492, Albert Jasper Foster, 'D' Coy., 1/5th (City of London) Bn. (London Rifle Brigade) The London Regt. (T.F.): late of Catford, London, S.E.6: *s.* of Albert Foster, of 61, Silverdale, Sydenham, by his wife Mary: killed at St. Jean in company with three other men, 28 April 1915, when the house in which they were breakfasting was hit by a shell: Age 22. *unm.* See also L/Corpl. J.W.C. Reading (Panel 52), Rfn. J.G. Newell (below), and R.S.M. A.G. Harrington, King's Royal Rifle Corps attd. London Rifle Brigade (Addenda Panel 57).

(Panel 54) Pte. 1201, Geoffrey William Freeman, 1/5th (City of London) Bn. (London Rifle Brigade) The London Regt. (T.F.): eldest *s.* of William Edward Freeman, of 77, North Side, Clapham Common, London, S.W., L.D.S., R.C.S. Eng., Dental Surgeon, by his wife Maud, *dau.* of the late John Hopkins, of Sydney, N.S.W.: *b.* Narrabri, New South Wales, Australia, 11 September 1896: came to England with his parents 1903: *educ.* Manor House School, Clapham Common, and when war broke out was studying to enter Guy's Hospital: volunteered and joined London Rifle Brigade, 4 November 1914, trained Crowborough and Haywards Heath, proceeded to France 12 March, 1915. Pte. Freeman wrote home regularly and cheerfully, his last letter being dated 8 May when the battn. was resting from a long spell in the trenches. A day or two later they were rushed up to take part in the 2nd Battle of Ypres, and he was one of the gallant band of nine who were with Sergt. D.W. Belcher when he won his V.C. on 13 May. Sergt. Belcher, with his handful of men, elected to remain and endeavour to hold a portion of an advanced breastwork south of the Wieltje-St. Julien Road, which was under heavy bombardment from the enemy's artillery, after the troops near him had been withdrawn, and there is little doubt that the bold front shown by Sergt. Belcher and the few men with him prevented the enemy from breaking through and making a flank attack on one of the divisions. They held on during the whole day, and at nightfall reinforcements came up and the position was saved. Unfortunately, however, Freeman was killed during the course of the day. He had volunteered to take a message under heavy fire to Capt. Somers Smith of the L.R.B.; the message was taken and delivered, but almost immediately a shell burst and he and all around him were killed. He was named in Battn. Orders, and a 2nd Lieut. A.G. Sharpe wrote, "He was always popular wherever he went, and everyone who came in contact with him liked him. During the whole time I knew him I never met one person who had anything but good to say of him. In his last term at Manor House he won the Gold Medal, and everyone who was with him during his short but glorious career in the Army says that they have lost in him a great pal. During his whole life he upheld the traditions of his school, which was very dear to him, and he died as every Manorian would wish to die. Truly when one thinks of him one is convinced that Manor House makes no idle boast when she says that all her sons are 'Sportsmen and true gentlemen.'" Age 17.

(Panel 54) Rfn. 9365, William Frank Galpin, 5th (City of London) Bn. (London Rifle Brigade) The London Regt. (T.F.): 2nd *s*. of William Henry Galpin, of 11, Montrose Terrace, Plymouth, Timber Salesman, by his wife Mary Elizabeth, *dau*. of John Hocking Francis, of Penzance: *b*. Plymouth, 1 September 1890: *educ*. Lipson House School, Plymouth; obtained honours in Cambridge Local Exam: Occupation – Quantity Surveyor; H.M. Office of Works, Westminster:: joined Duke of Cornwall's Light Infantry (Territorial Battn.), Bodmin, 1911; transf'd. London Rifle Brigade, 1913: volunteered for Imperial Service on the outbreak of war: went to France, 4 November 1914; attd. 11th Brigade (4th Division) there, and was killed in action, 13 May 1915, at Wieltje, during the 2nd Battle of Ypres, the same day Sergt. Belcher of his Battn. won the V.C. The London Rifle Brigade had been subjected to a terrific bombardment for nearly three weeks and its strength had been reduced to less than 200 men. He was buried near Ypres: Age 24. *unm*. Formerly a Scout Master, Rfn. Galpin received the Baden Powell Warrant, dated 7 June 1910.

On the outbreak of the Great War all the male staff of the Prudential Assurance Company were informed by the chairman, T.C. Dewey, that over 500 members of staff had already joined the forces; by 1915 70% of the clerical staff had enlisted. At the end of the war 9,161 Prudential staff had served with the Colours, 798 of them were killed.

Comrades! young warriors! Your country calls!
Calls on the eve of War and its alarms;
Bids you protect her, and maintain her walls:
To arms! To arms! To arms!

Comrades! Of whom we may indeed be proud!
Sons of those Eighteen-Sixty Volunteers;
Sons of those sires whom the heedless crowd
Greeted with ribald cheers'

Until at last their chance of glory came;
Britain had need of them. They asked no more
Beyond the right to win a need of fame
Far from old England's shore.

Be yours to follow – yours, the strenuous part:
Yours not to hesitate nor reason why,

But just to do your duty and depart
To fight – perhaps to die!

Vivat Prudentia! Prudential, long life!
Your hope and mine! And when, our troubles past,
God's Will is done, may He, through storm and strife,
Return you home at last!

'Ibis' The Journal of the Prudential Clerks' Society.

(Panel 54) Pte. 1906, Charles William Gates, 'D' Coy., 1/5th (City of London) Bn. (London Rifle Brigade) The London Regt. (T.F.): *s.* of William Henry Gates, Solicitor's Clerk; of 110, Manwood Road, Crofton Park, London, by his wife Caroline: *b.* 13 January 1886: *educ.* Alleyne's School, London, S.E.: Occupation – Clerk; Headquarters, Prudential Assurance Co. Ltd., Holborn Bars, London, E.C.: joined London Rifle Brigade, 6 April 1915: served with the Expeditionary Force in France and Flanders, and was killed in action 2 December following, while on guard duty. Buried at St. Eloi. Capt. A.T.B. de Colagan wrote, "He was universally liked and respected, and his loss to D Coy. is felt by all. Your husband made himself universally popular in the company, and his death came as a great shock to us all." Age 28. He *m.* St. Clement's Church, Dulwich, London, S.E.; Margaret May (273, Friern Road, East Dulwich), *dau.* of Walter Thomas Layton, Journalist; and had two children.

(Panel 54) Pte. 315179, Edwin Charles Grant, 1/5th (City of London) Bn. (London Rifle Brigade) The London Regt. (T.F.): *s.* of Walter James Grant, Printer; of Leadenhall Street, London, E.C., by his wife Ada Jane (73, Royal Road, Kennington, London, S.E.): *b.* Kennington Park, London, S.E., 1899: *educ.* St. Agnes' School, Kennington Park; and Borough Polytechnic School (Prize): Occupation – Compositor: joined London Rifle Brigade, 19 October 1916: served with the Expeditionary Force in France and Flanders. Reported missing after the fighting 15 August 1917; now assumed killed in action on or about that date. He was keenly interested in sport; particularly cricket and football: Age 19.

(Panel 54) Rfn. 862, John Edward Hewett, 'D' Coy., 1/5th (City of London) Bn. (London Rifle Brigade) The London Regt. (T.F.): only *s.* of the late George Hulbert Hewett, Mercantile Clerk; British India Steamship Navigation Co.; of 61, Rathcoole Gardens, Hornsey, London, N., by his wife Olivia, *dau.* of William Clarke: *b.* Highbury, London, N., 15 January 1894: *educ.* Hornsey County School: enlisted 9 September 1914; killed 28 April 1915. Buried at Fortuin: Age 21. *unm.*

(Panel 54) Rfn. 315183, George Albert Hewitt, 5th (City of London) Bn. (London Rifle Brigade) The London Regt. (T.F.): formerly no.6679, 11th London Regt.: *s.* of Polly Hewitt (221, Gray's Inn Road, London, WC.1): *b.* Holborn, 1895: enlisted Bunhill Row, London, E.C.: served with the Expeditionary Force in France and Flanders from 1916, and was killed in action 15 August 1917: Age 20. *Buried in Divisional Collecting Post Cemetery & Extension (II.F.2).*

(Panel 54) Rfn. 9432, Richard Henry James Moore, 1/5th (City of London) Bn. (London Rifle Brigade) The London Regt. (T.F.): *s.* of Sidney Herbert Moore, of Park School, 43, Park Avenue, Wood Green, London, by his wife Victoria: and brother to Sergt. 8557, S.A. Moore, London Rifle Brigade, died 8 May 1915, of wounds: *b.* Wood Green: enlisted London. Killed in action 30 April 1915: Age 20. *unm.* (*IWGC record R.H.T. Moore*)

His brother Sidney is buried in Boulogne Eastern Cemetery (VIII.C.1).

(Panel 54) Rfn. 282, John Gordon Newell, 'D'Coy., 1/5th (City of London) Bn. (London Rifle Brigade) The London Regt. (T.F.): *s.* of Charles Newell, of 3, Breakspear Road, St. John's, London, S.E.4, by his wife Sophia Elizabeth: enlisted London. Killed at St. Jean, 28 April 1915, in company with three other men when the house in which they were breakfasting was hit by a shell: Age 21. *unm.* See also L/Corpl.J.W.C. Reading (Panel 54), Rfn. A.J. Foster (above) and R.S.M. A.G. Harrington, King's Royal Rifle Corps attd. London Rifle Brigade (Addenda Panel 57).

(Panel 54) Rfn. 303184, Edgar Charles Newton, 'A'Coy., 2/5th (City of London) Bn. (London Rifle Brigade) The London Regt. (T.F.): *s.* of Charles Newton, of 61, Temple Sheen Road, East Sheen, London, by his wife Rebecca: *b*. 1894: Occupation – Clerk; London Stock Exchange: enlisted Wandsworth. Killed in action 9 September 1917: Age 23. *unm*.

(Panel 54) Rfn. 291, George Patrick Northam, No. 1 Coy., 1/5th (City of London) Bn. (London Rifle Brigade) The London Regt. (T.F.): *s*. of John Northam, of 27, Vicars Hill, Ladywell, Lewisham, London, S.E.13, by his marriage to the late Elizabeth Jane Northam: and elder brother to 2nd Lieut. J.McC. Northam, Prince of Wales's Own (Civil Service Rifles), who fell 15 September 1917, nr. Inverness Copse: *b*. Brockley, London, S.E.4: served with the Expeditionary Force in France and Flanders from January 1915, and was killed in action nr. Fortuin, 3 May 1915: Age 21. *unm*.

His brother John also has no known grave, he is recorded below.

(Panel 54) Pte. 793, James William Thomas Pepper, 1/5th (City of London) Bn. (London Rifle Brigade) The London Regt. (T.F.): only *s*. of James William Pepper, of 15, West Cliff, Whitstable, Local Secretary & Correspondent, Kent Education Committee (Whitstable); by his wife Emma Maria, *dau*. of John Harlow: *b*. Whitstable, co. Kent, 2 July 1891: *educ*. Simon Langton School, Canterbury, and Goldsmiths' College, London (B.A. 1912), and on leaving there was for several months Supplementary Teacher, Kent Education Committee; later certified Teacher, Bridge Road Council School, Harlesden, under the Willesden Education Committee who wrote highly of his influence and of his ability: volunteered on the outbreak of war August 1914; joined London Rifle Brigade, undertook Foreign Service Obligations, September: went to France with the first draft to join 1/5th Battn., on Active Service in Flanders, January 1915: served in the trenches January – April: retired to the rear after Easter for a rest, but was suddenly ordered up with his regt. to the support of the Canadians at the Ypres salient, and was killed in action there, 26 April 1915. Buried at Fortuin, nr. St. Julien. He obtained a Junior County Scholarship at ten years of age, and later a County Bursary: especially interested in history and languages; at the time war was declared was making a special study of Anglo-Saxon and Old English. During his last two years at College he played successfully as a member of the College Rugby Team, and was also interested in cricket: Age 23. *unm*.

Serving in the Ploegsteert sector during the winter of 1914, Pte. W.R.M. Percy wrote home to his family, describing the 'strange event' which occurred there between the opposing armies 24 – 25 December:– "...On Christmas Eve the Germans burnt coloured lights and candles along the top of their trenches, and on Christmas Day a football match was played between them and us in front of the trench. They even allowed us to bury all our dead lying in front, and some of them, with hats in hand, brought in one of our dead officers from behind their trench so that we could bury him decently. They were really magnificent in the whole thing, and jolly good sorts. I have now a very different opinion of the German. Both sides have now started firing, and are deadly enemies again. Strange it all seems, doesn't it?"

This 'strange event' would not occur again and Pte. Percy would never see another Christmas; he was killed near St. Julien two months later.

(Panel 54) Pte. 9755, William Reginald Minshull Percy, 1/5th (City of London) Bn. (London Rifle Brigade) The London Regt. (T.F.): *s*. of John Henry Percy, of Bod Meurig, Rhyl, by his wife Catherine, *dau*. of William Minshull, of Mold: *b*. Southport, 4 February 1895: *educ*. Epworth College, Rhyl, thereafter entered offices of the Prudential Society: joined London Rifle Brigade on the outbreak of war, August 1914. Killed in action nr. Ypres, 27 February 1915. Buried nr. St. Julien. His Capt. wrote of him as a great loss, "He was so cheery with a sort of Irish wit about him that made him excellent company." One of his comrades wrote, "The whole battn. was under heavy shell fire at the time, and you will be glad to know that Reggie behaved magnificently during the whole period. He was in fact one of the most popular fellows in the platoon." A writer in the '*Ibis*' said, "Clean-minded, high-spirited, with a charm of manner that captivated all with whom he came in contact, he was the embodiment of joyous youth. The cruel eclipse of this bright life has cast a shadow which only the years in their course can lighten." From the Headmaster of Epworth College, "Many old Epworthians will remember the skilful drawings he executed by W.R.M.P. His caricatures were the best this school have ever produced. All of us, masters and boys, at one time or another provided him with subjects for his friendly but critical pencil. The men of his company were fortunate in having a comrade so vivacious, and so full of kindly humour. Their testimony, and that of the officers of the battn., show the high regard in which he was held, and to this testimony we add our tribute of esteem and affection." Age 20. *unm.*

(Panel 54) Pte. 9563, Arthur Ronald Pigden, 'C' Coy., 1/5th (City of London) Bn. (London Rifle Brigade) The London Regt. (T.F.): *s.* of George Alexander Pigden, of 23, Albert Road, Stroud Green, Hornsey, Town Councillor, by his wife Matilda: *b.* Barnsbury, 25 December 1894: *educ.* Stroud Green School, Hornsey County School, and Clark's College: joined Boy Scouts, 1908; King's Royal Rifles Cadet Corps, 1911; London Rifle Brigade, May 1913: volunteered for Foreign Service on the outbreak of war, left England with L.R.B., 2 November 1914, and within a week was in the trenches where they remained over Christmas, fraternising with the Saxons who were in the trenches 80 yards in front of them that day. In April 1915, the regt. was resting at Armentieres, when the Canadians were gassed, and they were rushed up through Ypres to their support, marching seventeen and-a-half miles with full packs in four and-a-half hours. Writing home on 28 April, Pigden said, "Threw away all my souvenirs on march, only souvenir I am now anxious about is myself;" and the following day, "Am going out to repair telephone wire under fire, tonight, so cheer-oh!" He was on signalling duty in a dug-out at Fortuin with four others for fifteen days, and though all other parts of the line were being hit, their little dug-out escaped until 2 May 1915, when he was killed by the bursting of a shell. A comrade wrote, "We were sent up to relieve the Canadians when gassed, there was a heavy bombardment going on which lasted 15 days; as you can imagine our wires were continually being broken by the shelling and it was almost an hourly occurrence for one of our five to run out and repair them, and even deliver the message by hand, we five did this perilous work in rotation, and strange to say none of us were touched while on this task, although other stations were losing heavily meanwhile. Your son was hit by a shell in the left hand on the last day before retirement, and in the afternoon another shell burst among us, I was only stunned and ran for stretcher bearers, but it was too late, they declared your son dead on arrival." Age 21. *unm.*

(Panel 54) Pte. 90, James Reynolds, 'G' Coy., 1/5th (City of London) Bn. (London Rifle Brigade) The London Regt. (T.F.): eldest *s.* of the late James Reynolds, Solicitor, by his wife Annie Deletia (87, Anerley Road, Upper Norwood, London, S.E.), *dau.* of George Lowe: and brother to Lieut. C.E. Reynolds, Royal Air Force, died 23 October 1918, of accidental injuries sustained on crashing his machine on landing after a bombing raid: *b.* Southend-on-Sea, co. Essex, 18 February 1893: *educ.* Dulwich College, London, S.E., gaining his B.A. (London University) on leaving school: Occupation – Articled Solicitor: volunteered for Active Service on the outbreak of war; joined London Rifle Brigade, 6 August 1914: served with the Expeditionary Force in France and Flanders from November following, and was killed in action at the Second Battle of Ypres, 2 May 1915. Buried at Fortuin, nr. Ypres. His Commanding Officer wrote, "Would that I could write to all parents of the magnificent way their sons behaved the last ten days, but please accept this as my heartiest endorsement of all Gibson has said;" and Corpl. G. Gibson, "It may be some consolation to you to know that he died like a soldier during the very severe shelling to which we were subjected on Sunday afternoon last, and after he had rendered invaluable services in attending to wounded men under shell fire during the whole of the preceding week. He was always cheerful under all circumstances, and a great favourite throughout the company. I, his Section Commander, and his whole section feel his loss terribly." Age 22. *unm.*

His brother Charles is buried in Charmes Military Cemetery (I.C.19).

(Panel 54) Rfn. 304559, William Thomas Joseph Scutchings, 2/5th (City of London) Bn. (London Rifle Brigade) The London Regt. (T.F.): *b.* Hampstead, 1898: Occupation – Clerk; Messrs Coutts & Co., Lombard Street, London (1914 – 17): volunteered and enlisted Bunhill Row, January 1917: served in France from August following, and was killed in action north-east of Ypres, 20 September 1917; St. Julien: Age 19.

(Panel 54) Rfn. 898, Harold David Vallentine, 1/5th (City of London) Bn. (London Rifle Brigade) The London Regt., (T.F.): late of Stamford Hill: *s.* of the late James Vallentine, by his marriage to Christina Sarah Jane Warne, *née* Vallentine (The Grange, Kingston Hill, co. Surrey): and yr. brother to Rfn. 300282,

C.R. Vallentine-Warne, London Rifle Brigade, killed in action 7 April 1917, aged 27 years: enlisted Bunhill Row, London: Killed in action, 2 May 1915: Age 25. *unm.*

His brother Claude is buried in Agny Military Cemetery (G.44).

(Panel 54) Rfn. 315256, Cecil Chester Walsh, 1/5th (City of London) Bn. (London Rifle Brigade) The London Regt. (T.F.): formerly no.10024, Inns of Court O.T.C.: *s.* of the late Richard Walter Walsh, J.P., of Williamstown House, Castlebellingham, Co. Louth (High Sheriff, Co. Louth, 1905; *d.*1937); by his wife Ismay, *née* Chester (*d.*1937): *educ.* Stonyhurst College, from whence he joined Inns of Court O.T.C.: transf'd. L.R.B., late 1916: served with the Expeditionary Force in France, and was killed in action 16 August 1917: Age 19. His brother also fell.

(Panel 54) Rfn. 287, James Ernest White, 1/5th (City of London) Bn. (London Rifle Brigade) The London Regt., (T.F.): 2nd *s.* of James White, of 2, Woodside Road, Wood Green, London, N., by his wife Sarah Ann, *dau.* of Josiah Briscoe: *b.* London, N., 30 September 1885: *educ.* Higher Grade School, Wood Green, N., and Birbeck College: Occupation – Clerk; Oceana Land Co. Ltd.: joined London Rifle Brigade on the outbreak of war, August 1914: went to France, 13 March 1915, and was killed in action at Zillebeke, 27 April following. Buried at Fortuin. Rfn. White took part in many branches of Church work, was an enthusiastic cellist, and led a small orchestra: Age 29. *unm.*

(Panel 54) L/Corpl. 3218, Frederick J. Bailey, 1/6th (City of London) Bn. (London Rifles) The London Regt. (T.F.): late of Forest Hill, London, S.E.: *s.* of William Bailey, of 'Antrim,' The Glen, Minster, Sheppey, Sheerness, by his wife Mary Ann: and elder brother to Rfn. 4925, E.E. Bailey, 1/6th Bn. London Regt., who fell the same day. Killed in action 22 October 1916. Age 24. *unm.* See below.

His brother Ernest also has no known grave; he is recorded below.

(Panel 54) Rfn. 4925, Ernest Edgar Bailey, 1/6th (City of London) Bn. (London Rifles) The London Regt. (T.F.): late of Forest Hill, London, S.E.: *s.* of William Bailey, of 'Antrim,' The Glen, Minster, Sheppey, Sheerness, by his wife Mary Ann: and *yr.* brother to L/Corpl. 3218, F.J. Bailey, 1/6th Bn. London Regt., who fell the same day: *b.* Battersea, London, S.W.: Occupation – Gas Worker; South-Eastern Gas Co., Port Greenwich, London, S.E.. Killed in action 22 October 1916: Age 20. *unm.*

His brother Frederick also has no known grave; he is recorded above.

(Panel 54) Rfn. 323332, John Gordon Lewis, 1/6th (City of London) Bn. (London Rifles) The London Regt. (T.F.): *s.* of Rev. David Lewis, Rector; Llanbedr Rectory, Ruthin, co. Denbigh, and Caroline Lewis, his spouse: and brother to Chaplain Rev. I.M. Lewis, H.M.S. 'Goliath,' R.N., who lost his life when that ship was sunk in Morto Bay, off Cape Helles, 13 May 1915: Killed in action 7 June 1917.

With no known grave but the sea his brother Ivor is commemorated on the Chatham Naval Memorial (Panel 9).

(Panel 54) L/Corpl. 352067, John James Bloomfield, 1/7th (City of London) Bn. The London Regt. (T.F.): late of West Kilburn, London: enlisted Hammersmith. Killed in action 7 June 1917. Two months previously (10 April) the accidental discharge of his rifle in a trench near The Bluff caused the death of Pte. 350096, W.G. Bezley.

William Bezley is buried in Chester Farm Cemetery (III.D.2).

> *Can you hear them coming, the boys of London Town,*
> *The boys of the Post Office Rifles, the lads who won renown;*
> *The lads who faced the shrapnel, the bombs, and whizz-bangs too,*
> *And all they ever got to eat was Tickler's Jam and Army Stew.*

(Panel 54) Corpl. 374471, Thomas Bottomley, 1/8th (City of London) Bn. (Post Office Rifles) The London Regt. (T.F.): formerly no.17547, 1st Royal Berkshire Regt.: late of Todmorden, co. York: *b.* Stone, co. Stafford: enlisted London. Killed in action 7 June 1917; nr. Hollebeke, Battle of Messines. "The battalion being badly held up and suffering heavy casualties due to machine-gun fire from the White Chateau, just to the west of Hell-Fire Corner on the Menin Road. The chateau was one of the objectives of the Shiny Seventh on the left, this being a naturally strong position that was so well fortified a determined garrison might have held out for a long time. Some of the 1st./8th. Londons took part in the attack on the chateau and materially assisted in its capture. One deserving of mention Corpl. T. Bottomley, formerly of the Royal Berks, made his way into the place through the deadly machine-gun and rifle fire, and capturing one of the enemy machine-guns, which was doing so much damage to our attack, proceeded to use it to deadly effect on the enemy therein. Unfortunately he was not long to survive this heroic act for when our men finally made their way into the place Corpl. Bottomley was found slumped over the barrel of the machine-gun he had so gallantly captured and used." A few hours before his death in action he had remarked he had a premonition this day he was going to get a Victoria Cross or a wooden one. There being no witness to his actions he received no official recognition; his grave was lost in later fighting.

(Panel 54) L/Corpl. 372499, Francis John Pearson, 2/8th (City of London) Bn. (Post Office Rifles) The London Regt. (T.F.): *s.* of the late John Henry Pearson, by his wife Jessie Mary (91, Warham Street, Kennington Park, London, S.E.): *b.* Tenby, co. Pembroke, *c.*1896: enlisted Lambeth, London, N. Killed in action 20 September 1917, at the Battle of Wurst Farm Ridge, Alberta sector, Passchendaele: Age 21. *unm.*

(Panel 54) Pte. 371921, Robert Dudgeon Morris, 1/8th (City of London) Bn. (Post Office Rifles) The London Regt. (T.F.): *s.* of James (& Mrs) Morris, of 'The Cedars,' Northfield Road, Edinburgh: enlisted London. Killed in action 7 June 1917: Age 19.

(Panel 54) Rfn. 385154, Harold William Quibell, 1/8th (City of London) Bn. (Post Office Rifles) The London Regt. (T.F.): formerly no.5108, 18th London Regt.: *s.* of Joseph Quibell, of 180, Ashville Road, Leytonstone, London, by his wife Ellen: and elder brother to Pte. G/9768, L.S. Quibell, 11th Queen's Own (Royal West Kent Regt.), killed in action 7 October 1916: *b.* Leytonstone: enlisted there. Killed in action 20 September 1917: Age 26. He leaves a wife, Florence Mary Quibell (233, Cann Hall Road, Leytonstone).

His brother Leonard also has no known grave; he is commemorated on the Thiepval Memorial (Pier & Face 11C).

(Panel 54) Rfn. 373225, Wallace Bristow Riddiford, 1/8th (City of London) Bn. (Post Office Rifles) The London Regt. (T.F.): *s.* of George Riddiford, by his wife Emma: and brother to Gnr. 136845, F. Riddiford, Royal Garrison Artillery, died 2 February 1919: *b.* Ullcombe, co. Kent: enlisted Woking. Killed in action 26 August 1917: Age 34. He was married to Mabel Fanny Riddiford (Maybury Post Office, College Road, Woking, co. Surrey).

His brother Frank is buried in Cobham (St. Lawrence) Church Cemetery (south-west corner).

(Panel 54) Rfn. 372649, John Agar Wilson, 2/8th (City of London) Bn. (Post Office Rifles) The London Regt. (T.F.): *s.* of the late C. (& Mrs) Wilson, of Lealholm, co. York: *b.* Glaisdale, co. York: enlisted Whitby. Killed in action 20 September 1917; Wurst Farm: Age 26. *unm.*

(Panel 54) Major Thomas Prior Lees, 9th (County of London) Bn. (Queen Victoria's Rifles) The London Regt. (T.F.): 2nd *s.* of the late Alfred Lees, by his wife Rosa Matilda, *dau.* of Thomas Flood: *b.* The Old Priory, Bedford, 3 September 1874: *educ.* Bedford Modern School, and Clare College, Cambridge (M.A. and 8th Senior Optime). Entered the Home Civil Service, Senior Division; was Assistant Secretary, Civil Service Commission, Burlington Gardens. Joined the old Victoria & St. George's Rifles, 22 May, 1889: became Capt. March 1905; Major 15 August 1913: obtained Special Certificate, Chelsea Barracks; passed Army examinations for Field Rank (distinguished): volunteered with the officers of his regt. for Active Service during the South African War, but only a limited number were required, and he remained in England: volunteered for the European War, landed in France 5 November 1914. The battn. went straight into the trenches and was afterwards attached to 13th Infantry Brigade. On 17 April the Brigade was detailed for the capture of Hill 60. The fighting was so severe during the 17th, 18th and 19th that the West Kents, Scottish Borderers, Yorks L.I. and West Riding Regts., who had fought magnificently, were withdrawn and another brigade brought up. The Queen Victoria's had been occupied in carrying munitions to the front trenches, but miraculously escaped with few casualties. They were not relieved with their brigade. On the night of the 20th the enemy took the trenches on the top of the hill, and

Major Lees counter-attacked with two companies, the rest of the battn. being held in reserve in dug-outs near the foot of the hill, where they were subjected to a terrible bombardment lasting for hours. Major Lees' night assault was successful. He then found he was the senior officer left alive on the hill and reorganised the defence. The German artillery and machine-gun fire was continuous, save when they launched repeated infantry attacks against our trenches. About 5a.m. on the 21st, Major Lees had gone to the most exposed trench held by the Bedford Regt., in which there were nearly 300 of our killed and wounded. The enemy were assaulting, showering grenades into the trench and sweeping the parapet with machine-gun fire. It was at this critical moment that he was shot through the head and heart, only 10 yards from the Germans, while shouting orders to hold on. He fell off the parapet into the arms of a Sergt. of the Bedfords and never spoke again. The N.C.Os. and riflemen were heroic. Out of the 150 men with Major Lees all were killed and wounded, except 20 who were still holding on with 2nd Lieut. Woolley, V.C., when relieved by the Devons and Camerons. Lieut.-Col. Shipley, C.M.G., wrote to his brother, Major Lees, late 3rd South Wales Borderers,"He died like a hero, having retaken and made good a position of primary importance, which the enemy were on the point of re-occupying. His last gallant charge was, as he would have wished it, to the assistance of his county regt. the Bedfordshires. The last words I heard him speak as he led his company off into the trenches were, 'Now, remember, if anyone is wounded, the others must carry on. If I am hit, go on.' It was his initiative and courageous behaviour that has enabled us to hold on to the position. I cannot even attempt to tell you what a stupendous loss his is to the regt. and myself, but we must console ourselves by remembering and trying to emulate your brother's unswerving devotion to duty and the unflinching gallantry shown by him in all times of stress; his life so earnestly devoted to others will live in our memories for all time." Buried in the larch wood, nr. Hill 60: Age 41. Major Lees is remembered on a marble tablet in Elstow (St. Mary & Helena) Church, co. Bedford; his epitaph: *Immota Fides.*

(Panel 54) Lieut. Frederick Brian Arthur Fargus, 9th (County of London) Bn. (Queen Victoria's Rifles) The London Regt. (T.F.): *yr. s.* of Henry Robert Fargus, Solicitor; of 169, Queens Gate, London, W., formerly of Milton House, Strawberry Hill, Middlesex, by his wife Helen Mary: *b.* Strawberry Hill, 8 June 1887: *educ.* Rugby: admitted to the Roll of Solicitors, 1911, in which year he was gazetted 2nd Lieut. Queen Victoria's Rifles: promoted Lieut., December 1912: became partner in his father's firm, Messrs Clayton, Sons & Fargus, 1913. At the time of his death, 1 January 1915, he was in command of the machine-gun section of his battalion. His Commanding Officer wrote, "Your son Brian was in the trenches yesterday and was shot dead by a German sniper. One and all of us will miss his cheerful, bright presence, and his devotion to his duties has been an example to us all. Your son had endeared himself to us one and all, and as for his gun team, they absolutely worshipped him. He was so devoid of fear that he was invaluable in patrolling and reconnoitring." His recreations were cricket, football, golf, tennis, motoring and fishing, and he was keen and proficient in Freemasonry, being Master-elect of the Felix Lodge: Age 27. *unm.*

(Panel 54) Sergt. (Actg.) 2267, Walter John Clayton, 1/9th (County of London) Bn. (Queen Victoria's Rifles) The London Regt. (T.F.): *s.* of Charles H. (& Mrs) Clayton, of Hillside, Ditton Hill, co. Surrey: *b.* 1885: *educ.* Cheltenham College, where, being a fine athlete, he represented the college at both Cricket and Football: entered his uncle's firm Messrs Clayton & Aston (1902), later joining London Stock Exchange (Member), and Messrs Clayton & Sons: joined Inns of Court O.T.C. on the outbreak of war, but, anxious to get to the Front as soon as possible, enlisted Queen Victoria's Rifles and, after a brief period of training, went to France November following. Shortly after being promoted Sergt. (and on several other occasions) Mr Clayton was offered a commission but rejected the opportunity preferring to stay with his men. Served in the trenches throughout the winter 1914 – 15 and was killed in action at Hill 60, nr. Ypres, 19 April 1915: Age 29. A fellow Sergt. wrote, "I had been with him since the start and there was no more popular man in the Regiment. He will never be forgotten by any of us." The possessor of a fine voice, Sergt. Clayton did sterling work in organising sports events and concerts for his men.

(Panel 54) Sergt. 2349, Frederick Arthur Hooper, 9th (County of London) Bn. (Queen Victoria's Rifles) The London Regt. (T.F.): 2nd *s.* of the late William Joice Hooper, of 3, Duke Street, Grosvenor Square, London, W., by his wife Harriet Comins, *née* Hooper (15, Abbey Gardens, St. John's Wood), *dau.* of Henry Parsons: *b.* Duke Street, 3 September 1877: *educ.* Ardingley College: Occupation – Fruiterer & Florist: for many years a member of Queen Victoria's Rifles, and while serving with them was one of those selected to accompany H.M. King George (then Duke of York) upon his visit to Australia: volunteered for Foreign Service, and rejoined his old regiment, October 1914, after the outbreak of war: served with the Expeditionary Force in France and Flanders from 4 November 1914, and was killed in action nr. Ypres, 31 May 1915. Buried behind the trenches. Sergt. Andrews wrote, "He was admired and loved by us all. He was the hardest worker and the most reliable man in the company. A splendid soldier and a true friend. We shall all sadly miss as well as mourn his loss." He was mentioned in the order issued by Lieut.Col. R.B. Shepley, for 'invaluable service on Hill 60, and during the operations east of the Yser Canal.' Age 37. *unm.*

(Panel 54) Corpl. 1474, Howard Alan Farrar, 9th (County of London) Bn. (Queen Victoria's Rifles) The London Regt. (T.F.): *s.* of William David Farrar, of The Red Bungalow, Leckhampton, Cheltenham: *b.* Stroud, co. Gloucester, 1893: enlisted Cheltenham: served with the Expeditionary Force in France from 4 November 1914: took part in the fighting at Hill 60, and was killed by the bursting of a shell, 24 April 1915, on the St. Jan – Wieltje road. Buried nearby: Age 22. *unm.* See Rfn. P.G. Ford, D. Van Ryn and E.H. Wilson (below); also Rfn. W.O. Weedon, White House Cemetery (III.P.17).

(Panel 54) L/Corpl. 3457, George Clark Moncur, 9th (County of London) Bn. (Queen Victoria's Rifles) The London Regt. (T.F.): *s.* of John William Moncur, of Aberdeen, Hotel Proprietor (ret'd.), by his wife Elizabeth S.M., *dau.* of James S. Paterson: *b.* Aberdeen, 5 February 1894: *educ.* Ashley Road School: Occupation – Window Dresser: joined Queen Victoria's Rifles, volunteered for Foreign Service on the outbreak of war: went to France, February 1915, and was killed in action at Hill 60, 25 April following. Buried at Headquarter Farm (c.16-3, Reference Map, Belgium, 281/40,000) His brother, Sergt. Nicol Moncur, Dragoons, went to France with the Expeditionary Force in August 1914, and is still (1916) serving there: Age 21. *unm.*

(Panel 54) Rfn. 2181, Leonard Frederick Avila, 1/9th (County of London) Bn. (Queen Victoria's Rifles) The London Regt. (T.F.): late of West Norwood: *s.* of Joseph Avila, of 105, Exeter Street, Otley Road, Bradford, by his wife Annie E.: enlisted London. Killed in action 4 December 1914: Age 17.

Neglecting to mention the fact that Newhaven School was operating under difficult conditions, having been removed to alternative premises on the outbreak of war because the school buildings were being utilised as a military hospital, an inspection of the school, 17 April 1917, earned the following report:–
"The conditions under which school work is carried out at present no doubt renders the control of the boys more than unusually difficult, nevertheless it is disquieting to find that in all classes except the two highest a considerable section of the boys adopt an indifferent attitude towards their work. Discipline is especially unsatisfactory…It is doubtful whether an improvement can be looked for unless some changes are made in the personnel of the present staff."

The report also neglected to mention that the problems of indifference and indiscipline stemmed from changes already made in the personnel. The majority of the male staff were serving their country, their places having been taken up by female teachers whose brothers and husbands were also serving, the boys invariably found what was happening in France and elsewhere more interesting and mentally stimulating than schoolwork, and, if truth be known, the 'two highest' classes – the older boys – probably couldn't wait for the opportunity to enlist and 'do their bit.' Harry Bannister went to Newhaven School, he never had a problem with discipline; leaving the term before war broke out, Harry went to London, joined up, 'did his bit':–

(Panel 54) Rfn. 315080, Harry Patrick Bannister, 1/9th (County of London) Bn. (Queen Victoria's Rifles) The London Regt. (T.F.): *s.* of Harry James Bannister, of 14, High Street, Newhaven, by his wife Kathleen Mary: *b.* Newhaven, co. Sussex, 1898: *educ.* there: enlisted 1/9th London Regt., November 1914; aged 16 years: undertook Active Service obligations and served with the Expeditionary Force in

France from February 1915, and was killed in action nr. Glencorse Wood, at the Battle of Langemarck, 11 August 1917: Age 19. One of 127 names inscribed on the Newhaven War Memorial, dedicated – "To the glory of God and in undying memory of the men of this parish who gave their lives for King and Country and in grateful appreciation of those who took part in the Great War, 1914 – 1919." He is also remembered on the memorial recording 90 names in St. Michael's Church, Newhaven. See also Gnr. W.G. MacDonald, Royal Garrison Artillery, Dozinghem Military Cemetery (XIII.B.20).

(Panel 54) Rfn. 2376, Robert Cecil Brinton, 9th (County of London) Bn. (Queen Victoria's Rifles) The London Regt. (T.F.): late of Isleworth, London: enlisted August 1914. One of seventeen men killed, 24 April 1915, by a number of enemy shells which fell in the midst of the battalion between St. Jan and Wieltje. See Rfn. P.G. Ford, D. Van Ryn and E.H. Wilson (below); also Rfn. W.O. Weedon, White House Cemetery (III.P.17).

(Panel 54) Rfn. 2301, Horace Brian Brooker, 1/9th (County of London) Bn. (Queen Victoria's Rifles) The London Regt. (T.F.): only *s.* of Horace Sidney Brooker, Draper & Outfitter; of Queens Road, Weybridge, by his wife Kate, *dau.* of John Jonas Couzens: *b.* Weybridge, 20 June 1888: *educ.* St. James School, Weybridge: enlisted 9th London Regt., 21 August 1914, going into camp three days later. He was home only once subsequently, for a few hours, preceding his departure for the Front, on 2 November 1914. After a fortnight's training in France he went with his regt. straight into the firing line, and there he remained, with intervals of relief, right up to the memorable fight for Hill 60, where he was killed in action, 21 April 1915. In his last letter, dated 14 April, he referred to a visit of zeppelins which had dropped 11 bombs within 200 yards of the regt. making holes 24ft in diameter. A comrade, Rfn. Barry, wrote, "I have been closely associated with Brian since we came out in November last, and during the dreary months of bad weather in the trenches his cheery influence did much to keep us going. There is not the slightest doubt that the hill would have been lost but for the timely arrival of our regt. and the courage shown by both officers and men, who were determined to hang on like grim death, even when men of some other regts. were beginning to give way. No.1 platoon had to get out of the trenches and charge across the open and occupy a small German trench in front, and it was while doing this that Brian was killed." A well-known Surrey athlete, he had captained the Weybridge Football Club for several seasons, and achieved International A.F.A. honours, thrice accompanying representative teams to the Continent: Age 25. *unm.*

(Panel 54) Rfn. 3378, Harry Edwin Clegg, 1/9th (County of London) Bn. (Queen Victoria's Rifles) The London Regt. (T.F.): late of Harringay, London, N.: enlisted late September 1914. One of seventeen men killed by shellfire, 24 April 1915, on the road St. Jan – Wieltje. See Rfn. P.G. Ford, D. Van Ryn and E.H. Wilson (below); also Rfn. W.O. Weedon, White House Cemetery (III.P.17).

(Panel 54) Rfn. 2065, John Sewell Davies, 1/9th (County of London) Bn. (Queen Victoria's Rifles) The London Regt. (T.F.): enlisted August 1914. Killed by shellfire, 24 April 1915, on the road St. Jan – Wieltje. See Rfn. P.G. Ford, D. Van Ryn and E.H. Wilson (below); also Rfn. W.O. Weedon, White House Cemetery (III.P.17).

(Panel 54) Rfn. 3250, Percy Gorden Ford, 1/9th (County of London) Bn. (Queen Victoria's Rifles) The London Regt. (T.F.): 2nd *s.* of John William Fletcher Ford, Linen Merchant; of 57, Friday Street, London, E.C., and Rozel, Roydon, Essex, by his wife Catherine, *dau.* of Thomas Strout: *b.* Hornsey, London, 11 September 1891: *educ.* Tollingham School, and Christ's College, Finchley: Occupation – Traveller: joined Queen Victoria's Rifles on the outbreak of war, August 1914: went to France, 14 February 1915, and was killed in action at Hill 60, Flanders, 24 April 1915. A comrade wrote, "He was in hospital when we went up to Hill 60, but joined us up there in the dug-outs when we had been relieved from the firing line. I remember him, Claude, coming up to me and saying, as we shook hands, 'By jove, Ashford old man, I'm glad to see you; you fellows have had a rough time.' Not a word about the narrow escape *he* had had with our transport in Ypres. We left on the Thursday morning, 10 men at a time; they were shelling us and it was dangerous to offer too large a target. We assembled outside the Hospital at Ypres and Smith-Dorrien inspected us. We marched back to huts, as we thought to a well-earned rest. The huts were not completed and we had to bivouac. About 6.30 p.m. we saw the French coming pell-mell across country, a regular rout, we spoke to them and found they were retreating. We had to fall in and dig ourselves in by hedges in some fields near. We did not know which way the Germans were supposed to be coming, and had to change our position three times during the night. We were fagged out and had had no proper sleep since the Saturday previous – we couldn't get much at Hill 60. At about 2.30 a.m. we had orders to stop digging; marched back some way and spent the remainder of the night in a field. In the morning we had to sit in ditches along the road, in order to be out of sight of aeroplanes, awaiting orders. The cookers came up and we had some tea, I remember as well as if it were yesterday; Percy gave me some of his condensed milk, and I sat down beside him and we laughingly arranged to go to Golder's Green in the afternoon. Shortly afterwards we had to march off with the rest of the 13th Brigade, to which we were attached. We were in support on the banks of the Yser. The Canadians had driven the Germans back after the French retreat. During the night we had to go up to the firing line, but only for a few hours. The morning of the Saturday found us on the banks of the Yser, awaiting orders. We had dug ourselves in as protection against shrapnel. We moved off about 11 o'clock in single file along the banks of the Yser, towards Ypres, then we cut inland and gradually wound our way forward, moving in zig-zag manner, taking as much advantage of hedges, etc. as we could. Shells were flying all around, but Percy was there then, and that was Saturday. Amy, tells me you were told Friday; I feel certain that it was Saturday. Well, we must have marched 3 to 4 miles and we then got right into the thick of it, it was raining shells. We deployed and were told to take shelter behind some semi-circular parapets. The Germans seemed to have them taped and dropped shells right in amongst us. It was flat country and evidently they could see us approaching, and shelled us very heavily indeed, the air was thick with shells. We advanced by short stages about 100 yards, and then I got hit by a shell in the right shoulder, and missed Percy then; he was in the right half platoon and I was in the left half, so that we got separated. Those that were comparatively lightly wounded were the fortunate ones, Claude. I am sorry that I cannot give you more news of Percy, the last I saw of him he was coolly smoking a cigarette as we marched along over those fields in that awful hail of shells." He was a junior sides-man in the Wesleyan Methodist Church, Finchley: Age 24. *unm.* See also Rfn. D. Van Ryn (below); also Rfn. W.O. Weedon, White House Cemetery (III.P.17).

(Panel 54) Rfn. 2902, Edwin Samuel Fryer, 'B' Coy., 9th (County of London) Bn. (Queen Victoria's Rifles) The London Regt. (T.F.), 3rd London Infantry Brigade: only *survg.* child of Samuel Fryer, Beer Retailer; of The Harvest Home, Bury Cross, Alverstoke, co. Hants, by his wife Mary Anne, *dau.* of James Day, of Manwell, co. Somerset: *b.* London, 20 January 1887: *educ.* Archbishop Tenison's Grammar School, Kennington, London, S.E.11: after a short time in the Civil Service, left at the age of 21 to enter a private firm. On the outbreak of war he volunteered and joined Queen Victoria Rifles, 2 September 1914: proceeded to France, 4 November following, and was killed in action at Lindenhoek, 18 December 1914. Buried at Lindenhoek, Belgium. His Commanding Officer wrote, "He always did his duty well and cheerfully, under often very trying conditions, and showed a fine spirit, setting a splendid example to the rest of the men by whom he was much liked and respected, and who, in common with myself, will feel his loss very much." A Freemason, he was a highly esteemed member of the Equitable Friendly Society, having been Worthy Master during the year 1912: Age 27. *unm.*

(Panel 54) Rfn. 1053, Reginald Lionel Gibbons, 1/9th (County of London) Bn. (Queen Victoria's Rifles) The London Regt. (T.F.): late of Paddington, London, W.2: *s.* of the late Harry Gibbons, by his wife Caroline (79, Marylands Road, Maida Hill, London, W.9: joined Q.V.R., 1909: undertook Active Service obligations on the outbreak of war and served with the Expeditionary Force in France and Flanders from November 1914, and was killed by shell fire, 24 April 1915: Age 24. See Rfn. P.G. Ford (above), D. Van Ryn and E.H. Wilson (below); also Rfn. W.O. Weedon, White House Cemetery (III.P.17).

(Panel 54) Rfn. 392195, John Guilfoy, 1/9th (County of London) Bn. (Queen Victoria's Rifles) The London Regt. (T.F.): *s.* of William Guilfoy, of 22, Corunna Road, New Road, Battersea, London, by his wife Jane: and elder brother to Pte. G/9676, W.E.T. Guilfoy, 11th Queen's (Royal West Surrey Regt.), killed in action 1 August 1917: *b*. Clapham: enlisted London. Killed in action 16 August 1917: Age 23. *unm*.

His brother William also has no known grave; he is recorded on Panel 13.

(Panel 54) Rfn. 3368, Stanley Alfred Hall, 1/9th (County of London) Bn. (Queen Victoria's Rifles) The London Regt. (T.F): late of Forest Hill, London, S.E.23: enlisted London, October 1914. Killed by shellfire, 24 April 1915. See Rfn. P.G. Ford (above), D.Van Ryn and E.H. Wilson (below); also Rfn. W.O. Weedon, White House Cemetery (III.P.17).

(Panel 54) Rfn. 1767, Harold George Hart, 1/9th (County of London) Bn. (Queen Victoria's Rifles) The London Regt. (T.F.): *s*. of G.I. Hart, of The Gables, East Acton Lane, London, W.: *b*. Collingham, Newark, co. Nottingham, 16 January 1880: *educ*. St. Mark's, Windsor, and Salisbury School, Salisbury: admitted Member; Institute of Chartered Accountants, January 1914: enlisted 1 April 1908; discharged (time expired) 31 March 1914: re-enlisted (Queen Victoria's Rifles) on the outbreak of war, 5 August 1914: left with his regt. for the Front: served in France and Flanders, and was killed by a bullet wound received in a trench near Messines, Belgium, 8 January 1915. His Col. wrote to his parents, "Your boy was always splendid in his earnest endeavours to benefit the Coy. in every way. Not long ago a member of the Coy. got embedded in the mud of the trench and, whilst others waited to be ordered to help the man, your son got to work and largely by his exertions the man was released." Age 34. *unm*.

(Panel 54) Rfn. 2294, Francis Mackay Herford, 9th (County of London) Bn. (Queen Victoria's Rifles) The London Regt. (T.F.): late of Golders Green, London, N.W.: enlisted August 1914: took part in the fighting at Hill 60, and was one of seventeen men killed by shellfire in the vicinity of Wieltje while proceeding to the support of the Canadians, 24 April 1915. Buried near where he fell, S.E. of the St. Jan – Wieltje road. See Rfn. P.G. Ford (above), D. Van Ryn and E.H. Wilson (below); also Rfn. W.O. Weedon, White House Cemetery (III.P.17).

(Panel 54) Rfn. 1916, Francis William Hill, 1/9th (County of London) Bn. (Queen Victoria's Rifles) The London Regt. (T.F.): late of Shepherds Bush, London, W.: *s*. of Augustus Robert Hill, of 8, Hillersdon Avenue, Barnes, London, S.W.13, by his wife Ada: *b*. Birmingham, *c*.1890: enlisted London, early 1914: served with the Expeditionary Force in France and Flanders, and was killed at Ypres, 24 April 1915, by shellfire: Age 23. See Rfn. P.G. Ford (above), D. Van Ryn and E.H. Wilson (below); also Rfn. W.O. Weedon, White House Cemetery (III.P.17).

(Panel 54) Rfn. 393281, James Hunt, 1/9th (County of London) Bn. (Queen Victoria's Rifles) The London Regt. (T.F.): *s*. of Henry Hunt, of 139, Warren Street, Camberwell, London, S.E., by his wife Alice: *b*. Westminster, London, S.W., 1898: *educ*. St. John's School, London, S.E.: Occupation – Lift Attendant: joined London Regt., December 1914: served with the Expeditionary Force in France and Flanders: Reported wounded and missing after the fighting 16 August 1917; now assumed to have been killed in action about that time: Age 18.

(Panel 54) Rfn. 3857, Charles Joiner, 9th (County of London) Bn. (Queen Victoria's Rifles) The London Regt. (T.F.): late of Nelson's Square, London: enlisted London, December 1914. One of seventeen men of the battalion killed by shellfire on the approach to Wieltje, 24 April 1915. See Rfn. P.G. Ford (above), D. Van Ryn and E.H. Wilson (below); also Rfn. W.O. Weedon, White House Cemetery (III.P.17).

(Panel 54) Rfn. 2326, Frank Douglas Maisey, 1/9th (County of London) Bn. (Queen Victoria's Rifles) The London Regt. (T.F.): 2nd *s*. of the late Arthur George Maisey: *b*. London, 28 February 1893: *educ*. Commercial Travellers' Schools, Pinner: enlisted September 1914: went to France, March 1915, and was killed in action at Hill 60, 21 April following, on which occasion the Q.V.Rs. so greatly distinguished themselves, and 2nd Lieut. Geoffrey H. Woolley of that battn. won the V.C.: Age 22. *unm*.

(Panel 54) Rfn. 2364, Roland Newling, 'A' Coy., 1/9th (County of London) Bn. (Queen Victoria's Rifles) The London Regt. (T.F.): *s*. of Roland Newling, of 9, Fairlawn Avenue, Chiswick, London, W.4, by his wife Sophia: enlisted London, September 1914: served with the Expeditionary Force in France and Flanders from March 1915, took part in the fighting at Hill 60 where the Battalion so greatly distinguished itself, and was killed by heavy shellfire, 24 April 1915, nr. Wieltje: Age 21. *unm.* See Rfn. P.G. Ford (above), D. Van Ryn and E.H. Wilson (below); also Rfn. W.O. Weedon, White House Cemetery (III.P.17).

(Panel 54) Rfn. 2586, Harry William Purkis, 9th (County of London) Bn. (Queen Victoria's Rifles) The London Regt. (T.F.): late of Barnes, London, S.W.13: enlisted September 1914. Killed by shellfire, 24 April 1915. See Rfn. P.G. Ford (above), D. Van Ryn and E.H. Wilson (below); also Rfn. W.O. Weedon, White House Cemetery (III.P.17).

(Panel 54) Rfn. 3613, John Richard Reynolds, 9th (County of London) Bn. (Queen Victoria's Rifles) The London Regt. (T.F.): late of New Cross, London, S.E. 14: *s.* of James Reynolds, of Meadow Cottage, Higher Lympstone, co. Devon, by his wife Mary: enlisted London, November 1914. Killed in action, 24 April 1915, by shellfire: Age 26. See Rfn. P.G. Ford (above), D. Van Ryn and E.H. Wilson (below); also Rfn. W.O. Weedon, White House Cemetery (III.P.17).

(Panel 54) Rfn. 3448, David Van Ryn, 1/9th (County of London) Bn. (Queen Victoria's Rifles) The London Regt. (T.F.): *s.* of Mr (& Mrs) Van Ryn, of Willesden, London, N.W.: enlisted October 1914: served with the Expeditionary Force in France and Flanders from 23 January 1915: took part in the fighting at Hill 60. Two days after being relieved from the Hill (24 April 1915) the battalion were marching up to support the Canadians north-east of Ypres when, as they neared their destination, on the road between St. Jan and Wieltje, a number of shells dropped in the midst of the battalion; David Van Ryn was hit by a fragment and died almost instantly. Sixteen other men were also killed. Buried south-east of the Wieltje-St. Jan road: Age 20. *unm.* See also Rfn. P.G. Ford (above) and E.H. Wilson (below); also Rfn. W.O. Weedon, White House Cemetery (III.P.17).

(Panel 54) Rfn. 1874, Sydney William Smith, 1/9th (County of London) Bn. (Queen Victoria's Rifles) The London Regt. (T.F.): late of Harrow, co. Middlesex: *b.* Wembley, London, N.: enlisted London on the outbreak of war, August 1914: served with the Expeditionary Force in France and Flanders from November following, and was killed in action, 24 April 1915, by shellfire. See Rfn. P.G. Ford, D. Van Ryn and E.H. Wilson (above); also Rfn. W.O. Weedon, White House Cemetery (III.P.17).

(Panel 54) Rfn. 2056, Edward Henry Wilson, 1/9th (County of London) Bn. (Queen Victoria's Rifles) The London Regt. (T.F.): Officer's Servant: only *s.* of Henry Edward Wilson, of 45, Durham Road, East Finchley, London, N.2, by his wife Alice, *dau.* of Robert Pritty: *b.* Tufnell Park, London, N., 17 May 1895: *educ.* Owen's School, Islington, and, on leaving school, took up an appointment Head Office, London City and Midland Bank: volunteered on the outbreak of war, joined Queen Victoria's Rifles, August 1914: left for France, 4 November following, being attached battn. Machine-Gun section: took part in the capture of Hill 60, when the machine-gun section of the Q.V.R's rendered excellent service. Killed in action by shellfire nr. Wieltje, at the beginning of the Second Battle of Ypres, 24 April 1915. Buried in the garden of a cottage 200 yards S.E. of Battn. H.Q., Wieltje. His officer, Lieut. Brian Fargus, who was himself killed on New Year's Day, wrote (December 1914), "Wilson accompanies me voluntarily whenever I go out on a prowl round the lines or up to some dangerous point. He knows no fear and has turned himself into my bodyguard; he is a splendid fellow and I think no end of him." And the sergeant in charge of the machine-gun section wrote of his fearlessness of danger and conscientious attention to duty, and of the very good work he had done at Hill 60. He was a member of the Blackheath Harriers and had won a number of prizes at athletic meetings; he was also a keen cricketer and football player and an enthusiastic yachtsman. Age 19. See Rfn. P.G. Ford and D. Van Ryn (above); also Rfn. W.O. Weedon, White House Cemetery (III.P.17).

Lieut. F.B.A. Fargus also has no known grave; he is recorded above.

(Panel 54) L/Corpl. 452128, Patrick Lynch, 2/11th (County of London) Bn. (Finsbury Rifles) The London Regt. (T.F.): *s.* of Patrick Lynch, of 172, Trundley Road, Deptford, London, S.E.8, by his wife Ellen: *b.* Deptford, 1894: enlisted London. Killed in action 23 September 1917: Age 23.

(Panel 54) Rfn. 468006, Alfred Eke, 2/11th (County of London) Bn. (Finsbury Rifles) The London Regt. (T.F.): *s.* of Alice Eke (50, Kilmaine Road, Fulham, London): *b.* Camden Town, London, *c.*1896. Killed in action 23 September 1917: Age 21. *unm.* Remains recovered 'Unknown British Soldier,' (GRU

Report, Zillebeke, 5-293E) identified – Clothing, Titles, Boots (821391), Buttons, Division Insignia; reinterred, registered 5 October 1928. *Buried in Sanctuary Wood Cemetery (II.L.18).*

In Loving Remembrance Of My Dear Son Who Died For Us All
Never Forgotten
Mother

(Panel 54) Capt. (Temp Major) James Louis Foucar, 1/12th (County of London) Bn. (The Rangers) The London Regt. (T.F.): *yst. s.* of Mr (& Mrs) Foucar, of Blackheath, London, S.E.: *b.* 8, Tresillian Crescent, Parish of St. John, co. Kent, 15 October 1882: *educ.* Blackheath Proprietary School; London University, B.A. (Chemistry); also studied experimental physics and geology: formerly employed in research Beckton Gas Works, was, on the outbreak of war, employed in similar work in Italy: prior to departure to Italy was member of the Volunteer and Territorial Force (became Capt. in the latter, April 1910); returned to England (re-joined The Rangers) on the outbreak of war; undertook Imperial Service obligations; proceeded to France: served with the Expeditionary Force there and in Flanders from December 1914; promoted Temp. Major, February 1915: took part in some of the most deadly engagements and was reported missing / believed killed in Belgium, 8 May following, after the Second Battle of Ypres; all the other officers being killed, wounded or missing: Age 32. He married Beatrice Loveless, 12 December 1914: *s.p.* The author of a book on the properties of sulphuric acid (published posthumously) Capt. Foucar was well-known and respected as a scientist; his 'Certificate for Election to the Chemical Society' stated he was 'an earnest student of science in general and of chemistry in particular.' One of thirty members of the Chemical Society who made the supreme sacrifice:– '*Pro Patria.*'

(Panel 54) Lieut. Leonard Nithsdale Walford, 1/12th (County of London) Bn. (The Rangers) The London Regt. (T.F): only *s.* of Edward John Walford, of 12, Langford Place, London, N.W.: and *gdson.* to John Maxwell, a descendant of the Earl of Nithsdale, who escaped in disguise from the Tower of London where he was awaiting execution by beheading: *b.* 10 December 1896: *educ.* Mowden School, Brighton; member Brighton College O.T.C.: as a Law Student, London University (entered 1913), and the Middle Temple, he showed every promise of a brilliant legal career. A member of Inns of Court O.T.C., he passed from that body into 12th County of London (Rangers), June 1914: undertook Imperial Service obligations on the outbreak of war: promoted Lieut. September following; apptd. Transport Officer, 1914, but resigned the position shortly after arriving in France: served with the British Expeditionary Force, and was killed in action in Flanders, 8 May 1915. He was in command of 14th and 16th Platoons when the Rangers received orders to go to the support of 3rd Monmouth Regt. and, there being a slight ridge, Lieut. Walford went on some 100 yards in front for the purpose of reconnoitring. At this time shells were falling in hundreds, and on his attaining the crest of the ridge a line of shells fell either side of him, and one high explosive bursting within six feet of him ensured he would never be seen again. Lord Kitchener's Secretary wrote, "I had a very high opinion of him; he was a most interesting and keen boy, and full of intelligence, and would, I am sure, have got on well in any capacity he was called for. However, he has died a glorious death, and his country is proud of him." Age 18.

(Panel 54) 2nd Lieut. Charles Edward Beausire, 12th (County of London) Bn. (The Rangers) The London Regt. (T.F.): 3rd *s.* of Robert L. Beausire, of 15, Addison Crescent, London, W., and New York, by his wife Letitia: and brother to 2nd Lieut. H.A. Beausire, Royal Fusiliers, killed by the bursting of a shell, 15 March 1915; and Capt. F.R. Beausire, who, at the time of writing, is serving with the Artists' Rifles, after having served in France for five months as a Sergt. (2368) in the ranks: *b.* Iquique, Chile, South America, 20 June 1892: *educ.* Winton House School, Winchester, and Rugby, where he gained distinction for football and swimming: enlisted 23rd London Regt., as Private, immediately war broke out; shortly thereafter promoted Corpl.: gazetted 2nd Lieut. 12th London Regt., November 1914: served with the Expeditionary Force in France and Flanders from December following, and was killed Sunday, 14 February 1915 (St. Valentine's Day), with two of his men while holding a very exposed trench which had been heavily shelled all day. His Company commander wrote of him, "Your son's death was a severe blow to me and to his men, for he was a splendid officer and a friend." "Speaking from a professional point of view," writes the Adjutant, "I can assure you that I have seldom met a young officer who showed greater, or even as great, promise as Beausire. Bright and cheerful with his men, who loved him, yet always strict and conscious of his duty, he possessed just those qualities required to make a good officer. On the day he was killed the mud and wet also did their share to make the circumstances extremely trying. He was up and down amongst his men, putting heart into them, until a fatal well-burst shell took him." The Commanding Officer, in a letter to his parents, said, "I want to tell you how deeply we all feel the loss of your boy. During the few months he had been with us he had endeared himself to all ranks, and was one of my most popular and promising young officers. He was laid to rest near the place where he fell." Age 22. *unm.* (*IWGC record age 20*)

His brother Herbert is buried in La Chapelle D'Armentieres Communal Cemetery (E.3); Frederick survived the war.

(Panel 54) 2nd Lieut. Leonard Sampson Nicholson, 'E' Coy., 12th (County of London) Bn. (The Rangers) The London Regt. (T.F.): 2nd *s.* of John Nicholson, Matting Manufacturer; of Tanshelf Mills, Pontefract, co. York, by his wife Elizabeth (Westview, Ackworth Road, Pontefract), *dau.* of Leonard Sampson, of Humburton Grange, Boro'bridge, Yorkshire: and elder brother to Pte. 9592, G.W. Nicholson, 2nd Honourable Artillery Coy., killed in action 23 October 1918, at the Piave, Italy: *b.* Pontefract, 14 July 1880: *educ.* King's School, Pontefract: on leaving school, entered a wholesale iron and steel business; London: became a member of the Polytechnic, joined Rangers, March 1909: volunteered for Imperial Service on the outbreak of war, and left for France with his battn. Christmas Eve, 1914, holding rank of Platoon Sergt.: gazetted 2nd Lieut., 14 April 1915, and was killed in action at Verlorenhoek, during the Second Battle of Ypres, 2 May following. His Commanding Officer, Lieut.-Col. A.D. Bayliffe, wrote, "His death was a great loss to the Rangers; he would have made a very valuable officer had he been spared." He was greatly esteemed by his men and, to quote from a letter written by one of them, "...there was not a man in his platoon who would not have died for him if occasion had arisen. He faithfully upheld the honour of the British Army, and died doing his best for King and Country." Age 24. *unm.* Commemorated on Carleton (Wakefield) War Memorial.

His brother Geoffrey is buried in Tezze British Cemetery (III.D.15).

(Panel 54) Corpl. 932, Albert George William Hogg, 12th (County of London) Bn. (The Rangers) The London Regt. (T.F.): only *s.* of the late George Hogg, Merchant; of London, by his wife Julia (11, Cornwall Gardens, Willesden Green, London, N.W.), *dau.* of William Hill, of Nottingham Street, Marylebone: *b.* London, W., 3 January 1888: *educ.* Brondesbury College, and London Polytechnic, Regent Street, W.: joined The Rangers, 1909; was Secretary; Polytechnic Coy. of that Corps, ret'd. 1913; re-joined on the outbreak of war: went to France 23 December 1914, and was killed in action nr. Ypres, 21 February 1915. Buried in a little cemetery just outside Ypres. Lieut. G.F. Rickett wrote, "As an officer of the Polytechnic Coy. of the Rangers I am writing to tell you of some incidents that took place in the fighting of 20 and 21 February. We were ordered to go up some very exposed trenches at dusk and remain until just before daybreak. We succeeded in taking up our position and remained all night under a fairly heavy fire, but managed all right and got away quite safely to our dug-outs in rear just before dawn. We stayed in those dug-outs all day and again at dusk took up our position at the trench. We were relieved by another battn. during the night, and I regret to say our second attempt was not so successful as the first, for we had several casualties. Amongst those killed, I grieve to say, was your son and my friend. He was killed in action doing his duty, and I am thankful to say his death was instantaneous." Age 27. *unm.*

(Panel 54) L/Corpl. 2845, Sydney Langford Parr, 1/12th (County of London) Bn. (The Rangers) The London Regt. (T.F.): only *s.* of Thomas Parr, of 8, Vernon Gardens, Seven Kings, London, N., by his wife Caroline: *b.* Manor Park, East Ham, 8 January 1891: *educ.* East Ham Technical College: enlisted September 1914: went to France, 28 January 1915, and died of wounds at St. Julien, 26 April 1915: Age 24. (*IWGC record age 25*)

(Panel 54) L/Corpl. Cecil George Sandbrook Rawlings, 12th (County of London) Bn. (The Rangers) The London Regt. (T.F.): eldest *s.* of George Rawlings, of Rosemont, Salisbury, by his wife Ida, eldest *dau.* of William Sandbrook, of The Mount, Market Drayton, co. Salop: *b.* Salisbury, co. Wilts, 11 June 1894: *educ.* Salisbury School and Denstone College (O.T.C. member): sometime employee Messrs. Story & Co., Kensington; (later) Messrs. Waring & Gillow: joined London Rangers, October 1913: volunteered for Foreign Service on the outbreak of war August 1914: went to France, Christmas Eve following, and was killed in action near Ypres, 15 February 1915. Capt. Arbuthnot, in sending the news to his parents, wrote, "Just as it was getting light on the morning of the 15th, two platoons under Major V. Hoare were sent out to obtain information for the Brigade Gen., and to act as supports to some troops in front. It was not an easy task to move across the open in daylight, but Major Hoare's leading was skilful, and he found the way into the shelter of a trench. When he had got about three-quarters of the men in the trench a shell burst right in the trench, and I most deeply regret to say it killed Major Hoare and three men, one of those killed I grieve to say was your son. He was killed in action doing his duty. When darkness came on in the evening we buried him about 30 yards behind the trench. A Capt. of the King's Royal Rifles read the burial service, abbreviated, by the light of an electric torch, while we stood round in a half-circle to prevent the Germans seeing the light and firing on us. I can assure you that your son's death is a real loss to the company; he always did his work so calmly and efficiently, and at the same time he was a great favourite with the whole platoon." Age 20. *unm.* Remains (three) 'Unknown British Soldier. 12.T Londons' exhumed, identified – Clothing, Titles; reinterred, registered, 15 May 1923. Collective Grave. *Buried in Sanctuary Wood Cemetery (II.B.1/3).*

(Panel 54) Rfn. 1667, Edwin Ashton, 1/12th (County of London) Bn. (The Rangers) The London Regt. (T.F.): former Apprentice Engineer: *s.* of Edwin Ashton, Fancy Leather worker; of 116, Catford Road, Tooting, London, S.E., by his wife Eliza Jane: *b.* Peckham, 7 April 1895: a Scout and Patrol Leader from age 13 to age 18, when he joined the Rangers. Killed in action at Zonnebeke, 20 April 1915. Capt. Jones wrote, "He was hit by a bullet on the evening of the 20th, and died soon afterwards. We buried him that night in a small wood behind our trench. He was a man for whom I had a great liking; a good soldier, and he died doing his duty." Age 20. *unm.*

(Panel 54) Rfn. 2154, Ernest William Barge, 12th (County of London) Bn. (The Rangers) The London Regt. (T.F.): served with the Expeditionary in France from Christmas Day 1914: moved up to Ypres sector 8 February 1915, and was killed in action 2 March following; on which date his company had been sent forward for 24 hours to assist, and strengthen, the battalion then in the front line; 2nd Lieut. L.C. Wildsmith was also killed.

2nd Lieut. Wildsmith is buried in Ypres Town Cemetery Extension (III.A.6).

(Panel 54) Rfn. 2767, Carl Gorringe Carpenter, 1/12th (County of London) Bn. (The Rangers) The London Regt. (T.F.): *s.* of Charles Thomas Carpenter, of 'Maidworth,' 48, Shakespeare Road, Worthing, co. West Sussex, by his wife Edith: enlisted London: served with the Expeditionary Force in France from Christmas 1914; moved up to Ypres salient 8 February 1915, and was killed in action one week later, Monday, 15 February 1915: Age 20. *unm.* Remains (three) 'Unknown British Soldier. 12.T Londons' exhumed, identified – Clothing, Titles; reinterred, registered, 15 May 1923. Collective Grave. *Buried in Sanctuary Wood Cemetery (II.B.1/3).*

(Panel 54) Rfn. 2535, George Thomas Haffenden, 12th (County of London) Bn. (The Rangers) The London Regt. (T.F.): late of Regent's Park, London: *s.* of Philemon Spencer Haffenden, Bricklayer; of Westham, co. Sussex, by his wife Harriet Alice, *née* Isted: *b.* Westham, *c.*1887: Occupation – Chauffeur: enlisted London. Killed in action nr. Ypres 12 April 1915: Age 27. *unm.*

(Panel 54) Rfn. 2790, Fraser Hatcher, 1/12th (County of London) Bn. (The Rangers) The London Regt. (T.F.): 2nd *s.* of Leonard George Hatcher, Clerk in Charge, West Kensington Station, District Railway; of 7, Dorville Road, Hammersmith, by his wife Helen Johnston, *dau.* of Patrick Barry; Member of the Institute of Journalists: *b.* Shepherd's Bush, London, W., 2 November 1898: *educ.* William Street Central School: sometime member Lad's Naval Brigade (Hammersmith Branch): Occupation – Clerk;

Chief Accountant's Office, Great Western Railway Co. (joined March 1914): joined 12th London Regt., 1914, and showed so much keenness and energy in becoming efficient that he was selected for – and one of the first to join – the Service Battn.: went to France, 8 March 1915, and was killed in action, north-east of Ypres, 4 May 1915. Buried nr. Fortuin: **Age 16**.

(Panel 54) Rfn. 2869, Ronald Egerton Hedges, No.9 Coy., 12th (County of London) Bn. (The Rangers) The London Regt. (T.F.): 2nd *s*. of Frederick John Hedges, of The Shrubberies, George Lane, South Woodford, by his wife Charlotte Elizabeth, *dau*. of John Abraham, of Dunstable, co. Beds: *b*. South Woodford, co. Essex, 9 December 1896: *educ*. Woodford College and Loughton School: Occupation – Marine Engineer: volunteered on the outbreak of war, joined London Rangers, 9 September 1914: went to France, 9 March 1915, and was killed in action at the Second Battle of Ypres, 29 April 1915. Buried at Verlorenhoek. His Adjutant wrote of him, "He was brave and cheerful and one of our best, a keen soldier, eager at all times to do his duty." Age 18.

(Panel 54) Rfn. 2518, Paul James Hilleard, 1/12th (County of London) Bn. (The Rangers) The London Regt. (T.F.): *b*. St. Saviour, London, 1894: *educ*. Southend Boy's High School. Killed in action 24 April 1915. In a letter to his family, a comrade wrote, "We had finished an eight day spell in the trenches to the N.E. of Ypres and had retired to our former field containing open dug-outs and rested one night. Next morning many French and Canadian troops passed by in disorderly groups having been forced by gas fumes to flee. The order came to stand to and after lunch our Battalion received orders to go up and support the Suffolks in a big attack. This we did in extended order, as it was daylight. A machine-gun played upon us apart from shrapnel and shell fire above and Paul fell saying 'Arthur I'm hit!' I was ordered to go with the rest, but ran back to pull him into a less dangerous spot. To our delight we found the bullets had merely grazed the skin, and got just through the edge of his right-hand trouser pocket! Consequently we both caught up our company (which by now had separated from the Battalion and had also passed the Suffolk's, who were pack loaded) and took possession of an empty trench, only to find the Germans creeping along it from our left. They got another wretched machine gun to play, enfilade fashion, upon us and poor Paul was shot through the eye. He died instantly without any pain whatsoever. We cleared out the enemy with the help of the Suffolk's but had to relinquish the position at midnight, owing to insufficient men (38 out of well over 100). There was just time, however to see to burying and we laid your son to rest, together with many another poor 'Ranger.'" Age 21. A well-known cricket player, Rfn. Hilleard played for Essex 2nd XI, Minor Counties Championship, 1914. His name, with that of fellow Old Southendian Frank Osborne, was added to the School Roll of Honour in 2008.

(Panel 54) Rfn. 2657, Alfred Felton Mathews, 1/12th (County of London) Bn. (The Rangers) The London Regt. (T.F.): *s*. of William Felton Mathews, of Highworth, co. Wilts, by his wife Emily, *dau*. of John Shewry, of Southampton: *b*. 2 September 1894: *educ*. Carlton Road Council School, and Polytechnic, Regent Street: employee Messrs. H.J. Nicoll & Co., Regent Street, London, W., when war broke out, but was intending to enter a missionary college as a student: joined Rangers, 5 September 1914; went to France, Christmas Day following, and was killed in action nr. Ypres, 5 May 1915. At the time of his death he was acting as a stretcher-bearer when a shell burst close to him, wounding him in the arm, but he pluckily refused to give in until quite exhausted, when he laid his groundsheet down and fell asleep. Shortly afterwards another shell came and killed him. Buried in the grounds of the Asylum, Ypres: Age 20. *unm*.

(Panel 54) Rfn. 2754, Edgar Henry Mellin, 1/12th (County of London) Bn. (The Rangers) The London Regt. (T.F.): late of West Kilburn, London: *s*. of the late Max Louis Mellin, by his wife Fanny (Prendelstrasse 4III, Leipzig, Germany): enlisted London. Killed in action 8 May 1915: Age 18.

(Panel 54) Rfn. 3128, Herbert Pearce, 1/12th (County of London) Bn. (The Rangers) The London Regt. (T.F.): late of Norwood: *s*. of the late John Pearce, by his wife Emma (9, Longley Road, Harrow, co. Middlesex): and elder brother to Rfn. Z/2905, J. Pearce, 1st Rifle Brigade, killed in action 13 May 1915: *b*. Lambeth: enlisted London. Killed in action 8 May 1915: Age 31.

His brother John also has no known grave; he is recorded on Panel 48.

(Panel 54) Rfn. 2338, Frederick Thomas George Pulsford, 1/12th (County of London) Bn. (The Rangers) The London Regt. (T.F.): only *s.* of Frederick Luke Pulsford, of 10, Tradescant Road, South Lambeth Road, London, S.W., by his wife Blanche Bertha, *dau.* of George Hawke: *b.* London, 26 June 1897: *educ.* Westminster City School: volunteered and joined The Rangers after the outbreak of war, 8 September 1914: went to France, 9 March 1915, and was killed in action at Zonnebeke, 21 April 1915. Buried at the back of the trenches there. 2nd Lieut. H.H. Bentley wrote, "On 21 April your son and his friend Elvin were in a dug-out at Zonnebeke, tending to the pressing wants of a comrade who was dreadfully wounded. As they busied themselves with him, a German shrapnel fell into the dug-out and burst. The violence of the explosion, and the deadly hail of shrapnel bullets, annihilated all the occupants of the dug-out, and the Rangers lost two fine soldiers in the painless heroic deaths of your son and his friend Elvin. It gives me great pain to have to break this sad yet heroic news to you, because he was always a great friend of mine and one who always did the utmost of his duty." Age 17.

(Panel 54) Rfn. 1422, Sydney Walter Rush, 12th (County of London) Bn. (The Rangers) The London Regt. (T.F.): eldest *s.* of Walter Rush, Draper & Ladies Outfitter; of 27-29, Uxbridge Road, Shepherd's Bush, London, W., by his wife Annie Elizabeth, *dau.* of J.R. Collender, of Bow, London, E.: *b.* Paddington, London, W., 21 September 1890: *educ.* Mathematical School, Rochester: was partner in his father's business: a pre-war member of the Territorial Force (joined Rangers, February 1912), volunteered for Foreign Service on the outbreak of war, and enlisted Chenies Street, London, August 1914: went to France, 24 December, and was killed in action at St. Eloi, nr. Ypres, 15 February 1915. Buried behind the trenches nr. Menin Cemetery: Age 24. *unm.* His Capt. wrote expressing great regret at his loss, adding how devoted he was to his duty, and what a wonderful capacity he had for 'sticking it.' Remains (three) 'Unknown British Soldier. 12.T Londons' exhumed, identified – Clothing, Disc; reinterred, registered, 15 May 1923. Of the three sets of remains recovered, only those of Rfn. Rush could be identified with any degree of certainty. *Buried in Sanctuary Wood Cemetery (II.B.2).*

Till The Day Breaks
And The Shadows Flee Away

(Panel 54) Rfn. 1886, Sidney Herbert Whiles, 12th (County of London) Bn. (The Rangers) The London Regt. (T.F.): eldest *s.* of William Herbert Whiles, of 70, Northcote Road, Walthamstow, late Private No. 6824, Army Service Corps (served with the Expeditionary Force in France and Flanders; discharged, April 1916, owing to eye injury), by his wife Margaret, *dau.* of John Steuber: *b.* Leytonstone, 19 November 1896: *educ.* Forest Road Council School, Walthamstow, and Walthamstow Higher Elementary school, at both of which he gained prizes for mathematics, and also showed proficiency in Art and Divinity: Occupation – Clerk; National Amalgamated Insurance Society: joined The Rangers, January 1914, and volunteered for Imperial Service on the outbreak of war: went to France with the first draft for his battn. (part of 11th Brigade, 4th Division), and was killed in action near the village of Fortuin during the Second Battle of Ypres, 26 April 1915. His Commander wrote:– That he was a gallant soldier throughout and that he personally regretted his loss, as he frequently accompanied his officer on billet finding expeditions, in which his knowledge of French enabled him to act as interpreter. A brass plate to his memory was placed in the church of St. Michael & All Angels, Walthamstow (where he was a chorister for eight years), by his old comrades. Age 18.

(Panel 54) 2nd Lieut. Edgar Raymond Seabury, 13th (County of London) Bn. (Princess Louise's Kensington Rifles) The London Regt. (T.F.): *s.* of Edward Seabury, Engineer; of Garth, Broxbourne, co. Hertford, by his wife Emily, *dau.* of Charles Wyatt: *b.* Netteswell, co. Essex, 2 May 1898: *educ.* St. Catherine's, Broxbourne, and Harlow College: Occupation – Bank Clerk: joined 13th London Regt. May 1916: gazetted 2nd Lieut. 8 May 1917: served with the Expeditionary Force in France and Flanders from 5 July following, and was killed in action nr. St. Julien, 20 September of the same year. An officer wrote, "He was leading his platoon in an attack, and was doing splendid work when he was hit by a piece of an enemy shell and instantly killed. He had not been with us long, but had endeared himself to us in an extraordinary manner, and all of us, both officers and men, will never forget him and his wonderful charm. He was a most promising young officer, and had he been spared would have gone far, I am sure. He was the most popular officer in the company, and deservedly so. He was always cheery." He was a keen sportsman, and captained his college cricket and football teams. Age 19. (*IWGC record 21 September*)

(Panel 54) Pte. 613147, William Richard Piggott, 1/13th (County of London) Bn. (Princess Louise's Kensington Rifles) The London Regt. (T.F.): 2nd *s.* of Thomas Piggott, of 33, Sutherton Road, Hammersmith, London, W., by his wife Ellen, *dau.* of Richard Aldridge: *b.* Hammersmith, *c.*1897: *educ.* there: volunteered for Active Service on the outbreak of war, August 1914; joined London Regt.: served with the Expeditionary Force in France and Flanders for 12 months, and was killed in action 23 August 1917. Buried where he fell: Age 20. *unm.* (*IWGC record 1/19th Bn.*)

(Panel 54) Lieut. John Charles Lancelot Farquarson, 14th (County of London) Bn. (London Scottish) The London Regt. (T.F.): 7th *s.* of the late Lieut.Col. M.H. Farquarson, R.M.L.I., by his wife Emma ('Glengarry,' The Grove, Woking, co. Surrey): and brother to Lieut.Col. C.G. Farquarson, M.C., 2nd Royal Marine Light Infantry, died of wounds, 24 March 1918, at No.3 C.C.S, Dernancourt. Missing / believed killed in action 31 October – 1 November 1914, following the fighting at Messines: Age 33. Remembered on Horsell (St. Mary's) Parish Church War Memorial, and Woking First World War Roll of Honour. (*IWGC record Farquharson*)

His brother Cecil is buried in Dernancourt Communal Cemetery Extension (X.D.9).

(Panel 54) Sergt. 122, William Tindal Fitchie, 'B' Coy., 14th (County of London) Bn. (London Scottish) The London Regt. (T.F.): *s.* of T. Tindal Fitchie, of 79, Nightingale Lane, Balham, London, S.W.12, and the late Mrs M.A. Fitchie: *b.* Edinburgh, 1879: previously served with Gordon Highlanders in the South African Campaign: returned to the Colours on the outbreak of war, Buckingham Gate, London, 4 August 1914: served with the Expeditionary Force in France and Flanders from 16 September following, and reported 'Missing' following the charge of the London Scottish at Messines on the night of 31 October – 1 November 1914: Age 35. Any information regarding her late husband should be addressed to Mrs. Mary Edith Fitchie (42, Union Road, Clapham, London, S.W.4).

(Panel 54) Sergt. 17, Lionel Purvis, 'F' Coy., 14th (County of London) Bn. (London Scottish) The London Regt. (T.F.): *yst. s.* of John Prior Purvis, Surgeon; of 16, The Grove, Blackheath, London, S.E., by his wife Frances Mary, *dau.* of William Vaughan: *b.* Greenwich, S.E., 19 July 1873: *educ.* Roan School, Greenwich: Occupation – Furniture Manufacturer: joined London Scottish Rifle Volunteers (7th Middlesex), 12 November 1894: volunteered for Foreign Service, Buckingham Gate, on the outbreak of war, August 1914: proceeded to France, 14 September 1914, and was killed in action at Messines, 1 November following. Sergt. Purvis won many prizes at Bisley and elsewhere, coming 7th in the King's Prize Competition at Bisley (1904), and twice being a member of the winning team for the '*Daily Telegraph*' Cup: Age 41. *unm.*

(Panel 54) Corpl. Piper 139, Harry Gould Latham, 1/14th (County of London) Bn. (London Scottish) The London Regt. (T.F.): late of Russell Square, London: *s.* of the late Albert Latham, M.I.C.E.: *b.* Margate, co. Kent: enlisted London. Killed in action 16 November 1914, at Zillebeke: Age 29. *unm.* Corpl. Latham was a crack shot and had qualified for the final stages of King's Hundred at Bisley (1914). He was Mentioned in Despatches when, following the heavy casualties incurred at Messines in which he took a prominent part, the battalion pipers were employed in the ranks and due to his proficiency with a rifle he was employed as a sniper with much success.

(Panel 54) L/Corpl. 142, James Carey; Piper, 1/14th (County of London) Bn. (London Scottish) The London Regt. (T.F.): late of Charing Cross, London: *s.* of Jane Carey (Dunnichen Villa, Invergowrie, co. Dundee): *b.* Dundee: former employee London County Council Architects Dept.: a pre-war Territorial; joined London Scottish, 1908; volunteered for Overseas Service, Buckingham Gate, August 1914: served with the Expeditionary Force in France from September following. Died in enemy hands (prisoner), 1 November 1914, of wounds: Age 31. Remembered on Invergowrie (Longforgan Parish) War Memorial.

(Panel 54) L/Corpl. 785, James Roy Hamilton, 1/14th (County of London) Bn. (London Scottish) The London Regt. (T.F.): late of Highgate, London, N.6.: *s.* of James Hamilton, J.P., of West Bank, York, by his wife Jane Selkirk: Occupation – Clerk; Messrs Lloyds, London: *b*. St. Pancras, 1889: enlisted London. Killed in action 1 November 1914, at Messines: Age 25. *unm*. One of five brothers who served.

(Panel 54) Pte. 3085, Archibald Angus, 'C' Coy., 1/14th (County of London) Bn. (London Scottish) The London Regt. (T.F.): 2nd *survg. s.* of the late David Angus, M.Inst.C.E., former Consulting Engineer, by his marriage to Mary (9, Muswell Road, London, N.), *dau.* of the late Rev. Thomas Clark Wilson, E.C. Scotland, Minister of Dunkeld Cathedral (1846 – 77): and *yr.* brother to 2nd Lieut. S. Angus, Royal Engineers (T.F.), killed in action at Hebuterne, during the Battle of Gommecourt, 2 July 1916: *b*. Colico, Province of Arauco, Chile, 7 April 1897: *educ*. Edinburgh Academy, 1908 – 14, where he was pipe-major of the band during his last year: joined 2nd Bn. London Scottish, as Piper, 3 September 1914, after the outbreak of war: transf'd. 1st Battn. on its being ordered to the Front: served with the Expeditionary Force in France and Flanders from 15 September 1914. Reported wounded and missing after the fighting at Messines, 1 November following; assumed (1916) to have been killed in action on that date: Age 17.

His brother Stewart also has no known grave; he is commemorated on the Thiepval Memorial, Somme.

(Panel 54) Pte. 1903, Eldred Cole Banfield, 1/14th (County of London) Bn. (London Scottish) The London Regt. (T.F.): late of Dulwich: *s.* of Eldred Wilks Banfield, of Holy Vale, St. Mary's, Scilly, Penzance, by his wife Ellen Harvey: and elder brother to 2nd Lieut. C.B. Banfield, 8th Sqdn. Royal Flying Corps, killed in action 21 March 1918: *b*. Penzance, co. Cornwall, 1895: enlisted London. Killed in action at Messines, 1 November 1914: Age 19.

His brother Cyril also has no known grave; he is commemorated on the Arras Flying Services Memorial.

(Panel 54) Pte. 1547, Kenneth Barclay, 'G' Coy., 1/14th (County of London) Bn. (London Scottish) The London Regt. (T.F.): 3rd *s.* of Henry James Barclay, of 'Wapella,' Silverdale, Sydenham, London, S.E., by his wife Mary Allen, *dau.* of the late Allen Stoneham, Financial Secretary, Board of Trade: and yr. brother Lieut. A. Barclay, 170th Coy., Royal Engineers, killed in action 24 April 1915, at Givenchy; aged 28 years: *b*. Sydenham, 31 December 1892: *educ*. The Hall, Sydenham, and Dulwich College: joined London Scottish, May 1911: volunteered for Foreign Service on the outbreak of war, took part in the charge at Messines and the first battles of Ypres, and was killed in action, 12 November 1914. His Colonel, in writing, said, "No commanding officer could have had under his command a braver or more gallant soldier." The bell of St. Philip's Church, Sydenham, suitably inscribed, commemorates him, and a beautiful memorial in bronze and hammered ironwork was placed in the chancel of that church, where for years he sang in the choir: Age 21. *unm*.

His brother Allen also has no known grave; he is commemorated on the Le Touret Memorial (Panel 1).

(Panel 54) Pte. 1685, Maurice Steel Bryce, 'B' Coy., 1/14th (County of London) Bn. (London Scottish) The London Regt. (T.F.): *s.* of Alexander Bryce, of 8, Lessar Avenue, Clapham Common, London, and his wife Christian Stenhouse Bryce: Occupation – Clerk; London County Council Architects Dept. Missing / believed killed in action 31 October – 1 November 1914, 'when the 14th London won their laurels near Messines; the first occasion when a Territorial battalion had fought as a complete unit by the side of the Regular Army.' Age 23.

(Panel 54) Pte. 1745, Leonard George Coldwells, 'F' Coy., 1/14th (County of London) Bn. (London Scottish) (T.F.): *s.* of Joseph George Coldwells, of 'Glenalmond,' Egmont Road, Sutton, co. Surrey, by his wife Elizabeth: and brother to 2nd Lieut. F.B. Coldwells, Devonshire Regt., killed in action 1 July 1916, at the Somme; and 2nd Lieut. C.A. Coldwells, Royal Field Artillery, killed in action 28 September 1915, at Loos: *b*. Purley: enlisted London. Killed in action 31 October 1914, at Messines: Age 20. Inscribed 'This Sign Of The Great Sacrifice Is Raised In Honour Of Our Heroic Dead, Who Gave Their Lives For England In The Great War: Their Name Liveth For Evermore;' the brothers Coldwells are remembered on the Sutton War Memorial.

His brother Francis also has no known grave, he is commemorated on the Thiepval Memorial (Pier & Face 1C); Charles is buried in Dud Corner Cemetery (VII.F.16).

(Panel 54) Pte. 2160, Tom Crafter, 1/14th (County of London) Bn. (London Scottish) The London Regt. (T.F.): late of Forest Hill, London: brother to Lieut. J. Crafter, M.C., 20 Sqdn, Royal Flying Corps and 20th Bn. London Regt., killed in action 7 July 1917: Occupation – Clerk; London Stock Exchange: enlisted London: served with the Expeditionary Force in France from 15 September 1914, and was killed in action 12 November 1914.

His brother James also has no known grave; he is commemorated on the Arras Flying Services Memorial.

(Panel 54) Pte. 1818, William Francis Dunlop, Bugler, 'C' Coy., 1/14th (County of London) Bn. (London Scottish) The London Regt. (T.F.): *s.* of the late William Alexander Dunlop, of Thames Ditton, co. Surrey, by his wife Mrs R.L. Dunlop (119, Chadwick Road, Peckham, London, S.E.): and elder brother to Pte. 510716, J.V. Dunlop, 1/14th London Regt., killed in action, 7 October 1916, aged 19 years: *b.* Thames Ditton, 1893: joined 'C' Coy., London Scottish, 31 March 1913: volunteered for Foreign Service on the outbreak of war: served with the Expeditionary Force in France and Flanders from 15 September 1914, and reported missing / believed killed in action during the charge of the London Scottish at Messines on the night of 30 October – 1 November 1914. Col. A.J. Masterton, 12th Lancers, later recalled how, during a lull in the fighting on the night of Halloween 1914, he found a young bugler badly wounded. He gave him water and made him comfortable, then stayed with him until he died. A comrade, Herbert de Hamel, gave the following account, "All through the inferno I was held by the pluck of the man next to me; in the very worst moments he was as bright and cheery as was his usual habit of life. He must have felt afraid, as we all did, but he showed no sign of it. After one particularly lively outburst of assorted shells he remarked, 'I suppose that after a couple more days we shall go back into a reserve trench.' 'Probably this is a reserve trench,' I suggested 'and tomorrow we shall get the real thing.' 'You always were a cheerful blighter,' replied Bugler Dunlop and we both laughed. Two days later I was told of his death out in the open." After his death his bugle was given to the Officer Commanding, 12th Lancers, whose regiment treasured it for many years thereafter: Age 21. *unm.*

His brother John also has no known grave; he is commemorated on the Thiepval Memorial, Somme.

(Panel 54) Pte. 2006, Ernest Frederick Green, 1/14th (County of London) Bn. (London Scottish) The London Regt. (T.F.): *s.* of William George Green, of 7, High Road, Buckhurst Hill, co. Essex: *b.* Hackney, London, 1893: *educ.* City of London School; Gold Medallist (Gymnasia), 1911: volunteered for Active Service on the outbreak of war: served with the Expeditionary Force in France from 15 September 1914. Reported missing / believed killed 30 October – 1 November 1914, after the famous charge by the London Scottish at Messines: Age 21. *unm.*

(Panel 54) Pte. 1310, Leonard Percy Hewett, 1/14th (County of London) Bn. (London Scottish) The London Regt. (T.F.): *s.* of L.W. Hewett, Esq., of 10, Milton Road, Hanwell, London: *b.* Paddington: Occupation – Clerk; Securities Dept., Messrs Coutts & Co., 440, The Strand: a pre-war Territorial; joined London Scottish, 1910: volunteered for Overseas Service on the outbreak of war: served with the Expeditionary Force in France and Flanders, from 16 September 1914. Missing / believed killed in action 31 October – 1 November 1914, at Messines, Belgium: Age 20.

(Panel 54) Pte. 1781, Robert Bruce Kyle, 1/14th (County of London) Bn. (London Scottish) The London Regt. (T.F.): *yr. s.* of the late John Kyle, M.I.C.E., Resident Engineer, Harbour Works, Colombo, Ceylon, by his wife Agnes (100, Station Road, Barnes, London, S.W.): *b.* Colombo, 30 April 1893: *educ.* Kelvinside Academy, Glasgow; and Royal High School, Edinburgh: Member (Foreign Staff); Hong Kong & Shanghai Bank: joined London Scottish, January 1913: volunteered for Imperial Service on the outbreak of war: left for France, 15 September 1914, and was killed in action at the charge of the London Scottish at Messines, 1 November following. Initially reported missing, it was not until 15 February 1915 that definite news he had fallen was received: Age 21. *unm.*

(Panel 54) Pte. 2131, Theodore Laing, 1/14th (County of London) Bn. (London Scottish) The London Regt. (T.F.): elder *s.* of William Arthur Laing (an old member of the London Scottish), of Dalmahoy, Horsell, Woking, by his wife Lucy Glanvill, *dau.* of William Walters: *b.* Tooting Graveney, 16 May 1897:

educ. City of London School; two years member of the O.T.C.: enlisted in his father's old regiment the day before the declaration of war, 4 August 1914: went to France with the Expeditionary Force, 15 September 1914, and fell in the charge of the London Scottish at Messines, 1 November 1914. His Capt. wrote, "Your brave son was shot through the head, and death must have been almost instantaneous. He was one of our keenest soldiers in the company, and his loss will be greatly felt by all his comrades, with whom he was a great favourite. I, personally, shall miss him intensely." Though not 18, Laing was over 6 ft. in height, big and broad in proportion; he was also a first-class shot: Age 17.

(Panel 54) Pte. 1730, Alistair Allan MacGillivray Maclean, 1/14th (County of London) Bn. (London Scottish) The London Regt. (T.F.): 3rd *s.* of Alexander Maclean, Farmer; of Gordon Hall, Kingussie, co. Inverness, by his wife Margery, *dau.* of Finlay McGillivray: and elder brother to Pte. V.McG. Maclean, Royal Garrison Artillery, who fell 29 November 1917: *b.* Gordon Hall, 4 May 1894: *educ.* Kingussie Higher Grade School: Occupation – Clerk; London Branch, Bank of Montreal: joined London Scottish, 1913: volunteered for Foreign Service on the outbreak of war, August 1914: went to France, 15 September: severely wounded by shellfire at the First Battle of Ypres, 11 November 1914, during the intense and stubborn fighting in which the London Scottish nobly acquitted themselves, and died at Poperinghe three days later, 14 November 1914. Buried at Poperinghe: Age 20. *unm.*

His brother Victor lies nearby in Ypres Town Cemetery Extension (III.G.25).

(Panel 54) Pte. 2211, Allan Muir Morten, 14th (County of London) Bn. (London Scottish) The London Regt. (T.F.): *s.* of J.G. Morten, of 99, Newgate Street, London, E.C.1: and brother to 2nd Lieut. G. Morten, 1st King's (Liverpool) Regt., missing 16 – 19 May 1915, since confirmed as being killed in action on the former date: *b.* Sutton, *c.*1894: enlisted London: served with the Expeditionary Force in France from 15 September 1914. Killed in action 1 November 1914, at Messines: Age 20. *unm.*

His brother Galbraith is buried in Rue-Des-Berceaux Military Cemetery (II.E.6).

(Panel 54) Pte. 2093, George Edward Randall, 1/14th (County of London) Bn. (London Scottish) The London Regt. (T.F.): *yr. s.* of Charles William Randall, Merchant; of Barton Bendish, Alderton Hill, Loughton, co. Essex, by his wife Emma, *dau.* of Edward Witton, of South Lopham, co. Norfolk: *b.* Norwich, 29 February 1892: *educ.* Sidcup College: was engaged in his father's business as Managing Director of Hamburg (Germany) branch and Director of C.W. Randall & Co. Ltd., London: joined London Scottish, 15 June 1914: volunteered for Foreign Service on the outbreak of war August following: went to France 15 September, with the first batch of Territorials to leave for the Front, and was killed in action at Messines, 1 November following, during the famous charge of the London Scottish. Buried there: Age 22. *unm.* A window to his memory was erected in Woodford Parish Church.

(Panel 54) Pte. 3136, Ronald Edward Mackenzie Richards, 'D' Coy., 1/14th (County of London) Bn. (London Scottish) The London Regt. (T.F.): *s.* of the late Frederick Edward Richards, by his wife Lilian Annie (7, Meadway Close, Meadway, Golders Green, London, N.W.): *b.* Foo Chow, China, 13 March 1895: *educ.* Colet House, Rhyl, Wales; Berkhampstead School, co. Hertford; Trinity College, University of Toronto (Forestry), 1912 – 14: Occupation – Student. On the outbreak of war was in England on summer vacation and enlisted London Scottish, August 1914: proceeded to France (14 September), where he took part in the famous charge of his battalion at Messines (1 November), and was killed by a shell two weeks later, 14 November 1914, in a wood near Ypres: Age 19. Pte. Richards was the first University of Toronto student to fall in the Great War.

(Panel 54) Pte. 1328, Donald Hamilton Ross, 1/14th (County of London) Bn. (London Scottish) The London Regt. (T.F.): *b.* Lewisham, London, S.E.: enlisted Horseferry Road, London, S.W.1. Killed in action 1 November 1914.

(Panel 54) Pte. 2565, James Ross, 1/14th (County of London) Bn. (London Scottish) The London Regt. (T.F.): late of Chipstead, co. Surrey: *s.* of Richard Ross: *b.* Rutherford, co. Roxburgh, 1880: *educ.* Cargilfield, Trinity, Edinburgh, and Fettes College (played in the Hockey XI, Cricket XI, Rugby XV [Capt. 1897 – 89], and took several prizes): after leaving school took up a position with Messrs Renton Bros & Co. (1899), joining London Stock Exchange, 1905 (Member), continuing his sporting activities as time permitted. In the season 1901 – 02 he won his Scottish International Cap as forward, thereafter taking up rowing being sometime a member of Kingston Rowing Club, thereafter took up golf and after joining Raynes Park Golf Club transferred to Chipstead where he was resident and for which club he was playing at the time of his enlistment: served with the Expeditionary Force in France and Flanders from 15 September 1914. Reported missing after the fighting 31 October 1914, since which date no further word has been received of him: Age 34.

(Panel 54) Pte. 2233, James Methuen Ross, 1/14th (County of London) Bn. (London Scottish) The London Regt. (T.F.): late of Highbury, London, N.5: *s.* of Grace Ross (65, Cluny Gardens, Edinburgh, co. Midlothian): *b.* Dundonald, nr. Kilmarnock, co. Ayr: enlisted Horseferry Road, London, S.W.1: served with the Expeditionary Force in France and Flanders from September 1914. Reported missing / believed killed in action at Messines, 1 November following.

(Panel 54) Pte. 3135, Albert Brian Sarll, 'H' Coy., 1/14th (County of London) Bn. (London Scottish) The London Regt. (T.F.): *s.* of the late Albert Sarll, by his wife Margaret (6, Melody Road, Wandsworth, London): *educ.* Shillington Street School; Battersea Grammar School; Islington Training College: Occupation – Schoolmaster; London County Council Education Dept. (Gopsall Street School): volunteered and enlisted on the outbreak of war. Missing / believed killed in action at Messines, 1 November 1914: Age 23. He was a member of Roehampton & Mitcham Football & Cricket Club. Remembered on Graveney School War Memorial, Battersea.

(Panel 54) Pte. 2026, Herbert Ashford Walford, 1/14th (County of London) Bn. (London Scottish) The London Regt. (T.F.): eldest *s.* of the late Thomas Charles Walford, of Maidenhead, Mineral Manager, Great Western Railway, by his 1st wife, Mary Ann Ashford, *dau.* of Thomas Hobbs, of Tiverton: and elder brother to Pte. L.F. Walford, who was in the same battn.; wounded and taken a prisoner, 31 October 1914, and died the next day: *b.* Southall, co. Middlesex, 26 February 1889: *educ.* Maidenhead College: Occupation – Staff; Messrs Eveson & Co., Coal Merchants: joined London Scottish, February 1914: volunteered for Foreign Service on the outbreak of war: went to France, 15 September 1914. Reported missing after the charge of the London Scottish at Messines, 31 October following; assumed killed in action on that date: Age 24. *unm.* (*IWGC record A. Walford, 1 November 1914*)

His brother Leslie also has no known grave; he is recorded below.

(Panel 54) Pte. 2048, Leslie Francis Walford, 1/14th (County of London) Bn. (London Scottish) The London Regt. (T.F.): 2nd *s.* of the late Thomas Charles Walford, of Maidenhead; Mineral Manager, Great Western Railway, by his 1st wife Mary Ann Ashford, *dau.* of Thomas Hobbs, of Tiverton: and *yr.* brother to Pte. 2026, H.A. Walford, London Scottish, believed killed 31 October 1914: *b.* Southall, co. Middlesex, 6 August 1891: *educ.* Maidenhead College: Occupation – Clerk; Wm. Cory's, Mark Lane: joined London Scottish, May 1914: volunteered for Imperial Service on the outbreak of war: went to France, 15 September 1914. Wounded and taken prisoner during the charge of the London Scottish at Messines, 31 October 1914, and died the following day. Buried Messines – Wytschaete. Age 23. *unm.*

His brother Herbert also has no known grave; he is recorded above.

(Panel 54) Pte. 1112, George Watson, 'B'Coy., 1/14th (County of London) Bn. (London Scottish) The London Regt. (T.F.): only *s.* of the late George Watson (first Registrar to Royal Court of Music), by his marriage to Mary Ann Alma Watson (10, Baron's Court Road, West Kensington, London, W.14): *b.* Rochester, *c.*1880: *educ.* Colet Court, and St. Paul's School: employed Secretary's Office, Great Western Railway: enlisted London: proceeded to France September 1914. Reported missing 1 November 1914, at Messines; since confirmed killed in action: Age 34.

(Panel 54) Pte. 2168, Robert Theodore Morrison Wyllie, 1/14th (County of London) Bn. (London Scottish) The London Regt. (T.F.): late of Muswell Hill, London, N.: *s.* of William Lionel Wyllie, Artist; of Tower House, Portsmouth, co. Hants, by his wife Marion Amy: and brother to Capt. W.T. Wyllie, 1st Durham Light Infantry, killed in action 19 July 1916: *b.* Rochester, co. Kent, 1888: prior to enlistment Horseferry Road, London, was employee London County Council Architects Dept.: served with the

Expeditionary Force in France from 16 September 1914. Reported missing / believed killed in action 31 October – 1 November 1914, nr. Messines: Age 26.

His brother William is buried in Dantzig Alley British Cemetery (VIII.F.9).

(Panel 54) 2nd Lieut. John McClure Northam, 15th (County of London) Bn. The Prince of Wales's Own (Civil Service Rifles) The London Regt. (T.F.): *s.* of John Northam, of 27, Vicars Hill, Ladywell, Lewisham, London, S.E.13, by his marriage to the late Elizabeth Jane Northam: and yr. brother to Rfn. 291, G.P. Northam, London Rifle Brigade, who fell 3 May 1915, nr. Fortuin: previously served as Rfn., L.R.B., 1915 – 1916, and, after obtaining a commission, was killed in action 15 September 1917, nr. Inverness Copse: Age 22. *unm.*

His brother George also has no known grave, he is recorded above.

(Panel 54) Sergt. 531269, Abraham Hertz, 1/15th (County of London) Bn. (Prince of Wales's Own Civil Service Rifles) The London Regt. (T.F.): late of 40, Wenlake Buildings, Old Street, London, E.C.: *s.* of Isaac Hertz, of 1, Cranley Buildings, Holborn, London, E.C., by his wife Annie: Occupation – Civil Servant; Board of Trade, Labour Dept. In a period described by the Battalion History as 'three very unlucky days,' Sergt. Hertz was one of seven men of his battalion killed in action 3 July 1917: Age 21. *unm.*

(Panel 54) L/Corpl. 4615, Thomas John McAdoo, 'C' Coy., 1/15th (County of London) Bn. (Prince of Wales Own Civil Service Rifles) The London Regt. (T.F.): 3rd *s.* of the late Thomas McAdoo, Farmer; of Kilcreen, Selloo, Clones, Co. Monaghan, by his wife Elizabeth, *dau.* of William Waide: *b.* Kilcreen, Selloo, 24 May 1897: *educ.* High School, Clones, and Skerry's College, Dublin: Occupation – Civil Servant; Education Office, London: joined Civil Service Rifles, 15 November 1915: served with the Expeditionary Force in France and Flanders from 14 May 1916, and was killed in action 12 January 1917. Capt. H.D. Oliver wrote, "He was always bright and cheerful, and ever ready to do what was expected of him. I had just given him the first promotion, and in losing him I have lost a very good N.C.O." Age 20. *unm.* (*IWGC record Pte.*)

(Panel 54) Pte. 535425, Eric Percy Blaxland, 15th (County of London) Bn. (Prince of Wales's Own Civil Service Rifles) The London Regt. (T.F.): apptd. 1/9th Bn. (Queen Victoria's Rifles) London Regt.: *b.* Sandwich, co. Kent, 1896: enlisted Falmouth. Killed in action 16 August 1917: Age 21. Remembered on Sandwich St. Mary the Virgin (& St. Peter's) Parish War Memorials.

(Panel 54) Pte. 533219, Herbert Courtney, 1/15th (County of London) Bn. (Prince of Wales's Own Civil Service Rifles) The London Regt. (T.F.): *s.* of Mr (& Mrs) Courtney, of Richmond: and *yr.* brother to Corpl. 13288, E. Courtney, 9th Norfolk Regt., died 1 December 1918: *b.* Fulham, London: enlisted Richmond, co. Surrey. Killed in action 7 June 1917: Age 20.

His brother Ernest is buried in Premont British Cemetery (III.D.13).

Following a period of reorganisation and training at St. Omer after taking part in the capture of the Messines – Wytschaete Ridge, Civil Service Rifles returned to the front. There followed what the Battalion History describes as 'three very unlucky days': 'The weather was bad, the trenches were in a perfectly rotten state of repair, the men had no protection against persistent shelling ... the losses from shell fire amounted to about 40 all ranks." 30 June – 3 July 1917: 8 O.R. killed, 1 died of wounds. The only one to die on the first of these three very unlucky days – Rfn. Hartley. Very, very unlucky!

(Panel 54) Rfn. 532121, Ernest Hartley, 1/15th (County of London) Bn. (Prince of Wales' Own Civil Service Rifles) The London Regt. (T.F.): late of Chelsea, London, S.W.3: Occupation – Civil Servant; Abstractor, Board of Trade, Finance Dept.: enlisted Somerset House, Strand, London. Killed in action 30 June 1917. The only member of his battalion killed on that day.

(Panel 54) Pte. 532224, Alan Frank Pearson, 1/15th (County of London) Bn. (Prince of Wales' Own Civil Service Rifles) The London Regt. (T.F.): formerly no.4926, London Regt.: *s.* of Harry Pearson, of 'Woodruff,' Vicarage Road, Great Cornard, co. Suffolk, by his 2nd wife, Elizabeth: and half-brother to Pte. 55934, F.C. Pearson, Machine Gun Corps (Inf.), killed at Ypres, 31 July 1917; and Pte. 4812, W.H. Pearson, 8th East Surrey Regt., killed 1 July 1916: *b.* Upper Norwood, co. Surrey: *educ.* Bury St. Edmunds Grammar School, thereafter went on to college where, on the outbreak of war, he had just passed the first examination for the degree Bachelor of Science: enlisted Somerset House, Strand: served with the Expeditionary Force in France from March 1915: took part in the Battle of Aubers Ridge, Festubert, Loos, Flers-Courcelette, Le Transloy, and was reported missing / believed killed 22 December 1916, after failing to return from a successful bombing attack on the German trenches: Age 18.

His half-brother Frederick also has no known grave, he is recorded on Panel 56; William is buried in Delville Wood Cemetery (XVI.P.4).

(Panel 54) Pte. 535237, Gilbert Arthur Wagg, 1/15th (County of London) Bn. (Prince of Wales' Own Civil Service Rifles) The London Regt. (T.F.): *s.* of Arthur Thomas Wagg, of 166, North Street, Wolverhampton, co. Stafford, by his wife Ada: and brother to Pte. 421030, E.D. Wagg, Royal Army Medical Corps, died of wounds (gas) 10 May 1918, in the Base Hospital, Etaples: enlisted Wolverhampton. Killed in action 16 August 1917: Age. 19.

His brother Edward is buried in Etaples Military Cemetery (LXVII.B.27).

(Panel 54) L/Corpl. 2816, William Theodore Bushell, 'A' Coy., 16th (County of London) Bn. (Queen's Westminster Rifles) The London Regt. (T.F.): eldest *s.* of Arthur Forest Bushell, of 39, Moreton Place, Pimlico, London, S.W., and Biggin Hill, Westerham, Kent, by his wife Sarah Ann, *dau.* of William Cooper, of Milton, Kent: *b.* Pimlico, 17 July 1883: *educ.* Westminster Training College, and was for some 14 years in the employ of Messrs. J.W. Benson Ltd., Ludgate Hill: joined 1st Cadet Battn. Queen's Royal West Surrey Regt., 27 February 1899, age 15; leaving 11 January 1900: thereafter served with the Old 13th Middlesex Queen's Westminster Volunteers, 5 November 1900 – 8 December 1904: rejoined, 2 September 1914, after the outbreak of war: went to France late January 1915. The Westminsters were stationed at Houplines, near Armentieres, until 28 May when they were moved up to Ypres. At the Battle of Hooge they were in reserve and were heavily bombarded the whole time. Bushell was hit in the head by a piece of shrapnel shell, and was killed instantaneously at midnight on 16 – 17 June 1915. He was buried on the side of the Potijze-Hooge Road, about half a mile from Potijze. His Commanding Officer, Capt. Stanley Low, wrote, "He was killed by shrapnel whilst doing his duty nobly in the trenches. He was very popular and will be sadly missed by his comrades. I should like to say how well his brother (who recently joined us) behaved, by restraining his natural inclination to go to his brother's assistance, and remaining on sentry go until someone came to relieve him." Lieut. R.S. Dickinson wrote of him as "One of the best soldiers" in his platoon. His third brother, Harry George, joined the Warwickshires on the outbreak of war, and was later transferred to the Westminsters, being with his brother when he was killed. He is now (1916) a 2nd Lieut. in the 10th Suffolks. His next brother, Arthur Frederick, is serving with the Army Service Corps: Age 31. *unm.*

(Panel 54) Rfn. 1993, Athole Stanley Ford, 1/16th (County of London) Bn. (Queen's Westminster Rifles) The London Regt. (T.F.): only *s.* of Stanley Ford, of 1, Ardlui Road, West Norwood, London, S.E., by his wife Mary Elizabeth, *dau.* of William Armstrong: *b.* Dulwich, London, S.E., 9 March 1896: *educ.* Dulwich College (Corpl., O.T.C., and member of the 'Gym' Six): joined Queen's Westminsters for Foreign Service, 6 August 1914, the day following the Declaration of War: trained Hemel Hempstead: crossed to France, 1 November 1914, and was killed in action on the Menin Road, 9 August 1915, whilst carrying bombs to a captured German trench at Hooge. One of his officers wrote that he "made a fine, plucky little soldier and he was universally popular;" and his Corpl., "He was a good lad, a fearless soldier, a splendid comrade – one I was proud to call my friend. By his courage, sympathy and cheerfulness, even under the most trying circumstances during all these months, he endeared himself to us all and deeply we feel his loss." Age 24. *unm.*

(Panel 54) Rfn. 553194, Harold Ralph Holmes, 'D' Coy., 1/16th (County of London) Bn. (Queen's Westminster Rifles) The London Regt. (T.F.): *s.* of the late Frederick Holmes (*d.*1906), Publican, 'The Pomfret,' Colliers Water Lane, Thornton Heath, co. Surrey, by his marriage to Ellen A. Hardy, *née* Holmes (12, Godson Road, Waddon, co. Surrey): and brother to Pte. 34818, S.E. Holmes, 7th Royal Fusiliers, killed in action 13 November 1916, at the Somme: *b.* Croydon, August 1897: *educ.* Croydon

School: Occupation – Clerk; London City & Midland Bank, Head Office, Threadneedle Street, London, E.C.: enlisted Croydon, November 1914. Killed in action 16 August 1917: Age 20. *unm.*

His brother Sidney is buried in Ancre British Cemetery, Beaumont-Hamel (III.E.20).

(Panel 54) Rfn. 1910, William Austen Kerl, 1/16th (County of London) Bn. (Queen's Westminster Rifles) The London Regt. (T.F.): only *s.* of William James Kerl, Auctioneer & Surveyor; of Old Jewry, London, E.C., and Past Master of the Worshipful Company of Curriers (*d.* 17 February 1903), by his wife Emily (19, Solon New Road, Clapham, S.W.), *dau.* of the late Henry Jeffery Austen, of Wadhurst, co. Sussex, Auctioneer: *b.* Beckenham, co. Kent, 9 September 1893: *educ.* City Freemen's School, Brixton, and on leaving school entered the wholesale drapery warehouse of Messrs. John Howell & Co., Ltd., St. Paul's Churchyard, E.C.: volunteered on the outbreak of war, joined Queen's Westminster Rifles, 6 August 1914: went to France with his battn. 1 November 1914, and was killed in action 4 June 1915, by a shell bursting in the reserve trenches in front of Ypres while waiting to occupy the first line of fire trenches. Buried at 'Cross Roads', Potijze, Ypres-Zonnebeke Road. Letters from officers and men testify to his great courage and lovable disposition. A comrade wrote, "On Friday 4th June the Germans shelled us on three different occasions, the first two times doing very little damage, but during the third shelling one percussion shell fell right in the trench amongst the men of my Company and killed nine of my chums, wounded seven others and three sustained shell shock. The stretcher bearers went immediately to their aid and one of them, whilst carrying out his duties, was severely wounded by another shell. The shell which killed so many of these fine fellows went right through the parapet and the men were buried under the debris. They were dug out but, found to be beyond recognition, the names of the killed could only be discovered by calling the roll. This terrible result was the work of one single shell. Several other shells, to the extent of about 50, were fired at us, causing a number of casualties, more or less severe. During the night a burial party made a large hole just behind the trenches in the which to bury their remains, and whilst on this unpleasant task came across a number of other bodies, and as the morning light was about to appear, our men had to be buried in the same spot." Age 21. *unm.*

(Panel 54) Rfn. 554384, Cyril John Killick, 1/16th (County of London) Bn. (Queen's Westminster Rifles) The London Regt. (T.F.): eldest s. of Cyril (& Annie, *née* Lee) Killick, of 'Brewery House,' 1, Lion & Lamb Yard, Chelmsford: late *husb.* to Minnie Violet Killick, *née* Choat (21, Tower Avenue, Chelmsford): and brother-in-law to Sergt. 43637, S.J. Choat, M.M., 82nd Field Coy., Royal Engineers, killed in action 20 September 1917: *b.* Chelmsford, 22 July 1888: *educ.* King Edward VI Grammar School: Occupation – Mayor's Court Clerk: enlisted Finsbury, London. Missing, believed killed in action 16 August 1917: Age 29.

Stanley Choat is buried in Klein-Vierstraat Military Cemetery (III.D.9).

(Panel 54) Rfn. 553186, Richard Harold Treffry, 1/16th (County of London) Bn. (Queen's Westminster Rifles) The London Regt. (T.F.): *s.* of Thomas Alfred Treffry, of 16, Bensham Manor Road, Thornton Heath, co. Surrey, by his wife Helen: and brother to Pte. L/10105, B.T. Treffry, 1st Royal West Surrey Regt., killed in action 31 October 1914, at the First Battle of Ypres: *b.* Croydon, co. Surrey, *c.*1898: served with the Expeditionary Force in France and Flanders, and died at Langemarck, Belgium, 16 August 1917: Age 19.

His brother Basil also has no known grave; he is recorded on Panel 14.

(Panel 54) Corpl. 572696, George Otter, 1/17th (County of London) Bn. (Poplar & Stepney Rifles) The London Regt. (T.F.): *s.* of Edward (& M.A.) Otter, of Kirkstead, Woodhall Spa, co. Lincoln: *b.* Kirkstead, *c.*1890: enlisted Shoreditch, co. Somerset: served with the Expeditionary Force in France and Flanders from 1916, and died consequent to and abdominal wound while carrying out consolidation work in the trenches 19 August 1917. The Commanding Officer, Lieut.Col. Hughes, later wrote, "We marched from the Ramparts at Ypres to take over the front line which extended from the cross-roads at Westhoek along the front of Nonne-Boschen Wood to the corner of Glencorse Wood with three companies in the front line, and one in support with the H.Q. on Bellewaarde Ridge. The actual front line was a series of posts with a facing support line immediately in rear. There had obviously been heavy fighting in this area, and our trenches were full of our dead and had been vacated in a dreadful condition by the outgoing division. However, we made a great effort to consolidate our posts and the immediate support line, and succeeded to a wonderful degree. The conditions were all against us, being subjected night and day to an infernal fire with severe losses, but the men came through the ordeal with the greatest credit. Even the relief of this sector was a dreadful adventure, the roads were simply swept with fire during the hours of darkness, and I always felt that immediately I left the Menin Gate it was quite a toss up whether I could get my whole battalion or one man to our immediate objective. The Officers, N.C.O.'s and men knew the fact equally well and it was a pleasure to see them moving off in heavy marching order with their faces set with grim determination, full of courage, moving forward steadily under heavy fire with perfect order and neat formation." Age 27.

(Panel 54) L/Corpl. 593381, Albert Francis Gains, 18th (County of London) Bn. (London Irish Rifles) The London Regt. (T.F.): formerly no.4561, 4th Bn. The Buffs (T.F.): *s.* of W.A (& Mrs E.E.) Gains, of 34, Marshall Street, Folkestone, co. Kent: and elder brother to Rfn. A/200268, A.E. Gains, 16th King's Royal Rifle Corps, reported missing in action 12 October 1918, at the River Selle: enlisted Canterbury. Killed in action during a trench raid, 7 April 1917: Age 32.

His brother Arthur also has no known grave; he is commemorated on the Vis-En-Artois Memorial (Panel 9).

(Panel 54) Rfn. 593502, Richard Kemsley, 18th (County of London) Bn. (London Irish Rifles) The London Regt. (T.F.): formerly no.4444, 4th Bn. The Buffs (T.F.): only *s.* of Albert Victor Kemsley, of 98, William Street, Milton Regis, nr. Sittingbourne: Occupation – Paper Mill worker: enlisted Sittingbourne. Reported missing following a trench raid, 7 April 1917; since confirmed killed in action: Age 19.

(Panel 54) Rfn. 591853, Charles Edward Nicholls, 'C' Coy., 1/18th (County of London) Bn. (London Irish Rifles) The London Regt. (T.F.): *s.* of Joshua (& Mrs) Nicholls, of 16, Fransfield Grove, Sydenham, London, S.E.: enlisted Chelsea, London, S.W. Killed in action during a trench raid, 7 April 1917: Age 29. One of four brothers who served in the Great War.

(Panel 54) 2nd Lieut. Reginald Silvester, 20th (County of London) Bn. (Blackheath & Woolwich) The London Regt. (T.F.): *s.* of George Silvester, of 4, Canadian Avenue, Catford, London, S.E.6, by his wife Sarah: and yr. brother to Pte. 3045, P. Silvester, 'D' Coy, 20th Bn. London Regt., fell 26 September 1915, at the Battle of Loos. Killed in action 7 June 1917: Age 24. *unm.* Remembered on the Brockley (St. Peter's) Church War Memorial, London, S.E.4.

His brother Percy also has no known grave; he is commemorated on the Loos Memorial, Dud Corner.

(Panel 54) Pte. 6310, Frederick James Harvey, 20th (County of London) Bn. (Blackheath & Woolwich) The London Regt. (T.F.): *s.* of Daniel Harvey, Drainage Inspector; of 156, Westmount Road, Eltham, London, S.E., by his wife Mary, *dau.* of Charles Whitman Lock: *b.* South Hackney, London, E., 21 October 1879: *educ.* Eltham National School: Occupation – Builder's Clerk: joined 20th London Regt. 20 June 1916: served with the Expeditionary Force in France and Flanders from 24 October following, and was killed in action New Year's Day, 1 January 1917: Age 37. He *m.* Eltham Parish Church, 17 August 1907, Lillie Maud (15, Roper Street, Eltham), and had two children – Marjorie May, *b.* 1 May 1908; Douglas Frederick, *b.* 28 July 1909.

(Panel 54) L/Corpl. 701405, John Reginald Charles Edwards, 23rd (County of London) Bn. The London Regt. (T.F.): *s.* of John (& Louisa S.) Edwards, of 37A, Crimsworth Road, Lambeth, London: enlisted Clapham Junction. Killed in action, 7 June 1917: Age 21.

(Panel 54) Pte. 722604, Edwin Muggeridge, 1/24th (County of London) Bn. (The Queen's) The London Regt. (T.F.): *s.* of Thomas (& Mrs) Muggeridge, of 251, Brockley Road, Lewisham: *b.* 22 November 1897: Occupation – Shop Assistant; Messrs Sainsbury's: enlisted Deptford, November 1915: posted 3/24th Queen's, May 1916; transf'd. 1/24th Queen's, December following. Killed in action 7 June 1917: Age 19. Dedicated by the Rev. E. Davies, 5 December 1920; Pte. Muggeridge is one of nine men remembered on the St. George's Church War Memorial, Brockley.

(Panel 54) Sergt. 800454, Archibald Bernard Claridge, 30th (City of London) Bn. (Royal Fusiliers) The London Regt. attd. 26th (Bankers) Bn. Royal Fusiliers: formerly no.322, 5th London Regt.: *s.* of the late Henry Claridge, by his wife Mary Ann (12, Holland Terrace, Acton, London): and brother to Corpl. 316, A.A. Claridge, London Rifle Brigade, fell 13 May 1915; Corpl. Z/104, S.H. Claridge, 2nd Rifle Brigade, killed in action 3 March 1916; and Pte. L/13839, A. Claridge, 3rd Royal Fusiliers, killed in action 7 March 1915: *b.* Hammersmith, London, W.6, 1890: enlisted Bunhill Row, London, E.C.: served with the Expeditionary Force in France and Flanders from, November 1914, and was killed in action at the Battle of the Menin Road, 20 September 1917: Age 27. Sergt. Claridge leaves a wife, Edith (37, Cameron Road, Seven Kings, co. Essex). One of four brothers who made the supreme sacrifice.

His brother Albert also has no known grave; he is recorded on Panel 52; Sydney is buried in Rue-du-Bois Military Cemetery, Fleurbaix (I.C.26); Alfred, Kemmel Chateau Military Cemetery (G.46).

(Panel 54) Pte. 653583, Walter William Rickwood, 21st (County of London) Bn (First Surrey Rifles) The London Regt. (T.F.): *s.* of William Rickwood, Carman, by his wife Mary Ann: *b.* Peckham, London, S.E., September 1885: *educ.* Sumner Road School: Occupation – Decorator: joined 21st London Regt., June 1916: served with the Expeditionary Force in France and Flanders, and was killed in action at Messines 7 June 1917: Age 31. He *m.* Christ Church, Peckham, S.E., 12 September 1912, Edith Sarah (161, Commercial Road, Peckham, S.E.), now Mrs Martin (45, Rolt Street, Deptford, London, S.E.), *dau.* of Charles William Foster, and fathered two children.

(Panel 54) Rfn. 653437, William Alban Rogers, 1/21st (County of London) Bn. (First Surrey Rifles) The London Regt. (T.F.): *s.* of Richard Rogers, of Broad Haven, co. Pembroke, by his wife Mary Anne: following the Conscription Act, joined First Surrey Rifles, Upper Norwood, London, June 1916: served with the Expeditionary Force in France and Flanders from October following, and was killed in action at the Battle of Messines, 7 June 1917: Age 35. He leaves a wife, Nellie Rogers (9, Cintra Park, Upper Norwood, London, S.E.19), to whom all correspondence and effects regarding her late husband should be forwarded.

(Panel 54) Rfn. 652409, Kennedy Stinton, 21st (County of London) Bn. (First Surrey Rifles) The London Regt. (T.F.): 2nd *s.* of Harry Kennedy Stinton, Tobacconist, by his wife Kate: *b.* Hammersmith, London, W., November 1887: *educ.* Maidenhead Grammar School: Occupation – Tobacconist: joined First Surrey Rifles 29 May 1916: served with the Expeditionary Force in France and Flanders from the following October, and was killed in action 7 June 1917: Age 29. He *m.* at St. Mary's Church, Islington, London, N., 14 March 1915, Minnie (181, Rye Lane, Peckham, London, S.E.), *dau.* of Frederick Goodings, and had one child.

On the opening day of the Third Battle of Ypres, 31 July 1917, 1st Hertfordshire Regt., were in support for the attack on the 'Langemarck Line.' Commencing at 03.45 a.m. the attack had three objectives – the Blue, Black and Green lines – and, meeting relatively light resistance, units of the 116th Brigade captured the first two objectives; preparing the way for 1st Hertfordshire to move forward and take the third objective.

Leaving their assembly positions at 05.00 the battalion began the attack on their objective which lay over the crest of a ridge but, as they made their way forward, they came under concentrated fire from German machine guns and snipers. Slogging their way forward they eventually managed to eliminate a German strongpoint which enabled them to move towards St. Julien. Shortly thereafter, losing two of their supporting tanks bogged down in the mud in crossing the Steenbeek, the battalion's situation rapidly deteriorated from bad to worse. Due to the state of the terrain a pre-arranged artillery barrage never materialised because the guns were unable to move forward; and the German barbed wire defences, which were in places fifteen feet deep and still intact, brought the Hertfordshires to a virtual standstill. Any further advance could only be achieved by employing sectional rush tactics: Small units rushing forward supported by the fire of their unit comrades behind them. On the battalion's right flank were the Cheshires, but on their left – where the Black Watch would have been had they not got seriously held up themselves – there was a gap which the Germans fully exploited pouring a hurricane of fire into and onto the stricken Hertfordshires; followed at 10.30 by a strong counter-attack, any hope the Hertfordshires might have had regarding achieving their objective were finished.

In the space of a few short hours, and after reasonable initial progress, the Hertfordshires had all but ceased to exist.

(Panel 54) Capt. Sidney Henry Lowry, M.C., 1st Bn. The Hertfordshire Regt. (T.F.): *s.* of Henry Lowry, of Stevenage, co. Hertford, by his wife Alice: *b.* 1888: *educ.* Charterhouse, and Pembroke College, Cambridge: became Member; London Stock Exchange, and partner in his father's business, Messrs Lowry Bros, 1913: a member of the O.T.C. at both Charterhouse and Cambridge, on the outbreak of war joined Inns of Court O.T.C. from whence he was gazetted Capt., Hertfordshire Regt., 28 October 1914 ('*London Gazette*,' 27 October), and went to the Front, January 1915, where for a period of time his regiment was brigaded with the Brigade of Guards: served in France and Flanders for over two years during which time he took part in much heavy fighting and was decorated with the Military Cross: returned to England, Spring 1917, for a training course at Aldershot and, after being recommended for the post of Second in Command of a battalion, returned to France just before his regiment's part in the Third Battle of Ypres on the opening day of which, 31 July 1917, he was killed before St. Julien; an action in which the regiment earned great distinction. His Commanding Officer, in a letter to Capt. Lowry's parents, wrote, "Your son was killed in action, whilst gallantly leading his company against the final objective. I don't think a better officer or more gallant man is serving in the army. It is not only a splendid officer but as a friend that we, who had the privilege of knowing him intimately, will always remember him." Age 29.

(Panel 54) Capt. (Adjt.) Alexander Richard Milne, 1st Bn. The Hertfordshire Regt. (T.F.): only *s.* of Frank Alexander Milne, Barrister-at-Law; of 11, Old Square, Lincoln's Inn, London, W.C., and of Summerhill, Barnet, by his wife Alice Emily, *dau.* of the late T.S.H. Burne, of Loynton Hall, co. Stafford: *b.* Barnet, 13 June 1896: *educ.* Northaw Place, and Winchester (Sergt., O.T.C.; gained 'A' Certificate): joined Inns of Court O.T.C. on the outbreak of war: obtained a commission 2nd Lieut. 3rd Hertfordshire Regt. 28 October 1914; promoted Lieut. 6 September 1915; Capt. September 1916: served with the Expeditionary Force in France and Flanders from July 1915, attached to a trenching battalion: rejoined his regiment January 1916, and was killed in action at St. Julien 31 July 1917. Col. (now Brigadier-General) Sir H. Page Croft wrote, "I hear that our dear comrades died like heroes, after the most wonderful exhibition of dogged pluck and brilliant fighting seen in this war. I am so proud to have known your son. He and his brother officers have earned our undying gratitude;" and a brother officer, "I don't think a more gallant officer has served in the Army, and it is largely due to his ability and the work he has done as Adjutant that the battalion has reached its high state of efficiency. He was killed while taking up reinforcements in the most gallant manner, under heavy fire, to repel a counter-attack; his Commanding Officer having been killed just previously. He was always so cheerful and high-spirited that he was extremely popular with both officers and men, and it is as a friend that all of us who had the privilege of knowing him, will always remember him." Age 21. *unm.*

(Panel 54) Sergt. 265148, Hiram John Hammond, 1st Bn. The Hertfordshire Regt. (T.F.): *yst. s.* of Herbert Samuel Hammond, of 20 Crib Road, Ware, co. Hertford, by his wife Susan: Occupation – Postal Worker; Ware P.O.: joined Territorials, November. 1911; called up on the outbreak of war August 1914: promoted Corpl. 1914; Sergt. 1915: served with the Expeditionary Force in France and Flanders from November 1914, and was killed in action during the fighting at St. Julien, 31 July 1917, on which day Sergt. Hammond was Platoon Sergt., No.9 Platoon, under Lieut. Francis (since taken prisoner). Having successfully forded the Steenbeek and beaten off a German attack on the Poelcapelle – St. Julien Road, the platoon were in the process of advancing toward their final objective – the Green (Langemarck) Line when Sergt. Hammond was wounded. Lieut. Francis later wrote, "On going through a hedge lining the road, we had our first view of the Green Line – a great big trench on top of a rise, and what was worse, two thick lines of wire in front, but it was our objective and the Germans in front of us could be seen running away. It was at this point that Sergt. Hammond came up to me with a grin on his face and said something about at last getting at the Boche and that he would tell the men to get ready to go absolutely all out. Immediately afterwards a Private came up and reported Sergt. Hammond badly wounded in the leg. He died immediately I believe. I won't say much about Hammond, as anyone who was out in France with the Herts knew him, but I should like it to be known that he died just as he always carried on, absolutely fearless and looking as if there was no finer fun than going over the top." Later reports stated that Sergt. Hammond's wounds had not been of a serious nature, but seconds after being taken to an aid post for treatment it was hit by a shell and completely destroyed. Sergt, Hammond was a keen footballer, in 1912 –13 he played for Ware and was awarded two medals. Age 27. *(IWGC record Hirim)*

(Panel 54) Corpl. 2270, Arthur Ernest Boardman, 'E' Coy., 1st Bn. The Hertfordshire Regt. (T.F.): late of Herne Hill, co. Surrey: *s.* of Duncan Leonard Boardman, of 'Glenmaye,' 238, Croydon Road, Caterham, co. Surrey, and Eliza Ann, his spouse: *b.* Hove, co. Sussex: served with the Expeditionary Force in France from 6 November 1914, and was killed in action at Ypres on the 18th of that month; the battalion's second Active Service fatality (first N.C.O.) attributable to enemy action: 18 November 1914: Age 21. See Pte. F.J. Darlow, below.

(Panel 54) Corpl. 268052, Ernest Walter Izzard, The Hertfordshire Regt. (T.F.): formerly no.72761, Royal Army Medical Corps: *s.* of James (& Mrs) Izzard, of 35, Upper Culver Road, St. Albans, co. Hertford: and brother to Pte. 4/7118, A.A. Izzard, Bedfordshire Regt., died 30 January 1919, aged 24 years. Killed in action 31 July 1917: Age 31. He leaves a wife, Lily May Izzard (33, Kimberley Road, North Street, St. Albans), and children.

His brother Arthur is buried in Hatfield Road Cemetery, St. Albans (Mil.L.3).

(Panel 54) L/Corpl. 265463, John Hall, 1st Bn. The Hertfordshire Regt. (T.F.): *s.* of Martin Hall, of 4, Northgate End, Bishop's Stortford, co. Hertford, by his wife Esther Elizabeth: and brother to Ab/S. J/16257, S.C. Hall, HMS 'Princess Royal,' died 6 May 1915, consequent to wounds received at the Battle of Dogger Bank (January 1915): *b.* Linton, co. Cambridge: enlisted Bishop's Stortford. Killed in action 31 July 1917: Age 19.

His brother is buried in Bishop's Stortford Old Cemetery (B.12.14).

PANEL 54 ENDS – PTE. J.R. ALLWOOD, HERTFORDSHIRE REGT.

PANEL 56 BEGINS – PTE. R.W. AMBROSE, HERTFORDSHIRE REGT.

(Panel 56) Pte. 266041, Reginald Walter Ambrose, 1st Bn. The Hertfordshire Regt. (T.F.): *s.* of John (& Mrs) Ambrose, of 16, Austin Place, Hemel Hempstead, co. Hertford: and *yr.* brother to Pte. 266763, J. Ambrose, Hertfordshire Regt., died of wounds received before Passchendaele: prior to enlistment was employee Messrs John Dickinson & Co., Paper Manufacturers, Apsley Mill: enlisted Hertford. Killed in action on the opening day of the Third Battle of Ypres, 31 July 1917. Age 23. *unm.*

His brother Joseph also has no known grave; he is commemorated on the Tyne Cot Memorial (Panel 153).

(Panel 56) Pte. 270201, Percy Edgar Bixey, 1st Bn. The Hertfordshire Regt. (T.F.): *s.* of Edwin Arthur Bixey, of Valiant's Farm, Pebmarsh, by his wife Maria Elizabeth: *b.* Colne Engaine, co. Hertford. Killed in action 31 July 1917.

(Panel 56) Pte. 265841, James Cordell, No.4 Coy., 1st Bn. The Hertfordshire Regt. (T.F.): *s.* of John Cordell, of Bridge Foot Farm, Walkern, co. Hertford. Killed in action 31 July 1917, nr. St. Julien. Age 24.

(Panel 56) Pte. 2238, Frederick James Darlow, 1st Bn. The Hertfordshire Regt. (T.F.): *s.* of S. (& Mrs) Darlow, of 1, George Lane, Royston, co. Hertford: served with the Expeditionary Force in France from 6 November 1914; reported missing in action on the 18th of that month; later confirmed killed on that date. 1st Hertfordshire's second Other Ranks fatality attributable to enemy action: 18 November 1914: Age 18. See Corpl. A.E. Boardman, above.

(Panel 56) Pte. 266902, George Henry Edwards, No.4 Coy., 1st Bn. The Hertfordshire Regt. (T.F.): *s.* of George Edwards, of Froghall Lane, Walkern, co. Stafford, by his wife Emma. Killed in action 31 July 1917, nr. St. Julien. Age 24.

(Panel 56) Pte. 2518, George Edward Ellis, 1st Bn. The Hertfordshire Regt. (T.F.): *s.* of William Ellis, Publican; 'The Hen & Chickens,' 51, Clarke's Lane, Baldock, co. Hertford: and *yr.* brother to Pte. 17492, F.F. Ellis, 8th Bedfordshire Regt., killed in action 15 September 1916: *b.* Baldock: enlisted Hertford: served with the Expeditionary Force in France and Flanders from 6 November 1914, and was killed in action 19 November 1914. Age 30.

His brother Frederick also has no known grave; he is commemorated on the Thiepval Memorial, Somme.

(Panel 56) Pte. 265430, Albert Harrowell, 1st Bn. The Hertfordshire Regt. (T.F.): *s.* of William Harrowell, of Clarence Cottage, Clarence Road, Berkhampstead, co. Hertford, by his wife Lizzie: and *yr.* brother to L/Corpl. 55366, F. Harrowell (served as Lewis), Machine Gun Corps (Inf.), killed in action 6 May 1918: enlisted Berkhampstead. Killed in action 31 July 1917. Age 31. He leaves a wife, Florence Harrowell (25, Queen's Road, Berkhampstead).

His brother Frank also has no known grave; he is commemorated on the Loos (Dud Corner) Memorial (Panel 136).

(Panel 56) Pte. 2636, Philip James Robinson, 1st Bn. The Hertfordshire Regt. (T.F.): *s.* of Robert Robinson, Coachman; of 66, Vicarage Road, Ware, co. Hertford, by his wife Lottie: *b.* Cheshunt, 1892: *educ.* St. Mary's Elementary School; Hertford Grammar School: Occupation – Clerk: served with the Expeditionary Force in France from 6 November 1914, and was killed by shellfire eleven days later on the morning of the 17th., Menin Road, Ypres. Buried there: Age 22. *unm.* 1st Battalion's first Active Service fatality attributable to enemy action. See also Corpl. A.E. Boardman and Pte. F.J. Darlow, above.

(The battalion's first active service fatality, Pte. C. Castle, died at Le Havre, 7 November 1914, of sickness. Ste. Marie Cemetery, Div.14.D.3).

(Panel 56) Pte. 168, Robert 'Robbie' Appleton, Northumbrian Div. Cyclist Coy., Army Cyclist Corps: late of 5, Green Road, Skelton: *s.* of John Appleton, Ironstone Miner; of 8 Manless Green Terrace, Skelton-in-Cleveland, co. York, by his wife Annie: *b.* Skelton, 1896. Killed in action 24 May 1915: Age 19. '*The North Eastern Daily Gazette*,' In Memoriam,' 24 May 1916:–

> *He did his duty.*
> *He left his home in the flower of youth*
> *He seemed so strong and brave*
> *We little thought how soon he would*
> *Be laid in a hero's grave.*

Ever remembered by his ever loving Father, Mother and Sisters Emma, Edith and Winnie.

(Panel 56) Lieut. Walter Leverton Jessopp, Machine Gun Corps (Inf.): *s.* of Walter Budworth Jessopp, of 25, Park Avenue, Bedford, by his wife Emily Frances: and *yr.* brother to Temp. Lieut. A.J. Jessopp, General List attd. 56th Sqdn. Royal Flying Corps, killed in action 12 May 1917, aged 23. Killed in action 31 July 1917: Age 20.

His brother Augustus is buried in Orchard Dump Cemetery, Arleux-en-Gohelle (III.G.30).

(Panel 56) 2nd Lieut. William George Bown, 44th Coy., Machine Gun Corps (Inf.): *s.* of Frank George (& Constance Mary) Bown, of The Firs, Chapel Allerton: a pre-war member Army Service Corps (T.F.); served at Gallipoli with West Somerset Yeomanry: applied for and obtained a commission – trained Officer Cadet Training School, Grantham, transf'd. Machine Gun Corps, 2nd Lieut., 1916: proceeded to France and was killed in action there 31 July 1917: Age 24. His widow Jessie Bown (Manor Lodge, Wedmore, co. Somerset) to whom he married 1 July 1916 (shortly before his departure to France), never remarried; she remained true to her beloved William and – every fortnight – for the remainder of her life, never failed to place a bunch of flowers in his memory on the Wedmore Memorial.

(Panel 56) Sergt. 68301, Thomas Hollingsworth Tovey, 2nd Coy., Machine Gun Corps (Inf.): only *s.* of the late Thomas William Tovey, Secretary, by his wife Kate (78, West Street, Farnham): *b.* Farnham, co. Surrey, 10 July 1896: *educ.* Farnham Grammar School (O.T.C. member): Occupation – Apprentice Motor Engineer: joined 5th Bn. Queen's (Royal West Surrey Regt.), (T.F.), February 1914: called up on mobilisation August following: served with the Expeditionary Force in France and Flanders, transf'd. Machine Gun Corps Section, November 1916, and was killed in action at Hollebeke 5 August 1917. Buried where he fell. An officer wrote, "I feel his loss very much as he was always most cheerful, and proved himself a very capable Sergt. On August 5th, at the time of his death, he was with one of my foremost guns; it unfortunately happened that the Germans attacked us at dawn in a very thick mist. I regret to say that the Boche apparently crawled up to the gun and bombed them out. We could find no trace of him shortly after, and I presumed he had been taken prisoner. We have just heard from another battalion that he was killed." And the officer who found his body, "There is positive proof that he died bravely doing his duty in the advance we made early in August, by the fact that he was found in front of the line which we took up." Age 21. *unm.*

(Panel 56) Corpl. 15726, George William Biggs, 111th Coy., Machine Gun Corps (Inf.): formerly no.14365, Suffolk Regt.: *s.* of George Biggs, of Needham Hall Farm Cottages, Friday Bridge, nr. Wisbech, co. Cambridge, by his wife Emma: and elder brother to AB.R/1030, C. Biggs, Howe Battn. R.N. Divn., attd. 1st Bn. Royal Marine Light Infantry, fell 24 April 1918: *b.* Coldham: enlisted Wisbech. Killed in action 31 July 1917: Age 22. *unm.*

His brother Charles also has no known grave; he is commemorated on the Arras (Faubourg d'Amiens) Memorial (Bay 1).

(Panel 56) Corpl. 20589, Michael John Glancy, M.M., 17th Coy., Machine Gun Corps (Inf.): formerly no.9650, 2nd Bn. Leinster Regt.: *s.* of Michael Patrick Glancy, of 22, Allingham Street, Dublin, by his wife Mary Jane: *b.* Roscrea, Co. Tipperary, 1895: enlisted Drogheda. Killed in action 16 March 1916: Age 20. *unm. Commemorated in Sanctuary Wood Cemetery (Sp.Mem.).*

(Panel 56) L/Corpl. 21602, Robert William Stocker, 21st Coy., Machine Gun Corps (Inf.): *s.* of John Joseph Stocker, of 4, Gladstone Terrace, Sun Street, Biggleswade, co. Bedford, by his wife Sarah Rebecca: and brother to Corpl. 9474, H. Stocker, 2nd Bedfordshire Regt., killed in action 8 November 1914: enlisted Biggleswade. Killed in action 31 July 1917: Age 21. *unm.*

His brother Herbert is buried in Harlebeke New British Cemetery (XVI.A.6).

(Panel 56) Pte. 6156, James William Coupe, 50th Coy., Machine Gun Corps (Inf.): formerly no.19422, Leicestershire Regt.: *s.* of William Coupe, of Bondhay Cottage, Scotland Street, Whitwell: and brother to Pte. 306079, P.N. Coupe, Sherwood Foresters, died in a Base Hospital, 1 July 1917, of wounds: *b.* Whitwell, co. Derby: enlisted Worksop, co. Nottingham. Killed in action 2 March 1916: Age 28. He was married to Gertrude Fanny Harrison, *née* Coupe (Fir Vale, Harthill, Sheffield), who would be pleased to receive correspondence regarding her late husband from any of his comrades.

His brother Percy is buried in Longuenesse (St. Omer) Souvenir Cemetery (IV.C.41).

(Panel 56) Gnr. 57692, Frederick Charles Hopkins, 56th Coy., Machine Gun Corps (Inf.): only *s.* of the late Thomas Frederick Charles Hopkins, by his wife Charlotte Elizabeth (69, Royal Road, Kennington, London, S.E.), *dau.* of the late Charles William Bangs: *b.* Kennington, London, S.E., 23 April 1893: *educ.* St. Agnes' School: Occupation – Solicitor's Clerk: enlisted Cyclist Corps, 8 May 1916: transf'd. Royal Warwickshire Regt., thereafter Machine Gun Corps: served with the Expeditionary Force in France and Flanders, from the October following. Reported missing after the fighting, 31 July 1917; now assumed killed in action on or about that date: Age 24. *unm.*

(Panel 56) Pte. 90518, John Theodore Mitchinson Lewis, 122nd Coy., Machine Gun Corps (Inf.): formerly no.22849, Loyal North Lancashire Regt.: *s.* of the late Rev. William John Lewis, Rector of Eydon, late of Mount Sorrell Vicarage, Loughborough; by his wife Mary Darnell Lewis (26, Newton Road, Bayswater, London): and elder brother to Gnr. 197593, W.E.M. Lewis, Royal Horse Artillery, killed in action 30 March 1918, aged 19 years: *b.* Mount Sorrell Vicarage, co. Leicester, 1897: enlisted Liverpool. Killed in action 1 August 1917. Age 20.

His brother William also has no known grave; he is commemorated on the Pozieres Memorial.

(Panel 56) Pte. 44893, Thomas Gaskell Lindow, 73rd Coy., Machine Gun Corps (Inf.): formerly no.3753, King's Own (Royal Lancaster Regt.): *s.* of Mary Augusta Coward ('Rose Cottage,' Lowick Green, Ulverston, Manchester): and brother to Pte. 3894, W.A. Lindow, 23rd Royal Fusiliers, killed in action 30 April 1916: *b.* Ulverston. Killed in action 31 July 1917: Age 27.

His brother William is buried in Aix-Noulette Communal Cemetery Extension (I.B.11).

(Panel 56) Pte. 4593, Donald McIntyre, 58th Coy., Machine Gun Corps (Inf.): formerly no.18355, Cameronians (Sco.Rif.): *s.* of Thomas Peyman McIntyre, of 40, Latimer Road, Eastbourne, by his wife Elizabeth Emma: Occupation – Sailor: enlisted Canning Town, London. Killed in action at Messines, 10 June 1917: Age 22. *unm.*

(Panel 56) Pte. 55934, Frederick Charles Pearson, 25th Bn. Machine Gun Corps (Inf.): formerly no.1421, 5th London Regt.: 2nd *s.* of Harry Pearson, of 'Woodruff,' Vicarage Road, Great Cornard, Sudbury, co. Suffolk, by his 1st wife Mary: and brother to Pte. 4812, W.H. Pearson, 8th East Surrey Regt., killed in action, 1 July 1916; and half-brother (by his father's second marriage) to Pte. 53224, A.F. Pearson, 15th London Regt., killed at Ypres, 22 December 1916: *b.* Rotherhithe, *c.*1885: a pre-war Territorial, enlisted Brixton: served with the Expeditionary Force in France, and was killed in action at Ypres, 31 July 1917: Age 32.

His brother William is buried in Delville Wood Cemetery (XVI.P.4); Alan has no known grave, he is recorded on Panel 54.

(Panel 56) Pte. 206172, Arthur George Pigg, Machine Gun Corps (Heavy Branch): *s.* of John Pigg, of 1, Gower Road, Royston, co. Hertford: and brother to Rfn. 372861, E.J. Pigg, 2/8th London Regt. (Post Office Rifles), killed in action 30 October 1917: *b.* Royston: enlisted Hitchin. Killed in action 7 June 1917.

His brother Ernest also has no known grave; he is commemorated on the Tyne Cot Memorial (Panel 151).

(Panel 56) Lieut. Henry Paul Mainwaring Jones, Tank Corps: elder *s.* of Harry Jones, Editorial Staff member, '*The Daily Chronicle*;' of 'Allendale,' 29, Half Moon Lane, Herne Hill, London, S.E., by his wife Emily Margaret, *dau.* of Thomas Mainwaring: *b.* London, 18 May 1896: *educ.* Dulwich College (Jnr. & Snr. Scholarship winner: Brackenbury Scholarship winner – History & Modern Languages, December 1914); Balliol College, Oxford: obtained a commission, 2nd Lieut. Army Service Corps, 15 April 1915; promoted Lieut. 18 May 1916: served with the Expeditionary Force in France and Flanders from July 1915 – Requisitioning Officer, 9th Cavalry Brigade – later 2nd Cavalry Brigade, same capacity: transf'd. Tank Corps, February 1917: took part in the Battle of Arras, and was killed in action in Flanders, 31 July following. His Commanding Officer wrote, "He was efficient, very keen and a most gallant gentleman. I am certain he did not know what fear was." He was a keen athlete, and while at school was a member of the First Football XV during the years 1912 – 15; captain of football 1914 – 15, and editor of the School Magazine 1913-14. At school sports (March 1915), he won the mile flat rate, half-mile, steeplechase, and tied for the '*Victor Ludorum*' shield. Age 21. *unm.*

(Panel 56) 2nd Lieut. Eric Arthur Frank Coleman, Machine Gun Corps attd. Tank Corps: *s.* of Capt. George Drury Coleman, R.D.C., of Manor Cottage, Acle, co. Norfolk, by his wife Edith Isabel, *dau.* of James Evens: *b.* Coleshill, co. Buckingham, 3 December 1886: *educ.* Brighton, and Marlborough College: obtained a commission 3rd Norfolk Regt., January 1915: served with the Expeditionary Force in France and Flanders, and was killed in action at Wieltje 31 July 1917. Buried in the track of his tank. His Colonel wrote, "He was very keen and inspired every member of his crew with the same feelings. They would have done anything for him. Major Hawkins, his Company Commander, is writing to you, and will give you all such particulars as we have; for myself, I can only say that we have all lost a friend, and the battalion an officer whom we could ill spare – and one whom I cannot replace;" and one of his men, "I offer you my deepest sympathy in your sad loss and bereavement, and so do all the crew who had the pleasure of serving under such a gentleman and hero as Lieut Coleman was. When I sit and think of this awful tragedy that has befallen us, it makes me ill, as I lost an officer who was a chum to all – always merry and bright, ready for any danger when duty called. He respected all and sundry, and helped many in distress; worked hard for our comfort and benefit, and I can assure you every brother officer and man in the battalion respected him and would have followed him anywhere, as we did, for we had implicit trust and every confidence in such a brave gentleman, who fought game to the last. Although an officer and I his driver, we shared our confidence in each other, and had various views in common. I feel now I have lost a friend who was dear to me – a hero and a man. We crawled up on the 30th., at night, waiting for morning to go over the top and strafe a cunning, cruel foe. Lieut. Coleman and seven of us, his crew, slept near each other, waiting for the light of day to bid for victory or death. At the given time we went over merry as sand-boys, our 'Governor,' as we called him, leading the way. He never seemed to care what was falling around us. He just led us like a hero would. We did good work too, but it was a hot time and difficult." A brother officer also wrote, "I was not actually present when Eric met his death, which you will be glad to know must have been instantaneous, and that he cannot have suffered at all. He died in the execution of his duty, and that he had performed always to the satisfaction of his superior officers. In this, his first Tank action, he was working on the left of the company; was first over, and while advancing to push through the first waves of infantry, he had led his Tank on foot all the way. Consequently, he had reached his objective early on, and was rendering good assistance to the infantry, who were held up by machine-gun fire at the time, near a strong point at Spree Farm, east of Wieltje. Up till then he had been outside his tank, leading it over very difficult ground – sodden with rain, and aerated by shell fire. When summoned to the assistance of the infantry on his right, he got inside and went to their help; which he seems to have rendered satisfactorily. Then a shell hit the left track, breaking six track plates and stopping the Tank. He said, "What's that?" got outside to examine, and another shell came, hitting the Tank and killing him and wounding one of the crew. I may say that if all the junior officers in this action had shown the same devotion to duty and led their Tanks forward, the company would have done better than it did. He always worked hard and could be relied on to execute any duty to the best of his ability." Age 31. He *m.* Wakefield, August 1915; Lilian (5, St. John's Terrace, Wakefield, co. York), *dau.* of J. Harris, Chief Constable, Wakefield.

(Panel 56) Pte. 95272, Robert Handley, 'G' Bn., Tank Corps: *s.* of George William Handley, of 5, Heaton Road, Mitcham, co. Surrey, by his wife Emma: *b.* Camberwell, 1893: enlisted Duke of Cornwall's Light Infantry, no.12361, London: subsequently transf'd. Tank Corps with a number of other members of D.C.L.I., and was killed in action 2 August 1917, when, whilst supporting the attack by 39th and 51st Divisions attack on Pilckem, his tank came under heavy enemy fire after getting bogged down in the St. Julien sector: Age 23.

On the night of 11 February 1916, after spending most of the evening drinking in a nearby estaminet, Dvr. Thomas Moore and his friends returned to their hut at Busseboom where, after being requested to quieten down, Moore took up his rifle, loaded it and fired a shot through the roof. Shortly afterwards two NCO's and an officer sent to investigate were threatened by Moore. At this point Staff Sergt. James Pick, one of Moore's friends with whom he had been drinking, intervened advising Moore to curb his behaviour forthwith. In response to this advice Moore, in a fit of drunken rage, turned on his friend and shot him through the throat and, as Sergt. Pick fell to the floor, shot him again.

(Panel 56) Dvr. TH/040862, Thomas Moore, 4th Coy., 24th Divn. Train, Army Service Corps: Executed – Murder, 26 February 1916. Age 23.

Sergt. Pick is buried in Poperinghe New Military Cemetery (I.F.12).

(Panel 56) Pte. 22184, William Smith Diack Byres, 17th (Service) Bn. The Royal Scots attd. (no.115370) 193rd Labour Coy., Labour Corps: *s.* of Andrew Anderson Byres, of 47, Hutcheon Street, Aberdeen, by his wife Georgina (1, Hanover lane, Aberdeen): *b.* Aberdeen, 1 January 1896: *educ.* Middle Public School, Gallowgate, Aberdeen: Occupation – Apprentice Riveter: enlisted 16 March 1915: served with the Expeditionary Force in France and Flanders: took part in the Battle of Arras, and was killed in action 10 June 1917. Buried at Ypres. Age 21. *unm.*

(Panel 56) Pte. 80443, George Carter, 135th Coy., Labour Corps: formerly no.50457, Queen's (Royal West Surrey Regt.): late *husb.* to Eliza Mary Carter (9, Walrond Street, Streatham, London, S.W.16):

b. St. Pancras: enlisted Royal West Surrey Regt., Streatham, later transf'd. Labour Corps, and was killed in action 29 May 1917: Age 38. *(IWGC record 26 May 1915) Buried in Westhof Farm Cemetery, Neuve-Eglise (I.A.5).*

(Panel 56) Capt. Ernest Mure Glanvill, Royal Army Medical Corps attd. 2nd Dragoons (Royal Scots Greys): only *s*. of Henry Glanvill, late Registrar of the Inland Revenue Estate Duty Department: *b*. Edinburgh, 14 November 1877: *educ*. Edinburgh University, qualified, M.B., Medicine, 1901: gazetted Lieut. R.A.M.C., 31 August 1903; promoted Capt. 28 February 1907: passed through Army Medical College, Millbank, August 1911, with six months acceleration for promotion to Major, and would have attained that rank February 1915, had he not been killed: served with the Expeditionary Force in France and Flanders from August 1914 – Medical Officer, In Charge, Scots Greys – killed in action 2 November following. Age 26. Mentioned in Despatches (*'London Gazette,'* 17 February 1915) by F.M. Sir John (now Lord) French, for 'gallant and distinguished service in the field,' having shown great coolness and conspicuous bravery on many occasions. Capt. Glanvill left a widow and two children – a boy and a girl.

(Panel 56) Capt. Bentley Moore Hunter, M.B., Royal Army Medical Corps attd. 1/1st Bn. (57th Foot) The Cambridgeshire Regt.: 5th *s*. of Charles Hunter, of The School House, Dunragit, B.A., by his wife Susan, *dau*. of William Riddell, of Aldous, co. Ayr: *b*. Glenluce, co. Wigtown, 28 April 1888: *educ*. Stranraer High School, and Glasgow University, where he graduated M.B., Ch.B. (Prizeman and Medallist): Occupation – Assistant; Consett, afterwards Stevenston, co. Ayr: obtained a commission 15 May 1915, being attd. 1st Cambridgeshire Regt., and sent out to Mudros (Lemnos) and Egypt: subsequently served with the Expeditionary Force in France and Flanders, and was killed in action nr. Ypres, 31 July 1917. Buried at Steenbeek, Langemarck, north of Ypres. Age 29. *unm*. His Commanding Officer wrote, "Your son was killed trying to save the lives of others, as he had done so many times before. I, fortunately, had the satisfaction of telling him, some few days before, that I had recommended him for some sort of award." And his Chaplain, "His staff say they will never have another like him. He was so generous minded and willing to help others. I shall never forget the way he carried on down south when the other Medical Officer was killed. He was simply splendid." He was recommended for decoration by Brigdr.-Gen. E.Riddell, D.S.O.

(Panel 56) Capt. Michael Joseph Lochrin, Royal Army Medical Corps attd. 1st Bn. The Northamptonshire Regt.: *s*. of Owen Lochrin, of 'The Bull Ring,' Drogheda, by his wife Margaret: *b*. 27 May 1883: took his diploma L.R.C.P. and S. (Ireland), 1904: joined Royal Army Medical Corps, July 1906: promoted Capt. January 1910: served with the Expeditionary Force in France and Flanders, and was killed in action 23 October 1914, nr. Pilckem, Ypres: Age 31. *unm*.

(Panel 56) Capt. Angus Macnab, Royal Army Medical Corps (T.F.) attd. 14th (County of London) Bn. (London Scottish), The London Regt. (T.F.): M.B., F.R.C.S.: *s*. of Alexander Macnab, of Argyllshire, N.B.: *b*. Southland, New Zealand, September 1875: *educ*. Dunedin, and Edinburgh University (graduate): served in the South African War: joined Royal Army Medical Corps (T.F.), March 1911, being attd, London Scottish from that date: accompanied his regiment to France, and was killed in action at Messines, in the first engagement of the London Scottish, 31 October 1914. Age 39. Capt. Macnab, fond of rifle shooting and golf, was a member of the Royal and Ancient, and Sandy Lodge, co. Hertford. He leaves a widow Evelyn, *née* Calder.

(Panel 56) Lieut. Donald Campbell, M.B., Royal Army Medical Corps attd. 2nd Bn. (15th Foot) The East Yorkshire Regt.: 3rd *s*. of the late John Campbell, for 43 years Tenant of Blair Mills, by his wife Isabella (Fincastle, Bridge of Tilt, Blair Atholl), *dau*. of Alexander McBeath: *b*. Blair Atholl, 20 January 1887: *educ*. Blair Atholl Public School; Pitlochry Higher Grade School (County Council Bursary winner); George Watson's College (1904 – 06); Edinburgh University – Arts Student, (entered 1906, gained McDougal Bursary same year) – graduated M.A. (1909); M.B.Ch.B. (1913). In 1910 he shared the Vans Dunlop Scholarship with another student. On the outbreak of war was house surgeon Sheffield Royal Hospital, and receiving a commission in the R.A.M.C. 16 December 1914, went to France, January 1915, as Medical Officer attd. 2nd East Yorks Regt., and was killed 17 February 1915, nr. the village of Zillebeke while going to the assistance of a wounded man. Buried at St. Eloi. An officer of the 2nd East Yorks Regt. wrote, "He was only with me a short time, but it is no exaggeration to say that he left behind him not mere acquaintances, but real friends, who mourn his loss more than I can tell you. He lived always in the same billet with me and the headquarters staff, and shared all our rough food, delicacies and hardships just as they came, and for my part I find he has left a blank that will take a long time to fill. He met his death going up to the front to help a wounded man. A stretcher-bearer was with him at the time, and as they crossed an open space they came under the fire of the enemy in a house some 200 yards away, and both were shot dead." For two years he was joint secretary for the Edinburgh University Musical Society; a keen golfer, and for several years a member of the Edinburgh Northern Hockey Club: Age 28. *unm.*

(Panel 56) Lieut. George McCallum, Royal Army Medical Corps attd. The Duke of Cornwall's Light Infantry: *s.* of the late John McCallum, by his wife Emma (Thornby Park Terrace, Paisley). Killed in action at Hooge 30 July 1915. Age 25. *unm.* See also Sanctuary Wood Cemetery (I.C.4)

(Panel 56) Lieut. Martin James Richardson, 'C' Section, 21st Field Ambulance, Royal Army Medical Corps: *yst. s.* of the late Martin Richardson, Solicitor; of Roseville, Bridlington, co. York, by his wife Georgina: and nephew to Major-General George B. Heastey, Royal Marine Light Infantry: *b.* Bridlington, co. York, 1867: *educ.* Durham School, and Edinburgh University, where he took his medical degree: on the outbreak of war volunteered for Temporary Service: received his commission Temp. Lieut., August 1914: served with the VIIth Division of the Expeditionary Force in France and Flanders from October 1914, and was killed in action nr. Ypres, 4 November 1914, by the same shell that mortally wounded Capt. T.McC. Phillips, R.A.M.C.: Age 47. Lieut. Richardson *m.* Elizabeth Maud (1, Selwood Terrace, Onslow Gardens, South Kensington, London, S.W.), *yst. dau.* of Dr. Eagland, of Burleywood, Harrogate, and had three children – Norman Martin Heastey, *b.* November 1893 (gazetted R.M.L.I., Temp. 2nd Lieut. September 1914, promoted Lieut. January 1915); Dorothy Jennie Heastey, *b.* February 1896; Evelyn Joan Victoria Heastey, *b.* January 1901.

Capt. Phillips is buried in Poperinghe Communal Cemetery (I.B.6).

(Panel 56) Lieut. David Wylie Rintoul, Royal Army Medical Corps attd. 3rd Bn. Coldstream Guards: *s.* of David Rintoul, M.A., House Master, Clifton College, by his wife Catherine Barclay (42, Caynge Square, Clifton, Bristol): *b.* Clifton, 23 May 1889: *educ.* Clifton College, and St. Andrews University; graduated M.B., Ch.B.: joined Royal Army Medical Corps, January 1914: posted No.5 Field Ambulance, IInd Division, on mobilisation: afterwards apptd. Medical Officer, In Charge, 2nd Coldstream Guards: subsequently transf'd. 3rd Coldstream Guards, 19 September 1914. Lieut. Rintoul was killed not far from St. Julien, 21 October 1914, while advancing with the leading company. The Officer Commanding, 3rd Coldstream Guards, wrote of him, "He was brave and fearless, and most gallant. He had no idea what fear was, his one ideal being to assist the wounded." Age 25. *unm.*

(Panel 56) Lieut. Hugh John Sladen Shields, Royal Army Medical Corps attd. 1st Bn. Irish Guards: *s.* of the Rev. Arthur John Shields, Rector of Thornford, co. Dorset: *b.* Calcutta, India, 16 June 1887: *educ.* Loretto School, and Jesus College, Cambridge; graduated B.A. (Hons.), and M.B. (1910): commissioned Royal Army Medical Corps, July 1912: apptd. Medical Officer, In Charge, Irish Guards, on the outbreak of war: Mentioned in Sir John (now Lord) French's Despatch, 8 October 1914, 'for his services in the field.' Lieut. Shields was killed in action nr. Ypres, 26 October 1914, while attending to a wounded man in the firing line, and buried at Huize Berkershorst, Zillebeke. While at Cambridge he rowed in the Jesus College head of the river crew, and gained his Blue in 1910, when he stroked the Light Blues against Oxford. The same year, with Eric Fairbairn, he won the Lowe Double Sculls. He also rowed at Henley in the Jesus Grand Challenge Cup crew, which three years in succession were runners-up for that trophy, and won the Ladies' Plate (1908). He rowed No.2 in the Jesus crew, composed of past and present members, which was the first English crew to beat the Belgians, winning the International Race at Ghent (1911). At Jesus College he was captain of the Rugby Football Club, and when at Middlesex Hospital, where he was a scholar and prizeman, was captain of their XV. Played for United Hospitals *v.* the Army, Queen's Club; 1912. In that year he competed for the Army and Navy Boxing Championship, winning in the semi-finals of the middleweights, and being runner up in the light heavyweights (1913). He was keenly and self-denyingly interested in religious work and social work at Cambridge and in London, giving his evenings and Sundays largely to work among lads at the Magdalen College Union Club, Camberwell: Age 27. *unm.* (*IWGC record 25-26 October 1914*)

Leaving one sector for another could often be akin to 'jumping out of the frying pan and into the fire.' On 24 July 1917 1/2nd Highland Field Ambulance left Clairmarais for Lederzeele on the last leg of the journey that would, within a few hours, bring them to Gwalia Farm in time for the opening of the Third Battle of Ypres. The ambulance had already had plenty of experience under fire – they had been serving in France for two years – but nothing could prepare even the most battle hardened for the terrors of salient. Prior to the ambulance's arrival at Gwalia the stretcher bearers had gone on ahead to the Advanced Dressing Station at Essex Farm – 'a hot spot' – where, by way of welcome and warning to the rest of the ambulance, four of them were killed by a shell which crashed into their shelter at the nearby Willows Collecting Post; they were joined a week later by three of their comrades.

(Panel 56) Pte. 303238, Harry Cameron Badenoch, 1/2nd (Highland) Field Ambulance, Royal Army Medical Corps (T.F.): *s.* of the late James Badenoch, by his wife Bathie Johnstone: enlisted Aberdeen. Killed in action, Canal Bank sector, Ypres, 24 July 1917. Age 27. He was married to Janet Anderson, *née* Badenoch (166, Auchmill Road, Bucksburn, co. Aberdeen).

(Panel 56) Pte. 303072, William Mearns Clyne, 1/2nd (Highland) Field Ambulance, Royal Army Medical Corps (T.F.): *s.* of John Clyne, of 152, West North Street, Aberdeen: and elder brother to Pte. S/42582, A. Clyne, 6th Gordon Highlanders, killed in action 26 August 1918: volunteered and enlisted Aberdeen: undertook Foreign Serrvice Obligations, and served with the Expeditionary Force in France and Flanders from May 1915, and was one of three men of the ambulance killed by shellfire in the Canal Bank sector, 1 August 1917: Age 21. *unm.* See also Corpl. Brand, Gwalia Cemetery (I.G.23).

His brother Andrew also has no known grave; he is commemorated on the Vis-en-Artois Memorial (Panel 10).

(Panel 56) Pte. 2165, Richard Robert Douglas, 9th Sanitary Section, Royal Army Medical Corps: Killed in action 13 May 1915.

(Panel 56) Pte. 303067, William Duncan, 1/2nd (Highland) Field Ambulance, Royal Army Medical Corps (T.F.). One of three of the ambulance stretcher bearers killed by shellfire while at duty in the Canal Bank sector, 1 August 1917. See Corpl. Brand, Gwalia Cemetery (I.G.23).

(Panel 56) Pte. 303351, Williamson Davidson Milne, 1/2nd (Highland) Field Ambulance, Royal Army Medical Corps (T.F.): *s.* of Wiliam Milne, of 421, Clifton Road, Woodside, Aberdeen, by his wife Margaret: *b.* Old Machar, co. Aberdeen, 1893: enlisted Aberdeen: served with the Expeditionary Force in France and Flanders from May 1915; killed in action at Ypres, 24 July 1917: Age 24. *unm.*

(Panel 56) Pte. 303342, Charles Milne, 1/2nd (Highland) Field Ambulance, Royal Army Medical Corps: *s.* of the late Alexander Milne, by his wife Margaret (30, Nether Kirkgate, Aberdeen): enlisted Aberdeen: served with the Expeditionary Force in France and Flanders from 1 May 1915, and was killed by the explosion of a shell 27 July 1917: Age 22. *unm.*

(Panel 56) Pte. 303342, David Oliphant, 1/2nd (Highland) Field Ambulance, Royal Army Medical Corps: late of Montrose, co. Forfar: *s.* of James Oliphant, of 'Caerlee,' Innerleithen, co. Perth: enlisted Aberdeen. Killed in action 27 July 1917: Age 27.

On the morning of 4th August 1917, to the loud accompaniment of the gun batteries sited nearby, 7th Cheshire Regt. attended church parade before making final arrangements to depart to the fighting line. For even the hardest of men present the summing up of the chaplain's service, which always seemed to close with, "There are going to be extremely difficult and hard times ahead for all and for some there will be no coming back," there was something inexplicably comforting in these words of solemnity.

Later as the battalion prepared to move off Padre East, who had only recently come to the battalion and despite the unwritten rule that excused them from the front line, was heard to thank the Colonel for his kind consideration, expressing "My place is up there with these lads."

That evening as the battalion passed close by the crater at Hooge the Colonel stood silently watching his men pass by, beside him stood the tall figure of Chaplain East; for many this would be their last sight of him.

In the early hours of the following morning, shortly after making his way through the gloom to meet with his Company Commander, Capt. Wilkinson, Lieut. Lloyd found him engaged in visualising the dispositions thereabouts. About fifty yards away were some derelict tanks, the cover afforded by which had been taken up by German snipers. Bullets commenced humming and the cracking sounds about their faces told both men they were flying a little too close for comfort. Suggesting they move away to position of cover Lieut Lloyd felt a sudden knock on his arm as a round of lead passed through the fleshy part of Capt. Wilkinson's biceps. Quickly passing along the word for stretcher-bearers they soon appeared and administered first aid in the form of placing the damaged limb in a sling. Despite the wound Capt. Wilkinson insisted in carrying on with his duties until he was persuaded by Major Bowen to report to Battalion Headquarters in Chateau Wood. Here it was found the loss of blood necessitated his removal to the nearest dressing station, and the Padre volunteered to guide him in the dark, over the treacherous ground to the aid post on the Menin Road. Leaving Battalion H.Q. together, with two batmen, they were almost in sight of their goal when Capt. Wilkinson discovered his puttee trailing behind him. Owing to his injured arm, the adjustment took longer than usual, but the slight delay, trivial though it seemed, was enough to spell disaster. Just as Padre East stooped to fasten the spiral piece of cloth a shell pitched close by and killed all four members of the party.

(Panel 56) Rev. Herbert Hinton East, Army Chaplain 4th Class, Royal Army Chaplain's Dept. attd. 13th (Service) Bn. The Cheshire Regt.: *s.* of the late Francis Hyde Hinton East, and his wife Emma Jane East (284, Kew Road, Kew, co. Surrey). Killed in action 5 August 1917, Chateau Wood – Menin Road, Ypres: Age 30.

Capt. W.O. Wilkinson also has no known grave; he is recorded on Panel 19.

(Panel 56) Rev. John Kellie, Army Chaplain 4th Class, Royal Army Chaplain's Dept. attd. 6th (Service) Bn. The Queen's Own (Cameron Highlanders): *s.* of Robert Luin Kellie, by his wife Janet: late *husb.* to Margaret Orr Ramsay Kellie (30, Park Circus, Ayr). Killed in action, 1 August 1917: Age 34. A member of the Freemasons, at the time of his death Mr Kellie was in the chair of Lodge St. John Maybole No.11. Seven years earlier, on 19 June 1910, as the newly ordained minister of Kirkmichael, the Rev. Kellie assisted in the rescue of four of his parishioners who with seven others, despite warnings to the contrary, had taken an un-seaworthy boat out to sea. Witnessing the boat sinking he immediately went down to the shore and shouted to the people on board to strip and try to swim back; casting modesty aside and hastily divesting himself of much of his clothing that he might swim out to the sinking boat, but even as he entered the water he could see the boat had already sunk by the stern and saw only a few hands above the water. Swimming further out he came across local message carrier, James Findlay, who had sunk and after getting hold of him by the hand managed to turn him on his back and swam back to shore with him. The Rev. Kellie then re-entered the water and swam out for eleven year-old David Clowes, who was standing on the prow of the boat up to his chest in water. Informing the boy to turn on his back Kellie succeeded in getting him back to shore also. Reluctant to speak about his part in the event Kellie said "I felt that I wanted to go back." Five people died by drowning.

(Panel 56) Sergt. P/1, Arthur James Toole, Military Mounted Police, Military Police Corps: late of Clapham Common, London. S.W.: *s.* of Christopher Toole, of 127, Sugden Road, Battersea, London, S.W.11, by his wife Charlotte Emma: *b.* Dundalk, Co. Louth, *c.*1872: employee London County Council Education Dept.: enlisted Southampton: served with the Expeditionary Force in France and Flanders, and was killed in action 21 October 1914, nr. Zonnebeke, at the First Battle of Ypres: Age 42. Sergt. Toole held the South African War Medals – having served in that campaign with the Queen's Bays – and both the Long Service and Good Conduct Medals; he was the eldest of four brothers who served in the Great War. The first man to enlist in the Corps of Military Police, August 1914, he was the corps second Active Service fatality in France.

PANEL 56 ENDS – 2ND. LIEUT. A.H. PETRIE, GENERAL LIST.

(Addenda Panel 58) Capt. George Millais James, 1st Bn. (3rd Foot) The Buffs (East Kent Regt.) attd. 22nd Infantry Bde., 7th Divn. (Bde. Major): *s.* of Major W. James, Scots Greys, and the late Mrs E. James, *née* Millais: *gdson.* of the renowned painter Sir John Millais: *b.* London, 1880: *educ.* Cheltenham College; and Royal Military College, Sandhurst: joined Northumberland Fusiliers, December 1899, serving with them in the Boer War: present at operations in Orange Free State; Transvaal, including actions at Venterskroon (slightly wounded) and Rhenoster River: Twice Mentioned in Despatches (*London Gazette*, 9 July, 10 September 1901): Queen's Medal, three clasps; King's Medal, two clasps: promoted Lieut. February 1900; Capt. May 1904: transf'd. The Buffs, May 1908: entered Staff College, Camberley, 1910: after passing out apptd. Brigade Major, Pretoria District, 1912: accompanied the Expeditionary Force to France as Brigade Major, 22nd Infantry Brigade, VIIth Division, and, while on duty, was killed instantaneously by a sniper 3 November 1914: Age 34. Capt. James *m.* 1908, Hilda Madeleine Bates, *née* James (Oxenden Hall, Market Harborough, co. Leicester), *dau.* of Sir James Heath, Bart., and left two daughters; Aileen, age 4 and Daphne, age 2, at the time of their father's death.

(Add.58) 2nd Lieut. Arthur Herbert Rosdew Burn, 1st (Royal) Dragoons: eldest *s.* of Col. Charles Rosdew Burn, of 77, Cadogan Square, London, S.W., and Stoodley Knowle, Torquay, M.P. for Torquay, one of the Gentlemen-at-Arms, late Royal Dragoons, formerly A.D.C. to H.R.H. the Duke of Connaught, by his wife Ethel Louise, *dau.* of Alexander John Forbes-Leith, the Baron Leith of Fyvie: *b.* 30 June 1892: *educ.* Ludgrove, Eton, and Christ's College, Oxford: volunteered for service on the outbreak of war: gazetted 2nd Lieut. 1st Dragoons, 26 August 1914: served with the Expeditionary Force in France and Flanders, and was killed in action 30 October following: Age 22. *unm.* (*IWGC record A.H. Posden Burn*)

(Add.58) 2nd Lieut. Henry Gage Morris, 'C' Coy., 2nd Bn. (46th Foot) Duke of Cornwall's Light Infantry: only *survg.* child of Col. Henry Gage Morris, late comdg. 2nd Duke of Cornwall's L.I., and *gt.-gt.-gdson.* to Col. Roger Morris, of York, by his wife Maude, *dau.* of the late Preston Gilbert Wallis, of Park Hill, Bodmin: *b.* Bodmin, co. Cornwall, 14 August 1897: *educ.* Preparatory School, The Hoe, Plymouth; Marlborough College (September 1911 – July, 1914); and Royal Military College, Sandhurst: gazetted 2nd Lieut. Duke of Cornwall's L.I., 12 January 1915, aged seventeen and a half years: went to France, 15 February 1915, and was killed in action at the Second Battle of Ypres, 23 April 1915. Buried where he fell beside 2nd Lieut. G.J. Lunnon, and Lieut. H. Stewart, Durham Light Infantry. His commanding officer wrote, "He was such a nice boy, and a very brave and gallant lad, and died gallantly. He was killed in a counter-attack we made with the 13th Brigade, the East Yorks, York and Lancs, and 4th Canadians on the 23rd. I was commanding the Battn. at the time, and the last I saw of him he passed me with a platoon of 'C' Coy., which was in Reserve. He came past me with a very cheerful face, and laughing under a very heavy cross-fire from machine-guns, and sang out to me, 'Shall I push on?' and I answered, 'Go on, laddie, as hard as you can.' Poor lad, I did not see him again, but heard he was shot in the head, but he would not let anyone stay with him. He was such a good boy, always cheerful and always ready to do anything that was wanted. He was very popular with everyone – officers and men." And Private W. Board, 'C' Coy., Duke of Cornwall's L.I., "You must be proud to know that your son was as brave a man as anyone could wish to meet. I was his servant while he was in France, and a better master I never had. The men in the platoon loved him, and would do anything for him. He was always cheerful, and had friends everywhere he went. I was not with him when he got hit, but I heard he wanted to go on, and refused to be bandaged, as he said there were men who were hit more badly than himself." A writer in his School Magazine ('*The Marlburian*,' 19 May 1915) recorded:– "From his earliest days in the school – in 'A' House – his company was a real pleasure. Always bright and full of fun, and merry talk, he had from the first great personal charm, and, as he developed, one saw behind him those qualities of modesty, generosity, and straightness, which mark the perfect gentleman." Age 17.

Both 2nd Lieut. George Lunnon and Lieut. Herbert Stewart have no known grave; they are recorded on Panels 20 and 36 respectively.

(Add.58) Pte. 5315, Thomas Richard Dawes, 3rd (Prince of Wales' Own) Dragoon Guards att. 2nd Life Guards: *s.* of George Henry Dawes, of 48, Channel View Road, Eastbourne, co. Sussex, by his wife Sarah Jane: and yr. brother to Corpl. of Horse, 2350, H.W. Dawes, 1st Life Guards, missing and wounded (confirmed killed) in action at Zandvoorde the previous day: *b.* Langley, 1883: enlisted Eastbourne. Killed in action 31 October 1914; vicinity of Hooge: Age 31.

His brother Herbert also has no known grave; he is recorded on Panel 3.

(Add.58) Pte. 3/8725, James Egan, 2nd Bn. (76th Foot) The Duke of Wellington's (West Riding) Regt.: *s.* of John Egan, of 69, Garnett Street, Bradford, and Georgina, his spouse: *b.* Idle, co. York: enlisted Strensall. Shot and killed by a German sniper 9 November 1914, while digging trenches; vicinity Hermitage Chateau: Age 24. Ptes. V. Tuck and W. Plumb were also killed.

(Add.58) Pte. 3408, Joseph Nutley, 'B' Coy., 2nd Bn. (5th Foot) The Northumberland Fusiliers: 5th *s.* of James Nutley, of 35, Hargil Road, Howden-le-Wear, Co. Durham, by his wife Eleanor 'Ellen,' *née* Jolly: served in India with his battalion prior to the outbreak of war, August 1914; and in France and Flanders from 16 January 1915. Missing, believed killed, 21 February 1915: Age 27.

(Add.58) Pte. 8087, William Plumb, 2nd Bn. (76th Foot) The Duke of Wellington's (West Riding) Regt.: late of Keighley, co. York: *b.* Oxenhope: enlisted Halifax. Died of wounds, 9 November 1914, received in action, being shot by a sniper while digging trenches nr. Hermitage Chateau.

(Add.58) Pte. 16768, Clement Murray Pritchard, Stretcher-bearer; 'C' Coy., 4th Field Ambulance, Australian Army Medical Corps, A.I.F.: *s.* of F.W. (& E.A.) Pritchard, of Windsor, Victoria. Killed in action 21 October 1917: Age 25. Buried near where he fell. See Pte. E.A. Esdaile, Lijssenthoek Military Cemetery (XXII.D.10).

(Add.58) Pte. 10666, Victor Tuck, 2nd Bn. (76th Foot) The Duke of Wellington's (West Riding) Regt.: *b.* Tottenham: enlisted Stratford. Died of wounds being shot by a sniper while digging trenches nr. Hermitage Chateau, 9 November 1914. Col. E.G. Harrison wrote, "...Everything was fairly quiet whilst I remained with them with the exception of the continual sniping which goes on all day and all night incessantly in these huge woods, where the German sniper, who anywhere is a marvel at his job, gets well behind our lines, and very seldom gets caught...they are good shots, evidently picked men, and lie up in ditches or turnip fields and keep at it all the time..."

(Add.58) Pte. 11713, Cecil Peachey, 6th (Service) Bn. The Oxford & Bucks Light Infantry: brother to Pte. 11715, W. Peachey, 6th O.B.L.I., killed in action 27 October 1915: *b.* Churchill, co. Oxford: enlisted Oxford. Killed in action, 10 August 1917.

His brother Wilfred is buried in Rue-du-Bacquerot No.1 Military Cemetery, Laventie (II.C.27).

(Add.58) Pte. 777, Arthur Shinn, 2nd Bn. (76th Foot) The Duke of Wellington's (West Riding) Regt.: *s.* of the late Samuel Shinn, by his wife Julia (54, Catherine Street, Cambridge): and elder brother to Rfn. S/29441, E.C. Shinn, 8th Rifle Brigade, killed in action 12 April 1917, aged 19 years: enlisted Cambridge. Killed in action, 8 November 1917: Age 28.

His brother Ernest is buried in Hibers Trench Cemetery, Wancourt (C.12).

(Add.58) Pte. 260092, Andrew Smith, 1/5th Bn. The Gordon Highlanders (T.F.): *s.* of the late William G. Smith, by his wife Margaret M. (Dundee): enlisted Dundee. Killed by the blast of a shell which came through the doorway of 5th Gordon's HQ, Turco Farm, 26 June 1917: Age 26. *unm.* 2nd Lieut. Milne and 3 OR were also killed; Corpl. Webster attd. T.M.Bty., died of wounds the same day. See Poperinghe Nw Military Cemetery (II.A.32).

(Add.58) Pte. 3/10407, James Edward Soden (served as Parker), 2nd Bn. (76th Foot) The Duke of Wellington's (West Riding) Regt.: *s.* of Henry Stephen (& Mrs H.) Soden, of 196, Duncan Road, Aylestone Park, Leicester: and elder brother to Pte. 32490, W.T. Soden, 20th Hussars, killed in action 22 March 1918: Killed in action, 11 November 1914: Age 18.

His brother William also has no known grave; he is commemorated on the Pozieres Memorial (Panel 6).

(Add.58) Pte. 240446, William Strachan, 1/5th Bn. The Gordon Highlanders (T.F.): enlisted Fraserburgh, co. Stirling. Killed by the blast of a shell which came through the doorway of 5th Gordon's

HQ, Turco Farm, 26 June 1917. See Pte. A. Smith above; also Poperinghe New Military Cemetery (II.A.32).

(Add.58) Pte. 11050, Thomas James Williams, 2nd attd.1st Bn. (41st Foot) The Welsh Regt.: *s.* of George Williams, of Ffosyfedwen, Velindre, Henllan, Flannel Weaver, by his wife Hannah, *dau.* of William Evans: *b.* Ffrontywann, 15 November 1894: *educ.* National School, Velindre: enlisted Welsh Regt., December 1913: in training with 2nd Battn. in Hampshire when war broke out, and soon afterwards sent out to France. There he was a driver in the transport section of his regt., until he contracted rheumatic fever, thereafter lying for some weeks in hospital at Le Havre, and then returning to England on three weeks' leave. At the appointed time he reported himself at Cardiff Barracks, and was in a few days on his way back to France again to join the 1st Battn. He served with them for three months, and was killed in action, being shot in a bayonet charge, at Zillebeke, 25 May 1915. His brother Private William Williams, is now (1916) serving with the Devons: Age 21. *unm.*

(Addenda Panel) Pte. G/34626, Frank Richard Pratt, 16th (Service) Bn. The Duke of Cambridge's Own (Middlesex Regt.): only *s.* of Frank George Pratt, by his wife Catherine (132, Welbourne Road, High Cross, Tottenham, London, N.), *dau.* of Samuel Ball: *b.* Tottenham, 4 January 1889: *educ.* Page Green London County Council School: Occupation – Stock Room Hand; H. Lebus: enlisted Middlesex Regt., 7 November 1916: served with the Expeditionary Force in France and Flanders from 19 January 1917, and was killed in action at Ypres 8 August following. Buried where he fell: Age 28. He *m.* Trinity Church, Tottenham, London, N., 25 June 1911; Edith Myria (109, Welbourne Road, High Cross, Tottenham), *dau.* of Charles Wilkins, and had two children – Frank Samuel, *b.* 19 November 1912; Edith Catherine, *b.* 30 April 1914.

By lying about his age Herbert Burden enlisted in the Northumberland Fusiliers when he was just 16 years old and, after training, was drafted to the 1st Battalion of his Regiment – 24 March 1915 – just before his seventeenth birthday. Throughout the summer of 1915 the battalion was heavily engaged in the Ypres salient and in the latter part of June, while they were suffering enormous losses during fighting on the Bellewaarde Ridge, young Burden deserted. His freedom, however, was relatively short-lived and it was not long before he was arrested and charged. At his Court Martial, such were the horrendous casualties suffered by his battalion, no member of his unit could be found to supply even a character witness and, on 2 July 1915, he stood undefended before the Court charged with desertion in the face of the enemy and, after being found guilty, was sentenced to death and shot.

(Add.60) Pte. 3832, Herbert Francis Burden, 1st Bn. (5th Foot) The Northumberland Fusiliers: Executed – Desertion, 21 July 1915: Age 17.

After the war Herbert Burden's grave – like so many others – could not be located, but it was not until the 1990's that his name was added to the Menin Gate.

(Add.60) Bmdr. 690, John William Gregg, 4th Durham (Howitzer) Bty., Royal Field Artillery (T.F.): eldest *s.* of George Gregg, of 48, Gladstone Street, Hebburn, by his wife Emma Louisa, *dau.* of William Young: *b.* Jarrow-on-Tyne, Co. Durham, 24 March 1895: *educ.* Grange Board School, Jarrow: Occupation – Apprentice Boiler Maker; Messrs Palmer Boiler Works, Jarrow: joined Royal Field Artillery (T.F.), 23 October 1913: volunteered for Imperial Service on the outbreak of war, 4 August 1914: served with the Expeditionary Force in France and Flanders from 22 April 1915, and was killed in action nr. St. Julien, 8 May following: Age 20. *unm.* (At the time of writing CWGC record plans to add Bmdr. Gregg to the Addenda Panel)

(Addenda 57 – 60) Lieut. Col. Alexander Daniel Reid, D.S.O., 7th (Service) Bn. The Royal Inniskilling Fusiliers; Comdg. 1st Bn. (83rd Foot) The Royal Irish Rifles: *s.* of Capt. William Thomas Reid, J.P., of Ardmeallie and Hazelwood, co. Banff, by his marriage to the late Margaret Grieg Reid (Cowichan, Vancouver, British Columbia), *dau.* of James Grey: *b.* Edinburgh, 2 February 1882: *educ.* Westminster; and Royal Military College, Sandhurst: joined Indian Army, Lieut., 28 October 1902; served on Staff Corps; retired April 1909. Residing in Canada at the outbreak of war, August 1914, he rejoined: apptd. Major, 7th Royal Inniskilling Fusiliers; proceeded to France with this unit February 1915. Left out of the fighting at Leuze Wood, he came forward on the night of 5 September 1916 and, following the serious wounding of Lieut. Col. H.N. Young the following day, assumed command of the battalion. Major Reid was himself wounded shortly thereafter (8 September) and removed to the Base Hospital, Rouen. A War Office telegram sent to his mother (11 September) informed Major Reid had been admitted to hospital with a 'slight gunshot wound, right eye.' transf'd. and admitted London Hospital (12 September): rejoined his unit, 31 December 1916, as Actg. Comdg. Officer until the return of Col. Young; thereafter served (until 7 July 1917) as 2nd in Command 7th Battn.: Awarded Distinguished Service Order, 4 June 1917, but was not invested with it by the King, no warrant being issued due to the forthcoming offensive: assumed command 1st Royal Irish Rifles, 8 July 1917. Killed in action 31 July 1917: Age 35. Lieut. Col. Reid's mother administered his will; she requested his D.S.O. be forwarded to his brother Lieut. Henry Francis Reid, 7th Royal Inniskilling Fusiliers, currently serving somewhere in France. Mentioned in Despatches, 22 May 1917; awarded ('*London Gazette*,' 26 May) Silver Medal for Military Valour (Italy).

(Addenda 57 – 60) Pte. 22232, Thomas Jenkins, 1st Bn. (41st Foot) The Welch Regt.: *s.* of Stephen Jenkins, of 3, North Road, Newbridge, co. Monmouth, by his wife Sarah: and brother to Pte. 9593, W.J. Jenkins, South Wales Borderers, died Barrow-in-Furness Hospital, 1 July 1918, of wounds received in action in France: enlisted Newbridge: served with the Expeditionary Force in France and Flanders from January 1915, and was killed in action at the Second Battle of Ypres, 5 May following. Buried where he fell: Age 21. *unm.*His brother William is buried in Barrow-in-Furness Cemetery (III.406).

(Addenda 57 – 60) Pte. 7538, Edward Barron, 4th Bn. (77th Foot) The Duke of Cambridge's Own (Middlesex Regt.): *s.* of William Barron, and Susan, his spouse: late *husb.* to Martha S. Barron (Kempsford, Cirencester, co. Gloucester): served in the South African Campaign, and with the Expeditionary Force in France and Flanders, and was one of six men killed in action 15 December 1914, during heavy shell-fire of the battalion's position, Kemmel: Age 34.

The other five men killed, Ptes. W.T. Ardin, J.W. Jennings, R.H. Read, G.J. Rose and J. Steward have no known grave; they are recorded on (Panels 49-51).

Panel Index: Menin Gate (North)

South Portal (Right)

20)   Duke of Cornwall's Light Infantry
Duke of Wellington's (West Riding) Regt.
Royal Sussex Regt.

South Staircase (Facing)

22)   Cheshire Regt.
Royal Welch Fusiliers
South Wales Borderers
King's Own Scottish Borderers
Cameronians (Scottish Rifles)
Royal Inniskilling Fusiliers
Gloucestershire Regt.
24)   7th, 8th, 10th, 13th, 14th & 15th Battn. Canadian Infantry
26)   15th, 16th, 18th, 19th, 20th, 21st, 22nd 24th, 25th, 26th, 27th & 28th Battn. Canadian Infantry
28)   28th, 29th, 31st, 38th, 42nd, 43rd, 44th, 46th, 47th & 49th Battn. Canadian Infantry
30)   49th, 50th, 52nd, 54th, 58th, 60th & 72nd, Battn. Canadian Infantry
75th, 78th, 85th, 87th, 102nd & 116th Battn. Canadian Infantry
Canadian Mounted Rifles
32)   Canadian Mounted Rifles
Canadian Pioneers
Canadian Machine Gun Corps
Canadian Labour Corps
Canadian Army Service Corps
Canadian Railway Troops
Canadian Army Medical Corps
Canadian Y.M.C.A.
34)   Gloucestershire Regt.
Worcestershire Regt.
East Lancashire Regt.
East Surrey Regt.

South Loggia (Left to Right)

36)   York & Lancaster Regt.
Durham Light Infantry
38)   Durham Light Infantry
Highland Light Infantry
Seaforth Highlanders
Gordon Highlanders
Cameron Highlanders
40)   Cameron Highlanders
Royal Irish Rifles
42)   Royal Irish Fusiliers
Connaught Rangers
Argyll & Sutherland Highlanders
44)   Argyll & Sutherland Highlanders
Leinster Regt.
Royal Munster Fusiliers
Royal Dublin Fusiliers